Towards Freedom

ICHR: Towards Freedom

General Editor   Sabyasachi Bhattacharya

Volume Editor   K.N. Panikkar

Towards Freedom

Documents on the Movement for Independence in India
1940

PART 1

Edited by
K.N. Panikkar

With a Preface by the General Editor
Sabyasachi Bhattacharya

Indian Council of Historical Research

OXFORD
UNIVERSITY PRESS

OXFORD
UNIVERSITY PRESS

YMCA Library Building, Jai Singh Road, New Delhi 110 001

Oxford University Press is a department of the University of Oxford. It furthers the
University's objective of excellence in research, scholarship, and education
by publishing worldwide in

Oxford   New York
Auckland   Cape Town   Dar es Salaam   Hong Kong   Karachi
Kuala Lumpur   Madrid   Melbourne   Mexico City   Nairobi
New Delhi   Shanghai   Taipei   Toronto

With offices in
Argentina   Austria   Brazil   Chile   Czech Republic   France   Greece
Guatemala   Hungary   Italy   Japan   Poland   Portugal   Singapore
South Korea   Switzerland   Thailand   Turkey   Ukraine   Vietnam

Oxford is a registered trademark of Oxford University Press
in the UK and in certain other countries

Published in India by Oxford University Press, New Delhi

ISBN-13: 978-019-806078-9
ISBN-10: 019-806078-5

Typeset in Baskerville BE Regular 11.5/14 at Le Studio Graphique, Gurgaon 122 001
Printed in India at DeUnique, New Delhi 110 018
Published by Oxford University Press
YMCA Library Building, Jai Singh Road, New Delhi 110 001

Contents

General Editor's Preface

The agenda of an endeavour such as this series of volumes defines itself in part through editorial practice and partly through attempts towards a statement of objectives. The historical context in which this project developed initially is generally known. While it will be excessively deterministic to overestimate the influence of that historical conjuncture on the academic inputs which went into the making of the project's agenda, one has to take that into account as one of the formative factors. After the vertiginous years leading to 1947, there came a time when historians turned their attention to those years and archives began to acquire and provide access to source materials. The last years of 'British India' began to be addressed by professional historians and indeed the theme attracted national attention both in India and in Britain. In June 1967, the British Prime Minister Harold Wilson made an important statement in this regard in the House of Commons: 'in view of the great interest now being shown in historical circles in the last days of British rule in India', there would be published 'documents from the India Office records on the Transfer of Power and the events leading up to it.'[1] The announcement included the assurance that 'the editors will be independent historians who will be given unrestrained access to the records, and freedom to select and edit the documents for publication.' The outcome of the project thus framed at the highest level in England was the series known as *The Transfer of Power* edited by Nicholas Mansergh, Smuts Professor of the History of the British Commonwealth at Cambridge. In addition to the announcement made in Parliament, Mansergh, as 'the Editor-in-Chief', stated that the 'purpose of the series' was 'to make available to scholars in convenient printed form the more important British historical records relating to the transfer of power in India'.[2]

Arguably, there is an obvious inadequacy in the notion that all that happened in 1947 was a 'transfer of power'. In Indian perception the attainment of Independence was a significant moment in the history of the struggle against British rule in the subcontinent. The representation of the emergence of independent India and Pakistan as transfer of power, solely an alteration of constitutional relations, tended towards the occlusion of that history. The focus on the legalistic notion of power transfer and the discourse of modalities of transfer, marginalized the more significant part of the historical processes at work. Likewise, the self-imposed limitations of the British documentation enterprise left many issues unaddressed: the project was to select documents from British state papers relating to the constitutional arrangements from the Cripps Mission of 1942 to 15 August 1947. In that discourse, in the official archives and the Viceroys' papers the Indian voice was recorded only in so far as a few important spokesmen of political parties were among those present in negotiations with the British Indian government. The

---

[1] *Parliamentary Debates*, 5th Series, House of Commons, Vol. 749, 30 June 1967, cols 147–8.
[2] Nicholas Mansergh, ed., 'Foreword', *The Transfer of Power*, London, 1976, Vol. VI, p. viii.

Indian institutions, personalities and events were included in the documentation only to the extent the official papers took cognizance of them.

That is not to say that the task of documentation in the twelve volumes produced between 1970 and 1983 by the HMSO was not competently handled by Professor Mansergh and his editorial assistants. These volumes were products of the best of British scholarship. But the initial conception of the project was delimited to certain issues and historical sources. I recall that in 1971 when I invited Sir Penderel Moon, a brilliant officer of the Indian Civil Service and later a member of Mansergh's editorial team, to a seminar at St Antony's College, Oxford, a number of us questioned him about this and he pointed out that perhaps we had not paid attention to the subtitle of the Mansergh volumes, 'Constitutional Relations between Britain and India'. Clearly the agenda for any Indian endeavour towards the documentation of the years leading to independence in 1947 would be different. How it would be different was suggested by Professor Sarvepalli Gopal in a luminous editorial Preface to the first volume produced under the present project. He said that the projected volumes aimed to 'present, within limits set by the sources, documents relating to the activities, attitudes and ideas of the diverse classes and sections of Indian society, all of which contributed to the attainment of Indian independence with partition.'[3]

It is significant that the title chosen for this series was 'Towards Freedom'. While the subtitle emphasizes the focus upon the 'movement for independence', the title evokes discourses in other domains as well—the struggle for social justice, for economic empowerment against exploitation, and for cultural autonomy. These were also prominent discourses within the overarching framework of the Indian people's struggle for freedom. One is reminded of the words of Mahatma Gandhi in an essay he wrote in the *Harijan* a few days before his death, on 27 January 1948: 'the Congress has won political freedom but it has yet to win economic freedom, social and moral freedom.'[4] This awareness of different categories of freedom allows space for a conception of the freedom struggle far wider in amplitude than the textbook approach to the struggle for independence from British rule. It makes a struggle for freedoms of many kinds thinkable. And it broadens the idea of a history of freedom struggle. This is how I understand the choice of the title for this series: *Towards Freedom.*

To sum it up, the present series of volumes focuses upon not just the legal processes of the transfer of power and the overtly political activities which brought that about, but also the struggle for freedom in different domains—economic, social, and cultural. The agenda of the series, therefore, is open to the entry of themes relating to the struggle of the peasantry, the working classes, and different sections of people as well as to a broad spectrum of political organizations who in their own light worked towards attainment of freedom.

To any one interested in the craft of history a pertinent question will be how the documentation will reflect this agenda. The selection of appropriate documents is not an easy task. We are here looking at long term historical processes such as the slowly evolving ideas about nationhood or class solidarity, the dynamics of popular participation in political

---

[3] S. Gopal, 'General Editor's Preface', in Partha Sarathi Gupta, ed., *Towards Freedom 1943–44*, Delhi, 1997, p. vii.

[4] M.K. Gandhi, 'Congress Position', *Harijan*, 1.2.48, *Collected Works of Mahatma Gandhi*, Vol. 90, p. 497. Also see 'His Last will and Testament', *Harijan*, 15.2.48 where he spoke of economic, social and moral dimensions of independence, beyond the political independence which had been attained, ibid., p. 526. This document was written *c.* 29 January 1948, shortly before Gandhi's death, and it was also referred to in the AICC papers as 'Draft Constitution of the Congress'.

movements, the links being forged between movements of the peasantry, the industrial labour and the freedom struggle, the youth and student movements vis-à-vis the political parties, the changing social hierarchy in caste terms in relation to electoral and agitational politics, the gender relationships evolving from the traditional patriarchal structure towards developments that had liberating potentials, the anti-feudal and anti-British movement in the princely states, and the interface between all these trends in the ideational and cultural domains. The instantiation of these long-term processes through events as reflected in documents is the task at hand. The documents reflect fragments of the events which constitute links in the chain of certain historical processes of long duration.

It was decided years ago at an early stage of this project to distribute the work among editors on a purely chronological basis, that is to say each of the volumes in this series would relate to a particular year assigned to an editor. This opened the project to the possibility that the long-term processes would be lost sight of in the depiction of the particularities of the year each editor is taking care of. I incurred unpopularity in the Indian Council of Historical Research (ICHR) when I suggested many years ago that a thematic division of labour between the various editors, rather than a chronological one assigning one year to each, would have been a better organizing principle.[5] I will not elaborate that point again. Whatever the drawbacks or merits of the chronological frame for assigning editorial responsibility might have been, it has been in operation for twenty years and hopefully it will enable us to complete the task before us. For the volume editors the limitation of chronological framework has been probably an irksome constraint. On the whole, the volume editors, each a distinguished historian, bore with fortitude the limits set on their temporal range, and they situate the particular historical conjuncture of a given year in the broader perspective of the long-term processes as they see them in the Introduction to the volume. The Editor's Introduction is thus a bridge between the narrative of events and the narrative of the freedom struggle as he or she sees it. The editor's introductory observations also provide a space for the presentation of his or her approach to the themes and issues the volume addresses and the explication of that approach.

As regards the sources from which the documents are collected for the volumes in this series, Professor Sarvepalli Gopal, in his General Editor's Preface, remarked in 1997: 'Although some of the volumes contain documents drawn from regional language sources, a fully comprehensive selection from these sources merit a separate project.'[6] This was an accurate prediction of the future output, that is the volumes now coming out. In deciding on what non-English and regional language sources will be collected the volume editors have exercised their judgement in deploying the research assistance they were provided. Judging by volumes produced till now and the manuscripts now being received from editors and being processed in the editorial office at the ICHR, the editors possibly felt that on most of the themes addressed there exist sufficient source material in the English language and in translation. A more systematic search for and selection of non-English sources would have made this collection more complete, but it was evidently not found to be feasible. We are committed to a schedule which requires us to complete as early as possible the project undertaken in 1988–9 rather than to expand the scope of the editors' search to new sources.

---

[5] S. Bhattacharya, 'The Empire on Borrowed Time: Towards Freedom 1943–44', *The Book Review*, Vol. XXII, January–February 1998, pp. 24–5.

[6] S. Gopal, 'General Editor's Preface', in Gupta ed., *Towards Freedom 1943–44*, p. vii.

One more point needs to be made about the sources. Probably, in the last decade of the Raj, specially during the World War, perspicacious observers began to sense a debilitation of the imperial powers and the impending decolonization process on a global scale, and the consequent shift in the power relationships—this altered their perception of the politics of independence struggle radically. This was happening globally in old empires, among the people and leaders in the imperial metropolises as well as their colonial peripheries. On the latter process we do have some documentation in the present series, but not much on the shift in the imperial metropolis. This is because *ab initio* the project was meant to be mainly for the collection of sources in India. This was probably because it was clear from the beginning that we have our hands full if we look at the Indian archival sources alone. The mass and density of archival sources generated by the Government in India will be evident to even a layman who glances at the following pages. Moreover, as I mentioned earlier, unlike similar enterprises in England, Pakistan, and Sri Lanka to collect sources throwing light on the last days of the British Raj, this series includes a great many activities and events which are not overtly political or constitutional.

A few words on the editorial apparatus in these volumes may be in order. The chapters are thematically organized while the sequence of placement of documents in each chapter is strictly chronological. There are two guides for the reader, first the Calendar of Documents indicating the subject of each document and the source, and second, the Index at the end of the volume. An effort has been made to make the volumes as 'reader-friendly' as possible. In some collections of this nature the editorial practice has been to provide a synoptic account of the contents of each document. This has not been the pattern in this series chiefly because it would increase the size of the volumes. As it is the present volume is very bulky and the editors are to be applauded for trying to trim them down.

I would like to put on record the annoying delays this project was subjected to on account of political interference to the detriment of academic autonomy. One result of such interference was that the ICHR authorities appointed no successor to the General Editor, Professor Sarvepalli Gopal when he passed away in April 2002; in fact all work on the project was suspended for about five years. I was asked in March 2005 to take up the task initiated by Professor Gopal, my senior colleague at Jawaharlal Nehru University. Upon accepting this position, an honorary one, my first task was to assemble an editorial team at the ICHR and to request the editors of the different volumes to resume the work.

The disruption in the production of the volumes in the series for several years up to 2005 was tantamount to political censorship of academic work. It is interesting to note here that the British developed a system which prevented political parties' interference in such matters. The British project for the documentation of the Transfer of Power was processed through a mechanism which ensured inter-party consensus in parliament.[7] For this purpose a standing inter-party group of Privy Counsellors was appointed and it included a minister of the ruling party and representatives of the opposition parties, the Conservative and Liberal Parties; thus, once the project was passed by that committee, the task was left to experts duly appointed and no political interference occurred. In the light of what happened in our country on account of governmental changes, one might say that there was much that was commendable in the mechanism devised in Britain.

---

[7] *Parliamentary Debates*, 5th series, House of Commons, Vol. 733, col. 1706.

It is hoped that the agenda outlined above makes it amply clear what have been and remain the principles of documentation in the *Towards Freedom* series. The editors of the volumes have had the freedom to exercise their choice within certain parameters and they focus upon the themes which emerge from the selected documents. An editor of a volume in this series stated what most other editors would endorse: this is not 'an attempt to provide materials for an "official" or "definitive" statement on the history of the freedom movement.'[8] I accepted the responsibility of being the General Editor of this series since I believe that although the Government of India has funded this enterprise, like many other research projects and institutions in this country, the output of the project is the work of autonomous minds of scholars guided by standards of the discipline of historiography. As I have said in the beginning, not only agenda statements like the one I have attempted now, but practice has defined principles as well, and that is how an academic community works.

* * *

It will be pointless to discuss in this Preface the issues addressed adequately by the editor of this volume in his Introduction and in the documents relating to the impact of the Second World War on Indian political parties,[9] the constitutional negotiations,[10] the progress of the nationalist leadership towards civil disobedience and individual *satyagraha* during the year 1940,[11] and communal politics.[12] It may be more useful (since this volume and the series as a whole focus only upon documents on India) to try and situate these internal developments in the context of the World War which, needless to say, dominated the global scene.

The shadow of the Second World War looms large in the entire scene depicted in the documents in this volume as a whole. While documents gathered in Chapter 1, relate to the varied impact of the War on the attitude of various political leaders and parties, it may be useful to bear in mind the following brief account of the course of developments in the War since that was a factor which evidently influenced the political stance of the British Indian government as well as that of the political leadership in India. The year 1940 began with a strong wave of rumour in diplomatic circles that German invasion of Norway was imminent.[13] Documents revealed later indicate that Hitler had indeed issued instructions on 27 January 1940 to prepare such plans. Britain planned to plant mines in Norwegian waters to deter invaders. While Prime Minister Chamberlain dithered as usual, Hitler invaded Norway on 9 April 1940 and occupied Oslo and all the major ports. At the same time Germany also occupied Denmark and sent troopships into Copenhagen. This was followed up, on 10 May, with an advance across Belgium and attack on the Netherlands. By 12 May Germans were in the suburbs of Rotterdam. Resistance around Amsterdam was weak and the Queen and her government sought refuge in England on 13 May while the army surrendered to the Germans. As regards Belgium, the Luftwaffe did the job in conjunction with armoured corps. Meanwhile the French found that the much vaunted Maginot line was a necessary but not a sufficient

---

[8] Basudev Chatterjee ed., *Towards Freedom 1938*, Delhi, 1999, p. lvii.

[9] See Chapter 1, 'Response to the Second World War' in this volume.

[10] See Chapter 2, 'The Politics of Constitutional Negotiations' in this volume.

[11] See Chapter 3, 'Towards Civil Disobedience' and Chapter 4, 'Individual Satyagraha' in this volume.

[12] See Chapter 5, 'Communal Politics' in this volume.

[13] Sir Basil Liddell Hart, *History of the Second World War*, New York, 1999, a standard authority, has been used in constructing our highly abbreviated narrative.

defence measure. By 12 May the Germans had crossed the frontier between Belgium and France. The French troops, without anti-tank and anti-aircrafts guns, were no match for the German tank corps. Hence the German advance towards the English channel was unstoppable. The British expeditionary force and the French troops in that part of the battle front were in danger of being cut off by the advancing German troops. Dunkirk was the only port left from which the isolated troops of the Allied Powers could be rescued. From 26 May evacuation began, the day the defeated Belgium asked for an armistice. Up to 4 June about 338,000 French, British, and Belgian soldiers were evacuated from the beach of Dunkirk under constant bombing by Luftwaffe.

What were the consequences of these global developments for India? First, the British Indian government's topmost item on the agenda now was to use India as the war base to supply resources, human and material. Viceroy Linlithgow said so in his conversations later with W. Philips, President Roosevelt's emissary.[14] The Viceroy was also anxious that agitators in India should not rock the boat in those critical days of the War. He wanted to secure as much as possible support from the participants in Indian politics, particularly the Congress and the Muslim League. Therefore, it is not surprising that on 10 January 1940 he declared that the ultimate objective of His Majesty's Government was Dominion Status under the Statute of Westminster; while deploring the resignation of Congress ministries in the previous year, the Viceroy declared the intention to expand his Executive Council to include some representative Indian political leaders. The problem was a mismatch between this promise and what India expected. The Congress was keen on obtaining a promise of independent status for India in the near future. In the following pages we have documents showing how at the Ramgarh Session of the Congress on 20 March 1940 the demand for a Constituent Assembly based on adult suffrage and independence was asserted. Britain, the resolution said, was in the 'War fundamentally for imperialist ends and for the preservation and strengthening of her Empire which is based on the exploitation of the people of India, as well as of other Asiatic and African countries.'[15] The Muslim League found this to be the opportune moment to put forward their demand and thus the well-known Pakistan resolution was passed by the League on 23 March 1940.[16] Within a few days Germany invaded Norway and Denmark and this hardened British attitude to troubles in India. The retreat forced on the British at Dunkirk and their isolated position compelled attention mainly to war measures. On 21 May 1940 the Defence Plan of India was issued by the Commander-in-Chief: the Indian Army was to be expanded by six divisions, aircraft production in India was prioritized, Eastern Group Supply Council was created to mobilize supply from the colonies to the European war front. Secretary of State Amery's report to the War Cabinet exclusively focused upon these measures.[17] Indian politics was of marginal importance for Britain at that moment of crisis. This infuriated Jawaharlal Nehru, among others, and he wrote of the 'singular obtuseness of the English' in scathing words: 'Not even ... war and disaster has made any dent on their imperialist outlook or their

---

[14] *Transfer of Power*, vol. 3, p. 689, 19 Feb. 1943.

[15] 'India and the War-Crisis: Resolution Adopted at 53rd Session of Congress, Ramgarh, 19–20 March 1940', *Indian Annual Register*, 1940, Vol. 1, New Delhi, pp. 228–9. See Chapter 1, Document no. 3, p.4 in this volume.

[16] 'Muslim League's Lahore Resolution', *Indian Annual Register*, 1940, Vol. I, pp. 311–12. See Chapter 2, Document no. 43, p. 149 in this volume.

[17] S.N. Prasad, *Expansion of the Armed Forces and Defence Organisation, 1939–1945*, Calcutta, 1956, p. 58 et seq.

attitude to India.'[18] And again he stated on 10 May his opinion that 'the invasions of Holland, Belgium and Luxembourg mean that the war has now entered a new and Napoleonic phase'[19] while Britain seemed to be unaware of its implications. Britain on the one hand 'talks vaguely in terms of standing up for democracy in Europe and freedom of small nations and on the other hand it sticks like a leech to its empire'.[20]

By the middle of June the whole of northern France was in German hands. On 14 June they entered Paris. On 16 June Marshal Petain, the new head of a government which had abandoned Paris asked the Germans for an armistice. In the meanwhile Winston Churchill had succeeded Chamberlain on 10 May and he encouraged General Charles Gaulle to continue France's war, in the last resort from French North Africa. Two other consequences followed the fall of France. First, the depredations of the German submarines increased. Second, invasion of Britain became the next object of Hitler's attention. His plans of invading Britain, codenamed Operations Sea Lion, was resisted by the British air force very effectively. From 8 August Germany sent 1,500 aircrafts almost every day to destroy British air power and the city of London. This Battle of Britain intensified from 15 September but it failed against the Royal Air Force, while causing immense destruction.

Winston Churchill attained the status of a national icon during those days as the leader of British resistance. A man who declared that it was not his intention to preside over the dissolution of the empire was not inclined to be responsive to Indian grievances. He was not satisfied with the Viceroy's declaration of 10 January 1940 regarding the Dominion Status. Churchill thought that it was impossible to promise any constitutional arrangement before the conclusion of the War, and to pledge an advance to the Dominion Status in anticipation of what the Parliament would decide in future was a mistake.[21] Hence the so-called 'August Offer' by the Viceroy was a very limited one: he was, he said, authorized by His Majesty's Government to set up a War Advisory Council and to expand his own Executive Council to include 'Indian States [i.e. the Princely States] and other interests in the national life of India'; it was added that after the conclusion of the War a new constitutional order would be considered.[22] Congress rejected the empty promises in the August offer which the Working Committee described as 'wholly opposed ... to the principle of democracy as acclaimed by the British Government in the War...'.[23] The League rejected it likewise. The launching of the individual satyagraha movement by the Congress inevitably followed.

While these developments occurred, the Axis Pact was concluded between Germany, Italy, and Japan (27 September 1940), a formidable threat to Britain. Hitler drew Hungary, Romania, and Slovakia into the Axis Bloc. German and Italian penetration into East Europe, specially Yugoslavia and Greece, was accompanied by threat to Britain's position in north and east

---

[18] 'Jawaharlal Nehru to Rajendra Prasad, 16 May 1940', *SWJN*, Vol. XI, pp. 29–35. See Chapter 1, Document no. 5, p. 7 in this volume.

[19] 'The Fundamental Issues at Stake: Statement to the Press by Jawaharlal Nehru, 10 May 1940'. See Chapter 1, Document no. 4, p. 6 in this volume.

[20] Ibid.

[21] Anita Inder Singh, *The Origins of the Partition of India, 1936–47,* New Delhi, 1987, pp. 62–3.

[22] 'Viceroy's Statement on Expanding the Governor-General's Council and Establishing War Advisory Council, 8 August 1940', *Speeches by the Marquess of Linlithgow,* Vol. II, November 1938–December 1943, Government of India Press, Simla, 1944, Linlithgow Papers, Acc. No. 2329, NAI. See Chapter 2, Document no. 57, pp. 173–4 in this volume.

[23] 'Congress Working Committee Resolution on Viceregal Declaration, Wardha, 18–22 August 1940', *Hindustan Times,* 23 August 1940. See Chapter 2, Document no. 65, p. 186.

Africa from Italian forces. Sir Archibald Wavell, the British Commander-in-Chief in West Asia and in later times the Viceroy in India, led Allied operations in north and east Africa. Indian troops, along with forces from other countries under his command, fought in Africa mainly against the Italian army. Protection of the Suez Canal, strategically vital for British possessions in South Asia and for the war in the east, was secured by the end of 1940. The year 1940 ended with the destruction of the British air-base in Hong Kong, and the sinking of British warships *Repulse* and the *Prince of Wales* on 8 and 10 December. Thus a new front was opening up in the east and from 1941 that would more directly involve British India, just as Hitler's attack on Russia would soon draw her as well into the vortex of the expanding Second World War. That however is another story.

In these closing months of 1940 crowded with events on the war front, the nationalists' battle for the mind of the nation took the form of individual civil disobedience, as prescribed by Mahatma Gandhi who prevailed over dissenters in the Congress on the question of strategy. The resolution of the All-India Congress Committee on the issue, drafted by Gandhi and Nehru, was somewhat remarkable in that it expressed 'admiration for the bravery and endurance shown by the British nation in the face of danger and peril.'[24] This was written at a time when the Battle of Britain was indeed testing British endurance. At the same time, the resolution also reiterated the Congress agenda for non-violent resistance 'for the preservation of the liberties of the people.'[25] Gandhi's speech was an attempt to explain why, having repeatedly stated earlier that he 'would not be guilty of embarrassing the British people or the British government when their very existence hung in the balance'[26] in the War, he now recommended *satyagraha*. He argued that under the circumstances the Congress and the Indian people faced 'the virtue of self-restraint now becomes vice.'[27] At the same time he stated: 'there will be no mass civil disobedience because... [it] is not required on this occasion.'[28] There were many in the Congress sceptical of the efficacy of individual civil disobedience. There are reports that Jawaharlal Nehru was one of them. However, it was Jawaharlal Nehru who offered a persuasive rationale for that strategy in his statement to the Court which sentenced him to four years in jail in November 1940. He made the point that the British imposed on their Indian subjects a war in 1939 and this was inconsistent with 'freedom and self-determination and democracy for which, it was alleged, the war was being waged.'[29] He argued that an individual offering satyagraha was nothing but a 'symbol of Indian nationalism resolved to break away from the British Empire.'[30] And Nehru appealed to history: The British rulers of the Indian people had 'misjudged their present temper and read history in vain.... The future recorder of this history might well say that, in the hour of supreme trial the Government of Britain and the people of

---

[24] 'AICC Resolution on Satyagraha, Bombay, 15–16 September 1940', *Harijan*, 22 September 1940. See Chapter 4, Document no. 1, p. 410 in this volume.

[25] Ibid.

[26] 'Mahatma Gandhi's Speech in English at the AICC Meeting, Bombay, 15 September 1940', *Harijan*, 29 September 1940. See Chapter 4, Document no. 2, p. 411 in this volume.

[27] Ibid.

[28] 'Mahatma Gandhi's Speech in English at the AICC Meeting, Bombay, 15 September 1940', *Harijan*, 29 September 1940. See Chapter 4, Document no.2, p. 414 in this volume.

[29] 'Jawaharlal Nehru's Statement to the Court, 3–4 November 1940', *SWJN*, Vol. XI, 3–4 November 1940, pp. 486–90. See Chapter 4, Document no. 16, in this volume.

[30] Ibid., p. 444.

Britain failed because they were drunk with the wine of imperialism and could not adapt themselves to a changing world. He may muse over the fate of empires which have fallen because of this weakness, and call it destiny.'[31]

* * *

In the last year and a half ICHR has been able to publish the following volumes in the Towards Freedom series: Parts 1 and 2 of the volume on 1939 edited by Professor Mushirul Hasan, the complete volume on 1945 edited by Professor Bimal Prasad, and Parts 1 and 2 of the volume on 1946 edited by Professor Sumit Sarkar. The project to revive and publish *Towards Freedom* achieved in the past eighteen months a massive documentation of these years. I understand that the total output amounted to 4,496 pages of documents and 369 pages of descriptive calendars of documents and editorial matter in the volumes mentioned above. Any one with the slightest acquaintance with the nature of this sort of documentation project will appreciate the amount of time and energy invested to put the typed or photocopied documents into digital form, to compile or check the calendar of documents, to research and write editorial notes, and to make such additions as were deemed necessary in the final stage of production. I am grateful to the editors of the volumes published till now and to the editorial team at ICHR for their unstinted cooperation.

In the following pages the eminent editor of this volume, Professor K.N. Panikkar, has put together rarely used documents which throw a shaft of light on the freedom movement in its various aspects in 1940: the Indian response to the Second World War, the constitutional negotiations, the evolution of the strategy of individual *Satyagraha*, and developments in the area of communal politics. In the forthcoming second part of this volume the author addresses the issues in the peasant and labour movements, the struggle of the Dalit women's participation in politics, and the movment against feudal oppression and British hegemony in the Princely States.

In conclusion, I would like to thank Professor K.N. Panikkar, and acknowledge my indebtedness to the editorial team at the ICHR. In the latter half of 2005 as I was casting around for colleagues to work with me in the *Towards Freedom* project, I was fortunate to obtain as colleagues Professor Arjun Dev and Dr Amit K. Gupta; later Rajesh Kumar, Dusi Srinivas, V.I. Benaseer, and Satheesh P. joined us. Needless to say, the Editorial Committee which has met from time to time was of great help. My thanks go to my distinguished fellow-editors in charge of different volumes: Professors Partha Sarathi Gupta, Bimal Prasad, K.N. Panikkar, Sumit Sarkar, Arjun Dev, Mushirul Hasan, Basudev Chatterjee, Bipan Chandra, and Dr Sucheta Mahajan. I would also like to thank Oxford University Press, New Delhi, for their cooperation. Archiving is to historiography what brick-making is to architecture, and therefore our thanks also go to many unnamed archivists.

SABYASACHI BHATTACHARYA
General Editor

---

[31] Ibid., p. 444.

Editor's Introduction

The publication of the volume for the year 1940 in *Towards Freedom* series, which I was commissioned to edit by the Indian Council for Historical Research (ICHR) in 1989, has taken an unduly, and in a sense unpardonably, long time. What caused the delay was the concerted attempt of Hindu communal forces to stop its publication, which I attribute to their 'fear of history'. The controversy it generated, although germane to larger ideological debate in India in recent times, need not detain us. Yet, some facts deserve to be put on record in order to remove any possible misunderstanding. Despite being a massive and time-consuming work, undertaken along with the official academic responsibilities as a member of the teaching faculty of the Centre for Historical Studies, Jawaharlal Nehru University, the preparation of the volume was completed within the stipulated period and the manuscript was handed over in 1995 to Professor Sarvepalli Gopal, the General Editor of the series, and Professor Ravinder Kumar, the then Chairman of the ICHR. After the General Editor had approved it, the manuscript was with the ICHR for three years for 'processing' before it was sent for publication. What happened to the manuscript after that is a mystery. The ICHR, newly constituted by the government headed by the Bharatiya Janata Party (BJP), had decided to withdraw it in December 1999. Since there was no official communication from the ICHR the reason for the withdrawal was unknown.

After the BJP government went out of power and with the subsequent reconstitution of the ICHR, the manuscript was returned to me but now it had only 750 pages left from the 2500 pages of the original. The rest was reportedly missing. Or was it intentionally lost? The interesting fact is that the experts who were asked to review the manuscript by the ICHR during the BJP rule had done so with just about one-fourth of the original manuscript and yet, it was described by them as a 'massive collection of documents having immense historical value reflecting all shades of ideology' and recommended its publication, as 'it would make a significant contribution to the history of Indian Freedom movement'![1] One of them had suggested several additions to the manuscript, even when complimenting the Editor for not including a chapter on communalism! Since the ICHR had lost a major part of the manuscript I had to rework the volume and reconstruct it from the records available with me. The reconstructed volume was resubmitted to the ICHR in 2006, which is not substantially different from the original. However, the delay has afforded an opportunity to revise some chapters and add new material.

The project on *Towards Freedom* was conceived as a history of the movement for independence in India, during its last phase, from 1937 to 1947, as recorded in contemporary sources, reflecting the ways in which Indians perceived and participated in it. Being a mass

---

[1] Report of the Review of the Manuscript by the experts appointed by the ICHR, 1940, p. 28.

movement, perhaps the largest in the twentieth century, it has generated a variety of sources which shed light on its different dimensions. The colonial strategy of suppression of the movement, on the one hand and simultaneous negotiation and accommodation on the other— the details of which are carefully recorded and preserved in the official archives—form an important source of information, particularly about the intricacies of politics and constitutional negotiations. At the same time, the movement, seeking to establish its hegemony in society, generated a large amount of literature by the participants themselves. Bulk of it is in the form of speeches, writings, memoirs and private correspondence as well as the proceedings of political organizations and social institutions. Parts of it are now available in print in the form of selected works of prominent leaders like Mahatma Gandhi, Jawaharlal Nehru, Vallabhbhai Patel, Mohammad Ali Jinnah, Bhimrao Ambedkar and a few others. But a large amount of literature created by lesser known activists as well as institutional records has not received the same attention. An entirely different genre of documentation can be found in the reports in newspapers, with both national and local coverage and flavour. Professor Gopal, in his preface to the volume for the years 1943–44 edited by Professor Partha Sarathy Gupta, had indicated that the Series should not have an exclusive preoccupation with 'high politics', but should incorporate, 'within the limits set by the sources, documents relating to the activities, attitudes and ideas of diverse classes and sections of Indian society, all of which contributed to the attainment of independence'[2]. This principle informs the selection of documents and the apportioning of relative space to them. Coupled with that, the attempt has been to include as much unpublished and inaccessible material as possible and using already published material only when they are necessary for ensuring continuity, either in information or argument or when other sources are not available.

I

The outbreak of the Second World War on 1 September 1939, as a result of the invasion of Poland by Nazi Germany, and the unilateral decision of the British Government to make India a party to the War was a decisive factor influencing the course of the freedom struggle in 1940. Both the nationalist activities and the reaction of the colonial rulers were, to a large measure, guided by the compulsions of the War. The Government of India Act of 1935, which provided for a federal structure and limited devolution of power had paved the way for the participation of Indians in the administration of provinces. In the elections held in 1937 in pursuance of the Act, the Indian National Congress fared well, gaining clear majority in six out of 11 provinces and emerging as the single largest party in another three. In the remaining two provinces, Bengal and Panjab, Krishak Praja Party and the Unionist Party were the frontrunners respectively. The Muslim League fared poorly, particularly in Panjab and Bengal, where Muslims were a sizable population, thus undermining the claim of the Muslim League to represent the Muslims. Consequently, Congress ministries were formed in seven provinces and non-Congress ministries in the remaining four.[3] The participation in administration, however, was short-lived, as the Congress Governments in the Provinces resigned in protest against the declaration

---

[2] S. Gopal, 'General Editor's Preface,' in Partha Sarathi Gupta (ed.), *Towards Freedom, 1943–44*, New Delhi, 1997, p. vii.

[3] The Congress assumed office in Bombay, Madras, United Provinces, Bihar, Central Provinces, Orissa, and North Western frontier Province and non-Congress ministries in Bengal, Panjab, Assam and Sindh. Later Congress also formed the government in Assam. Pattabhi Sitaramayya, *History of the Indian National Congress*, Vol. ii, Delhi, 1969, p. 53.

of India as a belligerent country without consulting the Provinces. The co-operation of India being a crucial factor in the War efforts of Britain, both as a source of men and material; the Government of India was keen on arriving at an understanding with different political formations, so that mobilization for the War could be effectively accomplished. At the same time, Indians faced the difficult task of defining their position in relation to Imperialism, on the one hand and Fascism, on the other. They were keen to ensure that their opposition to Imperialism did not tantamount to support to Fascism, as they were alive to the danger posed by Fascism to democracy and freedom.

Although all political parties shared certain common ground in relation to their attitude towards Imperialism and Fascism, their response to the specific situation arising out of the War differed in details and in some cases even in approach. The Congress was keen to prevent the advance of Fascist forces, but at the same time was chary of the British which 'like a leach was sticking to its empire'.[4] Unwilling to come to 'the rescue of a tottering imperialism' the Congress ruled out any co-operation with the British War efforts.[5] The Congress Socialists took a similar view.[6] The Communist Party of India located the War in the contradiction within the capitalist world and highlighted its Fascist and imperialist character, choosing to oppose both.[7]

Apart from the Congress, the Socialists and the Communists, all other political opinion was in favour of supporting Britain in 'its hour of crisis'. The Muslim League, alarmed by 'the growing menace of Nazi aggression', promised wholehearted co-operation to the British in return for the trust in Muslim leadership.[8] The Hindu Mahasabha, which generally took a pro-government attitude, advocated active participation in War, not for anti-Fascist reasons, but for availing the opportunity, the War afforded, to militarize the Hindus and industrialize the country. The Hindu Mahasabha, therefore, offered co-operation to the government in all its War efforts by offering to participate in the proposed war committees.[9]

The response of the League of Radical Congressmen headed by M.N. Roy was influenced by its attitude towards Fascism which it considered a great threat. Since Britain was fighting an anti-Fascist war, it was of the view that supporting the War effort of Britain was a part of the struggle against Fascism without defeating which freedom was not possible.[10] The attitude of the political parties was fairly well-defined. While the Congress, the Socialists and the

[4] 'The Fundamental Issues at Stake, 10 May 1940, Statement to the Press by Jawaharlal Nehru', *Hindustan Times*, 11 May 1940. See Chapter 1, Document no. 4 in this volume on p. 6.

[5] 'Letter from Jawaharlal Nehru to Rajendra Prasad Regarding War Developments, 16 May 1940', *SWJN*, Vol. XI, pp. 29–35. See Chapter 1, Document no. 5 in this volume on p. 7.

[6] 'Jayaprakash Narayan's Justification of the Congress Socialist Party's Anti-War Stand', *Janata*, 1 February 1940 and 'Congress Socialists Explain their Attitude Towards War Efforts', *Pioneer*, 29 July 1940. See Chapter 1, Document nos 26 and 27 in this volume on pp. 55, 57 respectively.

[7] 'Forward to a Peoples' Constituent Assembly. Manifesto of the Communist Party of India', *Communist*, Vol. II, No. 4, January 1940, P.C. Joshi Archives on Contemporary History, JNU. See Chapter 1, Document no. 24 in this volume on p. 42.

[8] 'Conditional Support for War by the Muslim League Political Department', Secret Branch, File No. 11(24)/P-Sec/40, 18 June 1940, NAI. See Chapter 1, Document no. 14 in this volume on p. 22.

[9] 'Hindu Mahasabha's "Terms of Co-operation" All India Hindu Mahasabha Working Committee's Resolution, Bombay, 22 September 1940', Sir Maurice Gwyer and A. Appadorai, *Speeches and Documents on the Indian Constitution 1921–47*, Vol. II, Bombay, 1957, pp. 506–07; *Indian Annual Register*, 1940, Vol. II, p. 267. See Chapter 1, Document no. 17 in this volume on p. 25.

[10] 'Bombay Provincial League of Radical Congressmen: Resolutions Regarding India and War, and the Congress and the Present Crisis Independent India, 4 August 1940'. See Chapter 1, Document no. 20 in this volume on p. 32.

Communists chose to distance themselves from both Fascism and Imperialism, Muslim League and Hindu Mahasabha extended support to the colonial government. The politics during 1940 was to a large extent shaped by these differing attitudes towards the War.

II

Another important issue around which the politics during 1940 was organized was the nature of constitutional changes. If one of the aims of the War was to uphold the principle of democracy, as claimed by Britain, it was reasonable to expect that the same would be applied to the Indian situation. The cooperation of Indians in the War efforts, to a large measure, depended upon the extent to which this expectation was met by the colonial government. An initiative was therefore taken by the Viceroy on 10 January 1940 when he declared rather dramatically that the British government would confer on India Dominion Status of Westminster variety within the shortest practicable period. This was an extension of the federal scheme, which the Viceroy claimed, was designed as a stage on the road to Dominion status.[11]

The reaction to the Viceroy's declaration was a combination of appreciation, expectation and suspicion. The Congress saw it as a positive step, but inadequate to meet its declared aims. The Congress President, Babu Rajendra Prasad, welcomed it as the clearest of all 'declarations hitherto made'.[12] Mahatma Gandhi saw in it the substance of independence.[13] Yet, the offer of the Viceroy did not satisfy the Congress, as its declared goal was 'independence pure and simple'. A solution to the constitutional problem, the Congress held, was possible only through a Constituent Assembly. The moderates and constitutionalists within the Congress were, however, in favour of accepting the Viceroy's offer. The Muslim League also was opposed to the idea of Dominion Status, although for different reasons. Mohammad Ali Jinnah believed that the dominion status with a democratic constitution was totally unsuitable for a multi-religious country like India, as it would result in the rule of the majority community. The political fall-out of this view was the Lahore Resolution of 24 March 1940 which demanded the formation of independent states in Muslim majority areas in which 'the constituent units would be autonomous and sovereign'.[14] The most positive response came from the Hindu Mahasabha which welcomed the offer of Dominion status as 'practicable, clear and definite'. Responding to the Viceroy's statement, Vinayak Damodar Savarkar suggested that 'the British government should frame a Dominion constitution on the broad and universally acceptable principles of democracy after consulting all parties and interests in India'.[15]

Throughout the year discussions took place between the Viceroy and the leaders of different political parties, without, however, making any substantial advance. Disillusioned by the

---

[11] 'Viceroy's Proposal for Dominion Status', 10 January 1940, Speeches by the Marquess of Linlithgow, Vol. II, November 1938 to December 1943, Linlithgow Papers, Acc. No. 2329, NAI. See Chapter 2, Document no. 12 in this volume on p. 103.

[12] 'Congress President Rajendra Prasad's Response to Viceroy's Statement', *Statesman*, 12 January 1940. See Chapter 2, Document no. 13 in this volume on p. 105.

[13] 'Dominion Status Vs Independence', Editorial, *Amrita Bazar Patrika*, 31 January 1940. See Chapter 2, Document no. 25 in this volume on p. 122.

[14] 'Jinnah's Views on Constituent Assembly', reproduced from *Time and Tide*, London, 9 March 1940, in Waheed Ahmed (ed.), *Quaid-i-Azam Mohammad Ali Jinnah: The Nation's Voice—Towards Consolidation—Speeches and Statements, March 1935–March 1940*, Karachi, 1992, pp. 473–9. See Chapter 2, Document no. 41 in this volume on p. 146.

[15] 'Savarkar's Letter to Viceroy on Hindu Mahasabha's Policy of Responsive Co-operation, 19 August 1940', No. 125, Viceroy's Correspondence with Persons in India, 1940, Linlithgow Papers, Acc. No. 2307, NAI. See Chapter 2, Document no. 63 in this volume on p. 180.

reluctance of the government to take any positive step for fulfilling its demand, the Congress in its annual session at Ramgarh decided to launch a civil disobedience movement, as proposed by Gandhiji.[16] Instead of a mass civil disobedience movement, for which several leaders felt the situation was not opportune, the Congress decided, about six months after the Ramgarh session, to start Individual Satyagraha, the details of which were spelt out by Gandhiji. Vinoba Bhave, whom Gandhiji described as an 'out and out war resister', was selected to launch the Satyagraha.[17] The reasons for intensifying the struggle at a time when the British government was engaged in mobilizing its strength in fighting the Fascist forces were: the rejection of the demand for the formation of a national government, the denial of the freedom of speech against the war effort and the unilateral decision of the government to declare India as a belligerent country.

The wisdom of launching a civil disobedience movement at a time when Britain was engaged in a life and death struggle against Fascism was widely debated. Many, particularly the Liberals, felt that it was an inopportune moment and it would 'amount to stabbing Britain in the back'.[18] They believed that Britain was engaged in a struggle in defence of democracy and if she loses the War, freedom and democracy would vanish in thin air. Therefore India should desist from any agitation which is likely to weaken its power to overcome the Fascist forces. The Muslim League was also of the opinion that the Satyagraha would have serious consequences for the country. As to the Communists, they did not subscribe to the power of Satyagraha as a weapon of struggle for freedom. Yet, they decided to participate in it in order to transform it into a mass struggle. The Individual Satyagraha, about which there were initially reservations even within some sections of the Congress, turned out to be a major step forward in the freedom struggle. It greatly contributed to the spread of anti-colonial consciousness among the masses.

III

The growth of communal consciousness during 1930s, both among the Hindus and the Muslims, adversely impacted on the possibility of a united struggle against Imperialism in 1940. Chaudhury Rehmat Ali's idea of Pakistan had not too insignificant a following among the Muslims. The influence of the separatist and communal movement was reflected in what came to be known as the Pakistan resolution passed by the Muslim League at Lahore in 1940.

During the course of 1940, communal politics was further consolidated and communal riots erupted in different parts of the country. Both the Muslim League and the Hindu Mahasabha staked their claims to represent the Muslims and Hindus respectively. Objectively the positions taken by the Muslim League and the Hindu Mahasabha were remarkably similar: both sought to represent their respective communities and both discounted the national character of the Congress. Contesting these claims, the Indian National Congress stressed the importance of communal harmony, if *Swaraj* had to be won. The British perceived in these 'emphatic and uncompromising dissensions' the possibility of strengthening the separatist

---

[16] 'India and the War-Crisis: Resolution Adopted at 53rd Session of Congress, Ramgarh, 19–20 March 1940', *Indian Annual Register*, 1940, Vol. 1, New Delhi, pp. 228–9. See Chapter 1, Document no. 3 in this volume on p. 4.

[17] 'Mahatma Gandhi's Plan of Commencement of Civil Disobedience, 15 October 1940', *Harijan*, 20 October 1940. See Chapter 4, Document no. 6 in this volume on p. 420.

[18] 'Liberal Leader's Advice to Congress Leaders on Civil Disobedience Movement—Appeal to postpone it', *Amrita Bazar Patrika*, 2 May 1940. See Chapter 3, Document no. 56 in this volume on p. 314.

politics.[19] The Viceroy openly supported the creation of Pakistan as a possible solution to the communal problem.[20] The colonial state did not leave any stone unturned to exploit the communal differences for weakening the national movement.

The core of the communal argument was based on the cultural differences between the two communities. The Hindus and Muslims, it was held, belonged to two different races with different cultural identities and practices. Based on such an argument, Jinnah sought a separate political destiny for the Muslims and in the wake of the Lahore resolution took several steps to mobilize the Muslims all over India in support of the demand for Pakistan. Consequently, Muslim Independence Day and Pakistan Day were organized in several parts of India. But the two-nation theory had much earlier provenance. As early as 1924 Vinayak Damodar Savarkar had invoked it in his book *Hindutva: Who is a Hindu*, which later became the testament of Hindu communalism.

Although Muslim League made the two-nation theory the cornerstone of its politics with Jinnah as the 'sole spokesman', dissenting voices were not altogether absent among the Muslims, particularly in South India. For instance, in the Kerala Provincial Political Conference Muslim leaders took the view that the League was misleading the ignorant Muslim masses in the name of religion.[21] The All India Azad Muslim Conference, at which several Muslim organizations were represented, rejected the Pakistan scheme as impractical and harmful to the country's interest generally and of the Muslims in particular. The South Indian Nationalist Muslim Association was very critical of the Muslim League for being guided only by the interest of those Muslims in the provinces in which they formed a majority. The nationalist Muslims, therefore, opposed the agenda of the League and observed 20th April as anti-partition day.

The opposition to the Muslim League demand also came from other minorities. The idea of partition did not find favour with the Sikhs with whom the Hindu Mahasabha was trying to forge an alliance. The President of the Shiromani Prabandhak Committee, Master Tara Singh, did not approve of the League's claim to represent all minorities. He suggested a three-nation theory so that the Sikhs would be able to gain a homeland for themselves.[22] The Christians too were opposed to the Pakistan demand.[23] On the whole, however, resistance to the Muslim League's communal mobilization was weak. The communalization of society was not reflected

---

[19] 'Secretary of State on Viceroy's Interview with Indian Leaders, Letter from Secretary of State, 28 February 1940', Correspondence with Secretary of State, Vol. V, 1940, Linlithgow Papers, Acc. No. 2153, NAI; and 'Viceroy's Telegram to Secretary of State on his Assessment of the Communal Situation Secretary of State to Viceroy, 4 April 1940', Telegraphic Correspondence between Viceroy and Secretary of State, Linlithgow Papers, Acc. No. 2162, NAI. See Chapter 5, Document nos 1 and 3 in this volume on pp. 530, 531 respectively.

[20] 'Secretary of State on Muslim League's Attitude, Letter from Secretary of State to Viceroy, 24 April 1940', Correspondence with Secretary of State, Linlithgow Papers, Acc. No. 2153, NAI; and 'Viceroy's talk with Hindu Mahasabha leader B.S. Moonje', Editorial, *Tribune*, 25 September 1940. See Chapter 5, Document nos 4 and 5 in this volume on pp. 532, 533 respectively.

[21] 'Sikhs opposed to Muslim League Partition Scheme', *Hindustan Times*, 5 April 1940. See Chapter 5, Document no. 84 in this volume on p. 672.

[22] 'Repudiate Mr Jinnah and the League: A letter by a Nationalist Sikh to the Editor', *Hindustan Times*, 3 February 1940; and 'Sikhs opposed to Muslim League Partition Scheme', *Hindustan Times*, 5 April 1940. See Chapter 5, Document nos 83 and 84 in this volume on pp. 671, 672 respectively.

[23] 'Christian Leaders' Appeal to "Follow Mahatma Gandhi" in order to Abolish Communalism', *Hindustan Times*, 9 January 1940. See Chapter 5, Document no. 86 in this volume on p. 673.

in politics alone. Several incidents of communal tensions and riots occurred in 1940 which reflected the deterioration of inter-communal relations.[24]

IV

The movement for freedom, as evident from its different dimensions narrated above, was articulated through different streams, strategies and programmes, informed by different conceptions of freedom and nationalism. Implicit in the struggles, in the mode of their organization as well as their execution, was an effort to arrive at an understanding of what the struggle meant for future. Evidently the understanding was multilayered, reflecting the consciousness generated by different forms of experience and ideological persuasions. These differences, in a way, comprehended the internal dynamics of the freedom struggle and contributed to its complexity. Although the political struggle was explicitly for emancipation from foreign domination, freedom from external control, it was realized, would not necessarily ensure 'individual liberty of thought and action' without which freedom would remain incomplete.[25] A holistic view of freedom, transcending the political, found expression which would ensure an 'all-round emancipation of the country, an everlasting end to all methods of exploitation'. The concept of freedom, in this view, was not limited to political rights, but incorporated within it the notions of social justice and economic equality. The significance of these different conceptions, which documents in Chapter 2.A, highlight not only indicate the different streams within the anti-colonial struggle but also underlines contradictions within it.

On the concept of nationalism views differed even more sharply. The emergence of Fascism in Europe and the aggressive nationalism it represented had led to serious introspection in India. There was increasing realization about the dangers of 'narrow nationalism'. The need to go beyond the confines of patriotism was realized by many. Nationalism, it was felt, could be fulfilling only when related to the world order.[26] Yet, a sense of nationalism anchored in religious identity found articulation and elaboration, both among the Muslims and Hindus, a tendency which had its origin in the early part of the twentieth century and gaining considerable ground in the thirties. Some members of the Muslim intelligentsia questioned the very idea of Indian nationalism on the premise that nationalism was essentially a Western ideology. Moreover they held that Hindu society was incapable of nationhood due to its 'permanent and graded zones of superiority and inferiority'. According to them only the Muslims satisfied the requirements of nationhood, as they alone subscribed to 'the fundamental principles of human equality, liberty and citizenship'.[27] The Hindu communal conception of nationalism was akin to Mohammad Ali Jinnah's idea of two-nation theory on which he had based his demand for Pakistan. That the Hindus and Muslims belong to separate nations based on their cultural identities was first mooted by Vinayak Damodar Savarkar in 1924 in his book *Hindutva*. Such an argument became the ideology of the Rashtriya Swayam Sewak Sangh and the political creed of the Hindu Mahasabha. By 1930 this divisive reading of Indian nation had gained

---

[24] See Chapter 5, Document nos 86 to 92 in this volume.

[25] 'Independence I', Editorial, *Pioneer*, 23 January 1940. See Chapter 2, Document no. 1 in this volume on p. 80.

[26] 'Nationalism is a Process not the Goal: Mrs Naidu's Speech', *Tribune*, 5 February 1940. See Chapter 2, Document no. 3 in this volume on p. 82.

[27] 'Communist Party's Perspective on Constituent Assembly: Manifesto of the Communist Party of India (Extracts)', *Communist*, Vol. 2, No. 4, January 1940, P.C. Joshi Archives on Contemporary History, JNU. See Chapter 2, Document no. 8 in this volume on p. 88.

support from both communities. The president of Hindu Mahasabha, B.S. Moonje, identified two nationalisms in India: 'indigenous Hindu nationalism and foreign Muslim nationalism'. He also argued that 'the scientific and natural nationalism is the nationalism of the dominant religious community, organized into a system of disciplined militarism'.[28] Both of them were opposed to secular and territorial nationalism which emphasized equal citizenship, social justice and economic freedom. The internal differences within the freedom movement were informed by different conceptions of nationalism.

V

In collecting and editing these documents I had the able assistance of a research staff—Shipra Misra, Krishna Ananth, Ram Narayan and A.G. Lal—who were appointed by the ICHR at different points of time in the Project. Although the bulk of the documents were gathered by the National Archives of India from its repository in New Delhi and the archival holdings of different states, considerable work remained by way of collecting further materials, checking with the original and incorporating new documents in order to ensure the necessary continuity in each section. Their contribution in this regard has been substantial which I would like to acknowledge. The Towards Freedom Project Unit of the ICHR headed by Dr Amit Kumar Gupta and Professor Arjun Dev and well served by young scholars—Dr Rajesh Kumar, V.I. Benaseer, D. Srinivas and Satheesh P.—provided additional material wherever necessary, checked the documents with the original and prepared the manuscript for the press. I would like to place on record their contribution to the making of the volume.

The Towards Freedom Project was all but lost due to the unprofessional and politically-motivated attitude of the ICHR under the BJP regime. It was given up, at least I had, as a lost case, even though several institutions and publishers had volunteered to publish the volumes recalled by the ICHR from the press. In retrieving the Project and imparting to it a sense of urgency, the interest and initiative of Professor Sabyasachi Bhattacharya, the new General Editor, who was appointed to succeed Professor Gopal who unfortunately had passed away before the Project was revived, have been very crucial. I would like to acknowledge his positive contribution to the publication of this volume. Finally, to Professor Gopal whose friendly persuasion was responsible for my accepting this assignment, and under whose guidance and direction the major part of the work on this volume was completed, I dedicate this volume, with fond memories of his noble personality.

K.N. PANIKKAR

---

[28] 'B.S. Moonje's Concept of Hindu Nationalism as True Nationalism: Extracts from a Speech at Gorakhpur Hindu Mahasabha Conference, 2 September 1940', *B.S. Moonje Papers, Speeches and Writings*, Serial No. 42, 2 September 1940, NMML. See Chapter 2, Document no. 10 in this volume on p. 95.

Abbreviations

AICC	All India Congress Committee
AIHMS	All India Hindu Mahasabha
AIKC	All India Kisan Council
AIKS	All India Kisan Sabha
AILRC	All-India League of Radical Congressmen
AIML	All India Muslim League
AISF	All India Student's Federation
AISPC	All-India States People's Conference
AITUC	All India Trade Union Congress
AIVIA	All India Village Industries Association
AIWC	All India Women's Conference
AP	Associated Press
APCC	Andhra Provincial Congress Committee
	Assam Provincial Congress Committee
BJP	Bharatiya Janata Party
BPCC	Bengal Provincial Congress Committee
BPCC	Bihar Provincial Congress Committee
BPCC	Bombay Provincial Congress Committee
CA	Constituent Assembly
CID	Criminal Investigation Department
CLA	Central Legislative Assembly
CP	Central Provinces
CPI	Communist Party of India
CrPC	Criminal Procedure Code
CRR	Crown Representative Records
CSP	Congress Socialist Party
CWC	Congress Working Committee
CWMG	Collected Works of Mahatma Gandhi
DCC	District Congress Committee
DIR	Defence of India Rules
DPCC	Delhi Provincial Congress Committee
DSP	District Superintendent of Police
FB	Forward Bloc
GPCC	Gujarat Provincial Congress Committee
ICHR	Indian Council of Historical Research
ILP	Independent Labour Party
INC	Indian National Congress
IPC	Indian Penal Code
IRA	Indian Railwaymen's Association

JNU	Jawaharlal Nehru University
KPCC	Karnatak Provincial Congress Committee
	Kerala Provincial Congress Committee
LRC	Labour Representations Committee
MLA	Member legislative Assembly
MLC	Member Legislative Council
MPCC	Mahakoshal Provincial Congress Committee
	Maharashtra Provincial Congress Committee
NAI	National Archives of India
NMML	Nehru Memorial Museum and Library
NWFP	North-West Frontier Province
NWP	North-Western Province
PCC	Provincial Congress Committee
PPCC	Punjab Provincial Congress Committee
SDM	Sub-Divisional District Magistrate
SGPC	Shiromani Gurdwara Prabandhak Committee
SWJN	Selected Works of Jawaharlal Nehru
TNPCC	Tamil Nad Provincial Congress Committee
UP	Unionist Party
VPCC	Vidarbha Provincial Congress Committee

Calendar of Documents

Chapter 1: Response to the Second World War

Chapter 3: Towards Civil Disobedience

A. Independence Day Celebrations

Chapter 5: Communal Politics

A. British Attitude Towards the Communal Problem

Chapter 1. Response to the Second World War

A.   INDIAN NATIONAL CONGRESS

1.   No Chance of a Settlement: Jawaharlal Nehru's Letter to Mahatma Gandhi, 24 January 1940

SWJN, Vol. X, pp. 310–12.

My dear Bapu,

You asked me at Segaon about Molotov's speech about the war and I said something in reply which was rather vague. Since Molotov's speech was made much has happened and the position has grown very difficult. I have no doubt in my own mind that Russia has acted very wrongly in regard to Finland and she will suffer because of this. But what concerns us even more is the fact that behind the Anglo–French–German war, what is really happening is a consolidation of the imperialist and fascist powers to fight Russia. It is clearer now than it was even before that the war is a purely imperialist venture on both sides. Fine phrases are being used by politicians as they were used in 1914. It seems to me highly important and vital that we should not be taken in by these phrases and pious protestations. All this has an intimate bearing on our own position in India and any talks with the British Government. The object of the government is to gain our goodwill for their war. Under existing circumstances, quite apart from the question of India, I do not see why we should give our moral support to an imperialist war. Of course if Britain changed her attitude radically towards India and acknowledged our independence that in itself would mean that her imperialism has undergone a vital change. But what is more likely to happen is that this imperialism will fundamentally continue and the war will continue to be waged for its sake, though under stress of circumstances some vague declarations are made in regard to India. Even these declarations, it will be said, will be honoured at the end of the war. That seems to me a very dangerous position for us as we shall be involved, whether we want it or not, in supporting British imperialist policy in all manner of nefarious undertakings. I feel, therefore, that we must be very cautious and wary and should make it perfectly clear that we are not going to support these imperialist objectives of the war.

As I have mentioned above, the position is likely to grow much more complicated soon if the Western powers mobilize against Russia and their intrigue with Italy succeeds. They will call it a holy war against communism and under cover of that not only try to strengthen their own empire but break up the socialist state of Soviet Russia. That would be a calamity from every point of view, quite apart from our agreement with Russian policy or not. I would beg of you to bear this in mind and to view Indian talks in this perspective.

You will notice that one or two optimistic phrases in your article, as well as some minor occurrences like the [UP] Governor's visit to Anand Bhawan, have led to an extraordinary impression everywhere that some kind of a settlement is coming with Britain and that the Congress ministries will soon be back in office. Jinnah profits by this by making fun of our independence, the Muslim League gets an opportunity to raise its head a little, and as for our newspaper editors, they misbehave as usual. All this creates a wrong impression in the minds of the public in India as well as England. It makes even a possible settlement far less likely. What will happen again is that the Viceroy will complain that he was misled. The *Pioneer* has come out with a heading 'Congress Ministries' Resignation Bluff Called by Viceroy' and so on. Everywhere there is questioning, what is happening behind the scenes? Everywhere there is expectation of some big and sudden development.

All this not only does not square with the facts and with the existing situation, but creates a wrong atmosphere for any kind of mental or other preparations.

Personally, I feel sure that there is no real chance of a settlement, although the British Government would no doubt like it. But they are very far from agreeing to what is our minimum. The British Government today is more reactionary and imperialist than it has ever been and to expect it to give in to us is to expect something that cannot happen at this stage. To raise false hopes is unfair and inexpedient and may even weaken our position. I would suggest that it is fairer to lay stress on the other side so that the other party may know exactly how matters are and should adjust itself accordingly.

Yours affectionately,
Jawaharlal

2. 'An Atmosphere of Approaching Compromise': Jawaharlal Nehru's Letter to Mahatma Gandhi, 4 February 1940

SWJN, Vol. X, pp. 319–22.

My dear Bapu,

You will reach Delhi tomorrow and it appears that you are going to stay there for a week or more. I do not know what development there will be and whether it may become necessary for you to summon any of us. Personally I do not think there is the slightest chance of this happening as I do not see the least bit of a change in the government's attitude. In any event I wanted to inform you that it is exceedingly difficult for me to think of going to Delhi during the next two weeks. I am fully occupied all this time. Tonight I am going to Lucknow for two days. On the 7th I shall come to Allahabad for a day, leaving on the 8th morning for Bombay, where I have to attend important meetings of the Planning Committee which I have convened specially to consider certain matters. The whole meeting would be completely upset and would become infructuous if I did not go there. I shall be in Bombay from the 9th morning to the 12th night when I leave for Lucknow. On the 14th, 15th and 16th I shall be in Lucknow for our provincial Congress and delegates' meetings. During the next two days I expect to be in Gorakhpur for vast gatherings there. This is for the moment my programme for the next two weeks.

Everything that has happened during the last month or so confirms me in the belief that there is not the slightest ground for hope that the British Government will accept our position. In fact many things have happened which demonstrate that they are following a very definite imperialist policy. You must have seen that the British Parliament has just passed a bill amending the Government of India Act which limits the powers of provincial governments in regard to taxation. This was especially in view of the Property Tax in the UP which is thus vetoed. Apart from the demerit of such a decision which reduces the powers of the provincial assembly, the time and the method chosen for it are eloquent of the imperialist outlook of the British Government and indicate that this has in no way changed.

I wonder if your attention has been drawn to a recent social function in London, organized by the Royal Central Asian Society. Lord Zetland presided and a number of cabinet ministers were present. The ostensible object was to establish a centre of Muslim culture and religion in London; the real object was to encourage pan-Islamism and to exploit this sentiment in India and in the Islamic countries to the advantage of the Allies in the war. It is extraordinary how the war is developing along true-blue imperialist lines and how events are repeating themselves.

All this does not fit in with the notion that England is preparing to deliver up her empire. Nor is it at all encouraging to find that we are going to have again a procession of people headed by you to interview the Viceroy. The same old game is played again, the background is the same, the various objectives are the same, the actors are the same, and the results must be the same.

There are, however, some unfortunate indirect results also. An atmosphere of approaching compromise pervades the country when, in effect, there is no ground for it. It is enervating and depressing because it does not come out of strength but, in the case of many individuals, from the excessive desire to avoid conflict at all costs and to get back to the shreds of power which we had previously. Conflict is undesirable but obviously conflict cannot be avoided at all costs, for sometimes such avoidance itself is a more costly and harmful affair. For the moment, however, there is no immediate question of conflict. The question is of maintaining our position with dignity and not weakening it in any way. I fear that the impression is widely prevalent in England as well as in India that we are in no event going to have any conflict and therefore we are going to accept such terms as we can get. This kind of impression is demoralizing. I have noticed during the last fortnight that even our Congress delegates' elections have been influenced by this. Many people, who for fear of possible conflict were keeping in the background, have now pushed themselves in front again when the possibility of enjoying the plums of office and power seem to dangle again in front of them. The effort of several months to keep undesirables out of the Congress has partly failed because of this sudden change in the Indian atmosphere which has led them to believe that a compromise was imminent.

The British Government is also reacting in a way unfavourable to us, though it may use soft language. Of course it wants to come to terms with us because it wants our support in the war. But it is much more certain that it does not wish to give up any shred of real power or change its fundamental imperialist policy in order to come to terms with us. It is carrying on and will carry on its old intrigue on the communal issue, though occasionally it uses a few critical words against the Muslim League in order to soothe the Congress. So far as it is concerned, it will try to win us over, keeping its present position intact. If this is possible, well and good for it. If this does not take place, as seems likely even to it, then to carry on from time to time conversations with Indian leaders, to prolong the issue, to make it appear that we are on the verge of a compromise, and thus to soothe both world opinion and Indian opinion. This second policy has the additional advantage, from their point of view, of exhausting our energy and toning us down, so that, if ultimately a conflict does come, the requisite atmosphere is lacking for it. It is the general belief among official circles in England that their policy of parleys and postponement has had this result and the situation in India, which was threatening when the Congress ministries resigned, is much easier now and no dangers are to be feared.

It seems to me that while we cannot and must not precipitate a conflict and, while we need not bang the door to a possible and honourable compromise, because your methods are never to bang the door, still we must make it crystal clear that there can be or will be no compromise except on the conditions stated by us previously. As a matter of fact even these conditions have to be slightly reviewed from the point of view of developments in the war. We cannot now say, as we then said, that we want to know whether this war is imperialist or not. The British Government's answer to us as well as their consistent policy in the war and in foreign affairs has been one of full-blooded imperialism. We must therefore necessarily proceed on this admitted fact that it is an imperialist war, any profession to the contrary notwithstanding. The war and British policy grow more and more sinister every day and I would hate to see India entangled in any way in this imperialist adventure from which India can only lose, not only materially but spiritually. This point seems to me of vital importance today.

Thus it seems to me that the most important thing for us to do is to make our position perfectly clear to the world, to the British Government and to the Indian people. There is too much misunderstanding on this issue of compromise and this misunderstanding is entirely to our disadvantage and to the advantage of British imperialism which meanwhile is exploiting our resources for the war and even pretending to have a large amount of our goodwill. An approach by us to the British Government or to the Viceroy increases these misunderstandings and leads the British Government even further away from a right compromise.

Some recent speeches of Rajagopalachari have distressed me because they talk too compromisingly of Dominion Status and the like. The Congress speaks with too many voices and it is not surprising that confusion and embarrassment should result. On the question of independence at least there should be only one voice.

I have inflicted two long letters on you today for which I seek your indulgence and forgiveness.

Yours affectionately,
Jawaharlal

3.   India and the War-crisis: Resolution Adopted at the 53rd Session of Congress, Ramgarh, 19–20 March 1940

Indian Annual Register, 1940, Vol. I, New Delhi, pp. 228–9.

This Congress, having considered the grave and critical situation from the war in Europe and British policy in regard to it, approves of and endorses the resolutions passed and the action taken on the war situation by the AICC and the Working Committee. The Congress considers the declaration by the British Government of India as a belligerent country, without any reference to the people of India, and the exploitation of India's resources in this War, as an affront to them, which no self-respecting and freedom-loving people can accept or tolerate. The recent pronouncements made on behalf of the British Government in regard to India demonstrate that Great Britain is carrying on the War fundamentally for imperialist ends and for the preservation and strengthening of her Empire which is based on the exploitation of the people of India, as well as of other Asiatic and African countries. Under these circumstances, it is clear that the Congress cannot in any way, directly or indirectly, be party to the War, which means continuance and perpetuation of this exploitation. The Congress therefore strongly disapproves of Indian troops being made to fight for Great Britain and of the drain from India of men and material for the purpose of the War. Neither the recruiting nor the money raised in India can be considered to be voluntary contributions from India. Congressmen, and those under the Congress influence, cannot help in the prosecution of the War with men, money or material.

The Congress hereby declares again that nothing short of complete independence can be accepted by the people of India. Indian freedom cannot exist within the orbit of imperialism, and dominion or any other status within the imperial structure is wholly inapplicable to India, is not in keeping with the dignity of a great nation, and would bind India in many ways to British policies and economic structure. The people of India alone can properly shape their own constitution and determine their relations to the other countries of the world, through a Constituent Assembly elected on the basis of adult suffrage.

The Congress is further of opinion that while it will always be ready, as it ever has been, to make every effort to secure communal harmony, no permanent solution is possible except through a Constituent Assembly, where the rights of all recognized minorities will be fully protected by agreement, as far as possible between the elected representatives of various majority and minority groups, or by arbitration if agreement is not reached on any point. Any alternative will lack finality. India's constitution must be based on independence, democracy and national unity, and the Congress repudiates attempts to divide India or to split up her nationhood. The Congress has always aimed at a constitution where the fullest freedom and opportunities of development are guaranteed to the group and the individual, and social injustice yields place to a just social order.

The Congress cannot admit the right of the Rulers of Indian States, or of foreign vested interests to come in the way of Indian freedom. Sovereignty in India must rest with the people, whether in the States or the Provinces, and all other interests must be subordinated to their vital interests. The Congress holds that the difficulty raised in regard to the States is of British creation and it will not be satisfactorily solved unless the declaration of the freedom of India from foreign rule is unequivocally made. Foreign interests, if they are not in conflict with the interests of the Indian people, will be protected.

The Congress withdrew the Ministries from the Provinces where the Congress had a majority in order to dissociate India from the War and to enforce the Congress determination to free India from foreign domination. This preliminary step must naturally be followed by Civil Disobedience, to which the Congress will unhesitatingly resort as soon as the Congress Organization is considered fit enough for the purpose, or in case circumstances so shape themselves as to precipitate a crisis. The Congress desires to draw the attention of Congressmen to Gandhiji's declaration that he can only undertake the responsibility of declaring Civil Disobedience when he is satisfied that they are strictly observing discipline and are carrying out the constructive programme prescribed in the Independence Pledge.

The Congress seeks to represent and serve all classes and communities without distinction of race or religion and the struggle for Indian independence is for the freedom of the whole nation. Hence the Congress cherishes the hope that all classes and communities will take part in it. The purpose of Civil Disobedience is to evoke the spirit of sacrifice in the whole nation.

The Congress hereby authorizes the All India Congress Committee and in the event of this being necessary, the Working Committee, to take all steps to implement the foregoing resolution, as the Committee concerned may deem necessary.

4.   The Fundamental Issues at Stake: Statement to the Press by Jawaharlal Nehru, 10 May 1940

Hindustan Times, 11 May 1940; *SWJN,* Vol. XI, pp. 27–8.

The new developments in the European war, involving the invasions of Holland, Belgium and Luxemburg, mean that the war has now entered a new and Napoleonic phase. They are surprising only because we have got accustomed to the static phase during the last eight months. When the war started one almost expected some such thing to happen. It is clear that this extension of the war is going to have far-reaching and frightful consequences, and all of us must regret it deeply. There is no escape for the world now from an all-embracing war.

While a measure of admiration goes out to the efficiency and thoroughness of the military machinery of Germany, it is obvious that the menace of Nazi domination of Europe and to some extent other parts of the world is a real one. On the other hand, it is equally obvious that the British Government is continually falling between two stools, and it will continue to do so till it makes up its mind on fundamental matters affecting it, the British Empire and the world. On the one hand, it talks vaguely in terms of standing up for democracy in Europe and freedom of small nations and on the other hand it sticks like a leech to its empire, and is not prepared to divest itself of it. The result will surely be that events will divest it of that empire, and what might have been done with grace and advantage to itself and the goodwill of large numbers of human beings will be brought about by external forces which are too strong for it, because Britain cannot make up her mind. The clinging on to the empire and fight against fascism cannot go together with any effectiveness.

It has been an astonishing thing that the leader of this struggle in England could have been for all these months a person who must bear a great deal of the responsibility for the growth of the fascist menace. That in itself inevitably had to lead to England's incompetence in dealing with the situation. That leader may possibly be changed under the new stress of circumstances, but if the ideals he stood for remain and if Britain still thinks in terms of the empire, she will fail in her endeavour and fail grievously.

All of us, whether in England or in India, have to make this final choice. There is no room for halfway houses anywhere. While India is completely opposed to the idea of the triumph of Nazism, it is no good asking her to come to the rescue of a tottering imperialism which still presumes to speak of her with arrogance and in terms of domination. That language could have only one answer from India, and that answer has been given. Whatever happens, we shall cooperate with no person or country if we are ordered to do so, or if we are treated in any manner other than that as a free country.

The pace of events is so fast and the forces that have been unleashed are so great that individuals matter little now, and perhaps it is not possible to stop this avalanche till it has gone its way.

It is no good getting excited and losing our head and balance because events happen which we do not like. We shall face everything whatever befalls us, and let us be prepared for it.

⊧⊨═✶═⊨⊧

5. Letter from Jawaharlal Nehru to Rajendra Prasad Regarding War Developments, 16 May 1940

SWJN, Vol. XI, pp. 29–35.

My Dear Rajendra Babu,

... The new developments in the war situation are surprising and disconcerting in some ways, and yet they did not surprise me over much. Ever since the war began, and even earlier, I had given much thought to this matter and all these possibilities were before me. I have been convinced for a long time that the disruption of the British Empire must take place soon, and it is with this background that I have considered our problems. Hence all the talk of Dominion Status and the like seemed singularly unreal to me.

For some months past I have had a personal reason to try to anticipate events in Europe. My daughter is in Switzerland and I was concerned about her future programme. Long before the invasion of Holland, Belgium etc., I wrote to her and to her doctors putting these possibilities as well as others to them. After full consideration we decided that she should remain where she was, even if Switzerland became involved in the war.

I mention all this simply to indicate that the new development did not shock me or upset me. I had prepared for them. My mind had reasoned out the consequences and it was clear to me what our attitude should be. Subsequent events have justified abundantly the line we took up at the beginning of the war. That line must be continued without the least change. That line was dictated not only by the war situation but by what transpired between us and the British Government. Therefore the war in Europe made no essential or direct difference. Indirectly it might affect the attitude of the British Government but that was their concern, not ours. Our attitude and line of action must inevitably remain unchanged so long as no effective change took place on the other side.

What has surprised me more than the invasion of Holland etc., has been the quite singular obtuseness of the British. Not even the Nasmyth hammer of war and disaster has made any dent on their imperialist outlook or their attitude to India. The last debate in the British Parliament demonstrated that even the Labour members shared this outlook completely. I do not see how we can have any dealings with people who continue to think and treat us in this way.

To say that Nazism is worse than the present form of British imperialism is true in some respects, though I doubt if there is fundamentally much difference. But to say that because Nazism is worse therefore we must prefer the domination of the British is surely dangerous doctrine. It means that we are helpless people who must have a master and the little choice we have is to choose masters. To say this is to put an end to all our pretensions and to admit the fundamental basis of British rule. I think we can never do this, whatever the consequences. We stand for independence and we shall resist any and every foreign authority which seeks to dominate over us. If we fail, it is better that we perish than willingly put on a yoke which we think might be a lighter one than another.

But I don't think there is the slightest chance of a German or Japanese invasion of India. Hitler may win this war. This grows more likely. But Hitler will not dominate the world. He will fall as Napoleon fell. The real possibility of trouble in India is not from external invasion but from internal adventurism and conflict. That possibility has to be faced and we cannot seek the help of British imperialism to overcome it. Indeed British imperialism will hardly be in a position to help effectively. The only thing we can do is to add to our strength, in so far as we can do so, and to keep a nucleus going round which various elements can gather in time of need. The only possible nucleus is the Congress, and apparently the most effective way of gaining strength is to continue to prepare for satyagraha. That satyagraha is not immediately indicated even if we were ready for it. I think it would be wrong at this particular moment when Britain is in peril for us to take advantage of her distress and rush at her throat. That would be wrong from the larger as well as the satyagrahi point of view; it would also be wrong tactics. But we want the discipline and training of satyagraha to meet other perils also.

Any other course is full of dangers for us, apart from the great injury to our self-respect and dignity. Indeed such other course is likely to lead to that very internal commotion which we wish to avoid or provide against. The Congress would then lose the moral prestige it possesses and cease to be the nucleus round which the nation might gather. That other course might even facilitate external attack. In any event, whatever we may do will not make much difference from the military point of view. Modern warfare demands very special mechanized training and we cannot produce this, in large enough numbers, within a short time.

I am convinced that the British Empire has had its day. It will go to pieces and not all the king's horses and all the king's men will be able to put it together again. We surely are not going to indulge in the vain attempt to join together these pieces. If the British people are still imperialistic enough and proud enough to think of holding on to that empire, they deserve failure and no one can save them.

In any event I am quite clear that we cannot change our line of action in the least. Indeed we must resist the slightest variation of it and hold firmly to the recognition of Indian independence and the full and unfettered right of our people to frame our constitution through a constituent assembly. Every suggestion that a small body of men should do this must be rejected. Nor am I prepared to take any promises for the future. I do not understand why vital changes in India should wait till the war is over. The preparation for giving effect to them may take a little time but that has nothing to do with the ending of the war.

I would further add that even if all this is agreed to, it does not follow that we throw our manpower into the war. That will depend upon us, and our decision will no doubt be governed by the conditions then prevailing.

I do not myself like a negative attitude. I wish ours was more positive. Yet just at present I think a negative attitude has certain advantages—the positive side of course is preparation for satyagraha. I am glad that the Working Committee is not meeting for another four weeks. This period will help us to understand the situation better.

One other matter I might draw your attention to: so far as our newspapers are concerned, we get very one-sided and partial news. The radio helps in giving other viewpoints....

6. The Grim Progress of War, Disastrous Potentialities for India: Dr Khare Spells Another View, 21 May 1940

Hitavada, 22 May 1940.

Nagpur, May 21.

Dr N.B. Khare, Ex-Premier, Central Provinces and Berar, has issued the following statement to the Press:

At a time when the War has assumed a grim and serious aspect and when any serious reverses to the Allies may mean disastrous fate to the small and weak nations of the world and possibly a disaster to India, it is desirable for all right-minded Indians to consider seriously over the political stupor in which India has been placed by the mystic genius of Sewagram.

When the war broke out this Congress dictator[1] with his usual solicitude for Britain and every thing British advocated unconditional support to the Allies. His utterance however, did not fit in with the wild utterances of his disciples who demanded a declaration of war aims of Britain and its attitude towards India's demand for full-fledged independence, and the Mahatma Gandhi then followed his usual method of explaining away what he said. Unable to resist the growing demand of the left wingers in the Congress he appealed to their finer sentiments by giving a wailing description of what he would feel if Westminster Abbey were bombed. The Mahatma even went to the length of saying that freedom and democracy to India were of no consequence if France and Britain did not win the war. But strangely enough he wished success to the Allies though he could not advocate India's wholehearted participation in the war. To cloud the hypocrisy behind this technique the Ministries were asked to resign. Many of such ministries had already become unpopular and the shrewd saint of Sewagram used this opportunity of saving the faces of the Congress Ministers and leaving a free hand to the bureaucracy to deal freely with those who dared to advocate a policy of militant action for the freedom of the motherland.

But even here the Mahatma Gandhi was not satisfied, he issued a long spate of statements saying that Satyagraha was inevitable, but adding that the country was not imbued with the necessary spirit of non-violence and truth. The Ramgarh Congress was held in this atmosphere of vacillation and hypocrisy and it only passed a long winded resolution which advocated Satyagraha but asked the Congress workers to spin regularly and take to khadi, and thus advocated in actual practice no Satyagraha. The Ramgarh Congress was followed by a series of arrests of left wingers all over the country and men like Prof Ranga and others only received a certificate of breaches of discipline and harm to Congress for being more honest and straightforward in their views about war. The result has been a complete political stupor all over the country. The Congress Committee have in name transformed themselves into Satyagraha committees and are manned in many cases by persons who at the first sound of a shell will run in terror of their lives. It is no doubt true that Britain has by its foolish policy of keeping Indians unarmed left this country defenceless and weak, but the Mahatma is further emasculating even the spirit of defence of the country, and India stands in danger of being butchered by outsiders or even by the worst elements in the civil population of the country, if the situation worsens. Every Congress leader talks of spinning and the Charkha and proclaims the value of truth and non-violence from every house top and platform but none tries to reason out for himself, if the policy of the Mahatma is a part of a plan to sabotage all political agitation and Satyagraha during the continuance of the war. He has said in a number of statements that he does not want to embarrass Britain, then why talk of earnest wants, internal peace and no agitation in India at this time and the leader of the freedom movement in India also does not want Satyagraha just at this time. One can understand an honest policy of advocating wholehearted cooperation with Britain in this hour of peril but why should the Mahatma feel shy of his real feelings and fool the intelligentsia of this country by his political cant and quackery? The Congress leaders know and everybody knows that Satyagraha is as dead as cold mutton in India and yet when men, women and children of neutral countries in the west are being bombed and butchered in cold blood and when India also stands in the same potential danger, the Congress High Command headed by the Mahatma talks of spinning and charkha, and the mirages of Satyagraha. The ministries in the Congress governed provinces have gone handing over the reins of Government to irresponsible advisers and the disciples of the Mahatma spend their time in doing lip service to truth and non-violence. If those who do not see eye to eye with this mystic philosophy of inaction, speak otherwise or try to end this constitutional stalemate, the Gandhites consider this action as anti-national and inopportune. But the favoured few of the Mahatma men like Asaf Ali, Lala Dulichand and Satyamurthi can boast of their loyalty to Congress ideals and their nationalism, even if they advocate unconditional support to Britain for war or formation of coalition ministries.

How long young India, and educated India in particular, is going to tolerate this intellectual slavery, heaven alone knows, but even so the world situation demands that Indians must think and act seriously for the defence of their own homes and motherland.

No one can live only on tall talks of nationalism and freedom, and in this war humanity itself is threatened with all forces of slavery and destruction and it is the duty of all Indians, of all political parties to cast aside their differences, end the political stalemate and work in a manner which will ensure victory to the Allies. India has enough man power if only Britain gives up its foolish policy of mistrust in the Indians and even now arms them and mobilizes an army at least for the defence of India's own borders.

Britain should also immediately after the war give India complete freedom of the Westminster Status type and not show its imperialistic claws and prejudices, and if it does so, it will do so at its peril gravely endangering her own position and prestige in the world in the new situation in which she will find herself. Robust and honest nationalism and humanism demand this policy. This is the only way to extricate ourselves from the political quagmire into which we have been led by political cant and quackery and it will re-animate our jaded intellect for a renewed fight at the proper time, if and when it becomes necessary.

---

[1] The reference is to Mahatma Gandhi.

7.   The War and its Impact on India

Editorial, *Hitavada*, 7 June 1940.

It was expected by many people in this country that with the grave turn the events had taken in Europe, a fresh effort would be made by the British Government to solve the political dead-lock in India. But so far that expectation has not been fulfilled. The recent pronouncements of the Viceroy and the Commander-in-Chief[1] were only confined to appeals for unity and help. They did not make any contribution whatsoever to the solution of the political crisis. On the other hand we find a noteworthy change towards conciliation in the recent pronouncements of the Congress leaders. In the latest issue of the *Harijan*,[2] Mahatma Gandhi has expressed the opinion that the Congress should wait till the heat of the battle in the hearts of the Allied countries subsides and the future gets clearer than it is now. He further stressed that he and others of his way of thinking, do not seek independence out of Britain's difficulty. This statement of Mahatmaji should be sufficient to remove all doubts from the mind of British Government about the possibility of a civil disobedience movement by the Congress in the near future. Amplifying Gandhiji's statement further, Mr C. Rajagopalachari, the ex-Premier of Madras said in the course of a lecture that Mahatma Gandhi did not want to embarrass the British Government who were engaged in a life and death struggle.[3] He did not even demand a constitution now from Britain but only wanted a promise that India would be made free. He was willing to put trust once more in the words of the British Government. This elucidation of the Congress demand by the ex-Premier of Madras is another positive indication of the change that has come over the minds of the Congress leaders after the recent events in Europe. This is more amply demonstrated in the following statement by Mr C. Rajagopalachari made in his above mentioned lecture. He said, 'If the country is to be safe during times of trouble power should be transferred to responsible leaders of the people'. There can be no more eloquent proof of the desire of the Congress leaders to return to office than this statement of the Madras ex-Premier. We fail to understand why the British Government has so far failed to note this perceptible change in the recent pronouncements of the Congress leaders. In the course of a recent leading article the London *Times* writes that 'Indian opinion is steadfastly hostile to Hitlerism and all that it stands for but the present crisis and above all the possibility that war may soon extend to the Mediterranean region emphasize the need for translating that hostility into action'. When India is being asked to translate her hostility to Hitlerism into action, it should not be forgotten by the British statesmen that the time has also come to translate into action the war aims of Britain with regard to India. What India is asking today is not even translation of those war aims into action here and now, but only an assurance that Britain would grant self-determination to India at the end of the war. If the British Government desire to mobilize the entire man power and resources of India towards the destruction of Hitlerism, the only way to do it is to end the present deadlock in India. And there cannot be a more favourable opportunity to do this than the one which has now arisen.

---

[1] On 5 June 1940, the Viceroy announced the formation of war committees in each district as well as of a civic guard which was intended to be a voluntary organization affiliated to the police.

On 31 May, 1940 the Commander-in-Chief announced certain plans for the strengthening of the defence services.

[2] The article 'Not Yet' was published in *Harijan* of 1 June 1940. Also see *Hitavada*, 12 June 1940.

[3] For Rajagopalachari's speech, see *Hindustan Times*, 3 June 1940.

8. Congress View on War and Indian Problem: Statement by C. Rajagopalachari

Statesman, 10 June 1940.

Conditions for Full Cooperation

'We consider it our duty, however unpleasant and unreasonable it may appear on the surface, to deliberate with all the force we can command, our claim that Britain should at this supreme hour of her difficulty declare India once and for all time free and independent and then India should declare herself as a new-born ally on the side of England and France'. This statement was made by Mr C. Rajagopalachari, former Madras Premier, presiding over the Tinnevelly district political conference here today.

Mr Rajagopalachari said that it might seem ridiculous and utterly small-minded to harp on the Indian political issue when England and France are in the throes of a life and death struggle against a merciless enemy who had gained many advantages enabling him to pursue his relentless plan.

'Our political issues', he added 'being internal quarrels first between the Congress and the disgruntled elements in the body politic, and secondly between the people of India and the British Government must appear to be insignificant and meaningless in the eyes of the world, whose attention is reverted on the battle between England and France on the one side and Germany on the other. All the disadvantages of a superior culture and humanitarianism are hampering the movements of the Allies, while the very inhumanitarianism and the baser feelings of revenge and hunger for land and wealth are helping the German force to fight like savages but with modern weapons.

I feel it almost impossible to turn from this scene to our own problems. Yet every nation has its own life to look after, and India cannot afford to forget her own problems in the grim enactment of the Western struggle. We do not serve civilization by forgetting our rights. We cannot help the Allies by agreeing to be a subject people. On the contrary such surrender would help the Germans by furnishing both a justification and a motive and edge to their appetite.'

India's Defence

Mr Rajagopalachari asserted that the claim of the Congress for complete national independence had now been brought out in a tangible form. A country of the size and capacity of India could not be defended except by herself. To depend upon a hundred thousand European soldiers garrisoned in India with her own teeming millions crying for service, disarmed, was utter folly for both England and India. This was patent at all times but the march of events had brought to vulgar view the grave danger involved in the political status of subjection in which India had been kept with all its corollaries of helplessness when left to herself.

Mr Rajagopalachari explained that if the British Government declared India's sovereignty and right to self-rule, there was not the least doubt that all the innate capacity of Indians and of all communities for mutual adjustment would be brought into play under the stress of the present grave situation in the world.

The speaker then went on to say that he had said before on several occasions and still believed that the British Government, or at any rate those who thought and acted on their behalf, had no desire to set up any popular representative government for the duration of the war. 'At a time', he continued, 'when the future is fraught with grave potentialities of trouble and disturbances and even civil strife, if the British Government wish well by the people of India, they should hasten to constitute a strong and stable government in all the provinces that command the backing of the people behind them. It is a most inappropriate time to install or continue governments without stability, and wholly unrelated to popular feeling when stable governments commanding the enthusiastic and overwhelming support of the people are available for the asking, that is to say provided England has no objection to the freedom of India being clearly declared.

Popular Government

'In order to make up for the inherent weakness of the break down arrangements now prevailing, the Viceroy instead of seeking to resolve the deadlock proposes to set up war boards everywhere, and organizing civic guards for the preservation of order. It was our own intention when we were in office to raise an auxiliary police force if we could get over the departmental jealously. But coming as his proposal now does in the background of the non-cooperation of Congress ministries and of the electorate whom they represent, the civic guards plan is fraught with grave dangers of communal and political strife. The position requires the most anxious consideration before any step is launched in the direction proposed.'

Mr Rajagopalachari hoped the Congress Working Committee would take a decision on the matter.

Reiterating the plea for the establishment of a stable responsible government at the Centre and in all provinces as the most proper thing to do in the present anxious international situation, Mr Rajagopalachari said that he had no objection whatsoever to national government being formed in the place of party governments. But those who pleaded for national governments did not seem to be aware of the real meaning of national governments or of the amount of powers given to the heads of such governments.

'A national government is not the same thing as a composite government with scope for intrigue and obstruction,' he added. 'A national government would give no quarter to rift makers'. The first essential condition of a national government is the backing of a vast majority of the people, and no threat to its stability would be tolerated.'

9. Congress Working Committee Resolution on 'Political Situation', Wardha, 21 June 1940

National Herald, 22 June 1940; *Indian Annual Register,* 1940, Vol. II, pp. 175–6.

The Working Committee have been deeply moved by the tragic events that have taken place in Europe in startling succession and, in particular, by the misfortunes that have befallen the people of France. These events have already had far-reaching consequences, and they are likely to be followed by other happenings which will lead to novel situations and complex problems.

Ever since the commencement of the European war, the Congress has followed a policy which was based on its principles and on the attitude of the British Government towards the demand that India should function as a free and independent country. This policy was confirmed in the Ramgarh resolution. The manner of the application of this policy will necessarily depend on the situation which changes from day to day. The problems which were distant are now near at hand and may soon demand solution. The problem of the achievement of national freedom has now to be considered along with the allied one, its maintenance and the defence of the country against possible external aggression and internal disorder.

The war in Europe, resulting from a desire for imperialist domination over other peoples and countries, and a suicidal race in armaments, has led to human sorrow and misery on a scale hitherto unknown. It has demonstrated the inefficiency of organized violence, on however vast a scale, for the defence of national freedom and the liberties of peoples. It has shown beyond a doubt that warfare cannot lead to peace and freedom, and the choice before the world is uttermost degradation and destruction through warfare or the way of peace and non-violence on a basis of freedom for all peoples. Mahatma Gandhi has presented to the peoples of the world, crying for relief from the crushing burden of war, a weapon in the shape of organized non-violence designed to take the place of war for the defence of people's rights and freedom against armed aggression. He feels that at this critical phase in the history of man, the Congress should enforce this ideal by itself declaring that it does not want that India should maintain armed forces to defend her freedom against external aggression or internal disorder.

While the Working Committee hold that the Congress must continue to adhere strictly to the principle of non-violence in their struggle for independence, the Committee cannot ignore the present imperfections and failings in this respect of the human elements that they have to deal with, and the possible dangers in a period of transition and dynamic change, until the Congress has acquired non-violent control over the people in adequate measure and the people have imbibed sufficiently the lesson of organized non-violence. The Committee have deliberated over the problem that has thus arisen and have come to the conclusion that they are unable to go the full length with Gandhiji. But they recognize that he should be free to pursue his great ideal in his own way and therefore absolve him from responsibility for the programme and activity which the Congress has to pursue under the conditions at present prevailing in India and the world in regard to external aggression and internal disorder.

Many of the problems which the Working Committee have considered in this connection are not of the present, though they may be of the near future. The Committee wish to make it clear that the methods and basic policy of non-violence in the national struggle for freedom continue with full force and are not affected in the least by the inability to extend it to the region of national defence.

The War committees that are being formed are definitely aimed at increasing the war effort. In view of the Congress policy, they cannot be supported and Congressmen cannot participate in them or contribute to war funds. Nor can Congressmen associate themselves, under the present political conditions, with Government controlled Civic Guards.

Congress committees should organize, wherever necessary, people in villages and other areas for self defence and in order to maintain a sense of public security in their respective areas. This should be done on a non-communal basis and in full cooperation with all other groups interested in this task.

In view of the difficult times that loom ahead, it is essential that the Congress should function as an active and disciplined organization. Provincial Committees are enjoined to take necessary steps for this purpose. They should realize that it is of urgent and vital importance that the Congress should function in this way in these days of crisis, and should not be merely a roll of vast numbers of inactive members. All members of executive committees, in particular, are expected to take a continuous and active part in Congress work, and those who are unwilling or unable to do so are failing in their duty to the country, and are of no service to the organization.

The critical situation that faces the world today requires vigilant attention and action whenever needed. For this purpose the Working Committee will meet at frequent intervals, and all members must keep in readiness to obey an urgent summons. The All India Congress Committee should be summoned to meet in the last week of July.

10.   Congress President Maulana Abul Kalam Azad on Mahatma Gandhi's View of Non-violence and the Congress Position

Statement at AICC Meeting, Poona, 27 July 1940, *Indian Annual Register*, 1940, Vol. II, pp. 193–4.

It was hardly four months and two weeks since they met at Ramgarh but during this short period the world had changed almost out of recognition. This change was not only in respect of outward form but it had almost brought about a revolution in ideas and beliefs. It would not be possible for us not to be affected by all that has happened and, therefore, it becomes our duty to review our own position and take stock of the situation with a view to seeking what changes we should make in our own attitude.

Two important decisions of the Congress Working Committee are to be placed before you. One of these is known as the Wardha Statement. Although there is nothing new in it, as it relates to the basic policy of the Indian National Congress, it becomes our duty to consider it as this House represents the Congress.

It was not at the Wardha meeting in June last that Mahatma Gandhi raised the question of non-violence for the first time. He had raised it two years ago. In September 1938 the All India Congress Committee met at Delhi. At this meeting of the Congress Working Committee Mahatma Gandhi raised the issue of extending the principle of non-violence which the Congress had followed in regard to its internal policy for the last twenty years to other spheres.

Mahatma Gandhi wanted the Congress at this stage to declare that a free India would eschew all violence and would have no army to defend the country against aggression. The Congress should thus depend entirely upon non-violence for the purpose of dealing with internal disorders and external aggression. Mahatma Gandhi felt that he had to give the message of non-violence to the world and if he could not persuade his own countrymen to accept it, it would be difficult for him to preach it to others. The Congress Working Committee felt itself unable to accept his position and explained its difficulties to Mahatma Gandhi. The issue however did not assume any serious proportion then as the Munich Agreement postponed the war.

The question was again raised by Mahatma Gandhi when war broke out in September last. In November last when Gandhiji went to interview the Viceroy he asked me and other members of the Working Committee to relieve him of the responsibility of guiding the Congress policy and leave him free to pursue in his own way the policy of non-violence. The Committee, however, once again persuaded Mahatma Gandhi to postpone decision. At Ramgarh Mahatma Gandhi raised this question for the third time. On this occasion Mahatma Gandhi also referred to other weakness in the Congress organization and expressed a desire to be relieved of responsibility. This came as a shock to the Working Committee and if I had not practically forced Mahatma Gandhi to postpone decision of the issue once again, a crisis would have arisen as early as at Ramgarh.

You will thus see that this issue had been hanging fire for over two years and when we met in Wardha in June last Mahatma Gandhi wanted the Committee to make up its mind once for all as the international situation had become delicate and he felt that a decision on such a vital issue could not be postponed any longer. Even then I tried to persuade Mahatma Gandhi once again to postpone the matter as I knew the dangers and the difficulties of a decision. There is not a soul in the Congress who is not anxious to go the whole length with Mahatma Gandhi, if he can help it; but we cannot close our eyes to hard facts. We know that arms and ammunitions have not been able to save the freedom of France, Holland, Belgium and Norway but we also know that human nature even after realizing the futility of armed resistance is not prepared to give up force. We had not the courage to declare that we shall organize a State in this country without an armed force. If we did it would be wrong on our part. Mahatma Gandhi has to give the message of non-violence to the world and, therefore, it is his duty to propagate it but we have to consider our position as the representatives of the Indian Nation meeting in the Indian National Congress. The Indian National Congress is a political organization pledged to win the political independence of the country. It is not an institution for organizing world peace.

Honestly we cannot go as far as Mahatma Gandhi wants us to go. We admit that it is a weakness on our part but it is a weakness which we share with the entire humanity. Though we cannot go with Mahatma Gandhi the whole hog, we do not wish to stop him from pursuing his own path. Yet realizing the loss that the Congress would suffer on being deprived of Mahatma Gandhi's guidance, I was tempted to approach him once again to defer his decision on this issue. I had thrice succeeded in my attempt but this time, I failed because Mahatma Gandhi pointed out that it was no use postponing his decision on this vital issue for the moment was fast approaching when the Congress would have to take a final decision and therefore, it was better that each party decided to follow its own path. I placed the whole matter before the Working Committee and invited separately the opinion of each member. Most of us felt that we were not able to take up the grave responsibility of declaring that we would completely eschew violence when we had to deal with widespread internal disorder in this country or external aggression. But we all were quite clear in our minds that so far as the struggle for winning our independence was concerned non-violence would continue to occupy the same place in the Congress programme that it had occupied all these 20 years. We all felt that the slightest deviation in this respect will mean political suicide for the Congress.

Whatever success we have achieved in our struggle during all these years has been due to our unflinching faith in non-violence, and if we have not succeeded to the extent to which we ought to have succeeded, it is due to our inability to practice non-violence to the fuller extent. If we ever give up this idea, we shall be burying the Congress. I feel I must take you further in confidence and inform you that there are four members of the Working Committee, Babu Rajendra Prasad, Dr Prafulla Chandra Ghose, Mr Kripalani and Mr Shankerrao Deo who feel that they can go the whole length with Mahatma Gandhi. You already know about Khan Abdul Ghaffar Khan.

There are people who think that by passing the Delhi resolution[1] the Congress Working Committee has made a departure from past resolutions. I wish to emphasize that this is a wrong view. Even if we wished to take a new step we could not do so because we have behind us a series of resolutions and statements issued from time to time by the Congress Working Committee during the past few months. We cannot demolish all these. We have not the right to do so. We have not the power to do so. Changes in the international situation however are so serious that we cannot shut our eyes to them and proceed blindly. We have not abated our original demand in any way. We have demanded the unequivocal declaration of India's Independence. As a provisional measure we have asked for the establishment of a representative national government.

Although Mahatma Gandhi would not be responsible for the policy of the Congress any longer, his advice would always be available to the Working Committee and the Congress. Our relations will continue with him as long as he lives and I pray to God that he may be spared long to guide us. We must however realize that the nature of his guidance will not be the same as before and this adds greatly to our responsibility. We have a great objective to achieve; we have an ideal before us which is sufficient to inspire any group of people. There may be ups and downs and difficulties may beset our path but we need not be disheartened or dis-spirited by these.

We have to solve every difficulty that presents itself to us and we have also to recognize the hard fact of Mahatma Gandhi's separation from us. We must bear it bravely. In this difficult hour, it is our duty to be united. I therefore appeal to you to sink all differences and to face bravely the trials that lie ahead of us. This is what the country demands from us and this is what the Congress expects us to do. If we fail in this hour of trial, the world will have a poor opinion of us; but I am sure that we shall not fail.

---

[1] The reference is to the resolution on Political Situation adopted by the Congress Working Committee at its meeting in Delhi held from 3 to 7 July 1940. For text of the resolution, see Chapter III, Item No. 23.

11. 'The March of Mighty Events': Jawaharlal Nehru's Address at Lal Diggi, Gorakhpur, 6 October 1940

National Herald, 9 October 1940; *SWJN,* Vol. XI, pp. 156–60.

The war is changing the map of the world and will continue to do so. This war has many problems behind it which have to be understood. The world has never seen such a war. All previous wars were either political or religious or social and the revolutions that followed in their wake affected one or two nations. But the present war is something quite different.

The world has never been so closely linked as it is today. An important incident in one part of the world is bound to influence the entire world. It is indispensable for us to understand the history of the world as it exists today. We cannot blind ourselves to what is taking place in China or Japan or any other country of the world. The problems that the war is going to solve are problems of the world. These problems cannot be of one particular country. It is impossible to solve the problems of America or Japan individually and to leave apart the problem of India, because the world is so closely linked together that solving of one country's problems involves the solving of the problems of other countries. So the steps that we in India have to take must be firm and steady. The present revolution, which confronts the world, is not only political, but is also social and economic.

During the past few years Europe and America have accumulated immense wealth by draining the wealth of Asia. But at the same time unemployment has gone on increasing in those continents, so much so that today the registered figure of the unemployed in America stands at 12,00,000 and in England at 22,00,000. Unemployment always retards the progress of a country. This problem is one of immense importance. The present economic structure of the world has completely failed to solve this problem. It has no solution for it.

A great upheaval swept over Russia and it has changed the present economic structure of the world to a certain extent. That system has solved the problem of unemployment and the Russian Government has assured the people that it has sufficient work for its countrymen. There are many things in Russia with which I might not agree but I think that Russia has at least devised some means to solve the problem of unemployment.

It is true that Hitler has usurped the freedom of Germans but he too has driven unemployment out of his country. If we were to choose between freedom and starvation, we would certainly forego freedom than undergo starvation. That is why the whole German nation is behind Hitler today. Other countries, except Russia and Germany, have failed to solve the problem of unemployment. The progress of Great Britain has come to a halt before this wall of unemployment as the system of administration has no solution for it. This problem has to be solved and I think that some phases of it are disappearing in the present war.

We are living in a very eventful period of history and we have to face many odds. There are some among us who are terrified at the march of these events, but there are also those who welcome it. The events will march on whether we face them with a weak and timid heart or we face them boldly, and it is only natural that the strong will overpower the weak. But if we face them strongly we have the power to bend the trend of the revolution in our favour.

Big achievements demand equally big sacrifices. If we want to win freedom, we must make sacrifices worthy of that freedom. We must bear in mind that the march of the mighty events of the world will have to be faced and we cannot escape them. But at the same time we must see that we pay the price and do not fail to turn the hour to our advantage.

The war has made it quite clear that there is no place for small nations in the present-day world. We cannot go single-handed. We can no doubt exist in a federation of smaller nations. There is hardly any room for bigger nations. It is becoming impossible for any country to command an empire spread over the entire world. For to do so that country must command all naval bases and must rule over important sea routes; otherwise it might be challenged by other countries. The invention of aeroplanes cannot be ignored nor can we ignore the changes it has brought in the world.

However mighty a nation might be, it cannot command all air bases and sea routes of the world and so it is impossible for an empire to exist. But such empires as are linked together or federated can exist. Hitler succeeded in forming the European countries into a federation. Such a federation can exist, but empires like those of Britain cannot exist. That is why just before the surrender of France, Great Britain had proposed to link the two countries together.

The other important thing which has become quite clear is the changing economic structure of the world. Great Britain is spending a huge sum of between 15 to 20 crores of rupees a day on the war. Nations involved in the war are floating huge loans and borrowing enormous sums of money from other countries. How long can they do this? They can hold on for some time by introducing paper money and inflating the currency, but the way the war is proceeding a stage will soon come where things would become impossible.

This aspect of the war is bound to influence the economic problems of the world. May be it might entirely displace gold and silver out of the currency system of the world. What changes will take place cannot be forecast. But it is quite clear that the present system is bound to go out. The revolution which will follow the war will work many changes.

Perhaps to the common mind the word *inqilab* might connote the idea of freedom from British bondage, and no doubt this is included in it, but no *inqilab* can be a real *inqilab* if it cannot wipe out poverty once for all. What are we to do then? India has been dragged into the war unwillingly and in spite of protests. We could have refused to be dragged into it and we had every right to do so, but we restrained ourselves....

We are passing through a revolution and every step that we take forward must be steady. This question of India's participation in the war has been subjected to prolonged discussions and we have tolerated this insult for over a year, but we cannot tolerate it any longer. Mahatma Gandhi, who is a great man and whose views are also great, does not think it proper to embarrass the British Government at such a time. But our silence is interpreted as our weakness.

Attempts are made to aggravate communal matters and it is asserted that India is not fit for democracy, nay, every attempt is made to demolish the edifice of our nationalism. The British think that if their country is being ruined, they must ruin India too. We cannot sit silent when an attempt is being made to divide India. Thousands have been arrested and forced subscription is being levied for purposes of war. Things have become intolerable.

We did not want to resort to satyagraha. All these things came up for consideration before the Working Committee and the AICC and Mahatma Gandhi was empowered to lead the country. His talks with the Viceroy failed. The time for action has come. When the satyagraha will begin, I cannot say, but it is only a question of days.

The fight for our freedom will also become a part of the world up-heaval. It is being asked how the step taken by the Congress can be confined to a chosen few. When the movement starts, none of us know what form it will take. None knew that the Dandi march of Mahatma Gandhi would inaugurate a country-wide agitation. This time too, it will not be confined to a few. All of us will have to join it in some form or other. At such a juncture a question arises as to what will be the plight of the country if some other country invades India. This question has taken the form of a threat. Happen what may, we are not going to beg the Englishmen to come to our defence. It will be a matter of shame for us. They hold us in bondage and even at this hour of peril, when their very existence is threatened, they are unwilling to restore freedom to us. We will face all odds even if we perish in the attempt.

It is not easy for any country to step into India unless that country brings the whole world under its sway. Japan might try to invade India but bear it in mind, that the battles that are being fought will not be decided in India. They will be decided in the Pacific or in Europe and America. However, the fear that another country might enslave us cannot daunt us and keep us away from a fight to tear away the shackles of bondage.

I have undertaken my present tour of the eastern districts of the UP to bring this message of the Congress to every door. But there is a definite reason why I have selected Gorakhpur first of all. I have come to Gorakhpur so many times, because here I can see the most terrible picture of the poverty of the Indian masses. Nowhere in India are tenants so downtrodden. Anyone who looks at the abject poverty prevailing in this district can say that it betrays the worthlessness of those who are responsible for it and that they must be turned out of the country.

How can those, who raise communal issues, link this question of poverty with their communalism. Communal organizations of the country want to divide India into parts, they want to ruin its unity and even wipe out its name. The sacrifices that we have made for decades were made for unity and freedom and for effacing poverty. And the freedom of the country means the removal of the poverty of the tenants and the labourers of Gorakhpur. The question of India's freedom is related to the conditions of tenants and *mazdoors* and is in no way connected with a few seats on the Viceroy's Council....

B. ALL INDIA WOMEN'S CONFERENCE

12. War Resolution: All India Women's Conference, 14th Session, Allahabad, 27 January 1940

Indian Annual Register, 1940, Vol. I, pp. 350–2.

After the announcement of the office-bearers nominations, the Conference discussed the War resolution. Dr Natarajan moved:

'The Conference of Indian women once again expresses its abhorrence of war. It deeply regrets that in spite of the overwhelming desire on their part to avoid war women failed to exert that moral influence which was necessary to save their respective countries from plunging the world into the present grim struggle. As women we sympathize with the sufferings of the people in the warring countries and pray for a speedy cessation of hostilities and for a lasting peace.

'This Conference is convinced that there can be no world peace so long as any nation remains a subject people. It is of opinion that Great Britain should declare the terms upon which it would be willing to make peace and include among those terms the recognition of equality of race and of the rights and liberties of the individual and respect for the integrity of small as well as great nations. The women of India not only demand freedom for their own country, but desire it for all those people who are being exploited or oppressed or are the victims of aggression by the armed might of their stronger neighbours.

'This Conference reaffirms its faith in non-violence as the only means of ushering in a new era of peace and goodwill in the world, and calls on all women, in particular Indian women to try to realize it in their individual as well as their collective lives'.

Miss Zulfikar Ali seconded the resolution. She said that she had great pleasure in seconding the resolution not only because she was in entire agreement with it but also because she thought that it echoed the thoughts of the young women of her province (Punjab) on whose behalf she was speaking. Their hatred of modern methods of warfare, which entailed unimaginable sufferings, was intense and they heartily sympathized with the sufferers. At the same time they felt that the time had come for Great Britain which was fighting to restore the liberties of some of the nations of Europe, to make no further hesitation in recognizing the right of the Indian people to attain freedom. She added that [was] the best way in which Great Britain could prove to the world that it stood for liberty to India.

Miss Shah Nawaz supporting the resolution said that she had been asked to speak very mildly but it was very difficult for her to speak mildly because she was not under fifty years of age; because wanton bloodshed was going on; because the men of India and the men of the province she represented, were being sent every day to fight for the cause which was not theirs; because she saw that during the last few years Japan had invaded China, Italy had swallowed Abyssinia and so on. She asked how countries, which had deprived other nations of their liberty, could say to-day that they were fighting for democracy. She did not want to doubt their word but she wanted them to give proof of it and what better proof could be, she asked, than to give freedom to those countries whom they had oppressed. Therefore, the speaker said, on behalf of the younger generation and on behalf of the ladies of her province, she had great pleasure in supporting the resolution. Women in this world had always stood for peace; they would still be prepared for sacrifice for freedom but not for power politics. They should all unite and meet the charge that India could not get freedom because she was not united. She felt that in India their points of union were far greater than those of various nations in Europe. In Europe there was greater disunity. Therefore they could not possibly bring out the plea that Indians could not get freedom because they were not united. But since that challenge had been thrown, she appealed to women to meet it and get men united. If the women of the world who stood for peace insisted that there should be no more mutual quarrels, the war would end.

Rani Lakshmibai Rajwade, supporting the resolution, in the course of her speech, said that the resolution as it stood spoke for itself. She had only to point out that in framing the resolution pains had been taken to arrive at a sort of highest common multiple of the various groups within the Conference. That had been done with the idea to maintain the common front which that Conference had so far preserved. She knew that many of them, including herself, felt deeply on the issues involved—Nazism, international peace, self-determination, India's future, the close connection between Indian self-determination and participation in the war and so on. And she might even risk disagreement to express their full convictions. But the whole point was that such a stage had not arrived and above all the resolution as worded embraced all those issues and yet did not antagonize any other prejudices or preferences.

As to the general question of war the only reasonable attitude was more or less, she said, along the same lines as those followed in the Congress resolution. It seemed to her clear that

India should participate only in a war which was based demonstrably on the principle of self-determination and the only demonstration possible was the application of that principle to India. That much seemed to be clear. It was also clear that if that was not possible then India must devote herself to her reconstruction effort until self-determination was achieved by their national effort.

Mrs Chandrakali Sahi and Miss Chandrawati Tripathi also supported the resolution. Miss Shepherd moved an amendment suggesting that in the sentence 'Great Britain should declare the terms', '*Allies*' should be substituted for 'Great Britain' because both England and France were fighting in alliance. The amendment, however, fell through for want of a seconder. The resolution was passed unanimously.

C.   MUSLIM LEAGUE

13.   Resolutions on 'War Effort' and 'Enemy Aggression' Passed by the Working Committee of the All India Muslim League, 15–16 June 1940

Historic Documents of Muslim Freedom Movement compiled by Jamil-ud-din Ahmad, Lahore, 1970, pp. 383–4; *Indian Annual Register,* 1940, Vol. I, pp. 317–18.

War Effort

The Working Committee of the All India Muslim League, while being of the opinion that further clarification contained in the letter of His Excellency the Viceroy, dated the 19th of April, 1940 with regard to the assurances asked for by the All India Muslim League is not satisfactory, endorses the following from the statement issued by the President Mr M.A. Jinnah, to the press on the 27th of May, 1940.[1]

'Up to the present moment, we have not created any difficulty nor have we embarrassed the British Government in the prosecution of war.

'The Provinces where the Muslim League has a dominant voice have been left free to cooperate with the British Government, pending their consideration with regard to the assurances we have asked for and in particular that the British Government should make no declaration regarding the future constitutional problems of India and the vital issues that have been raised in that connection without our approval or consent.

'Nevertheless, without prejudice to the adjustment of the larger issues later on, we were even willing as far back as November last to consider the proposal of the Viceroy to bring about an honorable and workable adjustment in the provincial field, which would have been followed up with our representatives being appointed to the Executive Council of the Central Government to the extent permissible within the framework of the present constitution and existing law.

'But this proposal was summarily rejected by Mr Gandhi and the Congress. A similar attempt was again made by His Excellency early in February, which met the same fate. Since then it seems that the Viceroy has been waiting for the Congress to pass its word.'

'With regard to Mr Amery's statement and the broadcast appeal of His Excellency the Viceroy, may I say that it is up to the British Government to show trust in Muslim leadership there are many ways of doing so and, as confident friends seek our wholehearted co-operation and we shall not fail.'

Enemy Aggression

'The Working Committee looks with alarm at the growing menace of Nazi aggression which has been most ruthlessly depriving one nation after another of its liberty and freedom, and regards the unprovoked attack by the Italian Government against the Allies as most unwarranted and immoral at a time when France was engaged in a brave struggle against very heavy odds.

'The grave world situation demands serious efforts on the part of every Indian for the defence of his country and the Working Committee calls upon the Government of India to prepare the country in an organized manner to meet every eventuality. The Committee is constrained to state that the proposals for the defence of India indicated in the statements of their Excellencies the Viceroy and the Commander in Chief as well as the statements of some provincial Governors are wholly inadequate to meet the urgent requirements of the situation. The Committee, therefore, authorizes its President to enter into communication with His Excellency the Viceroy with a view to explore the possibility of devising adequate and effective measures to mobilize the country's resources for the purpose of intensifying war efforts and the defence of India. The Committee is of the view that unless a satisfactory basis for close cooperation is agreed upon on an All India basis, and not province-wise, between the Government and the Muslim League and such other parties as are willing to undertake the responsibility for the defence of the country in the face of imminent danger, the real purpose and objective will not be served and achieved.

'The Working Committee is of the opinion that in view of the immediate grave danger that is facing the country the real purpose will not be served by the Mussalmans and others merely joining the proposed provincial and district War Committees with their present scope and functions.

'In view of the numerous enquiries that have been received from the various provincial and district Leagues and individual members seeking guidance and instructions as to what course they should adopt towards the proposed War Committees announced by His Excellency the Viceroy and some Governors, the Working Committee is of the opinion that at present Mussalmans should not serve on these Committees and should await further instructions from the President pending the result of the communication with the Viceroy.'

---

[1] The Viceroy's letter to Jinnah, dated 19th April 1940 regarding the assurances sought by the Muslim League on various matters, e.g. that the British Government should not use Indian troops against Muslim powers or countries and they should consult the Muslims before convening a Constituent Assembly.

14.   Conditional Support for War by the Muslim League

Political Department, Secret Branch, File No. 11(24)/P-Sec/40, 18 June 1940, NAI.

The governing body of the Muslim League met at Bombay on June 15th. It has endorsed a statement published by Mr Jinnah at the end of May, which promised the British Government wholehearted cooperation in return for 'trust in Muslim leadership'. After expressing alarm at the growing menace of Nazi aggression and denouncing the unprovoked attack of Italy on the Allies, the resolution calls on the Government to organize the defence of India to meet every eventuality. It describes the measures already announced as wholly inadequate; and Mr Jinnah is authorized to enter into communication with the Viceroy with a view to intensifying the war effort. A satisfactory arrangement is demanded for close cooperation 'on an all India basis and not province-wise' between the Government on the one hand and on the other hand the League and such other parties as are willing to undertake responsibility for the defence of the country. Meanwhile and until Mr Jinnah issues further instructions after communicating with the Viceroy, Muslims should not serve on the war committees now being constituted.

This decision and a somewhat similar one announced by the Hindu Mahasabha (which however permits individuals to join the war committees and civic guards) shows that the international crisis has not yet cured in India that tendency of political manoeuvre which arises from communal distrust.

15. Viceroy's Rejection of Congress Demand—Nawab of Chhatari Explains

Star of India, 5 October 1940.

'His Excellency the Viceroy was right when he declined to agree to allow the Congress to spread anti-war propaganda in the country. No Government can afford to do so. Even in England this is not permitted,' says the Nawab of Chhatari in a statement.

He adds, 'As to the question of India's intentions towards this war, if there is anything on which there is complete agreement among Indians, it is the fact that they all sympathize with the British nation in her present struggle and that they wholeheartedly condemn Nazism. It was Mr Gandhi himself who had said that he was for unconditional support for Great Britain. If her cause was not based on truth and justice, why was the Mahatmaji ready for unconditional support?

Universal Support for Britain

'There is no political organization, no prominent Indian who has not come out with a statement sympathizing with Great Britain and condemning Germany and her accomplice, Italy. Therefore, Indian opinion is quite clear on the point.'

D.   UNIONIST PARTY

16. War and the Unionist Party

(a) Punjab Governor Sir Henry Craik's Letter to the Viceroy, 19 February 1940

> Correspondence with the Governor of Punjab and his Secretary, Linlithgow Papers, Acc. No. 2224, NAI.

[Private and Personal]
D.O. No. 211-F.L.

Dear Lord Linlithgow,

You may remember that I mentioned to you a plan of Sikandar's[1] to send out parties of students to tour the Punjab to do propaganda work in connection with the war in rural areas. I think you will be interested in the enclosed note by J.D. Anderson, describing the arrangements made for these parties. The idea is entirely Sikandar's own.

[Enclosure]

His Excellency asked me for a note, describing briefly the arrangements for the parties which will be sent out shortly to do publicity work in villages.

There will be five parties, one for each Division, but at present we are sending out three only because there is not money to buy the equipment for all five; each party is in charge of a Professor of whom two have recently been in Germany. The speakers are eight students selected by the Premier himself, as far as possible from the Division in which they are to tour. Each speaker is to carry the flag of one of the Allied Countries and is to represent that Country at meetings. They have received special printed and written material and coaching from the Provincial Secretary, Boy Scouts Association, and from D.I.B.'s office. They have also been drilled and dressed in a grey costume not likely to show dust.

Each Party is self-contained travelling with their luggage in a lorry bought by Government. They will sleep in schools and similar buildings. They have their own cook, tent-pitcher and general servant with them in the lorry, which also carried a trained man to look after the loud-speaker with which the expedition is equipped. The other members of the party are the lorry driver and his cleaner.

The party will spend a week in each district of the Division and suitable stages have been drawn up in consultation with the commissioners and Deputy Commissioners. They will hold, as a rule, one meeting a day at which we expect an attendance of not less then two thousand. We are sending them off the main roads to places beyond the reach of the daily papers. The proposal is for one speaker to open the proceedings in a general speech explaining why the Empire is at war with Germany and what the war aims of the Allies are; after he has done this it is hoped that there will be a general discussion in which each member of the party will answer questions relating to the Country which he represents. The choice of the speaker to open the meeting will depend to some extent on the composition of the audience. We are not sending projectors with these parties, as films can be shown in the open air only after dark, and we want to attract the villagers from some little distance round. It is not everyone who will walk three or four miles on a dark cold winter's night to sit in the open air and listen to a discussion. We intend to send parties in the summer with projectors and fewer debaters.

The parties will not be cheap; each lorry by the time it is licensed and insured will cost not less than Rs 4,000; the loud speakers have cost about Rs 13,000; the parties will have to be fed, and the servants and mechanics will get their wages. It is important that there should not be a charge on the countryside. I do not see how the total cost can be less than Rs 40,000 and it may well be more.

J.D. Anderson,
Joint Chief Secretary

16.02.40

---

[1] Sir Sikandar Hayat Khan, Premier of the Punjab.

(b) Punjab Governor Sir Henry Craik's Letter to the Viceroy

Correspondence with the Governor of Punjab and his Secretary, Linlithgow Papers, Acc. No. 2224, NAI.

[Private & Personal]

Dear Lord Linlithgow,

....

4. Sir Sikandar has taken the opportunity of this brief visit to the plains to hold several public meetings in the Jullander and Jhelam Districts. These were, I understand, attended by very large audiences and marked by great enthusiasm to co-operate in all war-efforts. The Premier has made some stirring speeches and has expressed his determination to deal sternly with any kind of internal disorder. He also announced his intention of himself joining the Civic Guards. Sir Chhotu Ram also recently had one or two successful meetings in other districts.

---

[1] Sir Henry Duffield Craik, 3rd Bart, GCIE, KCSI (1875–1955), Chief Secretary, Punjab, 1922–7; Commissioner; 1927; Member of the Executive Council, Punjab, 1930–4; Home Member of the Governor General's Executive Council, 1934–8; Governor of the Punjab, 1938–41; Political Advisor to the Viceroy, 1941–3.

E. ALL-INDIA HINDU MAHASABHA

17. Hindu Mahasabha's 'Terms of Co-operation': All India Hindu Mahasabha Working Committee's Resolution, Bombay, 22 September 1940

Sir Maurice Gwyer and A. Appadorai, *Speeches and Documents on the Indian Constitution 1921–47*, Vol. II, Bombay, 1957, pp. 506–7; *Indian Annual Register,* 1940, Vol. II, p. 267.

Resolved that in view of the opportunity that the present war offers for the general militarization of the Hindus and for the organization of the system of India on sound and up-to-date modern lines so that India be converted into a self-contained defence unit, the Hindu Mahasabha is prepared wholeheartedly to work out the schemes of the expansion of the Viceroy's Executive Council and the War Advisory Council, but on honourable terms of equity and justice as stated below:

1. In view of the declaration made by the Muslim League of its 'determination, firm resolve and faith' that the partition of India is the only solution of India's future Constitution, the Hindu Mahasabha urges the Viceroy to make a clear and definite declaration that the Government has not approved or accepted any such proposal or scheme.

2. (A) That in view of the reported understanding between the Viceroy and the Muslim League that the League would be given two seats on the proposed extended Executive Council and five seats on the proposed War Advisory Council, the Hindu Mahasabha claims representation of six seats on the extended Executive Council and 15 seats on the War Advisory Council on the population basis.

   (B) That out of these six seats one be given to the Sikhs and one to the Scheduled Castes and the rest be given to the nominees of the Hindu Mahasabha.

3. This Committee considers the demand of the Muslim League of 50 percent representation on the proposed Executive Council and elsewhere as undemocratic, unconstitutional, unreasonable and preposterous and it would urge the Viceroy to give an assurance to the Hindu Mahasabha that no such demand would be entertained.

18. V.D. Savarkar's Letter to the Viceroy Regarding Hindu Mahasabha's Attitude Towards War, 22 October 1940

Correspondence with Persons in India, Vol. V, Linlithgow Papers, Acc. No. 2307, NAI.

Dear Lord Linlithgow,

1. Your kind letter dated the 11th instant to hand. I thank you for the kind thoughts Your Excellency was pleased to express wishing me speedy recovery. At present recovery had definitely set in. But it will take at least a couple of months before I can face travels or take up active work.

2. I was glad to note that Your Excellency has communicated Hindu Mahasabha's Resolutions to His Majesty's Government. But the reference in your letter that 'the position will of course have to be considered in the light of those Resolutions,' is the very point to correct which I am hastening to write this letter.

3. A number of events have happened since the Resolutions were passed which have given a favourable turn to political situation from the Hindu Mahasabha point of view. Your firm reply to the League and refusal to grant a number of aggressive demands forwarded by the League such as 'the 50 per cent Ratio' or that 'the Government should get itself definitely committed to the Pakistan proposal', etc. your firm refusal has automatically eliminated a number of counter-demands which the Hindu Mahasabha had to make in its Resolutions. Consequently, now those resolutions must be considered not 'by themselves' alone but in the light of and in connection with this favourable turn events have taken.

4. Now, the position is simple. Almost all the Members of the Working Committee had an informal discussion with me and with Dr B.S. Moonje and both of us have already written to Your Excellency to the effect that the Hindu Mahasabha is firmly of the opinion that the proposal of the extension of the Executive Council must in no case be abandoned. Such a step on the part of the Government will be constructed as an abject capitulation to those reactionary forces which want to hinder constitutional progress by advancing impossible demands. Now even if the original proposal which Your Excellency had referred to during our interviews is definitely announced reserving one seat for the Hindu Mahasabha; one for the Scheduled classes; one for the Sikh or any other Hindu Party and the remaining one for the Muslim or any other non-Hindu if necessary, taking for granted that only four Members are to be added, such a proposal will meet the requirement of the situation and enable the Hindu Mahasabha to participate in the Council in as much as this scheme too does naturally meet the just contention of the Hindu Mahasabha that the representation the Hindus get must be in the proportion of their population.

5. Moreover, in this connection Your Excellency will note the fact that the most prominent Hindu Sabhaites in Bombay, United Provinces, Ahmedabad, Berar and several other

parts throughout India have already joined the War Committees and are extending whatever cooperation is possible and advisable in pressing on the war efforts. In case the Hindu Mahasabha is not given a representation in the Extended Councils on equitable terms, it will necessarily have an alienating effect on all the Hindu Sabhaites who are holding such prominent positions on most leading War Committees at Bombay, Amraoti, Lucknow, etc. But if the Hindu Mahasabha is enabled to send its representatives on the Extended Councils, such a step on the part of the Government will doubtless encourage these Hindu Sanghatanists all over the country and cement further the alliance between the Government and the Hindu Mahasabha, which it is my aim to bring about in the prosecution of the common cause of defending India against aggression from outside or from anarchy at home!.

Awaiting a definite announcement on the part of Your Excellency of the extension of these Councils on lines suggested above which are also more or less identical with those on which Your Excellency wished to base your proposal.

Yours sincerely
V.D. Savarkar,
President, Hindu Mahasabha

19. Participation in War Efforts for Militarization of Hindus: Extracts from V.D. Savarkar's Presidential Address at the 22nd Session of the Hindu Mahasabha, Madurai, 28 December 1940

Jayakar Papers, File No. 709, 1940, NAI.

... The first point to be noted is the fact that we are in no way morally bound to help any of the belligerents in this world-wide war whether it be England or Germany or Japan or Russia or China or any other country involved in the war, from only altruistic point of view as has been demanded from us not only by Great Britain and America but curiously enough by some of the Congressite leaders themselves, and some other sections of the Indian public. The Hindu Mahasabha has already made its position clear on this point in a resolution passed by its Working Committee in September, 1939, just within a month after the breaking out of the war, when Gandhiji, the *de facto* dictator of the Congress was proclaiming in a flattering mood to the effect that he was not thinking of Indian independence then but was chiefly concerned with the safety of England and France and proposed to offer them unconditional help in their crusade to save democracy in the world; when even Pandit Nehru was calling upon India to support these British and French democracies in the holy war they were carrying on against the imperialistic German aggression on Poland and other free nations and while the leader of the Forward Block, the Communists, the Royists and other parties too were swearing by the anti-imperialistic innocence free from all political greed on the part of Poland and Russia, the Hindu Mahasabha was about the only organized and outstanding political body in India which was far and far-sighted enough to give the correct lead to the country and to the Congress itself in ascertaining the real motives and objectives of the belligerents, by ascertaining that none of the belligerent powers in Europe whether England, Germany, Poland, France or Russia, etc. had been actuated by any moral, democratic or altruistic considerations apart from its own self-interest and self-aggrandizement. The Viceroy and the Secretary of the State for India have more than once wanted us to believe in their various speeches that the only objective which had actuated Britain to continue the war had been 'to resist aggression whether against England or others, to defend great democratic ideals and without seeking any material advantage to lay the foundation of a better international system and to secure a real and lasting peace'. No better proof can be adduced to disprove these declarations as to the altruistic objectives of Great Britain in going to the war than the fact that they provided an occasion for Hitler to retort when he was asked by Chamberlain to free Poland that he would do so as soon as Great Britain freed India. Verily does the adage say, 'thieves alone can trace the foot-steps of thieves best.'...

The Militarization and Industrialization of the Hindus Must Constitute our Immediate Objective under the War Conditions

Thus after taking stock of all other courses and factors for and against us, I feel no hesitation in proposing that the best way of utilizing the opportunities which the war has afforded to us cannot be any other than to participate in all war-efforts which the Government are compelled by circumstances to put forth in so far as they help in bringing about the militarization and industrialization of our people. Fortunately for us facilities are thrown open to us in this direction within a single year in consequence of the war which we could not find during the last fifty years and could not have hoped to secure in ordinary course by empty protests and demands for the next fifty years to come. Owing to the Gandhist lead, the Congress had neglected the question of fostering military strength of our people to such an extent that even the wordy resolutions which the Congress used to pass while it was under the lead of those who were called Moderates but who in this particular respect were more Extremists and far-sighted than this spineless school of Gandhist military non-resisters, used to pass demanding the repeal of the Arms Act and Indianization of the Army, were tabooed for the last twenty years under Gandhiji's pressure on the Congress Platform. Even when the Congress was in power it did not take a single step to promote or even to safeguard the military interests of our people. But throughout the last twenty years the Muslims, who cared a fig for any non-violence, non-resistance, non-cooperation nonsense in which the Congress kept indulging under Gandhiji's pressure, almost monopolized recruiting into the army and armed police. It was only a few Hindu Mahasabhaite leaders like our revered Dr Moonje and Bhai Paramanand who were trying their best to counteract this senseless policy of the Congress owing to which the Hindus alone had to suffer and lose whatever numerical strength they had in the army. Not only that, the sophisticated teaching of the so-called Satyagraha creed sought to kill the very martial instinct of the Hindu race and had succeeded to an alarming extent in doing so. That was the reason why throughout my tours as the President of the Hindu Mahasabha I made it my duty to put this point above all others and tried my best to give a fillip to military awakening amongst the Hindus by addressing thousands and thousands of Hindu youths from Punjab to Madras with no negligible success. But I was always at a loss to know how we Hindu Sanghatanists can find immediate ways and means to impart to our young Hindu generation the practical and up-to-date military training. Just then the war broke out and the British Government, to serve their own interests, were compelled to raise new military forces in India on a large scale. Naturally, the Hindu Mahasabha with a true insight in practical politics decided to participate in all war efforts of the British Government in so far as they concerned directly with the question of the Indian defence and raising new military forces in India, I emphatically maintain that the results of that policy even within a year of its trial are positively encouraging.

Results in Participating in War Effort Satisfactory

In examining these results we must bear in mind that the British are raising these Military forces and encouraging industrial development so far as it helps their war efforts with no altruistic motives of helping the Indians. They are doing whatever they have to do to help themselves. We are also participating in these war efforts or at any rate are not out to oppose them, with no intention of helping the British but of helping ourselves. I have put the situation almost bluntly in the above manner to disarm the political folly into which the Indian public is accustomed to indulge in thinking that because Indian interests are opposed to the British interests in general, any step in which we join hands with the British Government must necessarily be an act of surrender, anti-national, of playing into the British hands and that cooperation with the British Government in any case and under all circumstances is unpatriotic and condemnable. It is all the more amusing to find that this spirit of silly bravado is more rampant amongst those very Congressites who did not hesitate to serve the British Government by conducting their Provincial Ministries swearing loyalty and allegiance to the British Domination in the oath of allegiance which they had to take; who wept over the fancied destruction of Westminster Abbey only the other day and had served the British Government as their recruiting officers during the last war and are even now promising full cooperation to the British, if they get some of their faddist demands satisfied and assure the British that they would do nothing even as it is to embarrass the British. But the Hindu Sanghatanist at any rate must realize the difference between a senseless bravado and a real act of bravery.... In practical politics, alliances are to be based on any point of common interests in spite of the fact of the conflict in all other interests between the allied parties. Who can say that Hitler or Stalin can be wanting in bravery or can be silly enough to play into the other's hand and yet did not both of them join in alliance, in spite of their opposing interests on all other points, as soon as they found that their mutual interests coalesced on some points during this war? One who is always afraid of being duped by others must be a simpleton indeed deserving to be duped all round. The Hindu Sanghatanists are so conscious of their political wisdom and so self confident that they can take good care of themselves against being duped even by the crafty statesmanship of Great Britain and therefore feel no hesitation and ought to feel no hesitation in extending a wholehearted participation in the war efforts of Great Britain if it serves their own purpose better than any other course.

Examining from this point of view the results of the Hindu Mahasabha's policy of participating in the war efforts so far as the militarization of the Hindus is the enlistment of thousands of new recruits in the Indian Army. While in the old army the proportion of the Moslems had risen in some parts even to 75 per cent we find amongst these new recruits there are nearly sixty thousand Hindus and thirty thousand Moslems. The strength of the air force also is trebly increased and is being daily increased. It is very encouraging a fact that the Hindus are evincing a special interest and ability in the air craft and are getting themselves enlisted in large numbers on the air forces and many of them are already serving on the war front and partaking in actual air fight against the seasoned air forces of Germany. In the naval forces, it is regrettable to note that the Hindus counted for nothing up to this time. The very small number of Indians who was somehow connected with the navy, more than 75 per cent were Moslems. Consequently, strong representations were made by the Hindu Mahasabha during this year against this partiality of the Government. The sea-faring and sea-fighting Hindu castes on the Konkan coast in particular, who distinguished themselves so valorously in the days of the Maratha Empire as to inflict several serious defeats to the English sea-forces but who have been neglected of late by England near to them, were roused from their lethargy and were made to demand entry into the naval forces. Hundreds of meetings were organized by the Hindu Mahasabha this year in the villages and towns which were attended by very large numbers by these castes: the Agris, the Bhandaris, the Kolis and others, and petitions signed by thousands of them were submitted to the Government demanding entry into the naval forces and the opening of ship-yards and naval bases on the Konkan coast. In response to this agitation on the part of the Hindu Mahasabhaites on this point throughout India, the Government have promised to recruit Hindus in naval service without any distinction and have also admitted the fact that the Hindus are showing more inclination to take to that line than they were doing formerly. In order to meet large demand for technicians to work in the new factories started on a very large scale to manufacture military equipments, rifles and even tanks, the Government has already made arrangements for fifteen thousand Indian candidates to be trained immediately as technicians. All experts to train them who were available in India are called upon to take up the work and in addition to them, technical experts in up-to-date war crafts are requisitioned by the Indian Government from England as well. Besides this large numbers of Indian workers and technical hands are to be sent to England to receive the training in up-to-date methods. They will all stay together with the British technical hands and labourers, will receive pay on the same scale and will be treated on an equal footing. The cost of it will also be borne by the British Government. As the raising, equipping and training of the new army of a lakh of Indian soldiers is already substantially complete, the Government has only recently announced the expansion of the Indian Army to half a million men of the all arms. Thus nearly two lakhs of Indians would be immediately recruited and the ever increasing necessity under war pressure is sure to compel the Government to recruit some five lakhs of Indian soldiers before long, bringing up the total strength of the Indian army to a million soldiers properly trained, equipped and even mechanized to bring them up to an up-to-date efficiency. Then again we must take into consideration the large increase in the armies of the different Hindu States that has been sanctioned by the Government under the war pressure. Not less than forty battalions have already been sent to the different fronts of the war and are taking their lessons in actual fighting on modern lines. The old rusty outlook of the forces of Hindu States has already been transformed as to present a smart well-armed and well-equipped front.

The sudden increase in the army from some two lakhs to ten lakhs of Indian soldiers was bound to create an enormous demand for commissioned officers. So the old policy of army Indianization by the introduction of special Indianized units has been scrapped and all units have been opened to Indian officers' recruitment. The Viceroy's commissioned officers too have been reintroduced in the Indianized units and thus all units are placed on the same footing. There is consequently an enormous field opened out for Indians to serve as officers in the army in all capacities and on equal footing with the British officers who up to this time enjoyed a sort of monopoly in officering the army. Besides this expansion of the rank, file and officers in the regular army to a million men, the Indian territorial forces also are soon to be re-touched more efficiently equipped and expanded. So far as the question of the compulsory military education to be introduced into the high schools and colleges is concerned, the Indian Government is still following obstructive tactics. But it must be noted that the Senates of almost all leading Universities in India have demanded during the year that compulsory military training must forthwith be introduced and are already knocking at the gates of the Government which as the war pressure goes on increasing are sure to yield and get thrown open.

.... The manufacture of war materials on an enormous scale is also being introduced in India which has already afforded and is sure to afford as days pass by an opportunity for thousands of our artisans, craftsmen, workers, and technicians to get specialized in turning out up-to-date rifles, tanks, ammunition, and even machines required in connection with them.

Then again whatever be their reluctance, the Indian Government has at last been compelled to permit Sheth Walchand Hirachand[1] who must be specially congratulated on his untiring efforts and able lead in this respect, to open a shipyard at Visakhapatnam financed by Indian capital, worked by Indian labour under Indian management. Permission for opening a factory to manufacture aeroplanes on a large scale has also been granted to Sheth Walchand Hirachand who has already selected a site at Bangalore and is sure to set it going at full speed with his characteristic promptness and efficiency. The Government has already lodged orders for a crore of rupees of planes.

With regard to large industries other than the war industries, it suffices to say that this year has given a fillip to many a chemical industry, the paper industry, etc. Within a couple of years if the war pressure is continued we are sure to record an industrial progress which otherwise even a dozen years would not have enabled us to do as the Government stood always in our way to economic self-sufficiency. But now that military exigencies have forced England to raise India to a self-sufficient economical and military unit, a centre commanding the defences of the whole Eastern part of their Empire from Egypt to Australia they are compelled to see that key industries and even industries in general are started and flourished in this country to such a wide extent that if ever the connection of the Eastern part of their Empire is at least temporarily cut off from the Western Empire, they may be able to depend for all the sinews of war chiefly on India which abounds in the resources of men and materials.

A Serious Question

Now I ask you all whether you could have ever been able to bring about such rapid militarization and industrialization of the country within a year out of your own resources? Could have the Hindu Mahasabha or the Congress or any such public organization ever been able to recruit, train, equip half a million of our men and send them to learn real fighting on the field on the strength of its own resources? And even if you had aimed to do so would the British Government had ever allowed you to do so? We could not have conducted even lathi clubs on such a large scale. Last year, even to run half a dozen institutions to impart military education even to a few hundred Hindu youths was difficult. And now that the war has opened out an opportunity for us to send hundreds of thousands of Hindus to the army, the navy, the air services and to get them fully trained, equipped and armed as up-to-date soldiers and commanding officers and for building shipyards, aeroplane factories, gun factories, ammunition factories and get thousands of our mechanics trained into war technical experts, shall we turn our back on all these facilities, refuse to join the army, decline to participate in the manufacture of war materials simply because some fools will call it a cooperation with the Government, or some body will curse it as an act of violence? If we do so we shall but deserve even ourselves to be bracketed with the fool and the booby.

Let us note also that these half a million or million of men who are finding employment in the army and the thousand of workers and artisans and technicians and specialists who will get work and secure posts in the war material factories and the industries made possible by the war will bring food and clothing necessaries of life, to at least fifty lacs of persons belonging to the very class who is at present suffering most on account of chronic unemployment. Will it not lessen the unbearable burden that at present falls on our agricultural classes who have to depend on the proceeds of land in spite of its daily diminishing returns? ...

---

[1] Walchand Hirachand (1882–1953) was born in Sholapur in Maharashtra in a business family. He was deeply influenced by Dadabhai Naoroji in his early years. Critical of British economic policies, he was a staunch advocate of India's economic independence through industrialization of the country by Indians themselves. He was a leading figure in promoting and setting up industries in numerous key sectors including shipping, aircrafts, and automobiles.

F.   LEAGUE OF RADICAL CONGRESSMEN

20.   Bombay Provincial League of Radical Congressmen: Resolutions Regarding India and War, and the Congress and the Present Crisis

Independent India, 4 August 1940.

The recent developments in the international situation can no longer permit an attitude of neutrality towards the war on the part of progressive and freedom-loving elements in the world. The triumphant march of Fascism which is taking place with the active support or passive connivance of the ruling classes of many a country, can be arrested only by a mobilization of all democratic masses in a genuine anti-Fascist struggle. It is, therefore, the considered opinion of this conference that the Indian people should actively participate in the anti-Fascist struggle.

This participation can not be made conditional upon any declaration of Indian independence to be made by the British Government. In the first place, such a declaration can not be made by the British Government. And secondly even if any declaration is made it can be only of a formal character which can not confer any rights on the Indian people. Independence is not a thing which can be granted by one nation to another by a declaration. It has to be fought for and won as a result of revolutionary mass action.

The fight for Indian freedom can not be isolated from the larger fight for human freedom. It is only by actively participating in the latter fight that the Indian people can take effective steps towards the securing of their own freedom from the shackles of British Imperialism. India could have made a large contribution towards the growth of human freedom and the destruction of the dark forces of Fascism which today are seeking to destroy it, by striking a decisive blow for the destruction of imperialism. The given situation in the country does not allow that to be done immediately with any hope of success. The task, therefore, is to preserve the popular forces and prepare them for decisive action on a more favourable opportunity which may ensue before long.

The conditions for this can not be created by the present policy of non-cooperation which has resulted in a complete stalemate and demoralization and degeneration of the political life in the country. They can be neither created by following a policy of war resistance which is neither possible nor desirable. War resistance on the contrary will prove definitely harmful, to the interest of the world struggle against Fascism, and therefore to the Indian struggle for freedom. Nor can they be created by a sham 'struggle' of the Satyagraha type which always ends in a demoralization and destruction of the forces of struggle. Under the given circumstances, active participation in war is the only course open to the Indian people. They will not be thereby helping British Imperialism, but will on the contrary be weakening it by developing and strengthening the anti-Fascist forces in England and Europe. They will be also thereby working for their own freedom, for the opportunities created by the active participation in the anti-Fascist struggle, can be utilized for carrying to a successful end the anti-Imperialist struggle. This conference therefore appeals to the Congress to straight-forwardly and honestly adopt this course, which under the given circumstances is the only course that can be adopted with advantage to the interest of the national struggle. This conference also calls upon the Congress to address an appeal to all the anti-Fascist forces in the world, more particularly the Soviet Union, in order that a world anti-Fascist bloc may be built up for the complete destruction of Fascism.

Congress and the Present Crisis

In order to end the stalemate and the consequent stultification of our national politics, this conference calls upon the Congress:

1. To abandon its present futile and indecisive course of action.
2. To return back to offices on the basis of coalition ministries in provinces and at the centre.
3. To utilize the offices for developing a revolutionary movement and organization in the country, and with that object in view guarantee civil liberties and protect the large masses of the people from the oppressive effects of the war.
4. To prepare the country for the assertion of the right of self-determination by creating a country-wide network of revolutionary organizations which will secure for themselves the support of the masses by actively participating in all the struggles for the redress of their immediate grievances.
5. To prepare for the convening of the Constituent Assembly, and with that object in view take the initiative in calling together a meeting of all the elected members of the provincial assemblies for determining the fundamental principles of the constitution of the free Indian State. Once they are determined the Congress should, in cooperation with other organizations agreeing with them, carry on an intensive and extensive propaganda for their popularization, and for the creation of the peoples councils to serve as the electoral units for the election of delegates to the Constituent Assembly.

Plan of Action

On the basis of the analysis of the national and international situation, contained in the basic documents and the recent resolutions of the AILRC, this conference is convinced that the supreme task of the moment is the organization of a new leadership for the national movement, a leadership which will, with the objective of accomplishing a national democratic revolution in the country, lead the country step by step towards the goal of the capture of political power.

This conference therefore pledges itself to that task and resolves to devote itself to the following:

1. Creation of a cadre of revolutionary political workers.
2. Propaganda for exposing the futility of the Gandhian line and the acceptance by the general mass of people of the alternative revolutionary line of the AILRC.

3. Active participation in Congress Committees and other mass organizations with the object of winning the confidence of the people and their support to the League's line of action.

In order to effectively achieve these objects, this conference resolves to carry on the following activities during this year.

1. To raise the membership of the League to at least 100.
2. To raise the sale of *Independent India* to at least 1000 in the city of Bombay.
3. To push forward the sale of League literature.
4. To intensify our work in the Congress Committees, trade unions, students and similar other organizations and to carry on propaganda specially amongst Muslim, depressed class and non-Brahmin masses.
5. To organize Study Classes for the education of members and sympathizers, and to produce literature for that.
6. To activate every member and every local unit.
7. To organize volunteer corps in every ward under the guidance and control of the League.

21. M.N. Roy's Circular to Members of League of Radical Congressmen to Launch an Anti-Fascist Mass Movement in India, 17 August 1940

Independent India, 18 August 1940.

Dear Comrades,

It is very encouraging that a lively discussion is being carried on by Radical Congressmen throughout the country about the bold and truly revolutionary stand that we have taken regarding the war. The fundamental principles of our policy are stated in our Thesis 'India and War'. Those principles as well as the analysis of national and international situation in the light of which they are formulated, were reviewed and discussed at length during our summer camp at Dehra Dun. The All-India Conference of the League of Radical Congressmen reaffirmed the principles and policy formulated in 'India and War' by a resolution on the international situation. In pursuance of that resolution we have been trying to persuade the Congress leadership to adopt a course of action suggested by us from time to time. Unfortunately our efforts have not been successful.

Although the decision of the next meeting of the Working Committee may precipitate an undesirable and highly dangerous situation we shall have to keep on hammering our point of view hoping that sooner or later good sense will prevail and Indian politics will be conducted in a really honorable and fruitful course. We need not under-estimate the difficulties. Even today, ours may be a cry in the wilderness. Yet, we should have the courage of conviction necessary to swim against the current of set habits, political backwardness and prejudice.

I am decidedly of the opinion that the road to Indian freedom lies through an active participation in the struggle against Fascism. I have come to know that some of our comrades do not fully share this conviction. There can be only one reason for that. It is insufficient appreciation of the danger of Fascism. To talk of a choice between Imperialism and Fascism is altogether an erroneous approach to the problem. Those romantic Indian nationalists, who have been advising Imperialism to liquidate itself for the benefit of India, are blinded by their prejudice, and therefore cannot see that Imperialism is liquidating itself in as much as Fascism is becoming the politics of decayed Capitalism throughout the world. Therefore, the fighters for freedom, wherever they may be today, have only one enemy to face, that is Fascism.

The present is not England's war. It is a war for the future of the world. If the British Government happens to be a party to this war, why should the fighters for human liberty be ashamed of congratulating it for this meritorious deed, perhaps inadvertently committed, and recognize it as an ally in a noble cause? The old saying, that adversity brings strange bed fellows, is not altogether meaningless. If it was justifiable for the Soviet Government to make the non-aggression pact with Nazi Germany, why should it not be equally permissible for the fighters for Indian freedom to support the British Government so long as it is engaged in a war against Fascism?

All these obvious considerations are not seen by those who are not inspired with the ideal of the liberation of the oppressed and exploited throughout the world. Conscious or unconscious Fascist sympathy on the part of the average nationalist makes him blind to the dangers of the situation. Radical Congressmen should be free from such narrow-mindedness and prejudices. The realization of the danger of Fascism is the condition for the development of a truly democratic and progressive movement for the freedom of India. Those who have already realized that should take the initiative to make others conscious of the danger. An anti-Fascist mass movement is the crying need of the day. All the truly democratic and progressive elements in our country are bound to be crystallized in course of that movement. On the other hand, by developing such a movement, the fighters for Indian freedom will make their contribution to the world fight against Fascism.

September 1, the anniversary of the outbreak of the war against Fascism, should be the most propitious day for launching the movement. The League of Radical Congressmen is the only organized force in India today which can take the initiative in this respect. I hope you will approve of the proposition, and make of our next independent action as big a success as on the occasion of the anniversary of the French Revolution.

I shall issue a public appeal in this connection, and you will receive further directions from the Central Office. Meanwhile, I advise you to get in touch with all who are likely to cooperate in the demonstration and do all the other necessary preparations. Let the Anti-Fascist Day, celebrated by the League of Radical Congressmen, mark the beginning of a new stage in the struggle for Indian freedom.

M.N. Roy,
Dehradun, 17 August 1940

22. Develop a Broadbased Anti-Fascist Movement: M.N. Roy's Circular Addressed to Members of the League of Radical Congressmen

Independent India, 1 September 1940.

Dear Comrades,

I have noticed in the correspondence of our comrades and even in some contributions to *Independent India* a tendency of being apologetic for our stand regarding the war and the view that for the moment the concentration of the entire energy for helping the fight against Fascism is the correct thing for all the fighters for freedom to do, wherever they may be. This tendency expresses itself in associating the proposed anti-Fascist movement with the ideas of 'the final struggle' and 'seizure of power'. The analysis of the national and international situation, which had led us to our present position, excludes the possibility of realizing such ideas in the near future. Therefore, no useful purpose will be served by talking about them, when we should apply ourselves to an immediate task of supreme importance, which is to fight against Fascism. Even from the Bombay, Bengal and Maharashtra resolutions, as well as from individual correspondence, I gather that we are unanimous in that connection. Then, why all this star-gazing and fortune-telling? The reason for this repetition of certain stock-phrases can only be that we are not sufficiently convinced of correctness of our view that the supreme task of the movement is to organize an anti-Fascist movement; we want to reassure ourselves that we are much more revolutionary than 'mere anti-Fascists.' That is a wrong point of view and I am writing to urge that such unnecessary apologies and romantic ideas should not creep into our demonstrations on September 1.

To participate in the fight against Fascism being our task and responsibility, we must find the most effective way of doing so. We cannot imitate the Congress leadership and wait for the British Government to give us the chance. We know how to do it. We have undertaken the task of mobilizing popular opinion in support of the world struggle against Fascism. That task should have been undertaken by the Congress. It cannot be done by the present Government for obvious reasons. But there are numerous elements in the country who may be expected to join us in this task. We shall alienate them by introducing in our anti-Fascist propaganda the distant ideals and political ideas which may not secure their approval. A broad based mass movement can be created only on the basis of the largest measure of common agreement. Nothing should be done which would prevent our securing the largest possible cooperation in the Anti-Fascist movement. If we are not careful, our purpose will be defeated. That is not opportunism, it is a categorical imperative of political strategy....

However, the idea I anxiously want to convey is that we should do the first thing first. The present should not be spoiled by dreams about the future. Let us take care of the present, and the future will take care of itself. Let us have no vacillation or apologia interfere with our single-mindedness which will guarantee success regarding our immediate as well as the ultimate goal.

Yours sincerely,
M.N. Roy

23. An Article by Ellen Roy on Why the League of Radical Congressmen is Supporting the War

Independent India, 13 October 1940.

Com Roy will refuse to undertake the impossible task of producing evidence for the several things mentioned by you, but never maintained by him. Nowhere in his numerous writings and pronouncements, will you find any indication that he expects anything for India from either a victory of British Imperialism, or Mr Churchill, or from America, or from any other 'imperialist democracy' (which is a contradiction in terms). Com Roy does not expect anything or anybody to bring freedom anywhere. Freedom is not brought; it is conquered. That opinion is the main difference between him and the Radicals, on the one side, and the majority of the nationalist leaders, on the other.

We do not advocate support in this war because we expect Mr Churchill to give us something, nor do we wait for him to give us something before advocating support. It is not in his interest to give us what we want. But it is in our interest that we advocate support to this war. And that support does in no way prejudice our pursuing the achievement of what we want. There is no contradiction and no interference between the two.

The Congress leaders say that they would also like to give their support to the war, but only under certain conditions. We maintain that, on the one hand, these conditions are completely inadequate and their fulfillment of no avail for the attainment of Indian freedom; on the other hand, if the conditions are rejected, we should have to sit on our prestige and refuse support to the war, in spite of our professed opinion that it should be given. The Congress leaders desire 'transfer of power' from the British to Indians or at least the 'recognition of India's right of independence.' We maintain that transfer of power is an impossibility; and as for the recognition of the right of independence, only facts can be recognized. And India's independence is not yet a fact. Nor can this fact be established by the present Congress policy of 'semi-benevolent neutrality', which amounts to nothing in terms of the prosecution of the war, and self-immolation and stultification in terms of India's freedom struggle.

We do not mix up things. We do not maintain that India will gain freedom simply by a victory of the British arms, as you seem to suggest. But we do maintain that the cause of Indian freedom can be better promoted by supporting this war which as a war against Fascism, deserves support than by not supporting or even opposing it. Nor is this war likely to end just with the victory of this or that belligerent, with the *status quo ante bellum* returning only the scales tipped in favour either of Britain or Germany. That was so in the case of the previous war. Even for the small man in England or Germany, then, it made little practical difference who won the war. This time, we can assume that the small man in Britain knows what the difference of a victory of the Nazis would mean for him. And what quarrel do we have with the English man in the street? He is not an imperialist. And it is more likely that, if England wins this war it will be the democratic people who will have won it.

The European democracies do not want Fascism. They know today that only through defeat in this war can it be stamped out, and that, unless it is stamped out they are in for it. The European imperialists were not anxious to fight this war. They blundered on it. Mr Chamberlain might still have corrected the blunder by coming to (Hitler's) terms with Germany either after the fall of Poland, or of Norway, or of any one of the subsequent victims. Mr Chamberlain is indeed the better imperialist. But Mr Churchill does conduct a war against Fascism, which the democratic masses must see through if they want to survive even in their relative freedom, which is still better than an absolute slavery.

No sane man desires war. But pacifism in the face of Fascism is nothing short of grotesque. The common people suffer in the war; but they know they will suffer more when Fascism wins. The imperialists might have avoided the necessity of this war. But for their complacency and even connivance, Fascism would have never become the powerful menace it is today. That is another matter. They are atoning for past sin, and are paying dearly for it. No use sneering. History is taking its implacable course. Politics, which is the process of history in the making, cannot be done with emotions. Out of resentment against British Imperialism, we should not allow ourselves to act against our own conviction as regards this war. On the other hand, whatever our attitude towards this war in particular may be, it needs in no way interfere with our legitimate fight against imperialist injustice. Only, there are ways and ways of doing a thing.

But in order to define our attitude towards this war, we must have an opinion about it. If it is a 'bad' war and should not be fought, we should have the courage to say so and resist it, and see that our resistance becomes effective. Or, by analysing the character of the war, we come to the conclusion that the best thing that can happen, now that it is on our head, is to fight it to the finish and prevent Fascism from winning it. If we do come to this conclusion, we should also have the courage to say so openly and not shrink from acting according to our conviction because once in life the British Government is acting in a way which we could not object to.

When the Polish 'incident' was closed, we suggested that the Congress should appeal for an early termination of the war. We did so because the discrepancy in preparedness for a major war between Germany and the rest of Europe became evident already then, and the perspective of a complete Fascization of Europe was already opened up. Not much prestige was yet at stake on either side; and though return to the status quo could not have improved matters much, yet it would have closed, temporarily at least, that immediate and horrible perspective.

But the war went on. And peace now would mean voluntary Fascization of Europe, which is in effect no better than forcible Fascization. Therefore, this war must go on until the perspective of the Fascization of Europe, and with it almost inevitably, of the whole world, will disappear with the defeat and overthrow of Hitler. That is necessary in our own interest; and if it happens to coincide with the interest even of the British Government, should we therefore act against our own interest, only to spite the British? After all, anti-Imperialism is not an end in itself. We fight imperialism in so far as it encroaches upon our freedom. The Fascization of Europe is the greatest menace to our freedom. Therefore, we must do whatever we can to prevent it.

In analysing this war, one must of course agree on the premises. I start from the assertion that Fascism is the greatest and immediate menace to the forces of freedom and democracy throughout the world including India and including Germany. Nobody would reasonably maintain that the Fascization of Europe in general, including England in particular, would bring India freedom. Nor is it a matter of indifference to India. Fascism is more efficient and ruthless in suppression than Imperialism. And supposing Hitler wants to crush the British Empire it is not the small island or France that he covets; we can legitimately assume that India will be the prize. And if it was not possible until now for India to become an independent country, with Hitler on our neck, the perspective will vanish in dimmest posterity. On this question, we can only agree or differ, not argue; because the facts of Fascism are known. One may find them good, another bad, but nobody can dispute them. We find them bad, worse than anything, worse even than Imperialism! It is also a fact that it is not generally realized in this country, at a distance, how abjectly bad it is, although the facts are there to be known.

There are reasons for mental reservations; there is a traditional pro-German sympathy; and there is the radio propaganda from Berlin promising freedom to India. Such promises from Berlin are not new. M.N. Roy knows something about it. And there must be a reason why he warns unless you suggest that he does not care for the freedom of his country. I have also heard Hitler being praised because he had made Germany great and is he not a vegetarian and a bachelor, to boot! You will agree with me that, he who approves of the methods with which Hitler is supposed to have made his country great, must be a Fascist and imperialist, believing in the subjugation of other peoples by the cruellest means. (And if you only knew how much greater Germany was in its wretched post-war misery—Germany, the land of poets and thinkers, was never greater than in the period of painful and peaceful reconstruction after the last defeat) And why it should be virtuous if one eats no meat because of a liver disease, and is a bachelor for other medical reasons—I cannot see for the world of it.

The most facile retort to the contention that the defeat of Fascism is our foremost concern, is; 'What do we care? Fascism and Imperialism are one and same; let them quarrel and ruin each other; or do you want the victory of Imperialism?' No, we are not interested in the victory of Imperialism. Nor do we think that, the welfare of the English people is conditional upon a victory of Imperialism. We even think that there may be no Imperialism left if Fascism is finally crushed. But to be quite consistent, let us assume that British Imperialism will be victorious; Germany defeated and under British influence; we shall not have gained anything for India. Still, we would at least be left where we are today, while under Fascist domination, either through English Petain[1] or through direct agents of Hitler, we would be worse off. (We would be worse off between English Tommy and a Nazi–Prussian drill-sergeant—the Tommy, any day!) And as for those who think that Fascism and Imperialism are the same, but for my good heart, should wish them an experience of the difference. I have seen both.

Some argue that victorious Imperialism would be worse than pre-war Imperialism, would even go Fascist itself. But why should it? A country goes Fascist as the last Capitalist way out of perpetual economic crisis threatening with overthrow of the established system. Fascism is not the product of the wickedness or perversity of an individual, however 'great'; nor is democracy the attribute of virtuous people. Democracy is the luxury of a prosperous bourgeoisie which can afford this generous gesture for its own satisfaction as well as incidentally, for the benefit of those whose labour makes it prosperous. Fascism is the weapon with which a bankrupt bourgeoisie fights for its life. Therefore, it is so deadly. So, supposing England would come out of this war victorious and unscathed, the hegemony and patron of all Europe, the restorer of French, Dutch, Belgium etc. independence and recipient of their tributes in the shape of market monopolies, it would feel so safe and strong that the democratic gesture would be but the pat on its own back had not they fought for democracy? Fascism is inconvenient even for the Fascists, unless you assume that a whole section of a people can suddenly go sadist; it is an inconvenient necessity for a certain class of people to cling to their power and privileges. For that purpose, it is a necessity. Without that purpose, that is, if power and privileges are not threatened, it can only be a nuisance. A victorious British Imperialism would not feel the necessity.

For those who do not know to choose between a victory of England or Germany, that is the worst that can happen from 'victory of British Imperialism.' In the worst case, the status quo of to-day, minus Defence of India Rules, plus, of course, in the case of civil disobedience during the war, a demoralized movement and ruined organization and, on jail delivery, begin from the beginning all over again (if possible); but if all the strategic positions will be occupied during the war (which we have assumed has got to be fought anyhow) that will not only serve the purpose of democratizing certain administrative processes, but also that of strengthening the spirit and organization of the nationalist forces. We are to choose presently; and our decision will decide much of the future of India.

But certainly, if this war is bad and should not be fought, cooperation, even in the sense of occupying strategic positions conquered by the vote of the people, and in India's own interest, should not be extended if it also served a purpose; which we considered to be definitely undesirable. However, from no quarters this view has yet been openly expressed. Contrary, the Congress leaders have all expressed their sympathy with Britain in this war and abhorrence for Fascism as well as profound regret that Britain does 'not give nationalist India a chance' to throw in her lot on the non-Fascist side of this war. The position is queer. They would like (if they would like) Fascist Germany to be defeated without imperialist Britain being victorious.

Supposing this to be desirable, how can it be brought about, if it is true that British Imperialism is waging an imperialist war against Fascism?

We maintain that this is not an imperialist war, because, for the benefit of British Imperialism, this war was not a necessity. Nor is it subjectively an anti-Fascist war, because the British Government has not been consistently motivated by antagonism to Fascism; indeed, it has largely created the nuisance value. Still whatever the motive may be or may not be, it happens to be a war against the stronghold of Fascism, and in this sense, logically it is an anti-Fascist war. We think it is so by accident; if the British Government could have 'produced' a Polish representative before midnight on August 30 last year in Berlin to surrender Danzig and the Corridor, this war might never have happened at all. But now that it has happened, what are we to do about it?

Nationalist India wants to see Fascism defeated, but does not want to do so without serving its own freedom; that is the most natural and legitimate thing in the world. The question is only: How to do it? How will the purpose be served by non-cooperation of the Congress, which can only be gesture anyhow, since all are 'co-operating': from the princes who give lakhs and soldiers, the mill-owners who produce and sell to Britain all the latter's needs for the war, and profit greatly by it, to the workers who produce what the mill-owners sell, and get at least some more employment and slightly raised wages down to the rural unemployed, who flock to recruit in the army, where they get at least some full meals a day which they otherwise don't. How would the purpose be served, even if the Congress demand for a National Government at the Centre was accepted by the British Government? What is an Indian National Government with an English Viceroy, anyhow? It is a contradiction in terms. It is also quite meaningless, in the light of what Ex. Minister K.M. Munshi said only the other day in a meeting in Bombay, referring to the Poona resolution of the AICC. 'Congress offered friendship and active participation in the war, if a National Government was appointed at Delhi. By that resolution, Congress did not want to wrest power from the Viceroy, it did not want responsible Government ...'.

We are not against bargaining a moral turpitude. But we are against bargaining away our freedom to act according to our conviction for a chimeric mess of pottage. If this war is bad, let us say so and resist it. If it is not, and should be fought to the finish, it does not look well to stand by the wholesale slaughter and exclaim; 'Very good war this, indeed! Go ahead, boys and fight those nasty Fascists! We ourselves have no time just now, because we must go to jail, so that we may emerge from it as heroes in time for the next general elections. Therefore, good bye until after the war, then we shall administer your affairs in India again; and don't forget how well we did it!'

If this war has to be fought, not because the British Government happens to have declared it and incidentally declared India a belligerent party to it, but because Fascism is a menace to the world, and not to the world of the big imperialists so much as to the greater world of the oppressed and exploited in all countries (including Germany and including India), then we must have a place in it. It may sound very nationalistic to argue: 'What do we care for the Fascist menace to the peoples of the world, when the imperialist menace sits on our necks?' In reply, I would ask: 'Who told you to put up with the imperialist menace? If you can get rid of it, do it, by all means'! But nobody in the whole country has the illusion that India can strike for her freedom now. And how will the prosecution of the fight for Indian freedom be prejudiced by making India's participation in the war against Fascism, which is today an involuntary fact, a voluntary effort—provided, of course, that we are convinced that this war against Fascism must be fought till the end? On the other hand how will war-resistance or non-cooperation promote the cause of Indian freedom?

Another seemingly patriotic argument is: 'Why should India as an enslaved country help her rulers in this war against their enemy?' Well, firstly I maintain that Fascism is also the enemy of Indian freedom. And then, if a slave is locked up with his master in the latter's burning house, he will fight the fire together with the master, unless he prefers to die with him, thinking: It serves my master right if I die—why did he not make me free? That is what the Congress attitude amounts to today. Is it reasonable?

We maintain, from a knowledge of facts, that Fascism which the British Government only happens to fight today, while we opposed it since its very existence, is our own enemy as much as that of the English people and more our enemy than that of British Imperialism; and that, if Fascism is not defeated, we are in for it. Therefore, we advocate participation in the fight against it. We are of the opinion that, even if India were an independent country, she should join the fight against Fascism in the most effective way. Here arises the question which has been put to us repeatedly, namely, 'Why, if Fascism is the enemy of democracy, and Soviet Russia the champion of democracy, does not the latter join the fight against the former? And why, if Russia does not deem it necessary, should we go out of our way doing it?' Firstly, we need not go out of our way: the fight against Fascism lies on the road to Indian freedom. And then, has not Soviet Russia joined this war, and is he not playing quite a prominent and effective part in it, having afflicted the only defeats on the Nazis in this war otherwise so dangerously successful for them? But there are ways and ways of doing a thing. This war against Fascism is waged quite successfully on the Russian borders by means of 'neutrality'. If Com Roy's answers to your previous questions in this respect have not satisfied you, this is rather because of your anti-Soviet sentiments; because you find not only his arguments, but also undeniable facts, 'unconvincing'. You believe that the Soviet Union has developed into 'Red Imperialism', not into the highest form of democracy hitherto attained. You believe, flying in the face of facts that the Soviet Union is an 'ally' of Nazi Germany, that Stalin is a 'blood-brother' of Hitler. Therefore, you are bound to disagree with an opinion based upon different premises and a different outlook, a different standard of good and bad. So let us leave the Soviet Union apart. But if your question in this connection is honestly meant for information, and you are prepared to waste some space on it, it can be once again answered separately.

However, the effect of Soviet neutrality may be well appreciated by all anti-Fascists. English anti-Fascists even in this country have done so. Russia's anti-Fascism is proved beyond doubt. The rest must be left to their strategists, trusting that they know their job. If India was one of the three mightiest powers on earth and had common or near frontiers with a Fascist country, the right policy for her might also be a 'neutral' tiger's clasp like Russia's 'neutral' bear's embrace. But as she is not, the right policy for her must be something else, the aim of all truly democratic forces being the same, namely, defeat of Fascism by their own efforts. (Because one can expect to reap the fruit only of what one has sown oneself), Imperialism, being not a democratic force, cannot be expected to defeat Fascism ultimately. It has somehow got into this war and being a powerful military force, should be welcome as an instrument in the fight against Fascism. But having entered the war reluctantly in the beginning still with visible appeasement tendencies, the danger still remains that the defeat of Fascism may suddenly appear too big a victory of democracy for the conscious imperialists to stomach. If the democratic forces will want to carry on in such an eventuality, they can do so only if they are in the thick of the fight themselves.

The democratic forces cannot be sure of the outcome of this war, unless they are active agencies in its prosecution. In India, they can, besides what is being done anyhow, do little but mobilize and quicken the consciousness of the people, and prepare them for their role in any development that events may take. And developments may well happen nearer home. Already Hitler is *ante portas* of the East. This war cannot be fought successfully except on the strength of popular will to fight an enemy of the people; that is true for the people in India as well as England and elsewhere. If the expression of this popular will in India looks like support for the British Government, which happens to fight the same enemy, is that enough reason for us to act contrary to our conviction (provided we have it)? Can we not think except in terms of 'British Government'—some having needs to do the same, and others need to do the contrary, of what it does? That is to deny ourselves even our spiritual independence! And where the popular will to fight Fascism, is not there, it is for ignorance of what Fascism is; and it is the duty of those who know to make others understand. In India, that is quite a big task, it seems. But the task is urgent, for the danger may be nearer home than one dares think. Supposing that Hitler would defeat England, and an English Petain be found to sellout the Empire; are we going to be the slaves of a slave of Hitler? Are we to refrain from fighting in such an eventuality, for the mere reason that some Englishmen also may have enough sense to fight the same fight? Should we not rather try to prevent the dire emergency? If we are complacent now, and escape from the dilemma into jail (because we could not have an Indian 'National Government' with an English Viceroy) what are we going to do, if such a case should arise, with our crown of thorns in the jails?

---

[1] Henri Philippe Petain was a Marshal of France. After the German invasion of France, the government of France moved out of Paris. Petain became Prime Minister of France on 16 June 1940 and entered into an agreement with Germany. According to the agreement, about two-thirds of France was under direct German occupation while the remaining one-third was semi-independent with a government headed by Petain. After the liberation of France, Petain was tried for treason and convicted.

G.   COMMUNIST PARTY OF INDIA

24.   Forward to a Peoples' Constituent Assembly: Manifesto of the Communist Party of India

Communist, Vol. II, No. 4, January 1940, P.C. Joshi Archives on Contemporary History, JNU.

THE TENTH ANNIVERSARY OF THE INDEPENDENCE DAY FALLS IN THE MIDST of the Second Imperialist war. Imperialist Britain is at war with Nazi Germany. Enslaved India has been forced to accept this war to protect the Empire. Its resources and man-power are daily exploited to fight Britain's battles to uphold Britain's right to rule over the world. The slave is made to fight for the slave-driver and enslave other people.

TEN YEAR BACK, THE MEN AND WOMEN OF INDIA PLEDGED THEMSELVES TO win Indian independence. Little did they imagine that within a decade British Imperialism itself would create conditions, light conflagrations, which would ensure the success of the Indian struggle. And yet that is exactly what has happened.

BY DECLARING THE PRESENT WAR, BRITISH IMPERIALISM HAS EXPOSED ITS FLANKS. ITS EXISTENCE, ITS FATE, LIES HENCEFORWARD IN THE HANDS OF THE INDIAN NATION.

By declaring the present war, British imperialism has pronounced its bankruptcy, its decline as a decisive force in international politics. The war is the biggest measure of the defeat of British diplomacy.

British diplomacy consisted in making other powers fight its battles. Its treacherous designs were directed finally against the Soviet Union, the land of Socialism, the beacon light for revolutionary movements.

Its unscrupulous diplomacy massacred the Spaniards, it sold the Abyssinians, the Czechoslovakians and the Austrians; it attempted to sell the Chinese people to Japanese imperialism. It suppressed the Palestine Arabs with a ruthlessness unheard of in history.

It nourished Hitler on the blood of democracies, on the blood of thousands of innocent men and women, who loved freedom and fought for it. It perpetrated these crimes with only one object—to keep the Empire out of war and save it, save it at the expense of the Soviet Union, at the expense of the Independence of other nations.

Why did it follow this unscrupulous path to save itself? Why was it not prepared to meet the menace of other imperialist powers on the strength of its bayonets? Because, it was afraid of its own people, of the millions of Indians, who would refuse to wield the British bayonets. It knew that war would sound its death-knell. It was afraid of a mighty revolutionary wave sweeping over the world in the wave of war. Britain's treacherous blow against world freedom was defeated by Soviet Russia. Britain found itself at war with Nazi Germany. It found itself at the mercy of the Indian People, of the masses of Britain, of the oppressed Arabs.

ON THIS INDEPENDENCE DAY, LET THE TRUTH BE ANNOUNCED THAT BRITISH IMPERIALISM IS AT OUR MERCY. ITS DESTROYERS AND BATTLESHIPS, ITS AEROPLANES AND ARMIES, ITS FINANCES AND TRADE CANNOT PROTECT IT. WITH THE WAR, THE DECISIVE VOICE HAS PASSED OVER TO THE INDIAN PEOPLE.

What have we done to implement the oath of Independence when history itself has created conditions for our successful deliverance? What have the prisoners done when the prison walls are tottering? What has the national leadership done to assert the nation's right to freedom, to complete independence?

More than four months of war have passed. And yet the nation stands spellbound. The High Command weaves fine fabrics of compromise, dreaming in terms of peace with the enemy, just when he cannot withstand our united onslaught. A general who fails to rout the enemy's armies when they are breaking up, commits a crime against his own army. And the national leadership follows this very tactic with impunity. It advises calm and patience, when the most desperate and determined struggle is necessary. Utilizing his unique position in the country, Gandhiji advocates Charkha to meet a world historic situation.

Imperialist agents are busy in the recruiting centers. The Congress sits quiet and looks on. Indian sailors are drowned. Indian troops are despatched to enchain foreign peoples; the non-violent leadership continues to expect yet another call from the Viceroy. Prices soar high. Workers strike for better wages. Peasants loot the bazaars. The Congress leadership ignores all these happenings and says 'the masses are not ready'. Arrests of radicals continue. Civil Liberties are suppressed in Bengal. The High Command does not yet give the signal, fearing communal riots.

This is the way in which the sacred oath of Independence is being implemented. This is the way of people who are content to be slaves not of those who would fight for their freedom, no matter what the cost is. Just because of this bargaining, the communal agencies have reared their hand once more and threaten to submerge the country in communal riots.

The bargaining policy is undermining national unity, demoralizing the people, encouraging the Government to propagate the war with vigour and break up the resistance of the people. The oath of independence seems to have disappeared in thin air.

FOLLOWED TO ITS LOGICAL CONCLUSION, THE POLICY OF THE HIGH COMMAND WOULD LEAD TO THE SAME DISASTER AS IN 1914. Twenty-five years back India perpetrated a crime against humanity, world freedom and national emancipation by helping Britain in its war. Indian armies massacred other people; they acted as the base hirelings of the British Government. Indian leaders, unwittingly conspired in this atrocious conspiracy and increased the prestige and power of His Majesty's Government. Gandhiji in spite of all his non-violence, recruited hundreds of Indians for Britain's 'just' war.

History revenged itself. Soon after the war, imperialist terror was let loose. Thousands of unarmed people were massacred in Jallianwala Bagh. Women of Punjab were outraged by British soldiers. Men were openly flogged, children were tortured. General Dyer closed the whole chapter by giving the Crawling Order at Amritsar.

And yet to-day the same history is being repeated. Covert support through inaction has taken the place of open support. Immediate concessions are demanded in place of future promises. Indian freedom is being bartered for a mass of pottage.

Nonviolence has become the thinly-veiled excuse for ruinous compromise, for inaction. CHARKHA HAS BECOME THE SUBSTITUTE FOR STRUGGLE.

... The Independence Day comes as a reminder to us. Shall we go down in history as people who dared not strike for their own freedom, as people who repudiated their pledge? Shall we repeat the miserable performance of 1914–18, in spite of our colossal strength and our enemy's weakness? Shall the Congress be remembered by posterity as the instrument of ignoble compromise or as the deliverer of India?

ON THE INDEPENDENCE DAY, WE MUST PROCLAIM THAT INDIA CANNOT BE A PARTY TO ANY COMPROMISE ON THE ISSUE OF THE WAR. THE CONGRESS CANNOT BE A PARTY TO INACTION; THE PEOPLE WILL NOT BE A PARTY TO THE STALEMATE. PEOPLE'S OFFENSIVE AGAINST WAR, AGAINST FOREIGN DOMINATION, MUST BE DEMANDED ON THIS SACRED DAY.

The situation is ripe for this offensive. The time is ripe for a final onslaught.

The hope of a speedy end to war is no longer entertained by British diplomats. The economic blockade against Hitler has failed. British steamers are daily being sunk. Britain is no longer the mistress of the sea. The war threatens to prolong indefinitely.

But prolongation of the war means further isolation of the Government. In Britain itself the working class desires peace. The mad enthusiasm which was there in the last war is nowhere to be seen. Under stress of economic pressure, the British working class will become more and more opposed to war and paralyse its own government.

At the same time, Britain dare not contemplate the effects of a prolonged war on India. During the last war, the Indian masses groaned under the war burdens. They went through unspeakable miseries. British Imperialism transferred the burdens of war to the backs of the Indian people and won the war.

The situation is not the same today. The masses are no longer in a mood to tolerate the burden. Within the first months of the war, the Indian sailors demanded more insurance and got it. Thousands of Jute workers in Calcutta struck work and fought for increase. In Bombay the entire working class is preparing the war allowance offensive. Within three months of the war, high prices are forcing the peasants and workers to go in for food-riots.

THE ECONOMIC STRUCTURE OF IMPERIALISM IS COLLAPSING. THE MASSES ARE THE FIRST VICTIMS AND THEY HAVE ALREADY SEIZED THE INITIATIVE.

Besides, the recruitment campaign is not providing [proving] successful. The Indian peasant does not want to shed his blood for Britain's sake. Even Sikander Hyat Khan is finding it difficult to cheat the peasants. Desertions are reported from the Army. The last pillar of Imperialism is wavering, shaking.

What more do we want for a successful offensive? Why then this stalemate? Who wants compromise? Not the people of India. Who wants co-operation with the Government? Not the masses of Congressmen.

All we require is courage and daring to take the leadership and begin our final battle against Imperialism. The overthrow of the Government is imminent if only we will it.

Let this message be broadcast on 26 January Independence Day. The demonstrations and meetings must become the starting point for a big struggle. Every Congress Committee, every honest Congressman must passionately demand that the Congress launches immediate struggle and goes for uncompromising resistance to war and the government. The High Command must know the truth. The people can no longer wait. The loyalty of Congressmen cannot be strained to breaking point.

ON THE INDEPENDENCE DAY, EVERY CONGRESS COMMITTEE AND CONGRESSMAN MUST RESOLVE TO LAUNCH THE STRUGGLE AGAINST ORDINANCES, AGAINST REPRESSION, AGAINST RECRUITMENT IN HIS LOCALITY. AND ABOVE ALL, THE CONGRESS COMMITTEES MUST LEAD THE SPONTANEOUS STRUGGLE OF THE MASSES AGAINST ECONOMIC BURDENS, THE STRUGGLE WHICH WILL DECISIVELY THROW THE MILLIONS AGAINST THE GOVERNMENT AND THE WAR.

The stalemate can be broken through an intensification of this struggle. The national leadership can be brought to face the realities only through concrete demonstrations of people's readiness to fight against the war and the Government.

And above all, Independence Day must broadcast the fighting slogan of Constituent Assembly as the sovereign body of the Indian people. The High Command seeks to transform the Constituent Assembly into a docile instrument of compromise—a glorified edition of the Round Table Conference. But no Indian can accept this interpretation, this surrender before Imperialism. The Constituent Assembly will come as the result of a successful struggle, as the organ of power—after vanquishing the British Government. It will have earned the right to represent the people after the overthrowing of the present Government.

FOR STRUGGLE, FOR FINAL BATTLE, FOR A CONSTITUENT ASSEMBLY, AGAINST COMPROMISE AND STALEMATE—THESE MUST BE THE SLOGANS ON THIS INDEPENDENCE DAY:

We are not alone. Millions beyond our frontiers are preparing for the final battle. A world revolutionary crisis is maturing. The people of Germany are massing against Hitler. The British and French workers have begun their struggle. The colonies are seething with unrest. A triumphant phase has begun in China's war of independence. Having smashed the plans of imperialism, the Soviet Union stands more powerful than ever, prepared to aid the oppressed masses of all lands.

World reaction is fighting a losing battle. World revolution is on the offensive. Let us not forget that the whole world is watching us that for us to fail at this historic moment would be a crime against humanity.

LET THE INDEPENDENCE DAY MARK THE BEGINNING OF A NEW PHASE IN OUR HISTORY!

LET US CONGRESSMEN SHOW ENOUGH DARING TO LEAD THE PEOPLE!

VICTORY IS OURS, IF ONLY WE WILL IT.

25. 'Proletarian Path', CPI Policy Statement on Tactics during the Imperialist Phase of the War, 1940

File No. 1940/48, P.C. Joshi Archives on Contemporary History, JNU.

We are an illegal Party and cannot popularize our programme openly. Other parties are free to do so. We suffer under this disadvantage. After the outbreak of war, our legal press has been suppressed, the censor sits guard over the daily press terrorizing it to have no truck with us. In our legal publications, we can only criticize the policy of other Parties and vaguely indicate our own. Those who desire to know the Communist Policy in the present situation will find it outlined in this document. It will tell them why is it that the main fire of British Imperialism to-day is directed against us, Communists.

—Polit Bureau, Central Committee,
Communist Party of India.

British Imperialism occupies in present-day world a position similar to what Tsardom occupied at the outbreak of the last war. British Empire is the biggest prison of peoples. Consistent upholder of reaction in every land, abettor of Fascist aggression, destroyer of People's Front in France and Spain, instigator of war of intervention against the Soviet Union, the British ruling class is to-day the most serious enemy of human progress. India is the main colony of Britain and the main source of its imperial power. Hence, achievement of freedom by India will not only mean the liberation of 350 millions of people from the yoke of slavery, it will also be the most powerful blow against the strongest pillar of WORLD REACTION. National Revolution in India will create the most irreparable breach in the world Imperialist system, will enormously strengthen revolutionary movements in Egypt, in Middle East, in Africa, in every colony held by Britain and France. It will be the most decisive step towards the creation of a new world order.

The Two Camps

2. The world is in the midst of a deep crisis, the crisis of the Second Imperialist War. As in the last war, but on a much vaster scale, a new revolutionary wave is rising all over the world. Confronting each other stand two forces—the forces of Imperialism, Fascism and War; the forces of Socialism, Democracy and Peace. That is the basic conflict. One force drags humanity towards world conflagration and black reaction. The other, headed by the Soviet Union, fights to save humanity through world revolution. India cannot remain neutral in this conflict, nor can she support Britain. To do either would mean betrayal of the national movement, betrayal of the world revolutionary movement.

INDIA HAS TO MAKE REVOLUTIONARY USE OF THE WAR CRISIS TO ACHIEVE HER OWN FREEDOM. THAT WOULD BE HER REAL CONTRIBUTION. BY THAT ALONE SHALL SHE WIN A WORTHY PLACE IN THE CAMP OF THOSE FORCES THAT ARE STRIVING TO SAVE HUMANITY AND CREATE A NEW WORLD ORDER.

3. The Indian national movement has entered into a new phase—a phase full of the most glorious and unprecedented possibilities. This war has created for British Imperialism the biggest crisis it has ever faced. And that crisis shall deepen with every prolongation of the War. Provincial Autonomy has been destroyed. Ordinance Raj established. In order to forestall action by the people, imperialism has launched offensive against the last vestiges of democratic liberties, against rights of association, press and speech.

In order to finance her predatory war, Britain robs all sections of the Indian people, including the national bourgeoisie. The Excess Profits' Tax, the increased Railway fares and freights, the Excise Duty on Sugar—all these are indications of what is to come. The political discontent created by Ordinance Regime increases a hundred-fold because of these measures. Masses have started hitting back. Food riots took place all over the country in September and again in December. Mass strikes are developing on a scale like which India has never seen before. These actions will draw millions into active struggle.

Thus, every measure taken by imperialism, every effect of the war, drives the people more and more to the path of revolt. The crisis of imperialism is deepening and will deepen with every prolongation of the war.

General Strike—Armed Insurrection

4. In a situation like this, achievement of national independence, CONQUEST OF POWER BY THE INDIAN PEOPLE BECOMES THE IMMEDIATE TASK. It becomes a practical proposition. Our strategy, the strategy of the entire national movement has to be based with this task in view. How to raise the national movement to that level is the immediate question.

POLITICAL GENERAL STRIKE IN THE MAJOR INDUSTRIES together with COUNTRYWIDE NO-RENT AND NO-TAX ACTION constitute the first steps towards this objective. When such a situation has been brought about, when industries and transports have been, and are being paralysed, when the whole countryside has been engulfed by the rising wave of no-rent and no-tax struggle, when tens of thousands of students have come out in the streets, have spread to the countryside and are taking part in the daily clashes between the forces of the Government and the people—then the crisis created by the war and intensified by mass action during the war period, will begin to deepen into REVOLUTIONARY CRISIS. Confronting each other will stand two forces—the armed might of British Imperialism and the mightier forces of national revolution. The national movement will enter into a new and higher phase—the phase of ARMED INSURRECTION.

General Strike and No-Rent will have drawn millions into active struggle against the Government, will have demoralized the forces of the Government, will have disorganized and semi-paralysed the State machinery. That, however, will not OVERTHROW the Government. 'The combination of proletarian mass strikes in the city with the peasant movement in the villages' said Lenin in the *Revolution of 1905*, 'was sufficient to SHAKE UP the firmest and last prop of Tsarism—the Army'. In order, however, to SMASH the State machinery and not merely to paralyse it, in order to WIN over the rank and file of the Army and not merely shake it up, the movement will have to develop into nationwide armed insurrection. Storming of military and police stations by armed bands of national militia in rural as well as urban areas, destruction of Government institutions, actual OFFENSIVE against the armed forces of the Government on the most extensive scale—these will increasingly become the chief features of the struggle. That will be the culminating point of the mass movement, the point at which the last pillar of imperialism will begin to crack. Within the Indian Army a profound crisis will develop, the rank and file, the Indian soldiers, will increasingly come over to the people's militia. Under the smashing blow of the popular forces, the State machine will break down. The parties and bodies representing the victorious people's revolution will form the Provisional Revolutionary Government and summon the Constituent Assembly, which elected on the basis of universal adult franchise, will meet as the ORGAN OF POWER of the triumphant People's Revolution and frame the Constitution for Free India.

Basic Slogans of National Revolution

5. The Imperialist State will be supplanted by the Democratic Republic of the People; the existing mercenary army will be supplanted by the People's Army into which the revolutionary national militia will develop. The existing Civil Service and Police will be replaced by elected officials and armed guards who shall be servants of the people and not their masters. Landlordism shall be abolished and agrarian indebtedness cancelled. Eight-hour day and minimum wage shall be introduced. The Revolution shall sweep away the rotten, decayed, social structure artificially preserved by Imperialism and on its ruins lay the foundation of a new social order based on democracy and well-being of the people.

It is with this perspective and towards this culmination that the Communist Party, the revolutionary party of the proletariat shall work. It is this perspective that it shall strive to make the perspective of the ENTIRE national movement. As against the Gandhian programme of 'Constituent Assembly' meeting with the sanction of Imperialism, it will popularize the Constituent Assembly as the organ of power, meeting as the culmination of triumphant revolution. As against the Gandhian dreams of Dominion Status in which the foreign Army, the Civil Service, the imperialist police remain intact, the Communists shall place before the people the goal of People's Republic, People's Army, elected officials and armed National Guard. As against the Gandhian concept of Swaraj, in which the social structure undergoes no fundamental change and the system of rack-renting and debt-slavery remain intact, the Communists shall proclaim the programme of abolition of landlordism and cancellation of indebtedness. As against the Gandhian ideal of 'trusteeship' of the factory-owner, the Communists shall to-day fight for a social system in which the right to eight-hour day and minimum wage are guaranteed.

Thus, concretizing the programme of National Revolution through the basic slogans of (1) DEMOCRATIC REPUBLIC AND PEOPLE'S ARMY (2) ABOLITION OF LANDLORDISM AND CANCELLATION OF INDEBTEDNESS (3) EIGHT-HOUR DAY AND GUARANTEED LIVING WAGE, popularizing these slogans on the most extensive scale in every meeting, in every procession and in every conflict with the Government, EVERY STRIKE, EVERY DEMONSTRATION of workers, students, Kisans, Congressmen etc., the Communist shall strive to make these slogans THE SLOGANS OF THE NATIONAL MOVEMENT.

This perspective and this programme shall determine the strategy and tactics of the Communists in every conflict, their attitude towards every party, their slogans in every specific situation and on each issue.

Weapon of Mass Strike

6. In order to develop the national movement to this revolutionary level, the Communists shall make the most extensive use of the weapon of MASS STRIKE.

It was the use of this weapon—as Lenin points out—that in 1905 transformed 'slumbering Russia into the Russia of Revolutionary proletariat and revolutionary people'. It was through the use of this weapon that the proletariat of Russia became the leader of the democratic revolutionary movement. It was through the combination of POLITICAL and ECONOMIC strikes that the broad masses of the people of Russia were drawn into active struggle against Tsardom and the movement acquired extensive sweep and immense striking power. Events of the last six months—the great Anti-War Strike of 90,000 Bombay workers, the Independence Day Strike of 30,000 Cawnpore workers, the strike at Dehri, the organized participation of the working class of Calcutta, Coimbatore, Sholapur and other centres in the Independence Day demonstrations—have conclusively demonstrated that for the first time in its history, THE INDIAN WORKING CLASS IS EMERGING AS AN INDEPENDENT POLITICAL FORCE ON A NATIONAL SCALE. The gigantic strike struggles that are developing in Bombay, Cawnpore, Nagpore, on the basis of the demand for War-Allowance, are schooling the proletariat, steeling and unifying their ranks and preparing them for the decisive struggles that lie ahead. Through these struggles, the proletariat is exercising profound influence on non-proletarian masses. Its technique of action—mass strike—has already, under Communist influence, become the technique of the STUDENT MOVEMENT. The great Student strikes that took place on the Independence Day, the strikes organized by the Calcutta students against the arrests of working class and student leaders show this clearly.

This constitutes the most important and MOST SIGNIFICANT development of the last six months—the rapid growth of the political strike movement; mass strikes on the most extensive scale against the economic distress caused by the war; extensive use of the weapon of political strike by non-proletarian sections, particularly STUDENTS.

To intensify this development still further, to strengthen the proletarian base of the Communist Party, to develop the Communist Party into mass Party, to make the Party known to the masses of proletariat, the Party to which they look for guidance and whose lead they follow; to develop Trade Unions into mass unions; to organize Volunteer Corps with young militant workers, which shall develop into nuclei of the proletarian and national militia in the coming period—such are the immediate tasks.

In the period of storm and stress that lies ahead, in the period when political suppression shall be intensified and economic distress aggravated, in the period when the political crisis of imperialism shall deepen, the weapon of mass strike, strikes of workers and students shall be the most powerful weapon for preventing demoralization and disorganization in popular ranks, for imbuing them with revolutionary spirit, for demonstrating national hatred against imperialist rule, for forging national unity. Actions like students going on strike against arrests of working class leaders, workers downing tools against shooting of peasants and States' People—such actions would strengthen the bonds of fighting unity, make every section feel that it is a part of the united national army, make every victim of Government terror feel that he is not alone. It would demoralize the forces of the Government.

Revolutionary Alliance of Workers and Peasants

7. The factor that shall determine most decisively the course of our national movement shall be: with whom and under whose leadership will the Indian Peasantry act? Only the completion of the National Democratic Revolution—a Revolution that sweeps away British Imperialism and along with it landlordism, rack-renting etc., a Revolution that removes the crushing burden of debts, can solve the basic problems of the Kisans. The National bourgeoisie cannot lead such a revolution. Only the proletariat can. The national movement must land to defeat or compromise if the peasantry remain a reserve of the bourgeoisie and act under bourgeois leadership. Hence, forging revolutionary alliance with the peasantry, making decisive bid to win the leadership of the peasantry are tasks that confront the proletariat to-day, tasks by fulfilling which alone can the proletariat ensure the success of the National Revolution.

On the basis of the gigantic growth that the organized Kisan movement has attained during the last four years, the Communists shall prepare the Kisan masses for playing their role in the new phase. They will make the most extensive use of the weapons of Kisan marches, rallies, no-rent, no-tax struggles and militant action against the landlords and police. The attitude of criminal negligence of Kisan Sabha work that has been the most deplorable feature of the last six months, as clearly seen in the sharp fall of Kisan Sabha membership, shall be finally and decisively given up. The sharp rise of prices of agricultural goods has benefited the middlemen and not the Kisan. It has aggravated his misery. On the basis of the demands that the minimum price which Kisans get for such goods be fixed and that maximum prices of manufactured goods which Kisan have to buy be fixed, powerful Kisan movements shall be developed in every province. Resistance to forcible recruitment, resistance to forcible levies, shall be organized and the whole struggle directed towards countrywide no-rent movement. Immediate strengthening of the mass basis of Kisan Sabhas, their development into mass Kisan Sabhas, organization of Kisan Volunteer Corps that shall develop into Kisan and National Militia, strengthening of Party units in rural areas—such are the tasks of Communists in rural areas to-day.

Weapon of Satyagraha

8. Satyagraha cannot bring about revolutionary culmination of the national movement and hence Communists definitely reject it as a weapon in the struggle for freedom. Nevertheless, the organized forces of the workers, peasants and students are to day so mature and so powerful, that by their independent action, they can transform mass satyagraha into mass revolutionary movement. Therefore, far from OPPOSING mass satyagraha, Communists shall actively work to bring about such situation as makes the Congress give the call for MASS struggle—even of the Satyagraha variety. 'Call for nationwide satyagraha' however given by the CSP, Forward Bloc or even the United Left, will not draw the popular MASSES in, who continue to be under the influence of the Right and therefore, will not afford any such revolutionary possibilities. Hence, Communists shall OPPOSE such call. When MASS satyagraha is launched by the CONGRESS, the Communists shall actively participate in it. They shall be at the forefront of all clashes and conflicts with the forces of the Government. And they shall, by propaganda and by actual development of mass strike etc. demonstrate to the Congress masses the greater effectiveness of the proletarian method of struggle and thus win them over.

Anti-Struggle Policy of the Bourgeoisie

9. But the National Congress leadership too realizes this implication of mass satyagraha. It knows that in the period of profound revolutionary crisis that has begun with the war and because of the great strength and maturity that the mass movement has attained, mass satyagraha will inevitably flow into revolutionary channels. Hence, it strives to avoid any sort of struggle. Through the technique of stalemate and inaction, the Gandhian leadership is trying to demoralize the Congress masses and create the atmosphere favourable for 'honourable settlement'. Determined to reduce the Congress into an instrument for carrying out the policy of compromise, it has begun to make the Congress into an instrument for carrying out the policy of compromise, it has begun disruptive offensive against the Congress—as amply shown by its policy towards the Bengal Congress and by the Spinning Pledge. Afraid of the masses and their struggle, it has turned its face away from them and now bases its hope for 'compromise' on the increasing difficulties that the Government will face if the conflagration starts.

The fact that imperialism has intensified its offensive against all sections of the people, including the bourgeoisie (Excess Profits Tax, Railway Freight, Excise Duty on Sugar etc.) has not made the bourgeoisie pro-struggle. On the contrary, conscious of the explosive nature of the situation, the bourgeoisie is to-day more opposed to mass struggle than it ever was. As the crisis created by the war shall deepen and the situation will grow more and more revolutionary, this fear of struggle will more and more dominate the mind of the national leadership and determine its policy. But simultaneously the conflict between the bourgeoisie and imperialism will sharpen because imperialism will intensify exploitation of the whole country. Faced with such a situation, the national leadership will strive to frighten imperialism with the spectre of revolution, restrain the masses, restrict their struggles and use these very struggles to extract concessions from imperialism. With the growing explosiveness of the situation, the national leadership will grow more and more anti-struggle, its tactics will grow more and more disruptive of national unity.

Gandhism—A Disruptive Force

10. Permitting imperialism to decimate the revolutionary forces in isolation; seeking to cover its utter bankruptcy and cowardice with phrases about 'duties of a Satyagrahi'; coming out openly against political strikes, against even mass satyagraha; combining abject surrender to imperialism—on the issue of States, on the issue of War, on the issue of Ordinance—with ruthless offensive against the forces of struggle, Gandhism, with the outbreak of War has entered into its last and most reactionary phase. NO LONGER DOES IT PLAY ANY UNIFYING, ANY PROGRESSIVE ROLE WHATSOEVER. It is to-day the most disruptive, most demoralizing, most anti-struggle force within the National Congress, in the national camp.

Compromise on the issue of war is the essence of Gandhian policy to-day. Inaction, stalemate is the TECHNIQUE for carrying out that policy. Hence, STRUGGLE AGAINST STALEMATE, STRUGGLE AGAINST COMPROMISE MEAN SIMULTANEOUSLY STRUGGLE AGAINST GANDHISM.

Not declaration of faith in Gandhiji's leadership but ruthless EXPOSURE of that leadership. Not the tactic of 'inducing or pushing' the Gandhian leadership into struggle but of ISOLATING that leadership and smashing its mass influence. Not expression of surprise at the 'fade' of Gandhiji but tearing away the non-violent mask from the face of Gandhism and exposing it as the policy and technique of the compromising bourgeoisie. Not academic 'criticism' of Charkha, Khaddar and constructive programme as being 'economically wasteful' but their political exposure as technique of sidetracking the main issue and dividing the national forces. Not meaning that there is stagnation but criticizing stagnation as the technique of compromise. Not abstract criticism of the growth of 'authoritarianism' in the Congress but exposing the policy of 'homogeneity' as a policy of reducing the Congress into a docile instrument for carrying out the policy of compromise. In brief all-round and convincing political exposure of Gandhism— TO THIS TASK, THE COMMUNISTS SHALL SET THEMSELVES ENERGETICALLY.

This does not mean that Communists shall fight on 'two fronts'—against British Imperialism and against Gandhism. The front of the people is only ONE, the front against British Imperialism. Inside the national front, Gandhism represents the anti-struggle, disruptive trend. The more we EXPOSE this character of Gandhism, the more we mobilize the masses for ACTION against Imperialism, and its bloody barbarities, cruel exploitation, ruthless repression, the more we succeed in unifying the front of the people, as a fighting front, the more we expose and isolate the compromisers. The 'theory of two fronts' results in the tactic of verbal condemnation of compromise coupled with complete inaction as far as imperialism and its war measures are concerned. It results in refusal to fight imperialist terror; in refusal to mobilize masses FOR ACTION against Ordinance Regime, against economic distress. It strengthens compromisers and their policy. It results in disruption of the fighting front of the people. It is not the slogan of serious revolutionists. It is the slogan of factional—and not political—opposition of the present Working Committee.

Struggle against Compromise: The Slogan of Two Congresses

11. Communists categorically reject the slogan of Two Congresses given by Bose. POLITICAL ISOLATION of the bourgeoisie, of the compromisers, cannot be brought about by forces of struggle splitting away from the Congress and forming another 'Congress'. That would destroy the national unity that has already been achieved instead of strengthening it. That would isolate the forces of struggle and not the compromisers. That would intensify disruption instead of liquidating it.

The Congress leadership stands for a 'Constituent Assembly' which shall meet with the sanction of imperialism and which shall THEREFORE leave the Army, the Civil Service, the Police, the existing social structure INTACT. The policy of the Congress leadership is compromise. The technique is negotiations and in the extreme case Satyagraha—limited, restricted satyagraha, satyagraha that must end in defeat or compromise.

Political isolation of the bourgeoisie means weaning the masses away from this objective, from this policy, from this technique; and winning them FOR revolutionary objective, revolutionary policy and revolutionary technique. This winning over cannot be done by mere ideological exposure of Gandhism. It has to be done mainly by mass action, mass action of workers and peasants against political repression and economic exploitation, mass strikes of students against police terror, mass popularization of the basic programme of the National Democratic Revolution.

When the slogans of Democratic Republic, People's Army, cancellation of indebtedness, abolition of landlordism, Eight-hour day and living wage become THE slogans of the entire national movement, the slogans of every mass meeting, demonstration and conflict; when revolutionary utilization of the war crisis and overthrow of imperialism and convening the Constituent Assembly have become the perspective of the people's movement; when people reply to every act of Imperialist terror and of economic exploitation with the weapon of MASS STRIKE, mass actions, hartals and demonstrations; when every act of betrayal on the part of the Congress leadership is greeted—not by Bose threatening split or Congress Socialists launching satyagraha under their 'own' leadership—but by SIMILAR MASS ACTIONS—when such a situation comes about, THAT will signify POLITICAL ISOLATION of the compromisers. That will signify rejection of their policy, rejection of their technique by the masses.

For Communists, therefore, struggle against Imperialist War, struggle against compromise, struggle against Gandhism, struggle against stalemate are not SEPARATE struggles. They are all parts of the same struggle, the struggle to develop the national movement into mass revolution against foreign rule. At a stage when the Gandhian leadership is disrupting national unity, and destroying the heritage of the Congress, through SUCH struggle, the proletariat shall isolate the disruptors and come out as the unifier of the nation, upholder of the glorious traditions of the Congress. By fulfilling this role of unifier of the nation, by being the most consistent champion of national unity against imperialist rule, the proletariat shall realize hegemony in the national movement.

Such is the Communist way of struggle against compromise, against Gandhism. To the hypothetical question as to what they would do if even after the compromisers have been politically isolated, they retain control over the Congress by destroying all inner-Congress democracy, the reply of the Communists is: at such a stage the mass struggle will have reached so high a level and become so powerful that it will sweep away the present leadership and with it, the organization which remains in their pocket. New organs of struggle will have come into existence and new unity of the people on their basis would have been forged.

To raise the slogan of Two Congresses NOW is only a means of escaping IMMEDIATE implementing of the line of struggle, is to lack faith in the masses, in our own capacity to move them and PREVENT a compromise.

Through such a path alone can the stalemate be broken, compromise PREVENTED and if it comes about, SMASHED.

Slogan of Alternative Leadership

12. Communist policy of realization of proletarian hegemony in the national movement has nothing in common with the Royist slogan of 'alternative leadership'. The present leadership representing the national bourgeoisie cannot lead the national movement to revolution. The cleavage between ITS class interest and the interest of the nation is growing and shall grow sharper with the deepening of the war-crisis, with the growing explosiveness of the situation. Unifier of the national movement at one stage, this leadership will grow more and more disruptive as that cleavage widens. That class will have to increasingly assume leadership of the national movement which can maintain national unity which is the most consistent, revolutionary, whose interest corresponds to the interest of the overwhelming majority of our people, not only at this stage but even up to, through and after the overthrow of Imperialism. SUCH A CLASS IS THE PROLETARIAT.

The proletariat, however, shall become the leader of the national movement not by an organisational coup BEFORE struggle develops, not by disrupting the Congress. It will achieve that leadership by developing the weapon of mass strike to the utmost, by giving its own impress on the national movement, by being the most consistent champion of the full programme of the national democratic revolution. It will achieve that leadership by coming forward and fighting against every act of imperialist terror—no matter against whom it is directed. It will achieve that leadership by really ACTING as the unifier of the nation, of the Congress. THROUGH struggle against the Government and not BEFORE struggle, the proletariat shall PROGRESSIVELY and not at one STROKE, UNIFY the nation and THUS win leadership.

Roy's opposition to even MASS satyagraha by the Congress, and also to independent political action by the working class (Roy opposed the anti-war strike of Bombay workers) clearly demonstrate that by 'alternative leadership', Roy means not PROLETARIAN leadership, but an 'alternative' BOURGEOIS or PETTY–BOURGEOIS leadership. How the technique, the METHOD OF STRUGGLE of this alternative leadership will differ from that of the present leadership, to this ALL IMPORTANT QUESTION, Roy has given no reply. He has said that it will NOT be satyagraha but what it will BE, he has not said. And he cannot say, because the ONLY alternative to satyagraha, mass strike, mass no-rent, he rejects as 'dissipation of energy'. Roy considers compromise inevitable and believes that the only task of revolutionists to day is to carry on 'ideological struggle' and 'educate' (not struggle). He rejects the path of mass action.

Role of Independent Mass Action

13. In contradistinction to other Parties of the Left—CSP, Forward Bloc etc.—therefore, Communists do not consider compromise INEVITABLE nor do they frame ONE tactic for to-day and ANOTHER basically different 'when compromise comes about'. Independent mass action is the MAJOR weapon, through which compromise can be prevented, national unity maintained, compromisers weakened and isolated, and the Congress moved towards struggle. Independent mass action is the weapon by which satyagraha can be transformed into mass

revolution. Independent mass action is ALSO the weapon by which compromise, even if it comes about, can be smashed.

Congress as Organ of Struggle

14. While laying the utmost emphasis on independent actions by the class organizations of workers and peasants, the Communists shall strive to build up the Congress as the organ of people's movement. Without waiting for 'call for struggle' from above, they shall, wherever they influence the Congress organizations, undertake the formation of Congress Volunteer Corps, and place the Congress units on fighting basis, with cadres of trained organizers, apparatus for production and distribution of literature etc. The local Congress units must initiate struggle against suppression of political liberties. They must wholeheartedly support IN ACTION the struggles of workers and peasants for War-Allowance, for Fixation of Prices, against every economic distress. By thus identifying themselves with the EXISTING and DEVELOPING struggles and not by waiting for 'call' will the Congress units grow and draw strength from the masses and be able to influence the Congress leadership itself.

In the Thick of Every Struggle, at the Head of Every Clash

15. By thus struggling against the compromisers, by resolutely fighting for the full programme of national revolution, by developing the weapon of mass strike and mass action to the utmost extent, the Communists shall prepare the basis for mass revolutionary uprising against British rule. With this object in view, they shall strengthen their Party and develop it into a mass Party. With this object in view, they will work in the Congress, fight against all disruption and strengthen the Congress as an organ of struggle. With this object in view, they shall strengthen the class organizations, from Volunteer Corps of workers, peasants and Congressmen as the nuclei of the revolutionary national militia.

Conscious of the revolutionary nature of the new situation, conscious that in this period, every conflict unfolds revolutionary possibilities, the Communists shall be in the thick of every struggle, at the forefront of every clash between the people and the Government. Thus, in action and through action, they shall establish their claim to be the vanguard of the national forces. Through such action and through the fulfillment of this programme shall the Communist Party of India win a worthy place in the rank of the World Communist Movement.

What Communists Want

16. Such are the tactics of the Communists for the present period.

We, Communists, want to create a new India on the ruins of the present decayed and rotten structure of imperialism. We want our country to make the most decisive contribution ending this predatory war, for striking a mortal blow at the greatest enemy of human progress— British Imperialism. We want our country to play the glorious role of one of the builders of a New World Order—a world order based on PEACE, DEMOCRACY AND PROGRESS.

Join the Communist Party!

THE COMMUNIST PARTY OF INDIA is the political Party of the most exploited and revolutionary class in modern Indian society, namely the Working Class, the final aim of which is the attainment of socialism and ultimately completely complete Communism and classless society.

THE COMMUNIST PARTY OF INDIA seeks to achieve the political and organizational unity of the working class. It seeks to build the revolutionary unity between the working class and the peasantry. It seeks to unite the overwhelming majority of the Indian people in one single anti-imperialist national united front.

THE COMMUNIST PARTY OF INDIA stands for the following immediate programme:

  (a) Complete overthrow of British Imperialism;
  (b) A democratic state and army of the people;
  (c) Abolition of landlordism in all its forms, abolition of slavery and serfdom in all forms and the cancellation of debts;
  (d) 8-hour day and a guaranteed living wage to industrial workers;
  (e) Confiscation and nationalization of all key Industries, Banks, Railways, Sea and River Transport and Plantations owned by foreign as well as Indian Capital.

THE COMMUNIST PARTY OF INDIA considers that the role and historically tested means of winning independence, carrying out of the agrarian revolution (abolition of landlordism), achieving democratic reconstruction, is the path of the revolutionary struggle of the widest possible mass of the people developing into a general national armed insurrection against the British exploiters and their allies in our country.

THE COMMUNIST PARTY OF INDIA is a part of the organised world Communist movement— a section of the COMMUNIST INTERNATIONAL. The COMMUNIST PARTY OF INDIA calls upon all advanced workers and revolutionaries devoted to the cause of the working class to join ITS RANKS.

THE COMMUNIST PARTY OF INDIA in this period of war and revolutionary crisis concentrates all its efforts in making possible a national united struggle against the enemy of the Indian people, the chief war-incendiary, the main prop of World capitalist reaction, the inveterate foe of Socialism and the Soviet Union, namely British Imperialism. THE COMMUNIST PARTY OF INDIA fights against compromise, for national unity, for the PROLETARIAN PATH of mass revolutionary struggle.

(Published by the CENTRAL COMMITTEE of the COMMUNIST PARTY OF INDIA)

H. CONGRESS SOCIALIST PARTY

26. Jayaprakash Narayan's Justification of the Congress Socialist Party's Anti-War Stand

Janata, 1 February 1940.

The World War and the Congress Socialist Party

Here Mr Jayaprakash Narayan has given a befitting reply to the charges of the Communist Party—The editor.

We have to answer the propaganda against the party spread by the Communists that the party itself had devised the adventuristic plan of starting the Civil Disobedience Movement. In this connection and in connection with other matters, they have spread many false rumours. The first point which should be considered is that the party has never decided that it will do everything independently on its own. During our meeting, we had decided about the possibility of following the policies of the Congress and what should be the position of the Party regarding the implementation of these policies. Among these possibilities the first one was Congress Party's unconditional support to the government in this war and the other one was to pressurize it for sometime and then arrive at a settlement after some haggling. We had already informed the Congress Working Committee that the Party will not support the war efforts on any condition and if Congress takes such a step, it will oppose this activity of the Congress and the war. We should remember that we took this step after considering all these extraordinary possibilities. The Working Committee of the party had never thought that the Congress Working Committee will take sides with Imperialism as is shown through an article of the Community Party which has condemned us.

The overall belief of the Working Committee of the Party is that the Congress will fight in the end and therefore, it is our duty to strengthen its internal and external powers. Nevertheless, if the other possibilities become true in reality or the Congress takes more time in being firm about its decision and the Congress Ministries remain in power, then what should be our plans; we should clear these things through discussion. This is the decision of the Working Committee and also of the members of the Party that it should start the Civil Disobedience movement on its own. Still we should remember that the Working Committee had never thought that the Party will fight on its own and will uproot imperialism. When our activities had started, it would have accelerated the ordinary speed of the political movement. But this path was not chosen because we should be remembered as martyrs or we would satisfy our Gandhian hunger of going to jail, or we would reconstruct our Party. The result of our activity would have been to pressurize the Congress institution and the common public to move towards this revolution. Our activities would have got special strength because of the place of Congress Socialist Party in the Congress organization. It would have prevented the Congress from either cooperating in the war or keeping a neutral stand in regard to this matter. The Ministries should have resigned. We should remember that all this debate was started on behalf of the ministries. But these strict measures become unnecessary when there are certain changes in the Congress policy towards that direction, which we had decided for it—the resignation of ministries, non-cooperation in war efforts and the preparation for civil disobedience. The Communists called it adventurism and they used every known abuse for it. Besides calling us Gandhist, they call us Marxists or Gandhists according to their convenience. The most laughable fact is that the Communists are shedding tears because (according to them) the Congress Socialist Party is dangerous for the unity of the country.

I have already mentioned that the policy of the Congress has relaxed and many of us are anxious for the new activity. I have already stated that this is not the proper time for any activity. You should give your full attention to the above mentioned programme. You should always remember that all of us could not be fully prepared all at a time. There are seven lakhs villages in India. You should ask yourself as to how many villages are prepared for non-payment of rents and taxes. There are many factories, thousands of Congress Committees and lakhs of students. How many volunteers can you appoint and train? There are many kinds of work around us. You should start implementing your duties according to your strength and send its report to me.

I have to say something regarding the organisational measures which we have taken during this period. When the war started in Europe and many ordinances were proclaimed and it was quite uncertain as to which direction the country will take it seemed useful in every way to make our organization strong enough to face any kind of unnatural situations. According to this the Working Committee has appointed a War Committee to take the necessary action at the time of extraordinary situation. The committee had decided to cancel the constitution of provincial parties. But it did not mean the abolition of parties. It only meant that they should not function according to their ordinary rules and sections because during this extraordinary situation if the small committees are functional, then we can arrive at some decisions very fast and also keep them under the central control. Therefore, the provincial committees were instructed to turn themselves into war committees. Almost every provincial committee has followed these instructions. In some provinces—like Orissa and Gujarat—the All India War Committee had itself appointed such committees because there were intra-party conflicts. The Communists started protesting against it because it did not suit them. They have directed the members of the party to revolt against it. I am requesting and alerting all of you not to bow before these pressures. The Communist Party is following its policy of attacking the Congress Socialist Party and their false propaganda to defame the Party and create internal confusion within the Party, is spreading as usual. We cannot let them proceed with all this. But we cannot stop them from attacking us and we should not bother about it. We did not care for it even during 1934–5 when we were rather weak. Then, why should we care for it now. But we have admitted many Communists in our Party because of our concern about unity, [by the word Communist, I mean the members of the Communist Party of India] and these people are working like the agents of the Communist Party of India and they are wasting their energy in demoralizing the Congress Socialist Party. We will not allow them to disrupt our Party like this. We should reorganize our Party. I appeal to you to help me in discharging this difficult duty. Are you concerned about the unity of the Socialists? I have been worried for it since long time and had been working for it. We are not against the unity of the Socialists. But what should we do against the Communist attack? If we are reorganizing our Party, it does not mean to disrupt our unity if they really mean unity by it. Let there be two parties in real operation, whose opposition should be truthful and which should criticize and cooperate honestly with each other. If we can achieve it then we can achieve unity as well. But the present policy of the Communists is not only destroying the unity of the Socialists but they are bent upon destroying the aims/ambitions of this Party. The main reason behind their present policy is that they are thinking highly of their strength. Their leaders have openly talked about crushing the Congress Socialist Party. Let us make our Party a Thinkers' Party without the help of other individuals. We should not be worried about these petty Parties. We should shift our attention to the wider problems and work among the people with self-confidence in ourselves and our Party.

27. Congress Socialists Explain their Attitude Towards War Efforts
Pioneer, 29 July 1940.

The following is the text of the Socialist Party statement:

'The Executive Committee has noted with alarm the decision of the Congress Working Committee at the last meeting at Delhi, to offer support to the British Government in the prosecution of the war on certain conditions. It appeals to Congressmen to raise their voices against this decision and to strive to secure its reversal.

'For five years now, the Congress has at each successive session declared its uncompromising opposition to war, and its decision to resist actively any attempt to involve India in any Imperialist war.

'When the present war broke out in September 1939 and the British Government declared India to be a belligerent, the AICC meeting at Wardha recorded its protest against India being dragged into the war against her will. Still the Congress did not take any precipitate step at that time and invited the British Government to declare its war aims. Meanwhile, the Congress stood firmly by its policy of non-cooperation with the war efforts. At the Wardha meeting of the AICC in October 1939, the Congress Socialist Party moved an amendment to the resolution defining its attitude towards the war in which it was definitely indicated that only a free India could finally determine India's attitude towards the present war.

'The British Government true to its imperialist character, declined to respond to this invitation and the Working Committee felt compelled to call for the resignation of all Congress Ministries in the provinces as a first step in non-cooperation with the war.

'The resignation of Congress Ministries created a wave of popular enthusiasm and it was hoped by the mass of Congressmen that Ramgarh would set the stage for the coming struggle. That session reaffirmed India's opposition to participation in the Imperialist war and gave the call to the Congress organizations to prepare for a mass movement. The assumption of leadership by Mr Gandhi at Ramgarh was a clear indication that the Congress offer would not involve India actively in the war.

'Government repression has taken a heavy toll of Congressmen throughout the country and day by day repression is getting intense. At the Ramgarh session a statement was made on behalf of the party lending support to the Working Committee in the belief and hope that the call for preparation for mass civil disobedience would soon turn into direct action itself. The Working Committee's present stand shatters any hope of resistance to war, and opens up the prospect of actual support for the war which the Congress stands pledged to oppose.

'Despite any declaration that Britain would make regarding India, Britain would remain an Imperialist power and the war an Imperialist war. The latest illustration to prove that Britain is not fighting for democracy or for the freedom of nations against aggression is the crossing of the Burma Road to China, thus assisting an aggressor against a fellow member of the League of Nations which is being attacked.

Grave Concern

'The Congress had to make its choice. The temptation is irresistible. Congressmen can again become cabinet ministers. They may also be ministers or members at the Centre. They will have an insight into the war machine. They will watch from inside (again to the extent allowed) the Englishman at work when engaged in a life and death struggle. They will have to raise crores of rupees and dispose of them in the war effort.

'We cannot contemplate without grave concern the prospect of Congressmen taking their places in such a government. The various attempts of the Congress in seeking clarification and finally declaration on the part of the British Government during the last few months have resulted in our not being able to devote all our energies to the task of preparing the country for the struggle for independence. We feel it is time we cried halt to the policy of seeking satisfaction of our demands from the British Government and devoted all our energy to prepare the country to wrest power from Britain.

'Events are moving so fast on the international stage that India might be called upon to face a grave crisis at any moment. If she is to take full advantage of such a crisis it can only be done if the realization of the existence of such a situation is brought home to the Indian people and the means for facing the situation are created without delay.

'With this end in view, we suggest that immediate steps should be taken to create an effective organization of national guards throughout the country to reorganize the Congress committees in such a way that they become effective in any emergency; to prepare the people for the not too distant contingency when they will be called upon to summon a constituent assembly to frame the constitution of a free India'.

I. FORWARD BLOC

28. Extracts from Presidential Address by Subhas Chandra Bose at the All India Forward Bloc Conference, 2nd Session, Nagpur, 18 June 1940

Sisir Kumar Bose (ed.), *Crossroads: The Works of Subhas Chandra Bose, 1938–40*, Calcutta, 1981 (2nd edition), pp. 337–41.

... Let us now proceed to consider the international situation as we find it today and as it will probably be tomorrow. After reading the outspoken statements of Messrs. Winston Churchill and Paul Reynaud we cannot blink the prime facts of the situation as they emerge from the quick tempo of war. Everyday makes it more clear that M. Paul Reynaud's summing up of the situation in the Chamber of Deputies (that victory of the Allies could only be brought about by a miracle) was a true measure of the military conditions then obtaining. Dark as was the picture then, it has grown darker since. The prospect today is positively bleak. And when one remembers this is a totalitarian war, it dawns on us how impossible is the situation in which the losing side is placed.

We may also concede that Monsieur Reynaud's ringing resolution 'to intensify the struggle and not to give up' is brave and resolute, and his words not empty heroics. For all that, he fails to convince when he says: 'We will shut ourselves into one of our Provinces and if we are driven out we will go to North Africa and if necessary into our possessions in America.'

That is hardly the way to carry a war through to victory. If the Allies lose their foothold in Europe, they may conceivably fight on in Africa, in Asia, even in America; but it is for the ultimate aim of victory, useless.

Today we have every right to examine the stark realities of the War as it has developed until we see them in the white light of clarity. The leaders of the French and British peoples have been frank. We should also be frank with ourselves.

The cause of the Allies' continuous defeat seems today lodged somewhere in their system. It was a system which Mr Clement Attlee, speaking, I believe, for the last time from the opposition benches, said had failed to meet the needs of the crisis. It was the fundamental weakness of a system in which slavery and freedom existed side by side that had resulted in Britain being 'decisively beaten' on the propaganda front. This was what the *Daily Mail* said was happening. Propaganda radiocasts from the Reich, it wrote at the end of March, were 'influencing not only the civilian population of Britain, but also our armed forces. ...' 'Goebbels,' it asserted, 'has had a walk-over.'

But we are not so much interested in a particular method as in the basic principles of action. And we are not to be dissuaded from pressing home our demand for the admission of our fundamental rights by a clouding of the issues and cry of 'saboteur'! We have too long been taken in by the cleverest Imperialist propaganda.

We cannot but ask ourselves where we stand in this international flux. Following the sombre thoughts of Allied statesmen and strategists, we cannot but ask ourselves what we should do if British resistance collapses. This is by no means impossible. In fact, the Premier, Mr Churchill has already talked in terms of defeat for Britain. He talked much earlier in the strain in which Premier Reynaud has now talked—of dispersing to the far ends of the Empire to carry on the struggle. Some of our statesmen, it seems, have been possessed with the dream of India being converted into a bastion of democratic resistance against the dictators' hordes. What a grotesque picture!

Almost the whole of the English Channel coast on the French side is in the hands of the Germans, making ordinary communications difficult and hazardous and the transport of troops all but impossible. Some of the best industrial regions of France are in the hands of the invaders. Paris, the heart of France, has ceased to throb. In the Champagne region a powerful German drive is developing to isolate the Maginot Line from the rest of France. In the South-East the powerful and fresh Italian legions are pressing, and everywhere the retreating French forces are harried by the admittedly superior air-arm of the Reichswehr. Such is the gloomy picture of the Allied position in Europe. From the Northern Arctic regions to the Atlantic, the Nazi eagle has spread its wings in an unbroken line. It is not surprising we should be told that there is no cause for optimism.

When the Nazi hordes crossed the German frontier into Holland and Belgium only the other day with the cry of 'nach Paris' on their lips, who could have dreamed that they would reach their objective so soon? A miracle in military warfare has happened, as it were, before our eyes and for an analogy, one has to turn to the Napoleonic wars or to the catastrophe at Sedan in the Franco–Prussian war of 1870. Whatever the French High Command may say, in the face of mechanized transport, innumerable tanks and dive-bombers, no resistance worth the name is possible after the capitulation of Paris. The days of trench warfare are over.

But what next? It is clear that Reynaud's[1] Government will not make a separate peace with Germany, leaving Great Britain in the lurch. But how long will he be able to retain the confidence of the French people? The fall of his cabinet, a tempting offer from Germany and Italy, a new Cabinet ready to make peace on those terms—these are events not altogether beyond the domain of possibility. The British Premier, Mr Winston Churchill, made an ominous reference to this in his historic speech the other day. And England? What is she likely to do, with or without France? The answer to this question could be furnished by that inexplicable factor 'the public morale'. Unfortunately, the morale of the British people has been badly shaken and the speeches of the Premier and of other Ministers give ample proof of it. Why should it be necessary to tell the British people that they should not go about with long faces as if they were at a funeral? Why should it be necessary to tell the world that even if Great Britain is overrun by the Nazis, the Empire will go on fighting and in God's good time, the New World will come to the rescue of the Old World? The British people are famous for their dogged pertinacity and their unflinching nerves. They are now confronted with what is perhaps the severest ordeal in their history. Let us see how they will acquit themselves.

The Nazis have performed a miracle with the help of a new military technique, invented by the younger Generals and military strategists. The Allies have fallen back on their war-renowned, hoary-headed Generals who have been found wanting, however. Have the Nazi Generals exhausted their new technique? Have the Allies any military secrets or any new technique up their sleeves? Much will depend on the answers to these two questions.

We used to hear much of the chemical preparations of the Reichswehr (German Army). Have they really perfected a new technique of chemical warfare? If they have, then we shall get evidence of it in the days to come. And it will then be seen how men's nerves behave under those new conditions. Will they collapse as the nerves of the brave Abyssinians did when attacked by Italian aircraft? Or will the soul conquer matter?

Judged from the realistic point of view, it is difficult to realize how the war can continue, if Great Britain is overrun. The United States of America cannot go beyond a certain limit in helping the Allies, lest Japan should make trouble in the Far East. And there is no hope, whatsoever, that Sir Stafford Cripps will succeed in dividing Germany and Soviet Russia. It is more than probable that there is a definite agreement between Soviet Russia on one side and Germany and Italy on the other. If I were to make a guess as to the terms of that agreement, I should hazard a statement of this sort:

1. Germany will have a free hand on the Continent minus the Balkans.
2. Italy will have a free hand in the Mediterranean region.
3. The Balkans and the Middle East will be the Russian sphere of influence.
4. The resources of Africa should be shared by all the Big Powers.

Since both Germany and Italy and perhaps Soviet Russia now regard great Britain as Public Enemy No. 1, it is also likely that they have a plan of carving up the British Empire. In this task they may invite Japanese help and cooperation, knowing that Japan has always cast longing eyes on the entire Archipelago, from the Dutch Indies right up to Australia.

Such being the situation, if Britain cannot save herself and her Empire from the German–Italian attack, it would be idle to expect, like Mr Churchill, that the Empire would save itself and Britain on the top of it. Let us, therefore, cease talking of saving Britain with the Empire's help or with India's help. India must in this grave crisis think of herself first. If she can win freedom now and then save herself, she will best serve the cause of humanity. It is for the Indian people to make an immediate demand for the transference of power to them through a Provisional National Government. No constitutional difficulties can be put forward by the British Government with a view to resisting this demand, because legislation for this purpose can be put through Parliament in twenty-four hours. When things settle down inside India and abroad, the Provisional National Government will convene a Constituent Assembly for framing a full-fledged Constitution for this country.

Friends, these are some of my thoughts and suggestions today. I hope and trust that you will give them due consideration. In any case, I appeal to you not to leave Nagpur till you have in your pockets a concrete plan of action for winning Purna Swaraj in the immediate future.

Let us proclaim once again—'All power to the Indian people, here and now.'

---

[1] Paul Reynaud was Prime Minister of France from 21 March 1940 to 16 June 1940.

J. INDEPENDENT LABOUR PARTY

29. War and Independent Labour Party[1]

Bombay Chronicle, 4 September 1940.

Mr D.V. Pradhan, the General Secretary of the Independent Labour Party, has issued the following statement to the Press:

A meeting of the Executive Committee of the Party was held on Sunday, Dr Ambedkar presided. After having discussed the preliminarily matters, the President acquainted the committee of his interview with the Viceroy both at Delhi and in Bombay and also with the correspondence that has passed between him and the Viceroy. The Committee discussed at length the matter from various points of view and decided that the Party should give unconditional support to Britain and also desired that Dr Ambedkar should accept a seat on the Expanded Executive Council if such an offer came from the Viceroy.

---

[1] Formed by Dr B.R. Ambedkar in 1936.

K.   ALL-INDIA STATES PEOPLE'S CONFERENCE

30.   States' People's Conference Deplores Princes' Attitude

Statement issued by All-India States People's Conference Standing Committee, Bombay, 10–13 February 1940; *Indian Annual Register*, 1940, Vol. I, pp. 405–6.

The Standing Committee of the All-India States' Peoples' Conference which had been meeting at Bombay for the last three days, concluded the sitting on the 13th February 1940. The Committee issued a statement on the present situation.

Dealing with the war crisis, the statement says, the Committee considered the war crisis and pointed out the incongruity of Indian Rulers expressing support to the principle of democracy in Europe while maintaining 'undiluted autocracy in their own States'. The Committee declared that it was unable to accept the commitments of the Rulers regarding the war and urged them immediately to declare their acceptance of the objective of full responsible government in their States and give effect to this in the largest possible measure in the immediate future.

The Committee repudiated the claim of the Rulers to speak on behalf of the people of the States and took serious objection to the British Government taking shelter under treaties which were entered into between the East India Company and the then Rulers under special circumstances and for using the States as instruments and permanent safeguards against India's freedom and the spread of democracy in India. The Committee emphatically refuted the whole background of the theory and argument by which the Rulers attempted to defend 'their autocracy and separate themselves from India's progress'. The people of the States were no parties to the old treaties and they did not consider themselves bound by them. Nor would they recognize any new treaties or arrangements which limited their rights or came in the way of India's freedom. Their objective was full responsible government in the States within the framework of an independent and united India and everything that militated against that objective had to be rejected. Thus no constitution or convention which made progress dependent on the will of the Ruler could be acceptable. The essential conditions that must be observed were that the will of the people of the States must prevail in constitutional and other matters that civil liberty must be maintained and that the rule of law must be established.

The Committee had every wish to help in the peaceful settlement of the problem of the States and in any future arrangement to maintain the dignity of the Ruler as a constitutional head. But the Committee could not agree to autocracy in any shape or form or to the will of the people of the States being overruled by their Rulers.

—⧉—✳—⧉—

L. NATIONAL LIBERAL FEDERATION

31. An Appeal to Support the Allies in their War Efforts by Sir Chimanlal Setalvad, the Liberal Leader

Statesman, 14 May 1940.

Help for Britain in War—A 'Common Danger'

An appeal to all parties in India 'to bury the hatchet' and support the Allies in their war effort, is made by Sir Chimanlal Setalvad, the Liberal leader, in a press statement.

He welcomes the latest pronouncement of Dr Rajendra Prasad on the international situation and hopes that other Congress leaders would realize what the former Congress President had himself realized.

Sir Chimanlal adds that 'India for the moment should call a truce and support England against a real and serious common danger.'

Sir Chimanlal further expresses the opinion that 'if after the war is won, England failed to do the right thing by India, by all means let the Congress or any other organization forge such sanctions as it likes to compel England to yield to the wishes of India.'

Appeal to Congress

The following is the text of the statement:

'It is indeed refreshing to find so eminent a Congress leader as Babu Rajendra Prasad at long last realizing and publicly owning that in spite of all the wrongs England has done to India, England is any day better than the totalitarian States, and expressing genuine anxiety at the events that have happened in Europe during the last few days. I do trust that Babu Rajendra Prasad will exert all his influence with the other leaders of the Congress to realize what he himself has realized and stop them from turning Congress committees into satyagraha committees and hampering instead of assisting the Allies in winning the war.

'Months ago I pointed out that the Charge-Sheet that can be truly framed by India against England is long and grave and that her failure to make India ready and fit for her own defence was unpardonable. Why, even now with the war on, the training of all Indians irrespective of the artificial distinction of martial and non-martial classes for all arms of defence is not seriously undertaken on the necessary scale. But I repeat what I then pointed out that sheer self-interest dictates that India should whole-heartedly support England in the prosecution of the war. If England loses there will be an end to all freedom and democracy for India. It behoves all parties and interests to put aside for the moment all their domestic differences as well as their differences with, and grievances against England.

Coalition of Parties

'Take the promise of England to inaugurate Dominion Status in as short a time as practicable after the end of the war, at its face value. Let the Central Government and the provincial Governments be formed by coalition of important parties and interests on certain agreed lines, avoiding controversial party programmes and views in the same manner as the truly national Governments composed of all parties are at present formed in England and France. If after the war is won, England failed to do the right thing by India, by all means let the Congress or any other organization forge such sanctions as it likes to compel England to yield to the wishes of India and in such action they will secure general support in the country. But for the present let the hatchet be buried and let a united India support the Allies in their war effort for if Britain loses, India will be a prey to any ruthless aggressor from the west or east and freedom, independence, democracy will be idle dreams.

'The first instinct of Mr Gandhi to give unconditional support to England in the war was, I venture to think, the right one, and it is a great pity that he did not carry the Working Committee with him. At any rate now with the promises and offers that have been extracted from the British Government, India should for the moment call a truce and support England against a real and serious common danger'.

32. Tej Bahadur Sapru's Letter to Kailash Nath Katju Regarding the War and Political Situation, 27 May 1940 [Extract]

T.B. Sapru Papers, Series I, Vol. 12, File No. KI-K 91, 1922–47, NMML.

... Yes the War situation is very grave, perhaps much graver than we are permitted to know.... The real question for us to consider is as to what is going to happen to us if Great Britain should lose the war. I have not the least doubt as to the result though I know that good many of my countrymen differ from me and in their hatred of the British are prepared to take all consequences. ... But I have a fear of Hitler, I have a greater fear of Stalin and the so called Communists and Socialists of Russia.... I have never believed that Russia will refrain from laying its hands on us if it gets an opportunity. It is all very well for people here to abuse British Imperialism and to look upon Russia as their Mecca, but imagine to yourself how we shall have to start afresh if the system under which we have been living—however bad it may be— were torn to the roots. ... We may perhaps save the situation if we build up our strength in close cooperation with the British at this grave crisis, but if we go on telling, day in and day out as some of our friends have been saying, that imperialism must go, we shall be encouraging Hitler and Stalin and possibly Mussolini and Japan. The thing for us to do is to sink our differences and not to swear by individual or party views but to demand first, that our defences will be strengthened, and secondly, that during the period of the war National Government shall be formed, for take it from me this is not the time when any party, however strong it can be, can run a Government without evoking opposition from those who do not belong to it. ... If Indianization has not gone at a more rapid pace it is because the British have distrusted us and they have good reasons to do so when day in and day out we talk of finishing British imperialism and when we have been unable to compose our differences on the idle plea that it is the British who bring about these differences....

M. THE BUSINESS COMMUNITY

33. Sj. N.R. Sarkar Urges Extreme Caution in Planning during the War-Time Boom in Industries

Amrita Bazar Patrika, 6 March 1940.

Responsibilities of the State—Provision must be made for easy merging into peace time conditions.

Following is the speech of Mr N.R. Sarkar at the Commerce Society of the Calcutta University on 'War Economy from Indian Standpoint'.

Sometime ago I had occasion to develop in broad lines the subject of 'War Economy from the Indian Standpoint'. And I trust you will appreciate my desire on this occasion to go further on the lines I chalked out at the time. I was concerned at that time to indicate the nature of the problems, the difficulties and the opportunities which the war might create in our national economic life and the lines on which the utilization of these opportunities might be attempted. Now, however I propose to take a step or two further. I would like in the light of our experience of the last Great War and also of the developments in recent months to deal with some of the important aspects of our economy in greater detail as also to consider how the experiences, the efforts and achievements of the war period may be related to the future of our national economy.

The position of India in relation to the war, in other words, the economy of India as affected by the war is peculiar and needs to be distinguished from that of the countries actively engaged in war, though technically that is, according to international law, India is a belligerent country. The war economy of an active belligerent means the presence of compelling circumstances under which the resources of the country, sparing the minimum required for keeping up the morale of the nation, have to be directed almost entirely to war purposes. The normal industrial activities of the nation in such a country may have to be partially suspended or curtailed for facilitating necessary concentration on the emergency requirement of the war. The aim of war economy becomes for active belligerents one of widening the margin between civil consumption and limited national production and to canalize the margin into military consumption. Evidently India is not called upon to attune her economy to the same key as the active belligerents, and the contrast in this respect is indeed unmistakable. In the present war, as in the past the role of India is primarily to assist Britain by the supply of war materials which we are in position to produce. It is only a step further to say that our productive capacity must be improved so as to supply Britain with more things than we were able to produce before the war. In the process of this assistance to the Allied Powers in meeting some of their demands for war materials, India has been provided with an opportunity to increase the wealth of the nation, to accelerate her industrialization and to advance her national economy. The contrast in the aims as well as in effects implies a fundamental distinction that whereas the economic activities of active belligerents have to be restricted in many directions, the reactions of the war on the economy of India will be more on the side of expansion.

Threat of War

The threat of war in 1937 caused an upward swing in prices and profit. And again, during the last few months that we have been at war, prices and industrial profits have been increasing. These are no doubt rather encouraging facts. But I should deprecate undue optimism. The situation is full of possibilities, if wisely handled; but the exuberant optimism and fantastic anticipations of a certain class of people need to be curbed. Possibilities there are, but are they as great as we imagine? A boom there is, but are there in it all the elements of stable economic recovery and lasting economic prosperity?

The opportunity that faces India today is vastly different from that afforded by the Great War. In 1914 India was not so industrially advanced as she is in 1940, and therefore the scope for expanding existing industries and starting new ones was much greater. But in so far as India is industrially more advanced today than in 1914, she is so in a better position to take advantage of the opportunities offered.

Further, both the government and the people, here and abroad are better informed today, and have clearer ideas of the problems and situations arising out of the war. The art of financing war is better known, and the governments seem to have had their plans ready even before the war. They will not allow the burdens of the war to be heavier than they need be by permitting fantastic prices. Prices and profits are and will continue to be much better controlled than on the last occasion. In India the government are, besides, determined to finance the increased expenditure primarily by taxation. Even in the very first war budget there is an array of new impositions, Excess profits tax, increase in the excise duty on sugar, increase in import duty on petrol, increase in railway fares, both passenger and goods. In these circumstances, those who had expected the war to provide opportunities for making large profits met with an early disillusionment.

Different Situation

There is yet another factor that should serve as a check on unbraided optimism. Labour is much better informed and organized today than it was in 1914. Any rise in profits or cost of living is bound to be followed by a demand for higher wages, war bonuses etc. The demands are already being made and some of them are being conceded. When we take into consideration all these factors, the conclusion is inescapable that the situation is vastly different from what it was in 1914 and that our ideas of the opportunities for development and possibilities of making large war profits will require careful pruning.

The danger of quickened economic activity that is not based upon real economic demand (as distinct from the demand for war purposes) or arise in the consuming capacity of the country is obvious.

What the conditions require is that we should take the fullest advantage of the opportunities as and when they come; but in starting new ventures or carrying out new expansions of existing concerns, the conditions which the cessation of hostilities would bring about should not be lost sight of. The cost structure of industries started in the present conditions or of new expansions should be kept flexible, so that when the artificial stimulus will wear off the organizations may return to the conditions of normal times with the least difficulty and without severe financial loss. In other words, while the opportunities should be utilized to foster industrial expansion, the requirements for working under peace time conditions should be kept steadily in view. Much of the adverse reactions of India's economy, as much as on the economy of other nations which followed in the wake of the last war, was largely due to the absence of this necessary caution on the part of the people and the Government.

An analysis of the economic developments during the last war shows that they were largely haphazard. There existed no proper organization nor was there a conscious plan to take the fullest advantage of the opportunities that were opened up. Certain lasting results, it is true, were derived and along certain lines industries developed took firm root. But for want of a definite aim and rational plan, there also occurred much wastage of capital and effort which prospectus was avoidable.

The Present Prospectus

In order that the lack of a conscious positive plan and the prejudicial effects of the absence of it on the economy of India may not be repeated, it is desirable that the war time economic policies of both Government and businessmen on the present, occasion should be formulated with a full appreciation of the existing and future needs of the country, and with due regard to the changed conditions that may follow the termination of the war. Fortunately in the present emergency the business world seems to have met the situation with a clearer view of things, with the result that the confusion and panic that attended the outbreak of war in 1914 have been very much minimized this time. It may, therefore, be expected that the war economy of India will be susceptible to a more conscious planning. But to ensure a planned development, the essential pre-requisites are first a clear enunciation of the objectives and secondly the formulation of proper means for the achievement of those objectives. I shall try to offer some indications to you against an objective background of what should be the proper policy for us to pursue in some of the spheres of our economic activities during the present emergency.

Industrial Development

First, in regard to industries, the prevailing war conditions seem to bear tangible signs of an imminent boom. The rise in prices and increased demand have come as a boon to many struggling industrial concerns. Further the shrinkage of imports from both the belligerent and non-belligerent countries has proved a great opportunity for the establishment and expansion of various industries within the country. As against these adventitious factors should be reckoned the rising costs in production and the difficulties in obtaining certain essential raw materials and machineries which have to be imported from abroad. Even so, our industries will receive some undoubted stimulus from war conditions and the earnings of those industries which have been receiving a direct impetus from war demands are calculated to reach a very high degree of prosperity.

It would, however, be unwise on the part of our industrialists if they allow themselves to be carried away by the lure of large profits in certain lines. Our past experience would show numerous instances of rash enterprises which were prompted by the lure of war profits and eventually collapsed. The prospects of large profits have blinded many company promoters in the past to the need for a cautious policy, so much so that they freely indulged in extravagant borrowings for irrational schemes of expansion and pursued an unsound dividend policy. In considering schemes of expansion during and after the war, this danger must never be lost sight of.

The manner in which rash enterprises, prompted by the lure of boom profits, came to grief after the last war is best illustrated by the experience of industries like glass and iron and steel. Under the stimulus of the demands of the Munitions Board quite a number of glass factories were started in India with rather poor equipment for the manufacture of such articles as flasks, beakers and non-resistant tubes. In some other countries also the glass industry was developed to meet the demands and conditions arising from the war, but on a much sounder and secure foundation. The result was that while many of the latter steadily forged ahead even after the war to meet the growing demands for these articles in the export market in India, the factories had in many cases to be closed down under the pressure of foreign competition. In respect of iron and steel again we have had almost identical experience of the organization of inherently unsound concerns for the manufacture of such articles as hollow enamelled ware, wire and wire products, bolts and nuts which collapsed within a few years of the termination of the last war.

Total Cost Estimates

We must make a distinction between industries that can only thrive during the abnormal war conditions and others that can be established under the stimulus of war prices and profits and continue to operate, probably at a much reduced rate of profit, after facing severe competition in normal peace time. Industries of the former category should not be started unless they are essential for national economic life, in which case there must be a guarantee of State assistance after the war. In starting industries of the latter category care should be exercised in order to see that their cost structure is not loaded with such rigid factors as long-period contracts at war prices, extravagant provision for building and equipment etc. The cost structure should be kept as flexible as possible so that it may be automatically adjusted downward as soon as prices begin to move in the wrong direction.

The Government of India have a great responsibility in the present time especially the Supply Department. They are very large buyers, and form by far the most important group of consumers. They should keep in close contact with industries, and advise them regarding industrial opportunities for the production of the innumerable variety of commodities of which they are buyers. They possess accurate knowledge of the demand for certain products. They know from inside the nature and extent of their demand, their costs etc. This information should be placed at the disposal of those who intend to start industries and such persons should in all possible ways be encouraged to start working to meet the demand. Without the guidance of the Government in such matters, industrialists would find it exceedingly difficult to determine the new products that should be produced, their markets and prices. Unfortunately, our Central Government, not being a popular and responsible Government, appear to be entirely preoccupied with the immediate problems arising out of the War. But this is obviously a short-sighted policy that does not take a comprehensive view of the country's interests. Responsible Governments elsewhere are pursuing an entirely different policy. The Commonwealth Government of Australia, for instance, have established a Committee of five economists to advise on general economic policy in wartime. The task of this Committee is to think ahead about problems of post-war adjustment as well as considering immediate problems. The Australian Premier has also divided his cabinet into two sections, a war Cabinet and an Economic Cabinet, the latter having its own secretariat. The Department of Supply in Australia again is obtaining elaborate census regarding factories and private wealth, some of the information obtained having little direct relation to war purposes, but the information is of fundamental importance in relation to any plan for industrial development. From the information collected, the Department is in a position to provide details regarding the equipment of factories, the type of labour employed etc. and also to indicate the scope for extension.

Taxation Policy

There is then the question of taxation policy. I have only to mention it for all the wide ramifications of this factor to arise in one's mind. At a time like this, it is inevitable that all countries whether belligerent or neutral will have to spend an ever-increasing amount for purposes of defence. There are two methods by which war expenditures may be financed, viz. taxation and loan. And controversy has always raged acute and bitter as to which is better, often in complete disregard of actual objective conditions. For the present I am not considering the third and most reprehensible method, inflation.

In India, it appears that Government have decided to adopt the method of taxation to its utmost limit. A priori it can always be argued that unproductive war expenditure should be financed as much as possible by fresh taxation so that heavy burdens may not be shifted on to future generations as would happen if borrowings were resorted to. It may also be argued that this is the policy which is being followed by Great Britain, not other countries. Apart from the theoretical validity of this proposition, one important fact is that conditions in Great Britain and India are not on all fours. Nor are the objectives similar. One primary objective of India today is to forge ahead in industrial expansion. One important difference in economic conditions as between India and Great Britain is that India unlike Britain is a country which is industrially backward and possesses at the same time illimitable opportunities for further development. And a taxation policy has important and vital repercussions on prospects of industrial expansion. Unfortunately, it would appear that the taxation policy which the Government have adopted is likely to seriously hamper the growth and expansion of industries. I have already mentioned these measures of new taxation. Along with these there are the measures for controlling prices. The result of all this is that industries have to function and economic progress has to be achieved in conditions of deflation or profits. Further, the adverse psychological effect of the Government taxation policy cannot be over-exaggerated. This policy is likely to have two serious and unfortunate results. First, it will check the industrial expansion of the country, which will mean that the opportunities which have now been opened up to us will not be fully utilized. Secondly, it will in all probability also mean less revenue for the Government. For, if industry were allowed to expand, and capital were not given a shock by the injudicious taxation policy, it is quite probable that the accelerated expansion of industry and commerce would have brought in a larger revenue for the Government. From every point of view the need for a revision of the Government's taxation policy seems desirable and necessary.

Niemeyer Award

Another aspect of the Central Government policy to which I should like also to make a brief reference is the revision that has been effected in the Niemeyer Award in respect of allocation of revenues between the centre and the provinces. This revision to the detriment of the interests of the provinces is as unfortunate as it is unfair. The nation-building departments are, as is well known, in the charge of the provincial Governments while their scope for augmenting revenues is severely restricted. The share they obtain under the Niemeyer Award is of great importance to them. The revision of the Award would mean that the provinces would be deprived of money which they could utilize for financing schemes of mass amelioration. It would also probably mean that the provinces would be obliged to increase their taxes in order to escape the stigma of deficit budgets. Lest War conditions should engender a feeling of irresponsible drift both among the people and in the Government, I would like to emphasize the need of a complete reorientation of our attitude towards the necessity and significance of regularity in our economic activities on a planned basis, even during the emergency of a war. Both the Government and people must now take a long range view of things and give their thought to the formulation of suitable devices for minimizing the shocks of possible post-war reverses and conservation of economic prosperity which the war has brought to this country. These objectives would require an avoidance of uncontrolled rise in both prices and costs, suitable schemes to act as cushion for likely reverses, and stimulation of investment habit of the people.

Let it not be said of us that we welcomed the birth of prosperity by digging its grave with ominous forethought. In the life of nations as of individuals daring has its place. Enterprise has its risks, whether the beneficiary is a whole country or a small class of the businessmen. I have no doubt emphasized the need for caution but the keynote of our war economy should be enterprise. India never had greater need for enterprise than today. The present war has been described as the death throes of an epoch. It is an age that is dying and so far as we are concerned an age of supine indifference, poverty, slavery and humiliating inconsequence. Just as in the sphere of our war economy, we talk of profiting by the mistakes of the last war, the

Powers too especially those who are neutral are talking of profiting by the blunders of the last peace. The problem of war economy impinges in many a point on the problem of our political integrity. The latter is not my theme. But these distinctions are blurred on the realm of practical effort. Politically or economically, there is a common task of rebuilding a world order which faces all nations and peoples. And in that task our role is to do well by ourselves to raise India to the dignity that belongs to her. To have raised a fifth of the race from the depths of ignorance and poverty to the level at which it can support and sustain a rational world order is in itself a great achievement. A new world fit for India and a new India fit for the world that ought to be our ideal.

34.   War's Effect on Trade and Industry: Report on Chamber of Commerce Meeting

Statesman, 16 March 1940.

Chamber of Commerce Meeting

'Speaking for the economic life of the country as a whole, the immediate effects of the outbreak of hostilities in Europe cannot be said to be wholly beneficial,' observed Dr N.N. Law, President, Bengal National Chamber of Commerce, in his address at the annual general meeting of that body at 2, Royal Exchange Place, Calcutta, yesterday.

Dr Law said that the commercial community could hardly regard either internal or international unrest as ultimately beneficial to their interest. There was a widespread belief that the War had enabled trade and industry to earn abnormal profits. So far as there had been a restriction of imports from foreign countries owing to the trade with enemy countries, the manufacturers here of indigenous goods had benefited to some extent, and also trade, industry and commerce had taken some advantage of the general rise in prices which had been brought about by the War. It was, however, necessary for a proper appreciation of the effects of the War on trade and industry to take into account the fact that the War had also imposed considerable handicaps on them.

Openings had been created by the War for new industrial ventures, owing to the lessening of the keenness of competition from foreign countries in regard to a number of commodities.

War-time Trade Handicaps

But these advantages were to a great extent counter-balanced by the difficulties in importing raw materials, machineries and mill-stores and also by the absence of any clear declaration from the Government of India regarding the steps to be taken by them, on the cessation of the War, in protecting those industries which might not attain stabilization by that time. Suffice is to say that speaking for the economic life of the country as a whole, the immediate effects of the outbreak of hostilities in Europe could not be said to be wholly beneficial.

Policy Criticized

After criticizing the general policy pursued by the Bengal Government in their attempt to check even legitimate increase in prices, Dr Law said that the most important factor which seemed to have been totally ignored by the Government in controlling prices was that there had been only a few years ago a serious slump in the prices of all commodities, the effect from which the business concerns had hardly had time to overcome.

Further, the action of the Government of India in imposing fresh taxation in the shape of increased railway freights, excess profits tax, and the increases in the excise duties on sugar and petrol, was absolutely unfair to the tax-payer in general and in particular, to trade and industry which had to bear the burden directly.

They quite appreciated that the outbreak of the War had imposed on the Government of India an additional liability on account of defence expenditure. But apart from that the Government had not been able to prove that they had taken the utmost care to cut down their expenditure to the furthest minimum limit. The Chamber strongly objected to the measures adopted by the Government to meet their deficit about the size of which again they had their reason to disagree with the Government.

Capital and Labour

Turning to the serious situation arising out of the increased tension between capital and labour in this country. Dr Law pointed out that 'employers fully appreciate that increased allowances should be granted to their workers, to enable them to meet any increases in the cost of living that may have been brought about by the War, and I am sure everyone of us appreciate their needs and sympathizes with their condition. I have also no doubt that whenever possible, employers would readily grant a dearness allowance to all their workers, some of them having already taken some steps in this respect. At the same time, I have to point out with regret that there has not been an equal appreciation of our difficulties on the part of labour and that demands are being made for increased allowance in total disregard of our capacity to meet the same. In fact it seems that many are under the impression that trade and commerce are making abnormal profits and whether it be the Governments or the consumers or our workers—all are pressing their claims on our limited purse in such a manner as to make it absolutely impossible for us to accede to their joint demands.

The measures taken to control prices, the imposition of heavy taxes and the equally heavy demands which are being made by the labourers for increased wages are all to be traced to the mistaken notion that War has brought about a great economic prosperity. The prosperity that has come in the wake of the War is not only artificial but also temporary and has benefited trade and commerce only to the extent that it has enabled them to partially cover the losses which they had incurred in previous years. While, therefore, it is incumbent on the employers to recognize that some increase in their wages bill has to be made, it is at the same time the duty also of labour to realize that the demands they are making do not in all cases take into adequate account the capacity of the employers to meet the same'.

35. Industrial Policy Criticized at the Annual General Meeting of the Marwari Chamber of Commerce

Statesman, 1 September 1940.

India 'Weakest link in the Empire'

The Government of India's attitude towards the promotion of new industries in this country was criticized by Mr S.K. Bhatter, the retiring President of the Marwari Chamber of Commerce, Calcutta, at the annual general meeting of the Chamber yesterday.

'During the full year that the war has been in progress,' said Mr Bhatter, 'Government have not taken any pains to consider the question of promotion of new industries.

'The proposals for starting of new enterprises have been received coldly by the Government. It was only with the greatest difficulty that Mr Walchand Hirachand could procure a site for the ship-building yard near Vizagapatnam harbour after his efforts to establish the industry in Calcutta had failed.

'The short-sighted policy of the Government regarding this country's industrialization is proving to be a great handicap at the present moment. Besides this country not being in a position to take part fully in the Empire's war effort, the lack of ship-building facilities and shipping is greatly hampering the trade of this country. Not to speak of overseas trade, which is fully monopolized by foreign shipping, there is not sufficient tonnage even for the requirements of coastal trade. The neglect of the problems of defence and the absence of any facilities for mechanizing units has exposed the country to invaders and this country is at the present day, from the point of view of external defence, the weakest link in the Empire. I hope that in the forthcoming conference in Delhi, serious consideration will be given to the various questions involved and a satisfactory agreement reached.'

War and Industries

Mr Bhatter then described the effect of the war on the jute and cotton industries. With regard to the former, he said that although at the beginning the war set prices of jute goods soaring, the absence of any further large orders for sandbags and buying by overseas countries caused prices to slide down. Beyond the large profits made in the earlier months of the war, jute mills were now having a difficult time. Mills were trying to push up prices for jute manufacturers above the levels fixed in agreement between the Government and the Indian Jute Mills Association, but the pessimistic attitude of operators and the unhealthy technical position of the market, were preventing any sustained improvement in prices. The outlook, therefore, was far from satisfactory.

The same was the case with the cotton textile industry. At the beginning of the war, prices were stimulated owing to the placing of large war orders, but now depression had set in. This depression was also due to the fact that Japanese competition had continued undiminished in recent months. There was considerable resentment about the temporary increase in the Japanese quota without any corresponding increase in the off take of cotton. Mr Bhatter expressed the hope that in view of the many delicate problems at issue in the Far East, the Government would not be obliged to adopt a policy harmful to the interest of the country.

Mr Bhatter concluded by paying a tribute to Mr Kishorilal Dhandhania, the honorary secretary, for his steadfast and ungrudging work to which the Chamber owed its position of leadership among the Indian mercantile community

Self-Sufficiency Aim

Mr Mangturam Jaipuria, the new President in his address, said: 'The war that is now raging in Europe threatens to extend to the East and has indicated clearly the great part which our country can play at this juncture. It is being realized on all hands that the industrial potentialities of the country have not been explored to the fullest extent and that big gaps have to be filled up, especially in the field of the industries, necessary for the defence of the country. The proposals for the expansion of the armament factories and the erection of new factories for the production of automobiles and aircraft should go a long way in this direction. Restricted imports of foreign supplies of various other necessities have also indicated the various other industries which need development in our country. I hope that we will gain by experience and that our country will be self-sufficient in the matter of the foreign supplies at an early date.'

N. THE PRINCES

36. Indian Rulers' Pledge 'Every Possible Assistance': Annual Meeting of the Chamber of Princes, New Delhi, 11 March 1940

Statesman, 12 March 1940; *Indian Annual Register*, 1940, Vol. I, pp. 398–400.

Chancellor's Resolution in Princes' Chamber

A joint declaration of loyalty to the King-Emperor and pledge of support for Britain in the present war was made at the meeting of the Chamber of Princes in New Delhi today.

Moved in the form of a resolution, the declaration emphasized the determination of the Princes to give every possible assistance in men, money and material in the war which had been forced upon the Empire.

His Excellency the Viceroy, who opened the meeting, paid a warm tribute to the offers of service made by the Princes and assured them that these offers would be taken advantage of as soon as the opportunity arose.

His Excellency, opening the conference, said:

'Your Highnesses, it is, as you know a very great pleasure to me to see you here again today and to preside over your deliberations.

'Since our last meeting we have to mourn the deaths of two members of the Chamber, His Highness the Maharaja of Benares, and the Thakor Shaheb of Dhroli and of three members of the representative electorate the Thakur of Bija, the Maharaja of Kalahandi and the Raja of Miraj (Senior).

'It will, I am certain, be the wish of all Your Highnesses that we should take the opportunity of this meeting to express our deep sympathy with the relatives of the Rulers whose names I have mentioned, and that we should convey to their successors our sincere good wishes for the prosperity and the happiness of their States.

The War

'The most significant and the most important event since we met a year ago, an event of overwhelming concern to all of us here to-day, is the outbreak of the war. His Majesty's Government, as Your Highnesses so well know, continued till the last moment to spare no effort to resolve the difficulties that had arisen in the international sphere by peaceful means. If in the result their efforts were unsuccessful they can at least feel that they had left nothing undone and that responsibility for plunging the world into a conflict, the disastrous effects of which must last for many years to come, cannot rest upon them.

'The impact of the war has found the Princes of India, true to their traditions, staunchly loyal to His Majesty the King-Emperor. They have placed their forces, their personal services, and all their resources at the disposal of the Crown, and they have contributed in every way open to them to the Empire's cause.

'Those offers have, I can assure Your Highnesses, been most deeply and genuinely appreciated and as you are aware in every case in which it has been possible to accept them, they have been accepted with deep and real gratitude.

'Many of the Rulers of Indian States have expressed the utmost eagerness to be allowed to serve personally in the theatre of war. I sympathize sincerely with them in their disappointment that it has not as yet been found possible to take advantage of these offers of personal service.

Your Highnesses will be aware that, so far, the course of hostilities has differed very materially from that of the last war; up to the present, there has been no substantial call on the man-power of India. If conditions alter in this respect, Your Highnesses may rest assured that your officers, so deeply valued, will be remembered.

Poor Monsoons

'Since our last meeting, many of Your Highnesses have had to face difficult problems consequent on the succession of poor monsoons which have visited so many parts of India; and among those areas which have been particularly affected have been large tracts of Rajputana and Kathiawar.

'In the steps they have taken to meet this calamity, the Governments of all the important States concerned have made full and liberal use of their reserves, and they have devised widespread and well organized plans for the relief of suffering. It is my earnest hope that this year the States affected will receive timely and sufficient rainfall and that the sufferings of the people and the anxiety of the States' Governments will be brought to an end.

'As Your Highnesses are aware, His Majesty's Government felt on the outbreak of war that, in the conditions then prevailing and on a review of the probable course of hostilities, they had no option but to hold in suspense, however reluctantly, the work in connection with the preparations for Federation, while retaining Federation as their objective.

'But the suspension of those preparations does not mean that His Majesty's Government, to repeat the words which I used a month or two ago at Baroda, "have in any way modified their own view as to the necessity for securing Indian unity—a unity which can only be complete if in the constitutional arrangements of the future, the historic Indian States, with their great and special traditions, take the place which we have always looked forward to seeing them occupy".

Unity of India

'Your Highnesses are well aware of my views on the question of Federation and of its many advantages from the point of view not only of the Indian States but of India as a whole and in particular of the unity of India. I am confident that you will appreciate the importance of continuing to apply your minds to this vitally important problem and to the questions that arise in connection with it.

'When we last met I spoke very frankly and very directly to Your Highnesses on the subject of setting the houses of the States in order. I do not wish to repeat all that I said then. My view of the profound importance of action on the lines which I then indicated remains unchanged. Indeed, if anything, I regard it, in the light of developments over the last 12 months, as of greater importance now than I did when I addressed you in March 1939.

'I gratefully acknowledge that many Rulers have of late made earnest endeavours to improve their administrative standards, that various admirable reforms have been introduced, and that measures have in many cases been taken to ensure that all legitimate complaints on the part of State subjects receive due consideration.

'But I earnestly hope that Your Highnesses will not cease to give your continual and close attention to the perfecting of your administrative machinery. The value of administrative reform remains as great and as present as ever, and it would be rash to assume that troubles, where they have for the time being subsided, will not recur.

Crown Police Force

'That the Crown is anxious to give such help as it is properly incumbent upon it to give is clearly shown by the assistance rendered to various States in different parts of India, and by the establishment of the Crown police force to assist the States authorities should any situation pass beyond their control. But I am sure that it is fully realized by Your Highnesses that the maintenance of order in the territories of Indian States is primarily the responsibility of the Rulers concerned.

'I would like to draw particular attention to the view I expressed last year as to the desirability and the importance of the creation of joint services where small States in the same group are unable individually to maintain an adequate standard of administration. I can well understand and sympathize with the reluctance of individual Rulers to depart in such matters from the strict path of tradition. But the spirit of the times makes it essential for them in their own interests to take a longer view. A beginning has been made in the organization of joint services. It is, in my judgment, of vital importance that progress should be made in that direction and it is my sincere hope that this movement will develop, and that I can look up to you, gentlemen, who are members of this most important body, to do all in your power to encourage its growth. I have kept in the closest touch since we met last year with the action taken by States in various parts of India, consequent on my address to the Chamber. You may be certain that the interest which I have taken in this matter and the care with which I follow all developments in connection with it will not diminish in the time that lies ahead.

'Since the last meeting of the Chamber, the reforms in its constitution, so strongly advocated by the great majority of its members, have been carried into effect. I earnestly trust that those reforms will lead to greater harmony, to more effective work and to closer cooperation between all States, whether great or small, for the good of the Princely order and the prosperity and welfare of the subjects of the Rulers. Let me only add that I have under my consideration the proposals which have been submitted to me by the Standing Committee for the enlargement of the Chamber ....'.

Help for Britain

Chancellor Moves War Resolution: On the conclusion of His Excellency's speech, the Chancellor of the Chamber of Princes, His Highnesses the Jam Saheb of Nawanagar, moved the war resolution which read as follows:

'The Chamber of Princes request His Excellency the Crown Representative kindly to place before His Imperial Majesty the King-Emperor the firm determination of the Ruling Princes and Chiefs of India to render every possible assistance in men, money and material to His Imperial Majesty and His Government in their heroic struggle for upholding the cause of justice and for maintaining the sacredness of treaties and covenants, and prays that the united efforts of the Empire and the Allies may lead to the early and triumphant vindication of the high principles for which His Imperial Majesty has been forced to take up arms against the enemy.

'The Rulers had already given earnest proof of this by the spontaneous offer of their States' resources, supplemented in many cases by their personal services. These offers were not made in a bargaining or calculating spirit'.

There might be differences of opinion, said the Jam Saheb, in regard to some aspects of British imperial history in the past, but there were certain basic facts in the present international crisis which must be accepted by all impartial and disinterested persons. The present war was not of the seeking of Great Britain but had been precipitated by the godless aggression of the Nazi rulers. All assurances given by Germany that she would respect the sanctity of treaties had been falsified.

His Highness said that whatever be the sins of omission or commission attributed to the British Government in their treatment of India, surely no fair minded person could reasonably expect better treatment from the Germans to whom neither freedom, self-determination for nations nor pledges was sacred. To his mind, it would be a denial of the best traditions of the States and of the history of India of which they were all proud, if in the face of this clarion call of duty from suffering humanity, India faltered or hesitated.

There was another aspect of the question that could not be ignored and that was the serious threat to the country. The Indian States had made their choice to stand united with their resources in support of the King Emperor in the heroic struggle for the protection of humanity and the defence of the motherland.

The Jam Saheb thought that the present war would probably be a long one. He had every hope and faith that wiser counsels would prevail in India and that the best and patriotic elements would combine to contribute their utmost towards the successful prosecution of the war.

Grim Spectre

Seconding the war resolution, His Highness the Maharaja of Patiala said that they gathered today under the shadow of a grim spectre which threatened the very foundations of the world. They saw the spectacle of the ruthless culmination of the totalitarian cult which believed in war as the highest expression of national life. The whole fabric of civilization was threatened.

O.   THE JUSTICE PARTY

37.   War, Justice Party, and Depressed Classes

(a)   Madras Governor's Letter to the Viceroy, 17 March 1940

Report No. 5 of 1940, Correspondence with the Governor of Madras and his Secretary, Linlithgow Papers, Acc. No. 2204, NAI.

[Secret]

My Dear Linlithgow,

My first impression after seeing the Opposition leaders, Independents, etc. is that there is no chance whatever of any alternative Government here for a long time. Both the Justice Party leaders, Chattoer [Chattiar] and the Depressed Classes leader, M.C. Rajah, are hopeful that, as time goes on, they will detach former supporters from Congress, but say that it will take time, which I can well believe...

M.C. Rajah, the Depressed Class leader, is very anxious that his people should be open to recruitment in the event of any large extension of the Army. He says that in the past, they made good soldiers and that their later deterioration was due to bad officers; I have heard this in other quarters and think that if the question of extending the recruiting area arises, it would be a popular thing to reform the Madras Regiment ....

Yours very sincerely,
Arthur Hope

(b) Madras Governor's Letter to the Viceroy, 4 August 1940

Report No. 13 of 1940, Correspondence with the Governor of Madras and his Secretary, Linlithgow Papers, Acc. No. 2204, NAI.

[Secret]

My Dear Linlithgow,

I have not written to you for a month as when the last letter was due you were here. Nothing of much importance has occurred since you left. Nobody expected Congress to accept your offer and there is no surprise at their refusal. I do not think however that there is growing disgust at their attitude and many waverers are coming over. If only the opposition here were stronger, there would be a real chance of attracting a very large number of moderate Congressmen. But, although certainly improving, Justice Party has little organization and is still suspect on its past record. They do not see eye to eye with the main Liberal Party in India and all already are saying that they ought to have a representative on your expanded Council. I do not suppose for a minute that you intend to do this, but I do think that it is important to have the Kumaraja of Chettinad on the War Council. With all their faults they have been very loyal and helpful, and if they are not represented, it will be a terrible slap in the face, and will increase their present feeling that we ignore our friends.

Yours very sincerely,
Arthur Hope.

P.   BRITISH ACADEMICS' VIEW

38.   British Academics Support Indian National Congress

Harijan (Reproduced from *Cambridge Review*), 20 January 1940.

I

Sir,

To those who had watched the emergence and rise to power of the National Congress Movement of India since the last war, its transformation from a talking shop of nationally minded intellectuals into a mass movement with adherents of all classes and creeds, and drawing it strength particularly from millions of peasants, it was obvious even before the out-break of the present war—that a crisis in the relations of India and Great Britain was not far distant. That crisis has been precipitated by Great Britain's action in declaring India at war, and in appropriating to herself the power to suspend the constitution, and govern by ordinance.

We feel that the struggle in India is essentially one against indescribable poverty, the persistence of feudal anomalies, and Government by a narrow alliance of sectional interests. This struggle can be viewed by the vast majority of British people only with sympathy, and indeed with a sympathy which can be easily translated into willing and active co-operation with the Indian people. Particularly at the present time it is an acid test of the ability of the British people to maintain and extend democracy. We are therefore perturbed by the Indian policy of the National Government, as outlined by Sir Samuel Hoare in his Parliamentary statement of 24th October. This uncompromising attitude obstructs the path towards the achievement of democratic reforms long enjoyed in this country. The resignation of the representatives of two-thirds of the electorate, and the support they have received from the remaining third, is an indication of the determination of the wide mass of the Indian people to continue the struggle for the right to govern their own country, to embark on a programme of social reform, and to decide their own foreign policy.

There is in this country a great lack of information about India and its problems: the communal question, land-hunger, illiteracy, the Government of India Act, etc. We therefore welcome the setting up of an Indian Independence Committee in Cambridge to provide information about India, and to explain and advocate the Congress policy. We should like to draw attention particularly to the exhibition which is to be held during the course of the next term, to illustrate the economic, political and cultural development of India, and its present-day problems and aspirations.

We are, Sir, yours, etc.

Eileen Power   H.L. Elvin
Susan Stebbing   Harold J. Lasky
M.H. Dobb   Joseph Needham
David Hardman   J. Robinson

(*Cambridge Review*, 2-12-39)

II

Sir

We wish to take this opportunity of registering our opposition to the policy of the National Government towards India, outlined in the Viceroy's White Paper of 17th October, and reasserted by Sir Samuel Hoare in the House of Commons, 26th October. The Indian National Congress, which is supported by two-thirds of the Indian electorate and has a very wide support among the unenfranchised population (which number 330,000,000 out of 350,000,000), has stated its demand for India could make no concrete reply to this demand except to ask the Indian people to rely upon a promise of a conference to discuss the possibility of Dominion Status at the end of the war and to say that, in the event of the Indian people refusing these terms, the King's Government would be carried on, presumably by force.

The demand of the Indian people for democracy and national independence is a product of their poverty. This poverty in its turn is a product of the feudal oppression of a landlord and princely caste, the burden of maintaining a system of guaranteed profits on government stocks, railway shares and irrigation investments, and the legal inability of the people to control interest rates, exchange rates, wages and expenditure on social services. The Indian people demand freedom and democracy in order to overcome the economic and political backwardness which 150 years of foreign rule has done little or nothing to alleviate. No formula which does not grant these things can be satisfactory, nor can it produce anything but conflict and disorder.

The Indian National Congress proposes to introduce universal adult franchise without discrimination against any race, social class, religion or sex. A Constituent Assembly will determine the Constitution of an independent India. No minority in India which genuinely believes in freedom objects to this, and it is a demand with which the British people are in full sympathy.

The Indian people have no cultural, religious or racial ties with Britain, and Dominion Status can have no meaning for them. They are prepared, on the basis of independence, to co-operate with the people of Britain in the maintenance of freedom and peace.

The people of the world can have no confidence in the capacity of the British and French people to maintain peace, freedom and abundance so long as their Governments carry out a policy which deprives colonial peoples of their rights to political liberty, national independence and the control of the economic form of their society. There is very little distinction between Nazism and the National Government so long as both deny freedom and national independence to subject peoples. No war between them can be a just war so long as they both stand indicated as oppressors of people who desire to be free. It is for these reasons that we wish emphatically to protest against the whole Indian policy of the National Government.

R.R. Pittam,
President, Universities Liberal Club.
M.J.C. Hodgart,
President, University Socialist Club.

(*Cambridge Review*: 11-11-39)

Chapter 2. The Politics of Constitutional Negotiations

A.   APPROACHES TO FREEDOM AND INDEPENDENCE

1.   Independence I

Editorial, *Pioneer*, 23 January 1940.

'Independence Day' is to be celebrated by the Congress this week and it is, therefore, opportune to consider, in a calmer spirit than that of party politics, what exactly independence implies.

In India the word is almost always used in its first sense, 'freedom from external control or support'. But it has another meaning, 'individual liberty of thought or action' and the two are very far from synonymous. Germany and the USSR are nominally independent, in the sense that they enjoy complete freedom from foreign control. India, in this sense, is not independent. But so far as liberty of thought or action is concerned, individual Germans and Russians are in chains, while individual Indians are free men—much more free at the moment than, for example, the French. For in France there is now the most drastic censorship, not only of news but of views, and the second largest single political party has been dissolved.

There, indeed, liberty has been temporarily and in most cases voluntarily surrendered, even by the Communists, and no one would suggest that in normal times the French are not in every way independent. But whether a slave state properly be called independent merely because it is exempt from foreign control (or support) is a question we might well ask ourselves on Independence Day.

This is not an attempt to argue that the desire for national independence in the common sense is not a natural one or is one that ought indefinitely to be resisted. On the contrary, we are inclined to agree rather than to disagree with the saying that 'no man and no nation can be trusted to rule another when self-interest is involved'. But it does not follow that independence necessarily means an increase in happiness or prosperity or that foreign control is always pernicious.

Nevertheless, Indians will reply, they all fought to preserve it, even if the fight ended in the destruction of themselves and their independence together. If, therefore, India demands independence, it is no answer to say that she is better off without it. She may or may not be: that is for her to judge. Where Indians go wrong is in imagining that any but a tiny minority of Englishmen today dispute this claim. The minority is strongly represented in the Cabinet by Mr Winston Churchill and it is also strongly represented in those circles which take what might be called a professional interest in India. But the average Englishman has had such a 'sickener' over Ireland that his attitude is: 'If they want it, for Heaven's sake let them have it'.

The difference, even with officials, is merely as to time and method. To that aspect of the question we shall return tomorrow.

2. Independence II

Editorial, *Pioneer*, 24 January 1940.

Yesterday we said that the differences between the Congress and the British Government on the subject of *Swaraj* for India were differences regarding time and method. For the Congress, the time is now and the method a constituent assembly. What are the objections to accepting this demand without further demur? We submit that it is absurd to seek to reduce them to a mere desire on the part of the British people to keep the Indian people in a state of perpetual subordination. They are, in fact, substantial and it is of no use to adopt towards them the attitude of the old lady who looked at the rhinoceros and declared 'There ain't no such animal'.

In the first place, while Congressmen habitually draw a sharp distinction between complete independence and Dominion Status, such a distinction does not exist or exists only at one remove. Mr Baldwin may have spoken of the British Commonwealth of Nations being 'indissolubly linked together'. But as long ago as March 1920, Mr Bonar Law, speaking on behalf of H.M. Government, stated that the right to secede was inherent in Dominion Status. This contention was subsequently disputed by Mr Winston Churchill. Both houses of the South African Parliament, however, formally affirmed it, when accepting the Statute of Westminster in 1931, without protest from Great Britain, and Ireland has in fact seceded. 'Full Dominion Status', as has been promised, implies, therefore, at least the possibility of an early secession of India from the British Commonwealth.

Now it can hardly be denied that Britain has, inevitably, assumed certain obligations towards this country. In particular she has assumed the general responsibility for its defence and special responsibility, by treaty, for the defence of the Indian States. She may or may not have emasculated large sections of the people by excluding them from the armed forces, as nationalists allege. She may or may not have been unpardonably slow in implementing her promises regarding Indianization. We think that she has been—and still is. We are amazed, for example, that Indian pilots are not today being trained, on political as well as on military grounds, in thousands instead of in tens. This seems to us to show an almost criminal lack of vision in high places.

Nevertheless, the responsibilities are there. Mr de Valera and Mr Pirow have both admitted that foreign powers cannot be expected to respect a Dominion's neutrality, even if it declares it: an India which had seceded from the Commonwealth would invite attack. The Congress may announce that, it is willing to accept the risk. But there are tens of millions who are not willing and the result of one general election, based on an electorate of no more than 14 per cent of the population, does not give Congress a mandate to endanger the whole country. The handing over of defence must be, even technically a long process: to attempt it in the middle of a world war would be madness.

Congress leaders know this very well. Yet when the demand is made for a constituent assembly, at which Great Britain is not even to be represented but whose findings she is to agree in advance to accept, not a word is said about defence. Suppose that the constituent assembly, dominated by Congress, decided that satyagraha was a sufficient weapon and that all British troops and officers should forthwith be withdrawn, would the British Government be justified in withdrawing them? Would this not be an even more gross betrayal of those who look to it for protection and do not share the Congress creed than its alleged betrayal of Abyssinia, of Czechoslovakia and of China?

This one consideration alone seems to us to dispose of the contention that the Viceroy should commit himself unreservedly to the principle of a constituent assembly. It is, however, less than half the story. The internal question of the minorities also involves Great Britain and her representatives in certain special responsibilities, with which we must deal in a third article on independence and its implications.

3.   Nationalism is a Process Not the Goal: Mrs Naidu's Speech

Tribune, 5 February 1940.

Isolation has never been India's Ideal: Sarojini Naidu

'One word has obsessed us for the last twenty-five years and it is nationalism. The definition of nationalism is too narrow. We have to be something better than patriots. We must take the map of the world into consideration for every gesture of service to India,' observed Mrs Sarojini Naidu, addressing the commemoration day celebrations of the Ravenshaw College last evening.

'Let us, therefore, consider what the non-spiritual ideals of new India—but the spiritual and common ideals of the new world—are going to be', continued Mrs Naidu. 'I shall not be happy, if I believe that we do not visualize ourselves as something greater than can be defined within the narrow confines of nationalism.'

She asked them to cease thinking in terms of provinces, races and the country. That was the ultimate value of education. By education she meant that greatest quality that evolved out of itself a personality, character, initiative, and courage to dream and to do.

In India nationalism could only be a process, not the goal itself. It should be the only process by which Indians, who for centuries had forgotten freedom, should pass, so that we may emerge into the great ocean of liberty—but not that liberty by which India would be isolated. The spirit of isolation had never been India's ideal at any time.

In conclusion Mrs Naidu stressed the responsibility of the educated to spread knowledge among the masses, and also for communal unity.

4.   'Why We Ask for a Constituent Assembly': Jawaharlal Nehru

Extract from Foreword to *Constituent Assembly* by Jai Gopal Narang, 1940, *SWJN,* Vol. XI, pp. 5–7.

... I am convinced that there is no way out for us, if we aim at real democratic freedom, except through a constituent assembly. The alternatives are: (1) Continuation, in a greater or less degree, under the control of the British Parliament; (2) some kind of fascist or military dictatorship or dictatorships; (3) Soviet communism in some parts of India with disruption and chaos in other parts: (4) complete disruption and chaos.

For my part I would like to have a socialist economy all over India, and I think that the Soviet form of government, with certain variations and adaptations suited to India, may well fit in here. Thereby I do not mean that the Russian system or methods should be introduced here *in toto*. I disapprove of much that has been done there. I think that the soviet system can be allied to a vast deal of real democracy. But any attempt to introduce Sovietism in India would, I am sure, now and for some time to come, lead to terrible conflicts and disruption. Whatever the outcome might be, and the outcome would be doubtful, the cost would be almost unbearable.

Therefore, of necessity, I am led to the conclusion that the way of the constituent assembly is the only way. But let it be remembered that this way is not the way of advancing step by step to the haven of Dominion Status. It means the creation of a new state; it means the walking out and away from the economic foundations and structure of imperialism. This cannot be done by the wisest of lawyers sitting together in conclave; it cannot be done by small committees trying to balance interests and calling that constitution-making; it can never be done under the shadow of an external authority. It can only be done effectively when the political and psychological conditions are present, and the urge and the sanctions come from the masses. Hence the vital importance of adult suffrage.

Are these political and psychological conditions present today? No, obviously not, or else we would have got the constituent assembly already. But I cannot say about tomorrow or the day after, for we live in dynamic and swiftly-moving times and all manner of forces are at play.

Why do we ask the British Government for a constituent assembly? Strictly speaking, we are not asking for any gift. We are stating what we propose to have and are going to have sometime or other. We shall have it when we are strong enough for it, no sooner, and probably after a struggle. But, then, are we to refrain from saying what we want and aim at, because for the moment we cannot attain it? Surely that is not even the way of preparation. And then it is never wise to rule out the odd possibility of gaining our objective otherwise, for our strength and world events may force the pace. To envisage this possibility does us no harm, unless it leads us to complacency and a giving up of the idea of struggle.

Why do we ask the British Government to acknowledge the independence of India? Does that make any difference? Of course it does, though it does not mean that we have gained our objective or that the British Government will not go back on their word. The mere fact that they refuse to acknowledge it, itself shows what value they attach to such a declaration. If there was such a clear declaration of Indian independence, of the right of the Indian people to frame their own constitution through a constituent assembly elected by adult franchise and without any external interference, that in itself would create a psychological situation of revolutionary significance. That in itself will not take us to our goal but it will strengthen us enormously and bring the masses into play.

The question of a constituent assembly is an acid test for all of us. It shows where each one of us stands. Britain refuses because she will not give up her imperialism. The Liberals in India, or the Muslim League, or other protestants, oppose because they do not want real independence and they have no conception of a new state, or, if they can conceive of it, they dislike it. Howsoever much they might dislike things as they are, they prefer them to that new free state where the people can make or unmake. Hence the objection to adult suffrage, and even to large numbers of people being associated with this undertaking. Small committees of the elect are suggested whose chief function will be to move warily within the limits laid down by the British Government and to discuss interminably communal claims and counter-claims.

That is not our idea of Indian freedom or the state that we seek to build.

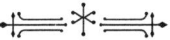

5.   What We Want to Do: Swami Sahajanand Saraswati

Janata, 4 April 1940.

It is stated that only a National Institution/Organization can announce the beginning of a national struggle for freedom. It will lose its meaning if anybody else starts it. In fact, this is quite true and it also impresses the general public. The intelligentsia also thinks in the same way. Therefore, if some people, tired of this nation-wide political stalemate, try to march forward, then they are not only showered (with criticisms) but are also pulled back. At the same time nobody provides any suggestion to save the country from this deadly deadlock and if anybody dares to suggest anything, these suggestions seem to be quite vulnerable. If we start a struggle on behalf of the daily problems and demands of the oppressed masses and promise to intensify it slowly but steadily, even then it is called dangerous. Those people who support this struggle even now say that if we linked this everyday struggle with the National Struggle and announce that it is a part of that struggle, a strong blow (of that struggle), it will prove destructive. Do everything but do not mention that it is the National Struggle or a part of it. Because we have not got the right to say/announce it. Only a National Organization can do so. It is a strange riddle—as soon as we announce the onset of a nation-wide peasant worker movement and struggle based on any country-wide problem, whether economic or not, then it will lead to destruction because it will mean that we have begun the national struggle for freedom. This is a strange case of political untouchability and we are being made a victim of it or at least they are trying to do so.

As long as slavery does not pinch us we can tolerate anything but as soon as we awakened ... our campaign against slavery had already begun whether we announce it or not ... since then our every activity will be directed towards rebellion. At that moment our whole 'being' becomes associated with rebellion and it continues as long as we do not get freedom; in-between, this rebellion could subside but it never dies out completely. In this situation there is no need to announce the struggle of freedom at intervals. It is always continuing, although we can intensify it if it becomes ineffective. The proposition that those who are to be set free should not participate in it and others should struggle for them is beyond comprehension. This freedom received through the efforts of others will be no better than slavery even if it is named otherwise. It will only prove to be mere political freedom, because real freedom is gained when there is no oppression anywhere.

When our country declared in one voice that 'self government is our birthright' from a higher platform, the struggle for freedom started at that very moment and it is still continuing. Therefore there is no question of starting it from beginning. One can only intensify it. One thing more—whatever effort has been made in this direction is only a curtain-raiser, an introduction and an effort to shift the total mentality of the masses towards freedom. It was successful and gradually the people have started recognizing and understanding freedom. Hence the true picture of the struggle will be used to end oppression whether domestic or foreign. It is also necessary to start and organize such struggles which were announced at Ramgarh by the Kisan Sabha.

In fact as long as the revolutionary sentiments are not awakened completely and their real image is not shown or developed, there will be no revolution and oppression will not end; and these matters could not be settled through mere political talks and other things like that. The toiling masses are always oppressed and tortured and in this way they become useless and depressed. They start thinking that there is no saviour for them and their life will be always full of sorrows. He becomes dependent upon God and Luck. It is our duty to end their disparity and make them hopeful and confident and it is possible only when we start the struggle for ending their oppression and involve them in it completely and make them victorious in their struggle. In this way the masses will recognize their power and feel it, only then we will be involved as leaders among them. We will become their active and real leaders. Without this it will never be possible. This is the crux of the Anti-Compromise and Palasa Kisan Sabha Resolutions.

We should remember that this struggle could not be started by the announcement of any great organization or person. It will develop and intensify slowly. Partial struggles can assume gigantic proportions. This partial struggle will become the foundation and structure of the national struggle. This is the real meaning of a partial struggle. As long as we consider the everyday struggle for bread and the national struggle as two different things it will be our mistake. Just like the engine acquires speed after running slowly for some time, we can transform our everyday struggles into a strong and powerful national struggle. The other way is that of deceit. This is the meaning of our programme for the celebration of National Week. In this way we are trying to create such a situation in this country when the sleeping powers of the country will awaken simultaneously and it will end the oppression and torture prevalent in the present society and lay the foundation of a peaceful humanity.

6. Jayaprakash Narayan's Proposed Resolution for the Ramgarh Congress, 15 March 1940

AICC Papers, File No. G–25/1940, NMML; *Harijan*, 20 April 1940.

The Congress and the country are on the eve of a great national upheaval. The final battle for freedom is soon to be fought. This will happen when the whole world is being shaken by mighty forces of change. Out of the catastrophe of the European war, thoughtful minds everywhere are anxious to create a new world—a world based on the cooperative goodwill of nations and men. At such a time the Congress considers it necessary to state definitely the ideals of freedom for which it stands and for which it is soon to invite the Indian people to undergo the uttermost sufferings.

The free Indian nation shall work for peace between nations and total rejection of armaments and for the method of peaceful settlement of national disputes through some international authority freely established. It will endeavour particularly to live on the friendliest terms with its neighbours, whether they be great powers or small nations, and shall covet no foreign territory.

The law of the land will be based on the will of the people freely expressed by them. The ultimate basis of maintenance of order shall be the sanction and concurrence of the people.

The free Indian State shall guarantee full individual and civil liberty and cultural and religious freedom, provided that there shall be no freedom to overthrow by violence the Constitution framed by the Indian people through a Constituent Assembly.

The state shall not discriminate in any manner between citizens of the nation. Every citizen shall be guaranteed equal rights. All distinctions of birth and privilege shall be abolished. There shall be no titles emanating either from inherited social status or the State.

The political and economic organization of the State shall be based on the principle of social justice and economic freedom. While this organization shall conduce to the satisfaction of the national requirements of every member of society, material satisfaction shall not be its sole objective. It shall aim at healthy living and the moral and the intellectual development of the individual. To this end and to secure social justice the State shall endeavour to promote small scale production carried on by individual or cooperative effort for the equal benefit of all concerned. All large-scale collective production shall be eventually brought under collective ownership and control and in this behalf the State shall begin by nationalizing heavy transport, shipping, mining and the heavy industries. The textile industry shall be progressively decentralized.

The life of the villages shall be reorganized and the villages shall be made self-governing units, self-sufficient in as large a measure as possible. The land laws of the country shall be drastically reformed on the principle that land shall belong to the actual cultivator alone, and that no cultivator shall have more land than is necessary to support his family on a fair standard of living. This will end the various systems of landlordism on the one hand and farm bondage on the other.

The State shall protect the interests of all classes, but when these impinge upon the interests of those who have been poor and downtrodden, it shall defend the latter and thus restore the balance of social justice.

In all the State-owned and State-managed enterprises, the workers shall be represented in the management through the elected representatives and shall have an equal share in it with the representatives of the government.

In the Indian States, there shall be complete democratic government established, and in accordance with the principle of abolition of social distinction and equality between citizens, there shall not be any titular heads of the States in the persons of Rajas and Nawabs.

This is the order which the Congress envisages and which it shall work to establish. The Congress firmly believes that this order shall bring happiness, prosperity and freedom to the people of all races and religions in India who together shall build on these foundations a great and glorious nation

7. Mahatma Gandhi on the Proposed Resolution of Jayaprakash Narayan, 14 April 1940

Harijan, 20 April 1940.

The following draft resolution[1] was sent to me by Shri Jaiprakash Narayan. He asked me, if I accepted his picture, to put it before the Working Committee at Ramgarh.

I liked it and read his letter and the draft to the Working Committee. The Committee, however, thought that the idea of having only one resolution for the Ramgarh Congress should be strictly adhered to, and that the original, as framed at Patna, should not be tampered with. The reasoning of the Committee was unexceptionable, and the draft resolution was dropped without any discussion on merits. I informed Shri Jaiprakash of the result of my effort. He wrote back suggesting that he would be satisfied if I could do the next best thing, namely, publish it with full concurrence or such as I could give it.

I have no difficulty in complying with Shri Jaiprakash's wishes. As an ideal to be reduced to practice as soon as possible after India comes into her own, I endorse in general all except one of the propositions enunciated by Shri Jaiprakash.

I have claimed that I was a socialist long before those I know in India had avowed their creed. But my socialism was natural to me and not adopted from any books. It came out of my unshakable belief in non-violence. No man could be actively nonviolent and not rise against social injustice no matter where it occurred. Unfortunately Western socialists have, so far as I know, believed in the necessity of violence for enforcing socialistic doctrines.

I have always held that social justice, even unto the least and the lowliest, is impossible of attainment by force. I have further believed that it is possible by proper training of the lowliest by the non-violent means to secure redress of the wrongs suffered by them. That means is non violent non-cooperation. At times non-cooperation becomes as much a duty as cooperation. No one is bound to cooperate in one's own undoing or slavery. Freedom received through the efforts of others, however benevolent, cannot be retained when such effort is withdrawn. In other words, such freedom is not real freedom. But the lowliest can feel its glow as soon as they learn the art of attaining it through non-violent non-cooperation.

It therefore gladdens me to find Shri Jaiprakash accepting, as I read his draft, non-violence for the purpose of establishing the order envisaged by him. I am quite sure that non-violent non-cooperation can secure what violence never can, and this by ultimate conversion of the wrong doers. We in India have never given non-violence the trial it has deserved. The marvel is that we have attained so much even with our mixed non-violence.

Shri Jaiprakash's propositions about land may appear frightful. In reality they are not. No man should have more land than he needs for dignified sustenance. Who can dispute the fact that the grinding poverty of the masses is due to their having no land that they can call their own?

But it must be realized that the reform cannot be rushed. If it is to be brought about by non-violent means, it can only be done by the education both of the haves and the have-nots. The former should be assured that there never will be force used against them. The have-nots must be educated to know that no one can really compel them to do anything against their will, and that they can secure their freedom by learning the art of non-violence, that is, self-suffering. If the end in view is to be achieved, the education I have adumbrated has to be commenced now. An atmosphere of mutual respect and trust has to be established as the preliminary step. There can then be no violent conflict between the classes and the masses.

Whilst, therefore, I have no difficulty in generally endorsing Shri Jaiprakash's proposition in terms of non-violence, I cannot endorse his proposition about the Princes. In law they are independent. It is true that their independence is not worth much, for it is guaranteed by a stronger party. But as against us they are able to assert their independence. If we come into our own through non-violent means, as is implied in Shri Jaiprakash's draft proposals, I do not imagine a settlement in which the princes will have effaced themselves. Whatever settlement is arrived at, the nation will have to carry out in full. I can therefore only conceive a settlement in which the big States will retain their status. In one way this will be far superior to what it is today; but in another it will be limited so as to give the people of the States the same right of self-government within their States as the people of the other parts of India will enjoy. They will have freedom of speech, a free Press and pure justice guaranteed to them. Perhaps Shri Jaiprakash has no faith in the Princes automatically surrendering their autocracy. I have. First because they are just as good human beings as we are, and secondly because of my belief in the potency of genuine non-violence. Let me conclude, therefore, by saying that the Princes and all others will be true and amenable when we have become true to ourselves, to our faith, if we have it, and to the nation. At present we are half-hearted. The way to freedom will never be found through half-heartedness. Non-violence begins and ends by turning the searchlight inwards.

Sevagram, 14-4-40.

---

[1] See the preceding item.

8. Communist Party's Perspective on Constituent Assembly: Manifesto of the Communist Party of India [Extracts]

Communist, Vol. 2, No. 4, January 1940, P.C. Joshi Archives on Contemporary History, JNU.

The Constituent Assembly and the Fight for Power

The Working Committee of the National Congress in its Allahabad session last month called upon the Congress organizations and Congressmen 'to explain to the people the message and policy and implications of the Constituent Assembly which is the crux of the Congress programme of the future.' We greeted the call. We girded our loins to popularize the slogan among the masses. When the National Congress declares that the stage is now reached when the slogan of the Constituent Assembly becomes 'the crux of the Congress programme' we could only draw one conclusion. That is, that the Nation has now to proceed to the final conflict, the nation-wide fight for the struggle for power. How can the nation proceed to the assertion and the realization of its will to self-determination and independence through a democratically elected Assembly based on free and equal adult suffrage unless it has also simultaneously created the sanctions to back its will? Merely moral and spiritual sanctions would not do. They have to be material. The brute force of exploiting and oppressing imperialism which stands pitted against our people has to be paralysed and overthrown. It is only then that the resolutions of the elected representatives of the people will become realities.

Mass Sanctions behind Constituent Assembly

The Constituent Assembly will proclaim the sovereign right of the Indian people to frame the constitution of a free, independent democratic and republican India. But Sovereignty cannot be established by the force of a 'proclamation' if it is not already a fact by force or other means. Where and when in the history of nations has a constituent assembly met that was not preceded by a mortal blow to the rule of autocracy? In the classical French example the Assembly met only after the monarch had fled and after the power of the landlords and priests was broken in fact. In Germany (1919), in Ireland and in Spain the Constituent Assembly came AFTER the people had delivered a mortal blow to the rule of the most reactionary class and its allies. We are not here concerned with the fact the developments which followed the establishment of the Constituent Assemblies in the cases cited did not lead to the further growth of democracy— to the flowering of a real people's democracy. The Constituent Assembly represents the assertion of the highest measure of bourgeois democracy against the will of feudal and reactionary classes which hold up bourgeoisie democratic development. In India it is British Imperialism and the reactionary classes on which it relies, that hold up this development. The Constituent Assembly representing the will of the Indian people including the progressive sections of the bourgeoisie, the will to free and unhampered political and economic development—the will to independence—can only arise when imperialism is uprooted. This is the lesson of history.

Real Implications

How did we popularize the slogan? The Congress challenged the British Government to prove its bona fides. 'If your pretensions about this "war for democracy" are true prove them by applying the democratic principle to India. Declare India independent.' Every one knows imperialism's insulting reply. That gilded halter of slavery—Dominion Status, would be put round India's neck at some unspecified, distant date. For the present our leaders would have the honour of being on the Consultative Committee to co-operate in Britain's war of aggrandizement against Germany. This has completely exposed Britain's real war aims and her designs against the Indian people. The Congress and the people have now to take up the challenge. The Working Committee has declared 'that the present war like the war of 1914–18 is being carried on for imperialist ends and British imperialism is to remain entrenched in India. With such a war and with this policy Congress cannot associate itself and it cannot countenance the exploitation of India's resources to this end' (Allahabad Resolution). The Congress has taken 'the first step towards non-co-operation' by withdrawing the Ministries. It has declared that it will 'resist all attempts to coerce the people of India along paths which are not of their choice and everything that is against the dignity and freedom of India' [Allahabad Resolution]. In the context of these declarations the raising of the slogan of the Constituent Assembly can have only one meaning. It must be the raising of the standard of revolt against imperialism and imperialist war. We linked up the slogan with the slogan of immediate preparation for nation-wide action through the Congress Committees, through kisan sabhas and through the trade unions.

Allahabad Resolution

This is how we explained the implications of the slogan to the people. But this is not how the National leadership visualizes the demand for constituent assembly. Look at the cautious wording of the Working Committee resolution:

'The Committee wish to declare again that recognition of India's independence and right of her people to frame their constitution through a Constituent Assembly is essential in order to remove the taint of imperialism from Britain's Policy and to enable Congress to consider further co-operation.' (Allahabad Session, November 23, 1939)

How has the Working Committee raised the slogan? Not as the banner of a nation-wide struggle. They have not put the slogan before the people. They have not called upon the people to forge the sanctions which alone would make the decisions of the Constituent Assembly a reality. No, they have addressed their demand to imperialism. In spite of repeated rebuffs and 'banged door' they 'continue to explore the means of arriving an honourable settlement.' Imperialism is called upon to concede the demand for a Constituent Assembly in order to 'enable the Congress to consider co-operation' in (what is not mentioned but obviously meant) 'Britain's just war.' In short the slogan is raised as a white-flag—as an offer for a compromise.

Gandhiji's Remedy for Preventing Struggle

If there was ambiguity on this point in the wording of the Working Committee resolution we have Gandhiji's HARIJAN article of the same week to place it beyond all doubt. 'All resources must therefore be exhausted to reach the Constituent Assembly before direct action is thought of. A stage may be reached when direct action may become the necessary prelude to the Constituent Assembly. That stage is not yet'. (*Harijan*, 25th November) Gandhiji says that it came to him as if in a flash that the Constituent Assembly could be the ideal.

'I knew for certain' he writes, 'that if I cannot discover a method of non-violent action or INACTION to the satisfaction of the Congress and there is no communal adjustment, nothing on earth can prevent an outbreak of violence resulting for the time being in anarchy and red ruin. I hold that it is the duty of all communities and Englishmen to prevent such a catastrophe. The only way out is Constituent Assembly'. (*Harijan*, 25th November)

Imperialism Not for Harakiri

Gandhiji wants the Constituent Assembly as a substitute for struggle. He wants it to meet with the sanction of and under the protection of British imperialism. Can such an Assembly be expected to produce 'a charter of Indian independence?' Has imperialism suddenly decided to commit Hara-Kiri—to destroy itself? Or is it that imperialism is willing to grant independence and self determination to India and it only wants to ascertain the real will of the Indian people through a universal adult vote? Nothing of the kind. Imperialism is not going to commit suicide nor is it going to allow even a country-wide mass election campaign where the straight issue of independence and British connection would be posed before the people. *The Times* (London), the mouth piece of the Chamberlain Government has said it in so many words:

'The convening of such an assembly now or even after the war, could only prove to the world the extent of Indian political disunity and many hold that an attempt to solve the communal problem on the simple majority basis would split India from top to bottom perhaps irrevocably.' (Reuter telegram dated 5-12-1939).

The meaning of these sinister words is clear. Imperialism would have nothing to do with a Constituent Assembly. If one is held on popular initiative as a moral demonstration of popular will—imperialism will use its feudal reactionary agents from both the communities to wreck it, to transform the election campaign itself into an orgy of communal riots. A virulent campaign against the Congress demand for a Constituent Assembly has already been started by Communal reactionaries.

Rajaji Abhors Vacuum

In this situation, the demand for a Constituent Assembly under the aegis of imperialism—and as a device to avoid struggle can only have one meaning. It would be a basis for bargaining and compromise with imperialism as well as with the reactionary communal leadership. The logic of the position taken by the National leadership leads irrevocably to this conclusion. Listen to Rajaji's argument:

'A regularly elected Constituent Assembly' Mr Rajagopalachari remarked 'could not come into being unless there was state help or a new state was created.' 'In a vacuum created by a revolution we can make a new state; but that is not the present condition, nor do we desire it. Just now we are trying to arrive at AN AGREEMENT WITH THE BRITISH GOVERNMENT. Unless the existing state consented to a nation-wide election campaign mere ad-hoc Committees and organizations would tumble down.'

Good old Rajaji, like nature, abhors vacuum that would be created by the evacuation of the British rulers from India after the revolution. He wants to arrive at an agreement with the British Government. He wants the existing imperialist state to convert to a nation-wide election campaign. It must be clear to the meanest intelligence that an assembly called with the consent of the oppressors, an election campaign run with the permission of the bureaucracy will be a farce and a mockery. It would be an all-parties convention or a conference of the representatives of the Congress, the Muslim League and 'other organizations', a Sikandar Hyat Khan to hatch out a joint formula of compromise with imperialism. It would have nothing to do with the conception of the Constituent Assembly as we know it in History.

Dr Pattabhi on the Reverse Gear

Dr Pattabhi Sitaramayya, an illustrious member of the Congress Working Committee has come out with three newspaper articles—popularizing the Allahabad decisions. The learned doctor herein attempts to present the case of the Gandhian conception of the Constituent Assembly 'in all its bearings, historical, legal, political and ethical.' The irrefutable evidence of history is brushed aside by this remarkable argument: 'In a scheme of violence', argues Dr Pattabhi, 'the Constituent Assembly naturally comes after the struggle. India, of course is a unique country. It has a unique destiny and a unique role to play. In India we work in accordance to "a scheme of non-violence" and in this scheme "history need not repeat itself, nay *take a reverse course*"' (Italics ours). We are told not to 'apply wrong standards because our movement is born in non-violence, is growing in non-violence and trying to reach its destination, its climax and culmination through non-violence. We claim that in the case of India the Constituent Assembly need not be the result of a knock out blow on either side' (*Bombay Chronicle*, 9-12-1939). We are frankly unable to understand the magic or the mystic process by which the Constituent Assembly makes the material brute forces of British Imperialism disappear without giving it 'a knock out blow.' Perhaps in the scheme of Dr Pattabhi it is not at all necessary to harm imperialism. 'History has to take a reverse course'—from independence to a vulgarized edition of a Dominion Status.

His Majesty's Constituent Assembly

'Whether direct action should lead to the Constituent Assembly or a Constituent Assembly should obviate all necessity for direct action is the real problem of the hour. The whole of the Indian issue reduces itself to this one question.' This is how Dr Pattabhi has posed the issue. We may agree with him. But in that case the choice before the Indian people is not between violence and non-violence but between fight and surrender, between struggle and compromise. Does anybody in his senses believe that British Imperialism because of the difficulties in the present war, has already been reduced to the state when it would agree without any struggle on our part to call Constituent Assembly and abolish its own rule? Sir Stafford Cripps may roam about the country regaling us with the story that the British Government is willing to accept the Congress demand for a Constituent Assembly. He may have his reasons for doing so. We refuse to believe that the imperialist lion which feeds on the blood and flesh of the colonial peoples and subject nations has suddenly turned into an innocent lamb. Those who place the slogan before country unrelated with struggle, those who present it as a non-violent panacea for our slavery, those who raise it as demand made upon imperialism—are straightaway leading the country towards a compromise and a surrender. The 'Constituent Assembly' which would meet with the benign permission of imperialism would be a farce of an all parties conference. The Congress would have only two alternatives—either to wreck it or to agree to a reactionary 'compromise solution' which would be offered by imperialism through its reactionary agents in the Assembly.

The Perspective and Task

But our national leadership would argue—we have put forward the demand for unadulterated Constituent Assembly—the one which would really implement and realize India's independence. We are not going to accept anything less. If imperialism refuses our moral case would be strengthened. The non-violent resistance which we would then put up would get the moral support of the whole world. If this is our position, then let the Working Committee stop this interminable drift and stalemate. Let it put a time limit before imperialism. Let it call upon the people to forge the sanction which alone would enable them to enforce the demand for independence and democracy. Let the call for nation-wide struggle ring out in every town, village and hamlet in India. The inane formula of 'spin for Swaraj' won't do. A grim mass struggle is ahead in which all sections of the people will participate. The industrial working class is on the move, demanding more allowances. The Kisans are fighting against the speculative fluctuation of prices. The people are resisting recruitments, and war loans. The discontent against the war, restrictions of civil liberties, the freedom of speech, press and organization is steadily rising. The people have sensed that their imperialist rulers have involved themselves in a war with a powerful rival. They know it is a war for world domination, for the perpetuation of their own slavery. They have sensed that a new period of revolutions is at hand. They know that this time the cause of peace and revolution has a powerful ally and a friend in the great Soviet people in the mighty Workers' and Peasant's Red Army. They have heard of the liberating role they have already played. The prospect is a protracted war—a deepening political and economic crisis. The exploited people of India are going to act. The question is whether the great Indian National Congress is to arise as the leader of a people in revolt—coordinating all the forces of struggle into one nation-wide offensive against the main enemy British Imperialism. This is the real task of the hour. Given a national initiative and lead to unite all the sections of the people which have already begun to move against the worsening conditions of war—against imperialist repression, the bogey of communal riots will disappear into thin air. Unshakable unity of the Hindu and Muslim masses would be forged in the fire of struggle—unity which would be the basis of a victorious national Assembly rising on the ashes of imperialist rule.

Raise the Banner of the Struggle for Power

Pandit Jawaharlal Nehru is reported to have stated that 'the alternative to the Constituent Assembly would be the continuation of British domination and the development sporadically or otherwise of Sovietism in India'. (*Times of India*, 18-12-1939). We do not know whether this is a threat or a promise—a threat to imperialism or a promise to the people. In either case, Panditji's pose is wrong. The threat of sporadic outbursts is not going to bully imperialism into conceding our demand for a Constituent Assembly; nor have we reached the stage when we can proceed to the organization of a Soviet revolution. To-day in the midst of the political and economic crisis created by the imperialist war, the basic conflict in our country, the one between imperialism and its reactionary feudal allies on the one hand and the people on the other has extremely sharpened. The moment has arrived for the National Congress to fulfil its historic mission of uniting the people and the communities of India in a final nation-wide fight against foreign imperialism and its native allies. It must inscribe on its banner the following simple demands:

1. End of foreign imperialist rule.

2. Constituent Assembly to frame the constitution of a free united India (through adult franchise).
3. Unity of all communities in joint struggle against common enemy.
4. Guarantee to all religious communities and races and language groups the full freedom for development of their culture and language and for their religion.
5. Guarantee of democratic rights and civil liberties to the people.

Here is the platform of the basic bourgeois–democratic demands which very nearly correspond to the present programme of the Congress. It is a platform which is in the interest of all the sections of the people who today stand behind the Congress—from the national bourgeoisie to the working class. A nation-wide struggle embracing mass actions of all sections of the people—strike action of industrial and transport workers, no-tax, no-rent actions of the kisans, resistance against the war measures, curtailing civil liberties, against suppression of the freedom of speech, press and association, resistance to recruitment and war loans—this is the urgent task before the nation to-day. The slogan of the constituent assembly has meaning only when the national leadership launches such a struggle. A popular mass struggle under the leadership of the Congress leading to a Constituent Assembly is on the agenda today. To talk of Sovietism either as a promise or a threat in the situation of to-day is to side-track the main danger to our national movement which comes from the compromise in our midst. THE WORKING CLASS AND ITS PARTY DEMANDS THAT THE SLOGAN OF CONSTITUENT ASSEMBLY BE RAISED AS A BANNER OF STRUGGLE FOR POWER and not as a white-flag of compromise and surrender.

9. 'Concept of a Separate Muslim State': K.S. Abdur Rahman Khan, MLA, Berar

Eastern Times, 26 April 1940.

The Prelude

In spite of our long association of past one thousand years with India, our countrymen still suffer from a lack of appreciation of our history and traditions, our psychology, the structure and the fabric of our society and our beliefs and aspirations. At times, it appears that we are being deliberately misunderstood and misrepresented. For the last century and a half, the Imperial Power and the Hindus seem to have conspired to bring about annihilation of the Muslims in India and be the coparceners in the exploits. It was a joint and co-operative concern with both and the advantages were reciprocal. Even the last vestiges of Muslim power, culture and influence were destroyed for one or the other reason and the Hindus never failed to offer voluntary services to fill up the gap. The relief of a change of masters was no small gain to them. The Muslims who were the rulers of the land a century and a half ago, are no better than paupers today.

Nationalism Born of Hatred

The Muslims never treated India as a land for exploitation and richly contributed to its wealth, progress and prosperity. India was 'Heaven on Earth'. But since the advent of British rule in India, they came to be treated as aliens and their rule of centuries is considered to have been a reign of terror, of bloodshed, of cow-slaughter, of destruction of temples, of forced conversions and of loot and plunder of the country. The country is portrayed to have been ruled by Timur, the tyrant, Alauddin, the debauchee, Tughlak, the mad, Babar, the drunkard, Humayoon, the opium-taker, Jahangir, the pleasure-lover, Akbar, the infidel, Shahjahan, the murderer of his own kith and kin, and Aurangzeb, the terror of Hindus. This is the compliment paid to us for our services to India and Indians which are unparalleled in the annals of the country. India of pre-British days knew no communal problem and history cannot provide us with a single instance when wars were waged on communal or religious basis during the time when the Muslims ruled. But Nationalism entered through the door of communal hatred in India and was nourished with the sentiments of ill-will and revenge towards the Muslims.

Nationalism in India is a borrowed ideology from the West. A plant of the Frigid Zone is trying to spread roots and branches on the hard rock of the Tropics. It is the Eighth Wonder of the World. No wonder the plant did not prosper and yielded no fruits. On the other hand, it threatens to ruin both the grafts and the main tree. This cross-breed child of Nationalism is the adopted son of British Imperialism and is now trying to oust the legitimate heirs from their rightful possessions.

Hollowness of Theory of Nationalism

Nationalism is the intellectual luxury of the Hindu intelligentsia. It is not the result of natural evolution nor the product of genuine local germination. Nationalism presupposes a Nation, a people, a country, common history, traditions and beliefs, common interests and aspirations. It is based on the fundamental principles of human equality, liberty and citizenship. Apart from Muslims, do the various sections of Hindus satisfy the requirements of Nationhood? India never thought in terms of nationalism during pre-British days. It was never a country and even today it is not a country. The Arya-varta did not extend beyond the boundaries of the Punjab, the Land of Five Rivers and the home of the Vedas, Bharat-varsha never crossed the barriers of the Vindhias, Magadha Desha was not India. During the Muslim period, it was divided into Ind, Sind and Dakhan. And what is India? Is it a country? No. It is a subcontinent. Is India a nation? It is congeries of nations. What is common between the Punjab and Bengal, Rajputana and Maharashtra, Dravid-Desha and Arya-Varta, Indian States and British India, Hindus and Muslims except the common administrative link of the British Government? India is not the name of a country or a nation but of the territory under British Rule, another name for British military occupation. One-third of the territory, viz., Indian India, does not subscribe to Indian nationalism and the rest is divided even under the Government of India Act of 1935 into autonomous provinces.

Indian nationalism is thus without its basic foundation of universal, social, religious, political and economical equality and liberty. The greatest barrier to the achievement of the cherished goal of nationalism is the structure of Hindu society which has created permanent and graded zones of superiority and inferiority. No Hindu is born an equal of other Hindus nor has he any chance in his life to attain the status of majority.

The Congress, which demands the democratizing of 600 States and asks the Muslims to merge their identity in the Indian Nationalism should first set its own house in order and dissolve Hindu Society to make India safe for democracy. Without this, Nationalism means only Brahmin Theocracy and Swaraj, Brahmin-cum-Bania Raj.

Growth and Development of Congress Nationalism

Like Nationalism, the very word 'Congress' is a foreign nomenclature. The Congress began by petitions and reaffirming its allegiance to the British Crown, from year to year. It started from a share in the service under the Crown to a share in local self-government. The next step was self-government interpreted as responsible government. It was followed by agitation for Home Rule meaning thereby Dominion Status. It was in 1920 that Dominion Status was replaced by Swaraj. Till Now, it was a plain political fight against foreign domination. But with the introduction of the mystical ideal of Swaraj and with the advent of diarchy, the seeds of communal misgivings were sown. Swaraj again came down to the level of Dominion Status in the Nehru Report and although the Congress made a high flight in the plain of complete independence, the impression that the Congress was out for Hindu Raj could not be removed from the Muslim mind. The introduction of provincial autonomy and the idea of a Federal Government have brought the issue to the surface and the Congress is making its last efforts for capturing the centre to install Hindu majority into power.

Since the advent of British rule in India, Muslims are being driven from every position of vantage. When they laid down the reins of power, they were not so low in the scale of nations as they are today. They lost their high place in the services. The Babus replaced the Muslims. The Indianization of services cost them too much, in the sense that not only their proportion in services was brought down but their language, culture, law and rules of administration, were also given the go-by. Their Jagirs, Inams and religious endowments were ruined. Their arts and crafts ceased to exist. The National Congress had not the charity to shed a tear in sympathy on the fate of Muslims who were the custodians of the national wealth. The Congress grew under the patronizing care of the British Imperialism and what was taken out from the hands of the Muslims was given to the 2% Brahmins in the name of Indian Nationalism....

10. B.S. Moonje's Concept of Hindu Nationalism as True Nationalism: Extracts from a Speech at Gorakhpur Hindu Mahasabha Conference, 2 September 1940

B.S. Moonje Papers, Speeches and Writings, Serial No. 42, 2 September 1940, NMML.

Ladies and Gentlemen,

I thank you heartily for the honour that you have done me in inviting me to preside over this conference.

The politics in India has become very complicated and there is now no hope of politics alone being able to find a solution for our difficulties and to lead us to our goal of Independence. First there is the wrong and quite unscientific conception of Nationalism. Next comes the spiritual philosophy, politics and programme of the Congress under the dictatorship of the spiritual Idealist, Mahatma Gandhi. Then there is the virtual domination of fanatic Moslem communalism which is inspired and encouraged by the policy of the Congress and which is sought to be enthroned in the public life and the public administration of the country by the shrewd Britishers and the British Government for perpetuating their hold on India. Finally comes the famous diplomacy of the British whose seeds were sown by Clive and Hastings in the past.

As for Nationalism, our present day conception of Nationalism having been originally injected into our minds by the late Mr Hume who may be said to be the founder of the Indian National Congress, is novel, suicidal and unnatural. If we look to our own history of our Nationalism, it will be found that we were working on the right track till the Mutiny of 1857 which we are proud to call as our War of Independence. At the time the East India Company, which had swallowed the Hindu Empire newly established and whatever remnant was still left of the foreign Moghul Empire, was consolidating its position and expanding its political authority throughout India. The protagonists of both the Hindu Empire and the remnant of the Moghul Empire had up to this time not entirely lost their hearts and cast in their lot together against the common foe in their attempt to regain their power. They, therefore, joined hands and became allies to fight the common enemy as they had done during the last Khilafat Agitation of Mahatma Gandhi; but it must be clearly understood that these allies were inspired by their own separate nationalisms, the Hindu Nationalism and the Moghul Nationalism in the hope that if the common enemy could be destroyed, they would again resume their fights among themselves for the annihilation of the one or the other for the final establishment of the one or the other Nationalism.

Thus from the very commencement of the struggle for Swaraj and Independence of Hindustan, there were two antagonistic forces struggling against each other for supremacy, that is the indigenous Hindu Nationalism and the foreign Moslem Nationalism of the Arabs, Turks, Afghans and Moghuls. Broadly speaking it may well be said that this struggle was initiated after the defeat of Prithviraj Chauhan, the last Hindu King of Delhi, and his murder in captivity. The leadership in the national struggle was assumed first by the Rajputs, the hereditary Hindu Rulers of India. It lasted in one continuous chain of alternating victories and defeats, until the death of Rana Pratap of blessed and inspiring memory. The struggle of Rajputs for regaining the independence of India is a most shining and energizing record of chivalry and indomitable bravery on numerous fields of battle.

After the extinction of Rajputs, this leadership passed on to Marathas who had the luck and the skill to subvert the Moghul Empire and to re-establish the independence of India and the Hindu Empire practically throughout the whole of India. The Marathas like the Rajputs were fighting single handed and in their struggle for reviving Hindu Nationalism had to fight against three enemies on three fronts simultaneously at one and the same time, that is the East India Company of the English in the East and the South, the Portuguese in the West and the Moghuls in the North.

Lately, the Sikhs organizing themselves in a separate warlike Panth of Hinduism, rose like a meteor and rid the Punjab right up to the River Sindh of the Afghan domination. Thus Hindu Nationalism was revived and re-established throughout the whole of India.

Every religion, that is, the Religious community predominant in a geographical unit, has its own Nationalism and it is this Nationalism when properly organized into a system of disciplined Militarism that is called the scientific and natural Nationalism. What is the Nationalism, say, in Afghanistan, Turkey and Arabia as well as Europe and America, if it is not the Nationalism brought about by the dominant religious communities in those countries? In those countries there are also Christians and Jews as in Arabia and Turkey, Hindus and Sikhs as in Afghanistan, living as separate religious communities. They do not formulate the Nationalism of those countries but they have to shape their lives according to the nationalism of the dominant ruling religious communities such as the Afghans, Turks and Arabs of those countries.

Similarly, is the case in Europe and America. So the Afghans rule in Afghanistan, the Arabs rule in Arabia and the Turks rule in Turkistan and formulate their own Nationalisms in their own countries. Are these not their National Governments under their own Nationalism? So where is the sin if there be Hindu rule and Hindu Nationalism in Hindustan, the land of the Hindus? That is natural, and appropriate and must be acceptable to all fair and just minds; but the Congress under the inspiration of the late Mr Hume and the British statesmen in India has conceived the idea that the Nationalism in India must be an exception to the general rule and therefore must be the composite conglomeratism of all the different religions existing in India. It is an impracticable absurdity but the Congress has been carrying on throughout the last 55 years, in the hope which is unrealizable of developing a United Nation of the Hindus, Muslims and Christians combined residing in India. This attempt has been particularly intensified during the last 20 years of Mahatma Gandhi's dictatorship in the Congress with the fervour of religious spiritualism. It ordained that there can be no Swaraj in India without Hindu–Moslem Unity, that is, the 28 crores of Hindus will not be able to attain Swaraj without the cooperation of, say, 6 crores of Moslems; as if the Hindu History of establishing our own Swaraj ..., not in the long past, fighting against three enemies, the Moghuls, the Portuguese and the East India Company of the British on three fronts at one and the same time, is of no account to Mahatma Gandhi whatsoever. In this way more than half a century has been wasted in the futile attempts of bringing together two mutually contradictory and antagonistic religions and civilizations of the Hindus and the Muslims for merging into one common nation and common Nationalism.

The credit however of giving the first rude and terrible shock to this Utopian Idea must go to the Muslim League of Mr Jinnah. He has often stated that 'One must be driven to the conclusion that the only solution of India's future lies in the division of India—Hindu India and the Muslim India', and that 'India has never been, could never be and is not a national state' and 'to contemplate a Government of such a vast sub-continent on the basis of one nation and United India is to pursue the will-o-wisp'. Quite apart from historic correctness or otherwise of such a statement from the President of the Muslim League, there is here no question that such are the ideas that are surging in the minds of the Muslims and influencing their thoughts and activities. It would not be wrong to say that these ideas have been inherited traditionally from the foreign rule of the Moghuls in India. These very ideas are being reinforced and preached and broadcast by the lesser leaders of the Muslim League in their own peculiar language. As an example, I may quote here from the presidential speech of Raja of Mahmudabad at the Bihar Provincial Moslem Conference. He says, 'We want to set up a state founded on Islamic principles of Government—what we want is Government according to the principles of Islam throughout India'. 'India is not a homogeneous country. The Hindus and Muslims are different National units hostile to each other. Democracy can never flourish in India due to Hindu–Muslim differences'.

Thus, these views of Muslim leaders of the Muslim League being so emphatically clear and unambiguous, is it any saneness on our part to still hug the idea of a common united nation of Hindus and Muslims to our bosom? But Mahatma Gandhi, the dictator of the Congress, will not forget anything and nor he will learn, I think, anything new.

The psychological and critical analysis of such a mentality of the Muslims may prove both interesting and instructive. The six crores of the Muslims of India are children of the soil as the Hindus are. They have not come from any foreign countries, though their religion has been imported from foreign countries. Besides, they are the children of those Hindus who have been converted to Islam by fair or foul means throughout the period of Islamic Rule in India of about 700 years. This process of conversion is still going on. Thus these six crores of Muslims of India are pure Hindus in blood and bones, though their religion is Islam. If this is so, then how are they different and separate from the Hindus of Hindusthan? If a Hindu or a Muslim is converted to Christianity by, say, a French Padri, or an English Padri or a German, will he become a Frenchman like Napoleon or Marshal Foch, or an Englishman like General Wellington or Admiral Nelson or a German like General Hindenburg or General Mackensen? Will the French or the English or Germans admit him among themselves as a French or an English or a German? He will remain and be recognized all the same as a Hindu of Hindusthan. Then how can a Hindu–Muslim become an Afghan or an Arab or a Turk? He will remain a mere Hindu of Hindusthan in spite of his being tempted to claim kinship with Afghans, Arabs or Turks. In fact he is every-where recognized as a Hindu outside India.

Such is the analysis of their mentality and it must appeal to all sensible persons. But we Hindus cannot afford to remain content with such an intellectual analysis. We have to take note of such a foreign mentality as it affects their thoughts and activities in the day-to-day affairs of the world. We must leave them alone and go on organizing true Nationalism in India, the Hindu Nationalism. I am hopeful—nay certain—that when we cease talking of Hindu–Muslim Unity and of no Swaraj without Hindu–Muslim Unity and go on organizing ourselves with the prime objects of ourselves undertaking the responsibility of defending our own Nationalism without the help of others or even in spite of them, the Muslim will then, of their own accord come to us and own kinship with us as they really are in blood and bones....

11. League of Radical Congressmen's Programme of National Reconstruction: Extracts from V.B. Karnik's booklet *The Road to Freedom*, 1940

Home Department (Special), File No. 379, Maharashtra State Archives, 1940.

League of Radical Congressmen

The object of the Indian National Congress is the attainment of complete independence. Notwithstanding the means prescribed in Article One of its Constitution, according to resolutions of the Congress, the object implies unconditional severance of all relations with the British Empire, and can be attained upon the capture of political power by the Indian people, and the establishment of a democratic State.

National independence is necessary for removing the obstacles from the path of economic development and general progress of the Indian people. Therefore, what is really needed is effective political power in the hands of the masses of the people.

But world experience has proved that formal democracy does not really vest effective power upon the masses. Therefore, the nature of the democratic State to be established upon the success of the nationalist anti-imperialist movement must be clearly defined. The definition is to be deduced from the programme of national reconstruction which is to take place upon the attainment of national freedom. But the programme of national reconstruction has not yet been clearly formulated. The Karachi resolution was a hesitating step. Even the inadequate and ill conceived reformist measures, visualized therein, did not find favour with the patrons of the Congress. Therefore, it has been quietly shelved.

In the absence of a programme of national reconstruction, political freedom is an empty ideal which can be differently interpreted. This has been done recently. Only the other day, a resolution of the Congress (Ramgarh) repudiated the novel doctrine that Dominion Status of the Westminster Statute variety is the same as complete independence. Nevertheless, today again it is said that, in the opinion of the Congress leaders, there need be no insistence about status, if the people of India will be granted the right of framing the Constitution on the basis of a previous agreement with British Imperialism. That shows that as long as the Congress remains committed to nothing more concrete than the vague idea of political freedom, nothing can prevent the growth of tendencies completely antagonistic to that idea. To be protected against such vulgarization, the ideal of national freedom must be given a concrete socio-economic content.

Economically, national reconstruction is visualized by the present leaders of the Congress, in so far as they are dominated by the Gandhist ideology, as a reactionary, revivalist, process. The idea that we can go back to the conditions of self-contained village economy is not only impractical, but positively reactionary. The economic life of the nation must be reorganized on the basis of the introduction of the modern mechanical means of production which will increase the productivity of labour. The industrial expansion and commercial prosperity of a country are limited by the power of consumption of its people. Rapid industrialization is the only remedy for the poverty of the Indian masses as well as for all the other evils eating into the vitals of the nation. It is an opinion, based on historical experience and proved economic theories, that the antiquated forms of non-productive (feudal, semi-feudal, sacerdotal, etc.) ownership of land are obstacles to the normal economic development of any country. A revolution in the relations of property in the main means of production is demanded for the promotion of national welfare and general prosperity. In India, land is still the main means of production.

Nevertheless, quaint economic ideas and utopian, if not consciously reactionary, ideals of social justice prevail among the bulk of Congressmen. That, naturally, creates confusion even about the real nature of the goal of political freedom. Unless the programme of national reconstruction is so conceived as to make evident the indispensable necessity of effective political power in the possession of the people, the struggle for national freedom is bound to end in a compromise. The realization of the economic programme of the Gandhist leadership of the Congress is admittedly not conditional upon the conquest of political power. On the contrary, it is maintained that the attainment of political freedom (whatever that may mean) is conditional upon the working of the so-called constructive programme. The deduction to be made from this is that political power is of no consequence, and that there is no relation between it and the economic reconstruction of the nation.

All this confusion about its object and romantic and reactionary ideas about national welfare have prevented the development of the struggle for political freedom in the right direction. This confusion must be cleared so that the road to freedom may be clearly visualized. With that purpose, the programme of national reconstruction must be concretely formulated.

The motive force of the nationalist movement is the urge for progress in all the departments of the life of the Indian people. The foreign domination has prevented the free play of that urge. Therefore, political freedom of the Indian nation is a necessity. That, however, is only a means to the end of social progress. Economic prosperity and physical well-being are the preconditions for any progress. To create those conditions, therefore, is the central point of the programme of national reconstruction, which must be concretely formulated as follows:

1. Abolition of private property in land which will be held only by actual cultivators on the payment of a tax not exceeding fifteen per cent of the net produce.
2. Nationalization of all natural resources.
3. Modernization of the economic life of the country through the rapid introduction of modern mechanical means of production.
4. State control of mining, mechanical transport and heavy industries ....

5. State financing of extensive public works and industrial undertakings for the productive employment of the huge mass of labour wasted today.

6. Minimum wages to guarantee an irreducible standard of living to those labouring in the fields, factories, mines, transport, office and schools.

7. Introduction of the system of seven hours working day, and of the leave for one day a week and one month a year with full pay.

8. State guarantee of employment or relief for every willing worker.

9. Protection of public health and sanitation to be an important item of State budget: Free medical aid stations in each village.

10. Introduction of free and compulsory secular education for all children up to the age of sixteen.

11. Constitutional guarantee for the freedom of press, speech and association.

12. Fullest freedom of religion and worship.

13. Complete cultural autonomy for all the communities.

14. Equal rights and responsibilities of citizenship for women.

To enforce this programme of national reconstruction will be the fundamental duty of the democratic State to be established in pursuance of the goal of complete independence. No State, however democratic formally, can perform the duty unless it is under an effective control of the masses. The democratic State to be established for reconstructing the nation on the above lines, therefore, must be a Government *of the people, by the people.* There will be no delegation of power. Such a State can be established only through the capture of political power by the masses, and their direct control of the Executive as well as the Legislative organs of the State. The failure of formal parliamentary democracy, and the world-wide experience that political power and economic protection are not necessarily associated with legal and formal rights, must compel all advocates of popular welfare and progress to visualize a more effectively democratic form of State organization.

Let all the Indian members of the Provincial Assemblies meet in a joint session to proclaim the Indian people's right of self-determination. Concretely, their task will be to enunciate the fundamental principles of the Constitution of the Democratic State which must be established with the object of undertaking the task of national reconstruction as outlined above. The Constitution of a new State legalizes the establishment of new social relations and rights, which is visualized in the programme of the movement for a far-reaching socio-political change. That being the case, the fundamental principles of the Constitution of the Democratic State of Free India are predetermined by the programme of national reconstruction. They can be formulated as the following:

1. The sovereignty belongs to the people and will be exercised through the direct control of the executive as well as the legislative function of the State by the elected representatives of the people.

2. Local People's Councils, created by the masses during the struggle for freedom from foreign imperialism and native reaction, are the basic units of the State. They will be elected, in future, by the universal franchise of the population under their respective jurisdictions, proportional number of seats being reserved for minority communities if so desired.

3. The members of the Provincial and National Legislative Assemblies will be elected by the local Councils which will thus function as the electoral unit.

4. India is a Federal Republican State, composed of a number of autonomous Republics, built on the basis of linguistic and cultural homogeneity as far as possible.
5. All the component parts of the Federation shall have a uniformly democratic Constitution.
6. All land as well as underground riches are the collective property of the nation.
7. Promotion of the productivity of labour through the introduction of modern mechanical means of production is the responsibility of the State.
8. Financing of public works and public utilities out of the Exchequer is permissible.
9. Heavy industries and banks are subject to State control.
10. Cultivators are entitled to hold land, without any disability, subject to the payment of a unitary land tax not exceeding fifteen per cent of the net produce. Small agricultural producers are free from all other taxation except local rates.
11. The promotion of large-scale co-operative agriculture through the cheap supply of modern machinery and credit is the responsibility of the State.
12. A minimum scale of wages, to provide an irreducible standard of living is guaranteed to all labouring in fields, factories, mines, transport, offices, schools, etc.
13. The State guarantees employment or relief to every willing worker, as a right of citizenship.
14. Nobody shall labour more than seven hours a day for six days a week, every worker shall be entitled to one month's leave with full pay every year and women workers to three months' maternity leave.
15. Free and compulsory secular education is guaranteed to all children up to the age of sixteen.
16. Promotion of public health sanitation is a charge of the State.
17. Freedom of press, speech and association is guaranteed to all but the enemies of the people.
18. The fullest freedom of religion and worship is guaranteed.
19. Women have the same rights and responsibilities of citizenship as men.
20. Complete cultural autonomy is guaranteed.
21. Rights of minorities will be protected through proportional reservation of seats on public bodies, if so desired.

Having declared that the above should be the fundamental principles of the Constitution of the State, to be established for promoting national progress and prosperity, the joint session of the members of the Provincial Legislative Assemblies should call upon the people to elect delegates to the Constituent Assembly to assert their sovereignty.

The programme of national reconstruction outlined above represents not only the interest of the entire nation, but also of the voters who elected the Indian members of the present Provincial Legislative Assemblies. In spite of the limited franchise, the majority of the electorate belong to the oppressed and exploited masses. Therefore, if there will be some among the members of those Assemblies opposed to the suggested principles of the Constitution of the Democratic State, they will forfeit the title of popular representatives and, therefore, should be declared to have betrayed their trust. Their opposition, thus being antagonistic to national welfare, will not make the joint session less representative, and will not affect its competence to take the next step toward the Constituent Assembly by endorsing the Draft Constitution and issuing the call for its election by the people.

The great merit of this procedure is the solution of the communal problem it offers. The issue of the Constituent Assembly ceases to be the demand only of the Congress. It becomes the demand of the vast majority of the Indian people, irrespective of religion, community or caste. Neither the Muslim League nor the organizations representing other communities can be opposed to the programme of reconstruction outlined above and the suggested fundamental principles of the Constitution of a democratic State under which effective political power will belong to the masses, and minorities will be afforded the fullest protection. If they do so, they can no longer claim to be the custodians of the interests of the masses belonging to their respective communities. A democratic State, constructed according to the principles outlined above, cannot possibly become the instrument in the hand of any one community, because it will be under the direct control of the masses, the identity of whose economic interests cuts across the superficial communal and religious differences. Cultural autonomy and freedom of worship constitutionally guaranteed, the identity of economic interests will prevail and the masses of the population will be welded into a united nation marching on the road of progress and prosperity. In a Federation of Autonomous Republics, the community constituting the majority of the entire population cannot possibly nullify the advantageous position occupied by other communities which constitute majorities of the populations in some of the constituent parts of the Federation.

That being the case, all popular representatives, even if they are actuated with the desire to protect and promote the welfare only of particular communities, are sure to participate in the joint session of the Indian members of the Provincial Legislative Assemblies. If the Congress, as the major political organization, takes the initiative, and appeals for the co-operation of other organizations, having recognized their nationalist bona fide and respective representative character, a favourable response can surely be expected from them all. There will be traitors and self-seekers in every camp. But let them be judged as such by the masses of their respective communities whom they claim to represent. To recognize the sovereignty of the masses is the first condition for asserting the sovereignty of the people.

The delegates to the Constituent Assembly will not be elected immediately upon the issue of the call for their election. There must be an intervening period of propaganda and agitation for the struggle in the midst of which the electorate will be created by the masses in the form of the People's Councils. The propaganda will be carried on the basis of the programme of national reconstruction which is sure to inspire the masses with a concrete picture of freedom and with the will to fight for it. The object of the propaganda will be to make them realize that capture of political power and the establishment of a State directly under their control, are the conditions for the attainment of their freedom as visualized in the programme of national reconstruction. Once the necessary political consciousness and the will-power have been created, local People's Councils will be set up throughout the country, composed of the representatives of the various classes and communities and groups actively engaged in the struggle for freedom. Finally, the People's Councils will begin to function as the electorate of the Constituent Assembly as well as the units of the rising Democratic State.

This is the only road to power which must be captured if the goal of national freedom is ever to be attained, if it is not to remain an empty ideal to be interpreted to suit the convenience of an anti-revolutionary, cowardly and opportunistic leadership. If the present leadership of the Congress fails to travel on this road to freedom, even after it is clearly indicated, they will forfeit the popular confidence and must be removed from their position for betraying the trust of the people. The fraud of glorifying a compromise with Imperialism, on the terms of an abject surrender, should not go unchallenged even if it is committed with the cry of a pseudo-internationalism and false hypocritical humanitarianism....

This conference condemns the reign of repression that has been let loose on the country since the outbreak of the War. It condemns the arrest and prosecutions of innumerable fighters for freedom and the suppression of civil liberties by the promulgation of orders restricting the freedom of press, speech, movement, assembly and organization. The conference protests in particular against the arrests of such members of the LRC as Coms R.D. Nigam, Bhupendranath Sanyal, Surendranath Panday, Birendranath Panday, N.N. Chandur, Murti, Anil Banerji, Swami Kumaranand and others.

B.   DOMINION STATUS AND ALTERNATIVES

12.   Viceroy's Proposal for Dominion Status, 10 January 1940

Speeches by the Marquess of Linlithgow, Vol. II, November 1938 to December 1943, Linlithgow Papers, Acc. No. 2329, NAI.

His Excellency the Viceroy made the following speech at the Luncheon given by the Orient Club, Bombay, on the 10th January 1940:

... When I had the pleasure of meeting you a year ago, gentlemen, I spoke of the working of Provincial Autonomy, and the success which the scheme of provincial autonomy under the Act of 1935 had achieved in this great Presidency. I said, too, that Provincial Autonomy was only one part of the scheme. I emphasized the importance of bringing into effect without any delay the scheme of Federation which was the coping stone of the constitutional structure embodied in the Act. I said that it was all the more important that we should secure Federation with as little delay as practicable because of the deterioration in the international situation, and I urged that we should press on with it with all the energy in our power, since, whatever its shortcomings, the federal scheme was the scheme that held out the best hope of swift constitutional progress and of the unity of India.

We meet today in very different circumstances. To my deep regret there has been in this province a temporary interruption in the normal working of the scheme of Provincial Autonomy. We have no longer in power, Ministers backed by a majority in the legislature; and the administration is perforce being carried out under the emergency provisions of the Act of 1935. No one regrets, I am sure, more than you do yourselves that this should be the case, or that at a time when the burdens and the responsibilities to be carried on behalf of the public are greater than they have ever been, Ministers should not be in power to assist in carrying those burdens. We can but trust that this interruption will be temporary, and that the re-establishment of the normal working of the constitution in the provincial sphere will before long be practicable.

But in the provincial field we have at any rate been able to bring into being, and to test by practical application, those portions of the Act of 1935 which devolve great powers and responsibilities on elected Ministers. We had not reached that point in the Centre when the war broke out, though our preparations were being pushed on with all possible energy. At the beginning of the war, which we had every reason to believe would develop on lines which would make it immediately necessary to concentrate every atom of our energy on the prosecution of the war to the exclusion of all other matters, the course of wisdom, much as all of us might regret it, was clearly for the time being to suspend the preparations afoot for the establishment of the Federation of India. I deeply regret myself that that should have been necessary, since whatever criticisms on one ground or another have been levelled against the scheme of federation in the Act, could it but have been brought into operation, it would, as I remarked recently elsewhere, have provided us with the solution of almost all the problems that confront us today—the presence of Ministers at the Centre; the association of the Indian States—a point of such vital importance to British India—in a common Government; the representation of all minorities on the lines elaborated after a full consideration of the claims and proposals of the minorities themselves; and the unity of India.

You know only too well how things have gone since September. I do not propose to dilate on that today. As you know, in response to requests for a clarification of the aims of His Majesty's Government and of the intentions towards India, His Majesty's Government has made it clear, both through statements issued by myself, and in Parliament, that their objective for India is full Dominion Status, Dominion Status, too, of the Statute of Westminster variety: that, so far as the intermediate period is concerned (and it is their desire to make that intermediate period the shortest practicable), they are ready to consider the reopening of the scheme of the Act of 1935 as soon as practicable after the war with the aid of Indian opinion: that they are prepared in the meantime, subject to such local adjustments between the leaders of the great communities as may be necessary to ensure harmonious working, and as an immediate earnest of their intention, to expand the Executive Council of the Governor General by the inclusion of a small number of political leaders: and that they are ready and anxious to give all the help they can to overcome the difficulties that confront us and that confront India today. But those assurances have not, to my profound regret, dissipated the doubts and the uncertainties which have led to the withdrawal from office of the Congress Ministers, and which have made it necessary in seven provinces to make use of the emergency provisions of the Act.

The pronouncements made on behalf of His Majesty's Government since the beginning of the war make clear, I think, beyond any question whatever, their intentions and their anxiety to help. The federal scheme of the Act was itself designed as a stage on the road to Dominion Status: and under that scheme, devised, I would remind you, long before there was any question of a war, very wide and extensive powers were to be placed in hands of the a Central Government representing the Indian States as well as British India, and constituted on a very broad basis indeed. There can be no question of the good faith and the sincerity of His Majesty's Government in the efforts they have made to deal with the constitutional future of India. I well know that there are many people who press for swifter and more radical solutions of the problems before us. I do not question the sincerity or the good intentions of those who feel that way. But all those of us who have to deal with problems of this magnitude know only too well how often we are attracted by apparently simple solutions; how often those apparently simple solutions, when more closely investigated, reveal unexpected difficulties, and difficulties, too, of unexpected importance, anxious as we may all be to take what seems to be the shortest course.

Short cuts, as many of us know to our cost, are too often prone in experience to lead to a considerable waste of time. Nowhere I fear is that truer than of the political problems of India, for there are difficulties, and real difficulties, of which we are all aware and which we all regret. But they will not be avoided or disposed of by ignoring their existence. The wise course is to face up to those difficulties and to try to find a solution of them that will result in the subsequent co-operation of all the parties and interests concerned. We are, after all, dealing not with one political party only, but with many. Nor must we forget the essential necessity in the interests of Indian unity, of the inclusion of the Indian States in any constitutional scheme. There are the insistent claims of the minorities. I need refer only to two of them—the great Muslim minority and the Scheduled Castes—there are the guarantees that have been given to the minorities in the past; the fact that their position must be safeguarded, and that those guarantees must be honoured. I know, Gentlemen, that you appreciate the difficulty of the position of the Viceroy and the difficulty of the position of His Majesty's Government, faced as they are with strong and conflicting claims advanced by bodies and interests to whose views the utmost attention must be paid, and whose position must receive the fullest consideration. Justice must be done as between the various parties, and His Majesty's Government are determined to see justice done. But I would ask my friends in the various parties to consider whether they cannot get together and reach some agreement between themselves which would facilitate my task, and the task of His Majesty's Government, in dealing with this vital question of Indian constitutional progress: and I would venture again to emphasize the case for compromise, the case for avoiding too rigid an approach to problems such as those with which we are dealing today.

As to the objective there is no dispute. I am ready to consider any practical suggestion that has general support, and I am ready, when the time comes, to give every help that I personally can. His Majesty's Government are not blind—nor can we be blind here—to the practical difficulties involved in moving at one step from the existing constitutional position which is represented by Dominion Status. But here again I can assure you that their concern and mine is to spare no effort to reduce to the minimum the interval between the existing state of things and the achievement of Dominion Status.

13. Congress President Rajendra Prasad's Response to Viceroy's Statement

Statesman, 12 January 1940.

'I admit that the Viceroy's declaration is the clearest of all declarations hitherto made. But there are some things which need to be said on behalf of the Congress. For instance, His Excellency the Viceroy refers to Dominion Status of the Statute of Westminster variety. But it should be clear that the Congress goal is independence, pure and simple.

'The Second thing that I would like to draw attention to is about the many parties and the Viceroy's appeal to them to arrive at some kind of compromise. I wish to point out that the party leaders are not full representatives of their communities. Thus though the Congress aspires and claims to represent the whole of India, legally I myself represent no more than the voters on the Congress register. Similarly Mr M.A. Jinnah although he is president of a very important All India Muslim organization, cannot legally represent the whole of Muslims in India. We know that there are rival Muslim organizations. Or take the Scheduled Classes. Dr Ambedkar, an eminent member though he is, in reality, represents a fraction of these classes.

'Therefore, when the Viceroy appeals to the parties he evidently ignores the inherent and fatal object I have pointed out. Such parties can never come to a just conclusion in a matter of tremendous importance as drawing up a charter of independence for India. So long as the British Government's attitude is not changed in this respect their assurance would seem to lose its force, accompanied as it is by a condition which I have shown to be incapable of fulfillment.

'It will now be seen that the Congress has not put forth the constituent assembly as the only solution without careful consideration. All Congressmen realize that short cuts are no cuts and so far as the rights of minorities are concerned it is a common cause that they should be clearly defined and scrupulously respected.'

14.   'A Clear Issue'

Editorial, *Times of India,* 13 January 1940.

If, as some complain, His Excellency the Viceroy's speech at the Orient Club contains nothing new, it certainly clarifies the Indian political situation. The Indian people have now received from Lord Linlithgow assurances which they cannot ignore. India's goal, said the Viceroy, is Dominion Status as defined by the Statute of Westminster; it is the intention of His Majesty's Government to reach that objective in the 'shortest practicable' time, and they are ready to consider the revision of the present constitution as soon as possible after the war with the aid of Indian opinion. They are prepared immediately—subject to an agreement to ensure harmonious working—to expand the Government of India by the inclusion of a small number of political leaders, and finally are anxious to help India to overcome her present difficulties. This plain and unequivocal statement calls for a response, and we are glad to note that Indian press reactions are not unfavourable. *The Hindu* of Madras, which represents moderate Congress opinion, welcomes the speech and advocates immediate steps to restore constitutional government in the provinces now that, on the Viceroy's assurance, the Congress objective has been conceded. Several prominent Madras public men have sent a telegram to Mr Gandhi inviting him to 'respond generously' to Lord Linlithgow's appeal.

Dr Rajendra Prasad, the Congress President, admits that the Viceroy's statement is the clearest of all declarations so far made, but qualifies his approval by emphasizing that the Congress goal is 'independence pure and simple' and by insisting on the Congress scheme for a constituent assembly. It is extremely unfortunate that the Congress President should pursue the hare of complete independence; we firmly believe that the great majority of the Indian people have no desire whatsoever to cut themselves adrift from the security, political as well as economic, which membership of the British Commonwealth of Nations gives this country. The trend of events in the world today clearly shows that unless they are safeguarded, weaker and smaller nations must inevitably succumb to totalitarian aggression. This fact is being demonstrated before our eyes. The other night at a dinner in Bombay to congratulate Mr Walchand Hirachand on his services to Indian shipping, the hope was expressed that India's mercantile marine would sail the seven seas in the near future. That is an admirable sentiment to which everybody can subscribe, but is India prepared to face the expense of a powerful navy to protect her shipping? We see on all hands what is happening to merchant craft; unless there is a lion to protect mercantile lambs, they are completely at the mercy of naval wolves in time of war. Complete independence carries responsibilities for defence which cannot be shirked by leaders whose ambition it is to cut India adrift from her present security to both by land and sea. Indian shipping today pursues its avocations peacefully because it is protected, and if our pandits argue that a 'free India' will be left unmolested by aggressor nations—East and West—they are living in a fool's paradise.

We have already explained—and everybody knows—why this country is coveted economically by Powers seeking political and economic expansion. Membership of the British Commonwealth of Nations gives independence which is appreciated by people like the Dutch in South Africa, and surely it is not suggested that they are less patriotic than the people of India. We suspect that Dr Prasad's insistence on complete independence is merely to show that the Congress is more heroic than other parties in its nationalist demands. But even if this is so, it dangerously complicates the situation and introduces needless difficulties in the way of a settlement. It goes flatly against the view expressed by Mr Gandhi that Dominion Status gives India the 'substance of independence' which he desires. Why, then, create a fresh obstacle which has no backing amongst the mass of the people?

Dr Rajendra Prasad, in commending the Congress constituent assembly idea, said that although the Congress claimed to represent the whole of India, legally he himself represented no more than the voters on the Congress register. The same status, he maintained, applied also to Mr Jinnah and Dr Ambedkar. This is a refreshing admission, but if pursued to its logical conclusion it could mean that nobody represented anybody and that Hitler, for example, represented God and not the German people. Is the coolie in the street to be invited to decide India's constitution? He may be and undoubtedly is, an excellent fellow, and at his own job he can give points to many Western porters, but he has not yet received—through no fault of his own—that training which makes him competent to decide big political issues. Our objection to a constituent assembly on the adult franchise basis demanded by the Congress is clear. It is that an appeal would be made to a vast mass of illiterate and ignorant people whose knowledge of constitutions is nil. It would also, as a correspondent recently pointed out in these columns, involve a vast mass of communally minded people, who could be swayed by a simple appeal to their religious susceptibilities. A constituent assembly based on these premises would, we are convinced, make confusion worse confounded. But this does not mean that a form of constituent assembly to consider the revision of the Government of India Act is ruled out; far from it. We have already urged that in British India a basis is already to hand in the electorate to the provincial legislatures, although care would have to be taken to prevent unwieldiness in the resultant body. Mr Gandhi has himself said that he is willing to consider alternatives to the Congress constituent assembly plan, and we ask the Congress in all seriousness to modify their scheme in order to make it practicable. At present it is not. The difficulty is that too many of our leaders, with no actual experience of administration, preach abstract political theories culled from books. What they must do is to come down from their Olympian heights and tackle the problem among living human beings struggling on the ground floor. They would then appreciate the real difficulties which beset India, communal and otherwise, and would be more able to suggest a practical solution.

The Viceroy's sympathetic and clear statement puts a simple issue before the Indian people. The time has come for moderate men to assert themselves—the men who represent that vast amount of commonsense and goodwill which permeates the Indian masses. Extremists, communal and otherwise, have clearly shown that they will lead this country into either civil war or a partition, which in both cases means goodbye to all hopes of unity and of India as a great and powerful nation playing her due part in world affairs. If the present impasse is serious for the British Government, it is no less serious for the Congress. Extreme Congress demands and an intransigent attitude are merely strengthening the opposition to that body which is showing signs of coalescing in the most surprising fashion. If Congress extremism can bring the Hindu Mahasabha and Mr Jinnah together, to what extraordinary results will it not lead? Millions of people of all communities believe, and rightly believe, that Mr Gandhi could settle this business with His Excellency the Viceroy in a few hours if he made up his mind to do so. We strongly suggest that Mr Gandhi should take the task in hand without delay; the country looks to him to get it out of its present political morass. The events of the past few months have shown clearly that Mr Gandhi's instincts were right, and that the advice of some of his friends to which he listened was wrong. Mr Gandhi has never been afraid to shoulder responsibility when he felt that it was his duty to do so, and the hour has again struck when he must live up to his reputation for the sake of India's political progress and communal peace. He has to deal with a sympathetic Viceroy who is ready and waiting for co-operation on reasonable and practicable lines. Will he rise to the occasion?

15.   *Indian Social Reformer* on Linlithgow's Speech

Indian Social Reformer, Vol. 50, Bombay, 13 January 1940, pp. 233–4.

Britain and India

Dominion Status for India is to our mind an etymological and political absurdity. One might as well speak of China enjoying Dominion Status in relation to Japan. Historically Dominion Status rests on the theory that the Englishman carries the right of representative government wherever he goes as an integral part of his personal law. This right of the English settler was subsequently extended to all White men who profess the Christian religion. The French in Canada, the Dutch in South Africa and, with much reluctance, the Irish, were recognized as fit for this right. All the Dominions have White populations numerically far smaller than Great Britain. The coloured people, of course, do not count. India is not a White man's land. The great majority of its people do not profess the Christian religion. The minority which professes it has no affinity with any White race. The tendency among them is towards Indian nationalism. India's population is several times the White populations of Great Britain and all the Dominions put together. If India is to remain in the Commonwealth she must be the predominant partner in it. The very first Parliament will vote for secession and the demand can be resisted only by armed force. If Great Britain can not make up her mind to unite India in complete comradeship to herself, it will be the wisest course for both to sever their present relationship which is humiliating to India and demoralizing to Britain. We are surprised to see the President of the Theosophical Society, Dr Arundale, saying that India can not remain independent for any appreciable period; she will be pounced upon by some strong power. What has the Theosophical Society been doing all these years? Even Babu Rajendra Prasad seems to admit this and he protests that India will seek an alliance with England so as not to be isolated in her Independence. For our part, we think it is quite possible for India to pursue a policy which will make her acceptable to all nations including the present Great Powers. But can not England and India find a way of cementing their present relations? We think they can if they sincerely desire to do so. Not, however, by way of Dominion Status.

Lord Linlithgow in Bombay

Lord Linlithgow pleaded in speech at a luncheon at the Orient Club for an early compromise of differences between communities and parties in order to facilitate the introduction of Dominion Status which His Excellency rather hastily assumed, has been accepted by everybody as the end of Indian politics. We do not share this view and have stated our reasons for our conviction that Dominion Status has no meaning in its application to India. We need not repeat these reasons. But when His Excellency pleads for compromise, we must premise that the compromise does not sacrifice the interests of the social and spiritual life to the exigencies of politics. This must inevitably happen if the progressive and forward looking elements are made subservient to the reactionary and retrograde elements. We fully realize that there can be no real progress if the latter are left behind in the march of progress. This is a good reason for moderating the pace but not for handing over the lead to elements which do not want to move at all. We should add that the principle of equal citizenship which is at the root of all just governments, whether democratic or autocratic, should form the basis of every compromise which it would be becoming in responsible statesmen to suggest or accept.

16. 'How to End the Deadlock'

Editorial, *Amrita Bazar Patrika*, 13 January 1940.

A number of prominent men in South India[1] have appealed to Mahatma Gandhi to accept the latest statement of the Viceroy as satisfactory and respond to his invitation to terminate the present deadlock and accept responsibility for office in the provinces once more. The signatories to the appeal are all prominent men. Their patriotism is above suspicion. We have, therefore, no doubt that their earnest request to the Congress authorities will be considered with the care and attention it deserves. At the same time we hope they and others who think like them will not in their turn fail to take into proper consideration the difficulties that stand in the way of the Congress feeling elated at the latest gesture from the Viceroy. There is no doubt, as Dr Katju, the former Congress Minister of Justice and Development in the United Provinces, has said, that 'the Viceroy's speech betrays for the first time a real anxiety for the termination of the present impasse'. That this pronouncement is also 'the clearest of all the declarations hitherto made' will also be readily admitted. The speech, therefore, constitutes in a sense the first definite sign on the part of the British Government of their realization of the fact that the Congress demand for the clarification of Great Britain's intentions about India is not unreasonable. Unfortunately, however, as is usual with statements issued from high quarters, the present one also falls short of the requirements of the situation.

Dr Rajendra Prasad has pointed out wherein this declaration of the Viceroy is defective from the point of view of the Congress. The Viceroy has declared that Dominion Status of the Statute of Westminster variety is the goal of British policy in India whereas the Congress demand is for independence pure and simple. Frankly speaking we do not consider this difference in the objectives of the two parties as an insurmountable barrier in the path of mutual understanding between them. No one will suggest that Independence and Dominion Status ever of the kind enjoyed by Ireland are one and the same. At the same time India, in her present position, is so far removed from either of the two that in the opinion of the majority of the people it will not make much difference to her from the practical point of view just now whether her goal is defined in terms of one or the other. Besides, Mahatma Gandhi has declared in clear and unambiguous terms that all that he cares for or insists on at present is the substance of Independence. Whether that status is to be obtained within or outside the British Empire will depend on the attitude of the British Government and other members of the Empire. In his now famous speech at Serajgunj the late Deshbandhu C.R. Das also spoke in the same train.

Although, therefore, the more ardent spirits among Congressmen would not remain perfectly satisfied with anything else than an assurance from the British Government that the latter would not oppose India attaining the status of an independent nation bound by the ties of voluntary friendship with Britain, we believe they will not also go to the extent of splitting the sincerity of the British offer of Dominion Status as defined by the Statute of Westminster. What is, however, essentially necessary is that this Dominion Status will have to be conferred upon India immediately with the termination of the war. Even in the latest statement of the Viceroy, the question of time as to when India is to obtain this status has been left untouched. This has virtually taken away all values of the pronouncement which would have otherwise gone a long way to appease progressive public opinion. This vagueness must be removed if the deadlock is to be ended.

But this will not be enough. The most outstanding defect of the Viceregal statement is the absence of any indication that the British Government will recognize India's right to self-determination. Dr Rajendra Prasad has conclusively shown why the Congress demand for a Constituent Assembly to frame India's Constitution becomes imperative even for the purpose of a compromise for which His Excellency has made a fervent appeal. The Viceroy has requested the party leaders to come to a sort of agreement among themselves to what they want. It ought to be clear to His Excellency and his superiors that as 'the party leaders are not full representatives of their communities, they can never come to a just conclusion in the matter of so tremendous importance as drawing up a charter of independence for India.' It is therefore necessary that the nation as a whole ought to have an opportunity to indicate its opinion as to what will satisfy it. Any agreement, for instance, that may be arrived at between Mr Jinnah and the Congress leaders is not likely to be acceptable to the Nationalist Muslims who have repudiated the leadership of the League or to the Hindu Mahasabha which has challenged the right of the Congress to speak for the Hindus. The Congress plan for the framing of the new Constitution including the clauses regarding the minority interests with the help of a Constituent Assembly would therefore appear to be the best from all points of view.

True, to Mr Jinnah His Excellency has spoken about the British guarantee to the minorities to safeguard their interest. But if the suggestion is good and reasonable, is it to be discarded simply to satisfy the whims of these reactionaries? Let Lord Linlithgow in whose intentions we have perfect confidence put his hand on his heart and tell us wherein this plan is open to any reasonable objection. Of course, if Great Britain does not want to concede to India the right to self-determination she will not support it. Otherwise there is no conceivable ground on which this can be rejected. His Excellency has spoken about the British guarantee to the minorities to safeguard their interests. No one asks the British Government to break this pledge. But if the guarantee is only for upholding the reasonable demands of the minorities and not to allow them to hold up the political and economic advance of the country demanded by the majority, they are not under any obligation to stand by Mr Jinnah and Dr Ambedkar in their opposition to this demand for a Constituent Assembly. On the contrary in view of the declaration of the Congress that the minority representation in the Constituent Assembly will be on the basis of special electorates and that the minority question will be solved not by majority votes but by a general agreement leaving any point of disagreement to be settled by an impartial tribunal, the British Government, if they are sincere in their desire for a communal settlement, should be prepared all the more to accept this plan.

We think, therefore, the Liberal leaders who have appealed to Gandhiji to terminate the present deadlock will be serving their country more if they address their appeal to the British Government.

---

[1] The reference is to Chimanlal Setalvad, P.S. Sivaswamy Iyer, C. Rajagopalachari and C.P. Ramaswamy Aiyer.

17. V.D. Savarkar on Linlithgow's Speech [Extracts]

Hindu Mahasabha Papers, File No. C–26/1940, 15 January 1940, pp. 130–2, NMML.

The following statement has been issued by Mr V.D. Savarkar to the Press regarding the speech delivered by His Excellency the Viceroy at the Orient Club, Bombay, on the 10th instant.

1. I feel no hesitation in noting that so far as promise goes, the announcement made by His Excellency Lord Linlithgow regarding the intension of the British Government of introducing a Constitution granting India Dominion Status as envisaged in the Westminster Statute at the earliest date practicable, was clear and definite.

2. The proposal of expanding the Central Executive Council by the inclusion of a number of political leaders 'as an immediate earnest of the Government's intention referred to above' is also not likely to be objected to by the Hindu Sanghatanist party in general. The policy of responsive co-operation implies that every inch of ground opened out on the path of constitutional progress must be occupied and utilized with a view to further progress. The immediate expansion of the Central Executive Council can be a step in that direction provided that some of the accredited spokesmen of the Hindu Mahasabha are included in the Executive Council with a genuine desire on the part of the Government to seek and give effect to their counsel.

3. But the condition which the Viceroy has laid down in connection with these constitutional changes is almost sure to frustrate the practicability of these proposals and it must be clearly pointed out that it has a ring of obstructive tactics about it. If the British Government is to wait till there is a harmonious and a full fledged unity amongst all the conflicting parties and interests in India and make it a condition precedent to the introduction of this constitutional reform, then they will have to wait forever. If the British Government is genuinely anxious to introduce a Dominion Constitution in India as His Excellency the Viceroy assures us in his speech, then the best and the most practical way to that end would be that the British Government should frame a Dominion Constitution on the broad and universally accepted principles of democracy after consulting all parties and interests in India in general, taking the greatest measure of agreement they arrive at as its basis and solving the vexed question of the minorities in the light of the rules laid down by the League of Nations and accepted by almost all Democratic and free states in the world to which Great Britain and the Indian Government as well had subscribed their consent and approval, and introduce that constitution with a stern hand in India at the earliest possible date.

   Why His Excellency should be so cherishing almost a religious reverence for securing a unanimous consent of the conflicting interests and parties in India only with regard to the introduction of the Dominion Constitution, passes understanding. When an undiluted autocracy was introduced in India under the emergency powers only the other day, was any plebiscite taken to secure a harmonious and united consent of the Indian people? Was the Federal scheme on whose relative virtues His Excellency is so eloquent based on any such harmonious and full fledged unanimity of Indian opinion when it was passed into an Act and brought into operation? If, when the British Government can thrust a course of an undiluted, alien autocracy of India, can they not thrust a blessing of a Dominion Constitution based on universally accepted principles of National Democracy and the rules laid down by the League of Nations in connection with the minority problem, even in spite of the dissent of any anti-National and aggressive party here and there?

18. Viceroy's Letter to Secretary of State Regarding his Talk with Dr B.R. Ambedkar, 12 January 1940

Correspondence with Secretary of State, Vol. V, 1940, Linlithgow Papers, Acc. No. 2153, NAI.

I had a long talk with Ambedkar also. I have touched on this in my letter of the 8th January, but would like to supplement what I said there in one or two respects. He made the point, which is important, that our tendency to concentrate the lime-light on Congress and the Muslim League was causing him a good deal of difficulty. On the one hand the Congress were actively trying to detach a section of his community from his leadership by the argument that His Majesty's Government were only anxious to settle with the Congress and that once that settlement was achieved the Scheduled Castes would be thrown overboard and would have cause to regret their not having come to terms with caste Hindus. From the other side, his own community tended to ask him where, in fact, the Scheduled Castes stood, and whether it was certain that His Majesty's Government would protect them. It was important that we should not lose sight of that. I thought there was something in this, and I accordingly mentioned the Scheduled Castes by name, bracketing them with the Muslims, in my speech at the Orient Club on the following day, but I suggest that you might also think it worth considering some reference to them when opportunity next offers. They are after all not only a very substantial minority, but one for the protection of which we have in the past been specially concerned. Ambedkar expressed great regret that there had been no opportunity given here of forming an alternative Ministry. But he admitted under cross examination that it would have taken him a little time in office to get a team together commanding a majority, and that he might have had to ask for his first budget to be certified.

19. Note of a Talk between Viceroy and Jinnah at Bombay, 13 January 1940 [Extracts]

Viceroy's Letter to Secretary of State for India, No. 4, Enclosure 2, 16 January 1940. Correspondence between Viceroy and Secretary of State, Linlithgow Papers, Acc. No. 2153, NAI.

Mr Jinnah came to see me today at my invitation, and we had a general discussion ....

2. I then thought it well to have a word with him about the Consultative Committee[1] and I asked him whether in his judgment it would be a good thing for us to go ahead with that idea which, as he knew, had for some time past been rather in cold storage. I said that there was, of course, no connection between the Consultative Committee proposed and the offer I had made for the expansion of my Executive Council.

3. Mr Jinnah said he fully appreciated that fact, and there had never been the least confusion in his own mind on the point, though he was aware that there had been confusion elsewhere. We must go to the roots of this business. He wished me to know that he had done his utmost during the November discussions at Delhi to persuade Gandhi and Nehru to accept my first

offer and he himself thought there was a good deal to be said for it, but they would not look at the proposal, or even begin to discuss it. They had made up their minds then to have a shot at the Viceroy and try to see what more they could get out of him and His Majesty's Government in just the same way at the present time, although they had been carrying on discussions with him (Mr Jinnah) for an agreement they had, as he was perfectly well aware, been simultaneously designing behind his back the disintegration of the Muslim League and preparing for war against it. Before leaving this subject I again pressed on Mr Jinnah the advantages of the Consultative Committee as consolidating the minorities and as providing an outlet for their energies. It was however, perfectly clear that so far as he was concerned that must be regarded as off the map for the present, and he told me that he could not come in until he had made up his mind to give unconditional support, which might be a long time.

4. I then described the general position as I saw it that while Section 93 was working smoothly at the moment we could not mark time on it indefinitely nor could we overlook the fact that there were signs of Parliamentary uneasiness, the importance of which he would fully realize and that there was a certain amount of criticism at Home. The Secretary of State equally had to keep his eye on these matters and it was essential to make allowance for the inevitable result at Home, whether in politics or on the public, of the Parliamentary tradition and outlook. Neither Ministers nor the public would like an indefinite postponement of return to normality. What way out was there? Mr Jinnah and Congress were both in the same difficulty and I must look to him for his help.

5. Mr Jinnah was perfectly clear on this. We could not, he thought, find a way. He quoted to me the example of Egypt. We had, after all kept Egypt waiting a long time and had achieved no inconsiderable success as the result of doing so. We must go on as at present and we must tell Congress that there was nothing doing. Until we did there was no prospect in his judgment of any headway being made. Nor should I ignore the fact that in South India the non-Brahmin feeling was as strongly anti-Congress as the feeling of any Muslims. Indeed, he had been almost appalled by its strength. He urged that I should see the speeches recently made by the Justice Party leaders in Madras which had been reported in the *Bombay Chronicle*, and which fully bore out what he said as to the attitude of the non-Brahmin element.

6. I then said to Mr Jinnah that I was anxious to get the position as clear as possible. If by any chance I was able to work a miracle and persuade the Congress to come some way to meet us, what in fact were his terms for an understanding with them?

7. Mr Jinnah said that the Congress were already well aware of his terms as he had given those terms to them in the course of conversations in Delhi. They were applicable to the period of the war only and were as follows:

First, Coalition Ministries.

Second, so far as Provincial Legislatures were concerned, no measure to be forced through if two thirds of the Muslim members of the Assembly objected to it.

Thirdly, the Congress flag not to be flown on public institutions.

Fourthly, *Bande Mataram* to be abandoned as a National Anthem.

Fifthly, Congress to abandon their wrecking tactics against the Muslim League.

8. I said that I took note of this but that it followed of course that on this basis collective responsibility went overboard. Was it his considered judgment that that was wise and desirable?

9. Mr Jinnah replied that his answer was definitely in the affirmative and that he could not hold to collective responsibility. He had himself been partly responsible for its original adoption, because he had dissuaded his friends from pressing for statutory inclusion of Muslims in Cabinets

because of the risk of blocking the machine. We had therefore moved from a statutory provision to a convention which took its shape in the Instrument of Instructions. His Majesty's Government however had, for the purpose of minority representation, stultified for the virtue of the Act taken with the Instrument of Instructions by inserting in the same Instrument of Instructions provision for collective responsibility, with the result, said Mr Jinnah, that we were left with a few dud Muslims who had joined the Congress in order to get jobs and who were 'worse than our enemies being as they were turncoats and renegades'.

10. I said that he would not dissent from my view that the whole position was very deplorable. We were bound to ask ourselves whither we were going and what is the future of all this going to be? Was I to understand that we were to abandon all hope of a democratic government at the Centre based on popular vote and on an executive responsible to the legislature? Mr Jinnah replied that that was the position. He agreed that it was most deplorable, and he fully realized the gravity of what he was saying. The fact remained, however little we might wish to believe it, that the Hindus were not capable of running a government, and we should find that out for ourselves before we had finished.

12. ... Our conversation, which was more friendly almost than any I have had with Mr Jinnah made it I fear perfectly clear that no move could be looked for from him at this moment. We did not discuss the points which he had referred to me in his letter of 5th November, but he told me that he had received my reply and that he proposed to put it before the meeting of the Working Committee of the Muslim League at Delhi at the end of the present month. He was somewhat disturbingly frank and fair. My speech to the Orient Club was, he thought, very good, and he knew that I was trying to keep the balance. But he was emphatic in his view that I would not succeed in doing so since the Congress would not have it. I commented on this that speaking not as a Viceroy, but as the ordinary man in the street, I was frankly frightened by the risk that the end of the war might find Great Britain exhausted and tired and in a disposition to hand over rope pretty freely to an Indian in no shape to take the strain. I found the possibility of the resulting case depressing to a degree and I could not reconcile myself to the thought that the great achievement represented by the 150 years for which we have administered this country should go by the board. Surely it was worth taking a few risks now in order to keep India together and to avoid a period of chaos such as I had referred to? Mr Jinnah replied that that was precisely what he had told Mr Gandhi but that Mr Gandhi had refused to play and had expressed the view that India could expect to go on getting Great Britain to do what was necessary. I expressed my interest in his view, and I said that I had the strong impression that many politicians here, however much they might talk of independence did not envisage an independence in which India was left without the support of His Majesty's Government. Mr Jinnah said he wholly agreed and that he had pressed that also on Mr Gandhi as an argument for accepting the offer which I had made to the communities in Delhi at the beginning of November last, but that Mr Gandhi had never even looked like doing any business on that basis.

13. Before we parted I said that I would like to say a word to him about publicity. He had clearly put the Muslims very much on the map both here and in the United States in the last few weeks and he would realize the importance of publicity from his own point of view. I showed him the article by Gunther on Nehru which has just appeared in *Life*, an article which of course completely ignores the Muslim position as well as many of the other difficulties which confront us in India today. Mr Jinnah's comment was that he only wished he had the funds to arrange for similar publicity. Congress could touch as much as they wanted whenever

they wanted. I asked him whether he thought that the financial supporters of Congress were moved by the thought not only by the very national desire to secure a greater share in the government of their own country but by the thought that they might be making a good business investment so far e.g. as fiscal control was concerned, but his definite view was that 90 per cent of these contributions were blackmail, and that the contributors did not dare to face the back door influence and indirect pressure brought to bear upon them if they failed to pay up.

14. I could not feel that I had made very much progress as the result of my talk with Mr Jinnah save to the extent that one now had a definite idea of his terms for accommodation with Congress. He clearly remains profoundly suspicious of that organization and very indisposed to make any advance himself unless he is certain that he can look for a readiness on the part of Congress to grant him his terms.

---

[1] Formed specifically for the purpose of war efforts, consisting of Indians to mobilize native public opinion in support of war efforts.

20. Secretary of State's Views on Viceroy's Proposals

Secretary of State's Letter to Viceroy, 17 January 1940. Correspondence between Viceroy and Secretary of State, Linlithgow Papers, Acc. No. 2153, NAI.

In my telegram of 10th January, in which I agreed with the line of approach you outlined in your secret and personal letter of the 21st December, I said that I felt some difficulty about the third part of your tentative plan and promised you a considered reply.

Your plan assumes, as a result of the small exploratory committee which I should gladly see brought into existence, accommodation between the Congress and the Muslim leaders as to the position of the Muslims under responsible government in the Provinces and at the Centre; your hope is that such accommodation can be reached and the Muslims are prepared on the basis of it to be parties to responsible government at the Centre: it will not prove impossible to get them, the Congress and the Princes to agree to the Central Government taking the form for the time being of the Federation provided for by the Act of 1935, subject, of course, to whatever modifications are required to give effect to the Hindu–Muslim concordat. So far so good. But it is hardly conceivable that the position so reached would remain stable beyond the end of the war at most. The statement you propose to make in regard to Dominion Status in (c) of paragraph 26 of your letter as I understand it is designed to give an acceptable indication of the next stage and your hope is that it would be accepted by all concerned in the small exploratory committee. You suggest that this statement should be a reiteration, approaching to a promise of attainment soon after the war, of Dominion Status as our objective, with an explanation that this is in effect independence; in other words, full self-government. There would, however, be implicit in this two conditions:

1. that the self-government to be acquired would be self-government within the Empire; and
2. that arrangements satisfactory to His Majesty's Government are agreed to by Indians and embodied in the Constitution for the future defence of India and for the preservation of British commercial interests.

My difficulty about this is that I am doubtful whether, assuming that a Hindu–Muslim modus vivendi has been reached, we could for long hold this position. 'Dominion Status' now means full self-government beyond dispute, and in the light of Eire's neutrality in the life and death struggle we are now engaged in, it has become more difficult than ever to deny that full self-government means, in practice, competence to secede. I admit that it might conceivably be necessary for us to compel a self-governing unit of the Commonwealth to remain within it as Lincoln did with the Confederacy, but that is not a matter of constitutional law. It is clear, however, that any admission of a right of secession would be very badly received by the States.

Apart from this, a promise of Dominion Status, subject to insistence by us upon incorporation in the *Dominion Constitution itself* of limitations of self-government so fundamental as the Defence and commercial limitations in question, can be represented as almost a contradiction in terms. Will it not lay us open to the old charge of insincerity?

I am well aware that in pointing out these difficulties I have not provided you with a solution for this stage of your problem. But if the Committee could be assembled without a fresh formal promise on our side, and any of the parties to it could be induced to make suggestions on the lines of which you are thinking, we should be in a much happier position.

If it has really come home to Congress, as seems possible, that without some sort of communal accommodation there is no peaceful escape from the present deadlock, cannot the leaders of the communities now put their heads together on the Sikander plan[1] with a view to finding a way out of their impasse and with a view, having found it to letting us know on what basis and what principles they are agreed in desiring the future government of India to be devised?

The foregoing is concerned with the tactics appropriate to the existing situation. On a long view, however, the considerations set out in paragraphs 14 and 15[2] of my letter of the 20/21 December still seem to me to hold good.

---

[1] The plan proposed in pamphlet, 'Outlines of the Scheme of Indian Federation', based on the Act of 1935 divided India (Princely States included) into seven regional zones.

[2] Refers to Zetland's view on Dominion Status as a final goal and the idea of Constituent Assembly as impractical.

21. 'Congress and Dominion Status'

Editorial, *Hitavada*, 17 January 1940.

The rejection by the Congress President of the Viceroy's offer of Dominion Status, within the meaning of the Statute of Westminster, has evoked criticism at the hands of Sir Chimanlal Setalvad and Sir P.S. Sivaswamy Iyer. Sir Chimanlal describes it as 'childish and suicidal' and Sir P.S. Sivaswamy Iyer as 'unpractical and foolish'. We are afraid that the eminent leaders referred to above have missed the distribution of the emphasis in Dr Rajendra Prasad's statement. It is true that Dr Rajendra Prasad referred to the Congress goal being Independence. But this mention was almost casual. What Dr Rajendra Prasad said referring to the Viceroy's statement was only a sentence, but it should be clearly understood that the Congress goal is independence, pure and simple. The emphasis of Dr Rajendra Prasad was on the demand for a Constituent Assembly, and it is on this aspect of the question that the Congress president has spoken at considerable length. The demand for a Constituent Assembly has been misunderstood in many quarters. It is argued that such an assembly will be a bear garden in which our communal differences will be exploited and which will finally land us in disgrace. But here again, we should not be misled by the phrase, 'constituent assembly'. The Congress, of course, insists on adult suffrage but we have reasons for believing that they will be prepared to accept modifications. What the Congress really has in mind is a National Convention, having an electoral basis provided the British Government accepts an agreed constitution. Let the election for the Constituent Assembly be on a suitable basis and let us call it by any name 'Convention or Constituent Assembly' provided the Government accepts its verdict. The term 'Constituent Assembly' has been much misunderstood but we have, as we have stated above, reasons for the belief that the Congress will agree to consider modifications, a point stressed by Mr Rajagopalachari in his reply to Sir Maurice Gwyer. What is wanted is the right of self-determination and the Congress is on thoroughly sound ground in taking this stand. We do not want another Round Table Conference with His Majesty's Government as an Arbiter because we know what fate overtook the memorandum of the Joint Indian Delegation which was rejected in toto. It is to obviate the repetition of such a rejection that the Congress asks for a Convention or a Constituent Assembly, whatever you like to call it, whose verdict will be accepted. As regards the objective of the Congress, we have reasons for stating that they will accept the goal of Dominion Status provided the 'modus operandi' for the making of the future constitution is self-determination. Gandhiji himself stated in a message to Mr Polak two years ago that he for his part will accept Dominion Status and we feel that if the offer is made with the acceptance of the right of self-determination, the Congress will contribute its share in the removal of the present impasse, which all of us deplore. After all, it is Gandhiji who is the Congress to-day and if Gandhiji says, he accepts 'Dominion Status', his writ will be honoured by his followers.

22. Viceroy on Mahatma Gandhi's Attitude

Telegram from Viceroy to Secretary of State, 19 January 1940. Telegram No. 12, Telegraphic Correspondence between Viceroy and Secretary of State, Linlithgow Papers, Acc. No. 2162, NAI.

Immediate Private & Personal. No. 75–5. My private and personal telegram No. 93–S.C. of January 16th. I subsequently wrote to Gandhi to say that I will be glad to see him at the end of the month or the beginning of February as might be convenient. This crossed a telegram from him asking me to postpone my reply until I had received a further letter which he was sending me. I have had the letter in question. It is dated 17th January and runs as follows:

'Since writing to you on the 14th instant I have had reports of the interviews you gave to Shris Bhulabhai Desai, Munshi and Kher. These reports convey an impression different from the one in your Bombay speech. If they are a correct reflection of your mind a settlement may be more difficult than your speech had led me to believe and perhaps the time has not yet arrived for our meeting. But of this you shall be the sole judge. I do not want to put you in a false position by your inviting me to meet you because of my letter of 14th instant. Somehow or other I feel that when we meet we should do so to come to a final settlement. But I must not anticipate'.

You will have had, in my letter of 12th January gist of my talks with Munshi and Kher, and note of my talk with Desai went by bag of 16th January. Gandhi's gambit is not wholly unexpected but I doubt very much whether it represents the whole story. I suspect myself that Rajendra Prasad and Nehru have stiffened his mind, but if he relapses to being their mere mouthpiece, it is not going to make it very easy for me to do business with him as profitably as might otherwise have been the case.

I think that on the whole the wise course would be to have a talk with him despite the risk that the position may be aggravated if the gap between us proves greater than might have been hoped; but I will wait a day or so before sending him a reply.

23.   Jawaharlal Nehru's Confidential Note on Congress Policy, 20 January 1940

SWJN, Vol. X, pp. 303–8.

In considering the present position and what should be put forward as India's demand, it is important that we keep in mind the complexities of the international situation and the war and the possible outcome of this war. All this is entirely uncertain and it is difficult to base any calculation on it, and yet it cannot possibly be ignored, or else we might get entangled with all manner of commitments which we find difficult or undesirable to accept. It was for this reason that the Working Committee laid stress in their statement of September 14, 1939 on these wider implications and the whole background of the war, and asked for a declaration of war aims. Any precise announcement of war or peace aims is perhaps difficult at this stage, but this difficulty does not arise in a general and somewhat vague declaration which may deal with the ending of the imperialist method of governing and exploiting countries and introducing the principle of self-determination to the largest possible extent in colonial and dependent countries. The cooperation of peoples and nations, both political and economic, on a democratic foundation and a world basis, should be aimed at. Disarmament would be essential.

There is at present a great deal of talk about a united states of Europe or a loose federation of democratic countries, including England, France, U.S.A., some minor European countries and some British Dominions. It seems almost inevitable that some such attempt will be made at the end of the war, if there is anything left then. But all such talk completely ignores Asiatic countries and colonial areas. It is confined to European peoples. It is thus a dangerous objective from our point of view, as well as that of China or other countries. It means European consolidation to hold on to and exploit Asia and Africa.

It is necessary therefore that we must insist now and continuously on the wider objective of world cooperation of free nations, including Asiatic nations, and ending colonial domination. Few thinking people imagine that the British Empire, as constituted today, will continue after the war. If, unhappily, it does continue, this will mean three or four vast groups in the world, hostile to each other and preparing against each other for political and economic conflicts. It would be unfortunate for us to be associated with such an empire.

For the present, the immediate and pressing problem for us is India and what should be done here. Is it possible to come to terms with Britain and, if so, what should these terms be? While this is the real problem for us, it would be unwise to separate it from the wider problem referred to above. We shall then see it in wrong perspective and this might lead us to wrong conclusions and dangerous entanglements. The war situation has all manner of sinister possibilities. It is safer for us not to commit ourselves at this stage unless that commitment is based on clear principles which we hold, and on our ability to prevent ourselves being dragged in directions we disapprove of. It must always be remembered that the present British cabinet is excessively reactionary in outlook and to expect good to come out of it, except under stress of circumstances, is to expect something that is beyond the bounds of probability or even of possibility. Nothing can be taken for granted by us, nothing can be left vague. Every loop-hole that is left will be used against us. Every possible misinterpretation of equivocal phrases will be made. The problem is not one of satisfying the Viceroy or of getting assurances from him. The Viceroy counts, as everything counts when the scales are evenly balanced, but the conflict is a far deeper one and individuals do not vitally affect it.

We desire a settlement of course, for the failure to have such a settlement will inevitably lead to conflict on a big scale and no one knows the consequences of such a conflict. Even if the British authority is weakened or eliminated, the internal forces of disruption may gain the upper hand and lead to chaos and anarchy. We want to avoid that. But a settlement on a wrong basis will be no settlement at all and might lead ultimately to that very chaos when even the central cohesive force of the Congress will become powerless to shape events, and adventurers and communalists will do as they like. It is better, therefore, not to have a settlement and to await the development of events than to accept something which is a feeble and a wrong settlement with the seeds of evil and conflict in it.

Coming to the particular problem that confronts us in India today, we must not view it merely as a disagreement between us and the British Government but as an integral part of a world problem. A settlement involves an ending of that disagreement but from that larger point of view. Both from the standpoint of England and India this is the right approach, and this approach will be understood and appreciated in other countries. Viewed as such, our communal problem falls into its proper place and does not dominate us, as otherwise it might.

The British Government should therefore make some general declaration about its aims and the future of its empire. In regard to India it should recognize the right of India to independence and self-determination, that is, the right of the Indian people to frame their own constitution as that of a free state, and to determine the relation of this state to England. So far as the British Government is concerned, it may express its own wish that a free India may continue as a partner in a British federation of free nations, but it will be for the Indian people to determine this and it will be open to them to sever this connection if they so wish. For the present, this connection inevitably continues till that decision is finally made.

Thus though we do not expressly deny the possibility of Dominion Status after the Westminster model, we cannot commit ourselves to it because:

(i) We do not know what the position will be at the end of the war and how this conception might develop.

(ii) We think that the ideal should be a larger world group and not one confined to the British group, which necessarily would mean other and possibly hostile groups. To this larger group we would gladly owe allegiance, as we hope England will.

(iii) We do not know what political or economic policy England or her Dominions will follow then. If this is not in conformity with our policy we cannot find a place in her group.

(iv) We cannot be parties to a group which denies us racial equality and treats our countrymen in the manner they are treated today in parts of the empire.

(v) The conception of Dominion Status developed as between England and her own people spread out in various colonies. There was and is much in common between them. These common bonds are lacking here and it is difficult to see how Dominion Status fits in with India.

(vi) Psychologically, Dominion Status is bitterly opposed in India and it cannot be accepted quite apart from its context because in many minds it is still a symbol of alien domination to some extent. A free India, deciding for itself, may choose its own way and may ally itself closely with England. But before it does so it must clearly have this freedom to decide. Not to have it itself means that something is being imposed upon her. Not to be called independent is itself significant as it means that something less is meant.

If the British Government make a proper and acceptable declaration then steps have to be taken to give effect to it. There is no reason why this process should be delayed till the end of the war. We should not agree to this postponement though circumstances may perhaps lead to that. In any event the process will take a year or so. A constituent assembly being agreed to, its details should be worked out. I think adult suffrage is essential both from the political and communal points of view. But, to avoid difficulties, indirect election should be accepted, the primary electors electing electoral colleges. Separate electorates for those recognized minorities as desire it.

Minority problems will be settled, as stated, by agreement and in case of no agreement, by arbitration. Even before the constituent assembly meets, the fundamental laws protecting the minorities and citizens generally should be agreed to, and the constituent assembly should not touch these. These laws may be those incorporated in the Karachi Resolution as well as possibly some others.

The constituent assembly will elect by proportional representation a committee to draft the constitution for its consideration. Proportional representation will enable minorities to be represented on it. The constitution as framed by the constituent assembly will be final. We need have no objection to the British Parliament passing it in any way it likes, provided that in doing so it divests itself of further authority over India and the constitution. The proper course, however, would be for the constituent assembly to elect representatives to confer with representatives of the British Government in regard to the many matters—defence, trade, finance, services, etc. which have to be settled by mutual agreement. This agreement will form the basis of a treaty between England and India and it may be for a period of ten years or so. It is this treaty, of which a part will be the Indian constitution, which will be ratified by the British Parliament on the one hand and the new Indian parliament on the other hand. How this will be done is a matter for lawyers to determine.

If there is such a treaty, it means naturally some kind of an alliance for that period. What legal relationship should subsist between us then will depend on world developments and cannot be decided now.

The financial part of the treaty will probably give rise to more trouble than the rest, especially the question of India's public debt. If this is not agreed to mutually, the matter to be referred to the arbitration of an impartial authority like the Hague Court.

The question of minorities will offer difficulties. Possibly some guarantees about them might be incorporated in the treaty with the proviso that if there is an alleged breach of the guarantee, either party can demand impartial arbitration.

British financial or vested interests cannot be given a privileged position over Indian interests. At the most they will be given the most favoured nation treatment.

If any such settlement is arrived at between the British Government and the Indian people, it should be made clear that our attitude to the war will depend upon us. They will have our moral support and such other support as India may consider desirable and within her power. But she cannot be dragged about in any direction by British foreign and war policy. Fundamentally

India's policy will have to be determined by India's representatives. At the conclusion of the war, India must have her own representatives at the peace conference.

A settlement involves numerous adjustments during the present transitional period so that in effect, if not so much in law, Indian opinion must prevail. These implications must be fully accepted and the Viceroy and his advisers must realize that their position will change considerably. The Viceroy's executive council should be largely composed of elected members of the Central Assembly. It will be desirable to have a composite cabinet under the circumstances so as to avoid communal trouble. The details of this can be considered separately. It would be much better for a fresh election of the Central Assembly to be held but on the provincial register.

It would be essential for the war committee—or whatever it is called—to have popular representatives whose decisions count. The committee would also of course have permanent heads of the defence departments.

There would be reversion to provincial autonomy. Ordinarily this would offer no difficulty, it being made clear that under the new circumstances, the governor must act purely as a constitutional chief, and the special ordinance, etc. will not function, unless the legislature decides in favour of any. The real difficulty will be the communal one. After all the shouting about the 'day of deliverance', the Muslim League will object strongly to the old ministries going back. They will demand coalition or composite ministries. I am entirely opposed to composite ministries and dislike the idea of coalitions unless there is real agreement about policies and discipline. It is possible to have a minorities department of each government and a committee elected by proportional representation in each assembly to safeguard the interests of the minorities....

The real point is that the whole outlook and basis of the Government of India must change completely if there is settlement, and it must be recognized that the new phase is entirely different from the past. It is a phase of popular government through popular representatives and popular goodwill. It is not possible for popular representatives to govern through repression.

In many respects the policy of the Government of India has been thoroughly bad in recent months in regard to the states, appointments, etc. This will naturally undergo a change.

The question of the states has not been touched in this note. I do not think we should raise it directly at this stage but indirectly they will be powerfully affected. The door of the constituent assembly should be left open to them but on the same democratic conditions as the others. If they do not choose to come, they can stay out for the present. We can deal with them later.

24. Secretary of State's Suggestions to Viceroy Regarding his Response to Mahatma Gandhi on the Position of Scheduled Castes

Telegram from Secretary of State to Viceroy, 26 January 1940. Telegram No. 22, Telegraphic Correspondence between Viceroy and Secretary of State, 1940, Linlithgow Papers, Acc. No. 2162, NAI.

Let me first give what seems to me to be answer to Gandhi if he raises questions you anticipate about treatment of Scheduled Castes. Present position of Scheduled Castes so far as special representation goes is determined by Poona pact. This was a contract which by its own terms is terminable only by mutual consent. Accordingly question whether or not position created by Poona Pact is to be carried on into any new constitution is not one either for you or for His

Majesty's Government at all: it is a question between Castes Hindus and Scheduled Castes. For it is inconceivable that His Majesty's Government and Parliament would attempt to impose, presumably if necessary by force, upon so considerable section of Indian population as Scheduled Castes (or Muslims) a constitution purporting to be based on principle of self-government by provisions of which that section declined to be governed. This being so in this matter no less than in that of relations between Hindus and Muslims *sine qua non* to any advance is that there should first be agreement between parties, in this case Caste Hindus and Scheduled Castes, as a condition of further progress.

25. 'Dominion Status vs Independence'

Editorial, *Amrita Bazar Patrika*, 31 January 1940.

It was not long after the Indian National Congress had declared complete independence to be our political goal that Mahatma Gandhi expressed India's readiness to be satisfied with the substance of independence. Of late a tendency has crept into Congress circles to regard Dominion Status as the 'substance of independence' that Mahatmaji had in his mind; and in spite of Dr Rajendra Prasad's declaration that the goal of the Congress was Complete Independence and not Dominion Status, responsible Congress leaders have from time to time expressed the opinion that Dominion Status as defined by the Statute of Westminster was as good as Complete Independence and might be accepted by India as such. This also is the opinion of Mr Nalini Ranjan Sarkar, ex-Finance Minister of Bengal, who in a recent speech at Mymensingh observed that 'Dominion Status of the Statute of Westminster variety was virtual independence since it recognized the right to secede'. If that status, contended Mr Sarkar, could be obtained as a result of negotiations, it was scarcely worthwhile to talk constantly of a fight for independence. 'A fight merely for its own sake,' he added, 'for just displaying an extremist attitude did not serve any useful purpose; on the contrary, it was likely to bring harm to the country'. In Mr Sarkar's opinion, Dominion Status, as defined by the Statute of Westminster, 'did not contain any impediment to the development and growth of the people to their fullest stature', and as a practical man of the world, he had no hesitation, therefore, in recommending that 'in the present state of things, keeping an eye on reality' they should demand as much as they stood a chance of getting, and that they should not insist on those things which, even if they get them, they would be unable to maintain just at present.

The consideration which weighed with Mr Sarkar in expressing the opinion that he did seem to be (1) that any struggle for Complete Independence was foredoomed to failure and (2) that even if it succeeded, India could hardly expect to maintain her independence against the attack of rapacious foreigners.

Whether any immediate struggle for independence would be premature and whether, even if successful, it would expose India to greater risks than she runs at present are certainly important considerations that should guide the policy of the Congress leaders; but whatever may be our immediate objective on grounds of expediency, the question whether Dominion Status is practically the same thing as Complete Independence and whether it contains no impediment to the growth and development of the people of India to their fullest stature requires careful and dispassionate consideration.

Dominions, as defined by the Statute of Westminster, mean 'autonomous communities within the British Empire, equal in status, in no way subordinate to one another in any aspect of their domestic or external affairs, and freely associated as members of the British Commonwealth of Nations'. It should be noted that in spite of the equal status which the Dominions enjoy amongst themselves, the British Empire continues to exist with Britain herself as the centre, and have no voice in determining the future of the other parts of the Empire. Dominion Status, therefore, does not mean equality of status with Britain. The Statute of Westminster does not transform the British Empire into a Federation of free and equal nations and does not therefore liquidate British Imperialism. It is idle, therefore, to pretend that membership of the British Empire with the status of a Dominion is practically the same thing as Complete Independence. The right of secession is as good as useless if we really stand in need of British protection against other imperialisms.

The legal status of the Dominions, practical politics may contend, is more or less a sentimental consideration which does not materially affect the substance of independence. Apart from the fact that sentimental considerations have played no inconsiderable part in the evolution of nations, we have our doubts whether the economic foundation on which the present relation between Britain and India is based will be appreciably altered by the acquisition by India of Dominion Status. A financier of Mr Sarkar's reputation surely knows much better than most people that modern imperialist States bind their dependencies by chains of gold which are not in any way necessarily weakened by changes in the legal status of the dependencies; and it is because Mr Sarkar is aware of the fact that he has mentioned the existing British interests in this country in so far as business, industry, etc. are concerned as the first question that has to be settled between India and Britain. The preservation of these interests intact, or in a slightly modified form if absolutely necessary, is obviously the main consideration for the recognition of India's Dominion Status.

The present relation between India and Britain results in the transfer of about two hundred and fifty crores of rupees yearly from India to Britain. This sum represents not only profit from trade, but interest on loans and income from capital invested in industrial enterprises in India. How this drain affects the poverty stricken masses of India is fairly well-known. And the question as to how far Dominion Status will enable India to stop this drain should furnish us with the answer to the question whether Dominion Status does really contain the substance of independence which the Congress demands on behalf of the Indian masses. Will India as a British Dominion have the legal right as well as the political power to break this chain of gold that ties her today with the City of London? Will it enable India to cancel those foreign debts that were incurred by the Indian Government to extend British influence in Asia? If not, Dominion Status may give Indian capitalists an opportunity of acting as junior partners of elder British brothers in the task of joint exploitation of the Indian people, but it can never mean for the masses of this country the economic freedom for which they hanker.

26. Secretary of State's Guidelines to Viceroy for Negotiations with Mahatma Gandhi

Telegram from Secretary of State to Viceroy, 2 February 1940. Telegraphic Correspondence between Viceroy and Secretary of State, No. 23, Linlithgow Papers, Acc. No. 2162, NAI.

Immediate, Personal. No. 104. Your telegram No. 140–S of January 30th. Cabinet after full discussion this morning authorize you to proceed in your conversation with Gandhi on broad lines which you propose namely—

(a) A further formal assertion of His Majesty's Government's fixed intention to enable India to attain Dominion Status at the earliest possible date.

(b) Participation by Congress in scheme previously mooted and rejected by them of addition of Hindu and Muslim politicians to Governor-General's Executive Council.

(c) The inauguration of Federation so soon as necessary number of States can be persuaded to accede and necessary preliminaries pushed through.

(d) At some time in the future at all events after the war consultation with Indians on revision of constitution using for choice new federal legislature as consultative body.

You should not go beyond this without further reference through me to Cabinet.

General feeling was that it would be unwise to use phrase 'independence within the Empire' as suggested in paragraph 4 of your telegram of January 28th, No. 127–S, and Cabinet would prefer that you should use the phrase 'self-government within the Empire' as descriptive of Dominion Status.

27. Viceroy's Response to Secretary of State on the Position of Scheduled Castes

Telegram from Viceroy to Secretary of State, 3 February 1940. Telegram No. 40, Telegraphic Correspondence between Viceroy and Secretary of State, 1940, Linlithgow Papers, Acc. No. 2162, NAI.

Immediate. No. 174–G. I have further considered general statement in paragraph 2 of your telegram of 26th January, No. 431, in respect of Scheduled Castes and in the result am in full agreement with it. Particular line Gandhi seems likely to take is to confront me with proposition that as from date of Poona Pact His Majesty's Government must be held to be now out of the picture in respect of any aspect of their constitutional position whether now or in future self-governing India. In other words Scheduled Castes are no longer to be regarded as in any sense our concern. Reply I would propose to give would be in sense generally of emphasizing recognition without reserve on our part of position of Scheduled Castes as section of general Hindu community from which they are not separate with object that in fullness of time they should be capable of maintaining their position within that community without political, social or other distinction. But I would propose to turn Gandhi's argument by putting it to him that provisions of Poona Pact are not specific to Government of India Act [of 1935] as now framed and that constitutional rights of Scheduled Castes under that Act which includes statutory confirmation of Poona Pact do not automatically disappear with any revision of constitution that may take place. As you have yourself observed Poona Pact is itself a contract which by its own terms is terminable only by mutual consent. If in course of revision of present constitution, Scheduled Castes were to be in complete agreement with Caste Hindus as to their future position either in terms of carrying forward Poona Pact as it stands or modifying or extending its terms I would agree that His Majesty's Government would have no concern to intervene with other conditions of their own making. But if there were no agreement His Majesty's Government could not be a party to imposing on Scheduled Castes conditions which they rejected, while on the other hand they could not be unconcerned if without agreement between the contracting parties the Pact were to be terminated by Caste Hindus. Kindly wire urgently whether you agree.

28. Viceroy's Note on his Talk with Fazlul Huq and Sikander Hyat Khan on 3 February 1940 [Extracts]

Viceroy's Letter to Secretary of State, No. 8, 6 February 1940. Correspondence between Viceroy and Secretary of State, Linlithgow Papers, Acc. No. 2163, NAI.

2. ... Mr Fazlul Huq opened the proceedings by a statement of his position, which was couched in very definite terms. He was, he said, a Muslim first and always, and his duty to his community was one which he could not at any stage forget (I thought that Sir Sikander, as a fellow Muslim Prime Minister, looked a little coy at this proposition). He proceeded to refer to the state of affairs in Bengal. The Hindu press had been granted, and had taken, the utmost license. The Muslims had throughout loyally supported His Majesty's Government though, other reasons apart, admittedly in sheer self-defence. The effect of their loyalty to His Majesty's Government had been constantly to antagonize the Hindus, but that had not shaken them in their attitude, though it appeared that His Majesty's Government gave them small thanks for it. He was bound to say that he felt that His Majesty's Government continued to let down their friends in the interests of flattering Congress.

3. Mr Fazlul Huq then made an excursion into past history by way of illustrating his points. The partition of Bengal had, he said, been effected without consultation with the Muslims, and its effect had been very definitely prejudicial to Muslim interests. In the period of post-war non-cooperation, though it was perfectly true that for a short period some Muslims had joined the Congress, he could fairly claim that Muslim support and loyalty had normally been with British rule. In the present war we were receiving the full support and cooperation of the Muslims, and it was impossible for the average Muslims such as himself to understand why we insisted on continuing to encourage those who had done their best and were doing their best to harm us. Great Britain, it was true, had nothing whatever to be ashamed of. She had done her utmost over the last 40 years to push political advance in this country, and that period had seen the most rapid movement possible towards political emancipation in India. The Congress, however, refused to face realities or admit the difficulties. They wanted undertakings of a binding character from His Majesty's Government in the light of which they could hold His Majesty's Government in subjection to themselves so that the British might be available to oppress the Muslims and the other minorities while the Congress consolidated their power.

4. Mr Fazlul Huq went on to say that he did not object to Congress resuming office. The question was on what terms they would resume it. The Muslim case had not been represented adequately or fully understood either here or at Home. He begged that we should not now conciliate those who make trouble; and it was essential that the minorities in Congress provinces should have some guarantee of a change for the better. If it was finally decided to accept the principle of coalitions with joint policies to carry out a common programme, and the understanding was strictly confined to the carrying out of that programme, Bengal would reciprocate, however inconvenient it might be to let in a Congress Minister.

5. He proceeded that the Muslims were in the constant difficulty of being on the defensive. They could not recommend any recession from the present position in regard to constitutional advance, or publicly reject the principle of Home Rule or Dominion Status. This made it very difficult to put their point of view, sincerely as it was held, before the public as they were constantly accused of standing in the way of India's progress. He concluded by saying that however small the encouragement which the Muslim community had in the past received in

return for their loyalty, he wished to assure me that I could rely on their holding of Britain's cause during the war.

6. I said that I would ask Mr Fazlul Huq and Sir Sikander Hyat Khan at this stage whether I had thrown away the Muslim or the minority case in any respect, and if so, how? They both replied at once 'No', Sir Sikander later amending his reply to 'Not yet'!.

7. I said that I had listened with interest to Mr Huq's exposition of the position as he saw it. I did not propose to deal with it in detail. I would take only one point which he had raised. He had made the complaint that the Muslim case had not been properly presented. Why was that? Who was to blame? It was not my fault that it had not been properly put forward. Mr Huq said that he quite agreed that that was so. I went on to say that if he and his friends could secure that the Muslim case was better understood nobody would be better pleased than I should ....

10. Sir Sikander went on to say that it would of course, as I would appreciate, take time to arrange a programme. There were divergent points of view and it might well be that not everyone would agree with all that might be recommended. I said I quite understood that, and that I too might find certain of the recommendations that would emerge difficult to accept. But the important thing was that there should be something put before the public of a reasoned and convincing character.

11. Sir Sikander proceeded that defence would be the crucial point, and that while ultimately the whole complex of constitutional advance would have to be considered, some interim arrangement seemed essential. What was the nature of that interim arrangement to be? He agreed with Mr Fazlul Huq that coalitions on some common agreed programme might be the solution. But he hoped that I would realize the nuisance and the set-back to him and to the Punjab which it would be to have Congress members in his Cabinet. For all that he was perfectly ready to do this if it was the only possible escape from the present impasse. As Mr Huq had pointed out, any such arrangement would be equally hard on Bengal, but there too the Prime Minister was ready to co-operate and make the sacrifice involved.

12. Sir Sikander proceeded that he did most earnestly hope that the Congress governments would not be allowed to return to office in the provinces, and at the same time secure some advance at the Centre, unless and until they had satisfied the minorities. He fully recognized that it would hardly be practical politics to reject a move by Congress to return to office in the provinces; but if Congress were not prepared to satisfy the minorities before returning to office in the provinces, then it was in his view essential that no concession should be made to them at the Centre. In other words, any advance at the Centre should be strictly conditional on satisfaction having been previously given to the minorities in the provincial field. (I gather that both he and Mr Fazlul Huq felt that were the Congress to secure concessions at the Centre without some offsetting concessions to the minorities in the provinces, the minorities would feel that they had suffered a permanent loss of maneuvering ground, and that they would risk being squeezed out at the Centre without securing any remedy for their existing grievances in the Provinces).

13. In conclusion Sir Sikander asked me to believe that on the matter of defence no compromise whatever would be considered by the Muslims. On that matter they would fight to the last ditch and they were not prepared to make any concessions. He added that the Working Committee of the Muslim League had today passed a resolution recommending Mr Jinnah to come back to me for further elucidation of various points arising out of my reply to his letter of the 5th November.

14. The general impressions left upon me by the conversation were:

 (a) The almost complete intransigence of Mr Fazlul Huq in the communal field, and the probable difficulty of doing business with him for a general settlement.

 (b) That Sir Sikander Hyat Khan was much more moderate and, I suspect, well content to allow his colleague to have an opportunity of stating his case as fully and frankly as he had.

 (c) That both of them undoubtedly were anxious to impress upon me the seriousness with which the Muslim League would view any concession of importance to the Congress if unaccompanied by some satisfaction of their own demand.

29. Viceroy's Note on his Conversation with Mahatma Gandhi on 5 February 1940

Viceroy's Letter to the Secretary of State, No. 8, Enclosure 2, 6 February 1940. Correspondence between Viceroy and Secretary of State, 1940, Linlithgow Papers, Acc. No. 2153, NAI.

1. Mr Gandhi opened the conversation by saying that while he could stay here till 11th February, he did not want to do so if it could be avoided, and that he was anxious to get off as soon as possible. After the usual compliments I asked him whether he had seen Sikander. He replied that he had done so, and that the conversation had ranged over various matters and had been friendly. This represented a resumption of touch and a preliminary approach after the months that had elapsed since he had last seen Sikander. As for Mr Jinnah, his reaction to Mr Gandhi's approach of a few weeks back had come as a shock to Mr Gandhi and had been entirely unexpected. In view of his general intransigence Mr Gandhi felt that he had no meeting ground whatever with him.

2. I said that I dared say that Sir Sikander had mentioned to Mr Gandhi the Muslim intention of undertaking propaganda at Home, and that perhaps he was aware that the Princes also were likely to combine in this. Mr Gandhi replied that he realized that, and that he could indeed claim to have appreciated the alliance between the Princes and the Muslims in this matter even earlier than I had myself. He had sensed it at Rajkot, and had realized also that the finance of this business was coming from the Princes. On all that let him make his position clear. He came to see me today not merely without the agreement of his colleagues, but despite the efforts which they had made to prevent him from doing so. He was alone, throwing himself on the mercy of God. His friends were indeed profoundly uneasy. Vallabhbhai Patel had sent him a letter which he opened only in the car as he came along, in which he begged him to give nothing away at his interview with me.

3. Mr Gandhi proceeded that he had communicated what he intended to say to me in a short time to Rajendra Prasad alone, and that he alone was aware of it. He had undertaken to Rajendra Prasad to make his approach purely exploratory and to come to no final conclusion or agreement. Neither was possible without consultation with the Working Committee. He had told them that he would come in his own name, but that they must recognize that with his status, he must not be checked in his impulse to come and see the Viceroy. He was coming to see me because he felt that if I, under instructions from the Cabinet, was in a position truly to reflect current British opinion, there was a chance of a settlement honourable to all, which might make it possible for Indians to feel about the Commonwealth as the British felt. His

friends rejected the possibility, but he still had hopes, or rather faith. He recognized that this might be a dream which would not come true. As for the Princes, let them spend their wealth on propaganda. Sooner or later they would dig their own grave. The Muslim League, when the crisis came, would not receive the support of the mass of the Muslim population. He, Mr Gandhi, could still stir those masses. They had not forgotten his actions and his attitude during the Khilafat agitation. Even in Tribal Areas or among the Moplahs he had support, and he was prepared to go unprotected amongst both, whether amongst the Moplahs or into the Tribal Areas of the North-West Frontier Province. It is true that there were some who claimed that they sought to kill him, and he was well aware that there was a Khaksar list of five, of which he was No. 1. But he slept peacefully in the open at Wardha. He had no guards or protection inside the Ashram. What happened outside was the business of the Government of the Central Provinces which he could not control. The turbulent forces of the Left listened to his voice, because alone and by themselves they were impotent, and they realized that the issue of peace or war was in his hands. Yet the Working Committee had not given him a blank cheque so far as negotiations were concerned. Of this he did not complain. It was right that no one man should be in a position to give away anything of the national cause.

4. As he came to examine the prospects of reaching a settlement or the reverse, he had no anxiety. Vallabhbhai Patel had wanted to accompany him on his visit lest he should require support. He had preferred to come alone. If indeed carnage must come, he would look on without flinching though he himself was a man of non-violence. He hoped that he might have strength to sacrifice himself along with his friends. It was true that non-violence in experience had not come up to his expectations. That was due to the weakness of human nature. His supporters in the various groups were all begging him to declare war and crying out that they could do nothing unless he was prepared both to commence hostilities and to lead them. But he had so far refused to declare war unless they gave him their hearts, and their complete obedience to the principles of non-violence. What mattered to him was that he should obtain a settlement which by its repercussions should raise the moral stature of India. At this stage, in his judgment, it was better to have nothing than a makeshift.

5. The Mussalmans and the Princes might disturb the Viceroy and confuse issues for a while by propaganda activities in Great Britain. If invited by us to do so, despite his age he himself would do his personal best to appeal to British public opinion.

6. At this stage I told Mr Gandhi that I noticed that he proposed to speak for himself only and that he was unable to commit his friends. I quite understood the circumstances in which on this occasion he was debarred from speaking for the Working Committee. He must realize however that it would not be possible assuming that a preliminary enquiry showed that we could usefully proceed with conversations, for me to continue to do business on that basis. It was essential that he should be in a position to speak for and commit, the Congress as such. He had mentioned his age. Neither I nor His Majesty's Government overlooked that factor, or the limitations that it inevitably placed on his opportunities. But I thought it only right to tell him that many of us felt very strongly that if a good issue was to come out of negotiations, it would be essential that he should not merely initiate, but that he should concern himself directly with implementing, any agreement that might be arrived at. His prestige, I thought had never been higher. As he was aware, I myself had found Jawaharlal Nehru attractive; but that gentleman now as Chairman of the War Committee of Congress had neither the experience of public affairs, the steadiness of vision, or the control of his own utterances which Mr Gandhi, possessed.

If any real advance was to be made, it was quite essential in my judgment that Mr Gandhi, while taking colleagues with him, should himself direct and maintain control over the activities of Congress. Indeed speaking for myself personally I could hardly contemplate accepting responsibility for my share of any agreement unless I could rely on a firm assurance from him of his personal direction of Congress and his comfort and support for myself.

7. Mr Gandhi in reply stated that he unequivocally undertook to give me his constant support. He himself, he might tell me, was, he thought, in a very strong position at the moment. The more difficult and combative elements in Congress felt that they could not dispense with his Generalship. As he had told me, he would not flinch if he thought the moment had come for giving the word. Meanwhile, he could assure me that he was in no hurry to declare war. If I thought it derogatory to the Viceroy's dignity or the prestige of His Majesty's Government to confer on him power to put through a settlement, we had only to say so, and he would not complain. But that indeed was the surest way to get the business put through. Would I care to hear his views about the general question of a settlement.

8. I replied that I should certainly be very glad to hear his views. With a less experienced negotiator I might have felt that it would be more conducive to a successful outcome, if my offer, which might conceivably be short of his requirements, came first. In his case I knew that he would not allow any sharpness of contrast between our positions to prejudice the chances of an understanding. I would like to put him in possession of my mind on one or two aspects of the case as I saw it. The task ahead might be divided into two parts. On the one hand, we were both concerned to satisfy what I might call the spiritual aspect of the Indian demand. On the other hand, we had to contemplate machinery to deal with the practical work-a-day problems. Thus, for example, to take the matter of defence, defence was a subject which could not easily be dealt with in time of war. No one knew how India and how Great Britain would stand at the close of hostilities. The subject was a vast and complicated one, in which with the best will in the world it was inconceivable that an arrangement to deal with it could be given practical shape without prolonged analysis and negotiations.

9. Mr Gandhi, who had evidently misunderstood a little the purport of my remarks, answered that he was of opinion that while the war lasted the British word should be final in military policy: but that even during the period of war, no secrecy as between Indian and English colleagues was justified. (I imagine he was thinking of an expanded Executive Council). If Indian Members or Ministers could not be trusted to keep official secrets despite their oath of secrecy, and the responsibility attaching to a share in administration, they must be traitors and would deserve to be ejected. Surely it would be better to assume that they would be loyal and to trust them ....

30. Government Communiqué Issued after Mahatma Gandhi's Meeting with Viceroy, 5 February 1940

Harijan, 10 February 1940.

In response to an invitation from His Excellency, Mr Gandhi today came to see the Viceroy. A prolonged and very friendly discussion took place in which the whole position was exhaustively examined. Mr Gandhi made it clear at the outset of the conversation that he had no mandate from the Congress Working Committee, that he was not empowered to commit it in any way, and that he could speak on behalf of himself only.

His Excellency set out in some detail the intentions and the proposals of His Majesty's Government. He emphasized in the first place their earnest desire that India should attain Dominion Status at the earliest possible moment, and to facilitate the achievement of that status by all means in their power. He drew attention to the complexity and difficulty of certain of the issues that called for disposal in that connection, in particular the issue of Defence in a Dominion position. He made it clear that His Majesty's Government were only too ready to examine the whole of the field in consultation with representatives of all parties and interests in India when the time came. He made clear also the anxiety of His Majesty's Government to shorten the transitional period and to bridge it as effectively as possible. His Excellency drew attention to the fact that as he recently repeated at Baroda, the Federal Scheme of the Act, while at present in suspense, afforded the swiftest stepping-stone to Dominion Status, and that its adoption, with the consent of all concerned, would facilitate the solution of many of the problems that had to be faced in that connection. He added that the offer put forward by him in November last of an expansion of the Governor-General's Executive Council on the lines and on the basis then indicated remained open and that His Majesty's Government were prepared to give immediate effect to that offer, subject to the consent of the parties affected. His Majesty's Government would be prepared also to re-open the Federal Scheme, so as to expedite the achievement of Dominion Status and to facilitate the settlement after the war of the issues to which it gave rise.

Mr Gandhi expressed appreciation of the spirit in which these proposals were put forward, but made it clear that they did not, in his view, at this stage meet the full demand of the Congress Party. He suggested, and the Viceroy agreed, that in the circumstances it would be preferable to defer for the present further discussions with the object of a solution of the difficulties which had arisen.

31. Mahatma Gandhi's Reaction to the Government's Proposal

Viceroy's Telegram to Secretary of State, 5 February 1940. Telegraphic Correspondence between Viceroy and Secretary of State, 1940, Telegram No. 43, Linlithgow Papers, Acc. No. 2162, NAI.

Most Immediate. No. 183–S. I had two and half hours with Gandhi today and put him the offer authorized by the Cabinet. He made it clear that this did not meet his case, and we agreed that conversations had better be adjourned *sine die* for the present, and that an agreed statement should issue this afternoon. I will get Reuter to cable text of it to you, and will report at greater length in a separate telegram. Atmosphere very friendly, but nothing doing. On status his view is that we ought to leave it to India to say what she wants and to take the consequences of her mistake if she makes one, rather than to 'limit' her freedom of choice by confining her to Statute of Westminster Dominion Status or any other specific proposal.

32. Viceroy's Telegram to Secretary of State on his Conversation with Jinnah, 6 February 1940

Telegram No. 47, Telegraphic Correspondence between Viceroy and Secretary of State, 1940, Linlithgow Papers, Acc. No. 2162, NAI.

Immediate, No. 196–S. I saw Jinnah today. He was clearly far from dissatisfied with the outcome of my interview with Gandhi yesterday, and raised two main points: (a) What was to be done by all parties other than Congress in face of the position which had now been reached and in view of the War? (b) What was to be done when we come to question of the future constitution of India? His own judgment was clear that examination of that question could only lead to preliminary stage, and that it was out of the question to go straight to Dominion Status or anything approaching it from existing conditions.

As regards the first point I admitted that my efforts to reach accommodation satisfactory to all parties had for the moment received a setback, but that did not mean that His Majesty's Government or I would in the least degree relax our endeavours to restore the normal working of the Act. It was most unsatisfactory that ex-Congress Provinces should be governed under conditions approximating to those of 1860: and neither public opinion at Home nor Parliament would for a moment, apart from that, acquiesce in the maintenance of Section 93 unless they were satisfied that we were continuing to do our utmost to escape from it.

Jinnah retorted by referring to what he called the dreadful effect of this suspense in India. I never appeared to break with Gandhi, and always left the impression that I was going to see him before long and that negotiations would be resumed. That naturally produced throughout the community the fear that Congress Governments might return to office at any moment. 'Fear' was the right word even among Congressmen. Allegiance to Congress three years ago would have been for love. But their power today was derived from their capacity to inculcate fear. We ought to make clear to Congress without undue delay that there was nothing doing. If the Congress Ministers did return to office under existing conditions, there would be civil war in India. I replied that that was a very grave utterance from a man in his position: but even if he meant what he said, the constitution was part of the law of the land and must be respected in its present form unless and until the law was altered. He must take it from me that no opportunity would be missed of persuading Congress Ministers to return to office where they could rely on a majority.

As regards Jinnah's second point, he explained that he was not yet able to let me have the considered views of his colleagues and himself. I again put to him the familiar arguments for formulating and publishing a constructive policy: and in the light of our discussion he said that he was disposed to think that it would probably be wise for his friends and himself to make public at any rate the outline of their position in good time. I warned him that it would be a great mistake to think that responsible opinion in any circle at Home would accept the view that to stand still, much less to go back in India was the right solution of our difficulties.

I then asked whether he wished to deal orally with the points raised in my letter of 23rd December and I suggested that a situation in which the public knew that my letter had been written and were aware of certain of the points in it, 'thanks' to the communiqués released by the Working Committee of the Muslim League, but in which they had not the text was hardly satisfactory. Jinnah agreed and expressed his readiness to release the correspondence forthwith.

33. Viceroy's Note on his Conversation with Jinnah, 6 February 1940

Letter of Viceroy to Secretary of State, No. 8, Enclosure 3, 6 February 1940. Correspondence between Viceroy and Secretary of State, 1940, Linlithgow Papers, Acc. No. 2163, NAI.

1. In response to an invitation from me, Mr M.A. Jinnah came to see me today. It was obvious that he was in very good fettle, and that the developments with Mr Gandhi yesterday had caused him no dissatisfaction. After the usual compliments he opened the proceedings by

asking me what we were now to do. Assuming that 'we' meant the Muslim League, I thought it well to encourage him to move into a constructive position, and I emphasized on the familiar lines the impossibility of maintaining a purely negative position, the propaganda value of a constructive plan, and the weakness of a long sight of the present situation.

2. He told me that he had listened with great interest to what I had said, and that the two specific questions which he would like to clear were first what 'we', by which he meant all parties other than Congress, were to do in face of the position which had now been reached and in view of the war. Second, the question, which he recognized was an entirely different issue, of what was to be done when we came to the question of the future constitution of India. On that point, in spite of the different view which he was aware that Mr Gandhi held, his own judgment was clear that such examination could only lead to a preliminary stage. It was out of the question to go straight to Dominion Status, or anything approaching it, from existing conditions.

3. I said to Mr Jinnah that as regards the first point he had raised, I had reluctantly to admit that my efforts to reach accommodation satisfactory to all parties had for the moment received a set-back. But even if that meant a postponement for the time being, and the persistence in the maintenance of the emergency provisions of the Act, he must not think that His Majesty's Government or I would for an instant relax our endeavours to return to the normal working of the constitutional scheme. Quite apart from the unfortunate position out here where the government of those provinces which had previously been administered by a Congress Ministry and in which no alternative arrangement had proved practicable now approximated to the conditions of 1860, we were faced with the fact that neither public opinion in Great Britain nor Parliament would for a moment countenance, or acquiesce in, the maintenance of a Section 93 position unless they were satisfied that we were making constant and active efforts to escape from it ....

6. Mr Jinnah said that that might be so, but that if the Congress Ministries did so return in existing conditions, there would be civil war in India.

7. I said that that was a very grave utterance to be made by a man in his responsible position: but that even if he meant what he said, the fact remained that the constitution, being part of the law of the land, would have to be respected in its present form unless and until the law was altered.

8. Mr Jinnah said that he found it quite impossible to understand our attitude towards Congress, in face of the fact that the pledge taken by Congress and its supporters on 'Independence Day' was, in his considered opinion as a lawyer, treasonable in terms of our own law.

9. I repeated that whatever the difficulties and the uncertainties of the present position, Mr Jinnah must take it from me that His Majesty's Government and I would miss no opportunity, subject always of course to due care for the legitimate interests of all minorities, of persuading Congress Ministries to return to office in those provinces in which they were supported by a majority of the Legislature.

10. Passing from this matter I asked Mr Jinnah whether he desired during our present conversation to deal with the points raised in my letter to him of 23rd December. Mr Jinnah replied that he would prefer to communicate his views in writing. I said that in this context I was not entirely happy about a position in which the public were aware that my letter had been written and in which they were seized of a certain number of points in it through the communiqués released by the Working Committee of the Muslim League, but in which the

text had not been released and so was not available to them. Mr Jinnah agreed that this was hardly satisfactory, and expressed his readiness forthwith to release the text of my letter of 23rd December together with the ancillary documents (his original letter to me of 5th November, and the interim correspondence regarding publication which had passed between us).

11. We then turned to Mr Jinnah's second point referred to in paragraph 2 above. Mr Jinnah asked if I wished to discuss this matter with him now; and I replied that I should very much like to hear his views. He said that he was not yet in a position to present in detail the considered opinion of his colleagues and himself on this very important subject, but that he would very shortly be ready to do so. Might he come and see me a little later on in the season and put me in possession of the formulated opinions of the Muslim League? He and his friends were disposed on the whole to take the view that to publish in full their formulated opinions as to the constructive steps to be taken for the future would at this stage from their standpoint be inadvisable since it would needlessly expose surface to criticism. They would prefer to wait until His Majesty's Government had reached the point at which they would say to the Muslim League 'What are your views?' He and his colleagues would, he could assure me, be ready to speak once such enquiry was made of them.

12. I said that that was all very well: that I fully understood the tactical convenience from his point of view of a purely negative attitude at this stage as opposed to an attempt to formulate and publish a constructive policy. But, if I might say so, this plan for postponing any announcement of the constructive programme of the Muslim League until the last moment failed altogether to meet the requirements of propaganda. With his great experience he would not disagree with me when I said that it was impossible to hope to be able to educate public opinion in Great Britain, and more particularly the 600 odd representatives of constituencies in the House of Commons, by the submission of a formal memorandum to His Majesty's Government, or by the leading of evidence before some committee on the eve of critical decisions. If he and his friends wanted to secure that the Muslim case should not go by default in the United Kingdom, it was really essential that they should formulate their plan in the near future. At the risk of wearying him I was bound to repeat what I had often said before that I was convinced that it was quite useless to appeal for support in Great Britain for a party whose policy was one of sheer negation. Many shades of opinion, as we both well knew, existed in that country. But beyond a very small number of ultra-conservative persons it was, I thought, true to say that no responsible opinion would accept the idea that standing still, much less going back, in India was the right way to solve our difficulties. There was much in this intractable problem that was open. But this much at least was clear, that there was no refuge for any of us in sheer reaction ....

34. 'Vital Difference' between Viceroy and the Congress:
Mahatma Gandhi's Statement [after his meeting with Viceroy]
Hindustan Times, 7 February 1940.

... The vital difference between the Congress demand and the Viceregal offer consists in the fact that the Viceroy's offer contemplates the final determination of India's destiny by the British Government, whereas the Congress contemplates just the contrary.

The Congress position is that the test of real freedom consists in the people of India determining their own destiny without any outside influence and I see no prospect whatsoever of a peaceful and honourable settlement between England and India unless the vital difference is obliterated and England decides upon the right course, namely, accepting the position that the time has come when India must be allowed to determine her own constitution and her status.

When that is done, the question of Defence, the question of minorities, the question of the Princes and the question of the European interests will automatically resolve itself.

The Minorities

Let me make this a little clearer. Safeguards for the rights of minorities is not only common cause [between the British Government and the Congress], but the Representative Assembly of Indians cannot evolve a stable Constitution without fullest satisfaction being given to the *legitimate* minorities. I use the word '*legitimate*' advisedly because I see that minorities crop up like mushrooms till there will be no majority left. By 'fullest satisfaction', I mean satisfaction, which will not militate against the progress of the nation as a whole.

I will, therefore, in the event of differences, refer the question to the highest and most impartial tribunal that can be conceived by human ingenuity. Its voice shall be final as to what will amount to the fullest satisfaction of minority interests.

Defence

So far as Defence is concerned, surely it will be the primary concern of free India to make her own arrangements. It may well be that India would want elaborate preparation and would want Britain's help, if it is given, in enabling her to do so. Thanks to Imperial policy, unarmed India is left wholly unprotected except by the British bayonets and Indian soldiers whom British power has brought into being. It is a position humiliating alike for British and for India. I am personally unconcerned because, if I could carry India with me, I would want nothing beyond a police force for protection against dacoits and the like. But so far as Defence is concerned, unarmed peaceful India would rely upon the goodwill of the whole world. But I admit that it is only a dream at the present moment.

European Interest

So far as European interests are concerned, emphasis on the word 'European' must be entirely removed. But that does not mean that a free India should be free to confiscate European interests or any other interests. There would, as there should, be provision for reasonable compensation for any existing interests which are legitimate and not harmful to the nation. It follows that there can be no question of favouritism which is being enjoyed today by European interests. I would, therefore, regard them as big zamindars or capitalists, and they would place on the same footing as these.

Princes

So far as the Princes are concerned, they are free to join the national assembly which will determine India's fate not as individuals but as duly elected representatives of their own people. As Princes being vassals of the Crown, I fancy they have no status apart from the Crown, certainly not superior to the Crown itself. If the Crown parts with the power it today enjoys over the whole of India, naturally the Princes have to, and it should be their pride to look up to the successor of the Crown, that is the people of India, for the preservation of their status. I hope this will not be regarded as a tall claim, for it is made by me on behalf, not of the Congress, not of any single party, but on behalf of the unrepresented dumb millions [of India].

No claim made on their behalf can be considered too tall. I am myself an insignificant being. But I am supposed to have some hold over these dumb millions. I know that in every fibre of my being I am absolutely one with them. Without them I am nothing and I do not even want to exist. I want on their behalf an honourable settlement with Britain without even a non-violent fight. My dictionary has no such expression as a violent fight.

Delhi Talks

Yesterday, I put this view before His Excellency in as courteous and friendly a language as I was capable of using. We approached the discussion as personal friends, each believing in the other's sincerity. We understood each other and both recognized that there still existed a wide gulf between the position taken by the British Government as explained by him and the position taken by the Congress which I put, though not as an accredited representative of the Congress but certainly as the self-appointed representative of the dumb millions.

We parted as friends. I have no disappointment in me that the negotiations have failed. That failure I am going to use, as I am sure H.E. the Viceroy is going to use, as a stepping-stone to success. But if that success does not come in the near future, I can only say Heaven help India, Britain and the world. The present war must not be decided by a clash of arms, but it must be decided by the moral strength that each party can show. If Britain cannot recognize India's legitimate claim, what will it mean but Britain's moral bankruptcy?...

35. Viceroy's Telegram to Secretary of State on Reactions from Madras Presidency, 8 February 1940

Telegram No. 50, Telegraphic Correspondence between Viceroy and Secretary of State, Linlithgow Papers, Acc. No. 2162, NAI.

Important No. 204–S. Following telegrams were repeated for information:

From Erskine, No. 24–M of 7th February

Begins. Your telegram No. 190–S of 6th February concerning reactions to failure of Gandhi's talks. The people who count in Madras Congress Party are all Brahmins and Right Wingers and they are panting to return to office, so naturally this set is exceedingly sorry that no agreement was reached. Unfortunately Madras has little influence with Working Committee which is mainly run by Northern India and even Rajagopalachari has ceased to have ear of Gandhi.

The Justice Party, the Muslim League, and other opposition groups are all delighted that conversations have broken down as last thing they wanted was an agreement and they feared that this time one might result.

36. 'Sir C.P.R. Iyer and India's Future'

Statesman, 8 February 1940.

Sir C.P. Ramaswamy Iyer, Dewan of Travancore, interviewed regarding the statements made and the communiqué issued relating to the interviews that took place between His Excellency Viceroy and Messrs. Gandhi and Jinnah recently, said:

'Like many others in India, I also deeply regret the inconclusive nature of the results achieved. I have perused Mr Gandhi's statement regarding what has been termed the vital difference between the Congress demand and His Excellency's offer and reading it with the statements issued after the interview with Messrs. Gandhi and Jinnah, one realizes to the full the distance that separates the parties *inter se*.

'In my present position it would be inappropriate to say anything about British Indian politics and their repercussions on the policy of the United Kingdom, but I may aver without hesitation that the demand for Dominion status is, in my opinion, conditioned to no small extent upon the speedy attainment of India's capacity for self-defence, an attainment to be worked for intensively by the government and the people alike. Without a solution of the problem of defence, Dominion Status of any variety whatsoever cannot under Indian conditions be achieved or maintained.

'As for independence of any kind, it is, in my humble view, so far beyond the range of practical politics that it cannot be seriously debated in view especially of what is taking place all over Europe and Asia.

The Princes

'With regard to the Princes, it is a matter of intense regret that Mr Gandhi's statement is not helpful and hardly likely to lead to a friendly adjustment. To state that the Princes will have to join the National Assembly not as individuals but as duly elected representatives of their people is to ignore the facts of history and even the present position of affairs. It is not correct to say that the States have no status apart from the Crown.

'Many States have maintained an independent existence for hundreds of years and some States, including Hyderabad and Travancore and many of the Rajput and other States have never been conquered or annexed.

'Undoubtedly, for purposes of defence against aggression and to secure mutual benefits, these states entered into alliances with the East India Company, alliances that have been confirmed and continued, by the British Government which acquired a dominant position in India. Many of these treaties are on a contractual basis although they are founded also on the theory of allegiance to the British Crown coupled with rights and obligations arising out of treaty and usage.

'It cannot be asserted that if the Crown parts with power today the Princes also have to do so. Nor can there be an automatic transference of allegiance or obligations or rights to some other political entity except on the basis of fresh understandings and new treaties.

'On the other hand, if the Crown withdraws from India, the Indian States presumably will reassume the position they occupied in India before the treaties were entered into.

'No argument based on non-recognition of this fundamental fact can possibly be accepted by the States whose adherence to the British Crown cannot be regarded as a matter for political transfer even without reference to the States and history of the Indian Rulers'.

37.   'Constituent Assembly for India': Mr Patel's Plan

Statesman, 9 February 1940.

The suggestion referred to by His Highness the Aga Khan was made by Sardar Vallabhbhai Patel last weekend at a public meeting in Surat. At that meeting Sardar Patel explained the Congress demand and said: 'What the Congress wants is the undiluted right for Indians to frame their own constitution through a constituent assembly.

'If a constituent assembly elected by an electorate based on adult franchise is considered impracticable, a substitute such as a constituent assembly elected on the basis of the present provincial franchise will do, provided that that assembly is given the sole right of framing India's constitution without outside interference and provided that in case of any difference arising out of any communal issue, there is a proviso that such differences should be settled by arbitration'.

38. V.D. Savarkar's Statement to Press on National Constitution, 22 February 1940

Hindu Mahasabha Papers, File No. C–26/1940, NMML.

The following statement has been issued by V.D. Savarkar, President, Hindu Mahasabha, for being released to the Press:

'I enter a strong protest against the proposal that is being discussed in the press and has been backed up, if not originally conceived and initiated by prominent Congressite leaders to the effect that the present members of the Legislatures in the country be authorized to form themselves into a sort of a Constituent Assembly to frame a National Constitution. Because:

Firstly, the present Legislative members were not elected on the mandate of authorizing them to frame such a constitution which should be binding on the whole Nation.

Secondly, the overwhelming majority in the present Legislature comprises of Congressite representatives. They cannot claim themselves as a Nation. The Congress is but one of the many parties in the country. It secured this large number of votes by raising a number of the other slogans such as, breaking the prevailing constitution by working it out and the like. There are several other parties and interests in the country representing crores of citizens, which being independent of the Congress have never empowered the Congressites to represent them. Nay, they have been definitely repudiating the claim put forward by the Congress to speak in the name of the whole Nation, so emphatically that the Congress leaders including their outgoing president Babu Rajendra Prasad, have themselves been recently compelled to admit that the Congress represents none else but the Congressite section of the public and is consequently but a party organization. Now, if the present Legislative members are allowed to assume the right of framing a National Constitution the presence of the overwhelming majority of the Congressite members in them will naturally succeed in getting passed a framework which can never be entitled to be deemed a national Constitution which could only be determined by the representatives of all parties and interests in the Nation elected with a clear mandate to frame such a fundamental National Constitution. Any constitution framed by the present members in the Legislative Assembly can only be a one party show, a Congress Constitution. It is a sly attempt to thrust on the Nation a "Congressocracy" under a deceptive mask of Democracy.

Thirdly, because apart from the non-Hindu Constituencies the very Hindu Constituency which voted for the majority of the Congress members in the last election has now ceased to have confidence in them. Events too glaring to be enumerated here in details have compelled millions and millions of Hindusthanis who rally round the Hindu Mahasabha Flag to denounce time and again the anti-Hindu and anti-national policy of the present Congressite party in the Legislatures and outside and to declare that their interests and trust have been betrayed by the Congress representatives. Consequently, the present Congressite majority in these legislatures have ceased to have any confidence of the Hindu Electorate as a whole which has in the main returned them to the Legislatures and has no right therefore even to pose as Hindu representatives with powers to frame a permanent National Constitution for Hindustan.

If a proposal to authorize the Legislatures to frame a constitution is to have any ring of sincerity about it, then the Congressites should first of all get the present Legislatures dissolved, go back to the Electorate to get a special and definite mandate authorizing them to frame a National Constitution and then only the representatives who may be returned to the Legislatures by the Electorate can be entitled to form themselves into such a Constituent Assembly as that.

In the meanwhile it must be made clear that no constitutional promise can be binding on Hindus as a whole unless and until it is arrived at in consultation with and with the consent of the Hindu Mahasabha.'

39. Secretary of State's Telegram Giving Suggestions to Viceroy, 5 March 1940

Telegram No. 57, Telegraphic Correspondence between Viceroy and Secretary of State, Linlithgow Papers, Acc. No. 2162, NAI.

Personal. No. 1063. Your telegram No. 323–G. and your private and personal telegram No. 327–S, March 2nd. In view of Working Committee's resolution, I must shortly report to Cabinet. I should like to have for the purpose a comprehensive appreciation of position as you see it. I note that your inclination is to take no action at present but I anticipate criticism here if we do nothing at all. Would it not be possible for you to renew your offer to set up a consultative committee and to expand your Executive Council, making it clear, although Congress will not participate you see no reason why other parties who are willing to co-operate should be deprived of opportunity of doing so by Congress refusal? This would doubtless be resented by Congress but they are themselves making it impossible for us to do business with them.

40. Viceroy's Telegram to Secretary of State on Congress Working Committee Resolution, 8 March 1940

Telegram No. 141, Official Telegrams between Viceroy and Secretary of State, (Governor-General's Series) July 1939–December 1941, Linlithgow Papers, Acc. No. 2335, NAI.

Immediate. No. 358–G. Following is my appreciation of position in light of Working Committee resolution passed at recent Patna meeting, full text of which will already be available to you:

2. Before discussing background of resolution and reactions to it here, I will comment briefly on its content. It is, as you will agree, wholly unsatisfactory from our point of view. It reiterates demand for independence and rejects Dominion Status (despite obvious practical difficulty of India's attaining independence even if she was internally united, which she is not, and strong opposition of the Muslims, to say nothing of Princes, to severance of connection at any rate at this stage with His Majesty's Government). It repeats demand for settlement of future constitution by the people of India alone, on the basis of the Constituent Assembly based on adult suffrage. Practical objections to this need not be stated. Political objections are equally obvious. Apart from the fact that we could not dissociate ourselves from any such deliberations, so far as British India is concerned, effect would be, thanks to superior quality of

the Congress machine, to submerge the Muslims and other minorities; while one has only to consider the level of education of the populations of e.g., the Eastern States, to appreciate the effect in the case of Princely India, even if Indian rulers were likely to be prepared to acquiesce in any such procedure. I do not believe that there is any misunderstanding as to our war aims, and resolution ignores efforts that we have made to clear that point.

3. Resolution further is completely at variance with general feeling in this country. India has as you know lent fullest and most generous support in the war. We could at this moment have ten times as many men recruited if we could use them and pay for them. So far as supply is concerned, we are working overtime, and Congress supporters themselves are deeply interested in financial results of orders we are receiving. There is general sympathy for the ideals animating the allies, and general condemnation of the stand taken by Hitler and Stalin. A friendly settlement with Congress, desirable as it is on other grounds, would be unlikely materially to improve our contributions in terms either of men or of supply, although it would dispose of the nuisance value internationally, and of the local nuisance value in the event of civil disobedience, which determined Congress opposition would undoubtedly represent.

4. So far as the minorities are concerned, the resolution presents a further stiffening. It refers in terms in the first place to 'recognized' minorities. This would be very likely to cut out the Anglo-Indians, and just conceivably the Sikhs. The position in relation to the Scheduled Castes equally is left obscure: but the Congress would, one would judge, be likely to be reluctant to accept them as a 'recognized' minority, and would press a claim to speak on their behalf as far as possible. Further the protection to be granted to minorities as a result of the Constituent Assembly is now to be based on agreement 'so far as possible', with arbitration in the event of disagreement on any point. I need not emphasize that these communal divisions will not admit of being settled for ever by any judicial or arbitral finding, and that the party against which the finding goes, even if it has submitted to the jurisdiction of the tribunal, will remain resentful, intransigent and as anxious to secure reopening as it is likely to find it difficult to control its followers.

5. The Princes are to be steam-rolled, no account being taken of treaty obligations of His Majesty's Government, and 'foreign interests' (without distinction between British interests and those of other countries) are to be protected only 'if they are not in conflict with the interest of the Indian people'.

6. The Working Committee have thus stated the Congress claim in a more extreme form than ever hitherto employed and one which denies the possibility of treating Dominion Status as consistent with India's freedom or independence; a form, too, which we can fairly I think hold takes no account of practical realities or difficulties, or of bare justice to others, and which is well calculated to disturb still further all minorities, including the Europeans and the Princes. The threat of civil disobedience which it then proceeds to make is however most carefully guarded, and no date is fixed. The decision to move into civil disobedience is made contingent on conditions indefinite or likely; so far as they are definite, to be difficult of realization. In a word the resolution gives Congress the political credit of threatening us, without any early need to perform.

7. I would judge that the carefully guarded form of the really important part of the resolution, viz. the threat of civil disobedience, is due to the influence of Gandhi, in whose frequently repeated reluctance willingly to contemplate civil disobedience I am still disposed to believe; and that the resolution, outspoken as it is, may be regarded as another effort on the one hand to maintain the solidarity of Congress to which he attaches so much importance, and on the

other to outbid, or bid up to the level of, the Left Wing. Nehru is reported to have taken an active part in the drafting, to have urged an active line in the interest of holding the support of the country against the Left Wing, and to have been very tolerant as usual of opposition. Steward reports a rumour (though other information received by the DIB throws doubt on it) that Patel advocated return to office, supported by Prasad and Rajagopalachariar, and was vehemently opposed by Nehru (supported by Azad), and that Patel seemed likely to carry the day when Gandhi intervened in time to prevent Nehru walking out and secured postponement of the decision.

8. Further contributory factors are doubtless: (a) the hope that a really strongly-worded resolution, with a threat of direct action, would shake His Majesty's Government (whom Nehru appears to believe still to be squeezable) and make them produce some further concession or statement before Ramgarh which would strengthen the hands of the Right Wing at that meeting: (b) the anxiety to offset possible local difficulty with Bose who is proposing to run an anti-compromise rally at Ramgarh. It appears that there is considerable probability also of a large demonstration of Kisans under Sahajanand and an aboriginal anti-Congress demonstration under Jaipal Singh. But whatever the underlying tactics, the fact remains that Congress is now committed publicly to threat of open resistance, and that negotiations in existing position would take place under that threat.

9. So much for the substance of the resolution. I turn now to the reactions to it. The Congress press has generally taken it without any critical comment that matters. It has, as might be expected, been ill-received by the Muslims, and the most significant feature of developments over the past month has been a marked and definite hardening of the Muslim attitude. Muslims are now for the first time, thanks to the intransigent attitude adopted by Congress, coming to analyse what is involved from their point of view as a minority community in the attainment not merely of independence, but even of Dominion Status. They are beginning to appreciate that, short of a series of safeguards which it might be very difficult to reconcile with the ordinary form of Dominion Status, the effect of it would be to enthrone the majority community at the Centre and to run a considerable risk of leaving the minorities at its mercy. The point has been taken too that a Dominion Government once set up will in practice have very considerable, if not indeed complete, powers of modifying the constitution (compare the case of Eire) and so, if necessary, of getting rid of paper safeguards embodied in it. And the *Hindustan Times* has unwisely in the last couple of days indicated in a leader that it is essential that any constitution to be acceptable should vest the right of such modification in the Dominion Government. I have had from one or two Muslim sources recently the suggestion that what Congress are really concerned to do is to get us deeply committed to the principle of Dominion Status of the fullest kind, with the implication that there shall be no interference by His Majesty's Government save such as may be provided for by any documents exchanged at the time of the recognition of the Dominion; that special powers and responsibilities of the Governor-General and Governors must disappear; that there shall be power in the Dominion Government to make alterations in the constitution; to control very largely the appointment of Judges; to use the forces at the disposal of the Dominion Government for the maintenance of law and order in such a manner as they may think fit; to handle appointments to services, and other things, without interference from outside, and the like. I should not be surprised as matters stand today to find the Muslims moving away not only from the idea of any early independence but from the idea of any advance as far as Dominion Status: and as you will have seen from Jinnah's letter to me of 24th February, repeated to you in my telegram of 26th February,

No. 292–S., the Muslims are becoming increasingly insistent, and I am satisfied that they are serious in this, that they will not accept any constitution that is not satisfactory to them. The practicability of devising a constitution satisfactory to Congress in its present frame of mind, and to the Muslims, calls for no comment.

10. Minorities other than the Muslims have not been very much in evidence, but I have no reason to think that they are not beginning to be as much disturbed as the Muslims at the possible implications of Dominion Status in face of the present claims of Congress, and at the risk that His Majesty's Government may acquiesce in those claims. The Princes equally have said little, but it is clear from the attitude of the Diwans of Kashmir, Hyderabad, Cochin, and Baroda, whom I have seen in the last couple of days, and whose impressions I shall be able to check when the Chamber meets at the end of this week from various of Their Highnesses, that they too regard with deep uneasiness the nature of the Congress claims and the prospect of any surrender to those claims by His Majesty's Government.

11. Meanwhile, despite this political ferment in higher quarters, the former Congress Provinces, so far as I can judge, are running very smoothly indeed. There is no sign of popular discontent or agitation, and one still gets the same feeling of relief at the lull in the political debate so far as the ordinary man in the street is concerned. Full weight in assessing the importance of this must be given to the professed anxiety of Congress to avoid a row. I give them full credit for that. But we must also give weight to the fact that if they thought it to their interest to have trouble, they would not hesitate to do so; and I have little doubt that a contributory factor, whatever they may say in their resolutions about their readiness to proclaim civil disobedience, is the uncertainty as to how civil disobedience would work out from their point of view. I should judge myself that it would be likely to lead to severe communal trouble, certainly in the United Provinces, possibly in Bihar and Bombay, and while an open breach with us would no doubt for the time being close the ranks, and consolidate the present Right Wing control of the machine, it would be bound as time went on to result in a movement more towards the left and a strengthening of the position of leftist elements which could not but tend to take control in an increasing degree out of the hands of the Right Wing, who, I am certain, are as reluctant to part with it as ever.

12. I ask myself in these circumstances:

    (a) What Congress think they can hope to gain?
    (b) What our tactics ought to be, both immediately and in dealing with them in terms of the remoter future.

13. On the first of these points I am frankly puzzled. But I am increasingly disposed to think that there is something in the Muslim suggestion referred to in paragraph 9 above in other words that they want to get us committed to a qualified acceptance of the implications of normal Dominion Status and then require us to hand over responsibility to a Dominion Government in which they will be in a decisive majority, under an agreement which (subject to an arrangement to cover defence) would reduce our power of effective interference in the Government of India as a whole to a minimum, leaving the problem of the minorities, and to some extent the problem of the Princes, to be dealt with by the new Dominion Government. There are indications that this consideration was presented to the Patna meeting, and that that meeting was perfectly content to allow Gandhi to continue to play the hand in his own way. If there is anything in what I suggest, the position is that Congress regard the stakes as high, and well worth playing for. We have fortunately always been cautious, for we have made it clear in

our declarations that an essential preliminary to progress is the necessary measure of agreement between the various communities, etc., in India. But it will be in my judgment more important than ever in such statements as we may in future make to continue to emphasize that point, and to bring out that anxious as we are to see India progress to the Dominion Status level, and ready as we are to give all possible help to her to do so, we cannot overlook the claims and the attitude of the great minorities and of the Princes, to whom we have formal obligations, and that it is essential that Indians should themselves reach that degree of general agreement between major interests and communities here which would make government by the resulting Dominion Government without our continual intervention a practicable proposition.

14. It is conceivable, again, that Congress think that if we suffer a severe reverse in the West, we shall be prepared to let them have what they want, and that, while now marking out their claim, they will continue to play for time till the position is clear. If that is the idea, it is, I should have thought, based on a completely false argument. Congress in such an event would be a nuisance to the extent that civil disobedience or the like on an extended scale might immobilize troops and might interfere with supply at a time when it might be of real importance that there should be no such impediment to our conduct of the war. But in the event of a reverse, the support in men of the Muslims, the Hindu fighting races, and the Princes would be even more important than before, and I should be surprised if the effect on supply were to prove to be really major in character. We should in any event in such circumstances be justified in taking action far more drastic against Congress and its supporters than we should contemplate at a time when there was still a prospect of agreement and when they did not constitute an active and immediate menace, and, as I see it, would be essential that we should not hesitate to take that action.

15. Finally, there is of course the ever present pressure of the Left Wing. Much as (on the assumption for what it is worth that they or certain of them may be prepared to be reasonable) one may sympathize with the Right Wing elements in Congress over such pressure, and desirable as it is not to break so long as we see hope of a settlement which we could regard as acceptable, there is a definite limit to the extent to which we can allow our sympathy to affect our actions. What I have always been afraid of has been (compare paragraph 4 of my telegram of 30th January No. 140–S) that we should do a deal with the Right Wing and then find that the Right Wing, as a result of Left Wing pressure, is unable to deliver the goods. What is in fact happening now in an increasing degree is that the Right Wing in order to preserve unity within Congress are being forced in public to support more and more leftist doctrines. The natural tendency in any political organization of this type is no doubt naturally to the left. But the right are coming perilously near, though they would not admit this themselves, to having the pace set for them by Bose and his friends.

16. Assuming then that the analysis I have endeavoured to make above of the position corresponds reasonably to the facts, the next question is what should be our immediate line? I feel bound to report in this connection that I have had in the last few days a series of representations from various quarters that we should take immediate steps to warn Congress in terms and officially that if they contemplate implementing their threat of civil disobedience, they would be dealt with most severely as impeding the progress of the war. The suggestion has also been made to me that we should warn Congress that resolutions of the type passed at Patna, if reaffirmed at Ramgarh, would make further negotiation impossible; that His Majesty's Government would not be prepared to conduct discussions under a threat of blackmail such as this, and that if endeavours are made to implement it, Congress as a political organization will

be proclaimed. Maxwell, my Home Member, is very strongly in favour of a formal communique in terms which I will telegraph to you separately. Hydari and Shanmukham Chetty have strongly urged that unless and until His Majesty's Government make their position in relation to Congress intentions clearer and show that they are not going to contemplate any settlement on the basis indicated in the Congress resolution, there is no hope of opposition to Congress developing or consolidating in the former Congress Provinces; but that once the necessary indication has been given, we need anticipate no delay in the development of such opposition. That view is also held by Mudaliar and by others in touch with political life in British India whom I have seen in the last few days.

17. Arthur Moore whom I interviewed on 6th March was also strongly in favour of something on these lines. (As you know, I do not place his judgment or balance very high, and am disposed to weight what he says pretty heavily. But he has wide contacts in India, and is the Editor of a leading paper). He puts it that it is our business now to show up Congress, to make it clear to the world that it is Congress that has destroyed the hope of Indian unity, had wrecked Federation, has lost the chance of Dominion Status, has alienated the minorities and the Princes, and as the result of two and a half years experience of government in the Congress Provinces, so alarmed the minorities about their position that there is little hope when the Act is reopened of the existing Provincial scheme, well as it may be working in the Punjab and Bengal, being allowed to stand.

18. I do not think that I am overstating it when I say that I get the very strong impression that the bulk of moderate opinion, whether European or Indian, in this country is losing or has lost sympathy with these exaggerated claims of Congress; while for the reasons I have given above, moderate opinion in non-Hindu circles is also gravely apprehensive that we may go some distance further to meet Congress claims; and is beginning to wonder whether what has already been promised by way of meeting the demands for self-government urged on us by all parties before the passing of the Act may not work out in practice to the serious detriment of the minorities.

19. Accepting all that, and feeling as one must some sympathy with the impatience and irritation of anti-Congress elements both at the exaggerated claims of Congress and at what they probably regard as our undue hesitation in dealing severely with them, we have, as I see it, to consider a variety of other factors in making up our minds as to a communiqué such as Maxwell suggests, or to any radical change in policy such as would be welcomed at this moment by Moore and probably too by the ordinary conservative elements in this country, more particularly as the burden of implementing it would fall on His Majesty's Government and not on them. It may be, as I have recognized before, that in fact experience will show that the democratic experiment will not work in this country. But, though with growing doubt, I still feel that it is essential that we should give it a further run. The considerations that weigh with me in hesitating to take any extreme step are first of all parliamentary reactions. I doubt if Parliament has yet caught up with the gradual movement of opinion here, and particularly among the Muslims, which I have reported above. Feeling at home is still in favour, as I see it of constitutional advance to Dominion Status, on the assumption that that can be secured without any major rupture in India. We should have some difficulty, I should have thought, in carrying conviction to Parliament at this stage of the case for any immediate and drastic reversal of policy; though that would not necessarily be the case as regards a warning to Congress.

20. Secondly, we have to consider the material afforded to hostile propaganda, and the effect likely to be produced in America, by what would certainly be represented as a reversion

in India to a policy of repression and coercion on a scale which would inevitably be grossly exaggerated. We may have to face that, but it is not a thing to take on lightly.

21. Thirdly, I have the feeling, which may of course be ill-founded, that there may be a certain element of bluff in existing Congress tactics. Their game is consistently to ask for far more than they can carry or than they really hope to secure. It is quite likely that as I said in paragraph 13 above, they may be prepared to take the risks involved in playing for very high stakes, and to take the chance of difficulty in avoiding losing face if they fail. I feel too that they are at the moment very lacking in a target. They cannot fail to be conscious that they are coming under a good deal of criticism in moderate quarters here; they must be aware of the hardening of Muslim opinion (which may of course make them all the more anxious to jockey us into acceptance of their claims before we take that hardening really seriously); while the tone of the home press, which was originally, thanks to their admirable publicity machine, so favourable to them, shows a change as the result of fuller realization of the complexities of this situation; and the latest American press reports suggest a certain lapse in active interest (though that I fully accept may be only temporary and would disappear with active anti-Congress measures on our part) in that country.

23. The picture which I have painted above is a disturbing one, as no one knows better than I do. But we can I think feel entirely clear in our conscience as to our own responsibility for it. We have done our utmost to bring people together. We have spared no effort to try to bridge differences between communities. It cannot fairly be represented as our fault if we have failed to do so. We could abdicate to Congress in conditions such as I have described above only at the cost of a quite definite betrayal of our responsibilities to the minorities and to the Princes. Nor, as I see it, would be able to clear ourselves of responsibility for the results to India and to the Empire of such abdication. Congress in any event cannot govern this country in face of Muslim and Princely hostility unless we are prepared to enable it to do, and I cannot conceive our holding the minorities in order as the agents of Congress. Nor can the Muslims or the Princes govern it without our help, and there are signs in the Muslim camp of a growing readiness to recognize that it may be necessary to retain the British in India for many years to come as the only means of holding the balance between conflicting interests here. I see nothing for it in the circumstances but to continue to reiterate our own readiness to help; our anxiety to help India as swiftly as practicable on the path of constitutional progress; but also the fact that the obstacles to advance are Indian obstacles which we cannot ignore and the necessity for agreement here as a condition of advance; that we should continue to resist Congress demands for any concessions other than those we have already offered, or for any overriding of the minorities or the Princes; and that if they do go into civil disobedience, we should deal severely with them.

24. Fully realizing the parliamentary and the propaganda aspects of this issue, especially in war time, I have not failed to ask myself whether there is any further move or gesture that could appropriately be made by us at this stage which would be calculated to ease the situation, either by giving Congress an opportunity to abate their claims, or if Congress are not prepared to abate those claims, by satisfying Parliament and public opinion at home and internationally that the fault does not rest with us, and that we are dealing with people with whom it is impossible to negotiate. My conclusion is, I fear, negative. We have already offered in the most public way everything that we have to offer. I am quite satisfied that on the important matter of machinery we could not do business by means of a Constituent Assembly, and that there would be no hope of the Muslims accepting such an arrangement. In any event, if we are to

take the Patna Resolution seriously, Congress might well demand, as a preliminary to participating in such an Assembly, its restriction to 'the people of India' and an undertaking by us to accept its conclusions (and the arguments which I gave against committing ourselves blindfold to accepting the conclusions of any such body, even if it contained a European or official element, in paragraph 7 of my telegram of 28th January, No. 127–S still seem to me decisive), or might require other unacceptable conditions.

25. Two possibilities of a minor order are the establishment of the Consultative Committee which we discussed last year, or the expansion of my Council, in either event leaving Congress to stay outside if it did not want to come in. I should myself be opposed to either. To both there is, in my judgment, the same general objection that any further move at this stage on our part towards Congress would be interpreted by Congress as an encouragement to think that they have only to shout loud enough and they will bring us all the way (their tactics have of course been to drown with abusive language any comment on the situation such as your recent speech which exposed the weakness of their position, and to reiterate, in complete disregard of the arguments advanced in various quarters against them from time to time, their earlier claims in all their plentitude). The effect too, I am satisfied, on the Muslims and on other more moderate elemen's in this country would be very disturbing. They equally would feel that it was only a question of time till, probably at their expense, we would come to terms with Congress. Further, were we to take action on these lines and leave Congress to remain in the wilderness, we should provide them, whether in the Consultative Committee, or in the expanded Executive Council, with the sort of target which they are so anxious to secure. They would be able to point to the unrepresentative character of both in the absence of Congress and in the case of the Executive Council to suggest that that body had ceased to be as at present a purely administrative governing organ, taking an objective view, had assumed a political character, and was packed with political nominees entirely hostile to Congress whose influence would be felt in the day-by-day government of the country. The lack of substance for any such suggestion would not in the least prevent Congress from broadcasting it as widely as possible and from turning it, I suspect, to account.

26. My own provisional conclusions at this stage on the picture as set out above are as follows. I am not disposed, on a balancing of arguments, to challenge the Congress positively before Ramgarh by any warning so definite as Maxwell would favour. I do not want, so far as there may be any division of opinion in the Working Committee (not that I attach much importance to that, for Gandhi's prestige and his skill in keeping that body together are too great) to cement them by the appearance of a threat. Secondly, there is always the possibility, though I do not rate it high, that counsels of greater commonsense may prevail at Ramgarh, or that the trend of discussion there may better enable us to appreciate Congress tactics and strategy. Thirdly, my personal relations with all parties being still friendly, and that fact holding out some hope, so far as Congress are concerned, of maintaining contact and of resuming conversations later, I think that there would be disadvantage from the wider point of view of too positive and categorical a warning or threat unless forced upon us, which would make those contacts impossible or difficult for some considerable time to come. The furthest I should therefore be disposed to go before Ramgarh would be an arranged parliamentary question as to the steps, if any, which were contemplated to deal with the Congress threat of civil disobedience. The answer to that might be that His Majesty's Government were fully alive to the importance of that issue; that as would be observed, the suggestion of civil disobedience in the Patna resolution was entirely contingent, but that if the consistent efforts of His Majesty's

Government to bring about peace in India between the communities, and to secure the unity of India, unhappily failed, and if the Congress implemented their threat appropriate action would be taken without a moment's delay to deal with it.

27. As regards the general position Ramgarh may help us to see our way more clearly, and I should prefer to report again once it is over. But it may help you to have my present view. Subject to its outcome, and on the assumption that Congress take no steps to implement their threat of civil disobedience, and keep within the law in their speeches and activities, I am, as you will have gathered from paragraph 24 above strongly in favour of taking no action, and of lying back. I should greatly regret it if as I recognize is quite possible, that policy, if approved by His Majesty's Government should expose you and His Majesty's Government to difficult passages in Parliament. I have shown above that I am fully alive to the possible embarrassment in propaganda and in the international field of a period of severely strained relations, or of a break necessitating coercive measures, with Congress. But my considered judgment is that we should now make no further move towards Congress beyond repeating our readiness to help (cf., paragraph 23 above), etc., and that we should be ready, if Congress make a break inevitable, to deal with civil disobedience resolutely and without delay, to use to the full powers of censorship and press control so far as Congress is concerned, and to spare no effort of propaganda to bring home to Parliament and the public that the responsibility for the fact that India has not advanced to the point, and now seems unlikely to advance to the point, to which we have been and are anxious to bring her, is not ours, and that the predominant responsibility rests with the Congress and with the intransigence of its present attitude, and the profound uneasiness which that attitude has caused to the Indian minorities as well as the Princes.

41. Jinnah's Views on Constituent Assembly

Reproduced from *Time and Tide*, London, 9 March 1940, in Waheed Ahmed (ed.), *Quaid-i-Azam Mohammad Ali Jinnah: The Nation's Voice—Towards Consolidation—Speeches and Statements, March 1935–March 1940*, Karachi, 1992, pp. 473–9.

The constitutional maladies from which India at present suffers may best be described as symptoms of a disease inherent in the body-politic. Without diagnosing the disease, no understanding of the symptoms is possible and no remedy can suggest itself. Let us, therefore, first diagnose the disease, then consider the symptoms and finally arrive at the remedy.

What is the political future of India? The declared aim of the British Government is that India should enjoy Dominion Status in accordance with the Statute of Westminster in the shortest practicable time. In order that this end should be brought about, the British Government, very naturally, would like to see in India the form of democratic constitution it knows best and thinks best, under which the Government of the country is entrusted to one or other political party in accordance with the turn of the elections.

Such, however, is the ignorance about Indian conditions among even the members of the British Parliament that, in spite of all the experience of the past, it is even yet not realized that this form of Government is totally unsuited to India. Democratic systems based on the concept of a homogeneous nation such as England are very definitely not applicable to heterogeneous countries such as India, and this simple fact is the root cause of all of India's constitutional ills.

Even as Under-Secretary of State for India, the late Lt Col Muirhead failed to appreciate this fact for deploring the present communal tension, he expressed the opinion that the tendency on the part of both, those in power and those in opposition, was to consider that what the position now was would be the position always. He deplored the failure of Indians to appreciate an essential feature of democratic Government, namely, the majority and the minority are never permanent, and he therefore, felt that the minorities' opposition to Federation on the assumption that from the outset power would be in the hands of an irremovable majority was untenable. But he forgot that the whole concept of democracy postulates a single people, divided however much economically, and he might well have started his study of Indian problems by consulting the report of the Joint Select Committee on Indian Constitutional Reforms, (Sessions 1933–34, Vol. 1, para 1).

Let us consider briefly the implications of this nebulous and impracticable Constituent Assembly. To commence with, the question arises, why is this demand made at this particular time? The answer is obvious. The war is to the Working Committee a heaven sent means of increasing its rule from over eight provinces to over the whole of India, State and Province. If the British Government are stampeded and fall into the trap under stress of the critical situation created by the war, India will face a crisis the result of which no man could prophesy, and I feel certain that Muslim India will never submit to such a position and will be forced to resist it with every means in their power. And of what type of constitutionalists will this Constituent Assembly consist? There are in India roughly 400 million souls who, through no fault of their own, are hopelessly illiterate and consequently, priest and caste ridden. They have no real conception of how they are being governed even today, and it is proposed that to the elected representatives of such, should India's future constitution be entrusted. Is it too much to say that since the vast majority of the elected representatives will be illiterate Hindus, the Constituent Assembly will be under the influence of Mahatma Gandhi and the Congress leaders, and the constitution that will emerge will be as the Working Committee directs?

Thus, through the Constituent Assembly will the Working Committee attain its ends? British control and commerce will disappear, the Indian States will be abolished! Minority opposition will be stifled and a great Hindu nation will emerge, governed by its beloved leader, Mahatma Gandhi, and the Congress Working Committee.

The British Government should review and revise the entire problem of India's future constitution *de novo* in the light of the experience gained by the working of the present provincial constitution and developments that have taken place since 1939 or which may take place hereafter.

While the Muslim League stands for a Free India, it is irrevocably opposed to any Federal objective which must necessarily result in a majority community rule, under the guise of Democracy and a Parliamentary system of Government.

No declaration regarding the question of constitutional advance for India should be made without the consent and approval of the All-India Muslim League, nor any constitution be framed and finally adopted by His Majesty's Government and the British Parliament without such consent and approval.

To conclude, a constitution must be evolved that recognizes that there are in India, two nations who both must share the governance of their common motherland. In evolving such a constitution, the Muslims are ready to co-operate with the British Government, the Congress or any party, so that the present enmities may cease and India may take its place amongst the great countries of the world.

‡═✳═‡

42.   Secretary of State's Impression of Ramgarh Session[1]

Secretary of State's Letter to Viceroy, 20 March 1940. Correspondence between Viceroy and Secretary of State, 1940, Linlithgow Papers, Acc. No. 2153, NAI.

3. ... Since I last wrote I have received a printed copy of your letter to me of February 27th, the original of which was lost in the ill-fated Hannibal and I have also received your letter of March 5th. I have read all that you say, particularly with regard to the best use of handling the major political problem with which we are confronted, with immense interest but there is nothing that I can add on this question just now, since as I told you in my last letter, the Cabinet postponed any decision on the matter pending the receipt of a further appreciation by you after you have had the time to sum up the results of the meeting at Ramgarh and the reactions throughout the country to it. With the aid of different reports, and more particularly with Stewart's[2] report in Bihar, I have been able to picture the vast temporary city which has been thrown up like a mushroom in the night in the neighbourhood of Ramgarh and the character of the gathering which must now be in full swing there. The All India Congress with their followers, Subhas Bose with his army of dissentients, Swami Sahajanand with his Kisans, and Jaipal Singh with his 20,000 Aboriginals armed with bows and arrows, are soon to make up between them the ingredients of a multitudinous and lively concourse. I can also picture the possibilities which Stewart indicates of the havoc which the torch bearers may all unwillingly create of the temporary city of bamboo, wattle and straw, as also the distractions which may be caused as the traffic-shy bullock of Chota Nagpur lurches along the single road with a lumbering bullock-cart in tow. The procession of a thousand of these cumbrous vehicles would indeed present a traffic problem which even those experts in traffic control in London, namely, the Metropolitan Police, would be likely to shy away from. It seems, however, if the telegrams which I have so far seen may be believed, that all risk of a physical conflagration was disposed of by a wholly unprecedented flood, for I gather that, as in the days of Noah, the heavens were descended upon the city of Ramgarh, reducing it to a swamp and preventing the President of Congress from even delivering his speech. There is really something half comic and half pathetic in the picture of this immense array being reduced by rain to a draggled mob and I shall look forward with interest to reading the more detailed accounts of what happened which will no doubt in due course reach me.... I have just seen in this morning's papers a short telegraphic message containing brief extracts from observations made by the Mahatma. I was happy to see that he declared that he was willing to see you fifty times if necessary. He also appears to have referred sympathetically to the ordeal which he assumes I underwent at the Caxton Hall[3], but adds that they must nevertheless continue to fight my reactionary policy. The suggestion rather seems to be that a reactionary and stiff-necked Secretary of State is preventing a sympathetic and willing Viceroy from meeting the just and legitimate claims of India as put forward by the Congress. In the view of the circumstances known to you and me this interpretation of the situation is not without its humorous aspect! It certainly looks as if the Working Committee had no intentions of embarking upon any immediate campaign of civil disobedience and I shall be interested to see whether or not Gandhi does suggest you in due course a further interview. I am bound to say, however, that in view that terms of the resolution which I presume has by now been passed at the meeting of the whole Congress it will be difficult to provide any plausible reason for further discussion between you and him.

---

[1] For the text of Ramgarh Resolution, see Chapter 1, Document no. 3.

[2] Sir Thomas Alexander Stewart, Governor of Bihar.

[3] The reference is to the shooting incident in Caxton Hall in which Michael O'Dwyer was killed and Secretary of State hurt.

43. Muslim League's Lahore Resolution

Indian Annual Register, 1940, Vol. I, pp. 311–12.

Text of the Resolution on 'Constitutional Problem'[1] moved by Fazlul Huq on 23 March 1940 at the twenty-seventh annual session of the All-India Muslim League, Lahore and passed on 24 March 1940:

'While approving and endorsing the action taken by the Council and the Working Committee of the All-India Muslim League, as indicated in their resolutions dated the 27th August, 17th and 18th September and 22nd of October 1939 and 3rd of February 1940 on the constitutional issue, this session of the All-India Muslim League emphatically reiterates that the scheme of Federation embodied in the Government of India Act, 1935 is totally unsuited to and unworkable in the peculiar conditions of this country and is altogether unacceptable to Muslim India.

'2. It further records its emphatic view that while the declaration dated the 18th of October 1939 made by the Viceroy on behalf of His Majesty's Government is reassuring in so far as it declares that the policy and plan on which the Government of India Act, 1935 is based will be reconsidered in consultation with the various parties, interests and communities in India, Muslim India will not be satisfied unless the whole constitutional plan is reconsidered *de novo* and that no revised plan would be acceptable to the Muslims unless it is framed with their approval and consent.

'3. Resolved that it is the considered view of this session of the All India Muslim League that no constitutional plan would be workable in this country or acceptable to the Muslims unless it is designed on the following basic principles, viz, that geographically contiguous units are demarcated into regions which should be so constituted with such territorial readjustments as may be necessary that the areas in which the Muslims are numerically in a majority, as in the North-Western and Eastern zones of India, should be grouped to constitute "independent states" in which the constituent units shall be autonomous and sovereign.

'4. That adequate, effective and mandatory safeguards should be specifically provided in the constitution for minorities in these units and in the regions for the protection of their religious, cultural, economic, political, administrative and other rights and interests in consultation with them and in other parts of India where the Mussalmans are in a minority adequate, effective and mandatory safeguards shall be specially provided in the constitution for them and other minorities for the protection of their religious, cultural, economic, political, administrative and other rights and interests in consultation with them.

'5. This session further authorizes the Working Committee to frame a scheme of constitution in accordance with these basic principles, providing for the assumption finally by the respective regions of all powers such as defence, external affairs, communications, customs and such other matters as may be necessary.'

---

[1] This Resolution came to be known as the 'Pakistan Resolution'.

⊹⎯⎯✳⎯⎯⊹

44. Viceroy's Assessment of the Political Situation after the Ramgarh Session of the Congress and the Lahore Session of the Muslim League

Extracts from Viceroy's Telegram to Secretary of State, 6 April 1940, Telegram No. 121. Telegraphic Correspondence between Viceroy and Secretary of State, 1940, Linlithgow Papers, Acc. No. 2162, NAI.

Immediate. No. 517–S. My appreciation of the position in the light of the Working Committee resolution passed at the meeting in Patna is contained in my telegram of 8th March, No. 358–G. Since its issue the main developments have been:

(a) Discussions in the Chamber of Princes on 11th/12th March.

(b) The Ramgarh resolution (in terms identical or practically identical with that passed at Patna) of 20th March;

(c) the resolution of the Muslim League on 24th March....

3. There is however no sign of any modification in the stiffness of Gandhi's attitude, or the excessive nature of Congress claims as embodied in the Ramgarh resolution, with which there is no reason to doubt that he identifies himself. It is clear, on the other hand, that there is a good deal of uneasiness in the minds of more moderate Right Wingers such as Birla, & c., who are disturbed at the clear evidence of hardening on the part of other communities. But I would not judge it at all likely that any such uneasiness will manifest itself in a breakaway, or in anything but rather plaintive private remonstrances to Gandhi on which he will take such action as he thinks fit.

4. My estimate of the hardening of the Princely attitude has been confirmed by the line of the resolution passed in the Chamber and the tone of the speeches there made. These were in certain cases outspokenly critical of the Congress and of Gandhi personally. And while the speakers continued to pay lip service to the ideal of Dominion Status, they were more insistent than in the past on the necessity for His Majesty's Government discharging their treaty obligations to the States, and on the necessity for their being fully associated with any constitutional changes. The Patna resolution was in my judgment clearly responsible for this stiffening in their attitude....

6. I am myself disposed to regard Jinnah's scheme as very largely in the nature of bargaining. I think he has put forward this scheme, the many objections to which I need not set out here, partly to dispose of the reproach that the Muslims had no constructive scheme of their own; partly to offset the extreme Congress claims to independence, & c.; and the Congress contention that Congress is the mouthpiece of India; and that a Constituent Assembly on the basis of adult suffrage is the only machinery for deciding future progress, as put forward in the Ramgarh resolution. That many Muslims are unhappy about the partition scheme I have no doubt, more particularly Muslims in the minority Provinces. That it may lose some non-Muslim support for Jinnah is clear from speeches by, e.g., Chhotu Ram in the Punjab and by Sikh protests that they will not readily submit to Muslim domination. But at the present stage my impression (confirmed by the reports from Governors referred to in paragraph 7 below) is that, while the scheme will be much criticized and rightly so, there is a good deal of feeling that it is bargaining in character, and very considerable doubt apart from that whether many Muslims of substance could face up to Jinnah over it. Sikander, I am certain, does not like the scheme: but he is not in a strong enough position in the light of the Khaksar incident to fight Jinnah.

I would myself agree with Craik's[1] estimate that the effect of Lahore has been to a remarkable degree to increase Jinnah's prestige and to consolidate his position as an All-India Muslim spokesman, and with the view reported by Steward that unsound as the partition idea may be, it is one which will get into the heads of very large numbers of Muslims, and may prove increasingly difficult to dislodge. I get the general impression that the Muslims in the light of Lahore and despite the internal dissensions connected with the Khaksar movement are in a far more confident and resolute mood than they have hitherto been. I am perfectly clear as to the seriousness of the factor which this hardening on their part represents: and I am confirmed in the view expressed in my telegram of 8th March of the difficulty of ignoring or overriding it, and the necessity for giving full consideration to Muslim claims.

7. Before sending my present appreciation I thought it well to give all Governors an opportunity to express their views. I consulted them on a personal basis in general terms. The text of my reference to them went to you by the mail of 29th March. I am telegraphing their replies in full so as to put you fully in possession of their views. I need not therefore summarize these telegrams here. But I think it not unfair to say that they appear to accept my own appreciation of the position as substantially justified: that they bring out (a) the increased hardening and importance of the Muslim element and attitude (cf., in particular views expressed by United Provinces, Punjab, Bihar, and Bengal and the relevance of the fact that the Punjab and Bengal are working Provincial Autonomy); (b) that an immediate outbreak of civil disobedience appears on the whole unlikely, given the absence of terrorism, the absence of economic crisis, the fact that there is no very strong and compelling motive behind civil disobedience which will appeal to the public generally, though the general sense of the Governors' replies is that Congress constituents would rally to an appeal for Civil Disobedience even though without enthusiasm, and Hallett[2] thinks that it is bound ultimately to come: (c) that Civil Disobedience is very likely to involve communal trouble where minority community is of any size. Hallett anticipates that it would be serious: Craik that it would almost certainly lead to communal trouble; as does Stewart, though he does not think that trouble would be widespread: Lumley[3] regards it as probably likely to create conditions in which there might be outbreaks: Herbert[4] that if it was not soon crushed it would lead to communal trouble; and communal trouble would be likely in Madras, though not on a very serious scale: (d) that desirable in principle as some gesture on our part might be if circumstances were favourable, the wise course, (subject to remarks in paragraph 13 below on Lumley's views) is for the present to continue to lie back.

8. I have again most carefully reviewed the whole position in the light of developments since my telegram of 8th March and of the views expressed by Governors. I have had particularly in mind (i) the arguments for and against formal warning to Congress (a) that civil disobedience in time of war will not be permitted and/or (b) a formal warning to them that they will not be permitted to proceed with preparations for civil disobedience: (ii) the question discussed in my telegram of 8th March, viz., whether the better course would be to lie back, or whether any move or gesture on our part, and if so what, is practicable and desirable: (iii) the extent to which any modification in general Congress attitude is to be looked for now that Ramgarh is over and that we are on the point of going to Parliament for an extension of the Section 93 Proclamation: (iv) points which might be of assistance to you in any debate on Section 93.

9. My views in the outcome are as follows: As regards point (i) (a) I put this in terms to Governors. I indicated to them as you will see that I was myself doubtful for the reasons set out in my telegram to them of 29th March as to the case for a warning to Congress: and I said that

a pretty broad hint, preferably given in Parliament, in a debate on Section 93 that civil disobedience will not be permitted in war-time would be the furthest I would myself be disposed to go. I think it fair to say that the Governors' replies, (I await Wylie's[5] comment only, but in view of urgency have not delayed issue of this appreciation for it), show that their general sense is averse from action. Bihar, Orissa and Madras would, as I read it, be prepared to go as far as I suggested to them, viz., a broad hint in Parliament. Hallett is strongly opposed, and thinks that not even a hint is called for so far as India is concerned, and that any reference necessary from the point of view of Right Wing opinion in Parliament should be carefully guarded. The Punjab take the line that any hint would be better privately given than public. Sind equally is opposed to a parliamentary announcement, and thinks any hint had better be private. The North-West Frontier Province and Bombay are against any action.

10. On the other hand, my Home Member remains in the light of Governors' replies of his previous view that there would be advantage in making it definitely and positively clear to Congress that civil disobedience will not be tolerated in war-time. A statement on these lines would, in his judgment, do much to counteract Congress efforts to create an atmosphere for civil disobedience, and while making our attitude clear to moderate elements and the services, give a lead to public opinion and show that we were not on the defensive, or likely to let ourselves be driven from point to point. I must of course pay the greatest weight to Maxwell's judgment, given his great experience and his balance. But with the utmost reluctance to differ from him and after full consideration, I adhere, in agreement with Hallett, now that I have had the benefit of the Governors' views, to my view that a broad hint of a non-provocative character in a debate on Section 93 such as Hallett suggests, viz., the inherent character of civil disobedience as shown on the last occasion; and the necessity of allowing no interference with the conduct of the war, is the further we could wisely go. I think that Governors generally are right in thinking that it is pretty widely accepted that we could not tolerate civil disobedience in war-time; and I am impressed by their references to that fact, and by the almost unanimous feeling of the unwisdom of anything that could be represented as a challenge, or used as a pretext by Congress for a break. There is a good deal in Cunningham's[6] point about the skill of Congress in misinterpreting any announcement by us.

11. As regards a warning against preparations, again in the light of Governors' views, I am myself satisfied that the wise course would be to give no warning continue to keep the closest watch on all action preparatory to civil disobedience, and to make full and prompt use of the law in suppressing unlawful activities. There is, as you will see from their replies, considerable identity of view among Governors as to the case for dealing with this side simply by picking up offenders as they transgress the law. As in the case of the alternative discussed in the preceding paragraph, there is widely expressed acceptance of the objections to throwing down any challenge to Congress, or providing them with a target. I have given full weight to the argument that action on our part might hearten non-Congress elements, and to the arguments for positive action by us. But having most carefully examined them with the assistance of the Governors' views, my own conclusion is as stated above.

12. To turn to point (ii) in paragraph 8 above, I need not say how concerned I have been to satisfy myself in again reviewing the situation whether there is any action, and if so what, which we could at this stage profitably and wisely take. The general sense of the Governors' replies supports my own earlier view that we should be wiser to make no move in the political field. Specific suggestions in the political field have been made by Craik and Lumley. As for Craik's suggestions, I of course wholly agree that it must be our policy to continue to try to

promote agreement here. But there will have to be a considerable easing off on the part both of Congress and the Muslim League before we should be justified in moving activity. I regard Craik's comment as more important as bringing out from the point of view of the Muslim Province the type of concession which he thinks would be called for to make accommodation between the Muslims and the Congress possible. It would clearly involve a very substantial sacrifice by Congress even on the basis of the Act of 1935.

13. Lumley's suggestion for a further endeavour to get a conference together is, as you know, one which has been very much in my mind from time to time, and I have again done my best to consider objectively whether there might not be something to be said for it. He advances good tactical reasons for making the move, and I accept their force. For all that, giving the suggestion the best consideration I can, I remain definitely averse from any move of this type at the present stage. I by no means exclude consideration of action on these lines at some later point. But I am certain that if we move in this field before conditions are favourable to our doing so, we shall merely make matters worse rather than better. A premature attempt of this nature, particularly if one or both parties decline to participate save on terms unacceptable to the other, or to us, might be of assistance from the propaganda point of view, but on a longer view would in my judgment be likely to set matters back as regards any arrangement between the parties, and to do no good to our prestige. There is already a good deal of suggestion that His Majesty's Government are concerned only to come to terms with Congress; that they will run after Congress in almost any circumstances; and that they will at any time be ready to sacrifice the remaining interests in the country if they can only conciliate Congress opponents. That is not the case. But the fact that the idea is in people's minds is relevant to the course to be adopted by us.

14. Nor am I, having again considered the matter, at this stage in favour of considering for the present before reaching agreement with Congress either the expansion of my Council or the establishment of a Consultative Committee. I do not believe we shall get Congress to play on either. Both (and more particularly the first) represent valuable concessions, and to throw them into the pool without some certainty of Congress taking advantage of them would be to leave us with still less to bargain with when the time comes for getting down to business with Congress. I will consult Governors separately as regards case for non-official advisers now that Section 93 looks like being prolonged, but rather anticipate that they will be against (cf., remarks in Hallett's telegram of 31st March, and Hope's of 3rd April). My considered opinion in these circumstances, and in the light of the views expressed by Governors, is that for the present we should continue to mark time. We should however continue equally to maintain such private contacts as are open to us, and be ready to take advantage of any improvement in the situation, or any change in the attitude of the principal parties, which holds out a hope of bringing them more closely together and of producing agreement. I repeat how greatly I regret that this should be the case. But equally, and with a full sense of responsibility, I feel it my duty to bring out the strength of the argument as I see it against any early move. I suspect that this situation has got to develop still further as between the parties before there is much likelihood of either coming to their senses: and a series of ineffective attempts at intervention on our part is likely, if anything, to reduce the value of our intervention or our assistance to secure agreement when circumstances favourable for that present themselves.

15. As regards point (iii) in paragraph 8 above—possibility of a modification in general Congress attitude—I fear that as mentioned in paragraph 3 above, I see no present sign of this. I think Lumley is probably right in his suggestion in paragraph 2(b) of his telegram of 2nd April

that Congress by their present threats hope to blackmail us into further concessions while hoping not to have to implement their threats, though I agree with him also that they are creating an atmosphere in their own ranks in which it will be difficult for them to climb down. There may well, too, be something in the suggestion that they hope that if we suffer a reverse, or become deeply engaged, in the West, we shall be more pliable, though for the reasons given in paragraph 14 of my telegram of 8th March I do not regard that argument as well founded. I suspect Gandhi of conducting at the moment of war of nerves in which he will return an entirely polite but completely negative answer to any forward move on our part short of his full demand, hoping that if he can keep this up long enough we shall get rattled and that other communities and interests in this country will be all the more shaken by any concession or move which we may be persuaded to make and all the more convinced of the capacity of Congress to squeeze us.

16. As regards point (iv) in paragraph 8 above you are of course the best judge of what arguments are likely to be of value in any debate. But I may perhaps indicate briefly my own views of the consideration which might be worth emphasizing from the standpoint of reactions here. As a preliminary point, there is I think force in Sarkar's suggestion to me that, if that could be secured, sorrow rather than anger should be the note of the discussion. I think it important to bring out again by a quotation in both Houses (perhaps the terms of the communiqué issued after my talk with Gandhi on 6th February) as well as in the White Paper which I have separately suggested to you if you accept that suggestion, the nature of the offer we have made and its great generosity that with the best will in the world to reach Dominion Status as early as possible, His Majesty's Government cannot ignore or override the views and interests of the minorities, particularly the Muslims, and the Princes; that the impasse which has now been reached is not due to any failure on the part of His Majesty's government who have nothing whatever with which to reproach themselves in the eyes of India or of the world; that we did indeed succeed in bringing the leaders of the two principal parties together last November, but that the intransigence of one party then made further progress impossible; that since then increasing demands by Congress have made the position still more difficult, and have resulted in a definite strengthening of the critical opposition of two elements who cannot be ignored and whose feeling must be given fullest weight to in any settlement which may be reached, viz., the Princes and the Muslims; that there is no reason to think that the minorities such as Scheduled Castes, & c., are not equally disturbed by the Congress claim; that these more recent developments have brought out more clearly than ever the lack of any substance for the Congress claim to be accepted as the mouthpiece of India; and that it is obvious that any settlement which is to last and any constitutional progress for India must be preceded by internal agreement and a greater readiness on the part of the principal parties in this country to strike a balance.

17. It is, I suggest, important also (from the USA point of view as well as generally) to bring out that we have never at any stage demanded 100 per cent agreement between the parties as a condition of advance, and that in connection with the proposals put to Congress and the Muslims in November it was made clear in terms that it ought not to be necessary absolutely to resolve any detail of such differences as may exist in the provinces, and that we asked the parties to reach such resolution of those differences as would make the devising of a scheme for harmonious cooperation at the Centre possible. I suggest that (as in your broadcast of 3rd April) we should play up to middle position opinion here, and in particular

assure India that the present difficulties will in no way diminish the desire or intention of His Majesty's Government to establish at the earliest possible moment self-government within the Commonwealth of Nations: should reiterate our own readiness to lend any help, make some play with the extent to which we have already tried to bridge the widening gulf between the communities, and while expressing our regret that normal constitutional working of the scheme of Provincial Autonomy should be interrupted in many provinces and that its interruption should now have to be further prolonged through circumstances outside our control, bring out that it is working smoothly and well elsewhere and that though it may contain defects, experience has shown that they are not fundamental in character.

18. As for the future Government of India as a whole, that we should draw attention to our continued insistence on the importance of Indian unity which you and I have repeatedly stressed and express our regret that the widening gap between the communities and interests, consequent on the attitude which Congress has adopted towards Minorities and towards the Princes should constitute so serious a threat and a setback to that unity. There is much that could be said in criticism of Jinnah's partition ideas and we clearly could not accept or endorse them. But quite apart from the fact that we have left the whole scheme and policy of the Act open for discussion after the war, and that Jinnah's scheme itself has I suspect largely been provoked by the unreasonable demands of Congress, any condemnation of Jinnah's scheme will at once irritate Muslim feeling and will be seized on by Congress. In present tempers here I would myself therefore think it preferable to quote it as illustrating the extent to which the gulf has widened between the parties, and to take the line that His Majesty's Government attached all the more importance in such circumstances to reaching a solution, with the agreement of all parties, which would secure the unity of India...

---

[1] Sir Henry Duffield Craik, Governor of Punjab
[2] Sir Maurice Garnier Hallett, Governor of United Provinces
[3] Sir Lawrence Roger Lumley, Governor of Bombay
[4] Sir John Arthur Herbert, Governor of Bengal
[5] Sir Francis Verner Wylie, Governor of Central Provinces
[6] Sir George Cunningham, Governor of North-West Frontier Provinces

45. Viceroy's Views on Future Constitutional Discussions

Telegram to Secretary of State, 8 April 1940. Telegram No. 127, Telegraphic Correspondence between Viceroy and Secretary of State, 1940, Linlithgow Papers, Acc. No. 2162, NAI.

Immediate. No. 530–G. My appreciation had been prepared before receipt of your telegram containing your suggestions as to the line to be taken in debate, Paragraphs 16 to 18 of my telegram of 6th April, No. 517–S, largely cover the ground as I see it. I send however the following supplementary comments on points taken in your telegram of 4th April, No. 1610:

(a) While fully appreciating your feeling with which I entirely sympathise as regards the Muslims partition plan, I would again emphasise the great importance of saying nothing which will antagonize the Muslims and of avoiding any direct attack on them. I think myself that this matter could best be handled on the line suggested in paragraph 18 of my telegram of 6th April; but I am confirmed by enquiries I have made here in my feeling that any overemphasis on unacceptability and faults of Muslims' scheme would be politically unfortunate. We have after all made it clear already that whole scheme and policy of the Act is open to consideration at the end of the war, and we cannot exclude the possibility that something of the nature of the Muslims scheme would then be put forward and possibly strongly pressed. We cannot well rule out any proposition of this nature in advance and I think you will probably feel with me that wise tactics would be to keep our hands free until critical moment is reached in future constitutional discussions and we can make clear our true attitude towards it in light of circumstances then prevailing.

(b) I would urge most strongly that no suggestion or reference to British rule in India ceasing should be made. I am quite clear that effect here of any such suggestion would be deplorable; and in present circumstances I should myself judge that date of a severance of our connection or substantial reduction of our influence in India has receded materially within the last six months.

(c) I agree that there is a good deal to be said for putting on Indian political parties themselves the onus of producing a constructive plan and for bringing out that we are the only people who have made constructive and practicable suggestions so far. I suggest at the same time that it would be well to walk warily so as to avoid the reply that the true answer to all this is the Constituent Assembly with representation for the minorities. Equally I should on the whole depreciate a request for willingness to cooperate in discussion which would have some chance of producing a plan. Here again we might be met by an expression of readiness to come in so long as Independence was the basis of discussion or the like, and I think we should do better to avoid committing ourselves in any way.

Two additional points which might be useful to you are (a) that one-third of the population of British India, nearly 90 million people by the 1931 census, occupying over 300,000 square miles, are still enjoying the benefits of Provincial Autonomy. If a kind word could be said for the Punjab, Bengal, Sind and Assam in the debate on behalf of His Majesty's Government, it would, I am sure, be greatly appreciated.

(b) Consistently with the line of argument suggested in my telegram of 6th April, No. 517–S, it would, I think, be possible to bring out that apart from the necessity of avoiding interference with the conduct of the war, there is the necessity of safeguarding the peace of India, since it is certain that civil disobedience would lead to disorder and probable that in some parts of the country it would act as provocation with serious communal strife.

3. I have now had, and am repeating to you, Wylie's thoughtful appreciation of the position. I have considered it very carefully, but having done so, I do not wish in any way to modify the appreciation in my telegram of 6th April. I doubt if he gives full value to a further period of silence. I should myself be wholly against interference with European recruitment, and I am not disposed to get ahead with administrative arrangements for introducing Dominion Status until we can see more clearly where we stand. I am certain that any statement would best be made in Parliament at this stage, and the general line of phrase which he suggests might be employed fits in pretty well with what I have suggested in paragraphs 16 to 18 of my telegram of 6th April. I should myself be averse from seeing Gandhi at this moment.

4. Hubback[1] has written in amplification of his telegram. Nothing of great importance emerges, but he emphasizes his feeling that Congress are waiting for us to make a false step of

which they can take advantage. I have little doubt that that is true, and am all the more anxious that we should expose no avoidable surface.

---

[1] Sir John Austen Hubback, Governor of Orissa

46.   Secretary of State Zetland Blames Congress for Moslem Apprehensions: Statement in the House of Lords

Statesman, 19 April 1940.

Key to Unity in India
Hindu–Moslem Accord
Future Rests with Congress
Allaying Fears of the Minorities

Lord Zetland reviewed the position in India at length yesterday during a debate in the House of Lords

THE debate was occasioned by Lord Zetland's request that the proclamations under Section 93 of the Government of India Act by which the Governors assumed the powers of government in seven provinces when the Congress Ministries resigned be extended for 'such further period, not exceeding 12 months, as developments may show to be necessary.'

Lord Zetland paid a tribute to the provinces of Bengal, the Punjab, Sind and Assam, where the popular ministries had continued to function. This was a matter of satisfaction to those anxious to see India progressing smoothly towards her goal, he said.

Referring to Mr Gandhi's accusation that he had closed the door on the Congress position, Lord Zetland said 'I have never desired to close any doors.' However, it was only too apparent, he said, that the door was being closed by others.

'A substantial measure of agreement among the communities of India is essential if the vision of a united India is to become a reality', he said. 'I shall labour for a reconciliation between those two great communities—Moslems and Hindus.'

'But the fact of the matter is that the Congress Party has raised in the minds of many Moslems apprehensions which only they themselves can allay.... Will the Congress refrain from closing the door upon unity in India?.... Upon their answer hangs the future fate of that country.'

Rule by Governors
Continuance Requested by Lord Zetland

Opening the Debate in the House of Lords on proclamations in the provinces under section 93 of the Government of India Act, Lord Zetland, Secretary for India said:

'No one regrets more than I do the necessity for the motions, which stand in my name. They relate to the present position in 7 of the 11 provinces of British India.

'It must, at least, be a matter for satisfaction for all those who are anxious to see the people of India progressing smoothly towards their goal that in the provinces of Bengal, the Punjab, Sind and Assam, embracing as they do not less than one-third of the population of British India and governing 300,000 square miles, parliamentary government is functioning successfully and I have little doubt that your lordships will wish to associate yourselves with me in offering the governments of those provinces our congratulations on their achievement in the past and our warm good wishes for still greater successes in the future.

Cause for Regret

'But when we contemplate the sort of affairs in the remaining provinces we find cause, not for satisfaction, but for very real regret. It is now nearly six months since the Ministers acting on the instructions of the Working Committee of the Congress Party, withdrew from the responsibilities which they had assumed towards both the legislatures and their constituents, thereby obliging the governors to assume powers of government. And since it is provided by section 93 (3) (B) of the Constitution Act that a proclamation conferring such powers upon the governor shall cease to operate at the expiration of six months, I have no option but to ask Parliament to approve, in accordance with the provisions of the Act, the continuance in force of the Act, the continuance in force of the various proclamations for such further period, not exceeding 12 months, as developments may show to be necessary.

Viceroy–Gandhi Talks

'Let me recall to mind briefly the course of events in India since I last had occasions to address the House on matter. On January 10 the Viceroy delivered a speech in Bombay which was intended to be, and was widely accepted as being, a gesture of conciliation and goodwill towards those who were pressing for more rapid progress in the constitutional field. It was followed by a meeting between the Viceroy and Mr Gandhi at Delhi on February 5. The announcement of this meeting undoubtedly created a feeling of optimism in India and it was, I think, contrary to general expectation and certainly to hopes entertained in many quarters that the discussion proved barren of results and was adjourned *sine die* at the end of an exchange of views lasting for two and half hours. Your lordships will find in the White Paper which I have circulated the text of the official communiqué which was agreed between the Viceroy and Mr Gandhi and issued after the meeting.

'It will be seen that the Viceroy emphasized the desire of His Majesty's Government that India should attain Dominion Status at the earliest possible moment and their desire to facilitate that object by all the means in their power; that he drew attention to the fact that while federal scheme of the Act afford the swiftest stepping stone towards Dominion Status, His Majesty's Government were only too willing when the time came to examine the whole field in consultation with all parties and interests in India. The Viceroy further explained that His Majesty's Government were prepared to give immediate effect to the offer, which had already been made to associate political parties in India with the Central Government on conditions which had been laid down in November.

Hopes Dashed

'It will further be seen that Mr Gandhi's response to this approach was a mere statement to the effect that it did not meet with the full demand of the Congress Party. That seemed to me to be a very unfortunate outcome of the meeting which had been undertaken with such high hopes and I expressed the fear that if the Congress Party maintained their attitude the obstacles in the way of an honourable settlement would be greatly increased.

'I said that because the reports which were reaching me from many quarters made it abundantly clear to me that the opposition of Moslems—and not of Moslems only—was increasing and the strength of their determination to resist the two main items in the demand of the Congress Party, namely for a declaration by His Majesty's Government that India should become a completely independent country and for the drafting of the future constitution of the country by a constituent assembly, elected on the basis of adult suffrage was rapidly growing. And it seemed to me that further efforts must be made to persuade the leaders of different communities to meet and discuss their respective difficulties if the gulf between them was to be prevented from widening disastrously.

No Closed Door

'Mr Gandhi thereupon accused me of closing the door on the Congress position. I have never desired to close any doors. From the first it was my desire to keep open the door, which it was only too painfully apparent to me was being closed by others. Let me repeat what I said: "I believe that only by means of discussion between those who can speak with authority for their followers, informal and in confidence in the first instance, is a helpful appreciation of their respective standpoints and the difficulties inherent in them to be hoped for. If such discussion is to be fruitful, there must be on all sides a genuine will to succeed and a real spirit of compromise. The British Government cannot compel these things. They can only plead for them, as I most earnestly do."

'I used those last words because the Viceroy had already attempted to bring the leaders of the Congress Party and the All-India Moslem League together and for the time being, at any rate, had failed. Unhappily, as I think, the suggestion met with little encouragement from those primarily concerned for Pandit Nehru is reported to have said in reply that he thought that it was futile to try to solve a problem by what he described as 'Sweet talks' between individuals. Yet a similar course has been urged by men so differently placed as the Chief Justice of the Federal Court of India and the Prime Minister of the Punjab and I adhere to my view that it would be a most helpful first step towards ending the present deadlock.

Scheduled Castes

'I said a moment ago that it was not Moslems only who were viewing with growing concern the rigidity of the attitude of the Congress Party. Men like Dr Ambedkar and Rao Bahadur M.C. Rajah who speak for the Scheduled Castes have given expression to their fears, and I think that in order to give your lordships a balanced picture I should call attention to the views expressed by the council of the National Liberal Federation of India in their most recent pronouncement on the position for the Council of that body contains many distinguished public men, who have rendered much service to their country and whose patriotism is unquestioned.

'They (the Liberals) stated categorically, in a public resolution on February 18, that in their view it is impracticable in the present circumstances to talk of complete independence and that they equally reject the idea of a constituent assembly based on adult suffrage as being a suitable body to devise a constitution. They suggest as much more practical the calling of a small conference, representative of several parties, communities and interests in the country, to determine the principles of the future constitution.

Moslems' Demand

'I now come to the events which followed upon the abortive meeting between Mr Gandhi and the Viceroy—events which have unhappily proved my fears to have been only too well founded. At their annual meeting at Ramgarh in the middle of March, the Congress reiterated their command [demand]. This was followed by a meeting of the All India Moslem League at Lahore at which a resolution was adopted unanimously putting forward a scheme for the future Government of India involving the partition of the country into separate Hindu and Moslem states.

'I am bound to say that while I fully appreciate the grounds on which this proposal is based, I cannot but regard it as constituting something not far short of a counsel of despair, since its acceptance would be tantamount to an admission of failure of the devoted labours of Indians and Englishmen alike over a long period of concentrated effort, for, those labours have been based upon the assumption that even in the admitted diversity of India, a measure of political unity could be achieved sufficient to enable India as a whole to take its place as an integral unit in the British Commonwealth of Nations.

Parties Concerned

'This then is the position in which we find ourselves and when I say we, I do not mean His Majesty's Government and Parliament only, for we are only one of the parties concerned. I mean also the Congress, the All-India Moslem League and the Princes, who, let it not be forgotten, constitute an element in the situation, which can not be ignored or brushed aside. It is all the more tragic because the interests and sympathies of the contending parties in that still greater struggle which we are waging against Nazi Germany are identical. And I ask myself, can we not even now find a golden path that leads to reconciliation?

'Are these differences between various parties in reality so great as unhappily they appear to be? I can speak neither for the Congress nor for the All-India Moslem League nor for the Princes. I can speak only for His Majesty's Government and I can not but think that in the dust raised by the controversy the significance of what we have undertaken to do as our contribution towards a solution of the problem has not been fully understood.

'Let me, therefore, repeat what it is that we have proposed. Though I attach real importance to it, I do not now dwell upon the offer which we have made with a view to securing the co-operation of political parties in the Central Government, since this offer may be regarded, apart from its intrinsic merits, as an earnest of our intentions with regard to the future. Let me explain. We realize that for varying reasons the three main parties to the controversy—the Congress, the All-India Moslem League and the Princes—have serious objections to the federal provisions of the Act. And we have, therefore, said that we are desirous of consulting those interested with a view to ascertaining the lines on which they wish to see these provisions altered.

A Result of History

'We have made that offer because we accept the reasonableness of the claim that Indians themselves should play a vital part in devising the sort of constitution which they deem best suited to the circumstances of their country. But we have also said that we cannot wholly disassociate ourselves from the shaping of the future constitution of the country and I should have thought that our reasons for saying that would have been both understood and accepted as valid. But since that is not apparently the case, let me state them once more.

'They are rooted in the history of the past 200 years and, however, much you might like to do so, you simply cannot wipe out history and treat events recorded in its pages as if they had never occurred.

'Let me merely, by way of example, take the case of the Princes to illustrate what I mean. Mr Gandhi has described the Princes of India as things of our creation. I feel sure that on reflection so fair-minded a critic as Mr Gandhi will be willing to agree that circumstances of the time, the force of events, their interaction and their consequences, which are things of which the content of history is made up bear far greater responsibility for the existence of the Princes than do His Majesty's Government.

The Minorities

'We made treaties with them certainly, but we could not have done so if they had not been there. Then too, we have a stake in the country which is equally the outcome of historical forces and there is the question of defence of the country which for the time being at any rate and possibly for many years to come an independent India wholly disassociated from Great Britain would admittedly not be in a position to secure. And there are the minorities, to whom we are under obligations which once more are embedded in the very texture of the tapestry of history, in that they have enjoyed their peaceful evolution as a result in part of the restoration of order by the British after the confusion and civil war which attended the dissolute of the Moghul Empire and, in part, of the administrative unity established during the long term of British rule throughout the land.

'These are, in the main, the reasons why we cannot disassociate ourselves from the shaping of the future constitution of India. But that does not mean that the future constitution of India is to be a constitution dictated by the Government and Parliament of this country against the wishes of the Indian people. The undertaking given by His Majesty's Government to examine the constitutional field in consultation with representatives of all parties and interests in India surely connotes not dictation, but negotiation.

Congress Holds the Key

'Admittedly a substantial measure of agreement amongst the communities in India is essential if the vision of a united India which has inspired the labours of so many Indians and Englishmen is to become a reality, for I cannot believe that any Government or Parliament in this country would attempt to impose by force upon, for example, the eighty million Moslem subjects of His Majesty in India a form of constitution, under which they would not live peacefully and contentedly.

'So far as it lies within my power to do so I shall labour for reconciliation between these two great communities. Moslems and Hindus, who after all whatever their differences of religion, of culture and of outlook upon life, have lived side by side in India for nigh upon a thousand years. But I realize how restricted is my own power for influence for the plain fact of the matter is that the Congress Party have raised in the minds of many Moslems apprehensions which only they themselves can allay and the question of vital import so far as the future of India is concerned is this—Will the Congress refrain from closing the door upon that unity of India, which they themselves so passionately desire?

'It is not too such to say that upon the answer which the Congress Party will give to that question hangs the future fate of India.' (Cheers)

47. Mahatma Gandhi's Letter to the Viceroy, 24 April 1940

CWMG, Vol. LXXII, pp. 21–2.

Dear Lord Linlithgow,

This is going to be a complaining letter. I was tempted to write to the Press on Lord Zetland's speech. But I restrained myself. What I wanted to say was too serious to be given to the public. Hence this letter. I am carrying on my head a tremendous responsibility. I want to avoid mistakes.

There is a ring of reluctance to [do] the right thing by India. He may say 'we don't want to do the things by way of settlement, you will have to fight for it or take what we offer.' That would be a straight answer. Why does he bring up against the Congress things which are common ground? Hindu–Muslim question, minorities and the like are common ground. The Congress claims that they can be truly settled only by a constituent assembly or its equivalent. On British admissions, Princes are your creation. That they were there before you came is true.

So were many other institutions. You kept what was necessary for your existence and destroyed what you thought were a hindrance. It is a thankless task to prolong this tale. I can if you want me to. I feel sure this sample should enable you to infer the rest.

Will you please convey my complaints to Lord Zetland in any way you think best? If I have misinterpreted him, you will oblige me by correcting me.

I know your and his preoccupations. But this Indian question is an integral part of the task in hand, is it not?

I am,
Yours sincerely,
M.K. Gandhi

48. Viceroy's Proposed Reply to Gandhi

Viceroy's Telegram to Secretary of State, Telegram No. 152, 28 April 1940. Telegraphic Correspondence between Viceroy and Secretary of State, Linlithgow Papers, Acc. No. 2162, NAI.

Immediate. No. 268–S. Following is text of my proposed reply to Gandhi:

Begins. Many thanks for your letter of the 24th April. I have read it carefully and, as you ask me to do, I am sending a copy of it to the Secretary of State. Let me only say this: that if you read the full text of the Secretary of State's speech in the House of Lords, you will I think appreciate more fully than may have been possible from the more condensed reports in the press the genuineness and sincerity of his desire (quite as deep as mine) to advance matters and to get over the difficulties here that have stood in the way of progress. We may all of us regret—I myself most certainly do—the existence of the Hindu–Muslim question and the problem of minorities which you mention, and we are indeed on common ground in doing so. But I am sure you will not misunderstand me if I say that I feel myself that they are matters which do exist, however much we may regret them, which are directly relevant to the solution of our common problem, and which we cannot hope to ignore if any lasting or generally acceptable solution of that problem is to be found. Equally that is the case of Princely India. And I am sure that the Secretary of State had not the least intention of conveying an impression misleading in the very slightest degree by what he said. You and I, I think, know him too well to think for a moment that he would be capable of such action. But it does seem to me, too, that we cannot refuse to face the historical facts of this matter or the historical setting in which the relationship of His Majesty's Government with the Princes is enshrined, or the treaties and the like by which it is to so large an extent governed.

That the difficulties of the situation before us should be there, I as you know, deplore; but all I can do is try to do my best to find some way out of them; and to find some way out of them of such a character as to carry with it the general support of all parties and communities and interests in this country. And that, as I have said more than once before in my public speeches, inevitably means some degree of compromise and a readiness for adjustment. We have not so far realized our hopes: in fact, one of the things that have depressed me most over the last three or four months is the fear that so far from advancing towards a solution, we are advancing into a still more intricate tangle. But the goodwill of His Majesty's Government, and of the Secretary of State and myself, remains there, and one can but hope that we may yet be able, with the help of those so directly affected in India, to turn the corner....

C.   CONSTITUTIONAL STALEMATE

49.   India's Stand: Constituent Assembly to Shape Structure— Article by Ram Manohar Lohia [Extracts from Part II]
Hitavada, 1 May 1940.

Complete Independence Stand

... A review of the position of the Congress and Mahatma Gandhi with regard to the social and economic ties that bind India to Britain shows that they stand for complete independence of the nation and it is but proper that the various implications of this position should be grasped in all detail by Congressmen and the Indian people as a whole. Again, the draft resolution for the Ramgarh Congress has authoritatively summed up this position. 'Indian freedom cannot exist within the orbit of British Imperialism and Dominion Status or any other Status within the Imperial Structure is wholly inapplicable to India and is not in keeping with the dignity of a great nation and would bind India in many ways to British politics and economic structure.'

Constituent Assembly

The Indian people are to be their own architects and masons and owners and dwellers. The contours of their structure are also generally indicated. 'A Constituent Assembly elected on the basis of adult suffrage' will shape these contours. Whatever other angles and curves and general form the Constituent Assembly might give to Indian freedom, it can in the nature of things permit no blockages or dark corners for British Imperialism to operate. The Constituent Assembly will consist alone of people's representatives; Knights, Rajas and Nawabs as such will have no place in it. This characteristic of the Constituent Assembly is decisive not alone from the view point that internal social justice can be worked out by people's representatives and not by vested interests, it is also decisive in regard to the relation between India and Britain and the complete freedom of Free India from foreign control. People's representatives are not only likely to ensure social justice and economic equality to the masses but also to wrest India completely from foreign domination of Knights. Rajas and Nawabs are not likely to line their own pockets at the expense of the mass of the people but also to ensure to British Imperialists their profits from India. In accepting the programme of a Constituent Assembly of people's representatives, the Congress has proclaimed its adherence to the twin ideals of international social justice and complete freedom from foreign control. The substance is to obtain its appropriate form, independence will be shaped in the Constituent Assembly.

Absurd Reasoning

Critics and carpers suffer from the habit of putting on wise smiles. In this case they ask that if the Congress position has been one of complete independence before and since the outbreak of the European war, why should a period of six months have been allowed to elapse and why should there still be delay in launching upon a struggle. Surely, the British Government should be expected to commit political suicide in India and that is what the Congress, with its goal of complete independence and its method of negotiations, wishes. The recurrent readiness, therefore, of Mahatma Gandhi to converse with the Viceroy shows that the Congress was and is still perhaps willing to compromise with the British Government on something less than independence. The reasoning is absurd. It is undoubtedly true that at the outbreak of the war two ways lay open before the Congress. One was the way of civil disobedience immediately upon the outbreak of war. The other way has actually been followed. It would serve little purpose here to compare the advantage of the two ways, but it may not be forgotten that urgent consideration both of the internal strength and discipline of the Congress and of the external necessity to give the British Government a chance to prove itself guiltless or otherwise, prevailed. To suggest that in letting these considerations prevail, the Congress was prepared to compromise on something less than independence is to suggest that every exchange of notes and visit of envoys or attempts at legal arbitration and political conciliation between two governments is a climb down. Before it actually goes to war, a government organizes itself on war-footing and presents its case before the whole world including the people of the enemy government. It would be senseless to detect in such activity of a government a desire to give in and to surrender the rights of its people. Moreover, the Congress did not content itself with a mere exchange of notes; it carried out what would be called a diplomatic rupture in the realm of inter-governmental relations. In withdrawing itself from provincial administrations at a fairly early stage of the war, the Congress declared its non-corporation with the British Government and its war-measures. Since then the Congress has been trying to put itself on struggle-footing and to present its case before the world including its own people and the people of Great Britain.

Viceroy's Declaration

Such consequences have in some measure, flown out of Congress activity during six months of the European war. Let us examine the single much debated link in the chain of happenings which began with the Viceroy's speech promising conferment of Dominion Status upon India early after the war. Mahatma Gandhi declared that, although there were snags, he saw germs of settlement in this speech. Then came the meeting between Gandhiji and the Viceroy, the agreement as usual to differ. Mahatma Gandhi once again stated wherein this difference lay and the proceeding flow of events enabled him to outline, in yet clearer detail and more convincing way, the Congress attitude on European interests, princes, minorities and defence. This single link, viewed as a whole, reveals itself and no explanation of its inner significance should be necessary. Nevertheless, it is instructive to elaborate one aspect. The Viceroy's speech was abandonment of an old position. Through its promise of Dominion Status, the British Government took up a new position. This was a change for all the world to see, for the Indian people, the British people and the world at large, and it also expressed a sentiment of the British Government. The Congress as Leader at once acknowledged the change in the position of the British Government and saw in it possibilities that might grow and develop into a settlement, naturally, on the basis of the Congress position. If these possibilities existed well and good, if they did not, his meeting with the Viceroy and the subsequent communiqués and statements would only enable Gandhiji to demonstrate that the new position of the British Government yet fell far short of the Congress position. Later, Mahatma Gandhi stated that these possibilities did not exist and that he was mistaken in detecting germs of settlements in the Viceroy's offer. Let a point of vital import be not missed. In confessing his own mistake Gandhiji invited those small sections in the world and, of course, the British people and their Government who might have likewise appreciated the Viceroy's offer, to feel with him that they were mistaken. This was a case of harmony between the great individual and the big world outside him, Gandhiji first reflected the experiences to the outside world. It was indeed unfortunate that this result was achieved at some cost. The highly favourable reaction of Gandhiji to the Viceroy's offer added to the indolence of the already indolent and the impatience of the already impatient. Whether this was due to the comparatively immoderate language of Gandhiji or the comparative immaturity of Congressmen both of the so-called right and the so-called left is not at all instructive to discover. Gandhiji's language being what it is, Congressmen must learn to know better.

50. Hindu Mahasabha Supports Dominion Status: Hindu Mahasabha Working Committee Resolution, Bombay, 19 May 1940

M.S. Aney Collection, File No. 7, NMML.

In accordance with the resolution passed by the Working Committee last February at Delhi the Government should immediately announce that Dominion Status under the Statute of Westminster will be granted to India immediately on the cessation of the war guaranteeing the indivisibility of India as a political unit and a Central Government strong enough to maintain it. This grant of Dominion Status should not be made conditional on any Hindu–Muslim pact as an indispensable pre-requisite, nor should the future constitution of India be based on the present Communal Award.

The Working Committee reiterates that it is prepared to accept Dominion Status as the immediate step towards the attainment of its goal of absolute political independence.

Whereas the Viceroy, the Secretary of State and other responsible Government authorities have recently persisted in stating again and again that if the Congress and the League arrive at an understanding it may form the basis to determine their status in any future constitutional framing and whereas such statements clearly imply that the Government persists in believing, in spite of the repeated protests by the Hindu Mahasabha to the contrary, that the Congress can speak in the name of the Hindus just as the League represents the Muslims; the Hindu Mahasabha calls upon the Government to give a definite understanding that no pact entered into by the Congress and the Moslems between themselves to which the Hindu Mahasabha is not made a party and which is not sanctioned by it, can be binding on the Hindus as a whole.

51.　Secretary of State Amery[1] on Political Dead-lock in India,
23 May 1940

Newspaper Report of Debate in House of Commons *Statesman*, 24 May 1940.

Indian's Part in Devising New Constitution
Britain's Promise Re-iterated
Negotiation—Not Dictation
Plea for Provisional Solution
Mr Amery on Support for Allied Cause

London, May 23.

'The attainment by India of free and equal partnership in the British Commonwealth is the goal of our policy', declared Mr L.S. Amery, Secretary of State for India, replying to questions today in the House of Commons.

Mr Wedgewood Benn (Lab–Gorten) asked Mr Amery whether he could indicate the attitude of the government towards problems facing them in India.

Mr T.V. Harvey (Independent), asked whether, in view of the 'encouraging pronouncement of Mr Gandhi and Pandit Jawaharlal Nehru', measures had yet been taken to promote a small conference of representative Indian leaders of all parties to agree upon the next step towards a solution of the constitutional deadlock.

Mr Amery, replying, said, 'I am glad to have this early opportunity of explaining, so far as I can within the limits of an answer to a question, the attitude of the Government to the present regrettable deadlock in India. The attainment by India of the free and equal partnership in the British Commonwealth is the goal of our policy as it was that of the late Government.

'We recognize that, as my predecessor made clear in his speech on April 18, it is for Indians themselves to play a vital part in devising a form of Constitution best adapted to India's conditions and India's outlook. The promise already given that the present scheme of the Act of 1935 and the policy and plans on which it is based are to be open for re-examination at the end of the war necessarily implies discussions and negotiations, and not dictation.

'We have no desire to delay any of the steps that may pave the way towards an agreed settlement that will take account of the legitimate claims of all communities and interests. On the contrary, we have been, and are only too anxious to make our contribution towards such a settlement.

'The difficulty at the moment lies in an acute cleavage of opinion in India affecting issues fundamental to the character of the future Constitution and even to an approach to the problem.

Provisional Solution

'I refuse to regard the cleavage as unbridgeable I cannot think it beyond the resources of Indian statesmanship to find at any rate such provisional accommodation as would admit the resumptions of office with general consent by Ministers in the provinces and appointment to the GG's Executive Council of representatives of the public on the basis already offered. I believe that such a solution of the present deadlock, provisional no doubt but still easing the way to an eventual agreement would be eagerly welcomed by an overwhelming body of Indian Public opinion.

'India from the outset of the war has made manifest her sympathy and support for the Allied cause and her anxiety to lend to that cause all aid in her power and it is the sincere and earnest hope of the British Government that in the situation which faces the whole civilized world today, the existing differences may be put aside and leaders of the great political parties in India will come together in an agreement in support of the common effort.

'The Viceroy, with the approval of the government, has spared no effort to bring the parties together and endeavour to find a basis for progress which will be generally acceptable. His own readiness to help in anyway he can remains unabated.'

Visit to India

Further questions followed: Mr R.W. Sorensen (Lab W. Hyton) asking if the Secretary of State could confirm the report that Pandit Nehru had declared that in the existing circumstances, civil disobedience was to be suspended, and if so would he express appreciation of the action of Pandit Nehru.

Further he asked, whether the Secretary of State would pay a personal visit to India.

Mr Amery replied that a visit to India could only be considered if circumstances made it feasible. He did not understand that civil disobedience had been suspended but that Pandit Nehru had declared that he would not take advantage of our difficulties ... We appreciated that ...

---

[1] L.S. Amery became Secretary of State for India on 10 May 1940 replacing Zetland.

52. Jawaharlal Nehru's Statement to the Press on Amery's Statement, 24 May 1940

SWJN, Vol. XI, pp. 45–6.

'No Provisional Solution'

We live in a rapidly changing world and astonishing things are happening from day to day, but one of the most astonishing of these happenings is the continuing attitude of the British Government towards India. Perhaps it is this very static and unchanging view that has brought so many difficulties and dangers to England.

The past few years of peace and war have been a succession of the most amazing blunders on the part of the British Government in foreign policy, in their Indian policy, and in other directions. The law of cause and effect is now having its revenge.

The new Secretary of State for India speaks in a tone which is no doubt meant to be conciliatory but the content of his utterances has no relation to facts in India or in Europe. We know the difficulties of the Indian problem. We know that there are differences of opinion here. We know that there are reactionaries here and communalists and feudal rulers and enormous vested interests. We do not underrate the complexity of this problem, no problem in the world today is free of difficulty and complexity. But in spite of this, it is completely out of place for Mr Amery to talk of a revision of the present Act and of what may be done after the war is over, or of provisional solutions and the like. There can be no provisional solution of the problem, nor can there be any solution within the orbit of British imperialism. There is no question, so far as we are concerned, of amending this act or that act. Nor do we want a part in devising our form of constitution.

The British Government must give up completely its conception of being the patronizing overlord of India, generously allowing us to have a say now and then. They must recognize the complete independence of India and the right of the Indian people alone to do what they like in regard to their future constitution as well as in regard to the problems arising from the war. We should try to settle our internal problems however difficult they might be. We shall strain every nerve to come to a settlement which is agreeable to various groups in India and to the vast majority of the people. If we fail, that will be our look-out and we shall face the consequences of the failure. But on no account and under no circumstances can we accept any interference with our future from the British Government or any other foreign authority. We realize fully the serious implications of the present world situation and its possible consequences in India. I wish the British Government would realize this also as well as we do and fashion their course accordingly, giving up all idea of empire and domination.

I said the other day that I thought it against the dignity and honour of India, just to take advantage of England's present difficulty. We are not out to bargain because one does not bargain about one's freedom. We are not out to embarrass at a moment of peculiar difficulty, because that has not been India's way. But we are out to assert and gain our freedom and we cannot give that up because the war situation has developed to England's disadvantage. Our internal policy must be governed by one consideration only—the freedom of India and the attitude of Britain towards that freedom. Any other course would be against the honour and dignity of India.

It must be remembered also, in spite of everything that is happening abroad, there has been no change in British policy in India. Many of our comrades are in prison and they continue to be sent to prison. We are treated as a hostile people and then it is expected that because of fear of consequences we should help in the maintenance of the British Empire. Whatever the consequences, we cannot help an empire to maintain its hold over us.

53.   'Who Can Save India?'

Editorial, *Sunday Amrita Bazar Patrika*, 26 May 1940.

We have seen that Mr Amery's statement in the House of Commons by itself is no solution of the deadlock in India. No party is satisfied with it, and with a few not very notable exceptions public men who have so far expressed an opinion on it are not satisfied. The Nationalist Press is equally dissatisfied. Mr Amery still talks of Dominion Status as the goal of British policy in India. Pandit Jawaharlal Nehru rightly says that 'the Secretary of State for India speaks in a tone which is no doubt meant to be conciliatory but the content of his utterance has no relation to facts in India or Europe'. It is an astonishing failure of the grasp of essentials to talk of the goal of British policy in India or elsewhere, when the very existence of the British Empire is in great peril.

It is for India to take action. The first action that Indian leaders have to take is to meet and discuss matters among themselves with the utmost goodwill and with the determination to end the deadlock. It should be clear to them that it will not do now to depend on the British Government to end our domestic quarrel. When British politicians like Mr Amery can talk in this vein even now, it should be clear to the meanest understanding in what language they are likely to speak after the crisis is over.

Sir Sikandar Hyat Khan has put a certain concrete proposal with a view to end the present deadlock. He suggests that the Premiers and the ex-Premiers of the Congress provinces in addition to representatives of all important interests in the country including the Congress, the Muslim League, the Hindu Mahasabha, the Scheduled classes, the European and Anglo-Indian Associations, the Chamber of Princes and three members to be nominated by the Viceroy, in all 31 persons, should meet with the Viceroy as Chairman in a Conference to hammer out the essentials of a Constitution and the safeguards for minorities. Mr Satyamurti, prior to that, made a similar suggestion. The conference will of course include Mahatma Gandhi and Mr Jinnah.

Sir Sikandar is not dogmatic about the personnel of the conference or the *modus operandi*. He offers his suggestion as a basis for immediate consideration by the leaders. We would however suggest a somewhat different personnel. In our opinion the Viceroy should not be invited now nor the Chamber of Princes. Let the conference be constituted somewhat on the basis of self-determination. The Premiers and ex-Premiers of the Congress Provinces and the representatives of the political parties and interests mentioned by Sir Sikandar should constitute the conference. Instead of the Viceroy presiding it, let Sir Sikandar be the Chairman. Let this conference reach an agreement the maximum agreement possible. It will then be time, if necessary, to approach the Viceroy to give the finishing touches and the Chamber of Princes. Let the representatives of British India, that is, the men who command considerable following in the country first try to reach an agreement.

It was thought even the other day that it might be practicable to elect a Constituent Assembly. But we are afraid the time is not propitious for it. In fact, the feasible solution of today becomes impossible the day after—such are the kaleidoscopic changes in the world situation. A small conference like the one suggested by Sir Sikandar is feasible now. It may not be possible a few days after. But we think it will be generally agreed that the dignity and interest of India require that her people should shake off the present feeling of helplessness and assert themselves. A conference of representative Indians should draw up not in detail for there is no time for it but in outline a Constitution for India, to be presented for acceptance by the British Government. The Constitution may be provisional, and we think it cannot be of a permanent character till a Constituent Assembly elected on the widest suffrage has considered and accepted it with or without modifications.

The Constitution framed by the conference may however be placed for approval before the Provincial and Central Legislatures in the same manner in which the British Parliament endorsed the revolutionary changes proposed by the ministers the other day.

If the Congress approves of this procedure the Congress ministers may return to office immediately, as it is on the mandate of the Congress that they resigned. They may return after the acceptance of the Provisional Constitution by the legislatures. We think however that it would be better if they did so on the acceptance of the conference idea by the Congress.

The time for airing complaints and grievances is gone. It is for the leaders of India to take the initiative and cease to look to the Viceroy or the British Government for assistance to solve the difficulty. There might have been some meaning in looking for that help till the other day. But now the international situation makes it incumbent on every people to devise measures for their own safety. If Mother India is to be saved, she can be saved by her own children.

54.   Mahatma Gandhi's Reply to a Question on Pakistan and Constituent Assembly

Harijan, 29 June 1940; *CWMG,* Vol. LXXII, pp. 200–2.

[...]

Pakistan and Constituent Assembly

Q. The two nations theory is by way of a counterblast to the demand for a Constituent Assembly which is about as absurd as the other thing. To me the idea of a Constituent Assembly ignores the existing conditions. 95 per cent of our people are illiterate, and nearly cent per cent are swayed by religious prejudices; and then there is the additional factor of corruption. And the fatal objection to a Constituent Assembly is that without a genuine desire on the part of the majority to give effect to safeguards the best of these are bound to prove unreal.

A. Surely you cannot speak of the Constituent Assembly side by side with Pakistan. The latter is wrong, as I conceive it, in every way. There is nothing wrong in the idea of a Constituent Assembly. At its worst, dangers surround its formation. Every big experiment is beset with dangers. These risks must be taken. Every effort must be made to minimize them. But there seems to me to be nothing like a Constituent Assembly for achieving the common purpose. I admit the difficulty of illiteracy. Indeed adult suffrage was introduced at the instance of Muslim nationalists including the late Ali brothers. The danger of corruption is also there. The greater the organization the less felt is the effect of corruption because it is so widely distributed. Thus in the Congress there are much corruption and jealousy, but they are confined to those few who run the machinery. But the vast body of Congressmen are untouched by these defects, though they profit by the good the Congress does. The danger you mention about safeguards will be reduced to the vanishing point if they come through a Constituent Assembly. For safeguards laid down by the representatives elected by the adult Muslim population will depend for their safety not on the goodwill or honesty of the majority but on the strength of the awakened Muslim masses. Fatality really attaches to your wrong conception of the majority, not to a Constituent Assembly. There is a majority of Hindus undoubtedly, but we observe that in popular political assemblies parties are not rigidly divided according to religious opinions, but they are according to political and other opinions. The curse of communalism became intensified by the introduction of separate electorates. The cry for partition is the logical outcome, but it is also the strongest condemnation, of separate electorates. When we have learnt wisdom we shall cease to think in terms of separate electorates and two nations. I believe in the innate goodness of human nature. I therefore swear by the Constituent Assembly. The Muslim vote will surely decide the issue so far as their special interest is concerned. Arguing communally, therefore, the fear, if there is any, about a Constituent Assembly, should surely be on the part of the Hindus. For if the Muslim vote goes in favour of partition, they have either to submit not to one but many partitions or to a civil war. As things are, all satisfy themselves by passing resolutions and seeing their names in print. In practice all of us remain where we are in a state of subjection. A Constituent Assembly is a reality. It will not be a debating or legislative irresponsible body. By registering its final decision it will decide the fate of millions of human beings. You may oppose it. If you are successful in your opposition, there is the dread prospect of anarchy, not an orderly civil war. There seems to me to be no solution of the painful deadlock except through a Constituent Assembly.

55. Congress Working Committee's Proposal for Provisional National Government

Resolution on 'Political Situation' Passed at Congress Working Committee Meeting, Delhi, 3–7 July 1940. *Indian Social Reformer*, 13 July 1940; *Indian Annual Register*, 1940, Vol. II, pp. 176–7.

The Working Committee have noted the serious happenings which have called forth fresh appeals to bring about a solution of the deadlock in the Indian political situation; and in view of the desirability of clarifying the Congress position, they have earnestly examined the whole situation once again in the light of the latest developments in world affairs.

The Working Committee are more than ever convinced that the acknowledgement by Great Britain of the complete Independence of India, is the only solution of the problem facing both India and Britain and are, therefore, of opinion that such an unequivocal declaration should be immediately made and that as an immediate step in giving effect to it, a provisional National Government should be constituted at the Centre, which, though formed as a transitory measure should be such as to command the confidence of all the elected elements in the Central Legislature, and secure the closest cooperation of the responsible government in the provinces.

The Working Committee are of opinion that unless the aforesaid declaration is made, and a National Government accordingly formed at the Centre, without delay, all efforts at organizing the material and moral resources of the country for defence cannot in any sense be voluntary or as from a free country, and will therefore, be ineffective. The Working Committee declare that if these measures are adopted it will enable the Congress to throw in its full weight in the efforts for the effective organization of the defence of the country.

56. On Congress Working Committee Resolution

Indian Social Reformer, 13 July 1940.

We publish in another column the resolution passed at its meeting at New Delhi last Sunday by the Working Committee of the Congress after prolonged deliberation. The first and fundamental requirement is that India should be assured of Independence, a declaration to this effect to be made immediately. The second is that, as a first step, a National Government should be installed at the Centre. These two conditions must strike every impartial observer as perfectly reasonable in the present circumstances. The declaration as regards Independence, is reasonable because, without such an assurance, India as a dependency has no *locus standi* in a war whose principal aim is to restore the Independence of Czecho–Slovakia, Poland, Holland, Belgium, Norway, Luxemburg and France, which has been lost owing to German aggression. The only argument against Indian Independence is that India can not defend herself. But the countries whose Independence the War is intended to restore, have proved by their collapse that they too were not able to defend themselves. It may be urged that the War is also intended to destroy Nazism and when that is achieved, these countries will have nothing to fear from Nazi or Fascist aggression. In that case, India too will be safe for the same reason. There can be no aggression without an aggressor. We wrote three weeks ago of the 'distressing dilemma' of the Indian who is called upon to support a war to restore their lost independence to several European countries, while he himself has been crying for it in vain all these years. A declaration of the kind contemplated by the Working Committee's resolution will go far to relieve him of this dilemma. It will also be of great moral advantage to Great Britain which is now open to the charge of proclaiming herself to be the world champion of Independence, while she herself is denying Independence to India. The plea that she is under obligation to certain interests to maintain her dominion over India will be of no avail. If she really believes in Independence as the supreme need of nations, to which everything else should be subordinated, she must act up to the faith which is in her by refusing to violate it in the case of India. Every conflict between precept and practice must straighten itself out before truth can prevail and error be vanquished. Of the two Britain and India, the former will be the greater gainer by such a declaration. The Congress would have stultified itself, after having all these years proclaimed Independence as the goal of India's political aspiration, it had flung away the present opportunity when the loss of Independence by several countries has made it the central issue of our time.

The issue now transcends politics. It is whether there should be one rule for white-skinned races and another for brown and yellow-skinned peoples. Pandit Jawaharlal Nehru's declaration that it would be undignified to start civil disobedience at this time when Britain is engaged single-handed in its fight for the cause of independence, has been applauded in the British Press and in Parliament. But surely it is not to be interpreted as meaning that the Pandit values the dignity of his Party above Independence for his country. We still hold the view which we have repeatedly expressed that closer cooperation and not Independence is the true solution to the Indo–British problem. But this is possible only if there is the will on both sides to work together as equals. It is recognized by many writers that absolute national sovereignty is incompatible with world peace and that, in the future world order, every country should surrender a part of the rights now held inviolable. India, too, will have to do the same, and she will do it cheerfully at the proper time.

The Working Committee has adopted a wise and statesmanly course in not insisting on the convening of a Constituent Assembly as in its former resolutions on constitutional reform. The transitional arrangement which it has proposed is reasonable. It is the constitution immediately of a provisional National Government at the Centre, which should be such as to command the confidence of the elected elements in the Central Legislature, and to secure the closest cooperation of the responsible governments in the provinces. The essentially moderate character of this proposal is obvious. The Working Committee has not asked immediately for responsible Government at the centre. It has asked only for a National Government, which in the conditions of the country can only mean a Government in which minority communities, especially Muslims, have adequate representation. It may consist of nominated as well as elected members. Only it should be such as to enjoy the confidence of elected members of the Central Legislature. Nominated and even official members of the Legislature are not precluded by the resolution. The Communal Award will not be disturbed. There should be no difficulty in adapting the Governor-General's offer to extend his Executive Council by the appointment of additional members, to satisfy the Working Committee's plan for the Provisional National Government. The next condition, namely that the Provisional Government should be such as to secure the closest cooperation of the responsible Governments in the provinces, presents a more difficult problem, if the autonomy of the provinces is to be left intact as under the Act. It would mean that the Central Government can not move hand or foot unless it has secured the previous consent of eleven provincial Governments. If an understanding is reached between the Congress and the Muslim League, the accord of the Provinces can be ensured by nominating some members of the high command of the two organizations to the Central Government. The other minorities the most important of which are Sikhs and Indian Christians may also be similarly accommodated. The Working Committee has not made it clear whether it assumes that the Legislatures, Central and Provincial, should be given an extended term or whether there should be fresh elections. We think that the latter course is to be preferred. The present legislatures were elected under totally different circumstances and may not represent the public mind as it is today. We are sure that the Congress Party and the Muslim League will gladly consent to fresh general elections. The resolution says that, if the measures recommended by it are adopted it will enable the Congress 'to throw in its full weight in the efforts for the effective organization of the defence of the country.' The Government of India has been acting on the hypothesis that the frontiers of India are in Egypt and Malaya and that the defence of India includes the defence of these territories. The Provisional National Government will have to decide whether it can accept this position.

57. Viceroy's Statement on Expanding the Governor-General's Council and Establishing War Advisory Council, 8 August 1940

Speeches by the Marquess of Linlithgow, Vol. II, November 1938–December 1943, Government of India Press, Simla, 1944, Linlithgow Papers, Acc. No. 2329, NAI.

India's anxiety at this moment of critical importance in the world struggle against tyranny and aggression to contribute to the full to the common cause and to the triumph of our common ideals is manifest. She has already made a mighty contribution. She is anxious to make a greater contribution still. His Majesty's Government are deeply concerned that that unity of national purpose in India which would enable her to do so should be achieved at as early a moment as possible. They feel that some further statement of their intentions may help to promote that unity. In that hope they have authorized me to make the present statement.

Last October His Majesty's Government again made it clear that Dominion Status was their objective for India. They added that they were ready to authorize the expansion of the Governor-General's Council to include a certain number of representatives of political parties, and they proposed the establishment of a Consultative Committee. In order to facilitate harmonious cooperation it was obvious that some measure of agreement in the Provinces between the major parties was a desirable pre-requisite to their joint collaboration at the Centre. Such agreement was unfortunately not reached, and in the circumstances no progress was then possible.

During the earlier part of this year I continued my efforts to bring political parties together. In these last few weeks I again entered into conversations with prominent political personages in British India and the Chancellor of the Chamber of Princes, the results of which have been reported to His Majesty's Government. His Majesty's Government have seen also the resolutions passed by the Congress Working Committee, the Muslim League and the Hindu Mahasabha.

It is clear that the earlier differences which had prevented the achievement of national unity remain unbridged. Deeply as His Majesty's Government regret this, they do not feel that they should any longer, because of these differences, postpone the expansion of the Governor-General's Council, and the establishment of a body which will more closely associate Indian public opinion with the conduct of the war by the Central Government. They have authorised me accordingly to invite a certain number of representative Indians to join my Executive Council. They have authorized me further to establish a War Advisory Council, which would meet at regular intervals, and which would contain representatives of the Indian States, and of other interests in the national life of India as a whole.

The conversations which have taken place, and the resolutions of the bodies which I have just mentioned, make it clear however that there is still in certain quarters doubt as to the intentions of His Majesty's Government for the constitutional future of India, and that there is doubt, too, as to whether the position of minorities, whether political or religious, is sufficiently safeguarded in relation to any constitutional change by the assurance already given. There are two main points that have emerged. On those two points His Majesty's Government now desire me to make their position clear.

The first is as to the position of minorities in relation to any future constitutional scheme. It has already been made clear that my declaration of last October does not exclude examination of any part either of the Act of 1935 or of the policy and plans on which it is based. His Majesty's Government's concern that full weight should be given to the views of the minorities in any revision has also been brought out. That remains the position of His Majesty's Government. It goes without saying that they could not contemplate the transfer of their present responsibilities for the peace and welfare of India to any system of Government whose authority is directly denied by large and powerful elements in India's national life. Nor could they be parties to the coercion of such elements into submission to such a government.

The second point of general interest is the machinery for building within the British Commonwealth of Nations a new constitutional scheme when the time comes. There has been very strong insistence that the framing of that scheme should be primarily the responsibility of Indians themselves, and should originate from Indian conceptions of the social, economic and political structure of Indian life. His Majesty's Government are in sympathy with that desire, and wish to see it given the fullest practical expression subject to the due fulfillment of the obligations which Great Britain's long connection with India has imposed upon her and for which His Majesty's Government cannot divest themselves of responsibility. It is clear that a moment when the Commonwealth is engaged in a struggle for existence is not one in which fundamental constitutional issues can be decisively resolved. But His Majesty's Government authorize me to declare that they will most readily assent to the setting up after the conclusion of the war with the least possible delay of a body representative of the principal elements in India's national life in order to devise the framework of the new constitution and they will lend every aid in their power to hasten decisions on all relevant matters to the utmost degree. Meanwhile they will welcome and promote in any way possible every sincere and practical step that may be taken by representative Indians themselves to reach a basis of friendly agreement, firstly, on the form which the post-war representative body should take, and the methods by which it should arrive at its conclusions, and secondly upon the principles and outlines of the constitution itself. They trust however that for the period of the war (with the Central Government reconstituted and strengthened in the manner I have described and with the help of the War Advisory Council) all parties, communities and interests will combine and cooperate in making a notable Indian contribution to the victory of the world cause which is at stake. Moreover, they hope that in this process new bonds of union and understanding will emerge and thus pave the way towards the attainment by India of that free and equal partnership in the British Commonwealth which remains the proclaimed and accepted goal of the Imperial Crown and of the British Parliament.

58. The Constitutional Future of India: Editorial on Viceroy's Statement of 8 August 1940

Indian Social Reformer, Bombay, 10 August 1940.

We publish elsewhere the statement issued by Lord Linlithgow on behalf of His Majesty's government indicating the limits of Britain's readiness to conciliate Indian National sentiment. In accordance with British political traditions, the latest pronouncement is linked up with the previous constitutional offer made last October. There are, however, important modifications in the British position as enunciated by Lord Linlithgow in his present declaration. The three essential points of the October declaration were the reiteration of Dominion Status as the objective, the expansion of the Viceroy's Council and the establishment of a Consultative War Committee, and the right to re-examine any part of the Reforms Act of 1935 when the constitutional position is revised after the war. On two of these points the present declaration indicates marked progress. While those who derive a certain satisfaction from the phrase, 'Dominion Status' might still continue to do so, it is clear from the statement that the objective now declared by His Majesty's Government is the more comprehensive and to our mind more definite, concept of 'free and equal partnership in the British Commonwealth'. His Majesty's Government have been wise in cutting free from the tyranny of a phrase which has little application to Indian conditions. If the present Secretary of State of India does no more for bettering Anglo-Indian relations, he may well be pleased to removing out of all controversy the Dominion Status–Independence wrangle. After the experience of Eire, there is little point in insisting on a 'Dominion Status' which is bound to culminate in Independence. Indian politicians, for their part, would do well to realize that Britain cannot confer Independence on any of her dependencies. At the most she can, by recognizing India as a Dominion, set her on the path to Independence.

If this were the only point at issue in regard to India's status, we would have no hesitation in accepting the Viceregal pronouncement as a satisfactory end to a twenty year controversy. But, though the question of setting up a representative body of Indian opinion to devise the framework of the new constitution is to be taken up with the least possible delay after the War, there is little to show whether this constitution is to be based on the ideas of equality and freedom in the Empire or whether it is entirely unconnected with the objective for the attainment of which no time limit is placed. We are reluctant to raise doubts at a critical time like the present but no good can come out of suppression of fears born of past experience. The construction placed by British politicians on phrases like 'responsible government' after the last war, render caution doubly imperative in assessing British declarations. For our part we fail to see why the discussion of the constitutional position should be deferred till the war ends. If the Governor's regime could carry on for the first eight months of the War and if they can still carry on, what is there to prevent Indian politicians with nothing important on their hands, from conferring on Indian reform in India? The presence, here if the need arises, of British leaders, representative of the mind of the present Government in Britain would bring a double benefit. It will reflect to some extent the revolutionary changes brought about by the replacement of Mr Chamberlain's cabinet and Mr Chamberlain's policies by the Churchill–Labour Coalition. And it will probably increase the Indian response to War appeals. An immediate Conference will have a greater measure of reasonability to work on than a post-war conference.

By leaving out all but the most formal reference to the Hoare's scheme of Reforms, the Viceroy's statement recognizes the complete breakdown of the 1935 Act. By the decision to leave the constitution work to 'a body representative of the principal elements of India's national life', His Majesty's Government repudiates the discredited tactics of the Round Table Conferences held as a preliminary to thrusting an unsatisfactory scheme on India. The second important gain from India's point of view, therefore, is the shaking off of the Hoare incubus after five years of determined opposition. Unfortunately the effect of Britain's sympathy with Indian nationalism is marred by the qualification, 'subject to the due fulfillment of the obligations which Great Britain's long connection with India has imposed upon her.' This unfortunate clause undoes any good effect which the statement as a whole might have had on the country. The Viceroy's communication is primarily a statement calling on Indians to trust Britain's sincerity and honesty of purpose in dealings with India. Yet it shows itself the gravest distrust of Indian leaders when it insists on the need for reserving its own interests from the Indian representatives who are to confer after the War. In short, the British Government is prepared to concede Indian demands so long as it is involved in no sacrifices. The reservation is the more deplorable since neither in peace nor in War has the Congress, the largest and most effectively extreme of Indian parties, ever set out to repudiate Britain's 'obligations'. In fact, Congress Working Committee members have been at great pains to declare that they were perfectly willing to endorse Britain's foreign policy and by taking over the defence commitments of the British Indian Government, to continue without question the military policy of the past administration. Apparently this sign has been lost on the Churchill Government.

59.   Mahatma Gandhi on Viceroy's Statement, 13 August 1940

Harijan, 18 August 1940.

In response to *The News Chronicle's* request Gandhiji has cabled the following statement:

Having retired from participation in Congress politics, I have refrained from expressing opinion on the recent Viceregal pronouncement. But pressure from friends in England and fellow workers here demands response from me. The Viceregal pronouncement is deeply distressing. It widens the gulf between India, as represented by the Congress, and England. Thinking India outside the Congress, too, has not welcomed the pronouncement. The Secretary of State's gloss sooths the ear, but does not dispel suspicion. Neither does the pronouncement take note of the smouldering discontent. My own fear is that democracy is being wrecked. Britain cannot claim to stand for justice, if she fails to be just to India. India's disease is too deep to yield to any make-believe or half-hearted measures.

60.   Sapru's Call for Support to the Viceroy's Offer

Statesman, 13 August 1940.

Dominion Status Compatible with India's Dignity

Sir Tej Bahadur Sapru in a statement on the Viceroy's recent pronouncement on India's constitutional advance hopes that Lord Linlithgow's appeal will meet with a helpful response from the country. The declaration on the whole, he says, opens a new vista, and the large interests of the country and the immediate question of the safety of India's demand that it should meet with public approval.

Referring to the plan for the formation of a War Advisory Council, he says that the Viceroy has provided a wide platform and is justified in the hope that all parties and interests may cooperate in making a notable contribution to the victory of the common cause. Sir Tej Bahadur expressed the opinion that it will be a misfortune if at this juncture consideration of prestige on theoretical discussions are allowed to outweigh practical considerations.

On the question of Dominion Status Sir Tej Bahadur Sapru does not agree that the question is dead or that it is incompatible with the dignity of India.

He says: 'The statement of the Viceroy issued four days ago marks a definite stage in the weary and by no means fruitful process of negotiations and interviews which while they were encouraging to some were equally discouraging to others.

'I also feel that a statement like this if issued say eight months ago might have made a great deal of difference in the situation. Nevertheless it was perhaps necessary that the Viceroy should fortify himself by exploring as wide a field of opinion as he possibly could. The outstanding fact, however, remains, as stated by His Excellency and that dominates the whole situation—that the earlier differences which had prevented the achievement of national unity remained unbridged. It is against this background that the proposals of the Viceroy should be examined.

Basis of Settlement

'For one thing it is clear that the basis of settlement is going to be Dominion Status and not independence. If by independence is meant a complete severance of the political and constitutional ties that have hitherto united India to England then I have at no time thought that it could form the basis of a settlement between India and England.'

Sir Tej Bahadur Sapru says that while he does not wish to attach any exaggerated importance to the phrase 'Dominion Status' as it has no fixed meaning in law, he does not agree that the idea is dead or that the status it connotes is incompatible with the dignity of India or that it will not 'give us the fullest freedom to control our defence or foreign policy or regulate our tariffs or manage our finance or pass our laws generally as do Canada and Australia today.' The fact is that the whole conception of Dominion Status has changed from decade to decade and it is by no means unlikely that as a result of the war, it will still undergo some radical changes.

'Speaking for myself, I maintain that though we might use the expression Dominion Status as a convenient expression for the purpose of discussion, yet our aim ought to be to secure for India a constitutional status and political and legal powers in no way inferior to those of any of the existing self-governing dominions such as Canada and Australia. If the Statute of Westminster is to be changed after the war so as to enlarge the sum total of the powers of other Dominions, I think we should insist that the benefit of those changes will not be limited to Canada and Australia and South Africa but will also be extended to us.'

Expansion of Council

Coming to the positive proposals of the Viceroy especially with regard to the expansion of the Governor General's Council. Sir Tej Bahadur Sapru says, 'I would give this proposal a fair trial though, personally, I think that in actual working the official members who under the law will be constitutionally responsible to the Secretary of State and the non-official members who though equally responsible to the Secretary of State, will look up to their respective bodies for their guidance and support, may find it somewhat difficult to work as a harmonious whole. Personally I should have been glad if a truly national Government could be established at present, but I realize the truth and the force of the Viceroy's statement that differences remain unbridged. A national Government does not mean the Government of any majority party and of those of the other parties who are merely the yes-men of the former. The basis of a national Government in times of emergency in particular, is the sinking of party differences and the readiness to cooperate with each other on vital issues affecting the safety, security and material interests of the country. This basis is lacking at present, and I think that the proposal to expand the Governor-General's Council is the only proposal which was possible under the circumstances.'

Referring to the Congress provinces he suggests that if responsible ministries were out of question a certain number of representative non-officials should be appointed as advisers to the Governors.

Referring to the question of a constituent assembly, Sir Tej Bahadur says: 'Personally I think in the existing circumstances a mere majority vote in determining our constitution for the future is not at all likely to be accepted by large sections of the people. How the Viceroy is to compose the representative body for devising the framework of the new constitution is a matter on which it is necessary for Government to throw light.'

The Time-Limit

Continuing Sir Tej Bahadur Sapru says that some disappointment has been felt and expressed in some quarters that no time-limit has been set for the establishment of the new order. But he says when it is for the body representative of the principal elements in India's national life to devise the framework of the new constitution, the fixing of a time-limit might easily be found to be impracticable.

It will be for us to set the pace and to determine the speed, he added. 'When such a body has been set up our real difficulties—like the problem of the Indian States and their relation with British India, the question of defence and British interests—will begin. We must show by practical conduct that our shoulders are broad enough to bear the burden'.

It is true, he continues, that the War Advisory Council is an advisory one but it may be hoped that its advice will be sought on everything affecting the defence of India and the building up of big industries directly or indirectly related to defence. The Viceroy has invited to this Council representatives of the Indian States also. He has thus provided a broad platform and is justified in the hope that all parties, communities and interests may combine and cooperate in making a notable Indian contribution to the victory of the united cause which is at stake. It would be a misfortune if at this juncture considerations of prestige or loyalty or fine logical distinctions or theoretical discussions or distrust of the British were allowed to outweigh practical considerations.

On the whole, concludes Sir Tej Bahadur, the Viceroy's statement is one which opens a new vista and the larger interest of the country and particularly the immediate question of the safety of the country require that it should meet with a helpful response from the country.

61.   Editorial on Secretary of State Amery's Speech

Tribune, 16 August 1940.

... By far the most important speech in the two debates was, of course, the speech of the Secretary of State[1] and however deeply one may regard that it marked no advance upon either the Viceroy's statement or the Secretary of State's own speech at Blackpool, it must be admitted by all fair-minded persons that it was unexceptionable in tone and temper....

But when the Secretary of State went on to say that the Congress's 'claim to speak for India is utterly denied by very important elements in India's complex national life' and cited the cases of the Muslim community and the scheduled castes in support of his allegation, and, what is more, made this alleged denial of the claims of the Congress by 'very important elements in India's complex national life' the ground of British Government's own unwillingness or inability to accept the Congress demand he fell into two grievous errors. In the first place, he exaggerated the strength and authority of those who deny the claim of the Congress. It was wholly and considerably untrue for instance that the entire Muslim community, constituting a majority in north-western and north-eastern India, but scattered as a minority over the whole sub-continent denied the claim of Congress to speak for India. Mr Amery is new to the India Office, but even that fact can be no excuse for his ignorance of the elementary and universally known fact that there are a large number of Muslims in the Congress, that the present President of the Congress is himself a Muslim leader and theologian with a large following in the country, that in one of the four Muslim majority provinces the Congress actually captured a majority of Muslim seats at the last Provincial elections, with the result that it succeeded in forming a Congress ministry with a Muslim Premier, that in another province with a Muslim majority there was a pro-Congress ministry with a pro-Congress Premier, that in all Congress majority provinces the Congress ministries contained Muslim members, some of these members having defeated their rivals, mostly belonging to the Muslim League, by large majorities, and that only recently a huge conference, representing a large number of Muslim organizations claiming to represent a majority of the Muslim community, was held at Delhi, which definitely supported the Congress demand and unequivocally repudiated the claim of the Muslim League to speak for the Muslim community.

What is true of the Muslim community is substantially true of the scheduled castes as well. It is doubly wrong to say that 'the scheduled castes as a community feel that they stand outside the main Hindu body, which is represented by the Congress.' The scheduled castes have their grievances against the Hindus, but it is wholly untrue that they as a community or the large majority of them feel that they stand outside the main Hindu body. The Poona Pact, as well as the repeated utterances of many Scheduled Caste leaders are a complete refutation of that view. Secondly, the Congress has never claimed to represent the Hindus as a community. The Hindus as a community are represented by the Hindu Mahasabha. The Congress represents members of all communities in India, but it represents them only as Indians, the numerical preponderance of Hindu in the Congress membership being due partly to the fact that the Hindus are an overwhelming majority of the population of India and partly to the fact that owing to a variety of causes, including their educational advancement, they as a community were the first to imbibe the spirit of nationalism.

The other mistake made by Mr Amery consists in his ignoring the fact that in putting forward its demand the Congress has asked for nothing for itself. It has, in fact, effaced itself completely. All that it has demanded is that the people of India as whole should have the right to complete independence which is claimed by every self-governing Dominion in the Commonwealth as well as by Britain herself. The constitution for a free India, according to the Congress demand, is to be framed not by the Congress itself or its nominees, but by a Constituent Assembly elected by the people of India as a whole on the basis of adult franchise or as near an approach to it as may be found practicable. To oppose this demand is not to deny the right of the Congress to speak for India, but to show one's complete distrust either of one's own representative character or of India's common nationality and the democratic principle. It is open to Mr Jinnah, who has publicly propounded the two-nation theory and denied the applicability of democratic principles to India, to declare himself against the Congress demand. But it is utterly incomprehensible to us how any British statesman, who proclaims himself an advocate of Dominion Status for India, can reject the Congress demand because Mr Jinnah is against it. If Mr Jinnah's opposition is to be the governing factor in the matter then not only the Congress demand for complete independence, but the British Government's own decision to confer Dominion Status on India must fall to the ground, for you cannot build a Dominion India on any other basis except that of democracy and of the recognition of India's common nationality. We have made no secret of our belief that Mr Jinnah does not represent more than a small fraction of his community. But if Mr Amery and the Government he represents believe otherwise, and if their acknowledgement of India's right to frame her own constitution is contingent on Mr Jinnah's support, then it will be franker and more straightforward on their part to declare publicly that it is impossible for India ever to attain Dominion Status and that she shall never attain it. To declare Dominion Status for India to be the immediate objective of British policy and at the same time to say that India shall have no constitution, whether of the Dominion or any other pattern, which does not command the support of Mr Jinnah, who has publicly and repeatedly rejected both the idea of India's common nationality and the idea of applying democratic principles to India, is manifestly a contradiction in terms.

---

[1] L.S. Amery's speech on 14 August 1940 in the House of Commons.

62.   Dr B.R. Ambedkar Conveys Willingness to Serve on the Viceroy's Executive Council, 18 August 1940

Dr B.R. Ambedkar's Letter to Viceroy, No. 123, Correspondence with Persons in India, 1940, Linlithgow Papers, Acc. No. 2307, NAI.

I am deeply grateful for the offer of a place in the Viceroy's Executive Council made to me by Your Lordship when I met Your Lordship in Bombay on the 13th instant.

I had then asked for a week's time to consider the offer and Your Lordship had been pleased to grant the same. I have thought over the matter and am now in a position to say that I am prepared to accept Your Lordship's kind offer.

63.   Savarkar's Letter to Viceroy on Hindu Mahasabha's Policy of Responsive Co-operation, 19 August 1940

No. 125, Viceroy's Correspondence with Persons in India, 1940, Linlithgow Papers, Acc. No. 2307, NAI.

May it please Your Excellency,

I extremely regret that I should have been unable to interview Your Excellency a third time as you had proposed to do on the 20th instant. But the sciatic pains in my legs and the consequent exhaustion have confined me strictly to my bed down to this day. Hence all I can do is to write to Your Excellency this letter as short as possible only touching the leading points. As soon as I am better, I hope that Your Excellency will make it convenient to hold the postponed interview wherein I may discuss a number of details which, however important, will render this letter too bulky and taxing my health if I touch them all here.

I. The deputation sent by the Nagpur Working Committee of the Hindu Mahasabha to acquaint me their decisions, saw me. They had kindly permitted me to take final decision in my own discretion after going through all their diverse instructions and views.

II. The millions and millions of Hindu Sanghatanists throughout the land have appreciated the recognition on the part of the Government of the fact that the Hindu Mahasabha represented the interests peculiar to Hindus as Hindus and the Congress represented but the Congressites. This recognition was brought out in Your Excellency's speech beyond cavil or criticism. Although you must have noted that Mr Amery has not as yet forgotten the old category summing up Indian World 'as the Congress and the Muslim League' more out of routine than intention. Your Excellency will kindly impress upon Mr Amery's attention that it is the Hindu Mahasabha now, that represents the special interests of the Hindus in India and the Congress has definitely forfeited its claim to do that.

III. The extension of the Advisory Council is looked upon by the Hindu Mahasabha as a step in the right direction taken together as the Government's promise to grant the Dominion Status immediately after the War. In accordance with the sound policy of the Hindu Mahasabha of responsive co-operation, of occupying every point of vantage with a view to march on further or at any rate to stop the vantage points from being abused in the hands of inepts or anti-Hindus, the Hindu Mahasabha has decided to participate in and utilize every war effort on the part of the Government which is genuinely calculated to contribute to Indian Defence and to further on, in the long run, Hindu interests.

IV. Consequently the Hindu Mahasabha will send those gentlemen to work on the extended Executive Council as Your Excellency will be pleased to select out of the panel I have already forwarded to Your Excellency in one of my letters.

Nevertheless to refresh Your Excellency's memory and also to add one important name I reproduce the panel below:

1. Dr B.S. Moonje, Vice-President of the Hindu Mahasabha.
2. Dr Shyama Prasad Mookerji, ex-Vice-Chancellor, Calcutta University; Vice-President, Bengal Provincial Hindu Sabha, Calcutta.
3. Sir Manmath Nath Mookerji, ex-Law Member to Government of India; President, Bengal Provincial Hindu Sabha, Calcutta.
4. Mr Jamnadas Mehta, BAR-AT-LAW, ex-Minister, Bombay.
5. Mr B.G. Khaparde, BA, LLB, MLA, ex-Minister; President, Berar Provincial Hindu Sabha, Amraoti (Berar).
6. Mr L.B. Bhopatkar, MA, LLB, ex-leader of the Legislative House, Vice-President, Hindu Mahasabha.
7. Sir Jwala Prasad Shrivastav, MLA, ex-Minister, President, Hindu Sanghatan Committee, Cawnpore.

If Your Excellency wishes to add to or substitute any names of any of these prominent Hindu Sabhaits you will kindly wire to me to that effect. The Hindu Mahasabhaits as a body are all of one mind in participating in the extended Council. I shall accept any two or three names which Your Excellency selects out of this panel or proposes any one in addition to this.

I assure that it will be our honest endeavour to render to the extended Council every possible patriotic help so that it may pave the way to an united Indian front in the Dominion Status to come.

I hope you will let me know, telegraphically if necessary, the names you select or any new names you propose from Mahasabha platform in advance of the final announcement.

Any name of the Hindu Mahasabhait representative, of course Your Excellency will please note, should have a formal acceptance on my part as the President of the Hindu Mahasabha. I do not mind whom you select from other parties.

V. So far as Your Excellency's proposal regarding the War Committee is concerned, it is also fully appreciated by me and the Mahasabha has decided to participate in it, as whole-heartedly as possible, to render the question of Indian Military Defence effective.

I suggest that those prominent Hindu Sabhaits who have already joined the War Committees in different Provinces should form the panel. For example—

1. Sir Jwala Prasad Shrivastav, MLA, Cawnpore.
2. Mr Hari Ram Sheti, BA, LLB, Taluqdar, Secretary, Hindu Sanghatan Committee, Unao, Lucknow.
3. Mr B.G. Khaparde, MLA, Amraoti (Berar).
4. Mr S.R. Kanitkar, BA, LLB, Buldhana (Berar).
5. Rao Bahadur S.R. Bole, JP, President, Bombay Provincial Hindu Sabha, Dadar Bombay–14.
6. Dr P. Varadarajulu Naidu, President, Tamil Nadu Provincial Hindu Sabha, Madras.
7. Mr Jamnadas Mehta, BAR-AT-LAW, MLA, Bombay.

And such others who are already on the War Committees should be taken up as first choice in the Central War Committee. Of course Dr B.S. Moonje's choice on War Committee would please all Hindu Mahasabhaits and make them feel that their cause lies in safe hands. Mr Nirmal Chandra Chatterji, BAR-AT-LAW, General Secretary, Bengal Provincial Hindu Sabha, Calcutta will also be powerful addition.

Anyhow on the Central War Committee Your Excellency should have some of these gentlemen so that the Committee may have the moral support of the Hindu Mahasabha party as such.

Your Excellency will of course let me know beforehand, telegraphically if necessary, whom you select.

Please note that any gentleman who is taken up on the War Committee should not form a Member of the extended Executive Council too. But some other names out of the panel provided for that in paragraph IV should be substituted in his place in the extended Executive Council.

VI. So far as the promise of granting Dominion Status is concerned, I for one am satisfied— and am going to issue a public statement to that effect—that the phrases used by Your Excellency and by Mr Amery are as convincing as any other sentences could have been. To me it is not now the question of the clarity of words. It is now only a question of sincerity with which the words are carried into effect and that could only be judged by the result. The beginning is well-made. I hope the end will not falsify the hopes.

VII. So far as the question regarding reference of minorities is concerned, it is a pity that the Government should have deliberately chosen terms too alarming to the Hindus in particular. Your Excellency will remember that the cause of the minorities which the Government and especially Mr Amery seem to have espoused with such rhodomontades of the type of the Knights of old imply and cannot but imply the cause of the Hindu minorities in Punjab, Bengal and Sind too and I sincerely hope that if but an honest defence is extended to those minorities which are really minorities which are in danger at the hands of fanatical majorities, the announcement regarding the minorities will have more cause to disillusion the Muslim Pakisthanis whom the Government seems to please too much than anybody else. But I leave the discussion for the future and only note in this short letter that any attempt to cut at the root the indivisibility of India as a political unit from Indus to the Seas and with a strong Central Government, to maintain it cannot fail to evoke an undying opposition from Hindudom as a whole. The Muslims or the Government have not now to count with the colourless Congressites or their Pseudo-Nationalistic innuendos but with the organic racial forces of genuine Hindudom for whom India, this Hindusthan, constitutes not only an indivisible Father Land but as Indivisible Holy Land too.

VIII. You will kindly note some of the following day-to-day points too:
   (a) In Bengal the Huq Government should be asked to stay the introduction of the three anti Hindu bills, at least during the war time, to avoid any unnecessary communal upheaval which may weaken our united efforts towards Indian defence.
   (b) In Sind Governor should be called upon to take up the Administration in his own hands as the Government has proved absolutely incapable to prevent anarchy.
   Just think, if life and property of Europeans had been victimized purposely in so many riots, broad day murders, etc., in Sind, would the Government have watched with folded hands that kind of anarchy which is now threatening Hindu life and property in that Province?

IX. In the end I thank your Excellency for the shipyard, the aero-plane factories, the increased out put of up-to-date ammunitions, the increase in the recruitment in the Military, Naval and Aerial to which Indians are allowed without any distinction of religion or Caste.
   The beginning is well made, though halting. But I hope everything will be put right as the Central War Committee sits shaping day-by-day on straightening and intensifying these war efforts.

I beg to remain,
Your Excellency's most obedient servant,
V.D. Savarkar

64. A Word to Hindu Mahasabha: S. Satyamurti

Tribune, 19 August 1940.

[...]

Concession to Jinnah's Intransigence

What ought to alarm the Hindu Mahasabha and made them distrust the Viceroy's statement that the British Government can be no party to imposing any constitution on India which large and powerful elements in India's national life are opposed, nor could they be parties to the coercion of such elements into submission to such Government. This is really a concession to Mr Jinnah's intransigence. It means that the constitution for India as a whole will be determined, not by the people of India, nor even by the British Parliament, but by vocal and powerful minorities, however small in numbers they may be. Far from tyranny of the minority by the majority, as they have been complaining, this is frankly tyranny of the majority by the minority. Do the Hindu Mahasabha agree to that? I want them to read, ponder and inwardly digest these ominous words in the Viceroy's statement.

The Viceroy's statement runs as follows:

'It goes without saying that they would not contemplate the transfer of their present responsibilities, for the peace and welfare of India, to any system of government whose authority is directly denied by large and powerful elements in India's national life. Nor could they be parties to the coercion of such elements into submission to such Government'. This gives the go-by to all conceptions of democracy and the Hindu Mahasabha will stand to gain nothing, even from their own point of view, let alone the point of view India as a whole, by accepting the implications of the statement which they will do, if they accept the Viceroy's offer in whole or in part.

What is Worrying Mr Jinnah?

I see the President of the Hindu Mahasabha, Mr Savarkar is authorized to seek clarification on this point, first and foremost. Is India's future constitution to be decided by the people of India in consultation, of course, with the representatives of all minorities, both Muslims and Hindus elected by separate electorates if necessary, and deciding their own safeguards for religious and cultural rights, but accepting the principle of democratic Government, that is government of the majority representatives of the electorates of the country? If the British Government can give no guarantee on that basis, the Hindu Mahasabha will be betraying the Hindu cause, let alone the Indian cause, in submitting to the Viceroy's statement.

Another matter which I should like the Hindu Mahasabha to consider most carefully is another point in the Viceroy's statement: 'The conversations which have taken place and the resolution of the bodies which I have just mentioned, make it clear, however, that there is still in certain quarters doubt as to whether the position of minorities, whether political or religious, is sufficiently safeguarded in relation to any constitutional change by the assurance already given.' For the first time, His Majesty's Government contemplates safeguards for political minorities. That is the end of all democracy in this country. Does the Hindu Mahasabha accept this? I do hope, therefore, that the Hindu Mahasabha in spite of its resentment against what it considers the neutral attitude of the Indian National Congress towards the communal award will not agree to cut nose to spite the face. Nothing is to be gained by sitting in the Viceroy's Executive Council by the Hindu Mahasabha, while the Muslim League is there with its avowed object of dividing India on the basis of Pakistan which it continues to reiterate, *now bloated* because of the surrender of the British Government to this intransigent minority. By all means, let Hindus have proper safeguards wherever they are in a minority. Let them also fight for a democratic constitution for India. But let them not make the path of even Muslims more difficult by accepting this impossible demand which cuts at the root of democracy.

Let me conclude this article by saying what is worrying Mr Jinnah and equally the British Government now is the fact that the Hindus are in majority in this country as a whole. Who can help it? Certainly the Indian National Congress does not want a Hindu or Muslim Government in this country. As it is, the Hindu Mahasabha does not. We all want democratic Government. The real solution for this is the substitution of joint electorates for separate electorates. That must come. Without this democracy is impossible. We must all work for that. But if we evolve any system of Government now based on separate electorates and based on impossible concessions to intransigent minorities, the Hindu Mahasabha will not bring that day nearer. I do hope this point will be considered most carefully and the Hindu Mahasabha will decide to reject the Viceroy's offer pending on a settlement on a broad democratic future for India and the establishment of a truly National Government at the Centre.

65.   Congress Working Committee Resolution on 'Viceregal Declaration', Wardha, 18–22 August 1940

Hindustan Times, 23 August 1940; *Indian Annual Register,* 1940, Vol. II, pp. 196–7.

The Working Committee have read the statement issued by the Viceroy on the authority of the British Government on the 8th of August and the report of the speech of the Secretary of State for India in the House of Commons explaining the Viceroy's statement. They note with deep regret that the British Government have rejected the friendly offer and practical suggestion contained in the Poona resolution of the AICC on 28th July framed for a solution of the deadlock and to enable the Indian National Congress to withdraw its non-cooperation and to secure in the present crisis the patriotic cooperation of all the people of India in the governance of India and the organization of national defence.

The Working Committee have read with deep pain and indignation the declarations and assumptions contained in the statements and speeches made on behalf of the British Government which seek to deny India her natural right of complete national freedom and reiterate the untenable claim that Britain should maintain herself in a dominant position in India in the discharge of the higher functions of the State. These claims render false and empty even their own promise to recognize India at an early date, as a free and equal unit in the British Commonwealth. Such claims and recent events and developments in the world have confirmed the Committee's conviction that India cannot function within the orbit of an imperial power and must attain the status of a free and independent nation. This does not prevent close association with other countries within a comity of free nations for the peace of the world.

The Working Committee are of opinion that the assertion contained in the statements made on behalf of the British Government that they will not part with power and responsibility in favour of the elected representatives the people of India, and that therefore, the present autocratic and irresponsible system of government must continue so long as any group of people or the Princes, as distinguished from the people of the States or perhaps even foreign vested interests [raised] objections to any constitution framed by the elected representatives of the people of India, is a direct encouragement and incitement to civil discord and strife, and amounts to a fatal blow to all willingness to compromise and adjustment of claims.

The Committee regret that although the Congress has never thought in terms of coercing any minority, much less of asking the British Government to do so, the demand for a settlement of the constitution through a Constituent Assembly of duly elected representatives has been misrepresented as coercion and the issue of minorities has been made into an insuperable barrier to India's progress. The Congress has proposed that minority rights should be amply protected by agreement with elected representatives of the minorities concerned. The Working Committee therefore cannot but conclude that the attitude and assertions contained in these statements made on behalf of the British Government confirm the prevailing feeling that the

British authority has been continually operating so as to create, maintain and aggravate differences in India's national life.

The Working Committee note with astonishment that the demand for the constitution of a Provisional National Government composed of persons commanding the confidence of the various elected groups in the present Central Legislature, formed under the 1919 Constitution of India has been described by the Secretary of State for India as one that would raise the unsolved constitutional issue and prejudge it in favour of the majority and against the minorities. The Working Committee are of opinion that the rejection of this proposal unmistakably indicates that there is no willingness on the part of the British Government to part with any power and authority even for the immediate purpose of securing cooperation in war efforts. The British Government would gather together and carry on with such dissentient groups and individuals as oppose the wishes of the majority of the people of India and without any coordination with elected legislatures at the Centre or in the Provinces, rather than concede anything that would work towards the recognition of the rights of the people of India to rule themselves democratically.

For these reasons the Working Committee have come to the conclusion that the statements referred to are wholly opposed not only to the principle of democracy as acclaimed by the British Government in the War, but also to the best interests of India, and they cannot be a party to accepting the proposals contained in the statements or advising the country to accept them. The Working Committee consider that these declarations and offers not only fall far short of the Congress demand but would be impediments to the evolution of a free and united India.

The Working Committee will call upon the people to condemn the attitude adopted by the British Government by means of public meetings and otherwise, as also through their elected representatives in the provincial legislatures.

66. Viceroy's Telegram to Secretary of State on Savarkar's Letter, 24 August 1940

No. 309, Telegraphic Correspondence between Viceroy and Secretary of State, Linlithgow Papers, Acc. No. 2162, NAI.

No. 1669–S. Constitutional position. I have now received Mahasabha reply. They are prepared to cooperate and make no embarrassing demands, though Savarkar's letter makes it clear that there are a number of issues on which they are not wholly satisfied. Savarkar adds that so far as the promise of granting Dominion Status is concerned, 'I for one am satisfied, and am going to issue a public statement to that effect, that the phrases used by Your Excellency and Mr Amery are as convincing as any other sentences could have been. To me it is not now the question of the clarity of words. It is now only a question of sincerity with which the words are carried into effect, and that could only be judged by the result. The beginning is well made. I hope the end will not falsify the hopes.'

His letter suggests that the Mahasabha may hope for two or three seats in my Council. That is of course out of the question. But I do not propose to argue the point with Savarkar, and will in due course and after consultation with you let him know the name of individual we contemplate for the Executive Council and the names (probably two, I think) to be selected for the War Advisory Council.

67. Muslim League Welcomes Statements of Viceroy and Secretary of State: Resolution Passed by Muslim League Working Committee, Bombay, 31 August–2 September 1940

Hindustan Times, 3 September 1940; *Indian Annual Register,* 1940, Vol. II, pp. 243–4.

1. Viceroy's Declaration

The Working Committee of the All India Muslim League have given their most earnest and careful consideration to the statement issued by His Excellency the Viceroy on the 8th of August, 1940, and the authoritative amplification and clarification of it by Mr Amery, the Secretary of State for India, on behalf of His Majesty's Government in the course of the India debate in the House of Commons on the 14th of August 1940. The committee consider that these pronouncements constitute a considerable progressive advance towards the approach of the point of view and the position taken up by the All-India Muslim League on behalf of the Muslim India regarding the problem of the future constitution of India, and the committee also note with satisfaction that His Majesty's Government have, on the whole, practically met the demand of the Muslim League for a clear assurance to the effect that no future constitution, interim or final, should be adopted by the British Government without their approval and consent.

2. Unity of National Life

The Working Committee place on record that some of the observations made in the statement of His Excellency the Viceroy and also in the speech of the Secretary of State for India, with regard to the theory of unity of national life which does not exist are historically inaccurate and self-contradictory. Such observations are calculated to raise apprehensions in the minds of the Mussalmans of India, and therefore, the committee deem it necessary to reaffirm and make the position clear once more that the committee stand by the Lahore resolution and the basic principles underlying the terms thereof, proposing the division of India and the creation of independent states in the north-western and eastern zones of India where the Muslims are in a majority, and the committee declare their determination, firm resolve and faith that the partition of India is the only solution of the most difficult and complex problem of India's future constitution and are glad to state that the vital importance and the true aspect of this question are being fully realized by the British Parliament; and that His Majesty's Government are now fully appraised and seized of the realities of the situation.

The Muslim League again makes its position clear that the Muslims of India are a nation by themselves and will exercise their right to self-determination and that they alone are the final judges and arbiters of their own future destiny.

3. Viceroy's Executive Council

The Working Committee appreciate that His Majesty's Government have conceded the principle urged upon them by the Muslim League that in order to secure genuine and full support of Muslim India and such other parties as are and have been ready and willing to undertake the responsibility and are prepared to make every contribution to the intensification of the war efforts and for the defence of India with a view to meet any external danger or aggression and to maintain internal security and peace they should forthwith associate the representatives of the Muslim League with authority and power as partners in the central and provincial Governments and establish a War Council which will include the Indian princes and thus secure their cooperation also.

The committee, therefore, are glad that His Majesty's Government provisionally and during the prosecution of the war have decided upon the expansion of the Executive Council of the Governor General and the establishment of a War Advisory Council on an all-India basis, although they regret that His Majesty's Government have declared that they at this stage do not contemplate non-official advisors in the provinces which are at present administered by the Governors under section 93 of the Government of India Act. The committee, however, find that the specific offer now made as embodied in the letter of the Viceroy dated August 14 purporting to give effect and implement that principle of cooperation with authority in Government as partners is most unsatisfactory and does not meet the requirements nor the spirit indicated in the resolution of this committee of June 16 which was communicated by the President to the Viceroy by his letter of that date nor does it meet the memorandum that was submitted to his Excellency by the president on July 1.

In these circumstances the committee find it very difficult to deal with this offer for the following reasons: (1) Neither the President nor the committee were consulted as to the number of the proposed increase of additional members of the Executive Council of the Governor-General, (2) The committee are not yet aware of the manner in which the entire Executive Council will be reconstituted, (3) The committee have no information as to which are the other parties with whom the Muslim League will be called upon to work, (4) The committee understand that the President has not been informed as to what portfolios will be assigned to everyone of these additional members. The committee are merely asked without any further knowledge or information, except that the total number of members of the expanded Executive Council will be in the neighbourhood of 11, to send a panel of four out of which two will be selected for appointment as members of the Governor-General's Executive Council. (5) The committee have considered the system of panel suggested and they are of the opinion that it is open to many objections, is not desirable and does not commend itself to them. (6) As regards the proposed War Advisory Council the committee do not know its constitution, composition and functions beyond the information that it will probably consist of about 20 members and the committee are asked to submit a panel out of which four will be nominated by the Viceroy. In these circumstances the committee consider the offer unsatisfactory and request the Viceroy to reconsider the matter and hereby authorize the president to seek further information and clarification....

6. Association with War Committees

The resolution of the working committee at Bombay on June 16, 1940, requesting the Mussalmans generally and in particular the members of the Muslim League not to serve on the war committees and to await further instructions from the president pending the result of the negotiations with the Viceroy was not a decision that adopted the policy of non-cooperation with the Government as has wrongly been represented by the enemies of the Muslim League but on the contrary was intended to urge upon the Government a line of action and policy which they should adopt to secure more effective cooperation in the prosecution of the war. Two very vital points were raised for which the committee have been pressing the Government, namely, (1) that no constitution either interim or final would be adopted by His Majesty's Government without the approval and consent of Muslim India and (2) that in order to secure the wholehearted support of the Mussalmans, it was imperative that within the framework of the present constitution Muslim India leadership should be associated as a partner in the realm of the central and provincial Governments forthwith.

As a result of the negotiations the working committee are glad to state that the first point has now been practically met by the statement of his Excellency the Viceroy of August 8, 1940, and the amplification and clarification of that statement by Mr Amery, the Secretary of State for India, in the course of his speech on August 14, 1940, in Parliament, and the committee note with satisfaction that the Government have accepted the principle of the second point that was urged upon them, namely 'cooperation with authority and power' in the Governments in order to prosecute the war successfully.

In view of these circumstances the working committee leave those Mussalmans who think that they can serve any useful purpose by merely associating themselves with the war committee free to do so.

The committee are of opinion that the Government should, in fact and not merely in principle, take without delay the Muslim leadership into their complete confidence and associate them as equal partners in charge of the reins of the Government in the centre and in the provinces in order to secure a genuine and wholehearted cooperation of Muslim India in the prosecution of the war successfully.

68. Dr Ambedkar to Join Viceroy's Cabinet if Invited

Bombay Chronicle, 4 September 1940.

Mr D.V. Pradhan, the General Secretary of the Independent Labour Party, has issued the following statement to the press:

A meeting of the Executive Committee of the Party was held on Sunday. Dr B.R. Ambedkar presided.

After having discussed the preliminary matters, the President acquainted the Committee of his interviews with the Viceroy both at Delhi and in Bombay and also with the correspondence that has passed between him and the Viceroy.

The Committee discussed at length the matter from various points of view and decided that the Party should give unconditional support to Britain and also desired that Dr Ambedkar should accept a seat on the Expanded Executive Council if such an offer came from the Viceroy.

Report on Pakistan Scheme

The Committee further discussed the report of the Special Committee appointed in June last to make a critical and detailed study of Pakistan scheme adumbrated by the Muslim League. The Executive Committee agreed in general on the various points on the report of the Special Committee, and decided to publish the same as a publication of Independent Labour Party Research Bureau.

Constitution Sub-Committee

The Executive Committee further discussed the constitutional question and decided to appoint a Sub-Committee of the Party to study and report on that question in all its aspects and prepare a constitution for the country with particular reference to safeguarding the rights and privileges of the Depressed Classes. The report is intended to be a basis for formulating an All India scheme, after ascertaining the views of the Depressed Classes all over the country. The Sub-Committee is also empowered to take into consideration the rights and privileges of all other minorities in general and others' interests.

69.   Hindu Mahasabha Revises its Position
Hindu Mahasabha Working Committee's Resolution, Nagpur, 21–23 September 1940

Indian Annual Register, 1940, Vol. II, pp. 266–8.

'The Hindu Mahasabha urges that the Governor General should not commit himself to any distribution of portfolios before the expanded Executive Council is constituted. This committee further urges that the distribution of portfolios when made should be made on an equitable basis with due regard to the importance and interest of the Hindus'.

'(1) In view of the attitude taken up by the Muslim League and the altered political situation brought about thereby, the committee requests the president without meaning any disagreement about the personnel of the panel, to withdraw the panel that has been submitted by him to his Excellency the Viceroy on behalf of the Hindu Mahasabha in deference to the wishes of the Viceroy.

(2) The Hindu Mahasabha urges that a sub-committee of the expanded Executive Council be formed, with the Viceroy and Governor-General, as chairman, to be in charge of the Defence portfolio and that the Hindus should be given adequate representation on the sub-committee.'

Mahasabha's Political Demands

'Resolved that the statement made recently by H.E. the Viceroy and the Secretary of State for India are highly unsatisfactory and disappointing, in that they make no reference to India's right to independence which has been declared to be the goal of Hindu Mahasabha; reference made to the grant of dominion status as an immediate step in constitutional advance is vague and uncertain. The Hindu Mahasabha claims dominion status of the Westminster type within a definite time limit not exceeding a year after the war.

'That the statement made to the effect that the British Government will not agree to hand over the Indian administration to a system of Government which will not be acceptable to large and powerful elements of Indian life, requires clarification as it is capable of the interpretation that if the Muslim League, the princes or the other vested interests oppose the recognition of the legitimate rights of the majority in India, the further constitutional advance will be held up or the rights of the majority will be surrendered to them which will mean the negation of the principle of democracy and incitement to minorities to obstruct and revolt.

'The temporary expedience suggested, namely, the expansion of the central Executive Council and the institution of the War Advisory Council will succeed only if a convention grows that the Viceroy will act as the constitutional head of the administration and all real power and responsibility is granted to these bodies.

'The Hindu Mahasabha notes with regret and disappointment that the British Government even at this crisis should not be prepared to give up its old imperialistic policy and states that its latest proposal is hardly of a nature to satisfy the demands of the Indian people. In the Mahasabha's opinion a great opportunity has been lost by the Government. The Hindu Mahasabha makes it clear to the people of India and particularly to the Hindus that in all its actions and activities it will be guided by a policy, whereby the Hindu interests will be furthered and no elements will be permitted to dominate the public life of India to the detriment of Hindu interests. The Hindu Mahasabha is determined to fight every inch of ground both inside and outside the Government to achieve the above object. The Hindu Mahasabha will accept any reasonable and honourable offer made by the Government, only if it will stimulate and advance the Hindu cause and prevent any encroachment being made on the rights of the Hindus by the reactionary elements in the country, and this acceptance of the offer will not be considered to constitute a bar to the Hindu Mahasabha carrying on the agitation for further advancement of the Hindu cause and interest.

'The Hindu Mahasabha hereby calls upon all Hindus to support the Hindu Mahasabha by joining it in large numbers and otherwise supporting it in the policy stated above, to organize themselves with all speed and offensiveness and to be prepared for the struggle, if necessary.'

70. Muslim League Rejects Viceroy's Offer of 25 September 1940

Text of Muslim League Working Committee Resolution, 28 September 1940. *Indian Annual Register*, 1940, Vol. II, p. 246.

The Working Committee of the All-India Moslem League at their meeting at Bombay on September 2 last, after considering the letter of His Excellency the Viceroy, dated August 14 last and addressed to the President, containing, a specific offer in regard to the proposed expansion of the Governor-General's Executive Council and the establishment of a War Advisory Council, requested His Excellency to reconsider the matter and authorized the President to seek further information and clarification, particularly on the points set out in the resolutions, before the committee could deal with the offer.

As a result of the communication of these resolutions to the Viceroy, His Excellency invited the President to meet him on September 24, and after a full and free discussion of the points arising out of those resolutions, His Excellency was pleased to send a formal reply, dated September 25. After giving their most earnest and careful consideration to the whole matter, the Committee, notwithstanding their desire from the very beginning to help in the prosecution of the war and the defence of India, regret that they are unable to accept the present offer for the following reasons:

That the inclusion of only two representatives of the Moslem League in the proposed expansion of the Governor-General's Executive Council of which neither the total strength nor the number of additional members has so far been definitely determined does not give any real and substantial share in the authority of the Government at the Centre;

That no indication has been given as to what would be the position of the Moslem League representation in the event of any other party deciding at a latter stage to assist in the prosecution of the war and the Government agreeing to associate it with the Executive Council—a situation which might involve a substantial modification and re-shuffling of the executive;

That, so far, the Government do not propose to appoint non-official advisors in those provinces which are being administered by the Governors under section 93 of the Government of India Act, 1935. The Committee feel that without the association of the Moslem League representatives in the administration of those provinces, it would not be possible to secure real and effective cooperation of the Mussalmans;

That the proposed War Advisory Council is yet in its embryo form and no information is available as to its constitution, composition and functions, except that it will be considered after the expansion of the Executive Council is complete; and

That out of the various points raised in the resolution of the Committee of September 2, only one relating to a panel, has been satisfactorily met.

71. 'Stalemate in Indian Politics'

Editorial, *Indian Social Reformer*, Bombay, 10 October 1940.

On Sunday the Muslim League decided that the Viceroy's offer of August 8 had failed to satisfy Muslim opinion, and therefore, left the League no option but to refuse the seats offered to its representatives on the Viceroy's expanded Council and on the Advisory War Council. Mr M.A. Jinnah the League President has made public the correspondence which he had exchanged with Lord Linlithgow with a view to clarifying the Government position. In a further statement explaining the League position, Mr Jinnah declared that the Muslim League had to reject the offer because the British Government appear to have no intention to part with power. In making the present offer, they are trifling with ninety millions of Muslims who are a nation. The long drawn out negotiations which the Viceroy has been carrying on with various parties lead only to one conclusion, namely, that the British still wish to continue the relationship of master and servants. We will not submit to this position.

In one of his letters to Lord Linlithgow, Mr Jinnah struck an ever sharper note. He told his Excellency.

> We are constrained to state that Your Excellency is unnecessarily over-anxious about the interests of other communities. It has never been our desire unjustly to harm any community. The issues that have been raised by us are due to apprehensions that the British Government may be stampeded by other powerful organizations in the country into adopting a course or agreeing to a settlement in the matter of India's constitution which may prove not only highly detrimental to the interest of the Mussalmans but may be disastrous for them.

The very language of this paragraph reveals that Mr Jinnah has been adroitly drawn by the Viceroy on to dangerous ground and that he is conscious of the pitfalls lurking there for the Muslim League. If the British have seemed to champion the Muslim cause as against the nationalist standpoint, they have no intention of admitting the Muslim League into partnership with them in wielding authority in India. In refusing the Muslim League demand, the Viceroy reminds Mr Jinnah that there are 'parties other than either the Congress or the Muslim League'.

Mr Jinnah's assertion that the British wish to continue the relationship of master and servant, bears all the appearance of a discovery. But surely he must have gathered from the various statements of the Viceroy and of the Secretary of State for India that there was to be no change in the political position till after the war. Then again, his declaration that 'we will not submit to it', seems to display a warmth completely unwarranted by the admission that it is merely a 'continuation' of a relationship to which the Muslim League has submitted in the past, is submitting at present and proposes to continue submitting for the duration of the war. For though the Muslim League will not send representatives to serve on the two Councils, yet members of the League will be free to cooperate in Britain's war effort. Mr Jinnah concedes equality with the League to the Congress in his letters to Lord Linlithgow. He demands equal representation for the Muslims with the Hindus if the Congress accepts seats on the Viceroy's Council and on the Advisory War Council, majority representation if the Congress non-cooperates. What if the Congress nominated a majority of non-Hindus to the Councils? No more successful than his attempt at constructing Executive Councils, has been Mr Jinnah's endeavour to present Pakistan as the 'universal faith of Muslim India'. Immediately after the

Muslim League session, Sir Sikandar Hyat Khan, Premier of the Punjab and one of the League leaders, issued a statement that to attribute the authorship of the Pakistan scheme to him was 'incorrect, unwarranted and mischievous.' Mr Jinnah has apparently failed to convert his leading lieutenant.

In one of his letters to Mr Jinnah, Lord Linlithgow stressed the need for reaching quick decisions. He wished to announce the names of members of the expanded Executive Council by the end of August, and to complete the personnel of the Advisory War Council by the middle of September at the latest. His reason for protracting negotiations with the Muslim League beyond that period, was his anxiety in the words of Mr Amery, to go ahead without the Congress 'prepared to work with those who will work with him and with each other'. The League decision has turned the tables on the Viceroy. But the ways of the Government of India are inexplicable. The Government of India Act of 1935 was thrust upon the people of this country against their wish and it took the British five years and a major war to discover that it was unworkable as a constitution and impossible as a basis of political reform. The obvious next step for the Viceroy is to give up his futile efforts at devising a formula which will preserve the constitutional *status quo* and at the same time satisfy any political party in his country. All parties in India, now that it is beyond doubt that the British have no intention of setting up any sort of national Government at the Centre during the War, will welcome such a decision. The only excuse we can think of for Lord Linlithgow's initiating his fruitless and protracted negotiations with political leaders is that he was himself in the dark about Britain's policy towards India. In view of the wide-spread confusion in both Britain and India it would be wise to avoid fundamental changes at the moment. The scheme Lord Linlithgow had put forward is nothing more than a patched up unity between various parties in which each party had to seek to score against the others. The emphasis naturally is more on how much one can get out of the scheme, than on what contribution one can make towards national unity and political progress. Such an atmosphere is unfavorable to any constitutional discussion.

72. Viceroy's Declaration 'Unsatisfactory' and Congress Position 'Unrealistic' Hindu Mahasabha Working Committee's Resolution, New Delhi, 12–13 October 1940

Indian Annual Register, 1940, Vol. II, pp. 268–9.

The Working Committee having given their anxious consideration to the Viceregal announcement of August 8 and the statements made by the Viceroy and the Secretary of State from time to time in elucidation and clarification of the same and having carefully noted the reactions to the same in this country have no hesitation to declare that the scheme and the proposals outlined therein have failed to give any satisfaction to the progressive political parties in the country, in as much as it holds out neither any tangible and definite promise of the inauguration of the dominion government immediately at the end of the war, nor the introduction of the element of responsibility in any form in the present central Government immediately.

The committee characterizes the principles laid down in the assurance given to the minorities or to certain important sections of national life as reactionary, and anti-national and anti-democratic. They virtually negative the promise to recognize the principle of self-determination in the case of the people of India in the matter of framing their constitution given in the first part of the announcement and are even calculated to incite and encourage the minorities to insist on impossible and anti-national demands and effectively impede the progress of the entire nation towards the goal of political emancipation.

The committee hope that the Viceroy will take note of the criticisms of the scheme by important sections of the Indian public and soon come out with a liberal scheme of reform in the existing system of central government as a transitory measure and a definite unconditional announcement in unambiguous and unequivocal terms recognizing the right of the Indian people to frame their constitution of the future Government of India on the basis of Dominion Status for India in the Commonwealth of British nations.

The committee desire to express their satisfaction at the firm stand taken by the Viceroy in dealing with the extravagant and arrogant demands made by Mr Jinnah, the leader of the Muslim League in regard to the representation of the League on the stillborn expanded Council and the advisory council proposed in the announcement.

The committee deeply regret to express their difference from the opinion of the Congress Working Committee embodied in the resolution passed at Bombay.[1] The Congress Working Committee have in the opinion of this committee failed to take a realistic view of the situation and give a correct lead to the country at this critical hour. The hope of the political emancipation of the Indian people depend on the defeat of totalitarian forces and the success of the British people with whom their fate is indissolubly bound. The war has now reached a stage when the Indian people can no longer afford to be indifferent to the vital problem of India's defence. The adequate preparation of the Indian nation for her national defence is a matter of vital importance to them. The committee ask them in all earnestness to urge on the Government of India to fully arm and equip the country for their defence by raising a strong national army, navy and air force, promising the Government active cooperation and participation in their effort of India's defence. In this connection the committee desire to invite the attention of the Government of India to the frequent complaints published in papers that the claims of the Hindus do not receive adequate recognition in the matter of recruitment to certain branches of national defence activities. The committee emphatically insists on the elimination of all arbitrary and artificial classification of the Indian people as martial and non-martial and deliberate attempt should be made to enlist in the defence forces recruits of all classes in proportion to their numerical strength in the population of the country as far as possible.

---

[1] The Congress Working Committee had passed a resolution on Satyagraha at its meeting held in Bombay from 13 to 17 September 1940. The resolution was subsequently approved by the AICC.

Chapter 3. Towards Civil Disobedience

A.   INDEPENDENCE DAY CELEBRATIONS

1.   Congress Working Committee Resolutions on Observance of Independence Day, Wardha, 18–22 December 1939

Harijan, 30 December 1939.

The Working Committee have studied with regret the recent pronouncements of the Secretary of State for India. His reference to the communal question merely clouds the issue and takes the public mind off the central fact that the British Government have failed to define their war aims especially with regard to India's freedom.

In the opinion of the Working Committee the communal question will never be satisfactorily solved so long as the different parties are to look to a third party, through whose favour they expect to gain special privileges, even though it may be at the expense of the nation. The rule of a foreign power over a people involves a division among the elements composing it. The Congress has never concealed from itself the necessity of uniting the various divisions. It is the one organization which in order to maintain its national character has consistently tried, not always without success, to bring about unity. But the Working Committee are convinced that lasting unity will only come when foreign rule is completely withdrawn. Events that have happened since the last meeting of the Committee have confirmed this opinion. The Working Committee are aware that the independence of India cannot be maintained, if there are warring elements within the country. The Committee are therefore entitled to read in the British Government's raising the communal question reluctance to part with power. The Constituent Assembly as proposed by the Congress is the only way to attain a final settlement of communal questions. The proposal contemplates fullest representation of all communities with separate electorates where necessary. It has already been made clear on behalf of the Congress that minority rights will be protected to the satisfaction of the minorities concerned, difference, if any, being referred to an impartial tribunal.

Congressmen must have by now realized that independence is not to be won without very hard work. Since the Congress is pledged to non-violence, the final sanction behind it is civil resistance, which is but a part of Satyagraha. Satyagraha means goodwill towards all, especially towards opponents. Therefore it is the duty of individual Congressmen to promote and seek goodwill. Success of the programme of khadi as an accepted symbol of non-violence, harmony and economic independence is indispensable. The Working Committee, therefore, hope that all Congress organizations will, by a vigorous prosecution of the constructive programme, prove themselves fit to take up the call when it comes.

The Working Committee draw the attention of all Congress committees, Congressmen and the country to the necessity of observing properly and with due solemnity Independence Day on January 26, 1940. Ever since 1930 this day has been regularly observed all over the country, and it has become a landmark in our struggle for independence. Owing to the crisis through which India and the world are now passing and the possibility of our struggle for freedom being continued in an intenser form, the next celebration of this Day has a special significance attached to it. This celebration must, therefore, not only be the declaration of our national will for freedom, but a preparation for that struggle and a pledge to disciplined action.

The Working Committee, therefore, call upon all Congress committees and individual Congressmen to take the pledge prescribed below in public meetings called for the purpose. Where owing to illness or other physical disability or to being in an out of way place, individual Congressmen are unable to attend a public meeting, they should take the pledge in their homes, individually or in groups. The Working Committee advise organizations and individuals to notify their Provincial Congress Committees of the meetings held as well as the individual or group pledges taken. The Committee hope that none who does not believe in the contents of the pledge will take it merely for the sake of form. Those Congressmen who do not believe in the prescribed pledge should notify their disapproval, stating reasons therefore, to the Provincial Congress Committee, giving their names and addresses. This information is required not for the purpose of any disciplinary action but for the purpose of ascertaining the strength of disapproval of anything contained in the pledge. The Working Committee have no desire to impose the pledge on unwilling Congressmen. In a non-violent organization compulsion can have little place. The launching of civil disobedience requires the disciplined fulfilment of the essential conditions therefore.

PLEDGE

'We believe that it is an inalienable right of the Indian people, as of any other people, to have freedom and enjoy the fruits of their toil and have the necessities of life, so that they may have full opportunities of growth. We believe also that if any Government deprives a people of these rights and oppresses them, the people have a further right to alter it or to abolish it. The British Government in India has not only deprived the Indian people of their freedom but has based itself on the exploitation of the masses, and has ruined India economically, politically, culturally and spiritually. We believe, therefore, that India must sever the British connection and attain Purna Swaraj or COMPLETE INDEPENDENCE.

'We recognize that the most effective way of gaining our freedom is not through violence. India has gained strength and self-reliance and marched a long way to Swaraj following peaceful and legitimate methods, and it is by adhering to these methods that our country will attain Independence.

'We pledge ourselves anew to the Independence of India, and solemnly resolve to carry out non-violently the struggle for freedom till Purna Swaraj is attained.

'We believe that non-violent action in general, and preparation for non-violent direct action in particular, require successful working of the constructive programme of khadi, communal harmony and removal of untouchability. We shall seek every opportunity of spreading goodwill among fellowmen without distinction of caste or creed. We shall endeavour to raise from ignorance and poverty those who have been neglected and to advance in every way the interests of those who are considered to be backward and suppressed. We know that though we are out to destroy the Imperialistic system we have no quarrel with Englishmen, whether officials or non-officials. We know that distinctions between the Caste Hindus and Harijans must be abolished, and Hindus have to forget these distinctions in their daily conduct. Such distinctions are a bar to non-violent conduct. Though our religious faiths may be different, in our mutual relations we will act as children of Mother India, bound by common nationality and common political and economic interest.

'Charkha and Khadi are an integral part of our constructive programme, for the resuscitation of the seven hundred thousand villages of India and for the removal of the grinding poverty of the masses. We shall, therefore, spin regularly, use for our personal requirements nothing but khadi, and so far as possible products of village handicrafts only, and endeavour to make others do likewise.

'We pledge ourselves to a disciplined observance of Congress principles and policies and to keep in readiness to respond to the call of the Congress, whenever it may come, for carrying on the struggle for the Independence of India.'

2. Mahatma Gandhi's Article on 'The Pledge', 24 December 1939

Harijan, 30 December 1939.

The Pledge

It is to be hoped that Congressmen will learn by heart, not merely store up in their memory, the resolution of the Working Committee containing the pledge for 26th January next. The pledge was first taken in 1930. Ten years is not a short time. If Congressmen had honestly lived up to the constructive programme of 1920, there would be Purna Swaraj today. There would be communal harmony, there would be purification of Hinduism and smiling faces in India's villages. These together would produce such a momentum that Independence could not be resisted.

But the painful fact must be admitted that Congressmen have not carried out the programme as they should have. They have not believed that the triple programme is non-violence in action. They have not believed that civil disobedience could not be successfully carried out without fulfilling it.

Therefore I have not hesitated to remark in these columns that our non-violence has been non-violent conduct born of impotence. Hence we witness the sorry spectacle of us confessing that, though this non-violence of the weak may bring us freedom from English rule, it cannot enable us to resist foreign invasion. This fact—and it is a fact shows that, if the English yield to the non-violence, miscalled, of the weak, it would prove that they had almost made up their mind to surrender power and would not hold on to it at the cost of creating frightfulness. Congressmen should not be surprised, if I would not declare civil disobedience unless I was morally certain that they had understood the full significance of non-violence and that they were carrying out the triple programme with as much zest as they would offer civil disobedience, so called. They would perhaps now understand why I call the three items of the programme essentials of non-violence.

What do I mean by communal fellowship? How is it to be obtained when the Jinnah–Nehru talks have failed? They may or may not have failed. Pacts are meant for big people. They do not affect men in the street, the ground-down millions. In cultivating fellowship among these, written pacts are not needed. Do Congressmen cultivate goodwill towards all without political motive? This fellow-feeling should be natural, not born out of fear or expedience, even as fellowship between blood brothers not being born out of any ulterior motive, is natural and lasting. Nor is it to be applied only as between Hindus and Muslims. It has to be universal. It must be extended to the least among us. It is to be extended to Englishmen. It is to be extended to political opponents. Removal of untouchability again has deep significance. The very idea of high and low among Hindus should be rooted out. Caste solidarity should give place to national solidarity. In Congress ranks these distinctions should be relics of the past.

Then the charkha. For nearly twenty years now it has adorned the National Flag which is made of khadi. And yet khadi has not become universal. Khadi having been adopted by the Congress, Congressmen may not rest till it has penetrated every home in the remotest part of India. Only then will it become a mighty symbol of voluntary cooperation and one purpose. It is a symbol of identification with the poorest in the land. Hitherto Congressmen have played with khadi. They have not believed in its message. They have used it often unwillingly, for mere show. It must become a reality if true non-violence is to permeate us.

Let Congressmen note the preamble to the Working Committee's resolution on the pledge. Those who do not believe in it are not bound to take the pledge. Indeed those who have not the belief, are bound not to take it. For the pledge this time is to be taken for a definite purpose. A grave responsibility rests on my shoulders. A vast organization like the Congress will not move in the direction of civil resistance unless I give the word. It is no matter of pride or joy to me. I should break under the weight of that responsibility, if I were not conscious of the fact that I am nothing. Congressmen have trust in my judgment which is dictated by the living Law of Truth and Love which is God. God speaks through acts of men and women. In this case acts of Congressmen and Congresswomen have to speak.

Segaon, 24-12-39.

3. Mahatma Gandhi's Article in Response to Criticism on Charkha, 9 January 1940

Harijan, 13 January 1940.

The Charkha
'THE EAST BOWED LOW BEFORE THE BLAST
IN PATIENT DEEP DISDAIN,
SHE LET THE THUNDERING LEGIONS PAST
AND PLUNGED IN THOUGHT AGAIN.'

I congratulate the Socialists, the Royists and others who have spoken out their minds on spinning. The situation that faces the country is most serious. If civil resistance is declared in right earnest, there should be no suspension unless there is a proper settlement. It therefore follows that, if the fight is to be non-violent, the non-violence must be unadulterated. I must not be weak in my statement of the requirements. If I hesitate, I would betray the national cause. I dare not lead an army that does not answer the qualifications which I regard as essential for success.

No half-hearted allegiance will do. Divided allegiance will lead to disaster. The critics should realize that I have not imposed myself on the Congress. I am no dictator though I have been given that nickname by unkind friends. I have no sanction for imposing my will on any person. Therefore I call myself truly a servant of the people. The public should know that

I have not even been formally appointed 'Generalissimo'. Not that the Working Committee would not give me the formal appointment. But I suggested and the members agreed that there was no necessity for it. Thus if ever there can be a bond of unmixed love and confidence between a general and his men, this is such a one. There is nothing to prevent the Congress from ignoring me and passing any resolution it likes. There is nothing so far as I am concerned to prevent any person or any province or district from declaring civil disobedience at his or its own risk. They will be guilty of indiscipline towards the Congress. But I can do nothing in regard to such insubordination.

Hence it should be unnecessary for me to argue out the case for spinning. It should be enough that it is the requirement that every satyagrahi has to fulfil.

But I must continue to argue till I convert opponents or I own defeat. For my mission is to convert every Indian whether he is a Hindu, Muslim or any other, even Englishmen and finally the world, to non-violence for regulating mutual relations whether political, economic, social or religious. If I am accused of being too ambitious, I should plead guilty. If I am told that my dream can never materialize, I would answer 'that is possible,' and go my way. I am a seasoned soldier of non-violence, and I have evidence enough to sustain my faith. Whether, therefore, I have one comrade or more or none, I must continue my experiment.

The first thing I would like co-workers to realize is that I have no hate in me for a single Englishman. I am not interested in driving him out of India. I am interested in converting him into a servant of India instead of his being and believing himself to be a ruler or a member of the ruling race. I feel towards him precisely as I feel towards an Indian, no matter what his faith may be. Therefore those who do not share this elementary quality with me, cannot become co-satyagrahis.

My love of Englishmen is not of the drawing room type. No one has painted their imperialism in more lurid colours than perhaps I have. But then I have done likewise in my domestic as also political circle. The love of my conception, if it is as soft as a rose petal, can also be harder than flint. My wife has had to experience the hard variety. My eldest son is experiencing it even now. I had thought I had gained Subhas Babu for all time as a son. I have fallen from grace. I had the pain of wholly associating myself with the ban pronounced on him. Time was when Dr Khare[1] and Vir Nariman[2] used to say that my word was law for them. Alas, I can no longer claim that authority. Anyway I was party to the disciplinary measures taken against them. I maintain that I have acted towards them as I have acted towards those who are considered nearest and dearest to me. In all my dealings love has dictated my actions. Even so have I acted towards Englishmen. Of course they have called me all kinds of names when I have fought them. Their bitter criticism of me had as much effect on me as their praise. I say all this not to claim or expect any certificate of merit. I want to show that because I have said hard things about British rule and methods ill-will against Englishmen must not be imputed to me. Those, therefore, who are filled with ill-will against them will find me a misfit in the end.

I am enunciating no new ideas here. They are to be found in *Indian Home Rule* (*Hind Swaraj*) which was written in 1908 when the technique of satyagraha was still in process of formation. The charkha had become part of this programme of love. As I was picturing life based on non-violence, I saw that it must be reduced to the simplest terms consistent with high thinking. Food and raiment will always remain the prime necessities of life. Life itself becomes impossible if these two are not assured. For non-violent defence, therefore, society has to be so constructed that its members may be able as far as possible to look after themselves in the face of an invasion from without or disturbances within. Just as a domestic kitchen is the easiest thing in such circumstances, the takli or at most the spinning wheel and the loom are the simplest possessions for the manufacture of cloth. Society based on non-violence can only consist of groups settled in villages in which voluntary co-operation is the condition of dignified and peaceful existence. A society which anticipates and provides for meeting violence with violence will either lead a precarious life or create big cities and magazines for defence purposes. It is not unreasonable to presume from the state of Europe that its cities, its monster factories and huge armaments are so intimately interrelated that the one cannot exist without the other. The nearest approach to civilization based upon non-violence is the erstwhile village republic of India. I admit that it was very crude. I know that there was in it no non-violence of my definition and conception. But the germ was there. All I have said may be pure folly. It behoves me as a faithful servant of the nation not to hide my folly. There is no doubt that we are on the eve of a big change. I hope it will be for the better, but it may be also for the worse. I must have the courage to share with my co-workers my innermost thoughts even though I may risk the loss of their co-operation.

To resume the argument. It is from that germ that I have developed the technique of non-violence. If the charkha can bear the ample interpretation I have put upon it, it becomes the most effective weapon in the armoury of satyagraha. The weak thread from the wheel binds the millions in an unbreakable cord. One yard of the thread may be useless, but millions of unending threads spun by willing and knowing hands will make a cord strong enough to bear any strain that may be put upon it. But between 1908 and 1914 the ideal remained dormant. The whole scheme was conceived for India. Nevertheless the spirit of it was worked out even in South Africa. The life of the satyagrahis there was reduced to simplest terms. Whether barristers or others, they learnt the dignity of labour. They accepted voluntary poverty as their lot in life and identified themselves with the poor. On my arrival in India I began single-handed to work for revival of the charkha. In 1921 khadi became one of the chief items of the constructive programme of the Congress. The charkha occupied the centre of the Congress flag with its vital connection with non-violence. I am, therefore, today saying nothing new. But as has often happened people have passed by what I have said until they have been compelled to take action.

I have great regard for all the comrades who have been writing against the charkha and its implications. They are rendering a service by guiding the country according to their lights. I do not want their mechanical assent to my requirements. I should take it if it served the national purpose, but I know that it cannot.

I must here consider Sir Chimanlal Setalvad's letter to *The Times of India*. I know we have had political differences practically since my return to India in 1915. He is an eminent lawyer. But that no more entitles him to give an authoritative opinion on the economy of the charkha than on the use of infantry in modern warfare. I invite him to study the literature that has grown round it. I promise that he will revise his opinion on its potency. May I also remind him that I claim many mill-owners among my friends? They know my views about mills. They know too that I have had a share in promoting the prosperity of our mills in relation to foreign mills. Sir Chimanlal should also know that I am guiding the policy of the largest and most powerful labour union in all India. My opposition to the mills is unbending and uncompromising. But it is wholly non-violent, and I make bold to say that the mill-owners will be the first to give me that certificate. My connection with the mills is a happy and complete illustration of non-violent resistance. I need not be reminded that they pamper me because they know that my activity cannot touch them. I flatter myself with the belief that they know better. They know that, if with my fixed views about mills I had violent intentions about them, my activity could cause so much trouble that they would be obliged to treat me as an enemy and to summon the assistance of the law against me.

But I like Sir Chimanlal's challenge to the ex-ministers. Let them speak. Segaon, 9-1-40.

---

[1] Dr Narayan Bhashan Khare was the Premier of CP and Berar for a little over a year during 1937–38. He was removed from the Premiership and expelled from the Congress. During the war, he was a supporter of the war effort and became a member of the Viceroy's Executive Council in 1943. After independence, he joined the Hindu Mahasabha and became its President.

[2] Khurshedji Framji Nariman, popularly known as Vir Nariman, was one of the foremost leaders of the Congress in Bombay in the 1930's. In 1937, he was elected to the Bombay Legislative Assembly but due to differences with the Congress leadership, he was not taken in the Ministry which was set up under the Premiership of B.G. Kher. He was critical of the Congress Ministry in Bombay and in subsequent years, his importance as a Congress leader declined.

4. Mahatma Gandhi's Article on Socialist Critics of Constructive Programme, 16 January 1940

Harijan, 20 January 1940.

The Dissentients

Shri Jaiprakash Narain and Shri Sampurnanand have spoken in no uncertain terms against the addendum to the pledge to be taken on the 26th inst. I have great regard for them. They are able and brave and have suffered for the country. I should count it a privilege to have them as companions in arms. I should love to win them over to my viewpoint. If the battle is to come and I am to lead it, I should not be able to do so with half-convinced or doubting lieutenants.

I am not spoiling for a fight. I am trying to avoid it. Whatever may be true of the members of the Working Committee, I wholly endorse Subhas Babu's charge that I am eager to have a compromise with Britain if it can be had with honour. Indeed Satyagraha demands it. Therefore I am in no hurry. And yet if the time carne and if I had no follower, I should be able to put up a single-handed fight. But I have not lost faith in Britain. I like the latest pronouncement of Lord Linlithgow. I believe in his sincerity. There are undoubted snags in that speech. Many *i*s have to be dotted, many *t*s have to be crossed. But it seems to contain germs of a settlement honourable to both nations. Those, therefore, who work with me have to appreciate this side of me. Perhaps from the standpoint of the dissentients this compromising nature of mine is a disqualification. If it is, the country should know it.

Shri Jaiprakash Narain has done well to clear his and the Socialist Party's position. He says of the constructive programme: 'We have never accepted it as the only or even as an adequately effective weapon in our struggle .... Our views regarding these matters have remained unchanged. Rather they have been strengthened by the helplessness of the national leadership in the present crisis .... Let students come out of their schools and colleges on that day and let workers lay down their tools.'

If the majority of Congressmen entertain the views that Shri Jaiprakash propounds on behalf of the Socialist Party, I can never hope to lead such an army to success. He has no faith either in the programme or in the present leadership. I suggest to him that he has quite unconsciously discredited the programme he would carry out merely 'because the nation's High Command desire it'. Imagine an army marching to battle without faith in the weapons to be used and in the leaders who have prescribed them. Such an army can only bring disaster to itself, its leaders and the cause. If I were in Shri Jaiprakash's place and if I felt able to tender discipline, I would advise my party to remain indoors and silent. If I could not, I would preach open revolt and frustrate the designs of an ineffective leadership. Again, he would have the students come out of their colleges and schools and workmen lay down their tools. Now this is a lesson in indiscipline. If I had my way, I would invite every student to remain in his school or college unless he got leave or the Principal decided to close the college or school in order to take part in the celebration. I should give similar advice to the workmen. Shri Jaiprakash complains that the Working Committee has given no details about the work to be done on the Independence Day. I thought that with the programme of fraternizing and khadi there was no need for detailed instructions. I should expect Congress committees everywhere to arrange spinning demonstrations, khadi hawking, and the like. I observe that some committees are doing so. I had expected Congress committees to make preparations from the day the Working Committee resolution was published. I shall measure the strength of the nation's response not merely by the quantity of yarn spun but mainly by the khadi sales throughout the country.

Finally Shri Jaiprakash says: 'We advanced for our part a new programme, that of labour and peasant organization, as the foundation of a revolutionary mass movement.' I dread the language used. I have organized both but not perhaps in the way Shri Jaiprakash has in mind. The sentence demands further elucidation. If they are not organized on a strictly peaceful footing, they may damage non-violent action as they did during the Rowlatt Act Satyagraha and later during the hartal in Bombay over the Prince of Wales' visit.

Shri Sampurnanand has raised a spiritual issue. He thinks that the original pledge should not have been tampered with though as he says, and rightly, it was discursive. I was its author. I wanted the people not merely to repeat the *mantra* of Independence but to educate the people as to its why and wherefore. It was later amended when certain portions of the original had become meaningless. I admit the sacredness of the *mantra* of Independence. That was given to us when the Lokamanya first uttered 'Swaraj is my birthright.' It was caught by thousands and is gaining strength from day to day. It is now enshrined in the hearts of millions. I hold that the addendum this year was necessary. It adds to the sacredness of the original and tells the people how everyone can contribute to the realization of national freedom.

I feel, therefore, that Shri Sampurnanand's objection really arises from his disbelief in the constructive programme. Thus he says: 'If making it an integral part of the pledge means that we are definitely committing ourselves to a policy of village industries as opposed to mass production, then I, as a socialist, cannot accept it.' Of course I cannot give the legal interpretation of the pledge. It can only be given by the Working Committee. But as the general responsible for declaring and conducting a non-violent war I am bound to say that this mentality must interfere with mass propaganda. A leader like Sampurnanandji can either throw himself whole-heartedly in the struggle or not at all. He will create confusion in the mass mind by being half-hearted in his exposition of the addendum. If khadi has not an abiding place in the national programme, it should have no place in the addendum. If there is anything more effective, it should be put before the nation. There need be no hush hush policy because a big fight is said to be impending. It is not necessary for all to be of one mind. But it is absolutely necessary that those who have to be in charge, as he would have to be, have a living faith in the programme they have to work out. No make-believe will answer the present requirements.

It has been suggested to me by a Congressman wielding great influence that as soon as I declare civil resistance I would find a staggering response this time. The whole labour world and the kisans in many parts of India will, he assures me, declare a simultaneous strike. I told him that, if that happened, I should be most embarrassed and all my plan would be upset, I must confess that I have no positive plan in front of me. Let me say that God will send me the plan when He gives the word as He has done before now. He has been my unfailing Guide and has sustained me throughout my stormy life. This, however, I know that no plan that I may put before the country will admit of unregulated and sporadic strikes, because that must lead to violence and therefore automatic suspension of the non-violent struggle. It would amount to my dismissal. I am sure the socialist leaders and other dissentients do not expect me to embark on a struggle which I know beforehand is likely to end in disaster. I ask for lieutenants and men who will act as one mind.

Even if somehow or other we achieve nominal independence, we cannot conduct national affairs with any degree of success unless we have won the struggle in the manner prescribed by me. Without real non-violence there would be perfect anarchy. I hope I am not expected knowingly to undertake a fight that must end in anarchy and red ruin.

Segaon, 16-1-40.

5. Jayaprakash Narayan's Reply to Mahatma Gandhi's Article

Sangharsh (Hindi daily), 29 January 1940.

What the Congress Socialists Want?

Mr Jaiprakash Narayan's answer to Mahatmaji. The answer which Mr Jaiprakash Narayan has written in response to Mahatma Gandhi's article 'The Dissentients', published in last week's *Harijan*, is given below:

We have to clear our position because of Gandhiji's article, 'The Dissentients', published in the *Harijan*. Some time ago, when Gandhiji had written that your objection is right and you have no other way than this one, I thought that Mahatmaji had understood our point of view. But his article shows that we had misunderstood him.

Mahatmaji has raised many important question in his article and when the different viewpoints of Gandhism and Socialism come in contact with each other, there are many chances of crash. I will take up only important points here.

Discipline and Faith

We have shown our inability to accept many clauses of the new pledge. Because of it we cannot maintain discipline. But discipline and faith are two different things. Non-violence is a democratic method and until one has faith in it, nobody can pressurize one to accept it on the basis of discipline. If the clause which has been attached to the independence pledge, means that we have to spin and work on the constructive programme only because of maintaining discipline, then we should have followed the whole pledge quite happily. I have said the same thing in my statements also. I had written, 'There is no need to affirm it that whatever meaning we have derived from the pledge, if it is wrong, then we will happily repeat the whole pledge with our friends'. We could not have made our position clearer or easier than this. But no responsible person took the effort of telling us that our explanation of the new pledge is wrong, and there was no need to believe in the policy of spinning, it had to be undertaken only in the name of discipline. Only one word from either Mahatma Gandhi or Rajendra Prasad could have cleared the position and there is still need for it. I know that Pandit Jawaharlal Nehru had understood the pledge in a different way and whatever Gandhiji wrote had further affirmed our thinking that a classification regarding different viewpoints is going on and our explanation of the new pledge is closer to truth.

Mahatma Gandhi had written that if he was in my position and could maintain discipline then he would have preferred to sit at home. I don't think that he could have done so. If he had understood the meaning of the pledge in the same way as I have done, then he would have done the same. As he had written in his letter that there would have been no other way in this situation.

The Question of Leadership

As far as there is a question of announcing open revolt against the bad policies of nincompoop leaders, I do not want to jump into such a struggle because I know that I can maintain discipline. Only a small number of Socialists could not attain self-government all by themselves. The whole Congress has to fight for self-government and only Gandhiji could lead this struggle.

Gandhiji has advanced some conditions for his leadership. We are ready to accept them without any hesitation. But if there is an insistence on changing our faith and leaving our thinking, then it will be an impossible condition. We accept the economic importance of Charkha in the present context. We want to promote communal unity and destroy untouchability. We consider 'Khadi' as the sign of Indian independence and unity. We will spin, but we cannot accept that spinning will make alive the seven lakhs of villages of India and neither are we going to accept the 'Indian Self-government' scheme of Gandhiji.

No Need to Revolt

Only people like Subhas Babu can talk of open revolt. For us, it will mean disunity and division because we know that we cannot replace the destroyed thing with some other constructive thing. We believe that we can work together keeping in mind each other's benefit and the need to work together. But if there is no programme of struggle in the future and there is a settlement which pushes back our independence, then there is no need to keep discipline and we will be independent to choose our future path.

Our Policy

This is not the proper time to discuss the spinning and constructive programme in detail. We had a detailed discussion with Gandhiji in Delhi some weeks after the Tripuri Session of the Congress in which we discussed the opinions of the two groups—Gandhists and Socialists—of the Congress formed on the basis of their different viewpoints. We found each other very close after the talks of three days and even Gandhiji had said that he was drawn nearer to us. Gandhiji was afraid that our programme to organize the workers and the peasants could become violent. We told him that we are also concerned about making this movement peaceful and he was satisfied with our policy at least. There is no doubt that he believes that there are such persons in every movement who are so narrow minded that they will always promote violence. But he was assured in regard to us that we will use our influence to make this movement peaceful and organized. Gandhiji has given a prominent place to my views in his article that we have proposed a new programme in the shape of the revolutionary movement of the peasant and workers' organizations and he says that he is afraid of the use of this language.

A revolutionary like Gandhiji who had played with fire and has encouraged lakhs of people to struggle, should not be afraid of these words. I do not mean the spread of violence and disorder by these words. The revolution is not always horrible. We had told Gandhiji in clear words in Delhi and later in Abbotabad that our aim is to prepare the workers all over India for the movement of non-payment of rents and taxes and the general strike of those working in different industries, rail, shipping and other means of transport. We believe that we can start a peaceful and organized but powerful mass struggle throughout this programme which will paralyse and destroy the British Government. We had made it clear to Gandhiji that in order to awaken and organize the peasants and the workers of different industries, it is necessary to organize them into peasant unions and workers unions on the basis of their immediate and the last economic rights.

The Incompetency of Charkha

We have always believed that in order to prepare the masses enthusiastic for the great works of bravery and sacrifice it is necessary that we should tell them that they are going to get economic benefits and freedom out of it. Spinning does not fulfill this criteria or it fulfills it to a lesser extent. It is worth remembering that we have never opposed the programmes of Gandhiji while keeping in mind our programme although we have often criticized it. If there was any opposition to Gandhiji's programme then it was only in the beginning. After that, our experience has taught us that we should not oppose the constructive programme, on the other hand, we should incorporate some parts of it into our programme. During the Lahore session of our party, I had drawn the attention of the party members working for the kisan movement towards sanitation in villages, abolish illiteracy, open library for youngmen, promotion of village industries and the improved means of cultivation, etc., constructive work and had instructed them to incorporate these in their programme. I had told that no peasant activist could always be absorbed in economic struggle. He should make himself even more indispensable to the peasants by adopting this programme.

It seems that Gandhiji has misunderstood my statement regarding the limitations of the National leadership at this hour of struggle. I did not mean that our leadership was incapable, but I could not help feeling that if Congress had accepted our programme and had implemented them during these five years then our leaders should have faced the present crisis in a more firm and confident way. The fear of the unknown, bloody murders and the movement of the oppressed masses had not stopped them from working as it is seen nowadays. Neither had we feared the conspiracy of the Communalists. I request Gandhiji that the Congress had not adopted our programme out of the fear of violence but because this programme could have been unprofitable to the class of those Congressmen who form the majority in the Congress organization. It is my opinion that our organization has got the power and ability to control the rightless masses of this country.

6. Mahatma Gandhi: 'The Independence Day', 22 January 1940

Harijan, 27 January 1940.

The Independence Day

Though questions regarding the forthcoming Independence Day pledge should be properly addressed to the Congress Secretary and though the President alone can give authoritative answers, they are continually being addressed to me; and as I have undertaken the duty of declaring civil resistance and leading the army should a struggle become necessary, it becomes incumbent on me to answer certain questions before 26th January.

1. Let it be remembered that, if civil resistance is to be declared, it will have to be more civil and more non-violent than ever before, if only to show the warring nations of the earth that a big people like that of India can fight non-violently for regaining their freedom. Therefore I shall resolutely refuse to fight unless I have sufficient confidence that Congressmen will render implicit obedience.

2. There is as much valour in self-denial as there is in rushing into the furnace, provided that the motive is the same in either case.

3. The Independence Day is an annual feature in the Congress programme and is unconnected with civil resistance. Hence the forthcoming celebration must not be mistaken for declaration of civil resistance. Nevertheless it would serve as an index of the discipline among Congressmen and those millions who have hitherto answered the Congress call. There should on the one hand be the largest demonstration of all the previous ones we have had, and on the other it should be of a character so peaceful as to disarm all criticism and induce and enable women with babes, little children and aged people to join the demonstration. Such was the demonstration on 6th April 1919 in Bombay.

4. Students have asked me what they should do. I would expect them individually to take the pledge, for it means their determination to win independence for India through truthful non-violent means symbolized in the constructive programme in which the charkha is the central activity. The other items are harmony among different communities and eradication of untouchability. These do not constitute the struggle but their fulfillment is indispensable for it. If the struggle comes, the students will not strike. They will leave their schools or colleges for good. But the students will not strike on the 26th. It will be good if the authorities themselves, as they well might, close their institutions and lead their staff and students in processions and other items of the programme. The same thing applies to labour. Those who without leave absent themselves from their work will in my opinion be guilty of indiscipline and render themselves unfit for enlisting as soldiers in the Satyagraha army. Non-violence is all discipline, wholly voluntary. It is clear from the foregoing that those who do not believe in and use khadi cannot take the pledge.

5. The pledge is not designed, as some fear, to eliminate strikes and no-tax campaigns. But I must at once confess that I have in my mind neither strikes nor no-tax campaigns as parts of the forthcoming struggle, if it comes at all. In my opinion the present atmosphere is not conducive to non-violent strikes and non-violent no-tax campaigns on an extensive scale.

6. I expect the whole weight of the Congress organization to be devoted to popularizing khadi and clearing the existing stocks.

7. For me Satyagraha is a method of self-purification. The word was first used in the AICC resolution of 1921. The constructive programme has been designed for that purpose. Though the word has fallen into disrepute, I as the author of the programme must have the courage to repeat it. We began Satyagraha with a 24 hours' fast in 1919. I propose to observe one myself on the 26th beginning in the evening of the 25th. And those who believe in its efficacy will do likewise.

8. Though I am preparing myself in the best manner I know and inviting the country to join me for a struggle for the overthrow of the imperialistic spirit and all it means, I am making a desperate effort to avoid the struggle. I believe that the best mind of England, nay of the world, is sick of the exploitation by the strong of the less strong. I believe in the sincerity of Lord Linlithgow. In the immediate carrying out of policies it is the individuals who count. I have worked with faith and hope. And I have not lost the hope that we shall have an honourable

settlement without a struggle which, no matter how non-violent, must involve considerable suffering. I therefore invite all communities, all parties, including Englishmen, to join the effort.

Segaon, 22-1-40.

7. Bombay Forward Bloc Not to Join Congress Meetings
Bombay Sentinel, 25 January 1940.

Messres H.V. Kamath and K.F. Nariman have sent the following: On January 26 the citizens of Bombay will have to demonstrate their unflinching determination to wage an uncompromising struggle against British Imperialism and for India's independence at this gravest crisis in our history. They will have plainly and firmly to tell those who are attempting to sidetrack the issue of the struggle that they are wrong. They will have to assert in unmistakable terms that they are prepared for freedom's battle.

The Bombay Forward Bloc has accordingly decided not to join the meetings organized by the Bombay Provincial Congress Committee on Independence Day. They will participate in the Girni Kamgar Union and thus show their solidarity with the exploited masses of India.

We appeal to the citizens of Bombay to do their duty by their country in this hour of trial. The Mother is calling. May we not prove deaf to her call!

We appeal to all our friends and sympathizers to muster in their thousands at Kamgar Maidan; Parel at 5-30 p.m. on January 26, and renew their resolve to fight relentlessly until victory is ours.

8. Newspaper Editorial on Independence Day
Bombay Chronicle, 26 January 1940.

The inauguration of the Independence Day ten years ago was an important landmark in the country's march to freedom, and the celebration of the Day to-day bids fair to be a still more important landmark. When the idea of substituting complete independence in place of the undefined 'Swaraj' of the Congress creed was first mooted, it was pooh-poohed by Britishers but the celebration of the first Independence Day in 1930 did much to inspire the national struggle of that year and its celebration annually since then has enthused the masses, millions of peasants and workers for the cause of complete independence. The Britishers no longer ridicule the celebration of the Day but earnestly hope that there may be an honourable settlement between India and Britain before it is too late.

Need for Discipline

The special significance of this year's celebration is by now obvious to all Indians. The celebration has to be followed either by an amicable settlement or a struggle which cannot end till independence is won. As the Congress Working Committee put it, 'this celebration must not only be the declaration of our national will of Freedom but a preparation for that struggle and a pledge to disciplined action'. In view of this fact the pledge invariably taken on this occasion, has been amplified this year so as to include a solemn undertaking to make special efforts to carry out the well-known constructive programme of the Congress including khadi, communal harmony and removal of untouchability. But the Working Committee has made it clear that it has 'no desire to impose the pledge on unwilling Congressmen, as in a non-violent organization compulsion can have little place". At the same time the Committee has stated that 'the launching of civil disobedience requires the disciplined fulfilment of the essential conditions thereof.' And Gandhiji, who alone can lead the struggle to victory, has definitely declared that it will be impossible for him to lead the country unless the conditions prescribed by him are substantially fulfilled.

Make History

To-day's celebrations in the city promise to be an unqualified success. Many mills and educational and business institutions are to be voluntarily closed and the celebrations in every part of the city will attract tens of thousands of men and women. Not the least impressive feature of these celebrations will be the participation therein of a large number of Muslims. An appeal was issued on Wednesday to Muslims 'to participate in their thousands in the celebration that will be held in Bombay and elsewhere on that day and thus prove to the world that they are in no way behind their fellow-countrymen of other communities in their desire for freedom and in their readiness for a struggle to win it'. In response to this appeal as also to that of the Bombay Provincial Congress Committee a large number of Muslims have decided to participate in the celebrations. They will first hold a National Flag salutation ceremony at Madanpura after which they will march in a procession headed by Red Shirt volunteers to join the main procession and finally join the mass meeting at Azad maidan. It is also gratifying to note that the Punjab Muslim Students' Federation has adopted a resolution urging Muslim students all over the province to join in the Independence Day celebrations. Press reports from other parts of the country also promise rousing celebrations by all classes of people. To mention only one such report from Patna, Bihar Socialists and Kisan Sabhaites have finally decided to make common cause with the local Congress Committees in the celebration of the Independence Day. Altogether, there is ground for hope that this year's celebration will be, as Gandhiji desires, larger than all previous ones. If the people will follow them up with appropriate action they will not fail to make history. Let to-day's observance mark the beginning of a new chapter in India's history.

9. Newspaper Reports of Country-wide Observance of Independence Day

Bombay Chronicle, 27 January 1940.

NATIONAL RALLIES TO CALL TO FREEDOM
People's Firm Resolve to Redeem Pledge
TREMENDOUS RESPONSE TO CONGRESS CALL
Millions Join Demonstrations on Independence Day

The call of freedom found the Indian nation rally to a man on the Independence Day all over the country. There was no distinction of class, community, creed or sect and, to judge from the reports pouring into the 'Chronicle' office from all corners of the country millions of people took the pledge of independence afresh on Friday in huge rallies and mammoth meetings.

Despite the controversy raised over portions of the pledge, the enthusiasm and earnestness that accompanied the demonstrations by every section of the people show that in the demand for National Independence the Indian people as a whole stand united and determined.

The Independence Day demonstrations passed off without any untoward incident and according to the directions of the Congress Working Committee and Mahatma Gandhi....

Country's Faith in Congress Leadership
Millions Pledge to Independence
'MAHATMA AS PILOT, GUARANTEE OF SUCCESS'

Processions and Public Meetings Demonstrate People's Determination to Be Free.

Reports from all provinces indicate that the Independence Day has been observed with due éclat in response to the special appeal of the Congress Working Committee and Mahatma Gandhi this year.

Mahatma Gandhi and Babu Rajendra Prasad observed a twenty four hours fast to inaugurate the Independence Day.

THE SIND ASSEMBLY WAS ADJOURNED AND THE PREMIER AND SIR GULAM HUSSEIN HIDAYATULLAH WHO APPEARED IN GANDHI CAPS WERE CHEERED BY THE CONGRESS MEMBERS.

PATNA'S RECORD

AT PATNA, THE STRIKE OBSERVED BY STUDENTS AND MILL WORKERS WAS SO PEACEFUL AND NON-VIOLENT THAT THE POLICE ARE REPORTED TO HAVE BEEN ASKED TO REMOVE THEMSELVES FROM THE PREMISES OF FACTORIES AND COLLEGES.

At Madras two huge public meetings were held side by side at the High Court beach when the Independence pledge was taken by over a lakh of people.

A large number of Harijans, Muslims and students participated in Nasik demonstrations.

'GUARANTEE OF SUCCESS'

At Poona, the new Congress House was opened by Sjt N.V. Gadgil, Sjt Shankerrao Deo addressing the gathering on the occasion said, that the fact that they had chosen Gandhiji as their generalissimo was a guarantee of success.

Similar reports have been received from Peshawar, Lahore, Calcutta, Delhi, Lucknow, Ahmedabad, Nagpur and several other places.

JAWAHAR HOISTS FLAG
Celebrations at Allahabad

Allahabad, Jan. 26. Independence Day celebrations in the Mohallas, City and Civil Lines of Allahabad were on a unique scale.

The entire programme beginning with Prabhat Pherries in the early hours of the morning was gone through. There were meeting and processions. There, were street decorations with flags and festoons. Shops and markets hoisted the national tricolour. The E. Wing of the University, the Christian College and other educational institutions also obscured the occasion with solemnity and enthusiasm.

Two Meetings at Madras High Court Beach

Two meetings were held at the High Court beach to-night in celebration of the Independence Day, one convened under the auspices of Andhra District Congress Committee presided over by Mr T. Prakasam, and the other under the auspices of Madras City Forward Bloc presided over by Mr N.G. Ranga, MLA (Central)....

Birth Right of Every Indian

Calcutta, 26 January—It was the birth right of every Indian to be free, said Maulana Abul Kalam Azad, speaking at Mohammad Ali Park on the significance of the Congress Independence Pledge.

The Maulana said that those, who did not agree to the pledge, as read out at the meeting, should stand aside and then report the views to their respective District Congress Committees, who would forward them to the AICC in due time. He reminded the audience that once they had taken the pledge, they were morally bound to carry out its terms. Merely to follow the reader of the pledge was not what was wanted of them. They must draw an inspiration from it, and try to follow it in their every day lives. He emphasized that their struggle was a non-violent one, and the non-violence must be observed in thought, word and deed.

Concluding, Maulana Azad requested every member in the gathering to take the oath in the spirit in which it had been drafted.

A large number of Muslims participated in today's celebrations in the city—A.P.

CELEBRATIONS IN FRONTIER

Peshawar, Jan. 26. The 'Independence Day' was celebrated throughout the Frontier Province to-day when Frontier men including Khan Abdul Gaffar Khan and Dr Khan Sahib, ex-Premier, took the Independence Pledge afresh under the Congress banner and held numerous meetings and red-shirt rallies.

In the afternoon a huge procession to the accompaniment of drums, flutes and bag-pipes and with shouts of 'Hindusthan Azad', 'Inquilab Zindabad' was taken through the main streets of the city.

In the evening a mass meeting was held under the presidency of Mian Jaffar Shah, MLA, President of the District Congress Committee, who unfurled the tricoloured flag....

LAUNCH FIGHT FOR INDEPENDENCE
Bose's Exhortation at Lucknow

Lucknow, Jan. 26. Lucknow observed the 'Independence Day' with great éclat. Prabhat Pheries were taken out and several meetings were held when the Congress Pledge was reiterated.

Addressing a meeting of more than 40,000 people organized by the Provincial Forward 'Bloc', where the pledge of 1930 was read out, Mr Subhas Chandra remarked that Swaraj could not be achieved through the plying of Charkha and using Khadi. It would come only through mass organizations and sacrifices.

'We do not want power, position and office. We want the Congress to launch a fight for Independence and the moment that fight is launched our differences would vanish.'

Referring to the projected compromise talks he remarked how could there be any compromise between slavery and freedom, and that too with honour.

The Congress Committee also observed the 'Independence Day' with great pomp by taking a procession, and holding a meeting where the new pledge was read out—United Press.

CELEBRATIONS IN DELHI
Several Mills and Factories Closed

New Delhi, Jan. 26. In spite of rains the 'Independence Day' was celebrated here with great enthusiasm. After Prabhat Pheriaes, flag-hoisting was performed in every ward of the city. In

Chandni Chowk and many other business quarters, National flags were hoisted on the shops, many of which remained closed....

Premier and Hidayatullah Wear Gandhi Caps

Karachi, Jan. 26. The Sind Legislative Assembly which met at three in the afternoon after eight months was adjourned owing to the 'Independence Day'.

The House met in a calm atmosphere although subdued excitement owing to the resignations of Mr Nichaldas Vazirani and Mr Dialmal Doulatram, Hindu Ministers, and the decision of the Hindu Independent Party to sit in the Opposition, was evident.

Sir Gulam Hussain Hidayatullah, Home Minister, wore a Gandhi cap to-day and had a tricolour flag in his button-hole. The Congress members warmly shook hands with him.

When the House met, Miss Jethi Siphimalani, Deputy Speaker of the Assembly, requested the Speaker to adjourn the Assembly to enable the members to participate in the 'Independence Day' procession. As Khan Bahadur Allahbux, Leader of the House, had no objection the Speaker adjourned the House which meets again to-morrow morning.

Later, Khan Bahadur Allahbux, Premier, and Mr Nichaldas Vazirani participated in the Independence Day procession—United Press.

SIND PREMIER LEADS PRABHAT PHERI

Karachi, Jan. 26. Independence Day is being observed throughout the city with great enthusiasm. All markets, Municipal offices, Colleges, and Government and Municipal schools are closed. Premier Khan Bahadur, Allah Baksh and the Minister Mr Nichaldas Vazirani donning Gandhi caps attended flag hoisting ceremony performed by Prof. Ghansham at Congress Bhavan this morning.

Earlier besides others the Premier and Mr Nichaldas led Prabhat pheries which paraded the streets. National flags are hoisted also on all schools and colleges—A.P....

Imposing Processions in Patna
(From Our Correspondence)

Patna, Jan. 26. Over a hundred thousand people, 'Rightist' and 'Leftist', Hindus and Muslims, Harijans and Momins mustered strong to-day at Patna and jointly pledged themselves for the liberation of their motherland at two meetings held at Bankipore Lawn and Patna City; when the Charkha and Khadi Clauses were read at the meetings the gathering repeated them with redoubled voice. There was complete hartal in city students observing a successful strike. The police were asked to remove themselves from the College gates as the atmosphere was peaceful and non-violent. Early in the morning, a cycle procession of about 1,000 students was taken out. The effigies of 'Dominion Status' and 'British Imperialism' and 'Slavery' were burnt this morning. Ten processions of students numbering over 3,000 paraded the streets. A procession of 1,000 girls with tricolour was taken out. Yet another auspicious procession of about 1000 bullock-carts with tricolour aloft was taken out....

Lakh of People Take Pledge of Independence
BOMBAY'S BIG RALLY AT CALL OF FREEDOM
Flag Salutations, Processions and Public Meetings

Bombay, Friday. With two main mass meetings, one at the Azad Maidan attended by over a lakh of citizens and another at Parel where 30,000 workers mustered strong and a number of public meetings in different wards, with prabhat pheries, processions and flag salutations in every part of the city, Bombay witnessed one of the biggest demonstrations of recent years, on the 'Independence Day'.

As the vast concourse of people gathered at the main meeting at Azad Maidan and took the pledge in low yet determined tones, resolving to attain complete independence, two national tri-colours, flown as kites by young volunteers, soared in the sky, symbolizing the aspirations of the Indian people.

A Unique Feature

A unique feature of the day's celebrations was the participation of a large number of Muslim citizens and associations including the Nationalist Muslim Party, Darul Mutalia, Anjuman Mujahedin, Majlis-e-Ahrar, Afzal-e-Payambarl, Mahfil-e-Subhani and the Young Muslim Azad Party. After paying their homage to the National Tricolour at Willingdon gardens at 2-30 p.m., a large number of Muslim citizens joined in a mile-long procession which started from the Congress House and terminated in a public meeting at Azad Maidan. The procession was led by Messrs S.A. Brelvi, Abid Ali Jafferbhai, Harris, Salehbhai Hakim Ikrami and other prominent nationalist Muslims.

63 Organizations Participate

The day's celebrations in the city and suburbs were held under the auspices of as many as 63 organizations including the Bombay Legislature Congress Party, Bombay Municipal Congress Party, All-India States' Peoples' Conference, the Nationalist Christian Party, Bombay Akali Dal, Goa Congress Committee, Nationalist Harijan Party, Marwari Sammelan, Bombay Kamgar Sangh and almost all the mercantile associations of Bombay.

CITY WAKES UP TO TUNE OF 'VANDE MATARAM'

The city woke early to the shouts of 'Vande Mataram' followed by the singing of 'Prabhat Pheries' led by saffron clad 'Desh Sevikas' under Mrs Safia Khan.

Children and adults were seen everywhere vying with each other for climbing up their house tops and soon the National tri-colour was flying triumphant everywhere in the city.

Business was at a standstill, shops in practically all the Hindu localities were closed; so also were all the chief markets in the city

All but ten out of the 62 textile mills in the city were closed and all the workers enthusiastically joined in the processions and demonstrations.

MILLS PICKETED

The Sassoon group of mills which remained open were picketed by volunteers of the Girni Kamgar Union.

Most of the private schools and colleges had declared a holiday, while the Government colleges had to be closed as the students kept out.

STUDENTS PROCESSION STOPPED

The students of the Elphinstone college and Law college took out a procession but it was stopped by the police near Dhobi Talao and a student was taken into custody.

By 7 a.m. hundreds of cyclists with waving tri-colours tucked on front of their cycles, were seen wending their way along city streets, raising national slogans and calling on the people to observe the Day in a fitting manner.

Two mammoth meetings, were held in the morning, one on the Chowpatty sands, and the other at Matunga, where thousands thronged to pay their homage to the national flag. The symbol of their infinite yearning for complete freedom.

FLAG SALUTATIONS

Hoisting the flag at Chowpatty Mr Bhulabhai J. Desai said that the observance of the Independence Day had a special significance now when the whole world was plunged in a struggle and when India had to play her part in refashioning it.

India he said pointed the way to a new order through the Gandhian philosophy of non-violence.

In the north of Bombay Mr B.G. Kher, hoisting the national flag at the gardens near Nappoo Hall exhorted the audience to prepare for a struggle, to recreate society on the basis of love—a society not based on the exploitation of the many by the few....

BR. PREMIER'S EFFIGY BURNT

The various processions and demonstration of students on the Independence Day in the north of Bombay, in which large number of girl-students participated in their school uniforms, culminated in a huge meeting held at Nappoo Hall Gardens at mid-day. Mr B.T. Ranadive presided. Mr S.A. Brelvi unfurled the National Flag. An effigy of Chamberlain, the British Premier, was burnt on the occasion.

Mr S.A. Brelvi unfurling the National Flag amidst deafening cries of 'Inquilab Zindabad' said, that at Lahore 10 years back, the Independence Flag was unfurled by Pandit Jawaharlal. Since then much water had flown below the bridges and they had achieved so much as to be confident of winning Independence very soon. They were now in the throes of a final struggle. It remained with Gandhiji to declare the struggle. That day would mark a winning point in their history. It was the day on which they resolved not to rest themselves or to let others rest until they had won Independence. They would gain their object either as a result of negotiations by Gandhiji with the Viceroy or through a final struggle. They did not wish to quarrel over words. They were determined to be as free in their country as the Britishers were in theirs. Gandhiji would give them the call. They should be ready to answer the call. They should realize the importance of khaddar in their national struggle. In the long struggle they had waged, it had acquired the status of a national uniform.

Concluding Mr Brelvi exhorted the students to keep the flag flying. He strongly disapproved students crossing the boundary of non-violence in their enthusiasm and burning the effigy of Mr Chamberlain.

Mr A.K. Ghosh also addressed the gathering.

Mr Kurape read out the Independence Pledge.

B.   INDIAN NATIONAL CONGRESS

I.   Ramgarh Session of Indian National Congress

10. Extracts from Presidential Address by Maulana Abul Kalam Azad, Ramgarh Congress, 19 March 1940

Hindustan Times, 20 March 1940; *Indian Annual Register,* 1940, Vol. I, pp. 290–5.

In 1923 you elected me President of this National Assembly. For the second time, after seventeen years, you once again conferred upon me the same honour. Seventeen years is not a long period in the history of national struggles. But now the pace of events and world change is so rapid that our old standards no longer apply. During these last seventeen years we have passed through many stages, one after another. We have a long journey before us and it was inevitable that we should pass through several stages. We rested at many a point no doubt, but never stopped. We surveyed and examined every prospect but we were not ensnared by it and passed on. We faced many ups and downs but always our faces were turned towards the goal. The world may have doubted our intentions and determination but we never had a moment's doubt.

Our path was full of difficulties and at every step we were faced with great obstacles. It may be that we did not proceed as rapidly as we desired but we did not flinch from marching forward. If we look back upon the period between 1923 and 1940, nineteen-twenty-three will appear to us a faded landmark in the distance. In 1923 we desired to reach our goal but the goal was so distant then that even the milestones were hidden from our eyes. Raise your eyes today and look ahead. Not only do you see the milestones clearly but the goal itself is not distant. But this is evident that the nearer we get to the goal the more intense does our struggle become. Although the rapid march of events has taken us further from our old landmark and brought us nearer our goal, yet it has created new troubles and difficulties for us. Today our caravan is passing a very critical stage. The essential difficulty of this period lies in its conflicting possibilities. It is very probable that a correct step may bring us very near our goal, and on the other hand, a false step may land us in fresh troubles and difficulties.

At such a critical juncture you have elected me President and thus demonstrated the great confidence you have in one of your co-workers. It is a great honour and a great responsibility. I am grateful for the honour and crave your support in shouldering the responsibility. I am confident that the fullness of your confidence in me will be a measure of the fullness of the support that I shall continue to receive.

The Real Problem of the Day

I think that I should now come straight to the real problem before us without further delay. The first and the most important question before us is this: Whither is the step taken by us in consequence of the declaration of War on the 3rd September, 1939, leading us? And where do we stand now?

Probably in the history of the Congress, the 1936 session at Lucknow marked a new ideological phase, when the Congress passed a long resolution on the international situation and placed its viewpoint clearly and categorically before the public. After this a consideration of the international situation, and a resolution thereon, became an essential and integral part of the annual declarations of the Congress. Thus this decision on this subject was arrived at and placed before the world with full deliberation. These resolutions embodied at one and the same time, two declarations to the world: Firstly, we stated, what I have described as a new ideology in Indian politics, that we could not remain in isolation from the political events of the outside world, even in our present state of helplessness. It was essential that while we forged our way ahead and fashioned our future, we must not confine ourselves merely to our own surroundings but should keep a vigilant watch on the conditions of the outside world. Innumerable changes in the world have brought countries and nations nearer to one another; so that the waves of thought and action, rising in one comer of the world, flow and produce immediate reactions in other places.

It is, therefore, impossible today for India to consider her problems while confining herself within her own four walls. It is inevitable that events in the outside world should have their repercussions in India; it is equally inevitable that our decisions and the conditions prevailing in India should affect the rest of the world. It was this consciousness and belief which brought about our decisions. We declared by these resolutions against reactionary movements like Fascism and Nazism which were directed against democracy and individual and national freedom. These movements were gaining strength day by day and India regarded this as the greatest danger to world progress and peace. India's head and heart were with those people who were standing up for democracy and freedom and resisting this wave of reaction.

But while we were considering the dangers arising from Fascism and Nazism, it was impossible for us to forget the older danger which has been proved to be infinitely more fatal to the peace and freedom of nations than these new dangers, and which has in fact supplied the basis for this reaction. I refer to British imperialism. We are not distant spectators of this imperialism, as we are of the new reactionary movements. It has taken possession of our house and dominates over us. It was for this reason that we stated in clear terms that if new entanglements in Europe brought about war, India, which has been debarred from exercising her will and making free decisions, will not take any part in it. She could only consider this question when she had acquired the right of coming to decisions according to her own free will and choice.

India cannot endure the prospect of Nazism and Fascism, but she is even more tired of British imperialism. If India remains deprived of her natural right to freedom, this would clearly mean that British imperialism continued to flourish with all its traditional characteristics, and under such conditions, India would on no account be prepared to lend a helping hand for the triumph of British imperialism. This was the second declaration which was constantly emphasized through these resolutions. These resolutions were repeatedly passed from the Lucknow session onwards till August 1939 and are known by the name of 'War Resolutions'.

All these declarations of the Congress were before the British Government when suddenly, in the third week of August 1939, the war clouds gathered and thundered and, at the beginning of September, the war began.

At this stage I will ask you to pause for a moment and look back. What were the conditions prevailing in August last?

The Government of India Act of 1935 was imposed upon India forcibly by the British Government and, as usual, resorting to the old stratagem, it tried to make the world believe that it had conferred a big installment of India's national right upon her. The world knows the decision of the Congress to reject this Act. Nevertheless the Congress decided to avoid a conflict at that stage and preferred a respite. It resolved to take charge of Provisional Governments on a certain definite condition. After this decision the Congress ministries were functioning successfully in eight out of the eleven Provinces, and it was in the interest of Great Britain herself to maintain this state of affairs for as long a period as possible. There was yet another factor. So far as the war was concerned, India had clearly condemned Nazi Germany. Her sympathies were with the democratic nations, and this was a point in Britain's favour. Under such circumstances, it was natural to expect that if the British Government had changed its old imperialistic mentality in the slightest degree, it would, even though as a measure of expediency, change its old methods at this juncture and afford an opportunity to India to feel that she was breathing in a changed atmosphere. But we all know how the British Government behaved in this matter. There was not even a shadow of change discernible in its methods. Its policy was dictated exactly in accordance with the habits of an imperialism a hundred and fifty years old. It decided its course of action and, without India being afforded in any manner and in the slightest degree an opportunity to declare freely her opinion, her participation in the War was announced. It was not even considered necessary to give those representative assemblies, imposed upon us by British diplomacy for purposes of show, an opportunity of expressing their opinion.

The whole world knows, and so do we, how all the Empire countries were given freedom of decision; the representative assemblies of Canada, Australia, New Zealand, South Africa, Ireland, all of them arrived at an independent decision, in regard to their participation in the War, without the least outside interference. Not only this but when Ireland decided to remain neutral, no surprise was shown nor was a single voice raised against it in Great Britain. Mr De Valera, in the very shadow of England, refused to extend his help to Britain in the War unless the question of Ulster was settled to his satisfaction. But what place did India occupy in this picture of the British Commonwealth? India is being told today that the generous hand of Britain will confer upon her the precious gift of Dominion Status in the near but unknown future. When the War began, a war which will probably be one of the greatest in the world, India was pushed into it suddenly without her even realizing that she was entering it. This fact alone was sufficient to show us which way the wind was blowing. But there was no need for us to hurry. Other opportunities were to come and the time was not distant when we could see the face of British imperialism even more unmasked and at closer quarters.

When in 1914 the first spark was ignited in a corner of the Balkans, England and France raised the cry of the rights of small nations. Later President Wilson's fourteen points came into view; their fate is well known to the world. On that occasion the situation was different. After the last war, England and France, intoxicated with victory, adopted a course of action which necessarily resulted in a reaction. This reaction grew. It took the shape of Fascism in Italy and Nazism in Germany, and unrestrained dictatorships, based on brute force, challenged the peace and freedom of the world. When this happened, inevitably the world aligned itself in two rival camps: one supporting; democracy and freedom; the other encouraging the forces of reaction. And in this way a new picture of the coming war began to take shape. Mr Chamberlain's Government, to which the existence of Soviet Russia was much more unbearable than the existence of Fascist Italy and Nazi Germany and which considered Russia to be a living challenge to British imperialism, continued to watch this situation for three years. Not only this, but by its attitude it clearly and repeatedly encouraged Fascist and Nazi ambitions. Abyssinia, Spain, Austria, Czechoslovakia and Albania, disappeared as free countries, one after the other, from the map of the world. And Great Britain, by her vacillating policy, continually assisted in the destruction of their freedom. But when this course of action produced its natural and ultimate result and Nazi Germany marched ahead unchecked, the British Government found itself compelled to enter the arena of war. Had it not done so then, the power of Germany would have become an intolerable menace to British imperialism. Now the new slogans of freedom, world peace, democracy, took the place of the old cry of saving the smaller nations, and the whole world began to ring with these cries. The declaration of war on the 3rd September by Britain and France was made to the accompaniment of the resounding echoes of these slogans. The peoples of the world were bewildered and harassed by the brutal trial of strength and the worldwide unrest created by these new reactionary forces, and they lent a willing ear to the siren voice of these slogans.

The Congress Demand

War was declared on the 3rd of September and on the 7th September the All India Congress Working Committee met at Wardha to deliberate upon the situation. What did the Working Committee do on this occasion? All the declarations of the Congress made since 1936 were before it. It had also to face the action taken by the British Government in declaring India as a belligerent country. Undoubtedly the Congress could not have been blamed had it come to a final decision in accordance with the logic of the situation. But it continued to keep vigilant watch on its mind and heart; it resisted the natural urge of the moment for an acceleration of pace; it deliberated upon every aspect of the matter, unemotionally and dispassionately, and took the step which today entitles India to raise her head and say to the world that this was the only correct step which could have been then taken. The Congress postponed its final decisions and asked the British Government to state its war aims, for on this depended not only peace and justice for India, but for the whole world. If India was being invited to participate in this war, she had a right to know why this war was being fought. What was its object? If the result of this grim tragedy was not to be the same as that of the last war, and if it was really being fought to safeguard freedom, democracy and peace and to bring a new order to the world, then in all conscience, India had a right to know, what would be the effect of these aims on her own destiny.

The Working Committee formulated this demand in a long statement which was published on the 14th September 1939. If I express the hope that this statement will occupy an outstanding place in recent Indian history, I am sure I am not claiming too much of the future historian. This is a simple but irrefutable document, based on truth and reason, and it can only be set aside by the arrogant pride of armed forces. Though this cry was raised in India, in fact it was not of India only, but it was the agonized cry of wronged humanity, whose hopes had so often before been betrayed. Twenty-five years ago the world was plunged into one of the biggest infernos of death and destruction known to history, and yet this was a preparation for a still bigger catastrophe. The world was bewitched and its hopes were kindled by cries of freedom for small nations, collective security, self-determination, disarmament, League of Nations and international arbitration, and of similar high sounding phrases. But what was the result in the end? Every cry proved false; every vision that seemed so real to us, vanished as a dream. Again nations are being plunged into the blood and fire of war. Should we part with reason and reality so completely as not even to ask why this is being done and how this affects our destiny before plunging into this deluge of death and destruction?

The Answer of the British Government and the First Step of the Congress

In answer to this demand of the Congress a regular series of statements were made on behalf of the British Government, both in England and in India. The first link of the series was the Delhi declaration of the Viceroy, dated the 17th October. This lengthy statement is perhaps a finished example of that peculiarly involved and tiring style which characterizes the official literature of the Government of India. After reading page after page of this statement, the curtain is at last lifted with hesitation. We have a glimpse. We are told then that if we want to know the war aims we must read a speech by the Prime Minister of Britain, and this speech deals only with the peace of Europe and with the adjustment of international relations. Even the words 'Freedom' and 'Democracy' are not to be found in the Viceroy's statement. So far as India is concerned, it only reaffirms the policy laid down in the preamble of the 1919 Act, which is now embodied in the 1935 Act. Today that policy continues to be the same; there is nothing to add to it or to improve it.

On the 17th of October, 1939, the statement of the Viceroy was published and the Working Committee met to deliberate upon it on the 22nd October at Wardha. Without any discussion it came to the conclusion that this reply could under no circumstances be considered satisfactory, and that it should now unhesitatingly give the decision, which it had postponed till then. The decision of the Working Committee was as follows:

'In the circumstances, the Committee cannot possibly give any support to Great Britain, for it would amount to an endorsement of the imperialistic policy which the Congress has always sought to end. As a step in this direction, the Committee call upon the Congress ministries to tender their resignations.'

As a result of this decision, the Congress ministries in eight provinces resigned.

This was but the first step which the Congress took in the series of events. Now we have to see to what these events led. The communiqué of the Viceroy issued on the 5th February from Delhi giving the resume of the talk between him and Mahatma Gandhi's statement of the 6th February may be regarded as the last of this series. We all know the substance of the Viceroy's statement. The British Government, it is stated, fully desires that India should, in the shortest time possible under the circumstances, attain the status of a British dominion, and that the transition period should be as short as possible. But it is unwilling to concede to India the right of framing her own constitution and deciding her own destiny through her own elected representatives without outside interference. In other words, the British Government does not accept the position that India has got the right of self-determination.

At the first touch of reality the structure of make-belief fell to pieces. For the last four years the world resounded with cries of democracy and freedom. The utterances of the responsible spokesmen of England and France in this regard are so fresh in our memory as not to need recall. But the moment India raised this question, the reality behind these utterances was unveiled. Now we are told that, without doubt, safeguarding the freedom of nations is the aim of this war but that this is confined within the geographical limits of Europe. The peoples of Asia and Africa should not dare to have any such hopes. Mr Chamberlain has made this even more clear in his Birmingham speech of the 24th February, though we never had any doubts about the matter. He confirmed the British Government's action by his words. Proclaiming British war aims, he stated that they were fighting to secure that small nations in Europe shall henceforth live in security, free from the constant threat of aggression against their independence.

Though this answer about war aims has been given through a British spokesman, yet in reality it interprets the real mentality of Europe as a whole, which has been known to the world for the last two hundred years. In the eighteenth and nineteenth centuries whatever principles were accepted for individual and collective human freedom, the right to claim them and to benefit from them was limited to European nations. And even amongst them, its application was confined to the Christian nations of Europe. Today, in the middle of the twentieth century, the world has so changed that the thoughts and actions of the last century read like ancient history, and appear to us as faded landmarks in the distance. But we will have to admit that there is at least one distinctive landmark of Europe emphasizing human rights, which has not faded and is still with us. We have not passed it yet, or achieved those rights.

This reality has been brought home to us again by the problem of our political and national rights in India. When, after the declaration of war, we raised the question of war aims and their effect on India's destiny, we were not forgetful of British policy in 1917 and 1919. We wanted to know how in the year 1939, when the world was covering the track of centuries in the course of days, England looked at India. Had that look changed? We were given a clear reply that it had not; even now there was no change in that imperialist outlook. We are told to believe that the British Government is very desirous that India should attain the status of a dominion, in the shortest period. We knew even before that the British Government had expressed this desire. Now we know that they are very anxious indeed.

But it is not a question of the desire or of the measure of the desire of the British Government. The straight and simple question is of India's rights; whether she is entitled to determine her own fate or not. On the answer to this question depend the answers to all other questions of the day. This question forms the foundation-stone of the Indian problem; India will not allow it to be removed, for if it is displaced the whole structure of Indian nationalism will collapse.

So far as the question of war is concerned our position is quite clear. We see the face of British imperialism as clearly now as we did in the last war, and we are not prepared to assist in its triumph by participating in the war. Our case is crystal clear. We do not wish to see British imperialism triumphant and stronger and thus lengthen the period of our own subjection to it. We absolutely refuse to do so. Our way lies patently in the opposite direction.

Where do We Stand Today

Let us return to our starting point and consider once again whither the step that we took after the declaration of war on the 3rd September is leading us. Where do we stand today? The answer to both these questions is by this time apparent to your minds and is hovering on your lips. It is not even necessary that your lips should tell me for I feel the quivering of your hearts. The step of temporary and partial cooperation which we took in 1937, we withdrew after the declaration of war. Inevitably we inclined towards further steps in non-cooperation. As we stand today, we have to decide whether we should march forward in this direction or go backward. When once a step is taken, there is no stopping. To cry halt, is to go back, and we refuse to go back. We can only, therefore, go forward. I am sure that the voice of everyone of you joins mine when I proclaim that we must and will go forward.

Mutual Settlement

In this connection one question naturally faces us. It is the verdict of history that in a struggle between nations, no power forgoes its possessions unless compelled to do so. Principles of reason and morality have affected the conduct of individuals but have not affected the selfish conduct of Powers that dominate. Today even in the middle of the twentieth century, we witness how the new reactionary forces in Europe have shattered man's faith in individual and collective human rights. In place of justice and reason, brute force has become the sole argument in the determination of rights. But while the world is presenting this depressing picture, there is another side, the hopeful side, which cannot be ignored. We see countless millions all over the world, without any distinction, awakening to a new consciousness which is spreading everywhere with great rapidity. This new consciousness is tired of the utter hopelessness of the old order, and is impatient for a new order based on reason, justice and peace. This new awakening which arose after the last war and took root in the deepest recesses of the human soul, has now come to dominate men's minds and their utterances. Perhaps there is no parallel in history to the speed of this awakening.

In these circumstances, was it beyond the realm of possibility that history should, contrary to its old record, take a new step? Was it impossible that two great peoples of the world, who had been tied together by the course of events as rulers and the ruled, should create a new relationship between them, based on reason, justice and peace? If that had been possible, the sorrows born of world war would have given place to a new-born hope; and the new order of reason and justice would have ushered in a new dawn. If the British people could have proudly said to the world today that they had added such a new example to history, what a vast and unparalleled triumph this would have been for humanity. Certainly this was not an impossibility, but it was an amazingly difficult thing to do.

In the prevailing darkness of the times, it is faith in the bright side of human nature which sustains the great soul of Mahatma Gandhi. He is always prepared to take advantage of every opening which might lead to a mutual settlement without feeling that he is weakening his unassailable position.

Since war began, several members of the British Cabinet have tried to make the world believe that the old order of British imperialism has ended, and that today the British nation has no other aims except those of peace and justice. Which country could have more warmly acclaimed such a declaration than India? But the fact is that in spite of these declarations, British imperialism stands in the way of peace and justice today exactly as it did before the war. The Indian demand was the touch-stone for all such claims. They were so tested and found to be counterfeit and untrue....

11.   M.N. Roy's Speech while Moving his Amendments to the Resolution on 'India and the War-Crisis',[1] at Subjects Committee, Ramgarh, 18 March 1940

A.M. Zaidi and S.G Zaidi (Chief Editors), *The Encyclopaedia of the Indian National Congress,* Vol. XII, Delhi, 1981, pp. 304–10.

Friends, it is practically impossible for me to move these amendments and explain why these amendments are necessary in five minutes. But the President says that the time at our disposal could not permit me to speak for more than five minutes. I shall not try to do anything more than move these amendments formally. I believe the amendments have been distributed to you in print. In five minutes I shall not be able even to read them. The object of the amendments is to add a vital part to the resolution which is absent. The resolution has no operative part. It is a declaration of various principles, and even the declarations are not new. It is only a repetition of declarations which the Congress has made from time to time. Therefore, it is not necessary for us to assemble in the annual session of the Congress to repeat declarations that have been made so many times. The amendments remove the defect of the resolution by adding an operative part. They will improve the resolution. That is why I wish to move the amendments. But within five minutes it is not possible for me to give any explanation.

If we are only to dot the *i*'s and cut the *t*'s, it is not necessary for us to assemble here. The main object of the annual session is to discuss the problems that arise in course of our experience during the year and take serious decisions. Therefore, it is only proper and desirable that not only every member of the AICC but every delegate should be given opportunity to express his opinion fully and freely.

But then there are difficulties, and certainly I shall be last person to question the legitimacy of the President's ruling. I shall be bound by it. It seems that we have come to this session for nothing. Since our voice will not be heard, the decision that will be made at the session will not be the result of the collective judgment of the delegates assembled here.

The President has been very kind to give me some additional time so that I may explain my amendments, of course, as briefly as possible. The amendments have been read out to you. The first amendment concretizes the declaration that is made in the resolution. The declaration is a repetition. But experience has proved that a simple declaration does not take us very far. Ever since 1929 the object of the Congress has been defined as complete independence. Nevertheless it is recent memory that there was a tendency, represented by not a few of our outstanding leaders, to interpret what is called dominion status of the Westminster variety as identical with complete independence. The resolution drafted by the Working Committee and submitted for your endorsement clearly and categorically rejects that tendency. But the fact remains that in spite of the self-same declaration having been made on innumerable occasions in the past, the growth of such a tendency, the tendency of deviating from the declared goal of the Congress, could not be checked. The object of my amendment is to create a guarantee against any such deviation in the future.

I want to draw your attention to one thing. Noting is farther from my mind than to question anybody's motive or to insinuate that there has been any wilful deviation. Since the goal is not clearly defined, everybody can make his own inference and the Congress being an organization of a large number of people, the danger of interpreting the vaguely defined goal differently will always be there unless it is more concretely stated. I am moving this amendment only as a guarantee against that danger, the danger which was actually before us in the recent past. I do not believe anyone of you will object to this amendment. I dare believe or hope that the Working Committee will see to it that such a declaration or a specific formulation of our goal is included in the resolution.

What is the implication of the amendment? We have been talking about Purna Swaraj or complete independence. In the Working Committee's resolution it has been clearly stated that independence of India, as desired and visualized by the Congress is incompatible with any status within the Empire. I propose that we go a little further and state the thing in a positive way. Any status within the British Empire would not be the complete independence we want. Let us go further and clearly define what status we do want. I am proposing nothing more than a concrete formulation of the ideal. I think that it goes without saying that complete independence means severance of all connections with the Empire. I know, as well as you do, that even as a free nation we shall have relations with other countries including England but that will be diplomatic relations. For the moment our relation is with the British Empire, which may be re-named the Commonwealth of British Nations. That relation must be severed, if we are to be free. Let us declare that without any ambiguity.

In the official resolution it has been visualized that even after the disappearance of political bondage India my be bound to Great Britain by all sorts of other ties. The main bondage is financial. Even the so-called self-governing Dominions, such as Canada and Australia, are bound down by financial operations. In the case of India it may be worse. Therefore, we want to make our goal very precise.

Secondly, there has been much discussion and difference of opinion about the way of attaining the goal of complete independence. I personally believe and my belief, I trust, is shared by many here—that complete independence can never be attained unless the Indian people are so organized as to capture power. Politics is always a question of power. We are subjects of a foreign Government, because the foreigners are in power. We shall be free from foreign rule when we have seized that power. There is no use of visualizing complete independence unless we think in terms of power; without that conception of power politics is meaningless.

These are the two concrete formulations I recommend. One is complete separation from the British Empire and the other is that complete independence will mean capture of power by the people. If the Congress goal of complete independence, as defined by the Lahore resolution and repeated since then on various occasions and once more reaffirmed by the resolution adopted by the Working Committee, is to be achieved, there should be no objection to amending the Working Committee's resolution in the manner I propose.

Now I come to the second amendment. The object of the second amendment is, as I said in the beginning, to add an operative part to the resolution. The resolution as it has come before us is not a resolution. It is only a declaration. As a declaration it is very important. But we are not to make a declaration, but to pass a resolution that we want to do certain things. A resolution sets some task before us and that task must be clearly defined. The task itself results from the declaration.

In the centre of the declaration of the Working Committee stands the demand for a Constituent Assembly. We shall do well to ponder what it means. We have declared that no constitution will be acceptable to India which is not framed by a Constituent Assembly. Nobody among us can share the delusion that the British Government will ever call a Constituent Assembly or will allow us to call one, or recognize a constitution framed by such an assembly if that constitution will be the constitution of a really free India. Others say that first we must be free, and the Government of free India will convene the Constituent Assembly. The task immediately before us then is to be free. What is the means, the instrument, for attaining our goal of complete independence? Those who maintain that the convention of the Constituent Assembly must be deferred until after the attainment of complete independence simply beg the vital question of power.

In that case, the demand of the Constituent Assembly ceases to have any bearing on the real politics of today. But it is our immediate demand. Therefore our task is to find out how that demand can be enforced. We reject the delusion that the British Government will allow us to call a Constituent Assembly? How can we then call a Constituent Assembly? In my amendment the process has been outlined. It is not possible that suddenly we call upon every single Indian adult to cast his or her vote and elect a Constituent Assembly. We are not living under normal conditions. The Constituent Assembly will challenge the authority of the British Government. We cannot expect the British Government to tolerate the rise of such an Assembly.

Therefore, we should be prepared to face resistance from the British Government. The Constituent Assembly will not rise in normal conditions and by normal means, such as adult franchise, through legal and legitimate method of ballot boxes, etc. That will not happen.

We shall have to create an electorate which will elect the Constituent Assembly. In order that the Assembly may be representative of the people of India, that section of the people of India which is engaged in the struggle of independence, which is working for the liberation of the oppressed and exploited masses, must create the electorate, so that it will be in a position to reflect their opinion. So our task is to organize their opinion. What kind of instrument should be created which will be able to express their opinion? We thought that in course of time the Congress organizations would be able to embrace the entire population of India and the local Congress Committees would eventually become the electorate for the Constituent Assembly and in course of time a special session of the Congress could declare itself the Constituent Assembly. But we have all sorts of communal differences which arrest that process. Therefore, the creation of some other organ of popular power and will, which, under the guidance of the Congress as the premier political organization of the country will be more representative of the various sections of the masses and thereby act as units of the Constituent Assembly representing the majority of the Indian people, has become necessary. For that, I have suggested the creation of People's Councils. The People's Councils cannot be created from today to tomorrow. It will grow out of struggle. How that struggle will develop has also been suggested in the amendment. Under the guidance of the primary Congress committees local struggles should be started for the redress of the burning grievances of the oppressed and the exploited masses. Experience of the struggle will convince the masses that even their daily grievances, their economic demands, are intimately connected with demand for political independence. From that experience they will feel the necessity of the conquest of political power. For fulfilling that necessity they will develop the will for political power. When that will is developed, we shall see how to enforce it. You have to create your local instruments in every village which will administer local affairs, according to your necessity and under your control and guidance. When these local instruments have functioned for some time, an atmosphere will be created in which these organs of popular power and will can be transformed into the local units of a new State. When such an atmosphere has been created throughout the country, then on the basis of these units we will build up the free democratic State of India. Upon the creation of these local units of popular power will the time come for the rise of the Constituent Assembly through which we would assert the sovereignty of the Indian people as against the sovereignty of a foreign authority. If we do not visualizes Constituent Assembly in that way, we shall be only talking about it.

The last point I want to make out is this. The constitution of a new state is made not by a handful of lawyers. It is the collective creation of the entire mass of a people involved in the struggle. We shall have to organize the masses of the people in this collective effort of creating the constitution. As the leader of the struggle for freedom, the Congress must place before the masses the principles of the constitution. As the leader of the Indian masses, as the organization which is fighting for the freedom of the Indian masses, the Congress will have to formulate such principles as will appeal to the masses, as will meet the needs of the life of the millions of the oppressed masses. Those principles will eventually be endorsed by the masses of the people. Then they will have a sanction behind them. A Constitution of a country is always made that way.

It grows out of a movement which has a programme. When these principles have secured the support of the people, then a new sovereignty is created by the people which gives sanction to the principles adopted by the masses of the people. Therefore, I propose that the principles should be formulated by the Congress which must declare what the constitution will be for which we are fighting. They should be submitted for mass discussion and endorsement. The masses must say that they approve these principles.

These are the two stages of constitution making. First of all, we shall have to work through local Congress committees and awaken among the masses political consciousness. We shall have to place the picture of the State which will give them real freedom. Finally when the masses give support to the principles on which the constitution should be based, we shall create the organizational conditions. Then the time will come when the Congress will be in a position to call upon the Indian people to elect a Constitution Assembly by free election, and the Constituent Assembly will have power.

I believe that my amendments are not foreign or repugnant to the resolution. Time has come when we must think clearly and we must have clear ideas before us. Let the Congress set before the country some concrete task. Let us make a resolution not merely a declaration. If you adopt the resolution as recommended by the Working Committee, you will be simply repeating a declaration. I am asking you to make a firm resolution, to give a lead to the country. I hope you will rise up to the occasion.

---

[1] The Congress Working Committee at its meeting held at Patna from 28 February to 1 March 1940 had adopted the Resolution which was recommended to the Subjects Committee on 18 March 1940 at its meeting at Ramgarh prior to the 53rd Session of the Indian National Congress held on 19–20 March 1940. The Resolution was passed by the Subjects Committee after all the amendments were voted upon and rejected. The text of the Resolution has been reproduced as Document no. 3 in Chapter 1.

12. R.D. Bhardwaj's Speech while Moving his Amendment to the Resolution on 'India and the War-Crisis' at Subjects Committee, Ramgarh, 18 March 1940

A.M. Zaidi and S.G. Zaidi (Chief Editors), *The Encyclopaedia of the Indian National Congress,* Vol. XII, Delhi, 1981, pp. 310–13.

Sir, I want to move the following amendment. Delete the whole sentence beginning from 'This preliminary step' to 'crisis' and replace it by the following in paragraph 5:

'The Congress declares that the stage is reached when this preliminary step must now be followed up by the launching of nation-wide mass civil disobedience in British India as well as in the Indian States.'

Friends, the resolution that has been placed before you on behalf of the Working Committee has got certain very important points clarified. It makes clear that the Congress will be satisfied only with complete national independence and not with any status within the structure of imperialism. It makes clear that the Constituent Assembly elected on the basis of adult suffrage is the proper course for the shaping of the Indian constitution and formulation of her foreign relations. The resolution also makes it clear that India asserts her right of self-determination and to have a constitution framed through the Constituent Assembly. Thirdly, the resolution also clarifies that the democratic regime of Indian India is to be established not only in British India but also in the Indian States, so that the integrity and unity of India are maintained.

Well, these three important points have been made clear by this resolution. We must go forward to the other part of the resolution, namely, the operative part of the resolution to which my amendment relates. You will find that in the preamble it is stated that the pronouncements of the British Government and of the representatives thereof have been absolutely unsatisfactory, and it is declared that the present war is meant to be an imperialist war carried for the purpose of continuing exploitation of India and of the Asiatic and the African countries and continuing imperialism. While all these things have been made clear, in the operative part all that we find is that civil disobedience is inevitable if circumstances so shape themselves as to precipitate a crisis, and when Congress organization is considered fit enough for it. I want to put before you me earlier statements with regard to these points. They have been clarified to a great extent. It was being stated that Dominion Status is equivalent to Independence. The resolution now placed before you, however, declares that nothing short of complete independence can be acceptable to the people of India. But in the resolution itself there is nothing whatsoever which gives a programme of action, the means, the instrument and the method of working whereby we may be able to achieve the high objectives that have been embodied in it. It is from the point of view of the operative part that we must judge this resolution.

After all, what is it that we have assembled for unless it be that the National Congress may be able to discuss things and give a call to the entire country to go forward and put that operative part into practice? Having said that civil disobedience has become inevitable, the resolution says, immediately in the next part of the sentence, that Congress will resort to civil disobedience when the Congress organization is considered fit or when a crisis is precipitated by imperialism. Let us try to understand what is the meaning of these two terms. Who is to judge the fitness of the Congress organization to launch civil disobedience? When are we to take it that a crisis has been precipitated by imperialism? Gandhiji has made it clear that unless communal harmony has been established, that unless he finds that Congressmen have pledged themselves to strict non-violence and that unless he finds there is strict discipline in the Congress rank, he will not consider the Congress fit enough for mass civil disobedience.

He has also laid great emphasis on the constructive programme of the Congress by which its fitness is to be tested. So the two conditions of imperialism precipitating a crisis and Congress being considered fit enough make this sentence of launching a civil disobedience movement absolutely useless, because the conditions of Mahatma Gandhi, in accordance with his interpretation, cannot be fulfilled in the near future. Those who believe that this resolution makes a declaration for starting civil disobedience or that it gives an order for marching forward or that it means any immediate struggle are absolutely wrong. If you read the articles of Mahatma Gandhi, you will find that they make it perfectly clear that he does not think in terms of a mass civil disobedience movement. He says the country is not ready. Can we today, at this moment when the entire forces of the country have gone forward ready to plunge in the battle for the achievement of the objective for which the country has been fighting for the last fifty years, believe that we are not ready, that we are not prepared and that there is going to be no mass civil disobedience movement?

Yesterday, Pandit Jawaharlal Nehru said that for any struggle great preparations were necessary and that we must make those preparations. We want there should be preparations. I want that the country should be prepared for the objective we have in view. If we want to launch a nationwide mass civil disobedience, we must give the call to the country to prepare for it and give a concrete programme of action so that within the shortest time we may be ready for civil disobedience. But there is no such declaration in the resolution. The resolution lays down certain conditions and eventualities on which alone civil disobedience will become inevitable. I assert with emphasis that those who believe that the resolution contemplates an immediate mass civil disobedience are wrong. There is [no] civil disobedience in the offing. The resolution, analysed in the proper perspective, means continuation of the stalemate that has been going on for the last six months.

The other day Gandhiji said that he still believed that without any struggle we could get complete independence. What is the basis of that stand-point? It appears they are harping on the belief that as the war crisis deepens, British imperialism will get increasingly involved in difficulties and then a situation may arise when it will not be necessary to launch any struggle for getting complete independence. That is the idea behind this resolution. That is the main basis of the resolution. I would like you to sit down and consider very coolly whether that is the correct line of argument which can appeal to you. We have for the last many years followed a policy the course of which is wholly inconsistent with this theory. Pandit Nehru at the Lucknow session stated that we must present a united front for fighting so that we may be able to achieve complete independence. I would ask you to consider whether we have given up that programme and course of action and whether we are going to get independence without any struggle? Do conditions warrant such a change in our policy? If you look at the world conditions, if you correctly analyse them, you will realize the importance of quick action. I would like to point out that if we do not move with the times, if we do not launch any struggle now, serious consequences are sure to follow.

Imperialism which is now in the midst of war, when it gets over its difficulties, will tighten its grip over the national movement and smash it and ultimately smash the Congress if it attempts to launch any movement later. Already it has turned its attention to the revolutionary forces in the country and the arrests and orders of internments and externments here and there, should not be taken as isolated cases. It is just beginning to attack the national movement. So if this stalemate continues, imperialism and communal and reactionary forces will gather force and smash the national movement. Besides, inside our own organization disruptive forces are at work. That section of the Congress which wants a revolutionary lead to be given and immediate action to be started are growing impatient and there is talk even of two Congresses. The unity that has been achieved by the Congress during all these years of struggle is threatened with disruption unless we go forward. Consider the whole background and the position to which we have been driven. The honour of the Congress is at stake. If you feel that any struggle is necessary to achieve the goal we have in view, today is the time when we should start the civil disobedience movement. To continue any longer the stalemate would mean disaster. It would allow imperialism and reactionary forces to smash our movement.

If my amendment is not accepted, and I apprehend it is not likely to be ultimately accepted, I make it clear that because the resolution means continuation of the stalemate and the consequent smashing up of national forces; and because it lacks an operative clause, communists are not going to vote for it.

13. Yusuf Meherally's Speech on the Resolution on 'India and the War-Crisis' at the Subjects Committee on Behalf of the Congress Socialist Party, Ramgarh, 18 March 1940

A.M. Zaidi and S.G. Zaidi (Chief Editors), *The Encyclopaedia of the Indian National Congress,* Vol. XII, Delhi, 1981, pp. 327–9.

Mr President, now that all the amendments are before the House. I want to indicate very briefly the position that the Congress Socialist Party proposes to take up vis-à-vis this resolution. It is known that we have decided to support this resolution. (Cries of 'shame' from a small section of the audience) The reasons why the Central Executive of the Congress Socialist Party has decided to support this resolution may be briefly indicated.

There is, of course, the obvious reason that we are in agreement with its essential points. Complete dissociation with the imperialist war is enjoined on all. Dominion Status has been categorically rejected. The demand for Constituent Assembly, elected on adult suffrage, is reiterated. The sovereignty of the people in the states is upheld against the pretension of the feudal Princes. Civil Disobedience as the next step is envisaged. We feel that what are important at this stage are not our differences but unswerving determination to march together in this hour of crisis. In a comprehensive resolution like this it is possible to detect things that one would phrase differently and points that are not fully covered. For the party whose role is that of parliamentary opposition, amendments are easy and even natural. But for a party of action at this critical time to differ over details, however important, is inexcusable. Since its inception the Congress Socialist Party has believed in the policy of a united front. We have recognized that the responsibility of a united front falls particularly on the shoulders of the Left. It is important, therefore, to contradict the impression that is being skillfully circulated, both in India and abroad, that the Congress is a house divided against itself and is in no position to make its will felt effectively.

On us lies the responsibility of checking and combating the disruptive tendencies. The situation is developing in a manner that we may find ourselves in the midst of a nationwide struggle at any moment. The interval between today and the actual commencement of the struggle cannot be long and must be utilized to speed up our final preparations and forge the necessary sanction for the fight. We feel that for this preparation, in addition to the constructive programme, the seven-point programme put forward by our party is necessary. Activization of Congress Committees, laying special stress on the position of the Congress on the question of the imperialist war and need for resisting utilization of Indian resources in men, money and material, clarification of our attitude towards a Constituent Assembly, enrolment and training of volunteers, development of labour and peasant struggles, particularly on the basis of the economic problems created by the war, boycott of British goods and intensive work in select areas in each district for civil disobedience, including no-rent and no-tax campaign, and to mobilizing workers for mass political action, are some of the plans, to which our immediate efforts must be directed.

There are only two things more on which I would like to speak to you. The first is about the amendment of Mr M.N. Roy. We cannot support it as it seeks to delete from the resolution that part of it which visualizes struggle against imperialism in the near future and he has been careful to remove the portion that the next step after resignation of the ministries would be civil disobedience. In so far as Mr Roy suggests incorporation of fundamental principles that should govern the constitution of free India, our party is in general agreement with him, and, as a matter of fact, a number of those items form part of our Party's ultimate programme. We feel it would find universal support in the Congress. But as we feel it is not desirable to divide the house on ideological issues and as we feel w that it is absolutely essential to preserve the unity of the Congress at this stage, we are unable to support the amendment of Mr Roy.

Communists have also moved some amendments. They have said that they would oppose the resolution if their amendments are not accepted. That attitude seems to be inexcusable. What can be the meaning of their stand that they would oppose the resolution when, on their own admission, it is a great advance on the existing position and it clarifies many issues of vital importance and when it says that the preliminary step must be followed up by civil disobedience? I wish to point out to them that, in effect, their policy would result in weakening those very forces whose assistance they themselves so strongly desire.

Finally, Sir, Government has embarked on a policy of severe repression. On a number of political workers orders of internment or externment or imprisonment have been passed for carrying out the anti-war programme of the Congress. The most effective reply to this repression would be intensification of the war resistance activities by every Congressman and starting a nation-wide campaign of civil disobedience. That will take India right to her goal of freedom.

14. Mahatma Gandhi's Speech at the Subjects Committee After it had Passed the Resolution on 'India and the War-Crisis', Ramgarh, 18 March 1940

Harijan, 30 March 1940.

To Find Out Where I was

Since I went out of the Congress at Bombay, there has been an understanding between me and the Working Committee that I should not be asked to speak at the AICC or the Subjects Committee or the open session, and should be allowed to conserve the little strength that is left in me. I have usually been attending the meeting of the Working Committee. On this occasion, I myself suggested that I should address the Subjects Committee and also the delegates. The Working Committee agreed to this and, although I wanted to address you before the resolution was adopted, the Committee suggested that I do so after the resolution was disposed of.

It was my desire to see the faces of you all, and also to give you an opportunity of looking at me and finding out if there had been any change in me since my retirement in Bombay. Fifty years of public life have given me the capacity to read your faces. I have A during these years created many institutions, met thousands and tens of thousands of people, and it should not therefore be difficult for me to get at the back of your minds. But my desire to see you was in order to find out where I was.

Difficulties

You have, I see, made considerable progress in the art of debate and I congratulate you, for in a democratic organization powers of persuasion and a high level of debate are essential. I have also seen that the number of amendments you move has also increased, and it is well that you should all be anxious to press new points of view, though I cannot congratulate you on some of the amendments which were either frivolous or absurd.

You have adopted the resolution practically unanimously as there were only seven or eight dissentients. That adds to my responsibility, for I have been witness to the debate. If I had so desired, I should have warned you before voting, but I accepted the suggestion of the Working Committee that I should not address the house before the resolution was passed.

I do not want to reply to what has been said by some of you in the course of the debate. But I do want to say that, though there was a time in my life when I launched movements even if some of my conditions had not been fulfilled, I am now going to be hard, not for the sake of being hard, but because a General who has to lead the army must let the army know his conditions beforehand.

Let me then tell you that I do not see at the present moment conditions propitious for an immediate launching of the campaign. We are hemmed in with difficulties greater than those we had to face in the past. They are external and internal. The external difficulties are due to the fact that we have declared unmistakably what we want and the Government have also declared their intentions as clearly as possible. Then there is the fact that the British Government are engaged in a world war and naturally, if we engage them in a fight, we ask for enough trouble.

What, however, appeals me is our internal difficulties. I have often said that external difficulties need never frighten a Satyagrahi. On the contrary, he flourishes on external difficulties and faces them with redoubled zeal and vigour. Today the situation is almost the reverse. Our external difficulties do not find us stronger and more united. Our internal difficulties are increasing. Our Congress registers are full of bogus members and members who have swelled them because they know that getting into the Congress means getting into power. Those who therefore never before thought of entering the Congress have come into it and corrupted it. And how can we prevent people from coming into a democratic organization because they come from selfish motives? We have not that discipline, and not the strength and purity of public opinion which would compel such people to stay out.

And this strength and purity cannot come so long as we approach the primary members only once in a year for the vote. There is no discipline in our ranks, they have been divided up into groups which strive to gain more and more power. Non-violence as between ourselves does not seem to us to be necessary. There may be groups, but they should strengthen and not weaken and destroy the organization.

No Democracy in an Army

Ours has been both a democratic organization and a fighting one, ever since we reorganized it in 1920. We have used even military language, though in a non-violent sense. Well, then, I want to repeat what I have said times without number that, if you will be soldiers in my army, understand that there is no room for democracy in that organization. The army may be a part of a democratic organization, but there can be no democracy in it, as there can be none in its rank, as there is none in our various organizations AISA AIVIA and so on. In an army the General's word is law, and his conditions cannot be relaxed.

My Conditions Inexorable

I am supposed to be your General, but I do not know a more feeble General in history. My only sanction is the love and affection in which you hold me. But it has its weakness as it has its strength. I know that you love me. Does your love translate itself into action? If it does not, if it does not mean ever-increasing discipline and ever-increasing response to what I say, let me declare to you that I cannot launch civil disobedience, and you must select another General. You cannot make me your General on your terms. Know, therefore, that I will insist on my conditions. They are inexorable, and if you do not observe them, I will automatically withdraw.

The General of a military army insists on strict discipline. I go on arguing with you, because my only sanction is love. I say to you, therefore, that unless you accept my conditions, unless you have faith in them as you have in me, you should not think of going to jail. If you will go to jail, you have to pay the price. Ours is a civil fight, and imprisonment as a civil prisoner has got to be earned by strict observance of the programme. Otherwise even thieves and dacoits also fill the jails, but they do not carry the country to freedom.

Well then I laid down the conditions in 1920 and have never ceased to repeat them. You may not believe in the programme, you may have grown wiser since then, but I have not. My faith in it has increased with the years. I see more virtues in it than I saw before.

I turned a rebel against this Government in 1919, but before that I was as loyal to it as any Britisher. It is that unique loyalty that gave me the unique power of civil disobedience, and the unquenchable spirit of search. I therefore go on making my experiments and also go on declaring my mistakes whenever I discover them. I am an erring mortal like you. I have never even in my dream thought that I was Maha-atma (great soul) and that others were Alpa-atma (little souls). We are all equal before our Maker—Hindus, Mussalmans, Parsis, Christians, worshippers of one God. Why then do we fight among ourselves?

We are all brothers—even the Quaed-e-Azam is my brother. I have meant all that I have said about him, never has a frivolous word escaped my lips, and I say that I want to win him over. A speaker said that I would not fight until I had won him over, and he was right. There was a time when there was not a Muslim whose confidence I did not enjoy. Today I have forfeited that confidence and most of the Urdu press pours abuse on me. But I am not sorry for it. It only confirms me in my belief that there is no Swaraj without a settlement with the Mussalmans.

You will perhaps ask, in that case, why am I talking of a fight. I do so in order to have a Constituent Assembly which means agreement and settlement. But if the Mussalmans will have nothing to do with it, I will understand that there is no settlement. I am also a reader of the Koran like them, and I will tell them that the Koran makes no distinction between the Hindus and the Mussalmans. But if they feel that they should have the Heaven without the Hindus, I will not grudge it to them.

Ever for Compromise

I have no ill-will towards Englishmen. When I heard that Lord Zetland was wounded, my heart was wounded. That is my temperament. I therefore always work with and for goodwill for them. That I want to destroy British Imperialism is another matter, but I want to do so by converting those who are associated with it. If non-violence has the power that I attribute to it, it is sure to react on the opponent. If it does not, the fault will be mine, not that of non-violence.

You must therefore understand that you have to deal with a dangerous man who will land you in unexpected situations. Compromise is a part and parcel of my nature. I will go to the Viceroy fifty times, if I feel like it. I went to Lord Reading whilst non-cooperation was going on. I would not only go to the Viceroy when invited, but I would even seek opportunities to go to him, if necessary. You must know that, if I do so, I do it in order to strengthen our cause and not weaken it. It happened so with General Smuts. At the last moment I telephoned to him. He put the receiver down in anger, but I thrust myself on him. As a result he relented and

I was in a stronger position. Today we are friends. I could not have fought the Dutch and the English without love in my heart for them, and without a readiness for compromise. But my compromises will never be at the cost of the cause or of the country.

One of the amendments was to the effect that the word 'mass' be inserted before 'civil disobedience'. Well, if it is not mass civil disobedience, is it to be the civil disobedience of a handful? In that case I should not have come to you. It is the thought of mass civil disobedience that keeps my mind awake all the twenty four hours. Why should a man of 70 trifle with a thing of this kind?

Therefore let me tell you that there is no civil disobedience until I feel that you are ready. You have therefore to purify every Congress Committee and make it a Satyagrahi unit. To that extent it will have to cease to be a democracy, because my word will be law. But if it does not become such a unit, millions of our dumb countrymen will be sacrificed. None of my campaigns has crushed or ruined the masses. They have increased their stature, and it is in order to take it still higher that I want to live. There was in the earlier campaigns enough of violence of thought and word, but there was non-violence in act, and therefore the masses were saved. I would not light-heartedly imperil those masses today, and that is why I insist on strictest non-violence and the fulfillment of my conditions. For that is the only link that binds them and me.

If I am your General, your pulse should be in my hands. Otherwise I cannot fight through you. I can fight single-handed, but for that fight I need not come and argue with you.

One last word before I close, I do not want to stand in the way of those who want to fight at once. But if they have any sense of honour, I should advise them to do so after getting out of the Congress. Let me assure them that, if they put up a non-violent fight and carry it through, I shall follow their lead.

Of course it is open to them to remain in the Congress and to defy it, but it will not be Satyagraha. Those who are impatient today do not know the power of Satyagraha.

The resolution does not bind you. If you do not accept the conditions, you can still say you do not accept them, and you can have the resolution reversed. That will free you and me both. But if you accept the conditions and will all observe them, you may be sure that it need not take me a month to launch the struggle.

15. Mahatma Gandhi's Speech at the Open Session of the Indian National Congress, Ramgarh, 20 March 1940

Harijan, 30 March 1940.

We are not Ready

I was glad to have the opportunity of listening to the speakers who moved the amendments. The name of Satyagraha was on their lips, and it reminded me of the Biblical phrase 'Not those who say "Lord" "Lord" but those who do the will of God will find Him.' (Cheers) I do not need your cheers. I want to win your hearts and your intellects, and cheers and acclamations stand in the way of winning them. Let me therefore warn you that not those who shout 'Satyagraha', 'Satyagraha', will do Satyagraha but those who will work for it. And the essence of Satyagraha is to carry out in letter and spirit the word of him whom you have chosen as your general, and to eschew the things he asks you to avoid. For without Satyagraha carried out in the proper spirit, there is no victory and no Swaraj.

I believe with some of you who said that it is our duty to shake ourselves free from slavery. But how are we to do it? Supposing a few dacoits come and take possession of our house and drive us out, it is of course our duty to fight the dacoits and get our house back from them. But how can we do it? We have to plan and prepare for it. Therefore when I saw you acclaiming the speaker who said that we were ready, I was shocked. For I know that we are not ready. And knowing this, how can I ask you to fight? I know that with such as you I can only have defeat. And defeat I do not want, and defeat I have never known, not even in Rajkot, whatever you may say to the contrary. The word 'defeat' is not to be found in my dictionary, and everyone who is selected as a recruit in my army may be sure that there is no defeat for a Satyagrahi.

One of the speakers said that he had no quarrel with the charkha, but he wanted the charkha to be divorced from Satyagraha. Well I tell you, as I have been telling you these 20 years, that there is a vital connection between Satyagraha and charkha, and the more I find that belief challenged the more I am confirmed in it. Otherwise I am no fool to persist in turning the charkha, day in and day out, at home and even on trains, in the teeth of medical advice. I want you too to be turning the charkha with the same faith. And unless you do it and unless you habitually use khadi you will deceive me and deceive the world.

Final Warning

I shall of course die with non-violence on my lips, but you are not wedded to it in the sense I am, and so it is open to you to have another programme and to make our country free. But if you will not do this, nor turn the charkha, and want me to fight, it will be an impossible situation.

I know that you will not fight unless you have me with you, but then you must know that I am here and I would fight only as a representative of those dumb millions for whom I live and for whom I want to die. My loyalty to them is greater than any other loyalty, and it is for them that I would not give up the charkha even if you were to forsake me or kill me. For I know that, if I were to relax the conditions of the charkha, I should bring ruin upon those dumb millions for whom I have to answer before God. If, therefore, you do not believe in the charkha in the sense I believe in it, I implore you to leave me. The charkha is an outward symbol of truth and non-violence, and unless you have them in your hearts you will not take to the charkha either. Remember, therefore, that you have to fulfil both the internal and external conditions. If you fulfil the internal condition, you will cease to hate your opponent, you will not seek or work for his destruction, but pray to God to have mercy on him. Do not, therefore, concentrate on showing the misdeeds of the Government, for we have to convert and befriend those who run it. And after all no one is wicked by nature. And if others are wicked, are we the less so? That attitude is inherent in Satyagraha, and if you do not subscribe to it, even then I would ask you to leave me. For without a belief in my programme and without an acceptance of my condition you will ruin me, ruin yourselves and ruin the cause.

II.   Preparations for Satyagraha

16.   Mahatma Gandhi: 'Every Congress Committee a Satyagraha Committee', 25 March 1940

Harijan, 30 March 1940.

When I said at the Subjects Committee meeting at Ramgarh that every Congress Committee should become a Satyagraha Committee, I meant every word of what I said, as I meant every word of everything else I said. I would like every Congressman who desires to serve in the Satyagraha Sena to read my two speeches made at Ramgarh as well as whatever else I may write in *Harijan* on the struggle, and to carry out the instructions meant for him or her.

In the coming struggle, if it must come, no half-hearted loyalty will answer the purpose. Imagine a general marching to battle with doubting, ill-prepared soldiers. He will surely march to defeat. I will not consciously make any such fatal experiment. This is not meant to frighten Congressmen. If they have the will, they will not find my instructions difficult to follow. Correspondents tell me that, though they have no faith in me or the charkha, they ply the latter for the sake of discipline. I do not understand this language. Can a general fight on the strength of soldiers who, he knows, have no faith in him? The plain meaning of this language is that the correspondents believe in mass action but do not believe in the connection I see between it and the charkha, etc., if the action is to be non-violent. They believe in my hold on the masses, but they do not believe in the things which I believe have given me that hold. They merely want to exploit me and will grudgingly pay the price which my ignorance or obstinacy (according to them) demands. I do not call this discipline. True discipline gives enthusiastic obedience to instructions even though they do not satisfy reason. A volunteer exercises his reason when he chooses his general, but after having made the choice, he does not waste his time and energy in scanning every instruction and testing it on the anvil of his reason before following it. His is 'not to reason why'.

Now for my instructions.

Every Congress Committee should become a Satyagraha Committee and register such Congressmen who believe in the cultivation of the spirit of goodwill towards all, who have no untouchability in them in any shape or form, who would spin regularly, and who habitually use khadi to the exclusion of all other cloth. I would expect those who thus register their names with their Committees to devote the whole of their spare time to the constructive programme. If the response is sincere, these Satyagraha Committees would become busy spinning depots. They will work in conjunction with and under the guidance of AISA branches in a businesslike manner so that there remain, in the jurisdiction of the Committees, no Congressmen who have not adopted khadi for exclusive use. I shall expect businesslike reports to be sent from provincial headquarters to the AICC as to the progress of the work of the Satyagraha Committees. Seeing that this registration is to be purely voluntary, the reports would mention the numbers both of those who give their names for registration and those who do not.

The registered Satyagrahis will keep a diary of the work that they do from day to day their work, besides their own spinning, will consist in visiting the primary members and inducing them to use khadi, spin and register themselves. Whether they do so or not, contact should be maintained with them.

There should be visits paid to *Harijan* homes and their difficulties removed so far as possible.

Needless to say that names should be registered only of those who are willing and able to suffer imprisonment.

No financial assistance is to be expected by Satyagrahi prisoners whether for themselves or their dependants.

So much for the active Satyagrahis. But there is a much larger class of men and women who, though they will not spin or court or suffer imprisonment, believe in the two cardinal principles of Satyagraha and welcome and wish well to the struggle. These I will call passive Satyagrahis. They will help equally with the active ones, if they will not interfere with the course of the struggle by themselves courting imprisonment or aiding or precipitating strikes of labourers or students. Those who out of overzeal or for any other cause will act contrary to these instructions will harm the struggle and may even compel me to suspend it. When the forces of violence are let loose all over the world and when nations reputed to be most civilized cannot think of any force other than that of arms for the settlement of their disputes, I hope that it will be possible to say of India that she fought and won the battle of freedom by purely peaceful means.

I am quite clear in my mind that, given the co-operation of politically-minded India, the attainment of India's freedom is perfectly possible through unmixed non-violence. The world does not believe our pretension of non-violence. Let alone the world—I, the self-styled general, have repeatedly admitted that we have violence in our hearts, that we are often violent to one another in our mutual dealings. I must confess that I will not be able to fight so long as we have violence in our midst. But I will fight if the proposed register is honest and if those who courageously keep out will not disturb the even course of the struggle.

Non-violent action means mobilization of world opinion in our favour. I know that a growing number of thinking men and women of the world are sick of the war spirit, they are longing for a way of peace, and they are looking to India to point that way. We cannot have that opinion on our side if we are not honestly non-violent. Let me repeat what I have said in these columns that I shall be able to fight with a very small army of honest Satyagrahis and shall feel powerless and embarrassed if I have a huge army in which I can have no trust or as to whose behaviour I am not always sure.

I expect the AICC to organize Satyagraha Committees and report to me from time to time of the progress made. If there is an enthusiastic response, inside of one month it should be possible to forecast the exact period required to put the Satyagraha Committees in working order.

Sevagram, 25-3-40

17. Congress General Secretary's Circular on Satyagraha Committees, 29 March 1940

Indian Annual Register, 1940, Vol. I, pp. 238–40.

In connection with my circular letter No. 1, P–l/8 dated 23rd March, 1940. I send you herewith copy of an article contributed by Gandhiji in the columns of the Harijan dated the 25th March, 1940 containing detailed instructions for all those who would participate and help to the forthcoming Satyagraha struggle. Gandhiji divides the army into active and passive Satyagrahis. For the former he has prescribed 5 conditions; (1) they must believe in the cultivation of the spirit of good will towards all communities and sections of people without distinction of caste, creed and colour and sex; (2) they must have no untouchability in them in any shape or form; (3) they must spin regularly; (4) they must habitually use Khaddar to the exclusion of all other cloth and (5) they must not expect in case of imprisonment any financial assistance either for themselves or their dependents.

The passive Satyagrahis are those men and women who 'though they will not spin or court or suffer imprisonment, believe in the two cardinal principles of Satyagraha (Truth and non-violence) and wish well to the struggle'. They will help the movement best 'if they will not interfere with the course of the struggle by themselves courting imprisonment and aiding or precipitating strikes of labourers or students'. They will, however, it is hoped, actively help in the prosecution of the constructive programme so far as it is not against their principles.

If Gandhiji's instructions are faithfully followed, every unit of Congress organization must convert itself into a Satyagraha Committee. It is, however, possible that the majority of the members and office bearers of a Committee are not active Satyagrahis. In that case, a separate Satyagraha committee may be created consisting of active Satyagrahis. The Congress Committee must help and co-operate with such Satyagraha Committees. The latter may carry on the work for the preparation of the struggle, while the former may go on with routine Congress business. I have already asked the provincial Congress Committee to have 4 departments of work namely: (1) the Charkha; (2) Minority; (3) Harijan; (4) Publicity Departments. If there be need for more departments they may be added. Funds must be provided for each department. Permission under necessary safeguards may be given to the departments to raise money for their respective activities. All the departments created must co-operate with each other.

At Ramgarh, Gandhiji was assured that the country was ready for a fight.

The only thing needed was the word of command. I have no doubt that this is the prevalent feeling in the country. In that case, given the will for Satyagraha, there should be no difficulty in fulfilling the conditions laid down by our Leader. Let every man and woman feel that he or she is already in jail. Let them combine under a Congress organization or Satyagraha association, or Sabha and establish ashrams, shibirs and camps where the members carry out in daily routine the programme that is prescribed. Let us even from now suspend our private normal activities and devote ourselves to the work of preparation. In such shibirs, ashrams and camps additional items of work may be undertaken, such as volunteering and first aid to the injured. Let such camps continue till the inmates find themselves in jail. Let the camps be conducted with as much voluntary 'sanyam' (restraint) and simplicity of life as are compulsorily the lot of the Satyagrahi after he is convicted and finds himself in jail. If this is done the order to march may be given even inside one month as Gandhiji hopes.

It is necessary for the active Satyagrahi to pledge himself about the main principles of Satyagraha and the chief items of the programme. Each provincial Congress Committee will therefore draw up a pledge on the lines of the one attached herewith. It is based upon the pledge drawn up and adopted at the open session of the Congress in 1921 at Ahmedabad.

It will not be out of place here to remind you what Gandhiji said at Ramgarh. He told his audience that this time when the struggle is likely to be final and therefore severe and prolonged, he will not be satisfied with doubtful material. He has also warned us that if he smells violence he will unhesitatingly call halt. It is a hazardous and delicate experiment that he is out to perform. If it succeeds, it means peace and goodwill for a tired nerve wrecked and war-weary world. Those whose faith in non-violence is not as bright as Gandhiji would wish it, will,

I hope, have the patience to allow Satyagrah[a] a chance, specially when with almost one voice the nation has reposed its faith and confidence in Gandhiji's leadership. After all those who work for peace and justice in this country or for the world, may not be impatient. They are bound to try every method that saves humanity from war, violence and bloodshed. When Satyagraha fails, after it has been given a fair trial in terms of the conditions laid down by its author and initiator, it will be time to use the orthodox way of violence, if the national so wishes. We must remember that the way of violence is ever with us. In the meantime, to interfere with the work of the Congress under Gandhiji's lead would not be to advance the best interests of the revolution we wish to achieve but to work for reaction and counter-revolution. Let therefore all earnest minds either close up the ranks by being active Satyagrahis or help the movement by remaining passive. 'They also serve who stand and wait.'

May I request you to carefully study the present statement of Gandhiji and any other instructions in this behalf that may be issued by him from time to time? You will ask your subordinate organizations to do likewise. The Office must get fortnightly reports containing facts and figures about the progress of the work undertaken.

Pledge

To

The Satyagraha/Congress Committee.

....

I desire to enroll myself as an active Satyagrahi.
I solemnly declare that,

1. So long as I remain an active Satyagrahi I shall remain non-violent in word and deed and shall earnestly endeavour to be non-violent in intent, since I believe that as India is circumstanced today, non-violence alone can help and result in the attainment of Purna Swaraj and consolidation of unity among all the races and communities of India whether Hindu, Muslim, Sikh, Parsi, Christian or Jew.
2. I believe and shall endeavour always to promote such unity.
3. I believe in the justice and necessity of removing the evil of untouchability and shall on all possible occasions seek personal contact with, and endeavour to render service to, the submerged classes.
4. I believe in Swadeshi as essential for India's economic, political and moral salvation and shall use hand-spun and hand-woven khaddar to the exclusion of every other cloth. I shall so far as possible use the produce of hand and village industries.
5. I shall spin regularly.
6. I shall carry out the instructions of my superior officers and all rules and regulations not inconsistent with the spirit of this pledge prescribed by any superior Congress organization or the Working Committee or any other agency established by the Congress.
7. I am prepared to suffer imprisonment or even death for the sake of the cause and my country without resentment.

8. In the event of my imprisonment I shall not claim from the Congress any support for my self, my family and dependents.

Signed
Full name ....
Address ....
Date ....

Note: Nobody who is not above the age of 18 may take this pledge.

18. Congress General Secretary's Circular, 5 April 1940
Indian Annual Register, 1940, Vol. I, pp. 241–2.

In continuation of my circular No. 4 dated March 29, 1940, I have to request that in recording the names of active satyagrahis, there need be no anxiety to add to numbers. Every care should be taken to see that the full implications and the requirements insisted upon by Gandhiji and given in the pledge are clearly understood and appreciated. Nobody who consents to the terms of the pledge from considerations of expediency for participating in the struggle, should be encouraged to join the ranks. Even in a violent fight, it is not merely numbers but the moral quality of the units comprising an army, that is of importance. This is much more true of a fight based upon principles of truth and non-violence. Here the moral quality of individuals is of utmost importance. Therefore it is not so much in numbers as in the quality of those who join the ranks of active satyagrahis, that our strength shall die. If we are in any way slack in this matter and if the future conduct of satyagrahis belies the conditions laid down, advantage will be taken of our slackness by the Government and the communal and other forces arrayed against us at present. It may even mean the suspension of our movement. If however, we stand firm on our principles and if no lure of temporary political advantage or speedy success deflects us from the course we have chalked out for ourselves in consonance with our high aims and noble and pure means, nothing in the world can resist us.

In making the list of active and passive satyagrahis Congress committees must confine themselves to recording the names of Congressmen. No general census of those in sympathy with us is to be compiled. It is quite possible that non-Congressmen may want to enlist themselves as active satyagrahis. In that case they must be asked to join the Congress and become primary members.

I have already written to you about camps, shibirs and ashrams that may be advantageously established for active satyagrahis. But this may not be possible everywhere. In that case in every locality, urban or rural, active satyagrahis must meet in batches regularly and carry out, in common, items of the programme. They will find this the easiest method of doing the allotted work. For instance, in every ward of a city or every village or group of villages, where there are enough active satyagrahis enrolled, they may meet together and appoint one from among themselves as Captain or Leader and under his guidance meet periodically if not daily, for plying the Takli or the Charkha. They will thus find that they may not need a separate teacher for spinning. They can also fix particular days in the week on which they may learn simple drill and first-aid to the injured. They may, in batches of 2 or 3, visit the Harijans and members of the minority communities in their homes and establish personal contacts with them. If they work together and in groups they will find that they can carry out the programme with ease and convenience. Each group must keep a diary of the work done and send it periodically to the Committee superior to it. The consolidated report of the activities in the province should be prepared in the Provincial Congress Committee Office every fortnight and forwarded to the All India Congress Committee Office.

19. Congress President Maulana Abul Kalam Azad's Statement in Connection with the National Week

Indian Annual Register, 1940, Vol. I, pp. 242–3.

The General Secretary of the All India Congress Committee has drawn the attention of the Congress organization [through circular No. 3, 25th March] towards the approach of the National Week, and reminded them of their tasks. I am confident that on this occasion all Congress Committees will fully demonstrate their capacity for action. In this connection I expect of every Congressman and woman, every supporter of the Congress cause to contribute in a practical manner towards the success of the week.

For the last 20 years this week has come to stay as the season of our constructive efforts. Like the natural seasons of our land this one also recurs every year, and after influencing us for a while, passes on. Our natural seasons affect us physically, while this one reacts on our intellect and emotions. It provides us with a rare opportunity for self-introspection and self-purification in order that we I examine afresh our hearts and our minds. It comes to gauge how far our professions of service, sacrifice and non-violence which we repeat so often, have penetrated into the depths of our hearts. For us this year the approach of the National Week has a special significance.

Only a few days back we have announced to the world from the Congress platform at Ramgarh, our new passion for freedom and our determination to achieve it. The National Week is thus the first stage of testing the value of these announcements. If at this stage, we live up to the true ideal of our constructive programme it would provide us with those inner resources without which it would be difficult for us to acquit ourselves with honour in the coming struggle.

How then do we expect to fulfil the requirements of the constructive programme? The constructive programme implies Hindu–Muslim unity, removal of untouchability and extensive popularization of Khadi. Do we imagine that by holding a few meetings and delivering speeches, we would fulfil the task assigned for the National Week? Does it suffice for us that we go about hawking khadi for a week in the streets and bye-lanes of the towns, and then come back to our normal occupations with the feeling that we have done our duty to the constructive programme?

Of course, all these are necessary items of the programme, and we must carry them out. But this alone would not do. These activities undoubtedly give shape and form to our efforts, but we require something more to put life into it. We Congressmen profess to shoulder the great burden of our national movement in India today, and ours undoubtedly is the responsibility in every phase of thought and action. If we imbibe the true spirit of the constructive programme, I have no hesitation in affirming that every atom of this land will respond to the call of national life.

But do we expect to carry warmth to others if our own hearths grow cold? No, we must kindle our own fires first. The National Week provides us with that opportunity.

⊢—✳—⊣

20. Congress Working Committee Resolution on Satyagraha, 15–19 April 1940

Indian Annual Register, 1940, Vol. I, p. 244.

The Working Committee have given full consideration to the situation in the country as it has developed since the Ramgarh Congress and to the necessity for preparing the Congress organization for Satyagraha which the Ramgarh Congress declared was inevitable in the future. The Committee welcomes the steps taken by the Provincial Congress Committees in pursuance of the directions issued by Gandhiji to function as Satyagraha Committee and to enroll active and passive satyagrahis. The Committee trusts that all Congress Committees throughout the country will pursue this programme with all earnestness and thoroughness and will put their affairs in order for such action as may be required of them. The Committee recommends that those members of Congress executives who are unable to take the prescribed pledge and shoulder the burden of a struggle under the disciplined guidance of the Congress, will withdraw from their executive positions. The Committee lay stress again on the fulfillment of the conditions laid down by Gandhiji, compliance with which is essential for Civil Disobedience.

21. Congress General Secretary's Circulars, 10 April–4 May 1940

Indian Annual Register, 1940, Vol. I, pp. 244–6.

Circular No. 1—10th April

One of our chief tasks is to inform our countrymen of the stand taken by the Congress during the present war and the consequences that flow out of it. This task should be so done that not a single Indian may be unacquainted with the Congress viewpoint and what is expected of him. It is true that Congressmen in the various districts are doing this work. But there ought to be better planning, more system and thoroughness. I suggest that this can be done if we decided to work out a programme of at least one meeting for every village.

There are on an average 2,500 villages to every district in our country. We must decide to hold public meetings in the district, one in each village. The District Congress Committee should for this purpose select a band of about 40 speakers. Each speaker, if necessary, can address two meetings in two different villages in the course of a day. Group of villages when near enough can be combined. In this manner, our programme can be worked out inside of a month.

Care should be taken in the selection of speakers. They must be active Satyagrahis, should have understood the Congress stand in its various aspects and must be able to put it across in simple and dignified language. The bases for these speeches should be: (1) Ramgarh Congress Resolution, (2) Mahatma Gandhi's instructions given in his article in the '*Harijan*' of 30th March entitled 'Every Congress Committee a Satyagraha Committee', (3) the AICC Circular No.4, dated the 27th March, explaining these instructions, and (4) the implications of the pledge. The speakers should aim at making clear and comprehensive speeches. It would be best if, at these meetings, the authorized speaker alone made a detailed and comprehensive speech.

I suggest that District Congress Committees be asked to take up this work at once, select a band of speakers and map out a plan of meetings.

In order to save time, copies of this Circular are being sent direct to such District Congress Committees whose address is with the AICC Office. You will please see to it that this work is properly organized and speedily carried out.

Circular No. 2—10th April

About the formation of the Provincial Election Tribunal in terms of the Congress Constitution, the Working Committee at its present meeting here have decided that 'For the purposes of Art VIII (b) May 5, 1940 is fixed as the last date for the appointment of the Tribunal.'

It is hoped that if you have not already appointed the Tribunal for the year you will do so now. If however by the 5th of May, 1940 no new Tribunal is appointed the Working Committee will be constrained to appoint one in terms of Art VIII, Clause (b).

I may also inform you, that till the new Tribunal is appointed, last year's Tribunal is to function.

Circular No. 3—23rd April

I am sending you herewith copies of the two resolutions passed by the last meeting of the Working Committee at Wardha. The resolution on Satyagraha is self-explanatory. You are directed to carryon the activities you have already undertaken in pursuance of Gandhiji's directions with all possible thoroughness. You will please bear in mind the necessity of sending to this office a fortnightly report of the work done.

Shri R.S. Pandit will soon undertake inquiries into the condition of the volunteer movement in the various provinces. He will communicate with you direct and may also visit your province. You are requested to render him full assistance and cooperation.

Circular No. 4—3rd May

Before the Ramgarh Congress you were requested to supply to this office the figures and all other information regarding suppression of civil liberties in your province, since the commencement of the war. I am sorry to say the most of the Provinces have not supplied us with the information asked for. When some provinces have given us information, they have contented themselves with sending it once only. We have, therefore, no up-to-date information in this behalf. May I request that up-to-date information about prosecutions, arrests, prohibitory orders, etc., in your province since the commencement of the war be supplied to us immediately. The information asked for is to be placed before the next meeting of the Working Committee which is likely to be held by the end of this month. If the information is supplied by the third week of May, at the latest, it will enable the office to arrange and tabulate it for presentation before the Working Committee.

Circular No. 5—3rd May

The President wants information from you on the following points. This information is to be supplied immediately. This letter must therefore be considered as urgent.

1. Is proper discipline maintained in the Congress organizations in your province?
2. If there is any indiscipline, what are the causes therefor?
3. What groups, if any, are there in the Congress organization in your Province?
4. What are their activities?
5. How far do their activities hamper Congress work in the province?

I would also remind you once again that you have to send to this office fortnightly reports about the progress of work in your province in connection with Satyagraha.

Circular No. 6—3rd May

In my circular letter No.4 dated March 29, 1940 I had said that where the majority of the members of the executive of a Congress Committee are nd1: active Satyagrahis, a separate Satyagraha Committee be formed for carrying on activities in connection with Satyagraha preparation and the Congress Committees in such cases should attend to the other routine business of the organization. The Working Committee at their meeting held at Wardha last month, decided that no separate Satyagraha Committee be formed and that every Committee of the Congress must necessarily transform itself into a Satyagraha Committee and carryon in addition to its ordinary routine work, the work of Satyagraha preparation. The Working Committee also decided such members of the Committees as could not for any reasons sign the Satyagraha pledge should resign their seats on the Committee and allow their seats to be filled up by active Satyagrahis. You will therefore please see to it that these latest instructions of the Working Committee are carried out in your Province.

This change was necessary because it was thought that it would be undesirable if people who were not in tune with the present policy of the Congress should yet continue holding offices in the organization. It was also felt that the question of relation between the Congress Committees and separate Satyagraha Committees may cause friction and indiscipline in the Congress organization at a time when unity of purpose and effort is absolutely necessary.

I am sure those who refuse to sign the Satyagraha pledge will see the wisdom and the necessity of voluntarily resigning their seats, thus allowing Congress organization to carry out the official policy smoothly and without friction.

Circular No. 7—4th May

I am sending you herewith the questionnaire in terms of which information has got to be collected in your province and submitted to this Office. You will please expedite the collection of information. Whenever you send this information you will keep in view the questionnaire. Enclo. 1

1. Number of Satyagrahis enrolled. Are they fulfilling the conditions prescribed in the Pledge? Do they meet periodically?
2. What steps have been taken to popularize Khadi?
3. What steps have been taken to establish contacts with the (1) Harijans, (2) Minorities.
4. The Office of the PCC (1) Hours of work, number of employees, salary, (2) Departments, quantity and quality of work, (3) Accounts, (5) Propaganda.
5. The meetings of the PCC and the Executive. How often do they meet? Matters dealt with by them after the Ramgarh Congress, instructions issued to the DCCs.
6. How many members of these bodies have signed the Satyagraha pledge?
7. District and City Congress Committees. The number of these committees and their total members. Have they turned into Satyagraha councils? How are the District Offices functioning? Do they keep contact with the subordinate committees?
8. What steps have the DCCs taken to organize the preparatory work for Satyagraha. The number of satyagrahis enrolled.

9. Are Mandal committees functioning? Details as to the number of members of these committees, satyagrahis enrolled, and their activities?

10. Have group rivalries within the Congress declined or disappeared? What is the strength of the dissentient groups and what are their activities?

11. How is the public reacting to our preparations for Satyagraha?

12. Training camps held in the Province. Details as to the number of persons who participated in them, their daily routine, the kind of training received, results obtained and other things.

13. Number of public meetings held since Ramgarh to popularize the Ramgarh resolution, Gandhiji's instructions and the AICC circulars.

14. What measures have the PCCs taken or propose to take for seeing that the conditions of the pledge and the programme they lay down from time to time are carried out by the Satyagrahis?

15. Are the members of the Congress Executive Committees and Congress members of Local Boards fulfilling the condition about Khadi as prescribed in Art. VII (b) of the Congress Constitution? What is done in the case of defaulters?

III.   Congress Resolutions After Ramgarh

22.   Congress Working Committee Absolve Mahatma Gandhi of Responsibility: Text of the Resolution Passed at its Meeting, Wardha, 17–21 June 1940

Harijan, 29 June 1940.

The following is the full text of the Working Committee's declaration of policy:

The Working Committee have been deeply moved by the tragic events that have taken place in Europe in startling succession and in particular by the misfortunes that have befallen the people of France. These events have already had far-reaching consequences, and they are likely to be followed by other happenings which will lead to novel situations and complex problems.

Ever since the commencement of the European war the Congress has followed a policy which was based on its principles and on the attitude of the British Government towards the demand that India should function as a free and independent country. This policy was confirmed in the Ramgarh resolution. The manner of the application of this policy will necessarily depend on the situation which changes from day to day. Problems which were distant are now near at hand and may soon demand solution. The problem of the achievement of national freedom has now to be considered along with the allied one, its maintenance and the defence of the country against possible external aggression and internal disorder.

The war in Europe, resulting from a desire for imperialist domination over other peoples and countries and a suicidal race in armaments, has led to human sorrow and misery on a scale hitherto unknown. It has demonstrated the inefficacy of organized violence, on however vast a scale, for the defence of national freedom and the liberties of peoples. It has shown beyond a doubt that warfare cannot lead to peace and freedom; and the choice before the world is uttermost degradation and destruction through warfare or the way of peace and non-violence on a basis of freedom for all peoples. Mahatma Gandhi has presented to the peoples of the world, crying for relief from the crushing burden of war, a weapon in the shape of organized non-violence designed to take the place of war for the defence of a people's rights and freedom against armed aggression. He feels that at this critical phase in the history of man the Congress should enforce this ideal by itself declaring that it does not want that India should maintain armed forces to defend her freedom against external aggression or internal disorder.

While the Working Committee hold that the Congress must continue to adhere strictly to the principle of non-violence in their struggle for independence, the Committee cannot ignore the recent imperfections and failings in this respect of the human elements they have to deal with, and the possible dangers in a period of transition and dynamic change, until the Congress has acquired non-violent control over the people in adequate measure and the people have imbibed sufficiently the lesson of organized non-violence. The Committee have deliberated over the problem that has thus arisen and have come to the conclusion that they are unable to go the full length with Gandhiji. But they recognize that he should be free to pursue his great ideal in his own way, and therefore absolve him from responsibility for the programme and activity which the Congress has to pursue under the conditions at present prevailing in India and the world in regard to external aggression and internal disorder.

Many of the problems which the Working Committee have considered in this connection are not of the present, though they may be of the near future. The Committee wish to make it clear that the methods and basic policy of non-violence in the national struggle for freedom continue with full force and are not affected in the least by the inability to extend it to the region of national defence. The War Committees that are being formed are definitely aimed at increasing the war effort. In view of the Congress policy, they cannot be supported, and Congressmen cannot participate in them or contribute to war funds, nor can Congressmen associate themselves, under present political conditions, with Government-controlled Civic Guards.

Congress committees should organize, wherever necessary, people in villages and other areas for self-defence and in order to maintain a sense of public security in their respective areas. This should be done on a non-communal basis and in full co-operation with all other groups interested in this task.

In view of the difficult times that loom ahead, it is essential that the Congress should function as an active and disciplined organization. Provincial Committees are enjoined to take necessary steps for this purpose. They should realize that it is of urgent and vital importance that the Congress should function in this way in these days of crisis, and should not be merely a roll of vast numbers of inactive members. All members of the executive committees, in particular are expected to take a continuous and active part in the Congress work, and those who are unwilling or unable to do so are failing in their duty to the country and are of no service to the organization.

The critical situation that faces the world today requires vigilant attention and action whenever needed. For this purpose the Working Committee will meet at frequent intervals, and all members must keep in readiness to obey an urgent summons. The All India Congress Committee should be summoned to meet in the last week of July.

23. Congress Working Committee Resolution on 'Political Situation': Working Committee Meeting, Delhi, 3–7 July 1940

Indian Annual Register, 1940, Vol. II, pp. 176–7.

Political Situation

The Working Committee have noted the serious happenings which have called forth fresh appeals to bring about a solution of the deadlock in the Indian political situation; and in view of the desirability of clarifying the Congress position they have earnestly examined the whole situation once again in the light of the latest developments in world affairs.

The Working Committee are more than ever convinced that the acknowledgment by Great Britain of the Complete Independence of India, is the only solution of the problems facing both India and Britain and are, therefore, of opinion that such an unequivocal declaration should be immediately made and that as an immediate step in giving effect to it, a provisional National Government should be constituted at the Centre, which, though formed as a transitory measure, should be such as to command the confidence of all the elected elements in the Central Legislature and secure the closest co-operation of the Responsible Governments in the provinces.

The working Committee are of opinion that unless the aforesaid declaration is made, and a national Government accordingly formed at the Centre without delay, all efforts at organizing the material and moral resources of the country for Defence cannot in any sense be voluntary or as from a free country, and will therefore be ineffective. The Working Committee declare that if these measures are adopted, it will enable the Congress to throw in its full weight in the efforts for the effective organization of the Defence of the country.

24. Congress President Maulana Abul Kalam Azad on Basic Policy of the Congress—Statement at AICC Meeting, Poona, 27 July 1940

Indian Annual Register, 1940, Vol. II, pp. 193–4.

President's Statement

It was hardly four months and two weeks since they met at Ramgarh but during this short period the world had changed almost out of recognition. This change was not only in respect of outward form but it had almost brought about a revolution in ideas and beliefs. It would not be possible for us not to be affected by all that has happened and, therefore, it becomes our duty to review our own position and take stock of the situation with a view to seeking what changes we should make in our own attitude.

Two important decisions of the Congress Working Committee are to be placed before you. One of these is known as the Wardha Statement. Although there is nothing new in it, as it relates to the basic policy of the Indian National Congress, it becomes our duty to consider it as this House represents the Congress.

It was not at the Wardha meeting in June last that Mahatma Gandhi raised the question of non-violence for the first time. He had raised it two years ago. In September 1938 the All India Congress Committee met at Delhi. At this meeting of the Congress Working Committee Mahatma Gandhi raised the issue of extending the principle of non-violence which the Congress had followed in regard to its internal policy for the last twenty years to other spheres.

Mahatma Gandhi wanted the Congress at this stage to declare that a free India would eschew all violence and would have no army to defend the country against aggression. The Congress should thus depend entirely upon non-violence for the purpose of dealing with internal disorders and external aggression. Mahatma Gandhi felt that he had to give the message of non-violence to the world and if he could not persuade his own countrymen to accept it, it would be difficult for him to preach it to others. The Congress Working Committee felt itself unable to accept his position and explained its difficulties to Mahatma Gandhi. The issue however did not assume any serious proportion then as the Munich Agreement postponed the war.

The question was again raised by Mahatma Gandhi when war broke out in September last. In November last when Gandhiji went to interview the Viceroy he asked me and other members of the Working Committee to relieve him of the responsibility of guiding the Congress policy and leave him free to pursue in his own way the policy of non-violence. The Committee, however, once again persuaded Mahatma Gandhi to postpone decision. At Ramgarh Mahatma Gandhi raised this question for the third time. On this occasion Mahatma Gandhi also referred to other weakness in the Congress organization and expressed a desire to be relieved of responsibility. This came as a shock to the Working Committee and if I had not practically forced Mahatma Gandhi to postpone decision of the issue once again, a crisis would have arisen as early as at Ramgarh.

You will thus see that this issue had been hanging fire for over two years and when we met in Wardha in June last Mahatma Gandhi wanted the Committee to make up its mind once for all as the international situation had become delicate and he felt that a decision on such a vital issue could not be postponed any longer. Even then I tried to persuade Mahatma Gandhi once again to postpone the matter as I knew the dangers and the difficulties of a decision. There is not a soul in the Congress who is not anxious to go the whole length with Mahatma Gandhi, if he can help it; but we cannot close our eyes to hard facts. We know that arms and ammunitions have not been able to save the freedom of France, Holland, Belgium and Norway but we also know that human nature even after realizing the futility of armed resistance is not prepared to give up force. We had not the courage to declare that we shall organize a State in this country without an armed force. If we did it would be wrong on our part. Mahatma Gandhi has to give the message of non-violence to the world and, therefore, it is his duty to propagate it but we have to consider our position as the representatives of the Indian Nation meeting in the Indian National Congress. The Indian National Congress is a political organization pledged to win the political independence of the country. It is not an institution for organizing world peace.

Honestly we cannot go as far as Mahatma Gandhi wants us to go. We admit that it is a weakness on our part but it is a weakness which we share with the entire humanity. Though we cannot go with Mahatma Gandhi the whole hog, we do not wish to stop him from pursuing his own path. Yet realizing the loss that the Congress would suffer on being deprived of Mahatma Gandhi's guidance, I was tempted to approach him once again to defer his decision on this issue. I had thrice succeeded in my attempt but this time, I failed because Mahatma Gandhi pointed out that it was no use postponing his decision on this vital issue for the moment was fast approaching when the Congress would have to take a final decision and therefore, it was better that each party decided to follow its own path. I placed the whole matter before the Working Committee and invited separately the opinion of each member. Most of us felt that we were not able to take up the grave responsibility of declaring that we would completely eschew violence when we had to deal with widespread internal disorder in this country or external aggression. But we all were quite clear in our minds that so far as the struggle for winning our independence was concerned non-violence would continue to occupy the same place in the Congress programme that it had occupied all these 20 years. We all felt that the slightest deviation in this respect will mean political suicide for the Congress.

Whatever success we have achieved in our struggle during all these years has been due to our unflinching faith in non-violence, and if we have not succeeded to the extent to which we ought to have succeeded, it is due to our inability to practice non-violence to the fuller extent. If we ever give up this idea, we shall be burying the Congress. I feel I must take you further in confidence and inform you that there are four members of the Working Committee, Babu Rajendra Prasad, Dr Prafulla Chandra Ghose, Mr Kripalani and Mr Shankerrao Deo who feel that they can go the whole length with Mahatma Gandhi. You already know about Khan Abdul Ghaffar Khan.

There are people who think that by passing the Delhi resolution the Congress Working Committee has made a departure from past resolutions. I wish to emphasize that this is a wrong view. Even if we wished to take a new step we could not do so because we have behind us a series of resolutions and statements issued from time to time by the Congress Working Committee during the past few months. We cannot demolish all these. We have not the right to do so. We have not the power to do so. Changes in the international situation however are so serious that we cannot shut our eyes to them and proceed blindly. We have not abated our original demand in any way. We have demanded the unequivocal, declaration of India's Independence. As a provisional measure we have asked for the establishment of a representative national government.

Although Mahatma Gandhi would not be responsible for the policy of the Congress any longer, his advice would always be available to the Working Committee and the Congress. Our relations will continue with him as long as he lives and I pray to God that he may be spared long to guide us. We must however realize that the nature of his guidance will not be the same as before and this adds greatly to our responsibility. We have a great objective to achieve; we have an ideal before us which is sufficient to inspire any group of people. There may be ups and downs and difficulties may beset our path but we need not be disheartened or dis-spirited by these.

We have to solve every difficulty that presents itself to us and we have also to recognize the hard fact of Mahatma Gandhi's separation from us. We must bear it bravely. In this difficult hour, it is our duty to be united. I therefore appeal to you to sink all differences and to face bravely the trials that lie ahead of us. This is what the country demands from us and this is what the Congress expects us to do. If we fail in this hour of trial, the world will have a poor opinion of us; but I am sure that we shall not fail.

25. Congress Working Committee Resolution on 'Compulsory Levies', Poona, 25–27 July 1940

Indian Annual Register, 1940, Vol. II, p. 195.

The Working Committee have received reports from many parts of the country that compulsion is being applied on a considerable scale, on the part of subordinate officials for the purpose of realizing contribution for war purposes. Collections ordered to be made by officials from peasants and wage earners are bound to result in considerable harassment, coercion and distress.

Compulsory levies are not only against the existing law of the land as well as the emergency laws but are also opposed to the declared policy of responsible officers of the Government. All compulsory levies and coercion in the collection of funds should be immediately stopped, and, where such compulsion is applied, people should refuse to submit to it.

26. Report on the Ban on Military Drills Following the Declaration of Satyagraha

Times of India, 6 August 1940.

The following orders are issued in a Gazette Extraordinary today:

Order under Rule 58 of the Defence of India Rules:

In exercise of the powers conferred by sub-rule (1) of rule 58 of the Defence of India Rules, the Central Government is pleased to prohibit the performance within British India of any exercise, movement, evolution or drill of a military nature, with or without arms or articles capable of being used as arms:

Provided that the prohibition herein before imposed shall not apply to the performance of any such exercise, movement, evaluation or drill:

1. By members of His Majesty's Naval, Military or Air Force or of an official police force or of any force constituted under any law for the time being in force in the exercise of their duty as such.
2. By members of the Association commonly known as the Boy Scouts Association in India or of the Association commonly known as the Girl Guides Association in India in their capacity as such;
3. Within any province by members in their capacity as such of any organization specified in an order in writing by the Provincial Government of that province, or
4. Within the precincts or premises of any government school or college, or of any school or college recognized by Government in this behalf, by persons whose participation in such exercise, movement, evolution or drill is part of the ordinary curriculum of such school or college.

Order under Rule 59 of the Defence of India Rules:

Whereas the Central Government is satisfied that the wearing in public of any dress resembling a uniform required to be worn by a member of His Majesty's Forces or by a member of any official police force or of any force constituted under any law for the time being in force is likely to prejudice the public safety, the maintenance of public order and the defence of British India;

Now, therefore, in exercise of the powers conferred by sub-rule (1) of Rule 59 of the Defence of India Rules, the Central Government is pleased to prohibit the wearing in public of any such dress by any person who is not a member of the said forces or a member of an Association which has been authorized by the Central Government as respects the whole of British India or the Provincial Government as respects the province to wear a specified uniform associated dress.

27. Congress Working Committee Resolution on 'Struggle' and 'Volunteers', Wardha, 18–22 August 1940

Indian Annual Register, 1940, Vol. II, pp. 197–8.

The decision of the British Government to enforce their will in India in opposition to the will of the great majority of the people and regardless of consequences has produced a situation of the utmost gravity. The rejection of the Congress proposals is proof of the British Government's determination to continue to hold India by the sword. In order to compass this end they have been endeavouring to undermine the strength of the Congress by picking up and arresting hundreds of public workers, including some of the best workers of the Congress, under the Defence of India Act which has no popular sanction whatever. The desire of the Congress not to embarrass the British Government, at a time of peril for them, has been misunderstood and despised. They are imposing on the Congress a struggle to vindicate its position and to act for the preservation of the liberties and honour of the people. The Congress can have no thought but that of the supreme good of the dumb and toiling millions of India and through them of the whole of submerged humanity.

In view of the gravity of the situation, the Working Committee have decided to convene a meeting of the All India Congress Committee on Sunday, 15th September.

The Working Committee call upon all Congress organizations to carry on their activities with full vigour and, in particular, to explain the Congress position and recent developments to the public. Satyagraha Committees must see that those who have taken the pledge act in terms of this pledge and carry on the constructive and other activities of the Congress.

The Working Committee have considered the recent Ordinance of the Governor-General relating to volunteers. The Committee are not in a position to understand the real purpose underlying this Ordinance and consider it as too widely and vaguely worded and liable to abuse in its application. The time chosen for its promulgation and the terms thereof are such as to lend some justification to the interpretation that it has been issued to prevent and hamper the normal activities of Congress volunteers.

The Working Committee fully agree that private armies organized for furthering political or communal objectives by intimidation or force are objectionable and should not be permitted. But there is no analogy between such private armies and the training by drill, exercise and otherwise of volunteers for peaceful national service. Congress resolutions and instructions, issued in respect of its volunteers make it clear that these volunteers are organized for the constructive activities of the Congress; for promoting communal harmony; for preserving order at its meetings, conferences, and the like; for teaching discipline and raising physical standards of fitness; and for the service of the people. Such volunteers are pledged to non-violence and they were never intended, nor are they expected to seek to enforce by intimidation or otherwise the political views of the Congress on others. They cannot be mistaken by dress or otherwise for the military or the police.

The Working Committee trust that the ordinance was not intended and will not be misused to suppress the lawful and peaceful work of such volunteers, or to interfere with their distinctive dress, drill, exercise and peaceful activities.

The Committee therefore direct that the normal activities of the Congress Seva Dal and other Congress volunteers should be carried on and that all such volunteers should continue the national service which they are privileged to perform.

28. Report on Government's Press Communiqué on Congress Volunteers

Bombay Chronicle, 26 August 1940.

In reply to the Congress Working Committee's resolution on the recent ban relating to volunteers, the Government of India have issued Press Communiqué containing a laboured justification of the ban. Referring to the drilling of a military nature and the wearing of uniforms resembling military or official uniforms, the communiqué says: 'In general terms these activities may be described as imitation of military methods. These methods are followed by the army and police for a definite object. That object is the use or display of disciplined force. Those who imitate military methods must be presumed to have similar objects in view'. This is fallacious reasoning and, in the present case, it is dangerous, too. Government's object in drilling and using uniforms may be the use or display of disciplined force. But it is utterly wrong to presume that others who drill or use uniforms must necessarily have the same object merely because their drilling and uniforms may resemble those of the army. Drilling, some what of the military type is common in schools and for scouts, and some of the latter use uniforms resembling military ones. But nobody with a head on his shoulder will argue that the schools and scout organizations aim at using or displaying disciplined force. Government themselves have admitted this and have exempted these bodies from the operation of their ban. They are right in doing so because these bodies aim only at discipline and physical fitness. But there are many other institutions which value discipline and physical fitness and use drilling to achieve these aims, and there is no sense in presuming that their objects are other than those of the schools and scout organizations.

Unfair Distinction

Some volunteer institutions may also aim at enabling their volunteers to use disciplined force lawfully, say, in maintaining discipline at big meetings, conferences, or fairs. That has never been regarded as an offence. It is true that some volunteer organizations may abuse their disciplined force or so display their drills and uniforms as to overawe the people and create in their minds anxiety at the possibility of unlawful force being used at any moment. If any institution does this, it becomes a public nuisance and deserves to be brought to book. But to put a ban on all volunteer institutions pursuing their normal time-honoured activities and methods is as unfair as to ban physical culture because some of the men trained to be strong may misuse their strength. It may be argued that the ban in question is only on military drilling and military uniforms. But almost all forms of drilling and many common volunteer uniforms resemble those of the military. That is precisely why schools and scout organizations are being exempted. Why ban other bodies which are as inoffensive and serviceable as these and which have been recognized as such all these years?

Reconsider the Decision

Referring to the use and display of disciplined force, Government's communiqué also says: 'No Government (as is recognized by the Congress Working Committee) can tolerate the growth of non-official organizations which have such objects in view. Equally no body of persons which has NOT such objects in view, can reasonably claim that such methods are necessary to its existence. This applies with even greater force to an organization which is openly pledged to non-violence'. The views of the Congress may not be acceptable to

Government but they must not be misinterpreted. Congress certainly recognizes that private armies meant to coerce or intimidate people are objectionable. But Congress does not admit that drilling such as it has been resorting to for years is in any way a source of danger to the public or otherwise objectionable. It reasonably claims that such drilling is as necessary for its service of the republic as it is necessary for bodies like scout organizations. Congress adhesion to non-violence does not prevent it from using methods necessary for training in efficiency, discipline and physical fitness. We trust that Government will reconsider their decision and see that the orders issued by them will not be used to suppress the work of Congress volunteers.

C.   'LEFT' PARTIES AND OTHER GROUPS

I.   (a) Forward Bloc and its Allies

29.   Subhas Bose's View on Forthcoming Congress Session at Ramgarh

Editorial, *Forward Bloc*, 13 January 1940. Sisir K. Bose (ed), *Crossroads: The Works of Subhas Chandra Bose, 1938–1940*, Calcutta, 1981 (2nd edition), pp. 272–4.

The darkest hour is ahead of the Forward Bloc. It has from its inception been fighting on a double front, namely, alien Imperialism and Indian Counter-revolution. The path it had selected was not an easy one, but it is doubtful if anybody had expected Indian counter-revolution to be so determined, ruthless and vindictive as it has in fact proved to be. We all know from personal experience that very often it is more difficult to combat reaction at home than Imperialism imposed from without. We have seen in recent months how so many comrades who would have fought foreign Imperialism bravely have succumbed to the onslaught from the Right.

Looking at the scene quite dispassionately for a moment, as a student of History would, one cannot but admire the Rightists who with all their lip-homage to Non-violence and Toleration are fighting a political game in a most downright manner. This is 'Real-Politiks' as History knows it and the game is bound to thrill all political fighters even those who are being subjected to persecution at present.

One of the immediate objectives of the Forward Bloc was the consolidation of all the Leftist elements in the Congress and in the country. Since this could not be achieved on the platform of the Bloc, the Left Consolidation Committee was brought into existence. The Committee has had a chequered career. The moment it showed its strength at the meeting of the All-India Congress Committee, held in Bombay in June 1939, the onslaught from the Right began—the first occasion being the 9th July demonstrations. Since then some of the Leftist elements have been steadily dropping off from the Left Consolidation Committee. The astute Rightist leaders have been pursuing a dual policy in their handling of the Leftists. Some of the compromising and 'reasonable' elements are being systematically wooed. But the harder nuts are being dealt with ruthlessly. The result has been a gradual thinning of the ranks of the Leftists. To make matters more difficult for the latter, governmental persecution has been steadily going on in several provinces and it was first resorted to under the Congress regime. Today, doubts are being raised as to whether Left-Consolidation is at all possible any longer.

Left-Consolidation can be achieved in either of two ways. The Leftist elements on a common platform and on the basis of a common minimum programme. If this method fails, then another method is still open to us. The events of the last few months have put Leftists to a severe test— they have had to pass through a fiery ordeal. Some have succumbed in the process, but not all.

Those who have stood the test bravely have proved to be genuine Leftists and Left-Consolidation will now mean their consolidation. In nature, floods are often preceded by a drying up of the rivers. A thinning of the ranks is often a prelude to a dynamic expansion. This will happen to the Left movement in this country. Those who have not lost faith during the course of the past struggle, will agree with us that the darkest hour that is ahead of us will be followed by the rosy dawn.

The role of the Forward Bloc in Indian history is not that of His Majesty's Opposition. We have seen remarks to the effect that the aim of the Forward Bloc is merely to ginger up the present policy and programme of the Congress. There could be no greater misunderstanding than this. The Bloc stands for something positive and dynamic. The role of the antithesis in the Dialectic of History is not a negative one. It is something positive and dynamic which had to carry us swiftly along the path of progress.

It is not outside the domain of possibility that as we approach the darkest hour, some of the elements in the Forward Bloc may quail before the ordeal. But there can be no going back for us—nor any marking time. Forward Bloc has to move forward without a pause, without a break. That is its historical role. Determination has to be met with greater determination and persecution with unflinching heroism. Only then shall we survive the ordeal—only then shall we succeed in our fight on a double front. Our cause is just and our role historic. Let us not therefore lose faith and courage, even if unrelieved darkness overcomes us for a while.

There are moments when reason fails to rend the veil of the future and on such occasions men who are weak in faith sometimes lose courage and self-confidence. But where reason fails, intuition steps in. Intuitive insight can pierce through impenetrable darkness and give us a glimpse of what is to come. Today, intuition tells us that no power on earth can vanquish us and our cause. The tremendous mass-response that greets us everywhere has but one meaning. Despite persecution on a double front, people realize that we are moving with the times—that we are thinking their thoughts and acting in consonance with them.

The air is thick with rumours of a compromise with the Government. Some fancy that the endeavour to conclude a settlement will be made before the annual session of the Congress meets at Ramgarh in March next. Others opine that the Ramgarh Congress will vest plenary powers in the Congress Executive and that the final attempt at a compromise will be made after March. So-called English friends of India have been advising the Rightist leaders to mark time till March next, when an agreement will become possible. There is not the least doubt that in the Rightist plan, Ramgarh Congress occupies an important place. How else can you explain the determined and ruthless attempt that is being made to exclude Bengal, real Bengal, from the Ramgarh Congress? The Rightist plan has to be put through at Ramgarh and Bengal with her contingent of 544 delegates may prove inconvenient to the Congress High Command. Therefore Bengal has to be eliminated by hook or by crook.

But this is not so easy. You can exclude Bengal from the Ramgarh Congress, but you cannot exclude her from the public life of India.

For the Leftists, Ramgarh may not have much importance—but the month of March will be important in the history of India. Leftists should therefore gather together during this month and prepare to meet the counter-revolutionary and compromising tactics of the Rightist leaders. In this connection it may be necessary to hold an All-India conference somewhere in Bihar at about the same time as the Ramgarh Congress. Among others, Leftists who have been expelled from the Congress or subjected to disciplinary action for their political convictions should attend this conference and make a success of it. Such a Conference will have a salutary effect on both the Congress Right-Wing and on the British Government and will tone up the militant Leftists in the country. Members of the Forward Bloc need not be so anxious about attending the Ramgarh Congress. With so many Leftist leaders under disciplinary action and with real Bengal out of the Ramgarh Congress, there will be little chance of influencing the decisions of that Congress. Members of the Bloc should rather concentrate all their energies on the task of winning Purna Swaraj as soon as possible.

30. Newspaper Report of Subhas Bose's Views on 'Future Programme'
Bombay Sentinel, 13 January 1940.

A broad hint about the future course of action to be pursued by the Forward Bloc was given by Babu Subhas Chandra Bose in the course of a special interview to the 'Sentinel' to-day.

The Executive of the Forward Bloc, it is expected will not meet during this month as was originally expected, but a larger meeting of the workers of the Forward Bloc will probably be held in the beginning of the next month to take important decisions to meet the present political situation in the country.

The 'Independence Day' will be of course a day of significance. But it is understood that if the Forward Bloc does not launch upon direct action on that day, it will be only with the intention of not breaking a butterfly on a wheel but nevertheless to prepare the country for a fight. Things then, as far as the Forward Bloc is concerned, will move fast according to present indications.

Babu Subhas Chandra Bose will leave for Patna to-night; he will stay there for a day and entrain for Calcutta where he will reach on January 16.

In the course of a special interview to the 'Sentinel', the leader of the Forward Bloc said:

'In the Rightist camp there is feverish activity going on to make the Ramgarh Congress safe for them. What is now happening in Bengal is but part of this activity.

'But we are not bothering ourselves about Ramgarh because by the time the Rightists assemble there, the Indian scene will have changed beyond recognition.'

The following is the full text of the interview given by Babu Subhas Chandra Bose to a representative of the *Sentinel*:

'I may say without any exaggeration that wherever I have toured—North, South, East or West—my experience has been the same. The sympathy of the masses has been entirely with us and there can be no doubt that the Forward Bloc has a much larger mass appeal than the Congress High Command.

'But our following in the country is not properly reflected within the Congress organization.

'We have been receiving reports from several Provinces that unfair and unscrupulous methods are being adopted by the Rightists in order to suppress our growing strength or to keep us out of the Congress machinery. This is a recent and unexpected development which is forcing the members of the Forward Bloc to do some hard thinking.

'However, one thing is certain. Whatever our position within the Congress machinery may be and even if we are expelled or disaffiliated we shall not allow ourselves to be diverted from our main task of fighting imperialism.

'Before we take the final step we intend informing the Congress High Command and the British Government and the public at large so that there may be no misunderstanding as to who is launching the struggle and with what objective.

'Once the struggle is launched, we shall follow our own course of action and on the major questions of "War and Peace" we shall not be bound by any decision of the Congress High Command.

'To-day the air is thick with reports of attempts that are being made to arrive at a compromise with the British Government. In the Rightist camp, there is feverish activity going on with a view to making the Ramgarh Congress safe for them.

'What is now happening in Bengal is but an item in their activity. But we are not bothering ourselves about Ramgarh because by the time the Rightists assembly there the Indian scene will have changed beyond recognition'.

31. 'The Bengal Tangle'—Subhas Bose's Editorial in *Forward Bloc*, 17 February 1940

Sisir Kumar Bose and Sugata Bose (eds), *Netaji: Collected Works, The Alternative Leadership*, Vol. 10, Calcutta, 1998, pp. 76–9.

Friends who are not in intimate contact with Congress affairs are often bewildered at the recent developments inside the Congress. This is particularly the case with comrades in remote parts of the country. Commonsense logic argues as follows: 'The Congress stands for Independence. The members of the Congress Committee and of the Bengal Provincial Congress Committee are all public servants who have set out to achieve Independence for their country. Why then this family quarrel?'

Others speaking in quite a naive manner, appeal in the following terms: 'Please make up you differences with the enemy.' As if it is we who have picked up a quarrel with the Working Committee!

Public memory is proverbially short. Hence a brief recapitulation of past events is called for.

In April 1939, when the All-India Congress Committee met in Calcutta under my Presidentship and the question of the constitution of the new Working Committee came up, we were confronted with the Gandhian theory of a homogeneous Cabinet. We were told in effect that in future, the Rightists could not work in cooperation with the Leftists. In fact, this non-cooperation had begun in February 1939, after my re-election as President, when the members of the Working Committee sent in their resignation.

Not only were we confronted with non-cooperation, but we were told by no less an authority than Mahatma Gandhi himself that a national struggle in the immediate future was out of the question.

In such a crisis, Pandit Jawaharlal Nehru argued that in spite of all internal differences, I should neither resign nor start a new organization within the Congress, in view of the international crisis that was looming in the horizon. I argued that since an international crisis was unavoidable in the near future and there was no hope that the Congress High Command would rise to the occasion when it came, we should lose no time in setting up an organization of our own. This organization would enable us to face the international crisis boldly, even if the Working Committee then failed us.

So the Forward Bloc and the Left Consolidation Committee came into existence.

Let us next refer to the demonstrations of 9th July 1939. Under the auspices of the Left Consolidation Committee, public meetings were held all over India in order to protest against two obnoxious resolutions of the All-India Congress Committee passed at its Bombay meeting in June 1939. One of these resolutions virtually robbed individual Congressmen of the right to offer Civil Disobedience. The other resolution sought to make Provincial Ministries more powerful than the Provincial Congress Committees concerned. Following my lead, the Bengal Provincial Congress Committee participated in the 9th July demonstrations.

This was the signal for the onslaught on the BPCC. I was removed from the Presidentship of the BPCC by a fiat of the Working Committee. The BPCC did not take this lying down and a long controversy ensued. During this controversy it became clear that a solid majority in the BPCC would adhere to me despite the frowns of the High Command. And this majority was a Leftist majority.

The above developments since June 1939, demonstrated that even if the AICC passed by a majority a resolution which was objectionable on grounds of principle, the minority would not hesitate to revolt against it. In other words, there would not be smooth sailing for the Rightists as in the case of office-acceptance in the provinces, when the oppositionist minority silenced itself as soon as the All-India Congress Committee decided on office-acceptance by a majority.

The Rightist leaders, looking ahead, decided that the minority should from now on be forced into loyalty and discipline—so that when ultimately a compromise with British imperialism was arrived at by a majority—no discordant voice would be raised by dissenting Leftists. As a matter of fact, the same consideration was responsible for strenuously opposing my re-election as President.

There was another source of anxiety for the Rightists. They wanted to have an easy time at the next Congress at Ramgarh in Bihar and were eager to avoid the uncertain atmosphere which had prevailed at the Tripuri Congress in March, 1939. It was clear to them that Bengal would send a strong contingent of Leftist delegates to the Ramgarh Congress—perhaps 450 in number. This had to be frustrated at any cost.

People who are not acquainted with Congress affairs in other provinces are under the impression that it is only the Provincial Congress Committee of Bengal that is fighting the Congress High Command. The contrary is, however, the case. The Forward Bloc being an All-India organization, we are in touch with what is happening in every corner of the country. We are, therefore, in a position to state authoritatively that the Leftists in general, and the Forward Bloc in particular, have been the target of attack on the part of the Working Committee in every province. The attack has been harder where the position of the Leftists and of the Forward Bloc is comparatively stronger. And because our position is the strongest in Bengal, the Bengal PCC has incurred the maximum wrath of the High Command.

Successive steps have been taken by the Working Committee to curb and humiliate the BPCC but to no avail. On a flimsy ground, a partisan Election Tribunal was foisted on the Bengal PCC. The rules for the Tribunal framed by the BPCC came in for special attention and interference at the hands of the Working Committee, unlike what happened in the case of other provinces. It was then discovered by the High Command that these devices would not help to reduce our majority in the new PCC. Then the Working Committee adopted the drastic and desperate step of virtually superseding the BPCC by handing over to a partisan ad hoc Committee the entire responsibility of running the election of delegates for the Ramgarh session of the Congress to be held in March 1940[1]. Once Leftist Bengal was out of the way, the Rightists would have an easy time at the Presidential election and at the Ramgarh Congress.

As an interesting interlude, an auditor was sent by the Working Committee to examine the accounts of the BPCC. But his Herculean efforts ended in smoke. The Working Committee had been misinformed by its agents in Bengal who had reported that the All-India Forward Bloc was being financed by the funds of the BPCC and of the Bengal Parliamentary Party.

We have no doubt in our mind that the drive and the vendetta against the Leftists and the Forward Bloc will continue so long as the Rightists entertain hopes of a compromise with British Imperialism or of getting back to power in the provinces. At present we are witnessing an exhibition of power politics and no one need be surprised at what is happening.

Whatever steps we taken in self-defence or as a reply to the onslaught from the Right, must be on an All-India front. The Forward Bloc offers an All-India front if no other organization will. Let everybody rest assured that Leftist Bengal is not going to be isolated from Leftist India.

The conflict in Bengal is thus a conflict on an All-India plane—a conflict between the forces of reaction and of progress—a conflict between the Right and the Left—a conflict between the policy of compromise and of no-compromise. The ultimate solution of such a conflict cannot take place in the local or the provincial sphere. The solution will come only when reaction is overthrown—and when the policy of compromise is discarded in favour of an uncompromising struggle with imperialism. Till then, let us go on fighting bravely and boldly on a double-front, with the firm conviction that we are going to win and to win soon.

---

[1] The Congress Working Committee at its meeting held from 18 to 22 December 1939 had passed a resolution which, *inter alia*, stated: 'The Working Committee resolve therefore that an ad hoc Committee consisting of the following persons with Maulana Abul Kalam Azad as Chairman be formed to make arrangements for and conduct elections of delegates to the next Congress and all other elections....' The Bengal Provincial Congress Committee requested the Working Committee to reconsider this resolution and deputed Sarat Chandra Bose to argue its case before the Congress Working Committee at its meeting held from 19 to 21 January 1940. The Working Committee considered the matter and in their decision stated that they were 'unable to alter their previous decision'.

32. Subhas Bose on Achievements of Forward Bloc: Presidential Address at the Second Session of the All-India Forward Bloc Conference Held at Nagpur, 18 June 1940

Sisir Kumar Bose and Sugata Bose (eds), *Netaji: Collected Works, The Alternative Leadership*, Vol. 10, Calcutta, 1998, pp. 115–19.

Comrades,

Early in May 1939, the Forward Bloc of the Indian National Congress was inaugurated in Calcutta following a momentous session of the All-India Congress Committee. In the last week of June 1939, the first session of the All-India Conference of the Forward Bloc was held in Bombay and the constitution and programme of the Bloc were adopted there. Since then, a year has rolled by—a year which will be memorable not only in the history of India, but in the history of the whole world. We are, therefore, meeting at a most opportune moment and not a day too soon. We shall have to do a great deal of heart-searching as well as stock-taking. We shall then have to determine our course of action in the crisis which has overtaken India and the world—the crisis which is deepening and worsening, not only from day to day but also from hour to hour.

The first question which I shall pose before you is: 'Have our policy and line of action been a correct one? And have we acted in the best interests of the country by launching the Forward Bloc? To that my reply is: 'Most certainly, yes.' I shall remind you that we were constrained to start the Forward Bloc in the light of four consideration. The Right Wing had definitely told us that they would not work in co-operation with the Leftists in future and they had rejected the proposal of a Composite Cabinet which was our demand. Secondly, Mahatma Gandhi and the Right Wing had told us that a national struggle in the near future was out of the question. Thirdly, the attempt to consolidate the anti-imperialist and radical elements in the Congress under the name of the Left Bloc had been given up by the Socialists and Communists. Consequently, a further attempt at Left-consolidation could be made only by us and for that the Forward Bloc had become indispensably necessary. Fourthly, the Gandhites or Right Wingers had already consolidated themselves under the aegis of the Gandhi Seva Sangha and any further delay on our part would have meant the strangling of the Leftist elements in the Congress by the Rightists.

It was clear in 1939 that most of those who had entered the Congress as Leftists in 1920 and 1921 and had retained the leadership of the Congress in their hands for well-nigh two decades, had ceased to be revolutionary or even radical. Any further political progress under such circumstances presupposed a consolidation of all anti-imperialist, radical and progressive forces in the country and particularly in the Congress.

Towards the end of April 1939, when I was seriously considering the idea of resigning the Presidentship of the Congress and inaugurating the Forward Bloc, I had an interesting and important discussion with a very prominent Leftist leader of the Congress who has since then thrown himself into the arms of the Gandhites. He advised me to refrain from either course and he added that since an international storm was brewing, we should avoid everything in the nature of a split within the Congress. I replied saying that since a war was inevitable in the near future, it was all the more necessary that the Leftists should be organized and prepared in advance, so that in the event of the Rightists developing cold feet in a war-situation, we at least could do something off our own bat. Differences had become so fundamental between the Right Wing and the Left Wing that a split, whether permanent or temporary, had become inevitable. That being the case, it was desirable that the internal crisis should come and should be transcended before the external or international crisis overtook us. I added that if I accepted my friend's advice and lay low for the present, the consequences would be far worse for us when the international crisis appeared. In such a crisis, we would never agree with the Rightists. But many people would blame us for causing a split, if we attempted to act on our own at that time. Moreover, if we did want to act independently, then we would have no organization behind us to fall back on. Consequently, the argument of my friend only strengthened my case.

Looking back on the last twelve months, can we not claim that events have justified our policy and line of action? Barring the Kisan Sabha of Swami Sahajanand (and Prof. Ranga, Comrade Yajnik, and others) and Forward Bloc, who is there to stand up to the Rightists today? The Left Consolidation Committee which came into existence in June 1939, after the formation of the Forward Bloc, has disintegrated by now. The Royists (or Radical Leaguers), the Congress Socialists and the Communists (or National Fronters) have in turn deserted the Left Consolidation Committee and only the Kisan Sabha and the Forward Bloc have been functioning as the spearhead of the Left Movement in this country. This was evident when we held the All-India Anti-Compromise Conference at Ramgarh in March 1940. There we found that the Royists, Congress Socialists and National Fronters boycotted that Conference and threw in their lot with the Gandhites.

There can be little doubt today than if there had been no Forward Bloc and Kisan Sabha, no voice would have been raised against the policy and line of action pursued by the Gandhites during the last twelve months.

We shall consider another question: What has been our actual achievement during the past year?

In the first place, we can claim to have successfully resisted the tendency toward Constitutionalism and compromise within the ranks of the Congress. Thanks to our efforts, the Congress ministries had to vacate office as a protest against the policy of the British Government. If they had not done so, they would have been carrying out the War policy of the Government of India, as agents of British Imperialism. In spite of all efforts made hitherto, no compromise has yet been made with the British Government and for this, we can legitimately claim some credit.

Secondly, we have so far frustrated all attempts to secure the co-operation of the Congress in the prosecution of the War. Friends will remember that in September 1939, when His Excellency the Viceroy invited Mahatma Gandhi for a talk at Simla on the War situation, the latter gave out that he was of the view that India should give unconditional help to Great Britain during the present war. This was reiterated by Mahatmaji in a press statement issued soon after the above interview. Nevertheless, until now, the Congress Working Committee, which usually follows Gandhiji blindly, has ignored his views on such an all-important issue. Would the same thing have happened if there had been no Kisan Sabha and no Forward Bloc?

Thirdly, we can perhaps claim that we have succeeded in creating an atmosphere of struggle. Today, we find Congress leaders drilling in shirts and shorts and Congress committees being converted into 'Satyagraha' Committees. Moreover, the Rightist leaders have been constantly talking of a struggle. Would all these have taken place, if there had been no Forward Bloc and if the Anti-Compromise Conference at Ramgarh had not shown which way the wind of public opinion was blowing? There is no doubt that today the talk of a struggle is everywhere in the air and the more our people talk of it, the more will they move away from a compromise.

Lastly, we can claim that at Ramgarh we launched our struggle with such strength and resources as we possessed. During the last three months, a large number of our fellow-workers, including men of outstanding influence in the country, have been arrested and incarcerated. Nine members of the All-India Working Committee of the Forward Bloc are at present in prison or internment. In addition to them, leaders of the Kisan Sabha headed by Swami Sahajanand Saraswati, Prof. Ranga and others, are behind the bars.

The National Struggle we launched at Ramgarh has been steadily gaining in strength and volume. The campaign has made considerable headway in Bihar and the United Provinces. In Bengal, the struggle was launched as early as January 1940, over the question of civil liberty, which had been violated by the drastic ordinances promulgated by the Government in September 1939. Thanks to the Civil Disobedience movement launched by Bengal Congress, we have restored in a large measure the 'status quo' which existed prior to September 1939. The special Session of the Bengal Provincial Political Conference which met at Dacca on 25th and 26th May 1940, took stock of the situation in the province and formulated a plan for intensifying the struggle and widening its scope. The Bengal Provincial Congress Committee will give effect to this plan....

33.   Subhas Bose's Views on Congress Leadership

Editorial, *Amrita Bazar Patrika*, 11 December 1940.

It gives us no pleasure to enter into a controversy on political issues with Srijut Subhas Chandra Bose whose timely release from the prison cell in circumstances of utmost gravity has not yet been able to restore him to his normal vigour of body and mind. But persons supposed to be in the full confidence of Srijut Bose have thought fit at this hour to acquaint the public with his views on men and things thereby forcing the hands of those who would not sacrifice principles to personalities or subordinate the large interests of the country to the whims or caprices of a political caucus. The whole country is passing through critical and anxious times and nothing is more deplorable than a systematic campaign deliberately designed to undermine the influence of the Congress and bring into public contempt its leadership.

In this connection we venture to make a present to the public of a letter addressed by Srijut Bose on the 29th October last from Presidency Jail to a chosen lieutenant of his in his unceasing but devastating campaign for national and social liberation and published yesterday by newspapers enjoying the patronage of Srijut Bose himself. Attention may also be invited to an expression of views by Srijut Bose in the course of a bed-room conversation with the acting general secretary of the *Forward Bloc* which has found its usual place in the columns of those newspapers. If the epistle and the Testament are read together—and these are days when there is a general disposition to revive the Biblical terminology despite our unflinching devotion to all *Leftist causes*—one is confronted with unending threats on one side and prayerful supplication on the other. There is a threat to Maulana Abul Kalam Azad, to the Congress High Command and to those loyal Congressmen in Bengal who act upon instructions from the Command. The humble petition is of course addressed to Mahatma Gandhi who only several months ago had to carry from Bengal on his slender shoulders the dirty shoes flung at him by a zealous protagonist of the cause of *Forward* liberation. The epistle and the Testament remind us of an interesting American story of what has been humorously described as the 'Petition of the Left Hand'. The petitioner was a modest girl in her teens neglected at home and not treated with respect and consideration abroad. She addressed herself to all the friends of youth—and Srijut Bose argues in his letter in question that he has youth on his side as well as infinite patience—and conjured them to direct their compassionate regards to her fate in order to remove the prejudices of which she was the victim. The girl accused her parents of partiality for her sister. She alleged that she was suffered to go up without the least instruction, while nothing was spared for her sister's education. Substitute 'political preferment' for 'education' and you get the story of the girl told so aptly and graphically by our friend, Srijut Subhas Bose. That petition of the left hand, be it further noted, was submitted in all solemnity on the eve of the American War of Independence and the girl's question was—if any indisposition perchance attacked her sister, without making mention of other accidents known in law as acts of God, what would be the fate of her aged parents and, what is more, of the War of Independence? The girl herself gave the answer. Must not the regret of her parents and the fighting forces of the revolutionary army, she asked by way of a clear suggestion, be excessive at having placed so great a difference between humans who were so perfectly equal? Alas, she exclaimed, the whole American people would perish from distress and defeat and dishonour.

There is one vital difference between the petition of the girl and Srijut Bose's epistle. It is not an epistle of the left hand but of the seasoned *leftist* always in the right but using both his right and left hands for the purposes of self-defence. Indeed in self-defence our friend treated

Mahatma Gandhi's historic Rajkot fast as a huge fraud and cruel joke. In self-defence he let his colleagues down by bracketing them with Imperialists and all their allies and agents. In self-defence he carried on from day to day 'a raging and tearing campaign' against newspapers that had the courage of their convictions and dared intervene in his thoughtless and suicidal politics. In self-defence perhaps an editor was 'sacked' from his rightful job and sent into the wilderness. In self-defence again Srijut Bose concluded a holy pact with the Moslem League for the better administration of the Calcutta Corporation and with a view to purging it of all undesirable Congress and non-Moslem League influences. 'Self-defence' is a great human virtue in private life no less than in public behaviour and even the much condemned Indian Penal Code puts it in the category of extenuating circumstances in charges of murder. Gandhiji is great for whom our friend has condescended to cherish deep personal regard and love, but the Gandhites are not of the Mahatmic make. They are a troublesome and perverse lot. Like the girl in the American story who was a victim of her sister's perpetual contempt due to discriminatory treatment by their common parents, our friend has suffered and is suffering at the hands of the unscrupulous Gandhian gang. The tallest among them for the time being is Maulana Abul Kalam Azad who is the elected President of the Congress and guides and controls its affairs. And the Maulana is a leader without a following, a leader's perspective and vision and courage. It is, however, no new story. Mr Jinnah told us so long ago. Perhaps Maulvi Fazlul Huq would proclaim it at a League meeting in a proper communal setting. Srijut Subhas Bose is in alliance with the League in Calcutta to be expanded at his own leisure and at the sweet will of the League stalwarts into a larger and more abiding communal fraternity embracing other and wider spheres of our national life. So great men think and speak and act alike.

If anybody has any doubt about Srijut Bose's historically necessary Leftist role in the politics of India (with all apologies to Marx and Lenin), he may just look up his defence in support of his candidature for a seat in the Central Legislative Assembly. Our Leftist friend with a Leftist thunder on all fronts disapproves of the policy of abstention from the legislatures adopted by the Congress. And why?—because the Defence of India Act and like measures could not be passed in their present form with the Congressmen shouting leftist slogans at the top of their voice on the floor of the Assembly. It was in the considered judgment of the Leftist philosopher and guide, a criminal neglect of public duty on the part of the Congress Party to have deserted their posts 'during such a momentous period in our nation's history' when he was engaged in a grim Leftist campaign for revolutionary seizure of power through the legislatures. A Leftist indeed of the purest ray serene—nothing right in his technique, his philosophy and his conception of home-brand revolutionary Swaraj! To go back to the entertaining American story, the War of Independence was won in spite of the unfortunate girl and her unhappy fate.

(b) Anti-Compromise Conference

34. Report on the Preparations for Anti-Compromise Conference, Ramgarh

Hindustan Standard, 12 March 1940.

Sj Dhanaraj Sharma, General Secretary, Reception Committee of All India Anti-Compromise Conference at Ramgarh writes under date 11-3-1940.

The All India Anti-Compromise Conference is going to be held at Ramgarh at a distance of about ten minutes walk from the Congress Nagar. While the Ranchi Road Station (EIR) is at a distance of about three miles, Ramgarh Town Station is quite nearby about five to seven minutes walk.

Facing all difficulties and against all odds on account of the hostile attitude of and the propaganda carried on by the Rightist group of the Congress as also by a section of such people who claim to be Leftists the work of the Anti-Compromise Conferences has been in progress and it is hoped that it will be completed by the 15th instant.

Accommodation for one thousand delegates, three hundred volunteers, fifty lady volunteers, fifty press representatives, twenty-five leaders, some hotels and restaurants, two hospitals, etc., is being provided and satisfactory progress is being made at a rapid speed.

Two flags, one the Tricolour National Flag and the other Red Flag will fly at the height of one hundred and five feet in the Jhandha Chawk.

A Kisan yard had been provided where *shamianas* will be pitched for accommodation of Kisans who have already started marching afoot from Daltonganj, Giridih, Purulia, Monghyr and other places. Fuels, *Pattals* and earthen pots are being stocked for their use.

Saheed Park

A Saheed park is under contemplation and organizations have been registered to send in names of martyrs who laid down their lives in the cause of freedom and lamps will be lighted at their altars.

The site on which the Conference will be held has been named as Kisan Nagar while the *Chawk* where flags will fly as Mazdoor Chawk. Gates of the *chawk* and the Pandal will be named in memory of great martyrs.

While the Pandal will accommodate one lakh and twenty thousand people, the Mazdoor Jhanda will provide a space for one lakh and fifty thousand people.

While the Reception Committee office is working day and night receiving letters, telegrams and telephonic messages and disposing them of in time, the Bengal Provincial Congress Committee have deputed Sj Ramesh Acharya and Rasamay Sur, to cope with the heavy work. Two more offices have been started at Kisan Nagar, one on behalf of the Labour Party of Bengal in charge of Comrade Suresh Roy and the other on behalf of the Students Federation of UP under the leadership of Comrade Ansar Harvani, the President of the United Provinces Students Federation.

Kisan Nagar

The Kisan Nagar is situated in the Ghurkunda Road and it is decidedly a better site than that of the Mazaherpuri. Vile and malicious propaganda have been carried on and are being carried on by the Rightist Group in which Government propaganda cars have been freely used against this Conference. Sj Jaiprakash Narain also issued statements from time to time explaining futility of a conference of this nature. Some other friends of the Kisan Sabha have made efforts to show that the Kisan Rally and the Conference are two different things. It is so no doubt, but Kisan Mazdoors and others who belong to the exploited class and the Anti-Imperialist Class are sure to rally round the banner of this conference. It is they whom the compromise hits and it is they who are likely to be vanguards of any freedom battle that might come ahead.

Momentous Conference

This Conference is a momentous one and will decide once for all the future course of Mother India. As it appears by now Gandhiji is not going to start a fight on the issue of complete Independence but this Conference is sure to find out a way out of this impasse.

Swami Sahjananda Saraswati who is Chairman of the Reception Committee of the All India Anti-Compromise Conference has been touring in the Chotanagar area and has already visited a number of places. He has addressed large meetings of Kisans in the area and Kisans in large bands have started on foot for Ramgarh. In the Chota Nagpur and the Bihar districts, great enthusiasm is evident among the peasant population and the leftist Congress workers.

35. Text of the Principal Resolution to be Passed at the Anti-Compromise Conference

Hindustan Standard, 17 March 1940.

From indications available at the Kisan Nagar camps it appears that the main resolution that will come up before the anti-Compromise Conference will deal with the questions of resisting the efforts on the part of Congress leaders to come to a compromise with British Imperialism on the issue of National independence of India.

It is stated in this connection that if nothing emerges out of the Ramgarh Congress in the matter of giving a lead to the country at the present moment, the Leftists who are opposed to the compromise move would feel it their duty to march forward with their fighting programme.

It is gathered from information to hand that the Conference will adopt a resolution condemning the repressive policy of the Government with special reference to recent arrests and externments of leaders and workers.

By another resolution the Conference will press the demands of peasants and workers. The present international situation with particular reference to the latest developments in Finland may also form the subject-matter of another resolution. The conference is also likely to take up consideration of the resolution on War, adopted by the Congress at the Haripura session and insist on the Congress acting up to it.

The principal resolution for the All India Anti-Compromise Conference, to be moved by the Bengal Labour Party delegates and which with possible slight, technical changes, will, it is confidently believed in well-informed Conference circles be adopted unanimously reads: 'This Conference reaffirms the inalienable right of Indian people to Independence. It refuses to recognize the right of the British Imperialist Parliament to dictate or frame a constitution for India and reaffirms the vows of Indian people to fight for severing all connections with British rulers.

This Conference is of opinion that this right of the people cannot be exercised in the teeth of Imperialist opposition unless it is backed by organized mass effort on a national scale. Any attempt to arrive at a 'Reapproachment' with Imperialism behind the back of the masses and without a decisive struggle on their part will achieve not independence but merely another name for this slavery. To win Independence and hold it against a possible combination of Imperialists, the masses must fight their way to power and at all stages of struggle dispute the right of individuals or narrow groups to call halt to struggle without a definite mandate from the fighting masses themselves.

This conference welcomes the resurgence of the wave of struggle in India with the struggle of the workers for a War Bonus at its head. These struggles fought by the masses of workers on their initiative in the face of hundred disabilities, absence of Civil Liberties, arrest of their leaders, shows vitality which would be foolish to underestimate. To allow these and other struggles to fade away for want of coordination and national support, would in the opinion of the Conference, constitute a treason against the Country.

This Conference resolves immediately to create a nation-wide organization which must (1) rally the support of the whole country for every struggle waged by the masses such as for War Bonus, for a reduction of rent and for moratorium of debt of the satisfaction of land hunger, for Civil Liberties and release of political prisoners for political rights in States; (2) provide a focal point of all struggles, so that all struggles are fought (and initiated where necessary) by a centralized collective leadership; (3) provide collective affiliation to the workers, peasants, students and other organizations as a guarantee that the organization shall be a common property of the fighting masses as a whole and that the fighting tradition of all these organizations should become the assets of this organization; (4) popularize and initiate a struggle among all sections of people, locally and nationally on a basis of charter for a Free India; (5) create a nation-wide movement to ensure peace between India and her neighbours by agitating for Pacts of non-aggression between India and her border States.

36. Swami Sahajanand Saraswati's Address as Chairman of the Reception Committee at the First All-India Anti-Compromise Conference, Ramgarh, 19 March 1940

Swami Sahajanand Saraswati Papers (IInd instalment), Serial No. 4, English Publication, 1940, NMML.

Comrades,

I deem it my singular honour and privilege to accord you, dauntless and distinguished sons and daughters of Mother India and seasoned soldiers of freedom's fight, a humble, but hearty welcome on behalf of the Reception Committee of the 1st, and let us hope the last, All India Anti-Compromise Conference. I am painfully aware of the all round glaring shortcomings in making you feel at home here. But, circumstanced as we are, this could not be otherwise, and as all of you know it well, and this is my only excuse to be forgiven for these. I am, therefore, sanguine, you will not mind the inconveniences confronting you at every step and proceed composedly forthwith with the work in mind.

Present Situation

You are assembled here at a time when our checkered national history of the long drawn freedom's battle is about, I am afraid, to take a most violent turn, which may make or mar our assured and systematic onward march at least, for some time to come, and it is your profound duty to see here and how that this turn is entirely in favour of that march and accelerates it. It pains one extremely to recollect the fact that a nation in bondage, which has consistently and uninterruptedly, for these twenty long years, fought, tooth and nail, in a most marvelous manner ever known to the history, the mightiest empire in the world with a considerable success, is now under the deadly grip of a terrible inertia and stalemate at this most critical juncture fraught with immense potentialities when the enemy is confronted with an equally formidable foe at his own home and fighting a desperate battle for safety and existence. Is this the time for us even to think of a compromise with him? Is it not the most opportune moment to strike a fatal blow at him and win our emancipation, we are hungering and thirsting after. British imperialism, although struggling hard and attempting desperately for its very existence under the dreadful danger of being eclipsed fully and wiped out completely, treats our demand for even the full-fledged Dominion Status, with unusual contempt and yet we talk and think in the terms of an honourable settlement with it and that too, to achieve complete Independence! Is this the way of any honourable nation which has challenged more than once the British Imperialism successfully? Do you not feel the pinch of this shameful move of our national leadership, bent upon dishonouring, may be unconsciously, still more mother India? We are so seized with this idea of compromise, the atmosphere is so thoroughly charged with it and we are so objectively under its poisonous influence that even in our ordinary talks on politics we cannot do without its idea, and yet we do not realize, I am afraid, its soul killing influence on us, so much so that some of us, who are taken as pucca revolutionaries and intellectual giants, feel in their heart of hearts that the complete and undiluted independence may be established here as a result of the talk of compromise. Our political bankruptcy and national downfall cannot go farther.

To instance Ireland on this score is the height of ignorance. Ireland used the last great war to the best of her advantage, gave all possible kicks to her neighbour master and never approached him with folded hands and did perform pilgrimages to viceregal lodge and London. She always stood erect and remained ready to kick whenever opportunity afforded itself to her. She is so even no. Hers has been the constant fight and nothing but fight and hence the freedom on Ireland is the direct result of fight and not of the talk of compromise and settlement. And yet that freedom is not full and complete as desired and required by the Irish masses. The Irish masses are still under the social and economic bondage and theirs is the mere political freedom which alone we do not require here. We want to establish here complete emancipation of the masses from the triple bondage and exploitation, we want the masses to wrest for ever from the hands of our masters the very power which enables them to exploit economically, socially and politically the kisans, the mazdurs and other producers of wealth, and thus desire to end this exploitation for all time to come by making these same masses the custodians of that power and hence of peace, progress and fraternity. Can anything but an uncompromising struggle achieve it?

Patna Resolution

After the election of Maulana Azad to the Presidentship of the National Congress he made a vague mention in a press-interview of a new form of civil disobedience and this was too much for some of our revolutionary friends, who went into hysterics over it and their excitement and joy knew no bounds. But to the piercing eyes there was nothing like this in that interview, which was a sheer diplomatic move on the eve of the Ramgarh Congress with the set purpose of smooth sailing in it, and therefore a preparatory instrument for that. First of all this new type of civil disobedience was sure to lead the nation nowhere. It seemed somewhat mystic and the nation is tired already of the mysticism of Mahatmas and saints. We have had enough of this and to spare. Then, again the mention of the possibility of coalition ministries, although in a diplomatically guarded language, in the same breath had nothing to do with a serious fight and it pointed clearly, if still clarity was needed at all, that all this was a clever move to prepare the ground for compromise.

Then came the Patna Resolution of the Working Committee which is meant for the Ramgarh session of the Congress. The same shrewdness, all round vagueness, past mastership in a diplomatic drafting and non-committal attitude is again to be found in it and there is nothing said unequivocally final here. The dimmest prospect of fight is of course, there. But then the door for compromise has also been kept purposely open in that resolution. It is evident beyond a shadow of doubt from the statements, press interviews and speeches of High Command after passing that resolution. The retiring Rashtrapati has said that there is still time for the British Government to make amends and concede our demands. The Sardar has told clearly that if our masters concede our demands for Constituent Assembly there will be no need for fight and we all are aware by now what sort of Constituent Assembly he has in his mind. It is nothing but a joint session of all the Assemblies elected under the Constitution Act of 1935. And the great Premier of Madras has declared that the resolution does not contemplate at all an immediate fight.

But why go so far and grope in dark? The author himself of the resolution, the saint of Shegaon, has thus given the authoritative interpretation of that resolution, 'the question has come from London whether the Congress has closed the door to negotiation and compromise. My interpretation of the resolution is that the Congress has not closed the door. It has been closed by Lord Zetland.' It is evident from above that although Lord Zetland closed the door unceremoniously and contemptuously months back, yet even now the resolution passed at Patna has not deemed it advisable and proper to bang it on behalf of the Congress, and the nation is thus still made to look with eager and expectant eyes to the high and mighty British Imperialism to condescend to throw the crumbs of Dominion Status as a result of the change of heart, though it has no heart at all, consequent upon the unbound love and perfect non-violence displayed towards it by the Indian masses led by Mahatma, Deputy Mahatmas, Asst. Mahatmas and their staunch followers. Indeed we are seriously advised by comrades and others that the compromise has been given the to-by and buried fathoms deep once for all by this resolution and the stage for fight has been set up. But anyone reading between the lines is bound to reach only one conclusion that the en as yet does not rule out Dominion Status or the like only if such a status is ever possible and existent, although history sets its face against it.

And as regards the fight, it is hinted at no doubt in the fifth paragraph of the resolution, but at the time it has been bound down by almost impossible conditions to be fulfilled. The first of these is that if and when 'the Congress organization is considered fit for the purpose'. And who will judge this fitness and enoughness thereof and how? It is clarified in the next sentence. 'The Congress desire to draw the attention of Congressmen to Gandhiji's declarations that he can only undertake the responsibility of declaring civil disobedience when he is satisfied that they are strictly observing discipline and carrying out the constructive programme described in the independence pledge'. This is the second condition, which again is impossible of fulfilment, as the nation as a whole has already shown by not taking that pledge on the Independence Day and by contemptuously disregarding Gandhiji's and Rashtrapati's advices to students and the workers not to leave their classes and not to resort to strikes that day. Our comrades themselves, who are extremely enthused over the prospect of an immediate fight, have declared unequivocally that they can never be a party to that pledge. And the third condition is in the shape of an alternative which too should deceive none. It is 'or in case circumstances so shape themselves as to precipitate a crisis.' But the fact of the matter is that the independence—fight is not or has never been a thing caused by circumstances, which precipitate a crisis. Rather those who wage this fight are invariably in search of the means how to precipitate such a crisis and they never commit the grave blunder of leaving this crisis to be created by the circumstances. But here our leadership clearly shirks this responsibility and, to be frank, is afraid of this crisis otherwise the present being the most opportune occasion they ought to have taken resort to means which have now presented themselves to these leaders and brought them to the nation. Moreover, our masters are clever enough to take the time by forelock and in no case to allow the circumstances to cause such a crisis. Therefore, it is totally wrong to expect any fight from our leaders in the near future and to those who say that the Patna Resolution is a great advance over the prevailing conditions, I make bold to submit humbly that it is an advance no doubt, but surely not over the prevailing conditions. It is an advance in the art of an almost clever and diplomatic draftsmanship, in which our leaders are unparalled, I admit. Of course, I shall be very glad and happy if I prove wrong and the real fight starts. But the latest pronouncement by Gandhiji in the Harijan has dashed to the ground any such die-hardism in hoping for a fight. Indeed personal leadership, and that too on the part of a single individual, cannot but result in a fiasco in the end and for a nation to depend on such a leadership for freedom fight is a calamity.

Plea of Unpreparedness

It is baseless and absurd to say that the country is not prepared for fight while previously it was and Gandhiji had no hesitation in declaring repeated fights against the British Imperialism on the basis of this very preparedness. And what are, pray, the reasons of its deterioration since 1934 as far as the fight is concerned and how to ascertain them? There is an all-round tremendous consciousness among the masses and they have waged marvelously many a successful struggle on various fronts throughout the country. This phenomenon was almost nonexistent prior to 1934 and instances of it were few and far between, while today there are thousands. Even the princely India is in the midst of a ferment and there is a tremendous mass upsurge there which was formerly untraceable. The kisans, mazdoors, youths and students are making history and forging ahead. They have established their solid organizations. The hunger poverty, helplessness and the nakedness are growing rapidly in the masses, taking their heavy tolls and rendering them impatient and desperate to get rid of their present hellish condition. The deterioration in their material conditions has reached its limit and they know fully that even jails, bullets and gallows are any day preferable to this death of theirs by inches. What is then the justification in dubbing them as unprepared? This is rather a most uncalled for insult hurled at them. Surely it is the leaders who are not ready for fight and they hide their unpreparedness under this false plea.

The fact is that the dire economic distress has touched and adversely affected the broad layer of the masses and the storm of the political awakening has swept over them giving them a new life and vigour. The result is that the lowest and the most oppressed stratum of the society has been rendered fully fit for a violent stir and spontaneous action. Then there are middle and upper strata too of the society resting for centuries over that most suppressed and oppressed stratum, and above all there is the British Imperialism. Now any mass movement on a nation-wide scale is bound to give a violent shake to that lowest layer, unleashing its mass energy and setting it in an uncontrollable motion with the clear result that all the middle and upper layers together with the British Imperialism are destined to be forcibly thrown away and torn into tatters. Our leadership consisting of the middle class is painfully aware and mortally afraid of its impeding doom if it once starts fight. Hence this excuse of unpreparedness, this excessive emphasis on non-violence and this constant slogan of keeping blindly an implicit faith in the Gandhian leadership! Otherwise if the fight is started once, Gandhiji or the present leadership will not be able to stop it in the middle, when they sense danger to their very existence and their cry for halt will simply prove their crying in the wilderness.

Where We Differ?

We too are not opposed to Khadi, Charkha and village industries and admit their place in the present national economy of our country. But unlike Gandhian School of thought we are not ready to accept them as the basis of the future society. Rather we believe that these will vanish from that society never to return and will adorn museums. So here our differences with that school are basic and fundamental and not practical and it is why we are opposed to the fourfold Gandhian Programme.

And as regards non-violence we are ready to accept it as a policy. Circumstanced as we are we can progress towards our aim through peaceful means alone and to that extent we are ready to pledge ourselves to it as practical men. My experience of the fight for the day to day demands of the Kisans has taught me this policy we are ready to give our national leadership full and unrestricted scope for the trial of the peaceful means to win complete independence with the full liberty to take recourse to other means if and when they fail to liberate the masses from the triple bondage. Here Gandhiji insists that we should accept non-violence as the only means to achieve our aim. It is just only then that he will lead the fight. But it is like the insistence of a doctor before he begins to serve a patient to pledge to him that he would approach no other doctor whether he is cured by him or not, while the ailing persons want to reserve for himself the right to requisition the services of other doctors too, in case he fails. Here we follow simple logic and history and hence our differences are basic and not immediately practical.

Then comes the problem of change of heart and transformation of the society by love and Ahimsa. Frankly speaking, I never believe in these and it is only on the Marxian line, I maintain, that the society can be rebuilt in order to be free from Himsa and exploitation of all descriptions. Therefore, here we stand poles apart vis-à-vis the Gandhian School.

In a nutshell we stand for an all round resolution, which is the only result, sooner or later of a national fight, while the other school stands for reformism in every sphere of our life. It is why it is so anxious for the compromise. The compromise is the very essence of reformism and it can exist and flourish on that alone.

Task Before Us

In the circumstances our task is clear. If we do not awake betimes, seize upon every opportunity, make desperate attempts, take concerted steps and move with a dashing spirit to thwart every effort to the contrary, this detestable compromise will shortly become, a fear, a settled fact that the country will be committed to it in the name of the National Congress. Political stalemate and inaction serve only those who want to profit by deterioration. It is why they always favour delay in a decisive and swift action. We must learn in this respect from the office acceptance episode when indecision and delaying tactics failed us and served the purpose of office-wallas. Therefore, there is no time to lose and we, while vigilant enough to detect and check in time every retrograde move should take the risk of an immediate plunge for direct action. Then and then alone we shall be able to save the nation from an ignoble surrender and capitulation.

Conclusion

But I am sorry, I have transgressed my limit and encroached upon the duty of our president of this conference. It is his duty and right to discuss threadbare the knotty problems staring us in the face and show us the way to their solution. My duty is only to welcome you all and crave your indulgence to excuse me and the reception committee for its various failings in proving for your comforts and bare necessities of life. Once more therefore I thank you for the patience with which you have tolerated large heartedly not only this uncalled for speech inflicted upon you but also our shortcomings in your reception and welcome. I now request you to elect your president and proceed with work awaiting your attention and deliberation.

Inquilab Zindabad

37. Subhas Bose's Presidential Address at the First All-India Anti-Compromise Conference, Ramgarh, 19 March 1940

Sisir K. Bose (ed.), *Crossroads: The Works of Subhas Chandra Bose 1938–40*, Calcutta, 1981 (2nd edition), pp. 289–94.

Comrades,

You have done me a very great honour by inviting me to preside over the deliberations of the All-India Anti-Compromise Conference at Ramgarh today. At the same time the responsibility you have thrown on my shoulders in onerous to a degree. This Conference is intended to focus all the anti-imperialist forces in the country that are now determined to resist a compromise with Imperialism. To preside over such a Conference is by no means an easy task. This task becomes all the more serious and arduous when the Chairman of the Reception Committee is no less a person than Swami Sahajanand Saraswati. It is in response to Swamiji's clarion call that we have assembled here today.

Comrades, I shall fail in my duty if before proceeding to discuss the problem of the day, I do not pay a tribute to those who are responsible for organizing this Conference. I happen to know something of the obstacles and the difficulties that had to be overcome before this Conference could meet and I can, therefore, speak with a certain amount of authority. These obstacles and difficulties were of a twofold character. In the first place, there were physical and material obstacles and difficulties to be overcome at Ramgarh before adequate arrangements for the Conference could be made. In the second place, persistent hostile propaganda all over country had to be faced and counteracted by the organizers of the Conference. The most surprising and painful of this propaganda was the determined endeavour of a section of Leftists (or shall I say pseudo-Leftists) to make this Conference impossible by openly condemning it and also by trying to sabotage it. As a matter of fact, during the last few months it has become more and more evident that a number of Leftists have begun to play the role of apologists of the Rightists—but such a phenomenon is not new in history. Man lives to learn and the longer he lives, the more does he realize the aptness of the oft-repeated truism that history repeats itself.

It has been argued by the apologists of the Congress Working Committee that the Congress is itself the biggest Anti-Compromise Conference and that such a Conference is, therefore, unnecessary. The resolution of the last meeting of the Congress Working Committee which met at Patna is held up before our eyes in order to demonstrate that the Congress has adopted an uncompromising policy. One cannot but admire the naiveté of such an argument, but is it meet and proper for politicians and political workers to be so very naive?

One has only to go through the whole of the Patna resolution and particularly through the latter portion of it in order to realize that there are loopholes which detract from the intrinsic value of that resolution. No sooner was this resolution passed than Mahatma Gandhi came forward with the statement that the door had not been banged on future negotiations for a settlement. Mahatmaji's subsequent lengthy remarks on Civil Disobedience do not assure us by any means that the period of struggle has commenced. In fact, what has distressed and bewildered us during the last year and a half is the fact that while on the one hand red-hot resolutions are passed and statements issued by members of the Congress Working Committee, simultaneously other remarks are made and statements issued either by Mahatma Gandhi or by other Rightist leaders which create a totally different impression on the average mind. Then there is the moot question as to whether the Patna resolution would have been passed at all, but for the pressure exerted by the Left during the last six months.

The country eagerly awaits a clear and unequivocal declaration from the Congress Working Committee that the door has finally been banged on all talks of a compromise with Imperialism. But will the declaration be forthcoming? If so, when?

Comrades, those who aver that the Congress is the biggest Anti-Compromise Conference perhaps suffer from shortness of memory and their brains consequently need refreshing. Have they forgotten that as soon as the War began, Mahatma Gandhi proceeded to Simla without caring to consult the Congress Working Committee and informed His Excellency the Viceroy that he was in favour of rendering unconditional help to Great Britain in the prosecution of the War? Do they not realize that Mahatma Gandhi being the sole Dictator of the Congress, his personal views necessarily have a far-reaching implication? Have they forgotten that since the outbreak of War, the Congress Working Committee has side-tracked the main issue—namely, our demand for Purna Swaraj—by putting forward a demand for a fake Constituent Assembly? Have they forgotten that some prominent Rightist leaders, including members of the Congress Working Committee, have been continuously whittling down the implications of a Constituent Assembly and that they have gone so far as to accept separate electorate and the existing franchise for the Legislative Assembly as the basis for electing the Constituent Assembly of their dreams? Have they forgotten that after the resignation of Congress ministries several Congress Ministers have been showing an inordinate desire to get back to office? Have they forgotten the consistent attitude which Mahatma Gandhi has adopted during the last six months in the matter of a compromise with the British Government? And do they not know that behind the smoke-screen of hot phrases, negotiations for a compromise have been going on apace.

Unfortunately for us, the British Government have ceased to take the Congress seriously and have formed the impression that however much Congressmen may talk, they will not ultimately show fight. Since September, 1939, there has not been any dearth of resolutions and statements. Some members of the Congress Working Committee opine that these resolutions have impressed the world. But whether they have impressed the world or not, they have certainly not impressed the British, who are essentially a realistic race. During the last six months we have offered them only words and words and we have received the time-worn reply that so long as the Hindu–Muslim problem remains unsolved, Purna Swaraj is unthinkable.

Since September last India has been passing through a rare crisis when men's minds have fallen a prey to doubt and vacillation. The first to fall were the leaders themselves and the demoralization that seized them has been spreading as a contagion throughout the land. A determined and widespread effort is needed if we are to stem the rot. To make this effort really effective, our activities should be focused at an All-India Conference of all those who are determined to have no truck with Imperialism.

The crisis that has overtaken us may be rare in Indian history, but it is nothing new in the history of the world. Such crises generally appear in periods of transition. In India we are now ringing down the curtain on an age that is passing away, while we are at the same time ushering in the dawn of a new era. The age of Imperialism is drawing to a close and the era of freedom, democracy and socialism looms ahead of us. India, therefore, stands today at one of the crossroads of history. It is for us to share, if we so will, the heritage that awaits the world.

It is not to be wondered at that men's minds should be bewildered when the old structure is crashing under its own weight and the new is yet to rise out of the ashes of the old. But let us not lose faith in ourselves, or in our countrymen or in humanity in this hour of uncertainty. To lose faith would be a calamity of the first magnitude.

Such crises constitute the supreme test of a nation's leadership. The present crisis has put our own leadership to the test and the latter has been unfortunately found wanting. It is only by analyzing and exposing the causes of its failure that we can learn the lesson of history and lay the foundation of our future effort and achievement. But such analysis and exposure will necessarily be painful to all concerned, though there is means of avoiding it.

I may digress at this stage and draw an analogy with similar crises in other climes and ages. When the October Revolution broke out in Russia in 1917, nobody had a clear conception as to how the revolution should be directed. Most of the Bolsheviks were then thinking in terms of a coalition with other parties. It was left to Lenin to denounce all coalitions and give out the slogan—'All Power to the Soviet.' Who knows what turn Russian history would have taken but for this timely lead of Lenin's during a period of doubt and vacillation? Lenin's unerring instinct (or intuition) which ultimately proved to be prophetic, saved Russia from disaster and from a tragedy similar to that which overtook Spain the other day.

Let us now take a contrary case. Italy in 1922 was all intents and purposes, ripe for Socialism. All that she needed was an Italian Lenin. But the man of the hour did not arrive and the opportunity slipped out of Socialist hands. It was immediately seized by the Fascist leader, Benito Mussolini. By his march to Rome and his seizure of power, Italian history took an altogether different turn and Italy ultimately went Fascist instead of going Socialist. Doubt and vacillation had seized the Italian leaders and so they failed. Mussolini had one supreme virtue which not only saved him but brought him the laurels of victory. He knew his mind and he was not afraid to act. That constituted the essence of leadership.

Today our leaders are wobbling and their vacillation has demoralized a section of Leftists as well. 'Unity,' 'National Front', 'Discipline'—these have become cheap slogans which have no relation to reality. Befogged by such attractive slogans, they seem to have forgotten that the supreme need of the hour is a bold, uncompromising policy leading us on to a national struggle. Whatever strengthens us for this purpose is to be welcomed. Whatever weakens us is to be eschewed. Unity which ties us to the apron-strings of Rightist politicians is by no means a blessing. We might as well induce the Congress to effect unity with the Liberal Federation—if unity is to be desired under all conditions and circumstances.

In the present crisis, the most distressing phenomenon is the disruption within the ranks of those who were hitherto regarded as Leftists. The immediate future will prove to be the acid test of Leftism in India. Those who will be found wanting will be soon exposed as pseudo-Leftists.

The members of the Forward Bloc, too, will have to demonstrate by their work and conduct that they are really forward and dynamic. It may be that in the ordeal that is ahead of us, some of those who are branded as Rightists today, will prove to be genuine Leftists in action, I mean.

A word is necessary here in order to explain what we mean by Leftism. The present age is the anti-imperialist phase of our movement. Our main task in this age is to end Imperialism and win national Independence for the Indian people. When freedom comes, the age of national reconstruction will commence and that will be the Socialist phase of our movement. In the present phase of our movement, Leftists will be those who will wage an uncompromising fight with Imperialism. Those who waver and vacillate in their struggle against Imperialism—those who tend towards a compromise with it cannot by any means be Leftists. In the next phase of our movement, Leftism will be synonymous with Socialism—but in the present phase, the words, 'Leftist' and 'Anti-imperialist' should be interchangeable.

The problem of the hour is—'Will India still remain under the thumb of the Rightists or will she swing to the Left, once for all?' The answer to this can be furnished only by the Leftists themselves. If they adopt a bold, uncompromising policy in their struggle with Imperialism, regardless of all dangers, difficulties and obstacles; then the Leftists will make history and India will go Left.

To those who may still be thinking of a compromise, the recent history of Ireland and the sequel to the Anglo–Irish Treaty should prove highly instructive and edifying. A compromise with Imperialism will mean that an anti-imperialist national struggle will soon be converted into a civil war among the people themselves. Would this be desirable from any point of view?

In the event of a compromise being effected with Imperialism in this country, Indian Leftists will in future have to fight not only Imperialism, but its new-fangled Indian allies as well. This will necessarily mean that the national struggle with Imperialism will be converted into a civil war among the Indians themselves.

Let us take time by the forelock and let us act while it is not too late. Swami Sahajanand Saraswati has sounded the clarion call. Let us respond to it with all the strength and courage that we possess. From this Conference let us send out a warning to both Imperialism and its Indian Allies. The success of this Conference should mean the death-knell of compromise with Imperialism.

Before we part, let us also set up a permanent machinery for implementing the resolutions of this Conference and for waging an uncompromising war with Imperialism. Everybody now realizes that if the Working Committee of the Congress does not give the call for launching a national struggle, others will have to do so. It would, therefore, be in the fitness of things for this Conference to set up a permanent machinery for undertaking this responsibility—should the Working Committee fail us in this crisis. I hope and trust that the deliberations of this Conference will be a prelude to work and struggle on a nation-wide scale and on an All-India front.

38. Swami Sahajanand Saraswati: What We Want to Do

Janata, 4 April, 1940.

It is stated that only a National Institution Organization can announce the beginning of a national struggle for freedom. It will lose its meaning if anybody else starts it. In fact, this is quite true and it also impresses the general public. The intelligentsia also thinks in the same way. Therefore, if some people, tired of this nation-wide political stalemate, try to march forward, then they are not only showered (with criticisms) but are also pulled back. At the same time nobody provides any suggestion to save the country from this deadly deadlock and if any body dares to suggest anything, these suggestions seem to be quite vulnerable. If we start a struggle on behalf of the daily problems and demands of the oppressed masses and promise to intensify it slowly but steadily, even then it is called dangerous. Those people who support this struggle even now say that if we linked this everyday struggle with the National Struggle and announce that it is a part of that struggle, a strong blow (of that struggle), it will prove destructive. Do everything but do not mention that it is the National Struggle or a part of it. Because we have not got the right to say/announce it. Only a National Organization can do so. It is a strange riddle—as soon as we announce the onset of a nation-wide peasant worker movement and struggle based on any country-wide problem, whether economic or not, then it will lead to destruction because it will mean that we have begun the national struggle for freedom. This is a strange case of political untouchability and we are being made a victim of it or at least they are trying to do so.

As long as slavery does not pinch us we can tolerate anything but as soon as we awakened... our campaign against slavery had already begun whether we announce it or not ... since then our every activity will be directed towards rebellion. At that movement our whole 'being' becomes associated with rebellion and it continues as long as we do not get freedom; in-between, this rebellion could subside but it never dies out completely. In this situation there is no need to announce the struggle of freedom at intervals. It is always continuing, although we can intensify it if it becomes ineffective. The proposition that those who are to be set free should not participate in it and others should struggle for them is beyond comprehension. This freedom received through the efforts of others will be no better than slavery even if it is named otherwise. It will only prove to be mere political freedom, because real freedom is gained when there is no oppression anywhere.

When our country declared in one voice that 'self government is our birthright' from a higher platform, the struggle for freedom started at that very moment and it is still continuing. Therefore there is no question of starting it from beginning. One can only intensify it. One thing more—whatever effort has been made in this direction is only a curtain-raiser, an introduction and an effort to shift the total mentality of the masses towards freedom. It was successful and gradually the people have started recognizing and understanding freedom. Hence the true picture of the struggle will be used to end oppression whether domestic or foreign. It is also necessary to start and organize such struggles which were announced at Ramgarh by the Kisan Sabha.

In fact as long as the revolutionary sentiments are not awakened completely and their real image is not shown or developed, there will be no revolution and oppression will not end; and these matters could not be settled through mere political talks and other things like that. The toiling masses are always oppressed and tortured and in this way they become useless and depressed. They start thinking that there is no saviour for them and their life will be always full of sorrows. He becomes dependent upon God and Luck. It is our duty to end their disparity and make them hopeful and confident and it is possible only when we start the struggle for ending their oppression and involve them in it completely and make them victorious in their struggle. In this way the masses will recognize their power and feel it, only then we will be involved as leaders among them. We will become their active and real leaders. Without this it will never be possible. This is the crux of the Anti-Compromise and Palasa Kisan Sabha Resolutions.

We should remember that this struggle could not be started by the announcement of any great organization or person. It will develop and intensify slowly. Partial struggles can assume gigantic proportions. This partial struggle will become the foundation and structure of the national struggle. This is the real meaning of a partial struggle. As long as we consider the everyday struggle for bread and the national struggle as two different things it will be our mistake. Just like the engine acquires speed after running slowly for some time, we can transform our everyday struggles into a strong and powerful national struggle. The other way is that of deceit. This is the meaning of our programme for the celebration of National Week. In this way we are trying to create such a situation in this country when the sleeping powers of the country will awaken simultaneously and it will end the oppression and torture prevalent in the present society and lay the foundation of a peaceful humanity.

II.   Congress Socialist Party

39.   Acharya Narendra Dev's Appeal to Celebrate Independence Day
   Aaj, 18 January 1940.

The Importance of Independence Day

What should the peasants do?

An appeal by the president of All India Kisan Sabha, Acharya Narendra Dev: The peasants should always be ready to bear difficulties and sacrifice selfishness.

Lucknow 8 January: The President of the All India Kisan Sabha, Mr Narendra Dev has appealed to the peasants of India to celebrate Independence Day on 26th January. He says:

Every year crores of Indians pledge for independence. We have sacrificed selfishness and have borne many difficulties in order to proceed on the path (of freedom) but a lot of things has to be done.

This year, the importance of independence has increased even more because the European War has proved that one cannot establish peace in the world without the end of Imperialism and Fascism.

Britain is not granting freedom to India, therefore, India, is not supporting it in its war efforts and the Congress has already made its representatives resign from the Government Ministerships. This is only the first step of civil disobedience. All of us have to prepare for the satyagraha. Peasants are the life of nation but there is no limit to their exploitation under the foreign rule and their basic existence seems to be in danger. The peasants have no rights left with them. They have been compelled to live under the pressure of the money-lenders.

As long as the present condition is not changed on India does not get the rights of introducing total reorganization of the social and economic systems, the villages of India cannot make any progress. Therefore, the question of India's Independence is more important for the peasants.

The peasants are awakening. They have supported the Congress in the Independence struggle. They are the foundation pillars of Congress, they have won many of their battles. I am requesting them to support the Congress in great numbers and work for making the Independence Day a success.

This time we have to make a serious commitment. We have to be ready for non-payment of rents. This time we will erase our defame of many centuries.

The future is bright, A full of hopes. The polluted system has to be demolished. A new arrangement has to be made based on peace, democracy, international cooperation, etc. We have to establish the Government of peasants and workers in India.

40. Jayaprakash Narayan's Statement on Anti-Compromise Conference, 29 February 1940

Bimal Prasad (ed.), *Jayaprakash Narayan: Selected Works*, Vol. 3, (1939–1946), Delhi, 2003, pp. 38–9.

The Congress Socialist Party is against compromise but so is the Congress. The Ramgarh session of the Congress will in itself be the biggest anti-compromise conference in the country. The recent statement of the Congress President has also made this clear. This does not mean that strong influences for compromise are not at work. We must oppose these. But in opposing them we must not oppose the Congress itself. Mass demonstrations against forces of compromise are necessary. But these demonstrations should not be against the Congress, nor aspire to become its rivals. They must contribute in a positive manner towards national solidarity. I am afraid the proposed anti-compromise conference does not fulfill these requirements. Its basic assumption is that the Congress Working Committee is going to enter into an alliance with imperialism and has relinquished the task of winning independence. Any action based on this assumption would logically and necessarily disrupt the Congress and destroy national solidarity. The entire background of the conference is disruptive. Among the elements that make up this background are the piqued revolt of Subhas Babu against the Working Committee, the breach in the National Front in Bengal and the threat to carry this breach forward beyond the frontiers of Bengal, the talk of a parallel Congress, the talk of a neo Swarajist Party, the encouragement given to communal organizations such as the Hindu Sabha and the Muslim League, and others. Added to all this is the recent statement of Subhas Babu that the anti-compromise conference if successful would eclipse the Congress. I cannot conceive how any Congressman can desire to eclipse the very organization to which he belongs. These considerations make it impossible for us to associate ourselves with the proposed conference.

41. Joint Statement by Narendra Dev and Jayaprakash Narayan on the Working Committee's Draft Resolution for the Ramgarh Congress, 4 March 1940

Searchlight, 5 March 1940; Bimal Prasad (ed.), *Jayaprakash Narayan: Selected Works*, Vol. 3, (1939–1946), Delhi, 2003, p. 305.

The draft resolution prepared by the Working Committee for the Ramgarh session of the Congress must mark a turning point in current Indian history. A distinct break with the policy of stalemate has been made. Dominion Status has been definitely rejected; complete independence and Constituent Assembly based on adult suffrage have been reiterated; complete non-cooperation with the Imperialist War has been enjoined upon all who would answer to the call of the Congress; the inevitability of civil disobedience has been unequivocally proclaimed. No other obstacle to resumption to civil disobedience remains, except indiscipline within the Congress. The British attempt to use communal differences and the Princes as obstacles has been finally put out of the way by pointing out that both these problems are British creations and, therefore, could be solved only when the British power has been overthrown.

We hope that in view of these fateful decisions. those who in the name of leftism have of late been trying to disrupt the Congress and lower its prestige will realize now that the time has come when we must put our house in order and repair the breaches that have been made in the national front. Their sole justification for all their actions has been that the Congress would not fight any more and that the Working Committee was soon to enter into a pact with Imperialism. These deductions as we often endeavoured to show, at some risk of misunderstanding, were based on a false reading of Congress policy and perhaps a certain amount of wishful thinking. The anti-Right vendetta must be based on some thing and what better basis could be found than the scare of a dishonourable deal with Imperialism. However, the draft resolution leaves no doubt about a national struggle. Its perspective is no longer dim or distant. Our duty, therefore, is also clear. Let not false notions of prestige stand in the way of duty. Differences may remain, as they must, but internal chaos and indiscipline must cease. The greatest responsibility in this connection lies on Shri Subhas Chandra Bose who, we hope, will rise to the occasion. The unseemly quarrel within the Congress in Bengal must cease. Let all our efforts be directed now to the sole end of preparing for the national struggle about which no uncertainty remains any longer.

42. Jayaprakash Narayan on Mahatma Gandhi's Leadership and the Congress Socialist Party

'Congress Socialist Tract No. 1', *National Herald,* 4 March 1940; Bimal Prasad (ed.), *Jayaprakash Narayan: Selected Works,* Vol. 3, (1939–1946), Delhi, 2003, pp. 39–45.

The policy that the Congress Socialist Party has followed in recent months with regard to the Congress has come in for a good deal of criticism. I believe, however, that a little dispassionate thinking would show the correctness of its policy. Unfortunately, the prevailing atmosphere is not too conducive to dispassionate thought. There is mutual distrust and ill-will, deliberate confusion of issues, empty heroics. In certain quarters it is the fashion to attribute motives to whoever disagrees with you. Thus, it has been suggested by some of my leftist friends that my recent policies have been dictated by my desire to be elevated to the Congress Working Committee. This way of political understanding throws some light on the depths to which a section of the left movement has descended. If my friends find such a motive behind my policies, it is little wonder that in every move of the Congress Working Committee they sense a deal with imperialism!

It is in public interest to refer—even at the risk of indecorum—to a personal matter. Since my membership of the Congress Working Committee is on the brain of some of my friends, I should like to tell them that the doors of the Working Committee have, since the time we were first appointed on it [1936], been always open to me and to some other leading members of the CSP. I resigned my membership in 1936 of my own accord, and since have refused a seat every time it has been offered to me. At the Haripura Congress Acharya Narendra Deva and Achyut Patwardhan refused their seats that were offered again by the then President, Babu Subhas Chandra Bose. At Calcutta, Dr Rajendra Prasad again invited us to serve on the Committee, which offer he repeated at Bombay, but Acharya Narendra Deva again declined the offer on behalf of the Party.

I should add that our refusal of membership never implied any disrespect to the Congress Working Committee, to be a member of which is a great honour. Nor did it imply our deviation from the principle of composite leadership which we have always held as we hold it even today.

Surrender to Gandhism?

To turn now to the subject-matter. Our present policy has been attacked on the ground that it is a surrender to Gandhism. Socialism versus Gandhism is not the present issue, however. We are faced with the task of preparing for and launching a national struggle against imperialism. This is not a socialist but a nationalist task to be carried out by Socialists, Gandhians and others. Our only crime, therefore, is that we continue to insist on the unity of the Congress as the only guarantee of national unity and a national struggle. Our further crime is that we insist that unity of the Congress involves the unity of its leadership, because we cannot, particularly in such a crisis as the present, split the leadership and keep the Congress together. Our still further crime is that we are being guided not by what is good for the Congress Socialist Party or for that heterogeneous and vague thing called the Left, but by what is good for the whole, the left and right together. We believe that we have reached a dangerous point when certain sections of the left have begun to look upon themselves not as a wing of a body, but as a whole body itself, with interests distinct and separate from the body of which they are a part.

The Congress Socialist Party was formed not to develop into a rival to the Congress, but to work within the Congress, to strengthen it, to mould and shape its policies. In the five years that the Party has functioned, it has succeeded appreciably in influencing Congress policy. A number of Congress decisions bear clearly the impress of our propaganda. Due to the pioneering work of the Party, since the depressing days of 1934, when civil disobedience had to be called off, and all through the upsurge of parliamentarianism, a vigorous left wing developed in the Congress which even penetrated the ranks of the leadership. The programme of peasant organization which we placed before the Congress, though unaccepted officially by it, yet won the approval of quite a number of provincial and other Committees and a large number of Congressmen. But inspite of all our efforts the official programme of the Congress is still Gandhiji's programme of 1920. Also, while a new leadership has arisen, the predominant leadership is still in the hands of the Old Guard. The old leaders have been at the helm for twenty years. During this period they have led three major struggles and numerous partial ones. They have brought new life, new strength, and new consciousness to the masses. They represent a vital national force—still the most influential in the country.

The Mistake of Subhas Bose

In these circumstances, what are we to do, particularly when a world crisis demands immediate action? Conceivably, given another five years the balance of influence within the Congress and the country could have been changed and the old, as always, would have given place to the new. I should interpolate a remark here that even today the influence of the left leadership would have been much greater had Sjt Subhas Bose followed the advice of our Party and had the communists and other leftists the guts to tender the same advice to him, We advised Subhas Babu, inspite of all that had happened, not to resign from the Presidentship of the Congress. Had he followed our advice we would not only have escaped all the sorry developments of the past months, but we would have also had a Working Committee with a large leftist voice, Subhas Babu himself would have been the President, Pandit Jawaharlal Nehru would have been the General Secretary, Sjt Sarat Chandra Bose and two leftists would have been among the members. It will be remembered that this was the minimum arrangement to which the Old Guard was agreeable. Unfortunately, for reasons best known to him, Subhas Babu thought it better to resign and organize his Forward Bloc. In what manner his resignation helped the country only he and his supporters can tell. I think there would be few impartial observers who would deny that his resignation and subsequent activities have delivered disastrous blows at leftism within the Congress.

Through Uncoloured Glasses

Let me revert to the question, in the present circumstances, what is our duty? To answer it, first let me ask whether we have any other instrument than the Congress for waging a national struggle and maintaining national unity? Throughout history we have had to contend with disintegrating factors and sometimes they have even overwhelmed the forces of national unity. Even today, excepting the Congress there is no other consolidating factor in our social or political life. The Congress represented and still represents, and from all appearances, will continue to represent (much as the communists and the Forward Bloc may dislike the prospect) the widest, the strongest front against imperialism in India. If India goes to war with imperialism with any chance of success, that war has to be waged under the tricolour flag. People talk loosely of kisans, mazdoors, youths and students, as if they stand outside of the Congress. What are meant by these generic terms, however are the Kisan Sabha, the Trade Unions Congress, and the Students' Federation. These bodies have potentiality for the future, but at present, except in a few provinces, their organization is elementary. Their role in our national struggle will be important, and it must be the task of Socialists as well as of other progressive elements to make that role even more important by strenuous organizational work. Their role is, however, clearly of an auxiliary character. The Congress must lead the struggle and the active cooperation and participation of these bodies will be an added factor of strength. But it is crystal-clear that today, neither the Kisan Sabha nor the Trade Union Congress in their present stage of development can hope to fight imperialism with, any degree of success. That task unquestionably belongs to the Congress.

This is the situation facing us when looked at through uncoloured glasses. The Congress alone is the country's salvation. And let us remember that Congress means the whole and not a part of it. A limb torn from a body does not have its proportionate strength and ability. It merely dies.

Gandhiji and National Struggle

I have said above that we are faced today with preparing for and launching a national struggle. I have shown that this struggle can be launched by the Congress alone. Now, let us examine another set of facts. The effective leadership of the Congress is in the hands of Gandhiji. It is obvious that if the congress starts a struggle today it would be in accordance with the programme that Gandhiji lays down. We can influence that programme but we cannot determine it. The technique of the struggle would therefore naturally be the old Gandhian technique, whether anyone likes it or not.

An acceptance of these facts does not mean surrender to Gandhism. We have not ceased to propagate Socialism. We have not stopped working in the Kisan Sabhas and Trade Unions and developing the peasant and labour movements. The first strike for a War-bonus was led by the CSP in the Gaya Cotton Textile Mill and the first War-bonus victory was won by the

Dalmianagar workers under the CSP's leadership. In Bihar, the UP, Bombay, Bengal and elsewhere members of the Party have been as active as before in the struggles of the workers. The same is true of the peasant movement. Where work has suffered in these spheres, it has been due to the withdrawal of Party cadres into the new activities of preparation for the national struggle—such as intensive organization of the Congress Committees and intensive propaganda, volunteer organization, and other things.

However, the situation in which we find ourselves is not such that we can expect to develop the national struggle out of our own, plan of action. We carryon our own work and propagate our platform, but at the same time, we desire an immediate struggle, When we know that there is no prospect of a struggle being started under any other leadership but the present, is it not a mistake to attack the leadership, to seek to discredit it, to weaken it? Shall we thereby bring the struggle nearer or push it away?

United Front and National Struggle

All these years we have heard the theories of United Leadership and United Front propounded. Now, when the hour has arrived to put these theories into practice, to act up to them, gutless revolutionaries are scurrying away from their implications. United leadership, was held to be necessary in the interest of a united national struggle, This theory was mouthed incessantly by our communist friends, at a time when the Congress was engaged in parliamentary work and struggle seemed distant. Now when the parliamentary work has been given up and the Congress is on the eve of struggle, our communist theorists have thought it wise to fling their theory to the wind and concentrate on attacking the present leadership. In this manner they will only contribute to the sabotaging of the struggle. The other day, I heard a Communist comrade, who holds an office in a provincial Congress organization declaim vehemently at a Kisan Conference against the Congress creed of peaceful means. It is fortunate that there are not many persons in the Congress foolish enough to repeat such folly. There is no surer way to sabotage struggle today than for Congressmen to go about decrying peaceful means.

I think it is necessary for us to realize the limitations in which we have to work. By disregarding them we only strengthen them. A fight against the leadership now is not only inadvisable, it is positively harmful. If a national struggle as opposed to sectional factional or partial can be launched by Mahatma Gandhi alone it is suicidal to fight him. It is necessary to lend him our fullest cooperation and loyalty in everything that is preparatory for struggle. If, then there is no struggle we may part company with him and then take the responsibility of the struggle ourselves if we have the strength. Revolt against the present leadership in the manner of Subhas Babu, or attack on it, in the manner of the Communists, both are harmful and are proving to be so.

Communist Bungling

Some people believe that in these circumstances, the Congress Socialist Party becomes superfluous. I should like to remind friends that we are to be guided by what is good for the whole movement and not by the necessity of blowing our own trumpet at all times. If our policy is correct, the CSP will draw strength from it and as in 1934 show again that of all the groups mouthing Marxism, it is the only one that understands how to apply Marxism to India. This is not the place to go into the matter here, but it would be interesting to show how at every critical stage in the last five years the Congress Socialist Party showed the way and others followed or proved their folly. In 1934, the wise Communists were out of the Congress and were out to destroy it. We were in it and to build and strengthen it. In 1936 they too filed in, to build or to destroy history alone will show. In 1936 the CSP opposed the acceptance of Ministerial Offices by the Congress. The communists were first for accepting them with a radical programme. Later, when they found that the anti-ministry cry was becoming popular in the Congress left, they veered round to it so that they may not be isolated: During the General Elections, the CSP supported the Congress wholeheartedly. The communists opposed the Congress in one constituency, to repent at leisure. At Tripuri they spoke passionately of unity and united leadership but again the fear of isolation drove them to action which could lead only to contrary results. At Calcutta the CSP boldly advised Sjt Subhas Chandra Bose to withdraw his resignation from the Presidentship; the communists lost their guts and kept mum. Coming to recent events, the CSP did not subscribe to the addendum to the Independence Pledge; the communists swallowed it. One hopes that they are faithfully carrying out their vow; otherwise there is danger that fraud may be discovered and Mahatma Gandhi may refuse to launch the struggle after all!! The CSP supported Maulana Abul Kalam Azad, the communists were neutral. The Communists declared in a public statement that voting for Maulana Azad would mean supporting the policy of the Working Committee. Strange argument! When the communists voted for Roosevelt in America, did it mean that they supported the whole of Roosevelt's policy? In such a thing as a presidential contest one votes for the candidate whose election would advance the nation's cause generally. If one must have a president with whose policies one must always be in agreement, one has only one course open, that is to set-up a candidate every time, from one's own Party or Group. There are thousand and one ways of expressing one's difference from the Working Committee and this both the CSP and the communists have been doing. Voting for Maulana Azad could never nave prevented Communists from pointing out their differences from the Working Committee. I agree that it would have prevented them from calling Maulana Azad an agent of imperialism! Then a last instance. The CSP clearly dissociated itself from the Anti-Compromise Conference the communists were neutral to it. Their growing neutrality is an index to their growing political impotency.

I had not intended to devote so much space to this matter. The list can be enlarged, more so when we leave the realm of policies and enter into that of tactics.

To return to my point. Far from becoming superfluous, the Congress Socialist Party has to be in the forefront of the struggle and the preparations for it. It must remain, as it has been so far, the active element in the Congress Committees, guiding them in organizational and agitational work. It must, by carrying on its mass work continue to prepare that basis for struggle that is ore important than anything else. It must influence Congress policy by criticism and propaganda as it has done so far. The time has come for the Congress Socialist Party to work out what it has preached so far, even more vigourously in the future.

43. Jayaprakash Narayan's Appeal to the Left Wing to Maintain Unity in the Congress, 7 March 1940[1]

> *Searchlight*, 9 March 1940; Bimal Prasad (ed.), *Jayaprakash Narayan: Selected Works*, Vol. 3, (1939–1946), Delhi, 2003, pp. 45–6.

It is a matter of deep regret to me that in this hour of crisis when National and Congress unity is so essential, there are so many disruptive tendencies at work. The task of maintaining unity in the Congress rests on the shoulders of the Leftists much more than those of others. Unfortunately, Left Wing infantilism is dragging the Congress to min. It is the duty of Congress Socialists, above everything else, to fight this disruption unmindful of the calumny that a section of the Left may heap upon them. Since its birth, the Congress Socialist Party has stood for balanced and sane policies. The necessity of adhering to the principles of united front and composite leadership is greater today than ever before. Let these principles guide our actions.

Acharya Narendra Deva and I have already commented upon the draft of Congress resolution. Mahatma Gandhi and Dr Rajendra Prasad's later statements have only confirmed our interpretation of the resolution. Let petty bickerings cease and let us close up the ranks. The Congress is in dead earnest about civil disobedience. This will be the country's final struggle for freedom. I hope that every Congressman will rise to the occasion and will not rest till freedom is achieved.

---

¹The appeal was issued just before his arrest on 7 March 1940.

44. Jayaprakash Narayan's Statement Before the Court
Harijan, 30 March 1940.

A Brave Statement

[Shri Jaiprakash Narayan sent me a copy of his statement before the court which is printed below. It is worthy of him, brave, brief and to the point. It is an irony of fate, as he himself has said, that his patriotism should be penalized. What tens of thousands think and thousands say in their talks, Shri Jaiprakash has said in public and before the very men who are producing war material. It is true that, if his words take effect and they are repeated, the Government would be embarrassed. But such embarrassment should set them thinking about their treatment of India instead of punishing a patriot for his open thinking.

The concluding portion of the statement proves the author's intense humanitarianism. He has no malice in him. He wants to end Imperialism and Nazism. He has no quarrel with Englishmen or Germans and says truly that, if England were to shed imperialism, not only India but the freedom-loving people of the whole world would exert themselves to see the defeat of Nazism and the victory of freedom and democracy.

Sevagram,
26-3-40
M.K.G.]

The Statement

I have been charged with trying to impede the production of munitions and other supplies essential to the efficient prosecution of the war, and with trying to influence the conduct and attitude of the public in a manner prejudicial to the defence of British India and the efficient prosecution of the war. I plead guilty to these charges.

These charges, however, do not constitute a guilt for me but a duty which I discharge regardless of the consequence. That they also constitute an offence under certain laws of the foreign Government established by force in this country, does not concern me. The object of these laws is diametrically opposed to the object of nationalist India of which I am but a humble representative. That we should come in conflict is only natural.

My country is not a party to this war in any manner, for it regards both German Nazism and British Imperialism as evils and enemies. It finds that both the sides in this war are driven by selfish ends of conquest and domination, exploitation and oppression. Great Britain is fighting not to destroy Nazism, which it has nurtured, but to curb a rival whose might can no longer be allowed to grow unchallenged. It is fighting to maintain its dominant place in the world and to preserve its imperial power and glory. As far as India is concerned, Great Britain is fighting to perpetuate the Indian Empire.

Plainly, India can have no truck with such a war. No Indian can permit the resources of his country to be utilized to buttress up imperialism, and to be converted through the processes of the war into the chains of his country's slavery. The Congress, the only representative voice of nationalist India, has already pointed out this sacred duty to the people of this country. I, as a humble servant of the Congress, have only tried to fulfil this duty.

The British Government on the other hand, in utter disregard for Indian opinion, has declared India a belligerent power and is utilizing Indian men, money and materials for a war to which we have pledged our uncompromising opposition. This is in the nature of an aggression against India, no less serious in the circumstances than German aggression against Poland. India cannot but resist this aggression. It therefore becomes the patriotic duty of every Indian to oppose the attempt of the British Government to use the country's resources for its imperialist ends. Thus the charge framed against me of trying to impede the efficient prosecution of the war is only the fulfillment of a patriotic duty. That the British Government should consider what is a duty for patriotic India to be an offence, only proves further its imperialist character.

Regarding the speech for which I am being prosecuted, I cannot say how far it succeeded in achieving its ends. But nothing would please me more than to learn that it did have some success in impeding the effective prosecution of the war. I shall deem the heaviest punishment well earned if I am found to have succeeded in this.

As for the charge of endangering the defence of British India, I think the irony of it cannot be lost upon us. A slave has no obligation to defend his slavery. His only obligation is to destroy his bondage. I hope we shall know how to defend ourselves when we have achieved our freedom.

I consider it fortunate that I have been prosecuted for a Jamshedpur speech. This important industrial centre, which I consider the most important in the country, is peculiarly backward politically and from the point of view of the labour movement. I shall derive some satisfaction in prison, where I expect inevitably to find myself, from the thought that my arrest and incarceration for a speech delivered there has attracted to that city the notice of the political and labour leaders of my country. It seems scandalous to me that the country's most vital resources should be so wasted in a war to which we are so firmly opposed. And it seems no less scandalous to me that while labour throughout the country should be reacting vigorously to the conditions created by the war, Jamshedpur labour should carry on as if nothing extraordinary has happened. May, at least, the demand for a war bonus gain some momentum from this prosecution.

Before concluding I should like to add that, lest as an Englishman you should misunderstand me, I should make it clear that in impeding the prosecution of the war I have no desire to help Germany or to see Germany victorious. I desire the victory neither of Imperialism nor of Nazism. Yet, as a Congressman and a socialist I have nothing but goodwill for the British and German people. If India's opposition to Britain's imperialist war ensures a Nazi victory, it is for the British people to decide whether they would have Nazi hegemony or victory, with real democracy at home and in India. If the people of Great Britain remove their present rule and renounce imperialism with its capitalist rulers, not only India but the freedom-loving people of the whole world would exert themselves to see the defeat of Nazism and the victory of freedom and democracy. In the present circumstances, however, India has no alternative but to fight and end British imperialism. Only in that manner can it contribute to the peace and progress of the world.

I am conscious, Sir, that I have made your task easier by this statement. I do not regret it. In the end I thank you for your courtesy and consideration during this trial.

45. Congress Socialist Policy Towards Satyagraha

Sangharsh (Hindi), 6 May 1940.

Satyagraha Committees and the Policy of the Congress Socialist Party (A Congress Socialist)

There is a lot of confusion regarding the question of the left-wingers of the Congress joining the Satyagraha Committees or not. This article explains the policy of the Congress Socialist Party very nicely. Editor (Sangharsh)

The independence struggle for which we have been waiting for so long has started. We can see it through the enlisting of active and passive Satyagrahis. We were organizing war committees and admitting volunteers to participate in the war since a long time. Now the whole Congress has adopted this programme. We should not get excited because the war committees are being called Satyagraha Committees and the volunteers are called active Satyagrahis. We should not refrain ourselves from joining these war committees because of our disapproval of the constructive programme and spinning of the Congress.

Deadly Confusion

It is being said that some of those people who had been coaxing Congress to start the struggle, are hating these Satyagraha Committees. They do not want to be related with these committees because they have no faith in Satyagraha, spinning or the like. Non-participation in Satyagraha because of working among labourers and peasants and having such a viewpoint are two different matters. He must be a fool who believes that the struggle which will be started in 1940 will be different from the usual concept of Gandhi's struggle. We have started our struggle believing the same point. It was not our conclusion that we will not participate in the struggle or in its preparation when it will be started because it is different from our viewpoint and programme.

The Congress Socialist Party had taken up the programme of organizing and mobilizing the labourers and peasants as a part of preparations for the struggle. They had a certain concept of the nature of this struggle. According to this plan, the movement of non-payment of rents and taxes, general strike of the labourers, and the organization of a parallel government in the form of revolutionary Panchayats and volunteer's police by the Congress were all part of this national struggle.

The Congress rejected this proposal or one cannot say anything definitely as to how much part of this programme is the Congress going to accept because the actual form of this struggle has not been decided yet. In fact, our programme is neither original nor is it opposed to the programme of Gandhiji. Some parts of this programme have been used in earlier struggles.

Still we have never tried to start the struggle according to our thinking in opposition to the programme of the Congress if it does not accept our programme. Congress is the united front of the Indian people. Its decisions show the strength of its various parts and they are arrived at in a democratic way. When the time to debate has passed and the time for actual action has arrived, then we should follow its instructions by all means. Therefore, it will be detrimental both to us and in national interest to say that we do not believe in the policy of the Congress and we cannot participate in it. It will result in our dissociation from other forces which are participating in the national struggle and our efforts will bear no fruits.

The Policy of the Congress Socialist Party

Our policy has always been to be ready to spin for discipline and do whatever is necessary for the struggle. The time has come to test the truth of this policy. Many Congress Socialists are holding responsible positions in Congress Committees. They should enroll themselves as active Satyagrahis and their committees should turn themselves into Satyagraha Committees.

According to the present programme of the Congress we should not only spin and participate in the constructive programme of the Congress but also do other important political work among the masses. Many of our friends are associated with labour movement. They should not become active Satyagrahis because they have to work among the labourers. Still, they should maintain close contact with the Satyagraha committees. They should provide help to them. It would not obstruct their work if those who are associated with the peasant movement become Satyagrahis. Besides this, many of them are also Congress workers; therefore, it seems inappropriate for them to keep themselves away from the Congress programme. So they should become active Satyagrahis and work with all their strength to make the Congress programme successful. The future of this struggle depends on the result of our work done during Gandhiji's appointed period of one month. They will get sufficient time for peasant conferences besides the work of active Satyagrahis; they should only do this work without opposing the Congress.

Now let us discuss the form of this struggle. Nowadays, there are many intelligent people who make fun of us that we will attain self-government through spinning and they criticize the Civil Disobedience movement. Still, no one has suggested an alternative to this struggle.... Therefore, we should decide regarding the programme of our party.

Our Programme

We have already mentioned that this programme is neither original nor is it strange to the Congress. This is true that the workers' strikes were not an indivisible part of the last Civil Disobedience movement. But strikes or general strikes do not depend upon the Congress. The workers' unions are independent to announce general strike when the time comes for it. This step is totally dependent on the Trade Union Congress, workers' organization and political organization, like Communist Party. If they think that the time to announce a general strike has come, they can do so.

Unfortunately the Trade Union Congress is totally under the patronage of the right wing group of N.M. Joshi, so that one cannot expect their support for the political general strike of the workers. The condition of the Railway Federation is also the same. There are strict restrictions for trying to end the movement of Jamshedpur workers. The worker activists are trying to impose their weakness on the Congress by blaming the Congress that it is not ready for announcing the general strike of the workers. If the workers' leaders are really interested in the general strike of the workers, then no power can stop them in this. It is doubtful that the Congress will become an obstacle in this way.

We have reasons for this assumption. During the last Civil Disobedience movement, those people who were in charge of the Central Organizational Committee, were lacking the enthusiasm to prepare the workers for the strike. In 1932, the secret centre of the Congress had tried for the strike of railway workers but it was not successful. It is worth mentioning here that the strike of the Railway workers was to be announced on the basis of their economic demands not on any political demands. The struggle committee of Bombay was successful in organizing the strike of the postal workers during Lord Lothian's visit to India but even this strike was not very successful.

We should not criticize those things for which there are no preparations. When the struggle will start then it will be difficult to decide or keep control on its terms. It is not Mahatmaji's nature to put restrictions on the movement; the only restriction which he wants and pressurizes for it is that the struggle should be non-violent. Whoever thinks seriously about this will realize that Mahatmaji's restriction in this regard is for our benefit only and any movement can become successful in this present time if it is peaceful.

The Concept of Non-Payment of Rents

Now we will take up the discussion of the movement of non-payment of rents and taxes. There is a lot of discussion that Mahatmaji had written in a recent article that he is not thinking about the non-payment of rents and taxes. Therefore, it is understood that it will never be an essential part of the struggle. But this thinking is wrong. The meaning of whatever he has said is that there is no proper environment for non-payment of rents or taxes all over India. It must be remembered that he was the first person to use the technique of non-payment of rents and taxes on a wide scale in the political field. The movement of non-payment of taxes or rents was started at many places during the last Civil Disobedience movement. The people got the permission of the Working Committee or the President wherever they had prepared to start such a movement. Therefore, the non-payment of rents movement in Allahabad, non-payment of taxes movement in Bihar, non-payment of taxes movement in Bardoli, Sini and Siddapur and forest Satyagraha in Maharashtra and Central Provinces. In many cases the permission was granted long after the commencement of these movements.

In this situation it is foolish to proclaim that non-payment of rents and taxes is the discovery of Socialists and the Kisan Sabhaites. Non-payment of rents is an important part of Congress programme. There is only one condition in starting this movement which is to make the Central Congress leaders realize that it is the right time to start this movement and there is no possibility of any kind of violence. Therefore, if the nonpayment of rents movement is not started in the beginning, it does not mean that it will never be started. Those of our friends, who can wait to work according to the policy of the United Front, should be provided with the opportunity to organize mass movements and through their participation all the difficult duties can be fulfilled quite easily. It is our only duty at this time.

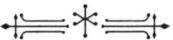

III. Communist Party of India

46. British Government's Orders for Communist Leaders' Detention, 15 March 1940

Indian Annual Register, 1940, Vol. I, p. 51.

A Press Note stated from New Delhi: 'The Central Government has had cause, for considerable time, to view with grave concern the activities of the Community Party of India. Although the party has been declared an unlawful body, there is ample evidence to show that it continues to operate through a widespread "underground" organization' .... 'Central government, in discharge of its responsibility for the defence of India and the prosecution of the war, has therefore, found it necessary to pass orders for the detention of the principal communist leaders under the Defence of India Rules'.

47. Communist Party's Critique of Congress Working Committee's Resolution for Ramgarh Congress

Editorial, *Communist,* Vol. II, No. 7, March 1940, P.C. Joshi Archives on Contemporary History, JNU.

Not a Forward Step

Six months after the outbreak of the War and on the eve of world historic events, the Congress Session will meet at Ramgarh. This will be the most momentous session in the history of the Congress, perhaps the last open session for the entire war-period.

There will be only one resolution before Ramgarh, that drafted by the Working Committee on the 1st March.[1] This resolution has been hailed by even Socialist leaders, Sjt Jaiprakash and Acharya Narendra Dev, as marking 'a turning point in Indian history', as denoting 'a distinct break with the policy of stalemate'. Is it really so?

The resolution declares this war to be an Imperialist war. It declares that India will not accept anything short of Complete Independence. Further, it declares that the preliminary step of withdrawal of Congress Ministries must naturally be followed by Civil Disobedience.

Every honest anti-imperialist will welcome these declarations. If the subsequent parts of the resolution—the parts that defined WHEN the Congress would resort to Civil Disobedience and laid down WHAT the Congress Committees and masses of Congressmen are to DO TO-DAY—if these parts indicated that a definite break with the policy of stalemate has been made and definite preparations for struggle will be undertaken, then it would be the duty of every Congressman to wholeheartedly support the resolution. The acid test as to whether this resolution marks a BREAK with the policy of compromise, lies precisely in this—What does it ask us to do TO-DAY?

Not only does the resolution not give any plan for struggle, it lays down such reactionary conditions BEFORE struggle can be undertaken, that the advance made in the declarations regarding War, Independence and inevitability of Civil Disobedience are rendered completely illusory. The resolution does not expressly vest Gandhiji with sole leadership of the movement but it lays down a plan of action completely in conformity with Gandhiji's present notions about 'discipline', about test of 'preparedness' about the need to fulfil the constructive programme as PRECONDITIONS for any struggle whatsoever. Thereby, it seeks not to unleash the forces of struggle but to impose further restraint upon them. It indicates not break with stalemate but continuation of stalemate in a new form. That is the essence of the resolution.

What is the Situation?

Let it not be forgotten that the Congress is meeting full six months after the outbreak of War—a period during which events of momentous importance have taken place. India groans under Ordinance Raj. Indian men and resources are being daily utilized for War. The British Government has rejected all demands made by Congress in a manner which leaves no room for any further negotiations. All meetings and processions have been banned in Bengal. Repression is taking daily tolls in every province. On the vary first day of the Bombay War-Allowance Strike, 47 persons—including 19 women—were arrested. The regimes of terroristic dictatorships in the States have been strengthened. 3,000 Congressmen of Mysore have been imprisoned. The Defence of India Act is being freely used in the States to crush all popular movements.

Masses are Ready

Let it not be forgotten that against the War, against suppression of Civil Liberties and against economic distress, the masses have already begun their struggles. The strike of 90,000 Bombay workers against the War, the strike of 30,000 Cawnpore workers on the Independence Day, the great strike of 1,60,000 Bombay workers that began on March 4th, the demonstrations that were organized by the Calcutta students in defiance of bans, the great Independence Day demonstrations this year which surpassed anything that the country had seen during the last ten years—all these indicate not only that masses Have Begun TO FIGHT, they also indicate that the nation is more PREPARED to-day than it ever was.

Finally, let it not be forgotten that Gandhiji has repeatedly declared that the nation is NOT prepared, that before there can be Civil Disobedience, the nation must conform to HIS test of preparedness which means carrying out of the constructive programme. It was political strikes that became the chief features of this year's Independence Day. But Gandhiji, a week before that day, openly condemned such strikes as acts of 'indiscipline'.

Against THIS background, what does the Ramgarh Resolution mean?

The New Technique

Does it mean a step from stalemate towards struggle? No. Under the name of struggle and on the plea of 'preparations', the stalemate is CONTINUED. There is declaration FOR struggle but no declaration of struggle. To-day, it is precisely THAT which makes all the difference. The situation demands immediate struggle. What we get is PROMISE of struggle. This difference tears away the veil and exposes the resolution as it really is—a desperate final attempt for compromise. This is the new Technique of compromise.

Why this strategy? The national leadership has failed to get any concession from Imperialism through constitutional pressure (the first six weeks of War) and through 'neutrality' (from the resignation of Ministries up to now). Imperialist offensive on the one hand—new Budget, Zetland's reply—and rising tide of mass discontent on the other is making the continuation of stalemate increasingly difficult. Therefore, declaration of the POLICY of struggle is made on the one hand to exert more pressure on Imperialism, on the other to ESCAPE immediate struggle.

The national bourgeoisie is attempting the most dangerous tight-rope walking in its history. It wants to avoid struggle, yet it fears that struggle cannot be long avoided. The situation grows more explosive every day, making struggle more and more dangerous. Yet, this very explosiveness of the situation makes avoidance of struggle more and more difficult. This resolution reflects fully the crisis in which the bourgeois leadership finds itself in such a situation. This resolution shows the way in which the bourgeoisie is seeking a way out of this crisis— avoidance of struggle as long as possible and a limited, restricted struggle when any further stalemate becomes impossible.

Even such a struggle, the Socialists and Communists must participate in, even such a struggle they must strive to transform into a mass movement against imperialism by independent action. But in order to be able to do THAT, it is essential that they entertain no illusion about this resolution, about what it aims at, about what it MAY lead to unless they are vigilant. Not to do that, as the CSP leaders do, means surrender to Gandhism, refusal to recognize its disruptive character.

A Suicidal Policy

This resolution means that the Congress will be kept isolated from the forces of struggle that are growing at tremendous pace, from the struggles that are breaking out in every part of the country. It means that the suicidal policy of permitting imperialism to decimate the national ranks, will be continued. It means that at a period, when masses of Congressmen should come out in defence of the people against Imperialist terror, should initiate and support every action against imperialist terror and against economic distress, and thus forge people's unity in action, thus carry forward the process of national unification, the national leadership calls upon Congressmen to ply Charkha and Takli and warns them that they must observe 'discipline' (political strike, according to Gandhiji, is 'indiscipline') BEFORE Civil Disobedience can be launched. This means disruption and not cementing of national unity. This amounts to giving free hand to imperialism to crush the existing and growing mass struggles. At a period when immediate nationwide struggle alone can frustrate imperialist plans and save national unity, the national leadership not only does not launch that struggle, it lays down such pre-conditions as mean weakening of forces of struggle and playing straight into the hands of imperialism.

'It all Depends on Britain'

The Resolution declares that Civil Disobedience will be declared if 'circumstances precipitate a crisis'. On the 3rd of March, replying to a question about struggle, Gandhiji declared. 'It all depends on Britain'. This means leaving the initiative in imperialism's hands. Imperialism will NOT precipitate a crisis, if by that term is meant, wholesale attack on the Congress organization. That is not imperialism's strategy. It will try to break up the national movement by bits. It will crush the mass struggles of workers and peasants. It will arrest the most militant sections of Congressmen—Communists and Socialists. It will 'precipitate crisis', provoke conflict, only when it feels confident that having decimated the national forces, having crushed the vanguard and having demoralized the masses of Congressmen, it is in a position powerful enough to smash the national movement at one blow. The calculations of imperialism may prove false, but this is precisely its strategy and the line put forward in this resolution facilitates the carrying out of this strategy.

The Path to Victory

Is there any reason why we should follow this policy: None at all. The Congress is mightier to-day than ever in its history. Let it declare unequivocally and without preconditions that mass struggle will be launched in the immediate future. All internal dissensions will disappear, and a united Congress will be leading a united people in the onslaught against the British Government which is in the midst of a crisis more serious than any it has ever faced. Let the Congress prepare for that movement by itself leading the struggles against repression and against economic distress, by supporting working class and peasant actions that are taking place everywhere. Millions will ally round the banner of the Congress immediately and millions more will join as the war is prolonged and distress increases. It will be a long and desperate struggle but victory is guaranteed if only the Congress dares and acts.

Shall THIS happen, or shall we pursue a half-hearted policy of waiting and watching while imperialism rains blows on the nation renders us impotent? Shall we seize the unique opportunity that the War has created or shall we go down in history as people who failed at the supreme juncture?

Ramgarh has to give the reply.

---

¹ The Congress Working Committee at its meeting held at Patna between 28 February–1 March 1940 adopted a resolution on 'India and War Crisis' which was to be placed before the Subjects Committee of the Indian National Congress at its forthcoming session at Ramgarh. The resolution was passed at the Ramgarh session.

48. Communist Party on Forthcoming Congress Session at Ramgarh

Communist, Vol. II, No. 7, March 1940, P.C. Joshi Archives on Contemporary History, JNU.

No Negotiation   **No Waiting**   **No Wavering**

Give Unconditional Call to Mass Civil Disobedience National Strikes No-Rent, No-Tax Campaigns to Destroy the Rule of Robbers and War-Mongers to Assert the Sovereignty of the People Forward to the Democratic Republic of India Manifesto of The communist Party of India.

In the midst of the darkening shadows of imperialist war, the Congress is holding the most momentous session of its history. The eyes of the people of India, of the whole world are on Ramgarh.

The war has entered into a critical phase. Realizing that its efforts have borne no fruits, realizing that its chances of victory are daily receding the mad dog of British Imperialism is planning new crimes against humanity. It is striving to light conflagration in every land. It is striving to create a world front for war against the Soviet Union.

Why this hatred against the Soviet Union?

It created in Finland a base for criminal war against the Soviet Union. But the Soviet Union by its firm and timely action smashed that plan too, thus inflicting on Britain the most severe defeats she has ever suffered in her history. Maddened by these defeats the British rulers are hatching new conspiracies.

It is the rulers of Britain who are today the main aggressors, the chief enemy of mankind. It is they who want to continue the war at all costs. It is they who pour arms, men and money into Finland while they did not lift a finger to save Poland because they had hopes that the Germans after conquering Poland would invade Soviet Union. It is the British rulers who are determined to reject every Peace offer. It is they who are trying to sell the Chinese people to the Japanese fascists in order to create an effective anti-Soviet front in the Far East. It is they who are conspiring with the monarchists and junkers of Germany against the German revolution. It is they who want to replace Hitler not by a Peoples Republic but by the Kaiser or a reactionary military dictatorship, thus putting back the clock by twenty years. It is their ally Daladier who has destroyed all democracy in France and flung tens of thousands of Communists and anti-fascists in prison. What Tsarism was in the 19th century, the bulwark of world reaction, so is British imperialism to-day. They are fighting this war not for democracy but for eliminating Germany as an imperialist rival, for creating a world front against the Soviet Union. Maddened by the set-backs they have received, they are striving to break the stalemate provoking neutrals, by dragging every nation into war, by setting the whole world aflame. 'After me the deluge' is their desperate motto.

Shall they succeed? Shall they succeed in destroying all that is noble in human civilization, in inflicting untold distress on humanity, in drawing the world into a blood bath?

More than ever before, the answer rests with the Congress, with every Congressman, with the Indian people. THE CONGRESS CAN SMASH BRITAIN'S MONSTROUS CONSPIRACY AGAINST HUMANITY. For the decision that we take at Ramgarh we shall have to answer before history, before humanity.

What is the reply of the Congress? What reply must the Indian people give? The Congress demanded clarification of British war-aims. Those aims have been clarified by every deed and every word of the British Government.

The Congress declared that Indian resources must not be used for imperialist war. The British reply is seen in the new budget, in the excess Profits' Tax, in, the increased Railway fares and freights.

The Congress declared that Indian blood must not be shed for Britain's war. Indian troops are being killed in France.

The Congress declared that it will not permit attack on the limited powers that the people won. The country groans under Ordinance Regime. In words, full of insolence, the British rulers have heaped humiliation on the Congress every time they have spoken on the Congress demand. Less than a month ago the Viceroy had the audacity to ask us to work the Federal Scheme.

What is our reply?

Six months have passed since the outbreak of war. Civil Liberties are fast disappearing. The Press has been gagged. The economic burden grows heavier everyday crushing our people. Fire has been concentrated against workers and Students because they have been the first to act. Working class, kisan and Student leaders are being thrown in prison in every province. THE GOVERNMENT IS TRYING TO CRUSH THE REVOLUTIONARY FORCES IN ISOLATION.

Yet the national leadership refuses to move. They dream of 'honourable settlement' with the enemy. They pin their faith in negotiations. They seem to hug the hope that when the war enters into a serious phase, the British Government will be prepared to make more concessions for securing Congress co-operation.

Stagnation is spreading demoralization in Congress ranks. Internal conflicts are becoming sharper. Communalist reactionaries are gathering strength in every part of the country. These are the disastrous results of the policy of 'wait and see'. The national movement is going to pieces. The leadership sees all this. It acts not against imperialism but against the Congress itself, against the forces of struggle, against those who demand action. By its disruptive attacks against the Bengal Congress, it throws one whole province out of the organized national movement. By all these measures it strives to reduce the Congress into a docile instrument of compromise. As a reaction to this the disruptive slogan of two Congresses rears its ugly head. Opportunists and careerists are utilizing this discontent of the rank and file for their aggrandizement for disrupting the Congress, for factional fight against the present leadership. While claiming to be radicals they enter into alliance with communalists and with anti-Congress reactionaries, thus spreading further demoralization. THUS, IN THE MIDST OF A WORLD HISTORIC CONFLICT, AT PERIOD WHEN WE STAND ON THE VERY THRESHOLD OF FREEDOM, WHEN WE CAN SMASH THE CHAINS OF SLAVERY AND PLAY A GLORIOUS ROLE IN BUILDING THE NEW WORLD ORDER, THE GREAT ORGANIZATION WHICH THE PEOPLE HAVE BUILT BY DECADES OF SACRIFICE STANDS IN DANGER OF UTTER COLLAPSE.

Is there any reason for this inaction? NEVER WAS THE BRITISH EMPIRE IN SUCH A CRISIS AS IT IS TO-DAY. All the bluffs and blusterings of the British rulers cannot conceal their panic. British ships are being sunk every day. Despite the vaunted blockade Germany is more powerful today than she was at the outbreak of war. Without spreading the war, without winning new allies, Britain cannot hope to win. The gangster tactics which she has now adopted shows the utter desperation of her rulers.

While such is the situation, while faced with her imperialist rival on the one hand and frustrated by the moves of the Soviet Union on the other, Britain is in a desperate position. Our national leaders are thinking in terms of 'honourable settlement'.

Can there be any honourable settlement short of the demand put forward by the Congress— the demand for Constituent Assembly and Complete Independence? No. Never.

Will imperialism grant these demands? Can the Constituent Assembly be anything but a glorified edition of the Round Table Conference as long as imperialism holds away? Will imperialism surrender world domination to maintain which it unleashed the war? No. Never. SETTLEMENT WITH THE BRITISH GOVERNMENT WILL LEAD NOT TO SWARAJ BUT TO MOCK-ERY OF SWARAJ.

What is the maximum we will get by settlement? Assurance of Dominion Status and some sort of Responsibility at the Centre. The British Army of occupation would remain. The Civil service would remain. The imperialist police would remain. The social structure would remain intact. Landlords, Money-lenders, Princes would continue to suck the life-blood of the people. The strangle-hold of British capital would continue. Workers would continue to live on starvation wages.

Such would be the 'Swaraj' that the Congress would get by negotiations, by the policy of wait and see. A leadership that expects more shows utter ignorance and bankruptcy or deliberately deceives the people.

Is that the Swaraj for which Congressmen have lived and died? Is that the vision which has inspired them to face lathis, prison and bullets?

WHO WOULD SUCH 'SWARAJ' BENEFIT? WHO WOULD WANT THE CONGRESS TO FOLLOW THIS POLICY? THE INDUSTRIALISTS, WHO WANT TO REAP WAR PROFITS, THE BIG MERCHANTS AND THE MILL OWNERS. NOT THE WORKERS, NOT THE PEASANTS, NOT THE PEOPLE OF INDIA.

Yet the Congress leadership that claims to represent the nation follows this policy, a policy that serves the interest not of the nation but of a handful of exploiters.

What do the people demand? What would correspond to their needs?

A DEMOCRATIC REPUBLIC WITH A PEOPLES ARMY,

CANCELLATION OF ALL DEBTS,

ABOLITION OF LANDLORDISM,

EIGHT HOUR DAY AND GUARANTEED MINIMUM WAGE.

These demands, which are the demands of the people, cannot be satisfied within the framework of imperialism, by negotiations with the British Government.

THEREFORE THAT FRAME WORK HAS TO BE SMASHED, THE BRITISH GOVERNMENT HAS TO BE OVERTHROWN AND ON ITS RUINS MUST BE RAISED THE EDIFICE OF THE DEMOCRATIC REPUBLIC OF THE INDIAN PEOPLE. FOR SUCH A STRUGGLE THE CONGRESS HAS TO PREPARE.

The people are ready. On the Independence Day 30,000 workers of Cawnpore went on strike, Mills in Bombay closed down. Lacs of Kisans rallied to celebrate the Day, tens of thousands of students in every part of the country came but on the streets. Down with war, down with imperialism and down with compromise, these slogans rent the air. That day revealed the depth of popular feeling, the eagerness of the people for struggle. THAT DAY SHOWED THE NEW WEAPONS THAT THE MASSES HAVE FORGED, THE WEAPONS OF MASS STRIKE BY WORKERS AND STUDENTS, THE WEAPON OF MASS ACTION BY THE PEASANTS, THE WEAPONS WITH WHICH IMPERIALISM MUST BE FOUGHT TO-DAY.

The nation is ready. The nation will fight for freedom with the weapon of mass actions. Such was the meaning of 26th January.

This is our final battle. WHAT THE NATION DEMANDS IS THE IMMEDIATE AND UNCONDITIONAL LAUNCHING OF MASS CIVIL DISOBEDIENCE BACKED BY NATION-WIDE STRIKES AND NO-TAX AND NO-RENT CAMPAIGNS. NOT A RESTRICTED LIMITED SATYAGRAHA STRUGGLE AS INDICATED BY GANDHIJI IN HIS STATEMENTS, a struggle which selected bands of Satyagrahis fight, while masses play the role of on-lookers. Such struggle can only end in defeat or compromise. The entire fighting resources of the country, of our nation, of every class will have to be hurled against the enemy in this final battle. The most powerful weapons forged by the masses in their numerous battles will have to be used. Workers to go on general strike. Peasants to withhold rents and taxes. Students and citizens to denounce imperialist terror by hartals, strikes and mass demonstrations. People to refuse to pay a pie to the Government. Mass Volunteer Corps of the Congress to defend the people against imperialist terror. Army to revolt against the British rulers. Such must be the weapons of to-day.

Such struggle alone will lead to freedom.

THE WORKING CLASS IS ON THE MOVE. On 2nd October 90,000 workers of Bombay struck against the war. Gigantic strikes on a scale, the like of which India has never seen are maturing in every Industrial centre. These struggles will draw lacs in active conflict with the Government. Against the terroristic regime of Huq the heroic students and Congressmen of Bengal have begun the fight. In defiance of bans they are coming out holding demonstrations.

FIRE IS SMOULDERING IN THE STATES AGAIN. The heroic struggle of the Mysore people has failed. But despite the arrest of over 3000, the people are not downhearted. The celebration of Independence Day in the States, the strike struggles that are breaking out in Gwalior and other States all these indicate that a new wave of States Peoples movement is about to rise, a wave far more powerful than the last one.

THE ARMY IS SEETHING WITH DISCONTENT. Within a month of the war 35 soldiers and 3 Indian officers deserted from the Sikh Infantry Regiment at Jhansi. 500 soldiers with their guns deserted from different regiments in the Punjab and took shelter in the jungles. If a nation-wide movement is launched such incidents will multiply. Soldiers will desert not to take shelter in jungles but to join the ranks of the people. The Government will find it increasingly difficult to use the Army against him people. The Soldiers will begin to turn their guns against the British rulers.

What more do we need? The Congress today is in a position to UNITE ALL THESE ACTIONS AND ON THEIR BASIS DEVELOP A MOVEMENT OF IRRESISTIBLE STRENGTH, A MOVEMENT WHOSE SMASHING IMPACT WILL SHATTER THE BRITISH EMPIRE.

Shall the Congress dare and act?

Ramgarh has to give the reply and on that reply shall depend the fate of the Congress, of India, of humanity. RAMGARH MUST DEMAND THAT ALL NEGOTIATIONS WITH THE BRITISH GOVERNMENT, NEGOTIATIONS THAT ONLY HUMILIATE THE NATION, MUST STOP. RAMGARH MUST DECLARE THAT BY RAISING A MASS VOLUNTEER CORPS, BY LAUNCHING STRUGGLE AGAINST IMPERIALIST TERROR, BY ACTIVELY SUPPORTING EVERY ACTION OF THE PEOPLE AGAINST THE ECONOMIC EFFECTS OF THE WAR, BY FORGING THE WEAPON OF MASS STRIKE, MASS NO-RENT, MASS ACTION OF EVERY TYPE, THE CONGRESS SHALL PREP ARE FOR THE FINAL BATTLE. This and not the fulfillment of the constructive program, will be real preparation for battle, battle for smashing British rule, for convening the Constituent Assembly, for raising on the ruins of the Empire the edifice of the Peoples' Democratic Republic.

History has placed before the Congress the task of freeing the people of India from bondage. History has placed before the Congress the task of freeing the world from the stranglehold of the monster of British imperialism. History has created for the Congress an opportunity that comes once in centuries.

If the Congress seizes the opportunity, if it fulfills its tasks, if it launches mass struggle against British rule, it will aid the world forces of revolution. It will aid the British people in their fight against Chamberlain. It will aid the Chinese people, whom Chamberlain is trying to sell to Japan. IT WILL AID THE PEOPLE OF FRANCE AND GERMANY WHO ARE FIGHTING AGAINST THEIR IMPERIALIST RULERS. IT WILL LIGHT REVOLUTIONARY. CONFLAGRATION IN EVERY COUNTRY HELD IN BONDAGE, TERSICRATE THE WAR AND THUS SAVE HUMANITY FROM DESTRUCTION.

And the Congress, the great and glorious organization of our people, shall lead India to this path.

This must be Ramgarh's verdict.

49. P.C. Joshi's Statement on Ramgarh Congress Resolution, 29 March 1940

Communist, Vol. II, No. 8, April 1940, P.C. Joshi Archives on Contemporary History, JNU.

Those who had hailed the Ramgarh Resolution as opening a new chapter in our national history and marking a definite break with the policy of statements must have read Gandhiji's latest article: 'Every Congress Committee into a Satyagraha Committee' with a sense of profound disappointment. What every Congressman wants to know today are firstly, when the national leadership is going to issue call for struggle, secondly, what will be the form of that struggle and thirdly, how effective and broad-based that struggle will be. On all these points, the replies supplied by Gandhiji are such as open out the perspective, not of an immediate nationwide struggle leading to victory, but of continuation of the present stalemate for an indefinite period and then an extremely limited, restricted struggle that is bound to end in utter defeat. Gandhiji does not tell the people what to do to-day in face of growing repression. He definitely ban workers' and students' strikes as parts of the struggle which he is to lead. He warns us that if such strikes take place, he may even suspend the struggle. Instead of welcoming the tremendous growth of the organized working class and student movements, in stead of enriching the national movement with the weapons that these have forged, Gandhiji wants to isolate the national struggle from the workers and students and their movements, their forms of struggle.

But by far the worst part of the new plan is the artificial division that is sought to be created among Congressmen and Congressmen. The Congress is the united organization of our people. People join it because they want to fight for freedom under its banner. It is now precisely this character of the Congress that is threatened with destruction, it is precisely this right to fight for freedom that is being denied to masses of Congressmen. They can join the Congress; they can remain its members; but the right to FIGHT for freedom, the right to participate in civil disobedience shall be enjoyed only by 'selected' Satyagrahis, who fulfil the constructive programme and spin daily.

This is an attempt to create castes among Congressmen, to raise a sect within the Congress, to transform the Congress from an organ of mass movement of the people into an organ of restricted, limited satyagraha, not by masses but by a handful of Gandhites. It is an attack on the very unity of the Congress, an attempt to have a 'homogeneous' Congress from top to bottom.

Denial of the right of participation in national struggle to the masses, even to masses of Congressmen, constitutes the essence of the new plan. If it is carried out, the Congress, as we know it to-day, will cease to exist. If it is carried out, it will mean the inauguration of a movement, in which No-Rent, No-Tax, General Strike and even mass demonstrations, will have no place, a movement which will and in defeat and demoralization. In fact, Gandhiji is refusing to have a movement even of the 1930 type.

Even in such a movement, the Communists shall participate. But they will carry on ceaseless and intensive campaign exposing the reactionary character of Gandhiji's new ban to make the Congressmen realize its dangerous consequences. A similar effort was made when the New Independence Pledge was published. On that occasion, a powerful expression of rank and file opinion had its effect. Once again, the masses of Congressmen have to rally to see that the national leadership gives us a plan of Mass Civil Disobedience movement, to be launched through existing Congress Committees and in which every Congressman participates and for which our entire nation is actively mobilized.

50. Communist Stand on the Ramgarh Resolution and the Impending Civil Disobedience Movement

Document of the Central Committee of the Communist Party of India: *Reality Vs. Myth*, April–May 1940, No. 1940/47, P.C. Joshi Archives on Contemporary History, JNU.

Comrades,

On the eve of a struggle that may decide the destiny of our nation, we Communists want to make clear where we stand and what our tactic will be.

We opposed the Ramgarh Resolution although that Resolution declared that Civil Disobedience is the next step. We have been raising our voice against the line put forward by Gandhiji although the Ramgarh Congress, by overwhelming majority, pledged implicit obedience to Gandhiji's directions. This has led many supporters of the present leadership as well as leaders of the Congress Socialist Party, to dub us as disrupters, as people who talked of unity in the past but have given up the line of United Front just when it is most needed, just on the eve of a struggle.

The Unity We Want

We claim that more than any other party or group we realize the urgent need for unity at this grave hour, the absolute necessity for complete solidarity and unanimity in Congress ranks. But we maintain that it must be unity for the achievement of freedom, unity for effective fight against the British Government, unity for defeating its war measures. Despite our ideological and political differences with Gandhiji and the present leadership we would have implicitly carried out their directions and submitted to their orders, if there were the slightest reasons to believe that the unity that would be achieved thereby would be unity for these ends.

Gandhiji's Conditions

In a serious of articles Gandhiji has specified his conditions, the conditions that we must fulfil in order that he may lead us. He demands:

Firstly, that only those Congressmen who have implicit faith in khadi and Charkha, who spin regularly and who enroll themselves as active Satyagrahis, should take part in Civil Disobedience.

Secondly, that there must be no secret work at all.

Thirdly, that there must be no strikes by workers and Students.

Fourthly, that there must be no Civil Disobedience in States.

Only one month has passed since Ramgarh and already these conditions have been imposed. Other conditions may follow. It is precisely because we knew that these were Gandhiji's conditions that we opposed the Ramgarh Resolution. They had already been specified by Gandhiji in his articles in the *Harijan*.

Their Disruptive Character

The Congress has grown into what it is today because it has been the leader of three mass movements and because every Indian has had the right to fight for freedom under its banner. To ban the participation of masses in the struggle on the plea that there is no non-violent atmosphere means to DESTROY THE CONGRESS AS A MASS ORGANIZATION. To demand that those Congressmen alone can be active Satyagrahis who have faith in constructive programme means to DESTROY THE UNITY OF THE CONGRESS.

We maintain that if Gandhiji's conditions are carried out the Congress will be disrupted. Also there will be no real struggle at all. Whatever attempt for struggle is made will be crushed in no time if the Government so desires.

Lessons of 1930–32 Forgotten!

In 1930 there was a mass movement more powerful than any in our history. The chief features of that movement were FIRSTLY that masses of people defied Government orders, faced lathi charges and bullets and SECONDLY that through shadow Committees, through secret publication of bulletins and their mass distribution, through illegal work in general, continuity of leadership was ensured and the tempo raised.

If masses of people had not been drawn into struggle, if masses had not held demonstrations in defiance of police orders, there would have been no movement at all.

If there had been no secret work, if shadow committees had not been formed and their composition kept secret, if secret offices of Congress War Councils had not been set up, if illegal publications had not been brought out, the movement, however big in the beginning, would have been crushed in no time.

What therefore Gandhiji is seeking today is to deprive the national movement of those very weapons which proved most effective in 1930. Thereby he is disarming the nation and fore-dooming the movement to failure.

The Possibilities of 1940

We can have today a movement a hundred times more powerful than what we had in 1930, a movement which the British Government, caught in the net of war, will not be able to defeat. We can have general strike in the transport and industries. We can have mass strikes in which lacs of students will take part. We can have no-tax and no-rent actions all over the country. We can have as powerful a movement in the States as in British India. The phenomenal growth of the movements of kisans, workers, students and States People have made all these possible today, have made it possible for us to develop a nation-wide movement of unprecedented sweep and intensity.

And if such a movement is developed there is no doubt today that it will profoundly influence the Indian Army. Already the Army is seething with unrest. Over 500 soldiers deserted from various regiments in the Punjab three months back. Similar desertions took place from the Sikh Regiment in Jhansi. At Dacca Indian Soldiers tried to shoot their Captain because they were refused permission to see Gandhiji.

Such are the possibilities of the present situation, possibilities that our leaders refuse to utilize.

The Choice of Weapons

They say that they will accept nothing short of independence, that they are fighting for freedom. Their deeds belie their words. What a fight will lead to depends not on what the leaders SAY they are fighting for but on the weapons they use. Without mass participation, without resort to illegal work, without strikes and no-rent actions, without any struggle in the states, the national movement can never lead to freedom. It can only lead to defeat and surrender.

Our Stand

Therefore we maintain that to submit to these conditions in the name of unity and discipline means to commit a crime against the Congress, against the national movement. Therefore, we will not submit to these conditions.

Many of us, particularly those who are in leading Congress Committees, will sign the Pledge and enroll themselves as Satyagrahis but that will be only because we want to take part in whatever struggle may be launched by the Congress and not because we have any faith in the Pledge.

While participating in whatever struggle that the Congress may launch we shall never cease to explain to masses of Congressmen and to the people that a struggle which is not a mass struggle is not a struggle that can lead to freedom and therefore it is our sacred duty to ensure that the movement breaks the bounds within which Gandhiji wants to keep it confined.

For a Mass Revolutionary Struggle

MASS CIVIL DISOBEDIENCE THROUGHOUT THE COUNTRY INCLUDING THE STATES, GENERAL STRIKE IN THE MAJOR INDUSTRIES AND RAIL WAYS ETC., MASS STRIKE OF STUDENTS AND NO-TAX AND NO-RENT ACTIONS IN EVERY PROVINCE—these must be the immediate features of a real struggle. For such a struggle we shall carryon incessant agitation.

We shall not confine ourselves to mere AGITATION for such struggle. We shall organize mass demonstrations against Government repression, we shall organize mass strikes—both political and economic, we shall prepare the basis for no-rent actions, we shall try to spread the movement to the States, we shall do everything in our power to develop a powerful mass movement against British rule. For such actions we shall strive our best to win the Congress masses, for with their active cooperation alone can such a movement be developed.

The tasks which we are setting before ourselves is heavy. It would be much easier to act as the Congress Socialists are doing—unreserved acceptance of Gandhiji's conditions, or as Bose is attempting to give 'call' on his own and launch through such call a movement under his own leadership. We reject both methods because we know that neither can lead to mass movement, that both will lead to destruction of the Congress as the organ of people's freedom movement.

Confident that that is the only correct policy to pursue, confident that we shall be able to win the support of rank and file Congressmen for carrying out this policy, with unbounded faith in the masses, we shall hold aloft the banner of the Congress, the banner of National Revolution.

Central Committee
Communist Party of India

51. Communist Party on Congress Socialist Party's Decision to Support the Congress Resolution

CSP: 'A Party of Action'?, *Reality Vs. Myth*, April–May 1940, No. 1940/47, P.C. Joshi Archives on Contemporary History, JNU.

A circular letter issued by the Secretariat of the All-India Congress Socialist Party on 30th March has reached our hands. It contains the major decisions that the National Executive took in its last two meetings held at Lucknow and Ramgarh and also the reason that led the CSP to support the Working Committee's resolution. Finally it draws the attention of the CSP Secretaries to 'one of the most important decisions' which is to have been taken by the National Executive 'unanimously'. That decision is that the Party should be made 'homogeneous' and Communists should be asked to resign from the CSP 'failing which they should be expelled'.

The political policy that a Party wants to pursue always determines its organizational decisions. Thus Gandhiji wants a 'homogeneous' Congress, a Congress of 'regular spinners', because the Congress as a MASS organization is not an instrument suitable for the carrying out of the political policy of compromise. In order, therefore, to understand the meaning of the slogan of 'homogeneous' CSP, it is necessary to analyse the political policy that the circular reveals.

The circular makes strange reading. It is as though we are not in the midst of an imperialist War; as though the national movement is not faced with gigantic tasks and tremendous possibilities; as though the policy that the Congress leadership is pursuing is a right except for 'details', as though all that a Socialist Party has to do in this situation is to declare that along with 'constructive programme', we must 'also' prepare 'no-rent campaign' and 'political general strike'.

Reading the circular as a whole, the conviction that becomes overwhelming is that these two bits: 'no-rent campaign' and 'political general strike' are put in there just to satisfy their Socialist CONSCIENCE. 'They lie who say we have become Gandhites. See ALSO "want" general strike and no-rent'—this appears to be the idea.

Why do we say so?

At its Lucknow meeting held on March 11, 12 and 13th, the National Executive hailed the Patna resolution of the Working Committee because it believed that that resolution brought the country 'on the threshold of mass civil disobedience' and that 'struggle was now inevitable'.

'Struggle is now inevitable', said the CSP leadership. What sort of struggle it would be, even when it came about, they did not care. They thought that all that was needed was to prepare a 'seven-point programme' of which two 'points' would be 'development of peasant and labour struggles' and no-rent, no-tax and general strike, and plead that 'in addition to constructive programme', these ALSO should be included.

We must be good Gandhites and also satisfy our Socialist conscience—this seemed to be the basic idea. That would be 'mutual adjustment' between Socialists and Gandhites, for which Jaiprakash pleaded so earnestly a month or so back.

This 'seven-point programme' was to have been moved as an amendment to the Working Committee's resolution. That was not done. Why? For the sake of 'unity'. Only a statement was read out at the Congress Session. That statement contains the following gem:

> 'In a comprehensive resolution like this, it is possible to detect things that one would PHRASE DIFFERENTLY or points that are not fully covered. For a Party whose role is that of Parliamentary opposition, amendments are easy and even natural. But for a PARTY OF ACTION, at this time, to differ over DETAILS, however important, is inexcusable'. (Our underline)

Comment is not necessary. All that was wrong in the resolution which embodied THE POLICY of the present leadership was that there were things that one would like to 'phrase differently'. The basic line was OK. Only some 'details' had to be supplied. But the CSP, as a 'Party of Action' would not like to differ even over those 'details'.

This meant UNCONDITIONAL support to the Working Committee's policy, UNRESERVED acceptance of Gandhiji's leadership, of his form of 'struggle', of his terms, of his preconditions. This meant being deceived and DECEIVING OTHERS by talks of 'struggle'.

Also, in the course of the statement, an attack was made on Communists. Their attitude was 'strange' and 'inexplicable'.

If the CSP leadership had not completely broken with Socialism and even Leftism, it would not have wondered at the Communist stand. That stand was very clear. Communists wanted the stalemate to be ENDED. They wanted MASS struggle to be launched. The resolution did neither. It continued the stalemate and through the clause about Gandhiji's conditions imposed such restrictions that mass struggle was rendered impossible. That is Why they opposed the resolution. The CSP leaders too would have done the same if they had not renounced Socialism.

This is the political policy that the circular reveals, the policy of subservience to Gandhism and renunciation of Socialism. Can one wonder at the slogan of homogeneous CSP. All who do not agree with this policy are suspected to be Communists or Communist sympathizers.

Therefore, they must be expelled. The presence of Communists, who have organized almost EVERY mass action during the last six months—both political and economic—cannot be tolerated in the CSP, the 'Party of Action'. A 'homogeneous' CSP, a CSP purged of Communists, will go into 'action', participate in 'struggle'.

Unfortunately, Gandhiji has already made clear what sort of struggle it will be, if it ever comes. No general strike, no no-rent, no mass defiance of Government as was in 1930, No Civil Disobedience of any sort in States. One would like to know how the CSP leadership reconciles whole hearted acceptance of Gandhiji's leadership with its 'seven-point programme'.

But one need not speculate. The answer has already been given. In an article written before his arrest, Jaiprakash wrote:

> 'If national struggle..... can be launched by Mahatma Gandhi alone, it is suicidal to fight him. It is necessary to lend him our fullest cooperation and loyalty in EVERYTHING that is preparatory for struggle. WE MUST SUBMIT TO HIS CONDITIONS. If then, there is no struggle; we may part company with him....' (*Hindustan Standard*, April 14th)

Nothing could be more banal, more ridiculous than this statement from a 'Socialist'. One must accept Gandhiji's leadership. For what? For struggle, Jaiprakash replies. But if Gandhiji's conditions THEMSELVES are such as rule out political strike, no-rent and even mass civil disobedience, if Gandhiji bans civil disobedience in States, should one even then lend him 'fullest co-operation and loyalty'? Yes, replies Jaiprakash.

THIS IS THE SOCIALISM OF THE CSP.

52. Communist Party on Subhas Bose

Communist Party of India, *Reality Vs. Myth*, April–May 1940, No. 1940/47, P.C. Joshi Archives on Contemporary History, JNU.

'The Man of the Hour'
Bose's Quest for 'Indian Lenin'

The National Week has come and gone. Bose had threatened the Congress leadership and assured his supporters that on the first day of this week, 'struggle on the all-India front' would be commenced, that is national structure would be launched. What actually took place was that in a few places separate National Week meetings were held by the Forward Bloc leaders. In Bombay, the police dispersed the meeting by lathi charge and arrested several of the organizers. In Allahabad also several arrests took place. After that a large number of Forward Bloc leaders have been arrested in Bengal.

Everyone would express solidarity with these victims of police terror. But the fact that the Government took these measures, cannot and does not by itself, mean that the tactic of giving the 'call' for national struggle was a correct tactic. The fact remains that except in Calcutta and may be one or two places more in Bengal, the Forward Bloc leaders failed to organize even effective and big mass meetings. Masses of Congressmen, masses of people were absolutely uninfluenced by the 'call'. It was a fiasco. It evoked no mass response.

Why then did Bose give the 'call'? Did he not know that it would evoke no response?

Bose has evolved a theory; the theory of 'man of the hour'. The tactic of 'declaration' of struggle, of giving 'call' for acting is the logical working out of that theory.

In the course of his Presidential address at the Anti-Compromise Conference, Bose said:

'The present crisis has put our leadership to the test and the latter has been found wanting. It is only by ANALYZING AND EXPOSING the cause of its failure that we can learn the lesson of history and lay the foundation of our future effort and achievement ....'

'.... When the October Revolution broke out in Russia in 1917, nobody had a clear conception as to how the Revolution should be directed. Most of the Bolsheviks were then thinking in terms of a coalition with other parties. It was left to Lenin to denounce all coalitions and give out the slogan: "All Power to the Soviets." Who knows what turn Russian history would have taken, but for this timely lead of Lenin during a period of doubt and vacillation? Lenin's UNERRING INSTINCT (or intuition) which ultimately proved to be prophetic saved Russia from disaster....'

'Let us take a contrary case. Italy in 1922 was to all intents and purposes ripe for Socialism. All that she needed was an Italian Lenin. But the MAN OF THE HOUR DID NOT ARRIVE and the opportunity slipped out of Socialist hands. It was immediately seized by the Fascist leader, Benito Mussolini... Mussolini had one supreme virtue which not only saved him but brought him laurels of victory. HE KNEW HIS MIND AND HE WAS NOT AFRAID TO ACT. That constitutes the essence of leadership.

'Today, our leaders are wobbling and their vacillation has demoralized a section of the Left as well....'

What do this 'analysis' and these conclusions mean?

They mean this: The old leaders are wobblers and vacillators. They do not know their mind. They are afraid to act. We need today an 'Indian Lenin', a man with 'unerring instinct or intuition', a man who will give a 'timely lead'. Such a man will be the 'MAN OF THE HOUR!' Round him will be formed a new leadership.

What will this 'man of the hour' do?

'If the Working Committee of the Congress does not give call for launching struggle, others will have to do so.' (Ibid)

Such things, however, happen only in fairy tales, in fictions. Never in real life.

Bose's 'Analysis' of Russian Revolution

And the irony is that Bose has attempted to draw a parallel from the history of the Russian Revolution, has attempted to place his 'call' for struggle in the same category as Lenin's slogan: 'All Power to the Soviets!'

It was not 'when the October Revolution broke out in 1917' (as Bose says) that Lenin gave the slogan: 'All Power to the Soviets!' It was in April 1917 that the slogan was given, and for six months, from April to October, the Bolsheviks won over the masses and made preparations to implement the slogan. It did not happen as though Lenin gave the call, masses rallied round his banner and there was, revolution. Nor was it 'instinct' or 'intuition' that enabled Lenin to give the slogan. Lenin who till then had advocated the slogan of Democratic Republic, made a MARXIST ANALYSIS, class analysis, of the situation as it had developed after the overthrow of Tsardom and because of the failure of the Provisional Government to make Peace, to satisfy the land-hunger of the peasantry, etc., and on the basis of this analysis came to the conclusion that conquest of power by the proletariat and the poorest strata of the peasantry was both necessary and possible and that the form of state of these classes must be a Soviet Republic.

All Power to the Soviets was not a slogan of 'call for action'. It was the CENTRAL POLITICAL SLOGAN of the Bolsheviks from April to October, just as Constituent Assembly and Democratic

Republic were their central political slogans in the previous period—and we may add, just as Constituent Assembly and Democratic Republic are our central political slogans today.

The SLOGANS OF ACTION by implementing which alone the Bolsheviks could implement this central slogan, corresponded at each stage, during the months of April to October, to the existing situation, the strength and influence of the Bolsheviks, the consciousness of the masses. Thus in April when the Bolsheviks were in a small minority, the task to which they set themselves, was the task of winning over the masses, of 'patient, systematic, persistent explanation', of 'criticizing and exposing', of 'preaching the necessary of transferring entire power to the Soviets'. (April Thesis)

In October, the Bolsheviks gave the slogan of UPRISING. That became the SLOGAN OF ACTION of the hour.

Thus while the slogan 'All Power to the Soviets' remained the central slogan of the Bolsheviks during this entire period, from April to October, the concrete slogans of the hour, the slogans of action, varied from stage to stage according to the maturity of the revolutionary crisis, the strength of the Bolsheviks, the degree of isolation of the parties of the bourgeoisie and other things. If Lenin had acted as Bose believes he DID act, then even in April, he would have given the slogan of armed insurrection, hoping that masses would respond, and that slogan would have been as much a fiasco as—and of course, far more disastrous than—Bose's slogan of 'national struggle' from 6th April.

It is needless to examine Bose's 'analysis' of the events in Italy that led to fascist triumph.

This 'Man of the Hour' theory has nothing to do with history, with reality.

Tasks of the New Leadership

It is obvious that the old leadership has failed and the national movement needs a new leadership. But wherein lies the failure of the old leadership? It is necessary to know that, for then only we can be conscious of our tasks and create a new leadership.

The failure does not lie in the inability of the old leadership to give 'call' for struggle IN GENERAL. It lies in its inability to develop and lead MASS struggle. Today the conditions are such that we can have mass civil disobedience all over the country including the States. We can have general strike and mass no rent actions. We can thus develop a powerful nationwide movement, a movement that will be a decisive step towards national revolution.

It is preciously SUCH a movement that the present leadership will not and cannot develop. It may—it WILL, if all efforts for compromise fail—give the 'call'. But it will not develop MASS struggle. Therein lies its failure. Therefore, the new leadership will be 'new' only in the measure in which it can make such a movement a possibility, a REALITY.

Such a new leadership does not 'come'. It is evolved. It is created in the midst of and through mass struggle and mass agitation. It launches mass campaign on a nationwide scale for the policy of mass struggle, its methods of mass action. It organizes MASS actions of workers, peasants and students and draws Congressmen into such actions. It decisively rejects opportunist alliances—alliance with Hindu Mahasabha today and Muslim League tomorrow—and all such methods as alienate honest anti-Imperialists. By its actions, by its methods, it creates respect for itself even among its opponents and wins confidence of the people.

Bose denies all this. His actions show that. He thinks that the first and most important task is to give the 'call'. If ten persons here and twenty persons there respond to the call, and defy the police, the struggle will have been launched, the 'Man of the Hour' will have done his job, will have given the 'lead'.

These may be the tactics of a Don Quixote but certainly not of a Lenin.

He Goes Forward

'The political stalemate is now broken' declares Shri Bose in a signed editorial in the FORWARD BLOC of 13th April. How? Because the Deshgaurab on 6th April, the first day (very auspicious!) of the National Week, has given 'the call for National Struggle'. And he is very much self-satisfied. 'There can be no doubt today that the masses are with us.' It does not matter to him if in a vast majority of places outside Bengal, the Forward Bloc could not even hold mass meetings on 6 April and if an overwhelming majority of the Forward Bloc leaders have not followed their leaders lead.

Shri Bose's ire is concentrated against the Communists:

'Is it not an irony of fate that the National Front Group are not coming forward to join the National Struggle? They could at least have come forward to intensify the local struggles and extend their scope, leaving it to others—to the Kisan Sabha and the Forward Bloc, to wit,—to work as they liked. But their present policy appears to be almost like a "dog in the manger" policy. They will neither join the struggle themselves nor permit others to do so.'

But Shri Bose is not bothered by it at all. 'The Caravan will march on, despite their indifference and possible obstruction. This is the time—not for wordy warfare or hairsplitting over the meaning of words'. To him, we are 'doctrinaire politicians' and 'bookish revolutionaries'. We will, therefore, not enter into a theoretical defence of our line as against his. We will let facts speaks for themselves. In judging political parties, it is not their claims but then deeds that matter. We readily give Sjt Bose his own home in Bengal, after Ramgarh.

Communists and Bose Separate

Before Ramgarh, the Communist split from Bose when after repeated efforts he refused to launch a struggle against the suppression of Civil Liberties in Bengal on the ground that he wanted to launch a 'national struggle'. We characterized his stand as being anti-struggle, using the slogan of NATIONAL struggle as a cover for escaping an IMMEDIATE and REAL struggle. When on top of this, he decided to carry on with a rival BPCC, we separated from him. We characterized his move as being disruptive of national unity, using 'left' phrases to hide his factional dog-fight against the dominant Right leadership. We had forecast that if inside the National Front, a leader advocates an anti-struggle and anti-unity line, it must lead him on to anti-national alliances. Events marched faster than we had imagined. Shri Bose had been proclaiming his eagerness to give the call for national struggle at Ramgarh, by mobilizing all genuine fighting elements through the Anti-Compromise Civil disobedience. But before this, he had entered into a pact with the Hindu Mahasabha for contesting the coming Corporation elections. We know who were Bose's fellow 'fighters', we knew how and with whom he meant 'to fight'. We decided to have nothing to do with the Anti-Compromise Conference.

And after Ramgarh, let us see what has happened in Bengal, who did what?

From the Hindu Mahasabha to the Muslim League

Sjt Bose had entered into a Pact with the Hindu Mahasabha NOT on the basis of a programme embodying clear-cut demands for the well-being of Calcutta Citizens but it was an unprincipled patch-up on the basis of division of seats. This corrupt alliance did not endure, they could not agree about the allotment of seats. Official Congress did not participate in the elections, Communists held aloof, Bose contested elections on behalf of his BPCC. Existing Congress majority was reduced to a minority under Bose's 'bold leadership', the Hindu Mahasabha exploited all the weakness of the situation and secured a large number of seats. Now came the Mayoral elections. But Shri Bose never loses heart, in some matters. Having failed at one end, he tried again at the other end. As suddenly he concluded a pact with the Muslim League, once again NOT on the basis of any civil programme but for the division of loaves and fishes of office and through intrigue. Bose's group was to have two Aldermen, Muslim League another two, a renegade Hindu Mahasabhite Sjt B.C. Chatterji, Vice-President of the Hindu Mahasabha, anti-Congress liberal in his views who had forsaken his colleagues and was now swearing by Bose was to be the fifth Alderman, and a Muslim Leaguer was to be the Mayor. From the time of Deshbandhu Das no non-Congressman had sat on the Mayoral seat. And this is where Bose had LED the Bengal Congress. When the present Muslim League Coalition Ministry introduced its Calcutta Corporation Amendment Bill introducing communal electorates and embodying other anti-democratic measures, Bose had vomited fire and thunder, pledged the honour of Bengal Congress to resist it to the last ditch. Just as the Right began to work the Constitution, they were pledged to wreck, Bose began co-operating with the framers of the very Act he had promised to fight and under the very provisions of that Act. Shri Bose defends this agreement on the ground that the Congress has always stood for an agreement with the Muslim League. Under the Muslim League Coalition Ministry of Bengal, under the Defence of India Act, 535 (almost entirely Congressmen) arrests have taken place, 61 meetings and 11 processions had not been permitted or prohibited, 21 orders had been served on newspapers (interpellation in Bengal Legislative Assembly on 27th March). Such is this 'leader of national struggle' but his checks do not blush.

So far the Congress masses in Bengal were used to see the whole Left—Forward Blockists, Socialists and Communists—stand together. The Right in Bengal had hardly any mass basis. By the end of the last year, the differences between Bose and the Communists began to grow and since they concerned the very fate and direction of the political movement of Bengal, headed by the BPCC, they became the talk of the day and began going down from leaders of Left parties to the rank and file as a whole. After Independence Day it became known to all that the differences were irreconcilable. We were convinced that Bose's line mean the sabotage of struggles and disruption of the Congress—the organ of struggle while ours was the line of immediate struggle and real unity. The issues could no longer be decided by debates, they had to be taken to the Congress rank and file. We proposed the convening of a really representative Congress workers' Conference. Bose without opposing it openly, did his very best to see that such a conference was not convened. In alliance with Socialists and several district Congress leaders we went ahead with the conference. It was a tremendous success. The Bosite line was put in the Conference by the 'Labour Party' delegates and overwhelmingly defeated. The Conference decided that similar conferences be held in the districts and of Congressmen still lower down. Let the Congress workers themselves decide whether it is necessary to disrupt the Congress to be able to give a 'call for national struggle' (Bose's line) which will be neither national nor struggle, or it was immediately necessary to launch actual mass struggles in defence of civil liberties, for the release of political prisoners and support working class and peasant mass actions against the ruinous effects of War (Communist Line). Whether it was necessary first to split the Congress and have a sham Satyagraha (as it has really turned out to be) or what was called for was to launch and support IMMEDIATE struggle of the people for their vital demands and create such an atmosphere and tempo of struggle as to hasten national struggle itself, with the actual participation of the masses in it, with the unity of the Congress preserved intact...

53.   Bombay Communist Initiative to Mobilize Congress Rank and File

> Report of 'Provincial Workers Conference', *Communist*, Vol. II, No. 9, July 1940, P.C. Joshi Archives on Contemporary History, JNU.

Though little publicity was given to it by the Nationalist Press, the Bombay Political Workers' Conference that was held on the 23rd June was an event of major significance. It was the first organized attempt made by Congress rank and file in this City to make its voice heard, to make Congressmen conscious of the unique opportunities and tremendous responsibilities before them; to fight against the disastrous notion that because of Britain's military defeats, freedom would come to India without any struggle on the part of her people, without any effort.

The initiative was taken by the Communists and they succeeded in getting the active support of quite a good number of rank and file Congressmen and militant conscious workers. The difficulties that they faced were simply terrific and men with less determination would have given up the job in despair. They had to contend against not only the prevailing demoralization but also active opposition on the part of the leaders of the Provincial Congress Committee. In their very first statement to the Press, issued in May, the organizers of the Conference made their object clear. At Ramgarh, the Congress had decided to launch Civil Disobedience and Rajendra Babu, Nehru and Gandhiji himself had declared that it would be MASS Civil Disobedience. Two months had passed since then. The war had entered into a decisive phase. Britain had suffered defeat after defeat. Determined to secure its rear in a period like this, the Government had launched a campaign of repression. Time was ripe for launching people's counter-offensive. Yet the Congress leadership had not done that. All idea of mass Civil Disobedience had been given up. Action in any form—even restricted Civil Disobedience— was being postponed. The Conference was to express opposition to this policy and demand nationwide action. Because it was to be a Conference of Congressmen alone, it would be called Congress Workers' Conference.

Threat of Disciplinary Action

In this move, the Secretary of the BPCC saw the danger of 'indiscipline and disruption'. The Conference was a 'stunt'. It was being organized by 'disgruntled' people who wanted to 'criticize the leaders'. Hence no Congressman holding Executive position must associate in any manner with the Conference. At one stage, it appeared that the objection was only to the name of the Conference, namely, that a Conference which was being organized by individual Congressmen and not by a Congress COMMITTEE could not call itself CONGRESS Workers' Conference. But that did not satisfy the Secretary. Another statement was issued on the same lines as the first one and Congressmen were asked not to attend Conference. All sorts of warnings and threats were given to those who dared disobey this 'fatwa'.

This talk of 'discipline' on the part of those who had thrown overboard every anti-war resolution of the Congress, who despite the AICC circular had not organized mass meetings to explains the attitude of the Congress towards war and were shamelessly declaring that they wished for the victory of the British—sickeningly hypocritical though it may be—can be easily explained. They did not want struggle and hence they wanted to stifle rank and file voice in the name of unity and on the plea of discipline. To give up the idea of the Conference because of this threat would have been the height of cowardice and would have created demoralization. So the organizers decided to go ahead.

Street-Corner Meetings

Street-corner meetings were held in every part of Bombay to explain the meaning of the war events, to emphasize the need for action at this hour, to popularize the conference and its slogans. Thousands of handbills were brought out. The response was greater than had been expected and showed clearly that even today things are not as bad as they are supposed to be and people CAN be rallied for a policy of action. Street-corner meetings began to draw larger and larger audience. One day a taxi was taken round the Dadar–Matunga areas—mostly middle class areas—and meetings were held in numerous places. Everywhere there was good response.

Of special significance was the work done by the working class comrades. They spread the message of the Conference and carried its slogans into chawls, they held numerous meetings in working class areas, they succeeded in getting hearing in predominantly Muslim areas. The general strike of March–April had galvanized the workers and raised their consciousness. Agitation for the Conference helped to develop that.

Government Strikes

The Government saw what was happening. The crop of arrests that had taken place during and after the strike had not killed 'subversive activity' in Bombay. So another blow was struck—again at the Communists and their supporters and sympathizers, many of whom were working for the Conference. On 5th June, eight comrades were arrested under the Defence of India Rules. No charge was framed against any of them. They were to be 'detained' in prison as long as the Government desired.

To these difficulties were added more. The Jinnah Hall which is always given on rent to anybody who wants to hold a meeting and even to marriage parties, was refused to the organizers of the Conference. This was done by the BPCC. Secretary who is in charge of the Hall. Having seen that all his exhortations and threats had borne no fruit, he now tried to prevent the holding of the Conference by this device. So another place had to be found. Then came another difficulty. Sjt Subhas Bose who had come to Bombay after the Forward Bloc Conference at Nagpore, conveyed to the organizers that he wanted to preside at the Conference. That had to be refused in view of Bose's slogan of 'two Congress', his alliance with reactionaries and his slogan of 'national defence'—his politics of the last ten months. Bose's supporters got so enraged at this that while knowing that they too would not be permitted the use of Jinnah Hall, they announced a meeting at Jinnah Hall at which Bose was to speak on the SAME DAY AND AT THE SAME TIME that the Conference was to meet. This was obviously done to draw people away from the Conference.

Then again there was the difficulty of getting a well-known Congress leader to preside over the Conference. That difficulty could not be solved. Most of the Communist and genuine left-wing leaders were in prison. Congress Socialists had completely fallen in line with the official leadership. So a President had to be selected from rank and file comrades themselves. Nature too was unkind. On the day of the Conference, it rained and rained as it does only in Bombay.

A Real Rank-And-File Conference

Despite all these difficulties and setbacks, over 500 delegates—all of them Congressmen—attended the Conference, workers came in procession, the hall was packed and on the whole, the Conference was a big success. The earnestness and enthusiasm that marked the proceedings, the businesslike way in which things were done—all these must be considered to be real successes. It was a real rank and file Congressmen's Conference.

In his Presidential address, Comrade Mahimkar made a powerful plea for immediate launching of national struggle. Pointing out the unique opportunity which the war-crisis created, stressing the need for mass action, he sharply criticized the policy of the Congress leadership.

The major political resolution of the Conference characterized the present phase of the War as 'a phase of cataclysmic changes, a phase in which events move and the crisis of imperialism, with lightning rapidity, a phase in which the national movement faces unprecedented opportunities and tremendous tasks.' It sought to dispel the illusion that because of defeats suffered in the War, the British Government would voluntarily also repression, precisely because of these defeats. It demanded 'mass civil disobedience backed by mass action of workers, peasants and students all over the country, including the States.' It condemned the action of those Congressmen who were declaring that India should not 'embarrass Britain' and those who were raising the slogan of defence. 'The slogan of Defence today means the defence of British Rule in India and the task of the national movement is NOT defence of that rule but EMANCIPATION of the nation from it'. It called upon Congressmen to organize mass actions against the economic distress caused by the war, against growing imperialist repression and through such action, prepare the basis for nationwide struggle.

The Slogan of 'Defence'

Comrade Vaidya moved the resolution. He made a most effective speech. When the situation was so favourable, when the enemy was reeling under the blows of its imperialist rival, our leaders were standing by helpless. This today was nothing short of treason. Instead of hitting out for freedom, they were dreaming of 'honourable settlement' which meant nothing but perpetuation of slavery.

Comrade Panikkar supported the resolution. He sharply attacked the slogans of 'National Government' and 'National Defence' and explained that they were just the slogans which imperialism wanted us to take up. 'We have nothing TO DEFEND. We have to WIN freedom. We have to destroy our slavery and British rule.'

The Slogan of Pakistan

Comrade Amin Hazien moved the resolution on Pakistan. The resolution had three parts. It exposed the slogan of Pakistan as given by the Muslim League as a slogan for perpetuating slavery of Hindus and also of Muslims—under Britain. It called upon the Congress to declare that the Congress stood for a free India that would be a voluntary federation of peoples and nationalities, a federation of which provinces where the Muslims form the overwhelming majority of population could form autonomous units and even have the right of session. Finally, it stressed that to bring about such freedom, Hindus and Muslims must join hands to fight against the common enemy, British Imperialism.

The significance of the resolution lay in the fact that it did not merely condemn the Pakistan Scheme as is usually done but was based on the realization that by making it appear as though Pakistan meant MUSLIM INDEPENDENCE, the League had succeeded in winning the support of a large section of Muslims for the slogan.

Comrade Amin Hazien ruthlessly exposed the Pakistan Scheme, as a scheme to disrupt unity and perpetuate slavery. Comrades Pawar and Mohiuddin stressed the need for immediate action by Hindu and Muslim masses.

The third resolution called for mass agitation against repression. It was moved by Comrade Valanju and supported by Sardar Makhan Singh and Comrade Karandikar. The speakers stressed the need for immediate counter-attack by the people, failing which there was the serious danger of defeatism and demoralization growing in our own ranks.

All the speeches were listened to with keen attention. There was enthusiasm and keenness. There was earnestness. There was the realization of the seriousness of the situation, of the havoc that stalemate was creating, of the glorious opportunity that was being lost because of the bankruptcy and cowardice of our leaders. Above all, there was the consciousness that we must explain and agitate and see that our slogans penetrate deep into the ranks of the Congress. We, the rank and file, have to ACT—this was the keynote of the speeches.

54. Communist Party's View of Subhas Bose's Position

Communist, Vol. II, No. 10, August 1940, P.C. Joshi Archives on Contemporary History, JNU.

'We believe that the establishment of national governments at the Centre and in the provinces will be a SOURCE OF STRENGTH TO THE BRITISH GOVERNMENT. Sjt Subhas Chandra Bose WAS WORKING FOR THIS OBJECT. Indeed so far as we know, HE WAS THE FIRST TO MOOT THE INDIA.' (Our emphasis)

This is not an extract from our earlier articles in criticism of Bose. This is an extract from the Editorial of *Hindustan Standard* (July, 4) a staunch supporter of Sjt Bose criticizing the action of the Government in arresting him. What this compliment to Sjt Bose implies, we leave it to the readers to judge. What we stress is that this compliment is not UNDESERVED:

This may seem strange to those who after Sjt Bose's launching of Holwell Monument Satyagraha thought that now at last he has taken to the path of uncompromising struggle No idea could be more illusory.

'National Government' and 'National Defence' are to-day the slogans of all those who want to strike a bargain with the British Government. This we have stressed again and again. No greater proof of this is needed than the fact that from Sir Tej Bahadur Sapru to Sir Sikandar Hyat and even the Anglo-Indian Press who condemned the Ramgarh Resolution of the Congress have acclaimed these slogans. The acid test of genuine anti-imperialism to-day lies precisely in one's attitude towards these slogans.

For Responsible Centre

On 8th June, Sjt Bose issued a statement in which he asked 'Hindus and Muslims' to 'PUT FORWARD A JOINT DEMAND FOR A PROVINCIAL GOVERNMENT'. He did say that this 'National Government' should have 'full sovereign power' but that was a mere eye wash. This is clear from his next sentence. 'THIS PROVINCIAL NATIONAL GOVERNMENT CAN FIT INTO THE EXISTING CONSTITUTION WITH CERTAIN CONSEQUENTIAL CHANGES IN THE GOVERNMENT OF INDIA ACT'.

Bose's demand, therefore, was in reality for RESPONSIBLE CENTRE, exactly the same demand as Rajaji's. on the same day, Bose issued another statement (See *Forward Bloc* 8th June) for the formation of a Defence Corps for maintaining 'INTERNAL PEACE'. Another slogan of Rajaji.

For Unconditional Surrender

A question that was put to Rajaji at the AICC meeting was: 'If the British Government refuses to concede our demand and thus makes the formation of 'National Government' at the Centre impossible, what should we do THEN? How long shall we wait'? To his question, Rajaji gave no straight reply, BUT BOSE HAD ALREADY ANTICIPATED THE QUESTION AND GIVEN THE REPLY. In a statement issued on 30th June, he said:

> 'A moot point in this connection is as to whether we should try the experiment of national cabinets in the provinces, even if we cannot set up a national cabinet at the Centre just now. TO THIS QUERY, MY ANSWER IS "YES". In the present dynamic situation, national cabinets in the provinces will be a great help not only in maintaining internal harmony, not only in establishing Hindu-Muslim unity—BUT ALSO IN WINNING POWER AT THE CENTER—should there be obstacles in the path of winning Swaraj' (*Hindustan Standard*)

The meaning is clear.

Even without a 'declaration' from the British Government, even without 'settlement', use would form 'National Cabinets', that is COALITION MINISTRIES IN the provinces. UN-CONDITIONAL GOING BACK TO MINISTRIES—that is his line'!

It is this line that masquerades as the line of 'uncompromising struggle'!

Pleading for 'Justice'

Finally, we shall quote a gem from the Editorial of the *Forward Bloc* of 29th June three days before Bose's arrest.

> 'Britain has avowed over and over again that one is fighting for the cause of the World—the cause of universal freedom and democracy.... India for her is the acid test....The act of bare justice to India to whose inherent idealism, fascist expansion is a startling menace, will not only win her over to the side of Britain but may induce wavering America to make a desperate bid in her favour....'

Could anything be more sickening, more nauseating? Could even Rajaji beat this? This piteous appeal for 'justices', this assurance that India will join Britain for the 'cause of universal freedom and democracy', this bait that if 'justice' is done to India then America too may join Britain—what do these show?

The 'Struggle'

But then what about Bose's 'struggle'—one may ask in wonder. Did he not launch the Holwell Monument Satyagraha? How is that consistent with this pathetic appeal for 'justice', this plea for 'National Government'?

There is no inconsistency. The decision to launch the Satyagraha was taken at the Dacca Conference of the BPCC which took place on 25th and 26th of May, at a time when the sweeping German victories on the Western Front had raised high hopes in the mind of every Congress leader that NOW the British Government would make concessions. 99 per cent of them thought that compromise was a matter of days It was IN THIS SITUATION, that Sjt Bose who for eight months had refused to launch struggle for civil liberties decided to begin the Satyagraha for removal of Holwell Monument, on the plea that 'all emblems of servitude should be demolished.' To say that it was a mere accident that the 'struggle' was begun at preciously this moment, is to be deliberately blind.

Bose's Successor

A word about Bose's successor. Sjt Bose on his arrest nominated Sardar Sardul Singh Caveeshar as leader of the All-India Forward Bloc. This gentleman on May 22nd had issued a statement that the 'Congress policy of non-co-operation' had become 'out of date'. Therefore, Congressmen should 'resume office immediately', 'National Government should be formed' and 'a strong Army of 10 lacs should be raised'!

There is no danger that he will fail to pursue the 'line' of the Forward Bloc. The above statement is sufficient guarantee.

55. Communist Party's View of the Poona Session of the AICC

Communist, Vol. II, No. 10, August 1940, P.C. Joshi Archives on Contemporary History, JNU.

A Sanction for Surrender

The session of the All-India Congress Committee, which concluded its sittings recently at Poona, approved of one more step in retreat which the national leadership had decided upon. In the teeth of a considerable and a vehement opposition, it endorsed the Wardha statement and the Delhi resolutions of the Working Committee. At a time when the British imperialist rulers reduced to desperate straits in Europe, are tightening their stranglehold on India by increasing war burdens, by intensifying repression—at such a time the national leadership makes a new offer for settlement. It has declared its readiness to co-operate in the imperialist war. It is ready to run the administrative and state machinery, the main business of which to-day is to force more men into uniform and squeeze more money from the people in the name of 'defence', and to beat and jail the fighters for freedom in the name of 'internal disorder'.

The Genesis of the Delhi Resolution

This is no sudden development nor an unexpected departure from the line adopted at Ramgarh as the CSP leadership thinks. As the Communist members of the AICC pointed out in their statement, it is 'the logical culmination of the policy of Constitutionalism and compromise which has always been there and which entrenched itself firmly in the period of Congress Ministries' (*We Warn*: p. 3). It was provided for in the policy of conditional co-operation for war, in the policy of stalemate, of waiting and watching, of sabotaging the preparations for struggle through the new Satyagraha plan. The Delhi resolution of July 7 makes explicit and concrete, what was implicit and nebulously worded in the Working Committee statement of September 14,1939. In fact it was immediately after the outbreak of the war that the national leadership gave up its position of resisting Imperialist War embodied in the Haripura Resolution. The Wardha Resolution of September 1939 shorn of its platitudes and revolutionary drapings already contained in an implied form the offer and the conditions for a compromise and for cooperation in war.

This Wardha Statement of the Working Committee of September 1939 stated:

'A clear declaration about the future, pledging the Government to the ending of imperialism and fascism alike will be welcomed by the people of all countries, but it is far more important to give IMMEDIATE EFFECT TO IT, TO THE LARGEST POSSIBLE EXTENT, for only this convince the people that this declaration is meant to be honoured. The real test of any declaration is its application in the present, for it is the present that will govern action to-day and give shape to the future.' (emphasis ours)

It was this under-lined phrase of the September statement which the Delhi Resolution translated in specific and concrete terms in the following way:

'An unequivocal declaration (by Great Britain of the Complete Independence of India) be immediately made and that as an immediate step in giving effect to it, a provisional National Government should be constituted at the Centre, which though formed as a transitory measure should be such as to command the confidence of all the elected elements in the Central Legislature and secure the closest co-operation of the responsible Governments in the provinces'.

Ist Class Aim

Thus the national bourgeois leadership is striving to take advantage of the new situation which has developed for Britain after the collapse of France. How? Not by placing before the people the issue of a nationwide fight against the tottering edifice of British Imperialism, but by placing before the British rulers the issue of settlement of sharing power with their class, so that they—the Indian bourgeoisie—may 'wholeheartedly' help them in the war and save British rule from collapse. It is not panic at the prospect of external aggression which determines this new move towards compromise. It is a cold-blooded move calculated to capitalize the weakening of Britain brought about by the developments in the European war. The fear of likely revolutionary developments which may be released by the collapse of Britain is the main driving force behind this new gesture for compromise. The reason why the national leadership has chosen this particular moment to lay its cards on the table and to ask for a compromise is two fold. Firstly, it thinks that this is the most opportune moment to put forward its demand in specific and acceptable terms, as the chances of British Imperialism conceding the same are the greatest. Secondly, it wants to be in a strategic position, sharing power with Imperialism so that it is able to forestall and suppress any revolutionary and untoward developments which may be released by the defeat of Britain.

Rift in the Gandhian Camp?

If the Delhi Resolution was a direct and inevitable corollary of the old Wardha Resolution (September 1939) on which the entire national leadership was united, why did differences arise in the Working Committee now? Why was the question of true and unalloyed non-violence raised in the Wardha Statement? Why did Gandhiji retire and why did certain Gandhian leaders of the Working Committee and the AICC remain neutral on the resolution? The Congress President in his opening speech gave an explanation of this. He said that ever since the beginning of the war, Gandhiji had been insisting that the Working Committee should base its stand on war, on the principle of 'true and unalloyed non-violence'. Gandhiji wanted the Working Committee 'to deny itself the opportunity of striking a bargain with England. It should make its contribution to world peace, to the defence of countries. Threatened by external aggression and to India's freedom by declaring to the world by its action that the way to peace with honour did not lie through mutual slaughter of innocents, but that it lay only and truly through the practice of organized non-violence even unto death'. He wanted the Working Committee to declare further that independent India would defend herself against external aggression or internal disorder only through the practice of non-violence unto death and that she would not organize any armed forces at all.

Maulana's Explanation

The Congress President as well as Pandit Jawaharlal Nehru, who moved the Wardha Statement on non-violence before the House, explained that it was Gandhiji's insistence on the unattainable ethical anarchic ideal that was responsible for these differences. The Working Committee, they said, was unable to take this position. They wished they had the moral strength to live up to and practice this ideal but the fact was that the bulk of Congressmen were not imbued with the spirit of non-violence and therefore they had to choose the traditional path. Maulana described how he pleaded with Gandhiji not to raise the question and stand with the Working Committee generally. Maulana succeeded in this till the war entered into its present phase and when the perspective of external aggression and internal disorder appeared on the horizon of India itself. Now Gandhiji could no longer be held back. He (Gandhiji) said that it was a question of principle with him which he cherished more than his life. He, therefore, insisted that the Working Committee take their decision and reject the principle and so free him from the responsibility of guiding that body.

Masking the Real Issue

This was the account which the Congress President gave of the genesis of the Wardha Statement of June 21st which was placed before the AICC as the first resolution for confirmation. The endeavour of Maulana and of the other Congress leaders who spoke on this question was to show that there was no real difference in the Gandhian camp on the political aspect of the question. They were all agreed that the only practical step possible under the circumstances was the one outlined in the Delhi Resolution. The difference lay only on the ethical principle of unalloyed non-violence, on the issue of Unattainable anarchic ideal.

This trick of separating principle from practice, the attempt to shift the controversy to the ethical plane, to focus the discussion on the artificial issue of the anarchic ideal, was a hypocritical manoeuvre to conceal the bankruptcy of Gandhism, to hide the disintegration inside the Gandhian leadership. The immediate issue before the Poona Session of the AICC was surely not whether independent India was going to have army or no, nor whether it was going to have an anarchic state. The issue was one of co-operation in the Imperialist war in order to gain political concessions. The issue was one of compromise with Imperialism, of giving up openly and without any subterfuge the Haripura Congress stand regarding war.

Stand of 'True Non-Violence' on War

What was Gandhism's stand on this issue from the viewpoint of 'unalloyed non-violence of the brave'? Mahadev Desai in a review published in *Harijan* (July 13, 1940) says that Gandhiji put forward this stand as early as in September 1938 at the time of the Czechoslovakian crisis. Gandhiji is reported to have persuaded the entire Working Committee then:

'to come to the conclusion that it would deny itself the opportunity of striking a bargain with England but would make its contribution to the world peace, to the defence of Czechoslovakia, and to India's freedom by declaring to the world by its action that the way to peace with honour did not lie through mutual slaughter of the innocents, but that it lay only and truly through the practice of organized non-violence even unto death.'

In private conversation Gandhiji is reported to have said at that time: 'For me even if I stand alone, THERE IS NO PARTICIPATION IN THE WAR EVEN IF THE GOVERNMENT SHOULD SURRENDER THE WHOLE CONTROL TO THE CONGRESS...' (*Harijan*, 3.7.40; italics M.D.'s) This position is in a way consistent with the Haripura stand. Politically it would lead to unconditional non-co-operation in imperialist war, though on the basis of non-violence. The acceptance of this stand by the Working Committee would have meant the acceptance of the policy of nationwide mass resistance to war, which could have been developed into an united national struggle for freedom.

Why Gandhiji Deserted It?

Why did not Gandhiji stick to this stand in September 1939 when the war actually broke out? Why was this apostle of the 'true non-violence of the brave' not able to persuade the Working Committee to adopt this position? Why did he run bleating to the Viceroy and offer him 'unconditional co-operation on the basis of non-violence' which in plain English meant moral support to imperialist war? Because Gandhism is nothing if it is not a political policy of the bourgeoisie. Because with Gandhism, in spite of its protestations to the contrary, non-violence is not an end in itself. It is for it a means and a mask, a means of pursuing the compromising politics of the bourgeoisie, a mask to hide its anti-popular character. The stand of unconditional non-participation in war might have been consistent with the principle of non-violence, but it was totally inconsistent with the practice of bourgeois leadership which during the recent period of Ministries has been to prevent and sabotage the nationwide struggle for freedom. Had not Gandhiji himself time and again said that a mass civil disobedience movement of 1930–32 was no longer possible in view of the growth of the forces of organized violence and revolution in the country? That is why the prophet of the non-violence of the brave did not put up any resistance to the Wardha stand (September 39) of the Working Committee, which as we have seen was one of conditional co-operation with imperialist war. Although he expressed his philosophical disagreement with it, he supported and lined up behind the Wardha Statement. (*Harijan*, 23.9.39).

Bankruptcy and Cowardice

Why then is this controversy raised once again? The Delhi Resolution is but the logical outcome of the Wardha stand. If he could make his peace with the Wardha stand of 1939, why not with the Delhi Resolution? Does it mean that he has now come to realize the disastrous political consequences of co-operation in war? His article entitled 'Some Vital Questions' written immediately after his interview with the Viceroy (*Harijan*: 6.7) does show that he considered the prospect of the Congress becoming a part of the war machine as a disaster of the first magnitude. In his 'appeal to Every Briton' (ibid) he admits that at the outbreak of the war, he had not the courage to take his stand by a policy aimed at ENDING THE WAR. He did express his approval of the Delhi Resolution. But in spite of all this, he has refused to throw in his weight against the Resolution. In his article in the *Harijan*, he says he could have stopped Rajaji bringing forward the Resolution but did not do so. The fact is that though Gandhiji and some Gandhists disagree with the Delhi resolution, they have NO ALTERNATIVE POLICY. The policy of unalloyed non-violence, of unconditional non-participation in war does not serve the compromising needs of the bourgeoisie. The mask of non-violence is cast aside The bulk of the Gandhists troop behind Rajaji, the farmer of the Delhi Resolution. The few Gandhists headed by Rajendra Babu, who still claim to adhere to 'unalloyed non-violence' offer no opposition to the Delhi Resolution. They vote against the Wardha statement. Thus the controversy on the question of non-violence becomes an artificial issue to screen the bankruptcy and the hypocrisy of Gandhism.

Debate on the Wardha Statement

The first resolution before the AICC namely the confirmation of the Wardha statement, as well as the speeches of the leaders on the same served merely to divert the attention form the main issue. This Resolution merely stated that the Congress cannot agree to adhere to the principle of non-violence in the contingency of defending the country against external aggression and internal disorder. It absolved Gandhiji of the responsibility for the programme and activities which the Congress may have to pursue in this eventuality. The real issue before the House was neither that of external aggression nor of defending the freedom of an independent India. The real issue was whether under the cover of 'defence of the country', Congress was to sanction a settlement with Imperialism and allow co-operation in imperialist war. That was the plain issue. If the test of non-violence was at all to be applied, it had to be applied to this issue.

Both Pandit Nehru who moved the resolution and Sjt Bhulabhai Desai who seconded it, laboured the obvious point that independent India must defend herself against external aggression with armed forces. Rajendra Babu speaking on behalf of the true non-violence wall as merely stated that it would have been better if the Congress Working Committee had declared its adherence to the principle of non-violence even in the field of national defence. He said Gandhiji did not come to Poona because he did not wish to influence the decision of the Committee. Jawaharlal Nehru in his, closing speech emphasizing once again the point that an independent state cannot be defended without an army and quoted Lenin to say that State is a coercive apparatus and is always based on force. The Socialist Pandit was not bothered about the incongruity of quoting Lenin and at the same time maintaining that independence could be won from imperialism through non-violence. When the proposition was put to vote, it was found that 91 voted for it and 63 against it, the Communists and Socialists remaining neutral. The Communist delegates were right in not moving amendments and in not voting on the resolution. But they ought to have demanded the floor to express themselves on the resolution and to expose the hypocrisy and bankruptcy of Gandhism and to show the real issue was being sidetracked.

Rajaji Poses the 'Real Issue'

Sjt Rajagopalachari who moved the main resolution put the case of the compromisers without mincing matters. He referred to the debate on the non-violence resolution as one creating an 'ultimate doctrine' atmosphere. Why this hullabaloo about a little inconsistency with the principle of non-violence, he asked. We are a political organization, not a missionary sect. Has not Gandhiji himself been inconsistent on occasions, he asked in an almost bantering tone, giving choice examples. Only Rajaji could allow himself such a filing at Gandhiji. Gandhiji aims at the anarchic ideal. It is not a 'practical proposition'. We are at the head of a great political organization which is on the eve of capturing power; that devolves certain responsibilities on our shoulders and we have to face them.

Recognizing in the Communists the most consistent and uncompromising opponents of the Resolution, he turned his fire mainly on them. Ridiculing them, he said, the Communists want to create chaos, destroy everything and then create something grand on the ruins. They stood for revolution. Not he. He stood for peaceful evolution. Coming to the main contention, he declared: We are not departing from the position at Ramgarh. Only the approach is changed. Why? Because the nature of the war has changed. Britain is now fighting a defensive war. This affects us. If our demands about declaration of independence and National Government are granted, we have to help in the war. This won't weaken us nor is it against any principle. Did not Gandhiji offer aid to Britain? Neither has Nehru taken up an attitude of untouchability towards war. Let us get away from the tyranny of phrases. We have a situation in which we can get independence by promising support and we must do it. There is no surrender in this as the Communists say.

Vallabhbhai's Pleading

Sjt Vallabhbhai seconding the resolution also put the case of the compromisers in a straightforward way. He said the anarchic ideal was unattainable. You have not run a State without an army. He admitted that even during the period of Congress Ministries, they had to use the military. He made another striking admission. The Wardha Resolution of September last, he said, assured help to the British Government in their war efforts, on certain conditions being fulfilled. That was why he resigned from the Gandhi Seva Sangh. He said it is no question of moral help. What Britain wants is material help and we are prepared to give it if our demands are satisfied. He frankly admitted that there was risk in the stand, but big issues like freedom could not be solved without taking risks.

Both the mover and the seconder pleaded straightaway for a participation in the war on condition that the demand of the National Government was granted. This would not give us independence immediately, but would be a strategic move towards winning independence. That was their argument. Several amendments were moved. Only two are worthy of note. One, moved by Pandit Balkrishna Sharma, said that the AICC noted the Delhi Resolution and called upon the Working Committee to place before the country a programme of national struggle. The amendment moved by the Royists showed that they had become open unashamed agents of Churchill. Their amendment suggested participation in the war as it was anti-fascist war, and unconditional resumption of Ministries.

Socialist Opposition

There were no Gandhites among the opposition speakers, who consisted mostly of Communists, Socialists and left nationalists. On the whole, the opposition was vehement and telling. The best speech was, of course, made by Dr Ashraf who spoke on behalf of the Communists. Yusuf Meherally's speech was also appreciated. The speeches of both Narendra Deo and Meherally followed the lines of the statement which they issued to the Press. The Congress Socialists interpreted the resolution as a departure from Ramgarh. They had pitched too much faith on the promises of Ramgarh. Now they were expressing disillusionment. Secondly they expressed a naive faith in Gandhiji. The leadership of Gandhiji was a guarantee against surrender. Finally though they opposed the resolution vigorously, they had no positive lead to give. They did not emphasize the need for launching national struggle. On the other hand, they followed in the wake of the Working Committee and Nehru in believing that an automatic collapse of imperialism was imminent and that no struggle would be needed. What was needed was merely to prepare the people to take advantage of 'the crisis'. Hence their 'positive lead' was: organize National Guards, strengthen Congress Committees and prepare the people for the calling of the Constituent Assembly.

Communist Speeches

Both Comrades Mahmud Ali and Ashraf who spoke on behalf of the Communists condemned the resolution as a great betrayal. They pointed out that the Delhi Resolution was not merely a departure from Ramgarh, but the culmination of the policy of compromise and stalemate pursued since the outbreak of the war. They corrected their mistake of remaining silent on the non-violence resolution, by exposing now that artificial controversy was used to cloud the main issue. They showed how the mask of non-violence was being cast aside as it proved a hindrance to co-operation in war and to compromise. They recounted how the situation had worsened since Ramgarh arid the most urgent need was the organizing of the struggle of the people against repression, war and for freedom. They concluded by declaring that the Communists would not accept the betrayal.

Dr Ashraf's speech was livened by flashes of biting rhetoric against the official speeches. He debunked Rajaji's formulation that the war for Britain was now one of defence. He reminded the mover of the resolution that Churchill still talked of final victory over Germany and of its annihilation. He showed how the declaration of independence if it ever, came, would give you at best SHAM independence like that of Egypt. He showed that the so-called National Government can be nothing else but an alliance of social reaction and that its function would be to prosecute war, carryon repression of the people. He pointed out the disastrous consequences of accepting Ministries in war time. He dealt with the hypocrisy of Non-Violence. He concluded by stating what the Communists demand.

Nehru's Revolutionary Drapings

Pandit Jawaharlal Nehru took it upon himself as usual to answer the opposition. His job usually is to attack the Left and especially the Communists and to hang revolutionary drapings round the resolution. This latter task was very essential in the present session. Both Rajaji and Vallabhbhai had talked too bluntly about giving material aid to Britain in her imperialist war. They had also stated that provisional National Government formed with the representatives of the various parties would fall short of complete independence, which was to emerge through a peaceful evolution. Constituent Assembly was not at all mentioned by them. To cover up these defects of the resolution, Nehru read out a written statement before the House. In this statement, he said that the independence of India was the foundation of the resolution and the provisional National Government would be soon replaced by a full National Government which would convene the Constituent Assembly. He expressed his impatience of the absence of any reply from the Government and stated that 'Congress could not stay its hand for long'.

Gibes at Communists

In his speech, Pt Nehru attacked the Communists. He hardly bothered to answer their arguments. He merely railed at them. He did not find it beneath his dignity to boast that he could any day hold his own among workers and peasants against the Communist Party. After this outburst against the Communists, he turned to the resolution, his attitude to which, he said, was a painful one. He did not like the idea of forming a provisional Government out of the Central Assembly. But for the time being, there was no alternative. The declaration of independence by Britain would change a lot. As for co-operation in war, he was against sending money out of the country but he would have no objection to sell goods to England. Rajaji confined his reply merely, to gibes at the Communists. He did not think it worth while to answer the points raised by the opposition. Pandit Nehru by his statement as well as by his speech had glossed over the ugly features of the resolution. Nehru's critical and impatient attitude had created a good impression on the audience, and the mover of the resolution did not want to spoil it.

The Vote and the Conclusions

Pt Balkrishna Sharma's amendment got 40 votes. This was made up of Socialists, Communists and their supporters. Royists did not vote. The main resolution was passed by 95 versus 47 votes, Gandhites and Royists remaining neutral. Thus the Poona session of the AICC has sanctioned a Resolution of Surrender with a big majority. What are the main conclusions to be drawn from this session?

1. Inspite of the decimation of the left by the Defence of India Act, the resistance to the resolution has been stubborn and heartening.
2. The bankruptcy and hypocrisy of Gandhian Non-Violence has been exposed. The Gandhites who claimed to adhere to 'true non-violence' voted against the First Resolution but remained neutral on the vital issue of co-operation in the war.
3. In the leading Gandhian group of the Congress, the leadership has now passed on to Rajaji, who is steering the course straight towards compromise and co-operation in war.
4. In the present situation, that is as long as new developments have not taken place in the European war (Hitler's attack on England), there seems to be little chance of a settlement. But the national leadership will not take any aggressive step but continue to wait and watch.
5. The danger of compromise is ever present. It is necessary to carry on a campaign of explanation among Congressmen debunking the deceptive arguments which are used to mask the surrender. These arguments are:
   (a) that the war has now become a defensive war, and ceased to be an imperialist one.
   (b) that the struggle would not now be necessary in view of the impending collapse of Britain. What is needed is preparation to convene a Constituent Assembly.
   (c) that the National Government formed out of the Central Assembly with the agreement of Britain would be a strategic weapon to win independence. ...

IV.   Liberals

56. Liberal Leader's Advice to Congress Leaders on Civil Disobedience Movement—Appeal to Postpone it

    Amrita Bazar Patrika, 2 May 1940.

Do not Launch Civil Disobedience—Dr Paranjpye's Appeal: Congress Leaders Urged to End Deadlock

An appeal to Congress leaders not to launch Civil Disobedience and to all parties to accept the offer by the British Government of Dominion Status, is made by Dr R.P. Paranjpye, President of the National Liberal Federation, in the course of a statement.

The Statement refers to the recent parliamentary debates and says that: The recent debates in both Houses of Parliament have clarified the position to a certain extent, there was nothing in it to which reasonable Indians can take any exception. It shows a real readiness to meet Indian aspirations as far as possible. The principle that an agreed solution arrived at by Indians themselves will be the determining factor in the future constitution is accepted by all parties in the Parliament. It is satisfactory that no support whatever was given by anybody to the Pakistan movement.

All that the official spokesmen urged was that Indians themselves should show a spirit of statesmanship, compromise and cooperation. Mention was also made of various practical considerations like defence, minorities and princes. But the mention of these matters appears to have incensed some of the Congress leaders. Mr Rajagopalachariar, who wields considerable influence in Congress circles, does not like to be reminded of them. Nobody contends that some measures taken in the past by the British might not have aggravated these difficulties.

Constituent Assembly

But it is not practical statesmanship to ignore them. The insistence on independence and a Constituent Assembly appears now to have become a kind of King Charles' head to the Congress leaders. They are even prepared to accept the Pakistan solution if a majority of the Muslims elected to a Constituent Assembly vote for it though all other sections and an appreciable minority of Muslims themselves might be against it.

Thus in an attempt to save this precious Constituent Assembly they are prepared to risk the unity of India. The Congress leaders think that the ballot box and the counting of heads are panacea for all evils and can solve all problems. Pure unadulterated democracy is not suited to present Indian conditions. Mere majority party rule has proved a failure. In France for a long time Government is carried on not by only one party but by a combination of different groups who agree on a certain programme and still France is nonetheless a democratic country. In England too Nationalist Government is functioning with a Cabinet composed of all parties. I think that Mr Rajagopalachariar unconsciously hits the nail on the head when he said that 'Great Britain and India were arguing with each other on the plane of reason and neither seemed to understand the heart of the other'. The tragedy of the Indian situation is that many of the leaders seem to have given a free rein to their hearts without the guidance and control of reason. Great thoughts originate in the heart but have to pass through the head. If the Congress and also the Muslim League leaders are prepared to argue on a rational plane, I think it will be possible to end the deadlock without great difficulty.

Even though the Congress is not prepared to consider realities I hope Government will act upon Mr Benn's suggestion to proceed at once with the enlargement of the Governor-General's Council so as to give it a non-official majority with an open offer to the Congress leaders to accept places on it and also set up a small body to devise a machinery for the purpose of solving the bigger political problem.

Terms of Settlement

The Secretary of State was right enough when he said that a wholly dissociated and independent India would admittedly not be in a position to secure the defence of India, but he forgot to mention that this is due to the long continued defence policy of the British Government itself. If he had announced a bold step in the matter of Indianization and of making the Indians more defence-minded he would have done a great deal to allay the feeling of suspicion among a large section of Indians about British intentions and at the same time enabled India to play a much bigger part in the war.

We realize that the settlement of a big political question like the constitution of India is not possible during the war time. The promise about the attainment of Dominion Status by India has been repeated; but a courageous policy on this matter of defence will rouse Indian enthusiasm far more than mere words of sympathy with our aspirations. It is possible, nay necessary, for such a policy to be enunciated and acted upon even while the war is going on.

I trust the Congress leaders will not launch Civil Disobedience and plunge the country into strife and disaster. Let all parties accept at its face value the offer by the British Government of Dominion Status and constitution at the end of the war as to the method by which this goal can be reached within the shortest time practicable and the enlargement of the Viceroy's Executive Council by the appointment of representative Indians. Having arrived at such an interim arrangement India should wholeheartedly support Britain in the war, for if Britain failed there will be an end of any prospect of democracy or independence for India.

57. Editorial on Mahatma Gandhi's Article—'Every Congress Committee a Satyagraha Committee'

Jam-e-Jamshed, Bombay, 4 April 1940.

The recent article of Mr Gandhi in the '*Harijan*' giving detailed instructions for organizing preparatory work for civil disobedience is having the effect desired by him. We now hear that the Executive Council of the UP Congress Committee has converted itself into a Supreme Satyagraha Council and is now preparing registers of Satyagrahis, both active and passive. We have no doubt the similar activity will shortly be undertaken by Congress Committees of different Provinces and their ramifications.

As we stated before, these activities clearly indicate that civil disobedience, notwithstanding Mr Gandhi's protest to the contrary, will shortly come. It is inconceivable that tens of thousands of men could be enrolled for active work as Satyagrahis and then be held back indefinitely. Matters are complicated and the situation precipitated by the recent programme of the Forward Bloc fixing April 6 as the day for commencing India's first war for independence. While there is nothing militant about Mr Bose's programme, it is clear that his suggestion of the 'Independence Week' activities include lectures to dissuade masses from participating in War. As such there is likelihood of many of these meetings all over India being banned, as they would conflict with the provisions of the Defence of India Act. Once the authorities take to suppression of the Forward Bloc's activities civil disobedience campaign would be automatically launched. Mr Gandhi will not be in a position then to prevent the hundreds of Satyagraha Committee's from active participation in the struggle.

Against this inevitable avalanche of mass lawlessness, some warnings are being sounded. One such warning comes from Dr Arundale who clearly tells Mr Gandhi that civil disobedience would very soon turn into civil war and that 'civil disobedience would be a crime at any time in India but never more so than now when the spirit of violence is abroad.' Dr Arundale makes it clear that failure of India to participate in War is to her own disadvantage. However, it is not enough to make a few protests against the coming political trouble. Today there are many sections of the public who strongly disapprove mass lawlessness in. any form, particularly when Hindu Muslim unity has been shattered to pieces both by the attitude of the Congress Governments and the extremism of the Muslim League. It is necessary that concerted action should be taken by these groups on an all-India scale. A rival organization with only one object, namely, preventing civil disobedience and minimizing its consequence to the country when it is launched, should be established. In such an organization all political parties can join since it is not designed to effect their distinctive political existence. An organization framed for one such basic object can afford a common platform to various political groups and help to stabilize Indian politics at a critical time.

For some time past the Liberals in India have watched closely the political developments in the country. Today they are best fitted to give a lead in constructing an organization which will pool the efforts of other political bodies in one common cause of saving India from the anarchy to which the Congress is slowly but definitely driving this country. The methods which an organization of this type can employ would include education of the masses in the dangers of civil resistance and the folly of India's neutrality in the present War even if she could maintain it....

D.   CAXTON HALL SHOOTING

58.   News Reports on Assassination of Michael O'Dwyer
Tribune, 14 March 1940.

Sir Michael O'Dwyer Shot Dead
Lord Zetland Wounded
Sir Louis Dane's Arm Broken
Lord Lamington Receives Injuries
Indian Commits Outrage

London, March 13.—Sir Michael O'Dwyer, Ex-Governor of the Punjab, was Shot Dead at a meeting of the India Association to-night by an Indian Gunman, who also wounded Lord Zetland, Secretary of State for India. Lord Zetland escaped with a slight Bullet Graze.

Sir Louis Dane, former Lieutenant Governor of the Punjab, was wounded and his arm was broken.

Lord Lamington, Ex-Governor of Bombay, also received arm injuries.

Brigadier General, Sir Percy Sykes, the well known authority on Middle East, who was standing next to Lord Zetland, escaped.

The shooting occurred at a crowded meeting in Caxton Hall, London.

59.   Newspaper Account of the Shooting
Tribune, 15 March 1940.

Lord Zetland Attends India Office
Lord Lamington has a Good Night
Sir Louis Dane Feels Fairly Comfortable
Mohammed Singh Azad Produced in Court
He Smiles and Chats with Police Officers

London, March 14. Lord Zetland attended the India Office at noon and performed his duties as normal.

The inquest on Sir Michael O'Dwyer is opening tomorrow.

Lord Zetland is quite well this morning. He was only bruised on the chest where a bullet glanced off his body. Two policemen were on duty outside his house.

Lord Lamington is reported to have had a good night and his condition is described as quite comfortable.

Sir Louis Dane stayed at the hospital where he was 'fairly comfortable'.

'Didn't Mean to Kill him'

The man, detained by the police, is named Mahomed Singh Azad[1] aged 37. Azad who is described as an engineer was charged at Bow Street with feloniously murdering Sir Michael O'Dwyer and remanded in custody for a week. A detective inspector said that Azad told him 'I did not mean to kill him. I just did it to protest. I did not mean to kill anybody.'

Azad was smiling and chatting to the two officers who accompanied him.

The police officers at the entrance of the Court examined the credentials of all who entered. While evidence was being given Azad stood almost non-chalantly in the docks with his legs crossed and one hand gripping the rail.

'Don't Want to Ask Questions'

At the conclusion of the evidence the Magistrate asked Azad, if he wanted to ask the Inspector any question.

Azad did not appear to understand and enquired: 'What?'

The Magistrate repeated the question and Azad said: 'No, Sir, I don't.'

The proceedings lasted only two minutes. The court was packed.

Azad remained in Bow Street for about quarter of an hour after he left the dock and then handcuffed to a detective and with another holding his arm, he was taken out through a side entrance and helped into a police service van and driven to Brixton.

The following are earlier messages giving details of the tragedy:

Lord Zetland fell by the side of his presidential chair and Lord Lamington and Sir Louis Dane were seen to be hit. A man clasping a gun was heard to shout 'Make way' and dashed down the crowded aisle towards the door.

For a moment there was a stampede, but two men jumped on him. No one in the audience of 150 was allowed to leave the meeting or telephone for two hours and a half. The police threw a cordon round the building and took statement from everybody present.

Lord Zetland told a reporter: 'I heard a bang close to me and then a sharp pain in my ribs. It knocked me out and, while I was down, I heard more shooting.'

A bullet was found in Lord Zetland's clothes at the hospital. The shooting occurred at a close, crowded meeting and a short, dark, thick-set Indian was seen to make his way towards the Press table. There were four shots in rapid succession and Sir M. O'Dwyer was seen to fall to the ground, bleeding profusely from a wound in the chest.

The Amritsar shooting affair[2], it will be recalled, occurred while Sir M. O'Dwyer was Lieut Governor of the Punjab.

Meeting in London

The High Commissioner for India has called a meeting of condolence for 4 p.m. at the India House to which all Indians resident in London have been invited.

'I am Not Worse for It'

Lord Zetland after his return to his Mayfair home from the hospital told Reuter, 'After the meeting was just over and I was moving away from the platform, there was a bang close to me.

It cannot have been more than two yards away. I felt a sharp pain in my ribs. It rather knocked me out and while I was lying down, I heard some other shooting going on but did not see what had happened. I was taken to St George's Hospital and X-rayed and nothing was found to be broken.'

Lord Zetland added: 'I do not think I am very much worse for it, though there are some bad bruises on my ribs. It was found afterwards that it was a bullet that struck me and there were marks in my clothes where it went through. The bullet was found in my clothes. My ribs are all bandaged up now so I do not know whether the bullet actually broke the skin.'

It was shortly after 19.00 that people were allowed to use the telephone or leave the meeting. Afterwards, the Assistant Commissioner of Police, Colonel Carter and high officials from the India Office arrived at the hall. Two doctors in the audience attended to Sir M. O'Dwyer and the wounded, but it was apparent that Sir M. O'Dwyer had died instantly.

It was learned that Lord Lamington had a part of his right hand shattered. After the shooting, Lord Lamington was leaning back on his chair bleeding from a forearm and in a state of collapse. Sir Louis Dane was bleeding from a hand.

Further details in hand show that Lord Zetland presided over the meeting and Sir Percy Sykes was on his right. Sir Louis Dane and Lord Lamington were at each side of the first row of the audience in the body of the hall.

Sir Louis Dane was taken to Westminster Hospital with slight injuries and it is stated that he would be detained for a few days.

It transpired that Sir Michael O'Dwyer had two bullet wounds in the region of the heart. His last words before leaving his Kensington Home were: 'Good bye, I shall be back in time for tea at 5 O'clock'.

Doctor Grace Mackinnon, a retired missionary doctor who has spent many years in India, was present in the Hall and she found Sir Michael O'Dwyer had died immediately.

The platform from which the meeting was addressed is about 8–12 feet high. Empty shells from the revolver were picked up and handed to the police....

Another eye-witness said that shots rang out in such quick succession that he thought it was an IRA bomb and added: 'I was surprised at the calmness of the people in the room and I did not hear any cries at all when the shots were fired except a shout for a doctor.'

Lady Lioneol Jacob, who was sitting in the third row, told Reuter that during the lecture she noticed an Indian acting in such a way that she commented on it to a friend. 'The vote of thanks had just been given when suddenly there were four or five shots. They were apparently made first at the platform and then at those in the front row. ...'

Another eye-witness stated there were about a dozen Indians at the meeting at which Sir Percy Sykes lectured on the history of Afghanistan. The meeting passed off quite normally until towards the end ....

Heroine of Tragedy

The heroine of the tragedy was an English girl, Miss Bertha Herring who valiantly tried to block the way of the assailant as, brandishing a revolver, he tried to push through the crowd, Sir Percy Sykes told Reuter.

Sir Percy, who had been delivering a lecture on Afghanistan, said, 'It was a very crowded meeting with about 400 people in the hall, about 50 standing at the sides. The meeting had just been declared closed and I was saying good-bye to Lord Zetland when shots rang out. At first I thought it was an IRA bomb. Then I saw Sir Michael O'Dwyer lying on the floor. I ran after his assailant. Just as I reached him, a very plucky English girl, Miss Bertha Herring, got hold of him and tried to bar his way.'

Sir Percy Sykes continued: 'It was particularly a plucky thing to do, as he still had the revolver. He knocked her aside but I do not think she was hurt. Then an Englishman, Mr C.W.H. Riches, jumped on the assailant's back. He was helped by Captain Banstead, a Deputy Commissioner in India. When I reached them, they were lying on the ground on the top of the assailant. Mr Riches handed me the man's revolver, a large service type of weapon. I think five shots been fired but I did not open it and handed it immediately to the police. I went back and saw Sir Michael O'Dwyer lying dead and Sir Louis Dane with a broken arm and Lord Lamington with a bullet in the hand, Lord Zetland lying apparently seriously wounded, but fortunately it proved only a graze.'

'The doctors who rendered assistance included Doctor Lawrence, brother of the "Lawrence of Arabia" and Colonel Reinhold of the Indian Medical Service.

'There was no panic at all and everyone behaved extremely well I am very proud of them. As far as I could see the assailant appeared to be a heavily built Asiatic, aged about 45. He created some attention during the meeting when he appeared to be taking some kind of pills. People were wondering who he was. Just before shooting he had his hand inside his waistcoat where the gun was apparently concealed'.

Indians Condemn Outrage

A statement issued by a number of Indians in London and signed by Doctors C.L. Katial, Sakir Mahmoodi, P.C. Bhandari and V.R. Bengeri, Secretary of the Hindu Association in Europe, expresses greatest regret at the news of the death of Sir Michael O'Dwyer and adds: 'Although we have disagreed with the political views of Sir Michael O'Dwyer, we must place on record our great sorrow at the tragedy. We have no doubt it will cause indescribable pain and anguish, as it has caused us, to leaders at the helm of the Congress and strong condemnation of this act is certain to be made throughout India.'

Parliamentarians' Condemnation

When the news of the shooting of Sir Michael O'Dwyer and the wounding of Lord Zetland and others reached the House of Commons in the evening, there were expressions of abhorrence on all sides. The general view was that it would elicit immediate repudiation in India and in this belief a number of prominent Parliamentarians, approached by Reuter, preferred not to elaborate their condemnation of the attacks.

Maulana Azad Expresses Sorrow

A Calcutta message says:

Maulana Abul Kalam Azad, President-elect of the Ramgarh session of the Indian National Congress, in an interview with the Associated Press said, 'We are very sorry for the tragedy. It is a relief to find that no political significance attaches to it.'

A New Delhi message says:

Sir Homi Mody, MLA, in the course of an interview said:

'The news of the outrage in London could not but be received with dismay in this country. If the motives were political in any sense, all that one can say is that the cause of freedom can never be advanced by crimes of this nature'.

Sir Mohammed Zaffrullah Khan, Law Member of the Government of India, has issued the following statement:

'I am sure that the whole country must have been deeply horrified, as I have been at the gruesome tragedy enacted in Caxton Hall, London, yesterday. I was greatly shocked and overwhelmed on reading the headlines in my morning paper and the sense of tragedy grew deeper and deeper as I read name after name of friends who had been wounded.'

Who is Mohammed Singh Azad

Our Special Correspondent wires:

According to Maulana Zafar Ali, the accused in the London outrage used to call himself even in India as Muhammad Singh Azad though he is a Sikh by birth. He was a Socialist worker about twenty years ago in the Punjab and was for some time in jail for making a seditious speech. Details of the outrage are being awaited with anxious interest, in lobbies where this is the only topic conversation.

While the resolution of sympathy was being discussed in the Council of State, it was noteworthy that Mr Brijlal Biyani, the only Congressman present in order to put in his token appearance under the Congress mandate, broke his silence and joined in the expression of abhorrence about the crime.

There was no such motion of condolence or sympathy moved in the Central Assembly which was more anxious to dispose of the general consideration stage of the Excess Profits Tax Bill....

---

[1] Ram Muhammad Singh Azad, an assumed name of Udham Singh (alias Ude Singh, alias Sher Singh, alias Frank Brazil), it is generally believed, was born on 26 December 1899 in a poor peasant family at Sunam in the present Sangrur District of Punjab. He is stated to have been a witness to the Jallianwala Bagh massacre and to the atrocities perpetrated on the people of Punjab under Martial Law in 1919. In the 1920s, he went to Uganda and subsequently to England and various other countries. While in USA, he came into contact with the Ghadarites. Back in India, he is believed to have been in touch with Bhagat Singh who greatly impressed him. In 1927, he was convicted under the Arms Act and sentenced to five years' imprisonment. In 1934, he went to England where he occasionally worked as a peddler and a carpenter. He is believed to have established contact with members of the Irish Republican Army. He was also in touch with the Ghadarites. He often traveled to Europe, including in the Soviet Union. On 12 March 1940, he had gone to the India Office where he saw a poster announcing a meeting of the East India Association and the Royal Central Asian Society to be held at Caxton Hall on 13 March 1940. He reached the venue of the meeting on 13 March 1940. Soon after the shooting, he was arrested. He was tried and was found guilty of murder. He was sentenced to death on 5 June 1940. The sentence was carried out on 31 July 1940.

[2] The reference is to the Jallianwala Bagh massacre.

60. 'London Shooting Outrage'

Tribune, 15 March 1940.

Indignation Felt in India

*New Delhi,
March 14.*

The news of the shooting outrage in London resulting in the death of Sir Michael O'Dwyer has aroused feelings of horror and indignation in official as well as unofficial circles and has for the moment thrown into the shade the more important news of the Russo–Finnish Peace Pact. The London outrage comes as a rude shock to the general confidence that a crime of this type was a thing of the past and that the happenings in the Punjab, which Sir Michael O'Dwyer's death recalls, were a forgotten chapter. In official circles profound regret is felt that an administrator of the standing and ability of Sir Michael O'Dwyer should have met with such a tragic end and anxious interest is shown in the possible repercussions of the crime in the Ramgarh deliberations.

Profound regret that such a dastardly crime should have been committed by an Indian was expressed by His Highness the Maharaja Jamsaheb of Nawanagar, Chancellor of the Chamber of Princes, in an interview. The entire Indian Princely Order deeply deplored the mad and meaningless action. It was not clear, said the Jamsaheb, what was the exact motive of the outrage, but whatever it was, the crime was such as to make the whole of India feel the deepest indignation. His Highness has sent the following cable to Lord Zetland:

'Have just heard shocking news of dastardly action at India Association meeting. My brother Princes join me in deeply deploring this cowardly and mad attempt. Every right thinking and sensible Indian should be ashamed of such an ignoble and meaningless action. Please accept my heartiest congratulations on your providential escape. Hope Your Lordship's injuries are only minor and you will soon recover from shock. Please also convey my deepest sympathies with which the entire Indian Princely Order associates to Sir Michael O'Dwyer's family.'—API

61. 'The Shooting Outrage'

Editorial, *Tribune*, 15 March 1940.

Anything more shocking than the outrage that took place at a meeting of the India Association in London on Wednesday night, when Sir Michael O'Dwyer, ex-Lieutenant Governor of the Punjab, was shot dead, Sir Louis Dane, another ex-Lieutenant Governor of the Punjab, was wounded and his arm was broken, Lord Lamington, ex-Governor of Bombay received arm injuries, and Lord Zetland, Secretary of State for India, was himself wounded, though slightly, cannot easily be imagined. Profoundly as all sections of public opinion in India will deplore the incident, no section of opinion will condemn it more strongly, more energetically or more unreservedly than the party of self-government between whom and the chief victim of the outrage there was little love lost during the period of his administration in this country. The reason is quite clear. Not only is that party irrevocably committed to non-violence, but it believes with the strength and favour of a religious conviction that violence is the weakest of political weapons, and that too often its only tangible effect is to retard the cause of freedom and progress. It was Lord Acton who once pathetically declared that twenty-five times in one century had the cause of political progress in Europe been interrupted by actual or attempted violence. In our own country anyone can recall repeated instances of such set-back during the last forty years. It is, indeed, a tragic irony of fate that these acts of violence have occurred with almost clock-like regularity exactly at those moments in history when they were calculated to do most harm to the cause of progress, when but for them the victory of that cause seemed almost assured. No wonder that the conviction has sunk deep in the hearts of the overwhelming majority of political-mined Indians that the complete eschewing of violence is the first condition of political advance.

Of course in saying this we are proceeding on the assumption that the assailant's motive was political. That assumption easily suggests itself in this case, because all the three principal victims of the outrage were subjected to severe criticism by progressive Indians for their measures and policy as provincial rulers in India. *Reuter's* message itself contains the suggestion, because it recalls the Amritsar shooting affair which occurred while Sir Michael O'Dwyer was Lieutenant Governor of the Punjab, while our local Anglo-Indian contemporary goes a step further and says that 'it was during Sir Michael O'Dwyer's last year as Governor that serious disturbances occurred at Amritsar, culminating in the Jallianwalla Bagh incident in which between four and five hundred people were killed during firing by the military under orders from General Dyer,' that 'the disorders in Amritsar then ceased but widespread disturbances took place in the Punjab, and martial law was proclaimed over a wide area,' and that 'considerable feeling was roused at the character of the measures taken to restore order in the province.' All this is quite true, but it took place twenty years ago, and these twenty years have witnessed great changes, both subjective and objective, in India. Subjectively non-violence, which was accepted as a policy by political India even then, has become almost an article of faith with it now, thanks to the unsurpassable emphasis laid on it by the greatest apostle of non-violence that our age has known. Objectively the Home Rule movement, which Sir Michael O'Dwyer so strongly disliked and which he sought by every means in his power to keep out of the Punjab, has now penetrated to the inner most recesses of the Punjab as of the rest of India and the British Government themselves have declared the establishment of Dominion Home rule to be the objective of their Indian policy. In the provincial sphere they claim to have established Home rule already, and in no Indian province has Home Rule in this limited sense been more successfully established, in their view, than in the province over which Sir Michael ruled and from which he sought rigidly to exclude all agitation for it. It is not at an easy to see why any person, whose motive was political, should have chosen such a moment for making a violent attack upon the principal protagonist or protagonists of a policy which is no longer the official policy of the British Government. Our own belief, indeed, is that the assailant drew his inspiration from and was misled by the example of the Irish Republican Army and wanted to produce an Indian counterpart to the sensation produced by that party in England by its recent acts of terrorism. But the question of motive does not and cannot affect one's judgment of the crime itself. Irrespective of the motive the people of India will condemn the crime not only with one voice but with all the strength and emphasis they can command, and will express their whole-hearted sympathy both with the family of the deceased ex-Lieutenant Governor and with the other victims of the outrage who happily have not been seriously hurt. In the case of Lord Zetland himself this expression of sympathy will be coupled with a note of thankfulness that he escaped with nothing worse than a slight bullet graze.

We do not for one moment believe that this outrage, which obviously was the work of an individual who is entirely out of touch with the ruling sentiments and ideas of India and particularly of all political parties and organizations in the country, will cause any change in the policy of the British Government. No one can have forgotten in this connection what happened twenty-eight years ago when no less a person than the then Viceroy of India was the victim of a similar outrage at Delhi. The very first words he uttered on regaining his consciousness were, 'No change of policy' and the policy which the Government followed fully reflected this attitude. It is inconceivable that they will adopt any other attitude in this case. They know that the cause of India is just and that the hands of those who are fighting for that cause are perfectly clean. They know, too, that by delaying the inevitable transformation they can only put themselves in the wrong, both in the eyes of India herself and of the world, and that at a time when they urgently need the sympathy and the moral support of civilized humanity. The only true policy for them is to go forward with courage and steadfastness and carry out as speedily as they can the policy enunciated by Lord Linlithgow in his latest statement. That is the best and most effective answer they can give to the crime, no matter by what motive it may have been inspired. That, we are sure, is only answer they will give if they are wise.

62. Congress Working Committee Resolution on O'Dwyer's Assassination, Wardha, 15–18 March 1940

Indian Annual Register, 1940, Vol. I, p. 237.

'The Working Committee has learnt with deep regret of the assassination of Sir Michael O'Dwyer and the wounding of Marquess of Zetland and others by a person said to be an Indian. The Committee does not attach any political significance to this unfortunate act of violence. Nevertheless, it wishes to reiterate its conviction that all such acts are injurious to the national cause.'

63. Extracts from Notes Brought into Court by Udham Singh (Mohammed Singh Azad) on 5 June 1940

Reproduced in Sikander Singh, *Udham Singh,* Amritsar, 1998, pp. 351–2.

...A 150 years English terrorism in India has shown it is impossible for the British to crush the Indian people. I did this to protest and uphold my country right even though I die. My greatest wish has not been fulfilled to see my country free again. I would rather die for the cause of my people than live in misery under the British terrorism. I nor my people were not born in this world to be ruled by the English Imperialism.

India will rise again....

...I am not afraid to die. I am proud to die for such a glorious cause to help to free my native land and I hope when I am gone that in my place will come thousands of my countrymen to drive you vultures until you not only free our country but also clear to hell out of it.

64. Udham Singh's Statement in Court After his Conviction

Cipher Telegram from Secretary of State to Government of India, Home Department. Reproduced in Sikander Singh, *Udham Singh,* Amritsar, 1998, p. 356.

5.6.1940

IMMEDIATE

No. 367   Begins Reference Udham Singh Case

Jury after absence of about 90 minutes returned verdict of guilty of murder/Stop/Before sentence was passed accused began reading a long violently-worded abusive statement directed against British Imperialism/Stop/Judge checked him and asked him to pass statement up for his perusal/Stop/accused refused to do this saying that he wanted the Jury and everyone in the Court to hear him/Stop/He expressed his detestation of British rule and said that the people of this country were also suffering under British Imperialism/Stop/He was allowed to read a little further but the Judge eventually told him to stop/Stop/As sentence was about to be pronounced accused shouted 'Inqilab' several times and loudly declared that he was quite ready to die for his country/Stop/As he was about to be removed he spat towards the Judge with some offensive reference to the Empire and the King/Stop/His statement has been secured STOP JUDGE GAVE DIRECTIONS TO PRESS THAT IT SHOULD NOT BE PUBLISHED ENDS.

E. HOLWELL MONUMENT AGITATION

65. Subhas Bose to Lead Campaign Against Holwell Monument

Subhas Bose's article in *Forward Bloc*, 29 June 1940. Sisir Kumar Bose (ed.), *Crossroads: The Works of Subhas Chandra Bose, 1938–40*, Calcutta, 1981 (2nd edition), pp. 344–5.

There has been unavoidable delay in bringing out this issue. In fact, we have been forced to miss one week, thanks to the kind attention of the Government of Bengal. Our office was searched and our security was forfeited. Fresh security to the tune of Rs 2000 had to be deposited before we could bring out the next issue.

This has been all to the good. It has put our back up. We have, therefore, to push on with our plan of work and put more zest and more zeal into it. The campaign against the Holwell Monument, which was the mandate of the Bengal Provincial Conference, has to be taken up at once. The third July, 1940, is going to be observed in Bengal as the Sirajuddowla Day—in honour of the last independent King of Bengal. The Holwell Monument is not merely an unwarranted stain on the memory of the Nawab, but has stood in the heart of Calcutta for the last 150 years or more as the symbol of our slavery and humiliation. That monument must now go.

On the 3rd of July next will commence the campaign against that monument and the writer has decided to march at the head of the first batch of volunteers on that day.

The second session of the All-India Conference of the Forward Bloc met at Nagpur on the 18th and 19th June. The Conference was a great success and a number of important resolutions were passed. The proceedings of the Conference have influenced public opinion throughout the country, including the mind of the Congress Working Committee, which was meeting simultaneously. Nagpur has virtually repeated the call of Dacca. The decisions at Nagpur may be summarized in the following manner.

1 Intensify the struggle and widen its scope under the slogan—'All power to the Indian people.'
2 Demand from the British Government immediate transference of full power to the Indian people through a provisional national government.
3 Work simultaneously for national unity and particularly for Hindu Muslim unity.
4 Organize Citizens' Defence Corps on a non-party basis with a view to preserving internal unity and solidarity during the transitional period.

Subsequent to and in furtherance of the Nagpur decisions, the writer has in a recent statement advocated the setting up of National Cabinet at the Centre, accompanied by National Cabinets in the provinces. The situation today is dynamic and in order to handle it properly, a dynamic policy is needed. History has put us to the test. Let us not be found wanting. It is for us now to make our country's future or to mar it.

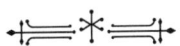

66. The Holwell Monument

Amrita Bazar Patrika, 2 July 1940.

Removal Urged
Premier Promises: A Decision This Month

A public meeting was held at Albert Hall on Monday evening when the demand for the removal of the Holwell Monument was reiterated and a hope was voiced that the Bengal Ministry would concede to this demand of the public immediately.

The meeting was presided over by Syed Muazzam Hossain, MLC of Faridpore and was addressed by a number of leaders belonging to both communities, Hindus and Moslems. The Holwell Monument, it was emphasized by the speakers, should have been removed by the present Ministry who described themselves as a popular Ministry. Moreover the Ministry, being a League Ministry, ought to have done away with this monument erected it was stated for the purpose of humiliating Bengalees as a nation.

It had been proved beyond any shadow of doubt, observed A. Waseq, President of the All-Bengal Muslim Students' Federation, that there was no historic truth behind the establishment of the monument. The story was invented and the monument was erected to blacken their national character. The Muslim students had been demanding its removal since the Ministry came into power but for some reason or other their demand had not been conceded. It was high time, the speaker observed, that the monument should be removed.

Sj Subhas Chandra Bose said that the agitation for the removal of the Holwell Monument had stirred the feelings of both the communities, Hindus and Moslems. This was a happy sign indeed and Sj Bose had no doubt of their success in the matter. The hour for action had struck and Sj Bose would call upon their youths to join in the agitation.

67. Newspaper Report of Subhas Bose's Arrest

Bombay Chronicle, 3 July 1940.

Calcutta,
July 2

Mr Subhas Chandra Bose, twice-President of the Indian National Congress and Founder-President of the All-India Forward Bloc, has just been arrested at his Calcutta residence in Elgin Road under Rule 129 of the Defence of India Rules.

Rule 129 of the Defence of India Act Rules runs as follows:
FURTHER POWERS OF ARREST AND DETENTION.

Any police officer not below the rank of Head Constable or any other officer of the Government empowered in this behalf by the general or special order of the Central Government may arrest without warrant any person whom he reasonably suspects of having acted, of acting, or of being about to act with intent to assist any state at war with His Majesty or in a manner prejudicial to the public safety or to the efficient prosecution of the war.

The decision not to change his programme regarding the removal of the Holwell monument in spite of the Chief Minister's appeal, is announced by Mr Subhas Chandra Bose, in a statement to the press.

Referring to the announcement made by the Chief Minister that the Government would declare its decision within a month Mr Bose says that the letter of the President of the Bengal Provincial Congress Committee (suspended) in this connection was delivered at the office of the Chief Minister on the 18th July (18 June).

'The Government have had plenty of time to consider the question but have not chosen to take any action so far.

The Chief Minister has not given us any indication as to what definite announcement he will make at the end of this month.

We have bitter experience of the delaying tactics of this Government in connection with our demand for the release of political prisoners.

In the circumstances the Chief Minister's statement is altogether unsatisfactory. If the Government feel inclined to respond to the public demand in this matter they can easily come to decision inside 24 hours and announce it to the public.'—AP.

68. Newspaper Report on the Commencement of Agitation for Removal of Holwell Monument

Amrita Bazar Patrika, 4 July 1940.

Four Satyagrahis led by Sj Nirmal Chandra Singh and including Sj Hirendra Nath Chakravarty were arrested by the Police on Wednesday afternoon while attempting to demolish (Block Hole) Holwell Monument situated on the north-west corner of the Dalhousie Square.

An agitation was recently launched by the suspended BPCC under the leadership of Mr Subhas Chandra Bose for the removal of the Monument and some time ago Mr Bose had announced his decision to lead the first batch of Satyagrahis on July 3 with that end in view.

In expectation of this move there was a very large concentration of Police Force round about the area. They included all branches of the police force mounted and foot. There were also armed police and police equipped with steel helmets, tear gas and gas masks. The force was headed by Rai Bahadur Bonbehari Mukherjee, Deputy Commissioner of Police, Rai Bahadur Pravat Nath Mukherjee, Assistant Commissioner of Police, South Division and some officers. Most of the forces were stationed inside the Customs House compound, Writer's Buildings and Dalhousie Square Tank compound.

The police were posted at about 3 p.m. By this show of police force naturally large crowds were attracted but the police did not allow the crowd to remain stationary but kept them moving. A very large crowd gathered on the steps of the General Post Office. The windows and balconies of the Government Buildings were also crowded.

The police had to keep a long watch. At about 5-20 in the evening four boys suddenly stepped down from the pavement near the comer of the General Post Office and proceeded towards the Monument with cries of Bandemataram. As they had gone a few steps and were about 10 yards off the Monument, they were stopped by the police. Rai Bahadur Bonbehari Mukherjee and Rai Bahadur Pravat Nath Mukherjee walked up to them. These boys had hammers and chisels in their hands. The Deputy Commissioner asked them, 'Why do you come here?' The tallest of them, apparently their leader, one Nirmal Sinha replied, 'To demolish the Monument'. The Deputy Commissioner ordered them to be arrested and sent to Lalbazar. Immediately a prison van appeared on the scene and the boys were taken to Lalbazar.

The police were stationed there till late in the evening but there was no further demonstration.

The Commissioner of Police, Mr C.S. Fairweather, visited the place at about 6 p.m.

Earlier, at 5 O'clock, Mr Sarat Chandra Bose in court dress was seen passing through the area in a covered car. He came from the south and went away towards the east rounding the Monument. Among others who were seen there just before the incident were Mr Narendra Narayan Chakravarti, Mr Anil Roy, Mrs Lila Roy. Mrs Bimal Prativa Devi came to the place shortly after the arrests had been made and parked her car on the west side of the Monument. She was asked by the police to move away her car which she did.

Sir Nazimuddin, Home Minister, was also seen touring round the area in a covered car.

More Arrests
Mr Hemanta Bose in Custody

Mr Hemanta Kumar Bose, a prominent member of the Provincial Forward Bloc, was arrested on Wednesday morning under Rule 129 of the Defence of India Rules.

It is understood that Mr Bose will be detained in one of the jails in Alipore.

Mr Krishna Kumar Chatterji, Assistant Secretary of the suspended Bengal Provincial Congress Committee and a prominent member of the Provincial Forward Bloc, was also arrested on Wednesday under Rule 129 of the Defence of India Rules.

'Forward Bloc' Press Searched Proof and Manuscript Copy of Sj Bose's Appeal Seized

Following a search of the Press, where the English Weekly, Forward Bloc, is printed, the keeper of the Press, the printer and a compositor, were arrested on Wednesday under the Defence of India Rules.

The proof copy and the manuscript of an appeal issued by Mr Subhas Chandra Bose soon after his arrest were seized by the Police. Another Assistant Secretary of the suspended Bengal Provincial Congress Committee, Mr Pannalal Mitra, was taken into custody on Wednesday afternoon under the Defence of India Rules.

Sardar S.S. Caveeshar Left for Lahore on Wednesday Night

Sardar Sardul Singh Caveeshar, President of the Forward Block was in Calcutta for the last few days and issued necessary instructions to the secretariat of the All India Office in Calcutta. He left on Wednesday night for Lahore by the Delhi–Calcutta Mail.

Nawab Sirajuddowla Commemoration Meeting at Town Hall

In Commemoration of Nawab Sirajuddowla, the last king of independent Bengal, Bihar and Orissa, there was a public meeting held at the Town Hall on Wednesday evening.

The efforts of Nawab Sirajuddowla to maintain independence were described by a large number of speakers belonging to both the communities, Hindus and Moslems, and by a resolution the meeting, which was largely attended, requested the Provincial Government, Universities and the Text book committees to delete 'all false accounts and mischievous statements' connected with the life-story of the Nawab.

Special stress was laid at the meeting on the question of the removal or demolition of the Holwell Monument based on a story known as the Black Hole tragedy and said to be an act of Nawab Sirajuddowla.

Expressing regret at the statement of the Chief Minister, Mr A.K. Fazlul Huq, on this question, so far as it lacked in any definite declaration as to whether it would be removed or not a resolution urging upon the Ministry to come to an immediate decision over the issue was unanimously passed at the meeting.

The meeting was presided over by Syed Baddurozzoha, MLA (a member of the ministerial party), rand was held under the auspices of the Sirajuddowla Anniversary Committee.

The Resolutions

The following resolutions were adopted at the meeting: 'This meeting pays its respectful homage to the sacred memory of Nawab Sirajuddowla, the last independent ruler and martyr-prince of Bengal, Bihar and Orissa.

'This meeting strongly condemns the foreign historians who with a view to serving a definite political motive painted the character of the illustrious Nawab in the darkest possible colour and call upon the historians of Bengal to vindicate the ill-fated Nawab by giving a true account of his life and work.

'This meeting requests the Government, Universities, and the Text-Book Committees to see that all false accounts and mischievous statements relating to the unfortunate Nawab be deleted from all Text Books.'

The other resolution *'inter alia'* expressed regret at the statement of the Chief Minister of Bengal so far as it lacked in any definite declaration as to whether the Holwell Monument would be removed or not and urged upon the Ministry to come to an immediate decision.

The meeting commenced deliberation in a calm atmosphere. The situation was found charged when the question of the Holwell Monument came up. While leaders of the Muslim Students' Federation expressed opinion that the Government should be given a chance to act on the issue for a fortnight, a section of the gathering protested dubbing the statement of the Chief Minister as wholly unsatisfactory. After some discussion the meeting adopted a resolution stated above.

Police Guard

From the beginning till the end of the meeting a large contingent of police force was stationed round about the Town Hall. All approaches to the Dalhousie Square where the Holwell Monument is, were guarded and no pedestrian was allowed to go in that direction. A few posters carried by some members of the All-Bengal Students Federation were taken away by the Police.

Among the large number of speakers who addressed the meeting were Mr Naharendu Dutta Majumdar, Mr Moazzem Hossain Choudhury, MLC, Syed Buddorozzoha, MLA, Mr Basanta Kumar Majumder, Miss Leela Roy, Mr Nurul Hudda and Mr A.W. Aeseque of the All-India Muslim Students' Federation.

A Lathi Charge

There was an incident at the close of the meeting. The police made a lathi charge on a batch of Muslim students in front of the Town Hall when they were proceeding towards the maidan after attending the meeting. A few of them were injured along with Messrs Marus Hossain, editor of 'Chhatra Sakti' and Nurul Hudda, Assistant Secretary of the All-Bengal Students Federation.

69. Newspaper Report of Holwell Monument Satyagraha

Bombay Chronicle, 4 July 1940.

Calcutta,
July 3

Satyagraha at Calcutta Batch of Four Marching to Holwell Monument Arrested

Nirmal Singh, a prominent member of the Provincial Forward Bloc, and three others, composing the first batch of Satyagrahis were arrested at quarter past five as they were approaching the Holwell monument.

Armed with hammers and shouting slogans, they came close to the monument when they were stopped by the police led by the Deputy Commissioner, South Section, about ten yards away.

The Satyagrahis were taken into custody and marched off to the Police Headquarters at Lal Bazar.—AP.

Police *Bundobust*

While the monument proper is being surrounded by a number of sergeants, its various approaches are lined by armed and lathi police. Mounted police are also standing by inside the Dalhousie Square in front of the monument.

The monument, standing as it does at the entrance of Clive street, the business quarter of Calcutta, has attracted a crowd.

Demand for Removal of Monument

Speeches demanding the immediate removal of the Holwell Monument were made by about a dozen Congress and Muslim leaders, including four MLAs at a public meeting held at Town Hall this evening in observance of the Sirajadulla Day. Mr S. Hadrudduja, MLA, presented.

The speakers also protested against the arrest of Mr Subhas Chandra Bose and criticized the policy adopted by the Government in regard to the question of the removal of the monument.

After the meeting a section of the audience formed a procession and attempted to march towards the monument from the Town Hal, but they were stopped by the police and dispersed—AP.

A joint notice of a resolution has been given for the Calcutta Corporation by Messrs Subhas Chandra Bose and Satish Chandra Bose requesting the Bengal Government to remove or demolish the Holwell Monument—United Press.

70. Bombay Socialists' Meeting on Subhas Bose's Arrest

Bombay Chronicle, 'Black Hole Tragedy, A Malicious Concoction', 5 July 1940.

Bombay Socialists Congratulate Bose on his Arrest

To congratulate Mr Subhas Chandra Bose on his arrest under the Defence of India Act a Public meeting was held on Thursday evening, under the auspices of the Bombay Congress Socialist Party.

Mr Meherally presiding over the meeting referred to the circumstances which led to the arrest of Sjt Bose. The arrest had not come as a surprise to them. Prominent political workers were daily being arrested under the Defence of India Act in all parts of the country.

Referring to the Holwell monument for whose removal Sjt Bose had started satyagraha, he said that the Black Hole tragedy was the malicious concoction of Holwell's imagination. Prominent historians had proved beyond a shadow of doubt that the 'Black Hole' had never existed. The story was given currency with a view to malign Indian people.

Sjt Bose was right in his decision to fight for the immediate removal of the monument which stood as a living insult to the self-respect of India. The speaker criticized the weak-kneed policy of the Bengal Government and in this connection made a reference to the bold step taken by Mr Rajagopalachari's Government in removing the Neil statue in Madras.

Among others who addressed the meeting were Messrs Ashok Mehta and Salehbhai.

71. Newspaper Report on Conviction: Attempt on Holwell Monument
Amrita Bazar Patrika, 5 July 1940.

Four Convicted
To Suffer 8 Days' R.I. Each

Nirmal Chandra Sinha, Birendra Nath Chakravarti, Satya Ranjan Mookherjee and Nitya Ranjan Ghosh have been convicted under Section 68 of the Calcutta police Act and sentenced to eight days' rigorous imprisonment each by Mr K.C. Law, Honorary Presidency Magistrate for having been riotous and disorderly conduct by creating a disturbance being armed with hammers and shouting slogans and forcibly attempting to break through the police barrier in order to demolish the Holwell Monument at Dalhousie Square at about 5-30 p.m. on July 3.

Sergeant Jolly, examined by Mr J.N. Lahiri, Chief Court Inspector, stated that they had information that people would be coming to break down the Monument in the afternoon of July 3. He was on duty there from 4 o'clock. A big crowd assembled there and at about 5-20 p.m. the accused came in a procession shouting 'Bande Mataram' and 'Subhas Bose-ki-Jai.' When they were about 10 feet away from the Monument, each having a hammer in hand, witness stopped them by putting his lathi across them. The Deputy Commissioner of Police asked them where they were going. They said they were going to demolish the Monument. They were then put under arrest.

Mr Lahiri—By their conduct, did you apprehend that there would be a breach of the peace among the people who had assembled there?—Yes.

Did you give them warning to disperse before arresting them?—The Deputy Commissioner asked them and they said they were determined to go to demolish the Monument.

Inspector A. Hyder deposed that he was also on duty near the monument and that the accused wanted, inspite of the police opposition, to forcibly go and demolish the monument.

Mr Lahiri prayed to the court for the maximum sentence provided under the law in view of the seriousness of the offence committed by the accused.

The accused pleaded not guilty and refused to take part in the proceedings as 'Satyagrahis'. They received the sentence with a smile.

72.   Views of a European Member of Central Assembly

Amrita Bazar Patrika, 6 July 1940.

'An Obstacle to Unity'
Mr Griffiths Urges Removal of Holwell Monument

The removal of the Holwell Monument, which he describes as an 'obstacle to unity', to the European cemetery, is suggested by Mr P.J. Griffiths, a retired LCS, and a member of the Central Assembly in a statement to the Press on Friday.

Mr Griffiths says, 'I have been somewhat surprised at the heat displayed in certain quarters regarding the proposed removal of the Holwell Monument. Controversy may always be expected to engender heat but in the present case there is no controversy; for as far as I am aware no responsible member of any community is opposed to the removal of the monument. For my part, as a European I cannot approve of the continuance of anything which tends to interfere with the good relations between Indians and ourselves. I am not concerned with the historical issues involved nor am I competent to discuss them. I am only concerned with the acts that this monument commemorates no event which is worth remembrance and that its existence is an offence to many of my Indian friends. If this monument does represent a historic fact let that fact be the concern of Dryasdust in his study. Let us who are concerned with the present and the future devote our energies to the more urgent task of uniting against the mechanized barbarians of Germany and in order that we may do so more firmly, let the Holwell monument be removed to the European cemetery.

I trust Government will not waste time on academic discussions but will at once remove this obstacle to unity. I am confident that such action will have the full support of the leaders of the European community'.

73.   Newspaper Report of Holwell Monument Satyagraha

Amrita Bazar Patrika, 10 July 1940.

Holwell Monument Satyagraha
20 Arrested, Eighteen Including Ten Sikhs on Trial

A large crowd collected near the Holwell Monument in Dalhousie Square on Tuesday afternoon when 20 Satyagrahis in three batches proceeded to the spot with hammers, shouting all sorts of political slogans at regular intervals.

The first batch consisting of six volunteers on arrival near the steps of the monument shouting 'Bande Mataram' were surrounded by the police and arrested.

About an hour after another batch of six Satyagrahis came and they were also similarly arrested.

There was a lull for some time and then at 5-30 p.m. the third batch consisting of eight Satyagrahis arrived and before they could proceed further the police arrested them and took them to thana in a prison van.

After the arrest of the third batch no other Satyagrahis were seen. The police guarded the monument till a late hour at night.

Accused Remanded to Custody

Eighteen Satyagrahis including ten Sikhs and one Moslem, who were arrested on Monday near the Holwell Monument, were prosecuted under the Defence of India Rules before Mr R. Gupta, Chief Presidency Magistrate, for holding processions without the permission of the Commissioner of Police.

The accused were remanded to jail custody and the hearing was adjourned to July 29.

74. Protest Meetings Against Subhas Bose's Arrest

Amrita Bazar Patrika, 11 July 1940.

Sj Subhas Bose's Arrest—Public Resentment—Immediate Release Demanded

Resentment at the arrest of Sj Subhas Chandra Bose was expressed at a public meeting held on Wednesday, evening at the Albert Hall. Moulavi A. Shiraji was in the Chair.

A resolution protesting against Sj Bose's arrest and demanding his immediate release was adopted by the meeting.

Moulavi A. Shiraji addressing the meeting said that their grievance was not Sj Bose's arrest, for they knew the latter had chosen in his life, a path which was not strewn with roses, but with thorns. Arrest and imprisonment were no terrors for him. But what they resented was his arrest and detention without trial.

The speaker appealed to all to forget party feuds. They should whole-heartedly support the cause for which Sj Subhas Bose stood. He hoped if support and sympathy were forthcoming from all sides, the present struggle which had already begun was sure to end in success.

Sacrifices Recalled

In moving the resolution Sj Jyotish Ghosh recalled Sj Bose's services and sacrifices in the cause of their country's freedom. He asked the countrymen to follow his lead.

Sj Anil Roy seconding the resolution said that arrests of this nature for an identical cause had been made in every country. Arrests and imprisonments in the struggle for freedom were not new things. Even the history of their country was replete with innumerable instances illustrating how lots of young men went through terrible hardships. Subhas Babu had set the ball rolling. Now it was their duty to carry it on. What Sj Roy would like to emphasize was that mere protests would not do. They had got to translate the resolve into action.

Sj Gopal Haldar said that a great moment in their life had arrived. It would be extremely unwise to let it go. They would be honouring Subhas Babu if they, utilizing the present moment, acted up to his programme.

Sjta Bimal Prativa Devi said that they should not rest content with making speeches only: The stage of delivering speeches was over. Now was the time for action.

Sjta Lila Roy said that they had made another protest meeting in this very hall. But protest after protest would yield no result unless they translated the protest into solid action.

Other speakers were Moulavi Ejabuddin Ahmed, Sj Aswini Ganguly, Sj Purushottam Roy, Bir Singh Sanjiban, Sj Asutosh Das, Sj Harnam Singh and Sj Basanta Kumar Majumdar.

Protest Meeting at Howrah

A largely attended public meeting held at the Howrah Town Hall on Wednesday evening passed a resolution protesting against the arrest of Sj Subhas Chandra Bose under the Defence of India Rules and congratulating him on his courage and patriotism.

75. Newspaper Reports on Holwell Monument Satyagraha

Amrita Bazar Patrika, 11 July 1940.

Holwell Monument Satyagraha—Wednesday's Situation—104 Satyagrahis Arrested Up-to-date

Holwell Monument Satyagraha situation remained unchanged on Wednesday when Satyagrahis, began to pour in at Dalhousie Square from noon, as usual, with hammers in hands.

Immediately after 1 O'clock shouts of 'Bande-Mataram' was heard from a distance and soon a batch of five Satyagrahis came up to the place where the monument is situated shouting all sorts of political slogans when they were surrounded by the police and arrested.

There was a lull for about four hours and just after 5 P.M. another batch of six Satyagrahis carrying tri-coloured flags rushed towards the monument and one of them actually reached the steps and struck a blow on the monument with a hammer with shouts of 'Bande Mataram'.

The police immediately secured the batch and sent them to the Police Station.

Two more batches consisting of four or five Satyagrahis respectively arrived again in quick succession and some of them attempted to throw hammers at the monument but they were similarly arrested.

No more Satyagrahis arrived at the place after 6.30 P.M. and the monument was guarded by the police as usual till a late hour at night.

Since the Satyagraha movement was started altogether 104 Satyagrahis have been arrested.

Students Federation Demands for Demolition of Holwell Monument

The Working Committee of the Bengal Provincial Students Federation at a meeting held on Wednesday supported the demand for the demolition of the Holwell Monument and protested the action of the Government of Bengal in arresting Sjt Subhas Chandra Bose and others in connection with the Satyagraha started for the purpose.

The meeting also urged for release of those arrested, and opined that a mass student movement must be created on this issue if this agitation is to achieve its object.

20 Remanded to Custody

Twenty Satyagrahis, who were arrested on Tuesday on their attempting to break Holwell Monument, were prosecuted before Mr R. Gupta Chief Presidency Magistrate, under the Defence of India Rules on a charge of taking part in processions at Dalhousie Square without the permission of the Commissioner of Police.

The accused were remanded to jail custody and the hearing was adjourned to July 30.

76. Muslim Students' League Demands Demolition of the Holwell Monument

Amrita Bazar Patrika, 15 July 1940.

Holwell Monument—Assurance for Immediate Demolition Urged— Muslim Students' Demand Demonstration Before Mr Fazlul Huq's Residence—Police on Scene

The Bengal Premier's residence at Park Circus was the scene of an unusual demonstration by the Muslim Students, about 250 in numbers, members of the Bengal Provincial Muslim Students' League.

For about a couple of hours, the students reinforced by fifty of their Hindu brethren, shouting 'Alla Ho Akbar' demanded of Mr A.K. Fazlul Huq a definite assurance for the immediate demolition of the Holwell monument.

The Premier appeared on the balcony of his house, delivered a harangue, tried to persuade the boys to return home like 'good boys'; but the youths continued to shout. Annoyed beyond measure Mr Huq retired inside.

Soon after, the police made their appearance on the scene but eventually withdrew following what might be regarded a dramatic gesture by Mr H.A.H. Ispahani, MLA and ex-President, Bengal Muslim Students' League.

At about half past six in the evening Muslims students, mostly residents of Baker, Carmichael and Eliot hostels and other members of the Muslim Students' League headed by Mr Nurul Huda, Joint Secretary of the League, began to assemble before the Jhawtalla residence of the Chief Minister. Half an hour later about fifty Hindu boys belonging to the Park Circus area also joined the assemblage.

Their shouts drew Mr Fazlul Huq out of his room. Standing on the balcony he demanded what the students wanted. They asked an assurance from the Premier that the Holwell Monument should be removed at an early date.

In reply Mr Huq bade them disperse like good boys. The boys refused to move. Thereupon, the Premier left the balcony and went inside.

At this stage Khwaja Nasirulla, a prominent member of the Coalition Party intervened and invited Mr Nurul Huda and four other students to have an interview with the Premier. They are reported to have found in that room Sir Nazimuddin, Mr Tamizuddin Khan, Mr M.B. Mullick and several other prominent coalitionists.

Premier Refuses to Give Assurance

The interview, however, proved abortive. Mr Huda repeated his demand that an assurance should be given by the Premier that the Monument would be removed within a definite period. Mr Huq repeated his request to the students to go home. The Premier, it is reported, refused to give any assurance in respect of the removal of the Holwell Monument.

By this time, at about half past eight, the Police were found to arrive; but the students did not leave the place although ordered by the Police to do so.

The situation was tense but at this moment Mr M.A.H. Ispahani appeared and it is stated, offered himself for arrest first if the boys were to be taken into custody. The Police eventually withdrew from the scene.

The students, it is learnt, would hold a meeting this (Monday) evening at seven on the Park Circus Maidan.

Ministry's Attitude Condemned

A public meeting held on Sunday evening at Sraddhananda Park under the auspices of the Bengal Provincial Students' Federation condemned the attitude which the Government of Bengal had adopted toward the agitation for removal of the Holwell Monument. Sj Arun Sen presided.

The meeting adopted a resolution condemning 'the adamant attitude of the Bengal Ministry in refusing to demolish the Holwell Monument' and demanding 'the immediate demolition of the same'.

By another resolution the meeting supported the stand taken in this respect by the Bengal Provincial Muslim Students' League.

After the conclusion of the meeting a procession was taken out and the processionists tried to proceed towards the Chief Minister's residence at Park Circus and join the Muslim students there with the intention of holding a demonstration before the Premier's house calling upon him to come to a final decision regarding the demolition of the Holwell Monument. But they were held up for some time by the Police at Sasi Bhusan De Street.

The police asked the boys to disperse peacefully which the processionists refused to do. They, about forty in number, refused to move and squatted on the street. After some time they were chased away by the police and one, it is reported, was arrested and taken to the Muchipara police station.

11 Satyagrahis Arrested

Eleven more Satyagrahis were arrested on Sunday on their attempt to break the Holwell Monument. This brings the total number of arrests made in this connection since July 3 when the Satyagraha was started, to 174.

77. Subhas Bose's Arrest: Why Working Committee Took No Notice
    Amrita Bazar Patrika, 14 July 1940.

Bombay, July 13

Why the Congress Working Committee had not taken notice of Mr Subhas Chandra Bose's arrest is examined by Mahatma Gandhi in an article in the 'Harijan' to-day.

Mahatma Gandhi writes: 'On the return journey to Wardha a young man at Nagpur Station asked why the Working Committee had not taken any notice of Subhas Babu's arrest. I was in silence and so gave no reply but took note of the reasonable question. I have no doubt that hundreds of thousands must have asked themselves the question the young man put at Nagpur. It is true that Subhas Babu is an ex-Rastrapati of the Congress twice elected in succession. He has a record of great sacrifice to his credit. He is a leader born. All these qualities alone will not warrant a protest against the arrest. The Working Committee would be bound to take notice of it, if it could be condemned on merits. Subhas Babu did not defy the law with the permission of the Congress. He has frankly and courageously defied even the Working Committee. If he had asked for permission to raise any side issue for battle at the present juncture, the Committee would, I think, have refused it. Hundreds of issues of greater importance can be discovered.

But the country's attention is for the moment riveted upon one single issue. Preparations are being made to take up direct action at the proper time on that issue. Therefore, if the Working Committee had taken any action, it would have been one of disapprobation. That the Committee would not do. I might also have ignored the youth's remark. But I felt that no harm could occur by my putting this arrest in its proper setting.

'The arrest of a big man like Subhas Babu is no small matter. But Subhas Babu has laid out his plan of battle with deliberateness and boldness. He thinks that his way is the best. He honestly thinks that the Working Committee's way is wrong, and that nothing good will come out of its "procrastination". He told me in the friendliest manner that he would do what the Working Committee had failed to do. He was impatient of delay. I told him that, if at the end of his plan there was Swaraj during my life time, mine would be the first telegram of congratulation he would receive. If while he was conducting his campaign I became a convert, I should whole-heartedly acclaim him as my leader and enlist under his banner. But I warned him that his way was wrong. My opinion, however, matters little. So long as Subhas Babu considers a particular course of action to be correct, he has the right, and it is his duty, to pursue it whether the Congress likes it or not. I told him he would be more in the right if he resigned from the Congress altogether. My advice did not commend itself to him. Even so, if success attends his effort and India gains her freedom, it will justify his rebellion, and the Congress will not only not condemn his rebellion but welcome him as a saviour.

'In Satyagraha a courted imprisonment carries its own praise. There can be no protest against an imprisonment for a breach of the current law of the land. On the contrary, the practice has been to congratulate arrested civil resisters and invite Congressmen to imitate them. It is obvious that the Committee could not do so in Subhas Babu's case. Let me remark in passing that the Committee has taken no notice of the numerous arrests and imprisonments that have taken place even of prominent Congressmen. It does not mean that the Committee does not feel anything about them. But in life's battle there is such a thing as a mute submission to many a wrong. If it is deliberate, it generates strength which, if the submission is well conceived, may well become irresistible'—(AP).

78. Subhas Bose's Arrest Raised in Bengal Legislative Assembly

Amrita Bazar Patrika, 16 July 1940.

Mr Santosh Kumar Basu wanted leave of the House to move an adjournment motion to discuss the action of the Government in arresting and detaining Sj Subhas Chandra Bose without any charge or trial.

Sir Nazimuddin opposed the motion saying that there was the law of the land under which a person could be arrested without charge and detained, so that there was nothing abnormal.

The Speaker held the motion to be in order and the requisite number of members supporting the motion, the adjournment motion was allowed.

No Justification

Mr Santosh Kumar Basu in moving the adjournment motion said that when Sj Bose was arrested he was engaged in an important political mission, namely, bringing about communal harmony. At this juncture the arrest of Sj Bose without any reason or justification came as a bolt from the blue. Only recently the Secretary of State for India in the House of Commons announced that the arrest of Sj Bose was in connection with the movement for the removal of the Holwell Monument in Calcutta.

Referring to the provisions of Rule 129 of the Defence of India Rules under which Sj Bose was arrested, Mr Basu remarked under no stretch of imagination any of the sub-rules could be made applicable to the crime which Sj Bose was supposed to have committed. Was the movement for the removal of the Holwell Monument a movement prejudicial to the public safety?

The Government were committed to the removal of this monument by the announcements of the Chief and Home Ministers on the floor of the House but they had not implemented their promise. The young men of this province, Hindus and Moslems, had thrown their hearts and had combined to remove this citadel of untruth. The Ministry's procrastination had led to the starting of this Satyagraha movement. The ministry were moving in a vicious circle and they were acting in a manner prejudicial to the public safety.

A Black Spot

Continuing Mr Basu said that the story of the Black Hole Tragedy was invented to meet the exigencies of political interest in this country. It had now been proved to be a myth. The people of this province were now wide awake and they were not going to tolerate any more the existence of a monument in the heart of the city which only served to represent a black spot in the nation's life.

Mr A.M.A. Zaman supporting the motion said that the Ministry called itself a Moslem Ministry. If so it passed his comprehension how could they tolerate the Holwell Monument which was a standing disgrace to the Moslems.

Rai Harendra Nath Chowdhury said that it was ridiculous to suggest that it was not possible to remove the monument because of the Satyagraha movement. All historical facts proved that the story of the Black Hole was an unmitigated lie. It was a fabrication of a first-class liar of the name of Holwell.

Mr Niharendu Dutta Majumder said that it was indeed a matter of deep surprise to all that Sj Subhas Chandra Bose could be arrested at a time when people of India were engaged to consider the India's position in the light of internal and international situation. It was well-known that Sj Subhas Chandra Bose was striving to bring about unity between the Hindus and Moslems. Mr Dutta Majumder continued that he should have thought that under the circumstances no Government who sincerely wanted to bring about a settlement and conciliation of the Hindu–Moslem question would have caused the arrest of Sj Subhas Bose.

In the face of it, proceeded Sj Dutta Majumder, the arrest of Sj Subhas Bose was due to action taken by the Commissioner of Police, Calcutta. Sj Dutta Majumder would like to know if the Commissioner acted according to the direction of the Ministry. If the Ministry had the consent in the arrest of Sj Bose let them come forward and declare that publicly.

Concluding Sj Dutta Majumder said that let the ministry respect the united voice of the people of the province and remove the monument without any further delay.

Premier's Explanation

The Hon. Mr A.K. Fazlul Huq speaking on the motion said that it was with sorrow and grief that they decided to arrest Sj Subhas Chandra Bose for whom they had admiration. He was one of the most lovable personalities in Bengal politics. But so far as the Satyagraha movement was concerned Mr Huq was afraid he could not see eye to eye with Mr Basu. The question that now confronted them was not the question whether the monument should be removed or not. The question was whether the Government should yield to an agitation. So far as the present movement was concerned Mr Huq stated that he was aware that there was a feeling in the country that the Holwell Monument should be removed and Mr Huq could tell the House that this Satyagraha movement stood in the way of the removal of this monument. Mr Huq would like to make it abundantly clear that so long as Satyagraha was there the Government could not consent to take any action whatsoever on the issue. 'Let Satyagraha cease, let this House have confidence in us. If we do not do anything within a reasonable time then the Satyagraha movement can be started again and lingered for any length of time.'

Proceeding Mr Huq said that he could tell the House that on July 1 last he had a long talk with Sj Subhas Chandra Bose. Sj Bose gave him the impression that if Mr Huq issued a statement on certain lines he would withhold his Satyagraha movement. At about 1 a.m. Mr Huq was told that Sj Bose had certain objections with regard to the statement and the next morning Mr Bose phoned Mr Huq to say that he considered his statement to be unsatisfactory and he would start the movement.

Government Not to Tolerate Agitation

Proceeding Mr Huq said that no Government could tolerate a movement like this at a time when perfect peace and tranquility should prevail in the country in order to enable the Government to take measures for the defence of the country and for the successful termination of the war. This was not the time for internal quarrel. It was obvious that when they were fighting an external enemy they could not afford to have internal dissensions. If the Defence of India Rules had to be applied, it was the case. 'I can tell this House,' Mr Huq asserted, 'that the Government will not budge an inch unless the Satyagraha Movement was called off first.'

Continuing Mr Huq said 'What is wanted to-day is that an attempt should be made to bring about peace. Let the satyagraha cease and everyone will find that within a reasonable time the Government will come to a decision, which will be satisfactory to all concerned. Everyone will understand that so far as the Bengal Government was concerned they are not obstructing a decision which will be acceptable and responsive to the dictates of public opinion.'

Mr Kshettra Nath Singh, (Independent schedule caste), accorded their sympathy to the movement for the removal of the monument.

Mr Abdul Hakim Bokhainagori said that the Ministry's first act ought to have been the removal of this monument. This was a great dereliction of duty on their part for which they must meet with the disapprobation of the public.

Scathing Remarks

Mr Abdul Hashim (Coalition) said that the removal of the monument was a holy cause but he failed to appreciate the Chief Minister's reference to the part played by Mr Subhas Chandra Bose. It is well known, he said, that Mr Basu had parted company with Mr Gandhi and he was looking forward for an opportunity to start satyagraha movement on an all India basis. But being outmaneuvered by a more astute politician Mr Bose failed to take hold of an opportunity for starting such a movement. The Holwell Monument gave him an opportunity. Mr Bose had raised a tempest over a tea pot. He was spoiling the boys of Bengal. His popularity was waning. So he wanted to use the Holwell monument as a spring boat to regain his popularity.

There were protests from the Congress bench on remarks of Mr Hashim.

Mr C.W. Miles on behalf of the European group said that he did not want to go into the merits or demerits of the Holwell Monument. In their opinion a great principle was involved, it was support for law and order. Under a threat of defiance of law and order no Government had any other alternative than to take strong steps. The arrest, in their opinion, was entirely justified. He could say without any fear of contradiction that whatever the Government they would find them (Europeans) always on the side of maintenance of law an order.

Mr A. Siddique said that he would appeal to the Hon. the leader of the Opposition to use his influence and his good office to call off the satyagraha because the Hon. the Chief Minister had told them categorically and very clearly that this satyagraha was standing between the removal of the monument and the release of Sj Subhas Chandra Bose. Mr Siddique hoped that his appeal would touch the heart of the Leader of the Opposition because it came out from his heart.

Clarification Wanted

Mr Sarat Chandra Bose said that the moment the Chief Minister made his statement he was trying to understand its implication and on that matter he was free to confess that unfortunately there was no agreement among the members of his party on this issue. But if as Mr Siddique had said what the Chief Minister said and meant was this that this Satyagraha Movement was standing in the way of the demolition of that outrageous monument, Mr Bose would certainly feel it his duty to consider the position here and now. Mr Bose would therefore request the Chief Minister once more to let them have a clear and unequivocal clarification of what he meant. He desired to make it clear that if what he (Mr Huq) meant was that this satyagraha movement was standing in the way of the removal of the Holwell Monument then Mr Bose would take it that the movement had served its purpose. But before Mr Bose expressed his considered opinion he would like to hear something more from the Chief Minister.

Objection to 'Demolition'

Mr C.E. Miles rising again pointed out that Mr Bose had used the words demolition and removal. The European group had no objection to the removal of the Holwell Monument but he was sure there would be whole-hearted antagonism to its demolition.

The adjournment motion at this stage came to a close and was defeated when put to vote.

79. Trial of Subhas Bose

Bombay Chronicle, 11 September 1940.

Subhas Bose Trial Opens—Speeches 'Likely To Influence Public Attitude Against War'.

Calcutta, September 10

Mr Subhas Chandra Bose was produced to-day before the Additional District Magistrate at Alipur to stand his trial under the Defence of India Rules. He is being prosecuted on a charge of having delivered two objectionable speeches at Deshapriya Park, Ballygunge and at Rajbagan maidan, Belliaghatts on February 22 respectively.

Mr Bose is now under detention in the Presidency Jail, having been arrested on July 2 in connection with the Holwell Monument agitation.

The court room was crowded by members of the Bar and public, long before the accused was brought before the Magistrate at 12-30 p.m. when the trial commenced.

Likely to Cause Dissatisfaction

The Public Prosecutor, Mr J.K. Mukherjee, said that two speeches delivered by Mr Bose contained materials which were prejudicial within the meaning of the Defence of India Rules. The speeches intended or were likely to cause dissatisfaction towards the Government or exciting hatred against the crown and also influence the conduct and attitude of the public against the War.

Intervening, Mr B.P. Jain, MLA, Defence Counsel, prayed adjournment of the hearing in view of the fact that the Defence knew nothing as yet about the complaints and the speeches on the basis of which the complaints had been made against Mr Bose. Counsel applied for copies of the speeches alleged to have been delivered by the accused on February 22 and 24, respectively.

Framing of Charges Delayed

The Magistrate observed that in order to give the Defence Counsel sufficient time for preparing his case, the Court was ready to delay the framing of charges, but the hearing would continue in the meantime.

After two sub-inspectors of the Special Branch Police and two official Bengali stenographers, who had taken down Mr Bose's speeches, were examined, the hearing was adjourned till September 30.

Mr Bose was taken back to the Presidency Jail. He is to be produced before the Chief Presidency Magistrate tomorrow in connection with another case.—AP.

80. Subhas Bose on Fast

Sisir Kumar Bose and Sugata Bose (eds), *The Essential Writings of Netaji Subhas Chandra Bose,* Calcutta, 1997, pp. 263–8.

'My Political Testament'

To H.E. the Governor of Bengal
The Hon. Chief Minister and
The Council of Ministers

26 November 1940

Your Excellency and Gentlemen!

I am writing this in connection with my letter of 30 October 1940, addressed to the Hon. Home Minister (copy of which was forwarded to the Hon. Chief Minister) and my confidential letters to the Superintendent, Presidency Jail, dated 30 October and 14 November, which were forwarded to Government in due course. Herein I shall recapitulate what I have to say regarding my own case and shall also put down in black and white the considerations that are impelling me to take the most fateful step in my life.

I have no longer any hope that I shall obtain redress at you hands. I shall, therefore, make but two requests, the second of which will be at the end of this letter. My first request is that this letter be carefully preserved in the archives of the Government, so that it may be available to those of my countrymen who will succeed you in office in future. It contains a message for my countrymen and is therefore my political testament.

I was arrested without any official explanation or justification on 2 July 1940, as per orders of the Government of Bengal, under Section 129 of the Defence of India Rules. The first explanation subsequently emanating from official sources came from the Rt Hon. Mr Amery, Secretary of State for India, who stated in the House of Commons quite categorically that the arrest was in connection with the movement for the demolition of the Holwell Monument in Calcutta.

The Hon. Chief Minister virtually confirmed this pronouncement at a sitting of the Bengal Legislative Assembly and stated that it was the Holwell Monument Satyagraha which stood in the way of my release. When the Government decided to remove the Monument, all those who had been detained without trial in connection therewith were set free, with the exception of Mr Narendra Narayan Chakravarti, MLA and myself. These releases took place towards the end of August 1940 and almost simultaneously an order for my permanent detention was served under Section 26 of the Defence of India Rules, in lieu of the original order under Section 129, which provided for temporary detention.

Strangely enough, with the new order under Section 26, came the news that prosecution was being launched against me under Section 38 of the D.I. Rules before two Magistrates—for three of my speeches and for a contributed article in the weekly journal of Forward Bloc, of which I had been the Editor. Two of these speeches had been delivered in February 1940, and the third one early in April. Thus the Government created a unique and unprecedented situation towards the end of August last by detaining me permanently without trial under one Section of the Defence of India Rules and simultaneously prosecuting me before judicial tribunals under another Section of the same Rules. I had not seen a similar combination of executive fiat and judicial procedure before this occurrence took place. Such a policy is illegal and unjust and smacks of vindictiveness, pure and simple.

One cannot fail to notice that the prosecution was launched is manifestly long after the alleged offences had taken place. Nor can it be overlooked that for the relevant article in Forward Bloc, the paper had already been penalized through forfeiture of the security of Rs 500 and deposit of a further security of Rs 2000. Moreover, the attack on the paper was made all of a sudden, after a long period during which no warning had been given to the paper in accordance with the practice of Government.

The attitude of the Bengal Government was further exposed when applications for my release on bail were made before the two trying Magistrates. Both these applications were stoutly opposed by the Government spokesmen. On the last occasion, one of the Magistrates, Mr Wail-ul-Islam granted the bail application, but was constrained to remark that this order would remain infructuous till the Government withdrew their order for my detention without trial under Section 26 of the D.I. Rules. It is thus as clear as daylight that the Government have been pursuing a policy which fetters the discretion of judicial tribunals and interferes with the administration of law. The action of the local Government appears all the more objectionable when it is remembered that they have given the go-by to the instructions of the Government of India with regard to such cases.

Another interesting feature of the Government's policy is my simultaneous prosecution before two Magistrates. If the intention was to place more than one speech of mine before a court of law, that could very well have been fulfilled without resorting to two Magistrates, for I have delivered any number of speeches during the last twelve months within the limits of Calcutta proper. The man in the street is, therefore, forced to think that Government are so keen on seeing me convicted that they have provided for a second string to the legal bow.

Last but not least. Government's action appears to an impartial man to be altogether mala fide, because proceedings were instituted so long after the alleged prejudicial acts had been committed. If the acts in question were in fact prejudicial, then action should have been taken by Government long ago, that is at the time that the alleged offences were committed.

May I request you to compare for one moment your attitude towards people like myself and towards Muslims arrested and imprisoned under the Defence of India Rules? How many cases have occurred up till now in which Muslims apprehended under the D.I. Rules have been suddenly released without rhyme or reason? The latest example of the Maulvi of Murapara is too fresh in the public mind to need recounting. Are we to understand that under your rule there is one law for the Muslim and another law for the Hindu and that the D.I. Rules have a different meaning when a Muslim is involved? If so, the Government might as well make a pronouncement to that effect. Lest it be argued or suggested for one moment that for my incarceration, the Government of India and not the Local Government are responsible, I may remind you that in connection with an adjournment motion concerning myself, tabled by Pandit L.K. Maitra before the Indian Legislative Assembly only the other day, it was stated on behalf of the Government of India that the matter should not come before the Central Assembly, since I had been incarcerated by the Bengal Government. I believe a similar admission was made in the Bengal Legislative Assembly on behalf of the Ministry.

And we cannot forget that here in Bengal we live under the benign protection of a 'popular' ministry.

My recent election to the Indian Legislative Assembly has raised another issue—that of 'immunity' from imprisonment for members of the legislature, while the legislature is in session. This is a right inherent in every constitution, no matter whether it is explicitly provided in the statute or not and this right has been established after a protracted struggle. Quite recently, the Burma Government allowed a convicted prisoner to attend the sittings of the Burma Legislative Assembly, but though I am not a convicted prisoner, I have been denied that right by our 'popular' ministry.

If apologists attempt to invoke the precedent of Captain Ramsay, MP, in support of the Government, I may point out that Capt. Ramsay's case stands on a different footing altogether. Serious charges have been preferred against him, but all the facts not being known to us, it is difficult to argue either way. One may, however, urge that if Capt. Ramsay has been unjustly imprisoned and no redress will be ultimately forthcoming, it would lend substance to what Mr Kennedy (American Ambassador to Great Britain) and others are reported to have said— namely, that democracy is dead in England. In any case, Capt. Ramsay has had the opportunity of getting his case examined by a committee of the House of Commons.

In dealing with my case generally, two broad issues have now to be considered. Firstly, have the Defence of India Rules any sanction—ethical or popular? Secondly, have the rules, as they stand, been properly applied in my case? The answers to both the questions are in the negative.

The D.I. Rules have no ethical sanction behind them because they constitute an infringement of the elementary rights and liberties of the people. Moreover, they are essentially a war-measure and, as is known to everybody, India was declared a belligerent power and was dragged into the war, without the consent of the Indian people or the Indian Legislature. Further, these Rules militate against the claim so vociferously made in Britain that she is fighting the cause of freedom and democracy. And lastly, the Congress Party in the Central Assembly was not a party to the adoption of the Defence of India Act or the Defence of India Rules. In these circumstances, it would not be improper to ask whether the Defence of India Rules should not more appropriately be called the Suppression of India Rules or the Defence of Injustice Rules.

It may be urged on behalf of this Government that the Defence of India Act being an Act of the Central Legislature, all provincial Governments are obliged to administer the Rules framed thereunder. But enough has already been said above to justify the charge that the Rules, even as they stand, have not been properly applied in my case. There has been manifest illegality and injustice. Only one explanation can, to my mind, account for such a strange conduct, namely that Government have been pursuing a frankly vindictive policy towards me for reasons that are quite inexplicable.

For more than two months, the question has been knocking at the door of my conscience over and over again as to what I should do in such a predicament. Should I submit to the pressure of circumstances and accept whatever comes my way—or should I protest against what to me is unfair, unjust and illegal? After the most mature deliberation I have come to the conclusion that surrender to circumstances is out of the question. It is a more heinous crime to submit to a wrong inflicted than to perpetrate that wrong. So, protest I must.

But all these days, protest has been going on and the ordinary methods of protest have all been exhausted. Agitation in the press and on the platform, representations to Government, demand in the Assembly, exploration of legal channels—have not all of these been already tried and found ineffective? Only one method remains—the last weapon in the hands of a prisoner, that is hunger-strike or fast.

In the cold light of logic I have examined the pros and cons of this step and have carefully weighed the loss and gain that will accrue from it. I have no illusions in the matter and I am fully conscious that the immediate tangible gain will be nil, for I am sufficiently conversant with the behaviour of Governments and bureaucracies in such crises. The classic and immortal examples of Terence Macsweeney and Jatin Das are floating before my mind's eye at the moment. A system has no heart that could be moved, though it has a false sense of prestige to which it always clings.

Life under existing conditions is intolerable for me. To purchase one's continued existence by compromising with illegality and injustice goes against my very grain. I would throw up life itself, rather than pay this price. Government are determined to hold me in prison by brute force. I say in reply: 'Release me or shall I refuse to live—and it is for me to decide whether I choose to live or to die'.

Though there may be no immediate, tangible gain—no suffering, no sacrifice is ever futile. It is through suffering and sacrifice alone that a cause can flourish and prosper and in every age and clime, the eternal law prevails—'the blood of the martyr is the seed of the church'.

In this mortal world, everything perishes and will perish—but ideas, ideals and dreams do not. One individual may die for an idea but that idea will, after his death, incarnate itself in a thousand lives. That is how the wheels of evolution move on and the ideas, ideals and dreams of one generation are bequeathed to the next. No idea has ever fulfilled itself in this world except through an ordeal of suffering and sacrifice.

What greater solace can there be than the feeling that one has lived and died for a principle? What higher satisfaction can a man possess than the knowledge that his spirit will beget kindred spirits to carryon his unfinished task? What better reward can a soul desire than the certainty that his message will be wafted over hills and dales and over the broad plains to every corner of his land and across the seas to distant lands? What higher consummation can life attain than peaceful self-immolation at the altar of one's cause?

Hence it is evident that nobody can lose through suffering and sacrifice. If he does lose anything of the earth earthy, he will gain much more in return by becoming the heir to a life immortal.

This is the technique of the soul. The individual must die, so that the nation may live. Today I must die, so that India may live and may win freedom and glory.

To my countrymen I say, 'Forget not that the greatest curse for a man is to remain a slave. Forget not that the grossest crime is to compromise with injustice and wrong. Remember the eternal law: You must give life, if you want to get it. And remember that the highest virtue is to battle against iniquity, no matter what the cost may be.'

To the Government of the day I say, 'Cry halt to your mad drive along the path of communalism and injustice. There is yet time to retrace your steps. Do not use a boomerang which will soon recoil on you. And do not make another Sindh of Bengal'.

I have finished. My second and last request to you is that you should not interfere forcibly with my fast, but should permit me to approach my end peacefully. In the case of Terence Macsweeney, of Jatin Das, of Mahatma Gandhi and in our own case in 1926, Government did decide not to interfere with the fast. I hope they will do the same this time—otherwise any attempt to feed me by force will be resisted with all my strength, though the consequences thereof may be even more drastic and disastrous than otherwise.

I shall commence my fast on 29 November 1940.

Presidency Jail

Yours faithfully

26 November 1940
Subhas Chandra Bose

81.   Newspaper Report on Subhas Bose's Release

Amrita Bazar Patrika, 6 December 1940.

Sj Subhas Chandra Bose, who was arrested on July 2, in connection with the Holwell Monument agitation under Section 129 of the Defence of India Rules, was released at 5 P.M. on Thursday from the Presidency jail and from detention.

Sj Bose was immediately taken to his Elgin Road residence in an ambulance, accompanied by the jail doctor.

It is recalled that Sj Bose who was ailing for sometime in the jail, went on hunger-strike on November 29.

Two cases under the Defence of India Rules in connection with speeches made by him at different times and places during the current year and also for the publication of an article entitled 'The day of Reckoning' in the English weekly 'Forward Bloc' are now pending against Sj Bose before the Additional Chief Presidency Magistrate, Calcutta, and the Additional District Magistrate, Alipore.

In view of the condition of his health, Sj Bose has been advised complete rest for some time and the public are requested not to disturb during the period of his illness.

Mr Bose, who was on hunger-strike for the past seven days broke his fast after coming out of the jail gate by asking glucose water offered by the Superintendent of the Presidency Jail.

Government Communiqué

The following communiqué has been issued by the Government of Bengal:

'Release of security prisoner Mr Subhas Chandra Bose for reasons of health:

Government Communiqué: Dated Calcutta the 5th December, 1940. Government were advised that continued persistence in his hunger-strike by security prisoner Mr Subhas Chandra Bose would involve serious danger to his health.

Government were not prepared to administer forcible feeding to Mr Bose and he was accordingly released from jail and taken to his own home on the afternoon of the 5th December 1940 upon the suspension of the orders of detention passed in his case under Rule 26 of the Defence of India Rules.

Government are advised that although Mr Bose is weak and has shown a tendency to nausea his condition gives no cause for anxiety provided that he breaks his fast. They accordingly accept no responsibility for the consequences to himself should he continue to abstain from nourishment'.

The following bulletin was issued through the 'Associated Press' tonight by Mr Bose's attending physicians:

'On examination after his arrival the doctors found Mr Bose's heart to be so weak that heart sounds were scarcely audible. His pulse is quick and intermittent and very soft. Blood pressure has fallen to a low figure. Extreme prostration is present and even talking is a strain. He is advised to remain in bed and consume small quantity of fluid diet very cautiously. It is essential that he should recover some little strength before he could think of any sort of activity mental or physical. Friends and well-wishers will be greatly assisting in his recovery if they kindly abstain from any direct interview as this would impede his progress'.

Maulana Azad's Satisfaction

Being informed of Mr Subhas Chandra Bose's release from detention the Congress President Maulana Abul Kalam Azad said 'I am glad to hear that Subhas Babu has been released'.

F.   SATYAGRAHA COMMITTEES AND BRITISH REPRESSION

I.   British Government's Policy Towards Satyagraha

82.   A Letter from the Viceroy to Secretary of State Regarding the Possibility of a Civil Disobedience Movement

Letter No. 20, To the Secretary of State for India, 26/27 April 1940, Correspondence with Secretary of State, Vol. V, 1940, Linlithgow Papers, Acc. No. 2153, NAI.

From Linlithgow to Zetland (Possibility of Civil-disobedience)

.... It is difficult to judge how we stand as regards civil disobedience. I still have considerable hope that we shall avoid it for some time to come, though here and there, there are disquieting symptoms. But I am sure that we shall do well to be prepared: and I am most anxious, if trouble forced upon, that we should be ready to strike at once and as decisively as possible. If we can deal a severe blow on the first day or in the first couple of days to the organization, the chances of an early collapse, given more particularly the hostility of the Muslims and the

Muslim League, would be immensely increased. I thought it well to ask Maxwell to consider the whole position before I left Delhi, and to satisfy himself that we were in good shape for a civil disobedience outbreak if it came, and that there was no outstanding points on which the Provinces would welcome advice, or which we might suggest to them; and I have indicated that we should aim at having our preparations, whether at the Centre or in the Provinces complete in all respects by 15th May if possible. I am satisfied that the ground is already well covered officially but there is no harm done by a further check over; and I thought in those circumstances that it might be as well if I sent out also a personal message from myself to Governors of a purely preliminary character warning them I may be addressing them more formally once I had recommendations from my official advisers, but with a view really to getting them on their toes. I am sending you a copy of this by the bag, with a copy of the replies which I have so far had, and of a most useful letter from Maxwell commenting on the general position with particular reference to his discussions with Lumley and officials in Bombay. The replies, and the points raised by them fully justify, I think this further precautionary reference to Governors. But I am still not without hope that may be a not considerable delay before trouble comes, unless there should be any serious and unexpected development in the west in which case Congress might feel tempted to take advantage of a situation in which they would judge us to be under markedly increased pressure.

83. Telegram from the Viceroy to Secretary of State Regarding Mahatma Gandhi's Article 'Civil Disobedience' and his Views on Satyagraha

Telegram No. 151, 28 April 1940, Telegraphic Correspondence with Secretary of State, Vol. V, 1940, Linlithgow Papers, Acc. No. 2162, NAI.

Viceroy to Secretary of State Telegram XX, 28th April 1940

Secret. Immediate. No. 267–S. I have telegraphed separately text of Gandhi's personal letter to me of 24th April and have repeated Lumley's telegram No. 325 of 26th April. According to press *Harijan* of 27th in fact contains passage in which the Mahatma writing under caption 'Civil Disobedience' is alleged to have declared that 'choice lies between individual civil disobedience on large scale, very restricted, or confined only to me' and to have added that so far as he could see at present mass civil disobedience is most unlikely as in face of lawlessness that prevails in country civil disobedience will easily pass for lawlessness: but that in every case there must be backing of whole of official Congress organization and millions who though not on Congress register have always supported organization. I would judge pressure on Gandhi to be fairly considerable. It is impossible to be quite certain what he means by civil disobedience confined to him only, but possibility of a fast is clearly inherent in this. My disposition is not to take this too seriously at the moment and leave it to Gandhi to define his meaning rather more precisely. My attitude in event of a fast would remain as already indicated to you. It is of course conceivable that he might contemplate using this weapon nominally against us, but actually to bring his more intransigent followers to make concessions which would make possible an understanding with Muslims, etc. such as we could accept as a basis for progress. But that is mere speculation.

I have carefully considered whether in replying to his present letter (envelope of which was marked 'personal') I should not in terms challenge him on the question whether he speaks for himself or for the Congress organization. I have, however, thought it wiser not to do so, or to question the 'personal' marking on his letter, though I do not propose to mark my reply personal, or confidential, or anything else. If of course any question arises of any statement of importance being made to him on behalf of His Majesty's Government in this correspondence (and I think there are very strong arguments against that despite the precedent of Jinnah) it would of course be essential first to clear up whether or not we were dealing with the matter on a personal basis, and the capacity in, and the authority with, which Gandhi claimed to be speaking in relation to Congress.

II.   Satyagraha in the Provinces

84.   Summary of Satyagraha Reports and Satyagraha Preparations from Different Provincial Congress Committees

Satyagraha Reports from PCCs, AICC Papers, File No. G–5 (Pt. I)/1940–41, NMML.

Summary of Provincial Reports Satyagraha Preparations

Andhra   *April 26, 1940*

At its meeting held on 6/4/1940 the Andhra Provincial Congress Committee set up the following sub-committees: (1) Charkha, (2) Harijan, (3) Minorities, (4) Publicity, and (5) Women.

The Sub-committees have been advised to draw up a programme of work and submit it to the PCC. All the members signed the pledge. The District Congress Committee converted themselves into Satyagraha Committees. The Satyagraha pledge has been sent to all the Congress members of the Provincial and Central legislature, presidents of District Boards, Chairmen of Municipal Councils and Provincial Congress Committee members. The PCC Office has received so far 196 pledges. PCC is organizing a volunteer captain's training camp at Madras from 1.5.40. It is proposed to train about 50 volunteer captains. Those trained will run volunteer camps in the districts. Camps have been already started in some districts.

Assam   *Up to 18-4-1940*

The Working Committee of the Assam Provincial Congress Committee has converted itself into Satyagraha Committee. Most of the members have signed the pledge. The District Congress Committees have been asked to do like wise. The DCCs have also been asked to hold meetings in villages to explain the Congress programme. A seven days programme of work has been decided upon for the members of the Working Committee, to begin from May 5.

Bengal

No report has been received from the Provincial Congress Committee.

Bihar   *Up to May 1, 1940*

The total number of Satyagrahis enrolled is 2000. A Provincial Satyagraha Training Camp was started at Sonepur from April 20 which lasted for a week. The total strength of the campers was 291 of whom 147 were interested and active. There were no servants, sweepers, cooks etc. All work in connection with the camp was done by the members themselves. The inmates of the camp showed remarkable discipline. The daily routine was strictly adhered to. Drill and prayer were optional. The main features of the camp were spinning and political week celebration. The camp attracted a continuous stream of visitors. B. Rajendra Prasad delivered several discourses on charkha, technique of Satyagraha and like subjects.

Similar camps in the districts are being started. Champaran has already begun.

Karnatak   Up to April 18, 1940

The Council of the Karnatak PCC has converted itself into the Satyagraha Committee for the Province. The Council called upon the subordinate committees to do likewise.

2 district Congress committees, Dharwar and Mangalore have turned into Satyagraha committees.

The committees have been instructed to open Satyagraha camps for the training of satyagrahis.

In the National Week *Khadi* hawking, spinning competitions and visits to Harijan colonies formed the principal features of the programme in the province.

Circulars from the AICC office and Gandhiji's instructions have been printed in Kannada and distributed to the committees.

Kerala   *Up to April 23, 1940*

A resolution has been passed by the Working Committee of the Kerala PCC for bringing into being a Supreme Council representatives of various groups in the Congress Shri K. Kelappan and Janab M.K. Moiuddiri Kutti Saheb of the Kerala Congress Gandhi Sangham have been asked to serve on the Kerala's Satyagraha Committee.

Mahakoshal   *Up to May 1, 1940*

The Provincial Executive has converted itself into Satyagraha Committee consisting of 11 members of the Committee who have signed the pledge.

Out of the 14 District Congress Committees, 11 have converted their executive councils into Satyagraha Committees. The following table gives the number of members on these bodies who have signed the Satyagraha pledge.

1. Jabbulpore	15	7
2. Saugor	15	9
3. Kareli (Narasingpur)	15	12
4. Betul	15	6
5. Chindwara	15	2
6. Seoni	15	7
7. Handla	15	7
8. Balaghat	15	7
9. Durg	15	3
10. Raipur	15	10
11. Bilaspur	15	8

The total number of pledges received from districts up to 30-4-1940 is 455. The number of Passive Satyagrahis is 186. Some districts, such as Saugor, Raipur and Hoshangabad have enroled as many as 113, 83, 49 active Satyagrahis, but some districts such as Khandwa, Mandla, Seoni and Balaghat have enrolled only 1, 1, 7, 7 active satyagrahis respectively. Instructions have been issued to the DCCs to send a list of whole time active satyagrahis. *Charkha* and *Takly* Competitions were held in the National Week. Sales of Khaddar were organized. A Khadi and village industries exhibition was held at *Khandwa*. The Provincial Executive has decided to open a provincial satyagraha training on camp at Narsingpur for a week. The PCC members who have signed the pledge and five satyagrahis from each district have been invited. This provincial camp will be followed up by district and tahsil camps.

Maharashtra   *Up to April 18, 1940*

7 Circulars have been issued to the District Congress Committees regarding the preparatory work to be done in connection with Satyagraha. Leaders were touring in the districts and enrollment of Satyagrahis is proceeding satisfactorily. There is enthusiasm in the province. The atmosphere inside the Congress and outside is showing signs of improvement. Party rivalries have declined. Only the Royists are a right in the lute. There is some marked improvement in the discipline of Congressmen in local bodies. The PCC is in correspondence with the *Charkha Sangh* for the organization of spinning. The DCCs are making necessary arrangement for staring shibirs for active Satyagrahis.

The Executive Committee has converted itself into Satyagraha Committee of the Province. It appointed Shri Shankerrao Deo to guide the Preparations of Satyagraha in the Province.

North West Frontier Province   *Up to April 24, 1940*

Members of the PCC including of course the members of the Provincial Executive have signed Satyagraha Pledge and these bodies have converted themselves into Satyagraha Committees. The DCCs of Dera Ismail Khan, Bannu and Kohat have likewise converted themselves into Satyagraha Committees, all the members signing the Satyagraha Pledge. Training camps have been started in the districts of Peshawar and Bannu. A camp will be held on May 4, 1940 attended by all the important workers of the Province. Khan Abdul Ghaffar Khan has started a tour of the province, from April 8, in connection with the Satyagraha campaign. The tour will last for a month.

Sind   *Up to April 27, 1940*

The Executive Council has converted itself into the Supreme Satyagraha Council for the province. The Executive committees of all Congress Committees have been directed to function as Satyagraha committees as from the statement May, 1940 members not signing the Satyagraha Pledge are to resign. A Sind Satyagraha camp will be started at Karachi from the 5th of May. District political conferences will be held during the course of this month. The pledges received in the office so far total 250. 12 are Muslim and 7 ladies. Instructions have been issued to establish closer contact with Muslims. The Charkha department is functioning actively. Spinning demonstrations have held at several places in the province. Regular classes for spinning will be opened at Karachi, Hyderabad, Sukkur and other places. Steps to popularize the products of village industries other than khadi are also being taken. On the whole the response in the province is good, specially in towns and bigger villages. There is however, not much activity in small villages where Muslims predominate.

Tamil Nadu   *Up to April 16, 1940*

North Arcot DCC: The Committee has sent the office a list of 220 persons who have signed the Satyagraha pledge.

United Provinces

The UP Provincial Executive has converted itself into Supreme Satyagraha Council for the province. The DCCs have been instructed to turn into Satyagraha Committees. Instructions have been issued for each member of the Satyagraha Committee to spin and send his fortnightly report to the local Satyagraha Committee. Members of Satyagraha Committees have been put in charge of areas in districts. They will supervise the whole thing in the area, and prepare fortnightly reports.

In 22 districts out of 48 more than 65 per cent of the members of the DCCs have signed the Satyagrah pledge. 23 persons so far have refused to sign the pledge because they did not believe in one or the other item of the programme. The total number of Satyagrahis enrolled in province up to 20th April 1940 is 5400. Out of these roughly 1700 are members of the executives of district and city Congress committees. About 500 have promised to be whole time workers of the Congress. In most of the districts, local dissensions have disappeared with the formation of the Satyagraha committees. Sufficient information has not been received yet about the mandal Committees. The total number of mandal committee functioning in province is roughly 2,000. Half of these committees are considered to be active bodies. The 41 organizers on the national Service Board have been deputed, one to each district. They cooperate with the District Congress committee in their work. Satisfactory spinning arrangements have been made in 10 districts. They have employed separate instructors. Yarn collection has been commenced in 22 districts. Sri Vichitra Narayan Sharma, who has been entrusted by the Council to organize spinning in the province, has issued circulars to committees giving necessary details about spinning work. Khaddar Bhandars are assisting in the carrying out of the spinning programme. There were public spinning demonstrations in 7 places. A spinning demonstration is proposed to be held on a fixed day throughout the province.

Every Satyagrahi has been asked to report about his spinning to an officer appointed for the purpose. Some committees suffer from paucity of funds. They have been asked to launch a campaign for enrolling Congress members. This will give them some money. The programme of one meeting in each village is being organized in the districts.

Utkal

The Provincial Congress Committee of Utkal has, at its general meeting held on 15-4-1940 transformed itself into Satyagraha Committee of the province and has directed the subordinate committees to do likewise. Total number of active Satyagrahis enrolled so far is 108. Districts such as Cuttuck, Koraput account for 43 and 35 Satyagrahis respectively. Districts such as Singhbhum and Ganjam have enrolled only 1 and 1 Satyagrahis respectively. The PCC has opened four departments: (1) propaganda; (2) Harijan, (3) minorities; and (4) charkha. These departments have started functioning.

Vidarbha

Out of 29 district, nagar and taluka Congress committees, 23 committees have converted themselves into Satyagraha Committees. The PCC Office has received 250 pledges. Of the 17 MLAs 6 have signed the pledge. The number of women Satyagrahis is 7. Special attention is being paid to propaganda. Conferences are being held in the province. A provincial camp of Congress workers will be held at Akola from 5th to 7th May. A volunteer camp will be held from the 5th to 20th May. Steps have been taken to popularize khadi and spinning. The work about Harijans uplift is also receiving attention. There is enthusiasm in the province. Workers are showing keener appreciation of their responsibilities.

85. Report of the Ajmer–Merwara Provincial Congress Committee
AICC Papers, File No. G–5 (Pt. I)/1940–41, NMML.

1. 72 Satyagrahis have been enrolled in the province so far. The office as not received any report about the work of the Satyagrahis but it is believed that a majority are fulfilling the conditions. The Satyagraha council of the PCC met at Ajmer for full five days. Spinning demonstrations were organized at two public meetings in Ajmer after Ramgarh.

2. National week was utilized to increase the sales of *Khadi*. An exhibition was held in Ajmer. Two exhibitions are also being held in Jaipur and Khargaon. It is estimated that khadi worth Rs 20,000 was sold during the week. *Charkhas* were also sold in large numbers. The Satyagraha Council has, after consultation with the provincial branch of' the AISA prepared a scheme about khadi which will be considered at the next meeting of the Satyagraha Council.

3. A sub-committee for minorities has been appointed with Sj Balkrishna Kaul as Convener. Harijan Sevak Sang is assisted by us in its activities.

4. ... The PCC office has no separate departments for separate items of programme. 14 circulars have been issued from Ramgarh. The accounts are properly kept. Propaganda work is carried on by the city Congress Committees. A scheme is being prepared for work in villages, which will include enrolling of Congress members, Satyagrahis, popularization of Ramgarh resolution, and other things.

5. The PCC met in February last and the executive in April .... The PCC converted itself into Satyagraha committee soon after the Ramgarh and circulars were issued to subordinate committees to do likewise.

6. The office has not received information as to how many members of the committee have signed the Satyagraha pledge. Of 21 members of the Ajmer Town Committee, 11 have signed the pledge. In Kekri only one member has signed the pledge. A reminder has been sent to the Committees to expedite the sending of necessary information. No replies have been received yet.

7. We have no District or Mandal Congress Committees. We have only primary Congress Committees, whose total number is 14, of which 8 are in the British territory and 6 in Indian states. Of these committees in British area, the one in Ajmer only has converted itself into Satyagraha Committee. A meeting was to be held in Mewar for this purpose, but no information has been received yet.

8. Only the Ajmer city Congress Committee has converted itself into Satyagraha Committee. It has also organized two meetings in the city to popularize the Congress programme.

10. Group rivalries had declined but they have revived with the arrival in the city of Sj Ramnarayanji Choudhury. As a result Sj Durga Prasad Choudhury has sent you some complaints about us which are motivated by party spirit....

11. Public reactions are favourable. There is enthusiasm in the public. When the proper time comes, some funds may also be made available to us.

12. No training camps have been held so far for the following reasons (i) The Ajmer–Merwara province is a non-regulated area and it is therefore not so easy to get a suitable site for the camp (ii) The number of satyagrahis is too small and they are scattered (iii) there is insufficiency of funds. An effort, however, is being made to hold a camp.

13. 8 meetings have been held in the province.

86. Assam Provincial Congress Committee's Report on Satyagraha Activities

AICC Papers, File No. G–5 (Pt. I)/1940–41, NMML.

A report on the preparations for Satyagraha in Assam up to June 15 1940

Enrollment of Satyagraha—The number of Satyagrahis enrolled up to 15th June is 1576, out of whom eleven are Mussalman and fifteen women. It may be noted that most of the Satyagrahis belong to villages. The DCC report that they are generally fulfilling the conditions prescribed in the pledge. The Tezpur District Congress Committee tops the list of District Congress Committees with 500 Satyagrahis enrolled within its jurisdiction.

The Executive of all the District Congress Committees excepting that of Khasi and Jaintia Hills DCC have converted themselves into Satyagraha Committees. There are thirteen District Congress Committees under the Assam PCC.

Forty six members of the PCC out of 59 at present have signed the pledge and the others are also likely to sign it. Only two members, namely, Shri Kiritibhusan Chaudhury and Kshirode Ranjan Deb have refused to sign the pledge on political grounds.

Propaganda

In spite of heavy and continuous rains, numerous meetings are being held allover the province. Only three District Congress Committees have sent us the numbers of meetings held after the last report was sent to the AICC Office on 22-5-1940. Between them, these DCCs have held eighty meetings.

The Minority Department of the PCC has begun Congress propaganda amongst the Muslims and the tribal peoples. It is gratifying that the number of Satyagrahis belonging to the tribal peoples is on the increase.

The Publicity Department has published two pamphlets on the present situation containing the Ramgarh resolution, Gandhiji's writings, instructions of the General Secretary, AICC.

The Assam PCC has opened a Women's Department and placed it in charge of three educated ladies, namely, Shrimati Amalprava Dass, MSc; Pushpalata Saikia, MA, and Girijabala Barooah.

Volunteer Corps and Training Camps

Seven District Congress Committees have so far opened Satyagraha Camps and in four camps alone 192 Satyagrahis are undergoing training. The number of Satyagrahis receiving training in the other camps is not known as reports from them are yet to come.

The Assam PCC has decided to organize a Provincial Volunteer Corps and has entrusted Shri Rajendra Nath Barua to raise new Volunteers and to coordinate the already existing district volunteer units. He has been directed to see that uniformity in all matters including command and dress is maintained in the corps.

A training Camp has already been started at Golaghat under his supervision to train a few important Congress workers from each district who, after the completion of their training will train the volunteers in their respective districts. Thirty eight persons are receiving training in this camp. A few DCCs have volunteers of their own, the Tezpur DCC alone having 350 trained volunteers.

Khadi Work

Spinning has made visible progress. Arrangements have been made by some DCCs either independently or in cooperation with AISA for the supply of Charkhas, Cotton and Slivers. Spinning forms a part of the daily routine in the Camps.

Besides the local branches of the AISA, the Assam Khadi and Rural Reconstruction Association, which owes its existence to the handsome gift of Rs 14,000 by Dr H.K. Das, is doing good work. This Association which was started with the object of working in cooperation with the AISA opened a Khadi production centre at Baihata in Gauhati sub-division a little more than a month ago. The Secretary of the Association reports that during this short period more than 500 spinners have been enrolled and that their number is on the increase.

Congress House,
Gauhati

General Secretary

87. Intelligence Report on Satyagraha Activities and Preparations in Bihar

Political Department, Special Section, 4 January 1940, Bihar State Archives, Patna.

Political—Congress: The first phase of the Satyagraha campaign has now come to an end and there will be an interval until January 5th when Satyagraha by members of subordinate Congress Committees and local bodies will start. Up to date 74 satyagrahis have been arrested and convicted. The lists submitted by district Congress Committee of those who have volunteered for the second phase which contain 2,370 names, have been returned by Dr Rajendra Prasad, who in a circular points out that sufficiently full information has not been given to enable recommendations to be made to Mahatma Gandhi and requires district committees to take advantage of the Christmas interval to revise the lists and to note against each name how far these conditions are being observed. The circular adds that quality is more desirable than quantity and that anyone volunteering in the hope of future preferment or for fear that failure to volunteer will count against him is to be discouraged.

Another problem which is exercising the mind of Dr Rajendra Prasad is the situation likely to be created if most of the members of the executives of local bodies, practically all of which have a substantial, and some an overwhelming, Congress majority, are allowed to do Satyagraha. In asking for instructions from the Congress High Command, Dr Rajendra Prasad has instructions from the Congress High Command. Dr Rajendra Prasad has pointed out the existence of internal Congress factions and anticipates that the better sort of Congressmen will join the movement, while those left behind will take advantage of the absence of their opponents to consolidate their position. He has suggested three possible courses. The first is to allow those who wish to join the movement to do so and let the remainder carry on as best they can, which may involve seats becoming automatically vacant owing to non-attendance at meetings and Government ordering fresh elections. The second alternative is to select only a limited number of Satyagrahis and leave the rest to run the administration. This would involve difficulties in making a choice and would probably result in the better men going and their inferiors staying behind. The third is to make all Congress members of the executive resign, which would result in district boards and municipalities passing into the hands of non-Congressmen. Options on these points have been asked for in a circular issued by Dr Rajendra Prasad to leaders of local bodies.

Opinion in certain non-Congress political circles is that individual Satyagraha has ensured the success of a future mass movement as Congress is fast regaining its lost grip on the masses. Had the policy of non-arrest been adopted, the movement might, they consider, have fizzled out Congress circles agree trial Gandhi has chosen a most suitable time for the Satyagraha campaign as the release of the leaders, most of whom had been awarded one year's imprisonment, will coincide in point of time with the next elections which Congress will then contest with added prestige. It is interesting to note that Dr Mahmud, ex-Minister, who had written to Mr Gandhi informing him that he was all right now and would like to offer Satyagraha during January, has been told by Mr Gandhi that he was not listening to him and he has been ordered to confine himself to his house. Amongst the notable Satyagrahis who have recently gone to jail may be mentioned the name of Mazhar Faridpuri, son of the late Mr Mazrul Haque, and one more member of the landed aristocracy, has also gone to jail for Satyagraha in the person of Kalika Prasad Singh who is closely related to the Gidhaur family.

88. Bihar Provincial Congress Committee's Report on Satyagraha Activities and Preparations

Satyagraha Report from PCCs, AICC Papers, File No. G–5 (Pt. I)/1940–41, NMML.

Bihar   *May 27, 1940*

All the 16 DCCs in the province, except of Singhbhum have turned into Satyagraha committees. The total number of Satyagrahis enrolled up to middle of May is 1991. Their number district-wise is as follows:

Muzaffarpur	180	Santhal Parganas	25
Champaran	209	Manbhum	285
Bhagalpore	253	Purnea	274
Gaya	147	Darbhanga	115
Monghyr	166	Patna	220
Hazaribagh	82	Palamau	35

Training camps have been held in the districts of Muzaffarpur, Champaran, Hazaribagh, Monghyr, Purnea, Manbhum, Darbhanga, Bhagalpore, SP Patna, Palamau. The total number of Satyagrahis joining these camps is 460. Figures from SP Darbhanga, Manbhum training camps are not available yet.

Bihar Provincial Congress Committee, Sadaquat Ashram, PO Dighaghat, Patna

Telegram: Congress
Dated 27-5-40

Ref. No. 936/11B
The General Secretary,
All India Congress Committee
Allahabad

Dear Sir,

I beg to submit herewith a fortnightly report of the work done in our province till the 15th May 1940 in connection with the preparation for Satyagraha movement.

Out of the 16 DCCs in this province, all, with the exception of district of Singhbhum, have been transformed into Satyagraha Committees and have taken up the task of enrolling by the middle of May, 1940, is 1991. The number of Satyagrahis enrolled in the various districts of Bihar is shown separately as follows:

1.	Muzaffarpur	180
2.	Champaran	209
3.	Bhagalpore	253
4.	Gaya	147
5.	Santhal Pargana	25
6.	Monghyr	166
7.	Hazaribagh	166
8.	Manbhum	82
9.	Purnea	274
10.	Darbhanga	115
11.	Patna	220
12.	Palamau	35

Reports from the remaining four districts (including Singhbhum) namely, Saran, Bhahabad, Ranchi and Singhbhum have not reached our office as yet.

Let us now deal with each of the above DC as one by one:

Muzaffarpur

The Satyagraha Training camp was started in this district at Miskaut from the 11th May 1940 which opened by Babu Srikrishna Sinha, Ex-Premier of Bihar and came to a close on 17th May after a week's training. The strength of the camp was 89 and the total quantity of thread spun by the campers during the training period was 128 miles, 559 yds. Their routine work was the same as that of Provincial campers at Sonepur.

Champaran

The satyagraha training camp was started in district at Brindaban from the 16th April 40 under supervision and guidance of Pt Prajapati Misra and dissolved after a week's training. 89 Satyagrahis joined the camp who followed in the footsteps of the provincial Satyagraha campers.

Hazaribagh

The Satyagraha Training was started in district at Ramgarh from the 29th April to the 5th May 1940. The strength of the camp was 66 and their daily routine work was the same as that of the PCC campers at Sonepur.

Manbhum

The report of the Satyagraha camp in this district has not reached our office as yet.

Purnea

The Satyagraha training camp was started in this district at Tikapatti Ashram. The number of Satyagrahis who joined the camp was 76 and the total quantity of thread spun by them was 227478 yds.

Darbhanga

The report of the Satyagraha training camp is not yet available.

Bhagalpore

The Satyagraha training camp was started in this district at Tilakpur which was dissolved on 10-5-1940. The strength of the camp was 63 and the thread spun by the campers was 58 miles and 1243 yds in length. They followed the same routine of work as that of the Provincial campers, report of which has already been sent to your office.

Gaya

The Satyagraha training camp has not started as yet.

Santhal Pargana

The Satyagraha training camp was started in this district at Deoghar from the 19th May 1940 and came to a close on the 26th May after a week's training. The detailed report is not yet available in our office.

Monghyr

The Satyagraha Training camp was started in this district at Khangarhia from the 11th and lasted till the 17th May 1940. The total strength of the camp was 87 and the total quantity of thread spun by the inmates of the camp was 133155 yds.

Patna

The Satyagraha Training camp was started in this district at Khangaul from the 15th May 1940 and was dissolved on the 21st May after a week's training. The number of Satyagrahi campers was 44 and the daily routine work was just in the same line as set up by the provincial campers at Sonepur.

Palamau

The Satyagraha training camp was started in this district at Lesliganj on the 12th and lasted till the 19th May 1940. There were 35 Satyagrahis in all in the camp and they are reported to have spun 25 miles of thread in length.

Further reports will be sent to you as soon as they are available.

Yours sincerely
(Jagjivan Ram)
Secretary

89. Intelligence Reports on Arrests and Convictions in Connection with Congress Activities

Political Department, File No. 42/1940, Serial No. 10 of the list, Bihar State Archives, Patna, 13 June 1940.

Activities of the Congress in this District up to date

Out of the 19 thana Congress Committees in district the following have been converted to Satyagraha Committee.

1. Monghyr Town Congress Committee
2. Khangaria   "   "
3. Chautham   "   "
4. Manjhaul   "   " (Begusarai)
5. Tarapur   "   "
6. Kharagpur   "   "
7. Baraihya   "   "
8. Teghra   "   " (Begusarai)
9. Ballia   "   "
10. Monghyr District Congress Committee

The workers of Chautham Committee have decided to open a Satyagraha camp at village Kaitha from 15/6/40 to 21/6/40 where they would organize a permanent volunteer corp. Brisk collection of fund is also contemplated to maintain the corp. and to construct a Congress building. Mahendra Narayan—a staunch follower of Suresh Misra is taking the lead. He has been elected as the Secretary of the Chautham Thana Congress Committee and Raghubir Singh has been elected President.

Similarly at Manjhaul thana camp organization is in progress and Jaladhar Singh Secretary has enrolled 18 Satyagrahis.

At Teghra a Satyagraha camp will be opened on 20th June and will operate till 27/6/40 near Teghra Railway Station.

Babu Nand Kumar Singh, District Secretary, has issued circulars to all thana Congress committees—that those Congressmen who have enrolled as Satyagrahis on the 30th May are to form Satyagraha Committee the member of which must strictly follow the undertakings of the Satyagraha pledge. The progress however of the enrolment of Satyagrahis in this district is slow and not encouraging to them. Up to 8th May the total number of Satyagrahis came to 166 for which time has been extended by Nand Kumar Babu. 7 more have been enrolled till May 1940 and more enlistment is in progress.

List of organizers for the Satyagraha Committee

1. Babu Nand Kumar Singh
2. Babu Bageshwari Singh
3. Kumar Kalika Pd. Singh
4. M. Saiyid Rafi Uddin Rizvi
5. Babu Ramrijhan Prasad Singh
6. Babu Raghubir Singh (Chautham)
7. Babu Janki Prasad Singh

8. Babu Ramkishore Prasad Singh—Manjhaul
9. Babu Nemdhari Singh
10. Babu Dwarka Prasad Singh
11. Babu Brahmdeo Narayan Singh
12. Babu Mitan Chaudhuri—Teghra
13. Hirday Narayan Prasad

Jamui—No progress—Jagdish Prasad Secretary reports that the workers are not interest in Satyagraha, Committee could be formed.

Babu Jagjiwan Ram, Secretary BPCC (Ex-Parliamentary Secretary) asked the local organizers to extend time for other thana Congress committee to become Satyagraha Committee and directed that no disciplinary action might be taken against any thana committee members. Secretary Gogri Thana Congress Committee reports that up to 27/5/40, 150 four Anna members have been enrolled and only three members have signed the Satyagraha Pledge. Suresh Misra has become the President with his lieutenant Bhutaneshwar Singh Bose as Secretary. (I am enclosing the circular issued by Babu Jagjiwan Ram regarding women's department.) Out of 11 women workers 5 come from Suresh Misra's Asram.

BIHAR PROVISIONAL CONGRESS COMMITTEE

Circular No. 38
Sadaquat Ashram

Patna 25/5/40

All the District Congress Committees
Dear Friend,

Perhaps you are aware that a women's department has been started by the AICC. This department is trying to collect information about the part women have played and are playing in our national movement.

I am sending you two questionnaires on the line of the questionnaires sent to us by the secretary, Women's Department, AICC. The first questionnaire should be replied to us within a week or so. The questions in the second questionnaire are of nature that will require some study and collection of facts and figures before they can be replied. I would suggest that the replies to this be sent to us in installments, if it is not possible to collect all the information at once.

Yours sincerely
Jagjiwan Ram
Secretary

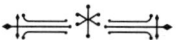

90. Bihar Provincial Congress Committee's Report on Satyagraha Activities

AICC Papers, File No. G–5 (Pt. I)/1940–41, 27 August 1940, NMML.

Bihar Provincial Congress Committee Sadaquat Ashram PO Dighaghat, Patna

Dated 27-8-40

The General Secretary
All India Congress Committee
Allahabad
Dear Sir,

I beg to send herewith the fortnightly report of the Satyagraha work done in our province up to the 10th August 1940.

All the Dist. Congress Committees in the province have been transformed into Satyagraha Committees and the total number of Satyagrahis enrolled till the 10th August 1940 in the whole province is 4376. The number of Satyagrahis enrolled by the various DCCs is given below against their names:

Patna	500
Gaya	175
Shahabad	227
Darbhanga	608
Muzaffarpur	481
Saran	76
Champaran	458
Bhagalpore	306
Monghyr	342
Purnea	405
Santhal Pargana	209
Palamau	35
Ranchi	100
Hazaribagh	94
Manbhum	334
Singhbhum	26

Let us illustrate them one by one:

Patna

The number of Satyagrahis which was 220 only has swelled up to 500. The Satyagrahis have shown great zeal and energy by starting four Satyagraha camps in the district. Sub-divisional camps have been opened in all the subdivisions of the district. And preparations are afoot to open Satyagraha camps in the various Thanas of the district also. The Satyagrahis are carrying on the constructive programme of the Congress successfully.

Gaya

Nothing fresh has been received in the office.

Shahabad

Nothing fresh has been received in the office.

Darbhanga

The number of Satyagrahis has increased from 584 to 608.

Muzaffarpur

The number of Satyagrahis has increased by two only.

Saran

No report is available now.

Champaran

The number of Satyagrahis has risen from 445 to 458. A Satyagraha Conference was held at Brindaban (Champaran) with great éclat in which about 300 Satyagrahis took part.

Bhagalpore

No fresh report is available as yet.

Monghyr

Nothing afresh except that the number of Satyagrahis has risen from 265 to 342.

Purnea

No further report is available.

Santhal Pargana

No fresh news is received.

Palamau

No fresh news is received.

Ranchi

No fresh news is received.

Hazaribagh

No fresh news is received.

Manbhum

No fresh news is received.

Singhbhum

No fresh news is received.

Yours sincerely
S.O. Munemi
Secretary

91. Bombay Provincial Congress Committee's Report on Satyagraha
     Activities and the Decision of Maharashtra Provincial Congress
     Committee on Satyagraha Activities
     AICC Papers, File No. G–5 (Pt.-I)/1940–41, pp. 177–9 and 189, NMML.

Bombay Provincial Congress Committee, Congress House
Vithalbhai Patel Road, Bombay

Date: 19th May 1940

The General Secretary,
All India Congress Committee
Swaraj Bhawan,
Allahabad
Re: Satyagraha activities in the City

Dear Friend,

This is to report the Satyagraha activities in the City of Bombay.

The BPCC had prepared a Satyagraha pledge as far back as January last, that is before the Ramgarh Session of the Congress. The Pledge in its material particulars was almost the same as has been now issued from your office. Even before the Ramgarh Session we had about 35 Satyagrahis in the City who had signed the pledge. After the Ramgarh Session this number is steadily increasing. Today the number of these Satyagrahis who have signed the pledge and put themselves at the disposal of the Congress is 166.

The BPCC has, of course, transformed itself into a Satyagraha Committee for the Province of Bombay, and has also elected a small Council of Action for carrying out the Satyagraha activities. Out of 31 members of the BPCC as many as 26 have already become Satyagrahis. One or two are out of Bombay due to sickness and their forms will be received when they come back to the City. There is one Royist on the Committee who refuses to sign the pledge and also refuses to resign. I have referred this case to you in a separate letter.

Of the 7 DCCs in the City, three have already transformed themselves into Satyagraha Committees. 3 more will do so in a few days. The Committee elections have not been held in one ward owing to election dispute but when these are held, this Committee also will become a Satyagraha Committee.

Out of 14 members of the Bombay Legislature Congress Party, as many as 11 have signed the pledge in Bombay, and others must have done so in Maharashtra, because their constituencies were composite ones coming under the jurisdiction of more than one Congress Province.

Out of 59 members of the Bombay Municipal Congress Party 28 members have already become Satyagrahis. We are expecting pledges from others and as soon as they are received, they will be communicated to you.

As to the holding of camps or Shibirs, it is felt that this kind of activity would not be of any material advantage in the City. Our PCC consists of a compact urban area and Satyagrahis can meet whenever they want. You can however advise us whether we can also usefully undertake this activity.

There have been two or three meetings of Satyagrahis for the exchange of views. During the National Week, Satyagrahis in Bombay undertook a non-stop spinning demonstration

(Akhanda Sutra Yagnya) during the eight days of the National Week. On an average 50 persons used to put in their appearance regularly. We are now thinking of making a rule that every Satyagrahi must contribute 5000 yards of evenly spun yarn every month to the BPCC. This will be decided at the meeting of the BPCC.

Several meeting have been held to explain to the people the political situation, especially with reference to the Congress attitude towards the present war.

At the headquarter of the PCC and also at the offices of the DCCs spinning classes are conducted for the last two months.

These are in brief the Satyagraha activities in the city.

Yours sincerely,
General Secretary.

Maharashtra

The Executive of the Maharashtra PCC met on May 22. The following decisions were taken:
1. Satyagraha camps were opened in each district.

92. Report on Satyagraha and Related Activities in Central Provinces and Berar during the Second Half of April 1940

Fortnightly Reports, File No. 18/4/40, Home Department, Political Intelligence Section, Government of India, NAI.

General Political situation: Complete reports of the observance of the 'National Week' which ended on the 13th, have now been received. The audiences at the meetings held in connection with the 'Week' were generally very small and nowhere exceeded 500, except at meetings held at Nagpur, Jubbulpore and Amraoti on the 13th. The Nagpur and the Jubbulpore meetings were organized by the Forward Bloc. The attendance at the Nagpur meeting is estimated at between 1,500 and 2,000 at the Jubbulpore meeting at 1,000, and at the Amraoti meeting at 7,000. The Amraoti meeting attracted a large attendance as Mrs Sarojini Naidu was the principal speaker. It is the unanimous impression of all district officers that the celebrations were generally devoid of any enthusiasm or active interest. At the Nagpur meeting, Mr Shyamlal Nai, a dismissed head-constable extolled the murder of Sir Michael O'Dwyer but, as he is a man of no status, it was decided not to prosecute him. Orders have, however, issued to warn him for his speech. Portions of the speech of Mr P.Y. Deshpande at this meeting were also objectionable. He has not come to notice before. It was, therefore, considered sufficient merely to issue orders that he should be formally and stringently warned by the District Magistrate. The speeches at Jubbulpore were not actionable, while the speeches at Pachmarhi, Khandwa, and Burhanpur, to which reference was made in the last report, are under examination. It is probable that orders would issue for warning speakers for their objectionable speeches. There has been very little political activity in the Nagpur district. It is said that local leaders are anxious to keep out of jail, and evidence of this is furnished by the fact that only 7 out of 15 members of the Provincial Congress Committee have signed the Satyagraha pledge. Orders have now issued for warning Messrs P.Y. Deshpande and B.N. Mukerjee for their speeches at a meeting held at Nagpur on the 17th March, to which reference was made in the fortnightly report for the second half of March 1940. In Betul, the Forward Bloc held a meeting at a village called Bhounra on 20th April. Mr Anandrao Lokhande presided at the meeting and the audience, which numbered 200, consisted mostly of Gonds. Mr Lokhande advised the people not to help Government on the present war either with men or money. It is reported that the speech had little effect. The Working Committee of the Betul district Forward Bloc has been abolished, and Mr Lokhande has been appointed as a sole dictator to carry on the work. The activities of Mr Lokhande are being carefully watched. A Congress Satyagraha camp was to have been opened on the 28th April near Betul and about 200 Congressmen, including a few ex-Ministers, were expected to attend. It is not yet known whether the camp has actually been opened. It is reported from the Jubbulpore division that 399 Congressmen from Mahakoshal have signed the pledge of active Satyagrahis and that those from the Jubbulpore district include Pandit Dwarka Prasad Misra ex-Minister, Pandit Kashi Prasad Pande and Mr Kunjilal Dube. The Congress proposes to hold a Satyagraha training camp near Jubbulpore sometime this month. The original idea was to hold this camp in the Mandla district from the 29th April, but the local response was apparently not encouraging. The camp near Jubbulpore is expected to be under the supervision of Thakur Chhedilal, president of the Mahakoshal Congress Committee, and the idea is that 100 Congressmen should be trained in that camp and then be posted to various places in the interior of Mahakoshal to train other Satyagrahis for the coming non-violent fight. Mr Shankerrao Deo, a member of the Working Committee of the Congress, who visited Jubbulpore in connection with an election dispute, addressed a meeting attended by about 400 persons on the 21st. Pandit Dwarka Prasad Misra appealed to the audience to obey Mahatma Gandhi and to register themselves as satyagrahis. Mr Deo detailed the stages leading to the present situation in which Congress was preparing for non-violent action. He accused Britain of fighting an imperialistic war and declared that Hitlerism cannot be destroyed so long as Imperialism flourishes. Acharya Narendra Deo addressed a meeting at Khandwa on the same day under the auspices of the district Congress Committee. He explained that the Congress stood for the independence of India as a whole. The Congress was against Nazism, but it was also out to destroy British imperialism. Finally, he appealed to all genuine Congressmen to be prepared for the Satyagraha which was bound to be started as soon as Mahatma Gandhi gave the lead. The president of the district Congress committee said that, in the coming struggle, Nimar would not lag behind other districts, and that within a month local Congressmen would tour the whole of the district and take the message of the Congress to the villages. In the Chhatisgarh division, Pandit Ravishanker Shukla, ex-Prime Minister and Mahant Laxminarain Das toured in Baloda bazar tahsil. They asked the people not to help the British Government during the war and to be ready for civil disobedience. The general idea in the Raipur district appears, however, to be that Mahatma Gandhi's conditions are too strict to make civil disobedience likely. The Raipur district Congress committee is said to have issued instructions to Congress workers to carryon propaganda in the interior to dissuade people from subscribing to the war fund, and it is further reported that district council teachers are also being utilized for this purpose. A report from the Commissioner is being called for. In the Durg district, Mr Sarju Prasad Agarwal has again been active. He addressed two meetings in Panabaras Zamindri on the 14th and 15th. The main object of these meetings was to pass a resolution of 'no confidence' against the Hon'ble Mr G.S. Gupta. It is not unlikely that Mr Sarju Prasad will again stir up agrarian trouble in the Dondi–Lohara zamindari. In the Bhandara district, Mr Chaturbhujbhai Jasani has been organizing Satyagraha committees and touring to enlist Satyagrahis, though with little result. In Berar, the public appears to be generally tired of politics. Mr Rajagopalachariar, ex-Prime Minister of Madras, was able to attract only an audience of about 2,000 persons at Akola, while a newspaper report states that the Hon'ble Mr Brijlal

Biyani was hooted at a meeting at Khamgaon. At the same time, preparations are being made by the Congress all over the province in anticipation of a struggle with the British Government though, according to the latest pronouncement of Mahatma Gandhi, mass civil disobedience is not likely to be started. As a precautionary measure, Government has now issued orders giving discretion to the local authorities to secure full and accurate reporting of speeches made at political and quasi-political meetings. The general situation is also being constantly reviewed by Government.

93. Fortnightly Report on Satyagraha and Other Political Activities in Central Provinces and Berar

Fortnightly Reports, File No. 18/5/40, Home Department, Political Intelligence Section, Government of India, First Half of May 1940, NAI.

General political situation: The speeches at Pachmarhi, Khandwa and Burhanpur in connect ion with the observance of the 'National Week', to which reference was made in the last report, have been examined. Orders have issued for warning Messrs Chaurasia and Jaiswal for their speeches on the 6th and the 13th April. Mr Chaurasia is a person of very little status, and it has been decided that both speakers should be prosecuted if the warning is not heeded. The speeches at Khandwa were not actionable, while Mr Fakirchand Kapoor has been ordered to be warned for his speech at Burhanpur.

All District Congress Committees have now been converted into Satyagraha Committees, and the enrolment of active and passive satyagrahis continues. Altogether 456 persons are reported to have enrolled as active satyagrahis in Mahakoshal. Of these, 45 are reported to belong to the Jubbulpore district. 100 Satyagrahis have been enrolled in the Raipur District. In the Bilaspur district, 29 persons have joined as active Satyagrahis. The number enrolled in Durg is 400, of whom only 12 are for active Satyagraha. Information about the total number of Satyagrahis enrolled in the province is being collected. The Mahakoshal Satyagraha train- ing camp, which was to have been held in the Jubbulpore district, was eventually held at Narsinghpur from the 8th to the 15th May. No report has yet been received of the number of persons attending the camp or about the activities at the camp. A training camp for satyagrahis was also held at Akola from the 5th to the 7th May. About 220 primary school teachers are said to have attended the camp under the orders of the Chairman, district council, and about 50 others. A Satyagraha training camp is also proposed to be opened at Raipur.

In the Nagpur district, a political conference was held at Umrer on the 28th April 1940. Speeches were delivered at the conference by Messrs Saoji, Mote, Dandekar and Bhise. Mr Bhise's speech was objectionable and orders have been issued for warning him. In Betul, the Multai Tahsil Congress Conference was held at Sainkheda on the 28th April under the presidentship of Mr Dipchand, MLA. The conference was addressed, amongst others, by three teachers presumably of district council schools. The speech of Mr Balaram, one of the teachers, was anti-British and anti-war. Orders have been issued for warning him. The speech of Mr Bakarama Khade, president of the Kisan Sabha, was also objectionable, and orders have been issued for warning him. A revolutionary pamphlet, the details of which are given in appendix A, was distributed at two places in the Betul district. The pamphlet has been banned under section 99 A of the Criminal Procedure Code, and the District Magistrate has been asked to prosecute the author, the printer and the distributors of the leaflet under the Defence of India Rules. In the Jubbulpore division, political activity was confined mostly to the recruiting of satyagraha volunteers by Congress workers. In the Hoshangabad district, Mr Shankerlal Choudhari, MLA, and one or two others have been touring in the villages and, at a fair in Seoni–Malwa, Mr Chaitram addressed about 150 villagers and asked them to volunteer for Satyagraha in the coming fight and not to help Government in the war. A belated report states that, at a meeting held at Damoh on the 20th April, which was attended by 400 persons, Mr D.P. Misra, ex-Minister, suggested that the War Relief Fund should not be supported and exhorted the audience to become active or passive Satyagrahis. A further belated report states that Mr Babulal Seth made an anti-war speech at a small meeting held at Garhakota in the Saugor district on the 14th April. Orders have been issued to warn the speaker. In the Chattisgarh division, the Raipur District Congress Committee has asked the district council to give leave to the teachers, who wish to become active Satyagrahis, and at a meeting held at Sihawa early in April, school teachers are said to have stated that they are ready to take part in civil disobedience. Schoolmasters are active in that district in organizing progress meetings and meeting Congress leaders on tour. They are said to have been asked to do propaganda against subscriptions to the War Relief Fund and recruitment, and it is reported that the school teachers are carrying on secret propaganda against the War Relief Fund. The Mahasamund tahsil political conference was held on the 25th April under the presidentship of Pandit R.S. Shukla, ex-Prime Minister. In the course of his speech, he said that people should be so trained in non-violence that they should not give way even if fired on by the authorities. In Bilaspur also, district council teachers are being used for Congress propaganda. An ashram is being built for the training of volunteers. It is reported that the officials of the Matin Zamindari, who are Congressmen, are trying to stir up trouble in Pendra by encouraging non-payment of rent and grazing dues and by inciting the tenants to clear up forests. The Deputy Commissioner is being asked to be in close touch with the situation. In Durg, Mr Sarjuprasad, who has often figured in these reports, is continuing to agitate against the orthodox Congress party and is showing signs of an intention to start Satyagraha. He has been told that, if he does so, he will be dealt with promptly.

94.   Confidential Reports on Political Activities in Central Provinces and Berar

> Madhya Pradesh Secretariat Records, General Administration Department, Government of CP and Berar, Mahakoshal, File No. 411, Acc. No. 2144, Madhya Pradesh State Archives.

Congress propaganda meetings were held at Mohpa, Khapa, Bori, Katol and Jalalkheda in the Nagpur district between the 6th and 14th instant. Bhikulal Chandak addressed the meetings at Mohpa, Katol and Jalalkheda. He described the policy of the Congress since the outbreak of the war and stated that it had refused to co-operate in the prosecution of the war until independence was granted. He added that Government announced India's belligerency without their consent because they were slaves but it had failed to influence Ireland and Egypt as these countries were free. He referred to the withdrawal from British Somaliland and stated that if Britain had no intention of defending India she should make over defence to them.

Speaking at the Khapa meeting, which was attended by 150 persons, one Agnihotri (definite particulars under enquiry) said that they would only be able to solve the problems of un-employment and agriculture after ejecting the British from the country and that it was only on account of disunity among themselves that enabled the small local police force to control them.

Narayanrao Balaji Neral, speaking at a meeting of 300 at Armori(Chanda) on the 7th October, criticized Government's failure to construct irrigation tanks in areas affected by drought and in attention to the widespread unemployment. He said that, unless they took over the reins of government, they would always be slaves.

A Congress Sainik Dal has been started at Magbhir (Chanda).

G.R. Trivedi, who has been appointed Dictator for the Chhindwara district, spoke at the first of his whirlwind tour meetings at Lodikhera on the 9th instant. He deplored the lack of enthusiasm shown towards the Congress, which was working for the freedom of the country and pointed out the benefits of the Congress regime. Referring to the war he said that the Congress merely wanted Britain to apply to India the principles for which she was supposed to be fighting.

In the Betul district meetings were held at Ramli and Chicholi only. At the former Ramrao, Kalar, a student of Pattan, who has been warned previously for objectionable utterances, advised his audience not to help in the war but to concentrate on the formation of Gram Rakshak Dals. At the other Kunjilal Kalar, a school master characterized British rules as tyrannous and stated they needed a government on the Soviet model. Satyanarayan Pande, a relieving schoolmaster, who also spoke, accused Government of ruining India's culture and prosperity and said it was not a sin to slay an enemy.

Pandit Jawaharlal Nehru addressed a meeting of 4,000 at Hoshangabad on the 16th October. In a guarded speech he dwelt on the international situation and the attitude of the Congress towards the war. He said the Congress had decided to resort to direct action as it was unable to tolerate the collection of subscriptions for the prosecution of a war in which it had decided not to cooperate. He explained that swaraj did not signify the substitution of European bureaucracy by an Indian but a complete revision of the administrative policy.

A series of well-attended to meetings were held in the interior of the Raipur district in connection with the threatened scarcity, at which Congress workers conducted Congress propaganda but seemed to make little impression on their audiences.

In the Bilaspur district a series of meetings in the mofusil has been announced between the 20th and 27th October. These meetings are advertised as measures to allay the scarcity but they will, it is understood, cloak Congress propaganda. A list of persons who will address these meetings has been prepared and instructions issued about the matter to be discussed.

Meetings began on 22nd and on that day were held in Khokhrash (attendance 800), Kargi–Khurd (500) and Bilaspur town (300). The speaker praised Congress and asked for whole hearted support of its measures. The audience was also told to ask Government for help during the scarcity and that Congress would see that Government took action. Certain speakers infringed the Defence of India Rules, particularly Bhuwan Bhaskarsingh of Akaltara at Khokhrash, whose references to Jallianwalabagh and its consequences, the present condition of Great Britain and the Government's present policy were objectionable. Sirpalsingh a 15 year old nephew of Thakur Chhedilal also made a violently abusive and anti-British speech in Bilaspur until checked by Mirza Ahmad Ali Beg, Diwan of Kargi Zamindari who was in the audience.

On the 10th October R.G. Tiwari opened the Satyagraha Ashram at Mungeli and in his speech urged the audience to make the ashram a bulwark in the coming fight with Government by joining it and being ready to die for their country.

At a *Ramayan* recital at Pendra on the 14th instant, Kranti Kumar dwelt on the freedom of speech and their inherent right to speak against the war which was none of their making.

Chaturbhujbhai Jasani addressed two meetings of about 500 and 1,000 at Mundhari-Kalan and Angaon (Bhandara) during the week. He referred to British rule as a curse and pointed out that a very small quota of the revenue of the country was utilized for their benefit and that liquor shops were maintained for their demoralization.

Small anti-war meetings were held at Nandgaon, Seoni and Kholapur in the Amraoti district at which Purushottam Kashinath Deshmukh, Mahadeo Namdeo Kubde and Raghunathmal Sarvasukhdas Kochar urged their audiences not to assist.

B.G. Kher, former Prime Minister of Bombay, addressed large meetings at Amraoti, Karanja and Telhara (Akola), Akola and Khamgaon (Buldana) between the 14th and 16th October. He spoke in justification of the attitude of the Congress towards the war as the help rendered in the last war was not only not recognized but followed by repression. He declared that the cordial relations, which had sprung up between Government and the Congress during the latter's tenure of office, were dissipated when India was involved in the war. He criticized the despatch of Indian troops overseas and said that the army maintained by Indian revenues, was obviously meant for the purpose of preserving bureaucracy both inside and outside India.

At meeting of 400 held at Akola on the 13th instant under the presidentship of the Hon'ble Mr Brijlal Biyani to mark the conclusion of 'Labourer's Week', organized by the Congress Mazdur Sangh, Members of the Textile Workers' Union spoke opposing the formation of the Sangh. The president denied that he was influenced by the mill-owners or that the Sangh was a political body, formed to secure votes for the Congress. He explained that the Sangh had not been able to do anything for the workers as it had only just been formed.

At a small Congress meeting held at Narwal (Buldana) on the 13th October, Vithal Gopal Korde stated that Britain's position was precarious and that she, after extracting their wealth, had ignored their claims to independence.

95   Report of the Delhi Provincial Congress Committee

AICC Papers, File No. G–5 (Pt. IV), 1940 [October ?], NMML.

The number of Satyagrahis so far enrolled in the province is 10 including 4 lady workers. Out of them 4 signatories who have signed the pledge are not spinning regularly. It has been arranged to hold weekly meetings of the Satyagrahis every Sunday.

A full fledged Charkha club has been started at a central place in Chandni Chowk and it is contemplated to open its branches in different wards of the city. The central club has on its rolls about 50 members including 20 ladies and daily spinning classes and demonstrations are held in the afternoon. In addition to this nearly all the members of the Charkha Club meet every Sunday and bring their Charkhas and slivers with them and spin for an hour. No other step is being taken just at present to popularize khadi.

No special steps have been taken this year to establish contacts with the Harijans and minorities.

The PCC and its executive has already met twice in May and the reorganization of various committees has engaged their attention. For various reasons the Delhi DCCs has been suspended and its functions have been taken over by the PCC.

As already stated only 10 members have signed the Satyagraha pledge. They are mostly members of the PCC.

The preparatory work relating to the Satyagraha has just been taken up by the reconstituted PCC.

Since there are very little preparations for Satyagraha, the question of reaction on the public does not arise.

Officially the Congress committee has not held any training camp in the province but some old and trained Congressmen are starting training camps both in the city and in the rural area on their own initiative.

A number of public meetings were held during the National Week and one or two more meetings later on, at which Ramgarh resolution was explained to the public.

A strict eye is being kept on those who have signed the Satyagraha pledge. In one instance it was discovered that condition regarding spinning and wearing Khadi was not being strictly adhered to and the fact was brought to the notice of the persons signing the pledge with the result that the pledge was withdrawn.

Officially there are no Congress members in the local boards. As regards the members of the Congress Executive instances have come to our notice that the khadi clause is not being rigidly and scrupulously obeyed.

96 Repression in United Provinces: Jawaharlal Nehru's Letter to Mahatma Gandhi, 10 August 1940

SWJN, Vol. XI, pp. 275–7.

My dear Bapu,

I have just received your letter of the 8th. About Hyderabad, I can make no suggestion. So much depends on the strength of the people and their organization. I think, however, that it is far better for them to concentrate on the rural areas where the chances of communal clashes are probably less. I do not see how they can remain passive under the circumstances. Yet it may be perhaps better not to precipitate a big crisis immediately in view of the rapid developments of the political situation in India as a whole. When this all-India situation advances further, Hyderabad people might be in a better position to assert their right.

In a sense I am not sorry at the developments in Hyderabad. The impossible attitude that Bahadur Yar Khan and others have taken up will react on them. It may of course lead to a great deal of trouble and bloodshed. In any event the state Congress people should make it perfectly clear that they cannot reduce by an iota their demand for responsible government.

I understand the Working Committee is likely to meet in Wardha in eight or nine days time. I hope to meet you then.

About the exactions for war funds, I have written to the secretary of the UPPCC to send you some particulars. Some have been published in the press and are clear enough. Some others, though equally clear, might be explained differently. For instance, a usual case is for a person to be approached for a donation. He refuses or offers a smaller sum than what is demanded. Immediately or a day or two after he is arrested on the charge of preventing others from subscribing to the war funds, and thereby coming in the way of war efforts.

I have just had a case like this from Allahabad district. A poor village shopkeeper was asked to give Rs 151 or Rs 201. He said the most he could possibly give was Rs 51. He was cursed and sworn at and immediately a notice was given to him to appear to show cause why he should not be proceeded against under the Defence of India Rules. His case is up today in a court here. Usually this kind of thing is not done with full-fledged Congressmen who are expected to refuse anyhow. Another case which has come to me today is from Kasgang in Etah district. A *Naib Tehsildar* went to the shop of a Congressman on 2nd of August and demanded money for the war funds. This was refused and the man stated that as a Congressman he could not do so. Thereupon the *Naib Tehsildar* threatened to take action and had the name of the person noted down. On the next day this man, who is the nephew of a well-known Congressman in the district, was suddenly arrested for non-payment of a punitive police tax. He was put in the lock-up and for 30 hours he was not given any food or facilities for bathing etc. This arrest was completely illegal as punitive tax can only be recovered by attachment of property and the person concerned, whose name is Omprakash, has considerable moveable and immoveable property. The amount of punitive tax concerned was only Rs 6 which could easily have been realized by attachment. Omprakash's uncle, Manpal Gupta, thereupon created a lot of fuss and ultimately Omprakash was discharged. That is how the matter stands now.

Another interesting case is that of Thakur Surendra Bahadur Singh, Taluqdar of Simri in Rae Bareli district. He is Congress MLA. His father, the Taluqdar, recently died and thereupon, at his own request, his taluqa was taken under the court of wards. The Deputy Commissioner informed him that he should contribute Rs 1500 to the war fund. He refused to do so as a Congressman. He was then told that he held his taluqa on conditions of loyalty and good service and the court of wards has a perfect right to give the donation out of the revenues of the taluqa. Thereupon he sent a registered notice to the Deputy Commissioner protesting against this imposition and saying that it was wholly illegal. His case was that it might or might not be open to the government to confiscate his taluqa for want of loyalty to them. But it was certainly not open to them to give a donation on his behalf and against his will. In spite of this the Deputy Commissioner has already paid or is going to pay this sum to the war fund and Surendra Bahadur Singh is thinking of bringing a declaratory suit in a court of law.

I am getting complaints from various districts of pressure being brought on kisans to pay eight annas or a rupee or more per plough. It is obvious that they do not want to pay but are compelled to do so.

Petty government servants and minor officials dare not say no when they are asked to contribute. A recent case which came to my notice informally but nevertheless correctly was that of a steno-typist of a district magistrate. He was asked to give Rs 200. His salary was Rs 125 a month. He pointed out hesitatingly that he had a large family and it was entirely beyond his capacity to pay that sum. He was then told that in any event he and his family would have to starve if the British lost the war. So this was a kind of insurance that he had to pay. A curious thing is that one does not hear very much about donations from higher officials. They think it is enough for them to serve the cause by giving their very efficient service at a high rate of payment.

The number of new appointments at high salaries grows from day to day. Probably a very large proportion of the funds that are being collected go towards the payment of these high salaries. Simla, I understand, is crowded with this type of officials serving the great cause by drawing a fancy salary for little or no work. There was a recent case of an English official who was till recently drawing Rs 750 a month suddenly being pushed into some war work and is being given Rs 2500 a month. It was stated that he had accepted this new job at considerable sacrifice to himself.

Yours affectionately,
Jawaharlal

97. Report of the Frontier Province Congress Committee

AICC Papers, File No. G–5 (Pt. IV), 1940 [May ? 1940], NMML.

1. According to reports received in the office from the subordinate committees, 6,000 Satyagrahis have been enrolled so far. They are all members of the Congress Committees. The work of enrolling members of primary Congress Committees as Satyagrahis has now commenced.

2. Three big Satyagraha Training camps were held in the province, which proved very successful. A provincial Satyagraha camp is in progress from May 8 in which all important workers and officers of the Khudai Khidmatgars are participating. It is proposed to follow up this provincial camp by district camps.

3. Lectures are being arranged to popularize Khadi. We have a spinning demonstration at every public meeting. A scheme for opening a Khadi centre in the province is under consideration.

4. (a) Harijans are a small number in the province. Most of them are with the Congress (b) Sub-Committee for minorities have been set up in important areas.

5. ... Departments for (i) propaganda (ii) minorities (iii) Charkha have been opened. On an average the office issues 10 circulars a month For propaganda the circulars resolutions! instructions and the utterances of Mahatma Gandhi are translated into Pushto and published in the form of pamphlets and public meetings are organized. The camps have been very successful.

6. The PCC met twice after fresh elections for the current year. The Working Committee meets every month. The matters discussed were (a) preparation for Satyagraha, enrolment of active Satyagrahis, ... (e) district and provincial camps for Satyagrahis, (f) Gandhiji's instructions ....

7. There are 7 district Congress committees in the frontier. The total membership of these committee is 428. They are all Satyagrahis.

8. The District Committees have turned into Satyagraha Committees. The work of training the Satyagrahis to enable them to fulfill effectively the conditions prescribed in the pledge has not begun. This is done through camps and public meetings. 6000 active Satyagrahis have been enrolled so far. The primary members will be tackled now. Details about this will be sent later.

9. The Ward Committees are doing their job well. Their members are active Satyagrahis.

10. All the members of the PCC have signed the pledge, including the members of the Forward Bloc who are there in small numbers.

11. ... The public is reacting very favourably to the preparations for Satyagraha. We, however, see to it that the Satyagrahis are not enrolled indiscriminately.

12. Four big training camps have been held so far in the province. They will now be followed by district camps; the daily routine in the camp is (1) physical exercise, (2) digging, (3) round making, (4) filling ditches, (5) spinning, (6) discourses and discussion. The results are very satisfactory.

13. 40 meetings have been held under the auspices of the PCC after the latter's conversion into a Satyagraha Committee. It is difficult to form an estimate of the Ward and Village Committees. We have now drawn up a programme of 'one village one meeting'. At these meetings the resolution of the Congress are explained and the people exhorted to act up to them.

The speeches and instructions of Gandhiji as also the circulars of the AICC are widely broadcast in Pushto.

98. Letter to the Secretary, All India Congress Committee Regarding Satyagraha Activities and Related Information in Gujarat

AICC Papers, File No. G–5 (Pt. IV), 1940 [May ? 1940], NMML.

To
The Secretary
All India Congress Committee
Allahabad

Dear Friend,

With reference to your letter No. P–1/598 dated 4/5/40 I am sending herewith the information required by you.

1. The number of members who have signed the Satyagraha Pledge is 1791. Some in Ahmedabad city signed in the hope that Satyagraha will be started at once. They think that their hopes are not fulfilled and therefore they withdrew their pledge. But their number is very small. Most of those who have signed the pledge are trying to fulfill its conditions. Those who have taken to spinning for the first time find it very difficult and they have not made much progress. These are mostly members of Municipal and Local Board Congress Party. Satyagrahis in a Taluka at present tour the Taluka and thus they are in constant touch with each other.

2. People have been asked to take to spinning and different spinning centres have been organized in each taluka, where every one spins for oneself. But on account of bad economic conditions of villages the progress is slow....

6. All the GPCC members numbering 114 have signed the Satyagraha pledge. 18 members of the District, Talukas City and Committees Congress have not signed the pledge. About 11 of them refused to resign their seats.

7. There are 5 District Congress Committees, 2 City Congress Committees and 31 Taluka Congress committees. All of them have been turned to Satyagraha Committees. The District Congress committees control and guide all the activities of the city and Taluka Congress committees within their jurisdiction.

8. ADCD does not take any step by itself but it works through Taluka Committees. Each taluka committee is organizing parties to tour the taluka to carry and explain the message of Mahatma Gandhi to the public.

9. There are very few village committees. They assist the Taluka Committee in organizing propaganda work.

10. There are following groups in the Congress (1) Socialists (2) Communists (3) Royist and Forward Bloc (4) Kisan Sabha group. The socialist group has practically accepted the Congress Programme. The other groups have no faith in the constructive programme of the Congress and try to ridicule it. They have not signed the pledge and refuse to resign their seats. Those who have refused to resign their seats belong to these groups.

12. No training camps are held in the province.

Yours sincerely,
B.D. Lala
Secretary
Gujarat PCC

99. Report of the Karnatak Provincial Congress Committee on Satyagraha and Related Activities
AICC Papers, File No. P–10/1940–41, NMML.

Dharwar: August 16, 1940

Dear Brother,

I am herewith sending you a short summary of the work done in the province for the last two months.

1. The total number of active Satyagrahis in the province as it stands today is 696, that is 98 more than when last reported on 28-5-1940. More are expected.

2. Last month two more Satyagraha camps were conducted one in Bailhongal in Belgaum District by the Belgaum District Congress Committee and the other in Ron in Dharwar District by Ron Taluk Congress Committee. The former trained 425 Satyagrahis while in latter 18 were given training. On the whole seven camps have been conducted and 201 Satyagrahis have been given training.

3. In order to organize and inspect the present condition of the Congress Committees I toured the Districts of Belgaum and Dharwar. I visited 64 towns and villages in Belgaum District in my tour then for 14 days.

4. The several Departments namely, the women, harijan, khadi, and others appointed by the Provincial Satyagraha Council are working to the best of their ability. The detailed reports of their working will be sent sometime later.

5. In connection with the Muslim mass contact everything had been arranged to have Shri Ali Bahadur Khan tour this province. He had agreed to tour this province in the third week of this month. But, unfortunately, as a case has been foisted on him the tour has to be indefinitely postponed. However, this office is in communication with other Nationalist Muslim workers in this connection.

6. The provincial Satyagraha council in its meeting of 25-7-40 considered the reports wherein officials were using coercion to collect the war fund. The council issued a publication explaining the real position and advising the people as to what they had to do in such circumstances. 4000 copies of this publication along with the Wardha statement of the Working Committee were printed by the Provincial Satyagraha Committee and circulated through out the province. Then an instant was brought to the notice of this office when the education inspector had warned some teachers of Dharwar District School Board who had refused to cooperate with the local officials in the war fund collections. The Dharwar District School Board condemned this action of the Education Inspector in its meeting of 4-8-1940.

..... Taking this instance as an example another publication was issued by the provincial office asking the people to be alive to their rights. The latest Working Committee's resolution on compulsory levies are being printed in the provincial language and distributed by the District Congress Committee concerned.

7. Before concluding I would like to bring to your notice that there is a growing impression in the minds of the people of the province that Government is taking undue advantage of the Congress policy of not precipitating matters. In this critical hour of Britain that these compulsory levies and coercion in war fund collections and repressive policy in general do show how the Government view our gesture and that it is high time that Congress takes a forward step and

counteract this. So I would respectfully suggest that the Working Committee considers this aspect of the question also.

Your brother,
Gen. Secretary

To
The General Secretary,
All India Congress Committee
Swaraj Bhavan,
Allahabad

100.   Kottayam Taluka Political Conference

Mathrubhumi, 16 May 1940.

Kottayam Taluk Political Conference flays Gandhian ideology and approach in freedom struggle. Congress has adopted a suicidal path ever since war broke out. Gandhi's unconditional offer of support to Congress is unjustifiable. Now people have to spend their resources to fight for the imperial dreams of the British. Gandhi's statement that there will be no movement like that of the Dandi March of 1930 is significant. He is indirectly helping the British.

The following appeals were made to Congress:

1. Propagate the Congress stand on war, democracy
2. Efforts for propagating Satyagraha through Satyagraha samiti.
3. Oppose vehemently the price rise, taxes etc owing to war.
4. Oppose rule by ordinance, oppression etc.
5. Actively participate in the war of peasants, labour etc.
6. Strengthen primary committee/volunteer corps to carry out these activities.

101.   Report on Satyagraha Activities in Madras

Fortnightly Report, File No. 18/4/40, Home Department, Political Intelligence Section, Government of Madras, Second Half of April 1940, NAI.

My dear Conran Smith,
Fortnightly Report for the Second Half of April 1940
Political: Congressmen have been active in forming themselves into Satyagraha Committees, in collecting signatures to the pledge, and in holding meetings to popularize the idea of a civil disobedience movement and to encourage volunteers. Orthodox Congress men are however by no means whole heartedly in favour of Satyagraha and are content with Mr Gandhi's view of the matter, and even office bearers in Congress organizations have shown little enthusiasm. Mr Satyamurthy, MLA (Central) at first avoided signing the pledge by leaving the Committee meeting early. He has however since signed it. An MLA in Chittoor refused to sign on the ground that there was no sense in it. The Secretary District Congress Committee, Chingloput has resigned in protest against the Congress attitude in time of this war. There has certainly been no rush of would-be Satyagrahis and some of those who have signed the pledge evidently believe that any Civil Disobedience movement that may be launched will be confined to a particularly favourable locality and that all those who have signed the pledge may not be

called upon to make 'sacrifices'. At the same time the preparations have led to an increase in Congress meetings. There were the usual occasional anti-war and communist speeches, and a few persons have been prosecuted or restricted to their villages and one more detained in Jail. Details will be found in the Appendix. At present Mottupalayam in Coimbatore District is the worst centre, as adherents of the Youth League have been fairly active both in making speeches and in distributing leaflets. A proposal to burn an effigy of Sir Michael O'Dwyer there was stopped by an order under Section 144 Criminal Procedure Code. At Pollachi in the same district an MLA made an objectionable speech in the course of which he said that England is not going to win the War. He will be warned by the District Magistrate.

102. A Report on Malabar Disturbances

File No. 5/22/40, Home Department, Political Intelligence, Government of Madras, NAI.

Describing the occurrences at Tellicherry, where printed notices were issued on 14th September announcing a meeting for the 15th, the press note says:

The joint Magistrate accompanied by the police inspector and Tahsildar went to the Congress office where some nine or ten local leaders were assembled. The joint Magistrate reasoned with them for about fifteen minutes and warned them of the consequences of defying the prohibitory order. They replied, in the words of the joint Magistrate, that 'they had orders from their headquarters to hold the meeting at all costs.' The joint Magistrate then instructed the inspector to arrest the nine leaders. This was done in the case of eight, the ninth escaping.

These eight persons were at once removed to Kuthuparamba eight miles away in order to avoid the possibility of demonstration.

In the meantime a crowd had gathered at the meeting place on the beach. A head constable with four constables had been posted there and the head constable had warned the crowd, to disperse but to no effect. Then the ninth person who had escaped arrest arrived and began to address the crowd. As soon as the main Police Party appeared, the crowd estimated at 1,500 strong began to throw stones and sand. The police party consisted of the joint Magistrate, the inspector, one sub-inspector 16 local police and 12 armed reserve summoned from Cannanore that morning. Nine constables were hit with stones and the joint magistrate was hit in the mouth and on the wrist. The crowd was warned but continued to throw stones and a lathi charge was ordered. This had no effect. The crowd became more riotous and stonethrowing continued. Some members of the crowd had short sticks and one a hammer, and three lathies were wrested from the police. The joint Magistrate again shouted a warning to the crowd in Malayalam that unless they dispersed and stopped throwing stones he would be compelled to order firing. This warning had no effect and the attitude of the crowd became more menacing. After a final warning the joint Magistrate ordered the police to open fire. Seventeen rounds were fired and the crowd then dispersed. Eight members of the crowd were wounded by the firing. Two have since died, one is in a critical condition and two are seriously wounded. A ninth member of the crowd is in hospital with a lathi blow. Of the eleven constables hit by stones three were admitted to hospital.

The two deceased persons were a school teacher and a beedi labourer. Five of the six wounded persons are beedi labourers.

Describing the occurrences at Pappinesseri the press note states the crowd did not disperse and some sixty uniformed volunteers formed themselves into two lines. The sub-inspector thereupon ordered a lathi charge. Immediately the crowd rushed from all sides and began to stone the police heavily. All members of the police party were hit by stones and a hand-to-hand fight began. The sub inspector, Taliparamba, fired two shots with his revolver, wounding one member of the crowd but was then felled to the ground by a big stone.

The sub inspector, Baliapatam and four constables were struck to the ground by stones and incapacitated. The remaining constables, the sub-Magistrate and the sub-inspector, Taliparamba then made their escape. The sub-inspector Baliapatam who was by this time unconscious was thrown on the side of the road where more stones were thrown at him. When a party of armed reserve arrived from Cannanore about two hours later he was lying dead amid a heap of stones. The four seriously injured constables had been moved to a verandah by sympathetic villagers and given water. One of these constables died that night in hospital.

At Mattannur six members of the police party of seven received substantial injuries and were removed to the Cannanore hospital, one of them has died.

103.   Riots and Disturbances—Celebration of 'Protest Day' by Kerala Provincial Congress Committee

File No. F5/18/40, Home Department, Political Intelligence, Government of Madras, NAI.

Political Agitation—'Protest Day'—Defiance of Prohibitory order against meetings—Report Submitted.

The Working Committee of the KPCC called for the observance of 15-9-1940 as 'Protest Day' to protest against the repressive policy of the Government under the Defence of India Rules and against the recent statement of the Secretary of State for India on constitutional affairs. Under Rule 56(1) of the Defence of India Rules I prohibited all meetings and processions in pursuance of 'Protest Day'. This order was issued on 12-9-1940 and was given wide publicity being served on local leaders in various places.

Calicut—Notice issued by the Secretary of the Calicut Town Congress Committee and dated 12-9-1940 were circulated in the town in the morning, saying that a procession would start from the Mananchira Maidan and proceed to the Beach where a public meeting would be held. Four subsidiary processions started, evidently with the view of joining up at the maidan, and the leaders totalling 17 were arrested. The processions broke up but the processionists made their way to the beach and at 6-30 the public meeting was attempted. H. Manjunatha Rao, who was restricted to a specific area by an order under the Defence of India Rule, broke the order and attempted to make a speech. He and the President were arrested. The crowd then began to throw stones and the Inspector, the Sergeant and some constables were hit, though not seriously injured; some passers-by were also hit. The crowd was warned and then dispersed by a lathi charge. The crowd began to run as soon as the Police charged and no serious injuries have been reported. The crowd is reported to have been very large.

Cannanore—A meeting was attempted and one person began to speak. The crowd was warned to disperse but refused to do so. A lathi charge was then ordered. The crowd began to run as soon as the Police charged and no serious injuries have been reported. There was no stone throwing or any attempt to attack the police.

Pappinisseri (about 6 miles north of Cannanore). In this case the prohibitory order defied was an order under Sec. 144. A so-called peasants' meeting was called for 15-9-1940, the same day as 'Protest Day', at short notice. The object of this according to Police information was to circumvent the ban against 'Protest Day'. Pappinisseri is the place where in April last a strike among the labourers of the Aaron Spinning and Weaving Mills gave rise to breaches of the peace and an assault on the Police. It was also a centre of peasants' agitation in 1938. The Sub-Magistrate decided therefore to prohibit the meeting under Sec. 144, apprehending that the holding of a meeting in this locality in circumstances amounting to defiance of the ban on 'Protest Day' might lead to a disturbance of the public tranquility. Upon being served with this order, the organizers of the meeting arranged to hold it in the next village just across the boundary to which the Sec. 144 order did not apply. (It should be explained at this point that the first order under Sec. 144 was issued by the Sub Magistrate, Cannanore in respect of Pappinisseri, Kalliasseri and Baliapatam the area from which the employees of the Aaron Mills come. The village of Morazha to which the meeting was shifted is in the jurisdiction of the Sub-Magistrate, Taliparamba, but within the jurisdiction of the Sub-Inspector of Baliapatam). The Sub-Inspector thereupon moved the sub-Magistrate, Taliparamba who apprehending in the circumstances a disturbance of the public tranquility, passed an order under Sec. 144 applicable to the village of Morazha.

The Police party consisting of the Sub-Inspector, Baliapatam, one Head Constable and seven Police constables accompanied by the Sub-Magistrate and the Sub-Inspector of Taliparamba proceeded to the meeting place reaching it about 4 PM. They found a large crowd gathered; among conflicting estimates I would put the number at 700–1000. There were also about 60 volunteers clad in green shirts. (They were not regular volunteers but appear to have been arranged for the occasion and included labourers of the Aaron Mills who were not re-instated after the April strike). The order was read out to the crowd and a copy served on the most prominent man present, K.P.R. Gopalan Nambiyar. (He is a member of the Working Committee of the KPCC and is said to have arranged the meeting together with V. Bharatheeyan, recently released from jail after serving a sentence imposed during the peasants' agitation). The Sub-Inspector, Baliapatam warned the crowd to disperse in five minutes. One leader argued that the order did not apply to them. The Sub-Inspector arrested him and warned the crowd that if they did not disperse he would disperse them by force. The crowd did not disperse and the volunteers formed themselves into two lines. The Sub-Inspector thereupon ordered a lathi charge. Immediately the crowd rushed from all sides and began to stone the Police heavily. K.P.R. Gopalan Nambiyar is said to have called on the crowd to 'smash the Police'. All members of the Police party were hit by stones and as a party overpowered, and a hand-to-hand fight began. The Sub-Inspector, Taliparamba fired two shots with his revolver, wounding one member of the crowd but was then felled to the ground by a big stone. The Sub-Inspector, Baliapatam appears to have been held by one man while others struck him with stones held in their hands. Four constables were struck to the ground by stones and incapacitated. The remaining constables, the Sub-Magistrate and the Sub Inspector, Taliparamba then made their escape. The Sub-Inspector, Baliapatam who was by this time unconscious was thrown on the side of the road where more stones were thrown at him. When a party of Armed Reserve arrived from Cannanore about two hours later, he was lying dead amid a heap of stones. The four seriously injured constables had been moved to a verandah by sympathetic villagers and given water. One of these constables died that night in hospital. The Reserve party found the place deserted, the offenders having taken to hiding. A similar situation prevailed when I arrived with another detachment of the Armed Reserve the following morning.

Mattanur (about 15 miles east of Cannanore) Three processions met at a central place forming a crowd of some 500 or more. The Sub-Inspector accompanied by a Head Constable and five constables warned the crowd to disperse. They refused to do so and the Sub-Inspector ordered a lathi charge. The crowd immediately began to throw stones. The sub-inspector appears to have been knocked out at a very early stage by a stone in the face; the small police party became dispersed and each man was attacked individually. One constable managed to get away and ran to the Police station about 200 yards away and returned with two muskets and ammunition. These were however snatched from him by the crowd. Six members of the Police party of seven received substantial injuries and were removed to the Cannanore hospital; one of them is in a very serious condition. A small party of Armed Reserve was sent there the next morning and found everything quiet. By the time I arrived in the afternoon, five arrests had been effected.

Badagara. At Badagara a very large crowd met following a procession and one man began to speak. The Sub Inspector warned the speaker and the crowd upon which stones were thrown and the Sub-Inspector was hit with a stick. Two constables were also hit wit a stick. The Sub-Inspector and four constables defended themselves with lathies and eventually succeeded in dispersing the crowd.

Payyanur. A meeting was held and the speakers and others were arrested after the meeting. The Police did not attempt to disperse the crowd by force.

Azhiyur (8 miles north of Badagara). A meeting was held attended by about 75 and addressed by one speaker. One Police constable was present.

Kuthuparamba (9 miles east of Tellicherry). Here there appears to have been no organized meeting but a crowd which had gathered to watch a religious procession became unruly when the persons arrested in Tellicherry arrived in the town. This developed into an impromptu meeting and was addressed by a local agitator. The crowd is estimated at about 1000. The speech delivered was objectionable. No action was taken against the crowd, which finally dispersed, but arrangements were made to guard the Police station and sub-jail.

All the places referred to above are in the north of the district. Meetings were also held in a few places in the south of the district but no disturbance of the peace is reported.

It seems clear that these several instances of defiance of the prohibitory order sprang from general instructions issued by the Working Committee of the KPCC. The attitude of the Tellicherry leaders was quite clear that they intended to hold the meeting in spite of the prohibitory order because of instructions to that effect from the KPCC and in Cannanore the attitude of the leaders was that unless they received instructions from the KPCC to the contrary they must hold the meeting. The actual instructions issued by the KPCC are not yet available; but that body must have realized there was a possibility of Protest Day being banned, as Civil Liberties Day had been banned. The degree of resistance to the Police varied. In Tellicherry, Pappinisseri and Mattanur it was determined; the difference between Tellicherry and the other two places is that at Tellicherry the Police were in sufficient strength to deal with the situation. In Calicut, Cannanore and Badagara the resistance was less determined and collapsed as soon as the Police showed that they were prepared to use force. It is noticeable that at four places (Tellicherry, Pappinisseri, Mattanur and Calicut) stones were thrown at the Police immediately they showed an intention to use force.

Clear instructions were issued in advance to the subordinate Police by the District Superintendent of Police, in consultation with me, as to the manner in which any attempt to defy the prohibitory order was to be handled. These instructions were first issued in connection with the ban on civil liberties day and were repeated when protest day was prohibited. It was realized that sufficient police could not be provided in every possible meeting place to enforce the order. The instructions accordingly were that (1) if the police were present in sufficient force the order was to be enforced and the meeting dispersed if necessary by force; (2) if the Police had not sufficient strength to enforce observance of the order, then the name of leaders and speakers were to be taken and they were to be prosecuted after the event. As regards Tellicherry, where objectionable speeches were delivered to a large meeting on Anti Repression Day in July and a disorderly procession took place, the Inspector was instructed to obtain a detachment of the Armed Reserve from Cannanore if he anticipated disobedience of the order. This was in fact done, a detachment of 12 being summoned on the morning of the 15th.

Of the unfortunate occurrence at Pappinisseri and Mattanur where the police were overwhelmed; it can only be said that the Police thought they could deal with the situation but events proved them to be wrong. It is clear that neither Sub-Inspector anticipated such resistance as he met. After warning the crowds they both acted without hesitation, doing their duty in an attempt to enforce the law. They had not thought it necessary to provide their men with muskets. They clearly thought that after a few lathi blows the crowd would disperse and run away. In April last the Sub-Inspector at Pappinisseri had dispersed, with only four constables, a crowd which had been throwing stones at his party and he was commended by the Inspector General for his determined action. On this occasion he had 8 men with him, and another Sub-Inspector. He was a determined man of fiery temper. It is clear that personal animosity figured in the attack upon him, no doubt because of the incidents in April last to which I have referred; and there is reason to suppose that many members of the Pappinisseri crowd were concerned in the labour troubles in April last. The attack on him was savage; he was badly battered about the head, face and neck.

At Tellicherry the situation was in my judgment correctly handled. The Joint Magistrate did his best to persuade the local leaders to observe the law. He and the Police were continuously stoned up to the time of firing in spite of repeated warnings. A lathi charge failed; the ground was unsuitable, being sandy, and the crowd recklessly defiant and aggressive. Seventeen rounds were fired and eight persons hit; this cannot be regarded as excessive in the circumstances. In my opinion no more force was used than was necessary to deal with the situation.

Cases have been registered and investigation is proceeding. The investigation at Pappinisseri has already established the names of some 30 participants in the riot. At Mattanur 5 persons have so far been arrested but the two muskets have not been recovered. Arrests have been made at other places and enquiries are proceeding. One platoon of the MSP together with a small detachment of the Armed Reserve have been stationed in the Pappinisseri area and will remain until the investigation is complete. Another platoon of the MSP with a small detachment of the Armed Reserve is at Tellicherry and from there will visit Mattanur, Kuthuparamba and Badagara. The situation has remained quiet since the events of the 15th. Special arrangements were made in Tellicherry for the burial of the two persons killed in the riot and this passed off without incident. Orders under Sec. 144 prohibiting processions or meetings for one month have been passed in Tellicherry, Cannanore, the Pappinisseri area, Mattanur, and Calicut.

As Government are aware Civil Liberties Day arranged for 18-8-1940 was prohibited under the Defence of India Rules and no attempt was made to disobey the order. On that occasion the Working Committee of the KPCC directed that the order should be obeyed. On this occasion they issued no such instructions and it is clear that they intended that the order should be defied. The question arises why they respected the order on 18-8-1940 and defied it on 15-9-1940. In this interval of four weeks the All India Congress Committee has decided to reject the Secretary of State's offer and its attitude has noticeably hardened. Secondly Mr Rajagopalachari has delivered a series of speeches in the south of the Presidency expounding this stiffening attitude of the Congress. Thirdly, Dr Pattabhi Sitharamayya has delivered a similar series of speeches in this district. Fourthly, while 'Mathrubhumi' said not one word about the order banning Civil Liberties Day, it published a leading article on the morning of 15-9-1940 which criticized the order banning Protest Day as an unbearable denial of civil rights and other things. Fifthly, no right-wing Congressmen in the district has taken any part in anti-war agitation, but on 14-9-1940 Mr Madhava Menon, MLA and Chairman of the Calicut Municipal Council is reported to have said in a speech that Britain will lose the war and that Germany cannot be blamed for wanting her colonies back.

Items (4) and (5) are no doubt the result of items (1), (2) and (3). The KPCC has evidently been similarly influenced by these Congress utterances.

From the District Magistrate of Malabar Camp, Tellicherry No. CC/252/40 dated the 21st September 1940.

Political agitation 'Protest Day'—Defiance of Prohibitory Order against meetings.

My report C.C.250/40 dated 17-9-1940

In continuation of my letter cited above, I regret to report that the constable who was severely injured in the rioting at Mattanur died on 19-9-1940.

The member of the crowd at Tellicherry who was critically wounded is now reported to be out of danger.

Investigation of the various cases is proceeding vigorously and practically complete at Pappinisseri where the Sub-Inspector was murdered. The investigation establishes a clear case against 32 participants in the riot. Of these, 10 have so far been arrested, including 2 ring-leaders who actually struck the Sub-Inspector. K.P.R. Gopalan Nambiar has not yet been apprehended.

At Mattanur 8 rioters have so far been arrested. A group of 30 rioters is said to be in hiding in neighbouring foot-hills and 2 platoons of the MSP are engaged in special measures with a view of their apprehension.

At Tellicherry 33 persons have been arrested.

At Calicut 19 persons have been arrested including H. Manjunatha Rao; at Badagara 6, at Payyanur 7, and at Cannanore 2.

The situation remains quiet. Suitable Police dispositions have been made. In addition to the 2 platoons of the MSP, at Mattanur, a third platoon is at Pappinisseri together with two sections of the Armed Reserve. Two sections of the Armed Reserve are at Tellicherry, one section at Badagara and one section at Mattanur.

In connection with the investigations various Congress offices have been searched. In the KPCC office at Calicut a letter was found signed by J.B. Kripalani, General Secretary of the AICC, addressed to Manjunatha Rao of the KPCC. The letter is dated 27-8-1940, in reply to a letter from Manjunatha Rao dated 18-8-1940, which obviously referred to the ban on 'Civil Liberties Day' in August. I enclose a copy of this letter for the Government's information. This letter requires no comment from me.

104. Mahakoshal Provincial Congress Committee's Report on Satyagraha Activities

AICC Papers, File No. G–5 (Pt. I), 1940–41, NMML.

Madan Mahal, Jubbulpore
Dated: 4th June 1940

Fourth Quarterly Report Ending 31st of May 1940
1. Number of Satyagrahis:

District	No. up to 15-5-40	No. up to 31-5-40	Total
1. Jubbulpore	73	7	80
2. Damoh	x	10	10
3. Saugor	113	14	127
4. Narsinghpur	54	28	82
5. Hoshangabad	60	20	80
6. Khandwa	28	9	37
7. Betul	82	4	86
8. Chhindwara	36	x	36
9. Seoni	11	2	13
10. Mandla	36	x	36
11. Bala Ghat	7	x	7
12. Durg	15	x	5
13. Raipur	101	36	137
14. Bilaspur	41	6	47
15. Baghelkhand	58	87	145
		Total	**948**

During the period of report two more PCC members have signed the active pledge.

Two more Legislature have also signed the pledge, this brings their number of active Satyagrahis to 33.

Some of the Forward Blocist have signed the active pledge to retain their seats and positions on the various committees that they have been hither to holding. This will be clear from the report of an interview that they gave to a local press reporter giving their reasons why they signed the pledge. They have put it clearly that had they not signed the pledge they would have to resign their seats in the committees which they cannot afford to lose which may result that other may occupy them. Therefore, they have thought it proper to sign the active pledge and thus stick to their seats or retain them.

Shivirs have been started and opened in the districts of Betul and Hoshangabad while Raipur, Durg, Bilaspur, Saugor, Mandla and Narsinghpur are holding on the first week of June. Rest of the District Congress Committees have not yet reported.

Charkha and Takli competitions have been held in Raipur, Saugor, Hoshangabad, Khandwa, Betul, Mandla, Durg, Narsinghpur and Jubbulpore periodically in various places of the Districts. As regards the Harijan work, Harijan meetings and visits in groups to their houses have been arranged in almost all the Districts periodically.

Repression and its toll

Till lately this province was regarded rather strangely fortunate as to have no sign of activity on the part of the Government but on the advent of the third week of May this proverbial lull that prevailed so far had witnessed a nice sudden break of storm: Repression. The province has now fallen into the line with other provinces in respect of the ruthless and mad repression. Coming directly from the Arabian sea the repressive monsoon shoots and covers the Western part which is nearer to Bombay. Burhanpur being on the frontier gets its first light showers in warning to Mr Fakirchand Kapoor, President, Town Congress Committee, Burhanpur. He has been warned by the Government for his past speeches and not for the present activities. Then comes the thunder showers to Betul adjoining to it.

Warning, Searches and Arrests

Brisk inquiries and investigations were made in connection with the publication of a leaflet 'Inquilab Zinda Bad, which has been under distribution, as reported, for the last fortnight in the District of Betul. On the 20th May Shri S.N. Tiwari's house was searched and nothing incriminating was found save to the speeches of Shri Bose and Sahajanand and some copies of resolution of the Anti Compromise Conference. Similar searches were also made in Multai one of the Tahsil Head Quarters of the District. On the same morning Shri Anandrao Lokhnade's house was raided and searched. He was put under arrest under 23(2) Defence of India Act. Mr Laxminarayan Dixit, Ex-Nagpur conspiracy case prisoner has also been warned. The house of Mr Kishanlal Sarsode, bookseller, Betul was searched. A lot of Sasta Sahitya Mandal Delhi, publications have been removed and copies of 'Jalianwalabagh', a booklet, have also been taken away. His residence was also searched. Subsequently Shri Namdeo Falke, Shurao Dhote and two other Gond workers were arrested under Defence of India Act.

Information received so far goes to say that these Forward Blocists of Betul have started so called CD movement by pulling up the alarm chain of passenger train. Three Gond women courted arrests in this attempt. Two more Gond Workers have also courted arrests by occupying the Magisterial Chairs at Bhainseehi Tahsil Head Quarters, District Betul.

Shri Bakaram Khande, member PCC from Betul and Shri Belaram Hain, Headmaster, Ambu School, a Congress worker have also been warned.

President Pachmarhi, Nagpur Congress Committee in the Hoshangabad District has also been warned and one Jubbulpore Forward Bloc member has been warned for his May Day inflammatory speech. Messrs Shrikarrao and Chunnilal of Bilaspur were warned and subsequently arrested and challaned.

Arrest and Trial

So far one dozen Forward Blocists from Betul and 8 Congressmen from Bilaspur totaling 20 arrests have been made and tried. Betul people are being tried under Defence of India Act while Bilaspur Congressmen are challaned under Section 117, 120B, 319 and 195.

Convictions and Sentences

Report received so far says that Mr Anandrao Lokhande, Betul Forward Bloc leader has been convicted under Defence of India Act 32 (2) and sentenced to two years R.I. and fined Rs 100. Shri Namdeo Falke has also been convicted under the same Act and sentenced to one year's concurrent sentence under two counts.

Government is trying to raise war-relief funds by adopting various methods through its petty officials such as Tahsildars and others. At some places it has given out that if Kisans contribute their mite they will not be required to pay their Takabi while at other places they have arranged wrestling tournaments, Carnivals, Dramas and other things.

During this period of report 56 Harijans and 4 Muslims have signed the active pledge: thus 103 Harijans and 20 Muslims have so far been enrolled as active Satyagrahis.

Secretary

105. Report of the Punjab Provincial Congress Committee
AICC Papers, File No. G–5 (Pt. IV), 1940, NMML.

The Punjab Provincial Congress Committee, Lahore.

The General Secretary,
All India Congress Committee
Allahabad

Dear Sir,

In reply to your letter No. G–28/670 dated 10th May, I am sending you herewith the following information's asked in your questionnaires.

The Punjab Provincial Congress Committee since Ramgarh Session has been busy with the primary tahsil and district elections. This was done so that the new Committees may be so formed as to include those persons, who In the light of Ramgarh session and the instructions of Mahatma Gandhi may take the responsibilities of holding office. This will facilitate the work of Satyagraha and will add impetus to the movement.

The District elections will end by the 20th of May. Every new committee will then be asked to transfer itself into a Satyagraha Committee.

On the other hand, a Central Training Camp for Satyagrahis is going to be opened in Lahore by the strenuous efforts of Mian Iftakhar-ud-din. The invitations for this camp have been extended to those persons who will sign the Satyagraha pledge from amongst the PPCC delegates, Congress MLAs, Congress Municipal Commissioner of the District and Tahsil Congress Committees, and distinguished Congress veterans.

The provincial machine for pushing Satyagraha preparation is ready and well set. It will be put into motion for mass enlistment after the 31st May when the Central Training Camp will terminate.

The information asked for in the questionnaire is as follows:

1. The office has received 314 signed Satyagraha pledges. Besides this 104 forms are lying with Hissar District Congress Committee and a large number of such pledges are lying with other primary Congress Committees to whom we are sending instructions to send these forms to the office. The office has not yet begun to supervise the fulfillment of the conditions prescribed in the pledge. No arrangement has yet been made to see that the Satyagrahis meet together. The reason for this is that the office is busy in election work.

2. The steps to popularize khadi since the Ramgarh session are:
   (a) The workers are sent from the province to address gathering arranged in the rural areas, who emphasize the use of khadi as a step towards the self realization of India.

(b) Circulars are issued to all the Primary Congress Committees numbering 2900 to popularize khadi during the celebration of the National Week from 7th April to 13th April.

(c) All India Spinners Association (Punjab Branch) has utilized the services of Miss Mira Ben in conjunction with some District and Primary Congress Committees to push the sale of khadi in the province. The office will direct more of its energies to accomplish this end after 31st May.

(d) The Charkha Department has been established with a view to popularize khadi and spinning and to devise means and method to do it.

3. The Working Committee of the Punjab PCC has established two Departments, namely:

(a) Harijan Department

(b) Minorities Department

This Harijan Committee had one meeting already on 17th April 1940. This Committee has suggested some ways and means for the removal of the social evil of untouchability and at the same time of improving economic status of these poor people.

All the instructions issued by Mahatmaji and the Secretary of the AICC along with suggestions of the Harijan Committee have been circulated to each Primary Congress Committee.

(b) The Minority Sub-committee consisting of representatives from the minorities of the province has been formed....

This sub-committee had its one sitting. It has given some useful suggestions for creating an atmosphere devoid of communal bickerings and bitterness.

5. Publicity—For publicity work a strong committee has been set up. It includes Congress minded journalists of the party.... The publicity Committee issues weekly statements.

6. The number of persons who have signed the Satyagraha pledge is small at present but as stated above the delay has been caused by the elections. Every member of the PPCC has been asked to join the Satyagraha Camp, hence it is expected that an overwhelming majority sign the pledge before that camp meets.

Number of the PPCC members who signed the pledges are 44. 16 members of the Working committee have signed the Satyagraha pledge. But others, some of whom were absent, are expected to sign it in the next meeting which will be held on 22nd May.

7. There are 31 District Congress Committees and 144 City Congress Committees. Their total membership, that is for the province 192, 495. The number is small on account of the new elections but as soon the new Committees are formed they will quickly turn themselves into Satyagraha Councils.

Some districts function very efficiently and others are made to work with constant reminders. The new Congress Committee will be pressed to keep contact with the Primary Congress Committees. The PPCC office sends quite a large number of circulars directly to the Primary Congress Committees.

8. The DCCs have not yet taken any special step but the new committee will make up the deficiency shortly.

9. The tahsil Congress Committee have been formed only this year. They have just taken up work. No report of their work can now be given.

10. The factional rivalries among the rank and file are definitely on the decrease in the face of impending struggle. The district elections did revive certain bitterness, but it is

hoped that it will soon vanish when the work for Satyagraha will be pushed ahead. Our Rashtrapati rendered a very valuable service to our province by bringing these groups together and contrary to expectations the Congress work is going on ever so smoothly.

11. Public appreciates step taken in the direction of enrolling Satyagrahis and the preparation for the final struggle of achieving complete independence. Public receives every activity of our leaders in this direction with enthusiasm. But the public is getting a bit impatient and wrongly suspicious that no struggle may be launched.

12. Two training camps were opened during the last year. One camp ended just before the elections of the PPCC. Total number attended that camp was 100.

   A provincial Satyagrahi training camp will be held from the 23rd to 30th of May at Lahore. The camp shall include courses in constructive work, and the various problems facing the country will be discussed daily. The life in the camp will be rigorous and strictest Satyagrahi discipline will be observed. Only active Satyagrahis from among Congress MLAs, Congress Members to local bodies, office bearers to District and Tahsil committees, delegates to the PPCC and other promised congressmen. It is then intended that the Satyagrahis attending this camp will hold similar camps in each district and train more Satyagrahis.

13. During the national week meetings were held allover the province explaining the Ramgarh Resolutions and implications of the struggle. The meetings have been held haphazardly since then but no exact number can be given.

14. No steps have yet been taken, but we are thinking of having a batch of inspectors visiting and helping various Satyagraha Committees in their day to day work.

Yours sincerely,
Sd—Partap Singh
General Secretary
Punjab Provincial Congress Committee,
Lahore

25-5-1940.

106. Fortnightly Report on the Enrolment of Satyagraha Volunteers and Related Activities in Sind during First Half of May 1940

Fortnightly Reports for the First Half of May 1940, File No. 18/5/1940, Home Department, Political Intelligence Section, Government of Sind, NAI.

My dear Conran-Smith,

Political—The enrolment of 'Satyagraha' volunteers and the conversion of Congress committees into 'Satyagraha' Committees continue to be the main activities of the Congress. District Congress Worker's Conferences were held at various places during the fortnight. The Executive Committee of the Provincial Congress Committee has been converted into a 'Satyagraha' Supreme Council in preparation for an impending Civil Disobedience movement. Members of the Executive Councils of the various District and Primary Congress Committees, who did not sign the 'Satyagraha' pledge, have been asked to resign. Only 'Satyagraha' Committees have been permitted to carry on Congress activities within their respective areas, other Congress Committees having ceased to function. All elections of office-bearers to the various Congress Committees were at first postponed sine die because of the coming 'Satyagraha' struggle: but it now appears that it is intended to hold them before the end of June. The 'Satyagraha' Committee of Karachi has decided to open a 'Satyagraha' Camp on 19th May, and the work of constructing the 'pandal' has started: they had leased a site for it at a nominal rent from the Karachi Municipal Corporation, but Government have suspended the operation of this decision of the Municipal Standing Committee, and the ground will have to be vacated. No doubt some other site will be found, though it is reported that an attempt may be made to defy the order. It is said that invitations are being issued to Maulana Abul Kalam Azad and Pandit Jawaharlal Nehru to attend the opening ceremony. It has been explained that the object of organizing a 'Satyagraha' Sena was to keep a big army in readiness for any eventuality and that a large and well-trained force may unnerve the British, whose rule in India was already breathing its last and that it was a matter of a few years only before it would be dead and buried. Wherever 'Satyagraha' Committees have been formed, the members have taken to *takli* and *charkha* spinning, and carrying out other tasks required of true 'Satyagraha' volunteers. *Charkha* classes have been opened at some places. The various local Congress Committees have received circulars from the Sind Supreme Satyagraha Council calling for reports regarding the number of 'Satyagraha' Committees formed and members enrolled, the arrangements made for spinning and for enlisting the sympathy of Harijans towards the 'Satyagraha' movement. The response to these efforts has been meagre indeed, and differences of opinion on the subject of the pledge have weakened the Congress still further. In some villages even the members of the committees have preferred to resign rather than sign the 'Satyagraha' pledge, while at one place the response was so poor that the President, Vice-President, Secretary and Joint Secretary of the Congress Committee refrained from signing the 'Satyagraha' pledge and had to resign. Speeches, appealing to the public to join the 'Satyagraha' Sena and describing British war aims as false and insincere, have been made in abundance by Congress leaders, who alleged that the Muslim League was a foster child of British Imperialism and that unemployment and poverty would remain in India so long as British rule endured. People were exhorted not to give any war help to Britain, and the redoubtable Dr Choithram announced that Europe was in such a state that it could not be said with any certainty whether the King-Emperor would be alive or not after a month. This same speaker, however, has since expressed his horror of the Nazi invasion of Holland and Belgium, and wondered how long India would be safe. He said that unity was the great need of the country. That the British were deceiving Indians, that their promise meant nothing, that no reliance can be put on their word, that democracy and the protection of weak neighbours were hollow phrases, that anti-British feeling in Europe was so strong that it had imperilled the security of the British Empire and that the British had to plunge into the war in order to save their own skins, were some of the sentiments expressed at Congress meetings.

107. Vidarbha Provincial Congress Committee's Report on Satyagraha Activities

Satyagraha Reports from PCCs, AICC Papers, File No. G–5 (Pt. I), 1940–41, NMML.

Rajasthan Bhawan,
Akola, May 16th, 1940

The General Secretary,
All India Congress Committee
Allahabad

Fortnightly Report

Dear friend,

Following is the short report with regard to the activities of the Vidarbha Province during the last fortnight.

Satyagraha Committees

The last report showed that one District Congress Committee and five Taluq Congress Committees had remained to be changed into Satyagraha Committees. In this fortnight the one remaining District Congress Committee and two more Taluq Congress Committees have turned into Satyagraha Committees. One Taluq Congress Committee is suspended as none from the Executive body has signed the Satyagrahi Pledge-form. Two Taluq CCs are still remained as non-Satyagraha Committees. Elections are to be held there and therefore the delay. Elections are being held on the basis of Satyagrahi Volunteers and the two Taluq Congress Committees will soon begin to function as Satyagraha Committees. Attention is being paid to start working of the one suspended Taluq Congress Committee.

Enrolment of Satyagrahis

Enrolment of Active Satyagrahis is going on. In this fortnight about hundred more Satyagrahis have enrolled. This brings a total of 350 Satyagrahis in the province.

Propaganda

Active Propaganda is going on, on an extensive scale, Conferences are being held where the message of the Congress is being explained.

Volunteers' Camp

Volunteers' Camp which was opened on the 5th May is going on. It would be closed on 20th of this month.

Constructive work is being attended to.

With regards,

Yours sincerely,
Brijlal Biyani
President

Number of active Satyagrahis enrolled in every District, Nagar and Taluq Congress Committee up till 12-5-1940.

Provincial Congress Committee

Strength	Enrolled
45	32
Congress MLAs Strength	
17	6
Akola District	114
Akola Nagar CC	20
Akola Taluq	7
Mangrul Pir	11
Murtizapur	21
Basim	7
Balapur	19
Akot	29
Total	114
Amraoti District	
Amraoti Nagar	60
Amraoti Taluq	1
Daryapur	12
Ellichpur	11
Morshi	7
Chandur Railway	1
Total	60
Buldana District	80
Khamgaon Nagar	10
Khamgaon Taluq	14
Chikhli	16
Malkapur	29
Jalgaon	11
Mehkar	0
Total	80
Yeotmal District	32
Yeotmal Nagar	1
Yeotmal Taluq	5
Wun	6
Darwa	2
Kelapur	8
Pusad	10
Total	32

III.   Repressive Measures Against Press and Political Leaders

108.   Public Protest Against Attack on Press Liberties

Amrita Bazar Patrika, 25 February 1940.

The Press cannot be terrorized—Protest from Public—Unfair Attempt at Boycott of A Particular Paper Condemned—Joint Statement by Leaders—Any Attack on Liberty of Press and Freedom of Expression of Opinion to be Resisted.

Mr Nishit Chandra Sen, Mayor of Calcutta, Acharya Sir P.C. Ray, Mr Ramananda Chatterjee, Dr Pramatha Nath Banerjee, Mr B.C. Chatterjee, Dr Syama Prasad Mookerjee, Mr Tulsi Chandra Goswami, Mr Pramatha Nath Banerjee, Sir Sarvepalli Radhakrishnan and Dr Radha Kumud Mookerji have issued the following statement to the press:

'For several months past an organized attempt has been made in Bengal to curb the civil liberties of the people by various methods. The liberty of the press and freedom of expression of opinion constitute the most elementary civil rights and any attack on them should be resisted. It is extremely unfortunate that in these extraordinary circumstances a controversy should arise as to the freedom of the press between different sections of public opinion who are agreed on the sanctity of civil liberties. We are not concerned with the differences that have in recent months manifested themselves between different wings of the Indian National Congress. All that we can say is that in the present national emergency these differences should be removed or at least minimized.

'Whether there are differences or not, there can be no question as to the necessity for the freedom of expression of opinion on the problems of the day. We may agree to, or differ from, the views now and then expressed by the nationalist press on any particular question, but we think it is unfair that an attempt should be made by any section of the public to gag any particular newspaper or terrorize it into a surrender of its judgement or boycott it. Should the present atmosphere of strife and mutual hatred be allowed to continue there would be an end of the freedom of the press and, indeed, of all civil liberties which all of us hold dear. We hope that in the heat of the hour we shall not so forget ourselves that any of us should be party to the undermining of the elementary decencies of social and corporate life.'

109.   Nehru's Views on Press Censorship

Letter to the Editor, *Hindustan Standard;* 4 March 1940, *SWJN,* Vol. XI, p. 365.

Allahabad
March 4, 1940

Dear Sir,

I have your letter of February 24th. I am sorry I am unable to send you special articles at present, as I am overburdened with work. I should like to tell you, however, that I learnt with regret and amazement of the order served upon your newspaper by the Government of Bengal. I think this order, asking you to submit all editorial matter to the censor before publication, was highly objectionable and I am glad you did not submit to it. No self-respecting newspaper can accept such a pre-censorship of articles. This is a matter of importance not only to you but to the newspaper press in general in India as well as to the public at large.

I have today sent a long letter dealing with this and other questions, relating to the liberty of the press, to the President of the Journalists Association of India, who had addressed an enquiry to me. I have asked him to release this letter to the press for publication and I trust that you will get it soon.

Yours sincerely,
Jawaharlal Nehru

To Tushar Kanti Ghosh[1]

Allahabad
March 4, 1940

Dear Friend,

Your telegram reached me late as it missed me in Patna.

I am certainly of opinion that it was unfortunate and unwise for the BPCC Executive to pass a resolution boycotting the *Jugantar* newspaper. I am not personally aware of the articles or other matters that have been appearing in the *Jugantar* and can say nothing about them. But I am a strong believer in the freedom of the press and consider that the fullest latitude should be given to it to express opinions and criticize policies. This of course does not mean that any newspaper or individual should indulge in malicious attacks on anyone, or should indulge in the low type of journalism which has been a feature of some of our communal organs. But it is my firm belief that public life should be built up on the foundation of a free and independent press. I therefore regret greatly the attempt to boycott the *Jugantar*.

I should like to add that the recent order of the Bengal Government on the *Hindustan Standard* to submit all editorial matter for censorship before publication, seems to me an amazing misuse of official authority. If this kind of thing is to be permitted, there will be a complete end of independent editorial writing in newspapers. Their leading articles will not be theirs, but the censor's, and nobody wants to read what the censor thinks about a particular matter. A government has every right to express its own opinion and to place it before the public directly as coming from it. But the indirect way of giving publicity to its own opinions through the editorial columns of newspapers, or of suppressing criticisms of its own actions, is something that has always been considered vitally wrong to the working of a newspaper. It is far better for a newspaper not to have any editorial matter than to submit to this degradation or surrender of its soul. I am glad that the *Hindustan Standard* preferred this course and stopped giving editorial matter. Every journalist and newspaper man in India, as well as every person who is interested in the vital question of having a free press, must condemn the action taken by the Bengal Government in this matter.

I understand that the Bengal Government has also tried to suppress newspapers by asking securities from them. A recent case has been brought to my notice of the demand of the Bengal Government of security from the *Rozana Hind*, a nationalist Urdu daily of Calcutta. A security was taken from this paper and now again further securities have been demanded both from the *Daily Hind* and the *Weekly Hind*. Apparently one of the offences of these papers was to publish a bulletin issued by the UP Provincial Congress Committee. It may be that the Bengal Government does not agree with or disapproves of the views of the UPPCC but I can say with confidence that this PCC has issued no bulletin or pamphlet which any person can call in the slightest degree, irresponsible. The UPPCC speaks and writes with dignity and deals with problems impersonally. In regard to the communal problem especially it has always maintained a high level and has never sunk to the level of just controversy and criticism. If even the bulletins of the UPPCC are enough to upset the Bengal Government and to induce it to demand security from newspapers publishing them, it does not speak well for the Bengal Government.

Famous nationalist newspapers which have established their position are, to a large extent, able to look after themselves. Anything that happens to them draws public attention and public support. Smaller and less known papers often have to suffer from government interference because they are not so well-known. It is dangerous, however, to allow even the smallest and the weakest of our journals to fall victim to official interference and suppression. For this habit grows with use and gradually the public mind gets accustomed to the misuse of its powers by the government. Therefore it is necessary for the Journalists' Association, as well as for all newspapers, not to allow even such cases relating to the lesser known papers to go by default. If they are at all anxious to retain the liberty of the press, they must be vigilant guardians of this liberty and must resist every encroachment from wherever it might come. This is not a matter of political views or opinions. The movement we acquiesce in an attack on a newspaper with which we happen to disagree, we have surrendered in principle, and when the attack comes on us we have no power left to resist it.

The freedom of the press does not consist in our permitting such things as we like to appear. Even a tyrant is agreeable to this type of freedom. Civil liberty and freedom of the press consist in our permitting what we do not like, in our putting up with criticisms of ourselves, in our allowing public expression of views which seems to us even to be injurious to our cause itself. For it is always a dangerous thing to seek a temporary advantage at the cost of the larger good or of the final objective. If we set wrong standards and adopt wrong means, even in the belief that we are furthering a right cause, that cause itself will be affected and prejudiced by those standards and those means. The end in view will itself be governed partly by these standards and means and may ultimately become something different from what we had envisaged.

If our aim is democracy and freedom, then we must keep that in view always in our work and our activities. If this work and activity is carried on in a way which is opposed to democracy and freedom, then surely the end will not be democracy and freedom but something different.

It is true that it is easy to lay down high principles which are logical and which sound well. It is more difficult to put them into practice. For life is not very logical and the standard of human behaviour is not as high as we should like it to be. We live in a jungle where, often enough, predatory individuals and nations roam about at will and seek to injure society. Crises arise, like wars or struggles for national freedom, or class struggles which upset the normal course of events. It becomes very difficult then to adhere, in their entirety, to the high principles we lay down which presume a certain standard of human behaviour. During these crises or revolutionary times, it becomes necessary to reconsider, to some extent, the ordinary freedom of the individual or the group. Even so, it is a dangerous thing and likely to have had consequences unless the greatest vigilance is exercised. Otherwise we succumb to the very evil we fight against.

When we talk of democracy and freedom as well as of civil liberties, we must always remember that they involved responsibility and discipline. Without discipline and responsibility in the individual or group, there is likely to be no true freedom. In the change-over from a state of subjection and denial of liberties to a free state, a certain tendency towards licence is perhaps inevitable. This is regrettable but it is not difficult to understand, for it is the reaction from long

392 Towards Freedom: 1940 (Part 1)

continued suppression. To some extent this should be tolerated, for to suppress it is to emphasize the very complex that produces it. Nevertheless, we have all to be on our guard to prevent freedom from degenerating into licence and irresponsibility and indiscipline.

In India we have a magnificent record of tolerance. No country in the world, excepting China, has this record. While Europe and other countries were deluged in blood in wars of religion and in the attempt to suppress this opinion or that, India and China, with the assurance of millennia of culture behind them, opened their doors wide to ideas and religions from abroad. This tremendous background of toleration and culture is a precious inheritance for us.

Today passions are roused on other issues which affect us vitally. It is right that we should feel deeply about these issues, for on their outcome depends the future of our country and of the world. It is right that we should put all our strength in the advancement of the cause that we hold dear. But it is not right that we should give up or tone down the very principles which have been the glory of Indian civilization in the past and which are, in a somewhat different sense, the foundations of democratic freedom. Above all we should try to combine freedom and civil liberty with discipline and responsibility.

As this letter of mine to you may be of interest to newspapers and the public, I would suggest to you to issue it to the press for publication.

Yours sincerely,
Jawaharlal Nehru

---

[1] Tushar Kanti Ghosh was the founder of *Jugantar*.

110. Ban on the Publication of Any Literature Connected with 'National Week' Programmes

Advance, 6 April 1940.

BAN ON NATIONAL WEEK PROGRAMME ORGANIZED BY SUSPENDED BPCC PUBLICATION OF ANY LITERATURE CONNECTED THEREWITH PROHIBITED

Calcutta, April 5.

By a Notification in the Calcutta Gazette Extraordinary issued under the Defence of India Rules, the Governor of Bengal has prohibited absolutely the printing or publishing within the Province of Bengal of:

1. Any document containing a reference by way of statement, advertisement, notice, news, comment or otherwise to—
   (a) the whole or any part of any programme for the so-called 'National Week, 1940' issued by or on behalf of the (suspended) Bengal Provincial Congress Committee or any body affiliated thereto or connected therewith or Mr Subhas Chandra Bose and Swami Sahajananda or either of them or any organization with which they are or either of them is connected, or any programme identical with, or based on, or substantially similar to, or reproducing part or the whole of, any such programme; and
   (b) any procession, meeting, assembly or demonstration held, speech delivered, or thing done or committed to be done in connection or in accordance with or for the

furtherance of any programme referred to in sub-clause (a) or part of such programme; and

(b) any document containing a reference by way of comment to this order.—United Press.

111. Rambriksha Benipuri's Statement before the District Magistrate

Janata (Hindi Daily), 13 May 1940.

'My press and Office was the home of revolution. We, the revolutionaries, live there.' Mr Benipuri's statement before the Magistrate.

Dear Magistrate,

It seems that the present government is specially benevolent towards me. The play which was being staged against me had not ended and the second one has already started on a bigger scale, whose results will also be wider than ever before.

I am a journalist. I try to discharge my duties with honesty and truthfulness. An honest journalist should always strive to put the true feelings of the public before the world. It will be beneficial both for the public and the government. Such journalists are revered in free countries. The government gets the opinion of the public in their writings and tries to amend its mistakes so that these do not occur again and again. Such government also pays respect to these journalists.

Both those things which are considered supreme qualities in a free country become an offence. My case presents one of these examples.

First of all I was convicted for an offence in which I was not involved. On the other hand I tried to help the police officers like a true civilian when they asked for help.

Still, I could not be saved from the clutches of law, but I did not get the required punishment as expected by the government. It was their bad luck.

But every bureaucracy and government has the right to change its fate. Within a week of this incident, I got a notice that I and my press had to deposit a bail of Rs 5000 otherwise I have to close the publication of the newspaper. Again within a week of this notice of bail, I was arrested under the Defence of India Act and I am produced before you.

I do not know if my friends are happy about my luck but I am proud of myself. The question is why is such a great imperialist power concerned about a 'nobody'. It is really surprising.

At the same time, it is not surprising at all. Whether our countrymen realize the power of newspaper and press or not, but the government is well aware of its potentialities. Again my newspaper and press was not an ordinary one. Only recently a police officer had jokingly said—this office is the home of revolution, as long as it is not destroyed, we cannot rest in peace at Patna.

My press and office is really the home of revolution. But it was not a home created in secrecy. It was prominently situated on one of the important roads of Patna. And we believe that we—its residents—are revolutionaries. Of course, the meaning of 'revolution' could be different. We consider revolution as the total transformation of the old infrastructure and the evolution of a new social system. Government is only a superstructure of the society. We cannot realize our aim by changing governments. It will only amount to be a mean interest. We could not rest as long as the society is not totally transformed. We want the power of the government in order to realize this ambition.

I can ask as to who is satisfied with the present system? The system where there are a lot of disabilities, communal fights and the like. Where on the one hand there are only a few places—full of quilts and carpets and luxury and full of facilities.

On the other hand, there are thousands of huts—full of skeletons, where they sell self-respect for food and do other kinds of menial work for making two ends meet. Over and above it there are religious and communal feelings. One person slaughters another in the name of God or Allah. The most dangerous and horrible face of this society comes before us when only a few people start a world war in order to procure markets for their goods and increase their profits under the capitalist system and involve millions and billions of people in a life and death war. The present war is only one of its examples.

Magistrate Sahib, I believe that there is no just man who will not try to destroy this system or imagine about building a new society in place of it. (If it is not so) I will not consider him a man he must be a hornless, tailless animal or we can call him a sub-man as well.

We are complete men; we are revolutionaries. We had built a home. My friends had obligingly made me the master of that house. The government thinks—evict the master of this house and destroy this house. They have got a good reason for it in the name of the World War.

When the war started, a Press-Adviser was appointed in the Districts as well Just like the provincial governments. Once, he sent for me in his office. Among other things he also said that it is our duty to see and advise you if you are not breaking the law by mistake; the aim of the government is not to suppress or destroy the newspapers or the Press. I thanked him for his hearty advice. But today, I am asking—where is the Press Adviser? What is his work now? The bail which they have demanded from my newspaper and office is for an article, which was published some seven months ago and other article, which was published two months ago. Was it not his duty to advise me regarding those articles during all these months before asking for a bail? I really deserved a warning if not advice regarding it. If we had not heeded those warnings then the government was free to do whatever it considered proper.

But No, their only interest was in destroying that home and the World war was the most suitable excuse for it.

Even consider that charge for which I am standing here in this court. The world is really getting strange nowadays. There are a lot of parties, and there are a lot of.... In such a situation, if the government had been wise and just it would have tried other methods before summoning the editors to the court for a technical mistake after seeing the name of a press on a pamphlet and considering only one objectionable line in it.

Sometimes, I think if the European War had not disturbed the balance of its mind. It seems, it is trying to compensate its failure in the European War by arrests in India.

I am charged that my conduct is harmful to the successful prosecution of war. But Mr Magistrate, please allow me to speak that this charge is more suitable for those who are standing against us; or their brethren who have unleashed the rein of repression all over India. Books are being confiscated, news papers are being closed. The citizens' rights to hold rallies and meetings are suspended. Searches and arrests are carried out every-where. (People are) getting rigorous and long terms of imprisonment. A reign of terror is imposed all over the country.

Does the government believe that the people will be afraid of this repression and they will keep quiet or they will surrender and it will use the wealth and manpower of this country according to its will? It is wrong in thinking so. It has to turn the whole India into a concentration camp. At this moment, it is worried about the four or five European fronts of war, but what will it do when the seven million villages of India will become a front?...

There was only one way left for England at this moment—it should respect Indian Nationalism. It should have surrendered before the symbols of this Nationalism—the Congress and Gandhiji. It should have allowed the resurgence of free India and in this way it could have acquired a powerful friend nation for itself and moral support in the eyes of the world which would have defeated thousands of Hitlers. But the mind is perverted when ruin approaches; it seems so to me.

I believe—whatever be the result of this war—it is certain that it will result in the destruction of the greatest imperialist power of this world, just like the previous war resulted in the destruction of Europe's ugliest dictatorship—the Tsarism....

112. Editorial on Suppression of Civil Liberties

Mathrubhumi, 10 March 1940.

In the name of Defence:

Numerous arrests are taking place in various parts of the country on the pretext of defence. Whatever public service which does not enjoy the nod of the authorities may be classified under this category—so wide is the scope of D.I. Act. The action taken against 'Modern Review', 'Hindustan Standard' bear testimony to this Press censorship has been severely imposed on these and several other newspapers.

It will be good for the government if it understands that India will not lend a blind eye to such wanton suppression of civil liberties. Even after the Congress had undertaken not to embarrass Britain in the ongoing war, it is ironical that many Congress leaders are serving prison terms.

The arrest of Jai Prakash Narayan for his speeches is hardly reasonable and worth all condemnation.

113. An Attack on Civil Liberties

Indian Express, 10 March 1940.

The significance of Mr Jai Prakash Narain's arrest is well brought out in Pandit Jawaharlal's comment.[1] The arrest signifies the determination of Government to declare war on the Congress. Ever since the declaration of belligerency by the Government of India, India, harassment of workers engaged in questioning the wisdom of India's participation in the war has been the order of the day in almost every province, but Mr Jai Prakash is the first leader of outstanding all India status to be marked out for Government's repression policy. The administrative wisdom of singling him out for penal action from all the array of available leaders is open to question since his guidance of the Socialist party has made invariably for moderation and balanced decisions. But for his restraining influence the Socialists world undoubtedly have carried their dissatisfaction with Rightist Congress leadership to more effectively than the most have done and the neogen of anti war demonstrations under Socialist auspices would have been very much more pronounced even during the pendency of Congress decisions on the subject. The arrest of a leader of the temperament of Jai Prakash will be interpreted throughout the country as an attack on civil liberties in the guise of war emergency, and it is likely to discredit the professions of high sounding concern for freedom and democracy which the British Government have been proclaiming to the world for the bolstering up of their war aims. It hangs the door against Indo–British settlement more extreme limits than the provocativeness of Lord Zetland's utterances can be said to have so far done, and its net effect must be to send down the stack of Britain's progressiveness in the world market of disinterested public opinion. The authorities responsible for it have just played into the hands of Hitler, for they have given sanction to a piece of Hitlerism in India. It is a bad way of prosecuting the war against Hitler to patronize Hitlerism.

---

[1] Nehru's statement to the Press on the arrest of Congressmen, *Hindustan Times*, 9 March 1940: '... Now comes news of Jai Prakash Narayan's arrest in Patna. That is vital news, for Jai Prakash is one of the dearest and most valued of our comrades and his arrest has a deep significance. It means the determination of the government to declare war on the Congress. We do not regret or protest against this as against other arrests. But we realize what it means and we are prepared for it. It is fitting that this arrest should have taken place in the province where the Congress is going to meet soon for it is that Congress that will give answer to British Imperialism.'

114. Repressive Policy of the Government in Bihar
Janata, 18 March 1940.

Repression

Repression is increasing day by day. Two important people working for the students of Bihar, Mr Ali Ashraf and Mr Sunil Mukherjee, have been arrested. Both of them were the members of the Communist Party of Bihar and were committed workers. Bombay's workers' leader Mr Dange, Mr Mirajkar and Ranadive have been also arrested. News has just arrived regarding the arrest of Mr Sajjad Zahir, member of the Working Committee of the All India Congress Socialist Party, in Lucknow. Mr Rahul Sukrityayan, the president elect of the fifth All India Kisan Sabha to be held at Palasa (Andhra) at the end of this month, has been arrested in Prayag. According to the section of the Ordinance under which he has been arrested, the Central Government is empowered to intern him anywhere in India for an unlimited period. Who knows how many people will form the list of martyrs. It seems that the Government has unleashed its repressive policy on the progressive forces (of India). One by one, everybody is being prosecuted. But, history tells that just like the sphinx, these Martyrs will become alive out of their ashes and at the end, victory will kiss their feet.

115. Repression in Bihar
Janata, 4 April 1940.

The Nazist policy of Bengal Government. Nothing should be printed concerning Swamiji and Subhash Babu.

Repression has exceeded its limits. One and a half years imprisonment for Mr Ranga.

The Bengal Government has issued a special statement and has banned the printing and publication of any news, comments, concerning Mr Subhash Chandra Bose, Swami Sahajanand Saraswati and the suspended Bengal Provincial Congress Committee, their activities and programmes and their activities during the 'National Week' under the Defence of India Ordinance within the province of Bengal. It is further notified in the statement that nothing should be published concerning any institution related with the two or either of them or any institution accepting the programmes of these two (people). The scope of this ordinance is so wide that even the printing of the names of Mr Subhash Chandra Bose and Swami Sahajanand Saraswati will be considered an offence. Nobody is supposed to criticize this Ordinance of the Government.

Repression

Three hundred and two people in Punjab up to 2nd March and five hundred and thirty five in Bengal have been arrested under the Defence of India Ordinance. The Madras government had interned the Vice-President of All. India Kisan Sabha, Professor N.G. Ranga in his village Naidubol. But he declined to accept this order. Hence, he was arrested and imprisoned for one year and has been fined Rs 500. Commenting on this arrest Swamiji said that the government has challenged the Kisan Sabha by arresting Mr Ranga, Rahulji and other friends, so we should answer it through our deeds not words. The Bihar government has prohibited the Secretary of Indian labour Union, Mr Niharendra Dutt Mazumdar and the Vice President of All India Trade Union Congress Mr Mukundalal Sarkar from entering Chota Nagpur Commissionery.

116. Reports on Searches and Arrests in Different Parts of India

Aaj, 17 April 1940.

Repression

Searches, arrests of Communist and Socialist workers; booklets, pamphlets forfeited, the publication of 'Viplav' closed; the list of Congress Workers in police's hand in Ajmer.

Ajmer, 12 April. The local police searched many houses under the Defence of India Act. The offices of Ajmer Merwara provincial Congress Committee, Ajmer city Congress Committee; and the houses of the Secretary of the Khadi exhibition, Mr Krishnagopala Garg, and many important Congress workers and the press of Mr Jagdish Prasad 'Deepak' was searched. The police forfeited many books, pamphlets and private papers. They have also taken away the list of the four anna members of the Congress from the office of the city Congress Committee.

It is reported that there has been searches in five or six places in Bevar also.

Search in Ganga Press. The police took away the proof

Lucknow, 12 April. The Ganga fine arts press was searched for several hours on Thursday. It is reported that the United Provinces Forward Block Party had sent the resolution of the Anti-Compromise Conference of Ramgarh for publication which was not printed. The police took away the copies of its proof.

Socialist Interned

Nandhal (Madras) 12 April. The Madras Government has ordered the interment of Guntur's important Socialist leader Mr Dubhavenkat Krishnamurthy in his own village under the Defence of India Ordinance.

He will get Rs 10 per month.

Congress Socialist Arrested

Madura, 12 April. The Congress Socialist leader, Mr K. Rajagopalan was arrested while delivering a speech at a meeting at Sialguri last night under the Defence of India Ordinance.

Socialist gets 18 months Imprisonment

Tirupattur, 12 April. The Congress Socialist worker of Vellur Mr T.N. Balasubramanyam Ayyar gets 18 months rigorous imprisonment for delivering a speech on 14th March under the Defence of India Act.

Arrests in Tripura State—of Gana-parishad Members

Akhaura, 12 April. The Vice-President of Ganaparishad, Mr Shachindralal Singh and its members Messrs Ravindra Mitra, Vimal Roy, Nani Chakravarti, Jyotisha Bhattacharya, Satya Chakravarti, Balai Saha, Yogendra Singh, Hiralal Saha, Manindra Seal, Sudhir Chandra Bhaumik and Shamsher Ali have been arrested at Akhaura under the Defence of India Act and were released on a bail of five hundred each.

Two people were debarred from delivering speeches in Azamqarh

Azamgarh, 13 April. Mr Shyam Sundar and Mr Umrao Singh have been ordered to deliver no speeches in public meetings under section 144.

Arrests in Kumilla

Kumilla, 13 April. An important member of District Forward Bloc Mr Ashutosh Bhati has been arrested under the Defence of India Act this evening for delivering an anti-war speech in yesterday's public meeting. The hearing of his case will be held on third day.

The President and Secretary of Navadweep Student's Onion fined.

Krishna Nagar, 13 April. The Sadar Sub-divisional off leer has ordered the imprisonment of the President, Mr Kumaresha Chandra and Secretary Mr Gaur Goswami of the Navadweep students union till the court is adjourned and fined them sixty rupees each failing which they will be imprisoned for two months each.

Ban on Congress Meetings. The order of the Magistrate of Jhansi

Jhansi, 13 April. The Sub-divisional Magistrate of Chiragaon has issued an order under section 144 that the Congress party and Zamindars' party should not hold any meetings, rallies and should not carry any arms up to 16 April.

It is reported that this order has been issued because of tensions between the Zamindar's Party and the Congress party.

Searches in Lucknow for Confiscated Literature

Lucknow, 14 April. The local secret police and the inspector of Alambagh police station has searched the house of Mr Surendra Balupuri and had confiscated, 1500 copies of a proscribed book, 'Krantikari' (Revolutionary), written by Mr Manmathanatha Gupta.

Mr Ramamurthi Arrested

Madras, 14 April. The Forward Block leader, Mr K. Sriramamurthi has been arrested under the Defence of India Act.

Bail of Congress Leaders is Not Accepted

Delhi, 14 April. The members of the Indian National Congress, Messrs Bahal Singh, Baba Ramchandra and Ismail who were arrested under the Defence of India Act for possessing objectionable literature were produced before the Magistrate. The Magistrate had refused their bail application and ordered them to be remanded into custody for two days.

Workers' Leader Arrested till Further Orders

Jamshedpur, 14 April. An important member of the Bengal labour union, Mr Shrinarayan was interned till further orders. He was arrested recently under the Defence of India Act. He had come here to participate in the Labour Conference to be held on 19th April.

Many Booklets and Pamphlets Confiscated

Patna, 14 April. The Bihar Government has forfeited six booklets and several pamphlets published by the Communist institutions and a book and a pamphlet published by Bombay's S.G. Volker under the Defence of India Ordinance.

The Publication of 'Viplav' suspended

Lucknow, 14 April. It is reported that Mr Yashpal has suspended the publication of 'Viplav' and other newspapers because of heavy fines imposed on them; and has filed a new declaration for starting a new monthly Hindi and Urdu magazine, named, 'Sathi'.

One newspaper had published the false news of Mr Yashpal's arrest.

Restrictions Imposed on a Worker's Leader in Barrackpore Subdivision

Calcutta, 15 April. The Sub-Divisional Magistrate of Barrackpore has ordered the leader of Bengal Labour Union, Mr Muhammad Moosa Khan, not to indulge in any such activity which can excite the workers under the Government of India Act.

Case on Workers' Leader. Rs 1000 fined

Sholapur, 15 April. The workers' leader, M. R.G. Katekar, who was arrested in Barasi under the Defence of India Act, has pleaded not guilty before the Sub-divisional Magistrate (Sholapur). He was charged for delivering objectionable speech. The Magistrate has released him after taking a fine of Rs one thousand.

Nasik, 15 April. The district Magistrate has further extended the restrictions for fifteen days on the Punjabi and other truck drivers. The period of the earlier restriction ended on 11 April.

117. Repression in Andhra

AICC Papers, File No. G–25/1940, 11 May 1940, NMML.

Andhra Provincial Congress Committee

Swarajya Bhawan,
Masulipatnam,
1 Gopaldas Road,
Mount Road, PO Madras
11-5-1940

The General Secretary,
All India Congress Committee,
Swaraj Bhawan,
Allahabad

Dear Friend,

Information received so far from the Districts goes to show that 52 persons have been subjected to the operation of the Defence of India Act.

16 persons have been arrested and sentenced rigorously the sentence varying from one month to twenty months and above.

18 persons have been warned.

5 persons have been bound over for good conduct.

13 persons have been interned in their villages. A few of them receive an allowance of Rs 10 each from the Government.

One Congress, MLA (Central), one member of the Madras Legislative Assembly, one General Secretary of a DCC, one Joint Secretary of a DCC, one manager of a DCC are among those affected. A number of members of the PCC and the DCCs are affected.

Yours sincerely,
General secretary

118.   Ernad Taluka Satyagraha Committee Meeting Against the Repressive Policy

AICC Papers, File No. G–19 (Pt. I) 1940, 6 July 1940, NMML.

Ernad Taluk Congress Committee

Feroke, 6th July 1940
All India Congress Committee
Receipt No. 1122
Date 10-7-40
File no. G–16

From:
The Secretary,
Ernad Taluk Satyagraha Committee
Feroke

To
    The All India Congress Working Committee

Sirs,
    At a meeting of the Ernad Taluk Satyagraha Committee held at Feroke on 30/6/40 under the presidency of Janab K.C. Koya Kunhi Naha Sahib, the following resolution moved by Jana K.T. Alavi and seconded by Shri P. Sankara Varier was unanimously passed.

    This meeting of the Ernad Satyagraha Council wishes to bring to the notice of the All India Congress Working Committee, the repressive measure taken by the Government throughout the Province under the guise of the Defence of India Act, thus disregarding the civil liberties of the citizens.

    The Congress Workers including members of the provincial Congress committee are arrested and sent to prisons daily, Prohibitory orders are served on Congress Workers, the Police are searching many Congress committee offices including the office of the provincial Congress Committee and the Ernad Taluk Committee. The residence of the Congress Workers including that of the Secretary of the Ernad Taluk Committee have also been searched. In this atmosphere of repression, it is impossible to carry on even the routine work of the Congress and the holding of public meetings is also not possible in these circumstances.

This committee therefore strongly recommends that a 'Repression Day' may be observed throughout the Presidency to protest strongly against these actions of the Government and earnestly request the AIC Working Committee to grant permission to the KPCC to do so.

119. Punjab Assembly Holds Secret Session Following Arrest of Communists and Socialists

Communist, Vol. II, No. 11, August 1940, P.C. Joshi Archives on Contemporary History, JNU.

'The Secret Session'

On 15th July, the province of Punjab had a unique honour. It was the first province in India to have a Secret Session of the Legislative Assembly. Irreverent people called it 'Purdah Session' but that was because they did not realize the gravity of the situation. A huge conspiracy had been unearthed. Over 40 Communists and Socialists from allover the province had been arrested—five of them members of the Punjab Assembly including Comrade Sohan Singh Josh and Master Kabul Singh, members of the Provincial Congress Working Committee. This bold and timely action of the Sikandar Hayat Ministry had saved the province from chaos and bloodshed. Startling revelations about the activities of v 'Fifth Columnists' were going to be made by the Premier at this historic session. Naturally, the Press and the public could not be permitted to attend the Assembly on that day.

What were the Congress MLAs to do? There was no unanimity. Mian Iftikharuddin, the President of the PCC wanted that Congress MLAs should walk out in protest against the procedure. The Government had a clear majority. If the opposition could not make its protest against the arrests known to the people, what was the purpose of their attending the session? But the majority of Congress MLAs did not agree. They argued that the Premier must be heard. After all, the charges that he would bring against those arrested MIGHT BE TRUE!

So the Session began. Congress MLAs at the very outset protested against the procedure. The five arrested MLAs had not been brought to the Assembly. Charges were going to be made against them without their getting any opportunity to give replies. Even interviews with them had not been granted, not even to Congress MLAs. This secrecy business was clearly a stunt to justify the Government's action. But these arguments had no effect. The Speaker ruled out all discussion on the issue and the resolution to have a Secret Session was carried.

Sir Sikandar Reveals the Conspiracy

Amidst pin-drop silence Sir Sikandar rose. He started with the statement that these arrests were not made with the object of weakening the Congress. He quoted Congress Ministers' statements and also those of some CSP leaders to 'prove' that Communists were not Congressmen. Communists alone were the real criminals whom the Government wanted to crush. He quoted from Communist publications to prove their criminal designs. He gave life-sketches of some of the arrested comrades but refused to give their names. A man had recently come from Nairobi in East Africa and was now carrying on subversive propaganda among Sikh troops. Another had come from Hankow and was now in the Executive of the Provincial CSP. He waxed eloquent and went to the length of saying that people who indulged in such activities SHOULD BE SHOT. They were 'agents of Russia' and were trying to get the Russians invade India! These Communists were not Congressmen. But they were everywhere and used all platforms Congress, CSP, Labour, Kisan and student.

THAT WAS ALL. He spoke for two and a half hours but this was all he had to say about the activity of the 'Fifth Column'. These were the 'startling revelations' which could not be made public in the interest of 'law and order'. It was, however, a profound disappointment to those who had expected to hear some real blood curdling stories.

CHAUDHARI KRISHNA GOPAL DUTT, a Congress MLA said that the Government might have had some reason for arresting the Communists but why had some other people been arrested? Arrest the Communists if you think necessary but don't touch OTHERS—this seemed to be the opinion of this stalwart Congress leader. He perhaps 'forgot' that Comrade Sohan Singh Josh was the Secretary of the Provincial Congress Committee last year and he and Master Kabul Singh were members of the Provincial Congress Working Committee at the time of their arrest. Also that most of the others were active Congress workers.

Who are the 'Fifth Column'

MIAN IFTIKHARUDDIN, the President of the PCC made one of the most vigorous and effective speeches ever made in the Punjab Assembly. The Government had charged these people with 'Fifth Column' activities and the Premier had gone to the length of saying that such people should be shot. The question was AGAINST WHOM were their activities directed? Against the British Government or against the country, that is against the people's movement for freedom? If against the British Government, then he too was proud to plead guilty to the charge. If the charge was that they were working against the country, then none could be more guilty of the charge than the Premier, his colleagues and his supporters. If the Premier thought that traitors should be given the maximum punishment, then the whole ministerialist benches would become empty. For IT WAS THEY WHO WERE THE ACTIVE FIFTH COLUMNISTS OF A FOREIGN POWER, of British Imperialism.

As a matter of fact, those gentlemen had got the chance to occupy their present position because of the struggles and sacrifices of those whom they dared to call 'fifth columnists'. Sir Sikandar himself had given the life history of some of those arrested—a history of struggle for freedom dating back in some cases to 25 years. Hitler did not exist then and Russia was under Tsarist regime. How could these people be fifth columnists and whose? Of course, they had opposed the war. So had he. So had the Congress. The attitude of Congressmen towards the war was clear. It was an Imperialist War, a war between rival robber powers fighting for empire and world domination. India's duty was to win her own freedom and she would win it despite all attempts of imperialism and its agents and lackeys—among them some sections of Punjabis.

What is their Crime?

These people whose only crime was that they were working for the freedom of the country had been arrested without any charge. And what was the treatment that was being meted out to them? They had been shoved in one room in this terrible hot season. Enemy aliens like the Italians and Germans were being sent to hill stations, by the Madras Government, for comfort. And this was how fighters for freedom were treated! The Government had made the astounding assertion that they were trying to bring about 'Russian invasion'. Surely if the Russian Government decided to invade India, it would not depend on the activities of Sohan Singh or

Kabul Singh. It would rely on its own forces. All these bogeys had been worked up to justify repression. That was the reality.

The members should carefully consider the whole thing. Who were the enemies of the country? Those who had helped to establish foreign rule in this country and were still helping it or those who were sitting among them till yesterday and were now rotting huddled in one room in the heat of Muzaffargarh?

These gentlemen of the Unionist Party boasted about their 'loyalty' and expressed horror at the activities of 'fifth columnists'. Did not many of them listen to the German Radio and like ill-treated hirelings get happy when they heard reports of British defeats? These were not good signs. They showed the real state of affairs.

'No matter what you do, you cannot stop the march of events. India will be free and soon' Mian Iftikharuddin concluded amidst applause in which a number of Unionist Party members too joined.

After this, Dewan Chamanlal spoke but he said little except the inadvisability of having Secret Session.

The Government then moved that the Speaker IN CONSULTATION WITH THE GOVERNMENT ALONE, should issue a Communiqué on the Session. The opposition was not to be consulted. In protest, the Congress MLAs walked out.

Thus ended the Secret Session. Its report has appeared nowhere. We alone are publishing it.

120. Figures of Suppression of Civil Liberties

AICC Papers, File No. G–25/1940, 31 August 1940, NMML.

Delhi Provincial Congress Committee, Delhi

31st August, 1940

The General Secretary,
All India Congress Committee
Allahabad

Figures of suppression of Civil Liberties

Dear Sir,

During the last fortnight there has been a lot of Police interference in various wards of the city at the flag salutation ceremonies. Obstruction to traffic has been made an excuse for Police presence and at one occasion a Mandi which is the private property of several persons was raided by the Police and senior Police Officers and Magistrates overawed the shopkeepers. The situation was averted by holding flag salutation ceremony at another place but the shopkeepers are still being threatened by the Police.

Another notable incident is the arrest of Maulana Hifz-Ulrahman, member of the executive of the UPPCC and a member of the AICC which took place on the 21st August under the Defence of India Rules. The charge against him is that on the 16th August 1940 he delivered a speech in Jama Masjid Delhi, which contained prejudicial matter.

Sita Ram Bharty who was being tried has been sentenced to one year R.I. under Rule 38 of the Defence of India Rules.

Yours sincerely,
General Secretary

121. Confidential Govt Circulars Regarding Measures to be Taken During CD Movement

File No. 50/1921–48, Bihar State Archives.

From:

Y.A Godbole, Esq, ICS,
Chief Secretary to Government

To

All Commissioners of Division,
All District Officers, including the
Additional Deputy Commissioner, Dhanbad
The Inspector-General of Police
All Deputy Inspectors-General of Police
All Superintendents of Police
Ranchi, the 17th/30th September, 1940

Sir,

1. I am directed to invite attention to my circular No. 2389–C dated the 21st August 1940, on the policy with regard to subversive movements. In view of the developments that have since occurred, Government consider it necessary to give more precise directions as to the measures to be taken in the event of a Civil Disobedience or other subversive campaign.

2. As stated in paragraph 6 of the letter above referred to, the general policy will be immediate action in all directions to nip any such movement in the bud and to prevent it from developing. The trend of events indicates that any movement of this nature will be initiated by the Congress and, therefore, action will be primarily directed against it and the Congress Socialist Party which is part of it. Other organizations such as the Kisan Sabha and Forward Bloc will presumably join in and will be dealt with as soon as they do so.

3. The procedure to be followed in carrying out that policy will depend upon whether the movement starts on one or other of two possible lines.

Possibility X—If the launching of Civil Disobedience is preceded by a period of preparation:

All activities directed towards preparation for a subversive movement will be watched as at present and action should be taken immediately under the Defence of India Rules against any one committing prejudicial acts. Large scale arrests are not desirable and action will be mainly against leaders or organizers. In this matter local officers will use their own discretion. Meetings, rallies and speeches will probably be a prominent feature of this preparation stage. These meetings will not be banned at the outset. They should be watched, reporters should attend and individual speakers should be prosecuted if they preach any incitement to or preparation for civil disobedience or any prejudicial act. If such propaganda becomes widespread the situation should be reported promptly to Government who will then decide when to issue orders for the banning of meetings. When that stage comes Government will delegate powers to District Magistrates under Defence of India Rule 56 to enable them to prohibit, restrict or impose conditions on meetings. Such meetings and rallies should then be prohibited. Where a meeting is prohibited, it should not be allowed to be held. If possible, the speakers should be arrested before hand and the place of meeting occupied by police. If the order is defined, the meeting should always be dispersed unless the police force is inadequate to do so. Arrests should be made before or after rather than at meetings.

While any such action will be the sublect of a report in ordinary course, a telegraphic report should be sent to Government when any important development takes place. It is important that Government should have full and early news of developments in order that they may be in a position to decide at what stage it is advisable that action should be taken to proscribe the movement under section 16 of the Criminal Law (Amendment) Act.

Possibility Y—If, as is possible, the Congress makes a declaration that it will embark on Civil Disobedience without launching any preparatory campaign, the active stage would be reached at once. In that event the Emergency Powers Ordinance would probably be brought into force immediately and the bodies participating in the movement would be declared to be Revolutionary Movements. This Ordinance will supplied offices at the local be to appropriate moment.

4. Whether action is taken under the Criminal Law (Amendment) Act, or the Emergency Powers Ordinance it will be necessary to cover the main organization such as the Indian National Congress and all its provincial and district or local branches and committees. Two notifications will therefore issue whichever Act is applied. One of the notifications will declare the main organization such as the Indian National Congress and all branches and committees thereof and all associations which aid or assist it, in general terms, as unlawful bodies or as revolutionary movements. The other notification will refer to a schedule and declare all associations described therein as unlawful or as revolutionary movements. All local branches, committees, and others which are known to Government will be named and included in the schedule. But it is possible that new local organizations may be brought into existence apparently having connection with the main organization proscribed under the criminal Law (Amendment) Act or declared as Revolutionary movement but in reality constituted in furtherance of the same object. It will therefore be the duty of District Officers to be on the look out and to report to Government without delay the names and addresses of all such new organizations or committees. Government will then issue additional notifications in respect of such new organization so that no loophole may be left for any organization to evade the law.

5. Whether the situation develops on line X, that is, with a preparatory stage, or line Y, that is, without a preparatory stage, once a declaration is issued either under section 16, Criminal Law (Amendment) Act declaring the participating bodies to be unlawful associations or under the Emergency Powers Ordinance declaring them to be revolutionary movements, the measures to be taken will be same, namely:

(i) Leading members of the organizations will be arrested at once and interned. Instructions regarding these arrests are contained in a sealed cover enclosed. The sealed cover is not to be opened until you receive a telegram beginning with the word 'ADOLF' or 'BENITO', If recalled by Government the sealed cover should be returned in tact.

(ii) Government will issue a notification ordering the seizure of places or buildings used by the unlawful associations. On receipt of the notification these places are to be seized at once. Reports should be submitted to Government promptly as soon as any new places or buildings are brought into use by any unlawful association so as to enable Government to notify them immediately.

(iii) Government will issue a notification ordering the seizure of funds of the unlawful associations or suspected to be held or used or intended to be used in aid of them. Appropriate orders for carrying out these measures will issue simultaneously with the notification.

(iv) All meetings in support of the movement will become unlawful and should be banned by the District Magistrate.

(v) Meetings of committees, etc., in support of the movement will be stopped where known and the members arrested and prosecuted.

(vi) The instructions issued with regard to drill and uniforms will continue to be strictly carried out.

(vii) Orders will issue under Defence of India Rule 59 (or under the Emergency Powers Ordinance) banning emblems such as Congress Flags, and other things.

(viii) It may be necessary to exercise some control on the publication of news connected with the movement. Separate instructions will issue on this point.

It is essential that action should be taken on (i), (ii) as rapidly as possible.

Other possible developments are non-rent or no tax campaign or picketing of foreign cloth and excise shops. Picketing will be dealt with under section 7 of the Criminal Law (Amendment) Act. Separate orders will issue in the case of a no-rent or no-tax campaign. Special instructions will also issue when necessary to deal with subversive activities of local bodies.

6. The powers that will be available will differ according to whether the Emergency Powers Ordinance is brought into operation at once or there is a preliminary period in which we shall have to rely on the Criminal Law (Amendment) Act and the Defence of India Rules. The powers under the Emergency Powers Ordinance are in some respects wider, but in substance the two sets of laws agree fairly closely; the main difference being that under the Emergency Powers ordinance many powers are vested direct on District Magistrates to enable them to act quickly, whereas under the Criminal Law (Amendment) Act and Defence of India Rules most of the powers vest in Government and require an order of Government before they are put into action.

Gandhi's claims. Mr Gandhi does not promise independence for the first time in the history of the Congress. In the past he has repeatedly done so and failed. Today there are leaders within the Congress itself who clearly ridicule Mr Gandhi's recipe of charkha winning political independence. At a time when Congress was united civil disobedience movement failed disastrously. Now that it is a house divided in itself there is hardly likelihood of its succeeding.

It is necessary that commercial bodies, political organization institutions pledged to social uplift and associations interested in the progressive political development of the country should act and procedure immediately an organization capable of counteracting the mischievous movement for which the Congress is now preparing.

⊹≡✳≡⊹

122.   Extract from Nehru's Speech, Bombay, 14 September 1940

Bharat Jyoti, 15 September 1940; *SWJN,* Vol. XI, pp. 137–9.

... As soon as the war started the Congress asked the British Government to declare their war aims and the reply given was so vague that it became clear that they were not fighting for freedom as declared by them. After that the Congress ministries resigned and the Congress passed resolutions in favour of satyagraha. ... British imperialism is bound to come to an end whether Britain wins the war or not. The Delhi resolution was passed in the hope that it could be given effect to easily and immediately. But it was rejected, and we were told that no settlement could be arrived at till we came to an agreement with the minorities and the princes. Even in these troubled times British policy towards India remains unchanged After all what was the Congress demand? It did not ask for independence or power for the Congress; but all that we demand is a constituent assembly chosen by the people irrespective of caste and creed. The British Government's reply seemed calculated to ridicule us as it is impossible that all the interests in India, especially the princes and the English traders will ever stand united on a common point. By this attitude the government has tried to put down the Congress through the communal organizations and those other organizations who are opposed to India's freedom. When Britain seeks to divide our country into hundreds of small bits we cannot remain idle. Thousands of Congress workers have been arrested in various provinces. It is our duty to fight back when the nation's unity and integrity are in danger. We have tried our level best to come to an agreement with Britain, but we did not manage to satisfy the Liberals. Britain is not prepared to part with power even when faced with a life and death struggle. If we do not face the offensive of the government now, then all the progress that has been made by us during the last fifty years will be retarded.

What are we to do in order to achieve our goal of independence? India can launch satyagraha. Some people are of the opinion that we should not start satyagraha now when Britain is in difficulties. Satyagraha has never been launched in order to embarrass the adversary found in a tight corner. But the point is that Congress is the victim of aggression and is likely to be annihilated if it does not stand up and fight. We have not the least sympathy with the Nazis. Supposing we were free and even if we sympathized with Britain we need not necessarily join the war. America sympathizes with Britain and is giving her all aid but hasn't actually joined the war. But India has been involved in the war without even being consulted. The question before us is how to protect India and how to achieve our freedom. When demands are being made on India and men and money are being taken by force, it has become our duty to resist this. We have tried our best and have given every kind of chance to the British Government to come to some settlement on the question of India's freedom. We were prepared to tolerate many things, which in the ordinary course we could not have tolerated, merely because Britain was in trouble.

Our struggle is not against the English nation or the German nation but our fight is against British imperialism as well as all other imperialisms and because the British Government wants to maintain her imperialistic policy, we have to make a stand against the British Government and achieve our country's freedom. Various kinds of attacks are being made on the activities of the Indians. Recently a new order was enforced to suppress the activities of the Congress volunteers who were pledged to non-violence. It was said that this banning order was meant for the Khaksars, but that is not true as a settlement had been arrived at between the Khaksars and the government when this order was issued and there was no necessity to issue such an order? The British Government has tried its best to strengthen all those forces which are against the Congress. The task before us is twofold. We have not only to achieve our independence but we must also concentrate on counteracting the anti-nationalistic tendencies and strengthen the forces of Indian nationalism.

The reasonable demands of the Congress have been rejected by the government. We have no other alternative but to start satyagraha and in what form it should be started is still to be decided. Mahatma Gandhi is our great leader and he will lead the satyagraha because this weapon was introduced by him. In what form he will start satyagraha will come to light shortly. He will of course in accordance with his usual practice give sufficient notice to the opponent. When satyagraha is started it will affect the whole world. The British Government would do its utmost to crush the movement as they are already involved in war and are risking their lives. We should also be prepared to risk our lives if we want to carry on the fight for freedom; it cannot be done by timidity and cowardliness. We must be prepared to pay the price of freedom which cannot be paid in gold or silver but by laying down our lives. The question is now before the All India Congress Committee and when a great organization like the Congress takes a step it will have its effect on millions of people and hence it has to consider the issue not only from one point of view but from a hundred points of view. The Congress is a democratic organization and hence it requires the support of the people. The people too must realize their responsibility and be prepared to do their duty.

Chapter 4. Individual Satyagraha

A.   CONGRESS DECISION TO LAUNCH SATYAGRAHA

1. All India Congress Committee Resolution on Satyagraha, Bombay,
    15–16 September 1940

    Harijan, 22 September 1940; *Indian Annual Register*, 1940, Vol. II, pp. 212–13.

On Satyagraha[1]

'The All India Congress Committee has given its careful attention to the events that have taken place since its last meeting held in Poona on July 27, 1940 and to the resolutions passed by the Working Committee at Wardha in August last. The Committee approves of and endorses these resolutions.

'In order to end the deadlock in India and to promote the national cause, in cooperation with the British people, the Working Committee, even at the sacrifice of Mahatma Gandhi's co-operation, made a proposal to the British Government in their Delhi resolution of July 7, which was subsequently approved by the AICC at Poona. This proposal was rejected by the British Government in a manner which left no doubt that they had no intention to recognize India's independence, and would, if they could, continue to hold this country indefinitely in bondage for British exploitation. This decision of the British Government shows that they will impose their will upon India, and their recent policy has further shown that they will not even tolerate free expression of public opinion in condemnation of their associating India in the war against Germany, against the will of a vast body of the people of India, and of exploiting her national resources and man power for this purpose.

'The All India Congress Committee cannot submit to a policy which is a denial of India's natural right to freedom, which suppresses the free expression of public opinion and which would lead to the degradation of her people and their continued enslavement. By following this policy the British Government have created an intolerable situation, and are imposing upon the Congress a struggle for the preservation of the honour and the elementary rights of the people. The Congress is pledged under Gandhiji's leadership to non-violence for the vindication of India's freedom. At this grave crisis in the movement for national freedom, the All India Congress Committee, therefore, requests him to guide the Congress in the action that should be taken. The Delhi resolution, confirmed by the AICC at Poona, which prevented him from so doing, no longer applies. It has lapsed.

'The AICC sympathize with the British people as well as the people of all other countries involved in the War. Congressmen cannot withhold their admiration for the bravery and endurance shown by the British nation in the face of danger and peril. They can have no ill-will against them, and the spirit of Satyagraha forbids the Congress from doing anything with a view to embarrass them. But this self-imposed restraint cannot be taken to the extent of self-extinction. The Congress must insist on the fullest freedom to pursue its policy, based on non-violence. The Congress has, however, no desire at the present moment to extend non-violent resistance, should this become necessary, beyond what is required for the preservation of the liberties of the people.

'In view of certain misapprehensions that have arisen in regard to the Congress policy of non-violence, the AICC desire to state this afresh, and to make it clear that this policy continues, notwithstanding anything contained in previous resolutions which may have led to these misapprehensions. This Committee firmly believes in the policy and practice of non-violence not only in the struggle for Swaraj, but also, in so far as this may be possible of application, in free India. The Committee is convinced, and recent world events have demonstrated, that complete world disarmament is necessary, and the establishment of a new and juster political and economic order, if the world is not to destroy itself and revert to barbarism. A free India will therefore throw all her weight in favour of world disarmament and should herself be prepared to give a lead in this to the world. Such lead will inevitably depend on external factors and internal conditions, but the State would do its utmost to give effect to this policy of disarmament. Effective disarmament and the establishment of world peace by the ending of national wars, depend ultimately on the removal of the causes of wars and national conflicts. These causes must be rooted out by the ending of the domination of one country over another and the exploitation of one people or group by another. To that end India will peacefully labour, and it is with this objective in view that the people of India desire to attain the status of a free and independent nation. Such freedom will be the prelude to the close association with other countries within a comity of free nations for the peace and progress of the world'.

---

[1] The resolution was passed by the AICC on 16 September 1940. It had been earlier approved by the Congress Working Committee at its meeting in Bombay held from 13 to 17 September 1940 and recommended to AICC.

2.   Mahatma Gandhi's Speech in English at the AICC Meeting, Bombay, 15 September 1940

Harijan, 29 September 1940.

I know that you have listened to me with the greatest patience. I am specially grateful to you today, for the simple reason that I have said many things which may have displeased you. But it was never my intention to displease those whom I want to harness for the great work that lies before you and before me. I have to speak to you at length because I have to shoulder this burden. I have not come with a prepared speech at all. The thoughts will come as I proceed.

Let me begin with a thought which has been weighing with me for a considerable time. When the war broke out and I went to Simla to see the Viceroy I issued a statement the next day, not in a representative but in my individual capacity. A friend has now reminded me how good it would have been if I had simply hung on to that statement although I could not take the Congress with me; and on the eve of my shouldering this responsibility, he prayed that I should be guided by God to take up that original position and retire. I have very great regard for him. I have not forgotten that statement, nor have I any regret or apology to offer. If such a thing occurs—and history often repeats itself—and I happen to go to another Viceroy, I should make the same statement.

Although I spoke only for myself, deep down in me there was the Congressman speaking. The Viceroy also did not send for me because I was M.K. Gandhi. M.K. Gandhi has absolutely no place in his books. The man who wields the sceptre can have no room for individuals. He sent for me because he thought I would represent the Congress view and I would be able to carry conviction to Congressmen.

I withdrew from that position, not as an individual but as a Congressman, and because I failed to carry conviction even to a single Congressman. Happily you have got on the Working Committee men with sterling honesty who had the courage to tell me that, although it was my statement, they did not feel like accepting it. They added that they had had bitter experience behind them, and that therefore they would not be able to take that position. Thus you had the resolution that was passed by the Congress immediately after the war. And I agreed with the resolution as a representative, although I said to them that, if I could carry conviction, my original position was the best possible one to take up. If I had pressed the members of the Working Committee to accept my position, they would have done so, but it would have been only mechanical. The statement was not made to deceive the Viceroy or, for the matter of that, a single soul. It came straight from the heart. It was not a theatrical display. It was the opening up of the secret recesses of the heart before the world, the Viceroy and the Congress. If these words of mine could not find an echo in their hearts, they would have been of no use whatsoever to the Viceroy, to the great English nation or to India. That still remains my sentiment. If I could not convince the Congress of my attitude, it would not carry us further. It would have been a wrong step to take, and hence it was not taken. With that background I approach this resolution.

I have made repeated statements that I would not be guilty of embarrassing the British people or the British Government when their very existence hung in the balance, that I would not be true to my satyagraha, would not be true to non-violence, would not be true to the truth, which I hold dear if did so, and therefore could not do so. That very man now stands before you to shoulder the burden of satyagraha. Why? There comes a time when a man in his weakness mistakes vice for virtue; and virtue itself, when taken away from its context and from the purpose for which it was dedicated, becomes vice. I felt that, if I did not go to the assistance of the Congress and take the helm even if it be in fear and trembling, I would be untrue to myself.

I feel that in taking the step that we are doing we are rendering a great service not only to the Congress but to the whole of India. And we are rendering a service not only to the whole of India. History will record—and Englishmen will be able to grasp this statement some day— that we rendered help to the English nation, and they will find that we were true to our salt and had the same bravery and fearlessness of which the Englishman is proud and for which he is renowned. I, who claim to be a fast friend of the British people, will be guilty of unfriendly conduct if, under a false sense of modesty, or because people may think otherwise about me, or because Englishmen themselves will be angry with me, I do not issue a warning that the virtue of self-restraint now becomes vice, because it will kill the Congress organization, and it will kill the very spirit which is exercising this restraint.

When I say this, I am speaking not only for the Congress, but for all who stand for national freedom—Muslims, Parsis, Christians and even those who are against the Congress, so long as they represent the aspirations of India, namely, unadulterated independence. I should be untrue to all of them, if at this time I said, 'no embarrassment to the British'. I must not repeat parrot-like 'no embarrassment'. Then that repetition would be just as useful for my salvation or for the guarding of my virtue as the repetition by a parrot of God's name which cannot bring him salvation, because it is only a mechanical and vocal effort without any intelligence behind it. Therefore, if I exercise that suppression at this critical moment in the history of the nation, it would be useless. I should be perfectly untrue to myself if I hid myself in Sevagram and said, 'No, I have told you, "no embarrassment".'

The language of this resolution is in the main mine; It appealed to Pandit Jawaharlal Nehru. I used to be the Congress draftsman. Now he has taken my place. He saw it was inevitable, if we were to be true to non-violent resistance to the extent to which we wanted to go. The working Committee has accepted this phraseology deliberately, well knowing its implications. The result is this: If we can get a declaration from the British Government that the Congress can carry on anti-war propaganda, and preach non-cooperation with the Government in their war effort, we will not have civil disobedience.

I do not want England to be defeated or humiliated. It hurts me to find St. Paul's Cathedral damaged. It hurts me as much as I would be hurt if I heard that the Kashi Vishvanath temple or the Juma Masjid was damaged. I would like to defend both the Kashi Vishvanath temple and the Juma Masjid and even St. Paul's with my life, but would not take a single life for their defence. That is my fundamental difference with the British people. My sympathy is there with them nevertheless. Let there be no mistake on the part of Englishmen, Congressmen, or others whom my voice reaches, as to where my sympathy lies. It is not because I love the British nation and hate the German. I do not think that the Germans as a nation are any worse than the English or the Italians are any worse. We are all tarred with the same brush; we are all members of the vast human family. I decline to draw any distinctions. I cannot claim any superiority for Indians. We have the same virtues and the same vices. Humanity is not divided into water-tight compartments so that we cannot go from one to another. They may occupy one thousand rooms, but they are all related to one another. I would not say, 'India should be all in all, let the whole world perish,' that is not my message. India should be all in all, consistently with the well-being of other nations of the world. I can keep India intact and its freedom also intact only if I have goodwill towards the whole of the human family and not merely for the human family which inhabits this little spot of the earth called India. It is big enough compared to other smaller nations, but what is India in the wide world or in the universe?

Let there be no mistake as to what I am about. I want my individuality to remain unimpaired. If I lose it, I would be of no service to India, much less to the British people, still less to humanity. My individual liberty is the same as the nation's, convertible with national liberty. I do not claim any greater liberty for myself. Hence my liberty is equal to the liberty of all of you and no greater. I feel that, if my liberty is at stake, yours is also at stake. I claim the liberty of going through the streets of Bombay and say that I shall have nothing to do with this war, because I do not believe in this war and in this fratricide that is going on in Europe. I admire the bravery. But what is the use of this bravery? I deplore the foolishness and the crass ignorance. These people do not know what they are fighting for. That is how I look at this war that is going on across the seas. I cannot possibly take part in it. Nor do I want the Congress to do so.

The part that I would like to take is the part of peace-maker. If the British people in their wisdom had recognized the independence not of the Congress but of all India, and if other parties in India had also co-operated with us, we would have taken the honourable place of peace-makers between these nations. Such is my ambition. But today I know that it is a day-dream. But sometimes a man lives in his day-dreams. I live in mine, and picture the world as full of good human beings—not goody goody human beings. In the Socialist's language, there will be a new structure of society, a new order of things. I am also aspiring after a new order of things that will astonish the world. If you try to dream these day-dreams, you will also feel exalted as I do.

And now I come to our 'tin-pot' Congress—tin-pot in the estimation of others, not my own. If we do not take care, the Congress will disappear, and if the Congress disappears, the national spirit disappears. One after another Congressmen are being selected and jailed. It is not satyagraha to watch people being taken away. It is much better for all of us to rush into the jaws of the opponent. After all, as the Maulana Saheb once said, India is a vast prison. Let us get out of this slave-prison by breaking the prison bars. He said to the Sikhs at the time of the Nankana Saheb tragedy: 'You may protect one gurdwara; but what about the vast gurdwara that is India? We have to deliver it from bondage.' Those words ring true even today in my ears. If this liberty of the nation or the movement for freedom is likely to be choked, then I say that the virtue of self restraint is going to become a vice. That virtue of restraint cannot be carried to the extent of the extinction of the national spirit wherever it may reside, whether among Congressmen or non-Congressmen.

I do not want to hurl civil disobedience or anything in the face of the Government without making my meaning clear, the meaning I attach to the sum total of Government actions— actions beginning with the declaration of the Viceroy, the statement of the Secretary of State for India, and the series of actions and the policy that the Government have pursued since. The sum total of all these has left an indelible impression on my mind that there is something wrong, some injustice, being perpetrated against the whole nation, and that the voice of freedom is about to be stifled. This is implied in the resolution, not in the exact language which I am using now, but you will see the meaning clear as daylight.

In order completely to clarify our position, I propose to approach the Viceroy with a request that he will be good enough to see me, and I have no doubt that he will. I will place my difficulties before him; I will place the Congress difficulties before him. I will approach him in your name. I will tell him that this is the position to which we have been reduced: We do not want to embarrass you and deflect you from your purpose in regard to war effort. We go our way, and you go yours, undeterred, the common ground being non-violence. If we carry the people with us, there will be no war effort on the part of our people. If, on the other hand, without your using any but moral pressure, you find that the people help the war effort, we can have no cause for grumbling. If you get assistance from the Princes, from the zamindars, from anybody high or low, you can have it; but let our voice also be heard. If you accept my proposal, it will be eminently honourable; it will certainly be a feather in your cap. It will be honourable of you, although you are engaged in a life and death struggle, that you have given us this liberty. It will be honourable of you that you take this great step, although you have limitless powers to choke our voice, and that you give us the fullest possible freedom, consistently with the observance of non-violence, to tell the people of India not to join the war effort.

Let the people use any reasoning they like for refusal to help the war effort. My reasoning is the only one which will sit well on Congressmen's lips. But I do not expect all to restrict themselves to that reasoning. Those who have conscientious objection, as I have, will adopt my reasoning. Those who are tired of British imperialism will use that argument. There may be others who will have other arguments. All these should be covered under this freedom of speech, provided, however, that they all accept non-violence, provided also that what they say is said openly and not secretly. These are the implications of my generalship. If these do not satisfy you, you must reject this resolution summarily. So long as you can preach non-cooperation with war effort in men and money, there should be no civil disobedience. But if you have not that liberty, there is no Swaraj but perpetual bondage. I would like the British people and the Viceroy to be able to tell the world that they have given the leaders of the Indian people liberty to preach to their people what they like. The British can then say to the world: 'Judge us by our conduct. Here in India we are playing the game.'

I do not mind the British not responding to the Delhi resolution. They may say, 'At the present moment you cannot interfere with the management of affairs as they stand. Deliverance will come to you in its own time. At this critical juncture do not worry us.' I will understand that argument. I will sympathize with it. I will hold my hand so long as there is no fraud or falsity in what they say. It is impossible for them to give us freedom. If freedom has got to come, it must be obtained by our own internal strength, by our closing our ranks, by unity between all sections of the community. It cannot descend from heaven, nor can it be given as a gift from one nation to another. I do not know whether I am representing the feelings of the members of the Working Committee, because I have not discussed these things with them. But you have to take me with all my limitations, with the workings of my mind.

The Viceroy may say, 'You are a visionary'. I may fail in my mission, but we will not quarrel. If he says he is helpless, I will not feel helpless. I will make good my position. I cannot sit still when I see Ram Manohar Lohia and Jaiprakash Narain in jail, than whom I do not know braver or straighter men. They have not preached violence, but simply carried out the behests of the Ramgarh resolution. It was a point of honour with them.

I have restrained myself, and will restrain myself. I will not seek imprisonment. I do not want to offer civil disobedience. I will not place myself in peril. In this battle I will not expose myself to imprisonment. But if the Government chooses, it will not be difficult to take me away. I will not be able to seal my lips or restrain my pen. It will be difficult for them to keep me in prison, not because India will rise in rebellion. India will be wrong if it does so. My own instinct is that they will not be able to keep me in jail.

I will place my argument before the Viceroy. I may fail in my mission. But I have never approached a mission in despair. I may have approached it with the consciousness that I may be faced with a blind wall. But I have often penetrated blind walls. I shall approach the Viceroy in the confidence and hope that he will understand the great reasonableness of the request of the Congress for full liberty to preach 'no war' in India. Everyone should have perfect liberty to preach by pen and tongue, 'we cannot aid imperialism, we cannot help spoliation.'

I shall strain every nerve to avoid satyagraha in your name. What shape it will take, when it comes, I do not know. But I know that there will be no mass civil disobedience, because mass civil disobedience is not required for this occasion. I have impenetrable darkness before me regarding the future course of action. I have no mysteries. I do not know how I shall lead you, what action I shall put before you. I hope that any action that we may take will be worthy of the Congress traditions and of the occasion.

I have often said that I do not know the Congress mind as I have buried myself in Sevagram. It is because of the Congress difficulty that I have dragged myself to Bombay, and immediately I am released from this duty you will find me in Sevagram. But I have got strength and resourcefulness enough to lead this battle, although I am buried in Sevagram. I shall do better and clearer thinking in Sevagram than anywhere else, simply because I have built up there an atmosphere for my growth. With the march of time my body must decay but, I hope, not my wisdom. I seem to see things more clearly with the advance of age. It may be self-deception, but there is no hypocrisy. Self-deception is good sometimes in that it helps one to remain cheerful and not to give way to despair. It will be, therefore, wrong of you to drag me from Sevagram; and I promise that I shall give a good account of my stewardship.

There are many parties in the Congress. We are not all of the same opinion. There is indiscipline in the Congress. I know it is inevitable in a mass organization which is growing from day to day. If it is all indiscipline and no discipline, the organization is on the downward path. Let it not be said of you that you come to the Congress although you do not believe in non-violence. How can you possibly sign the Congress pledge with violence in your breasts? I want complete obedience to the policy of non-violence. While the policy lasts, it is the same as though it was a creed, for so long as it holds good it is as good as a creed. My creed holds me for life: yours so long as you hold it. Resign from the Congress and you are free from it. Let us be clear regarding the language we use and the thoughts we nurture. For, what is language but the expression of thought? Let your thought be accurate and truthful and you will hasten the advent of Swaraj even if the whole world is against you. You will have won Swaraj without having to spend nine million pounds a day or without burning a single home. If you are true to your policy, I am sure that without doing any of these things you will build up the majestic edifice of freedom.

Now for the violence party. Do not mix up the methods if you can help it. You have restrained yourselves for some years. Restrain yourselves for some more years. Ours is not a small battle. If you restrain yourselves, you will lose nothing.

Freedom of speech and pen is the foundation of Swaraj. If the foundation-stone is in danger, you have to exert the whole of your might in order to defend that single stone. May God help you.

3.   Viceroy–Gandhi Correspondence, 30 September 1940
Harijan, 6 October 1940; *Indian Annual Register*, 1940, Vol. II, pp. 227–8.

Viceroy's Letter

Dear Mr Gandhi,

I think it will be convenient if I record very briefly in writing the origin of the talks we have had on the 27th and 30th September and their outcome.

As you will remember, you wrote to me on the 18th September to ask that I should grant you an interview, and explained in your letter that you were anxious to discuss the situation covered by the recent resolution of the All India Congress Committee not only in your capacity as guide of the Congress but as a personal friend. I was, I need not say, most ready to talk things over with you, and we have now had the advantage of two conversations.

In the course of these conversations the situation has been exhaustively discussed, with particular reference to the question of free speech in time of war. On that matter, while professing yourself most anxious to avoid in any way embarrassing His Majesty's Government in the prosecution of the war, you made it clear to me that you regarded it as essential that the Indian National Congress and other members of the public should be in a position to give full expression to their views in relation to war effort provided only that such expression was fully non-violent.

I indicated to you the nature of the special treatment laid down by law in the United Kingdom for dealing with conscientious objectors, which I may broadly describe as an arrangement under which, while the conscientious objector is absolved from the duty of fighting and is allowed even to profess his faith in public, he is not permitted to carry his opposition to the length of endeavouring to persuade others, whether soldiers or munition workers, to abandon their allegiance or to discontinue their effort.

You made it clear to me that you would not regard treatment of that nature as adequate in the conditions of India, and that you regarded it as essential that in India, where in your judgment conditions were wholly different from those existing in Great Britain, the Indian objector, either to all war as such, or to the participation of India in the present war, should be untrammeled in the expression of his views.

It emerged further from our conversation that while you would not yourself preach to workers engaged on war work at the actual works, in the endeavour there to dissuade them from working on war equipment, you would regard it as essential that it should be open to Congressmen and non-Congressmen alike to deliver addresses and otherwise to call upon people throughout the country to refrain from assisting India's war effort in any way which would involve India's participation in bloodshed.

I listened with the utmost care and attention to your argument, and our examination of the situation has been full and close. I felt bound, however, in the outcome to make it clear to you that action such as you suggest would certainly amount not only to the inhibition of India's war effort, but to that embarrassment of Great Britain in the prosecution of the war which the Congress state that they are anxious to avoid; and that would clearly not be possible in the interest of India herself, more particularly at this most critical juncture in the war, to acquiesce in the interference with war effort which would be involved in freedom of speech so wide as that for which you had asked.

Gandhiji's Reply

Dear Lord Linlithgow,

I have your letter of even date.

It fairly sets forth the Congress position as I placed it before you. It is a matter of deep regret to me that the Government have not been able to appreciate the Congress position, meant just to satisfy the bare requirements of the people, whether Congressmen or others, who felt a conscientious objection to helping a war to which they were never invited and which they regard, so far as they are concerned, as one for saving the imperialism of which India is the greatest victim. Their objection is just as conscientious as mine as a war resister. I cannot claim greater freedom for my conscience than for that of those I have named.

As I made it plain in the course of our talks, the Congress is as much opposed to victory for Nazism as any Britisher can be. But their objection cannot be carried to the extent of their participation in the war. And since you and the Secretary of State for India have declared that the whole of India is voluntarily helping the war-effort, it becomes necessary to make clear that the vast majority of the people of India are not interested in it. They make no distinction between Nazism and the double autocracy that rules India. Had His Majesty's Government recognized the freedom required in the special condition of India, they would have justified the claim that they were receiving from India only such effort as they could voluntarily. The war party and the no-war party would have been placed on an equal footing so far as each worked fully non-violently.

As to the last paragraph of your letter, I wish to remind you that it was never contemplated to carry non-embarrassment to the point of self-extinction or, in other words stopping all national activities which were designed to make India peace-minded, and show that India's participation could not benefit anyone, not excluding Great Britain. Indeed, I hold that if India were left free to make her choice, which freedom of speech implied, India would probably have turned the scales in favour of Britain and true liberty by the moral prestige which Britain would have then gained.

I must, therefore, repeat that the Congress does still want to refrain from embarrassing the British Government in their war effort. But it is impossible for the Congress to make of the policy a fetish by denying its creed at this critical period in the history of mankind. If the Congress had to die, it should do so in the act of proclaiming its faith. It is unfortunate that we have not been able to arrive at an agreement on the single issue of freedom of speech. But I shall hug the hope that it will be possible for the Government to work out their policy in the spirit of the Congress position.

I should like to touch upon the other points I raised in our talks. But for fear of burdening this reply, I refrain. I shall hope to make a public statement on them as early as I can.

In conclusion, let me thank you publicly for the great courtesy and patience with which you listened to my very long statement and argument. And though our ways seem to diverge for the moment, our personal friendship will as you have kindly said at the time of saying farewell, bear the strain of divergence.

As arranged, I am handing our correspondence to the press for publication.

4. Mahatma Gandhi's Statements 'To Satyagrahis' and 'The Breach', 2 October 1940

Harijan, 6 October 1940; *Indian Annual Register*, 1940, Vol. II, p. 228.

To Satyagrahis

Mahatma Gandhi issued the following statements:

Satyagrahis will not be impatient with me and argue with me or with themselves and say 'When will you give the word? You have had your interview with the Viceroy. You have got what many of us had told you would get'. Your telling me this or that mattered little. The attempt was worth making. I had told you that even if I did not get what I wanted from the Viceroy I would bring from Simla added strength for myself. Who knows that to have added strength is not better than weak success? But my wisdom will be tested by the manner in which I use the strength.

The Maulana Saheb has called the Working Committee for the eleventh instant. I hope I shall be ready then with my plan of action. But whatever it is, it will be good only if it carried with it the united will of all Congressmen if not the whole nation. Then the visible action even of one man will be enough for the purpose intended. Meanwhile, please remember that there is to be no civil disobedience, direct or indirect. Any breach of this will weaken the cause because it will unnerve your general who is susceptible to the slightest indiscipline. A general in action has no strength but what is given to him by his people.

The Breach

It is my firm conviction that British statesmen have failed to do the right thing when it was easy to do it. If India is wholly in favour of participation in the war, they could have easily disregarded any hostile propaganda. But the determination to gag free expression of opinion, provided it was not in the least tainted with violence, shatters Britain's claim that India's participation is voluntary. Had the Congress proposal been accepted, such aid as Britain would have got from India would have been an asset of inestimable value. The non-violent party would have played an effective part for honourable peace when the proper time for it was in sight, as it must be some day. I have been shown *The Times* comment on the breach. I accept the compliment about my resourcefulness. But great as I believe it to be, I own that it has its limitations. There must be willingness on the other side. I regret to have to say I wholly missed it at the interview. The Viceroy was all courtesy but he was unbending and believed in the correctness of his judgment and as usual had no faith in that of nationalist India. 'The Britisher is showing extraordinary bravery on the battle-field in a marvelous manner. But he lacks bravery to take risks in the moral domain. I often wonder whether the latter had any place in the British politics.

5. Mahatma Gandhi's Statement on his Meetings with Viceroy, 5 October 1940

Harijan, 13 October 1940; *Indian Annual Register*, 1940, Vol. II, pp. 229–30.

In the correspondence between HE the Viceroy and myself announcing the breakdown in the talks, I have said in my letter that I would make a public statement covering matters not referred to in my letter.

Before I do so I think it is necessary for my purpose to say a few words regarding Lord Linlithgow. He is straight in his talk and always deliberate and economical in his language. He is never equivocal, never leaves you in doubt as to his meaning. He conveys the most unpalatable decisions with a calmness and courtesy which for the moment make you think that you have heard no harsh or hard decision. He listens to your argument with a patience and attention I have never known any other Viceroy or high functionary to show in an equal measure. He is never ruffled and never discourteous. With all this however, he is not to be easily moved from his position. He meets you with his decision on the matter under discussion already made. He takes care not to let you think that it is so. But there is no doubt about it that his decision is unchangeable. He is not receptive. He has amazing confidence in the correctness of his judgment. He does not believe in a gentleman's or any other agreement. I have always felt that after the Gandhi-Irwin pact, British satraps decided that there should be no more pacts. Whatever they wanted to do, they should do independently. It shows either a high sense of justice or boundless self-assurance. I think it is the latter. He and I have become friends never to be parted, be the differences between us as great as they can be.

Holding such an opinion about the Viceroy it pains me to have to relate what I must of my impression of the talks which have ended in a divergence which in my opinion was wholly avoidable. Acceptance of my proposal would have been no less beneficial to England than to India.

I went to Simla in the capacity of a representative and as a friend. As a friend, I presented him with my doubts as to certain acts of the British Government. To have them dissolved was necessary to enable me to determine my mental attitude which to me is more than any visible act. I felt that the putting up by the Viceroy, and then the Secretary of State of want of agreement by the Congress with the Princes, the Muslim League and even the Scheduled Classes as a barrier to the British recognition of India's right to freedom was more than unjust to the Congress and the Indian people.

I told the Viceroy that these three represented class or communal interests, whereas the Congress represented no particular class. It was a purely national organization striving to represent India as a whole. And therefore, the Congress had always maintained that it would abide by the verdict of a national assembly elected on the basis of the broadest franchise. It had further declared its intention to abide by the vote of the separate Muslim electorate so far as special Muslim rights were concerned. Therefore, it was wrong to speak as if Muslim rights needed special safe-guards as against the Congress. The same thing applied to the Sikhs.

The Princes of the present day were a creation of the British Government to subserve the British interest. As against the plea that the British were bound by special treaty obligations, I contended that the Congress did not ask the British Government to disregard them. Only they could not be used to bar Indian progress and it was wholly wrong to expect the Congress to produce an agreement with them. The Princes were not like other parties free to conclude any agreement with the Congress even if they wished. Moreover the treaties, if they oblige the British Government to protect the Princes, equally compel them to protect the rights of the people. But it has been abundantly proved that the British had rarely interfered with the Princes purely on behalf of the people. If they had been as careful of the peoples' rights, as they were bound by treaties to be, the peoples' condition would not have been as miserable as it is today. Had they been true to the treaties of their own making, the people of the States in India should be more advanced than those of British India. I cited some telling illustrations of this neglect of duty.

The introduction of the Scheduled Classes in the controversy has made the unreality of the case of the British Government doubly unreal. They know that these are the special care of the Congress and that the Congress is infinitely more capable of guarding their interests than the British Government. Moreover the Scheduled Classes are divided into as many castes as the caste Hindu society. No single schedule class member could possibly and truthfully represent the innumerable castes among them.

I had sought the interview with the Viceroy to see if my interpretation of the British argument had any flaw. I failed to get any satisfaction on the points raised. The Viceroy would not be drawn into a discussion. I can have no grievance about his disinclination to enter into any argument. He had every right to rely upon the fact that that was a matter of high policy not admitting of argument.

There is a certain cold reserve about the British official world which gives them their strength and isolation from surroundings and facts. They do not want to be too frank. They politely refuse to enter into an embarrassing argument. They leave you to draw what inference you like while they continue to maintain their inflexible attitude. I suppose that is what is meant by the steel frame. For me this side of the British policy has been the least attractive. I had hoped against the warning of friends that I must be able to break through this steel wall of reserve and get the naked truth. But the imperialist Britisher is firmly fixed in his saddle.

Nevertheless I will not accept defeat. I must strive to have the truth admitted by the British people that the bar to India's freedom lies not in the Congress or another party's inability to produce an agreement which is in its nature impossible, but that it undoubtedly lies in the British disinclination to do the obviously right thing.

The unreality of the British reasons for refusal to treat India as a free country was not my only grouse. I drew the Viceroy's attention to certain irregularities in the prosecution of the war policy.

There was agreement between us that there should be no compulsion as to war contribution. He has promised to examine all cases of hardship and all other difficulties.

My purpose was to leave no ground for misunderstanding and to fight, if there was to be a fight, only on well-defined issues and without bitterness. I want to enter upon the fight with the hope that its very fairness will compel the recognition that India deserves better treatment, not merely from the British but from all the nations on the earth.

Lest it might be said that the Congress fights because it has failed to get power, I told his Excellency the Viceroy in the plainest words possible that the Congress had no desire to mount to power at the expense of a single national interest. It seeks no power save for the whole nation.

Therefore, he will have no opposition from the Congress if he forms a cabinet composed of representatives of different parties. The Congress would be content to be in opposition so far as the war effort is concerned and so long as the Government machinery has to subserve Imperialist ends.

The immediate issue is not independence. The immediate issue is the right to exist, that is, the right of self-expression which, broadly put, means free speech. This the Congress wants not merely for itself but for all, the only restraint being complete observance of non-violence. I hold that the condition answers all the difficulties by whomsoever raised.

6. Mahatma Gandhi's Plan of Commencement of Civil Disobedience, 15 October 1940

Harijan, 20 October 1940; *Indian Annual Register*, 1940, Vol. II, pp. 230–3.

I have had three days' discussion with the Working Committee [11–13 October 1940]. During it, I unfolded my plan of civil disobedience in so far as I was able to envisage it. Although I have sole charge of the campaign, I could not think of taking the fist step without consultation with the members of the Working Committee. In non-violent action one has to carry the co-workers with one, through the mind and the heart. There is no other way to enforce discipline or obedience to instructions. I must admit that it was not plain sailing for me. There was stubborn dissent from two members. I tried hard to carry conviction to them but, I fear, I failed. They will, however, yield to obedience so far as it is possible for them for the sake of discipline. The difference of opinion solely centered round the quantity of civil disobedience and the restriction with which it was hedged.

I disclose this part of the discussion to show that my plan will fall short of the expectations of those whom the dissenters represent. I would simply say to them: Wait patiently and see what happens. Carry out instructions to the best of your ability. Do nothing to thwart the plan. If your reason rebels against it you will serve the cause by seceding and educating the people along your own lines. That would be straight, brave and stimulating in that the people will learn to appraise the value of different methods. You will cause confusion by preaching from the Congress platform anything contrary to the official programme, especially when the whole organization becomes like an army. It matters little whether one person offers civil disobedience or many. The rest have to render such support as they may be called upon to do.

The plan is simply this. Direct action will be commenced by Shri Vinoba Bhave and for the time being confined to him only. And since it is to be confined to individual civil disobedience and that too of him only, it will be so conducted by him as to exclude others directly or indirectly. But since it is concerned with freedom of speech, the public will be involved to an extent. It is open to them either to listen to him or not. But much will depend upon what the Government wishes to do. In spite of all attempt to confine civil disobedience to individuals and for the moment to one only, they can precipitate a crisis by making it a crime to listen to him or read anything written by him. But I think and believe that they do not want to invite any trouble though they hold themselves in readiness to cope with every trouble that may face them.

I have discussed with Shri Vinoba various plans so as to avoid all unnecessary friction or risks. The idea is to make all action as strictly non-violent as is humanly possible. One man's violence, veiled or open, cannot go beyond a certain limit, but within that limit it would be effective. One man's non-violent action would be despised and ridiculed by the non-believer in it. In truth while the effect of a given violent action can be reduced to mathematical terms, that of non-violent action defies all calculation and has been known to falsify many that have been hazarded. How far I shall be able to present an example of unadulterated non-violence remains to be seen.

Who is Vinoba Bhave and why has he been selected?

He is an under-graduate having left college after my return to India in 1916. He is a Sanskrit scholar. He joined the Ashram almost at its inception. He was among the first members. In order to better qualify himself he took one year's leave to prosecute further studies in Sanskrit. And practically at the same hour at which he had left the Ashram a year before, he walked into it without notice. I had forgotten that he was due to arrive that day. He has taken part in every menial activity of the Ashram from scavenging to cooking. Though he has a marvelous memory and is a student by nature, he has devoted the largest part of his time to spinning in which he has specialized as very few have. He believes in universal spinning being the central activity which will remove the poverty in the villages and put life into their deadness. Being a born teacher, he has been of the utmost assistance to Ashadevi in her development of the scheme of education through handicrafts.

Shri Vinoba has produced a text-book taking spinning as the handicraft. It is original in conception. He has made scoffers realize that spinning is the handicraft *Par excellence* which lends itself to being effectively used for basic education. He has revolutionized takli-spinning and drawn out its hitherto unknown possibilities. For perfect spinning probably he has no rival in all India.

He has abolished every trace of untouchability from his heart. He believes in communal unity with the same passion that I have. In order to know the best mind of Islam he gave one year to the study of the Quran in the original. He therefore learnt Arabic. He found the study necessary for cultivating a living contact with the Muslims living in his neighbourhood.

He has an army of disciples and workers who would rise to any sacrifice at his bidding. He is responsible for producing a young man who has dedicated himself to the service of lepers. Though an utter stranger to medicine, this worker has by singular devotion mastered the method of treatment of lepers and is now running several clinics for their care. Hundreds owe their cure to his labours. He has now published a handbook in Marathi for the treatment of lepers. Vinoba was for years the director of the Mahila Ashram in Wardha. His devotion to the cause of Daridranarayan took him first to a village near Wardha and now he has gone still further and lives in Paunar, five miles from Wardha from where he has established contact with villagers through the disciples he has trained.

He believes in the necessity of the political independence of India. He is an accurate student of history. But he believes that real independence of the villagers is impossible without the constructive programme of which *khadi* is the centre. He believes that the *charkha* is the most suitable outward symbol of non-violence which has become an integral part of his life. He has taken an active part in the previous Satyagraha campaigns. He has never been in the lime-light on the political platform. With many co-workers he believes that silent constructive work with civil disobedience in the background is far more effective than the already heavily crowded political platform. And he thoroughly believes that non-violent resistance is impossible without a heart-belief in and practice of constructive work.

Vinoba is an out and out war resister. But he respects equally with his own the conscience of those who, whilst not being out and out war resisters, have yet strong conscientious objection to participation in the present war. Though Vinoba represents both the types, I may want to select another who will represent only one type, namely, conscientious objection to participation in the present war.

It was necessary to introduce Vinoba at length to the public in order to justify my choice. This will perhaps be the last civil disobedience struggle which I shall have conducted. Naturally I would want it to be as flawless as it can be. Moreover, the Congress has declared that it will avoid all avoidable embarrassment to the Government consistently with its own existence. For that reason too, I had to strive to produce the highest quality irrespective of quantity.

But Vinoba must fail, as I must, if we do not represent the Congress, let alone the whole nation. And we shall certainly not represent either if they do not give full-hearted co-operation which is ceaseless prosecution of the constructive programme. It is not vocal co-operation that is required. It is co-operation in work that is needed. The signs of such co-operation will be phenomenal progress in spinning, complete disappearance of untouchability and increasing sense of justice in every walk of life. Unless rock bottom justice and equality pervade society, surely there is no non-violent atmosphere. Above all, there should be no civil disobedience but what is sanctioned by me. This is a peremptory obligation binding on every Congressman. If it is disregarded, there is no co-operation.

The representative character belonging to Vinoba and me is then challenged, and I can say with confidence that if the full-hearted co-operation I want is forthcoming, not only will the issue of freedom of speech be decided in our favour but we shall have gone very near Independence. Let those who will, take me at my word. They will have lost nothing and will find that they had contributed greatly to the movement of freedom through truthful and non-violent means.

Let me repeat the issue. On the surface, it is incredibly narrow–the right to preach against war as war or participation in the present war. Both are matters of conscience for those who hold either view. Both are substantial rights. Their exercise can do no harm to the British if their pretension that to all intents and purposes India is an independent country is at all true. If India is very much a dependency in fact as it is in law, whatever the British get from India can never be regarded as voluntary, it must be regarded as impressed. This battle of life and death cannot be won by impressed levies, however large. They may win if they have the moral backing of an India truly regarded as free.

Non-violent Congress cannot wish ill to Britain. Nor can it help her through arms, since it seeks to gain her own freedom, not through arms but through unadulterated non-violence. And the Congress vanishes if, at the crucial moment, it suppresses itself for fear consequences or otherwise by ceasing to preach non-violence through non-violent means. So when we probe the issue deep enough we discover that it is a matter of life and death for us. If we vindicate that right all is well with us. If we do not, all is lost. We cannot then win Swaraj through non-violent means.

I know that India has not one mind. There is a part of India that is war-minded and will learn the art of war through helping the British. The Congress has no desire therefore to surround ammunition factories or barracks and prevent people from doing what they like. We want to tell the people of India that if they will win Swaraj through non-violent means, they may not co-operate militarily with Britain in the prosecution of the war.

This right of preaching against participation in the war is being denied to us and we have to fight against the denial. Therefore while that right will be exercised only by those whom I may select for the purpose, all the other activities of the Congress will continue as before unless the Government interfere with them.

A question has been asked why, if I attach so much importance to quality, I do not offer civil resistance myself. I have already said that unlike as on previous occasions I do not wish to do so for the very good reason that my imprisonment is likely to cause greater embarrassment to the authorities than anything else the Congress can do. I want also to remain outside to cope with any contingency that may arise. My going to jail may be interpreted as a general invitation to all Congressmen to follow suit. They will not easily distinguish between my act and speech. Lastly, I do not know how things will shape. I myself do not know the next step. I do not know the Government plan. I am a man of faith. My reliance is solely on God. One step is enough for me. The next He will make clear to me when the time for it comes. And who knows that I shall not be an instrument for bringing about peace not only between Britain and India but also between the warring nations of the earth. This last wish will not be taken for vanity by those who believe that my faith is not a sham but a reality greater than the fact that I am penning these lines.

7. Chimanlal Setalvad's Appeal to Congressmen to Postpone Satyagraha

Tribune, 14 September 1940.

Satyagraha will Embarrass British Government—It will amount to stabbing them in the back

The view that the launching of 'Satyagraha' by the Congress at the present juncture will create a greater gulf between the various communities and retard the object of creating a powerful and united India, is expressed by Sir Chimanlal Setalvad in the course of a statement to the Press.

Sir Chimanlal says that Congress leaders have been repeatedly professing that they do not want to embarrass the British Government in their present critical situation. He holds the view that if 'Satyagraha' is started now, it will not only be embarrassing to the British Government but it will amount to 'stabbing them in the back'.

In his view, if the Congress started Civil Disobedience now, many thinking people will feel that such an action is dictated by a desire to maintain and improve the position of the Congress Party over the unthinking masses. 'Whatever India's quarrel and grievances with Britain are,' concludes Sir Chimanlal, 'the fact must be faced that if, Britain loses this war, all hopes of freedom and democracy for India will vanish for a long time.'

The following is the full text of the statement:

'The Working Committee of the Congress at their Wardha meeting having rejected the offer of the British Government, as announced in the Viceroy's statement, meetings of the Working Committee and the AICC are to be held in Bombay from tomorrow to decide what further action the Congress should take and Mr Gandhi has arrived in Bombay to take part in the deliberations. It is necessary shortly to recall the offer of the British Government and the final demands of the Congress. The offer conceded that India was to attain Dominion Status on the same footing as Canada and Australia. Further, the framing of the future constitution should primarily be the responsibility of Indians themselves and should originate from Indian conceptions of the social, economic and political structure of the Indian life and that at the end of the war a representative body of Indians should be called together for that purpose and that in the meantime, Indians should reach among themselves a basis of friendly agreement on the form which this representative body should take and the methods by which it should arrive at conclusions and, secondly, upon the principles and outlines of the constitution itself. Further, certain number of representative Indians were to be invited to join the Executive Council of the Viceroy.

The Working Committee of the Congress at its Wardha meeting again insisted on a declaration of independence for India and the immediate formation of a national Government at the Centre, responsible to the Legislature. It has been repeatedly pointed out that full Dominion status, as promised by the British Government, is much better than independence in the present state of the world. As regards the demand for National Government at the centre, responsible to the Legislature immediately, it will really be rejudging the form of the future constitution of India, the framing of which is to be undertaken at the end of the war by Indians themselves. Moreover, the Congress leaders have been repeatedly professing that they do not want to embarrass the British Government in the critical situation in which they are placed at present. Do they seriously think that starting Civil Disobedience at this juncture would not be an embarrassment to the British Government? According to Mr Gandhi, the weapon of Satyagraha is to be used for the purpose of melting the heart of the opponent by our suffering. Is it conceivable that the heart of the British people will be melted by the Congress not only refusing to help in the war but actively embarrassing its prosecution? When they are being attacked in a deadly manner by a ruthless enemy, will they not feel that the Congress is stabbing them in the back? From all points of view it is not in the interest of the country to start Civil Disobedience at this juncture. If the Congress does so, many thinking people will justly feel that such action is dictated by a desire to maintain and improve the influence of the Congress Party over the unthinking masses. If satyagraha is started and leaders go to jails and thus pose as martyrs, they expect to be in greater favour with the people. It is hoped that leaders now assembled in Bombay will think more of the real and vital interests of the country than of maintaining the prestige and position of their Party. Whatever grievances and quarrels are grave and many, the fact must be faced that if Britain loses in this war, all hopes of freedom and democracy for India will vanish in the air for a long time.

8. Editorial on Congress Working Committee's Decision to Start Individual Satyagraha

Tribune, 15 October 1940.

What may turn out to have been the most fateful meeting of the Congress Working Committee held in recent years concluded its sittings at Wardha on Sunday last. The resolution it passed had a humdrum look, and amounted to little more than a renewal of its vote of confidence in Mahatma Gandhi's leadership, but in reality it was of tremendous importance. 'The Working Committee,' says the resolution, 'met at Gandhiji's instance and listened to the account of his talks with the Viceroy and the plan of campaign in so far as he had been able to envisage it. The Working Committee approve of what he has done and repeat the instructions given to Congressmen and Congress Committee by the AICC at its last meeting in Bombay that they should give him the fullest cooperation possible in all he may require or expect them to do.' After the AICC resolution investing the Mahatma with supreme dictatorial power there was hardly any occasion for the Working Committee to approve of any decision that the Mahatma might make, but as we said in a recent issue both the Mahatma and the Working Committee were probably anxious that the forms of democracy should be observed even though its substance had been discarded. In point of fact the Working Committee has now become a purely advisory committee whom the Mahatma may consult whenever he thinks it necessary to do so, but whose counsel he is not bound to accept or abide by. In the present case it is not known whether the members of the Committee or any of them expressed dissent from the plan of campaign envisaged by the Mahatma. It is difficult to believe that all of them share the Mahatma's view. Some of them, at any rate, must be clear sighted enough to see that even if the present is the right time for starting a campaign of Satyagraha, freedom of speech and action with regard to the war is hardly the issue over which to start such a campaign.

But whatever may be the feeling of individual members of the Committee and whether they gave free expression to their feeling or not, the die for the moment is cast. The Mahatma has made his decision and the Working Committee has, though unnecessarily, put its seal of approval on that decision. The exact nature of the decision is not known and will not be known until the Mahatma issues his statement on the subject, which he is expected to do sometime today. All that we have before us is rough outline of the Mahatma's plan of campaign contained in a Bombay telegram, which says that 'Satyagraha will be started as a protest against the Government's refusal to permit freedom of speech regarding their war effort' and that the first band of satyagrahis who will court arrest will not include any member of the Working Committee. The first satyagrahi according to the United Press, will be Mr Vinoba Bhave, a 'saintly ashramite,' and the Mahatma, it is said, has communicated or is about to communicate to the Viceroy the date, time and place where he will offer satyagraha by exercising the right of freedom of speech against war efforts in India. The general public knows little about this 'saintly ashramite,' nor can it anticipate the drift of his speech. If his speech will be a purely pacifist speech and will condemn war and violence in general, we have it on the authority of the Viceroy himself that no attempt will be made to interfere with him. And it need clearly not be anything more than a general condemnation of all wars, unless his object is not merely to assert his freedom of speech but to court imprisonment; for a general condemnation of all wars naturally and necessarily includes a condemnation of participation in the present war itself and a condemnation of participation in the present war necessarily includes an exhortation to all who are within the range of the speaker's influence not to participate in the war.

But obviously this would not serve the professed purpose of the Congress which is not merely to condemn war and violence, but to give a fight to the British Government over the Issue of freedom of speech with regard to their war effort, and this necessarily means saying and doing things which the Viceroy told the Mahatma in the course of his talk and his letter that the Government would not tolerate. It is, therefore, certain that the Satyagrahis chosen by the Mahatma will not only assert their freedom of speech with regard to war and violence generally, but so assert it with regard to participation in the present war itself as to make it impossible for the Government not to interfere with them, unless they are prepared to abandon the position which the Viceroy took up in his talk with and his letter to the Mahatma. The object here is clearly not merely to assert freedom of speech but to bend the Government to the will of the people as represented by the Congress. But satyagraha in this sense, in order to serve its purpose, must obviously be spectacular, both as regard the number and the position, influence and authority of those arrested. We remember an orthodox Congress organ saying some time ago that it would be impossible for the British Government to ignore the effect both on Indian and on British and world opinion of the arrest and imprisonment of Mahatma Gandhi, the members of the Congress Working Committee and hundreds of other influential Congress leaders in all parts of the country along with tens of thousands of ordinary Congressmen and possibly the suppression of the Congress as an organization. If, this is, indeed, the effect which the campaign of satyagraha is intended to produce, then clearly the method said to have been initially devised by Mahatma Gandhi is hardly calculated to produce it. The arrest and imprisonment of a number of selected individuals of whom the general public, whether in this country or in the world generally, knows next to nothing, no matter how perfect may be their moral worth or their sense of discipline, is hardly likely to make much impression, especially at a time when men's attention is engrossed by the big events that are happening on the several war fronts.

And yet it is difficult to see what other method of Mahatma can follow consistently with his declared intention of not causing embarrassment to the British Government at a time when they are engaged in a life-and-death struggle. By general consent the war has reached its most critical phase. The fate of England and allied countries, of democracy and civilization is hanging in the balance. Defeat for them would mean a tremendous set back to the forces of progress and a tremendous impetus to the forces of reaction. It is his realization of this truth that has led the Mahatma to declare repeatedly, a declaration which he has made in the current issue of *Harijan* itself, that he does not certainly wish victory to Nazism or defeat to Britain. But if that is not his wish how can he cause the maximum embarrassment to Britain that it is in his power to cause, by either courting arrest himself or asking other men of commanding influence and authority in the Congress and the country to court arrest at the present time! So far as the Mahatma himself is concerned it has been stated with considerable emphasis by those who ought to know that he has no intention of courting arrest on the present occasion. If the statement is correct, no decision could have been wiser or more statesmanlike, and we have no doubt in our mind that it will be welcomed equally by the British Government and the Indian people. But the decision would be robbed of much of its value and all its grace if instead of courting arrest the Mahatma would, as stated in a recent telegram from Wardha, resort to a fast. A fast by the Mahatma as a protest against the Government's policy would be as embarrassing to them as the courting of arrest by him, while to his countrymen it would be even more embarrassing and painful than the courting of arrest by the Mahatma, because while in the latter case it would be open to such of them, as so desire, to take their own share in that struggle, in the former they would have to remain mere passive onlookers while the most precious life in the country, perhaps in the world, was threatened with destruction. It is, therefore, sincerely to be hoped that the report about the Mahatma's intention of resorting to a fast in connection with the impending struggle is incorrect. Regarding the general situation we can only repeat the hope we have already expressed that even at the eleventh hour wiser counsels will prevail on both sides and that the catastrophe with which the country is threatened will yet be averted.

9. Communist Party's View of Bombay Meeting of All India Congress Committee

Communist, Vol. II, No. 12, October 1940.

Bombay AICC and After

Bankruptcy and hypocrisy—these two words sum up the results of the Bombay AICC.

The Devil and the Deep Sea

For twelve months, the national leadership had carried on the policy of stalemate, of postponing and putting off the struggle, of manoeuvring for a suitable compromise. At last, the decisive turn in the war—after the collapse of France and before the attack on Britain itself—had enabled it to put down in rupees, annas and pies its conditions for surrender to Imperialism, for cooperation in the war. But Imperialism had spurned that capitulatory offer. Emboldened by the weakness of the leadership, Imperialism had launched a frontal attack upon the Congress as a whole. The leadership was faced with a dilemma. It could not yield to the devil, British Imperialism, which demanded abject and unconditional surrender. That would even put an end to its pressure politics through which it sought to gain concessions for the bourgeoisie. On the other hand, it dared not jump into the deep sea of mass struggle. Even a restricted Satyagraha—let alone a struggle of the 1930–32 type could no longer be controlled—could no longer be used for the politics of compromise. The organized forces of the workers' and peasants' struggle though unable yet to lead a national struggle on their own, were strong enough to push a national offensive led by the Congress on to revolutionary rails especially in the present extremely favourable situation of the war. A leadership which was determined to put the narrow interests of a class before that of the whole nation, had no other alternative but to find new devices for continuing the stalemate, new excuses for postponing and sabotaging the struggle. Bankruptcy was writ large on the Bombay decision. The chosen leader, admitted it in so many words: 'I am a pilot without a chart and a compass.... I see impenetrable darkness before me'.

Hypocrisy

Just because it was a bankrupt policy, it became all the more necessary to conceal it. Just because it was a policy of continuing the stalemate and what is more, of repudiating mass struggle for the entire war period, it became all the more necessary to make the pretence that it was a policy of struggle, of 'going back to Ramgarh'. Just because it was a policy which kept alive the spirit and mentality of the Delhi and Poona Resolutions, which had evoked wave of resentment and disapproval among Congressmen, it was necessary to dress up the policy as a break with the Delhi offer. That is where hypocrisy came in. A deception had to be practised upon the people, upon the mass of Congressmen. On the one hand, Imperialism had to be assured that there was not going to be any mass struggle, no 'embarrassing of the Government engaged in a life-and-death struggle'. On the other hand, the people and Congressmen had to be told that there was going to be some sort of struggle to vindicate the nation's rights and demands. While there was going to be no mass resistance to war and no hindering of Imperialism's 'war-effort', a position had to be taken which would appear to meet the strong anti-war sentiments of the people. The door for compromise had to be kept open while telling the people that the leadership was now on the war path. Who could practise this huge deception and create this mass illusion at such a critical moment? None else but the master-magician, the Mahatma. The lesser luminaries like Pandit Jawaharlal Nehru and the Congress Socialist leaders would, of course, be required to play the accompanying melodies but the main theme and the lead had to come from the Master himself!

'Delhi Resolution Dead'!—Its Spirit Lives

The resolution before the Bombay AICC, we are told by Nehru, was drafted by Gandhiji himself who 'produced one draft and then another and then a third, until he saw that he had met the considerations advanced by each one of us and was not content until the result was a resolution that was as far as possible the collective reflection of the minds of us all' (quoted by Mahadev Desai in *Harijan*, 22.9.40). The resolution certainly did this. While it declared that 'the Delhi Resolution confirmed by the AICC at Poona.... No longer applied, it has lapsed'; it, at the same time, kept alive the spirit of that resolution. The basis of the Delhi offer and the Poona Resolution was the denial of the imperialist character of the war and the putting forward of the thesis that the war Britain was waging NOW was a defensive one. The implication was that it was a just war and it was right for India to co-operate in it provided Britain conceded certain minimum demands. The position the Congress had adopted since the outbreak of this war and which was maintained upto Ramgarh was this: 'We think this is an Imperialist War and as such India is pledged not to co-operate in it and even to resist enforced war measures. If Britain claims that it is not so, she must prove it by recognizing India's independence'. The question of co-operation and the form it was to take in case Britain recognized India's independence was not specified. Even this position of the partial and conditional recognition of the imperialist character of the war was repudiated at Poona and the war was admitted to be a defensive, therefore, a just war, and this became the basis of that disastrous offer.

Policy of Non-Embarrassment

The Bombay resolution does not go back to the Ramgarh position vis-a-vis war, but in reality, shifts the Congress position on war permanently on to the Poona basis. Let us see how. Imperialism has categorically rejected the demand made by the Congress since the outbreak of the war. If the Working Committee's statement of Wardha (14th September, 1939) and the Ramgarh Resolution had any meaning, this ought to have led straight to the confirmation of the imperialist character of the war. The Bombay Resolution on the other hand, says nothing positive about the character of the war. What is placed in the foreground is that we are denied the right 'of condemnation of their associating India in the war against Germany, against the will of the vast body of the people of India' etc. The Bombay Resolution not only tacitly denies the imperialist and unjust character of this war but in reality puts forward, by the backdoor, Rajaji's theory that it is a defensive and just war on the part of Britain. 'Congressmen' it says, 'cannot, withhold their admiration for the bravery and endurance shown by the British nation in the face of danger and peril. They can have no ill-will against them, and the spirit of Satyagraha forbids the Congress from doing anything with a view to embarrass them'. Here for the first time, is made explicit in a resolution the so-called 'policy of non-embarrassment'. This by implication means FIRSTLY that Congress would not launch any mass struggle either against enforced war-measures or for independence and SECONDLY that Britain is fighting a just war and not an imperialist war.

Meaning of Gandhiji's Demand

Here we come up against a riddle. If the Bombay resolution implies that Britain is fighting a just war, then what is the meaning of Gandhiji's demanding freedom for carrying on anti-war propaganda? What anti-war propaganda is possible when you recoginse the war to be just, when you already bind yourself not to 'embarrass the war-making Government'? It is useful to pose the question in this way because it at once enables one to see the hollowness behind the demand which Gandhiji is going to make to the Viceroy. The anti-war propaganda consistent with the implications and restrictions of the Bombay resolution has nothing to do with POLITICAL agitation or action against IMPERIALIST war and its effects on the people. The anti-war propaganda a la Gandhi is pure pacifism which is consistent with the thesis that Britain is fighting a just and a defensive war. The Gandhian position is as follows: Britain is defending herself against an aggressor, hence she deserves moral sympathy. But Britain is defending herself violently. That is why the Gandhite who is conscientiously opposed to all violence even when it is used in self-defence, cannot co-operate with it materially. In other words, the freedom of anti-war propaganda which Gandhiji demands consistent with his ethical attitude is nothing more than that of conscientious objectors. In Gandhiji's own words, his demand is that 'everyone should be free to refuse all co-operations in war and preach that non-co-operation to everyone he comes across' (*Harijan*: 22.9.40).

The Crux of the Bombay Resolution

The meaning of the Bombay Resolution may now once again be summed up. Its bankruptcy consists in this that it

   (a) repudiates the imperialist character of the war
   (b) smuggles in the implication that the war is just on the part of Britain and therefore, deserving our moral sympathy
   (c) repudiates, therefore, the idea of asserting India's independence during the pendency of war
   (d) repudiates the launching of any mass civil disobedience during the duration of the war
   (e) reduces the anti-war position of the Congress to one of pure pacifism.

   The hypocrisy of the Resolution consists in this that in spite of all this, it seeks to create the impression as if the national leadership has finally broken with the policy of compromise and that it is going to give a fight to the Government on the issue of insisting for the Congress 'the fullest freedom to pursue its policy based upon non-violence' and 'for the preservation of the liberties of the people'.

Revolutionary Drapery

In his closing speech, Mahatma Gandhi used all his persuasive power to bring out what he called 'the revolutionary message' in the resolution. He said, 'the present resolution was a great step towards "swaraj".... If they held fast to it, their desire would be fulfilled and that was that the right of free speech and civil liberty must be available to everyone. That was the root and foundation of Swaraj....' (*Bombay Chronicle*: 17.9.40). 'It is our duty to fight for that right. If they resist it and we have to fight and they are embarrassed, they will have invited the embarrassment themselves' (*Harijan*: 22.9.40). Referring to the demand for mass civil disobedience and no-tax campaign, he said 'he wanted to assure them that mass civil disobedience and no-tax campaign were within the ambit of the resolution. If only they accepted the resolution, they might see action in it. They might also see the new order of which the Socialists spoke'. (*Bombay Chronicle*: 17.9.40)

Pandit Jawaharlal Nehru whose role is to bark at Communists and to hang revolutionary drapings round the Working Committee resolutions, declared that 'as far as he was concerned, the Poona Resolution was dead and gone'. Comrade Yusuf Meherally, the spokesman of the Congress Socialist Party, was mightily pleased that 'Gandhiji had drafted the present resolution and helped the Congress to go back to Ramgarh position'.

Communists Expose

It was only the Communists who almost single-handed stood up against this resolution and exposed its anti-struggle and compromising character. Their amendments were moved not with a view to improve the resolution. It was impossible to do this by one or two amendments. Their amendments were moved with a view to express their firm and uncompromising opposition to two main features of the resolution, that it finally set its seal to the repudiation of the imperialist nature of the war and that it categorically rejected mass struggle for independence for the entire period of the war. They tore up the hypocritical arguments that it was a return to Ramgarh and Delhi-Poona offer was dead. They opposed Gandhiji's leadership which was meant to cover the sabotaging and circumscribing of any struggle whatsoever. The Communists ... refused to withdraw their amendments, when after Gandhiji's second speech all other opposition to the resolution collapsed. It was only their seven solitary hands which went up to vote against the resolution as a whole. At this point, it is reported, Pandit Nehru jumped up to his feet and demanded almost in a fury: 'Take down the names of those who voted against'. The names were taken down and appeared the next day in the entire all-India Press. They were the names of those who warned the nation against the pitfalls that were ahead!

Compromisers' Strategy

What the leadership seeks to achieve through this resolution is to mark time, waiting for something to happen in the war in the West, for a favourable situation for a compromise and a settlement with Imperialism. While it waits, the Resolution enables it to keep up the illusion among the people and among the Congress masses that the Mahatma is now in charge and if the Viceroy were to turn down the demand for freedom of speech as demanded by the Resolution, he is sure to start some sort of struggle. Of course, there is no preparation for struggle even of the most restricted type, no lead to carry on a mass campaign for the struggle for civil liberties. On the other hand, there is a deliberate and planned effort to stop all the resistance which the people and Congress organizations are putting up to the wholesale repression carried out by the Government. The Working Committee passed a resolution immediately on the conclusion of the AICC Session calling upon all Congress organizations to stop all civil disobedience, individual or other, pending definite instructions from Gandhiji. Imperialism is proceeding to crush the Congress organizations in those provinces where it has mass basis, where it is Left and better organized, as in the case of United Provinces and Malabar. Mahatmaji's *fatwa* would mean that the resistance which these bodies are putting up in defence of their right to exist and fight should cease. The glorious way in which the Congressmen in Malabar defended their right to carry on Congress activities against the bullets and lathis of the police, has elicited a comment from Mahatma, which shows that he wants to make another 'Chauri-Chaura' out of the events of 15th September in Tellicherry and other places in Malabar. 'I am thankful', he says, and 'that the unfortunate events in Malabar have come as a warning to the country and a pointer to me also'. (*Harijan*: 22.9.40). A pointer for what? Obviously, a pointer that 'the people have not yet imbibed the true spirit of non-violence' and that a 'struggle' of any kind, therefore, is dangerous.

Ghastly Perspective

What is the perspective? Would Imperialism too play a waiting game hoping to bring down the national leadership to surrender on the Viceroy's terms? Or will it precipitate a crisis by speedily turning down Gandhiji's demands? It is quite impossible that the Viceroy would accept Gandhiji's 'claim for freedom of speech no matter by whom exercised so long as it does not promote violence in any shape or form' (*Harijan*: 22.9.40). If after this rejection, Gandhiji or the Working Committee proceeded to show signs of a preparation for some sort of resistance even though restricted, the Government would promptly hit out and clap the entire leadership in jails and Concentration Camps and immediately set up the Enlarged Executive Council with the other parties. The result of this *blitzkrieg* would be far more disastrous than in the beginning of 1932. Then, the skeleton fighting organization of the Congress, with whatever illegal apparatus it had, built up during the 1930 struggle was intact. The Congress cadres everywhere were trained to look at the 'Delhi truce' as a temporary cessation of struggle. The fight could then be maintained in spite of the demoralizing and disorganizing tactics of the leadership. Today the mass influence of the Congress is far greater but there is no fighting organization of any kind, except in one or two provinces. The Gandhian ban on any type of secret or underground activity has been enforced upon the Congress organization so effectively that the result of the Government 'blitzkrieg' would be far more disastrous. A complete smash-up and collapse of the national organization, and the people and working masses left defenceless to their own devices to carry on the struggle against the brutal and ruthless war-machine of Imperialism: that is the grim perspective before the nation. This is where the bankrupt, blind class-policy of the national bourgeois leadership has led the nation. This is the result of the deliberate disarming and disruption of the fighting forces of the people caused by the last 12 months of the policy of stalemate.

The Tasks

What are our tasks, the tasks of the militant Congressmen, Communists and of the working class in this situation? While time is being wasted by Gandhiji over the negotiations and its aftermath, our job is to initiate a campaign of explanation among Congressmen and the people. Explain the real meaning of the Bombay AICC Resolution, laying stress on the two essential features, the final repudiation of the stand that it is an Imperialist War and hence must be resisted and the final refusal of the national leadership to launch any mass struggle during the pendency of the war. Explain the grim perspective which faces the nation in view of this stand. Expose the bankruptcy and the narrow selfish class outlook of the leadership which has brought this calamity on the head of the nation.

Secondly, the campaign of exposure and explanation must be accompanied by a positive lead. Gandhiji's demand for freedom of speech for the preservation of civil liberties is in itself a demand with revolutionary possibilities. Did not our national movement take its birth out of the mass struggle against the Rowlatt Bills and for the assertion of freedom of speech and Press? Today we have 20 years of strength, experience and organization behind us. In the conditions of today, a nationwide fight for civil liberties, can be nothing short of a mass resistance to war and war-measures, can be nothing less than a prelude to the final struggle for freedom. This is just what Gandhiji does not mean and want. He has made this amply clear. That is why we must explain to the people that the freedom of speech, press, organization and person cannot be won unless the masses are prepared to fight for its assertion, unless they are prepared to use EVERY MEANS for this fight. The freedom of press and speech cannot be won just by landing a selected band of Satyagrahis into jail. What is needed is a mass fight for these rights. To start such a mass fight and to maintain it in the face of repression, we must be prepared to use illegal methods of propaganda and organization. That is why we must strive to get the support of militant Congressmen for intensifying illegal anti-war propaganda, through printed sheets, posters, slogans written on walls and streets. The truth about this war must be told to the people in spite of the Government ban. 'Down with War-Funds and War-Loans', 'Not a Pie from your pay for this bloody war', 'Not a Man' etc—these slogans must appear in every village, in every factory, in every street!

Slogans

Our main slogans are: (1) Intensify illegal propaganda through posters, slogans and Bhui Patrikas against the war and against repression, (2) Win the support of militant Congressmen for this purpose—form unofficial broad groups and committees to carry out this campaign, (3) Prepare for Protest Strikes of students against every act of Government repression, (4) As against Gandhiji's idea of restricted Satyagraha, we must prepare for unleashing a genuine struggle for civil liberties, by mass dissemination of anti-war propaganda and agitation through illegal means, by mass demonstration, strikes and Hartals.

Our aim is to transform even the restricted and sham struggle of Gandhiji into a full-fledged mass struggle for the freedom of the country.

10. Intelligence Report on Preparations for Civil Disobedience in UP

Criminal Investigation Department, United Provinces, Report of the Week Ending 11 October 1940, UP State Archives.

Political—With the exception of the Congress leaders' tours described below, the week was outwardly extremely quiet, but behind the scenes Congress preparations for civil disobedience continued unabated. Lists are being prepared of persons prepared to take an active part in civil disobedience, Congress offices are being reorganized and in a number of cases records from these offices have already been removed to places of safe-keeping in private houses; Satyagraha committees are in some cases being elected, while further reports of the election of Congress dictators have also been received; finally, house to house canvassing for the enlistment of volunteers and Satyagrahis is increasing. Jawaharlal Nehru is reported to have written to responsible Congress workers throughout the province, asking for information regarding possible financial support for civil disobedience and lists of such persons are to be prepared and forwarded direct to Pt Nehru himself.

In accordance with the PCC programme, Pt Jawaharlal Nehru, Pt Govind Ballabh Pant, Dr Kailash Nath Katju and Mrs Vijay Lakshmi Pandit spoke at meetings during the week. Jawaharlal was the only one of these, however, to undertake a regular tour and he alone attracted real attention.

Jawaharlal left Allahabad on October 5 addressing several rural meetings, at which he repeated the objectonable anti-war remarks referred to in last week's appreciation. He then toured Ballia, Ghazipur and Gorakhpur districts, addressing some 20 meetings all of which were largely attended. His largest audiences were in Gorakhpur itself (10,000) and at Deoria (12,000).

Pt Pant spoke in Bareilly and Agra, both meetings being comparatively poorly attended. His Bareilly speech was on the usual lines, describing the present situation, repeating his well-known remark that a slave India could not cooperate in a war to liberate other countries and urging preparations for civil disobedience in the usual terms. In Agra, he presided over the 'opening ceremony' of the *Sainik* newspaper, the Sainik Press having recently been returned to its owners by Government. The paper has celebrated its revival by a repetition of its criticism of the District Magistrate.

Kailash Nath Katju spoke in Bareilly and Allahabad. The Bareilly meeting was small and his speech of little account. In Allahabad, however, the audience numbered 4000 and Dr Katju made an objectionable speech, condemning British policy in India since the war, particularly the present repression, and urging his audience to refrain from helping the war effort.

Mrs Pandit visited Cawnpore, where her reception must be considered disappointing, as the largest audience she attracted only numbered about 1000. Her speeches were on the usual lines, urging preparation for civil disobedience and describing the reconstruction which would follow the attainment of their goal, they call for no comment. At one of the meetings, however, Chhail Behari Kantak, Raghubar Dayal Bhat, Ganga Datt, and Ganesh Jog made somewhat violent anti-Government speeches.

At the request of the Secretary of the International Peace Committee, Pt Nehru has issued circular instructions to local Congress bodies throughout the province for the observation of October 15 as 'Peace Day'.

The school recently organized by the party in Ghazipur came to an end on October 3. Of the leaders invited, only Balkrishan Keskar and Rama Kant Srivastava actually came and gave lectures, and some 16 youth constituted the audience. The object of the organizers, however, is believed to have been the inculcation of a revolutionary spirit in the local youth and it would appear possible that the seeds of a future revolutionary cell have been sown.

B.   SATYAGRAHA BEGINS

11.   Report on Vinoba Bhave's Satyagraha Activities
Hindustan Times, 18 October 1940.

Anti-War Speech at Paunar

Mr Vinoba Bhave, under instruction from Mahatma Gandhi, today addressed here a meeting of about 300 which included Seth Jamnalal Bajaj, Mr Mahadev Desai and about fifty women from the Mahila Ashram at Wardha.

Paunar is about five miles from Wardha and Mr Vinoba Bhave arrived here at 8 this morning accompanied by Mr Desai and Seth Jamnalal Bajaj. Torrents of rain poured incessantly during the meeting, Mr Bhave was offered a number of Khadi garlands before he delivered his speech.

Mr Vinoba said that the Congress could not help Great Britain on ethical grounds in her war effort. He wondered why Great Britain claimed to fight for democracy which she denied to India. He said that it was necessary to carry on agitation against the war because the Congress demand for the formation of a National Government was rejected, secondly, because freedom of speech against the war effort was denied and, thirdly because the Government was not prepared to declare India a belligerent country of her own free will but belligerency was forced upon her.

Mr Vinoba said that the war was an uprising of Christian nations fighting among themselves. We were being asked to fight against some of them who were not our enemies and Christianity taught one to love even one's own enemies. India should not help in the war either out of fear or for personal gain which two motives were utilized by the Government to get help in this war. Our religion taught us not to resort to these sinful methods.

Mr Vinoba added that he would confine himself to verbal preaching and would not come in the way of those who wanted to help Britain in spite of his advice.

Concluding Mr Vinoba said that villagers should not content themselves with non-participation in the war but should carry on the constructive programme of spinning khadi, village uplift and Hindu-Muslim unity ....

12. Editorial on Individual Satyagraha

Tribune, 19 October 1940.

Our Allahabad correspondent has sent us a somewhat sensational account of what passed behind the curtain at the Wardha meeting of the Congress Working Committee. 'When Mahatma Gandhi put forward his scheme of individual civil disobedience,' he says 'several members of the Committee were opposed to it.' That there was stubborn dissent from two members the Mahatma himself admits in his statement. 'I tried hard to carry conviction to them,' he says, 'but I fear I failed'. Our correspondent says that the two members referred to by the Mahatma were none else than Pandit Jawaharlal Nehru and the Congress President. He adds: 'Maulana Azad at one time offered to resign the Congress Presidentship. Both Pandit Nehru and Maulana Azad, it is reported, bluntly told Mahatma Gandhi that the Working Committee should be allowed to frame its own scheme of satyagraha and if the Mahatma did not like to take up the responsibility for it he could once again be relieved of leadership. But this time Gandhiji refused to swallow the advice. He is reported to have argued as follows: "The All India Congress Committee has appointed me dictator, and the Working Committee which is a subordinate body, cannot dismiss me from that position. If the members of the Committee do not approve of my scheme it is for them to surrender their leadership."' We cannot of course, vouch for the correctness of the report, but there is nothing intrinsically improbable in the story. It cannot have been forgotten that in an article in *Harijan* Mahatmaji said that it was his weakness that he had allowed Working Committee to pass the Delhi resolution when he could easily have prevented it from passing it by asserting himself. That Maulana Abul Kalam Azad's position in this matter is fundamentally different from that of the Mahatma we know from his recent statement that 'the Congress is not a pacifist society but a political organization with a definite political objective.' That statement was doubtless made sensibly as a reply to the Viceroy, but it was in reality a vigorous expression of dissent from the Mahatma's own position. As regards Pandit Jawaharlal, we need not go beyond the statement he has just issued from Allahabad to see now radically he differs from the Mahatma's views in the present case. 'Mahatma Gandhi's approach to many problems,' he says 'is often a non-political approach. Some of us, including me, view these questions from a political angle only, though all of us, I hope, keep in mind the moral aspects of every question. I have sometimes found it difficult to understand Gandhiji's approach, because my mind functions differently. While fully appreciating the political aspects of non-violence in our struggle, I have been unable to appreciate many of its implications.' Again, 'In many matters I have ventured to disagree with Mahatma Gandhi and probably I may continue to disagree with him.' Lastly, 'The immediate issue has been raised by the war. It is not an issue of civil liberty or freedom of speech except in so far as these are related to the war issue. The issue is India and the war. And this is intimately related to our right to independence. The objective today and till we achieve it is unadulterated independence'.

It is necessary to say that the difference between this position and that of the Mahatma is fundamental, that while the Mahatma thinks primarily and almost exclusively in terms of non-violence, Pandit Jawaharlal thinks primarily and almost exclusively in terms of independence. The question of freedom of speech with regard to the war is of value to Pandit Jawaharlal simply in so far as it is intimately related to India's right to independence. To Mahatmaji, on the other hand, it is a part of his basic creed, in fact, his very being and he would have raised the question with the same vigour and earnestness even if India had been an independent country and her Government had been wholly responsible to her people. Why, then it may be asked, have Pandit Jawaharlal Nehru and men of his way of thinking entrusted the destiny of the Congress and the country to one who differs so fundamentally from them and from the overwhelming majority of political-minded Indians? The answer is contained in the following words of Pandit Jawaharlal's statement: 'Mahatma Gandhi has developed a certain technique of action which has yielded great results to our movement for freedom. It is clear that the Congress and the country want that technique to be continued and it is obvious that Gandhiji is best fitted to lead a movement with that technique.' Our own reading of the situation is somewhat different from that of Pandit Jawaharlal. We see little evidence that the Congress and the country want the Mahatma's technique to be continued out of any sincere and reasoned conviction. A large part of the country and at least a section of the Congress do not want it to be continued at all. Even among those Congressmen who do want it to be continued the large majority have simply been hypnotized into the belief that so great and saintly a man as the Mahatma can never be wrong when he speaks with such apostolic ardour. We have before now seen the hypnotic power of the Mahatma's saintly character and his transparently sincere and apostolic utterances. Everyone knows that with one single exception every political leader of the first rank was ranged against Gandhiji at the special Congress in Calcutta where he first unfolded his new technique. And yet within four months practically all those leaders rallied round him and supported his technique. They did so, not because they were convinced that the technique was right but because they reposed the same faith in the Mahatma as Pandit Jawaharlal reposes in him and because the Mahatma told them what he is telling their successors today. 'I would simply say to the dissenters,' he said in his recent statement, 'wait patiently and see what happens. Carry out instructions to the best of your ability. Do nothing to thwart the plan.' 'If you do all this,' he said in effect, 'the movement is sure to succeed.' If an appeal like this overcame the opposition of men like C.R. Das and Lajpat Rai, it is no wonder that it should hypnotize men of a weaker calibre. But the duration of hypnotism varies according to the nature of history that within less than two years some of the foremost leaders of the Congress revolted against the Mahatma's technique. That history is bound to repeat itself in the present case. We cannot for a moment believe that men like Jawaharlal Nehru, Abul Kalam Azad and Rajagopalachariar will for long acquiesce in the virtual conversion of the Congress into a pacifist society and the relegation of the fight for political independence to a secondary place.

13.   Commencement of Satyagraha—Arrest of Vinoba Bhave: Congress General Secretary's Circular, 21 October 1940

Indian Annual Register, 1940, Vol. II, pp. 226–7.

You know Shri Vinoba commenced Satyagraha on the morning of the 17th by delivering an anti-war speech in the village of Paunar where he resides. Paunar is about 5 miles from Wardha. The meeting was therefore attended not only by the villagers, but also the members of the various national institutions at Wardha. Among those present were Shris Kishorilal Mashroowala, Jamnalal Bajaj and Mahadeo Desai.

One of the possibilities open to the authorities to stop Satyagraha was to declare the meeting at Paunar illegal. If this was done Gandhiji's instruction were Shri Vinoba would ask such of the audience as were not prepared to break the law and court imprisonment to withdraw from the meeting. After their withdrawal he would address the prohibited meeting. This would naturally turn individual into collective civil disobedience. For such an emergency Gandhiji had made provision. In his first statement he said: 'In spite of all attempt to confine Civil Disobedience to individuals and for the moment to one, they (the Government) can precipitate a crisis by making it a crime to listen to him (Shri Vinoba) or read anything written by him.'

However neither was the meeting prohibited nor was Shri Vinoba arrested. Instead the press throughout India was warned against giving publicity to Vinoba's speeches or announcing his activities and programme. It is believed that this will leave him isolated. No reports of his first or his subsequent speeches have, therefore, been reported in the papers. The cryptic notices of his activities wired out by the news agencies are misleading. One such message says that Shri Vinoba emphasized the constructive programme as if that was the main burden of his speeches. At Paunar he spoke for full one hour. The constructive programme was mentioned only at the end. Almost the whole of his speech was devoted to the theme of non-participation by India in the present war. He emphasized equally the two points of view of the out and out believers in non-violence and those who object to this war on the ground that it is an imperialist war in which India has been dragged without her consent. I would, therefore, request you to warn Congressmen and the public against drawing any adverse conclusions about the progress of satyagraha from the reports appearing in the daily press.

Gandhiji is devising ways and means to counter this move of the Government. It is hoped that soon it would be possible to send you correct reports of what is happening. Till then you will advise Congressmen to carry on the usual work of the Congress, emphasizing the constructive programme, in the belief that our Leader will leave no stone unturned to spread the movement he has inaugurated after much prayerful waiting and deliberation.

From Paunar Shri Vinoba has been moving from village to village on foot addressing previously arranged meetings. The authorities are kept informed about his programme and movements. The latest report is that he has been arrested today at 4 a.m. and brought to Wardha. His trial begins at 11 a.m. today.

The next step will be decided upon by Gandhiji soon. You may learn of it before this reaches you.

14. Mahatma Gandhi Considering Going on Fast, Jawaharlal Nehru Decides to Follow Vinoba

Record of Jawaharlal Nehru's Conversation with Mahatma Gandhi, Wardha, 29–30 October 1940.
SWJN, Vol. XI, pp. 192–9.

Conversation with Mahatma Gandhi[1]

29 October 1940

Jawaharlal Nehru: Why did you not foresee that they would gag the press? They did more than this last time.

Mahatma Gandhi: I may foresee and be prepared for all events. But nevertheless it may be a surprise for me. I had hoped they would not behave in this manner. Therefore I can say your repression knows no bounds. I can do my worst too—for example mass civil disobedience. But I may not do this yet. The government still have the capitalists and the princes with them.

JN: I don't see why you should change your whole plan of action because what was probable has happened.

MG: I must because I did not think they would go so far. They won't allow us anti-war propaganda. I accept his interpretation of what I want. He should admit that if I have the power to convert people they should have India out of the war. We are not independent but we are 'at war' with you. We must assert ourselves as far as we can.

JN: You can't isolate your case in this way. It would be better now to say we want independence; nothing limited in the sense of free speech.

MG: I have said independence is not in their hands. They are struggling for their own independence.

JN: But it is there still. When they are defeated it will be another matter.

MG: If they have failed to give us independence, I say at any rate let us not join them in a war against our wishes. I say this according to our strength and internal position today. If they seize my own weapon of non-violence I must fight for it. I leave independence because they say they cannot discuss that today. So I say all right. I prepare myself for non-violence for the time being. They won't allow me. Our case is not weakened by the position I have taken up. My civil disobedience as I had envisaged it is not being allowed to proceed. The effect on the government is that they stiffen. Even one man offering civil disobedience has made them harsh. Vinoba Bhave was an unknown quantity outside my and his circle. Now I have to think if I send the next man I don't think I shall get the same result as from the उपवास [fast].[2] The latter will get at world conscience in a way which nothing else can. Take the example of salt satyagraha.

JN: The case is not analogous. Here is a case of their empire going. The step they have taken against Vinoba Bhave is a step against a symbol. They wanted to nip our protest in the bud. Your step of 'limitation' put them in a false position. I do not understand, even if you did not expect this development, why should you be driven to your last resort straightway?

MG: I can't explain.

JN: I understand there is no matter for logic or reasoning. One must think impersonally. I can only judge from what I imagine will be the result. I want to ask you whether in the excitement of the movement you have taken a premature step.

MG: I want to avoid it really. I won't hasten it. I am nervous of it. Yet I shall fulfil it if it comes on me. I am fighting against my desire. But I see no other way at the moment.

JN: Leave your non-violence aside for the moment. Aero-planes have altered everything. No frontiers left—no safety left. Either every nation must be armed to the hilt or else air warfare be banned. Whither are we going, is the question. We have to find a way out. The solution can even come from Linlithgow, Halifax and Churchill etc. God knows when the war will end. There can only be a world peace. Or else we shall all be nervous wrecks. Linlithgow personally can't help however much he may want to. The solution lies deeper. Inevitable revolution in the world. Britain fighting it. In a way Hitler is more in tune with it. The fabric of their society must change. I feel your step is very premature. You have only started the movement 12 days ago.

MG: I must tell you one thing. You say the face of the world is changing. I agree. It may be pride in me. But I feel this is the opportune movement not only for us but for the world. I am known all over and I feel I ought to sacrifice myself now. If it is pride in me, nothing will come of my sacrifice and I am then really a drag on you. If my last resort shakes the world, then I feel there will be a great result fraught with much good. I am therefore placing the best weapon in my armoury to see what I can do with it. I can go to jail also.

JN: All this doesn't make much difference. I have to think what I am to do before and after your fast. It is impossible for me to remain outside jail if you fast.

MG: That brings them still more in the wrong if they do that. Our policy has been never to take a wrong step. Always let them do the wrong. This happened in salt satyagraha too.

JN: You cannot compare salt satyagraha with this. The issues are different.

MG: They have to swallow a great deal. They are bound to as time goes on.

JN: You are premature-I maintain. You must see what happens. I am clear in my mind that I have to go. There is such confusion in people's mind. They imagine all kinds of foolish things. Granted your step may have a tremendous effect on India and outside. What do we do?

MG: You must watch. You must carry on agitation. Explaining the fast is one thing. Out of my 21 days fast was born the All Parties' Conference. While the fast goes on either you do nothing or else you go to jail straightway.

JN: We must explain to the people. If we do it on a big scale we shall be stopped. If we are stopped are we to submit or not?

MG: I feel while I am alive they will not stop explanations. But they may send you to jail. You go. After me you must carry on the fight. Individual civil disobedience presumably.

JN: Tell me. You fast. Then what do we tell the public to do?

MG: My manifesto will be there.

JN: Positive?

MG: One—constructive programme.

JN: Supposing meetings, etc. are banned?

MG: Then you must take the decision. Mass civil disobedience will be born out of it.

JN: Supposing they decide to let you fast. They will seize us all. Then what?

MG: If they become callous—fast goes on—all of you in jail, I feel crores will die refusing to help them. That is my belief. The other thing is that decent millions of the world are veering towards non-violence. I may be wrong. But all this will be made plain and if it is my pride that tells me all this, then too I shall be happy that I as a drag will be removed from the world. I have worked for 50 years—not a short time—result will be seen after I have gone. I have not so far ever done anything premature. It may be so. I am averting it as long as I can. I have always felt this to be the strongest weapon in my satyagrahi armoury. There is *hara-kiri* and there is *sati* of Rajasthan. History gives glorious instances of the latter. In Junagadh even Muslims died rather than submit to *zulum.*

JN: But this is not non-violence.

MG: Of course not. I only say the courage to die is in our bones. I want to do it non-violently. I feel the face of India will change. How I can't say. But I shall die in that hope. I can't think of anything else that can be effective at this stage.

Mahadev Desai: You don't want to embarrass them. Won't your fast be a terrific embarrassment to them?

MG: Yes and no. But India's non-violent strength grows. That is my mission. Any embarrassment born of non-violence will serve them. Mass civil disobedience will give birth to violence. They have no room for lakhs of prisoners. I am embarrassing them. I cannot reduce my strength by not embarrassing them. If they are callous there will be no embarrassment to them. I have used all my strength to convince them. I have no other weapon except this fast wherewith to teach non-violence to my people.

JN: The embarrassment question is but one of motive.

MG: Yes. But my motive is pure.

JN: I feel I must follow Vinoba.

MG: All right. But we'll talk of it tomorrow.

JN: When?

MG: All right. Supposing you leave here tomorrow, you can do it on the 4th or 5th.

JN: Yes-it must be after *Id* which is on the 3rd. But on 4th we have a conference of workers. Would it matter if they were all there?

MG: If I give notice they won't allow conference, i.e. you won't be there. So have the conference and you go on 8th or so. I would prefer a village because of the significance of that step. History will record the importance we gave to the village in this our last fight-at least the last conducted by me.

JN: I wanted Allahabad. But if you insist on a village I will select a village. How can we send notices to the people? And what about your notice?

MG: I will wire the date and time to the village for the people?

JN: We shall have to duplicate and distribute. It will require 5 or 6 days.

MG: If you are arrested before the meeting you will leave a message.

JN: Will the man who reads my message be arrested?

MG: He will only stress the constructive programme. After some talk—date to be 7th or 8th—after the conference in Allahabad.

30 October 1940

JN: I still feel, after sleeping over it, that I must go to jail. But your fast—the last resort, so to speak, is inopportune. It will create confusion in the mass mind. It will be interpreted by the government that individual civil disobedience had failed. I feel you ought to get the members of the Working Committee to offer civil disobedience.

MG: I do not think this is right. I cannot mix up issues. My own idea was not to send more than three. The fast was always in my mind. What the effect of it will be on the minds of the people or the government does not bother me. If I send the Working Committee it will defeat my whole purpose. I have always felt that Vinoba was to go and you and then I have felt one woman should represent her kind. Someone wholly fitted—a believer in non-violence who will remain steadfast to the end. While I am alive the question of leadership does not arise. I do not want the Working Committee in jail. I want the Working Committee to restrain themselves. In any case I do not want them to go to jail and I fast afterwards. They must go on working. I will keep on directing them so long as I am alive. I feel I shall not become senseless even this time. My fast is a substitute for everything—an integral part of satyagraha. I have been prepared specially for it. I have specialized in fasting previous to any reference to politics. I feel the masses will understand the fast and respond as they should.

JN: What is the response to be?

MG: Go on with the constructive programme, keep to non-violence and give no help to Britain in war. They must be prepared to die rather than pay. I feel my fast will awaken people too. It is terrible the way our people allow themselves to be wronged and forget and go on being suppressed. I would like you to stay out too.

JN: That cannot be. I must go. It is possible my arrest may have repercussions. How is one to guide it in the right channels?

MG: By what you say to them previously.

JN: In effect—every man who becomes a ·'walking newspaper' is really committing civil disobedience. He can be held up under the Defence of India Act. And the sentence is much heavier than it has ever been.

MG: But this is illusive. It would be difficult to arrest people. I don't agree with you that it will be converted into an offence. Duplication of statements is another matter. That comes under the Act. Therefore I have said we don't want to do anything secretly. But of course a certain amount has to come in. Have you any idea of instructions you want to give? I will have to give instructions to Kripalani—may be daily—for Working Committee members and other addresses too. If they intercept these even we will have to employ 4 persons. We may not have meetings but we can talk as you and I are talking.

JN: Why?

MG: For the reason that we do not want people to be arrested wholesale. They won't allow meetings for publicity. We should not invite the restriction and we strengthen our people—no newspapers, no meetings and yet our work goes on.

JN: After getting there I am to inform you—confirm my programme by phone or wire. When will you inform Vallabhbhai?

MG: I am preparing him for it in my letter today. And I will send him a wire later. You can announce on arrival in Allahabad regarding the meeting on 7th. No harm even if it goes to the papers. Just that you are addressing a meeting. You can announce at the meeting of 4th that you are offering civil disobedience on the 7th.

JN: Till now I have avoided the press. But can I now tell them?

MG: Yes—you may.

---

[1] Rajkumari Amrit Kaur had prepared this transcript of the conversation.
[2] Mahatma Gandhi had been considering going on fast.

15. Letter from Viceroy to Secretary of State About Mahatma Gandhi's Plans to Go on Fast and the Government's Action to Counter Civil Disobedience, 3 November 1940

Letter No. 50, Correspondence with Secretary of State, Vol. V, 1940, Linlithgow Papers, Acc. No. 2153, NAI.

To the Right Honourable L.S. Amery, PC, His Majesty's Secretary of State for India.

The Viceroy's House,
New Delhi
November 3rd, 1940

(Private & Personal)

1. We are still without any letters from home—the interval between receipts of air mails here being now something in the neighbourhood of a fortnight, though two or three bags may arrive on occasion together. But I think I had better carry on as before letting you have my impressions of how things are going whenever I have any news to give you, for some of this

comment may get home more rapidly than we anticipate, and in any case it gives a background to which you and I can relate our telegraphic correspondence.

2. I telegraphed to you on the 24th October the text of the somewhat stiffer reply which I sent to a letter received by me from Gandhi[1], and you will since have had by telegram the text of his reply, dated the 30th October. I felt obliged to take a rather stiffer line in my letter of the 24th, for whether one likes Gandhi or dislikes him the fact remains that he is now quite definitely out in opposition to us and inciting his followers to break the law. I cannot run any risk of allowing myself to be manoeuvred, into the position of an assistant of the Working Committee, or of allowing Gandhi to think that merely because he and I are on friendly terms, I can or ought to suspend the operation of the sanctions of the law in cases in which his followers, acting on his advice, choose to infringe the law. Finally things have of course now reached a point at which, given the fact that he is, as I have said above, openly out against us and encouraging his followers to break the law, I do not think I can wisely or properly continue to correspond direct with him. I have therefore sent him an acknowledgement of his letter of the 30th October through my Private Secretary and as Birla has just arrived here and has asked to see my Private Secretary, it will be possible to convey a hint to the old man that with no desire to bear hardly on him, I do find myself in a position of difficulty in present circumstances and that he must not expect to receive replies to any letters he may send signed by me. It is delicate business, for one does not want too lightly to throw away the position of friendly correspondence and friendly exchange of views which has been so laboriously built up and maintained over the last four years. But I do not see any answer other than that I have suggested above. I do not think that the hint will be lost on him or that a little stiffness on my part at this stage will hinder the resumption of more friendly relations later on, if happier conditions are restored.

3. His letter of the 30th October is very interesting. I need not bother you with any comment on the didactics in its earlier part, and I fear that by arresting Nehru for his bad speeches in the United Provinces before he had time to take up the mantle of Mr Bhave we may again have interfered with the Mahatma's plans (secret correspondence shows that he and his friends were a good deal disappointed that Bhave was not arrested on the spot when he started to make his speech and that we should have waited for four or five days before taking action against him). But the important thing of course is the question whether or not he is going to fast. It is obvious I think that he would be. Bhave's speeches have fallen very flat indeed. Bhave clearly had not the appeal to the popular imagination which was required, and had it not been that his action was a deliberate defiance of the law incited and presided over by Gandhi himself such as we could not ignore, there would have been a good deal to be said for letting him go on talking and kill himself by ridicule. It is very difficult to follow Gandhi's mind. But in my experience he is always exceedingly careful in the wording of his letters, and anything that those letters contain is worth careful examination. I get in the first place the impression that he has not really yet made up his mind as to whether or not to try a fast. Secondly, and this is the important thing, I note with great interest that he speaks of a 'prolonged fast' 'or even a fast to death'. Whenever in the past he has used this sort of threat, I think, I am right in saying that he has spoken of a fast to death, and the room for manoeuvre left in this new phrase of his is very considerable. As you may well imagine a fast by Gandhi is the very last thing I want to have to deal with. It is likely to stir up very considerable feeling in this country and to disturb many people who have little sympathy with Gandhi's politics, and it will lay us open to very serious misunderstanding abroad, more particularly if it should end fatally. But be that as it may, I am quite clear that if he does now decide to fast, whether the fast

be a 'prolonged' fast or a 'fast to death', he must be let go through with it and that we cannot submit to being blackmailed even when the threat held over us is something so serious and so significant as the life of Gandhi himself. We cannot possibly, as I see it, however sorry may be to see him in this way immolate himself, concede his claims (nor indeed am I too clear at the moment on what claim he would propose to stake his life—if it is freedom to preach against the war, he would put himself on pretty bad ground and would, I should have thought, get little real sympathy from public opinion here). But he is of course in a desperately tight corner. The failure of Bhave, followed by the loss to the Working Committee of Nehru (though important elements in the Working Committee, and even Gandhi himself, may be glad to have Nehru comfortably out of the way for a little while, the effect of the Press Ordinance which deprives him of the publicity of which he is such a master, and the clear disinclination in the country to take on a fight unless that is quite inevitable—are all factors which we cannot ignore and which cannot be too consoling from his point of view. Nor, I would have said, can he wholly ignore the risk that if the tall poppies such as Nehru are lopped off by sentences of imprisonment, and he himself—the only man who holds Congress together—does a fast to death, the prospect of Congress disintegrating is immensely strengthened. We can but wait and see how things develop.

---

[1] In a letter dated 24 October 1940 the Viceroy, Lord Linlithgow wrote to Mahatma Gandhi:

'I can, of course, appreciate your desire for freedom to conduct a civil disobedience movement in the way that commends itself to you and I can understand that for that purpose you wish to enjoy unrestricted access to the public through the ordinary channels of publicity .... I must credit you personally with the desire that it should succeed in its avowed object, that of persuading the public to withhold all support from India's war effort.... In so far as you ask for my cooperation in such a plan, I must once more make it plain to you... that both I myself as the representative of His Majesty's Government in this country and the Government of India as responsible for its security have a very definite obligation to perform, and it would be disingenuous of me were I to leave any doubt that activities, the effect of which may be prejudicial in terms of the prosecution of the war and which infringe the law, cannot but attract the provisions of law; and that it would not be possible for me or for the Government of India, consistently with the formal obligations falling upon us, to acquiesce in them....' (collected works of Mahatma Gandhi, Vol. LXXIII, p. 456).

In response to this letter Mahatma Gandhi wrote back to him (dated 30th October 1940) that he has misinterpreted the real message of his letter of the 20th October and telegram of the 21st October. He had only provided him all the information regarding his plans of the civil disobedience movement and nothing else. But he had accepted his verdict for the moment. According to him the civil disobedience movement cannot be conducted secretly and he intended to undertake a fast for this purpose. (For text of Mahatma Gandhi's letter, see collected works of Mahatma Gandhi, Vol. LXXIII, p. 137).

16.   Jawaharlal Nehru's Statement to the Court, 3–4 November 1940

SWJN, Vol. XI, 3–4 November 1940, pp. 486–90.

[Extract]

Statement to the Court

... Ever since the Congress came to the conclusion that, in order to give effect to the Congress policy, satyagraha or Civil Disobedience should be started, I have endeavoured to check myself in my utterances and to avoid what might be termed satyagraha. Such was the direction of our chief, Mahatma Gandhi, who desired that satyagraha should be confined to particular persons of his choice. One such person was selected and he expressed in public utterances the Congress attitude to the war, laying some emphasis on the Congress policy of non-violence. It was my good fortune to have been selected to follow him and to give expression to the Congress viewpoint, with perhaps greater emphasis on the political aspect. It had been decided that

I should do so, after giving due notice to the authorities, from November 7, onwards, in the district of Allahabad. That programme has been varied owing to my arrest[1] and trial, and the opportunity to give frank and full expression to the Congress policy in regard to the war has come to me earlier than I anticipated.

If I was chosen, or before me Shri Vinoba was chosen for this purpose, it was not to give expression to our individual views. We were symbols of the people of India. As individuals we may have counted for little, but as such symbols and representatives of the Indian people, we counted for a great deal. In the name of those people we asserted their right to freedom and to decide for themselves what they should do and what they would not do; we challenged the right of any other authority, by whomsoever constituted, to deprive them of this right and to enforce its will upon them. It was monstrous that any individual or group of individuals, deriving no authority from the Indian people and not responsible to them in any way, should impose their will upon them and thrust the hundreds of millions of India, without any reference to them or their representatives, into a mighty war which was none of their seeking. It was amazing and full of significance that this should be done in the name of freedom and self-determination and democracy, for which, it was alleged, the war was being waged. We were slow in coming to our final conclusions; we hesitated and parleyed, we sought a way out honourable to all the parties concerned. We failed and the inevitable conclusion was forced upon us that so far as the British Government or their representatives in India were concerned, we were still looked upon as chattels to do their will and to continue to be exploited in their imperialist structure. That was a position which we could never tolerate, whatever the consequences....

I stand before you, Sir, as an individual being tried for certain offences against the state. You are a symbol of that state. But I am also something more than an individual. I too am a symbol at the present moment, a symbol of Indian nationalism resolved to break away from the British Empire and achieve the independence of India. It is not me that you are seeking to judge and condemn, but rather the hundreds of millions of the people of India, and that is a large task even for a proud Empire. Perhaps, it may be that though I am standing before you on my trial, it is the British Empire itself that is on its trial before the bar of the world. There are more powerful forces at work in the world today than courts of law; there are elemental urges for freedom and food and security which are moving vast masses of people, and history is being moulded by them. The future recorder of this history might well say that, in the hour of supreme trial the Government of Britain and the people of Britain failed because they were drunk with the wine of imperialism and could not adapt themselves to a changing world. He may muse over fate, of empires which have always fallen because of this weakness, and call it destiny. Certain causes inevitably produce certain results. We know the causes; the results are following inexorably in their train.

It is a small matter what happens to me in this trial or subsequently. Individuals count for little; they come and go, as I shall go when my time is up. Seven times I have been tried and convicted by British authority in India, and many years of my life lie buried within prison walls. An eighth time or a ninth, and a few more years, make little difference. But it is no small matter what happens to India and her millions of sons and daughters. That is the issue before me and that, ultimately, is the issue before you, Sir. If the British Government imagines that it can continue to exploit them and play about with them against their will, as it has done for so long in the past, then it is grievously mistaken. It has misjudged their present temper and read history in vain ....

The government advocate has taken a lot of trouble for nothing in proving what is already proved. What I wanted to prove has been said in my statement. I assert that the Government of India Rules are the greatest insult that can be inflicted on the country and are monstrous and I want to break such a government.

---

[1] Jawaharlal Nehru was arrested on 31 October 1940 while on his way back from Wardha to Allahabad. He was tried, convicted and sentenced to four years rigorous imprisonment.

17. Journalists' Protest Against Government Measure

Amrita Bazar Patrika, 24 October 1940.

Liberty of the Press—New Menace—Journalists' Protest Against Government Measure

At an extraordinary meeting of the Executive Council of the Indian Journalists' Association held on 23rd October at the office of the 'Insurance World' (11, Dalhousie Square, Calcutta).

Sj Mrinal Kanti Bose presiding the following resolutions are unanimously adopted.

1. That this meeting places on record its deep sense of sorrow at the untimely death of Sj Kisori Mohan Santra of the 'Viswabharati,' a member of Association, who as a devoted worker had earned the esteem of all and conveys its condolence to the members of the bereaved family.
2. That a copy of this resolution presented to the family of the deceased.
3. That this meeting of the Indian Journalists' Association places on record its emphatic protest against the imposition of fresh fetters on the Press by an Amendment of the Defence of India Rules, published in the Gazette on 21st October empowering the Government of India and the Provincial Governments to require, in the name of public safety and prosecution of the War, printers, publishers and editors to submit for scrutiny to a Government officer any matter relating to a particular subject or class of subjects before publication; to prohibit or regulate the printing or publishing of any document or class of documents or of any matter relating to a particular subject or class of subjects or the use of any printing press.

   The Association notes that even before the publication of the Amendment in the Gazette the Government of Bengal through its special press office has directed the press by an order dated the 17th October not to publish accounts of incidents relating to the Satyagraha by Mr Vinoba Bhave or any developments in that connection without previous reference to the Chief Press Adviser, Delhi and has directed the Editor 'Burdwan Barta' a Bengalee weekly of the district of Burdwan, to submit for scrutiny to the district press office, Burdwan, all matter intended to be published in that paper.

The amendment lays down conditions which are impossible of the fulfillment particularly in the case of daily newspapers and cannot but be harassing in its operation to the press in general and they do completely take away, without the slightest justification what had remained of the liberty of the Press. The measures taken by the Government of Bengal even before the Amendment came into force are reprehensible and show an utter disregard of the liberty of the press.

By another resolution the Secretary was directed to send copies of this resolution to Mahatma Gandhi, the Government of India and Government of Bengal and the Press.

18.   Mahatma Gandhi's Article 'To the Reader' on the Suspension of the Publication of *Harijan*, 31 October 1940

Harijan, 10 November 1940.

To the Reader

You must have seen through my press notice that the publication of *Harijan* and the other two weeklies had been suspended. In it, I had expressed the hope that the suspension might be only for a week. But I see that the hope had no real foundation. I shall miss my weekly talks with you, as I expect you too will miss them. The value of those talks consisted in their being a faithful record of my deepest thoughts. Such expression is impossible in a cramped atmosphere. As I have no desire to offer civil disobedience, I cannot write freely. As the author of satyagraha I cannot, consistently with my professions, suppress the vital part of myself for the sake of being able to write on permissible subjects such as the constructive programme. It would be like dealing with the trunk without the head. The whole of the constructive programme is to me an expression of non-violence. I would be denying myself if I could not preach non-violence. For that would be the meaning of submission to the latest ordinance. The suspension must, therefore, continue while the gagging lasts. It constitutes a satyagrahi's respectful protest against the gag. Is not satyagraha giving an ell when an inch is asked for by the wrong-doer, is it not giving the cloak also when only the coat is demanded? It may be asked why this reversal of the ordinary process? The ordinary process is based on violence. If my life were regulated by violence in the last resort, I would refuse to give an inch lest an ell might be asked for. I would be a fool if I did otherwise. But if my life is regulated by non-violence, I should be prepared to and actually give an ell when an inch is asked for. By so doing I produce on the usurper a strange and even pleasurable sensation. He would also be confounded and would not know what to do with me. So much for the 'enemy'. I, having made up my mind to surrender every non-essential, gain greater strength than ever before to die for the defence and preservation of what I hold to be essential. I was therefore wrongly accused by my critics of having advised cowardly surrender to Nazism by Englishmen when I suggested that they should lay down external arms, let the Nazis overrun Britain if they dare, but develop internal strength to refuse to sell themselves to the Nazis. Full surrender of non-essentials is a condition precedent to accession of internal strength to defend the essential by dying.

But I am not writing this to convert the English to my view. I am writing this to suggest to you that my surrender to the framers of the gagging ordinance is an object-lesson to you, the Reader, in satyagraha. If you will quietly work out in your own life the implications of the lesson, you will then not need the weekly aid from the written word in *Harijan*. Even without your weekly *Harijan* you will know how I shall myself work out the full implications of giving an ell when an inch is wanted. A correspondent pleads with me that on no account should I suspend *Harijan*, for he says his non-violence is sustained by the weekly food he gets therefrom. If he has really done so, then this self-imposed restraint should teach him more than a vapid continuation of weekly *Harijan*.

One word as to the practical question. You are a subscriber to one of the weeklies. I do not know when, if ever, they will be resumed. You are entitled to the return of the unused balance of your subscription. On receipt of a post card from you to the Manager *Harijan*, Poona for a refund, a money order for it will be sent to you. Those who do not ask for a refund will have their paper sent to them if it is resumed. If it is not, the unused balance will be spent in covering any loss that may be caused in winding up. And then the balance, if any, will be sent to the Harijan Sevak Sangh for use in the service of Harijans. If *Harijan* is not resumed within six months, it will be deemed to have been finally wound up. Meanwhile good-bye.

Sevagram, 31-10-40

19. Fetters on the Press

Hindustan Times, 8 November 1940.

Meerut Journalists' Resolution

The Executive Committee of the Meerut District Journalists' Association met here on Tuesday evening with Mr Sam Ernest Devalal, President of the Association, in the chair to consider the ever-increasing restrictions being imposed by the Government on the freedom of the Press. It adopted unanimously the following resolution.

'Since the general tone of the Indian Press has been quite healthy in the matter of serving the best interest of the country, the ever-increasing restrictions put on the freedom of the Press by the Government are looked upon with alarm. It is urged upon the Government that before undertaking any such measure the accredited Journalists' Associations in the country should be consulted and hasty decision in the matter avoided.'

20. Mahatma Gandhi's Instructions to his Party Workers Regarding Satyagraha

P.D. Tandon Papers, 1940–41, File No. 79, Sr. No. 753, 9 November 1940, NMML.

1. Under the extraordinary situation created by the Government I have, after consultation with the Working Committee, extended the scope of Civil Disobedience and I propose to select for the time being, resisters from among the members of the Working Committee, the Congress members in the Central and Provincial Legislatures and the members of the AICC.
2. Those only will be selected who conform to the conditions I have laid down, who are themselves willing to offer resistance and who are otherwise free to do so.
3. The method of selection is as follows. The members of the Working Committee will send me lists of such members in the first instance and no one will offer Civil Disobedience whose name I have not passed. No list should contain names of those who are physically unfit to undergo prison life. I may supplement the lists by making selection out of the names I have already received or may receive hereafter.
4. The names should be sent through messenger to ensure delivery.
5. No one will offer Civil Disobedience without first informing the District Magistrate of his district of the time when, the place where, and the manner in which it is to be offered.
6. It is advisable not to hold public meetings for the purpose in cities. Meeting may be held in villages. The best and easiest way is to repeat the following slogan to passersby as the resister walked on in a particular direction until he is arrested. My preference is

for this last method. It is harmless, economical and effective. No argument is necessary. It rivets attention on the single issue of war. The idea is to prevent the movement from lapsing into mass Civil Disobedience. This is the slogan. 'It is wrong to help the British war effort with men or money. The only worthy effort is to resist all war with non-violent resistance.' The slogan should be translated into the language of the Province in which Civil Disobedience is to be offered.

7. Civil Disobedience is to be offered singly. It need not be simultaneous. The whole of this programme should, if possible, be finished in one month.

8. All demonstrations should be avoided when Civil Disobedience is offered.

9. The ordinary channels of publicity being closed, we must rely upon everybody becoming his own newspaper. Satyagraha is and must be independent of the ordinary channels. We must not feel helpless when these are closed, and they are for the most part even now closed against us. It should be realized too that the repetition of the slogan while walking in one direction reduces the movement to its simplest terms.

10. Secrecy should be avoided. Therefore, cyclostyles and the like should be used only when the owners are prepared to lose them. The cheapest multiplying method is to use composition trays. The formula for making them may be got locally. (The AICC office shall try to send it later).

11. Congress funds need not be kept secretly. If the Government choose to confiscate them they may do so. In this life and death struggle we must be prepared to lose all funds and other property. We must learn to depend upon the nation financing the movement from day to day. Our wants must therefore be reduced to the minimum. No one need expect monetary assistance from the Congress.

12. Our policy should be to avoid classification of prisoners. In no case should any attempt be made to ask either for a higher or a lower class. An 'A' class prisoner is not bound to take advantage of the special facilities offered to him. Nor need he be ashamed of availing himself of them if thereby he retains his health.

13. Jail rules and discipline should be strictly observed so long as they are not inconsistent with human dignity. No labour should be avoided because it is labour. One should know its dignity.

14. Hartals should be rare. They lose their force if resorted to too often. They are likely to be prohibited. It is better to anticipate the prohibition. Our Civil Resistance is strictly limited. It is not general.

15. Should the Congress be declared an illegal organization, it should make no difference. I shall conduct the movement so long as I am left free. In the event of my being arrested, it will become self acting if the people have imbibed non-violence. Congressmen should remain calm and unperturbed. Each one will act on his or her own initiative. If he or she feels like offering Civil Disobedience the way is clear. If he or she is unable, they will devote themselves wholly to one or more items of the thirteen fold constructive programme. I do not propose to appoint a successor. Whether I am in or out those who belong to the Congress constructive organizations may not offer Civil Disobedience.

16. While the Congress functions as legal organization, the Provincial committees will elect their President if the present one is arrested. The person elected should seek confirmation from me. I shall be unable to work through him if he does not fulfil my conditions.

17. In the provinces where there is no Working Committee Member, the Provincial President will put himself in touch with me and send me his recommendations.

18. If I am impelled to fast, I expect Congressmen not to feel paralysed but to be stimulated to more intensive effort in the direction of constructive work. The fast, if it comes, must result in Khadi and village manufactures generally becoming universal, untouchability being a thing of the past and communal unity a settled fact.

19. Congressmen should make it clear in their speech and their action that they are neither pro-Fascism nor pro-Nazism but that they are opposed either to all war or at least to the war conducted on behalf of British Imperialism. They sympathize with the British in their effort to live but they want also to live themselves as members of a fully free nation. They must not therefore, be expected to help Britain at the cost of their own liberty. They bear ill will to no nation. They want to play their part in establishing lasting peace in the world.

M.K. Gandhi
Sevagram, Wardha
9-11-1940

21. Press Order Withdrawn by the Government

Hindustan Times, 11 November 1940.

Announcement by Government of India

A Communique says:

'The Government recently felt it necessary to make it plain, by an order under the Defence of India Rules, that they could not permit the publication of any matter calculated to foment opposition to the successful prosecution of the war or the open support of any movement designed to that end.

'In doing so, they intended no reflection upon the Press, whose consistent support, since the outbreak of the war in the struggle against the totalitarian powers they readily and gratefully acknowledge.

'As the result of friendly conversations in Delhi with representatives of leading newspapers, who have given them an assurance that they have no intention of impeding the country's war effort and that any deliberate or systematic attempt by newspapers to do so would be viewed with disapproval by the Press as a whole, the Government now feel, that the matter may well be left to the discretion of editors, in consultation with Press Advisers in cases of doubt.

'They are therefore pleased to withdraw the order in question.

'They are further pleased to accept a suggestion that a small Advisory Committee of representatives of the Press, resident in Delhi shall be set up to advise the Government on any matter affecting the Press and they will recommend to Provincial Governments the constitution of similar Advisory Committees in the provinces.'

22. Telegram from Viceroy to Secretary of State Regarding Mahatma Gandhi's Views on Satyagraha, 12 November 1940

Telegram No. 545, Telegraphic Correspondence with Secretary of State, Linlithgow Papers, Acc. No. 2162, NAI.

My Private Secretary has had the following letter from Gandhi dated November 11th, I repeat also the Satyagraha instructions enclosed in it despite length in view of their importance. It is interesting that Gandhi tacitly accepts that while relations are as they are, I cannot correspond direct with him.

Begins I have to thank you for your letter of the 2nd instant. I must not offer any apology for this letter. For in answer to the Govt. measures regarding the Press I have given up making public statements on the struggle between the Govt. and the Congress. And I want to avoid Secrecy regarding my plans. I shall, therefore, continue to send you periodical letters unless His Excellency desires otherwise.

I had hoped to be able to confine civil disobedience to two or three typical cases and supplement them; if necessary and if the call came, with a fast, limited or unlimited. But the members of the working committee were very much perturbed over the contemplated fast. Wires also pressed in upon me from all sorts of men and associations prevailing upon me not to fast. I felt that if I was not to fast, I must in some way answer the action of the Government in regard to Pandit Jawaharlal. My restraint depended upon a measure of reciprocity from the Govt. as I had hoped in my letter of the 30th September, in the following words. 'I shall hug the hope that it will be possible for the Govt. to work out their policy in the spirit of the Congress position'. But I do not complain. I feel I should explain my change of plan.

The changed plan consists in extending civil disobedience to qualified persons selected from particular groups. The groups touched at present are the members of the working committees, the legislators, the members of the All India Congress Committee and a few others. I felt that with the Pandit dealt with in the manner he was and the almost simultaneous arrest of Shri Achyut Patwardhan who has proclaimed his faith in non-violence I should not restrain members of these groups and the like if they satisfied my test as to non-violence and the constructive programme.

I send herewith a copy also of the instructions I have issued to Congressmen which you will please show to His Excellency.

There is one other matter to which I wish to draw his attention. My son, Devadas, has sent me notes of the recent interview with certain editors by the Hon'ble Home Member. In it the Hon'ble Home Member is represented as having said 'Mr Gandhi's object is to paralyse India's war effort and thus to help Hitler'. If Sir Reginold said these words, I can only say that he is wholly wrong. I claim that nothing that I have said can warrant Sir Reginold's extraordinary statement. Indeed, I have said repeatedly, and so have Pandit Jawaharlal and almost all the numerous Congressmen who have been jailed that we do not want to help Hitler. I have never said nor wished to paralyse Govt.'s war effort. But I have said that those of us who do not believe in war as war or in the war on behalf of British Imperialism, which they hold the present British effort to be, should be free to propagate their views in non-violent manner. What will, however, help Hitler is the irresponsible and repressive policy of the Government including the wholly unwarranted arrests and imprisonments. I have expected that those in high places would observe fairness and not go to the extent of putting into the mouths of humble workers like me words which they have never uttered.

Yours sincerely,
M.K. Gandhi

C.   REPORTS OF SATYAGRAHA ACTIVITIES AND ARRESTS

23 (a)   Report of Meetings, Demonstrations, Hartals, and Students Strikes in Madras Province, 19 November 1940

Fortnightly Report for the First Half of November 1940, D.O. No. P.4–21, Public (General) Department, Government of Madras to Secretary to the Government of India, Home Department, 19.11.1940, Tamil Nadu State Archives.

WAR—In a few districts there has been distribution of leaflets urging non-co-operation in War efforts and in some cases posters have been affixed in prominent places. Wherever it has been possible to trace those responsible, suitable action is being taken.

POLITICAL—The central feature of most meetings directed against Government's policy was the conviction of Pandit Jawaharlal Nehru and the sentence imposed upon him. Throughout the Presidency amongst Congressmen and their sympathizers the sentence was considered very harsh. In nearly every district meetings and other demonstrations to protest against his conviction were held. In addition to meetings there were numerous partial hartals and students' strikes. The strikes organized amongst students, particularly in Madras and Vizagpatam, at one stage threatened to assume serious proportions and a general strike was threatened for the 14th. The Government however issued a Communiqué expressing severe disapproval of the students' conduct and warning them that such conduct would debar the ringleaders from employment in Government Service at any future date and in the case of Government Colleges that Government would be prepared to take steps for the expulsion of those responsible for organising such demonstrations. This order was severely criticized in some quarters, but it had the desired effect of curbing the demonstrations; in Madras agitation is still continuing but the idea of striking appears to have been given up.

A number of local bodies have passed resolutions condemning the action taken against Pandit Jawaharlal Nehru, while others, less willing to risk infringing the law, have simply adjourned their meetings without giving any specific reason. In Malabar the orthodox Congress party is being revived by Mr Nandkeolyar who has been sent by the Congress High Command from Bombay for the purpose. The three persons who were appointed as a Committee of Enquiry into the atrocities alleged to have been committed by the police during their investigation in connection with the recent 'Protest Day' riots were persuaded by the District Magistrate to abstain from holding any enquiry and it was not necessary to issue any specific prohibition.

Yours Sincerely,

The Hon'ble Mr E.Conran Smith, CIEICS.,
Secretary to the Government of India,
Home Department.

(b)   Report on the Press for the First Fortnight of November

Statement of Action taken under the Indian Press (Emergency Powers) Act, 1931, and the Defence of India Act so far as it relates to the Press:

The Editor of 'Modern Times' published in the issue dated 26.10.1940 an article entitled 'The liberty, the Congress wants' wherein a passage occurred that what the Congress wanted was the liberty to speak out against Indians being drawn into a War which had no purpose for them and which meant the moral and material ruin of the nation. As the publication of this passage was contrary to the provisions of the order of the Central Government it issued under rule 41 of the Defence of India Rules, the Editor was warned.

The Editor of the 'Tamil Mani' was administered a severe warning for publishing in the issue dated 27.10.1940 certain objectionable matter calculated to incite violence.

24.   Report on Political Leaders' Arrests

Hindustan Times, 20 November 1940.

Dr T.S.S. Rajan Arrested—Bombay Ex-Premier's Intimation to Authorities

Fresh list of 1,000 Satyagrahis drawn up in Gujarat—Dr T.S.S. Rajan, a former Congress Minister, was arrested tonight under the Defence of India Rules, by Mr Martin, District Superintendent of Police, Trichinopoly and taken to the Central Jail.

With the permission of Mahatma Gandhi, Dr T.S.S. Rajan, a former Minister, offered a new form of Satyagraha by personally delivering anti-war effort letters this morning to 15 prominent persons, including members of the District War Committee and the Deputy Collector Trichinopoly, asking them to maintain India's honour and not to participate in the Government's war effort.

500 From CP List Being Sent to Mahatmaji

Five hundred persons are understood to have been recommended to Mahatma Gandhi to offer Satyagraha in the Central Provinces and Berar by the three Provincial Congress Committees in the province, namely, Mahakoshal, Nagpur and Berar, their respective numbers being 250, 150 and 100. The lists are expected to be approved by Mahatma Gandhi shortly.

In a circular letter addressed to all MLAs Mr V.R. Kalappa, Secretary of the Congress Party in the CP Assembly has asked them to communicate to him the date suitable for each to offer Satyagraha. He suggests that any date after November 21, but not later than December 21, should be chosen. On hearing from each MLA, Mr Kalappa will get the selected date approved by Mahatma Gandhi.

Giving instructions in regard to the manner in which Satyagraha is to be offered, Mr Kalappa says that the best and easiest way is to repeat anti war slogans in a selected village. He adds 'No argument is necessary'.

R. Agnibho's Arrest

In regard to the offering of Satyagraha by Mr Agnibho, MLA yesterday at Chhipabad it appears that he had been informed by Mahatma Gandhi to offer Satyagraha sometime ago but Mahatma Gandhi's subsequent instructions to await further communication did not reach him in time. His Satyagraha was thus unexpected.

Bihar List—Special Messenger Sent to Gandhi

A special messenger is being sent to Mahatma Gandhi from the Provincial Congress with a list of 150 Satyagrahis for his approval. The list is believed to include names of Ministers, Members of Legislature and members of the AICC.

Intimation signifying willingness to join the Satyagraha movement are believed to have been received from a large number of members of the Bihar legislature in response to a circular sent out by the Provincial Congress.

A list of 75 students desirous to join the Satyagraha movement is understood to have been prepared by the Bihar Provincial Students' Federation. The Federation will request Mahatma Gandhi to permit them to take part in the movement.

Madras Quota

90 prominent Satyagrahis selected—It is understood that Mahatma Gandhi has approved of a list of 90 Satyagrahis, being the first batch from Andhra and Tamil Nadu provinces. The list contains the names of Mr C. Rajagopalachari, ex-Premier and member of the Congress Working Committee. Dr Patabhi Sitaramayya, Bulusu Sambhamurti, Speaker of the Madras Legislative Assembly, Mr T. Prakasam, President, Andhra Provincial Congress Committee, Mr K. Kamraj, President, Tamil Nadu Provincial Congress Committee, Mr S. Satyamurti, MLA (Central). Mr V.V. Giri, ex-Minister, and eight other ex-Ministers. The Satyagraha commences on November 26.

It is learnt that the list also includes about five women members of the Madras Legislature, including Mrs Rukmini Lakshmipati, Deputy Speaker, Madras Assembly.

The selected Satyagrahis will offer Satyagraha in their respective constituencies by duly notifying the proper authorities about the place, time and method of their Satyagraha.

Satyagraha by Andhra Ex-Ministers

Mr V.V. Giri, ex-Minister, will offer Satyagraha in his constituency, Bobbili, in Andhra on November 20.

It is learnt that Mr B. Gopala Reddy, ex-Minister will offer Satyagraha in his village of Buchireddipalayam, in Nellore district, on about November 26.

Civil Disobedience—Situation Discussed by Punjab Congress Cabinet

The present situation in the country with particular reference to civil disobedience was discussed at a meeting of the Working Committee of the Provincial Congress Committee this afternoon. Dr Gopichand Bhargava, former Leader of the Opposition in the Punjab Assembly. Dr Satyapal and Lala Dunichand, MLA attended the meeting on special invitation. Further discussions were adjourned till November 22.

Later, a joint meeting of the Congress members of the Punjab Assembly, members of the AICC and office bearers of the District Congress Committees and Members of the Working Committee of the PPCC was held when Mian Iftikhar-ud-Din President of the Punjab Provincial Congress Committee spoke on the recent developments in India.

The nature of the extended Satyagraha and the immediate possibility of its further extension were then discussed, and representatives of the districts were given instructions in keeping with Mahatma Gandhi's plans.

The President of the PPCC is in touch with Mahatma Gandhi as to the time and manner of offering Satyagraha, details of which have already been dispatched to Wardha.

Bengal Satyagrahis

Satyagraha in Bengal, it is learnt, starts on November 29. A messenger starts today for Wardha with the first list containing the names of 100 Satyagrahis prepared by the Bengal Provincial Congress Committee to Mahatma Gandhi's approval. The first Satyagrahi in Bengal will be Dr Prafulla Chandra Ghose, a member of the Congress Working Committee while Mr Surendra Ghose, President, Bengal Provincial Congress Committee, will be the second Satyagrahi.

25.   Kelappan Arrested—Kerala

Mathrubhumi, 22 November 1940.

K. Kelappan was arrested in Quilandy at 10.30 this morning. Kelappan was the first Satyagrahi from Kerala nominated by Gandhi. He had informed the District Magistrate about his intention to offer Satyagraha this morning.

Kelappan who left Calicut by train at 8 a.m. was greeted all through his way at the stations.

In Quilandy, there was a big gathering to welcome him. He spoke for about 20 minutes in pandal constructed under a sprawling banyan tree. After the speech he appealed to the people to disperse peacefully.

Circle Inspector, Ananda Iyer and Sub-Inspector, Abdul Hamid Khan, who were stationed elsewhere later arrested Kelappan under DIR and took him to Quilandy station. From there he was taken to Badagara produced before the Sub-divisional Magistrate, who was then camping in the Travellers' Bungalow. Kelappan was remanded to a week's custody in Kozhikode sub-jail.

26.   Report on Satyagraha Activities of Political Leaders

Hindustan Times, 23 November 1940.

Satyagraha in Bihar

Ex-Premier and ex-Finance Minister to Initiate

Patna, Nov. 22—Patna will be the venue of the joint initiation of Satyagraha in Bihar by the ex-Premier and the ex-Finance Minister on November 27.

Mr Sri Krishna Sinha, ex-Premier, will speak at a meeting to be held in Bankipore, while nearly at about the same time Mr Anugrah Narain Sinha, ex-Finance Minister will address a meeting in Patna city.

Thereafter, Satyagraha will begin in the districts. Mr Sri Krishna Sinha is expected to arrive here on November 26, while Mr Anugraha Narain Sinha is already here.

Mr Satyanarain Sinha, whip of the Congress party in the Central Assembly, will offer Satyagraha at Darbhanga on November 30.

Women Satyagrahis

A list of women Satyagrahis from Bihar is understood to have been included in the list submitted to Mahatma Gandhi.

The list is believed to include three lady members of the Bihar Legislative Assembly.

Bihar Satyagrahis-List approved by Mahatma Gandhi

Wardha, November 22—Shah Qzair Muneimi, Secretary of the Bihar Provincial Congress Committee, arrived here today with a list of Satyagrahis. The list was approved by Mahatma Gandhi—United Press.

Nagpur Hartal

Nagpur, November 22—Shops remained closed today in connection with the arrest of the former Minister of the Central Provinces and Berar.

The *tongawallas*, who are on strike, paraded the streets in the city in a procession—United Press.

AICC Member Arrested

Jalgaon, November 22—Mr Vasant Bhagwat, a member of the All India Congress Committee from Amalner, who was arrested under the Defence of India Rules, has been brought over to Jalgaon where he is being detained pending trial—API.

Congress Secretary Sentenced

Noakhali, November 21—Mr Manindra Kumar Rakshit, Secretary of the Noakhali District Krishak Samiti and the Town Congress Committee, who was prosecuted on a charge of breach of the warning notice served on him by the district magistrate of Noakhali under the Defence of India Rules has been sentenced to six months rigorous imprisonment by Mr F. Rahaman, deputy magistrate—API.

Sylhet Congress Secretary Sentenced

Sylhet, November 21—Mr Biresh Chandra Mishra, Secretary of the Sylhet District Congress Committee, has been sentenced to one year's rigorous imprisonment under the Defence of India Rules on a charge of delivering an anti-war speech at Sylhet.

He is already serving two terms of imprisonment under Section 108 IPC and the Defence of India Rules.

Mr Mishra is also undergoing trial under Section 124 (A) IPC on a charge of delivering two seditious speeches. The argument has been concluded and the judgment reserved—API.

Woman Satyagrahis Trial

Akola, November 22—Mrs Oke, the woman Satyagrahi who was arrested yesterday was tried today before Mr Chowdhury, First Class Magistrate, Akola.

Three prosecution witnesses were examined, who deposed that Mrs Oke was arrested after she had shouted anti-war slogans.

Charges were then framed against Mrs Oke under Rule 34, Section 6 (D) and (K) to which she pleaded guilty and filed a written statement.

Judgement was reserved till tomorrow—API.

Home Internment

Chandpur, November 22—Orders of home internment under the Defence of India Rule have been served on four Congress and Student Federation workers of Tipperah by the district magistrate there. The orders prohibit them from conversing, communicating or associating with certain persons mentioned in them.

Suspended Bengal PCC—Decision to Join Satyagraha

Calcutta, November 22—The United Press understands that the suspended Bengal Provincial Congress Committee has decided to join the Satyagraha launched by Mahatma Gandhi informing him of the decision of the Committee under his direct leadership. A list of Satyagrahis is also being prepared and will be sent to Mahatma Gandhi shortly.

In this connection, Mr Tarakdas Banerjee, acting Secretary of the BPCC, made a tour of the districts in Bengal. He met Congress workers everywhere and discussed with them the present political situation in relation to Satyagraha.

Further, it is understood that the Committee intends to launch Satyagraha in the last week of November. A Council of Action with five members has been already formed—United Press.

Mr R. Thevar Sentenced

Trichinopoly, November 22—Mr Rathnavelu Thevar, Chairman of the Trichinopoly Municipality was today convicted by the Sub-Divisional Magistrate, Trichinopoly for an offence under Section 38 (5) read with Section 38-A (C) of the Defence of India Rules. Five witnesses were examined.

Mr Thevar was sentenced to one year's rigorous imprisonment and was placed in 'A' class. He will be taken to the Central Jail, Vellore—API.

Mrs Lakshmipathy Transferred to Vellore Jail

Vellore, November 21—Mrs Rukmani Lakshmipathy, Deputy Speaker of the Madras Legislative Assembly, who was sentenced to one year's simple imprisonment by the Chief Presidency Magistrate, Madras was brought this afternoon to Vellore for detention in the Presidency Jail for Women—API.

Mr Kirtane's Trial Postponed

Bombay, November 22—Due to illness, the trial, of Mr Vasudev Vishnu Kirtane, which was to have taken place this morning in the Thana Jail, has been postponed to tomorrow. Mr Kirtane is one of the 75 Satyagrahis from Maharashtra and was arrested yesterday in a village in Thana district—API.

Enrolling Satyagrahis—Punjab Congress Cabinets Decision

Lahore, November 22—A meeting of the Working Committee of the Punjab Provincial Congress Committee held at Lahore today decided to ask all Congress members of the district boards and municipalities and office-bearers and members of the executives of the primary and district Congress Committee in the province to enrol themselves as active Satyagrahis.

The committee also discussed the resolutions to be placed before the general meeting of the PPCC tomorrow to which members of AICC Congress members of the Punjab Assembly and leaders of Congress parties in municipal committees and district boards have been invited—API.

Sardar Mangal Singh to offer Satyagraha in Ludhiana District

It is learnt that Sardar Mangal Singh, MLA (Central), will offer Satyagraha in a village in Ludhiana district in the first week of December—United Press.

Kerala Satyagraha—PCC President's Reminder to Congressmen

Calicut, November 21—Mr R.K.L. Nundkeolyar, President, Kerala PCC, issued a statement yesterday reminding all Congressmen and all sympathizers of the Congress in Kerala that none other than those selected by Mahatma Gandhi should offer Satyagraha. He added: 'There should be an atmosphere of peace and non-violence in the country'—API.

Poona Arrests

Poona, November 21—Acharya Limaye, President of the City Congress Committee, and Mr B.N. Gupta, ex-Parliamentary Secretary who offered Satyagraha this evening by addressing a large meeting in front of the Congress Bhavan were arrested tonight under Rule 38(5) for committing a 'prejudicial act' as defined in the Defence of India Rules. They have been taken to Yeravada Jail.—API.

Madras Leaders to Offer Satyagraha

Mr C. Rajagopalachari and all other Madras ex-Ministers except one have been included in the approved list of Satyagrahis. They have decided to offer Satyagraha within the next few days—API.

27. Satyagraha and Political Leaders' Arrests

Hindustan Times, 24 November 1940.

One Year for Bombay Ex-Minister—Satyagraha Plans for Various Provinces

According to a report received here Mr L.M. Patil, ex-Minister for Local Self-Government, Bombay was arrested yesterday at Rahuri under the Defence of India Rules for offering Satyagraha, and tried by the District Magistrate, Mr Streetfield, at Miri today and convicted and sentenced to one year's rigorous imprisonment. Mr Patil has been placed in "B" class.

Poona Arrests—Satyagraha near Sonya Maruti Temple

Mr Popatlal Shah, ex-President of the Poona City Municipality, and Mrs Laxmi Bai Thuse, MLA, offered Satyagraha last night by addressing a public meeting near the Sonya Maruti temple.

Both were arrested this morning at 6 under Rule 38(5) of the Defence of India Rules and were taken to the Yeravada Central Prison.

More Satyagrahis

Dr Kazi Abdul Hamid, from Jalgaon, will offer Satyagraha on November 24 and it is understood that he has duly intimated his intention to the District Magistrate.

Messrs Tulsidas Jadhav, MLA, and Ramakrishna Jaju, both from Sholapur, will offer Satyagraha on November 25 at Sholapur.

It is also understood that Mr S.S. More, President of the District Local Board, Poona has fixed November 30 to offer Satyagraha.

It is understood that Mr H.V. Tulpule, MLA from Poona, S.N. Gavankar, MLA from Ratnagiri district, Mr Lalchand Hirachand, MLA from Nasik district, Mr Annasaheb Datane from Bhusaval and Mr Babaubhai Mehta from Dhulia, Mr Devakinandan Narayan, President of the East Khandesh District Congress Committee, Mr Vasant Rao Vedak, President of the Panvel Municipality and Mr Shamboosingh Saith from Alibagh will offer Satyagraha before November 30.

1 Year's RI—Poona Satyagrahis Sentenced

Mr B.M. Gupte, ex-Parliamentary Secretary, and Mr V.P. Limaye, President of the City Congress Committee, who offered Satyagraha in Poona on November 21 and were arrested the same night were tried to-day inside the Yeravada jail by Mr M.R. Reuben, Additional District Magistrate, Poona. They were convicted and sentenced to one year's rigorous imprisonment each under Rule 38 (5) read with Rule 38 (1-A) of the Defence of India Rules.

Mr Popatlal Shah, former President of the Poona City Municipality and Mrs Laxmibai Thuse, MLA who offered Satyagraha yesterday and who were arrested this morning were tried inside the Yeravada jail by the same magistrate who convicted and sentenced Mr Shah to one year's rigorous imprisonment and Mrs Thuse to a fine of Rs 200 in default to undergo three months' simple imprisonment.

Asaf Ali—Meetings Addressed in Seven Villages

Mr Asaf Ali, MLA (Central) President of the Delhi Provincial Congress Committee made a tour of seven villages in Delhi Province where he addressed meetings.

Mr Asaf Ali explained how and why the Congress Party voted against the Finance Bill which sought to impose fresh tax upon them. He said that so long as the Government of the country was not owned by the people their representatives could not allow the imposition of any tax intended for the successful prosecution of the war.

Meerut Plans—Laxmi Narain to Inaugurate Movement

An emergency meeting of the Working Committee of the Meerut District Satyagraha Committee which was also attended by the Congress legislators, discussed plans of Satyagraha in the district and decided that Mr Laxmi Narain, member UP Council and ex-Parliamentary Secretary should inaugurate the Satyagraha in the district on November 26 by delivering an anti-war speech in the village Shiampur Dadiara in Hapur tehsil. The District Magistrate would be duly intimated. Messrs Charan Singh and Raghukul Tilak both members of the UP Assembly are to follow on November 29 and 30 respectively. Mr Vishnu Saran Dublish was the fourth on the list. Three leading Congressmen of the district, Mr Pyarelal Sharma, ex-Education Minister, Mr Raghubir Narain Singh, Member, Central Assembly, Mr Baij Nath, member UP Council and President of the Meerut Bar are, I reliably learn, to offer Satyagraha in the second week of December.

Punjab Plans—Mian Iftikhar-ud-Din to Initiate Satyagraha

It is understood that Dr Gopichand Bhargava who is to offer Satyagraha on November 27 by making an anti-war speech in Machhi Hatta the centre of the city, will intimate to the district magistrate on November 25.

Mian Iftikhar-ud-Din, President of the PPCC will intimate to the district magistrate on November 25 ... (He) will initiate Satyagraha in Baghanpura a suburb of Lahore on November, 25.

Choudhri Krishan Gopal Dutt, Deputy Leader of the Congress Party in the Assembly, it is understood, will offer Satyagraha in Sialkot shortly.

The third Satyagrahi is likely to be Sardar Sampuran Singh, Leader of the Congress Party in the Punjab Assembly. Lala Chandiram Verma, one of the Secretaries of the Punjab Provincial Congress Committee, is likely to offer Satyagraha in the first week of December.

A messenger from the Provincial Congress Committee is proceeding to Wardha with a list of Satyagrahis from the province for Mahatma Gandhi's approval. In accordance with the instructions of Mahatma Gandhi the Provincial Congress Committee is enlisting women Satyagrahis.

The Provincial Congress Committee office has received letters from different District Congress Committees for permission to commence Satyagraha in their areas.

UP Ministers to offer Satyagraha

Hafiz Muhammad Ibrahim has left Nainital for Bijnor, where it is reported, he will offer Satyagraha. Mrs Vijayalakshmi Pandit and Sh Laxmi Devi are expected to offer satyagraha at Allahabad and Hardoi respectively, during the next two weeks after giving due intimation to the district Magistrates. Pandit Pant is leaving for Haldwani tomorrow at 2 pm to offer Satyagraha there.

Mr K. Bharathy, MLA Arrested

Mr Krishnaswami Bharathy, MLA, was arrested this afternoon at his residence by the town police and taken in a police lorry. Mr Bharathy will be remanded to Madura District Jail by the Madura Additional District Magistrate under the Defence of India Rules.

V.B. Ayyangar Arrested

A Tanjore message says that Mr V. Buvaraha Ayyangar, MLA was arrested today under the Defence of India Rules while distributing anti-war leaflets.

Mr N.G. Ramaswamy, Labour MLA was arrested this afternoon by the Police under Defence of India Rules for having distributed anti-war leaflets to some war committee members last night at Coimbatore.

Andhra Province—List of 80 Satyagrahis Approved

Mr Kala Venkatarao, General Secretary of the Andhra Provincial Congress Committee, announces that Mahatma Gandhi has approved a list of about 80 Satyagrahis in the Andhra Province. Mahatma Gandhi has however, asked him to request Mr Konda Venkatappayya, MLA not to offer Satyagraha in consequence of his old age and feeble health.

Mr Kala Venkatarao adds that he has communicated this message to Mr Konda Venkatappayya.

Arya Shivaji Arrested

Arya Shivaji, President of the District Congress Committee was arrested today at Barsi under the Defence of India Act.

Sathe's Intimation

It is understood that Mr V.K. Sathe, president of the Poona District Congress Committee, has intimated the District Magistrate, Poona of his intention of offering Satyagraha at Chinchwad on November 27.

Nine Months for D.G. Desai—Bhaktilakshmi Also Convicted

Mrs Bhaktilakshmi Desai and Darbar Gopaldas Desai, who were arrested at Ras village were tried and convicted today under the Defence of India Rules.

Mrs Bhaktilakshmi was sentenced till the rising of the court and to a fine of Rs 200 in default three months imprisonment. Darbar Gopaldas was sentenced to nine months' rigorous imprisonment and a fine of Rs 200 in default three months' further imprisonment. They did not pay the fines and were taken to Sabarmati jail.

Miss Maniben Patel—To Shout Anti-War Slogans on November 24

Miss Maniben Patel, daughter of Sardar Vallabhai Patel, has today intimated to the District Magistrate that she will shout anti-war slogans at a public place in the village of Bareja tomorrow.

Mrs Vijayagarvi Kanugo has similarly intimated that she will shout such slogans in Manek Chowk a public thoroughfare here tomorrow.

Desai at Bombay—Leaving for Wardha to Meet Mahatmaji

Mr Bhulabhai Desai, Leader of the Congress Party in the Central Assembly, arrived here this morning. He was received at the Bombay Central station by the officials of the Bombay provincial Congress Committee.

Immediately after his arrival Mr Desai met the Congress workers at the Congress House and discussed the Satyagraha plan.

It is understood that Mr Desai is leaving for Wardha on Monday to meet Mahatma Gandhi and get his approval of the list of Satyagrahis from Bombay Province. Thereafter the dates of Satyagraha by different Congress will be announced.

Mr Desai will address a meeting here tomorrow evening on the present political situation.

Mrs Oke—One year's sentence on woman Satyagrahi

Mrs Pramila Bai Oke was sentenced today to a fine of Rs 200 or in default to simple imprisonment of a term of three months.

Mrs Oke was charged under the Defence of India Rules in connection with Satyagraha.—API.

28. Report on Arrests of Pandit Govind Ballabh Pant and
     Maniben Patel

Hindustan Times, 25 November 1940.

Shouting Anti-War Slogans—Removed to Haldwani Lockup—
Miss Maniben Patel also Arrested

Pandit Gobind Ballabh Pant, former Premier of UP, was arrested today at 3-40 pm at Haldwani while he was shouting anti-war slogans before a gathering of more than 5000 people including many ladies.

The arrest was effected under the Defence of India Rules.

Pandit Pant has been lodged in the local lockup. He will be tried tomorrow.

The Superintendent of Police accompanied by two inspectors of police handed over the warrant to Pandit Pant and taking him into custody, drove him to the lockup.

The gathering gave Pandit Pant a hearty send-off.

Pandit Pant in his parting message urged the people to remain calm and quiet and follow Mahatma Gandhi's instructions to the very letter.

Miss Maniben Patel Arrested in Village near Ahmedabad

Miss Maniben Patel, daughter of Sardar Vallabhbhai Patel was arrested this morning at Bareja village about seven miles from Ahmedabad under Rule 38(1)A of the Defence of India Rules while she was moving about in the village raising anti-war slogans.

Miss Maniben Patel had gone to Bareja village yesterday afternoon and had delivered a lecture there on the constructive programme of the Congress.

Mrs Vijayagauri Kanuga, Congress MLA was arrested today under Rule 129 of the Defence of India Rules. She had intimated her intention to offer Satyagraha today by shouting anti-war slogans.

29 (a) Political Leaders Arrested

Statesman, 28 November 1940.

Dr P.C. Ghosh Arrested—Anti-war Campaign—Madras ex-Minister Sentenced

Dr Prafulla Chandra Ghosh, member of the Congress Working Committee, was arrested at 3 pm yesterday at Basudevpur (Midnapur District) on a charge of shouting anti-war slogans before a large crowd.

Dr Ghosh who is the first Satyagrahi, was immediately followed by Mr Kumar Chandra Jana, president of the District Congress Committee who shouted similar slogans and was also arrested. Their trial is expected to take place in Midnapur tomorrow.

Dr Sarat Chandra Mukherjee, MLA, president of the Birbhum district Congress Committee and Mr Mihirlal Chatterjee, a member of the AICC who initiated the Satyagraha movement in Birbhum yesterday by shouting anti-war slogans in a local bazar before a large crowd, were also arrested.

Bombay

Mr Bhulabhai Desai, President, Bombay Provincial Congress Committee leader of the Congress party in the Central Assembly and member of the Congress Working Committee and Mrs Sarojini Naidu, member of the Working Committee have informed the Commissioner of Police, Bombay that they propose to offer Satyagraha at 5-30 pm tomorrow in front of Congress House.

Mr Mangaldas Pakwasa, President, Bombay Legislative Council, has also informed the Commissioner of Police of his intention to offer Satyagraha on Monday evening at Kalbadevi.

These, it is learnt, will be followed by a dozen members of the Assembly on subsequent days. Among these are three former Ministers, Mr K.M. Munshi, Mr M.Y. Nurie and Dr M.D. Gilder.

Mr Shantilal Shah, MLC, secretary of Bombay Assembly Congress Party was arrested yesterday at the Khar Suburb Bombay for delivering an anti-war speech.

Mr Shankerarao Deo, Member of the Congress Working Committee will offer Satyagraha at Poona on December 1. Mr Deo it is understood has already informed the district Magistrate of his intention.

Madras

Mr V.V. Giri, former Minister for Labour and Industries, was arrested yesterday for offering Satyagraha by shouting anti-war slogans at the Panagal Park, Mambalam, Mr Giri was later sentenced to 15 months simple imprison

Mr D. Ramasubba Reddy, MLC, who offered Satyagraha at Alamkhanipalli yesterday by shouting anti-war slogans, was arrested by the police and produced before the Deputy Magistrate at Khajipet who sentenced him to one year's rigorous imprisonment and Rs 250 fine in default to three months' further imprisonment.

Mr K. Madhava Menon, MLC (chairman, Calicut Municipality) was arrested at his residence under the Defence of India Rules. He had announced his intention of making an anti-war speech at the Town Hall.

Mr S. Nagappa, a Harijan MLA, offered Satyagraha at Kurnool was arrested and later sentenced to one year's rigorous imprisonment and fined Rs 250 or in default to six months' rigorous imprisonment.

Delhi

Mr Asaf Ali, MLA (Central) and member of the Congress Working Committee was arrested in New Delhi yesterday under the Defence of India Rule. He was taken to the Delhi district jail where he was received by Mr E.S. Lewis, Additional District Magistrate and superintendent of the jail. The magistrate granted Mr Asaf Ali four days remand under section 34 and 38 of the Defence of India Rules.

Mr Asaf Ali had earlier addressed two public meetings, one at the Juma Masjid and the other at Gandhi grounds. He raised anti-war slogans and announced at the latter meeting that Mr Nuruddin Behri will offer Satyagraha on December 4, Mr F.H. Ansari on December 8, and Lala Deshbandhu Gupta on December 14.

Lala Desh Bandhu Gupta, MLA (Punjab), Maulana Nooruddin Behari, Mr Bhal Singh, Mr Faridul Haq Ansari and Maulana Khalillur Rahman, Dictator of Majlis-i-Ahrar-i-Islam-i-Hind were arrested today under the Defence of India Rules.

Punjab

Choudhri Krishan Gopal Dutt, Deputy Leader of the Congress Party in the Punjab Assembly is, it is understood, offering Satyagraha in the Sialkot district on December 9.

Dr Gopi Chand Bhargava, former leader of the Congress Party in the Punjab Assembly, who had intimated the District Magistrate of Lahore of his intention to offer Satyagraha was arrested at his residence yesterday.

UP

Mr R.S. Pandit has been arrested at Allahabad under the Defence of India Rules. The arrest is believed to have been made in connection with a speech delivered by Mr Pandit at Allahabad a few days ago.

29 (b) Political Leaders Arrested

Hindustan Times, 28 November 1940.

Following a police lathi charge on a crowd that had assembled outside the Bankipore Jail in which Mr Sri Krishna Sinha, the Bihar ex-Premier, has been lodged after his arrest, Dr Rajendra Prasad has postponed Satyagraha in Bihar. Mr Sinha offered Satyagraha last evening by shouting anti-war slogans near the Bankipore Maidan and was arrested shortly after 4-30 PM.

A United Press message adds that some persons were injured due to the police lathi charge.

Among those who were arrested yesterday in connection with the Satyagraha were—

Mr Sri Krishna Sinha, Former Premier of Bihar.

The Hon. Mr G.V. Mavlankar, Speaker of the Bombay Legislative Assembly.

Mr Maganlal Gujarthi, MLA, Bombay

Mr Kunwar Rukum Singh, MLA, Budaun, UP

Mr Hukum Chand, MLA, Budaun, UP

Mr Laxminarain, Ex-Parliamentary Secretary, UP

Mr B. Gopala Reddi, Ex-Local Self-Government Minister, Madras and

Mr T. Viswanadham, ex-Parliamentary Secretary, Madras

Mr Mahavir Tyagi, MLA, UP

Mr Jwala Pershad Jigyasoo, MLA, UP

Mr R.K.R. Reddiar, AICC Member

Mr Sri Krishna Sinha, former Premier of Bihar was arrested this evening shortly after 4.30 after he had shouted some anti-war slogans near the Bankipur Maidan. He was taken straight to Bankipur Jail where the trial will be held.

A big crowd had gathered near the western end of the Bankipore Maidan where Mr Sri Krishna Sinha began anti-war Satyagraha in this province.

Mr Sinha on arrival began to shout certain anti-war slogans but was presented with a warrant of arrest under Section 38(5) by the Superintendent of Police. He was removed to a waiting car and removed to the Bankipur Jail where he again shouted slogans.

Previous to going to the Maidan Mr Sinha paid a visit to Sadaquat Ashram, the Provincial Congress Headquarters, where he was presented with a garland spun of white *khadi* yarn.

A considerable crowd gathered in front of the jail and special police arrangements had to be made.

The Police had to resort to a mild lathi charge. The crowd had surged towards the jail gate and a few stones were thrown on a police van and two persons were slightly injured. Subsequently Mr A.N. Sinha urged the crowd to go away from the jail premises which it did.

Mr Sri Krishna Sinha is expected to be tried tomorrow.

A United Press report adds When Mr Sri Krishna Sinha was arrested this afternoon the crowd became excited and then marched to the jail gate where Mr Sinha had been lodged and flocked at the gate. They threw brickbats at a lorry standing by whereupon the police made a lathi charge, as the result of which some persons were injured.

Satyagraha Postponed

Following this evening's incidents after Mr Sri Krishna Sinha's arrest, Dr Rajendra Prasad, President of the Bihar PCC, has asked Mr A.N. Sinha, the second Satyagrahi to postpone the Satyagraha which the latter was to have offered tomorrow to a later date.

Accordingly to Mr A.N. Sinha has informed the District Magistrate that he will not be offering Satyagraha tomorrow as intimated earlier.

Dr Rajendra Prasad is issuing a statement in this connection.

Mr Satya Narain Singh, MLA (Central) will be the first to offer Satyagraha, from the District of Darbhanga. He will, it is understood, offer Satyagraha at Laherrasarai on December 2. Mr Singh came here today and discussed his plans with Dr Rajendra Prasad.

Bombay

Mrs Naidu and Desai to offer Satyagraha on November 29—Immediately after his arrival in Bombay this morning from Wardha Mr Bhulabhai Desai had informal discussions with the officials of the Provincial Congress Committee.

It is understood that Satyagraha will start in the city on Monday, December 2, when Mrs Sarojini Naidu and Mr Bhulabhai Desai will offer Satyagraha by addressing a public meeting at Chawpatty.

On Tuesday, December 3, it is further understood, Mr K.M. Munshi, ex-Home Minister, Mr A.B. Latthe, ex-Finance Minister, Dr M.G. Gilder, ex-Minister of Excise and Public Health, Mr M.Y. Nurie, ex-Public Works Minister, Mr Nagindas Master, Vice President of the Bombay Provincial Congress Committee. Mr S.K. Patil, General Secretary, Mr Bhawanji Arjunkhimji and Mr Ratilal Gandhi will offer Satyagraha in different parts of the city.

It is learnt about 150 Congressmen will have courted arrests in the city by December 10.

Speaker Arrested

The Hon. Mr G.V. Mavlankar, Speaker of the Bombay Legislative Assembly, who was to offer Satyagraha tonight by making an anti-war speech, was arrested early this morning by Mr C.S. Panday, C.I.D. Inspector under Section 129, Defence of India Rules, and was taken to Sabarmati Central jail.

The United Press learns that the Bombay list of Satyagrahis which numbered about 200 has been approved, by Gandhiji. The exact date and time of offering Satyagraha by them will be announced probably tomorrow after Mr Bhulabhai Desai has consulted Mrs Sarojini Naidu, ex-President of the Congress and ex-officio Member of the Bombay Provincial Congress Committee.

It is further learnt that Mrs Naidu will be the first to offer Satyagraha in Bombay from among the members of the Bombay Provincial Congress followed by Messrs Bhulabhai Desai, K.M. Munshi, S.K. Patil, Nagindas Master and others. Mrs Naidu is expected in Bombay on Thursday.

Poona Satyagraha

It is understood that Dr R.N. Datar, Mrs Laxmibai Vaidya and Mrs Laxmibai Patharker have intimated their intention of offering Satyagraha at 6 pm on November 28 by addressing a public meeting in front of the Congress Bhavan in Poona.

Mr Ratilal Mehta

Mr Ratilal Mehta, member of the All India Congress Committee and President of the Ghatkopar District Congress Committee, has intimated to the suburban District Magistrate today that he would offer Satyagraha at Ghatkopar tomorrow evening.

Maniben Patel's Trial

Miss Maniben Patel, daughter of Sardar Vallabhbhai Patel, was produced in court today and the trial was held in Sabarmati Central Jail. Sardar Vallabhbhai Patel was present at the trial at Miss Patel's request.

Two prosecution witnesses were examined. One was a Police Sub-Inspector and another was an Inspector of Police.

Miss Patel refused to take part in the proceedings. After the prosecution witnesses were examined, the Magistrate framed charges under Section 38 (1)-A of the Defence of India Rules.

Asked whether she pleaded guilty or not Miss Patel said that she did not want to say anything. Judgement will be delivered tomorrow.

Charges were framed also against Mr Hari Prasad Mehta, a Congress leader after two prosecution witnesses were examined.

Madras—Mr R.K.R. Reddiar—AICC Member Gets One Year's RI

Mr Vishwanadhan was sentenced to 18 months' rigorous imprisonment and to pay a fine of Rs 200 in default three months' further imprisonment. He has been placed in 'B' class.

Mr R.K.R. Reddiar

Mr R.K. Rajachidambara Reddiar, a member of the AICC who was arrested today near Lalgudi was convicted under Section 38 (1) (C), Defence of India Rules (distribution of anti-war letters), and sentenced to one year's rigorous imprisonment and to pay a fine of Rs 250 in default to three months of rigorous imprisonment. He was placed in 'B' class.

Mr Krishnaswami Bharathi

Mr Krishnaswami Bharathi, MLA who offered Satyagraha on Friday and was arrested, was convicted and sentenced today to one year's rigorous imprisonment and a fine of Rs 500, in default, to six months' rigorous imprisonment for an offence under Section 38 (5) read with Section 38 (1) of the Defence of India Rules and was placed in 'B' class by the Additional District Magistrate, Madura.

Mr K. Varadachariar

Mr K. Varadachariar, MLA, Secretary Andhra Mahasabha and Chittoor District Congress Committee offered Satyagraha this morning by shouting anti-war slogans in the premises of the local Congress Committee office before a large gathering. He was sentenced to one year's rigorous imprisonment by the Sub-divisional Magistrate.

He was placed in 'B' class and taken to Vellore Jail.

The accused pleaded not guilty–API.

Punjab—Mian Iftikhar-Ud-Din To Offer Satyahraha on November 29

Lahore November 27

Mian Iftikhar-Ud-Din, President of the Punjab Provincial Congress Committee, has informed the District Magistrate of his intention to offer Satyagraha on November 29.

Mian Iftikhar-ud-Din will address a public meeting at Bhagwanpura, a suburb of Lahore, at 8 p.m. on November 29.

A number of other members of the Congress Assembly Party, including Sardar Sampuran Singh, Leader of the party, will follow him by addressing meetings in their respective constituencies.

An emergency general meeting of the Congress Assembly Party has been convened for tomorrow when date and method of offering Satyagraha for each member of the party will be decided.

Dr Gopi Chand Bhargava will offer Satyagraha in Machihatta locality on November 30.

Subject to permission being granted by Mahatma Gandhi, Raizada Hansraj, MLA (Central), will offer Satyagraha in Jullundur in the first week of the next month. He is the oldest Congressman in the Doaba and will be the first Satyagrahi to court imprisonment in this politically advanced part of the Punjab. The exact place and the date of offering Satyagraha will be announced as soon as he returns from Wardha.

Kumari Sarla Parashar, official stenographer of the Bihar Assembly during the Congress regime, has received an intimation from Sevagram to the effect that her name has been included in the list of lady Satyagrahis. She will probably be the first lady to offer Satyagraha in the Doaba. She is at present staying with her nephew, Comrade Saligram Parashar, a prominent Socialist of Bahadurpur.

30. Report of Arrests in CP, UP and Punjab

Hindustan Times, 30 November 1940.

CP SPEAKER GETS ONE YEAR'S IMPRISONMENT
MR SAMPURNANAND AND PUNJAB PCC PRESIDENT ARRESTED

Mian Iftikhar-Ud-Din, President of the Punjab Provincial Congress Committee, was arrested near Lahore yesterday. While he was being removed to the jail somebody from the crowd that followed is alleged to have thrown a brick-bat at the police whereupon the Senior Superintendent ordered a lathi charge resulting in minor injuries to some people.

> Reports have also been received from the various provinces of the arrest of Congress MLAs, and others. Mr Sampurnanand, an ex-Minister, was arrested at Benares.
>
> Mr G.S. Gupta, Speaker of the CP Assembly, was sentenced to one year's rigorous imprisonment.

Mian Iftikhar-Ud-Din, President of the Punjab Provincial Congress Committee, initiated Satyagraha this evening at Bhagwanpura a suburb of Lahore.

He was arrested by the police while making a speech.

A strong police party, headed by Mr Scroggie, Senior Superintendent of Police was present. Mian Iftikhar-Ud-Din had not yet finished his speech when the police proceeded to the dais and effected his arrest. In the course of his speech, Mian Iftikhar-Ud-Din explained the Congress policy in connection with the war.

While Mian Iftikhar-Ud-Din was being removed in a lorry to the Central Jail a section of the crowd followed shouting slogans. A brickbat is also alleged to have been thrown by some one at the police whereupon Mr Scroggie, Senior Superintendent of Police ordered a lathi charge. A few people are reported to have received minor injuries.

After the arrest of Mian Iftikhar-ud-Din the meeting was addressed by two other speakers.

Sardar Sampuran Singh, Leader of the Congress Party in the Punjab Assembly, and a number of Congress MLAs were present.

Mian Iftikhar-Ud-Din has nominated Lala Dunichand, MLA (Lahore), as his successor.

Sardar Sampuran Singh, Leader of the Congress Party in the Punjab Assembly, will offer a Satyagraha in his constituency on December 3.

Besides, the following 31 Congressmen, including 16 members of the Punjab Assembly, three of the Central Assembly and members of the AICC and the Punjab Congress Working Committee will offer Satyagraha in their respective constituencies or localities on dates convenient to them between December 1 and 15.

Raizada Hansraj, MLA (Central), Mr Shamlal, MLA (Central), S. Mangal Singh, MLA (Central), Sardar Partap Singh, MLA, General Secretary, PPCC (December 4), Krishan Gopal Dutta, MLA (December 9), Seth Sudarshan, MLA (December 4), Bhim Sen Sachar, MLA (December 14), Ch. Mohd. Hussain, MLA, Munshi Harilal (December 4) Munilal Kalia, MLA (December 9) Sahib Ram, MLA (December 15), Kapur Singh, MLA, (December 7), Sardar Amar Singh, Maulvi Abdul Ghani, Sardar Basant Singh, Handi Ram Varma, Giani Gurmukh Singh, Musafir, Lala Achintram, Pandit Nekiram Sharma (December 5), Master Anandlal, Sardar Darshan Singh Pheruman, Sardar Balwant Singh Anand, and Lala Kedarnath Sehgal.

UP

Mr Sampurnanand, Ex-Minister Arrested at Benares

Mr Sampurnanand, former Minister of Education, United Province Government, was arrested at his residence at 3.30 pm.

The arrest was made by Mr Nigam, Deputy Superintendent of Police who drove Mr Sampurnanand in his car to the District Jail, Benaras.

The arrest of Mr Sampurnanand was made under section 36 (6) (Prejudicial Act) and 121 (attempt to contravene the Defence Rules) of the Defence of India Act.

Mr Sampurnanand had intimated to the District Magistrate that he would offer Satyagraha at 1 pm tomorrow at Shuddhipur village in Benares by shouting anti-war slogans. On hearing the news, the Benares Municipal Board adjourned without transacting any business.

Pandit Badri Datt Pande, MLA (Central) and Pandit Har Govind Pant, MLA, will offer Satyagraha at Almora on December 5 and 6 respectively by shouting anti-war slogans.

Mr Mohan Lal Shah, MLC, will start Satyagraha at Kashipur in District Naini Tal on December 10 after giving intimation to the District Magistrate, Naini Tal.

Mr Raghukul Tilak, MLA (UP) and President of the Meerut City Satyagraha Committee, has intimated to the District Magistrate that he would offer Satyagraha on November 10 at 3 p.m. in the evening in village Rihani on the Meerut-Delhi Road by shouting anti-war slogans.

Mr Vishnu Saran Dublish, an ex-convict in the Kakori case, it is understood, is to follow him in the first week of December. He is likely to offer Satyagraha in Mowana Tahsil.

Shri Dhoom Singh, Mandal Congress Secretary (Kusari) and member PCC and Shri Shive Raj Singh were arrested at Bareilly today under Rule 38 (a) of the Defence of India Rules for alleged anti-war speeches in a village. Both these gentlemen were brought hand-cuffed.

A crowded meeting of the citizens of Barellly under the auspices of the City Congress Committee was held to protest against the arrests of Pandit Govind Ballabh Pant, the ex-Premier of UP and a representative of Bareilly in the UP Assembly and Dr K.N. Katju,

Ex-Minister of Justice, Mr Naurunglal, Acting President, DCC, presided. A resolution congratulating Pt Pant and Dr Katju was passed.

Mr Mahavir Tyagi, MLA was sentenced to one year's rigorous imprisonment under Sections 34 and 38 of the Defence of India Rules. His trial was held inside the Dehra Dun District Jail.

Mr Tyagi filed a written statement but did not offer any defence.

The first Satyagrahi of Mainpuri, Syt. Mizazilal, MLA offered Satyagraha at Bewar on Thursday at 3 pm before a crowd of 600 by shouting anti-war slogans. He was later arrested.

Information has reached here from Hamirpur that Mr Sattribuvan Singh will court arrest at Midnight on December 1.

The trial of Mr Lakshmi Narain, ex-Parliamentary Secretary, UP, who was arrested on November 26 for offering Satyagraha will be held on December 3 in Meerut District Jail.

Mr Charan Singh, MLA, General Secretary of the Meerut District Satyagraha Committee was arrested this afternoon in village Tugana in Baghpat tehsil where he offered Satyagraha before a gathering of 4,000 shouting anti-war slogans. He was brought here and is lodged in the Sadar Bazar Police lock-up.

The trial of Mr Jwala Prasad Jigyasu, MLA who had delivered an anti-war speech at Dadoon took place in jail before Mr Amruddin, Sub-Divisional Officer. The accused pleaded guilty and was sentenced to one year's rigorous imprisonment and put under class "B". The city observed hartal yesterday and a public meeting was held in Edward Park, where Dr K.M. Ashraf spoke for an hour on the political situation of the country.

Mr Sura Prasad Awasthi, MLA (Congress), has given notice to the District Magistrate of his intention to offer Satyagraha on December 1 at 4 pm in village Narainpur by shouting anti-war slogans.

CP

One Year's RI for Speaker—Mr G.S. Gupta Sentenced

Nagpur, November 29—Mr G.S. Gupta, Speaker of the CP Assembly, who was arrested yesterday for offering Satyagraha at Durg was sentenced to one year's rigorous imprisonment under the Defence of India Rules and brought to the Nagpur Central Jail.

Mr Dharmaraj Kedar was convicted under the Defence of India Rules on Friday by Mr B.S. Choudhari, First Class Magistrate of Akola, for having distributed leaflets containing the Satyagraha programme and sentenced to one year's simple imprisonment.

Mrs Premabai Anish was tried and convicted by the same Magistrate under the Defence of India Rules for shouting anti-war slogans and sentenced to one month's simple imprisonment.

Bombay

Shankarrao Deo—To Offer Satyagraha on December 1

Poona, November 29—Mr Shankarrao Deo, Member of the Congress Working Committee, will offer Satyagraha on December 1 at 6 pm at the Congress Bhawan by addressing a public meeting.

Mr Deo, it is understood, has already informed the District Magistrate, Poona, of his intention.

Mr Laxmidas Srikant, MLA offered Satyagraha by delivering an anti-war speech at Dohad on Thursday night and was arrested there early Friday morning. He was brought to Ahmedabad where he was immediately tried and sentenced by the Additional District Magistrate to one year's simple imprisonment. He was taken to Sabarmati Central Jail.

Appasaheb Vedak, President of the Panvel Municipality, who was arrested on Wednesday under the Defence of India Rules for offering Satyagraha by addressing a public meeting was sentenced to one year's rigorous imprisonment.

Mr Harprasad Mehta, MLA President of the Daskrel Taluka Congress Committee was sentenced on Friday on Sabarmati Central Jail to one year's rigorous imprisonment under the Defence of India Rules.

Dr R.N. Datar, Mrs Laxmibai Vaidya and Mrs Laxmibai Patharkar offered Satyagraha on Thursday evening by addressing a public meeting in front of the Congress Bhawan in Poona.

Mr Mahajan, President of the Ratnagiri Congress Committee was tried for shouting anti-war slogans by the First Class Magistrate at Malwan and sentenced on two counts to eight month's rigorous imprisonment and Rs 25 fine, in default one month more and three month's rigorous imprisonment and Rs 25 fine or in default one month more. The sentences are to run consecutively.

Mr Mahajan, President of the Ratnagiri District Congress Committee, was arrested for offering Satyagraha at Malwan, where he is awaiting his trial. Mr Mahajan is the first Satyagrahi from this district.

Mr R.G. Gadre, an ex-member of the AICC was arrested at Nasik last evening under the Defence of India Rules for delivering an anti-war speech. His trial takes place tomorrow.

Mrs Parvatibai Shendye, the first woman Satyagrahi from Ratnagiri was arrested for offering Satyagraha. She was sentenced by the Sub-Divisional Magistrate to one day's simple imprisonment and a fine of Rs 200, in default three months' imprisonment.

With a view to offering Satyagraha, Mr V.B. Sathe has resigned the office of Honorary Magistrate. Mr Sathe is the President of the Sholapur Municipality.

Madras

CR's Plans—To Offer Satyagraha on December 2

As at present arranged Mr C. Rajagopalachari, ex-Premier and a member of the Congress Working Committee, will offer Satyagraha on December 2 in Madras city after duly notifying the Government of his intention to do so.

Mr Salem Subramaniam, MLA, was arrested on Friday morning under the Defence of India Rules for making an anti-war speech in front of the temple at Tirukkoyilur. He was later produced before the Magistrate who sentenced him to one year's rigorous imprisonment and Rs 500 fine, in default a further term of four months' imprisonment.

Mr D. Ramalinga Reddy, MLA, who offered Satyagraha at Vellore on Friday by shouting anti-war slogans was arrested and later sentenced by the Sub-Divisional Magistrate to nine months' rigorous imprisonment under Rule 38 (5) of the Defence of India Rules.

Mr Mallipudi Pallamraju, MLA, President of the East Godawari District Board, Cocanada was arrested on Friday morning for offering Satyagraha by shouting anti-war slogans. Later, Mr Pallamraju was produced before the sub-divisional Magistrate who convicted him under Sections 38(5) and 38(1) of the Defence of India Rules and sentenced him to one year's rigorous imprisonment, and to pay a fine of Rs 1,000, in default to undergo a further six months' imprisonment.

Dr P.S. Srinivasan, MLA and municipal chairman, Conjeevaram, who was arrested on Wednesday under the Defence of India Rules for distributing letters to members of the War Committee, was sentenced by the Joint Magistrate Chingleput, to one year's rigorous imprisonment and Rs 500 fine in default further six months' imprisonment.

Mr K. Madhava Menon, MLC (Chairman, Calicut Municipality), was arrested at 6.30 on Friday morning at his residence under Section 120, Defence of India Rules. He had announced his intention of making an anti-war speech at the Town Hall at 9 am on Friday.

Mr Kutty was later produced before the Sub-Divisional Magistrate Palaghat, who sentenced the accused to one year's rigorous imprisonment and a fine of Rs 500, in default six months' further imprisonment.

Bengal

Dr P.C. Ghosh—to offer Satyagraha on November 10—Dr Prafulla Chandra Ghosh, Member of the Congress Working Committee, will leave on Friday morning for Tamluk reaching there at noon. He will offer Satyagraha at Vasudevpur on November 30.

On the eve of his departure for Tamluk, Dr Prafulla Chandra Ghosh, member of the Congress Working Committee, said: 'Every one should strictly follow the instructions issued by Mahatma Gandhi from time to time, and no one should offer Satyagraha whose name is not approved by him. Nor should anyone offer himself unless he fulfils the conditions.

'Those who cannot offer Satyagraha should devote themselves to the constructive programme. Hindu-Muslim unity should be one of the main things in Bengal and I appeal to all those Congressmen who are not strictly following the directions of the Working Committee to forget everything and rise above all considerations and compose all differences.'

Pandit Jeewanlal, President of the Burra Bazar District Congress Committee, and a member of the AICC from Bengal has sent a notice to the Commissioner of Police, Calcutta, stating that he will offer Satyagraha at 12.20 p.m. on December 2 near the Calcutta Stock Exchange in Clive Street.

The names of eight more persons have been approved by Mahatma Gandhi for offering Satyagraha in Bengal. They include a Muslim and four members of the Provincial Assembly. It is learnt that according to the plan of Mahatma Gandhi, Congress MLAs and members of the All India Congress Committee belonging to the first batch will offer Satyagraha by December 9.

Assam

G. Bardoloi—Meeting with Mahatma Gandhi

Mr Gopinath Bardoloi, former Premier of Assam, is here. He is interviewing Mahatma Gandhi this afternoon when he will present to him the list of Satyagrahis from Assam for his approval and discuss with him the details of the plans of Satyagraha in Assam. He is expected to leave for Assam on Saturday.

Orissa

Mr Bodhram Dube—Ex-Minister to Offer Satyagraha

Cuttack, November 29—Mr Bodhram Dube, ex-Minister of Orissa, will according to present arrangements, offer Satyagraha on December 2 at Sambalpur.

Bihar

MLA Arrested—Mr R.P. Singh Sentenced to One Year

Patna, November 29—Mr Rameswar Prasad Singh, a member of the Bihar Assembly, was arrested this afternoon for shouting anti-war slogans. He was placed for trial inside the jail before the Sub-Divisional Magistrate and found guilty on two counts. The Magistrate sentenced him to one year's rigorous imprisonment on each count under the Defence of India Rules. The sentences will run concurrently.

The accused was recommended for 'A' Class.—API and United Press.

31. Fortnightly Report on the Commencement of Civil Disobedience Movement by Brijlal Biyani

Fortnightly Reports, File No. 11/11/40, Home Department, Political Intelligence Section, Government of India, Second Half of November, 1940, NAI.

The outstanding event of the fortnight was the inception of the second phase of Mahatma Gandhi's individual civil disobedience movement. The start was made by the Hon'ble Mr Brijlal Biyani at Akola on the 17th November. He shouted the following slogans:

(i) From the moral and political point of view, it is harmful to help the war by enlisting in the army

(ii) It is sinful to help the war by giving money

(iii) In order to establish the reign of non-violence it is our duty to oppose the war by non-violent means.

He was arrested when he repeated the above slogans four times in front of a crowd of about 5,000 which, though highly orderly and well-behaved, appeared to be in a highly demonstrative mood. Mr Rameshwar Agnibhoj, MLA, offered Satyagraha on the same day at a village in the Hoshangabad district by making a bad anti-war speech. Three ex-Ministers offered Satyagraha on the 21st, Mr Bharuka at Nagpur, Mr Gokhale at Arnraoti and Pandit D.P. Misra at a village four miles from Jubbulpore. Mr Bharuka's Satyagraha took the form of shouting before an audience of about 6,000 persons the slogan 'It is sinful to assist this war with money and men. The proper thing for us to do is to oppose this war by means of non-violent Satyagraha.' Mr Gokhale delivered to an audience of about 6,000 persons a speech in the course of which he advised the people not to assist the Government in the efficient prosecution of the war. Pandit D.P. Misra delivered a speech to an audience of about 3,000 persons, in which, among other things he said: 'Ours is not the duty to help in this war. He who believes in this should say that not a single man should go in this war, not a single man should get himself recruited in the army in this war, not a single rupee should be given to this war and not a single man should be allowed to join the army.' Mrs Pramila Bai Oke the first woman satyagrahi offered individual civil disobedience on the same day by reciting the slogans used by the Hon'ble Mr Brijlal Biyani before an audience of about 2,500 persons. The Hon'ble Mr G.S. Gupta, Speaker of the CP and Berar Legislative Assembly, offered Satyagraha by reciting anti-war slogans at Durg before an audience of about 5,000 to 6000 persons. Other Satyagrahis during the fortnight included Mr D.B. Naik, MLA in the Hoshangabad district and Dr Ekpote at Khamgaon in the Buldana district. Pandit Ravishankar Shukla ex-Prime Minister, who was to have offered Satyagraha on the 21st afternoon, was arrested under rule 129 of the Defence of

India Rules on the 21st morning in order to prevent undue excitement. He has now been detained under rule 26 for a period of one year. The arrest of Mahatma Gandhi's Satyagrahis led to partial local hartals. The public in general is not however unduly excited, and too much significance should not be attached to the size of the audience at the meetings, as the place and time of the Satyagraha were chosen with a view to attract as large a number of people as possible. A good many people must have attended these meetings in order to witness a spectacle.

There has been very little other political activity. Three or four public meetings were held at Nagpur to congratulate the Satyagrahis on their arrests and convictions, the largest audience being about 3,000. The Nagpur Nagar Congress Committee has put into force its scheme of 'walking newspapers' by oral dissemination of Satyagraha news at certain centres in the city at appointed hours. The centres are being carefully watched by the police. The news-carriers have so far done nothing except announcing the news of the arrests of prominent leaders. The anti-war agitation, which started in the Bilaspur district towards the end of last month, has now ceased. The demonstration marches of the troops through certain districts have had an excellent effect. The troops have been welcomed everywhere.

32.   Report on the Satyagraha Movement in United Provinces

Fortnightly Reports, File No. 11/11/1940, Home Department, Political Intelligence Section, Government of India, Second Half of November 1940, NAI.

The Satyagraha movement continues on its course. Mrs Pandit was arrested in Allahabad before she could leave for Cawnpore to perform satyagraha in a village of that district. Other prominent people who have been arrested since I last wrote for performing, or intimating their intention to perform, Satyagrahis are Messrs Mohan Lal Saksena and Jogendra Singh, both of the Central Legislature, and Husain Zaheer, a Lecturer at the Lucknow University and a son of Sir Wazir Hasan, formerly Chief Judge of Oudh. Mr R.S. Pandit who had intimated his intention to perform Satyagraha was arrested before hand on a charge of having previously made an objectionable speech. Mr Kidwai, ex Minister, whose satyagraha had been postponed in order that he might organize the movement, was arrested on December 13 in Lucknow and will be detained under rule 26 of the Defence of India Rules. Protest meetings and local hartals have generally followed the arrests, but the hartals have generally been partial and, except in Benares, where 5,000 people attended a meeting to congratulate Mr Sampurnanand (ex-Minister) on his arrest, the meetings have been small. The arrests caused no disturbance, and in the few cases in which the Satyagrahis were allowed to address meetings, the audience were small. In a village in Bahraich, however, 2,500 people assembled to hear a Satyagrahi who, however, was arrested before he arrived, and a farewell meeting arranged for a Satyagrahi in Meerut was attended by 2,000 people.

It is difficult to gauge the effect of the movement. Practically all District Magistrates agree that it has hardly touched the masses. On the other hand, it has undoubtedly set the politically-minded intelligentsia of all parties thinking. They are facing a sort of 'war of nerves.' 'What will the Mahatma do next? Suppose 100,000 people do go to jail, what then? Can we cope,' or alternatively 'is there a danger, of the Congress coming to an agreement with the Government before it is too late' are the sort of questions that are worrying them, and the *National Herald* is doing all it can to keep up the attack. Among non-Congress politicians there is the fear that when people see that, right or wrong, Congressmen are prepared to suffer, if not for their beliefs, at least for their leader, they may be asked what they are doing about securing independence which is as much their creed as that of the Congress. In a statement attributed to Dr Moonje, which appeared in the *National Herald*, he is reported to have said,

'Quite apart from the fact whether such Satyagraha at the present moment is justifiable or not, the mass mentality always leans in favour of such seemingly bold actions. It will, therefore, be not far from right if it could be said that it is a bid for winning the elections when they will be held in the near future. It is an attempt on the part of the Congress to rehabilitate itself in the mass mind.

The Hindu Mahasabha now sees the danger. It will, therefore, be compelled to find some solid, reasonable and just excuse for inaugurating a mass Satyagraha of its own.

How and when it will be thought out and organized is the duty of the annual session which will be held at Madura in the last week of this month. But it seems certain that in the interests of its very existence in competition with the Congress, the Hindu Mahasabha will have to chalk out some jail-going programme. If the Congress is sending to jail its best men who are likely to contest the next elections, the Hindu Mahasabha also will have to send its best men to enjoy the Government hospitality as His Majesty's guests in his jails.'

Dr Moonje gave a very similar opinion in an interview with His Excellency.

The fear that if they do not secure Mr Gandhi's blessing by going to jail they will not be re-elected at the next election is undoubtedly one of the most powerful factors inducing those members of the Legislature who are neither anti-war nor believe in non-violence to perform Satyagraha. A few Congress members of the Legislature may stand out, but if they do they will have practically to resign from politics. The Congress Socialists, who have so far been sitting on the fence, are now reported to have decided to come into line with other Congressmen.

Apart from the performance of Satyagraha, there was little Congress activity, but a certain number of meetings were held in the villages, generally with the idea of advertising and popularising the Satyagraha movement. The speeches have generally been mild, but a few were objectionable.

Mr Abul Kalam Azad has been in Allahabad and a large meeting attended by 5,000 people, including 2,000 students, was held in his honour in the Purshottamdas Park on December 13. He started by explaining that the Satyagraha would be extended to members of district and mandal Congress Committees and even to four-anna Congress members and said that even non-Congressmen could join if they were selected. There was no bar to anyone performing Satyagraha, but it was essential that discipline must be maintained. The British Government were foolish to think that they could stem the tide that would flow over India, but then they were the blindest ruling race in the world. The Secretary of State had said that the Congress agitation was artificial. They would show him whether it was artificial or not. There was no danger to be apprehended from the blind British Government: the only danger was from themselves, that they would not maintain a peaceful atmosphere. It was entirely wrong to think that this struggle was for freedom of speech the struggle was for independence, without which there could be no freedom of any sort. Not a man or a pie should be given to the war into which the British Government had dragged India for their own selfish Imperialistic ends. A full report on this speech is being sent to the Government of India.

As the result of the Satyagraha movement, Congressmen who are members of the District Rural Development Associations have resigned in many districts as have also many Rural Development Organizers, who were appointed by the Congress Government. These resignations have generally been welcomed by Collectors on the ground that until the Congress element is removed from the Rural Development Department it is impossible to do really effective war work in the villages. One or two honorary magistrates, who are Congressmen, have also resigned.

The Muslims have taken no part in the Satyagraha movement. The attempt by the Congress, to get the Ahrars to support them, mentioned in my last letter is now reported to have succeeded, Mr Abul Kalam Azad having persuaded both the Ahrars and the Jamait-ul-Ulema to join. Advances are also said to have been made to the Khaksars, the offer being that if they join the anti-war movement the Congress will shout for the release of the Allama. Except for a Pakistan delegation, which has visited two or three districts, the Muslim League has shown little activity.

33.   Report on Civil Disobedience Movement in Delhi

Fortnightly Reports, File No. 11/11/40, Home Department, Political Intelligence Section, Government of India, Second Half of November 1940, NAI.

Fortnightly Report for the Second half of November 1940

My dear Conran-Smith,

Civil Disobedience was inaugurated in Delhi on the 29th November by Mr Asaf Ali, MLA (Central), who made an anti-war speech in a meeting in the Queen's Gardens before an audience of some ten thousand. He was arrested next morning. The meeting was under the chairmanship of Maulvi Noor-ud-din Behri, who made an opening speech introducing Mr Asaf Ali. Several well known Congress men were on the platform and garlanded Mr Asaf Ali before he made his speech. Out of these it was decided to arrest Deshbandhu Gupta, MLA (Punjab), Farid-ul-Haq Ansari and Behl Singh Jain for abetting Mr Asaf Ali's offence. Noor-ud-din Behari, Deshbandhu Gupta and Farid-ul-Haq Ansari had been chosen as the next three Satyagrahis in Delhi, and their arrest has dislocated the Congress programme.

In the week preceding the 29th Mr Asaf Ali had addressed a number of Congress meetings in Delhi itself and in the rural area. The meetings in the town were well attended and undoubtedly had some effect in arousing interest in the civil disobedience movement but even so it is fair to say that the public are generally apathetic. Since the arrests were made Congress activity has been negligible.

In sympathy with the Congress, the Ahrars also commenced civil disobedience on the 29th November, a party of five volunteers going out to shout anti-war slogans in the city streets. The volunteers were arrested without fuss. The fact that five volunteers were being sent out had been announced by Khalil-ur-Rahman,

34.   Report on Satyagraha Activities in Orissa

Fortnightly Reports, File No. 11/11/40, Home Department, Political Intelligence Section, Government of India, Second Half of November 1940, NAI.

Political: The main item of Political interest has been preparation for Satyagraha. On the 18th November 1940, the Provincial Congress Committee held a private meeting at Harekrishna Mahtab's house. They decided to draw up a list of persons in the province willing to offer Satyagraha and to individually tour in certain areas in order to obtain the consent of the persons selected. A list of 40 names was sent to Mr Gandhi and was reduced by him to 27, and the name of the Hon'ble Shri Mukund Prasad Das, Speaker, was added at the latter's own request, bringing the total to 28. It is, however, understood that there has been little, if any, real enthusiasm and certainly two out of the three ex-Ministers were most reluctant to give their names. It is fairly obvious that the reason why the list of volunteers was fairly large was that Congress Members of the Legislative Assembly felt that, if they failed to obey the Congress High Command now, their political future might suffer. As a result, Harekrishna Mahatab, Radhakrishna Biswasroy (ex-Parliamentary Secretary), Sarala Devi, Loknath Misra and Dr Kripasindhu Bhokta, Members of the Legislative Assembly, intimated to the District Magistrates concerned that they would offer Satyagraha on the 1st December. District Magistrates have been instructed to try persons of any importance offering Satyagraha themselves, so that the odium which may attach to the trial of such persons shall not fall on Deputy Magistrates and make them apprehend possible victimization in future. Harekrishna Mahatab was sentenced by the District Magistrate, Balasore, to one year's simple imprisonment. He made an anti-war speech by way of Satyagraha which is reported to have fallen very flat and, to his disappointment, he was not arrested then and there, but on his return to the Congress Office. Biswasroy was sentenced to one year's rigorous imprisonment and a fine of Rs 500 and in default a further 2 months rigorous imprisonment, by the District Magistrate, Koraput. Sarala Devi was sentenced by the District Magistrate, Cuttack, to 3 months simple imprisonment and a fine of Rs 100 in default to undergo 4 months' further simple imprisonment. Dr Bhokta was sentenced by the Sub-Divisional Officer, Angul, to 4 months' rigorous imprisonment and Loknath Misra to 6 months rigorous imprisonment by the Sub-Divisional Officer, Kendrapara. Sri Bodhram Dube (ex-Minister) who offered Satyagraha on the 2nd December, was sentenced by the Deputy Commissioner, Sambalpur, to 9 months' simple imprisonment.

35. Delhi Congress Leaders Arrested

Hindustan Times, 1 December 1940.

Mr Asaf Ali, MLA (Central), Member, Congress Working Committee and five other Congress leaders, including Lala Deshbandhu Gupta, MLA (Punjab) were arrested in Delhi on Saturday.

Reports continue to be received of the arrests and convictions of congressmen in the various provinces. Among other Congress leaders arrested yesterday were Dr P.C. Ghosh, a member of the Congress Working Committee for Bengal, Lala Gopichand Bhargava, Leader of the Congress party in the Punjab Assembly, and Mr V.V. Giri, ex Minister, Madras.

Mr Asaf Ali, Member of the Congress Working Committee and first Satyagrahi from Delhi was arrested this morning at his residence at Daryaganj under the Defence of India Rules.

Later in the day five other local Congress leaders, namely, Lala Deshbandhu Gupta, MLA (Punjab), Maulana Noor-ud-Din Bihari, Maulana Khalil-ul-Rahman, dictator, Majlis-i-Ahrar-i-Islami-i-Hind, Mr Faridul Huq Ansari and Mr Bahl Singh were arrested under the Defence of India Rules.

L. Dina Nath, Inspector of CID Police accompanied by Mehta Kartar Singh in charge of the City Kotwali and a sub-Inspector in charge of the Faiz Bazar police station arrived at Mr Asaf Ali's residence at 7 am and told Mr Asaf Ali that he was under arrest. Mr Asaf Ali soon got ready and at 7.35 am he came out and took his seat in the police car. He was taken to the District jail.

A large number of Congressmen including L. Deshbandhu Gupta, Mr Farid-ul-Haq Ansari and L. Omkar Nath and Mrs Asaf Ali and others gave a hearty send-off to Mr Asaf Ali.

Mr Asaf Ali was received at the District jail by Mr E.S. Lewis, Additional District Magistrate and the superintendent of the Jail. The Magistrate granted four days' remand under Section 34 and 38 of the Defence of India Rules.

On the eve of his arrest, Mr Asaf Ali gave the following message: 'In free India alone will Indians realize their destiny. Live to win our country's freedom and make history.'

The police searched the house of Mr Bahl Singh and it is learnt removed a box containing some papers. The office of the local Majlis-i-Ahrar was also searched.

L. Deshbandhu Gutpa, on the eve of his arrest, gave the following message to his countrymen. 'In Mahatmaji we have a tried, trusted and brave general. We should follow him with implicit faith. That is the surest way of winning our objective'.

It is understood that the trial of Mr Asaf Ali will commence on December 4 before Mr A. Isar, who is shortly taking charge as the additional District Magistrate.

The other five leaders namely L. Deshbandhu Gupta, Maulana Noor-ud-Din Bihari, Mr Farid-ul-Huq Ansari, Mr Bahl Singh and Maulana Khalil-ul-Rehman were produced yesterday before Mr E.S. Lewis, Additional District Magistrate in the Delhi District Jail and were remanded for one week under Section 34 and 38 of the Defence of India Rules.

A big public meeting was held in connection with the leaders' arrest. There were loud-speaker arrangements.

Shops in Chandni Chowk and other quarters in Old Delhi remained closed on Saturday as a protest against the arrest of local Congress leaders.

At the request of the Delhi Provincial Congress Committee, Maulana Abul Kalam Azad, the Congress President has nominated the following six persons to the Delhi PCC.

Mrs Asaf Ali, Shrimati Satyavati Seth, Kedarnath Goenka, Mr Prem Jas Bai, Mr Ramcharan Agarwal and Mr Surendra Nath Johar.

Hartal was observed at Narela on the arrests of Mr Asaf Ali and other Congress leaders. A public meeting was also held in the evening.

36. More Satyagrahis Arrested

Statesman, 2 December 1940.

More "Satyagrahis" Arrested—Mr B. Desai and Mrs Naidu in Custody

Mrs Sarojini Naidu and Mr Bhulabhai Desai, both members of the Congress Working Committee and Mr Mangaldas Pakvasa, President Bombay Legislative Council, were arrested early yesterday morning in Bombay under Section 129 of the Defence of India Rules. They have been taken to Yerawada jail.

Mrs Naidu, Mr Desai and Mr Pakvasa had intimated the Commissioner of Police of their intention to offer Satyagraha this evening.

Mr Nagindas Master, Vice-President Bombay Provincial Congress Committee, Mr S.K. Patil, general secretary, and Mr Arjun Khimji, treasurer of the committee were also arrested early yesterday morning under Section 129 of the Defence of India Rules.

Mr Bhulabhai Desai was taken in his own car to Yerawada Central jail. Mr Bhulabhai's son, Mr Dhirajlal Desai, was permitted to accompany his father upto Poona.

New Office-Bearers

The police first went to Mr Mangaldas Pakvasa's residence at Malabar Hill where he was arrested and then moved to Warden Road to Mr Bhulabhai's bungalow. It was about 4.30 in the morning when the Deputy Commissioner of Police called on Mr Bhulabhai and said he had no objection to wait for an hour to enable him to get ready. Mr Bhulabhai said that in that case he would have another nap and went to sleep. He got up, however, in time and was taken to Poona.

Mr S.L. Karandiker, chairman of the Maharashtra Provincial Hindu Mahasabha, was arrested on Saturday night under the Defence of India Rules for a speech alleged to have been delivered by him on November 20.

Mr T.R. Neshur, ex-Parliamentary Secretary, Bombay was arrested on Saturday when he offered Satytgraha at Hannsbhavi (Dharwar district) by shouting anti-war slogans.

Mr Shanker Rao Deo, a member of the Congress Working Committee and Dr (Miss) Tarabai Joglekar offered Satyagraha this evening by delivering anti-war speeches.

The Bombay Provincial Congress Committee at an urgent meeting last evening elected office-bearers to fill the vacancies caused by the arrest of Mr Bhulabhai Desai and others.

Dr D.T. Anklesaria has been elected president, Mr S.R. Silam vice-president and Messrs P.R. Lele and B.N. Maheshwari, general secretaries.

Earlier, the meeting co-opted 11 Congressmen to fill the vacancies caused on the committee by the resignation of three members and the arrest of eight others.

37. Report of Satyagraha in Madras Province

Fortnightly Report for the Second Half of November 1940, D.O. No. P.4–22, Public (General) Department, Government of Madras to Conran Smith, Secretary to the Government of India, Home Department, 2 December 1940, Tamil Nadu State Archives.

Political: The main feature is the commencement of Mr Gandhi's individual satyagraha movement. So far, satyagraha has been effected in Madras City and eight districts. Preparations have been made for the offering of satyagraha in 12 more districts. The actual date prescribed for the Satyagraha to begin varies from district to district. The method adopted has, so far, been either by the writing and delivering of letters to selected persons, usually members of District War Committees, urging them to refrain from assisting British War efforts in any way, or by shouting slogans of a similar nature. The campaign was opened by Dr T.S.S. Rajan ex-Minister for Public Health. He was convicted and sentenced to one year's RI and to pay a fine of Rs 1,000 or in default to undergo six months' further imprisonment. This sentence has been followed with minor variations in the cases of other persons of importance who have so far been convicted. Notable among these are Mrs Lakshmipathy, Deputy Speaker of the Madras Legislative Assembly; Mr T. Prakasam ex-Minister for Revenue; and Mr Gopala Reddi, ex-Minister for Local Administration Department.

In my last report I referred to the agitation amongst students against the communiqué issued by this Government on account of their conduct in connection with Nehru's conviction. Meetings condemning the Government communique have been held in several districts. Affairs in the Annamalai University are of a more serious nature, there, information was received by the Police that a certain number of students were intimately connected with communist activities and with the circulation of communist literature. A party of police went to search the rooms of the students concerned. They asked for help from the University authorities, in conducting the searches, but this given only sparingly and not before much valuable time had been wasted in discussion. The Police then tried to make the searches without the full co-operation of the authorities. The delay, however, had given the students time to hear of what was afoot. Parties of students assembled and their attitude was so definitely hostile that the police withdrew without achieving their object in order to avoid any risk of a riot. Government have made careful enquiries into what happened and steps are being taken to deal with the leading members of the Communist 'cell' in the University under the Defence of India Rules.

There are signs that, in some parts, particularly in Madras City, a number of people gathered from the irresponsible and unemployed classes are preparing to offer satyagraha without specific orders from Mr Gandhi or any other leader. Government are trying to deal with this situation without gratifying the desire of these nonentities to appear as heroes or martyrs.

Defence of India Rules: Prosecutions under the Defence of India Act have occurred in Madras City and in following districts.—Anantapur, S. Arcot, Chittoor, Coimbatore, East Godavari and West Godavari, Chingleput, Kurnool, Madura, Malabar, Nellore, Ramnad, Salem, Tanjore, Trichinopoly, Tinnevelly and Vizagpatam.

38.   Report on C. Rajagopalachari's Arrest

Indian Express, 4 December 1940.

Mr C. Rajagopalachari has been arrested and sentenced to one year's imprisonment. An event so moving and also so challenging in the implications has not happened in South India since the assumption of India by the Crown for we see the role of South India's first Prime Minister being changed into the status of a Prisoner. About a year ago he was in charge of the police in the Presidency under whose custody he now lives. We ask the Government to reflect on the circumstance that it is a man of such antecedents who brought credit to the administration, who nonetheless appears preferring jail to the freedom outside. Mr Rajagopalachari may be in office as Prime Minister or in the wilderness as publicist or in the jail as a prisoner but no one will question the sincerity of his political faith and the wealth of his contributions to the reawakening of the province. To the last he strove for the construction of a National Government at the centre with joint representations for all parties and communities. He even offered to pledge the readiness of the Congress to function in subordination to the nominee of the Muslim League as Prime Minister provided the British Government would permit the course and declare their willingness to part with power. The response was a strident negative and all we hear is Mr Amery's notorious 'No' supplemented with tedious repetitions about the bait of manufacturing fresh portfolios on the Viceroy's Executive Council for the benefit of aspirants. When the present chapter of conflict is fatefully recorded in the history of our own times, we shall find C.R. standing out as a passionate intercessor for peace; tireless in his quest for the creation of a spirit of partnership in the war for freedom, which Government must not forget, requires harmony in the country for its efficient prosecution. Truly he fills the part of the happy warrior. We ask Englishmen to reflect on the reasons for the present topsy turvy conditions. Mr Rajagopalachari played his part with distinctions and zeal and as he passes into durance, all will wish him health and pray for the restoration of reason in the present acrimonious situations, so that before long he may again be enabled to promote the aim of a National

Cabinet, which alone would serve the interests of all classes and bring the deadlock to an end. As was stated in Parliament the present situation in India is an offence against reason and commonsense.

Mr P.M. Audikesavalu Naicker, MLA, member of the Corporation of Madras and President of the Mahajana Sabha was arrested this morning for offering Satyagraha in front of Sir Thyagarayachetti Park, Washermanpet and sentenced to undergo a term of 6 months' RI under the Defence of India Rules.

The Office of the Madras Mahajana Sabha, the Free Reading Room and Hindi classes are closed to day on account of the incarceration of Mr Naieker, President of the Sabha.

Salem: The Sub-Inspector of Police, Yercaud arrested Mr Jagannathan, a Merchant on the charge of having delivered four letters to the residents of Yercaud who are members of the District War Committee.

Vellore: Mr C. Perumalswami Reddi, MLC, President of the N. Arcot District Board, offered Satyagraha by pasting letters was arrested and later was produced before Sub-Divisional Magistrate and was sentenced to undergo 9 months RI.

Tindivanam: Mr K. Kulasekara Dass MLA (Harijan) offered Satyagraha today at about 9 AM near the Gandhi Chowk by shouting anti-war slogans in the presence of the large gathering. He was arrested by Dy. Superintendent of Police and was produced before the Joint Magistrate, Tindivanam who sentenced him to one year's RI under section 38 (1), 38 (5) of the Defence of India Rules.

Salem: Messrs K. Ramaswami Reddiar, S.P. Arjunan, A. Kannuswami and R. Chellam were arrested yesterday at Omalur on the charge of having delivered anti-war speeches.

Mr K. Venkataswami Naidu, Deputy President of the Madras Legislative Council, Ex. Mayor of Madras, Leader of the Congress Municipal Party and member of the AICC was arrested this morning under the Defence of India Rules for offering Satyagraha in Bashyan Naidu Park, Kilpauk. He was sentenced by the Chief Presidency Magistrate to 6 months' S.O. Appah and Company as also some other chemists and druggists' shops remained closed today.

Sankaridrug—Mrs Radhabai Subbarayan MLA (Central), Zamindarini of Kumaramangalam offered Satyagraha in her Zamin Village by distributing anti-war pamphlets and was arrested by the Triuchengode Police today.

Dr P. Subbarayan Zamindar, of Kumaramangalam, Minister for Law and President of the Board of Control for Cricket offered Satyagraha in Tiruchengode this afternoon by distributing anti-war pamphlets and was arrested by the police.

Both Dr and Mrs Subbarayan were sentenced to 6 months' RI each.

Vellore: Mr S.S. Srinivasa Rao, Member AICC, offered Satyagraha at Arni Bazaar this morning by shouting anti-war slogans. He was arrested and sentenced to, under RI, for 9 months and to pay a fine of Rs 200.

Salem: Mr M.G. Natesa Chettiar, MLA (Zamindar) and former President of the Dharmapuri District Board who offered Satyagraha by making an anti-war speech was arrested under the Defence of India Rules.

Mannargudi: Mr K. Santhanam, MLA (Central) offered Satyagraha today and was arrested. He was sentenced by Sub-District Magistrate to one year's RI.

Mr V.G. Munuswami Pillai, ex-Congress (Harijan) Minister of this Province, was arrested this morning while offering Satyagraha opposite Blackie's Garden, the new home of the Tamil Nad Congress Committee in Teynampet. He was sentenced to undergo 7 months' RI.

Mr M. Natarajan, Member of the Madras Congress Socialist Party, has been arrested under Rule 38 of the Defence of India Rules. 1-12-40.

Mr T.S. Avanashilingam Chettiar, MLA (Central) and Mr C.P. Subbiah, MLA (Madras) were arrested by Inspector when they offered Satyagraha by shouting anti-war slogans. 12-12-40.

Tenkasi: T.S. Chockalingama, MLA was arrested this morning under the Defence of India Rules for offering Satyagraha by shouting anti-war slogans on the Lajpat Rai Maidan. He was sentenced to 9 months' RI and a fine of Rs 3000. 12-12-40.

Chidambaram: About 30 students were injured in a lathi charge made this morning, when a large number of schools from the Annamalai University made demonstrations as protest against the arrest of six of their comrades under the Defence of India Rules, 8 students including a lady were taken to Vellore Jail. Sensation in the University.

Madras: Mr S. Satyamurthi, MLA (Central) and Ex. Mayer of Madras offered Satyagraha on 13th by making an anti-war speech at the maidan adjoining his residence in T. Nagar. He was arrested and sentenced to 9 months' RI by the Chief Presidency Magistrate.

Rajapalayam: Mr P.S. Kumaraswami Raja, MLA, member of the AICC, who was arrested at Rajapalayam, was sentenced to 9 months' RI and to pay a fine of Rs 300 by the joint Magistrate.

Coimbatore: Mr V.C. Palaniswamy Gounder, MLA, was arrested and produced before SDM was sentenced to 6 months' RI and a fine of Rs 500. 16-12-1940.

Madurai: Mr A.K.A. Ramachandra Reddy, MLA offered Satyagraha at his village Azathapatty and was immediately arrested. He was sentenced to 6 months' RI and a fine of Rs 300 on two counts.

Tuticorin: Mr A.R.A.S. Doraisamy Nadar, MLA was arrested today for shouting anti-war slogans in front of the Town Congress Committee office. He was sentenced to 9 month's RI and a fine of Rs 300. Shops were closed.

Madras: Mr Gadde Rangiah Naidu, 72 years old member of the Madras Legislative Assembly and the Nestor of the Council of the Corporation of Madras was arrested and taken to the Madras Penitentiary. 17-12-40.

Villupuram: Mr S. Chidambaram Ayyar, MLA Municipal Chairman was arrested this afternoon at his residence. He was sentenced to 6 months' RI.

Tanjore: Mr V. Nadimuthu Pillai, President, Tanjore District Board offered Satyagraha at Tilak Maidan making anti-war speech. He was arrested and taken to Sub-jail for trial.

Salem: Mr K.A. Nachiappa Gounder, MLA President, Salem District Board was sentenced to six months' RI under the Defence of India Rules.

Mr S.K. Satagopa Mudaliar, MLC was sentenced under the Defence of India Rules by the Salem Sub-Divisional Magistrate to 6 months' RI.

Mr P.T. Venkatachari, MLA, Krishnagiri offered Satyagraha by distributing pamphlets and was arrested. 20-12-40.

Mr Kamraj Nadar, President, TNCC who left yesterday morning by Grand Trunk Express for Wardha was arrested at Gudur. He was proceeding to Wardha to submit a list of 1,000 Satyagrahis for approval. The police seized from him the list of Satyagrahis.

Madura: Despite of ill health Mrs Lakshmi Bharathi, MLA, wife of L. Krishnaswami Bharathi offered Satyagraha by reading and distributing anti-war pamphlets at Tirupparankundrum. She was immediately arrested under Defence of India Rules. She was sentenced to 6 months' RI each on two counts.

Ambasamudram: Mrs Lakshmi Sankara Iyer, MLA offered Satyagraha at Kalidaikurichi. She was arrested and later sentenced to undergo simple imprisonment for 6 months.

Mr Mohan Kumaramangalam, son of Dr Subbrayan, was arrested this morning in Madanam village in the outskirts of the city. Along with him three others were arrested. He was wanted by the City Police under Rule 26 of the Defence of India Rules. 6-1-1941.

Madras: Mrs Rajam Raghuraja Bharathi, member of the Madras DCC, was arrested under Defence of India Rules for offering Satyagraha by shouting anti-war slogan and sentenced to 3 months' RI and a fine of Rs 250 or a further RI for three months. 7-1-1941.

Pattukotai: Mr S.K. Chidambaram Chettiar, Ex-President DCC, offered Satyagraha. He was arrested and sentenced to 3 months' RI.

Trichinopoly: Mr R. Maruthi, MLA and Mr Manickka Pathar were sentenced to one year RI each for offering Satyagraha. Srimathi Rajamani Devi was sentenced to 4 months' RI.

Madras: Mr Mohanlal M. Metha, Vice President of the Gujarathi Mandal was arrested for offering Satyagraha by shouting anti-war slogans. The Chief Presidency Magistrate sentenced him for 3 months' RI and a fine of Rs 250, in default further 3 months.

Srimathi N.S. Rukmini shouted anti-war slogans and she was arrested by the Flower Bazar Police. The Magistrate convicted and sentenced her to three months' S.I. and a fine of Rs 250. 8-1-1940.

Madras: Srimathi Balammal, daughter of Mr M.S. Subramania Iyer offered Satyagraha this morning at the Congress House. The Chief Presidency Magistrate sentenced her to undergo S.I. for 3 months and pay a fine of Rs 260.

Tanjore: Mr S.A. Sambasive Pillai who offered Satyagraha by shouting anti-war slogans was arrested and remanded into custody.

Trichinopoly: Mr V. Jayaraman, Mirasadar, Valadi, who offered Satyagraha, this morning, was arrested and sentenced to one year RI and a fine of Rs 200.

Coimbatore: Mr I.V. Kanati Naidu, Treasurer of the Coimbatore Taluk Satyagraha Committee, who offered Satyagraha was arrested and sentenced to 6 months' RI.

Tanjore: Mrs Sarathambal who offered Satyagraha yesterday was arrested and remanded to custody. She is the wife of Mr T.N. Sivanandam.

39. Report on Satyagrahis' Arrests

Statesman, 4 December 1940.

Mr C. Rajagopalachari, ex-Premier of Madras was arrested yesterday morning at his residence in Mambalam.

He was later convicted by the Chief Presidency Magistrate, Madras on a charge of having issued a prejudicial report within the meaning of Rule 34 (7) read with 34(6)E and K, Defence of India Rule punishable under Rule 38(5) read with 38 (1) and C and sentenced to one year's simple imprisonment. He was placed in 'A' class.

Asked by the court Mr Rajagopalachari made the following statement. 'The British Government has dragged India into the war without asking her legislature. All other parts of the British commonwealth with much smaller populations and better prepared for defence were allowed the choice of remaining neutral irrespective of the causes and motives of the war. I have as the Premier, left the Legislative Assembly of the Province which in October 1939 passed by an overwhelming majority of 153 against 22 a resolution claiming the right of India to be neutral media and therefore claiming the right to make such an appeal as I have now made and for which I am undergoing trial at the instance of the present administration in tendering Satyagraha. I am not fulfilling my moral responsibility as the leader of the Assembly whose unequivocal verdict has been ignored.

'I feel it is my duty to claim on behalf of every citizen that it is not only moral by right but perfectly lawful to make the appeal that has been made either in the form of the slogans that have been uttered in some cases or in the form of letters in others as long as the war effort in India is claimed to be on a voluntary basis. Otherwise the voluntary character claimed would be a mere deception. I admit all the facts alleged in the charge.'

Mr Rajagopalachari was taken to Vellore jail in the afternoon by the Bangalore Express.

Mr K.M. Munshi, ex-Home Minister, Bombay and Mr Yasin Nurie, ex-Public Works Minister have announced that they will offer Satyagraha this evening in Bombay.

Mr B.G. Kher ex-Premier of Bombay, has been removed from Thana to the Yeravada jail.

Seth Govinddas has been sentenced at Jubbulpore to one year's rigorous imprisonment and Rs 500 fine and placed in 'A' class. He pleaded guilty and filed a written statement justifying Congress policy.

Lahore Incident

Sardar Sampuran Singh, leader of the Congress Party in the Punjab Assembly offered Satyagraha last evening by shouting anti-war slogans. He was arrested and removed to the Central Jail.

While he was being taken by the police to the jail a crowd which consisted mostly of students, followed raising slogans. Some of them are also alleged to have thrown brickbats at the police as a result of which a few policemen sustained injuries. A brickbat also hit Mr Tylar, Deputy Superintendent of Police, the Police thereupon made a lathi charge and dispersed the crowd.

Mian Iftikhar-ud-Din MLA President of the Punjab Congress Committee, was sentenced yesterday to one year's rigorous imprisonment and Rs 6,000 fine under Rule 38(5) of the Defence of India Rules by the additional District Magistrate. He was placed in 'A' class.

Mr Anugraha Narayan Singh, ex-Finance Minister, Bihar was arrested yesterday afternoon at his residence under section 29 of the Defence of India Rule. He has been lodged in the Bankipore jail.

Mr Biswanath Das, ex-Premier of Orissa, as it is understood, intimated to the District Magistrate of Cuttack his intention to offer Satyagraha today in Cuttack.

Mr Sampurnanand former Minister of Education, UP was yesterday sentenced to 18 months' simple imprisonment under section 38 of the Defence of India Rules and was recommended to be placed in 'A' class.

40.   Political Leaders Arrested

Hindustan Times, 5 December 1940.

Mr Biswanath Das, ex-Premier of Orissa the Hon. M.B. Sambamurti, Speaker of the Madras Legislative Assembly, Mr K.M. Munshi, former Home Minister of Bombay, and Miss Khurshed Ben were among the prominent leaders arrested on Wednesday.

The police have attached two cars belonging to Mian Iiftikhar-ud-Din, President of the Punjab PCC who was fined Rs 6,000 besides being sentenced to imprisonment. He has been ordered to pay the fine within a fortnight, failing which the cars will be auctioned.

Mrs Vijayalakshmi Pandit has intimated to the authorities her intention to offer Satyagraha today at Chaubeypur, Bilhour tehsil, in Cawnpore district.

Mr K.M. Munshi, ex-Home Minister of Bombay, was arrested at his residence early this morning.

Mr Munshi had informed the Commissioner of Police yesterday of his intention to offer Satyagraha this evening at Congress House.

Mr S.G. Songaonkar, a member of the Bombay Legislative Assembly, was arrested this morning under the Defence of India Act.

Mr Dinkarrao N. Desai, a member of the Bombay Legislative Assembly and the third Satyagrahi from Broach was arrested at 3.30 am this morning under the Defence of India Rule.

He had intimated to the District Magistrate yesterday his intention to offer Satyagraha at 5 pm today.

He has been taken to the Sabarmati Jail by the Delhi Express.

Miss Joglekar Released

Dr Miss Tarabai Joglekar, who was sentenced by the Additional District Magistrate, Poona, to pay a fine of Rs 200, in default three months' simple imprisonment for offering Satyagraha by delivering an anti-war speech on December 1 in Poona was released last evening, her fine having been paid by an unknown person.

Mr Shantilal Shah, member of the Bombay Legislative Council and Secretary of the Congress Legislative Party was sentenced on Wednesday under the Defence of India Act to nine month's rigorous imprisonment and Rs 25 fine, in default to further one months' simple imprisonment, for writing anti-war letters to members of the Bombay Suburban War Committee.

Mr Raghunathrao Bhaurao Patil, President of the East Khandesh District Board, offered Satyagraha yesterday night by addressing a public meeting at his village Shendurni. He was immediately arrested and brought to Jalgaon. He was convicted this afternoon under the Defence of India Act by the Jalgaon City Magistrate and sentenced to six months' rigorous imprisonment.

41. Report on the Commencement of Individual Satyagraha by Mr V.J. Patel and Related Activities

Fortnightly Reports, File No. 11/11/40, Home Department, Political Intelligence Section, Government of Bombay, No. SD 4367, 5 December 1940, NAI.

Political: Public attention during the fortnight was focused chiefly on the Satyagraha movement. Individual civil disobedience was started in this province by Mr V.J. Patel, who, it is reported, prior to his arrest appealed to the Ahmedabad magnates, Ambalal Sarabhai and Kasturbhai Lalbhai, and the leading representatives of the Textiles Association and the Cloth Merchants Association in that city, to sink their differences and to support the fight for independence. It is understood that they pledged him their support. Patel informed the District Magistrate, Ahmedabad, of his intention to start Satyagraha on November 18th. He was however arrested on the preceding night under rule 129 and detained under rule 26 of the Defence of India Rules. There was no great excitement over the arrest, but it was followed by the closure of mills and markets in Ahmedabad City. In Bombay City no business was transacted on the 18th in the stock exchange and wholesale and forward markets. The Ahmedabad and Bombay

Municipal Corporations also adjourned without transacting any business. The meeting which Mr Patel was to have addressed at Ahmedabad on the 18th was addressed instead by the ex-Minister Mr Morarji Desai. There was an attendance of about 25,000 persons, but little enthusiasm and no demonstrations. The speech was confined to the coming municipal elections and the need for implicit obedience to Gandhi's instructions. Twelve more Satyagrahis, including Messrs B.G. Kher and Morarji Desai, ex-premier and ex-Minister respectively, the Honourable Mr G.V. Mavlankar, the Speaker of the Bombay Legislative Assembly were arrested under rule 129 after they had intimated their intention of offer Satyagraha and were later detained under rule 26 of the Defence of India Rules. On the arrests of Messrs Kher and Desai forward business in stocks and shares, cotton, seeds and grain was suspended in Bombay City and the Bombay Municipal Corporation adjourned without transacting business. Thirty-six other Satyagrahis including an ex-Minister Mr L.M. Patil and eight other members of the Legislative Assembly, were convicted under rule 38(5) of the Defence of India Rule for shouting anti-war slogans or making speeches and varying terms of imprisonment, details of which are given in Appendix III. It is learnt that Mr Gandhi has expressed a desire that women should join the movement in as large a number as possible, and, in fact, there were as many as 15 women among the 36 persons convicted. The arrest of one of the Satyagrahis, Dr Abdul Hamid Kazi, was made at a meeting addressed by him at Jalgaon, which was attended by 400 persons. After the arrest the crowd swelled to 4000, became restive, and abused and stoned the police, injuring one inspector and one constable. The Bombay Municipality adjourned again on the 25th on account of the arrest of Pandit Govind Vallabh Pant and the conviction of Mr L.M. Patil.

Mr S.L. Karandikar, MLA and President of the Maharashtra Provincial Hindu Maha Sabha, delivered a rabid and unbalanced antiwar speech in Poona after intimating to the District Magistrate his intention to do so. He advocated non-cooperation in the conduct of the war and prayed for the success of Hitler and the down-fall and harassment of the British. He informed the District Magistrate that his action did not represent any change in the policy of the Hindu Mahasabha and that it was an individual protest on his part against the failure of His Excellency the Viceroy to expand his cabinet. There is good reason to believe that his outburst was as unexpected by leaders of the Sabha as it was by Government. Government has ordered his prosecution.

At a private meeting of 125 Satyagrahis held at Bombay on November 18th, those who depended on the Congress for the maintenance of their families or who had other household difficulties were asked to withdraw their pledge. It was made clear to prospective Satyagrahis that it was their primary duty to carry out the constructive programme of the Congress when not yet in jail, that they should not clamour for special treatment when in jail, and that they should assist in the collection and dissemination of Congress news if publication of reports connected with the Satyagraha movement were prevented by Government. It is reported that 16 Congress leaders met at Dharwar on November 24th and decided to form a committee with the idea of raising funds to the extent of Rs 10,000 for the support of the families of active Satyagrahis who were going to jail. Addressing an audience of 2,000 persons at Bombay on November 24th on the occasion of the monthly flag salutation ceremony of the Bombay Provincial Congress Committee, Mr B.J. Desai stated that 'Representative Satyagraha' would be launched in Bombay City shortly. Later, it was announced that it would begin on December 2nd and that Mr B.J. Desai, Mrs Sarojini Naidu and the Honourable Mr M.M. Pakvasa had been selected to make anti-war speeches on that day, but these and four others, who were scheduled to make anti-war speeches on the 4th of December and who had intimated their intention to do so, were arrested under rule 129 of the Defence of India Rules on December 1st and detained pending further orders. Another report has it that Mr Jamnalal Bajaj informed a selected number of Congress workers at Ahmedabad that Mr Gandhi contemplated selecting some 1,500 persons for jail in the first instance and would follow them up by another band of 2,000 Satyagrahis. The time would then be ripe for his arrest and a fast upto death. On the whole there has been relatively little public reaction to the movement although the arrests undoubtedly engender a certain amount of sympathy. It is clear also that the Congress leaders are anxious at this stage, at least, not to let outbreaks of violence or rowdiness torpedo the movement. The speeches too, and the slogans shouted have, in general, followed the lines of moderation laid down by Mr Gandhi. The Congress Socialists are, of course, siding with the Congress, and their leaders, Y.J. Meherally and Ashoka Mehta, are ready to offer Satyagraha when called upon.

42. Gradual Extension of Congress Movement—Speech by Maulana Abul Kalam Azad

Hindustan Times, 9 December 1940.

Mrs Uma Nehru Taken into Custody—First list of Punjab Satyagrahis exhausted

How the present Congress movement would extend stage by stage to the members of the district Congress Committees and village committees was outlined by the Congress President. Maulana Abul Kalam Azad, at a largely-attended public meeting here this afternoon.

Maulana Azad said that the members of the provincial, district, thana and village Congress Committees would follow and after that those who offered themselves would be allowed to court imprisonment under the conditions of the Congress.

The Maulana also said that if India had tried to take advantage of Britain's difficulties, it would have been justified but the Congress had not chosen that method.

Surveying the course of events since the outbreak of the war, the Maulana said that the Congress had gone to the furthest limit by the Poona resolution, but unfortunately every gesture of its goodwill was rejected by the Government. That was the reason why the Congress was forced to take up the present attitude.

He observed that Britishers should have no cause for complaint against the Congress as the present position in which the Government was placed had been precipitated by the bad diplomacy of British statesmen. The Congress, as a national organization could not afford to remain passive any longer. It had a certain duty to perform at this particular juncture and it was following the only course left to it.

In conclusion the Maulana stressed the need for discipline and observed that the Congress mode of fight was not marked by diplomatic cunning. Its foundation was goodwill and honesty and it would continue to preserve those moral qualities.

Maulana Abul Kalam Azad, the Congress President, met members of the Bihar Provincial Congress Committee and Congress workers on Sunday afternoon when, it is understood, the Congress President explained the present plan of action of the Congress and the manner in which members should conduct the movement in their respective areas.

The meeting was not open to the Press.

Maulana Abul Kalam Azad arrived here this morning from Calcutta. He was accorded an official reception by the Provincial Congress Committee at the Patna Junction railway station where a large number of people including Provincial Congress leaders, were present. The Maulana was garlanded and cheered as he came down from the compartment. He drove to Dr Sachchidananda Sinha's residence where he will stay for the day.

Maulana Azad is leaving for Allahabad on Monday evening.

UP Arrests
More Congress MLAs Taken into Custody

A report from Farrukhabad states that Mrs Uma Nehru, MLA (UP) who was going to Farrukhabad from Cawnpore to offer Satyagraha there was arrested at Fatehgarh station under Rule 38 (5) of the Defence of India Rule read with Section 121.

Arrests of the following members of the UP Legislature have been reported today.

Mr Hukum Singh, ex-Parliamentary Secretary, UP Kunwar Bhagwan Singh, MLA (Pilhibit) and Mr Lotan Ram, MLA (Orai).

Mr Hargobind Singh, a member of the AICC, has also been arrested at Patti Narendrapur in the Jaunpur district.

A report from Fyizabad says that the judgement in the case against Mrs Sucheta Kripalani will be delivered tomorrow. Mrs Kripalani did not defend herself but read out a statement.

Dr Hussain Zaheer, Reader in Chemistry, Lucknow University, who was proceeding to village Bharose, about fifteen miles from Lucknow, to offer Satyagraha, was arrested near Saadatgunj at about noon by the Lucknow Police under Section 38(1) (A) read with Section 121 of the Defence of India Rules and taken to the District Jail.

It is understood that Pandit Pearey Lal Sharma, MLA (Central) will address the Meerut citizens on December 10 in the Town Hall grounds on 'Satyagraha—its importance and significance in the nation's struggle for freedom'. Mr Sharma is likely to offer Satyagraha in this week from some suburb of the seven cities which he represents in the Central Assembly.

First List Exhausted—Satyagrahis Arrests in the Punjab

Three Congress members of the Punjab Assembly and one of the Central Assembly were arrested in the Punjab on Sunday.

Sardar Mangal Singh, MLA (Central), who had announced his intention to offer Satyagraha at Rajpur in the Ludhiana district was arrested at Ludhiana under Rule 129 of the Defence of India Rules.

Chaudhri Krishen Gopal Dutt, Deputy Leader of the Congress Party in the Punjab Assembly, was arrested under Rule 38 of the Defence of India Rules at the village of Shahzada in the Sialkot district where he addressed a public meeting. Sardar Kapoor Singh, MLA (Punjab), and Bibi Raghbir Kaur, MLA (Punjab) were similarly arrested in the Ludhiana and Amritsar districts respectively.

No further Satyagraha will be offered in the Punjab pending receipt of fresh instructions from Mahatma Gandhi. The first list of Punjab Satyagrahis approved by Mahatma Gandhi was exhausted today, while the second list submitted to him is still under consideration.

The Punjab Congress Committee has received the following telegram from Mahatma Gandhi,

'Names in Iftikhar-ud-Din's letter to Mahadev Desai of November 28 are under consideration. Therefore none should offer Satyagraha until my approval.'

The Secretary of the Punjab Congress has telegraphically informed the Satyagrahis concerned that they should wait for further instructions pending which no Satyagraha should be offered.

Sardar Sampuran Singh

Sardar Sampuran Singh, Leader of the Opposition in the Punjab Assembly, it is understood, has been asked by the Congress President not to offer Satyagraha again unless he receives further instruction from the Congress President.

It is learnt that the Congress President has asked for further details of Sardar Sampuran Singh's trial and other connected matters from the Punjab after which he is likely to issue a statement.

Mr Satindernath Vidyarthi, Secretary of the Abohar Congress Committee has been arrested under Rule 38 of the Defence of India Rules on a charge of delivering an objectionable speech.

43. One Year for Ahrar Leader: Volunteers Get 6 Months Each

Hindustan Times, 11 December 1940.

One year for Ahrar Leader—Volunteers Get 6 Months, Each

Mr A. Isar, Additional District Magistrate, convicted yesterday Maulana Khalil-ul-Rehman, Dictator of the All India Majlis-i-Ahrar, and five Ahrar volunteers under Rules 34 and 38 read with Rules 121 of the Defence of India Rules and sentenced Maulana Khalil-ul-Rehman to one year's rigorous imprisonment and the remaining five Ahrar volunteers to six months' rigorous imprisonment each. Maulana Khalil-ul-Rehman was placed in 'B' class.

The judgement was delivered yesterday morning at the Delhi District Jail.

Maulana Khalil-ul-Rehman was arrested on November 30 for addressing a meeting in Jama Masjid and making an announcement to the effect that five Ahrars would march through the streets shouting anti-war slogans. The other five volunteers were taken into custody while they were raising anti-war slogans in front of the City Kotwali at Chandni Chowk.

While delivering judgement, the Magistrate observed: 'The case is simple. On November 29 after Friday prayers, a public meeting of the Ahrars was held in Jama Masjid which was presided over by the accused, Maulana Khalil-ul-Rehman. The Maulana delivered a speech in which he stated that as early as September 11, 1939, the Majlis-i-Ahrar had decided to launch civil disobedience on the lines of the present Satyagraha movement of the Congress and although at that time all the political bodies in India had called this premature, he was happy to find now that the Congress had at last decided on the same course. He then announced to the audience that five Ahrar volunteers would march through the streets of Delhi and raise anti-war slogans. The Maulana in his speech mentioned what these slogans would be and he further announced that this movement would now spread throughout India. The five accused were then introduced and garlanded. They were arrested as they were marching in Chandni Chowk. They admitted what was alleged by the prosecution and pleaded guilty as stated above.'

Regarding the punishment, the Magistrate remarked: 'Anything coming from the lips of a man of the position of Maulana Khalil-ul-Rehman and anything done by him in his position as Dictator of the All India Majlis-e-Ahrar would be of greater consequence than the saying and doings of volunteers of the position of the remaining accused. The leaders in these matters have greater responsibility and when, unfortunately, their acts contravene the law, their liability to punishment is also greater. The abettor in such cases does more harm than those who are pushed forward to commit the actual offence. I, therefore, sentence Maulana Khalil-ul-Rehman to one year's rigorous imprisonment and the remaining accused to six months' rigorous imprisonment each.

'I recommend that Maulana Khalil-ul-Rehman be placed in "B" class. The others are men of no position at all and will remain in "C" class.'

Home Internment—Order on Released Congress Workers

Of the 16 persons sentenced to six months' simple imprisonment for holding a Congress workers' conference without the necessary permission in March last, five persons namely Benoy Bose, Prasanta Sen, Susil Sarkar, Nepal Nag and Prafulla Chakraborty were released at noon today from the Local jail on the expiry of their full term of imprisonment.

When they came out of jail all were served with an order under the Defence of India Rules, restricting their movements for a period of six months within the limits of their respective homes. They were directed to report daily at the Thana.

Others are expected to be released in the course of the day.

44.   More Ex-Ministers Arrested

Hindustan Times, 11 December 1940.

More ex-Ministers Arrested—Mr Munuswami Pillai and Dr Gilder, Gandhiji's Secretary, offer Satyagraha—Mrs Lilavati Munshi taken into Custody.

Mr Pyarelal, Mahatma Gandhi's Secretary, left the Satyagraha Ashram this morning to offer Satyagraha in Wardha. Mrs Gandhi and Mr Mahadev Desai accompanied Mr Pyarelal as far as the Mahila Ashram Wardha.

Near the Wardha level-crossing, Mr Pyarelal explained to certain Government officials whom he met what he was going to say.

Walking through the town, Mr Pyarelal exhorted people in Tilak Chowk and the cloth market to work for Hindu-Muslim unity, removal of untouchability and uplift of village life.

By 10 a.m. Mr Pyarelal had passed beyond Wardha Limits.

Mr Pyarelal offered Satyagraha this evening by shouting anti-war slogans in the village of Anji, ten miles from Wardha. Earlier in the day, Mr Pyarelal, it is learnt, addressed a meeting of villagers in Elikeli, five miles from here and another meeting at Sukli.

Mr Ganeshrao Deshmukh, MLA (CP) was convicted and sentenced to six months' rigorous imprisonment and a fine of Rs 50, in default further two months' rigorous imprisonment by the sub-divisional Magistrate, Amraoti under the Defence of India Rules for shouting anti-war slogans on Monday at Badhera, six miles from Amraoti. The Magistrate recommended 'B' class for Mr Deshmukh.

Mr Bhikulal Chandrak, MLA, who offered Satyagraha at Paradshinga in Nagpur district has been sentenced to six months' rigorous imprisonment.

Mr Sampatrao Bhopale, President of the Akot Taluka Congress who offered Satyagraha on Monday evening at Hiwkahed in Akot Taluka was arrested under the Defence of India rules.

Bombay—More Arrests—Dr Gilder and Mrs Lilavati Munshi

Dr M.D. Gilder, formerly Minister for Excise and Public Health, Bombay, Mrs Lilavati Munshi, MLA and Mr Jinabhai P. Joshi, also a member of the Bombay Assembly, were arrested at about 5 on Tuesday morning at their respective residences under the Defence of India Act.

All the three had previously given intimation to the Commissioner of Police that they would offer Satyagraha.

The Bombay Municipal Corporation adjourned on Tuesday evening without transacting any business. The adjournment motion was moved by Mr Mohamedohai Rowje and was seconded by Mr Salebhoy Abdul Kader. The adjournment, it is presumed, was due to the arrest of Mrs Lilavati Munshi, Chairman of the Municipal Standing Committee. Dr M.D. Gilder (ex-Minister) and Mr Jinabhai P. Joshi.

It is learnt that Dr Gilder and Mrs Munshi who were arrested this morning have been taken to Yeravda Jail and Mr Jinabhai to Nasik.

Mr B.S. Hire, MLA (Bombay), former Parliamentary Secretary, was convicted today under the Defence of India Rules and sentenced to one year's simple imprisonment. He was recommended 'B' Class.

Mr P.S. Hosmani, member of the AICC from Karnatak, who was arrested on Monday for shouting anti-war slogans was sentenced today by the Sub-Divisional Magistrate to one year's simple imprisonment. He was placed in 'B' class and was taken to the Belgaum Central Prison.

Dr R. Naigan Gauda, President of the Karnatak Congress, was sentenced to one year's simple imprisonment and a fine of Rs 600 or in default three months' more for shouting anti-war slogans.

Dr Miss Tarabai Jogleker who was convicted and sentenced by the Additional District Magistrate, Poona to pay a fine of Rs 200, in default to undergo three months' simple imprisonment and who was subsequently released on payment of her fine by an unknown person will again offer Satyagraha on December 12 at 4 p.m. at Hadaspur, five miles from Poona, and it is understood, she has already informed the District Magistrate, Poona of her intention.

Dr Champaklal J. Ghia, MLA (Bombay) was sentenced on Tuesday to nine month's simple imprisonment for offering Satyagraha by shouting anti-war slogans. He was placed in 'B' class.

UP—MLAs' Arrests—One Year's Sentence on Mrs Uma Nehru

Mr Shivram Vaidya, MLA, offered Satyagraha at Nimsar in the district of Sitapur, on Saturday last and was immediately arrested by the Circle Inspector. He was taken to Sitapur Jail where he was tried on Monday under Rule 34 (6) (D) (K) read with Rule 38 of the Defence of India Rules and sentenced to one year's imprisonment and a fine of Rs 50 or in default six months' further imprisonment. He has been placed in 'B' Class.

Mrs Uma Nehru who was arrested under the Defence of India Rules, was sentenced to one year's simple imprisonment on Monday by the Fatehgarh Magistrate.

Pandit Lakshmi Shanker Bajpai, MLA, inaugurated the Satyagraha movement in the Rae Barelli district on December 8 at Lalgunj and was arrested.

Mrs Sucheta Kripalani was sentenced today under the Defence of India Rules to one year's simple imprisonment and a fine of Rs 100 or in default two months' further imprisonment says a report from Fyzabad where Mrs Kripalani was tried.

Pandit Dashrath Prasad Dwivedi, member of the AICC and Vice-member [President] of the Gorakhpur District Congress Committee, who was arrested at his residence on December 2 before offering Satyagraha, was sentenced today to one year's rigorous imprisonment under Rule 38(5) read with Section 121 of the Defence of India Rules by Mr Srinivas, a First Class Magistrate and was recommended to be placed in 'B' class.

Dr Sheokaran Lal, convener of the Gorakhpur Satyagraha Committee was also sentenced to one year's rigorous imprisonment by Mr Srinivas under Section 38(5) of the Defence of India Rules for having made three alleged prejudicial speeches in tahsil Sadar and has been placed in 'B' class.

According to information reaching Almora the sentence of two year's rigorous imprisonment and a fine of Rs 100 passed on Mr Krishna Chandra Joshi a practising lawyer of Lohaghat district, Almora, under the Defence of India Rules for delivering an alleged objectionable speech some time in August has been reduced to nine months' rigorous imprisonment and a fine of Rs 100 by Mr F.L. Smith, District and Sessions Judge of Kumaon.

Thakur Sher Singh, a Congress worker of Lohaghat, district Almora, who was convicted and sentenced to nine months' rigorous imprisonment and a fine of Rs 25 has been released as a result of his tendering apology.

Sjt Niranjan Singh, a member of the AICC, president of the District Congress Committee and Chairman of the District Council Narsinghpur who was arrested on December at Kareli, while offering Satyagraha has been convicted and sentenced to nine months' rigorous imprisonment and a fine of Rs 150 by the Sub-Divisional Magistrate, Narsinghpur. Mr Niranjan Singh was tried in jail and has been recommended to be placed in 'B' class.

45. Mr Gopinath Bardoloi, Ex-Premier of Assam, Arrested

Hindustan Times, 12 December 1940.

Mr Gopinath Bardoloi, ex-Premier of Assam was arrested in Gauhati by the Superintendent of Police, Kamrup at 3.30 this afternoon when he offered Satyagraha by shouting anti-war slogans on a public thoroughfare near the Post Office. He was immediately taken to the Gauhati Jail.

Mr Bardoloi left his home at Silpukhri at 2 pm for the Congress office, from where he walked to the Bar Library. After talking to his colleagues in the bar for over an hour, he came out to offer Satyagraha on the roadside where a big crowd had assembled. After he had shouted the slogans four times, the Superintendent of Police approached him, showed him a warrant and placed him under arrest.

Mr Gopinath Bardoloi was tried by the Senior Magistrate, Mr G.C. Bardoloi, inside the jail immediately after his arrest and sentenced to one year's simple imprisonment under Section 38 of the Defence of India Rules.

Pleading guilty to the charges, Mr Bardoloi said in a statement before the court that he believed in anti-war slogans as according to him this war was not for freedom and justice.

The accused who was offered a seat during the one hour trial was placed in Division I by the Magistrate.

Bihar—Jaglal Chowdhuri—Ex-Minister Remanded to Custody

Mr Jaglal Chowdhuri, ex-Minister Bihar, was arrested at Manihar and brought to Purnea today. He was produced before the Sadar Sub-Divisional Magistrate and remanded to custody.

Mrs Labanya Prova Ghosh, wife of Mr Atul Chandra Ghosh, President of the Manbhum District Congress Committee was arrested on Tuesday for offering Satyagraha at Bhutan before a gathering of villagers.

Mr Sarangadhar Sinha, ex-Parliamentary Secretary, who was arrested in Patna yesterday, was convicted under Section 38 (5) of the Defence of India Act and sentenced to one year's rigorous imprisonment by Mr Ali Ashraf, SDO today.

The trial was held in jail. Mr Sinha was placed in 'A' class.

'I expect every Indian to do his duty' said Mr Sarangdhar Sinha, ex-Parliamentary Secretary, who came to Bankipur to offer Satyagraha. A small crowd had been waiting for him. He walked through it shouting his anti-war slogans and then presented himself to a police officer, who approached him. He was taken into custody and removed to the Bankipur Jail.

Mr Jagat Narain Lal a former Parliamentary Secretary, who was arrested yesterday at Dinapore for offering Satyagraha, was produced before Mr G.M. Ray, SDO Dinapore and tried under Section 38(5) of the Defence of India Rules. Judgement was reserved and will be delivered tomorrow.

Mr Mukutdhari Singh, a local Congress and labour leader, was arrested on Tuesday by the Jharia Police in connection with an anti-war speech delivered by him at Loona on December 8. He was later produced before Mr A.W. Khan, Senior Deputy Magistrate of Dhanbad who sentenced him to nine month's rigorous imprisonment. Mr Singh was placed in 'B' class.

Madras—Satyamurti—Intimation to Police Commission

Mr S. Satyamurti, MLA (Central) has intimated to the Commissioner of Police, Madras today his intention of offering Satyagraha near his residence in Theyagaroyanagar on the morning of December 13.

Mr T.B. Avanashilingam Chettiar, MLA (Central) and Mr C.P. Subbiah, MLA (Central) were arrested this morning when they offered Satyagraha at Coimbatore by shouting anti-war slogans.

Mr K.V.R. Swami Naidu, MLA (Madras), who was arrested for offering Satyagraha at Katheru near Rajahmundry by shouting anti-war slogans was sentenced by the Joint Magistrate Rajahmundry to undergo one year's simple imprisonment and a fine of Rs 500, in default three months' further imprisonment. He has been placed in 'A' class.

Mr B.J. Deshmukh, member of the AICC, who offered Satyagraha at Jarud village in Amraoti was sentenced to imprisonment till the rising of the court and to pay a fine of Rs 200, in default further four months' rigorous imprisonment.

Addressing a meeting of the Ramnad District Congress Committee, Mr Kamraj, MLA, President of the Tamil Nadu Congress Committee, asked Congressmen not to precipitate matters by resorting to Satyagraha on their own accord without instructions from the Congress High Command. He announced that 25 names had been called for the second list.

Mr C. Suryanarayana, President of the Guntur Town Congress Committee and a member of the All India Congress Committee who was arrested at Guntur this morning for offering Satyagraha by shouting anti-war slogans, was convicted and sentenced by the Deputy Magistrate under the Defence of India Rules to one year's rigorous imprisonment.

MLAs Sentenced

Messrs T.S. Avanashilingham Chettiar, MLA (Central) and C.P. Subbia, MLA (Madras), members of the All India Congress Committee who were arrested at Coimbatore for offering

Satyagraha were convicted and sentenced by the Sub-Divisional Magistrate under the Defence of India Rules to six months' rigorous imprisonment each. Both of them were placed in 'B' class.

Rajahmundry Sentence

Mr K.V.R. Swami Naidu, MLA who was arrested for offering Satyagraha at Katheru near Rajahmundry by shouting anti-war slogans today was sentenced by the Joint Magistrate, Rajahmundry to undergo one year's simple imprisonment and pay a fine of Rs 500 or in default three months' further imprisonment.

He has been placed in 'A' class.

MLAs Sentenced—Mohammad Ismail Arrested

Maulana Mohammad Ismail, member of the Assembly, was arrested on the night of December 10 from his residence in Moradabad having informed the District Magistrate of his intention to offer anti-war Satyagraha at Ruknuddin Sarai, a suburb of Sambhal, today. The Maulana was to proceed to Sambhal this morning. The arrest was made at 11 o'clock in the night and so very few friends and co-workers of the Maulana could see him off.

Mr Kesho Gupta, MLA, member All India Congress Committee and President, Muzaffarnagar City Congress Committee is to initiate Satyagraha in this district by reciting anti-war slogans in Bhainsi near Khatauli. He has been touring his constituency and addressing meetings. He will give intimation to the District Magistrate on December 12.

Mr Chait Ram, a Harijan, MLA, offered Satyagraha at about 3 pm on Tuesday in the village of Dadra about eight miles from Bara Banki by shouting anti-war slogans and was arrested.

Moradabad MLA Sentenced

Pandit Shanker Dutta, MLA who was arrested on Sunday last at Moradabad was today sentenced to nine months' rigorous imprisonment under the Defence of India Rules. Dr Jawaharlal Rohtagi, MLA (Congress) of Cawnpore who was arrested on December 9 for shouting anti-war slogans in Jhinjhak has been sentenced to one year's simple imprisonment. He will be placed in 'B' class.

Pandit Kamalapati Tripathi, MLA (UP), Editor of the *Aaj*, Benares, has informed the District Magistrate that he will offer Satyagraha in the village of Syedraja in Chaundauli tehsil on December 13. Mr Tripathi is also President of the Benares District Congress Committee.

Mr Sulaiman Ansari, former Parliamentary Secretary UP, was arrested at his residence in Gorakhpur before he offered Satyagraha. He has been taken to the District Jail.

Ch Buddhu Singh, MLA (UP) was arrested on Tuesday at Bharthana in Etawah district, while he was proceeding in a procession towards the railway station to start Satyagraha there on the next day. From there he was taken to the District Jail in a car by the ASP. His trial took place in the jail compound and was sentenced to one year's further rigorous imprisonment. The Magistrate has recommended him to be placed in 'B' class.

A message from Mirzapur says that Mr Vishwanath Prasad, MLA has informed the District Magistrate of his intention to offer Satyagraha on December 12 in Kassawa village in Mirzapur district.

Another message from Basti states that Pandit Sitaram Shukla has been sentenced to nine months' rigorous imprisonment and a fine of Rs 100 or in default to undergo three months' further imprisonment. Mr Harnath Prasad, a Harijan, MLA has been sentenced to three months' rigorous imprisonment. Both have been recommended 'B' class.

Mr Hukumchand Bukharia, Secretary of the Lalitpur Motor Transport Union, was sentenced to four months' simple imprisonment under the Defence of India Act, states a Jhansi message.

In pursuance of the orders of the UP Provincial Congress Committee, Mr A.G. Kher, ex-Parliamentary Secretary has resigned membership of the Rural Development Association.

Bengal—Arrests and Sentences

Mr Sushil Chandra Palit, member of the All India Congress Committee and secretary of the Bankura Congress Committee who was arrested on Monday under the Defence of India Rules in connection with the Satyagraha was sentenced yesterday by the Sub-Divisional Officer of Bankura to three months' simple imprisonment. The Magistrate placed him in 'A' class.

Mr Kamal Krishna Ray, MLA, Treasurer of the Bengal Provincial Congress Committee, was arrested on Monday while offering Satyagraha at Sonamukhi. He has been taken to Bishnupur, where the trial will be held.

Mr Deven De, Secretary of the Central Calcutta Congress Committee (suspended), was sentenced to 4 months' rigorous imprisonment under the Defence of India Rules by the Chief Presidency Magistrate for holding a public meeting in Shradhanand Park on December 6 last in contravention of the order of the Commissioner of Police, Calcutta. The trial was held inside the Presidency Jail.

A sentence of detention till the rising of the court has been imposed by the Sub-Divisional Officer of Comilla, Dewan Naimul Huq on Miss Labanya Lata Chandra, member of the AICC, the first woman Satyagrahi at Bengal under the Defence of India Rules. She was arrested in the central part of the town.

According to a report received from Barisal, Mr Suresh Chandra Das Gupta, Principal of the Harijan School offered Satyagraha on December 9 by shouting anti-war slogans before a crowd of Congressmen and others in front of the Bar Library at Barisal. Mr Das Gupta is the first Satyagrahi in the district.

Mr Dhirendra Nath Gupta, MLA, has informed the District Magistrate of Tippera that he would offer Satyagraha at Brahmanbaria on December 14 by shouting anti-war slogans states a report from Comilla.

Mr Prafulla Chandra Sen, a member of the AICC and President of the Arambagh Sub-Divisional Congress Committee was convicted today by the Sub-Divisional Magistrate at Arambagh under the Defence of India Rules and sentenced to one year and six months' simple imprisonment on two different counts, the sentences to run concurrently. Mr Sen was arrested on December 9 for offering Satyagraha by shouting anti-war slogans.

Mr Nikunja Behari Maitra, MLA, President of the Sub Divisional Congress Committee, Centai, who inaugurated the Satyagraha campaign in this sub-division on Tuesday by shouting anti-war slogans, was sentenced to one year's simple imprisonment and to pay a fine of Rs 100, in default further imprisonment for two months.

Punjab—Mr Deo Raj Sethi Sentenced

Mr Deo Raj Sethi, MLA, was sentenced this morning to an aggregate rigorous imprisonment under Rule 38 (5) of the Defence of India Rules by Mr Henderson, District Magistrate, in connection with two speeches delivered by him at Lahore. Mr Sethi was placed in 'A' class.

'I cannot imagine any other Congressman from the highest to the lowest admiring the skill and courage of the German airmen who attempted to kill their Majesties, the King and Queen by bombing the Palace', observed Mr Henderson, District Magistrate in sentencing Mr Deo Raj Sethi, MLA.

The Magistrate said: 'Although Mr Sethi refused to have any statement recorded it might be possible for the accused to assert that the German airmen are brave and he was asking the crowd to emulate the spirit of bravery and not think that even this would make matters better. A bravery which is afraid to attack military objectives alone and which delights in raining bombs on women and children is not courage of the highest order. Had the accused wished to refer to some bravery he could well have referred to the bravery of countries, noble people in this world, and not to that of callous destroyers of harmless non-combatants. Again, in praying that the war should be a long one Lala Deoraj Sethi should be in a minority of one in the entire universe.'

Concluding, the Magistrate observed, 'I wish it were in my power to pass a sentence that either Lala Deo Raj Sethi should be transported to London for the rest of the war in order to admire the spirit of the German pilots or he should be attached to a bombing squadron for the same period in order to see something of their bravery at even closer quarters. Either sentence would be appropriate. In passing what sentence I am permitted by law, I take into consideration that the speech of Lala Deo Raj Sethi was no mere misguided Satyagraha but was a deliberate adulation of the destroyers of the world's peace.'

Sardar Gopal Singh Quomi, member of the Punjab Provincial Congress Working Committee and AICC was sentenced to one year's rigorous imprisonment by the Additional District Magistrate, Montgomery under the Defence of India Act in connection with a speech delivered by him at Okara.

Sardar Gopal Singh, it may be recalled, is already undergoing four months' imprisonment and the present sentence will commence on the expiry of the first one.

He has been placed in 'B' class.

Frontier—Satyagraha on December 14—Dr Khan Sahib and Others to Court Arrest

On December 14, Satyagraha will be offered simultaneously in ten different places in the Frontier. This decision was announced by Khan Abdul Ghaffar Khan after the termination of an emergency meeting of Congress MLAs and members of the AICC which he had called today. Satyagrahis consisting of twenty persons will court arrest on the 14th and 15th, ten persons defying the law each day. All District Magistrates have been intimated by letters today. Dr Khan Sahib, ex-Premier, Qazi Ataullah and Mr Bhanju Ram Gandhi ex-Ministers and Mr Abdul Qaiyum, MLA (Central) will shout anti-war slogans in Peshawar City, Landi Dera Ismail Khan and Charsadda, respectively, on December 14.

Khan Abdul Ghaffar Khan and Qazi Ataullah Khan addressed a Red Shirt meeting at Shahidan on Wednesday evening and later left for Charsadda to attend a meeting of the Red Shirts.

Khan Abdul Ghaffar Khan has issued the following statement:

'The first set of Satyagrahis is ready and is about to go into action. After considering individual cases I thought that it was advisable not to permit for the present Mr Abdul Ghaffoor, Mr Abdullah Khan and Mr Pirkamaran, MLAs on medical grounds and Sardar Ishar Singh,

MLA on account of the serious illness of his daughter. The President of the PPCC Mr Ali Gul Khan has not been allowed for two reasons, first his ill-health due to tuberculosis of the lungs and secondly as the General Secretary, Mr Abdul Qaiyum Swati is going in the first batch, his keeping out to work with me is an absolute necessity'.

Ajmer—One Year's RI & Fine—AICC Member Sentenced

Judgement in the case under the Defence of India Rules against Syt Bal Krishna Kaul, member of AICC who offered Satyagraha here by sending anti-war letters, was announced today by the Additional District Magistrate, Mr G.A. Faruqi. Syt Kaul was convicted and sentenced to one years' rigorous imprisonment and a fine of Rs 150, in default 3 months' further imprisonment.

Arrest at Beawar

Syt Purshottam Prasad Naiyer (Jodhpur), another member of the AICC was warmly received at Beawar on arrival from Ajmer. A party in his honour was arranged and was attended by some 50 persons including prominent Congressmen from Ajmer and Municipal members of Beawar. After the party and all along the road to the Dixon Memorial Syt Naiyer was profusely garlanded and was received at the Memorial by a large crowd. Here he offered Satyagraha by shouting anti-war slogans and was arrested by the City Inspector of Police. He was first motored to Kotwali from where he was sent to the Ajmer Central Jail the same night, Monday, December 9.

Syt Naiyer was produced before Mr Faruqi Additional District Magistrate today. After prosecution witnesses had been examined, the charge-sheet was framed against Syt Naiyer under the Defence of India Rules. Syt Naiyer took no part in the proceedings. The case stands adjourned till tomorrow. Prominent Congressmen were present in the court during both the cases.

Syt Naiyer is a landlord and business man and is the grandson of the late Munshi Devi Prasad, the famous historian of Jodhpur in whose memory prizes are given to Research Scholars every year and who donated several thousand rupees for the education of girls in Jodhpur.

46. Arrests and Convictions for Satyagraha

Hindustan Times, 13 December 1940.

Delhi Ahrar Leader Taken into Custody—Arrests and Convictions for Satyagraha—Mahatma Gandhi's Secretary Sentenced

Mr B. Abdulla Faruqi, President of the Delhi Provincial Majlis-i-Ahrar and editor of the *Mahshar-i-Khayal*, was arrested this afternoon at his office near Jama Masjid, Delhi, under the Defence of India Rules.

Choudhury Raghubans Narain Singh, MLA will offer Satyagraha on December 14 from his constituency.

CP—Mr Pyarelal—Mahatma Gandhi's Secretary, Sentenced

Mr Pyarelal, Mahatma Gandhi's Secretary, was sentenced to three months' simple imprisonment. He has been placed in 'B' class. The trial of Mr Pyarelal, who was arrested on

Wednesday at Anji village, commenced at 12 noon in Wardha Jail before the Magistrate. Mr Kunte, Mrs Kasturba Gandhi, Mr Mahadev Desai and Rajkumari Amrit Kaur were present.

Completing Vinoba Bhave's Mission

Mr Chaoji, a Sub-Inspector of Police, in his evidence stated that besides exhorting people at Elikhali, Sukli and Anji villages to follow the constructive programme of the Congress, Mr Pyarelal had explained anti-war propaganda and had declared that he had been deputed by Mahatma Gandhi to complete the mission of Vinoba Bhave who could not visit these places on account of his being arrested.

After Mr Chaoji had read the reports of Mr Pyarelal's speeches, Mr Pyarelal said that the rendering of the translation of the slogans was incorrect and he gave his own words. Thereupon Mr Chaoji said that Mr Pyarelal might be said to have expressed himself as follows:

It is wrong to help Britain in the war with men and money and the only worthy effort for resisting all wars would be non-violent resistance.

The witness also stated that Mr Pyarelal might be said to have expressed himself thus—it is only through non-violence that we can serve Britain and the whole world and end Hitlerism.

Anti-war Propaganda

Examined by the court Mr Pyarelal admitted having carried out anti-war propaganda. He filed along statement explaining why he had resorted to Satyagraha and said that Mahatma Gandhi had raised India's status by non-violence which alone would resist all wars and bring peace for the world by ending Hitlerism and Imperialism.

Asked by the court whether he wanted to cross examine the prosecution witnesses or to adduce defence, Mr Pyarelal said he did not want to add anything to his statement.

Pandit Dinkar Shastri Ranade, President of the Buldana Municipality and President of the Chikhli Taluk Congress Committee, was convicted and sentenced today to six months' simple imprisonment under the Defence of India Rules. He was placed in 'B' class.

Mahant Posudas, MLA (Drug), was arrested today and sentenced to six months rigorous imprisonment. He was placed in 'B' class.

Mr Deogiriker, the new President of the Maharashtra Provincial Congress Committee, who had been to Wardha on December 8 to see Mahatma Gandhi in connection with some constitutional difficulties in the MPCC and the constructive programme, returned to Poona after having had consultations with the Mahatma for half an hour.

Mr Deogiriker was nominated President of the MPCC by Mr N.V. Gadgil, MLA (Central), the former President, prior to his arrest on offering Satyagraha.

Seth Shivdas Daga, MLA (Central), was arrested today at Arang under the Defence of India Rules, says a report from Raipur, for offering Satyagraha by shouting anti-war slogans. He has been brought to Raipur jail to stand his trial.

A citizens' meeting consisting of thousands of people was held in Gandhi Chowk on December 10 to bid farewell to Pandit B.A. Mandloi, MLA, a member of the AICC, the first Satyagrahi from Nimar district. About 30 public institutions garlanded him. Great enthusiasm prevailed and addresses from various institutions were presented to him.

Mr Mandloi addressed the meeting exhorting the people to follow the Congress and Mahatma Gandhi. He then started walking for Shihada village, shouting anti-war slogans but the police immediately arrested him and took him to jail.

UP
Mr M.M. Upadhyaya, AICC Member, Arrested

Mr Madan Mohan Upadhyaya, member of the All India Congress Committee, was arrested while addressing a gathering of nearly 10,000 people about 24 miles from Ranikhet on December 9. He also shouted anti-war slogans.

It is understood that Seth Achal Singh, MLA, President of the Agra DCC will offer Satyagraha on December 15 by shouting anti-war slogans. It is further understood that he will inform the District Magistrate about it on December 13.

The latest batch of Congressmen to be arrested and sentenced included four MLAs, one MLC and two members of the AICC, besides Mrs Sucheta Kripalani.

Mrs Sucheta Kripalani was sentenced under the Defence of India Rules to one year's simple imprisonment and a fine of Rs 100, in default two months' further imprisonment.

Dr Jawahar Lal Rohtagi, MLA, who was arrested in Cawnpore district, was sentenced to one year's simple imprisonment and placed in 'B' class.

Chaudhri Buddhu Singh, MLA, was arrested in Etawah district while proceeding to a railway station to offer Satyagraha at Jaswant Nagar. His trial took place yesterday and he was sentenced to one year's rigorous imprisonment and a fine of Rs 200 or in default four months' further rigorous imprisonment. He has been recommended 'B' class.

Maulana Mohammad Ismail, MLA, was arrested on Tuesday night at his residence in Moradabad.

Pt Shankar Dutta

Pandit Shankar Dutta, MLA who was arrested on Sunday last was sentenced to nine month's rigorous imprisonment under the Defence of India Rules.

Pandit Sita Ram Shukla, who was arrested on December 2, has been sentenced to nine months' rigorous imprisonment and fined Rs 100, in default three months further imprisonment.

Mahashaya Harnath Prasad, a Harijan MLA who was arrested on December 8, has been sentenced to three months' rigorous imprisonment placed in 'E' class.

Mr Hargovind Singh a member of the AICC from Jaunpur, was tried and sentenced to one year's simple imprisonment and a fine of Rs 50 and placed in 'B' class.

Mr Mohan Lal Shah, MLC, was arrested under the Defence of India Rules at Kotabagh about thirty miles from Haldwani in Naini Tal district for shouting anti-war slogans.

Bombay—Mr V.V. Patil—to Offer Satyagraha Today

Mr Sadashivappa Korannavar, a Congress worker of Badami (Bijapur), was sentenced to six months' simple imprisonment and Rs 25 fine for distributing a statement by Pandit Jawaharlal, by the First Class Magistrate, Bangalkot.

Mr V.V. Patil, President of the Dharwar District Local Board and member of the AICC, has given notice to the District Magistrate that he would offer Satyagraha at Hubli on December 13.

Mr A.D. Dodmeti, MLA, who was arrested at Jakkali for offering Satyagraha on Monday was sentenced today by the Sub-Divisional Magistrate to one year's simple imprisonment and was placed in 'B' Class. He was taken to the Belgaum Central Prison.

Mr Jaganatha Methashet Mahadwala who offered Satyagraha on Tuesday has been arrested.

Bihar—Mr S.R. Rizvie—Board Vice-Chairman Sentenced

Mr Sukhlal Singh, MLA, Chairman of the Hazaribagh District Board has been sentenced under the Defence of India Rules to one year's rigorous imprisonment and a fine of Rs 5, in default further rigorous imprisonment for five days for having offered Satyagraha at Giridih.

Srimati Saraswati Debi, MLA, has been sentenced to one year's simple imprisonment in connection with the Satyagraha at Bhagalpur. She has been brought to the Hazaribagh Central Jail.

Mr Ramnarain Singh, MLA (Central), has been arrested for delivering a speech at Giridih. The case has been heard by Mr C.S. Jha, ICS, Deputy Commissioner and the Judgement will be delivered on December 14.

Two Congress members of the Bihar Assembly, Mr Raj Kishore Singh and Mr Yadu Bansh Sabay, former Chairman and Vice-Chairman of the Palmau District Board have been arrested for shouting anti-war slogans in furtherance of Satyagraha at two different places in the district.

Mr S. Rafiuddin A. Rizvie, MLA (Bihar) Vice Chairman of the Monghyr District Board, who was arrested on Tuesday for shouting anti-war slogans was sentenced by Mr N.K. Banerji, Sadar SDO, to eight months rigorous imprisonment. The trial was held in the jail. He was placed in 'A' class.

Mr Jagat Narain Lal, former Parliamentary Secretary, Bihar was convicted under Rule 38 (5) of the Defence of India Rules and sentenced today to one year's rigorous imprisonment by Mr C.M. Ray, Sub-Divisional Magistrate Dinapore. He was recommended 'A' Class. The trial was held inside the Bankipore Jail.

Madras—Harijan MLA Sentenced to 6 months' imprisonment.

Mr M. Marimathu (Harijan, MLA) offered Satyagraha on Wednesday at Pattukottai and was arrested by the local police. The Sub-Divisional Magistrate, Pattukottai, sentenced him to six months' rigorous imprisonment and placed him in 'B' Class.

Mr T.S. Chokkalingam, MLA, was arrested this morning under the Defence of India Rules for offering Satyagraha by shouting anti-war slogans at Tenkasi.

Mr V.J. Gupta, MLA, who offered Satyagraha at Yellamanchili was sentenced to six months' simple imprisonment and placed in 'B' class by Narasipatam Divisional Magistrate.

Bengal—Dr S.C. Banerjee—T.U.C. Ex-President, Offers Satyagraha

For the second time, Dr Suresh Chandra Banerjee, MLA, ex-President of the All India Trade Union Congress offered Satyagraha today in the city by shouting anti-war slogans.

Dr Banerjee walked along the main road in Belgatehia in the eastern part of the city for a distance of about half a mile shouting the slogans to crowd of labourers and Congressmen who followed him.

Restraint order on an Artist

Radhikaranjan Banerjee, an Artist of Barisal has been served with a notice under the Defence of India Rules directing him to leave the town immediately and to reside in his home village at Tarpasha. Banerjee is a member of the *Krishak Samity*.

Bankim Chandra Guha, keeper of the *Binapani* Press at Munshigunge (Dacca) has been sentenced by the Deputy Magistrate at Munshigunge to pay a fine of Rs 100 and to be detained till the rising of the court for printing an alleged Communist leaflet in his press. Guha, who was prosecuted under the Defence of India Rules, surrendered himself to the mercy of the court.

Santiranjan Shome of village Hashara (Dacca) alleged to be the author of the leaflet has been sentenced by the Magistrate to six months' rigorous imprisonment.

Mr Kamal Krishna Ray

Mr Kamal Krishna Ray, MLA and treasurer of the Bengal Provincial Congress Committee who was arrested on December 9 for offering Satyagraha at Sonamukhi has been sentenced by the Sub-Divisional Officer of Bishnupur to 4 months' simple imprisonment. He has been placed in 'A' class.

Mr Lakhuji Bhude

Mr Lakhuji Bhude offered Satyagraha yesterday at Dahigaon village near Akola and was arrested under the Defence of India Rules. He was brought to Akola jail last night. His trial is expected to take place on December 14.

Mr Nagagibhai, a merchant of Akot, offered Satyagraha at Akot this morning.

Launching Satyagraha—Baluchistan National Organization's Decision

The Working Committee of the Anjuman-i-Watan, a national political organization of Baluchistan, at a meeting held in Sibi, decided to launch Satyagraha with the permission of Mahatma Gandhi.

The meeting further decided to enrol Satyagrahis from various parts of Baluchistan and to put up the list of these Satyagrahis before another meeting of the Working Committee which has been convened for December 23.

Khan Abdus Samad Khan is in correspondence with Mahatma Gandhi in this connection. Mahatma Gandhi is reported to have advised Khan Abdus Samad Khan to train the people of Baluchistan in non-violence.

Punjab Congressmen Sentenced

Prof. Rattanlal Bhatia, S. Lachman Singh, S. Surjan Singh, S. Niranjan Singh and S. Shuhar Singh, prominent Congress workers were sentenced to two years' rigorous imprisonment for speeches on several counts but the sentences would run concurrently. Prof. Bhatia was placed in 'B' Class.

Ch Krishan Gopal Dutt

Choudhri Krishan Gopal Dutt, Deputy Leader of the Congress Party in the Punjab Assembly, was sentenced today by a Sialkot Magistrate to two years' rigorous imprisonment under Rule 38(5) of the Defence of India Rules.

47. Report on Satyagraha: Arrests in Provinces

Hindustan Times, 14 December 1940.

Rafi Ahmad Kidwai Arrested—Satyagrahi Sentenced to 9 Months' Imprisonment—Satyagraha in the Provinces

Mr S. Satyamurti, MLA (Central) was arrested this morning at 10 o'clock for offering Satyagraha by shouting anti-war slogans near his residence in Tyagarajanagar.

Mr Devadas Gandhi and a number of Congressmen and Councillors of the Madras Corporation were present at Mr Satyamurti's residence this morning when he offered Satyagraha.

Mr Satyamurti came to the road-side and spoke a few sentences in Tamil reiterating the reasons which led the Congress to launch Satyagraha. He then uttered a few anti-war slogans when Mr Yusuf Ali Syed, Deputy Commissioner of Police arrested him and took him in a car to the Chief Presidency Magistrate's Court where the trial took place.

The crowd shouted Congress slogans as the car moved on.

Later Mr Satyamurti, MLA (Central), was convicted under the Defence of India Rules by the Chief Presidency Magistrate and sentenced to nine months' simple imprisonment. Mr Satyamurti was placed in 'A' class. He was taken to the Vellore Central jail.

Mr V.S. Mani of Madura, who was arrested for shouting anti-war slogans in front of the Kandaswami Temple in George Town this morning, was sentenced to four months' rigorous imprisonment by the Second Presidency Magistrate. He was placed in 'C' class.

Mr T.S. Chokkalingam, MLA, (Editor of *Dhinamani*) who was arrested this morning for offering Satyagraha under Rule 38 (5) of the Defence of India Rules was produced before the Sub-Divisional Magistrate, Tinnevelly camping at Tenkasi. The Magistrate fixed December 18 for the trial.

A Guntur message says that Mr P. Subbiah (Harijan), MLA, who offered Satyagraha at Ponnur, Guntur district on Tuesday has been sentenced to six months' simple imprisonment.

Mr T.N. Ramakrishna Reddy, MLA and President of the Chittoor District Board, who was arrested on Friday for offering Satyagraha by shouting anti-war slogans, was convicted and sentenced by the Joint Magistrate, Madanapalle under the Defence of India Rules to six months' simple imprisonment. He has been placed in 'A' class. He was taken to the Vellore Central Jail.

Mr E. Kannan, MLA, Vice-President, Malabar District Board was arrested on Friday morning at Parappanangadi for offering Satyagraha. He has been taken to Palghat for trial.

Mr Govind Prodhan, MLA President of the Zemindari Ryot Association has been arrested at Aska in Ganjam District for offering Satyagraha by shouting anti-war slogans.

Six students of the Annamalai University including a lady student were arrested today under the Defence of India Rules. Five of them including the lady student were taken to Vellore Jail for detention. They are Messrs Venkataramani, Gurumurti, Sankaranarayan and Karim-ud-Din and Miss Minakshi. Mr Driviam, the other student was served with an order confining him to his residence in Madras. Earlier in the morning the police arrested Mr Ramamurthi, a former student of the University, under the Defence of India Rules.

UP

Mr Kidwai Arrested—Detained in Lucknow District Jail

Mr Rafi Ahamad Kidwai, former acting Premier and Revenue Minister, the Indian Province, was taken into custody this morning from his residence at the Councillors quarters.

Mr Rafi Ahmad Kidwai was talking with about half a dozen Congressmen when Mr Anjanibir Prasad, Deputy Superintendent of Police, City served him with the detention warrant and a warrant of search of his residence.

Mr Kidwai was driven in the DSP's car to the Lucknow District Jail where he is being detained. He was given a send off by the Congressmen present there.

Pandit Rain Chitra Pande, MLA (Haryana) was arrested on Wednesday before he could offer Satyagraha. Kunwar Bhagwan Singh, MLA (Pillibhit) has been sentenced to one year's simple imprisonment under the Defence of India Rules. He was awarded 'B' class.

A message from Kalpi says that Dewan Satrughan Singh, MLA of Hamirpur, who had been arrested when he offered Satyagraha has been sentenced to eighteen months' rigorous imprisonment and a fine of Rs 300.

Mr Sandho Singh, MLA (Shahjehanpur), has also been arrested at his residence before he could offer Satyagraha.

A report from Ghazipur states that Mr Inderdeo Tripathi, MLA, who had arrested in November sentenced to one year's rigorous imprisonment under the Defence of India Rules and placed in 'B' class.

Mr Kamalapati Tripathi, MLA, the second Satyagrahi from Benares, was arrested on Friday at 1 p.m. on his way to Savedraja to offer Satyagraha in accordance with the notice given by him to the District Magistrate.

His car was stopped near Dandi a village between Benares and Moghalsarai, by the police, who were standing on the road. He was arrested under Rule 34 and 38 of the Defence of India Rules and taken to the district jail.

Bhowali and Naini Tal observed complete hartal today as a mark of protest against the arrest of Lala Mohanlal Sah, MLC.

A Muttra message states that Shrimati Shanti Devi, wife of Acharya Jugal Kishore, ex-Parliamentary Secretary, UP Government was arrested at Brindaban on December 12 at her residence before starting Satyagraha and has been sent to jail.

Lala Mohanlal Sah, MLC who was arrested at Haldwani, was sentenced to one year's rigorous imprisonment under the Defence of India Rules. He was placed in 'A' class.

Mr Madan Mohan Upadhyaya, a member of the AICC was convicted at Almora under sections 34 and 38 of the Defence of India Rules and sentenced to one year's imprisonment on each count for shouting anti-war slogans before a large crowd.

Pandit Rama Kant Malaviya, MLC (UP), was arrested at Allahabad on Friday at his residence under Section 38, Defence of India Rules, read with Section 121 (Preparation for Prejudicial Act). Pandit Rama Kant Malaviya had intimated to the District Magistrate that he would offer Satyagraha today (Saturday) in the afternoon in Phoolpur tehsil of Allahabad district.

Mr Rameshwar Singh, MA, LLB, a Congress worker of Dehra Dun, and Mr Kedar Singh of Jaunsar-Bawar have been sentenced to 3 months' RI each under Rule 38 of the Defence of India Rules, for having made alleged objectionable speeches in Jaunsar-Bawar. Mr Singh has been placed in 'B' class.

Mr Keshav Gupta, MLA (UP) and a member of the All India Congress Committee was arrested this evening at his residence under the Defence of India Act. It would be recalled that Mr Gupta had intimated to the District Magistrate his intention to offer Satyagraha at village Bhainsi on December 14.

Seth Achal Singh, MLA who is going to offer Satyagraha tomorrow, has, it is understood, intimated to the District Magistrate his intention to do so between 3 and 5 pm in village Pirthinath Suburb of Agra. Seth Achal Singh was entertained by the citizens. The Seth advised the people to obey the commands of Mahatma Gandhi to wear Khadi and do other constructive work.

Mr Hari Lal, MLA (UP) was sentenced today by the City Magistrate, Allahabad, under Sections 38 and 121 of the Defence of India Rules to one year's simple imprisonment. He was recommended 'B' class.

It is reported that Mr Sampurnanand, a former Education Minister, UP who is undergoing imprisonment in connection with the present Satyagraha movement has been transferred from Benares Jail to Fatehgarh Jail.

Chaudhary Raghubans Narain Singh, MLA was arrested today at his residence in Asora village, Meerut district, under the Defence of India Rules. He was brought to Meerut District jail.

Chaudhary Raghubans Narain Singh had intimated the District Magistrate yesterday that he would offer Satyagraha on December 14 by making an anti-war speech at Machraon.

Chaudhri Paragilal, MLA offered Satyagraha by shouting anti-war slogans at Saimaholi yesterday at 3 p.m. amongst an audience numbering about 2000. He was arrested by the circle Inspector of Police.

Bihar
Second List—About 500 Persons to be Included

Mr Harekishore Prasad, Mr Rajendra Mishra, Mr Newa Lal Jha and Mr Shivadhari Singh all members of the Bihar Assembly have been convicted in connection with the Satyagraha in Bhagalpur district.

Mr Prasad, Jha and Singh have been sentenced to one year's rigorous imprisonment and Mr Mishra to one year's simple imprisonment. Mr Prasad and Mr Mishra have been placed in 'A' class and others in 'B' class.

Second List of Satyagrahis

The second list of Satyagrahis from Bihar, which is understood to be complete now, consists of about 500 persons including the members of the Provincial Congress Committee, District Congress Committee and local bodies. The list, it is further understood, will be sent to Mahatma Gandhi on December 20 through a special messenger for his approval.

The second phase of the Satyagraha in the province, it is stated, will begin early in January next.

Mr Jagjiwan Ram, ex-Parliamentary Secretary, who was arrested on December 10 for shouting anti-war slogans at the village of Pire in the district of Shahabad was convicted on Thursday at Arrah and sentenced to undergo one year's rigorous imprisonment. He was placed in 'A' class.

Pandit Prajapati Misra, former Chief Rural Development Organizer, was convicted and sentenced on Thursday at Bettiah (district Champaran) to undergo one years' rigorous imprisonment under the Defence of India Rules.

He was arrested on December 9 for shouting anti-war slogans.

CP—Merchant Sentenced—Warning to Nagpur Harijan MLA

Mr Lakhuji Bhode of Dahigaon was convicted today under the Defence of India Rules and sentenced to four month's simple imprisonment.

Mr Nagaji Bhai, a merchant of Akot was sentenced to four months' simple imprisonment.

Dr Shantilal, a local Congress worker, has been sentenced to one year's rigorous imprison-ment under the Defence of India Act by the Sub-Divisional Magistrate, Moga on a charge of delivering an objectionable speech.

Others arrested for offering Satyagraha are Srimati Rukhminibai Korde, a lady Congress worker of Malkapur and Mr P.D. Jatar, MLA Chairman of the District Council, Seoni.

Mr H.J. Khandekar, Harijan MLA, Nagpur, was warned by the District Magistrate in connection with a speech he delivered to the Youth Conference held at Chhindwara on November 12 and 13.

Assam
Mr B.C. Misra—Sylhet Leader, Sentenced

Mr Biresh Chandra Misra, ex-Secretary of the Sylhet District Congress Committee has been sentenced to 18 months' rigorous imprisonment under Section 124-A, IPC for an article published in a local weekly paper (now defunct). He had been previously sentenced to two years' rigorous imprisonment under the Defence of India Rules.

Mr Bisnuram Meddhi, MLA (Assam) and member of the All India Congress Committee was arrested at noon today at Hajo where he offered Satyagraha by shouting anti-war slogans. An inspector of police brought him in his car to Gauhati Jail. He was tried there by the Senior Magistrate and sentenced to one year's simple imprisonment under the Defence of India Rule and placed in 'A' class. Mr Meddhi made a long statement during the trial.

Mr Fakhruddin Ali Ahmed former Revenue and Finance Minister of Assam and member of the All India Congress Committee offered Satyagraha by shouting anti-war slogans at Ghograpara and was arrested this afternoon. The Deputy Superintendent of Police brought him to Gauhati by motor at 5 p.m.

The trial will be held inside the jail tomorrow.

Bombay—Tarabai Joglekar—Arrested for Second Time

Dr (Miss) Tarabai Joglekar was arrested for the second time this morning for offering Satyagraha yesterday at Handapsar.

On Tuesday last Dr Joglekar had been convicted and sentenced to pay a fine of Rs 200 or in default to undergo three month's simple imprisonment by the District Magistrate, Poona. An unknown person had paid the fine and she had been released.

Pandit B.A. Manoloi, MLA, member of the AICC was arrested in Khandwa when he shouted anti-war slogans. He will be tried tomorrow.

Frontier—Dr Khan Sahib to offer Satyagraha Today

The two Khan brothers had a long homely talk tonight.

Dr Khan Sahib will offer Satyagraha at noon tomorrow by shouting anti-war slogans at the Kissakhani Martyrs' Memorial in Peshawar city.

Khan Abdul Ghaffar Khan embarks on a ten-day tour of Kohat district tomorrow.

Dr Khan Sahib's Appeal

Dr Khan Sahib has issued the following statement,

'My message to the people of the Frontier is to give up all feuds and internal disputes and develop a feeling of love and friendship for each other; thus make themselves fit for independence and I am sure independence will be theirs. It is a matter beyond doubt that action is the only thing which brings about results. Theories are meant only for those nations who want to pass time and are free. A nation like ours must wake up and act enthusiastically so that we may be able to break off the chains of slavery. Discipline is the first principle which leads nations to the goal of victory and I am sure our people will always take our absence from amidst them very calmly and patiently and will never waste time in heated discussions.'

48.   Khan Sahib Arrested and Later Released

Hindustan Times, 15 December 1940.

Khan Sahib Arrested and Later Released—To Offer—Satyagraha Again–Mrs Sarojini Naidu at Sevagram Bombay Congress Plans discussed with Gandhi.

Dr Khan Sahib, ex-Premier, initiated Satyagraha in Peshawar today. Qazi Attaullah, ex-Minister Mr Abdul Qaiyum, MLA (Central), and Mr Arbab Abdur Rahman also offered Satyagraha in other parts of Peshawar district.

When Dr Khan Sahib started moving through crowds in Kissakhani Bazar shouting slogans, the Deputy Commissioner and the Senior Superintendent of Police approached him and drove him in a car to his residence.

Qazi Attaullah Khan, Mr Abdul Qaiyum and Arbab Abdur Rahman Khan were similarly removed by the authorities to their respective homes.

A later report says that Dr Khan Sahib and Mr Abdul Qaiyum conferred with Khan Abdul Ghaffar Khan at Peshawar.

Satyagraha to be Repeated

It has been decided following emergency conversations between the Khan brothers and other Satyagrahis that the Satyagrahis who were not arrested on Saturday will repeat Satyagraha today (Sunday).

Dr Khan Sahib, ex-Premier of the NWFP, Mr Abdul Qaiyum, MLA (Central) and Arbab Abdur Rahman, MLA (NWFP) who offered Satyagraha today and were set free have given fresh notices to the District Magistrate of Peshawar intimating their intention of offering Satyagraha again tomorrow. Dr Khan Sahib in the villages of Faturahim (near Peshawar) and both Mr Abdul Qaiyum and Arbab Abdur Rahman in Peshawar City in two different parts.

Mr Bhanju Ram Gandhi, ex-Finance Minister, Khan Amir Mohammad, ex-Parliamentary Secretary and Khan Kamdar Khan, MLA, offered Satyagraha at noon today at three different places. They were not arrested.

Mr H. Chatterji has received a wire from Mahatma Gandhi saying that 'Dr Ghosh must not court arrest.'

Khan Abdul Ghaftar Khan, accompanied by Mr Mohd Yunus arrived in Kohat and inaugurated his tour of Kohat district by addressing a public meeting in the Town Hall grounds. Mr Khair Mohd Jilali presided.

Addressing in Pushtoo, Khan Abdul Ghaffar Khan said: 'The days when we used to address meetings and take out processions are gone. The time for action has come and I am here to give you a lead and show the right path. Our actions today will be responsible for the fate of tomorrow. Therefore, we should be on guard'.

He referred to the Satyagraha movement in the Frontier and the Government action in arresting and later releasing Dr Khan Sahib and others and expressed his surprise.

'When we asked for liberty of speech it was declined by the Viceroy but today it is achieved.' He added that Satyagraha would be continued till arrests were effected.

Earlier Pir Shahinshah offered Satyagraha but was not arrested.

Khan Abdul Ghaffar Khan has sent telegraphic information to Mahatma Gandhi apprising him of the situation. Khan Abdul Ghaffar Khan is proceeding to Hangu tomorrow.

PCC Secretary Arrested

Mr Abdul Qaiyum Swad, Secretary of the Frontier Provincial Congress Committee, who offered Satyagraha at Baffa in Hazara district, was arrested on Saturday. He will be detained under Rule 129 of the Defence of India Rules.

Although 10 Congressmen offered Satyagraha at different places in the Frontier Province on Saturday, nine of them were removed by the authorities to their respective homes. They included Dr Khan Sahib ex-Premier, Qazi Attaullah, ex-Minister, Mr Bhanjuram, ex-Minister, Mr Abdul Qaiyum, MLA and Amir Mohammed, MLA, CP.

Mrs Sarojini Naidu—Informal Talks with Mahatma Gandhi

Mrs Sarojini Naidu arrived here this morning and proceeded to sevagram immediately. She is at present having informal talks which, it is understood, will be continued in the afternoon, when the future plans of the Bombay Congress Committee will be discussed. She will be leaving Wardha as soon as the talks are concluded.

Mrs Sarojini Naidu had a prolonged interview with Mahatma Gandhi today. She intends leaving tomorrow evening for Bombay.

Mrs Naidu had a long interview with Mahatma Gandhi today. After the interview, Mrs Naidu said: 'I discussed with Mahatma Gandhi my future plans as well as plans of further Satyagraha in Bombay. We also took stock of the political situation and Satyagraha activities. I shall again see him tomorrow morning as the talks were inconclusive.'

Mrs Naidu is leaving for Bombay tomorrow and after a few days there, she will proceed to Hyderabad.

Lala Dunichand also saw Mahatma Gandhi today.

Seth Shivdas Daga, MLA (Central), who was arrested at Arang yesterday, was convicted and sentenced to nine months' simple imprisonment and a fine of Rs 200, in default, two months' further simple imprisonment.

Mrs Rukminibai Korde, the first woman Satyagrahi from Buldana district, who was arrested yesterday was sentenced to a fine of Rs 50, in default, to undergo three months' simple imprisonment.

Mr B.A. Mandloi, MLA, Khandwa, and Mr G.C. Choudhury, MLA, Chhindwara, were arrested for offering Satyagraha.

Mahant Purandas, MLA, has been arrested today when he offered Satyagraha.

Mahant Laxminarayandas, MLA, Vice President of the Mahakoshal Provincial Congress, will offer Satyagraha at Nagri on December 18.

Beohar Rajendra Singh, MLA, representing the Landholders' Constituency of the Northern Central Provinces offered Satyagraha by delivering a speech at Budhagar, a village 15 miles away from Jubbulpore. When after finishing his speech, he proceeded towards his car, he was arrested by the Deputy Superintendent of Police and driven away amidst shouts of jails.

Mr Sampatrao Bhopale who was arrested at Hiwarkhed on December 9 was convicted today under the Defence of India Rules and sentenced to one year's rigorous imprisonment.

Mr Shankar Guhe, who was arrested at Dhotardi, was convicted today under the Defence of India Rules and sentenced to six months' simple imprisonment. Mr Pandurang More, who was arrested under the Defence of India Rules, tendered an apology and the case against him was allowed do be withdrawn.

Seth Mohanbhai Narayanji, a cloth merchant of Amraoti who offered Satyagraha today by shouting anti-war slogans, was arrested and taken to the District Jail.

Mr Ram Murthi Mishra, a Congress worker, who was disseminating news at Congress News centres in Nagpur, was arrested this morning under Section 38 of the Defence of India Rules.

UP

Pyarelal Sharma—To Offer Satyagraha Next Week

Pandit Pyare Lal Sharma, MLA (Central) a veteran Congressman of Meerut, is scheduled to offer Satyagraha next week. The exact date, time and place of his offering Satyagraha are not yet known to anybody except to himself or them who have fixed and approved his programme. All attempts of everyone to squeeze out from him the information have proved abortive so far. He simply told the *Hindustan Times* correspondent that he would most probably be in jail by the 20th of this month. Sharmaji abhors publicity, and he would not even like to be bid farewell on the eve of his offering Satyagraha or to be congratulated on his arrest. He will most probably offer Satyagraha from some suburb of one of the seven cities of the United Provinces which constituency he represents in the Central Assembly.

Pandit Madan Mohan Malaviya arrived at Allahabad on December 18 for a couple of days, probably to see his son Pandit Rama Kant Malaviya, who is due to offer Satyagraha on December 14.

49.　Report on Satyagraha Activities in Orissa

Fortnightly Reports, File No. 18/12/1940, Home Department, Political Intelligence Section, Government of India, First Half of December 1940, 16 December 1940, NAI.

Reports from District Officers indicate an absence of any real enthusiasm for the Satyagraha campaign and, as indicated in my last report, it appears that volunteers have been forthcoming because they felt that, if they did not volunteer, their political future would be jeopardized. A large crowd collected when Mr Biswanath Das, ex-Premier, performed his Satyagraha on the 4th December, but there was no disturbance at the time of his arrest. In a long statement in Court, he repeated his reasons for resigning office and those which led him to commit Satyagraha. He stressed the poverty of the people and deplored the large amounts which, he said, were being spent from India on war purposes. He alleged that, in spite of this, the British Government was not prepared to part with power and denied India her freedom. He described India as one vast jail and said that he was merely going from it into a smaller jail. He pleaded guilty to all the charges framed against him and requested the Magistrate to award him the highest sentence permissible and to place him in the lowest class. Mr Kanungo, ex-Minister, made a very much shorter statement in Court than Mr Biswanath Das. He stated that he had committed Satyagraha as a protest against the fact that India had been made a belligerent without consulting the representatives of her people. He ended by saying that disobedience of the law was normally repugnant to him, but he saw no other effective means of protest.

It is said that the next batch of Satyagrahis will consist of the Congress members and executives of local bodies and that their names have been sent to Mr Gandhi for approval.

The total number of Congress members enrolled upto date is reported to be approximately 51,000 as compared with 1,23,900 odd in 1939 and 1,98,325 in 1935. This figure confirms reports previously received that there has not been any great enthusiasm for enrolment.

Pandit Nilakantha Das, MLA (Central) has resigned from the Congress Party. It is reported that he did so in order to avoid unpleasantness when asked to explain his conduct in connection with the formation of a coalition ministry in this province. In an interview the other day, the editor of the *Janata*, a vernacular paper which was started to support the coalition ministry which was proposed some months ago, stated that he considered that, with so many orthodox Congressmen in jail, a further opportunity should be given for a coalition ministry to be formed in this province, since the coalitionists could now easily command a majority! He seemed disgruntled that no progress had been made in this direction, and referred in disparaging terms to 'the Rai Bahadurs' on whom Government relied for prosecuting the War effort. He said that, if the War effort had been organized by the Congress or even by the people of his party who had split from the Congress, what has been raised for the Orissa War Fund would be insignificant compared with what would have been raised in such circumstances. It was pointed out to him that Pandit Godavari Misra, the leader of his party in the Legislative Assembly, had been invited by His Excellency with other leading Congressmen to join the War Committee when it was first formed and that he, like them, had eventually refused. He said that it was useless for people to serve on War Committees who had not got real power, and it was only by making promises to the people that subscriptions could be raised from them. He said that, at the request of certain of the Rulers of the Orissa States, he had addressed large meetings in those States in support of the War effort.

50. Report on Congress Party's Satyagraha Activities and Arrests

Fortnightly Reports, File No. 18/12/40, Home Department, Political Section, Government of Punjab, First Half of December 1940, NAI.

Congress—The arrest of Mian Iftikhar-ud-Din, MLA, the Provincial President, on the 29th of November and of Dr Gopi Chand on the 30th of November created very little interest even in Lahore city. Congress has given further proof of its inconsistency by holding meetings to protest against the arrest of persons who voluntarily offered themselves for arrest. The protest meeting at Amritsar on the 30th of November, drew an audience of only 150 persons. Mian Iftikhar-ud-Din was sentenced to a year's imprisonment and a fine of Rs 6,000 a sum well within his capacity to pay. The imposition of the fine was bitterly criticized by Congressmen both on the platform and in the press and this leaves no doubt about the efficacy of the imposition of fines in suitable cases. Sardar Sampuran Singh, the Leader of the Opposition in the Punjab Legislative Assembly, was the next person to offer himself for arrest. He emerged from the Lajpat Rai Hall, Lahore, on the afternoon of the 3rd of December and at once began shouting slogans. His programme had been widely advertised and there was a large crowd present mostly consisting of students. When the police arrested him, the students stoned them heavily, and they had to be dispersed with lathis. A few persons sustained minor injuries. Congress leaders at the spot made a pretence of restoring order but failed miserably. Their efforts were mainly directed towards absolving themselves from the responsibility of the disorder and ugly scenes that they themselves had created. It is clear that Mr Gandhi himself has been exercised in mind about the violence displayed by his followers in the Punjab and he has already issued orders to those intending to offer Satyagraha not to make known their intentions to the public. In court Sardar Sampuran Singh made it very clear that he did not support Mr Gandhi's views on non-violence and that he had resorted to civil disobedience only for the sake of Congress discipline. The District Magistrate recorded in his judgement that the Sardar Sahib was absolutely insincere when he shouted slogans, that he was merely making a fool of the public by shouting slogans in which he did not personally believe. Such conduct was characterized as dishonest and the Sardar's position in the Satyagraha campaign as ridiculous. Accordingly a nominal sentence of imprisonment and a fine of one anna was imposed. This judgement brought ridicule upon Sardar Sampuran Singh himself and the whole Satyagraha movement in the Punjab and it caused a great stir in Congress circles. The leader of the Opposition was taken to task by Congressmen and urged to perform Satyagraha again. He gave notice to the District Magistrate of Lyallpur of his intention to write anti-war letters to various persons, but before he could do so, orders were received from Mr Gandhi suspending Punjab. Mr Gandhi in Satyagraha has announced that S. Sampuran Singh was not approved by him for offering Satyagraha and in the same message, he criticized 'empty and meaningless discipline'. The suspension of civil disobedience in the province, pending further examination, has caused much heartburning among Congressmen, who rightly feel ashamed. L. Duni Chand, MLA, who became President of the Congress Committee on Mian Iftikhar-ud-Din's imprisonment, has had lengthy correspondence with Mr Gandhi on the subject and eventually proceeded to Wardha to discuss the situation. Latest press reports go to show that civil disobedience will shortly be resumed on defined conditions requiring careful scrutiny, complete faith in non-violence and the Congress constructive programme, daily spinning and wearing of Khadi. Akalis are to be permitted to join the movement if they vow that they are opposed to recruitment to the Army. The Sampuran Singh episode has encouraged Dr Satya Pal to come forward and openly attack Dr Gopi Chand and his Akali supporters. He declares that there is ample proof to show that Congress subordination to the communalist Akalis has been responsible for this sorry incident that has done so much to discredit Congress in the Punjab. He claims that if Mr Gandhi entrust Satyagraha in the Punjab to him, he will make a success of it. Before civil disobedience was suspended a number of other leading Congressmen were arrested. S. Partap Singh, MLA made a prejudicial speech at Tarn Taran in the Amritsar district on the 4th of December and was sentenced to 1½ years' RI. The same day Munshi Hari Lal, MLA in a public meeting announced by beat of drum made an anti-war speech. He was at once arrested and has since been sentenced to one year's RI and a fine of Rs 300. On the 5th of December Nawabzada Mahmud Ali and Nawabzada Mazhar Ali, two brothers with communist leanings (the latter is the President of the Students Union), were arrested and sent for restriction on certain conditions to Palampur in the Kangra district. Both of them defied the order and left Palampur; one was arrested in Lahore and the other in the train on his way to Rawalpindi on the 8th of December. They are now detained under rule 26 of the Defence of India Rules. Students in Lahore held a protest meeting in which they indulged in some wild speeches. On the same day Master Nand Lal, a member of the All India Congress Committee, made a prejudicial speech at Jaranwala in the Lyallpur district; he has since been sentenced to one year's RI and a fine of Rs 200. Mrs Duni Chand, MLA of Ambala gave notice of her intention to break the law on the 5th of December by shouting anti-war slogans in Lahore City and she was arrested and detained under rule 26 of the Defence of India Rules. Pandit Neki Ram Sharma created temporary enthusiasm at Bhiwani in the Hissar district by making an objectionable speech and he has since gone to jail for a year and a half. S. Mangal Singh, MLA (Central) gave notice to the District Magistrate, Ludhiana, that he intended to shout anti-recruitment slogans in a recruiting area of the district on the 7th of December. He was proceeded against under rule 121 of the Defence of India Rules and has been sentenced to one year's RI. Lala Dev Raj Sethi, MLA who was to have offered Satyagraha at Jhang on the 11th of December, was arrested at Lahore on the morning of the 7th of December on his return from Dehra Dun. He had made two prejudicial and defeatist speeches on the 23rd and the 30th of November in Lahore. The following extracts from the District Magistrate's judgement are of general interest:

'With regard to his first speech, Lala Dev Raj Sethi had the effrontery to assert that his statements were made in good company including that of Mr Arthur Moore. I have yet to hear of Mr Arthur Moore or any other good company asserting that Britain could not win the war, and that she had no allies. I am also somewhat astonished to hear from the lips of a Congressman that in this world no one comes forward to help the weak. The second speech contains two passages, which to the mind of any right-thinking person of whatever party, can only be classed as wicked. I refer to the exhortation to the audience to emulate the spirit of the brave German pilots bombing London, and to the prayer that this war should be a long one. It seems incredible that these two utterances should have come from the mouth of any human being.... I cannot imagine any other congressman from the highest to the lowest admiring the skill and courage of the German airmen who attempted to kill their Majesties the King and Queen by bombing the Palace. I wish it were in my power to pass a sentence that either Lala Dev Raj Sethi should be transported to London for the rest of the war to admire the spirit of the German pilots or he should be attached to a bombing squadron for the same period in order to see something of their bravery at even closer quarters. Again in praying that the war should be a long one, Lala Dev Raj Sethi should be in a minority of one in the entire universe. I take into consideration that the speech of Lala Dev Raj Sethi was no mere misguided Satyagraha but was a deliberate adulation of the destroyers of the world's peace.'

The District Magistrate went on to sentence Lala Dev Raj Sethi to 9 months' RI on the first count and to two years' on the second count, the sentences to run consecutively. S. Kapur Singh, MLA has been sentenced to one year's RI for making a prejudicial speech in the Ludhiana district on the 8th of December and Chaudhri Krishen Gopal Dutt, the Deputy Leader of the Opposition in the Punjab Legislative Assembly, got two year's RI for a similar offence in the Sialkot district on the same day. In his letter to the District Magistrate announcing his intention of offering Satyagraha he said that he was strongly opposed to Hitlerism and Fascism and wished the British arms every success but he felt constrained publicly to oppose the war because India had not been consulted before being involved in it. Bibi Raghbir Kaur, MLA who had already been forbidden under rule 26 of the Defence of India Rules to make speeches or attend public meetings, was smuggled to a meeting at Naushera Panwan in the Amritsar district on the 8th of December and there was able to shout a few anti-war slogans before being arrested by the police. She has since been sentenced to one year's RI. There is no doubt that some Congress leaders earmarked for civil disobedience welcomed the suspension of the movement and hoped that it would not be resumed; there is little enthusiasm among them. Subordinate Congressmen of no standing and of the professional agitator type are, however, anxious to resume Satyagraha as early as possible. They are believed to have written to

Mr Gandhi, asking for permission and threatening to start it themselves if permission is withheld. The *Pratap* and the *Vir Bharat*, commenting on S. Sampuran Singh's case, said that many men were offering civil disobedience not in the cause of non-violence but to express their displeasure against the attitude of the British Government. The *Milap*, dealing with a recent speech of the Premier, wrote that every man having the slightest sense of understanding the truth would agree with the Premier that in order to maintain the freedom of any country no useful purpose could be served by non-violence. The Premier, however, perhaps forgot that non-violence was neither the cult of Congress nor of nationalist India, it was solely the belief of Mr Gandhi. The paper held that the salvation of India lay in possessing superior military power.

51. Report on Satyagraha Activities

Fortnightly Reports, File No. 18/12/1940, Home Department, Political Intelligence Section, Government of Bihar, First Half of December 1940, NAI.

Political: The Satyagraha campaign continues and a number of Members of the Legislative Assembly and leading Congressmen have been convicted and sent to jail. Notable exceptions are (1) Dr Rajendra Prasad who is evidently staying out for the time being in order to control the movement and suppress disorder, (2) Dr Mahmud who is still unwell but may offer Satyagraha later in the month, and (3) Babu Baldeo Sahay, the Advocate General, whose failure to resign and offer Satyagraha has been severely commented on by Maulana Abul Kalam Azad. Babu Anugrah Narayan Sinha who had postponed his Satyagraha to the 3rd December in consequence of the disorder which marked Babu Shri Krishna Sinha's arrest, was arrested before he could carry out his programme. On the day before his arrest he had addressed a meeting in Patna City condemning the behaviour of the crowd when Babu Shri Krishna Sinha was arrested and asking the public to observe Mahatma Gandhi's Satyagraha conditions. These conditions have recently been circulated in leaflet form by Dr Rajendra Prasad. There has, somewhat naturally, been less public enthusiasm in rural areas than in towns with their larger population and excitable student element. Even in towns, however, enthusiasm does not seem to have been very long-lived or particularly marked. Where the shouting of slogans has been well advertised beforehand and has taken place in towns, large crowds have collected and there has been much interest and occasionally enthusiasm. In general crowds have been well behaved though there have been two instances of disorder, one at Monghyr where the police who arrested M. Rafuddin Rizwi and were about to take him to jail in a car, were obstructed by a large and hysterical crowd, which took charge of the car and ran with it towards the jail shouting subversive slogans. The other instance was at Dinapore where bricks were thrown by some students at the car in which Babu Jagat Narayan Lal was being escorted to jail. It would probably be a mistake to assume that the comparative lack of enthusiasm will be allowed to continue.

Congress leaders seem to be satisfied that they are getting as much publicity for the campaign as they want, both through the medium of the Press and others. The removal of the ban on the publication of Satyagraha developments in the Press is enabling news of Congress arrests to be broadcast in the interior through vernacular newspapers. There has been a good deal of public speculation as to why Mr Gandhi has ordered Satyagraha in this particular form of shouting anti-war slogans. One opinion commonly held is that Congress leaders are being sent to jail to atone for their sins of omission and commission while they were in power. Another is that it is

Mr Gandhi's policy to fill the jails to overflowing and thus involve Government in expenditure which would otherwise be used for India's war effort. Yet another view is that it is his intention to make the mass mind gradually Satyagraha conscious and thus pave the way for mass individual Satyagraha. This development is foreshadowed by a circular issued by the Provincial Congress Committee asking for names of Satyagrahis belonging to subordinate Congress organizations. At a meeting of the Provincial Working Committee held on the 8th December Maulana Abul Kalam Azad informed the members that Gandhi proposed to extend Satyagraha from Members of the Legislative Assembly to members of district and thana committees and then, if Government did not give way, to Four Anna Congress members. There would not, however, be any no-tax or no-rent campaign. He laid emphasis on the importance of enlisting Muslim satyagrahis and suggested that vacancies in subordinate Congress Committees and local bodies should, if possible, be filled by Congress Muslims. At a public meeting held in Patna on the same day, he gave out that if Mr Gandhi were arrested, no successor would be appointed, and responsibility would pass into the hands of each individual member of the Congress who would then be free to act as his conscience dictated. Reporting on the movement the Collector of Patna comments that Mr Gandhi's move in selecting men at the top for Satyagraha is dangerous and is catching the imagination of the masses and may get a response from them if allowed on to join. It is apprehended by non-Congressmen that the Congress would regain most of the hold and prestige that it had lost while it was in power or before the Satyagraha movement started. It is reported that the second list of Satyagrahis is being drawn up including the members of Provincial, district and village Congress Committees; that it has 5,000 names on it and that these men will start early in January next. It is generally considered, however, that a mass movement will be a failure, if, as is thought likely, it is not backed by the Muslims and the minorities and Government take some repressive measures to deal with it.

Several local bodies have passed resolutions applauding the action of Satyagrahis and condemning Government policy and adjourned their meetings as an expression of their feelings.

Babu Shri Krishna Sinha (ex-Premier) and Babu Krishna Ballabh Sahay (ex-Parliamentary Secretary) who are both in jail declined to see their relatives in the presence of a Criminal Investigation Department officer.

The Provincial Press has taken up the question and is asking the Government to remove such a 'humiliating' restriction, which they say is quite unnecessary in the case of Satyagrahis.

One Divisional Commissioner reports what is perhaps a general fear that the launching of the satyagraha movement will encourage studied indifference to the war effort. In general Muslims do not sympathize with the movement and the Adibasis of Chota Nagpur are watching their opportunity to capture the local bodies when Congressmen resign their seats.

52. Raizada Hansraj Arrested

Hindustan Times, 19 December 1940.

Satyagraha Movement in Provinces—Expulsion of Sardar Sampuran Singh

Raizada Hansraj, MLA (Central) who had intimated the District Magistrate, Jullundur of his intention to offer Satyagraha tomorrow was arrested this evening at his residence in Jullundur according to a telephone message received here. The arrest has been effected under Rule 38 (121) of the Defence of India Rules.

Raizada Hansraj was produced before the Additional District Magistrate who remanded him to custody till December 20. He has been lodged in the District Jail, Jullundur.

53. Report of Satyagraha in Madras Province

Fortnightly Report for the First Half of December 1940, D.O. No. P.4–23, Public (General) Department, Government of Madras to the Secretary to the Government of India, Home Department, 20 December 1940, Tamil Nadu State Archives.

War—Allegations of coercion in making collections are still made but on a restricted scale. In one case investigated it was found that colourable pretext had been given to the complaint by the stupid wording of a circular issued by a subordinate official, but in no other case has any semblance of truth been discovered. In various districts special attention is being paid to propaganda designed to combat the subversive activities of Congressmen and others.

Political–Individual satyagraha has been continued in most districts during the past fortnight. The first part of the programme appears to be coming to a close but it is understood that Mr Gandhi will extend the scale of operations by nominating Congress Committee members, Members of Municipal Councils and others of the same status to offer Satyagraha. The Chief leaders who have been convicted or detained during the fortnight are C. Rajagopalaohari, ex-premier, Dr Subbarayan, V.V. Giri, V.I. Muniswamy Pillai, ex-Ministers, Mrs Subbarayan MLA (Central), S. Satyamurthi, MLA (Central), Avanashilingham Chetti, MLA (Central), Anantasayanam Ayyangar, MLA, Bulusu Sambamurthi, Speaker and K. Venkataswami Naidu, Deputy President.

From reports received it seems quite clear that many of those who have gone to jail have done so with very great reluctance in some cases simply through fear that if they disobeyed the mandate, they would be made to suffer for it when Congress returns to power at some future date. Public interest in the movement has been somewhat greater lately, but in no district has there been any disturbance, beyond a few partial hartals to protest against the arrest of or conviction of a particular leader. Efforts to organize an anti-Repression Day in Madras City were frustrated by the issue of Prohibitory Order by the Commissioner of Police and the prosecution of the publisher of the leaflet calling the meeting. The belief, to which I referred in my last report, that there would be a compromise before long seems to be gaining ground.

Various Students' organizations have been active in organising protests, in the form of meetings, processions and even minor strikes, against what is termed 'the repressive policy of Government' towards students and political leaders generally.

Last Fortnight I reported that action was being taken under the Defence of India Rules to deal with a Communist Cell in the Annamalai University. Seven of those concerned were arrested on 13th December 1940; six of them are being detained under rule 26 and one, a boy aged 15 is being restricted to his father's house under rule 26 (d) and (h). One of the wanted students absconded. The arrests occasioned a demonstration by a large number of students in front of the P.W.D. inspection bungalow where the District Magistrate and the District Superintendent of Police were camping. At one stage the attitude of the crowd became so threatening that the Police had to resort to a mild lathi charge in which 30 students out of the 400 present received minor injuries. The ringleaders of the demonstration were arrested... and the situation was quickly brought under control by the police action and there have been no serious repercussions either in the University or elsewhere.

Defence of India Rules–The attached statement shows the action taken under the various rules and it will be seen that there have been prosecutions in nearly every district. In a few districts there has been a tendency amongst irresponsible youths to offer satyagraha, though they are persons of no importance and have not been nominated by Mr Gandhi. Where possible they are being more or less ignored and treated with the contempt which they deserve. Detention orders under rule 26 have been issued in 17 cases. Mr Sambamurthi, Speaker of Madras Legislative Assembly was also detained to prevent his arrest causing popular excitement in Madras City. Anti-War Speeches and anti-recruitment propaganda have been dealt with under the rules in a number of cases....

Report on the Press for the First Fortnight of December.

I. Statement of action taken under the Indian Press (Emergency Powers Act, 1931 and the Defence of India Act so far as it relates to the Press.

Relates to Andhra and Kerala.

Comments in the Press

The withdrawal by the Government of India of the order under Rule 41 (1) (b) of the Defence of India Rules has been received with widespread satisfaction by all sections of the Press. There is still some doubt lingering in the minds of some papers as to whether any assurance was given on behalf of the editors of the newspapers as suggested in the Press communiqué, issued by the Government of India. Mr Mahadeva Desai's attacks on the President of the Editors' Conference held at Delhi has given rise to the controversy. But papers now agree that no more need be said on the subject and as Press Advisory Committees are being formed in the provinces and many of the Provincial Governments have adopted an attitude which evinces a desire to co-operate with the Press.

Mr L.S. Amery's speech at New Market has been sharply criticized by the nationalist press. Some papers see in it the desire on the part of the Secretary of State to encourage Mr Jinnah. His reference to the Eastern Group Conference which is presided over by an Indian as affording an example of dominion Status in practice is stated by one of the newspapers conducted in Tamil as offering a plantain fruit to a crying child and does not show a sense of responsibility in a responsible statesman. The Hindu says: 'if Mr Amery, like the foolish virgins of the Parable, 'who when they took their lamps, took no oil with them', is capable of nothing better than the easy irresponsibility he has so far displayed, Britain should see to it that someone more alive to his responsibilities takes his place before it is too late'. Serious objection has also been taken to Mr Amery's characterization of the agitation in India as artificial.

Nationalist papers warn Government that the political situation will deteriorate still further if nothing is done to bring about a settlement with the Congress. A golden opportunity was offered to the Government in this respect by the Poona resolution which was, however, rejected. In this connection emphasis is being placed upon Maulana Abdul Kalam Azad's statement that 'if really Great Britain had really been anxious to part with power, a settlement could have been reached in two minutes'. Commenting on the move of Sir Jagadesh Prasad, Sir Fazlul Huq and others for political settlement some nationalist papers doubt very much, whether, when the British Government is so strongly opposed to part with real power, anything can be done to ease the situation.

Statement of Action taken under the defence of India Act and the Rules thereunder, etc., during the first fortnight of December 1940.

S.No.	Name of person, document, etc., or other particulars	Nature of offence	Action taken (specifying rule or rules under which action is taken)
1.	M.R. Venkataraman, Advocate, Madras and detenue, Vellore C.J. (no. 58 in the statement for 2nd fortnight of Nov. 5)	Violated conditions of parole under rule 26(6) of the Defence of Indian Rules.	Convicted and sentenced to Simple Imprisonment for six months.
2.	Hon'ble Mr Balusu Sambamurthi MLA, Speaker, Legislative Assembly.	Acting in a manner prejudicial to the maintenance of public order.	Directed to be arrested and detained in the Central Jail Vellore, under rule 26.
3.	K. Venkatamanacharu of Tadpatri, Anantapur District.	Delivering a lecture and shouting anti-war slogans	Convicted under rule 38(5) of the Defence of India Rules and Sentenced to one year RI.
4.	R. Venkatappa Naidu, BA BL, MLA, of Gooty, Anantapur District.	-do-	Convicted under rule 38(5) of the Defence of India Rules and Sentenced to RI for six months.
5.	Ethirajulu Naidu, of Gudiyatham, N. Arcot District.	Anti-war speeches.	Prosecution approved under rule 34 of the Defence of India Rules.
6.	D. Ramalinga Reddi, MLA, Cheyyar, North Arcot District, (No. 34 in the Statement for 1st fortnight of August 1940 and No. 32 in the statement for second fortnight of October 1940).	Satyagraha	Convicted under rule 38(5) of the Defence of India Rules and Sentenced to under RI for 9 months.
7.	N. Annamalaipillai, M.D.A., Thiruvannamalai, N.A. District	-do-	Convicted under rule 38(5) of the Defence of India Rules and Sentenced to under RI for 9 months.
8.	V. Subbiah of Pondicherry, (No. 27 in the statement of 2nd fortnight of November 1940)	Satyagraha	Directed to be arrested and detained in Jail.

(Contd.) ...

... (*Contd.*)

S.No.	Name of person, document, etc., or other particulars	Nature of offence	Action taken (specifying rule or rules under which action is taken)
9.	C. Perumalsami Reddi, MLC, President, Dist. Board North Arcot	-do-	Convicted under rule 38(5) and sentenced to RI for 9 months.
10.	K.R. Kalyanarama Ayyar of Ranipet, North Arcot District	Anti-war Speeches	Prosecution under rule 34 approved.
11.	W. Srinivasa Rao, President, Panchayat Board, Arni, North Arcot District	-do-	Sentenced to undergo RI for 9 months and fined Rs 200 in default RI for 3 months.
12.	Sambasiva Asary, Pallikonda, North Arcot District	Anti-war speeches and distribution of anti-war leaflets	Prosecution approved under rule 34 and 38.
13.	Ayyamperumal of Villupuram, South Arcot (No. 15 in the statement of the 2nd fortnight of October 1940).	Anti-war propaganda	Convicted and sentenced to RI for six months under Defence of India Rules.
14	Srimathi M. Anjali Ammal, MLA of Cuddalore OT South Arcot	Satyagraha	Convicted under rule 38(5) and sentenced to SI for six months.
15.	P. Ramswamy Reddiar, MLC of Omandur, South Arcot	-do-	Convicted under rule 38(5) and sentenced to RI for one year.
16.	K. Kulasekaran Doss, MLA, South Arcot	-do-	Convicted under rule 38(5) and sentenced to RI for one year.
17.	K. Karimuddin of Tellicherry, Student	Acting in a manner prejudicial to the maintenance of public order	Detained in the Central Jail, Vellore under Rule 26.
18.	V. Ramamurthi of Sivapuri	-do-	-do-
19.	K. Gutumurthi, Student	-do-	-do-
20.	P.K. Sankaranarayanan, Student	-do-	-do-
21.	M. Venkataramani, Student	-do-	-do-
22.	M. Meenakshi, Student	-do-	Detained in the Presidency Jail for Women Vellore under rule 26.

(*Contd.*) ...

... (*Contd.*)

S.No.	Name of person, document, etc., or other particulars	Nature of offence	Action taken (specifying rule or rules under which action is taken)
23.	K. Draviyam, Student	-do-	Movements restricted to his father's residence.
24.	R. Ramakrishna Raju, MLA, Chittor District	-do-	Convicted under rule 38(5) read with rules 38(1)(a) and 34(6)(k) and sentenced to SI for one year.
25.	M. Doraikannu, MLA, Chittoor	-do-	Convicted under rule 38 and 34 and sentenced to SI for six months.
26.	M. Anantasayanam Ayyangar, MLA (Central), Chittoor	-do-	Convicted under rule 34 and 38 and sentenced to SI for 9 months.
27.	R. Kissan Singh, Coimbatore	Communist activities	Directed to be arrested and detained in the Central Jail at Vellore.
28.	N.G. Rangaswami, MLA, Coimbatore	Satyagraha	Sentenced to SI for one year.
29.	Periaswami Goundaih, Coimbatore District	For committing a prejudicial act	Prosecution approved.
30.	K.S. Periaswamy Gounder, MLA, Coimbatore District	Distribution of anti-war leaflets	Sentenced to SI for 6 months and to pay a fine of Rs 200 in default SI for 2 months.
31.	Krishna Kudumban, MLA, Coimbatore District	Distribution of anti-war pamphlets	Convicted under rule 38 and sentenced to RI for 4 months and to pay a fine of Rs 200 in default RI for 2 months.
32.	C.P. Subbiah, MLA, Coimbatore	! ! Satyagraha	Sentenced to 6 months' RI each.
33.	T.S. Avinashilingam Chetti, MLA (Central), Coimbatore	! !	
34.	S.C. Balakrishna Kudumban, MLA, of Palni, Mudura District	-do-	Sentenced to SI for 6 months and a fine of Rs 100 in default of to SI for a further period of one month.

(*Contd.*) ...

... (*Contd.*)

S.No.	Name of person, document, etc., or other particulars	Nature of offence	Action taken (specifying rule or rules under which action is taken)
35.	D. Ramasubba Reddi, BA, BL, MLC, Cuddapah	-do-	Sentenced to RI for one year and a fine of Rs 250 in default to undergo RI for 3 months under Rule 38.
36.	V.S. Mani, son of Viswanatha Ayyar of Palghat now at Madura	Anti-war speeches	Prosecution and convicted under Rule 38(5) and sentenced to RI for 15 months under each of two counts, sentences to run concurrently.
37.	K. Sakthi Vadivel Gounder, Periyakulam, Taluk, Madura District.	Satyagraha	Convicted under rule 38(5) and sentenced to SI for six months and fine of Rs 300 in default to SI for 3 months.
38.	K.M. Karupiah of Kannampatti now at Madura.	Anti-war speeches	Prosecuted and convicted under rule 38 and sentenced to RI for 18 months under each of two counts—sentences to run concurrently.
39.	M.S. Abdul Sathar Sahib, Dindigul, Madura District	Satyagraha	Convicted under rule 38 and sentenced to undergo RI for 9 months and to pay a fine of Rs 500 in default to further RI for 3 months.
40.	P.R. Ramanuja Ayyangar, Vakil, Sivaganga, Ramnad District (No. 32 in the 1st fortnight of August 1940).	Anti-war speeches	Acquitted under Section 253(1) Cr PC
41.	Jainallaudin of Alayangulam, Ramnad District (No. 20 in the statement for the 1st fortnight of September 1940).	-do-	Prosecuted, convicted and sentenced to SI for 9 months.
42.	Dorariraj Reddiyar.	-do-	Each convicted and sentenced to RI for one year.
43.	N. Ayyavu Thevar.	-do-	-do-
44.	R. Guruswami Khone	-do-	-do-

(*Contd.*) ...

... (*Contd.*)

S.No.	Name of person, document, etc., or other particulars	Nature of offence	Action taken (specifying rule or rules under which action is taken)
45.	S. Ramaswamy Thevar All of Virudunagar, Ramnad District (Nos 17 to 20 in the statement for the 2nd fortnight of September 1940).	-do-	-do-
46.	Ayyangar of Sivaganga, Ramnad District	Anti-war slogans.	Prosecution approved under Defence of India Rules
47.	Sankara Menon, Ramnad District	-do-	-do-
48.	Mania Pillai, Ramnad District	-do-	-do-
49.	I.M.P. Arumuga Mudali of Salem District (no. 29 in the statement for the 1st fortnight of November 1940)	Anti-war speeches	Convicted and sentenced to RI for 18 months.
50.	Kannu alias Kandaswami Mudali of Salem District (No. 30 in the statement for the 1st fortnight of November 1940).	-do-	Convicted; but released under section 562 Cr PC with a bond for Rs 200 with one surety for a like amount.
51.	Dr P. Subbarayan MLA, Ex.Minister.	Satyagraha	Convicted and sentenced to SI for six months.
52.	Mrs Radhabai Subbarayan, MLA, (Central)	-do-	-do-
53.	M.G. Natess Chettiar, MLA, Salem District.	-do-	Convicted under rule 38 and sentenced to RI for 6 months and to pay a fine of Rs 500 in default to RI for period of 3 months.
54.	M.P. Periaswamy, MLA, Salem District.	-do-	Convicted and sentenced to RI for one year and to pay a fine of Rs 500 in default to further RI for 3 months.
55.	Nagaraja Ayyangar, MLA, Salem District.	-do-	Convicted and sentenced to SI for one year.

(*Contd.*) ...

... (Contd.)

S.No.	Name of person, document, etc., or other particulars	Nature of offence	Action taken (specifying rule or rules under which action is taken)
56.	Seshadri of Salem.	-do-	Convicted under rule 38(5) and sentenced to SI for 18 months and fine of Rs 100 in default to SI for 2 months.
57.	Palaniswami Mudali, Salem District	Satyagraha	Convicted and sentenced to SI for six months.
58.	Samanna alias Mari Chetti, Salem District	-do-	Convicted and sentenced to SI for six months
59.	Govindaswami Chetti, Salem District	-do-	Convicted and sentenced to SI for six months
60.	S.M.R. Manickam, Salem District	-do-	Convicted and sentenced to SI for 18 months and fine of Rs 100 in default to SI for 2 months.
61.	M.A. Vajralingam, Salem District	-do-	Convicted under rule 38(5) and sentenced to RI for 12 months.
62.	Arjunan	Satyagraha	Each convicted under rule 38(5) and sentenced to RI for one year.
63.	R. Sellan.	-do-	-do-
64.	Kannuswami.	-do-	-do-
65.	Ramaswami Reddy all of Salem District	-do-	-do-
66.	Venkatachalam Chetty, Salem District	-do-	Convicted under rule 38(5) and sentenced to SI for 18 months and fine of Rs 100 in default to SI for 2 months.
67.	Krishnan, North Arcot District	-do-	Convicted and sentenced to SI for 18 months and fine of Rs 200 in default to SI for 3 months.
68.	Jagannadan Pillai, Salem District	Distribution of anti-war pamphlets	Sentenced to RI for two months

(Contd.) ...

... (*Contd.*)

S.No.	Name of person, document, etc., or other particulars	Nature of offence	Action taken (specifying rule or rules under which action is taken)
69.	V. Bhooravaha Ayyangar, MLA, Tanjore District.	Satyagraha	Convicted under Rule 38 and sentenced to RI for one year.
70.	Kolandai Velu Nayanar, MLA, Tanjore.	-do-	Convicted under Rule 38 and sentenced to RI for 15 months.
71.	Ammapet P. Venkataram Ayyar, MLA, Tanjore	-do-	Convicted under Rule 38 and sentenced to RI for 9 months.
72.	A. Vedarathnam Pillai, MLA, Tanjore	-do-	Convicted under Rule 38 and sentenced to RI for 9 months.
73.	K. Santanam, MLA (Central) Tanjore	-do-	Convicted and sentenced to RI for 6 months.
74.	K. Mariamuthu Pillai, MLA, Tanjore	-do-	Convicted under Rule 38 and sentenced to RI for 6 months.
75.	Somasundaram Pillai of Negapatam (Tanjore Dt.) No. 21 in the statement for the 1st fortnight of August 1940.	Disuading people from contributing to the War Fund and creating alarm.	Convicted; but released under section 562 of Cr PC on executing a bond for Rs 25 to be of good behaviour for one year.
76.	Ponniah of Avadiyapuram, Tinnevelly District.	Anti-war Speeches	Prosecution approved under rules 34 and 38.
77.	S. Ramaswami Pillai of Tuticorin, Tinnevelly District.	-do-	-do-
78.	Shanmugasundaram Thevar, Dhevarpuram, Tinnevelly.	Anti-War Speeches	Prosecution approved under rule 34. Directed to be dealt with under section 562 Cr PC.
79.	Venkatachalam Pillai, MLA, Trichinopoly District.	Satyagraha	Convicted under rule 38(5) and sentenced to RI for six months and a fine of Rs 500/-
80.	Kolar Gangayya, Madras City.	Prejudicial act	Convicted under Rule 38(5) and sentenced to RI for six months.

(*Contd.*) ...

... (*Contd.*)

S.No.	Name of person, document, etc., or other particulars	Nature of offence	Action taken (specifying rule or rules under which action is taken)
81.	P.N. Madurai, Madras City.	-do-	-do-
82.	Deenan Alias Deenadayalu Madras City	-do-	-do-
83.	C. Ratnam, Madras City	-do-	-do-
84.	K. Govinda Menon, Madras City.	-do-	Convicted under Rule 38(5) and sentenced to RI for 3 months.
85.	P. Vakil Pillai, Madras City.	-do-	Convicted under Rule 38(5) and sentenced to RI for 5 months.
86.	V.V. Giri, MLA, Ex-Minister	Satyagraha	Convicted under Rule 38(5) and sentenced to RI for 15 months.
87.	C. Rajagopalachari	-do-	Convicted under Rule 38(5) and sentenced to RI for 12 months.
88.	P.M. Adikesavalu Naicker, Madras City.	-do-	Convicted under Rule 38(5) and sentenced to RI for 6 months.
89.	N.S. Varadachari, MLA, Ex-Parliamentary Secretary.	-do-	Convicted under Rule 38(5) and sentenced to RI for 6 months.
90.	K.Venakatasami Naidu, MLC, Deputy President.	-do-	-do-
91.	V.I. Muniswami Pillai, MLA Ex-Minister.	-do-	Convicted under Rule 38(5) and sentenced to RI for 7 months.
92.	V.S. Mani Alias Venkata Subramanian, Madras City.	Prejudicial act.	Convicted under Rule 38(5) and sentenced to RI for 4 months.
93.	S. Satyamurthi, MLA, Central.	Satyagraha	Convicted under Rule 38(5) and sentenced to RI for 4 months.
94.	Adimoolam Servai, Ramnad District.	Distribution of anti-war leaflets	Prosecution under Defence of India Rules approved.

(*Contd.*) ...

... (Contd.)

S.No.	Name of person, document, etc., or other particulars	Nature of offence	Action taken (specifying rule or rules under which action is taken)
95.	M. Natarajan, Madras City.	-do-	Prosecuted and convicted under rule 39(1)(c) and (5) and sentenced to RI for 6 months
96.	Ramaswamy Thevan, Ramnad District.	-do-	Prosecution under Defence of India Rules approved
97.	Sethuraja Thevar, Ramnad District.	-do-	-do-
98.	M. Muniswami Chetty	Possession of Communist literature	No. 98 Four months RI under two counts.
99.	T.R. Subramaniyam.	-do-	No. 99-15 months RI under one count and one year's RI each under two other counts.
100.	M.K. Panduranga Mudali	-do-	No. 100-15 months RI under one count and one year's RI each under two other counts.
101.	M. Venkatachala Mudali of Madras City. Nos. 28 to 31 in the statement for 2nd fortnight of July 1940.	-do-	No. 101-9 months RI under two counts. All sentences to run concurrently.
102.	R. Ramakrishnan, Student, Benaras Hindu University.	Communist Activities	Directed to be detained in jail under rule 26.
103.	K. Muthiah, Student.	-do-	-do-
104.	V.S. Somasundaram, Madras City	-do-	-do-
105.	Veerabhadra Rao, Vizagapatam	-do-	-do-

No. of persons newly prosecuted during the fortnight   108
No. of Persons convicted during the fortnight   111

No. of person actually undergoing imprisonment in Madras Jail on the 15th December 1940 in connection with political and subversive movements:

Under Section 124-AIPC   Nil
Under Section 153-AIPC   Nil
Under Defence of India Rules, convicted   258
Under detention in jails under rule 26 of the Defence of India Rules   60

54. Report of Satyagraha in Madras Province during the Second Half of December 1940

Fortnightly Report for the Second Half of December 1940, D.O. No. P.4–1, Public (General) Department, Government of Madras to the Secretary to the Government of India, Home Department, 4 January 1941, Tamil Nadu State Archives.

Satyagraha has continued in most districts, but on a restricted scale as the first list of nominees is now almost completely exhausted. The action taken against the Satyagrahis is shown in the attached statement. There have been more cases of unofficial Satyagraha. Many of the persons concerned are persons of little importance or influence and efforts are being made to find a suitable method of dealing with them, particularly as this class of offenders appear to be on the increase. Several District Magistrates have reported that further lists of persons to offer Satyagraha between January 5th and Aril 5th have been prepared. These lists contain a large number of name, the number being as high as 85 in Kistna. From this it will be seen that Congress propose to try and flood the jails in the next three months with as a thousand satyagrahis a month from one part of the province.

There have been many meetings of students and other bodies to protest against the police action at Chidambaram the details of which I reported last fortnight. The situation at the University appears to be improving as a result of the strong action taken, and the firm stand taken by the University authorities in dealing with a threatened strike by the students has at last made the latter realize that defiance of authority will be heavily punished. Similar action by the authorities of the Hindu College at Masulipatnam in dealing with students' strike has had an equally satisfactory result though not without police intervention at one stage.

During the fortnight several agitators, chiefly communists, who have been out of view for some time, have been arrested and detained or, where possible they have been brought to trial and convicted for specific offences.

There was brief hunger strike from 21st December to 23rd December by 12 convicted prisoners at Vellore Jail. The reasons for the strike was the diet awarded by the convicting magistrates. All twelve are being prosecuted.

Report on the Press for the Second Fortnight of December 1940.

Comments in the Press: His Excellency the Viceroy's speech in Calcutta so far as the political deadlock is concerned has been commented upon by the nationalist press as making no advance whatsoever on the present position. The Anglo-Indian Papers take the other view and call upon the political parties to come together and present a joint scheme, but the nationalist papers adhere to the view that mere expansion of the Executive Council would not satisfy the people and that reiteration of this scheme betrays lack of grasp of the essentials of the situation. This method of dealing with the impasse would only increase bitterness and postpone the prospect of conciliation after the war.

The MP's appeal to India is welcomed for the good sentiments contained in it. The nationalist papers ask whether the British Government now ruling India are 'irrevokably resolved to give India full political freedom'. It may be that the idea of considering India less than an equal is foreign to the House of Commons. But does that sentiment, it is asked, represent the view of the present Government? The appeal further repeats the arguments of Mr Amery and the Viceroy regarding the difficulties. This only shows that there is yet no clear grasp in Great

Britain, even in quarters which may be considered sympathetic towards Indian aspirations, of the crux of the situation. The Government are unwilling to part with power to the people. That is the point which Britishers have got to grasp.

Statement of action taken under the defence of India act and the rules thereunder during the second fortnight of December 1940

Number of persons against whom action was taken during the fortnight is 128 as contained in the list.

Number of persons newly prosecuted during the fortnight	99
Number of Persons convicted during the fortnight	93

55. Seth Jamnalal Bajaj Arrested

Hindustan Times, 22 December 1940.

9 months' Imprisonment and Rs 500 fine—Second List of Lucknow Satyagrahis—Arrests and Convictions in Provinces—UP Raja's Bonfire of Foreign Cloth.

Seth Jamnalal Bajaj, a member of the Congress Working Committee, was arrested at Sevagram yesterday morning and was later tried and sentenced to nine months' simple imprisonment and a fine of Rs 500.

Reports of arrests and conviction continue to be received from the various provinces in connection with the Satyagraha movement.

Pandit Peareylal Sharma, an ex-Minister of the UP, was sentenced at Meerut to one year's simple imprisonment on Friday last.

Seth Jamnalal Bajaj was arrested at Sevagram at 5 a.m. today (Saturday) under Section 129 of the Defence of India Rules. He was to have offered Satyagraha at 9 this morning.

Judgement was later delivered by Mr B.N. Runte in the case against Seth Jamnalal Bajaj sentencing him to nine months' simple imprisonment and a fine of Rs 500.

Seth Jamnalal Bajaj was recommended to be placed in 'A' class. It is understood that he is being removed to Nagpur Jail either tonight or on Monday.

Seth Jamnalal Bajaj was brought to the Nagpur Central Jail this afternoon.

Seth Jamnalal Bajaj attended this morning's prayers at Sevagram while the police waited for him. When the prayers were over, they informed Seth Bajaj that he was under arrest. Mahatma Gandhi and other inmates of the Ashram bade him farewell and then he was taken to his Wardha residence and from there taken to Wardha Jail.

Seth Jamnalal Bajaj, member of the Congress Working Committee, has issued the following statement to the press on the eve of his offering Satyagraha:

'Mahatma Gandhi has made this province his home and conferred on it the proud distinction of initiating individual Satyagraha. It is both a privilege and a responsibility and the responsibility is greater of the two. We should, therefore, realize our heavy responsibility and approach our task in a spirit of humility.'

'The eyes of the whole world are naturally fixed on our province, which had the rare privilege of launching individual Civil Disobedience. Shri Vinoba Bhave, the first and foremost Satyagrahi has struck a high standard. He has increased the prestige of our province and won admiration even from the adversary. It is ours to acquit ourselves in a manner calculated to maintain that noble tradition. We can discharge our task only if we scrupulously follow Mahatma

Gandhi's discipline and work out his constructive programme more specially Hindu-Muslim unity, removal of untouchability and Khadi.'

Mr Chaturbhuj Jasani, Vice-President of the Nagpur Provincial Congress Committee, who was arrested at Gondia was sentenced to six months' rigorous imprisonment and a fine of Rs 200. He was brought to Nagpur .... Mrs Umratkar, who offered Satyagraha on Friday morning, was arrested under the Defence of India Rules and fined Rs 75.

Bahorilal Suryawanshi, MLA, who offered Satyagraha at Pamgad on December 19 and was arrested has been sentenced to six months' rigorous imprisonment.

Mr Dipchand Gothi, MLA, the first Satyagrahi from Betul, has been arrested.

Mrs Umaratkar of Pahoor in the Yeotmal District who offered Satyagraha was sentenced till the rising of the court and to a fine of Rs 75. On her refusal to pay the fine she was released.

Shaikh Ibrahim of Ghatladki, Mr Raghunath Singh Kiledar, president of the Mahakoshal PCC and Mr Onkar Dutta Rathi, President of the Malkapur Town Congress Committee who offered Satyagraha have been arrested.

Seth Khushal Chand, MLA of Chanda who offered Satyagraha today was arrested and sentenced to six months' rigorous imprisonment and placed in 'B' class.

UP

More Convictions—Second List From Lucknow—Second list of nearly a hundred Satyagrahis has been sent to the Provincial Congress Committee office by the Lucknow District Congress Committee. The list includes members of local boards.

Mr Bansagopal, MLA, was sentenced to one year's simple imprisonment and placed in 'A' class yesterday says a report from Fatehpur. Pandit Govind Malviya and Dr Thungamma, both MLAs have been sentenced to one year and four months' simple imprisonment respectively at Benares.

Ali Sardar Jafri, Secretary of the Lucknow University Student Union and Kazi Jalil Abbasi, President of the Lucknow Students' Federation were sentenced under the Defence of India Rules to six months' simple imprisonment each by Rai Sahib Anand Swarup, City Magistrate, Lucknow. Both of them were placed in 'B' Class.

The announcement that he would say something while offering Satyagraha, if he got a chance at Aonla on December 23 was made by Moulvi Abdul Wajid, MLA (Central), while presiding over a meeting at Moti Park, Bareilly. A resolution moved by Mr Siddique congratulating Mr Rafi Ahmed Kidwai, President, Dwarka Prasad, MLA President, Shanker, G.L. Gupta, Brijmohanlal Shastri and Hafiz Mohd. Ibrahim on their arrest and condemning the repressive policy of the British Government was adopted.

In spite of police vigilance Chowdhri Bhimsen, Harijan MLA, offered Satyagraha at the scheduled hour in his constituency in the village of Arnia. After a speech by the District Congress President and Secretary, Mr Bhimsen raised anti-war slogans and was arrested.

Pandit Peareylal Sharma Sentenced

Mr Peareylal Sharma, MLA, ex-Education Minister, UP, who had intimated to the District Magistrate of Meerut of his intention to offer Satyagraha on December 18 at village of Muhluddinpur by shouting anti-war slogans, but was arrested earlier, was tried on Friday by the City Magistrate in the district jail and found guilty under the Defence of India Rules and sentenced to one year's simple imprisonment and recommended 'A' class. Mr Sharma merely pleaded guilty to the charge and did not participate in the proceedings.

Madras—K.K. Nadar Arrested—President of Tamil Nadu Congress Committee

News has been received that Mr K. Kamaraj Nadar, President of the Tamil Nadu Congress Committee, who left Madras yesterday for Wardha, was arrested at Gundur under Section 26 of the Defence of India Rules and taken to Vellore. It is stated that Mr Nadar was proceeding to Wardha with a list of Satyagrahis for the approval of Mahatma Gandhi.

Mr D. Kadirappa, MLA (Harijan) who offered Satyagraha yesterday was sentenced to six months' rigorous imprisonment.

Mr Mattaparai Venkatarama Aiyar, MLA, Whip of the Congress Party in the Madras Legislative Assembly who was arrested on Friday morning for offering satyagraha was sentenced to nine months' rigorous imprisonment and a fine of Rs 100 on each count, in default to further three months' rigorous imprisonment under the Defence of India Rules.

Andhra PCC Decision

The executive committee of the Andhra Provincial Congress Committee which met at Guntur on Friday afternoon under the presidentship of Dr Pattabhi Sitaramayya decided that such of the Congressmen as were under disciplinary action were not entitled to offer Satyagraha.

56. Intelligence Report of a Conversation Between the President of Maharashtra Provincial Congress Committee and Mahatma Gandhi on Satyagraha and Related Activities

Home Department, Political Section (Intelligence), File No. 3/33/40, 24 December 1940, NAI.

Copy of a note regarding the talk between T.R. Deogirikar, President, Maharashtra, PCC and Mahatma Gandhi.

Mahatmaji was asked whether after the commencement of his fast the Satyagraha would stop. He became at once serious and said why should Satyagraha stop if he starts his fast. There is no connection between the two. Satyagraha would and must go on in spite of the fast. I showed him the list he asked me whether I have got full information of those whose names I had suggested. I said 'Yes, I have brought that'. Do you know the ages of those Satyagrahis? 'Sorry', I said, 'I have not that. But all of them are above eighteen.' 'That is not sufficient. Do you know how many persons are dependent on each of the Satyagrahis? Take for instance Mr Mahajan, How many persons are dependent on him?' I could not reply. He said, 'Some persons come to me and say that they have thirteen persons to support. Wherefrom can I or the Congress Committee give them money? They must not depend on the Congress Committee for the support of their families'. I said, 'in the pledges they have agreed that they would not ask for help. Is it not sufficient?' 'Yes, I want to know under what pressing conditions they are offering Satyagraha. Do you know in the Military for instance John's details are given in full. The Commander must know every detail about the person whom he asks to fight. When I went to R.T.C. the Government had full information about us. I want to prepare Who's Who. I want to publish a book giving details about the Satyagrahis. I want to show to the Britishers, nay, to the whole world what the caliber of our Satyagrahis is. Do you know Mr Young of the *Pioneer*? When he came here, he was a pauper, a beggar. He got a job in the *Pioneer*. He became Editor of the paper, but as soon as War commenced, he was taken on Rs 5000 by the

Government. He took all the Englishmen working in that paper with him, and gave them high posts, and high salaries. They are exploiting India as much as they can even now. This is the sacrifice of the English people at the time of the War. I want to show by contrast that whereas the Englishmen are fattening themselves on India's money, the sons of India having big families to support are courting jail for their country. I am going to lay before the world that the Satyagrahis who had thirteen men to support made supreme sacrifices for the country. Would it not be glorious?' 'yes' I said. I told him I would supply him all the details as soon as I go to Poona. 'Yes, do that'. 'The Andhra people have given me full details. You must give me details about your Province. You know this is not a mass Satyagraha. I do not want a large number of people going to jail. I want the choicest and the best men to offer Satyagraha, they must not only be the representatives but must be men of high standard. I want to have such men. They may be few, but must be the best. I am sending Pyarelal to jail. Do you know what hardships I would be put to. He is my hand, my foot, nay my brain. Without him I cannot work. But I am sending him on the 15th. I want to send Mahadev also, but I would be crippled if I send him now. But his turn is to come soon. In making selection keep this point in view.'

'Mahatmaji, what should be the form of the notice to be given to the Magistrate?' why, he asked me, don't you know it? 'Yes, I know, we were saying that we were selected by Mahatmaji'. 'Yes, that should be the form. You must write in the notice that you are selected by me for offering Satyagraha, there should be one form in the whole country. We must have a uniform notice. In the Civil Procedure Code, the Government has one settled form of summons, go to any distant part of the country and you will have the same language of the summons. We must have one uniform language in Satyagraha, be particular about it.'

'Some persons whom we don't select will also be giving notice to the District Magistrate and will be going to jail. How can we prevent it?' 'That will be a calamity,' said Gandhiji. 'They should not do that. They should not embarrass us.' 'Mahatmaji may I suggest one way to distinguish?' 'Yes, Yes' said Mahatmaji. 'How do you like the idea of submitting the whole list approved by you to the District Magistrate of the Government?' 'That is splendid, you do it. The Government must know who are our men and who are coming in our way to foil our attempt', said Gandhiji.

'What about the Provincial and District Congress Committee? What work should they do and where are the men to do that?' Mahatmaji said 'What normal activities can you do? You won't get good men to carry on the work. Let the whole constitution be suspended. Only one man should be at the head of the organization.'

'You have given, I am told, option to the Provinces to determine their policy, with regard to the Local Bodies. We have asked the local body members to resign'. Mahatmaji said 'No, no, you must not ask them to resign. Why should they resign? You did not take them on the congress ticket on the condition that they should either go to jail or should resign, if the political situation develops in the way in which it has done now. MANU SUBHEDAR has resigned. He wrote to me today that he was not taken on congress ticket on the condition of his going to Jail. He is right. I have just written to him not to resign, let the seats remain vacant, if the members go to jail, the local bodies, work must go on. Undesirable persons would capture the seats if you resign'.

'Should the Communists be included in the list?' 'No,' Gandhiji said, 'Should we open volunteer camps?' 'No', he replied. 'What about meetings? No meetings should be held for Satyagraha, that is creating violent atmosphere. Look at the Ghatkopar incidence. I don't want to give a lightest opportunity for the violence. Only slogans should be pronounced. Notice to the District Magistrate is sufficient. People should not be informed of your Satyagraha (left blank) this should be on everybody's mouth just as Ramnam has become universal. Does it require notification to the people? Every man, child and woman should repeat that. Let the whole atmosphere be surcharged with this 'mantra'. You can have meeting no doubt but they should not be for the purpose of Satyagraha'.

I told him that person arrested under section 129 would be served with restrain orders after they are kept in jail for two months. Should they break the order immediately? 'Yes, if their names are approved by me, they must disobey the orders', said Gandhiji.

'What about those who come out after their term of sentence is over?' 'I have selected them and I want them to go to jail again and again. They require no further permission from me to offer Satyagraha. This is the last fight, we must sacrifice all for it' said Mahatmaj.

'You don't offer Satyagraha soon', he told me. I said, 'how will it be possible, I am doing this work and any day I am likely to be arrested'. 'Yes, yes,' said Gandhiji, 'I am sitting on the mouth of death, anything may happen to you and to me. But instruct your successor to mind my order. The second list must not begin before January.' Gandhiji appeared full of hope and sure of success. I took his leave and departed.

57. Report on Satyagraha Activities During Second Half of December 1940 in CP and Berar

Fortnightly Reports, File No. 18/12/40, Home Department, Political Intelligence Section, Government of India, NAI.

The individual civil disobedience movement initiated by Mahatma Gandhi continued during the fortnight. Persons against whom action was taken during the fortnight include one member of the Central Legislative Assembly, viz. Mr Shambhudayal Mishra, one member of the Congress Working Committee viz. Seth Jamnalal Bajaj, and several members of the Provincial Legislative Assembly. Seth Jamnalal Bajaj and one MLA were dealt with under rule 121 read with rule 38 of the Defence of India Rules in view of the anticipation that the Satyagraha would attract large audiences and cause excitement. One member of the Legislative Assembly in the Raipur district was arrested for the same reason under rule 129 and then ordered to be detained indefinitely under rule 26. Other persons were arrested after commission of the offence. In some cases, crowds witnessing Satyagraha were large, but there is no reason to believe that the excitement was anything but temporary. The crowds were in every case well-behaved and there were no incidents. The movement has not yet captured the public imagination and there is not much genuine enthusiasm. Rural areas continue to be quiet, and Berar reports apathy towards the movement. The total number of convicted Satyagrahis beginning with Mr Vinobha Bhave is now 96, of which five are women and one a Muslim. Two persons are detained under rule 26 of the Defence of India Rules. The number of persons convicted upto date from the beginning of the war and undergoing imprisonment on the 28th December 1940 is 138. Of these, 14 are in A class, 65 in B class, and 59 in C class. During the fortnight a change was introduced in the technique of sentences on Satyagrahis. In Berar, about nine Satyagrahis were sentenced to imprisonment till the rising of the court and fines proportioned to means. In CP Seth Dipchand, MLA, Betul, was sentenced to a fine of Rs 500 and imprisonment till the rising of the court. Prior to his offering satyagraha, he had received numerous farewell parties in the expectation that he would be sentenced to a long term of imprisonment and it is reported that the announcement of the sentence made him look crest fallen. One Baburao Kamat, an inmate of the Village Industries Association (Maganwadi) Wardha under the control of Mahatma Gandhi offered Satyagraha as expiation for adultery on a Mahar woman. He was sentenced to imprisonment till the rising of the court, and a fine of rupee one. It is yet too early to gauge the results of the policy of imposing only fines. During the fortnight, the Provincial Government reviewed the question of the policy of dealing with the Satyagraha movement and shortly after the close of the fortnight detailed instructions, of which a copy is being forwarded separately to the Government of India, were issued to District Magistrates. In the first phase of the movement, Satyagraha was offered by members of the Working Committee, the All India Congress Committee and the Central and Provincial Legislatures with one exception, are now in jail. The only member of the working committee in the province is also in jail. Forty four out of seventy Congress members of the Provincial Legislative Assembly are in jail. The first phase is, therefore, not yet complete, but the second phase will begin immediately and will consist of offer of Satyagraha by members of provincial, district and tahsil Congress committees and local bodies. Reliable figures are not available but it is estimated that within the next three months about 1,000 persons may take part in the movement.

There has been very little other political activity. The number of political meetings has declined and the size of the audiences is also dwindling. The All India Students' Federation met at Nagpur on the 25th and 26th December 1940 and resulted in a split between the Communists and Congress-minded members, both wings holding separate conferences. The Communist wing was addressed by Dr K.M. Ashraf, Mr B.N. Mukherji, chairman of the reception committee, and Professor Hiren Mukherji, the president of the conference. Dr Ashraf said that the European war was an imperialistic one. He also criticized the Satyagraha movement characterising it as 'a parliamentary show'. He further criticized Mahatma Gandhi for advising students to leave schools and colleges, if they wanted to join the Satyagraha movement. Mr Mukherji also criticized Mahatma Gandhi for advising students not to strike but to sit down with folded hands. The students wanted to fight and also wanted mass action. Professor Mukherji extolled the Russian system and remarked that imperialism was keeping India in a state of 'planned backwardness' as an 'agrarian hinterland'. He accused that the self-appointed British trustees had criminally neglected India's interests. He concluded by exhorting the students to become whole time revolutionaries ready for discomforts, and further advised them to arrange demonstrations against the Madras and United Province circulars. The meeting of the Congress-minded section of the federation was held under the presidentship of one Mr Madan Mohan Prasad. The speeches were moderate. Owing to the split, there was rowdyism and altogether the whole show has created a very bad impression. In Berar, Dr Patwardhan addressed several meetings in the Buldana district on behalf of the Forward Bloc.

Chapter 5. Communal Politics

A. BRITISH ATTITUDE TOWARDS THE COMMUNAL PROBLEM

1. Secretary of State on Viceroy's Interview with Indian Leaders

Secretary of State to Viceroy, 28 February 1940, Correspondence with Secretary of State, Vol. V, 1940, Linlithgow Papers, Acc. No. 2153, NAI.

Your letter of the 6th reached me on the 22nd and your letter of the 13th on the following day. Along with them came full records of your talks with Sikander, Fazlul Huq, Jinnah and Gandhi, documents which, as you will readily believe, I have studied with interest. What a medley of conflicting interests, ambitions and apprehensions, sharpened by the grindstone of personal jealousies, aspirations and animosities. How on earth are we to extract from this seething cauldron any solid matter capable of providing foundation for a political edifice large enough and substantial enough to accommodate within its walls the representatives of the sub-continent?

A word as to the talks themselves. After reading your account of your talk with Fazlul Huq[1], with his fulminations against the Congress and his reproaches to His Majesty's Government for fawning upon their enemies, i.e. the Congress and flouting their friends, i.e. Muslim League, I found myself of your opinion that his rabid communalism will present a formidable obstacle in the way of doing business with him as a collaborator in any general settlement. Imagine, then, my astonishment in reading his effusion reported in the *Hindustan Times* as having been made within 48 hours of his interview with you—no community had the right to hold up the progress of the country; the deadlock must be resolved by immediate agreement between the warring parties; they should start with a clean sheet and march shoulder to shoulder to their goal of the country's freedom—all these capped with the confession of a contrite heart that his attack upon his Hindu brethren in his speech at Jubbulpore had been a wicked business for which he now pleaded for their forgiveness. I am not surprised to hear that Jinnah laughed aloud when his attention was called to this staggering apologia. The explanation is doubtless to be found in Fazlul Huq's own admission that he is an emotional man, carried away as he himself puts it, 'many a time'. This must, I think, have been one of the many times! Meanwhile, he appears to have extended an invitation to B.C. Chatterjee to discuss the communal award in Bengal. I shall be interested to hear the outcome of any discussion that may take place between them.

---

[1] See Chapter 2, Document no. 28.

2. Viceroy's Talk with Jinnah

Viceroy to Secretary of State, 16 March 1940, Telegraphic Correspondence between Viceroy and Secretary of State, Vol. V, 1940, Linlithgow Papers, Acc. No. 2162, NAI.

I saw Jinnah on 13th March. As regards his letter of 24th February I told him that I was in touch with you and was not yet in a position to make any communication to him. I asked him whether he was yet able to let me know about his constructive proposals. He said nothing positive in reply but urged strongly that both from the Muslim point of view and that of His Majesty's Government given the development of the war and the growing feeling of solidarity in the Muslim world (though he did not exaggerate the importance of the external Muslim community in the Indian problem) there was much to be said for our getting together. Muslims could work with us only on a basis of confidence and partnership. When we got to the stage of deciding what was next to be done in India, the Muslims would be very ready to tell us the right answer. Meanwhile if we wished their definite and effective help we must not sell the pass behind their backs. If we could not improve on our present solution for the problem of India's constitutional development he and his friends would have no option but to fall back on some form of partition. It was most desirable too that we should as early as possible relieve the present state of painful uncertainty of the Muslims as to our future policy in relation to Congress. He and his friends were clear that the Muslims were not a minority but a nation; that democracy for all India was impossible; and were anxious not to let us get ourselves into a position in which our hold over India was deliberately and progressively withdrawn so that in the end, control of the country as a whole would be handed over to a Hindu Raj while in the intermediate period His Majesty's Government would be in the position of having to uphold Hindu control with British bayonets to hold the Muslims down.

He was quite prepared to contemplate the possibility that we might have to stay here much longer than was anticipated for the job of keeping the ring, but returned again on that point to his apprehensions of what would happen in regard to functions (other than defence) which ex-hypothesis would in such a situation be handed over to a Central Government alias Hindu Raj during the intermediate period.

As you will see nothing of much value emerged from our talk, record of which goes by next bag, but I again got the impression of hardening of Muslim opinion and of growing depth of feeling in that community.

3. Viceroy's Telegram to Secretary of State on his Assessment of the Communal Situation

Secretary of State to Viceroy, 4 April 1940, Telegraphic Correspondence between Viceroy and Secretary of State, Linlithgow Papers, Acc. No. 2162, NAI.

To reiterate and emphasize not only that goal of our policy is attainment as soon as possible of Dominion Status but also our firm intention to do all we can to further this object and to emphasize at the same time the obstacles to practical progress in shape of the Indian dissensions which have become so emphatic and uncompromising in the last few weeks. I should go on to state my belief that first necessity for any progress towards goal is emergence from some Indian quarter of some constructive plan for self-government which would take account of and surmount difficulties inherent in Indian conditions or at all events a willingness to cooperate in discussions which would have some chance of producing such a plan. I would then contrast this with facts that from one side we have so far had a demand for examination afresh of the Indian constitution with no indication, until recent formal adoption of idea referred to in paragraph 3 below, of nature of result to be achieved, while constructive efforts of the other side have been confined to the assumption that a Constituent Assembly elected by adult suffrage will some-how by some magic produce a plan the possible nature of which has never yet been indicated. But I would abstain from any criticism of Congress [which] might be construed as a declaration of war or afford an excuse for resort to civil disobedience. Incidentally there is material of which use can profitably be made in debate in *Manchester Guardian* leading articles of April 2nd, full text of which has been telegraphed to you.

In particular, I feel, I must make this debate the occasion for pouring much cold water on the Muslim idea of partition formally advocated in the Lahore Resolution, though not necessarily at this stage conclusively rejecting it. I should emphasize that this would be a counsel of despair and wholly at variance with the policy of a united India which British rule has achieved and which it is our aim to perpetuate after British rule ceases.

I should be glad if you would deal in your appreciation with probable reactions to such a passage in Government speeches in the debate and I shall of course be glad to have any other comments you wish to make on anything else in this telegram.

3. As for the future Government of India as a whole, that we should draw attention to our continued insistence on the importance of Indian unity which you and I have repeatedly stressed and express our regret that the widening gap between the communities and interests, consequent on the attitude which Congress has adopted towards Minorities, and towards the Princes should constitute so serious a threat and a set-back to that unity. There is much that could be said in criticism of Jinnah's partition ideas and we clearly could not accept or endorse them. But quite apart from the fact that we have left the whole scheme and policy of the Act open for discussion after the war, and that Jinnah's scheme itself has, I suspect, largely been provoked by the unreasonable demands of Congress, any condemnation of Jinnah's scheme will at once irritate Muslim feeling and will be seized on by Congress. In present tempers here I would myself therefore, think it preferable to quote it as illustrating the extent to which the gulf has widened between the parties, and to take the line that His Majesty's Government attached all the more importance in such circumstances to reaching a solution, with the agreement of all parties, which would secure the unity of India.

4. Secretary of State on Muslim League's Attitude

Letter from Secretary of State to Viceroy, 24 April 1940, Correspondence with Secretary of State, Linlithgow Papers, Acc. No. 2153, NAI.

I hope that the terms of reply to Jinnah which I telegraphed to you a few days ago will be sufficient to keep him quiet, though I do not feel All India Muslim League seems to me to justify the fear which I expressed last summer, with what I am afraid you must have found somewhat wearisome reiteration, that we should find the Muslims the most formidable obstacle in the way of the Federation which we were then hoping to achieve. I am bound to say that if their present mood persists, I see little chance of our being able to bring them in, at any rate on any terms approaching those contemplated by the Act.

The Diehards over here are secretly delighted at the widening of the gulf between the Muslims and the Hindus, but taking a long view I should myself doubt very much if a cleavage between the Muslims and the Hindus as fundamental as that contemplated by the present leaders of the All India Muslim League, would prove to be to our advantage.

The Hindus have no particular affiliation outside India, whereas the call of Islam is one which transcends the bounds of country. It may have lost some of its force as a result of the abolition of the Caliph by Mustapha Kemal Pasha, but it still has a very considerable appeal, as witness for example, Jinnah's insistence on our giving undertaking that Indian troops should never be employed against any Muslim State, and the solicitude which he has constantly expressed for the Arabs of Palestine. And I recall a statement by Sikander in a speech at Karachi on October the 10th, 1938, which is all the more significant, coming as it did from a man of such broad-minded views and so tolerant an outlook, that he would rather be 'shot down' than agree to Indian troops being sent to Palestine. I cannot help thinking that if separate Muslim State did indeed come into existence in India, as now contemplated by the All India Muslim League, the day would come when they might find the temptation to join an Islamic Commonwealth of nations well-nigh irresistible. More particularly would this be the case with the North-West of India, which would in these circumstances be a Muslim State coterminous with the vast block of territory dominated by Islam which runs from North Africa and Turkey in the West to Afghanistan in the East. You may think that this is looking unnecessarily far ahead and that we can but devote our energies to endeavoring to solve our more immediate problems. I dare say that you would be right; yet I feel that one has to keep one's eye on the possible developments of a somewhat distant future if we are to come to right decisions in connection with the problems immediately confronting us.

5. Viceroy's Talk with Hindu Mahasabha Leader B.S. Moonje

Editorial, *Tribune*, 25 September 1940.

It is a most amazing statement which the Viceroy is said to have made in the course of his recent talk with one of the Hindu leaders.[1] While he would give due consideration to the Mahasabha point of view, His Excellency is reported to have said, the Pakistan demand could not be ruled out at this stage, as it would be open to all groups to place their respective schemes for consideration before the conference of representatives to be held after the war. It may be, as His Excellency said, that it would be open to all groups to place their respective schemes for consideration before the conference. But schemes for what? What the overwhelming majority of political minded Indians have been demanding with one voice and what the British Government themselves have now conceded in theory is that the conference of Indian representatives should consider schemes for the future constitution of India. Surely that is not the same thing as to say that it will be open to them to consider schemes for the division of India. The idea of a division of India into two or more separate and independent states is ruled out by India's long history including the history of the British connection itself, by India's physical and cultural unity and by the very composition of her population no less than by the repeated declaration of the British Government and its agents and the unalterable convictions of the overwhelming majority of political minded Indians including as we have always believed a large majority of the Muslim community itself. There was a clear and unmistakable repudiation of the basic idea of the Pakistan scheme in the Viceroy's own declaration of a few weeks ago as well as in the speeches made by the Secretary of State in the British House of Commons in amplification of that declaration.

Take for instance, the latest speech of Mr Amery. While referring to India's upbraided differences, Mr Amery said:

Underlying them there is after all the fact that India is a self-contained and distinctive region of the world. There is the fact that India can boast of an ancient civilization and of a long history common to all its peoples, of which all Indians are equally proud. Is there any Indian who is not proud to be called an Indian? Underlying them too is the unity not merely of administration but of political thought and aspiration, which we here can justly claim to have contributed to India's national life.

In the same speech Mr Amery quoted with energetic approval the concluding words of the Viceroy's statement which described India's free and equal partnership in the British Commonwealth as 'the proclaimed and accepted goal of the Imperial Crown and the British Parliament'. If India is a self-contained and distinctive region of the world with an ancient civilization and a long history common to all its peoples, if underlying all her superficial differences there is the unity not merely of administration but of political thought and aspiration, and if the proclaimed and accepted goal of the British Crown and the British Parliament is that India, viewed as a single and united country, should be a free and equal partner in the British Commonwealth, where is the room for a Pakistan in it? Is it not too late in the day in view of all this for the Viceroy or any other spokesman of the British Government to say that the Pakistan demand cannot be ruled out at this stage? Has it not, as a matter of fact, been completely ruled out already, not, indeed, as a demand, for every man or group of men is free to make what demand he likes, no matter how fantastic or absurd it may be in itself, but as a practical proposition? There is one thing which the Viceroy clearly forgot in making the statement attributed to him. What his Hindu interviewer wanted to know was not whether the Muslim League would be free to put forward its demand for the vivisection of India, but what the British Government's own attitude towards that demand would be? Could that question admit of two answers if the British Government were not prepared to go back upon all their past utterances and undo whatever good they had done in India whether consciously or unconsciously, and indeed to go against their own best interest and the best interest of all that they stood for in India for no other purpose than to placate a small number of communal extremists who have taken complete leave of their political unity and judgment under the influence of a mad passion for communal bigotry and separatism.

And what, after all, is this previous scheme which the Viceroy cannot rule out at this stage? Nothing less than that the provinces of India in which the Muslims are in a majority should be constituted into separate and independent states. There are four such provinces in India. These are the North-Western Frontier Province in which the Muslims constitute the overwhelming majority of the population, Sind in which they constitute about 70 per cent of the population and the Punjab and Bengal in which they have a small majority. In not one of these provinces did the Muslim League succeed in obtaining an absolute majority of even the Muslim seats in the Legislature at the last provincial election. In the Frontier Province it was the Congress Muslims, who were fundamentally opposed to the Pakistan scheme, that formed the Government and since the resignation of the Congress ministry the League Muslims have tried their level best to form a Government and have failed. In Sind a ministry, the first article of whose political faith was opposition to the Muslim League, held the reins of power for a long time and would still have been in office if the Congress Party had not unwisely refused its support to it and the ministry that has taken its place has loudly proclaimed its national character in spite of the fact that it contains two League members. In the Punjab the League sustained a crushing defeat at the polls, and in spite of the acceptance of the creed of the League by the Muslim members of the Unionist Party, the ministry is still a non-League ministry and there is not a single member of the Government and not a single important member of the majority party who is a Pakistanist. The Premier himself has repeatedly condemned the basic idea of the scheme and in his latest statement has lent half-hearted support to it only after declaring that it is not a scheme for the partition of India, entirely oblivious of the fact that if it is not a scheme for the partition of India it is nothing at all: while two of his ministerial colleagues, one belonging to his own party, have publicly declared that they have his authority for the statement that he will never accept office in a purely Islamic State. There remains Bengal ninety-five per cent of whose Muslim population are descended from the same stock as the Hindus, talk the same language and are inheritors of the same culture and traditions. The idea of a partition of India on a religious basis can never be anything but an abomination to them.

Apart from these indisputable facts, the very strength of the non-Muslim community in the last two provinces makes any proposal to constitute them into separate and independent Muslim states an utter and demonstrable absurdity. The Muslims of India who constitute less than 25 per cent of the population of India would not, we are told, live under a common Government with the Hindus, even though that Government might be non-communal, because the Hindus were likely to have a major voice in its affairs, and this in spite of the fact that the Hindus constitute more than two thirds of the population of India. And yet the advocates of this puerile scheme expect the Hindus of Bengal, who constitute forty-five per cent of the population of their province and the Hindus and Sikhs of the Punjab, who constitute a similar percentage of the population of this province, to consent to live in a purely Islamic State under a purely communal Government in spite of the fact that they constitute a much larger percentage of the population of their respective provinces than the Muslims do of the population of India as a whole. It is no answer to this argument to say that the Muslims are prepared to give all reasonable guarantees to the non-Muslim minorities for the preservation of their rights and interests. Are not the Hindus prepared to give exactly the same guarantees to the non-Hindu minorities in their majority provinces and in India as a whole? If those guarantees are insufficient or unacceptable in the one case, how do they become sufficient and acceptable in the other? And what about the millions of Muslims who under the Pakistan scheme would be destined for all time to live in non-Muslim States? If they can be left to look after their rights and interests in those States, why cannot the Muslim community as a whole do so in India as a whole? From whatever point of view the matter is looked at a more ill-conceived, more ill-digested or more thoroughly impracticable scheme has never yet been devised by the wit of man, and we deeply regret that the Viceroy should have given even indirect encouragement to this rotten scheme by saying that it cannot be ruled out at this stage.

---

[1] The Viceroy's talks with Hindu Mahasabha leader Dr B.S. Moonje took place on 16 September 1940. Dr B.S. Moonje placed before the Viceroy the Hindu Mahasabha position, laying special stress on the points made in the statement by the Mahasabha President, V.D. Savarkar on 14 September 1940 (For Savarkar's statement, see Document no. 40, in this chapter).

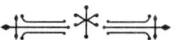

B.   ALL INDIA MUSLIM LEAGUE

6.   Release of Jinnah—Nehru Correspondence to the Press

Statesman, 8 January 1940.

The history of yet another attempt to compare Congress-League differences is set forth in a series of letters exchanged last month between Mr M.A. Jinnah, President of the All India Moslem League and Pandit Jawaharlal Nehru. Mr Jinnah has released the correspondence.

Mr Jinnah, while hoping for a solution, reiterates the League demand for recognition as the 'authoritative and representative organization of Moslems in India'.

Referring to the Congress demand for a declaration by Britain of her war aims, he says, 'that the League cannot endorse that demand as laid down in the Working Committee's resolution on the subject.'

Defining Congress's attitude, Pandit Nehru states that the Congress does regard the League as an influential organization of Moslems, but not as the sole representative of the Moslems of India.

Finally, the Pandit states that as he and Mr Jinnah have not found some common ground for discussion there can be no use continuing the negotiations.

Jinnah Explains Reason for Release of Correspondence

M.A. Jinnah, President of the All India Moslem League states:

'I regret to find that Pandit Jawaharlal Nehru, during his recent tour in the Punjab and elsewhere, has thought fit to attack me in a manner unworthy of any responsible leader[1]. He accuses me of being bent upon the preservation of British domination over India which I can only characterize as not only unwarranted, but mean. The reasons for his refusing to continue his talks with me, as given by him, are far from correct, are misleading and unfair.

'I would not further comment upon his reckless and irresponsible pronouncements, but I shall rest content with releasing the correspondence between us on the subject. This will show the true reasons for his refusing to proceed further in the matter, and I leave it to the public to judge the impossible attitude that is being taken up by him and the Congress'.

The Correspondence

The correspondence is given below:

From Pandit Nehru to Mr Jinnah, dated 1 December 1939 from Allahabad

My dear Jinnah—When we met last in Delhi, it was agreed that we should meet again to discuss various aspects of the communal problem. You told me that on your return to Bombay you would write to me suggesting some date for such a meeting. I have been looking forward to your letter since then. I hope that whenever it is convenient for you to fix a date you will kindly let me know.

Sir Stafford Cripps is coming to India soon and is likely to spend two or three weeks in this country. He is on his way to China. I do not yet exactly know when he will reach here but probably he will come in about a week's time. During his brief stay in India he would like to meet you, if that is possible. I do not know his programme at all nor do I know what cities he intends visiting. But I take it that he will go to Bombay. Could you kindly let me know if you are likely to be in Bombay about the third week of this month, or later? This information might help him to arrange his programme. He is coming by air and will land in Allahabad. Yours sincerely, Jawaharlal Nehru.

From Mr Jinnah to Pandit Nehru, dated 4 December

My dear Jawahar—I am in receipt of your letter of December 1, and thank you for it. As at present advised, I hope to be in Bombay for the next two or three weeks, and if it is convenient to you I shall be very glad to see you and fix up any date that may suit you. Please, therefore, let me know what date and time will suit you.

As regards Sir Stafford Cripps, I received a letter from him and I have already replied to him care of your address as directed by him and I have already stated I shall be here in Bombay and he is arriving at Allahabad on the 8th as I understand from his letter. I shall be very glad to see him when he is in Bombay. On hearing from him I shall fix up also the date and time that may suit him. Yours sincerely, M.A. Jinnah

From Pandit Nehru to Mr Jinnah, dated 9 December

My dear Jinnah—Two days ago, I sent you a letter informing you that I intended going to Bombay soon and hoped to meet you there. Yesterday morning, I read in the newspapers your statement fixing December 22 as a Day of Deliverance and Thanks-giving as a mark of relief that the Congress Governments have at last ceased to function.

I have read this statement very carefully more than once and have given 24 hours thought to the matter. It is not for me, in this letter, to enter into any controversy about facts, or impressions, or conclusions. You know my views about these, formed, I hope, in all earnestness and with all desire to find the truth. It may be that I am mistaken, but I have sought more light, and that light has not come.

But what has oppressed me terribly since yesterday is the realization that our sense of values and objectives in life and politics differ so very greatly. I had hoped, after our conversation that this was not so great. But now the gulf appears to be wider than ever. Under these circumstances, I wonder what purpose will be served by our discussing with each other the problems that confront us. There must be some common ground for discussion to yield fruit. I think I owe it to you as well as to myself to put this difficulty before you.

From Mr Jinnah to Pandit Nehru, dated 13 December

Dear Jawaharlal—I am in receipt of your letter of December 9th. I did not know where to address my reply to you as your movements were reported in the Press to be uncertain. The latest announcement is that you are arriving in Bombay on December 14 and I am, therefore, sending this letter to your Bombay address.

I quite agree with you that 'there must be some common ground for discussion, some common objective aimed at for that discussion to yield fruit'. That is the very reason why I made it clear in our conversation at Delhi in October last to Mr Gandhi and yourself first that so long as the Congress is not prepared to treat the Moslem League as the authoritative and representative organization of the Mussalmans of India, it was not possible to carry on talks regarding a Hindu–Moslem settlement as that was the basis laid down by the Working Committee of the All India Moslem League; and second that we cannot endorse the Congress demand for the declaration as laid down in the resolution of the Working Committee confirmed by the All India Congress Committee on 10 October, 1939 apart from the nebulous and impracticable character of it till we reach an agreement with regard to the minority problem. The Muslim League was also not satisfied with the declaration made by the Viceroy.

If happily we could settle the Hindu–Moslem question then we would be in a position to evolve an agreed formula for a demand of declaration by His Majesty's Government that would satisfy us. Neither the first nor the second suggestion of mine was acceptable to Mr Gandhi or to yourself at Delhi, but you were good enough to express your wish that you would like to meet me again and I said that I would be always glad to see you. In reply to your letter of December 1, expressing your wish to see me in Bombay, I inform you that I shall be in Bombay till the third week of December and I shall be glad to see you and I can only say that if you desire to discuss the matter further I am at your disposal.

From Pandit Nehru to Mr Jinnah, dated 14 December

My dear Jinnah—Thank you for your letter of 13 December which was delivered to me in the forenoon today on my arrival here. I sent you my last letter from Allahabad after reading and giving full thought to your statement about the celebration of 'Day of Deliverance and Thanksgiving' by Moslems. This statement had distressed me greatly as it made me realize that the gulf that separated us in our approach to public problems was very great. In view of this fundamental difference, I wondered what common ground there was for discussion and I put my difficulty before you. That difficulty remains.

In your letter you have emphasized two other preliminary conditions before any common ground for discussion can arise. The first is that the Congress must treat the Moslem League as the authoritative and representative organization of the Mussalmans of India. The Congress has always considered the League as a very important and influential organization of Moslems and it is because of this that we have been eager to settle any differences that may exist between us. But presumably what you suggest is something more and involves some kind of repudiation by us or dissociation from other Moslems who are not in the League. There are, as you know, a large number of Moslems in the Congress, who have been and are our closest colleagues. There are Moslem organizations like the Jamiat-ul-Ulema, the All India Shia Conference, the Majlis-e-Ahrar, the All India Momin Conference, etc., apart from trade unions and peasant unions which have many Moslems as their members. As a general rule, many of these organizations and individuals have adopted the same political platform as we have done in the Congress. We cannot possibly dissociate ourselves from them, or disown them in any way.

You have rightly pointed out on many occasions that the Congress does not represent everybody in India. Of course, not. It does not represent those who disagree with it whether they are Moslems or Hindus in the ultimate analysis. It represents its own members and sympathizers. So also the Muslim League, as any other organization, represents its own members and sympathizers. But there is this vital difference that, while the Congress by its constitution has its membership open to all who subscribe to its objective and methods, the Moslem League is only open to Moslems. Thus the Congress constitutionally has a national basis and it cannot give it up without putting an end to its existence. There are many Hindus, as you know, in the Hindu Mahasabha who oppose the idea of the Congress representing Hindus as such. Then there are the Sikhs and others who claim that they should be heard when communal matters are considered.

I am afraid, therefore, that if your desire is that we should consider the League as the sole organization representing Moslems to the exclusion of all others, we are wholly unable to accede to it. It would be equally at variance with facts if we made a similar claim for the

Congress in spite of the vastness of the Congress organization. But I would venture to say that such questions do not arise when two organizations deal with each other and consider problems of mutual interest.

Your second point is that the Muslim League cannot endorse the Congress demand for a declaration from the British Government. I regret to learn this for this means that, apart from communal questions, we differ entirely on purely political grounds.

The Congress demand is essentially for a declaration of war aims and more especially for a declaration of Indian independence and the right of the Indian people to frame their own constitution without external interference. If the Muslim League does not agree to this, this means that our political objectives are wholly dissimilar.

The Congress demand is not new. It is inherent in Article One of the Congress and all our policy for many years past has been based on it. It is inconceivable to me how the Congress can give it up, or even vary it. Personally, I would be entirely opposed to any attempt at variation. But this is not a personal matter. There is a resolution of the All India Congress Committee, endorsed by a thousand meetings all over India and, I am powerless to ignore it.

It thus seems that politically, we have no common ground and that our objectives are different. That in itself makes discussion difficult and fruitless.

What led me to write my last letter to you also remains—the prospect of a celebration of a Day of Deliverance by Moslems as suggested by you. That raises very vital and far-reaching issues, into which I need not go now but which must influence all of us. That approach to the communal problem cannot be reconciled with an attempt to solve it.

I feel, therefore, that it will serve little purpose for us to meet at this stage and under these conditions with this background. I should like to assure you, however, that we are always prepared to have free and frank discussions of communal or other problems as between the Congress and the League.

From Mr Jinnah to Pandit Nehru, dated 15 December

Dear Jawaharlal—I am in receipt of your letter of December 14, 1939, and I am sorry to say that you have not appreciated my position with regard to the second point. I did not say that the Muslim League cannot endorse the Congress demand for a declaration from the British Government. What I have said was that we cannot endorse the Congress demand for the declaration as laid down in the resolution of the Working Committee and confirmed by the All India Congress Committee on 10 October, 1939 for the reasons I have already specified in my letter.

If this resolution of the Congress cannot be modified in any way, and as you say that personally you would be entirely opposed to any attempt at variation of it and as you make it clear that you are wholly unable to treat with the Moslem League as the authoritative and representative organization of the Mussalmans of India may I know in these circumstances what do you expect or wish me to do. Yours sincerely, M.A. Jinnah.

From Pandit Nehru to Mr Jinnah, dated 16 December

My dear Jinnah—Thank you for your letter of 15 December. I realize the difference you have pointed out. Of course, the Moslem League cannot oppose the idea of any declaration. What the Congress had asked for was an enunciation of war aims and a recognition of India's independence and the right of her people to frame their Constitution, a right that must necessarily be inherent in independence. All these are basic principles which flow from our objective of independence, and as the Moslem League has the same declared objective, there should be no difference of opinion about them.

In the application of these principles many important matters will no doubt have to be considered. But so far as the basic demands are concerned, they are of the very essence of Indian nationalism. To give them up or to vary them materially is to knock down our case for independence.

In regard to the war also the Congress has repeatedly declared its policy during the last eleven years. The present declaration is a logical outcome of that policy. I have personally had some share in shaping this policy and I have attached importance to it. You will appreciate that it is exceedingly difficult, apart from the question of desirability to vary such long established and fundamental policies. These policies are political in their essence and I would venture to say, are the only policies which flow from a demand for Indian freedom. Details may be considered and discussed, their application should be worked out in mutual co-operation and in particular the interests of various groups and minorities should be considered carefully and protected. But to challenge the very basis of that declaration is to demonstrate that there is a great difference in political outlook and policy. This, as such, has nothing to do with the Hindu–Moslem problem. It is because of this that I feel that there is little in common in our political objectives.

May I say again that no one on our behalf, so far as I know, challenges or minimizes the authority, influence and importance of the Moslem League. It is for this reason that we have been eager to discuss matters with it and to arrive at a satisfactory solution of the problems that confront us. Unfortunately, we never seem to reach even the proper discussion of these problems as various hurdles and obstructions, in the shape of conditions precedent, come in our way. These conditions precedent as I have ventured to point out to you, have far-reaching significance. I do not know why they should be allowed to obstruct all progress or prevent us from considering these problems. It should not be difficult to remove these hurdles and come to grips with the subject itself. But as these hurdles continue and others are added to them, I am compelled to think that the real difficulty is the difference in political outlook and objectives.

At the present moment the decision to have an all India demonstration on 22 December has added a psychological barrier which effectively prevents mutual approach and discussion. I regret this exceedingly and have earnestly wished that you would see your way to remove the barrier which is leading and can only lead to ill-will. I still hope that you may be able to do so.

I do wish to assure you that, for my part, I do not want to leave any stone unturned which can lead to mutual understanding and settlement. But you will not have me as I do not want to have you, leave integrity of mind and purpose in pursuit of anything. Nothing worthwhile can be gained that way. I have deep political convictions and I have laboured in accordance with them these many years. I cannot leave them at any time, much less now when the world is in the throes of a terrific crisis. Yours sincerely, Jawaharlal Nehru. Associated Press.

---

[1] Jawaharlal Nehru had made these remarks in an interview with political workers in Amritsar on 30 December, 1939 during his tour in the Punjab. For a report of the interview, see *SWJN*, Vol. X, p. 421.

7. Fazlul Haq's Statement to the Press Regarding Congress and Hindu Mahasabha

Star of India, 8 January 1940.

'All dogs are equal. The only difference between them is that some of them do bark before they bite while the others do not,' with these remarks the Hon. Mr A.K. Fazlul Huq, Premier of Bengal, drew an analogy between the Congress and the Hindu Mahasabha, addressing the session of the C. P. and Berar Muslim League Conference here.

Mr Fazlul Huq declared that India was unsuited either for Constituent Assembly, or the Dominion Status, or Home Rule, because India was not a nation.

The Bengal Premier opposed the Governors of various provinces of partiality for their leaning towards the Congress and said that in some of the provinces the Governors had been mere puppets in the hands of the Congress.

Mr Fazlul Huq asserted that the Congress and the Hindu Mahasabha were one and the same thing and there was no difference between them. He appealed to the Muslims to stand united and help each other and assured the Muslims of the Central Provinces and the other parts of India, where they are in minority, of the fullest support of the Bengal Muslims who are 30 millions in strength. ...

In the Punjab and Bengal, Mr Fazlul Huq stated, the Hindus and the Congressmen are afraid of the Muslims and do not dare raise their heads there. He asserted that the Huq Ministry was a stable one, not because it was supported by the Government but because it was blessed by God and he was His torch-bearer.

He expressed his pleasure and satisfaction over the 'Exit' of the Congress Ministries, which he asserted was an ignominious one and hoped and prayed Congress Ministers would never return to power.

The Hon'ble Mr Fazlul Huq opposed the amendment of the India Act and supported the demand for the appointment of the 'Royal Commission' to enquire into the Muslim grievances. He declared that India is unsuited for the Constituent Assembly, or the Dominion Status, or the Home Rule, because it was not a nation and there were a lot of various communities living in it.

He advised the Muslims to keep themselves in readiness to face any ordeal and make any sacrifice, howsoever, bigger it may be for the cause of Islam. He asked them not to follow the footsteps of Mir Jaffar or to betray the cause of their religion so long as they are the Muslims. He also appealed to the C.P. Muslims to prepare a detailed statement about the acts of oppression and tyrannies committed upon them by the Congress and submit the same before him for his perusal and study. He called for the help of a band of selfless and ardent workers to carry out this work.

8. Jinnah 'lifting the Muslim League out of the Communal rut': Letter from Mahatma Gandhi to M.A. Jinnah, 16 January 1940

Syed Sharifuddin Pirzada (ed.), *Quaid-e-Azam, Jinnah's Correspondence*, Indian Edition, New Delhi, 1981, pp. 95–6.

The purpose of writing this letter is to send you the enclosed advance copy of the article I have sent to the *Harijan*. I have written it to further the end I have read in your recent messages and actions. I know that you are quite capable of rising to the height required for the noble motive attributed to you. I do not mind your opposition to the Congress. But your plan to amalgamate all the parties opposed to the Congress at once gives your movement a national character. If you succeed you will free the country from communal incubus, and in my humble opinion give a lead to the Muslims and others for which you will deserve the gratitude not only of the Muslims but of all the other communities, I hope that my interpretation is correct. If I am mistaken you will please correct me.

It is a purely personal, private, friendly letter. But you are free to make public use of it if you think it necessary.

Yours sincerely.
M.K. Gandhi

Enclosed article:

A Welcome Move[1]

On the Deliverance Thanks giving Day, declared by Jinnah Sahib, I had the following wire from Gulbarga Muslims:

'Deliverance Day greetings, Quaid-e-Azam Jinnah Zindabad'.

I took it was a message sent to ruffle my feelings. The senders little knew that the wire could not serve its purpose. When I received it I silently joined the senders in the wish 'Long Live Quaid-e-Azam Jinnah'. The Quaid-e-Azam is an old comrade. What does it matter that today we do not see eye to eye in some matters? That can make no difference in my goodwill towards him.

But the Quaid-e-Azam has given me special reason for congratulating him. I had pleasure of wiring him congratulations on his excellent Id-day broadcast. And now he commands further congratulations on forming pacts with parties who are opposed to the Congress policies and politics. He is thus lifting the Muslim League out of the communal rut and giving it a national character. I regard his step as perfectly legitimate. I observe that the Justice Party and Dr Ambedkar's party have already joined Jinnah Sahib. The papers report too, that Shree Savarkar, the President of the Hindu Mahasabha is to see him presently. Jinnah Sahib himself has informed the public that many non-Congress Hindus have expressed their sympathy with him. I regard this development as thoroughly healthy. Nothing can be better than we should have in the country mainly two parties—the Congress and non-Congress or anti-Congress, if the latter expression is preferred. Jinnah Sahib is giving the word 'minority' a new and good content. The Congress majority is made up of a combination of caste Hindus, non-caste Hindus, Muslims, Christians, Parsis and Jews. Therefore, it is a majority drawn from all classes, representing a particular body of opinion, and the proposed combination becomes a minority representing another body of opinion. This may any day convert itself into a majority by commending itself to the electorate. Such an alignment of parties is a consummation devoutly to be wished. If the Quaid-e-Azam can bring about the combination, not only I but the whole of India will shout with one acclamation: 'Long Live Quaid-e-Azam Jinnah'. For, he will have brought about permanent and living unity for which I am sure the whole nation is thirsting.

Segaon, 15.1.40

---

[1] Published in *Harijan*, 20 January 1940.

9. Gandhi Out of Touch with Reality: Jinnah's Reply to Mahatma Gandhi, 21 January 1940

Syed Sharifuddin Pirzada (ed.), *Quaid-e-Azam Correspondence*, Indian Edition, 1981, pp. 97–8.

I am in receipt of your letter of 16th January and the advance copy of the article you have sent to the *Harijan*.[1] I not only thank you for your courtesy but also for your anxiety to further the end you have been reading in my messages and actions. I, however, regret to have to say that your premises are wrong as you start with the theory of an Indian Nation that does not exist, and naturally, therefore, your conclusions are wrong. I should have thought, however, that you at least would not be led away by one-sided newspaper reports and canards. There is so much in your article which is the result of imagination. It is due partly to the fact that you are living a secluded life at Segaon and partly because all your thoughts and actions are guided by 'inner voice'. You have little concern with realities, or what might be termed by an ordinary mortal 'practical politics'. I sometimes wonder what can be common between practical politics and yourself, between democracy and the dictator of a political organization of which he is not even a four-anna member. But that is, I suppose, because you do not consider the Congress worthy of your membership.

I am glad to learn that you were not ruffled by the 'Deliverance Day' greetings sent to you from Gulbarga. It was indeed noble of you to join in the silent prayer 'Long Live Quaid-i-Azam Jinnah'. Although these are trivial matters, I nevertheless appreciate that you have realized the true inward meaning and significance of the 'Deliverance Day'.

It is true that many non-Congress Hindus expressed their sympathy with the Deliverance Day in justice to our cause, so also the leaders of the Justice Party and the Scheduled Castes, and the Parsis who had suffered. But I am afraid that the meaning which you have tried to give to this alignment shows that you have not appreciated the true significance of it. It was partly a case of 'adversity bringing strange bed-fellows together,' and partly because common interest may lead Muslims and minorities to combine. I have no illusions in the matter, and let me say again that India is not a nation, nor a country. It is a sub-continent composed of nationalities, Hindus and Muslims being the two major nations. Today you deny that religion can be a main factor in determining a nation, but you yourself, when asked what your motive in life was, 'the thing that leads us to do what we do,' whether it was religious, or social, or political, said: 'Purely religious!'. This was the question asked me by the late Mr Montagu when I accompanied a deputation which was purely political. 'How you, social reformer', he exclaimed 'have found your way into this crowd?' My reply was that it was only an extension of my social activity. 'I could not be leading a religious life unless I identified myself with the whole of mankind, and that I could not do unless I took part in politics. The gamut of man's activities today constitutes an indivisible whole. You cannot divide social, economic, political and purely religious work into watertight compartments, I do not know any religion apart from human activity. It provides a moral basis to all activities which they would otherwise lack, reducing life to a maze of "sound and fury signifying nothing"'.

More than any one else, you happen to be the man today who commands the confidence of Hindu India and are in a position to deliver the goods on their behalf. It is too much to hope and expect that you might play your legitimate role and abandon your chase after a mirage? Events are moving fast, a campaign of polemics, or your weekly discourse in the *Harijan* on metaphysics, philosophy and ethics, or your peculiar doctrines regarding *khaddar*, *ahimsa* and spinning are not going to win India's freedom. Action and statesmanship alone will help us in our forward march. I believe that you might still rise to your stature in the service of our country and make your proper contribution towards leading India to contentment and happiness....

Yours sincerely,
M.A. Jinnah

---

[1] See Document no. 8 in this chapter.

10. 'No Settlement can be Forced on Muslims'—Jinnah

Press Statement, *Civil and Military Gazette*, 30 January 1940, Reproduced in Waheed Ahmad (ed.), *Quaid-i-Azam Mohammad Ali Jinnah: The Nation's Voice—Towards Consolidation—Speeches and Statements March 1935–March 1940*, Karachi, 1992, pp. 445–7.

Ahmedabad: Regarding the British Government's attitude, as disclosed by Sir Hugh O'Neill[1] in the House of Commons, towards his demand for a Royal Commission to inquire into the treatment of minorities by Congress Governments, Mr Jinnah in a statement says:

We are informed that London 'scouts' our just demand to appoint an impartial judicial tribunal, namely a Royal Commission, to enquire into our charges of a very serious character about the tyranny and oppression practised over Mussalmans in Congress-governed provinces. Sir Hugh O'Neill is reported to have said that he could not believe that the interests of either party to the dispute or of the peoples of India as a whole would be served by a formal enquiry into the matter. Underline the word 'formal'. What does this mean? This unreasonable reply has imposed an additional task upon us. We shall try to remove his wrong belief when he says that it is not in the interests of the people to do justice. He is entirely mistaken when he says that such an enquiry would embitter Hindus and Muslims. It is a charge against the Congress High Command and the Congress Ministries which must be investigated in order to stop a recurrence or repetition of it.

'Ignorance'

Mr Jinnah added: 'My attention has also been drawn to an article in the London *Times*. This paper is generally well-informed, but when it says that the All India Muslim League is not an authoritative and representative organization of the Muslims of India, it is misled completely, showing ignorance of the actual position in India today. Of course, the League is not the only Muslim organization in the country, nor does it represent cent per cent of the Muslims in the country, which it is impossible for any organization to do in any country, but I venture to state without fear of contradiction that today it represents the Muslim nation more truly and effectively than His Majesty's present Government represents the British nation.

'The London *Times* is making a great mistake if it is under the impression that any settlement could be forced on the Muslims under the aegis of the British Government without their approval and consent. The Muslims are not prepared to leave their fate and future destiny in the hands of anybody. They alone are the final judges of what is best for them. They must be treated by all parties who play their part in shaping the future of India as a responsible and honourable people'.

Reply to Mr Gandhi

Referring to the latest article of Mr Gandhi in *Harijan*, Mr Jinnah said, 'Suddenly Mr Gandhi finds that my truthful and honest statement in reply to his letter recently published has dashed to the ground all hopes of Hindu–Muslim unity.[2] This was not the first time that I made the position clear. Why then begin to doubt now whether I represent the Muslim mind at all? I know it is not easy to convince Mr Gandhi of the reality of the situation. He feels that the picture I presented to him, if realized, would undo the efforts the Congress has been making for over half a century. The efforts of the Congress for the first thirty years have already been undone and Mr Gandhi is mainly responsible for that.

'It is the policy and programme Mr Gandhi has been pursuing blindly for two decades that is the cause of the present state of affairs. He is still under a delusion when he says that this is only a temporary phase in the history of the Muslim League and that the Muslims could never cut themselves away from their Hindu and Christian brethren. It is not a question of Muslims cutting away from their Hindu and Christian brethren. It is a problem of making our Hindu and Christian brethren understand that we are entitled to our proper place in the Indian sun.'

---

[1] Sir Hugh O'Neill, Parliamentary Under-Secretary of State for India and Burma, made these remarks in the House of Commons debate on 24 January 1940 when asked by Mr Edmund Harvey if the Indian Government is making any inquiry into the allegations made by Mr Jinnah, on behalf of the Muslim League with regard to the treatment of minorities by the Provincial Congress Ministries which had resigned office.

[2] See Document no. 46(a) in this chapter.

11. Jinnah's Appeal to All Indians—Abstain from Congress Independence Day Ceremonies on 26 January

Jinnah's Press statement, *Civil and Military Gazette*, 24 January 1940, Reproduced in Waheed Ahmad (ed.), *Quaid-i-Azam Mohammad Ali Jinnah: The Nation's Voice—Towards Consolidation—Speeches and Statements March 1935–March 1940*, Karachi, 1992, p. 439.

Rajkot, 23 January

Mr M.A. Jinnah has issued the following statement to the Press:

'I find that even Congressmen are realising that the Independence Day pledge as amended or with the addendum is a camouflage, is not genuine in its conception and is humiliating, and it must fail in its execution and its objective to achieve 'independence pure and simple'. The Congress High Command, from the latest writings of Mr Gandhi, are out for a compromise with the Viceroy under paramountcy in a manner such as would once more revive the gentlemen's agreement and the alliance with the British Government in order that Mussalmans and minorities and other interests may be placed at their mercy, once more for them to begin their process of crushing them downright. The Congress High Command directed the Ministries to resign as a bluff and they are dying to get back because the Viceroy has called the bluff.

'So far the trouble has been that Lord Linlithgow was perforce obliged to refuse, owing to the growing strength of the Muslim League, to treat the Congress as the only mouthpiece of India and therefore was unable to please the High Command as he realized that such a course would involve great risk to the British Government, especially at this juncture, if the Mussalmans and the minorities and other interests are to be ignored or sacrificed. Mr Gandhi having once tasted the power that was given to the High Command by means of assurances that special powers would not be used by the Governors or the Governor-General, would want more if he is allowed to cross the 't's and dot the 'i's in what he finds germs of settlement in the Viceroy's speech at Bombay.

'But I wish to strike a note of caution and I hope the Viceroy and the British Government fully realize that any repetition of such a position in which the guarantees already given to the minorities are not implemented, or are not honoured in practice, will create the gravest crisis in India; and Muslim India will resist it by all the means in their power and will not shrink from making any sacrifice. The British Government will be wholly responsible for the consequences if they yield or are stampeded by the threats and coercion by one party.

'I appeal to Mussalmans all over the country in particular and also to my non-Muslim countrymen not to have anything to do with the Independence Day on 26 January, as it is intended to deceive the people under the lure and guise of Independence. Mr Gandhi's meaning of Independence varies from time to time and I hope the Mussalmans will not fall into this trap'.—AP.

12. M.A. Jinnah's Presidential Address at the All India Muslim League Annual (27th) Session, Lahore 22 March 1940

India's Problem of Her Future Constitution, M.A. Jinnah (ed.), Lahore, 1940, pp. 1–15; A.M. Zaidi (Chief Editor), *Evolution of Muslim Political Thought in India*, Vol. V, *The Demand for Pakistan*, Delhi, 1978, pp. 198–213; Waheed Ahmad (ed.), *Quaid-i-Azam Mohammad Ali Jinnah: The Nation's Voice—Towards Consolidation—Speeches and Statements March 1935–March 1940*, Karachi, 1992, pp. 486–95.

Ladies and Gentlemen

We are meeting today in our session after fifteen months. The last session of the All India Muslim League took place at Patna in December 1938. Since then many developments have taken place. I shall first shortly tell you what the All India Muslim League had to face after the Patna session of 1938. You remember that one of the tasks, which was imposed on us and which is far from completed yet, was to organize Muslim League all over India. We have made enormous progress during the last fifteen months in this direction. I am glad to inform you that we have established Provincial Leagues in every province. The next point is that in every bye-election to the Legislative Assemblies we had to fight with powerful opponents. I congratulate the Mussalmans for having shown enormous grit and spirit throughout our trials. There was not a single bye-election in which our opponents won against Muslim League candidates. In the last election to the UP Council, that is the Upper Chamber, the Muslim League's success was cent per cent. I do not want to weary you with details of what we have been able to do in the way of forging ahead in the direction of organizing the Muslim League. But I may tell you that it is going up by leaps and bounds.

Next, you may remember that we appointed a committee of ladies at the Patna session. It is of very great importance to us, because I believe that it is absolutely essential for us to give every opportunity to our women to participate in our struggle of life and death. Women can do a great deal within their homes even under *purdah*. We appointed this committee with a view to enable them to participate in the work of the League. The objects of this central committee were (1) to organize provincial and district Muslim Leagues; (2) to enlist a larger number of women to the membership of the Muslim League; (3) to carry on an intensive propaganda amongst Muslim women throughout India in order to create in them a sense of a greater political consciousness because if political consciousness is awakened amongst our women, remember, your children will not have much to worry about; (4) to advise and guide them in all such matters as mainly rest on them for the uplift of Muslim Society. This central committee, I am glad to say, started its work seriously and earnestly. It has done a great deal of useful work. I have no doubt that when we come to deal with their report of work done we shall really feel grateful to them for all the services that they have rendered to the Muslim League.

We had many difficulties to face from January 1939 right upto the declaration of war. We had to face the Vidya Mandir in Nagpur. We had to face the Wardha Scheme all over India. We had to face ill-treatment and oppression to Muslims in the Congress-governed provinces. We had to face the treatment meted out to Muslims in some of the Indian States such as Jaipur and Bhavnagar. We had to face a vital issue that arose in that state of Rajkot. Rajkot was the acid test made by the Congress which would have affected one-third of India. Thus the Muslim League had all along to face various issues from January 1939 upto the time of the declaration of war. Before the war was declared the greatest danger to the Muslims of India was the possible inauguration of the federal scheme in the Central Government. We know what machinations were going on. But the Muslim League was stoutly resisting them in every direction. We felt that we could never accept the dangerous scheme of the Central Federal Government embodied in the Government of India Act, 1935. I am sure that we have made no small contribution towards persuading the British Government to abandon the scheme of Central Federal Government. In creating that mind in the British Government the Muslim League, I have no doubt, played no small part. You know that the British people are very obdurate people. They are also very conservative; and although they are very clever, they are slow in understanding. After the war was declared, the Viceroy naturally wanted help from the Muslim League. It was only then that he realized that the Muslim League was a power. For it will be remembered that upto the time of the declaration of war, the Viceroy never thought of me but of Gandhi and Gandhi alone. I have been the leader of an important party in the Legislature for a considerable time, larger than the one I have the honour to lead at present, the Muslim League Party in the Central Legislature. Yet, the Viceroy never thought of me before. Therefore, when I got this invitation from the Viceroy along with Mr Gandhi, I wondered within myself why I was so suddenly promoted and then I concluded that the answer was the 'All India Muslim League' whose President I happen to be. I believe that was the worst shock that the Congress High Command received because it challenged their sole authority to speak on behalf of India. And it is quite clear from the attitude of Mr Gandhi and the High Command that they have not yet recovered from that shock. My point is that, I want you to realize the value, the importance, the significance of organizing ourselves. I will not say anything more on the subject.

But a great deal yet remains to be done. I am sure from what I can see and hear that the Muslim India is now conscious, is now awake and the Muslim League has by now grown into such a strong institution that it cannot be destroyed by anybody whoever he may happen to be. Men may come and men may go, but the League will live for ever.

Now, coming to the period after the declaration of war, our position was that we were between the devil and the deep sea. But I do not think that the devil or the deep sea is going to get away with it. Anyhow our position is this. We stand unequivocally for the freedom of India. But it must be freedom of all India and not freedom of one section or worse still, of the Congress caucus and slavery of Mussalmans and other minorities.

Situated in India as we are, we naturally have our past experiences, and particularly the experiences of the past 2½ years of provincial constitution in the Congress governed provinces, we have learnt many lessons. We are now, therefore, very apprehensive and can trust nobody. I think it is a wise rule for everyone not to trust anybody too much. Sometimes we are led to trust people but when we find in actual experience that our trust has been betrayed surely that ought to be sufficient lesson for any man not to continue his trust in those who have betrayed us. Ladies and gentlemen, we never thought that the Congress High Command would have acted in the manner in which they actually did in the Congress-governed provinces. I never dreamt that they would ever come down so low as that. I never could believe that there would be a gentlemen's agreement between the Congress and the Government to such an extent that although we cried hoarse, week in and out, the Governors were supine and the Governor–General was helpless. We reminded them of their special responsibilities to us and to other minorities and the solemn pledges they had given to us. But all that had become a dead letter. Fortunately, Providence came to our help and that gentlemen's agreement was broken to pieces and the Congress, thank Heavens, went out of office. I think they are regretting their resignations very much. Their bluff was called off. So far so good. I, therefore, appeal to you, in all seriousness that I can command, to organize yourselves in such a way that you may depend upon none except your own inherent strength. That is your only safeguard and the best safeguard. Depend upon yourselves. That does not mean that we should have ill-will or malice towards others. In order to safeguard your rights and interests, you must create that strength in yourselves that you may be able to defend yourselves. That is all that I want to urge.

Now, what is our position with regard to future constitution? It is, as soon as circumstances permit or immediately after the war at the latest the whole problem of India's future constitution must be examined *de novo* and the Act of 1935 must go once for all. We do not believe in asking the British Government to make declarations. These declarations are really of no use. You cannot possibly succeed in getting the British Government out of this country by asking them to make declarations. However, the Congress asked the Viceroy to make a declaration. The Viceroy said, 'I have made the declaration'. The Congress said, 'No, no, we want another kind of declaration. You must declare now and at once that India is free and independent with the right to frame its own constitution by a constituent assembly to be elected on the basis of adult franchise or as low a franchise as possible. This Assembly will of course, satisfy the minorities' legitimate interests'. Mr Gandhi says that if the minorities are not satisfied then he is willing that some tribunal of the highest character and most impartial should decide the dispute. Now, apart from the impracticable character of this proposal and quite apart from the fact that it is historically and constitutionally absurd to ask the ruling power to abdicate in favour of a Constituent Assembly—apart from all that I suppose we do not agree as to the franchise according to which the Central Assembly is to be elected, or suppose we the solid body of Muslim representatives do not agree with the non-Muslim majority in the Constituent Assembly, what will happen? It is said that we have no right to disagree with regard to anything that this assembly may do in framing a national constitution of this huge sub-continent except in those matters which may be germane to the safeguards for the minorities. So we are given the privilege to disagree only with regard to what may be called strictly safeguards of the rights and interests of minorities. We are also given the privilege to send our own representatives by separate electorates. Now, this proposal is based on the assumption that as soon as this constitution comes into operation the British hand will disappear. Otherwise there will be no meaning in it. Of course, Mr Gandhi says that the constitution will decide whether the British will disappear and if so to what extent. In other words, his proposal comes to this: First give me the declaration that we are a free and independent nation, then I will decide what I should give you back. Does Mr Gandhi really want the complete independence of India when he talks like this? But whether the British disappear or not, it follows that extensive powers must be transferred to the people. In the event of there being a disagreement between the majority of the Constituent Assembly and the Mussalmans in the first instance, who will appoint the tribunal? And suppose an agreed tribunal is possible and the award is made and the decision given, who will, may I know, be there to see that this award is implemented or carried out in accordance with the terms of that award? And who will see that it is honoured in practice, because, we are told, the British will have parted with their power mainly or completely? Then what will be the sanction behind the award which will enforce it. We come back to the same answer, the Hindu majority would do it—and will it be with the help of the British bayonet or the Gandhi's *Ahimsa*. Can we trust them any more? Besides, Ladies and Gentlemen, can you imagine that a question of this character, of social contract upon which the future constitution of India would be based affecting 90 millions of Mussalmans, can be decided by means of a judicial tribunal? Still, that is the proposal of the Congress.

Before I deal with what Mr Gandhi said a few days ago I shall deal with the pronouncements of some of the other Congress leaders each one speaking with a different voice. Mr Rajagopalacharya, the ex-Prime Minister of Madras says that the only panacea for Hindu–Muslim unity is the joint electorates. That is his prescription as one of the great doctors of the Congress organization. Babu Rajendra Prasad on the other hand, only a few days ago says 'Oh, what more do the Mussalmans want?' I will read to you his words. He says, referring to the minority questions:

'If Britain would concede our right of self-determination surely all these differences would disappear'.

How will our differences disappear? He does not explain or enlighten us about it.

'But so long as Britain remained and held power, the differences would continue to exist. The Congress has made it clear that the future constitution would be framed not by the Congress alone but by representatives of all political parties and religious groups. The Congress has gone further and declared that the minorities can have their representatives elected for this purpose by separate electorates, though the Congress regards separate electorates as an evil. It will be representative of all the people of this country, irrespective of their religion and political affiliations, who will be deciding the future constitution of India and not this or that party. What better guarantee can the minorities have? So according to Babu Rajendra Prasad the moment we enter the Assembly we shall shed all our political affiliations, and religions and everything else. This is what Babu Rajendra Prasad said as late as 18th March 1940. And this is now what Mr Gandhi said on the 20th of March 1940. He says:

'To me, Hindus, Muslims, Parsis, Harijans are all alike. I cannot be frivolous'—but I think he is frivolous—'I cannot be frivolous when I talk of Quaid-i-Azam Jinnah. He is my brother'.

The only difference is this, that brother Gandhi has three votes and I have only one vote! He further said:

'I would be happy indeed if he could keep me in his pocket.'

I do not know really what to say to this latest offer of his. Mr Gandhi also said:

'There was a time when I could say that there was no Muslim whose confidence I did not enjoy. It is my misfortune that it is not so today.'

Why has he lost the confidence of the Muslim today? May I ask, ladies and gentlemen?

'I do not read all that appears in the Urdu Press, but perhaps I get a lot of abuse there, I am not sorry for it. I still believe that without a Hindu–Muslim settlement there can be no Swaraj.'

Mr Gandhi has been saying this now for the last 20 years.

'You will perhaps ask in that case why do I talk of a fight. I do so because it is to be a fight for a Constituent Assembly'.

He is fighting the British. But may I point out to Mr Gandhi and the Congress that you are fighting for a Constituent Assembly which the Muslims say they cannot accept—which, the Muslims say, means three to one, about which the Mussalmans say that they will never be able, in that way, by the counting of heads, to come to any agreement which will be real agreement from the hearts, which will enable us to work as friends and therefore, this idea of a Constituent Assembly is objectionable, apart from other objections. But he is fighting for the Constituent Assembly, not fighting the Mussalmans at all.

He says, 'I do so because it is to be a fight for a Constituent Assembly. If Muslims who come to the Constituent Assembly,' mark the words, 'who come to the Constituent Assembly through Muslim votes'—he is first forcing us to come to that Assembly and then says, 'declare that there is nothing common between Hindus and Muslim, then alone I would give up all hope, but even then I would agree with them because they read the Quran and I have also studied something of that holy book'.

So he wants the Constituent Assembly for the purpose of ascertaining the views of the Mussalmans and if they do not agree then he will give up all hopes, but even then he will agree with us. Well, I ask you, ladies and gentlemen, is this the way to show any real genuine desire— if there existed any—to come to a settlement with the Mussalmans? Why does not Mr Gandhi agree and I have suggested to him more than once and I repeat it again from this platform, why does not Mr Gandhi honestly now acknowledge that the Congress is a Hindu Congress, that he does not represent anybody except the solid body of Hindu people? Why should not Mr Gandhi be proud to say: 'I am a Hindu, Congress has solid Hindu backing'? I am not ashamed of saying that I am a Mussalman. I am right and I hope and I think even a blind man must have been convinced by now that the Muslim League has solid backing of the Mussalmans of India. Why then all this camouflage? Why all these machinations? Why all these methods to coerce the British to overthrow the Mussalmans? Why this declaration of non-cooperation? Why this threat of civil disobedience? And why fight for a Constituent Assembly for the sake of ascertaining whether the Mussalmans agree or they do not agree? Why not come as a Hindu leader proudly representing your people and let me meet you proudly representing the Mussalmans. This is all that I have to say so far as the Congress is concerned.

So far as the British Government is concerned, our negotiations are not concluded yet as you know. We had asked for assurances on several points, at any rate we have made some advance with regard to one point and that is this. You remember our demand was that the entire problem of future constitution of India should be examined *de novo*, apart from the Government of India Act of 1935. To that the Viceroy's reply, with the authority of His Majesty's Government, was—I had better quote that—I will not put it in my own words: This is the reply that was sent to us on 23rd December.

'My answer to your first question is that the declaration I made with the approval of His Majesty's Government on October the 13th last does not exclude'—mark the words—'does not exclude examination of any part either of the Act of 1935 or of the policy and plans on which it is based'.

As regards other matters, we are still negotiating and the most important points are: (1) that no declaration should be made by His Majesty's Government with regard to the future constitution of India without our approval and consent, and that no settlement of any question should be made with any party behind our back, unless our approval and consent is given to it. Well, ladies and gentlemen, whether the British Government in their wisdom agree to give us that assurance or not, but I trust that they will still see that it is a fair and just demand when we say that we cannot leave the future fate and the destiny of 90 millions of people in the hands of any other judge. We and we alone wish to be the final arbiter. Surely that is a just demand. We do not want that the British Government should thrust upon the Mussalmans a constitution which they do not approve of and to which they do not agree. Therefore, the British Government will be well advised to give that assurance and give the Mussalmans complete peace and confidence in this matter and win their friendship. But whether they do that or not, after all, as I told you before, we must depend on our own inherent strength and I make it plain from this platform, that if any declaration is made, if any interim settlement is made without our approval and without our consent the Mussalmans of India will resist it. And no mistake should be made on that score...

Then the next point was with regard to Palestine. We are told that endeavours, earnest endeavours, are being made to meet the reasonable, national demands of the Arabs. Well, we cannot be satisfied by earnest endeavours, sincere endeavours, best endeavours. We want that the British Government should in fact, and actually meet the demands of the Arabs in the Palestine.

Then the point was with regard to sending troops outside. Here there is some misunderstanding. But anyhow we have made our position clear, that we never intended, and, in fact, the language does not justify it, if there is any misapprehension or apprehension that Indian troops should not be used to the fullest in the defence of our own country. What we wanted the British Government to give us assurance of was that Indian troops should not be sent against any Muslim country or any Muslim Power. Let us hope that we may yet be able to get the British Government to clarify the position further.

This, then, is the position with regard to the British Government. The last meeting of the Working Committee had asked the Viceroy to reconsider his letter of the 23rd of December, having regard to what has been explained to him in pursuance of the resolution of the Working Committee, dated the 3rd of February, and we are informed that the matter is receiving his careful consideration.

As far as our internal position is concerned, we have also been examining it and, you know, there are several schemes which have been sent by various well-informed constitutionalists and others who take interest in the problem of India's future constitution and we have also appointed a sub-committee to examine the details of the schemes that have come in so far. But one thing is quite clear. It has always been taken for granted mistakenly that the Mussalmans are a minority and of course, we have got used to it for such a long time that these settled notions sometimes are very difficult to remove. The Mussalmans are not a minority. The Mussalmans are a nation by any definition. The British and particularly the Congress proceed on the basis, 'Well, you are a minority after all, what do you want'? 'What else do the minorities want'? Just as Babu Rajendra Prasad said. But surely the Mussalmans are not a minority. We find that even according to the British map of India, we occupy large parts of this country where the Mussalmans are in a majority—such as Bengal, Punjab, NWFP, Sind and Baluchistan.

Now the question is, what is the best solution of this problem between the Hindus and the Mussalmans? We have been considering and as I have already said, a committee has been appointed to consider the various proposals. But whatever the final scheme for a constitution, I will present to you my views and I will just read to you in confirmation of what l am going to put before you, a letter from Lala Lajpat Rai to Mr C.R. Das. It was written, I believe, about 12 or 15 years ago and that letter has been produced in a book by one Indra Prakash recently published, and that is how this letter has come to light. This is what Lala Lajpat Rai, a very astute politician and a staunch Hindu Mahasabhite said. But before I read his letter it is plain from that you cannot get away from being a Hindu if you are Hindu (Laughter). The word 'nationalist' has now become the play of conjurers in politics. This is what he says:

'There is one point more which has been troubling me very much of late and one which I want you to think carefully and that is the question of Hindu—Mohammadan unity. I have devoted most of my time during the last six months to the study of Muslim history and Muslim law and I am inclined to think it is neither possible nor practicable. Assuming and admitting the sincerity of Mohammadan leaders in the non-co-operation movement, I think their religion provides an effective bar to anything of the kind.

'You remember the conversation I reported to you in Calcutta which I had with Hakim Ajmal Khan and Dr Kitchlew. There is no finer Mohammadan in Hindustan than Hakim Ajmal Khan, but can any Muslim leader over-ride the Quran? I can only hope that my reading of Islamic law is incorrect'.

I think his reading is quite incorrect.

'And nothing would relieve me more than to be convinced that it is so. But if it is right then it comes to this, that although we can unite against the British we cannot do so to rule Hindustan on British lines. We cannot do so to rule Hindustan on democratic lines'.

Ladies and Gentlemen, when Lala Lajpat Rai said that we cannot rule this country on democratic lines it was all right, but when I had the temerity to speak the same truth about 18 months ago, there was a shower of attack and criticism. But Lala Lajpat Rai said 15 years ago that we cannot do so, viz., rule Hindustan on democratic lines. What is the remedy? The remedy according to the Congress is to keep us in the minority and under the majority rule. Lala Lajpat Rai proceeds further:

'What is then the remedy? I am not afraid of the seven crores of Mussalmans. But I think the seven crores in Hindustan plus the armed hosts of Afghanistan, Central Asia, Arabia, Mesopotamia and Turkey will be irresistible.

'I do honestly and sincerely believe in the necessity or desirability of Hindu–Muslim unity. I am also fully prepared to trust the Muslim leaders. But what about the injunctions of the Quran and the Hadis? The leaders cannot override them. Are we then doomed? I hope that your learned mind and wise head will find some way out of this difficulty.'

Now, ladies and gentlemen, that is merely a letter written by one great Hindu leader to another great Hindu leader fifteen years ago. Now, I should like to put before you my views on the subject as it strikes me taking everything into consideration at the present moment. The British Government and Parliament, and more so the British nation have been for many decades past brought up and nurtured with settled notions about India's future, based on developments in their own country which has built up the British constitution, functioning now through the Houses of Parliament and the system of cabinet. Their concept of party government functioning on political planes has become the ideal with them as the best form of government for every country, and the one-sided and powerful propaganda, which naturally appeals to the British, has led them into a serious blunder, in producing a constitution envisaged in the Government of India Act of 1935. We find that the most leading statesmen of Great Britain, saturated with these notions have in their pronouncements seriously asserted and expressed a hope that the passage of time will harmonize the inconsistent elements in India.

A leading journal like the London *Times*, commenting on the Government of India Act of 1935, wrote, 'undoubtedly the difference between the Hindus and Muslims is not of a religion in the strict sense of the word but also of law and culture, that they may be said indeed, to represent two entirely distinct and separate civilizations. However, in the course of time the superstitions will die out and India will be moulded into a single nation'. So according to the London *Times* the only difficulties are superstitions. These fundamental and deep-rooted differences, spiritual, economic, cultural, social and political have been euphemized as mere 'superstitions'. But surely, it is a flagrant disregard of the past history of the sub-continent of India as well as the fundamental Islamic conception of society vis-a-vis that of Hinduism to characterize them as mere 'superstitions'. Notwithstanding thousand years of close contact, nationalities which are as divergent today as ever, cannot at any time be expected to transform themselves into one nation merely by means of subjecting them to a democratic constitution and holding them forcibly together by unnatural and artificial methods of British Parliamentary Statutes. What the unitary government of India for 150 years had failed to achieve cannot be realized by the imposition of a central federal government. It is inconceivable that the fiat or the writ of a government so constituted can ever command a willing and loyal obedience throughout the sub-continent by various nationalities except by means of armed force behind it.

The problem in India is not of an inter-communal character, but manifestly of an international one, and it must be treated as such. So long as this basic and fundamental truth is not realized, any constitution that may be built will result in disaster and will prove destructive and harmful not only to the Mussalmans, but to the British and Hindus also. If the British Government are really in earnest and sincere to secure peace and happiness of the people of this sub-continent, the only course open to us all is to allow the major nations separate homelands by dividing India into autonomous national states. There is no reason why these states should be antagonistic to each other. On the other hand the rivalry and the natural desire and efforts on the part of one to dominate the social order and establish political supremacy over the other in the government of the country will disappear. It will lead more towards natural goodwill by international pacts between them, and they can live in complete harmony with their neighbours. This will lead further to a friendly settlement all the more easily with regard to minorities by reciprocal arrangements and adjustments between Muslim India and Hindu India, which will far more adequately and effectively safeguard the rights and interests of Muslims and various minorities.

It is extremely difficult to appreciate why our Hindu friends fail to understand the real nature of Islam and Hinduism. They are not religions in the strict sense of the word, but are, in fact, different and distinct social orders and it is a dream that the Hindus and Muslims can ever evolve a common nationality, and this misconception of one Indian nation has gone far beyond the limits and is the cause of most of our troubles and will lead India to destruction if we fail to revise our notions in time. The Hindus and Muslims belong to two different religious philosophies, social customs, literature. They neither inter-marry, nor inter-dine together, and indeed, they belong to two different civilizations which are based mainly on conflicting ideas and conceptions. Their views on life and of life are different. It is quite clear that Hindus and Mussalmans derive their inspiration from different sources of history. They have different epics, their heroes are different, and they have different episodes. Very often the hero of one is a foe of the other and likewise their victories and defeats overlap. To yoke together two such nations under a single state, one as a numerical minority and the other as a majority, must lead to growing discontent and final destruction of any fabric that may be so built up for the government of such a State.

History has presented to us many examples such as the Union of Great Britain and Ireland, Czechoslovakia and Poland. History has also shown to us many geographical tracts, much smaller than the sub-continent of India, which otherwise might have been called one country but which have been divided into as many states as there are nations inhabiting them. Balkan Peninsula comprises as many as 7 or 8 sovereign states. Likewise, the Portuguese and the Spanish stand divided in the Iberian Peninsula. Whereas under the plea of unity of India and one nation, which does not exist, it is sought to pursue here the line of one central government when we know that the history of the last 12 hundred years has failed to achieve unity and has witnessed, during the ages, India always divided into Hindu India and Muslim India. The present artificial unity of India dates back only to the British conquest and is maintained by the British bayonet, but the termination of the British regime, which is implicit in the recent declaration of His Majesty's Government, will be the herald of the entire break up with worse disaster than has ever taken place during the last one thousand years under the Muslims. Surely that is not the legacy which Britain would bequeath to India after 150 years of her rule, nor would Hindu and Muslim India risk such a sure catastrophe.

Muslim India cannot accept any constitution which must necessarily result in a Hindu majority government. Hindus and Muslims brought together under a democratic system forced upon the minorities can only mean Hindu Raj. Democracy of the kind with which the Congress High Command is enamoured would mean the complete destruction of what is most precious in Islam. We have had ample experience of the working of the provincial constitutions during the last two and a half years and any repetition of such a government must lead to civil war and raising of private armies as recommended by Mr Gandhi to Hindus of Sukkur when he said that they must defend themselves violently or non-violently, blow for blow, and if they could not, they must emigrate.

Mussalmans are not a minority, as it is commonly known and understood. One has only got to look round. Even today, according to the British map of India, 4 out of 11 provinces, where the Muslims dominate more or less, are functioning notwithstanding the decision of the Hindu Congress High Command to non-co-operate and prepare for civil disobedience. Mussalmans are a nation according to any definition of a nation, and they must have their homelands, their territory and their State. We wish to live in peace and harmony with our neighbours as a free and independent people. We wish our people to develop to the fullest our spiritual, cultural, economic, social and political life in a way that we think best, and in consonance with our own ideals and according to the genius of our people. Honesty demands— and the vital interests of millions of our people impose a sacred duty upon us to find an honourable and peaceful solution which would be just and fair to all. But at the same time, we cannot be moved or diverted from our purpose and objective by threats or intimidations. We must be prepared to face all difficulties and consequences, make all the sacrifices that may be required of us to achieve the goal we have set in front of us....

Anyhow, I have placed before you the task that lies ahead of us. Do you realize how big and stupendous it is? Do you realize that you cannot get freedom or independence by mere arguments? I should appeal to the intelligentsia. The intelligentsia in all countries in the world have been the pioneers of any movements for freedom. What does the Muslim intelligentsia propose to do? I may tell you that unless you get this into your blood, unless you are prepared to take off your coats and are willing to sacrifice all that you can, and work selflessly, earnestly and sincerely for your people, you will never realize your aim. Friends, I therefore, want you to make up your minds definitely, and then think of devices, and organize your people, strengthen your organization and consolidate the Mussalmans all over India. I think that the masses are wide awake. They only want your guidance and lead. Come forward as servants of Islam, organize the prople economically, socially, educationally and politically, and I am sure that you will be a power that will be accepted by everybody.

13. Reactions in Madras Province to Lahore Resolution

Appendix—I, Fortnightly Report for the Second Half of March 1940, Public (General) Department, Government of Madras, Tamil Nadu State Archives.

Report on the Press for the second fortnight of March, 1940. Statement of action taken under the Defence of India Act or the Indian Press (Emergency) Act, 1931.

...Comments in the Press: The proceedings of the Indian National Congress at Ramgarh and of the All India Muslim League in Lahore attracted widespread notice. The nationalistic press expressed the view that the attitude of the British Government and stated that Mahatma Gandhi will and take any hasty step and there was a great opportunity, therefore, for the Government to seek a settlement with him. The *Mail* regrets the resolution while the Muslim press and the *Viduthalai* of Erode condemned it outright. Mr Jinnah's plan adopted by the All India Muslim League of dividing India has come in for strong and bitter criticism at the hands of nationalistic press. Extreme Muslim opinion favours the division. The *Mail* expressed the opinion that the Scheme was impracticable, referring, in this connection to His Excellency Lord Linlithgow's view deprecating anything calculated to destroy the unity of India and called upon the Congress to be more realistic and arrive at a settlement with the Muslims.

There has been universal condemnation of the shooting to death of Sir Michael O' Dwyer at Caxton Hall. Papers in the city and the Muffassal have unhesitatingly expressed horror and indignation at the incident. *The Indian Express* while condemning the outrage had an article detailing the reasons why the late Sir Michael O' Dwyer had incurred great unpopularity of India.

14. Proceedings of All India Muslim League's Annual Session on 'Lahore Resolution', 23–24 March 1940

Indian Annual Register, 1940, Vol. I, pp. 312–14.

Moving the resolution[1] Mr Fazlul Huq said: We have stated definitely and unequivocally that what we want is not merely a tinkering with the idea of federation but its thorough overhauling so that the federation may ultimately go. This idea of federation must not only be postponed but abandoned altogether. On many an occasion on the platform of the Muslim League and the other day on the floor of the House in the Bengal Legislative Assembly, I made an emphatic and definite assertion that the Mussalmans of India will not consent to any such scheme which is framed without our approval. We will make such a constitution absolutely unworkable. I hope those who may have in their power to shape the future constitution of India will take the

Muslim feelings into consideration and not take any step which may be regretted. We have made our position absolutely clear. The problem is very simple. At present the Muslims constitute 80 millions scattered all over India. It may sound a big number but, as a matter of fact, the Muslims are in a weak position numerically in almost every province of India. In the Punjab and Bengal we are in an effective majority and are hopelessly in minority elsewhere. The position is such that whatever may be the constitution, Muslim interests are bound to suffer just as they have suffered during the last three years of the working of provincial autonomy.

Mr Fazlul Haq characterized as un-Islamic sentiments the recent statement of Maulana Abul Kalam Azad[2] in his presidential address that the Muslims should not feel nervous. Eighty millions was not a small number and they need not be afraid. Mr Fazlul Haq said even if a sufficient proportion of 80 millions had been congregrated in one province we would have had nothing to fear. Situated as we are, our political enemy can take advantage of the situation. Our friends will remember that even in the Punjab and Bengal our position is not very safe. In the legislatures we are not in such large majority; we have to seek the help of other interests and minorities to form coalition governments which are the weakest form of Governments known to constitutionalists. As regards the other provinces we are in a very weak position and are at the mercy of the majority. Until a satisfactory solution is found of this unequal distribution of Muslim population it is useless to talk of constitutional advance or of safeguards.

I earnestly appeal to my Muslim friends throughout India to remain united and exercise calm and sober judgment and remember that we have to stand on our own feet and cannot rely on anybody. It is a case of every one for himself and no one for Muslims of India. Mr Haq appealed to the audience to accept his motion and hoped the result would be good.

Seconding the resolution Choudhury Khaliquzzaman said that they should consider the circumstances which had forced the Muslims to demand separation and their own Government where they were in majority. Firstly, the responsibility of this demand rested on the British Government, who in order to exploit the Indians declared that India was one nation and started the majority and minority question. They opened the flood of such stupendous propaganda that the question came to be regarded as a real problem, whereas in fact, this question did not exist. After the British, Congress and the majority community were responsible for the Muslims' demand for separation. The working of the provincial part of the Act of 1935 in Congress provinces during the last three years had finally decided the question of separation. The treatment that the minorities in these provinces had received at the hands of the majority needed no comment. The Muslims had now realized that their existence was in danger, and if they wanted to maintain their identity they must struggle for it. Third and last, the responsibility was of those Muslims who tried to split the ranks of Muslims by setting up rival organizations or joining the Congress or other non-Muslim political parties. Continuing Ch. Khaliq-uz-Zaman said that he differed from Mr Abul Kalam Azad where he said that because the Muslims were strong enough to defend themselves they should not demand separation. He added that the responsibility of those Muslims who had damaged Muslim rights in India was great, for they were not only betraying the present generation, but the future generations also. If the Congress continued to act on the advice of Muslim Congressmen there was sure to be a civil war in India.

Supporting the resolution Maulana Zafar Ali Khan, MLA (central) said that he was feeling today as if he was speaking from a free India. For a long period he had been an advocate of Hindu–Muslim unity and had been in the Congress for a number of years. During all this time he had found that the Congress was not at all anxious to achieve freedom but in fact, wanted to suppress the minorities. The Congress had achieved its present high position as the result of the support lent by the Muslims in the past but now the Congress had adopted an indifferent attitude towards the Muslims. He as well as others of his school of thought had been criticizing the Muslim League for not doing any constructive work but today it had shown to the world its constructive programme. Referring to the Congress proposal for a constituent assembly, Maulana Zafar Ali Khan reiterated that they would not accept any constitution which had not been approved of and consented to by the Muslims of India.

Sardar Aurangzeb Khan, leader of the opposition in the Frontier Assembly said that he had the privilege of supporting the resolution which had been moved by the 'lion of Bengal.' It should be considered calmly and dispassionately. He congratulated the Muslims living in the Hindu provinces for lending their support to the resolution which sought freedom for six crores of Muslims. Speaking for the Frontier he said that his province was the gateway of India and he was there to assure Muslims living in the Hindu provinces that they were ready at all times to lay their lives for the sake of their co-religionists. The speaker expressed the opinion that it was absurd to declare Muslims a minority community when in four provinces in India they were in a majority.

Concluding Sardar Aurangzeb Khan said, 'We do not want British democracy which is nothing but counting of heads. Muslims are a separate nation; we want a home for the Muslim nation; our home is as indicated in the resolution'.

Sir Abdulla Haroon, MLA, (Central) said that it was a well-known fact that the Muslims came to India through Sind. Sind Muslims were the first to moot this question which was now before the League. In 1938 the Muslim League passed a resolution for establishing 'independent states' in the north-western and eastern zones. Since then various constitutional schemes had been framed and they were now being examined by a command that it was the duty of the Muslims to pass it without any hitch. Sir Abdulla Haroon warned the Hindus that if the Muslims in Hindu provinces were not justly treated, the Hindus in the Muslim provinces would be treated in the same way in which Herr Hitler had treated the Sudetans. The speaker hoped that the proposal embodied in the resolution would be acceptable both to the Hindus and the British as there was no better solution of the thorny problem.

Third Day—Resolutions—Lahore—24th March 1940

The third day's session of the League commenced on the 24th March at 11.15 a.m. As Mr Jinnah arrived a little late, the Nawab of Mamdot was voted to the chair to guide the proceedings which commenced with recitations from the Holy Quran. Discussion on the resolution on the constitutional problem was then resumed.

K.B. Nawab Mohd. Ismail Khan (Bihar), supporting the resolution said that he belonged to a minority province where Mussalmans did not enjoy freedom of speech. In this session which was being held in a 'free land' he had pleasure in speaking freely. He thanked the Muslim majority provinces for the offer of help to the Muslims of minority provinces if an attempt were made to suppress their rights, but he had full confidence in the ability of the Muslims of his own province to defend themselves in the hour of need. Referring to Maulana Azad's presidential address the Nawab said that he wanted to tell the Congress that Maulana Azad's voice was not the voice of the Muslims but that Mr Jinnah truly reflected Muslim opinion in India. (Cheers.)

Mr Mohd. Isa Khan (Baluchistan) assured his co-religionists in the minority provinces that when they had achieved freedom in majority provinces they would not forget them and would be prepared to render every kind of help in their power. He reminded the audience that like the Mussalmans of the NWFP, the Mussalmans of Baluchistan were also the gatekeepers of India, as they guarded the Bolan Pass. They were the trustees of a great charge and he hoped they would acquit themselves well in the eyes of their brethren in the minority provinces.

Mr Abdul Hamid Khan (Madras) declared that the All India Muslim League had been carrying on the fight for the freedom of India for the last 37 years. In this struggle they had co-operated with the Hindus in the hope that the freedom of India meant freedom for every inhabitant of this country. But their belief had been belied by the conduct of the Congress during its regime of two and a half years in seven out of the 11 provinces. Mr Abdul Hamid said that thanks to the Congress regime in the provinces the Muslims had been awakened and Muslim Leagues had been organized in every province. He expressed the hope that when the League prepared a new constitution the Muslims of minority provinces would be fully consulted.

Mr Ismail Chundrigar (Bombay) declared that Federation of the whole India in which the Mussalmans would be in a hopeless minority was entirely unacceptable to them. He maintained that the scheme embodied in the resolution was fair and just from all points of view. The Muslims in no circumstances were prepared to support the Congress proposal for a constituent assembly where the Muslims would be in a minority of one to three.

Syed Abdur Raul Shah (CP), said that he belonged to a province which had been the target of Congress oppression. In spite of the tyranny of the Congress ministry the Muslims did not lose patience.

Dr Mohd. Alam, MLA (Punjab), who recently resigned from the Congress, supported the resolution. Analysing the position of the Congress Dr Alam said that the Congress did not want independence but a Hindu Raj under the aegis of the British Government. This was why distinguished Muslim nationalists like Mohammad Ali had severed their connection with the Congress. It was not a fact, he asserted, that the Muslims had left the Congress but on the other hand, the truth was that the Congress had abandoned its original position and given up its goal of complete independence. Dr Alam related how before joining the League he went to Delhi to meet Mr Jinnah and enquired as to what sacrifice the Muslim League would be prepared to make to achieve the programme now outlined in the resolution. Mr Jinnah assured him, continued Dr Alam, that he would give his life for it and be the first to go to jail. Dr Alam appealed to the Muslims to organize branches of the League in all districts, towns, villages and mohallas and strengthen the hand of Qaid-i-Azam.

When the session met at 9 p.m., Syed Zakir Ali and Begum Mohd Ali supported the resolution. The resolution was passed by a show of hands.

---

[1] For the text of the resolution on 'Constitutional Problem', which came to be known as 'Lahore Resolution' and later as 'Pakistan Resolution', see Chapter 2, Document no. 43.

[2] The reference is to Maulana Azad's Presidential Address at the Ramgarh session of the Congress. For relevant extracts from the Address, see Document no. 47 in this chapter.

⊹⟨═⟩∗⟨═⟩⊹

15. Jinnah Explains the Full Implications of the Lahore Resolution
Amrita Bazar Patrika, 1 April 1940.

Partition of India
Exchange of Population not intended
Homeland for six crores of Muslims
Safeguards for Minorities in Hindu Provinces

An earnest appeal to the better mind of the Hindus and other communities to give serious consideration to the Lahore resolution of All India Muslim League is made by Mr Mahomed Ali Jinnah in a statement to the Press. Mr Jinnah says:

'I still hope that at any rate the better mind of the Hindus will give earnest and serious consideration to our proposals as therein lies the achievement of India's freedom at the earliest possible period. This freedom we shall be able to retain peacefully both internally and externally'.

Replying to the critics of the League's resolution, Mr Jinnah says, 'In the first place a wrong idea and false propaganda appear to be to set in motion in order to frighten the Muslim minorities that they would have to migrate "en-bloc" and wholesale. I wish to assure my Muslim brethren that there is no justification for this insidious misrepresentation of exchange of population, however, on the physical division of India as far as practicable will have to be considered. Secondly, the Muslim minorities are wrongly made to believe that they would be worse off and be left in the lurch in any scheme of partition or division of India. I may explain that the Mussalmans, wherever they are in a minority cannot improve their position under a united India or under one central government. Whatever happens, they would remain a minority. They can rightly demand all the safeguards that are known to any civilized Government to the utmost extent. But by coming in the way of the division of India they do not and cannot improve their own position. On the other hand they can, by their attitude of obstruction, bring the Muslim homeland and six crores of the Mussalmans under one Government, where they would remain no more than a minority in perpetuity.

Homeland Idea

'It was because of the realization of this fact that Mussalman minorities in the Hindu India readily supported the Lahore resolution. The question for the Muslim minorities in the Hindu India is whether the entire Muslim India of nine crores should be subjected to a Hindu majority raj or whether at least the six crores of the Mussalmans residing in the areas were they form a majority should have their own homeland and thereby have an opportunity to develop their spiritual, cultural, economic and political life in accordance with their own genius and shape their own future destiny, at the same time allowing Hindus and others to do likewise. Similar will be the position of the Hindus and other minorities in the Muslim homelands. In my opinion after the present tension created by the ambition of one community dominating over the other and establishing supremacy over all the rest is eased we shall find better understanding and goodwill created all round. The division of India will throw a great responsibility upon the majority in its respective zones to create a real sense of security amongst the minorities and win their complete trust and confidence'.

Sikhs' Apprehension

Mr Jinnah next dealt with the apprehensions created amongst the Sikhs by the Lahore resolution and said, 'I always have had an admiration and respect for the Sikh community and I want my Sikh friends to study thoroughly the constitutional problem of India as it stands today. I am sure that they would be much better off in the north-west Muslim zone than they can ever possibly be in a united India or under one central government for under one central government their voice would be negligible. The Punjab in any case would be an autonomous sovereign unit. And after all, they have to live in the Punjab. It is obvious that whereas in a united India they would be mere nobodies, in the Muslim homeland constituted of the western zone of the federated, autonomous states including the autonomous sovereign state of the Punjab, the Sikhs would always occupy an honoured place and would play an effective and influential role'.

Dealing with the Indian state Mr Jinnah said, 'The only important States which matter are not in the eastern but in the north-western zone. They are Kashmere, Bhawalpur, Patiala, etc. If these States willingly agree to come into the Federation of Muslim homeland we shall be glad to come to a reasonable and honourable settlement with them. We have however, no desire to force them or coerce them in any way.'

Relation with Britain

In regard to the relationship of the Muslim homeland with Great Britain Mr Jinnah referred to the Lahore resolution which said, 'This session authorizes the Working Committee to frame a scheme of constitution in accordance with these basic principles providing for the assumption finally by the respective regions of all powers such as defence, external affairs, communications, customs and such other matters as may be necessary'. Continuing, Mr Jinnah said 'As regards other zone or zones, that may be constituted in the rest of India, our relationship will be of an international character. An example already exists in the relationship of India with Burma and Ceylon'.

Proceeding, Mr Jinnah said 'One set of criticisms has come from some of the Congressite Mussalmans. Obviously they are speaking in their master's voice and I do not think anyone need worry about it. As to the criticism of some of the Congress leaders it is a parrot-like cry and thoughtless. The only person who has made any serious attempt to criticize the Lahore resolution is Mr Rajagopalachariar. He however, judges others by his own standards of political integrity when he said that we mean what we do not say, namely, 'What Mr Jinnah desires is a fuller aptitude for the so-called Muslim provinces to work out their progress without being hampered by a central government working under conditions necessitated by the composition of India's population and the play of political forces at such a centre. Surely he can ask for many things other than the cutting up of India into two parts based on a medieval conception in order to attain this laudable desire'.[1]

C.R. Criticized

Mr Rajagopalachari's arguments of dividing the baby and the parable of King Solomon has gone beyond the zenith of his intellectual powers. This analogy he wants to apply to our proposals. Surely India is not the sole property of the Congress and if the real mother was to be discovered it would be the Dravidians and still further the Aborigines. It would neither be the Aryan nor the Mussalman. The Aryan claim to India is no better than that of the Mussalmans except that they were earlier arrivals in point of time. What, however, is most astounding is Mr Rajagopalachari's talk when he says, 'Indeed not even Tippu Sultan or Hyderali or Aurangazeb or Akbar, all of whom lived during days when differences seemed more deep-rooted than now imagined that India was anything but one and indivisible. These great men might have differed from one another in many respects but they agreed in looking upon this precious land and this great nation as one and essentially indivisible'. Yes, naturally they did so as conquerors and parental rulers.

Is this the kind of government Mr Rajagopalachariar does still envisage? And did the Hindus of those days willingly accept the rule of these 'great men'?. I may or may not be suffering from a diseased mentality, but the statement of Mr Rajagopalachariar and his criticisms of the Lahore resolution indicate that in him there is no mind left at all. I hope he does not represent the true Hindu opinion and I doubt very much whether he represents the opinion of the Congress or its High Command, so far as his statement on Lahore resolution goes'.

---

[1] For Rajagopalachari's statement, see Document no. 49 in this chapter.

16. A Different Nation for Muslims: Statement by Chaudhury Rahmat Ali

Star of India, 11 April 1940.

The following statement has been issued to the Press by Choudhury Rahmat Ali, Founder President of the Pakistan National Movement, and, in view of its importance to the future of the Millat, we publish its original text in English.

In the thirteen centuries of our history we have known hard tests indeed, but surely, none so fateful as the one that confronts us today. A test of life and death, it summons us to make our final choice between slavery within 'India' and sovereignty inside Asia; between the meanest minority position under 'Indianism' and the noblest national status symbolic 11-year old Tricolour of the Jati—the paramount of our fate, and the historic thirteenth century-old crescent and Stars of the Millat—the protector of our destiny.

That, in essence, is the choice. It has to be one or the other. It cannot be both.

[I]f we once agree to live within 'India', we shall ever exist in subjection to 'Indianism' which is being cleverly canonized into a new cult by its creators—the Indians; screamingly accepted by its creators—the Muslim millions, and cruelly supported by its self-seeking suzerains, the British Imperialists. Bad enough indeed, but that is not all. As we all know, to this 'Indianism' even our own highest leadership tenders its homage in one form or the other.... The 'Indianism', whose supremacy they support will, in the name of democracy, create the Indian Government control its civil administration, and command its military arm. And if, and when, sure of its power—and of its prey—it will make use of it to coerce and crush us into complete captivity.

Such being the grim certainty, is it not the most imperative duty of all those Muslim individuals or institutions—including the All India Muslim League—who claim for the Millat a nationality distinct from the 'Indians' and yet accept 'India' as their common Motherland, to take note of the tragic consequences of their position—a position which is at once foolish, false and fatal.

This is not to deny that, for our sacred struggle, most of our institutions have now adopted the 'Bi-national Basis' which, for the first time in 1933, the Pakistan National Movement put before the Millat, rather it is to stress that being only the first half of the 'Movements

Fundamental' they must, if they want to preserve their heritage, adopt the other half too. For it is only a firm grasp of the Full Fundamental that the Millat can be saved.

What is the Full Fundamental? It is that we are Muslims, not Hindus; Asians not 'Indians'.

The whole world knows that the Pakistan National Movement has already led the way in this direction, and laid the foundation of the defence of 30 million Muslims living in Pakistan. And now that its work has borne fruit and made the Millat conscious of its mission, it takes the next decisive step and publicly calls upon the Millat to create its national status in Bengal as well as strengthen its sovereignty in Usmanistan—the two Milli strongholds outside Pakistan.

The Movement now, as ever, firmly maintains that, as in Pakistan, so in Bengal, we are in clear majority, and have, therefore, the God given right of 'Self Determination'—a right which none can question. But it is a right which we can only realize by the creation of a Milli movement which in the name of the Millat will first own the right itself, then declare it before the world, and finally inspire the people to work for, and demand, its recognition from others. That counsel comes to us from our history. We must pay heed to it. It is indispensable to our being and well-being.

May those who profess to serve the Millat fully realize its supreme importance—and their solemn responsibility before God and man; as on their realization hinges not only the immediate future of 30 million Muslims living in Bengal but also the fate of the Millat's entire mission in South Asia?

As for Usmanistan we derive our title to it from those canons of International law from which other nations do theirs to their respective domains. And it is by virtue of their sanction alone that we are, and have ever been, in possession of its *de jure* sovereignty—a sovereignty which has solemnly been acknowledged in the treaties originally entered into between the British Government and its 'Faithful Ally'. Inescapably, therefore, if in the bedeviled circumstances of today, we want it to survive as such we ourselves must stand for, and demand, the *de-facto* recognition of its *de jure* sovereignty from the British as well as from their presumptive heirs—the Hindus—both of whom profess to be great supporters of the sanctity of international treaties.

So much about the political aspect of the issue. Now let us turn to its historical side which must have supreme importance in the affairs of men and nations.

Looking at it from that standpoint, we find that both these territories are distinct lands, created by the forces of Nature which ever make the entities of nations. They have, therefore, been treated as such throughout the ages and, even to this day, remain different from Hindustan in character, culture and composition, as well as in geography, history and destiny....

It will, therefore, be the greatest injustice of modern times to incorporate Bengal and Usmanistan into 'India', especially when their rightful positions on the map involves no partition of 'India', no redistribution of territories, no fresh demarcation of provinces, and no exchange of population. All that it involves is the recognition of their historic status, born of measureless sacrifices of the Millat. Will the Indians do that?

Whatever their response to this call of justice may be, we must do all we can to recover our lost places in the world, for that alone can save our Millat from the serfdom of 'Indianism' and secure our lands from the shackles of 'provincialism' of India. Not only that, on their solid foundations we can, and will, build three independent nations larger, bigger, and more powerful than any that ever existed in the Muslim world.

This will naturally raise the question of co-ordination and consolidation of the three Millat strongholds by a central organization—an organization dedicated, both in name and in spirit, to the realization of the destiny placed before the Millat by the Pakistan National Movement.

At the moment, the only central organization of the Millat is the All India Muslim League, but, unfortunately, its very name bears the stamp of 'Indianism' and betrays our being to 'Indianism'. We must scrap it in its present form and recreate it as a league of the Muslim Nations of Pakistan, Bengal and Usmanistan and then unite under its flag and carry on the fight in the solemn conviction of our victory.

This is the only road to our destiny. May we take it while there is yet life and light.

Note: The name Usmanistan, coined by the Founder President of the Pakistan National Movement in 1937, is used here for the Dominions of Ala Hazrat the Nizam, which in his view, possess a territorial entity separate from Hindustan.

17. Liaqat Ali Khan on Mahatma Gandhi's Views on Partition

Pioneer, 16 April 1940.

Nawabzada Liaqat Ali Khan, Secretary of the All India Muslim League, has issued the following statement:

'Mr Gandhi's article in the *Harijan* in reply to my statement is to be welcomed for more reasons than one. The statement in M. Gandhi's previous article in the *Harijan* under the caption, "My reply to Quaid-e-Azam"[1], that if the vast majority of Indian Muslims feel that they are not one nation with their Hindu and other brethren, who will be able to resist them had created an impression that Mr M. Gandhi would not oppose the demand of the Mussalmans as laid down in the Lahore session of the All India Muslim League, if it was proved to his satisfaction that the Lahore resolution had the support of the majority of Mussalmans behind it.

'His latest statement[2] that "but I can never be a willing party to vivisection. I would employ every non-violent means to prevent it", removes any doubt or ambiguity about his attitude regarding the proposal for partition of India into more than one federation. The statement, shorn of all verbiage, shows that Mr Gandhi's attitude in the matter is exactly the same as that of Mr Savarkar and other Mahasabha leaders.

'While the Mahasabha leaders would not confine themselves to any particular method, Mr Gandhi would employ every non-violent means to prevent the 90 million Mussalmans from exercising the right of self-determination—a right which he and the Congress claims for the Hindus in the name of Indian nationalism. He would coerce them into accepting what he thinks is good for them'.

Method Not Important

'To my mind, the employment of a particular method is of little importance when the object is the same. While the object of the use of violence or brute force is to terrorize one's adversary into submission, the employment of non-violent methods is to paralyse the opponent into accepting one's terms. The object in both cases is the same-coercion of the other party.

'There is another significant point that emerges out of M. Gandhi's statement. The use of non-violent means is not to be made only against British imperialism to coerce it into accepting Mr Gandhi's demands but they are to be employed against the 90 millions of Mussalmans also if they dare demand something for their honourable and independent existence in this country, which is not approved of by Mr Gandhi.

'I wish to tell Mr Gandhi that the Muslim League was not unaware of the fact when it passed the Lahore resolution that opposition to it would come from those quarters that had been dreaming of the domination of the Hindus over every other nationality and the establishment of Ram Raj in the country. The Lahore resolution shatters all such hopes. In spite of threats of non-violence or otherwise the Mussalmans are determined to enjoy the same freedom, power and authority in this country as is demanded by the majority community. We shall have nothing less than a free Islam in a free India.

'Mr Gandhi accuses me of being hasty in what I said in my previous statement about the election of Maulana Abul Kalam Azad to the presidentship of the Congress and the policy that has been followed by the Congress. Thank God, I do not suffer from excessive emotionalism or making hasty declarations. What I stated is the confirmed belief of millions of people in this country.'

---

[1] See Document no. 48 in this chapter.
[2] See Document no. 51 in this chapter.

18. Jinnah's Call to Muslims—Confirm Lahore Resolution at Friday's Meeting

Bombay Chronicle, 16 April 1940.

Mr M.A. Jinnah, President of the All India Muslim League, has issued the following statement:

'I feel confident that the Muslims throughout India fully realize the paramount and vital importance of the resolution passed by the full session of the All India Muslim League at Lahore on 24 March, 1940. It was a red letter day in the history of Muslim India and of the sub-continent of India. The Lahore resolution has after the fullest and most careful considerations defined our goal in the clearest possible manner.

'It is to explain and confirm this resolution that the Muslim League has fixed 19 April, 1940, so that all the Provincial District and Primary Leagues should hold public meetings throughout the country to express their opinion so that no doubt should be left in the minds of anyone as to the verdict of Muslim India.

'I therefore, appeal to every Muslim throughout India with all earnestness I can command, to observe April 19, 1940 as the day "conforming the declaration of Muslims self-determination" and as the Muslims Independence Day.

'I Feel that Muslim India is whole-heartedly with us and will not spare any effort to demonstrate to the world that we have with all the solemnity set our goal in front of us and shall fight for it and are prepared for any and every sacrifice for achievement and realization.

'The secretaries of all primary and district branches of the Bombay provincial Muslim League have been requested by the Honorary Secretary, Bombay Provincial Muslims League, Mr M.M.S. Ispahani to hold public meetings on Friday, April 19, with a view to explaining and confirming the resolution passed at the Lahore session of the All India Muslims League.'

19. Criticism of Jinnah's Call for Pakistan Day Celebration

Aaj, 18 April 1940.

Horrible Imagination

Mr Jinnah has appealed to celebrate 'Pakistan Day' on 19th April. He has challenged Mr Gandhi that he should not think that only those fifty thousand Muslims, present at the Muslim League session at Lahore, were supporting the resolution passed by (them). We know that Mr Jinnah will be successful in this endeavour or whether he is successful or not, he will certainly boast of being successful. Some time ago, in the same way he had appealed to celebrate 'Deliverance day' after the resignation of the Congress Ministry. Now, he has taken the second step. We also know that Mr Jinnah's faithfuls are visiting every Muslim house to get the signatures of Muslims in order to show that innumerable Muslims are supporting the partition of India. Illiterate, unaware of the condition of the world and unaware of right and wrong, this kind of the general Muslim public could be easily swayed. It is not at all difficult to get their signatures after telling them false stories of oppressed Muslims, showing the danger to Islam, telling them about the possibility of the establishment of Hindu-raj, creating religious fanaticism and describing the imaginary but pleasant dream of Pakistan. Mr Jinnah is not worried about the results of this propaganda. He has neither the time nor does he want to think about it that these propagandas will further aggravate the already present fire of communalism and then it will be very difficult to extinguish it. If he is not bothered about the lives of the Hindus, then at least for the sake of the Muslims, for their safety and benefit, he should have turned away from this activity. But, he knowingly does not want all these factors to come forward. He wants to do only those things which will serve his self-interest irrespective of their results.

How treacherous, harmful and horrible is the plan of Pakistan, we do not want to explain it again through this article. We have written on it several times. This question is so clear that we need not debate or explain it. We only want to say that the establishment of Pakistan and partition of India are distant dreams, but Mr Jinnah is paving the path of a horrible destruction only through uttering these poisonous words. He should know that the partition of India is not a simple matter. If he hopes that British imperialism would implement this plan, then he is mistaken. Britain can keep India under its protection on the pretext of this demand and can benefit itself in this way but it is not possible for it to divide India. Mr Jinnah should know that the British Government does not possess the power to divide India into two parts. If Mr Jinnah is hoping for the division of India on the strength of the Muslims, then, again he is mistaken. He should remember that the pride of one's strength makes the others also realize their strength and it can have serious consequences. So, if Mr Jinnah utilizes his brains and thinks further, then he will realize that his plans to partition India could not be successful. Hence whatever he is saying is not workable. Yes it will have another repercussion. It will push back by many centuries the progress, civil war will spread in India, everywhere a state of destruction and anarchy will exist and the face of India will be blackened forever. At this moment if the attention of the country will be drawn to this destructive proposal instead of the main question of the day, it will prove fatal for the country and the nation would lose the opportunity to achieve freedom. Mr Jinnah will be successful if this is his only aim. The more you will talk about Pakistan and the partition of India, the more this matter will become complicated and we will be so entangled into it that it will become impossible to come out of it. The aims of independence and freedom from Imperialism will vanish on their own because nobody would have the time to look into these matters.

We are watching that slowly these circumstances are being created. Mr Jinnah, himself, is not sparing anything for its emergence and to make it more serious. The celebration of Pakistan Day is another step towards this. There is no doubt that these utterances of Mr Jinnah will have reactions. Nowadays, the sensation among Sikhs which we see, is also the result of these reactions. It is impossible that a permanent Muslim state is established in Punjab and the Sikhs also recognize it. Although Punjab is a Muslim majority state and the reins of government will also remain in the hands of Muslims, still, in democracy, despite the rule of the majority, everybody considers it his own because he has the same rights as the other. But when there is a suggestion for creating permanent Muslim government and Muslim India, then it will be unacceptable to the Muslims of Punjab and Bengal. It will be even more unacceptable to the Sikhs, because it will mean slavery under the Muslims and nothing else. Therefore, the Sikh Society has become depressed. Mr Jinnah should have thought about it because these reactions are spreading not only among Sikhs but among the Hindus as well. We are opposed to the policy of Mr Savarkar and have severely criticized him several times in these columns. But nowadays, Mr Jinnah himself is creating such situations where nobody would listen to those opposing the policy of Mr Savarkar, and he will create such a mental condition which will necessitate and facilitate the creation of different attitudes/view-points in the Hindu society. Only a few days ago, Mr Savarkar has said in a speech that if Muslims want to create Pakistan then they will also clearly talk about the establishment of Hindu raj in the whole of India. We will, of course, oppose this tendency, but Mr Jinnah should consider as to who is responsible for all this. He takes pleasure in calling themselves (Muslims) a separate nation, but does he realize that it will only arouse those sentiments about the incidents of past centuries among the Hindus which will make them consider their own fellow brethren as foreigners. The Muslims can look to the Arabs and Palestine but the awakened Hindus will see the reflections of its own past glory, history, culture and religion in every inch of the Indian land.

Will this Hinduism awakened out of the sorrowful incidents of the past, instead of Indianism, think about the welfare of the Muslims? The new attitudes and feelings which the Congress had been trying to create during this span of fifty years after burying the past, Mr Jinnah is trying to kill them and in this way he is not only harming the Hindus but the Muslims as well and even more. It is worth thinking if the interest of the Hindu society and India does not stop him from treading on this path. Can we hope that Mr Jinnah will listen to us in the wider interest of the country?

20. Report on Muslim Independence Day Celebrations
Star of India, 20 April 1940.

Never before in living memory did Calcutta witness a greater demonstration of enthusiasm and support of Muslim India's any one particular demand, as was witnessed on Friday evening at the Mohammed Ali Park, where speeches supporting and explaining the Muslim League scheme for the Partition of India into Hindu and Muslim States were made, in connection with the observance of 'All India Muslim Independence Day'.

Mr Syed Badruddoja, MLA, presided.

Amidst thundering cries of 'Alla-ho Akbar' a resolution was passed supporting the Lahore resolution of the All India Muslim League regarding the future constitution of India, and assuring the Muslim League Executive that the Muslims of Bengal would regard no sacrifice too great for the sake of 'freedom from the incubus of a permanent Hindu majority tyranny in the Federal centre, and for the building of independent and sovereign Muslim States as free homelands for the Muslim Nation in the sub-continent of India, and for securing adequate effective and mandatory safeguards for the protection of Muslim minorities in Hindu Zones.'

The meeting expressed the opinion that 'the misconception that India is a unitary "nation" and that future Indian Constitution should be based on territorial nationalism of the type of the uniform "nation-state" of Europe lies at the root of all the political ills of this sub-continent of India.' Mr Syed Badnuddoja, MLA, in his presidential speech, said that the demands of Muslim India could no longer be ignored. Assuring the great Hindu nation, he said: 'The vast majority of the Muslim nation have no intention of encroaching on the rights of Hindus or any other people'. Muslims' one and only insistent demand is that they should be merely allowed the right of self-determination without being coerced by the Congress or British Imperialism, to safeguard the rights, culture and religious entity of Muslim Nation and to achieve the consummation of an ideal of a free Islam and a free India.

At Patna
Muslims 'Would make every Sacrifice'

Patna, 19 April

'Muslims would make every sacrifice for the materialization of the Pakistan scheme of the Muslim League outlined in its resolution', declared Khan Bahadur S.M. Ismail, President of the Bihar Provincial Muslim League, presiding at a public meeting this evening held in the observance of 'Pakistan Day'.

Khan Bahadur Ismail added that it was wrong to suppose that Muslims in minority provinces would be left at the mercy of the majority community. The minorities in Hindu provinces would be entitled to the same protection which the minorities in Muslim provinces would enjoy.

At Noakhali

Noakhali, 19 April.

A mammoth meeting of the Muslims of Noakhali town was held under the presidency of Moulana Abdul Malekhan in the Jame Mosque today accepting the resolutions of the Lahore League, the only solution for the liberation of the Muslims of India. It further passed a no-confidence motion against the microscopic so-called Muslim organizations under the guidance and influence of the Congress and requested the Muslims of other parts of India to follow suit.

Implicit obedience and gratitude toward Haque—Nazimuddin Cabinet for championing and safe-guarding the rights and interests of the Muslims of Calcutta Corporation was also expressed.

21. Report on Muslim Independence Day Celebrations in Different Parts of the Country
   Pioneer, 22 April 1940.

In connection with the celebration of the Muslim Independence Day, in accordance with the instructions of Mr M.A. Jinnah, a public meeting of Muslims is being held this evening in Municipal Gardens outside Delhi Gate when the implications of the Muslim League resolution concerning the partition of India will be explained. Nawab Sir Shah Nawab Khan of Mamdot, President of the Punjab Provincial Muslim League, is expected to preside.

At Agra

A resolution supporting the Lahore resolution of the Muslim League was adopted at a mass meeting of Muslims held this evening under the presidentship of Mr Muhammad Faiyaz Khan,

MLC, President of the local Muslim League. The meeting expressed the view that the League plan for partition was the only solution to the prevalence of communal bitterness in the country.

At Moradabad

Two meetings were held today under the auspices of the Majlis-e-Ahrar and the Muslim League in observance of Anti-Partition and Partition Day. At the meeting of Ahrars at the Shahi Mosque, speakers expressed the opinion that the partition plan was impracticable and detrimental to the country's interests. Sir Raza Ali, who presided at the Muslim League meeting, observed that the proposal to convene a constituent assembly was absurd and involved perpetual slavery of the minorities at the hands of the majority community. He claimed that the Muslim League plan offered a better solution of the constitutional crisis facing the country.

At Benares

In observance of the Pakistan Day, a meeting of Muslims was held at the Town Hall this evening. About a dozen Khaksars in uniform and carrying *belchas* attended the meeting.

At Budaun

A meeting of the City Muslim League was held in the Juma Masjid presided over by Mr Muhammad Fariduddin Danishmandi. The Pakistan resolution, proposed by Hakim Fazalur Rahman and seconded by Maulvi Muhammad Yahaya was unanimously passed.

At Allahabad

A public meeting held under the auspices of the City Muslim League this evening celebrated the Pakistan Day as enjoined by the All India Muslim League. The Lahore resolution of the Muslim League was read out to the audience and implications were explained by several speakers. The resolution was adopted by the meeting unanimously.

Another meeting was held at Atala under the auspices of the Ansar Scouts and Volunteer Corps with Dr M.A. Ansari, Joint Secretary, All India Momin Conference in the chair to protest against the Muslim League proposal for the partitioning of India.

At Jaunpur

The Muslims observed the Pakistan Day after Juma prayers. At the Juma Masjid Maulana Azad Sahabni explained the Pakistan scheme as embodied in the Lahore resolution. At another meeting held in Atala the resolution was whole-heartedly approved.

At Hardoi

The Muslims observed the Pakistan Day by holding meetings in the town and in several parts of the district. The League resolution was unanimously approved at each meeting.

At Etawah

The Muslims held a meeting last night under the presidentship of M. Ghulam Mohiuddin Khan, Editor, the *Monis*, Etawah, and whole-heartedly supported the Lahore resolution and assured Mr Jinnah of their readiness to make sacrifices to attain the goal.

At Bangalore

In accordance with the direction of the All India Muslim League to observe 'Partition Day', a meeting of Muslims was held today at Sultanpet Mosque when the Lahore resolution of the Muslim League was adopted unanimously.

At Sultanpur

According to the instructions of the All India Muslim League public meetings of Muslims were held throughout the district and the Pakistan scheme was unanimously approved.

At Ghazipur

The Muslims took out a procession and held a meeting at the Town Hall to express their approval of the Pakistan scheme as passed by the Lahore session of the Muslim League.

At Peshawar

Scenes of great enthusiasm marked the celebration of the Independence Day organized by the Muslim League in Peshawar today.

Addressing a huge gathering of Pathans drawn both from the city and the neighbouring villages in Azad park, Sardar Aurangazeb Khan, member of the Working Committee of the All India Muslim League explained at length the Lahore resolution of the League and replied to the criticisms directed against it.

At Bijnor

Thousands of Muslims assembled at the Juma Masjid to endorse the Partition resolution of the League and to express their confidence in Mr Jinnah's leadership.

At Aligarh

A meeting of the local Muslims was held at the Juma Masjid under the presidentship of Professor Abdur Sattar to celebrate the Pakistan Day. The Ahrars, who were present at the meeting, tried to oppose the Lahore plan of partitioning India but the President dissolved the meeting without putting the motion to vote.

At Fetehpur

At a largely attended meeting of Muslims, the Pakistan scheme was whole-heartedly supported. A long procession was taken out with hundreds of placards and flags.

At Jabbulpore

Resolutions reiterating faith in Mr Jinnah's leadership and support for the scheme for India's partition were adopted at a meeting of the Muslims held here last night under the presidentship of Mr Burhanul Haque, Chairman of the District Muslim League. Nearly 7,000 Muslims attended the meeting.

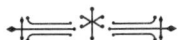

22.   Support to Pakistan Demand

Times of India, 22 April 1940.

Bombay Meeting: 'Separate Cultures will be Preserved'

Presiding over a mass meeting of Muslims of Bombay on Friday night on the occasion of the celebration of the Pakistan Day, Mr I.I. Chundrigar criticized the administration of the provinces by the Congress Ministries and pointed out that the opinion of the Muslims that their interests were not safe in the hands of the majority community had been confirmed.

At present, the minorities were often subjected to ridicule whenever they put forth even reasonable demands. To cite one example, in the province of Bombay, during the regime of the Congress ministry, text books had been prescribed in Urdu schools which were wholly unsuited to Muslim children. It was due to the persistent agitation carried on by the Muslim League Party in the legislature that the books were withdrawn. The Congress appeared bent upon destroying the language, culture and civilization of the Muslims. It was all due to the fear of the Congress that if the Muslims were left with the books of their own choice they would maintain their religious fervor and establish their sway over the whole of India some day. With the establishment of two separate states there would be no danger of one culture being annihilated by another.

Mr Chundrigar observed that the partition scheme had been misunderstood in certain quarters. It was suggested by critics that the Muslims in the provinces in which they were in a minority would leave their hearth and homes immediately and settle down in the Punjab or the Northwest Frontier Province. The scheme contemplated nothing of the kind. There would be safeguards provided for the minorities. The Muslims of Bombay, in any case, he asserted would not run away from the province although they formed only nine per cent of the population.

Sir Currimbhoy Ebrahim who moved a resolution endorsing the Pakistan scheme adumbrated at the Lahore Session of the All India Muslim League said that the time had come when the Congress itself would require the protection of British bayonets and the Muslims would only need to summon their own strength.

After several other speeches, the resolution was passed unanimously.

Muslim Women's Meeting: Pakistan Idea Supported

The Muslim League resolution regarding the Pakistan scheme was endorsed by a public meeting of the Muslim women of Bombay under the presidentship of Mrs Shuffi Tyabji on Friday evening. Mrs Tyabji said that the Pakistan scheme was the only solution of the communal problem in India. It was not altogether a new idea for it had been adopted with advantage by Turkey in solving her differences with the Balkan countries. She appealed to Muslim women to follow the lead of the Muslim League and to work for the realization of the scheme, which alone would ensure safety for Muslim culture, religion and interests.

Among those who addressed the meeting were Mrs K.S. Somjee, Mrs Al Haj Qasim Ali Jairazbhoy, Miss Suleka Cassum, Miss Meherbanoo M. Visram, Miss Aminabai J. Mohammad and Mrs Noorbanoo Zakaria Maniar.

23. Pakistan Day Celebrations in Madras Province

Fortnightly Report from Public (General) Department, 17th May 1940, Government of Madras to Secretary to the Government of India, Tamil Nadu State Archives.

Fortnightly Report for the Second Half of April 1940

...April 19th, Pakistan Day was celebrated with meetings by Moslem League organizations in nearly every district. In Salem, E.V. Ramaswami Naicker and other Justice Party Leaders participated in a meeting and there was a minor disturbance when a section of the crowd objected to Ramaswami Naicker's speech. E.V. Ramaswami Naicker supported partition and urged the need for a separate Tamil Nadu.

An attempt to hold a Nationalist Muslim meeting in Madras to oppose Mr Jinnah's proposal was abandoned owing to lack of support and fear of social ostracism....

24. Fazlul Huq and V.D. Savarkar Campaign in Madras Province

Fortnightly Report from Public (General) Department, 17th May 1940, Government of Madras to Secretary to the Government of India, Tamil Nadu State Archives.

Fortnightly Report for the First Half of May 1940

...The Hon'ble M. Fazlul Huq, Premier of Bengal, visited the Province at the end of April to preside over the District Muslim League Conference at Calicut on 28th and 29th April. He was enthusiastically received. The attendance on the first day was about 5000 and on the second day about half that figure. His speeches were in support of the Muslim League and in criticism of the Congress administration.

Mr Sarvakar of the Hindu Maha Sabha toured in Tinnevelly District and Madura and addressed meetings at which he deprecated the action of the Congress in endeavouring to compromise with the demands of the Muslims and urged Hindus to strengthen the Maha Sabha. The meeting at Madura was attended by about 5000 people. The Maha Sabha also held a moderately attended meeting in Madras on 5th May at which a resolution was passed expressing concern at the atrocities perpetrated by Muslims on Hindus at Bidar, condemning the indifference of the Hyderabad Government towards such happenings and suggesting that the Maha Sabha should consider the question of launching Satyagraha again....

APPENDIX I
Report on the Press for the First Fortnight of May 1940

...The Pakistan question continues to occupy wide attention.

Muslim opinion with regard to the All India Muslim Azad (Independent) Muslim' Conference at New-Delhi was not unanimous. A section of the Muslim press in the City held that the separate conference was an attempt by the Congress Muslims appearing in the new garb of the Independent Muslims, to divide the community. Another section held that the differences between the two bodies of Muslims are not fundamental and suggests that a conference between the representatives of the two sections may be held. As regards the conference in the Malabar district with Mr Fazal [Fazlul Huq] as President, the Hindu Press belittled its importance and took strong exception to the President's remark that if the Congress tried to impose its will on the Muslims, the Moplah population alone would deal adequately with the matter.

25. Jinnah's Message to the Bombay Presidency Provincial Muslim League Conference Held at Hubli on 26 and 27 May 1940

Jamil-ud-din Ahmad (ed.), *Recent Speeches and Writings of Mr Jinnah*, Lahore, 1942, pp. 162–6.

Let me say a few words to the Mussalmans of Southern Division. The All India Muslim League has given the Mussalmans of India the correct lead. It has given them a flag, a platform, a policy and a well-considered programme and finally it has defined the ideal and the true goal for Muslim India, by its resolution at Lahore last March, to fight for and achieve it at any sacrifice, for therein lies their true salvation. I am asked, will the British agree to the basic and fundamental principles of the Lahore resolution, namely, to create Independent Muslim States in the North-Western and Eastern zones of India? Whether they agree or whether they do not, we shall fight for it to the last ditch. I know that the British politicians, press and public are still holding on to the conception of unity and one India; but I am convinced that it is a self-deception and complete ignorance of reality. At the same time I am confident that when we have successfully dispelled the false propaganda and removed the delusion under which the British public are suffering, they with their sense of sagacity and the British politicians and Government, who are capable of handling big issues in a statesmanlike manner, will not fail to meet us; and they are sufficiently versatile to grasp the issues. If Muslim India is united and determined and carries on a vigorous propaganda to dispel the misconceptions that have been sedulously created so far, we are bound to succeed.

The conception of unity that the Congress High Command are preaching and hanging on to, is due to unworthy selfishness and is based on mean strategy. It is calculated and rests on the hope of exploitation of British ignorance of Indian conditions, and in fact, they look to the British arms for the realization and establishment of the Hindu raj in this country, but it is unthinkable that the British arms can ever be placed at the disposal of the Congress High Command to dominate Muslim India. This attempt at gamble on the part of the Congress is bound to fail and their hopes and aspirations in this direction have already been, to a certain extent, frustrated.

It is amazing that men like Mr Gandhi and Mr Rajagopalachariar should talk about the Lahore resolution in such terms as 'vivisection of India' and 'cutting the baby into two halves'. Surely, today India is divided and partitioned by nature. Muslim India and Hindu India exist on the physical map of India. I fail to see why there is this hue and cry. Where is the country which is being divided? Where is the nation which is denationalized? India is composed of nationalities, to say nothing about the castes and sub-castes. Where is the Central National Government whose authority is being violated?

India is held by the British power and that is the hand that holds and gives the impression of united India and the unitary Government. Indian nation and central government do not exist. It is only the convenient imagination of the Congress High Command. It is a pure intellectual and mental luxury, in which some of the Hindu leaders have been indulging so recklessly.

We are told that our demand is the quintessence of communalism. Why? Because we propose that the Hindus and Mussalmans should be provided with their homelands which will enable them to live side by side as two honourable nations, and as good neighbours and not Hindus as superior and Mussalmans as inferior nations, tied artificially together with a Hindu religious majority to dominate and rule over Muslim India.

We are told next that we may develop extra territorial affinity. Surely, when we have constituted our national homelands and developed our territorial sovereign government it is unthinkable that we shall not guard our frontiers, just as in the Middle East exist territorial Muslim States side by side. Next we are told that the scheme is impracticable; but the autonomous provinces are in existence, even under the present constitution, where the Mussalmans and the Hindus dominate respectively. Their reconstitution into geographical, contiguous, homogeneous, independent zones is a most feasible and practicable scheme, provided it is honestly examined. But this agreement can only emanate with the one and the only motive and desire on the part of the Congress, to coerce the Muslim India to submit to a central government with the Hindu majority and Hindu rule throughout the country. Our proposal is more practical than 'ahimsa' and 'charkha', or, for the matter of that, the ideal of Ram Raj or Swaraj and complete independence of Mr Gandhi's conception.

Further, it is not detrimental either to the Hindu or Muslim interests generally, and so far as the minorities are concerned in the respective zones they will be given safeguards which will be effective, adequate and mandatory. It is the only practical solution of not only communal but political problems confronting us. Both the nations would be in a position then to enjoy equal status, rights and privileges, free to develop their spiritual, economic, social and political life according to their own sentiments, culture, conditions and genius.

Lastly, it has been said that it is not in the interest of the Mussalmans themselves. Surely, that must be left to the self-determination of Muslim India. It is the same old hackneyed argument that our rulers have often advanced when all else has failed them whenever we have pressed our demands. It does not come with any grace from the Congress High Command or the Congress press.

Why talk of the civil war in connection with the League resolution? It is highly mischievous. There will be no conflict and should be no conflict unless the Congress desires it. There can be no chaos and confusion unless Mr Gandhi uses all his forces of non-violent methods to obstruct the achievement of the Muslim ideal. Our ideal presuppose Indian freedom and independence; and we shall achieve India's independence far more quickly by agreeing to the underlined principles of the Lahore resolution than by any other method.

In his latest article which appeared in the press on the 19th of May[1], Mr Gandhi says, 'Should it happen otherwise and partition becomes the fashion, either we shall have partition or partitions rather than foreign rule, or we shall continue to wrangle among ourselves and submit to foreign rule, or else have a proper civil war'. It is quite clear that Mr Gandhi understands or ought to understand that to wrangle over the imaginary one and united India can only result in our submission to foreign rule. I pray that Mr Gandhi's prophecy of 'proper civil war' will not come, but the better minds of Hindus and Mussalmans will come round to the only alternative embodied in the Lahore resolution.

In conclusion, I appeal to the conference to organize the Mussalmans and prepare ourselves by creating complete harmony and unity amongst us, that we may be ready to face any emergency, as and when it may arise.

The issues involve the future fate and destiny of ninety millions of Mussalmans and I am sure that Muslim India today is fully alive to the gravity of the situation both international and external that is facing us. Our ideal and our fight is not to harm or injure any other community or interest or block the progress but to defend ourselves. We want to live in this country an honourable life as free men, and we stand for free Islam and free India.

---

[1] See *Harijan*, 8 May 1940; *Hindustan Times*, 19 May 1940.

26.   Mr Jinnah Advises Maulana Azad to Resign

Tribune, 18 July 1940.

Mr M.A. Jinnah, President of the All India Muslim League has released to the press the following telegrams exchanged between him and the Congress President, Maulana Abul Kalam Azad:

From Maulana Azad to Mr Jinnah 'Confidential. Your July 9 statement. Congress Delhi Resolution definitely means by National Government a composite cabinet not limited to any single party. But is it the position of the League that she cannot agree to any Provisional arrangement not based on two-nation scheme? If so, please clarify by wire'.

From Mr Jinnah, to Mr Abul Kalam Azad: 'Your telegram. Cannot reciprocate confidence. I refuse to discuss with you by correspondence or otherwise as you have completely forfeited the confidence of Muslim India. Can't you realize you are made a Muslim showboy Congress President to give it colour that it is national and deceive foreign countries. You represent neither Muslims nor Hindus. The Congress is a Hindu body. If you have self-respect resign at once. You have done your worst against the League so far. You know you have hopelessly failed. Give it up'.

27.   Muslim League Working Committee Resolutions on the Viceroy's Statement of 8 August 1940, Bombay, 1–2 September 1940

Jamil-ud-din Ahmad (ed.), *Historic Documents of Muslim Freedom Movement*, Lahore, 1970, pp. 400–3.

The Working Committee of the All India Muslim League have given their most earnest and careful consideration to the statement issued by His Excellency the Viceroy on the 8th of August, 1940 and the authoritative amplification and clarification of it by Mr Amery, the Secretary of State for India, on behalf of His Majesty's Government in the course of the India debate in the House of Commons on the 14th August, 1940. The Committee consider that these pronouncements constitute a considerable progressive advance towards the approach of the point of view and the position taken up by the All India Muslim League on behalf of Muslim India regarding the problem of the future constitution of India, and the Committee also note with satisfaction that His Majesty's Government have, on the whole, practically met the demand of the Muslim League for a clear assurance to the effect that no future constitution, interim or final, should be adopted by the British Government without their approval and consent.

The Working Committee appreciate that His Majesty's Government have conceded the principle urged upon them by the Muslim League that in order to secure genuine and full support of Muslim India and such other parties as are and have been ready and willing to undertake the responsibility and are prepared to make every contribution to the intensification of the war efforts, and for the defence of India, with a view to meet any external danger or aggression and to maintain internal security and peace they should forthwith associate the representatives of Muslim League with authority and power as partners in the central and provincial Government and establish a War Council which will include the Indian Princes and thus secure their cooperation also.

The Committee, therefore, are glad that His Majesty's Government, provisionally and during the prosecution of the war, have decided upon the expansion of the Executive Council of the Governor-General and the establishment of a War Advisory Council on an All India basis, though they regret that His Majesty's Government have declared that they at this stage do not contemplate non-official advisers in the provinces, which are at present administered by the Governors under section 93 of the Government of India Act. The Committee, however, find that the specific offer now made as embodied in the letter of His Excellency the Viceroy dated the 14th of August 1940, purporting to give effect to and implement the principle cooperation with authority in the Government as partners is most unsatisfactory and does not meet the requirements nor the spirit indicated in the resolution of this committee of the 16th of June, 1940, which was communicated by the President to His Excellency the Viceroy by his letter of the 17th of June 1940 nor does it meet the memorandum that was submitted to His Excellency by the President of the 1st of July, 1940.

In these circumstances the Committee find it very difficult to deal with this offer for the following reasons:

1. Neither the President nor the Committee was consulted as to the number of the proposed increase of the additional members of the Executive Council of the Governor-General.

2. The committee are not yet aware of the manner in which the entire Executive Council will be reconstituted.

3. The Committee have no information as to which are the other parties with whom the Muslim League will be called upon to work.

4. The Committee understand that the President has not been informed as to what portfolios will be assigned to every one of these additional members. The Committee are merely asked without any further knowledge or information except that the total number of members of the expanded Executive Council will be in the neighbourhood of 11 to send a panel of 4 out of which 2 will be selected for appointment as members of the Governor General's Executive Council.

5. The Committee have considered the system of panel suggested and they are of the opinion that it is open to many objections, is not desirable and does not commend itself to them.

6. As regards the proposed 'War Advisory Council' the Committee do not know its constitution, composition and functions beyond the information that it will probably consist of about 20 members and the Committee are asked to submit a panel out of which 5 will be nominated by His Excellency the Viceroy.

In these circumstances the Committee consider the offer unsatisfactory and request His Excellency the Viceroy to reconsider the matter and hereby authorize the President to seek further information and clarification.

The Resolution of the Working Committee passed at Bombay on the 16th of June, 1940 requesting the Mussalmans generally, and in particular, the members of the Muslim League not to serve on the War Committees and to avail further instructions from the President pending the result of the negotiations with the Viceroy, was not a decision that adopted the policy of non-cooperation with the government as has wrongly been represented by the enemies of the Muslim League; but on the contrary was intended to urge upon the Government a line of action and policy which they should adopt to secure more effective cooperation in the prosecution of the war. There are two very vital points for which the Committee have been pressing the Government namely (1) that no constitution either interim or final be adopted by His Majesty's Government without the approval and consent of Muslim India and (2) that in order to secure genuine and whole-hearted support of the Mussalmans, it was imperative that within the framework of the present constitution Muslim India leadership should be associated as a partner in the realm of the Central and Provincial Government forthwith. As a result of the negotiations the Working Committee are glad to state that the first point has now been practically met by the statement of His Excellency the Viceroy of the 8th August 1940 and the amplification and clarification of that statement by Mr Amery, the Secretary of State for India, in the course of his speech on the 14th of August, 1940 in Parliament, and the Committee also note with satisfaction that the Government have accepted the principle of the second point that was urged upon them, namely 'cooperation with authority and power' in the governments in order to prosecute the war successfully.

In view of these circumstances the Working Committee leave those Mussalmans, who think that they can serve any useful purpose by merely associating themselves with the Working Committees, free to do so.

The Committee are of opinion that the Government should, in fact, and not merely in principle take without delay the Muslim leadership into their complete confidence and associate them as equal partners in charge of the reins of the Government in the Centre and in the Provinces in order to secure genuine and whole-hearted cooperation of Muslim India in the prosecution of the war successfully.

War Committee

The Working Committee passed a resolution appointing a committee with Nawab Mohd. Ismail Khan and Nawabzada Liaqat Ali Khan to examine the cases of those members of the Council of the All India Muslim League who joined War Committees in contravention of the League resolution and take such disciplinary action as it may consider appropriate.

The resolution reads as under:

'The Working Committee have carefully considered the notification of the Government of India of the 6th of August, 1940 together with the explanatory communique issued by the Government of India on the 24th of August, with regard to volunteer organizations. The Moslem National Guard Corps was started over two years ago and the aims and objects of the organization are defined in resolution No. 4 of the Working Committee passed on the 17th of June, 1940, which runs as follows: 'To train and discipline Moslems in coordinate activity for social and physical uplift of the Moslems and to maintain peace, tranquility and order in the country.

'Recently instructions were given to the provincial Muslim League to strengthen the Moslem National Guard Corps and to give them such training as would enable them to discharge their duty of maintaining peace, tranquility and order in the country worthy of the best traditions of Islam and to assist at and control the meetings of the Muslim League and generally for the purpose of social service and uplift. The Committee therefore, are of opinion that the ban imposed by the Government is not intended to prohibit or restrict such legitimate activities. In these circumstances the Committee direct the various provincial Leagues to exert every nerve to start, organize, and strengthen Moslem National Guards and the Committee trust that their activities will be carried on within the limits of the law'.

28. Punjab Premier and Pakistan

Editorial, *Tribune*, 11 September 1940.

Punjab Premier and Pakistan

In the course of an interview given by him to our representative on Sunday on the eve of his departure for Simla Sir Sikander Hyat Khan made the welcome statement that he was even today opposed to the division of India, that he still believed there should be no division of India on any communal basis, and that in the Punjab, for instance, there could be and should be the rule of no one community, but the rule of the Punjabis. When, however, Sir Sikander Hyat's attention was drawn to the statement made by Malik Barkat Ali that he (Sir Sikander) was in favour of the *Pakistan* scheme, Sir Sikander said that his position to-day was exactly what it had been after the Lahore resolution of the League, and that he held the view that even the League resolution did not contemplate any division of India. If our representative did not misunderstand this part of Sir Sikander's statement, as we have no reason to believe he did, we feel no hesitation in saying that either Sir Sikander or we must be mad. The exact words of the Lahore resolution were:

It is the considered view of the session of the League that no constitutional plan could be workable in this country or acceptable to the Muslims unless it is designed on the following basic principle, viz. that geographically contiguous units are demarcated into regions which should be so constituted with such territorial readjustments as may be necessary that the areas in which the Muslims are numerically in a majority, as in the north-western and eastern zones of India, should be grouped to constitute independent States in which the constituent units shall be autonomous and sovereign.

Again:

This session further authorizes the Working Committee to frame a scheme of constitution in accordance with these basic principles, providing for the assumption finally by the respective regions of all powers such as defence, external affairs, communications, customs and such other matters as may be necessary.

Can these words mean anything else except that India should no longer be a politically united country but should be divided into Hindu and Muslim India, each entirely independent of the other? Mr Fazlul Huq, who moved the resolution, left no room for doubt on the point. 'They were not going to tolerate Federation of any kind', he said. 'They did not want merely the postponement of the federal scheme; what they wanted was that it should be abandoned altogether'. Mr M.A. Jinnah himself expressed the same view in a still more emphatic and unambiguous form of words in the course of a statement made by him to Lahore journalists on the morrow of the passing of the above resolution. 'I firmly believe' he said, 'that the idea of one united India is a dream and given goodwill and a friendly understanding Muslim India and Hindu India can live as most friendly neighbours free from clashes and frictions in their respective spheres peacefully and develop the governments of their States to their own satisfaction respectively.'

Clearly these words, taken with the text of the resolution, can mean only one thing. India is henceforth to be one country only in a geographical sense. Politically Hindu and Muslim

India are to be entirely separate and independent entities. The constituent units of each of these entities may together form a Region or Federation, but between the Hindu and the Mahomedan Region or Federation there is to be no relationship except that of neighbours. Sir Sikander Hyat Khan must indeed, be a bold man if, after so many emphatic and unambiguous statements by Mr Jinnah and other eminent Muslim Leaguers regarding the absolute necessity of dividing India politically, he has the temerity to assert that the League resolution does not contemplate any division of India. If Sir Sikander is right, then either he or Mr Jinnah and his friends must be using common English words in a Pickwickian sense. As regards Sir Sikander's statement that there can be no rule of one community even in the provinces with a Muslim majority, one single quotation from the speech of the mover of the Pakistan resolution at the Lahore session of the League should be enough to show that here, as in the other case, his differences with the League are fundamental. 'In Bengal and the Punjab', said Mr Huq, 'the position of Muslims was very weak. They had to look to others for help and could not do without forming coalition Governments which history showed had proved to be the weakest Governments everywhere'. Does not this mean that while Sir Sikander is professedly at least, an advocate of coalition Governments, eliminating the rule of anyone community, the basic purpose of the League resolution as interpreted by its mover himself, was to make it possible for the Muslims in their own majority provinces to do without coalition Governments altogether and to carry on the administration without let or hindrance from any other community? Will Sir Sikander still maintain that he and the advocates of the Pakistan scheme mean the same thing and have the same end in view? If so, let him use a plainer form of words than he has chosen to use so far, so that the public in this province and especially the non-Muslim section of it may know where it stands. He must be labouring under a grave misapprehension if he imagines that he can pursue indefinitely the present policy of holding with the Unionist hare and hunting with the League hounds.

29. Jinnah and Hindu Mahasabha

Editorial, *Tribune*, 28 September 1940.

Our Bombay correspondent says that in the course of his talk with the Viceroy[1] Mr Jinnah is reported to 'have challenged the representative capacity of the Hindu Mahasabha', and to have expressed the opinion that 'the Congress was the only representative organization of the Hindus'. It suited Mr Jinnah's book to pat the Hindu Mahasabha on the back when the Hindu Mahasabha was engaged in a fight with the Congress. But now that the Mahasabha has entered the lists against himself and the League, it has naturally ceased to be in his good graces and lost its representative character. There is an additional reason for the alleged disparagement of the Hindu Mahasabha. Mr Jinnah knows full well that no consideration in the world would induce the Congress to join the expanded Executive Council in which he is anxious to have a lion's share of authority for his own nominees. It is different with the Hindu Mahasabha which is a serious competitor with the League for 'the lion's share of authority' and which would clearly have immeasurably greater right to it than the League the moment its representative character was acknowledged, because no Government that has not taken complete leave of its sense of justice and fairness could under any scheme of popular government deny to an organization representing a large majority of the population of the country a larger number of seats in the Executive Council than to one which at the outside represents less than a fourth of the population.

But Mr Jinnah is mistaken on the main issue. It does not matter whether the Hindu Mahasabha or the Congress more truly represents the Hindu community. As long as representation on the Executive Council is community-wise, the Council must contain a majority of Hindu members, no matter whether they belong to the Hindu Mahasabha or to the Congress.

---

[1] The talk between Jinnah and the Viceroy took place on 24 September 1940. Jinnah reiterated the Muslim League demand to have a fair representation in the expanded Executive Council of the Viceroy.

30. Jinnah's Speech at Delhi Muslim Students' Conference
Star of India, 25 November 1940.

Muslims not to be lured by any 'Bakshish'
Mr Jinnah restates demand for 'Pakistan'
'British authorities' opportunity to avail of offered help.

New Delhi, 24 November.

'The spokesmen of the British Government have recently declared that the door for negotiations is still open. We, the Muslims, also re-echo the statement and say that door for negotiations is still open,' thus declared Mr Mohammed Ali Jinnah, President of the All India Muslim League, in inaugurating the first Conference of the Delhi Muslim Students' Federation yesterday.

Mr Jinnah in the course of his address dealt with the position of the Muslims vis-a-vis the British Government, and the Congress and reiterated the demand for 'Pakistan'.

Mr Jinnah said: 'We feel that it is not only Great Britain alone but also India, which is in danger. Apart from other reasons, we do not want the Nazis to win the war. For that reason, we, from the beginning, did not place any obstacles in the way of Great Britain.

'For instance, in spite of the fact that 'Pakistan' is our sheet anchor, we did not demand 'Pakistan' as a condition precedent for our whole-hearted support to the British Government. We only asked for an assurance that the British Government would not let us down by entering into an agreement, either interim or final, with the Congress. It was to be purely a war contract without prejudice to the position of the conflicting parties now or in the future.

'We promise to give great deal in men, money and other materials, in fact, the whole-hearted support of 90,000,000 of the Muslims. I am prepared to bring to the common pool all this but real and effective share in the power. This is described as "uncompromising proposals of Mr Jinnah" by the apologists of the wooden and antediluvian Government of India. They want our support on the assurance that we shall be remembered as loyal servants after the war and will even be given a "Bakshish"'. Referring to Congress, Mr Jinnah said that every honest Muslim was now convinced that the Congress 'which is a Hindu body' and the Congress High Command has had only one objective in view, namely the establishment of a Hindu 'Raj' in India and domination of the Muslims and all other minorities. He referred to the statements of Dr Moonje and Dr Savarkar, who had declared that the Muslims were like Jews in Germany and should be treated as such, and said the Congress nationalism was a perverted nationalism. If it only gave up its pretence of nationalism, it would provide no place to so many 'show boys of other communities within its fold'.

The Congress wants independence, for which it demands a declaration from the British Government. 'Does history know of any country or nation, which has won its freedom or independence by the declaration by a foreign power? Independence can only be had by qualifying for it. It can only be wrested and captured.

The fact is that the Congress wants domination of India under the shelter of British bayonets. The Congress wants power, but for coercing other communities. Today it is attempting to coerce the British Government to surrender power to it. It is a process of blackmail. The Government knows it and we know.

But British Government dare not throw the Muslims at the mercy of the Congress or the Hindus. They will rue the day if they do so.

'The Hindus must give up their dreams of a Hindu Raj, and agree to divide India and leave three-fourths to them. If they continue to bargain, they may not be able to have this three-fourth. 'Pakistan' was our goal today, for which the Muslims of India will live for and if necessary die for. It is not a counter for bargaining'. He appealed to the Muslim young men to prepare themselves and to make themselves fit to achieve this goal. 'Our hope depends on the young men of the Muslim nation'.

C.   Hindu Mahasabha

31.   Hindu Mahasabha Working Committee Resolutions on 'Viceroy's Offer' and 'League of Nations to Settle Communal Issue', 10–11 February 1940

Indian Annual Register, 1940, Vol. I, p. 233.

The Working Committee of the All India Hindu Mahasabha commenced at New Delhi on the 10th February with the President, Mr V.D. Savarkar, in the chair, Dr B.S. Moonje and Bhai Paramanand were among the members present. The meeting adopted the following resolutions:

'In view of the facts (1) that the mischief sought to be created by Mr Jinnah and the Muslim League by their observance of the so-called 'Deliverance Day', has been nipped in the bud by the refusal of the Government to appoint a Royal Commission as desired by them[1]; (2) that H.E. the Viceroy has announced in clear terms that Dominion Status in terms of the Westminster Statute shall be the basis of the constitution for India to be achieved 'at the earliest possible moment[2]' and that he has further given the assurance 'to facilitate the achievement of that status by all means in their power'; and (3) that the Viceroy, the Congress and the Hindu Mahasabha are all of one opinion in making provision for safeguarding the legitimate interests of the minorities in any constitution that may be drafted;

'The Working Committee of the Hindu Mahasabha, in a spirit of responsive cooperation, is prepared to give its helpful considerations, as an immediate step to its goal of independence, to the proposals contained in the Viceregal communique, namely:

'(1) that His Majesty's Government were only too ready to examine the whole of the field in consultation with the representatives of all the parties and interests in India when the time came;

'(2) that the federal scheme of the Act, while at present in suspense, afforded the swiftest stepping stone to Dominion Status;

'(3) that the offer put forward by H.E. the Viceroy in November, 1939, of an expansion of the Governor-General's Executive Council on the lines and on the basis then indicated, remained open and that His Majesty's Government were prepared to give effect to that order'.

League of Nations to Settle Communal Issue

As regards the communal problem 'which is now the only hurdle in the way to further constitutional progress', the Hindu Mahasabha was of the definite opinion that it should be immediately referred for settlement to the League of Nations.

The Hindu Mahasabha welcomed the publication of the correspondence between Mr Jinnah and Lord Linlithgow 'in that it has brought into light the conspiracy which Mr Jinnah and the Muslim League are organizing to create facilities for the Moslem Powers and Moslem countries for aggression against India by demanding on the one hand, that Indian troops should not be used against any Moslem power or country and on the other, that the present proportion of the Moslems in the Indian Army should not be reduced'.

It was also resolved that a deputation of the Hindu Mahasabha be sent in time to England so that any agitation that might be started there prejudicial to the interests of the Hindus be effectively counteracted and an agitation be initiated for the annulment of the Communal Award.

Demand for Dominion Status after the War

The Hindu Mahasabha Working Committee passed a number of resolutions arising out of the international situation and the political situation in India, at its meeting held in Bombay on the 18th May 1940.

The committee reiterated that the Congress cannot speak on behalf of the Hindus and called upon the Government to give a definite undertaking that no pact entered into by the Congress and the Muslims between themselves, to which the Hindu Mahasabha is not made a party and which is not sanctioned by it, can be binding on the Hindus as a whole. The committee authorized the president, Sir M.N. Mukherji, Dr B.S. Moonje, Mr L.B. Bhopatkar and Dr Shyama Prasad Mukherji to place the committee's resolutions before the Viceroy, secure a definite reply to the issues raised and submit to the Working Committee, not later than July 31, a report, on receipt of which the committee would consider what further practical steps should be taken in case the Mahasabha's demands are not granted.

---

[1] 'Deliverance day' was observed by All India Muslim League on 22 December 1939 when the Congress Governments resigned.

[2] Viceroy's speech at the Orient Club, Bombay, on 10 January 1940. See Chapter 2, Document no. 12.

32. B.S. Moonje's Presidential Address at the Lucknow Hindu Youth Conference held on 3 March 1940

Pioneer, 5 March 1940.

In the course of his presidential address at the Lucknow Hindu Youth Conference Dr B.S. Moonje said:

'I have not been able to understand the propriety of youths insisting upon an old man of about 70 years like myself to preside over their Conference. But, personally speaking, I always like to be in the midst of Hindu youths for the reasons that I may be able to dispel from their minds wrong ideas and improper perspectives, unnatural philosophies and impractical programmes that have been impressed upon their minds during the last 20 years. In fact, I believe that the Hindu youths must forget most of what has been taught to them during the last

20 years and the sooner they do it, the better it will be both in the interest of their country and their religion and culture and civilization.

'By taking a detached and bird's eye view of the situation in the country it seems that we are now in the midst of changing times and the tide, that was favourable to Mahatma Gandhi and the Congress of his own conception during the last 20 years, has now definitely changed and we feel that, as an inevitable reaction the future will come more and more within the hold of the Hindu Mahasabha politics, particularly, if Mr Jinnah and his Muslim League were to keep on insisting on aggressive communal separation. Old men like us must soon retire to make room for younger and spirited men and the future, therefore, lies within the grasp of Hindu youths, if they are well prepared both physically and intellectually to take firm grasp of the situation in all its diverse implications.

'The Hindus are now rapidly awakening to the peril involved in Mahatma Gandhi's teachings and it seems the tide is changing and the people are looking about for new leadership.

'The Hindu Mahasabha now, finding the time more congenial, is boldly asserting itself and is calling upon the Hindus to hark back and rally round its banner. It says that this land, called Hindusthan implies by its very name that it is the land of the Hindus. Here in this land there is only one Nation, that is the Hindu Nation and there is one Nationalism that is Hindu Nationalism. It further says that we are all working for Swaraj, it will be a Hindu swaraj and it will be equally serviceable to all the various non-Hindu communities. Its replies are unambiguous and soundly broad-based on historical facts involved. The Congress has not the courage or the manliness to give the replies they deserve as the Hindu Mahasabha does give. Thus the time of the Congress is over and it has outlived its effective usefulness. It must now merge in the Hindu Mahasabha, so that the two together may give a bold lead to the country. What should be our conception of nationalism and our national policy and programme of action? They say we cannot have nationalism and therefore, we cannot evolve any policy because of our so-called communal disunity. The so-called disunity is made much of both by the Government and the Muslims for their respective imperial and communal vested interests. The Government wants the disunity to be kept ever green because without it, it will not be quite so easy for them to perpetuate their imperial hold on India. The Muslims on their part have never been able to conceive and evolve a national as opposed to communal outlook. The teachings of their leaders go even so far as to deprecate and decry even patriotism when it comes into clash with their communal interests.

Majority Community

'The first duty of the majority community is to shed this mentality of defeatism and remembering the doings of our forefathers before the British came to take courage in both hands and assert our right of a majority community to establish Swaraj and to maintain internal law and order and to defend the Swaraj from foreign aggression.

'To achieve communal and Hindu–Muslim unity, we require to develop a bond and manly mentality of self-confidence which it is hopeless to expect from the teachings and philosophy of Mahatma Gandhi and his Congress. It is here and for this special purpose that the Hindu Mahasabha, the Swarajists and the Nationalists have to step in. It is reserved for them, if they would foresee their noble destiny, to give a bold lead to the country in true and manly Nationalism. They must keep up the struggle for Swaraj by all legitimate means.

'While making up their mind to stand upon their own legs and disdaining to depend helplessly on others, they should respectfully invite and welcome the cooperation of all irrespective of their caste, creed or colour. They should combine and try and invade the Legislatures and by capturing the Government, should carry on the administration of the country on these principles with a firm hand, so as to lead the minorities feel and appreciate that their true interests lie not in separation from Nationalism and the Majority Community but in honest and loyal cooperation with them on perfectly equal terms.

'I feel sure that if we demonstrate our determination to carry on the administration on these lines, the Britishers are shrewd enough to amend the constitution of their own accord at the earliest opportunity thinking that discretion is always the better part of valour and will leave us free to manage the affairs of our own country as we like.'

Present Situation

Reviewing the present situation he said:

'Between two extremes there is complete stalemate in the political situation in the country— one extreme of Mahatma Gandhi demanding Complete Independence and the right of India framing its own constitution without interference from the British Government on the principles of self-determination. The other extreme is that of Mr Jinnah who has put on record, for the information of the Viceroy, his conditions of cooperation.

'Between these two extremes, people appear to be getting fed up.

'In agreeing to the Dominion Status, the British Government have gone to the extreme limit possible within their constitution and they cannot go any further. The Government should now very well ask the Congress to produce a Constitution, based, preferably, on the agreement, if possible, of all the parties concerned. It will then be impossible for the Parliament to refuse to recognize and give its sanction to it. If the Congress wants Independence, it can only be had by defeating England on a battlefield. Independence is a thing which cannot be given away nor can anybody ask for it.

'Now remain the two notorious hurdles—the Communal Problem and the problem of the Defence of India.

'To solve the communal problem, provisions of the League of Nations, Minority Treaties should be enforced or the Problem be referred to the League of Nations for solution. There is no possibility now of amicable settlement between the parties concerned.'

Hindu Minorities

Referring to the protection of Hindu minorities in Muslim majority provinces, he said:

'Particularly from the time the provincial autonomy has been established, it is becoming more and more evident every day that the Governors of the Provinces, having surrendered their authority for law and order to their ministries, are unable to give any kind of protection to the Hindus in provinces wherever the Muslims form the majority community, such as Sind and Bengal. Nothing could have brought the fact more vividly to us than orgies of murders, incendiarism, loot and kidnapping, indulged in by the Muslim dacoits practically with impunity in Sukkur and Shikarpur districts of Sind.'

Conclusion

'Taking into consideration all that I have said above my conclusions are as follows:

(1) 'That the Congress has now out-lived its mission and must make room for the Hindu Mahasabha, that is the Congress must now merge in the Hindu Mahasabha, so that the Hindu Mahasabha may merge in the Congress and both combined under the leadership of the

Congress may give a new and practical turn to the politics of the country. It can be very easily done. If the Congress were to cancel its resolution banning Congressmen from becoming members of the Hindu Mahasabha, the Congress will over-night discover that it is no other organization than actually the Hindu Mahasabha.

'I may here appeal to the Congress in another manner. Let us avoid internecine quarrels and competitions between the Congress and the Hindu Mahasabha, as they may turn out to be suicidal to both. Let us establish a convention of alternate provincial government of five years duration first by the Congress and then by the Hindu Mahasabha. The Congress is having its turn at present. Let the Hindu Mahasabha have its next time; so that by contrast it can be proved to demonstration whether the Congress policy of charkha, love and non-violence is more productive of good to the country, or the Hindu Mahasabha's policy of mechanical industrialism, militarism, and retaliation which includes love and non-violence.

(2) That, when the next general elections come, the Hindus, if they want to save themselves from extinction, must make up their minds to vote entirely for the candidates of Hindu Mahasabha rather than for those of the Congress.

(3) That, the Hindus should organize a Hindu militia—Rama Sena of their own, so that when a real emergency may come any time in the course of the recent European war affecting the integrity and solidarity of our motherland, the Hindus should be in a position to put into the field for the defence of India their own trained soldiers in proportion to their strength in the general population of the country as the Muslims are expected to do.

(4) That in view of the present mentality of separation and animosity as evidenced by Mr Jinnah and his Muslim League, the Hindus should start an India-wide agitation for pressing on the government the wisdom of entirely stopping or at least effectively curtailing the recruitment of Muslims in the Indian Army either as rank and fields or as officers in order to bring down their present strength in the Indian Army to level of their proportion in the general population of the country.

(5) That, training centres should be started all over the country in order to improve the physiques of the Hindu youths and to re-kindle militarism in them by wiping out the enervating effects created on their minds by the Congress propaganda of love and non-violence during the last 20 years.

Here it may be noted that hardly 25 miles beyond Peshawar where the brother of the Frontier Gandhi, the pre-eminent disciple of Mahatma Gandhi was until quite lately the Premier of the Province, factories for manufacturing rifles have been started and they are said to be busy working day and night. As a reply as it were to this practical exhibition of material love and non-violence Mahatma Gandhi is insisting upon charkhas without which he says he cannot lead the struggle for independence. But can you contemplate what will happen when the Pathans' rifles will come in conflict with Mahatma Gandhi's charkhas?

(6) That the Hindu–Muslim unity is the most welcome thing; nothing can be more welcome; but it is a fact that the Congress cannot bring it about. The Hindu Mahasabha hopes that, if a chance be given to it, the Muslims will of their own accord recognize the Hindus of Hindu Mahasabha as their equals both in love and non-violence as well as for retaliation. Thus the Hindu–Muslim unity will arise automatically.

(7) That in respect of taking decision on the problems of communal relations for facilitating the formation of a Constitution for India, the Congress does not represent the Hindus. It is the Hindu Mahasabha that alone does represent the Hindus.'

Resolution

The second day's open session of the Conference was also largely attended. Seven resolutions were passed in all.

The first resolution, which was moved from the Chair, criticized the policy pursued by the Congress for the last 20 years as a 'needless pro-Muslim policy' which had neither brought about Hindu–Muslim unity nor succeeded in influencing the Muslims to join the Hindus in the struggle for independence.

It further appealed to the Congress to revise its policy and cancel its resolution banning Hindu Congressmen from joining the Hindu Mahasabha and to help the Hindus in every way in regaining their strength in the Indian Army in accordance with their proportion in the general population and also to declare that it would join hands with the Hindu Mahasabha in carrying on the struggle for independence, irrespective of the consideration whether the Muslims would join or oppose this combined move.

By the second resolution, the Conference endorsed the resolution passed by the Hindu Mahasabha at its last annual session held at Calcutta for organizing a Hindu militia and called upon the Hindus of the province between the ages of 18 and 45 to sign the pledge and enlist themselves as the members of the militia. It also called upon the existing Hindu volunteer organizations working under different names to merge themselves in the militia...

.... The Conference also passed a resolution urging the Hindu youths to remove the blot of untouchability from the Hindu community and to protect the Hindu culture and civilization and to lay the foundation of a 'Hindu Raj'.

Another resolution expressed sympathies with the Hindu sufferers of Muslim riots at Sukkur in Sind and condemned the alleged 'atrocious acts' of Muslims which were encouraged by the agitation of the Muslim League in connection with Manzalgah buildings.

33 (a) 'Swaraj in India could only be Hindu Raj'—V.D. Savarkar's Address at Tamil Nad Hindu Mahasabha Conference, 23 March 1940

Indian Annual Register, 1940, Vol. I, pp. 335–7.

The first session of the Tamil Nad Hindu Mahasabha Conference was held at Salem under the presidency of Mr V.D. Savarkar, President of All India Hindu Mahasabha on the 23 March 1940, who in the course of his address said that the objective of the Hindu Mahasabha was the consolidation of the Hindus with the ultimate goal of absolute independence for India. Hindus did not mind if Moslems considered themselves a separate race, but the proposal to divide the country could not be permitted.

Mr Savarkar said that he had read with grief an extract of an article from the pen of Gandhiji, in which it was stated that he (Mahatmaji) would be ruled by them (Muslims) because it would still be Indian rule. Mr Savarkar deplored this attitude on the part of Gandhiji and the Congress. If Gandhiji would prefer to live in the divided India of the Muslims under Mr Jinnah's rule, why not, asked the speaker, live under the British! If the argument that Mr Jinnah's rule was Indian rule was quoted, it would be equally true to say that British rule was human rule. He could not understand this 'defeatist' mentality and he for one refused to allow the division of India into two. Mr Savarkar differed from Gandhiji fundamentally and added that the Hindu Mahasabha would never be a party to such arrangements. The Hindus too were Indians and why should the Muslims ask for their own part of the country?

The Congress might try to compromise with the League, continued Mr Savarkar, but the Mahasabha would not do it. No compromise which sacrificed the self-respect of the Hindus would be agreed to by the Sabha and he appealed to the Hindus to resist the proposals of Muslims who wished to restore Muslim rule through various means. Muslims had understood the weakness of the Congress and were bluffing. The Mahasabha was prepared to take up the challenge and to fight for the preservation of Hindustan. Let all minorities live in Hindustan and they would all receive equality of treatment. Let them not, however, arrogate any superiority of strength to themselves and try to befool the others who were equally wide awake and quite determined to safeguard their rights and privileges.

Mr Savarkar refuted the theory of Mr Jinnah that there were two major races in India. He pointed out that the Muslims had now come to regard themselves no longer as a minority, but as a major race and, perhaps, as the more powerful of the two major races. The Hindu Mahasabha was prepared to face this issue and would allow the Muslims no more rights than their population would justify. If they wished to fight out the issue, the fight would not be refused. He was very sorry that Mr Jinnah was becoming no better than Nadir Shah or Aurangazeb. Swaraj in India, Mr Savarkar concluded, could only be Hindu Raj since the Hindus were a majority and others could not object to it. It existed in other countries and Hindustan was no exception to the rule of the majority being in power. Mr Savarkar reiterated his point and added that the Hindus could not agree to Gandhiji's readiness to be under Muslim domination, even if it was Indian Raj. He appealed to the Hindus to join the Sabha and consolidate their ranks prepared for any fight which the Muslims might force on them encouraged by the British policy of 'Divide and Rule' and the weakness of the Congress in yielding to the Muslims and giving them a blank cheque in the name of nationalism which, however, was not true nationalism.

Proceeding, Mr Savarkar emphasized that Hindustan had a right to exist on the map of the world even as other countries existed, and he would exhort the Hindus to remember his appeal and to work for the Mahasabha. He could not see how Hindus of Hindustan could submit to Muslim rule. Hindus were awake to the real danger and were ready to fight any power to save their independence to the last drop of their blood. He was sorry for Gandhiji's statement, but felt amused by what Mr Jinnah had said in his speech at the League Conference at Lahore. Mr Savarkar also explained at the Conference the term 'Hindu' and defined the view of the Mahasabha as to who was a Hindu and what constituted the qualifications for being a Hindu.

Mr Savarkar observed that in South India there was some misunderstanding about the word 'Hindu'. The Mahasabha did not mean by the word 'Hindu' anything connected with mere religion or theocracy. Even those who did not believe in the Vedas were Hindus, as for instance, the Jains. The Sikhs, the Brahmos, the Reformers, the Sanatanists and others, who had their own special religious dogmas and books, were also Hindus. A Hindu was one who considered Hindustan as the land of his birth and as the land of his religion, whatever it might be. That India was his 'Pitribhommi' and 'Punyabhoomi' were the two essential constituents of the word Hindu. A Hindu ought to remember always that he was born in India and that India was his holy land, i.e. the land where his Gurus had their birth. The definition held good of the various denominations of the Hindu race, the Sikhs, the Jains and Lingayats. The Muslims, Christans and Jews, even if born in India, looked to Arabia as their Holy Land, therefore, they did not come within the meaning of the word 'Hindu'.

Mr Savarkar also touched upon the question of the Dravidian movement in South India and added that whether one was an Aryan or a Dravidian, he was a Hindu, since India had given birth to him and his religion had its origin in India. The Mahasabha was, therefore, for all Hindus, irrespective of all differences of caste or philosophy or other beliefs. He was glad to inform the audience that the Jains had agreed to be put under the main classification of Hindus in the ensuing census and he appealed to all Hindus—Aryan and Dravidian, Brahmin and Non-Brahmin, Mahratta, Madrassi or Punjabi—to join the Sabha and to consolidate its ranks.

Mr Savarkar then referred to Mr Jinnah's suggestion to bifurcate India into Hindu and Muslim India, and hoped that as a result of the efforts of the Hindu Mahasabha, the Hindus would all stand united in common cause, namely the preservation of their race, culture, religion and political rights in the land of their forefathers. That was what he called 'Hindu-dom' namely, the Hindu Nation, which comprised Hindu religion and all the other concomitants which were necessary to keep the race in a position of strength and influence. He appealed to Hindus to abolish untouchability, to relax the rigour of the caste system, to be united as one man and prevent the spoliation of Hindustan by any artificial division.

33 (b) Hindu Mahasabha Conference in Tamil Nad

Fortnightly report for the Second Half of March 1940, Public (General) Department, 4th April 1940, Government of Madras, Tamil Nad State Archives.

...The Hindu Mahasabha have been very prominent during the fortnight with their first Tamil Nadu Conference which was held at Salem on 23rd and 24th March with Mr Savarkar as President, Mr Savarkar made several speeches in Salem and Madras in which he sought to arouse the communal sentiments of Hindus here, which he seemed to consider insufficiently developed. He bitterly attacked Mr Jinnah's proposed partition of India and asserted that Hindus were ready to meet the Muslim challenge.

The attendance at the Salem Conference was about 2,000 persons but the attendances at Mr Savarkar's meetings in Madras were not large. The Justice party criticized the Mahasabha's activities as being in the interests of the Aryans as opposed to those of the Dravidians. Muslims were content to ignore the visit, while Congressmen kept aloof from the functions attended by Mr Savarkar....

34. Shyama Prasad Mukherjee's Presidential Address at the Bihar Provincial Hindu Conference Held in Ranchi, Bihar

Hindustan Times, 17 April 1940.

Presiding over the ninth Bihar Provincial Hindu Conference at Ranchi, Dr Shyama Prasad Mookerjee said:

Political power during the last 30 years has been transferred by the British Government to the representatives of the peoples of India through doses of constitutional reforms. But such transfer of power has been subjected to various conditions and restrictions which have retarded the growth of a full Indian nationhood. The administrative machinery has been so devised that today not only a large residue of powers but also the controlling forces in many directions are retained in the hands of authorities whose interests are not identical with those of the Indian people. The greatest apprehension of any foreign power ruling over a subject people arises through a possible unity among the people themselves. In India, thanks to the policy pursued by successive generations of British politicians, disunity and division specially between the Hindus and the Muslims have been successfully nurtured and fanned, and we witness throughout the country today the devastating result of this policy.

Disillusioned

Today we stand disillusioned. As Hindus we have been prepared to make sacrifices and forego many of our rightful interests in furtherance of a possible unity with the Muslims of India for the attainment of our goal. Our anxiety to obtain their support has been often misunderstood for weakness and helplessness. We have so failed to strengthen the social movement and have long laid stress on the religious basis of our own society, so essential for our progressive development. Not only do the Hindus and the Muslims stand divided but among the Hindus artificial barriers have been imposed and our dream of a united Indian nation is receding to the background. Distrust and hatred between one class and another, between the landlord and the tenant, between the capitalist and the labourer, between the employer and the employee, are of daily occurrence and we witness before our very eyes a possible breakdown of the entire social and economic structure. In provinces where constitutional powers have passed to the hands of Muslim Ministers reports of oppression and injustice daily pour in. I myself can bear testimony to a systematic policy pursued by the Ministry now in power in Bengal which is aimed at crippling the Hindus in every sphere of life—economic, political and cultural.

Hindu Unity

It is only when the Hindus have learnt to be united and consolidated, it is only when they are strong and resolute and refuse to barter away the liberty of their country, only then will the issues be clarified and the British realize the forces they have to fight against. It is only when the Muslims realize that 28 crores of Hindus have made up their minds to carry on a struggle for the political independence of India and that while the latter will gladly welcome the cooperation of Muslims and others in equal and just terms they are not prepared to allow them to bring about a deadlock, only then will the Muslims realize the supreme need for coming to an honourable understanding with the Hindus.

In the new order of society that we contemplate the Hindu Mahasabha must be the meeting ground of all classes and castes of Hindus, rich and poor, learned and ignorant, capitalist and labourer, employer and employee. It is only by means of frank and mutual discussions that we can appreciate each other's point of view and resolutely endeavour to solve existing difficulties. Our aim is to establish peace and harmony and this we can do if we can probe into the root causes of the present disaffection amongst different classes of the people.

World Belongs to the Brave

Non-violence is apt to mislead people and further weaken the weak and the vacillating. As Hindus we do not want that we should be guided by any lust of greed of power and possession or cultivate brute force for the purpose of oppressing and torturing the weak and the helpless. But we firmly believe that this world belongs to the brave—Virbhogya Basundhara. We must cultivate strength and courage not for any attack or aggression but when occasion arises, for defending our rights and liberties to the last drop of our blood. And this noble task of defence must be deemed a sacred duty on the part of every able bodied Hindu residing in this country.

Training in the art of self-defence must be specially imparted to the women folk whose position in some provinces is most precarious due to circumstances well known to all of us.

We can never expect to attain political freedom except through the enormous struggle.

35. V.D. Savarkar's Statement to the Press Regarding Hindu Mahasabha's Terms of Cooperation with Congress, 21 April 1940

Jayakar Papers, File No. 709, 1940, NAI.

The following Statement has been issued by Savarkar, the President of the Hindu Mahasabha:

Numerous Congressite Hindus have been questioning me throughout my tours with a well-meaning anxiety whether a way could be found to secure a hearty cooperation between the Hindu Mahasabha and the Indian National Congress instead of having these two great national bodies ranged into opposite camps. I promised to these friends that I would issue a public statement in general instead of replying to each individual so that it might reach a much wider circle of such well-meaning Hindus in Congress camp.

Is there a healthy and hearty cooperation between the Hindu Mahasabha and the Congress possible? Categorically I reply both Yes and No.

(I) The National Congress was based on principles which were on the whole so thoroughly National that had the Congress not lost its own moorings and continued in general to hold fast to these basic principles, the Hindu Mahasabha could have found no difficulty in offering a hearty cooperation with it. Under the able leadership of its early leaders like Messrs Dadabhai Naroji, Gokhale, Lala Lajpatrai, Lokmanya Tilak and others, The Indian National Congress tried its best to sail clear of all rocks and shoals of any perversely communal bias or short sighted anti-national vagaries. But ever since the grievous error of foisting the Khilafat agitation on the Congress was committed, the Congress rapidly lost its national moorings and began even to pride itself on serving as a hand-maid to the Moslems in India. As a symbolic expression more demonstrative than any substantial one could be, witness the fact that at the Kakinada Congress session[1], the Moslem Flag flew side by side with the Congress colours on the Congress Pandal—while the Hindu Flag continued to be discarded as something unclean, anti-national, communal. Can such a sight as that ever fail to egg on the idea in the Moslem mind that the Moslems are a separate political entity—a Nation by themselves and organically merged into and assimilated with the Indian Nation or the Indian National Congress? Treading on the heels of the Khilafat, came the stupid offer of blank cheques, the Communal Award, the meaningless and mendacious formulae of now 'neither accepting nor rejecting', now 'loyally accepting', then 'forgetting all about it' and still persisting in working out the Award. To cap it all the Congressites did not hesitate to contest the elections as Hindus on behalf of the Hindu electorate. A true 'Nationalist' of the Congress brand should not have offered himself to represent a Communal Hindu Constituency. If he did, he ought to have represented the legitimate Hindu interests. At any rate the least he should have done as an honest Nationalist and elected representative was not to suppress the legitimate grievances and betray the very Hindu electorate which returned him to the Legislature, which enabled him to exercise Ministerial powers. But the Congress Ministers and Members got themselves elected as 'Hindu' on communal tickets and as soon as they formed Governments began to pose as 'Nationalists' and betrayed and even oppressed that very Hindu electorate whenever the legitimate interests of the Hindus came in clash with the Moslem ones in the name of 'Nationalism'. Nay, the very Congressite

Governments vied with each other in issuing statements to provoke the Moslems that the Congress Ministries had always sacrificed Hindu interests to pander to the Moslem prejudices and loaded the latter with weightages, posts, positions at the cost of the Hindus and therefore, they pleaded, their 'Nationalism' ought to be above suspicion. If anyone wants to get this fact verified he need only refer to the Government communique issued by Mr Pant, the Congress Prime Minister in UP under his own Ministerial sign and seal wherein he cited instances after instances, as for example, how his Congress Government had ordered the Hindus not to blow conches or perform the *arties* even in private houses during the Mohurum week or given posts to Moslems in preference to the Hindus admittedly to please the Moslems and had even let go Moslems charged with murders because a certain secretary of the Moslem League wanted the Government to do so and all this is written down in black and white and issued with a brazen face as a Government communique to prove that the Congress Government was thoroughly 'National'!

The process was simple; the Congress coveted nothing more than the confidence of Moslems and hated nothing more than that it should be dubbed by Moslems as a Hindu body. This squeamish sentimentality was exploited by the Moslems quite methodically. They had only to call the Congress a Hindu body, and the latter was sure to dispose of the Hindus of some more of their legitimate rights and invest the Moslems anew with them, just to prove that it was not a Hindu body! The process continued as many times as the Moslems called the Congress a Hindu Body. The Congress leaders were nervous on this very account that they never displayed even that much anxiety about the horrible sufferings the Hindus had to undergo during the Moslem riots at Malabar, Kohat, Bannu, Sukkur, or the Nizam's fanatical rule, as they felt in solving the momentous question of the propriety of addressing Jinnah, whether he should be called Janab Jinnah Saheb or Quaid-e-Azam Jinnah Saheb! At last the Moslems got emboldened to demand that the Indian Nation itself should be cut into a number of independent Moslem States.

And here I sound a grave warning to all Hindus, whether Congressites or not, that a number of Congress leaders of eminence are very likely to go a long way in acquiescing even in this nefarious demand of the Moslems to break up the unity and integrity of India and the Indian States, if the Hindus do not repudiate in time the claim of the Congress to speak on behalf of Hindudom as a whole.

Consequently, so long as the Congress persists in hugging to this perverse conception of 'Nationalism', which practically amounts to the betrayal of the Hindu cause, there cannot and should not be any cooperation between the Hindu Mahasabha and the Congress. On the contrary, it will be the bounden duty of every Hindu who does not want to sell his birthright for a mess *pottage* to undermine the Congress and free Hindudom general and the Hindu electorate in particular from grip of the so called 'Indian National Congress'.

(II) Convinced by the above line of argument, hundreds of sincere Hindus who happen to-day to be in Congress camp but find it difficult through sentimentalism to cut off their connection from the Congress, suggest as a last lingering hope: 'Why not enter the Congress and bring it round to your views? Cannot the Hindu Mahasabhaites secure a majority in the Congress and overhaul it out of its anti-Hindu and anti-National policy?

It is enough to point out to such of our meaning but sentimental Hindu brethren in Congress that it is the Congress which has by a special resolution of the Working Committee banned the Hindu Mahasabhaites from entering the Congress and has anathematized the Hindu Mahasabha with bell, book and candle as a Communal organization too unclean to be associated with.

Secondly, in view of this insolent attitude on the part of Congress why should the Hindu Mahasabhaites care to enter the Congress at all when they find that the Congress 'Nationalism' can be brought to its senses far more effectively and quickly by coming out of the Congress rather than by entering it under humiliating conditions. The Indian National Congress cannot be superior to Indian nation itself and no Indian nation wherein Hindudom is not safe and cannot honourably claim to be an independent and powerful Nation in equal co-partnership with other non-Hindu constituents in India can be worth a brass farthing to a Hindu who is not a traitor to his own racial self. The Congress has banned and boycotted the Hindu Sabhaites for well and good. Let the Hindus who stand by their racial soul and honour come out of it. Let us see where does the Congress stand if the Hindus leave it; and the Hindu electorate does not vote for it in the elections. Is there then no way at all to secure a unity of aim and action between the Hindu Mahasabha and the Congress?

Yes, there is, and the condition also is the simplest one. It only lays down that the Indian National Congress should recover its own Self and be again a veritable Indian National Congress. There is always a paramount necessity in India to have a common National platform on which all patriotic Hindus, Moslems and Christians and all others who are genuinely loyal to the Indian State and the Indian State alone, can meet, unite and work in unison as sons of a common Motherland. The Hindu Mahasabha will always extend a hearty and healthy cooperation to any such National Organization. The Congress can even yet justify its claim of being such a National organization if it repudiates the Pseudo Nationalistic aberrations and takes up its stand on the following principles:

(a) India should be one and indivisible as a political unit with a strong and well-knit Central Government invested with such prestige and power as to enable it to maintain unity, integrity and freedom of the National Indian State and command a harmonious coordination of its different Provincial Constituents.

(b) All Indians should be treated alike as Indian citizens with equal fundamental rights and duties irrespective of caste or creed, race or religion so that there can be no question at all of a communal majority or a communal minority.

Failing which as the next best but the only one alternative may be resorted to, laying it down that all communities, not only the minorities but even the majority community should be granted explicit safeguards guaranteeing equal freedom regarding their respective religious, cultural and linguistic life; all political 'representation' will be based on the only definitely ascertainable and just principle of the proportion which their respective population bear to each other; the public services also may follow the same proportion but only in so far as it is consistent with personal merit and public efficiency.

(c) So long as there is no electorate based on one of the above National principles, insuring equitable share to all communities alike, the Congress should refuse to seek election on behalf of any communal constituency but should leave the Hindu and Moslem organizations to elect their respective representatives through their communal constituencies. The so-called general constituency under the present constitution is admittedly communal, because it implies a division of the National electorate into Moslems, Europeans etc. separate communal electorate; and is most intolerably humiliating, unjust and detrimental to the Hindus and even the Congress has to confess that it seeks to pamper the Moslems with all undue and undeserved weightages, reservations, statutory majorities and what not. Consequently, the Congress if it had to keep up its prestige as an Indian National Congress, should never have demeaned itself by seeking elections under such an anti-National and avowedly communal constitution.

If the Congress declares its adhesion to these fundamental National principles, pointing out sternly 'Thus far, but no further', and shapes its policy accordingly, the Hindu Mahasabha will ever be found prepared to extend a hearty and healthy cooperation to any such really National institution. Because the Hindu Mahasabha claims nothing for the Hindu which is not Nationally their due and it denies nothing to the Moslems which is Nationally due to them either on the principle of merit or population. But what the Hindu Mahasabha can never tolerate is to despoil the Hindu of anything which is justly and equitably and nationally theirs simply because they constitute the overwhelming majority in Hindusthan, their own Fatherland and Homeland.

Only if such an equitable cooperation is secured between the Hindu Mahasabha and the Indian National Congress and these two great National bodies can present a united front, they can save the Indian Nation from the challenge of any aggressions from without or treacherous designs from within.

Will the Indian National Congress take courage in both hands, accept the conditions laid down above and assume the role of a veritable 'Indian National Congress?' If it does, it deserves to survive; if it does not, it is bound to get dissolved as a National Congress.

---

[1] Kakinada Congress Session was held in 1923 and Mohamed Ali was its President-elect.

36. Savarkar's Speech Regarding Hindus as a Nation
Tribune, 17 May 1940.

The need for a separate Hindu organization to view political and economic questions through the perspective of Hindu interests was stressed by Mr V.D. Savarkar, President, All India Hindu Mahasabha, addressing a public meeting at the People's Park Maidan. Several addresses were presented to Mr Savarkar. Dr P. Varadarajalu Naidu presided.

Mr Savarkar said: 'Like the frog in the fable, which burst itself to death in trying to assume the dimensions of a bull, any minority which tried to convert itself into a majority would share the same fate. The best way for the minorities, therefore, was to be friendly with the Hindus. This was also the view of the Congress, the speaker believed, though they were not sufficiently strong in saying it.'

Mr Savarkar emphasized that they should have a separate Hindu organization. It was time, he declared, that India was a nation of the Hindus and the other communities were in the same position as the minority communities in countries like England, France and Germany. If they examined the political phraseology of any nation it would be clear that the majority was the nation and the minority the 'community'. The majority people could never be a 'community'. The Hindus were, therefore, a nation. The minorities would have equal rights according to their proportion and no more.

The Hindu Mahasabha's action in boldly asserting the claim of the Hindus to organize themselves, Mr Savarkar said, could not be considered anti-national. Because as a majority, which constituted the nation, the Hindus could not be anti-national. Nor could they be accused of communalism if they organized themselves for the purpose of setting right certain grievances. He was not sorry that the Congress movement was spreading rapidly for possibly the Congress itself might be helpful to their movement, but there was the necessity for a separate organization for the Hindus.

37. Savarkar on Mahatma Gandhi's Article, 'Two Parties', Published in *Harijan*, 15 June 1940

Jayakar Papers, File No. 709, 1940, NAI.

The following statement was issued by Savarkar, the President of the Hindu Mahasabha, in connection with Gandhiji's recent article in *Harijan*:

'In one of his recent articles in the *Harijan* under the caption of 'Two Parties', Gandhiji asserts that the Hindu Mahasabha would no doubt want favoured treatment for Hindus including Hindu States. Now, he knows perfectly well, at least he ought to have known by referring to its leading resolutions before he made such a sweeping statement regarding the Mahasabha that it never wanted any favoured treatment for the Hindus whether as to the Legislatures or services or safeguards beyond what was legitimately due to them either on the principle of the population proportion or merit or any other National test, provided it was applied equally to all. It is in the interest of the Indian Nationalism itself that the Hindu Mahasabha cannot tolerate that the Hindus should be deprived of an inch of their legitimate rights of citizenship, simply because they formed the majority, in order to bestow any undeserved, favoured treatment on the Moslems simply because they happened to be in a minority.

'But in spite of being fully aware of this attitude of the Hindu Mahasabha, Gandhiji had deliberately indulged in misrepresenting it as he wanted somehow to bracket the Hindu Mahasabha with the League as an anti-National body, so that the 'National' pose he now wants to arrogate to himself and the Congress may be brought into relief by contrast.

'That to ask a favoured treatment for a community over and above others is anti-national, constitutes a thesis on which, of all persons in the world, it is Gandhiji and his Congressite followers who ought to learn much from the Hindu Mahasabha instead of trying to teach it. Was it not Gandhiji himself who offered Blank Cheques to the Moslem Leaguers who he himself characterized as frankly communal? Who issued Government communiques on behalf of the seven Congress Ministries and especially a disgraceful one issued by Mr Pant, the Congressite Minister in UP, assuring the Moslems that the Congress Government did always treat the Moslems far more favourably than they did the Hindus, that he robbed the Hindus of their dues to pay the Moslems what was not due to them and paraded the fact as a 'National' achievement? Who abetted the treacherous designs of the Congressite Ali brothers to encourage the Amir to invade India? Who did not dare to embarrass the Nizam or certified that there was Rama-Raj in Bhopal, but did not hesitate to harass the relatively more progressive Hindu States alone? Who 'loyally accepted' the Communal Award which loaded the Moslems with favoured treatment and made the Hindus to pay the bill? Or does the Congress or Gandhiji mean that to ask favoured treatment for the Hindus and the Hindu States is alone anti-National, but to placate the Moslems with it constitutes the very kernel of Indian Nationalism? If the Hindu Mahasabha wants anything, it is not a favoured treatment for the Hindus but to lay the axe at the root of pseudo-Nationalism of the Gandhist brand.

'The claim advanced further on in that article by Gandhiji to the effect that the Congress can alone speak in the name of the Indian Nation as a whole, is also vitiated by facts which he has admitted in the course of the very same article. If a very large section of Moslems insists upon an independent representation and do not recognize the Congress as their spokesman on the one hand, and if millions of millions of Hindu Sanghatanists make it quite clear that they cannot trust the Congress to represent either the Hindu interests or the National interests and maintain that the Congress has consequently no right to represent them and if several other parties like the Democratic Swarajya Party or the Independent Labour Party of Dr Ambedkar or the Liberals and others, disown the Congress as definitely as possible, what credentials the Congress can have to arrogate to itself to represent All India or to speak in the name of India as a Whole?

'The fact is that the Congress can speak in the name of the Congressites alone. It is as much a party having no claim to speak on behalf of All India as any other party in the land. So far as the Hindu Mahasabha is concerned, we want to make it clear once and for all that no agreement arrived at between the Congress and the Government or the Congress and the Moslem League can be binding on Hindudom as a whole, unless and until the Hindu Mahasabha is made a party to it and secures its sanction. The Congress may deliver or accept goods which belong to the Congress. But it has no right to pilfer and deliver goods which do not belong to it but belong to Hindudom as a whole, nor to accept the delivery of any fancy products to its order like the Communal Award and call on the Hindus to pay the bill, unless the Hindu Mahasabha authorizes the transactions.

'Curiously enough Gandhiji says: 'It was an illusion created by ourselves that we must come to an understanding with all parties before we can make any progress'. It must be pointed out in this connection that the responsibility for his illusion cannot now be shifted on to others, by Gandhiji by so naive a trick. It is not 'we' but it is only your goodself, and the Congress who are responsible for this illusion. Who kept swearing by the suicidal slogan all along that there could be no political antidote to unite with us? It was the Hindu Mahasabha alone which dispelled the illusion by administering the virile antidote, 'If you come, with you but if, do not, in spite of' .... The struggle for progress, for a truly National Swarajya will and can continue till victory is won.'

38. Aney's Address at Hindu League Session Held at Lucknow on 27 July 1940

Pioneer, 28 July 1940.

The first open session of the All India Hindu League commenced yesterday at 4 pm in the Ganga Prasad Memorial Hall, Lucknow, under the presidentship of Mr M.S. Aney, MLA, leader of the nationalist party in the Central Assembly....

Aney's Address

It will be admitted on all hands that the future of the self-governing Dominions, dependencies and town colonies in the British Empire largely depends on the result of this war. It will be obvious even to the meanest intelligence that if Germany wins, she will dictate the peace terms which England shall have to submit to. If England wins, England comes out triumphant and very much stronger than before and the British people will be the sole arbiters of the destinies of dependencies like India. The history of the British connection with India during the last 150 years is indeed not a very creditable record. People of India have been demilitarized and disarmed and rendered entirely helpless in the matter of self-defence against internal disorder and external invasions. No serious attempt has been made in all these years to raise a real Indian army, build an Indian navy or create an Indian air force. We are thus left in a state of helplessness in the matter of defence.

In the government of the country itself the people of India have no real and effective voice as the Central Government is irresponsible and autocratic. The autonomy enjoyed by the Provincial Governments can do some lasting good to the people only if and when the Central Federal Government becomes a truly popular and responsible one.

The result was simply inevitable Provincialism, communalism, sectarianism and party spirit in the name of loyalty to party organization have been extremely intensified. Nationalism and national outlook have been at a discount.

The Indian National Congress which is undoubtedly the largest and the most representative political organization in the country, is being treated by the Muslim League as a purely Hindu body which has no right to represent the Muhammadans of India notwithstanding the fact that there are several thousands of Muhammadans on its rolls. The Hindu Mahasabha disgusted completely with the so-called pro-Muhammadan and anti-Hindu tendencies of the Congress flatly repudiates the claim of the organization to represent the Hindus also. With these disclaimers coming from two powerful organizations claiming to represent the two great communities of India, the position of the Congress is certainly weakened and undermined.

Thus we find ourselves completely divided at a time when the need of unity, mutual understanding and cooperative action is most urgent in the matter of national defence. Our helplessness can be overcome only by our determination to stand united and rise like one man. There is no time to lose. We must act immediately and make an attempt to shape our destiny or resign ourselves to fate and a state of persistent helotage and slavery.

Responsibility

But when we say that we must act, we have to bear in mind that the responsibility is to be mainly shouldered by the community which occupies the dominant position in the country on account of its numerical strength in the population. Let us not forget that our country is Hindustan the land of the Hindus who form nearly three-fourths of the entire population of the country. There are Mohammedans and Christians. But they are minorities whose religious and cultural interests it is the duty of the majority community to protect.

But it is unreasonable to expect that the minorities can take any effective initiative in a big enterprise to free the nation. I am not one of those who would like to quote them. No, on the other hand, I feel certain cooperation will be very useful, if not altogether indispensable, to expedite the success of the national movement for political freedom. But none the less the primary and essential responsibility must rest on the shoulders of the majority community itself to make a move. The question is whether this majority community in India feels itself sufficiently strong to take up this fight? Is it properly organized and adequately equipped for a fight of this kind?

The Hindus, who want to stand for the fulfilment of the ideal of the Indian nation 'Hindusthan' must also oppose with their strength every attempt to divide and vivisect the Indian nation.

The Princes

It is unfortunate that the growth of the conception of an Indian democratic state is viewed with great suspicion and fears by the ruling Princes of Indian States. The main reason for this fear is the socialistic and communistic bent of mind of some of the leading politicians who play a very important part in Congress politics. The landed aristocracy in British India also has been considerably agitated by some of the ex-proprietary [expropriatery] measures championed by certain Provincial Governments.

I have no hesitation to say that the sudden departure made by the Congress in its traditional policy of neutrality in regard to matters relating to the administration of native states was a blunder. And the direct participation of first rank Congress politicians like Sardar Vallabhbhai Patel, Mr Pattabhi Sitaramaiya and Seth Jamnalal Bajaj in the agitation carried on in certain States was a still greater blunder.

On the very day the political agitation carried on by the people of British India can secure the bold and brave backing of the Princes and the people of the Native States, I have no doubt that the problem of India's salvation will be solved. Is it an impossible feat to bring about some kind of reconciliation between the rulers of the Native States and the Indian leaders? If that aim is consistently kept in view and no encouragement is given to sinister activities inside the States by Public men in British India, we should be able to achieve success in this line much earlier than some of us may think.

Muslim League's Dream

This brings me to the question which has been most agitating the minds of all thinking people in this country during the last five months viz. the grievances of the Muslim League and the solution suggested by them, that is, the carving out of a Pakistan in India for the Muslims where they would be sole masters and arbiters. The conception of the Indian nation is definitely rejected by those who stand for the scheme of Pakistan.

Nothing will be more fatal to India's progress than the recognition in any form of the fratricidal scheme of Pakistan. It will be neither in the interests of the Muhammadans nor those of the Hindus. It will undoubtedly be the beginning of the end of both.

39. Pandit Malviya and M.S. Aney Condemn Communal Award

Pioneer, 1 August 1940.

Pandit Madan Mohan Malviya and Mr M.S. Aney have issued the following statement jointly:

The evils of the Communal Award, particularly of separate communal electorates, are much more widely recognized now than before. Those evils have reached the culmination in the claim of the Muslim League that the Muslims of India constitute a nation separate from all other Indians, and its proposal to carve out a state within India in the name of Pakistan.

Owing mainly to this Award, the relations between Hindus and Muslims are much more strained now than they were at any time before. The Award has done a grievous wrong, particularly to the Hindus of Bengal and also to the Hindus and Sikhs of the Punjab. Whatever may be the form of the constitution which will be framed for the India of the future, the system of popular election is likely to continue and those of us who are opposed to the Communal Award and separate electorates are justified in demonstrating the fact that their opposition to them remained unabated.

They are justified in reaffirming that separate communal electorates, weighted in excess of proportion of population, provision of the statutory majority and representation of aliens, are inconsistent with national responsible government and that the said government be based on a common roll of electors and uniform franchise.

We, therefore, approve the proposal of Bengal friends that August 17 should be observed as an Anti-Communal Award day, to emphasize the fact that the opposition to separate electorates and other evils implied in the Communal Award is not less but stronger than before, and that we should oppose its retention in the future constitution. We strongly hope that when a new constitution is framed for India the evils of the Communal Award and separate electorate will be eliminated.

40. Savarkar Advocates Pan-Hindu Front, 14 September 1940

Jayakar Papers, File No. 709, 1940, NAI.

The following statement has been issued by Barrister V.D. Savarkar, the President of the Hindu Mahasabha on the 14th September, 1940.

I have requested Dr Moonje Mahashay to officiate as a Working President during my illness and deputed him to continue the negotiations with the Indian Government on behalf of the Hindu Mahasabha which were suspended in the meanwhile owing to my inability to respond to the invitation extended to me some weeks ago by H.E. the Viceroy to have another personal interview with him. Dr Moonje will certainly record a protest as vigorous as justified in his representations to H.E. the Viceroy, against the preposterously anti-Hindu demands forwarded by the Moslem League.

It should also be noted that the Provincial Hindusabhas from Madras to Punjab and Bengal, Bombay to Sindh have already publicly condemned the Muslim League Resolutions and the speech of Mr Amery in particular, which more than anything else must be held responsible for egging on the Moslem minority in advancing such impossible claims.

But to be plain, the cause of Hindudom as well as the Indian Nation as a whole is not so much likely to be endangered by the unconsciously self-betraying mentality of some of the very Congressite leaders who are never tired of condemning 'communalism' and of pruning themselves up as nationalists of the truest breed. Witness for example, the speeches of the Sjt Rajagopalacharya who has tacitly assured the Muslim League that the Congress will not strain much to swallow even the Pakistan pill if that pleased the League and persuaded the Moslems to oblige the Hindus by joining into a 'National Government'. How curious it is to see that even the Congressite leaders like Sjt Rajaji should fail to perceive that the two terms 'Pakistan' and the 'Indian National Government' are in themselves self-contradicting and self-destructive and how typical it is of the Congressite conception of 'National Unity' that such eminent Congress leaders should have given an open assurance to the Moslems regarding the Pakistan long before even the British Government dared to do so. The 'sporting offer' of Sjt Rajagopalacharya are becoming as much a public nuisance as the 'Inner Voice' of Gandhiji are wont to be.

But whatever be the anti-Hindu demands of the Moslems, the Machiavellian policy of the British Statesmen in egging them on or the suicidal 'Blank Cheques' and 'sporting offer' strategies of the Congressite Pseudo-Nationalism, the Hindu Mahasabha at any rate cannot and will never accept any other principle to determine the representation of the Moslem Minority other than their population ratio.

And if only all Hindus who still live, breathe and have their being as Hindus, whether they happen to be in the Congress or otherwise, unite themselves as Hindus, demanding and defending that the Hindu Majority too must have its legitimate rights as zealously guarded and secured as the rights of anyone else, no one can deprive the Hindus of their representation in proportion to their population simply because they happen to be in majority or favour the Moslems as if they were a set of suffering saints simply because they happen to be a minority. Let all Hindus once and for all declare that the Moslems have not obliged the Hindus by being in minority and the Hindus are in majority because they proved themselves fit to survive and out-numbered anyone of those with whom they had to fight in the continued struggle for National existence. In fact, Democracy itself ought to assure the Hindus as the overwhelming majority in Hindustan to rule unchallenged. But even the spirit of compromise can never go further than the principle of representation in legislatures etc. in relation to population.

Let the Hindus know it for certain that if only the Hindus along with the Hindu States organized a Pan-Hindu front pledged to defend Hindu rights without let or hindrance, the Hindus will very soon be found far more powerful a factor in Indian political life than Mr Amery fancies today the Moslem minority to be and the Britishers will be compelled to placate the Hindus more desperately than they at present do the Moslem minority.

The Indivisibility and Independence of India, representation in proportion to population, and recruitment to public services by merit alone—these are the fundamental principles on which the Hindu Mahasabha has taken its stand ever since its formation and it will not budge an inch in future from it even if the worst comes to the worst.

41. Savarkar's Appeal to Sikh Leader

Tribune, 9 October 1940.

The following letter has been addressed by Mr V.D. Savarkar, President, Hindu Mahasabha to Master Tara Singh, President, Shiromani Gurdwara Prabandhak Committee, Amritsar.

You must have known from papers that I have been lying ill and I am still confined to bed owing to an acute sciatic attack. I can neither walk nor work.

But even in this painful condition I could not refrain from writing these few lines to you to convey my felicitations to you and to our Sikh brotherhood, on your refusal to get cowed down by the Congress threats which impudently demanded of you to betray the just and legitimate interests of our Sikh brotherhood in particular and Hindudom in general. I thank you for having cut off all connections from the Congress organization and freed yourselves from the shackles and servitude of the pseudo-nationalistic ideology of the Congress which has proved a death blow to the real racial, cultural and national being of us Hindus. You are now free, as never before, to serve and strengthen our Sikh brotherhood in particular, and Hindudom in general.

The letter which Gandhiji wrote to you must serve as an eye-opener to all our Sikh brothers for all time to come.[1] How impudent is its tone! And how self-arrogating withal! He poses as a nationalist and blames you for caring and safeguarding the interests of Sikhs as a community. But look at the slavish mentality of this very same unalloyed nationalist when he keeps dancing attendance on Mr Jinnah or for that matter of any Muslim who crops up in the political field. The Congressites are never tired of asking the Muslims what they would want, to safeguard their community. Nay, they would admire the uncompromising effrontery with which the Muslims are getting themselves organized as a community, declare the Muslims a nation by themselves and must convert this Hindusthan into a Pakistan and yet the Congressites are never tired of fawning on these Muslim Leaguers and would go on their knees before them if they would but join the Congress. They would raise Maulana Azad to the very presidential chair of the Congress though he openly declared that he was a Muslim first and would see to it that the Muslims were never deprived of the right to dictate to all, the special communal rights they wanted. And yet these very Gandhiites and Congress write to you. You must leave the Congress because you want to safeguard the legitimate interests of your community and are therefore, a communalist.

Well, dear Bhaiji, I may tell you in a few words: Shun the Congress ideology and the very institution which is fundamentally based on that ideology if you want to be true to your real racial and national self. The Muslims are right in declaring that they are a nation by themselves. We Harijans, Sikhs and *Sikhetars* must now boldly assert: Right you are! We Hindus also are a nation by ourselves. You want to convert this land into a Pakistan which your forefathers failed to do; we Hindus, true to our ancestral heritage and racial identity and mission, are also determined to see that this land continues to be Hindusthan.

With this clear-cut ideology please reframe the political movement and aspirations of our Sikh brotherhood in the Punjab and of the Hindus in general throughout India.

Try to get as many Sikh brothers recruited into the army as possible. Raise the Sikh martial spirit to its pristine intensity once more. Let us all remember that even in politics Shri Guru Gobind Singh is our Guru and no nincompoop can disarm the Sikhs of their 'kirpan'.

Please note that on the borders of the Punjab, the frontier tribes are breeding even today thousands of fanatics of that very blood-thirsty anti-Hindu type which flourished in the days of a Mahomed Ghori or an Aurangzeb. If they get a chance they would overrun Punjab in no time and annihilate our Hindus, Sikhs and *Sikhetars*, with the same ferocity. Under these circumstances woe to the Hindus, Sikhs and *Sikhetars* if they get themselves dosed with the psuedo-nationalistic opiates of the silly, spineless, mad, suicidal Congress ideology.

The Hindu Mahasabha has, time and again, passed resolutions that the number of the Sikhs in the army must not be allowed to fall below their pristine strength. I myself represented the cause to the Viceroy more than once. How foolish it would have been if some of the Sikh leaders themselves could have been doubted by Gandhiji and others to call on the Sikhs to boycott the army! That is why I was very glad to see that outstanding leaders like you, should have come out, boldly to dissociate yourselves from the Congress and its so-called non-violence fad which, in fact, is more likely to be responsible in theory and practice for inviting violence on the part of the enemies of Hindudom than anything else.

Now, friends, organize on military lines our brave Sikh brotherhood, occupy and utilize every point of vantage that we can get in the army, in the legislatures and in the services. Let us boldly assert that safeguarding and advancing the legitimate Hindu interests is the only patriotic duty we owe to our racial self and that we Hindus constitute the real nation in this land—Hindusthan.

This is my message to you and to all our Sikh brotherhood. If the Sikhs follow it, I again repeat that the Muslims who are indulging in the new dreams of Pakistan will find, in the Punjab when they wake up, a Sikhisthan instead. It is not even now, too late for us to be up and doing.

---

[1] For Mahatma Gandhi's letter to Master Tara Singh dated 16 August 1940 in which he had stated that he (Master Tara Singh) had nothing in common with the Congress, see Document no. 55(b) in this chapter.

42. B.S. Moonje's Views on the Jinnah–Viceroy Correspondence, 5 October 1940

B.S. Moonje Papers, Serial No. 39, NMML.

I have carefully read the correspondence, published between Mr Jinnah and H.E. the Viceroy[1]. The immediate impression left is that the correspondence makes alarming revelations about the motive and mentality of the Moslem Leaders. It may almost be said to be an attempt at conspiracy, by taking H.E. the Viceroy absolutely unawares, with the object of undermining the positions of the Congress and the Hindu Mahasabha, substantially in the case of Congress and completely in the case of the Hindu Mahasabha, and enthroning the Muslim League as the *de facto* ruler both at the Centre and in the Provinces under the sovereignty of His Majesty's Government in equal partnership with H.E. the Viceroy. I must, therefore, congratulate His Excellency the Viceroy of his having shaken off the shackles of the conspiracy with skill and caution.

These revelations are so alarmingly harmful to the position of the Hindus throughout the whole of India that I cannot resist the temptation of respectfully warning H.E. the Viceroy most solemnly that any flinching and giving in to the Muslim League will entirely ruin Britain's work of about a century and a half in India and encourage a strife jeoparadising the chances of the successful establishment of a strong Central Government for the whole of India. If encouraged or connived at, this mentality would become a menace—not only to the Hindus but also to the very name of the British in India.

This correspondence must open the eyes of the Congress—also, as it has of the Hindu Mahasabha—and must convince it that any attempt at Hindu–Muslim Unity is a wild goose chase and has not the least chance of success, as long as it is the Hindus that approach for such unity. If the Hindus were to demonstrate their strength and determination, they can still have the Moslems as their colleagues in the establishment of their Swaraj.

The Congress has already lost a great deal of its prestige, position and strength and unless it were to cease its spiritual aeronautics and to reconsider its policy on the basis of stern realism of the mundane world, it will sound the death-knell of the Congress, the great organization which has held the field practically unchallenged throughout the last more than half a century. It can, only if it can, shed its feeling of defeatism in respect of the Moslems certainly still maintain its prestige and usefulness inspite of the challenge of the Muslim League, however reinforced it may be by its attempt at what the League calls as a 'War Contract' with H.E. the Viceroy. The Congress cannot now fight single-handed against this challenge; it must seek an ally for its very existence. Can there be a more sure, honest, sincere and a faithful ally than the Hindu Mahasabha which, in view of the Muslim League's challenge to the Congress, is growing rapidly and tremendously in power and prestige by winning the hearts of the Hindu masses?

---

[1] Correspondence between Jinnah and the Viceroy was released to the press on 30 September 1940. Jinnah was not satisfied with Viceroy's decision to provide two seats to the Muslim League in the expanded Executive Council.

43. The Anti-Pakistan Conference at Lahore—Aney's Presidential Speech

Hindustan Times, 2 December 1940.

Presiding over the Anti-Pakistan Conference at Lahore yesterday, Mr M.S. Aney severely condemned the Pakistan scheme of the Muslim League as anti-national, reactionary and undemocratic and urged the different parties to form a united bloc to fight the 'unjustified demand of vivisection'.

Mr Aney said that the British Government had done nothing to create in the Muslims a will to unite with the Hindus to form themselves into one nation. The Government's indifference and, at times, deliberate connivance, he said, encouraged the growth of a spirit of a separatist mentality which ultimately led to the present demand for a communal partition of India.

It may be said with fair degree of accuracy that the Axis Powers are knocking at the eastern and western gates of India. The problem of India's defence has to be faced and solved jointly by the people of India and the Government of India, observed Mr M.S. Aney in the course of his presidential address at the Anti-Pakistan Conference this afternoon.

Mr Aney devoted a considerable portion of his address to examination of the recent pronouncements of the Viceroy and the Secretary of State for India. He said: His Excellency the Viceroy struck a right note asking the people of India to look upon this war as one that is being fought not merely for the cause of the Empire but for the cause of India also. But people there are who have doubts as to how this war is going to serve the cause of India. Frankly speaking, the Indian National Congress has by asking His Majesty's Government to enunciate and clarify their war aims raised this categorical issue. The reply given and the gesture made so far on behalf of His Majesty's Government have not satisfied them.

'I am sure,' added Mr M.S. Aney, 'that His Excellency did not want to repeat a mere platitude when he referred in the same sentence and the breath to the cause of India and the Empire. In order to understand the import of his Excellency's reference to the cause of India in his appeal to the Indian people, it is necessary to look back to the objects with which he has been strenuously trying to reconcile public opinion in India since the outbreak of war'. Mr Aney recalled the Viceroy's announcement that attainment of India of free and equal partnership in the British Commonwealth is the proclaimed and accepted goal of the Imperial Crown and the British Parliament and said, according to him, this consummation can be reached by India by the forging of '"new bonds of union and understanding" between the majority community and the various important elements in the national life of India by the combined' attempt on their part to defeat the totalitarian forces during the time of war as well as by taking counsels together to prepare the ground work for the framing of the constitution for a free India.

A Blunder

Mr Aney expressed the opinion that the Congress and the Muslim League committed a great mistake in rejecting the offer of the expanded Executive Council and the establishment of an Advisory War Council but pointed out that he was not without misgivings about the evolution of an abiding and genuine political unity as the result of the joint labours of a few leaders of the two different communities as members of the expanded Council and the War Council for the prosecution of the war which is a common danger.

Government to Cement Differences

Mr Aney said: When the misunderstanding exists between the two great communities in a nation, the task of restoring cordial relations between them has to be performed by those who hold the reins of administration and wield sovereign power in their hands. Private attempts at reconciliation can succeed only if there is a bona fide desire in those who happen to be at the helm of the political affairs to achieve that unity. Private peace-makers can act only as non-official agents of the Government which is ultimately responsible not merely for maintenance of peace and order but also for the preservation and creation of friendly relations between one community and another. In fact, it is the Government that alone can supply the cement to join the two. His Excellency the Viceroy and the Secretary of State in every one of their speeches express their deep regret at the fact that the differences between the two communities, Hindus and Muslims, are not bridged. I am sure that these great statesmen know too well that communal unity is not an achievement that can be had by any people like a gift from the easy-to-please heavenly gods for the mere asking of it or wishing it....

Pakistan

Mr Aney then criticized the communal award and said the anti-nationalist spirit of the Mohammedans has now found a free expression in what is known as the demand for 'Pakistan'. Various schemes have been formulated by leading Mohammedans to translate their vision of 'Pakistan' into a reality. There are differences among them about the details, but on main principles there seems to be a general agreement among the protagonists of these schemes.

Mr Aney characterized the Pakistan scheme as a conquest of India by the Mohammedans without a fight, and with the help and blessings of the British Government.

Mr Aney said:

'Hindus and almost the whole of non-Muslim India simply wondered at the audacity of the Muslim League when it openly declared itself as standing for the establishment of Pakistan in India.

Studied Silence of British Government

But the most surprising part of the situation was the studied silence of the British Government and the Government of India on the attitude of the Mohammedans as betrayed in the putting forth of the demand of partition. Mr Jinnah had declared times out of number that the Muslim League would fight for Pakistan and that they did not want even central Indian democracy to rule and govern India.'

'This demand', added Mr Aney, 'went counter to the very goal to which the British Government stood pledged. It was a negation of the very scheme of the Dominion form of Government of the Westminster type which they desired the Indian people to accept as their goal and work for'. Mr Aney wanted British statesmen to declare whether this proclaimed goal was compatible with the vivisection of India on communal consideration. If not, then it was their duty to condemn the idea publicly and shake the propaganda which was being carried on daily in the Press and on the platform by the Mohammedans.

Mr Aney said that the British Government must immediately declare that they are not going to entertain any scheme which strikes at the integrity of India as one indivisible nation. They must restate the war aims about which considerable doubts have been raised owing to the unreasonable emphasis on the interests and rights of minorities. In every civilized democracy, the nation means the power of the majority tampered with safeguards in the interests of minorities. This general rule must be followed and a guarantee given that British statesmen will not introduce the case of India as an innovation. This will appeal to the Indian youth and that will elicit a response from them to join fully in the cooperation for the war. Because in that case they will have no difficulty to see that they are fighting for the cause of India. With that cooperation they can build a national force, fully equipped and self-sufficient for the defence of India.

Resolution

The Conference adopted a resolution recording its unequivocal condemnation of the Muslim League plan for the dissection of India known as the Pakistan scheme and characterizing it as fantastic, impracticable, unpatriotic, vicious and fraught with grave consequences to the political, social and economic advancement of the country as a whole.

The Conference believed that despite diversities of religion and language, India was a complete, indivisible nation, the political and economic interests of the masses of her people were common and that any kind of partition was bound to create, accentuate and perpetuate constant friction among the various communities, leading to internecine civil war and thereby exposing the country to foreign aggression.

In any future constitution, stated the resolution, differential treatment of minorities should be avoided and the Communal Award be reversed and joint electorate introduced for all representative bodies, local, provincial and federal, with reservation of seats for minorities if necessary on one uniform principle for representation in the federal as well as provincial legislature.

The Conference suggested that in any future constitution the following principles should be borne in mind:

1. Safe-guarding of the interests of minorities by giving them unfettered freedom for maintenance of religion, culture and language.

2. Absolute equality of treatment in the acquisition of civic rights without allowing preferential treatment to any one on the basis of caste or creed.

The Conference drew attention of the Government to the fact that there were provincial minorities too and that redistribution of the existing provincial territories or compulsory exchange of population was no solution of the minority problem in India....

44. Shyama Prasad Mukherjee's Presidential Address (Extracts), Mahakoshal Provincial Hindu Sabha Conference, Bilaspur

Indian Annual Register, 1940, Vol. II, pp. 294–6.

The Hindu Mahasabha was founded twenty-two years ago through the efforts of patriotic Hindus who were prominently associated with the Indian National Congress. It did not perhaps originally aim at entirely independent political organization with a definite mission of its own— a role which the decree of Providence has assigned to it during the last few years. It had included within its main programme many an important item of social and economic reform of vital moment to Hindu interests, but its political outlook had not during the first decade of its existence captured the mind of the people at large. The dream of an Indian nationhood which would comprise within itself men and women professing different religions, who regarded

India as their common motherland, had fired the imagination of generations of political thinkers and workers in this country. I have nothing to say against this ideal for I believe that its consummation, if ever achieved, will be all to the good of our country.

But as a matter of actual experience we have noticed that at least one big community residing in this country, namely, the Muslim, has not openly identified itself to any appreciable extent with this movement; on the other hand, its demand for special treatment, which was readily acceded to, originally made on the ground of educational and political backwardness, has now, developed into an insistent call for the division of India on the basis of a 'two nations' theory and a claim for separate independent Muslim States within the boundaries of Hindusthan. If the Hindus of India during the last half of a century had not attempted to arrive at a patched-up peace with the Muslim leaders but had boldly laid down their political programme, fully recognizing the fundamental rights of citizenship of all communities inhabiting this land, the situation would not have perhaps developed in its present acute form. The last quarter of a century had unconsciously imbued some of us with the belief that Indian freedom was unattainable except with the support of the Muslims of India.

The time has now come when we should not only feel but declare unhesitatingly that the liberation of our motherland is capable of being accomplished with the united efforts of 28 crores of Hindus who regard this country as the holiest of holy land on this earth. If other communities join us on the basis of a clear-cut national programme, safeguarding the legitimate rights and interests of all, we shall welcome such cooperation. But if they refuse to join us, we shall regard them as a definite obstacle in the path of the achievement of our goal and must strenuously prepare ourselves to win back our freedom by our own efforts. Our outlook in brief should be the attainment of Indian liberty with the support of others if available on honourable terms, or without it, if the situation so demands. The infusion of strength into the Hindu mind on this basis has recently been and will continue to be a principal duty of the Hindu Mahasabha.

GOVERNMENT ATTITUDE

I do not for a moment ignore the fact that the present attitude of Muslims is largely due to the direct and indirect encouragement it has received from representatives of the British Government. Whatever pro-British historians may like to assert the fact remains that the policy of 'divide and rule' was astutely nurtured by British diplomats and has helped to embitter communal feelings in this country to a much greater extent than would otherwise have been possible. The answer to this will not be given by pandering more and more to unjustifiable communal demands. The answer which self-respecting India can give is to unite the Hindus and to make all parties feel that in spite of all diplomacy and separatist tendencies Indians are capable of reaching their goal by their own sacrifice and suffering.

The recent speeches of the Secretary of State for India give us an ample indication of the true spirit that pervades the minds of those in whose hands the destinies of India today lie. That spirit is clearly anti-Hindu in character. We are reminded of and on of communal disharmony in India as the stumbling block in the way of further political progress. But have we heard a single word of contrition or of apology for the introduction of separate electorates and accepting it as a basis for the present Indian political structure? The British Government is reluctant to transfer power to Indians for it apprehends that the Hindus, constituting 70 per cent of the Indian population, would then have the dominant voice which leading Muslims would not be prepared to accept. It is open to the Government to institute national electorates and leave administration in the provinces and at the centre to be run by majority parties who will be returned through such electorates with a mandate for giving effect to political programmes that transcend the bounds of sectional interest. It will not do that for it knows that the acceptance of joint electorates will ultimately reduce communal misunderstandings, lead to national solidarity and may sound the death-knell of British supremacy in India. At the same time it dare not allow representatives of the people coming through existing electorates to occupy positions of power and authority at the centre, for it knows that the majority of the people who will thus be returned to the legislature even through separate electorates must come from the Hindus who whatever their party allegiance will unite in removing the ever-tightening grip of the British Government on Indian affairs.

Crocodile tears are shed for the alleged welfare of the minorities in India. May I ask that if forcible disruption or hamstringing of the majority is a new democratic principle which British statesmen have learnt to appreciate, why should they not apply it to their own country and do away with the Parliamentary constitution that gives legitimate power to the party that is backed by the majority to rule over the destinies of England? Again, if an inordinate love of minority interests has temporarily absorbed the British mind, may I ask what persuaded Government to provide special electorates on a favoured scale for the Muslims in provinces where they were in a majority? May I ask, again, why does it hesitate to do the barest acts of justice to the Hindu minorities in provinces such as Sind, the Punjab and Bengal where rightful interests of the Hindus are being daily trampled under foot? When will British conscience be roused against the deliberately mischievous provisions of the Communal Award, designed to cripple the legitimate rights of the Hindus specially of the provinces I have just mentioned?

Will anyone dare deny that the deliberate acts of murder of Hindus in Sind are signs and portents of a spirit of complete lawlessness against which no adequate protection has yet been given by the Government of the day? If one single British life were lost through the acts of assassins, as hundreds of innocent Hindu lives have been lost during the last two years, not only would the British Lion have roared from one corner of India to the other but the whole Empire would have borne a witness to the shaking of its paws. In my own province acts of oppression affecting the honour of women, and the cultural, civic, religious and economic rights of Hindus are being systematically resorted to resulting in a recent demand by the Hindus for the suspension of the Constitution. The British Government is preserving an attitude of stolid silence and of unconcealed indifference that gives the lie direct to any genuine claim on its part for preservation of the interests of minorities. Today none can deny that even the Pakistan scheme has received at least indirect support from responsible and influential persons who speak on behalf of the British Government from time to time. It is significant that this nefarious proposal has not been disapproved much less condemned in any of the official pronouncements recently issued either from India or from England. Today, as I said, the policy is to curb and destroy the power and influence of the Hindus by depriving them of their legitimate rights and privileges.

CONGRESS AND MAHASABHA

There is much that is common between the ideal of the Congress and that of the Hindu Mahasabha; but there are also points of difference. Both believe that independence is our goal. The Hindu Mahasabha has, however, said that if India is treated as a full-fledged dominion just like Canada, Ireland and South Africa, it will accept that constitution as an immediate step towards the attainment of its goal of full independence. This does not narrow down the political goal of the Hindu Mahasabha; on the other hand, it puts England's sincerity to the test. It offers its hand of cooperation provided India's honour and self-respect are maintained intact. There are matters concerning India's welfare, specially in connection with defence, which may be solved peacefully if England and India acted on a basis of honourable cooperation. Of course, the way in which things are moving and the language in which British representatives are expressing their views about Indian aspirations make it extremely doubtful if full Dominion Status will come to India immediately on the termination of the war, even if England defeats Germany.

While fully prepared to co-operate with all other communities residing in India and to establish harmonious relationship with them on broad and statesman-like ideas of Indian nationalism, the Hindu Mahasabha genuinely aspires to instil in the minds of 28 crores of Hindus a sacred determination that it is possible for them, may incumbent upon them, to win back the independence of their country even though communities may refuse to offer the hand of honourable cooperation. The Congress attitude towards Hindu interest especially in respect of the communal award has been a regrettable episode in the history of Indian progress and the Hindu Mahasabha is determined to see that in future the case of the Hindus does not go by default. Where Hindu rights are violated as such, Hindus must learn to resist them with all their strength.

Lastly, the present creed of non-violence of the Congress as interpreted by some of its exponents is not the creed of the Hindu Mahasabha. Centuries of political subjection have almost blotted out the memory of Hindu valour and strength and broken the backbone of the people. Their power of resistance, their resolution to stand against evil even at the risk of death have been greatly weakened. The current doctrine of non-violence has further enervated the Hindu mind. The Hindu Mahasabha appreciates the need for Ahimsa. But it firmly believes that Ahimsa born of fear and cowardice is not consistent with India's great heritage nor have any people the right to preach the doctrine of non-violence unless they have the power, the courage and the valour to uphold truth and right, justice and equity by all possible means, peaceful or otherwise. A nation must first be physically strong and adequately armed before it can proclaim and defend moral doctrines. That nation is truly great which has force and strength at its disposal but never abuses from for the advancement of self-interest or self-aggrandizement.

D.   INDIAN NATIONAL CONGRESS

45.   Extracts from Jawaharlal Nehru's Speech, Ghaziabad, 10 January 1940

National Herald, 11 January 1940; *SWJN*, Vol. X, pp. 423–5.

...You live near Delhi, the centre of British imperialism. You have to show by your actions the influence of the great organization, the Congress, and tell the Viceroy, who wants to decide India's fate by calling 40 or 50 men, that the times are now changed and the real decision of India's problems lies in the hands of the villagers who constitute the masses.

Three years ago I made a tour in connection with the election campaign on behalf of the Congress. My real purpose was to see the picture of real India in the eyes of the masses that came to hear me. This picture aroused feelings both of satisfaction and disappointment....

The communal and other organizations in the country have discarded all limits of decency and are out to discredit and abuse the Congress. We have also to analyse the reasons why our repeated efforts for a communal settlement have failed. Swaraj today is within easy reach but our friends are pulling us away from grasping it.

Mr Fazlul Huq, the Bengal Premier, has gone out of his way to abuse the Congress. To win freedom for India I am prepared to crawl on my knees, but I will never stoop to meet Mr Fazlul Huq after what he has recently said. The Bengal Premier has made allegations against the Congress and then side-tracked the issue when called upon to substantiate the charges.

To win freedom for India we will have to fight not only the British Government but the organizations and interests created and backed by the British in this country. These interests will not bear to see power pass out of their hands, and in the name of religion are creating difficulties today. For instance, I am sure that free India cannot tolerate the Indian states for a day and yet the government, which professes to fight for democracy in the West, is backing the states to crush the life and liberty of those people. Some zamindars are sympathetic to the Congress, but as a group they are opposed to power passing out to the people. The same fear actuates the opposition to the Constituent Assembly proposal.

In order to allay the fears of minorities, the Congress has offered that if the minorities so desire they can send in their representatives to the Constituent Assembly by the method of separate electorates. Furthermore, decisions on communal issues are not to be taken by a majority vote but by common consent and, in the event of a deadlock, by such international bodies as the League of Nations or the International Court of Justice at the Hague....

46 (a) Mahatma Gandhi's Article 'Unity v. Justice', 23 January 1940
Harijan, 27 January 1940.

A visitor came the other day and said, 'You have done an irreparable injury to India by saying that there is no Swaraj without communal unity. You should say instead that there is no Swaraj without justice between and to the different communities'. I reasoned with my visitor but he would not be consoled. He said, 'You have offered to sell your soul to win the favour of your Muslim friends'. I protested and said, 'Surely you know, the world knows, that I would not sell my soul to buy India's freedom. And if I want Muslim friendship, it is not for personal gratification but for India's sake. You are unjust to me.' My visitor retorted with some passion, 'I know your love for the country. If I had not known it, I would not have come to you specially. But your love has blinded you to the mistake you have made and are making. You do not know what Hindus say and do. For fear of offending Muslims, they suffer because they believe in you. I do beseech you to replace "unity" with "justice".' It was no use my arguing with my friend. And I had no time. I promised to deal with the question in these columns. The promise soothed him. I do not know that my answer will.'

My belief is unshaken that without communal unity Swaraj cannot be attained through non-violence. But unity cannot be reached without justice between communities. Muslim or any other friendship cannot be bought with bribery. Bribery would itself mean cowardice and therefore, violence. But if I give more than his due to my brother, I do not bribe him nor do I do any injustice. I can disarm suspicion only by being generous. Justice without generosity may easily become Shylock's justice. I must, however, take care that the generosity is not done at the expense of the very cause for which it is sought to be done.

I cannot, therefore, drop the idea of unity or the effort for it. But what is wanted is not so much justice as right action. Qaide Azam Jinnah's reply to me[1], as published in the Press, however, dashes to the ground all hope of unity if he represents the Muslim mind. His repudiation of the natural meaning I put upon his action in making common cause with the different political groups has created a unique situation. His picture of India as a continent containing nations counted according to their religions, if it is realized, would undo the effort the Congress has been making for over half a century. But I hope that Qaide-Azam Jinnah's opinion is a temporary phase in the history of the Muslim League. Muslims of the different provinces can never cut themselves away from their Hindu or Christian brethren. Both Muslims and Christians are converts from Hinduism or descendents of converts. They do not cease to belong to their provinces because of change of faith. Englishmen who become converts to Islam do not change their nationality. I hope Qaid-e-Azam Jinnah does not represent the considered opinion even of his colleagues.

---

[1] See Document no. 9 in this chapter.

46 (b) Mahatma Gandhi's Response to a Question on His Article, 16 February 1940

Harijan, 24 February 1940.

Question Box

Q. In your article "Unity v. Justice" you say that, if you give more than his due to your brother, you neither bribe him nor do you do an injustice. You say 'I can disarm suspicion only by being generous. Justice without generosity is done at the expense of the very cause for which it is sought to be done. I submit that justice and generosity cannot go hand in hand. As Dryden has rightly observed, 'Justice is blind, it knows nobody.' Besides, you can be generous to the weak, meek and the humble, not to one who in the arrogance of his strength seeks to coerce you into submission. To give more than his due to such a person is not generosity but cowardly surrender. Though Hindus are numerically stronger, their majority, as you yourself have pointed out, is only fictitious and actually they are the weaker party. Besides, if generosity is to be shown to the Muslims, the only organization that is competent to offer it is the Hindu Mahasabha. What right has a third party to be generous to one of the two parties to a dispute at the other party's expense?

A. In my article referred to by you I have dealt with general principles, not with particular minorities. Even as justice to be justice has to be generous, generosity in order to justify itself has got to be strictly just. Therefore it should not be at the expense of any single interest. Hence there cannot be any question of sacrificing some minority or minorities, for the benefit of any minority. You are right again in contending that generosity has to be shown to the weak and the humble, and not to the bully. Nevertheless I would say, on behalf of the bully, that even he is entitled to justice, for immediately you brush aside the bully and be unjust to him you justify his bullying. Thus the only safe—not to put it higher—rule of conduct is to do generous justice, irrespective of the character of the minority. I am quite sure that where there is strictest justice the question of a majority and minority would not arise. The bully is a portent and is an answer to some existing circumstance, as for instance cowardice. It is often forgotten that cowardice can be unjust. The fact is that cowards have no sense of justice. They yield only to threat, or actual use, of force. I do not know that there is any question of choice between a coward and a bully. The one is as bad as the other, with this difference that the bully always follows the coward in point of time.

In a previous issue I have admitted that the proper organization to enter into settlements is the Hindu Mahasabha, so far as Hindus are concerned, or any such organization. The Congress endeavours to represent all communities. It is not by design, but by the accident of Hindus being politically more conscious than the others, that the Congress contains a majority of Hindus. As history proves the Congress is a joint creation of Muslims, Christians, Parsis, Hindus, led by Englishmen, be it said to the credit of the latter. And the Congress, in spite of all that may be said to the contrary, retains that character. At the present moment a Muslim divine is the unquestioned leader of the Congress and for the second time becomes its president. The constant endeavour of Congressmen has been to have as many members as possible drawn from the various communities, and therefore the Congress has entered into pacts for the purpose of securing national solidarity. It cannot, therefore, divest itself of that function, and, therefore, although I have made the admission that the Hindu Mahasabha or a similar Hindu organization can properly have communal settlements, the Congress cannot and must not plead incapacity for entering into political pacts so long as it commands general confidence.

On the train to Calcutta, 16–2–40.

47. Maulana Abul Kalam Azad on the Communal Problem

Extracts from Presidential Address at Ramgarh Session of Indian National Congress, 19 March 1940.
Indian Annual Register, 1940, Vol. I, pp. 295–308.

The Minorities and India's Political Future

I have briefly placed before you the real question of the day.[1] That is the vital question for us, all else are subsidiary to it. It was in relation to that question that the Congress put forward its invitation to the British Government in September last, and made a clear and simple demand to which no community or group could possibly object. It was not in our remotest thoughts that the communal question could be raised in this connection. We realize that there are some groups in the country which cannot keep step with the Congress in the political struggle or go as far as the Congress is prepared to go; we know that some do not agree with the method of direct action which the great majority of political India has adopted. But so far as the right of the Indian people to independence is concerned and the full admission of India's birthright to freedom, an awakened and impatient India has passed far beyond the early stages, and none dare oppose our demand. Even those classes, who cling to their special interests and fear change lest this might affect them adversely, are rendered helpless by the spirit of the times. They have to admit and to agree to the goal we have set before us.

A time of crisis is a testing time for all of us, and so the great problem of the day has tested us and exposed many an aspect of our present-day politics. It has laid bare also the reality that lies behind the communal problem. Repeated attempts were made, in England and India, to mix up the communal question with the vital political question of the day, and thus to confuse the real issue. Again and again, it was sought to convince the world that the problem of the minorities barred the way to a proper solution of India's political problem.

For a hundred and fifty years British imperialism has pursued the policy of divide and rule, and by emphasizing internal differences, sought to use various groups for the consolidation of its own power. That was the inevitable result of India's political subjection, and it is folly for us to complain and grow bitter. A foreign government can never encourage internal unity in the subject country, for disunity is the surest guarantee for the continuance of its own domination. But when we were told, and the world was asked to believe, that British imperialism had ended, and the long chapter of Indian history dominated by it had closed, was it unreasonable for us to expect that British statesmen would at last give up this evil inheritance and not exploit the communal situation for political ends? But the time for this is yet distant; we may not cling to such vain hopes. So the last five months with their succession of events have established. Imperialism, in spite of all assurances to the contrary, still flourishes; it has yet to be ended.

BRITAIN'S ATTEMPT TO EXPLOIT THE SITUATION

But whatever the roots of our problems might be, it is obvious that India, like other countries, has her internal problems. Of these, the communal problem is an important one. We do not and cannot expect the British Government to deny its existence. The communal problem is undoubtedly with us, and if we want to go ahead, we must needs take it into account. Every step that we take by ignoring it will be a wrong step. The problem is there; to admit its existence, however, does not mean that it should be used as a weapon against India's national freedom. British Imperialism has always exploited it to this end. If Britain desires to end her imperialistic methods in India and close that dismal chapter of history, then the first signs of this change must naturally appear in her treatment of the communal problem.

What is the Congress position in regard to this problem? It has been the claim of the Congress, from its earliest beginnings, that it considers India as a nation and takes every step in the interest of the nation as a whole. This entitles the world to examine this claim strictly and the Congress must establish the truth of its assertion. I wish to examine afresh this question from this point of view. There can be only three aspects of the communal problem: its existence, its importance, and the method of its solution.

The entire history of the Congress demonstrates that it has always acknowledged the existence of the problem. It has never tried to minimise its importance. In dealing with this problem, it followed a policy which was the most suitable under the circumstances. It is difficult to conceive of a different or better course of action. If, however, a better course could be suggested, the Congress was always, and is today, eager to welcome it.

We could attach no greater importance to it, than to make it the first condition for the attainment of our national goal. The Congress has always held this belief; no one can challenge this fact. It has always held to two basic principles in this connection, and every step was taken deliberately with these in view.

1. Whatever constitution is adopted for India, there must be the fullest guarantee in it for the rights and interests of minorities.
2. The minorities should judge for themselves what safeguards are necessary for the protection of their rights and interests. The majority should not decide this. Therefore, the decision in this respect must depend upon the consent of the minorities and not on a majority vote.

The question of the minorities is not a special Indian problem. It has existed in other parts of the world. I venture to address the world from this platform, and to enquire whether any juster and more equitable course of action can be adopted in this connection, than the one suggested above? If so, what is it? Is there anything lacking in this approach, which necessitates that the Congress be reminded of its duty? The Congress has always been ready to consider any failure in the discharge of its duty. It is so prepared today. I have been in the Congress for the last nineteen years. During the whole of this period there is not a single important decision of the Congress in the shaping of which I have not had the honour to participate. I assert that during these last nineteen years, not for a single day did the Congress think of solving this problem in any way other than the way I have stated above. This was not a mere assertion of the Congress, but its determined and decided course of action. Many a time during the last fifteen years, this policy was subjected to the severest tests, but it stood firm as a rock.

The manner in which the Congress has dealt with this problem today in connection with the Constituent Assembly, throws a flood of light on these two principles and clarifies them. The recognized minorities have a right, if they so please, to choose their representatives by their votes. Their representatives will not have to rely upon the votes of any other community except their own. So far as the question of the rights and the interests of the minorities are concerned, the decision will not depend upon the majority of the votes in the Constituent Assembly. It will be subject to the consent of the minority. If unanimity is not achieved on any question, then an impartial tribunal, to which the minorities have also consented, will decide the matter. This last proviso is merely in the nature of a provision for a possible contingency, and is most unlikely to be required. If a more practical proposal is made, there can be no objection to it.

When these principles are accepted and acted upon by the Congress, what is it that obliges British statesmen to remind us so often of the problem of the minorities, and to make the world believe that this stands in the way of Indian freedom? If it is really so, why does not the British Government recognize clearly India's freedom and give us an opportunity to solve this problem for ever by mutual agreement amongst ourselves?

Dissensions were sown and encouraged amongst us, and yet we are taunted because of them. We are told to put an end to our communal conflicts, but opportunity to do so is denied us. Such is the position deliberately created to thwart us; such are the chains that bind us. But no difficulties or constraints can deter us from taking the right steps with courage and fortitude. Our path is full of obstacles but we are determined to overcome them.

We have considered the problems of the minorities of India. But are the Muslims such a minority as to have the least doubt or fear about their future? A small minority may legitimately have fears and apprehensions, but can the Muslims allow themselves to be disturbed by them? I do not know how many of you are familiar with my writings, twenty-eight years ago, in the 'Al Hilal'. If there are any such here, I would request them to refresh their memories. Even then I gave expression to my conviction, and I repeat this today, that in the texture of Indian politics, nothing is further removed from the truth than to say that Indian Muslims occupy the position of a political minority. It is equally absurd for them to be apprehensive about their rights and interests in a democratic India. This fundamental mistake has opened the door to countless misunderstandings. False arguments were built up on wrong premises. This error, on the one hand, brought confusion into the minds of Mussalmans about their own true position, and, on the other hand, it involved the world in misunderstandings, so that the picture of India could not be seen in right perspective.

If time had permitted, I would have told you in detail, how, during the last sixty years, this artificial and untrue picture of India was made, and whose hands traced it. In effect, this was the result of the same policy of divide and rule which took particular shape in the minds of British officialdom in India after the Congress launched the national movement. The object of this was to prepare the Mussalmans for use against the new political awakening. In this plan, prominence was given to two points. First, that India was inhabited by two different communities, the Hindus and the Mussalmans, and for this reason no demand could be made in the name of a united nation. Second that numerically the Mussalmans were far less than the Hindus, and because of this, the necessary consequence of the establishment of democratic institutions in India would be to establish the rule of the Hindu majority and to jeopardize the existence of the Muslims. I shall not go into any greater detail now. Should you, however, wish to know the early history of this matter, I would refer you to the time of Lord Dufferin, a former Viceroy of India, and Sir Auckland Colvin, a former Lieutenant-Governor of the NWP, now the United Provinces.

Thus were sown the seeds of disunity by British Imperialism on Indian soil. The plant grew and was nurtured and spread its nettles, and even though fifty years have passed since then, the roots are still there.

Politically speaking, the word minority does not mean just a group that is numerically small and therefore, entitled to special protection. It means a group that is so small in number and so lacking in other qualities that give strength, that it has no confidence in its own capacity to protect itself from the much larger group that surrounds it. It is not enough that the group should be relatively the smaller, but that it should be absolutely so small as to be incapable of protecting its interests. Thus this is not merely a question of numbers; other factors also count. If a country has two major groups numbering a million and two millions respectively, it does not necessarily follow that one is half the other, therefore it must call itself politically a minority and consider itself weak.

If this is the right test, let us apply it to the position of the Muslims in India. You will see at a glance a vast concourse, spreading out all over the country; they stand erect, and to imagine that they exist helplessly as a 'minority' is to delude oneself.

The Muslims in India number between eighty and ninety millions. The same type of social or racial divisions, which affect other communities, do not divide them. The powerful bonds of Islamic brotherhood and equality have protected them to a large extent from the weakness that flows from social divisions. It is true that they number only one fourth of the total population, but the question is not one of population ratio, but of the large numbers and the strength behind them. Can such a vast mass of humanity have any legitimate reason for apprehension that in a free and democratic India, it might be unable to protect its rights and interests?

These numbers are not confined to any particular area but spread out unevenly over different parts of the country. In four provinces out of eleven in India there is a Muslim majority, the other religious groups being minorities. If British Baluchistan is added, there are five provinces with Muslim majorities. Even if we are compelled at present to consider this question on a basis of religious groupings, the position of the Muslims is not that of a minority only. If they are in a minority in seven provinces, they are in a majority in five. This being so, there is absolutely no reason why they should be oppressed by the feeling of being a minority. Whatever may be the details of the future constitution of India, we know that it will be an All India federation which is, in the fullest sense, democratic, and every unit of which will have autonomy in regard to internal affairs. The federal centre will be concerned only with All India matters of common concern, such as, foreign relations, defence, customs, etc. Under these circumstances, can any one who has any conception of the actual working of a democratic constitution, allow himself to be led astray by this false issue of majority and minority? I cannot believe for an instant that there can be any room whatever for these misgivings in the picture of India's future. These apprehensions are arising because, in the words of a British statesman regarding Ireland, we are yet standing on the banks of the river and, though wishing to swim, are unwilling to enter the water. There is only one remedy; we should take the plunge fearlessly. No sooner is this done, we shall realize that all our apprehensions were without foundation.

A BASIC QUESTION FOR INDIAN MUSLIMS

It is now nearly thirty years since I first attempted to examine this question as an Indian Mussalman. The majority of the Muslims then were keeping completely apart from the political struggle and they were influenced by the same mentality of aloofness and antagonism, which prevailed amongst them previously in the year 1888. This depressing atmosphere did not prevent me from giving my anxious thought to this matter, and I reached quickly a final conclusion, which influenced my belief and action. I saw India, with all her many burdens, marching ahead to her future destiny. We were fellow passengers in this boat and we would not ignore its swift passage through the waters; and so it became necessary for us to come to a clear and final decision about our plan of action. How were we to do so? Not merely by skimming the surface of the problem but by going down to its root, and then to consider our position. I did so and I realized that the solution of the whole problem depended on the answer to one question: Do we, Indian Muslims, view the free India of the future with suspicion and distrust or with courage and confidence? If we view it with fear and suspicion, then undoubtedly we have to follow a different path. No present declaration, no promise for the future, no constitutional safeguards, can be a remedy for our doubts and fears. We are then forced to tolerate the existence of a third power. This third power is already entrenched here and has no intention of withdrawing and, if we follow this path of fear, we must look forward to its continuance. But if we are convinced that for us fear and doubt have no place, and that we must view the future with courage and confidence in ourselves, then our course of action becomes absolutely clear. We find ourselves in a new world, which is free from the dark shadows of doubt, vacillation, inaction and apathy, and where the light of faith and determination, action and enthusiasm never fails. The confusions of the times, the ups and downs that come our way, the difficulties that beset our thorny path, cannot change the direction of our steps. It becomes our bounden duty then to march with assured steps to India's national goal.

I arrived at this definite conclusion without the least hesitation, and every fibre of my being revolted against the former alternative. I could not bear the thought of it. I could not conceive it possible for a Muslim to tolerate this, unless he has rooted out the spirit of Islam from every corner of his being. I started the *Al Hilal* in 1912 and put this conclusion of mine before the Muslims of India. I need not remind you that my cries were not without effect. The period from 1912 to 1918 marked a new phase in the political awakening of the Muslims. Towards the end of 1920, on my release after four years of internment, I found that the political ideology of the Muslims had broken through its old mould and was taking another shape. Twenty years have gone by and much has happened since then. The tide of events has ever risen higher, and fresh waves of thought have enveloped us. But this fact still remains unchanged, that the general opinion amongst the Muslims is opposed to going back.

That is certain; they are not prepared to retrace their steps. But again they are full of doubts about their future path. I am not going into the reasons for this. I shall only try to understand the effects. I would remind my co-religionists that today I stand exactly where I stood in 1912 when I addressed them on this issue. I have given thought to all those innumerable occurrences which have happened since then; my eyes have watched them, my mind has pondered over them. These events did not merely pass me by; I was in the midst of them, a participant, and I examined every circumstance with care. I cannot be false to what I have myself seen and observed; I cannot quarrel with my own convictions; I cannot stifle the voice of my conscience. I repeat today what I have said throughout this entire period, that the ninety millions of Muslims of India have no other right course of action than the one to which I invited them in 1912.

Some of my co-religionists, who paid heed to my call in 1912, are in disagreement with me today. I do not wish to find fault with them, but I would make appeal to their sincerity and sense of responsibility. We are dealing with the destinies of peoples and nations. We cannot come to right conclusions if we are swept away by the passions of the moment. We must base our judgements on the solid realities of life. It is true that the sky is overcast today and the outlook is dark. The Muslims have to come into the light of reality. Let them examine every aspect of the matter again today, and they will find no other course of action open to them.

ISLAM'S CONTRIBUTION TO INDIA

I am a Muslim and am proud of that fact. Islam's splendid traditions of thirteen hundred years are my inheritance. I am unwilling to lose even the smallest part of this inheritance. The teaching and history of Islam, its arts and letters and civilization are my wealth and my fortune. It is my duty to protect them.

As a Muslim I have a special interest in Islamic religion and culture and I cannot tolerate interference with them. But in addition to these sentiments, I have others also which the realities and conditions of my life have forced upon me. The spirit of Islam does not come in the way of these sentiments; it guides and helps me forward. I am proud of being an Indian. I am a part of the indivisible unity that is Indian nationality. I am indispensable to this noble edifice and without me this splendid structure of India is incomplete. I am an essential element which has gone to build India. I can never surrender this claim.

It was India's historic destiny that many human races and cultures and religions should flow to her, finding a home in her hospitable soil, and that many a caravan should find rest here. Even before the dawn of history, these caravans trekked into India and wave after wave of new-comers followed. This vast and fertile land gave welcome to all and took them to her bosom. One of the last of these caravans, following the footsteps of its predecessors, was that of the followers of Islam. This came here and settled here for good. This led to a meeting of the culture-currents of two different races. Like Ganga and Jumna, they flowed for a while through separate courses, but nature's immutable law brought them together and joined them in a *sangam*. This fusion was a notable event in history. Since then, destiny, in her own hidden way, began to fashion a new India in place of the old. We brought our treasures with us, and India too was full of the riches of her own precious heritage. We gave our wealth to her and she unlocked the doors of her own treasures to us. We gave her, what she needed most, and the most precious of gifts from Islam's treasury, the message of democracy and human equality.

HERITAGE OF OUR COMMON NATIONALITY

Full eleven centuries have passed by since then. Islam has now as great a claim on the soil of India as Hinduism. If Hinduism has been the religion of the people here for several thousands of years, Islam also has been their religion for a thousand years. Just as a Hindu can say with pride that he is an Indian and follows Hinduism, so also we can say with equal pride that we are Indians and follow Islam. I shall enlarge this orbit still further. Indian Christian is equally entitled to say with pride that he is an Indian and is following a religion of India, namely Christianity.

Eleven hundred years of common history have enriched India with our common achievements. Our languages, our poetry, our literature, our culture, our art, our dress, our manners and customs, the innumerable happenings of our daily life, everything bears the stamp of our joint endeavour. There is indeed no aspect of our life which has escaped this stamp. Our languages were different, but we grew to use a common language; our manners and customs were dissimilar, but they acted and reacted on each other and thus produced a new synthesis. Our old dress may be seen only in ancient pictures of bygone days: no one wears it today. This joint wealth is the heritage of our common nationality and we do not want to leave it and go back to the times when this joint life had not begun. If there are any Hindus amongst us who desire to bring back the Hindu life of a thousand years ago and more, they dream, and such dreams are vain fantasies. So also if there are any Muslims who wish to revive their past civilization and culture, which they brought a thousand years ago from Iran and Central Asia, they dream also and the sooner they wake up the better. These are unnatural fancies which cannot take root in the soil of reality. I am one of those who believe that revival may be a necessity in a religion but in social matters it is denial of progress.

These thousand years of our joint life has moulded us into a common nationality. This cannot be done artificially. Nature does her fashioning through her hidden processes in the course of centuries. The cast has now been moulded and destiny has set her seal upon it. Whether we like it or not, we have now become an Indian nation, united and indivisible. No fantasy or artificial scheming to separate and divide can break this unity. We must accept the logic of fact and history and engage ourselves in the fashioning of our future destiny.

I shall not take any more of your time. My address must end now. But before I do so, permit me to remind you that our success depends upon three factors: unity, discipline and full confidence in Mahatma Gandhi's leadership. The glorious past record of our movement was due to his great leadership and it is only under his leadership that we can look forward to a future of successful achievement.

The time of our trial is upon us. We have already focused the world's attention. Let us endeavour to prove ourselves worthy.

---

[1] For the earlier part of the Address, see Chapter 3, Document no. 10.

48. 'My Answer to Quaid-E-Azam' by Mahatma Gandhi, 26 March 1940

Harijan, 30 March 1940.

Quaid-e-Azam Jinnah is reported to have said:

'Mr Gandhi has been saying for the last 20 years that there cannot be any swaraj without Hindu–Muslim unity. Mr Gandhi is fighting for a Constituent Assembly. May I point out to Mr Gandhi and the Congress that they are fighting for a Constituent Assembly which we cannot accept? Therefore, the idea of a Constituent Assembly is impracticable and unacceptable. Mr Gandhi wants a Constituent Assembly for purposes of ascertaining the views of Muslims, and if they do not agree, he would then give up all hope and then would agree with us. If there exists the will to come to a settlement with the Muslim League, then why does not Mr Gandhi, as I have said more than once, honestly agree that the Congress is a Hindu organization and that it does not represent anything but the solid body of Hindus? Why should Mr Gandhi not be proud to say: 'I am a Hindu and the Congress is a Hindu body'? I am not ashamed of saying that I am a Muslim and that the Muslim League is the representative of Muslims. Why all this camouflage, why this threat of civil disobedience, and why this fight for a Constituent Assembly. Why should not Mr Gandhi come as a Hindu leader and let me meet him proudly representing the Mussalmans?'[1]

My position is and has been clear. I am proud of being a Hindu, but I have never gone to anybody as a Hindu to secure Hindu–Muslim unity. My Hinduism demands no pacts. My support of the Khilafat was unconditional. I am no politician in the accepted sense. But whatever talks I had with Quaid-e-Azam or any other have been on behalf of the Congress which is not a Hindu organization. Can a Hindu organization have a Muslim divine as President, and can its Working Committee have four Muslim members out of 15? I still maintain that there is no Swaraj without Hindu–Muslim unity. I can never be party to the coercion of Muslims or any other minority. The Constituent Assembly as conceived by me is not intended to coerce anybody. Its sole sanction will be an agreed solution of communal questions. If there is no agreement, the Constituent Assembly will be automatically dissolved. The Constituent Assembly or any body of elected representatives can alone have a fully representative status. The Congress representative capacity has been and can be questioned. But who can question the sole representative capacity of the elected delegates to the Constituent Assembly? I cannot understand the Muslim opposition to the proposed Constituent Assembly. Are the opponents afraid that the Muslim League will not be elected by Muslim voters? Do they not realize that any Muslim demand made by the Muslim delegates will be irresistible? If the vast majority of Indian Muslims feel that they are not one nation with their Hindu and other brethren, who will be able to resist them? But surely it is permissible to dispute the authority of the 50,000 Muslims who listened to Quaid-e-Azam to represent the feelings of eight crores of Indian Muslims.

---

[1] See Document no. 12 in this chapter.

49. 'Dividing the Baby': Rajagopalachari on Pakistan Demand
Hindustan Times, 26 March 1940.

'I consider it a sign of diseased mentality that Mr Jinnah has brought himself to look upon the idea of one Indian nation as a misconception and the cause of most of our troubles. It is not this conception of one Indian nation but the mischievous concept of two Indian nations that threatens to lead India to destruction, if those who are responsible for it fail to revise their notions in time', said Mr C. Rajagopalachari in the course of an interview to the *Hindustan Times*.

Examining the League scheme of partitioning India even from the 'quasi-tribal point of view' of Mr Jinnah, Mr Rajagopalachari showed it to be quite absurd and impracticable.

'I make bold to say' concluded Mr Rajagopalachari, 'that what Mr Jinnah desires is a fuller amplitude for the so-called Muslim provinces to work out their progress without being hampered by a Central Government working under conditions necessitated by the composition of India's population and the play of political forces at such a Centre. Surely, he can ask for many things other than the cutting up of India into two parts based on a medieval conception in order to attain this laudable desire'.

'It is open to a foreign invader to consolidate his conquests and frame a kingdom for himself in the North-West or North-East of India and from that base to seek to penetrate the rest of India. This is how India was conquered and brought under the sway of the various foreign invaders from time to time in her history. I do not, however, imagine that present-day India will ever agree to the reverse process of carving out kingdoms for the benefit of tribal leaders. Even if the Congress and the League leaders should for the sake of peace agree to partition India according to religious labels, none of them, not even the biggest, could possibly deliver the goods'. This was Mr C. Rajagopalachari's comment on the League resolution demanding the partition of India on a religious basis in the course of an exclusive interview to a representative of the *Hindustan Times*.

Analysing the issues raised by the League resolution in his characteristic manner, Mr C. Rajagopalachari said: 'The proposal to divide the country reminds me of the old story when one of the two claimant mothers was quite willing to divide the baby while the other claimant proved her case by agreeing to handing over the baby in entirety even as Gandhiji has offered in his latest article in *Harijan*. It is wonderful how these permanent truths embodied in old stories come up for recognition again and again in all our quarrels and difficulties. After all there is nothing new under the sun. The test for true love is ever the same namely, whether you would part with your own share, rather than agree to mutilate and kill the whole.'

Replying to Mr Jinnah's arguments, Mr Rajagopalachari said: 'Mr Jinnah's proposition is based on the fundamental conviction that it is impossible to harmonize the inconsistent elements in India. His conviction is so strong in this respect that he is surprised that leading statesmen of Great Britain seriously asserted and expressed a hope that the passage of time will accomplish such harmonization. Most congressmen in India remember a time when Mr Jinnah did not differ from themselves, either spiritually, economically, culturally, socially or politically. Hakim Ajmal Khan, Dr Ansari, Maulana Mohammed Ali, Badr-ud-Din Tyabji, and Nawab Sayyad [Syed] Muhammed, a descendant of Tippu Sultan, did not think that there were any fundamental or deep-rooted differences that could be solved only by a partition of India. Indeed, not even Tippu Sultan or Hyder Ali or Aurangazeb or Akbar, all of whom lived during days when differences should have seemed more deep-rooted than now, imagined that India was anything but one and indivisible. These great men might have differed from one another in many respects, but they agreed in looking upon this precious land and this great nation as one and essentially indivisible. I consider it a sign of diseased mentality that Mr Jinnah has brought himself to look upon the idea of one Indian nation as a misconception and the cause of most of our troubles. It is not this conception of one Indian nation but the mischievous concept of two Indian nations that threatens to lead India to destruction if those who are responsible for it fail to revise their notions in time. To take India to the condition of the Balkan states seems to be the proud aim and goal of Mr Jinnah. Surely he knows in what a state the people of the Balkan Peninsula are with Germany and Russia waiting for the convenient hour to take them over'.

Mr Rajagopalachari continued: 'We do not inter-marry or inter-dine, says Mr Jinnah, about the Hindus and the Muslims, but surely, he knows that the various castes among the Hindus do not inter-marry or inter-dine either. The very language for which he (Mr Jinnah) stands, i.e. Urdu, is born of Hindu and Muslim India combining. The poetry and the music and the architecture of India are results of combination, not of division'.

No Remedy at All

'Let us, however, put aside sentiment and patriotism, which may be foolish, in Mr Jinnah's opinion'. Continued Mr Rajagopalachari. 'Let us examine it from the quasi-tribal point of view only. All the minority problems as they are, and they have been exaggerated, will remain exactly where they stood even if the present so-called Muslim provinces are carved out into separate kingdoms or federated into a separate Muslim Indian democracy. The problems in the United Provinces and elsewhere will remain just the same. The minority problem, in the Punjab and Bengal will also remain just the same. What then is the object of cutting the body into two?

'It may be said that the cutting out of Muslim India is intended to be followed up by a drive against the minorities therein, to suppress them entirely or to drive them out in the name of expatriation to an artificially created homeland and that therefore, there will be no minority problems. What will this lead to even if it were possible, looking at it from the opposite end? Will the three taluqas of Malabar where the Moplahs live be a separate state or will these unfortunate people speaking Malayalam be removed from their homesteads to an Urdu country for the sake of religious contiguity? Will the Tamil Muslims of Tanjore and Tinnevelly and Trichnopoly have to be sent to the Punjab? Not even could love for the Muslim League reconcile them to such tyranny and strange oppression. Thus Mr Jinnah has hardly given us a remedy for the minority problem.

Impracticable and Absurd

'It is pleasant to think of provinces with a boundary-line drawn according to religion but it would cut across race, language, occupation and what is dearer than all else, house and land. We cannot expect the Muslims of seven or eight provinces of India to submit to transplantation for the sake of giving the Muslim leaders of the Punjab and Bengal the satisfaction of separatist autonomy. It is this conception of a most impracticable and unthinkable character that has furnished the reason for Mr Jinnah to characterize the Congress demand for Constituent Assembly as impracticable and historically and constitutionally an absurd thing to ask the ruling power to agree to. Were his own proposal less obviously absurd and impracticable, I have no doubt the ruling power would agree to it very gladly because if India were so divided its big boot could rest heavily on both Muslim and Hindu India. Yet Mr Jinnah in the same breath in which he makes his proposal of cutting India into two swears, 'We stand unequivocally for the freedom of India'. The cheers with which this declaration in favour of freedom is reported to have been received indicate the real mind of the audience which is fundamentally patriotic and stands for a united India whatever in their present misguided discontent they may say'.

Real Aims

'As I think I understand Mr Jinnah's mind', concluded Mr Rajagopalachari, 'I make bold to say that what he desires is a fuller amplitude for the so-called Muslim provinces to work out their progress without being hampered by a Central Government working under conditions necessitated by the composition of India's population and the play of political forces at such a Centre. Surely he can ask for many things other than the cutting up of India into two parts based on a medieval conception in order to attain this laudable desire'.

50. 'A Baffling Situation': Mahatma Gandhi's Article on Jinnah's Plan to Divide India, 1 April 1940

Harijan, 6 April 1940.

A question has been put to me:

Do you intend to start general civil disobedience although Quaid-e-Azam Jinnah has declared war against Hindus and has got the Muslim League to pass a resolution favouring vivisection of India into two? If you do, what becomes of your formula that there is no Swaraj without communal unity?

I admit that the step taken by the Muslim League at Lahore creates a baffling situation. But I do not regard it so baffling as to make civil disobedience an impossibility. Supposing that the Congress is reduced to a hopeless minority, it will still be open to it, indeed it may be its duty, to resort to civil disobedience. The struggle will not be against the majority, it will be against the foreign ruler. If the struggle succeeds, the fruits thereof will be reaped as well as the Congress as by the opposing majority. Let me, however, say in parenthesis that, until the conditions I have mentioned for starting civil disobedience are fulfilled, civil disobedience cannot be started in any case. In the present instance there is nothing to prevent the imperial rulers from declaring their will in unequivocal terms that henceforth India will govern herself according to her own will, not that of the rulers as has happened hitherto. Neither the Muslim League nor any other party can oppose such a declaration. For the Muslims will be entitled to dictate their own terms. Unless the rest of India wishes to engage in internal fratricide, the others will have to submit to Muslim dictation if the Muslims will resort to it. I know no non-violent method of compelling the obedience of eight crores of Muslims to the will of the rest of India, however powerful a majority the rest may represent. The Muslims must have the same right of self-determination that the rest of India has. We are at present a joint family. Any member may claim a division.

Thus, so far as I am concerned, my proposition that there is no swaraj without communal unity holds as good today as when I first enunciated it in 1919.

But civil disobedience stands on a different footing. It is open even to one single person to offer it, if he feels the call. It will not be offered for the Congress alone or for any particular group. Whatever benefit accrues from it will belong to the whole of India. The injury, if there is any, will belong only to the civil disobedience party.

But I do not believe that Muslims, when it comes to a matter of actual decision, will ever want vivisection. Their good sense will prevent them. Their self-interest will deter them. Their religion will forbid the obvious suicide which the partition would mean. The 'two nations' theory is an untruth. The vast majority of Muslims of India are converts to Islam or are descendants of converts. They did not become a separate nation as soon as they became converts. A Bengali Muslim speaks the same tongue that a Bengali Hindu does, eats the same food, has the same amusements as his Hindu neighbour. They dress alike. I have often found it difficult to distinguish by outward sign between a Bengali Hindu and a Bengali Muslim. The same phenomenon is observable more or less in the South among the poor who constitute the masses of India. When I first met the late Sir Ali Imam I did not know that he was not a Hindu. His speech, his dress, his manners, his food were the same as of the majority of the Hindus in whose midst I found him. His name alone betrayed him. Not even that with Quaid-e-Azam Jinnah. For his name could be that of any Hindu. When I first met him, I did not know that he was a Muslim. I came to know his religion when I had his full name given to me. His nationality was written in his face and manner. The reader will be surprised to know that for days, if not months, I used to think of the late Vithalbhai Patel as a Muslim as he used to sport a beard and a Turkish cap. The Hindu law of inheritance governs many Muslim groups. Sir Mohammed Iqbal used to speak with pride of his Brahmanical descent. Iqbal and Kitchlew are names common to Hindus and Muslims. Hindus and Muslims of India are not two nations. Those whom God has made one, man will never be able to divide.

And is Islam such an exclusive religion as Quaid e-Azam would have it? Is there nothing in common between Islam and Hinduism or any other religion? Or is Islam merely an enemy of Hinduism? Were the Ali Brothers and their associates wrong when they hugged Hindus as blood brothers and saw so much in common between the two? I am not now thinking of individual Hindus who may have disillusioned the Muslim friends. Quaid-e-Azam has, however, raised a fundamental issue. This is his thesis:

> It is extremely difficult to appreciate why our Hindu friends fail to understand the real nature of Islam and Hinduism. They are not religions in the strict sense of the word, but are, in fact, different and distinct social orders, and it is a dream that the Hindus and Muslims can ever evolve a common nationality. This misconception of one Indian nation has gone far beyond the limits and is the cause of most of our troubles and will lead India to destruction if we fail to revise our notions in time.
>
> The Hindus and Muslims have two different religious philosophies, social customs, literature. They neither intermarry, nor dine together and indeed, they belong to two different civilizations which are based mainly on conflicting ideas and conceptions. Their aspects on life and of life are different. It is quite clear that Hindus and Mussalmans derive their inspiration from different sources of history. They have different epics, their heroes are different, and they have different episodes. Very often the hero of one is a foe of the other and, likewise, their victories and defeats overlap. To yoke together two such nations under a single State, one as a numerical minority and the other as majority, must lead to growing discontent and final destruction of any fabric that may be so built up for the government of such a State.

He does not say some Hindus are bad; he says Hindus as such have nothing in common with Muslims. I make bold to say that he and those who think like him are rendering no service to Islam; they are misinterpreting the message inherent in the very word Islam. I say this because I feel deeply hurt over what is now going on in the name of the Muslim League. I should be failing in my duty, if I did not warn the Muslims of India against the untruth that is being propagated amongst them. This warning is a duty because I have faithfully served them in their hour of need and because Hindu–Muslim unity has been and is my life's mission.

51. 'My Position'—Mahatma Gandhi's Reply to Liaquat Ali Khan's Statement to the Press

Harijan, 13 April 1940.

Nawabzada Liaqat Ali Khan has, in his criticism of my reply to Quaid-e-Azam, put some questions which I gladly answer: I must adhere to my statement that I have never spoken to anybody on the communal question as a Hindu. I have no authority. Whenever I have spoken to anybody I have spoken as a Congressman, but often only as an individual. No Congressman, not even the President, can always speak as a representative. Big things have always been transacted on this planet by persons belonging to different organizations coming together and talking informally in their non-representative capacity. I fear that even the answer I am about to give must be taken as representing nobody but myself. In the present instance I have reason to say that probably I do not represent any single member of the Working Committee. I am answering as a peacemaker, as a friend (and may I say, brother) of the Mussalmans.

As a man of non-violence I cannot forcibly resist the proposed partition if the Muslims of India really insist upon it. But I can never be a willing party to the vivisection. I would employ every non-violent means to prevent it. For it means the undoing of centuries of work done by numberless Hindus and Muslims to live together as one nation. Partition means a patent untruth. My whole soul rebels against the idea that Hinduism and Islam represent two antagonistic cultures and doctrines. To assent to such a doctrine is for me denial of God. For I believe with my whole soul that the God of the Koran is also the God of the Gita, and that we are all, no matter by what name designated, children of the same God. I must rebel against the idea that millions of Indians who were Hindus the other day changed their nationality on adopting Islam as their religion.

But that is my belief. I cannot thrust it down the throats of the Muslims who think that they are a different nation. I refuse, however, to believe that the eight crores of Muslims will say that they have nothing in common with their Hindu and other brethren. Their mind can only be known by a referendum duly made to them on that clear issue. The contemplated Constituent Assembly can easily decide the question. Naturally on an issue such as this there can be no arbitration. It is purely and simply a matter of self-determination. I know of no other conclusive method of ascertaining the mind of the eight crores of Muslims.

But the contemplated Constituent Assembly will have the framing of a constitution as its main function. It cannot do this until the communal question is settled.

I still believe that there can be no Swaraj by non-violent means without communal unity. And eight crores of Muslims can certainly bar the way to peaceful freedom.

If then I still talk of civil disobedience, it is because I believe that the Muslim masses want freedom as much as the rest of the population of this country. And assuming that they do not, civil disobedience will be a powerful means of educating public opinion whether Muslim, Hindu or any other. It will also be an education of world opinion. But I will not embark upon it unless I am, as far as is humanly possible, sure that non-violence will be observed both in spirit and in the letter. I hope the Nawabzada has no difficulty in believing that whatever is gained by civil disobedience will be gained for all. When India gets the power to frame her own constitution, the Muslims will surely have a decisive voice in shaping their own future. It will not be, cannot be, decided by the vote of the majority.

Lastly, I suggest to the Nawabzada that he wrote in haste the lines about the President of the Congress. For they are contrary to the history of our own times. And he was equally in haste in suggesting that 'the sole objective of the Congress under Mr Gandhi's fostering care has been the revival of Hinduism and the imposition of Hindu culture on all and sundry'. My own objective is not the issue in the terrible indictment. The objective of the Congress is wholly political. Nothing is to be gained by making statements that are incapable of proof. So far as my own objective is concerned my life is an open book. I claim to represent all the cultures, for my religion, whatever it may be called, demands the fulfilment of all cultures. I am at home wherever I go, for I regard all religions with the same respect as my own.

52. Jawaharlal Nehru's Views on the Demand for Pakistan, 13 April 1940

Hindustan Times, 15 April 1940; *SWJN*, Vol. XI, p. 17.

All the old problems, associated with the so-called communal question, namely, separate electorates, composite cabinets and communal representations in different services pale into insignificance before the latest stand taken up by the Muslim League leaders at Lahore. There can be no more Hindu–Muslim problem that the Congress can talk with the League, because the latter's Lahore resolution precludes any such talks. There have been complaints in the press that the Congress leaders had not successfully negotiated with the League. The Lahore resolution has shown clearly the mentality of the League leaders and is an answer to such complaints.

The whole problem has taken a new complexion and there is no question of settlement or negotiation now. The knot that is before us is incapable of being untied by settlement; it needs cutting open. It needs a major operation. Without mincing words, I want to say that we will have nothing to do with this mad scheme. I do not know what the consequences to the country would be. Who can say?

The League is not interested in the Indian nation but in something else, and hence there can be no common meeting ground between the Congress and the League. On the other hand, it has become the clear duty of the Congress to fight out the League and its scheme of denationalizing India.

However, I welcome this stand of the League leadership in as much as it clears all misunderstanding that might have prevailed in some minds, and shows up the League leadership in its true colours. The latest attitude has simplified the issue without solving it.

Where has the League leadership drifted? There was a time when Sir Mohammad Iqbal, a prominent Muslim League leader, sang of the common motherland with pride. But today the League leadership feels itself to be an alien in this country, and thinks it has no roots in it. Look at the picture presented by the League leadership today, with its contempt for the country and its hymn of hatred. It has at last unmasked itself and left no room for misunderstanding. We will, of course, oppose the partition scheme, but our goal is clear and we will march on our path. A struggle is inevitable now.

53. 'Hindu Muslim Tangle': An Article by Mahatma Gandhi, 29 April 1940

Harijan, 4 May 1940.

The partition proposal has altered the face of the Hindu Muslim problem. I have called it an untruth. There can be no compromise with it. At the same time I have said that, if the eight crores of Muslims desire it no power on earth can prevent it, notwithstanding opposition, violent or non-violent. It cannot come by honourable agreement.

That is the political aspect of it. But what about religious and the moral which are greater than the political? For at the bottom of the cry for partition is the belief that Islam is an exclusive brotherhood, and anti-Hindu. Whether it is against other religions it is not stated. The newspaper cuttings in which partition is preached describe Hindus as practically untouchables. Nothing good can come out of Hindus or Hinduism. To live under Hindu rule is a sin. Even joint

Hindu–Muslim rule is not to be thought of. The cuttings show that Hindus and Muslims are already at war with one another and that they must prepare for the final tussle.

Time was when Hindus thought that Muslims were the natural enemies of Hindus. But as is the case with Hinduism, ultimately it comes to terms with the enemy and makes friends with him. The process had not been completed. As if nemesis had overtaken Hinduism, the Muslim League started the same game and taught that there could be no blending of the two cultures. In this connection I have just read a booklet by Shri Atulanand Chakrabarti which shows that ever since the contact of Islam with Hinduism there has been an attempt on the part of the best minds of both to see the good points of each other, and to emphasize inherent similarities rather than seeming dissimilarities. The author has shown Islamic history in India in a favourable light. If he has stated the truth and nothing but the truth, it is a revealing booklet which all Hindus and Muslims may read with profit. He has secured a very favourable and reasoned preface from Sir Shafaat Ahmed Khan and several other Muslim testimonials. If the evidence collected there reflects the true evolution of Islam in India, then the partition propaganda is anti-Islamic.

Religion binds man to God and man to man. Does Islam bind Muslim only to Muslim and antagonize the Hindu? Was the message of the Prophet peace only for and between Muslims and war against Hindus or non-Muslims? Are eight crores of Muslims to be fed with this which I can only describe as poison? Those who are instilling this poison into the Muslim mind are rendering the greatest disservice to Islam. I know that it is not Islam. I have lived with and among Muslims not for one day but closely and almost uninterruptedly for twenty years. Not one Muslim taught me that Islam was an anti-Hindu religion.

54. Mahatma Gandhi: 'Two Parties', 11 June 1940

Harijan, 15 June 1940.

Private and public appeals are being made to me to call all parties together and arrive at a common agreement, and then, they say, we shall get what we want from Great Britain. These good friends forget one central fact. The Congress, which professes to speak for India and wants unadulterated Independence, cannot strike a common measure of agreement with those who do not. To act otherwise would be to betray its trust. In the nature of things, therefore, there can be no 'all parties conference' unless all have a common purpose.

The British Government would not ask for a common agreement, if they recognized anyone party to be strong enough to take delivery. The Congress, it must be admitted, has not that strength today. It has come to its present position in the face of opposition. If it does not weaken and has enough patience, it will develop sufficient strength to take delivery. It is an illusion created by ourselves that we must come to an agreement with all parties before we can make any progress.

There is only one democratic elected political organization, i.e. the Congress. All the others are self-appointed, or elected on a sectional basis. The Muslim League is an organization which, like the Congress, is popularly elected. But it is frankly communal and wants to divide India into two parts, one Hindu and the other Muslim. I read an appeal by a Muslim Leaguer suggesting that the British Government should come to terms with the Muslims and depend upon Muslim aid. That would be one way of settling the question but also of perpetuating British rule. The Hindu Mahasabha will no doubt want favoured treatment for Hindus including Hindu States.

Thus for the present purpose there are only two parties—the Congress and those who side with the Congress, and the parties who do not. Between the two there is no meeting ground without the one or the other surrendering its purpose. The other parties must be presumed to be as constant in their purpose as the Congress claims to be in its. Therefore there is a stalemate. But the stalemate is only apparent. An agreement independently of evolving a common demand the Congress must seek and has always sought. It is the process of conversion. Its non-violence forbids the Congress from standing aloof and riding the high horse as the opponents say. On the contrary it has to woo all parties, disarm suspicion and create trust in its *bona fides.* This it can only do when it has cleaned its own stables. The process may take time. That time must be given. It will be no waste. But if the Congress loses hope and faith and comes to the conclusion that it must surrender its original position for the purpose of getting a common measure of agreement, it will cease to be the power it is. Today it is the sheet-anchor of India's hope and faith. It will be well with it, if it refuses to move away from its moorings, whether it is in a minority or a majority.

Sevagram, 11–6–40

55. Mahatma Gandhi Regarding Sikhs Joining the Army

(a) Master Tara Singh's Letter to Maulana Abul Kalam Azad Regarding Sikhs Joining the Army

Harijan, 29 September 1940.

Amritsar, 9 August 1940

Dear Maulana Sahib,

I feel it is impossible to ignore reality of war. Independence is synonymous with power. Only nations that are fully organized and have a disciplined army are able to preserve their independence. We who are seeking to secure independence cannot afford to neglect the opportunity which the war offers of entering the army and learning both the meaning of sacrifice, unity, command and obedience and art of offence and defence.

The fate of nations is in the balance. I trust you will agree with me, as we claim to be arbiters of our own future, that we must do all we can to help the mobilization of our manpower and our resources, with one object only that, whatever the result of war, we may be able to attain and maintain independence.

I am, therefore, of opinion that we should not only do nothing to prevent recruitment but demand that India should be in a position to produce the modern armament in factories under Indian control only. To leave the responsibility of defence to Britain is to accept continuance of dependence.

It is Britain's interest, at the moment, to prepare India for her own defence. England is no more in a position to spare any force for Indian Defence. It is a rare opportunity for us to raise India from a position of helplessness to a position to be able to help herself. It is the interest of England to defeat her enemies by raising India to a position which England could never have contemplated before. It is the interest of India to make the most of the opportunity which circumstances have created.

It is my considered opinion that, even if the Congress is compelled to have recourse to Civil Disobedience to exert moral pressure on the Government, it should do nothing to prevent recruitment to the army but confine its activities to spheres which do not infringe on the morale of our troops or dissipate our powers of defence.

In our present preoccupation of wresting power from Britain, we must not close our eyes to dangers internal and external to which our country would be exposed if England fails in the war. We must prepare ourselves for all contingencies. No other preparation can take place of an Indian army, offered by Indians, ready to meet all eventualities.

I am writing to you to make the position of my community and my own clear. I am definitely of the opinion that Sikhs should join the Army in as large a number as possible in the interest of their Motherland and their own. They can only then maintain their position in any Government. I cannot be a party to anything which is likely to weaken the position of my community. To be strong is the essence of independence.

In my anxiety to help the Congress and removing the last obstacle in the path of recruitment to the army I made a conditional offer to provide a hundred thousand recruits in case a Congress-Government agreement was reached. The chances of an agreement appear to be far from encouraging, while the world situation is worsening. I therefore, see no alternative but to support full and free recruitment of the Sikhs to the army. I am, therefore, inclined to give public expression to these views, unless otherwise advised by you and other friends.

Need I say that in all other matters you can rely on my full co-operation and support including Civil Disobedience?

I may add here that I have information that indiscipline is spreading in the Sikh army. There have been desertions and disobedience. Innocent people are suffering under wrong notions. Some of the deserters from the army have reached villages in the Punjab where they are committing murders and dacoities and are proving a terror to the countryside. This has alarmed us, and immediate action has to be taken. If we start civil disobedience without positively advising the army not to participate in such disobedience, the civil disobedience is apt to turn into military disobedience, which means bloodshed and mutiny. Under these circumstances civil disobedience will fail, and impending anarchy will be suppressed by the British with a strong hand, thus reversing the course of the progress of India.

I seek your advice and that of Mahatma Gandhiji, at this critical juncture, to whom I am sending a copy of this letter. I know Mahatmaji's views on non-violence, but I still hope he can give me valuable advice at this critical juncture.

Yours sincerely,
(Master) Tarasingh

To Mahatma Gandhiji for information with the request that the Mahatmaji may kindly give advice immediately. Tarasingh.

(b) Mahatma Gandhi's Letter to Master Tara Singh, 16 August 1940

Harijan, 29 September 1940.

Dear Sardarji,

I am glad you have sent me a copy of your letter to Maulana Saheb. As I have told you, in my opinion, you have nothing in common with the Congress nor the Congress with you. You believe in the rule of the sword; the Congress does not. You have all the time 'my community' in mind. The Congress has no community but the whole nation. Your civil disobedience is purely a branch of violence. I am quite clear in my mind that being in the Congress you weaken 'your community' and weaken the Congress. With your mentality, you have to offer your services to the British Government unconditionally and look to it for the protection of the rights of 'your community'. You do not suppose for one moment that the British will take your recruits on your conditions. They would commit suicide if they did. You have to be either fully nationalist or frankly communal and therefore, dependent upon the British or other foreign power.

This is the considered opinion of one who loves you and the Sikhs as he loves himself and in reality more. For I have ceased to love myself.

Yours sincerely,
M.K. Gandhi

Sevagram, 16–8–40.

E.   FORWARD BLOC, LIBERALS, RADICAL DEMOCRATIC PEOPLE'S PARTY, JUSTICE PARTY AND INDEPENDENT LABOUR PARTY

56. Subhas Bose's Editorial 'Towards Communal Unity' in *Forward Bloc*, 24 February 1940

Sisir Kumar Bose (ed.), *Crossroads: The Works of Subhas Chandra Bose, 1938–1940*, Calcutta, 1981 (2nd edition), pp. 285–6.

The annual session of the Congress is upon us and much depends upon what will transpire at Ramgarh when the Congress meets there. The Leftists will be in a hopeless minority in that Congress—thanks to the enforced absence of Bengal and to the drive against the Leftists conducted by the Congress High Command throughout the country during the past year. Bengal delegates, who would in normal circumstances, have attended the annual session of the Congress need not feel sorry for their enforced absence. Even if they could be present in full strength at Ramgarh, they would not be able to influence the decisions of the Congress. The heavens will not fall if the Leftists do not bother about the Ramgarh Congress. In fact, it may be better if they could help to convert the Ramgarh Congress into a Rightist Congress.

This year, more important than what will transpire inside the Congress is what will happen outside the Congress pandal. The Bihar Provincial Kisan Sabha has given the call for a mammoth peasants' rally to be attended by at least two hundred thousand peasants from the neighbouring districts. An All India Anti-Compromise Conference is also going to meet at Ramgarh about the same time as the annual session of the Congress. If this Conference proves to be a success, it may eclipse the Congress in its political importance. In any case, it will bury once for all, the talks and the efforts at a compromise between the Congress High Command and British Imperialism.

It is imperatively necessary for the political advancement of the country that the Congress High Command should be forced to give up their attempt to arrive at a compromise with British Imperialism. When this is done, there will be but one path open to the Congress—namely, the path of uncompromising struggle leading to Purna Swaraj. All those who stand for the Independence of India will then be obliged to launch a national struggle.

The call for a national struggle will be an appeal to all anti-imperialist elements in the country and to all patriotic men and women. When the bugle is sounded, all those who hunger after freedom will naturally fall in line and resume freedom's march regardless of their religious faith and denomination.

When people become 'comrades-in-arms' in the struggle for liberty, a new *esprit d'corps* will develop—and along with it, a new outlook, a new perspective and a new vision. When this revolution comes about, Indians will be a changed people and a revolutionary people at that. It will then be easy for them to solve many of the questions which to-day appear difficult to solve.

Under present conditions, it appears well-nigh impossible to destroy the canker of communalism and foster all-round nationalism in our public life. But how easy this task will become, once we develop a revolutionary mentality on a nation-wide scale.

Communalism will go only when the communal mentality goes. To destroy communalism is, therefore, the task of all those Indians—Muslims, Sikhs, Hindus, Christians, etc., who have transcended the communal outlook and have developed a genuine nationalist mentality. He undoubtedly has a genuine nationalist mentality who wages a war for national freedom.

In every fight a special responsibility devolves on the vanguard of the army. In the war against communalism, a special responsibility similarly falls on the shoulders of the front-fighters. It is their task to lay the foundation of intercommunal—i.e., national unity, Hindus and Muslims, Sikhs and Christians who fight for India's Independence must be specially commissioned to solve the communal problem. Once they solve this problem and announce it to the whole country—the atmosphere will automatically change and the death-knell of communalism will be sounded. If the front-fighters show the way, the nation will ultimately follow.

Let us not therefore, sit with folded hands waiting for the day when the High Command of the Congress and of the Muslim League will bring about a solution of the communal problem. Let us rather see to it that the real fighters for freedom get together and solve this problem. If they succeed, the first and the most formidable hurdle will be overcome and the general public—the entire nation—will follow in their footsteps. Those who love freedom and will die for it can solve the communal problem more easily than anybody else. Forward, therefore, all front-fighters and fulfil the mission that to-day is yours.

57. Subhas Chandra Bose's Views on the Bengal Provincial Congress Committee and Hindu Mahasabha Pact, 3 March 1940

Sisir Kumar Bose (ed.), *Crossroads: The Works of Subhas Chandra Bose, 1938–40*, Calcutta, 1981 (2nd edition), pp. 295–7.

The annual All India Conference of the Hindu Mahasabha was held in Calcutta towards the close of last year. As a conference it was a great success and it afforded considerable satisfaction to the Mahasabha leaders who began to hope that their organization would forge ahead in Bengal. At that time, it was whispered about that the conference was merely a preparation for the coming Municipal Election in Calcutta and subsequent events have not belied that report.

With a view to promoting the civic welfare and advancement of Calcutta and in order to avoid unnecessary friction and clash over the elections, the Bengal Provincial Congress Committee and the Bengal Hindu Mahasabha arrived at an understanding through their respective representatives. The terms of the understanding were duly published in the press.

The basis of the understanding was that the elections would be run in the name of the Joint Congress Corporation Election Board and that all those who would be elected would join the Congress Municipal Association. The Congress Corporation Election Board would co-opt six nominees of the Hindu Mahasabha and the Committee that would select candidates would have an equal number of representatives from both the organizations. But the elections would not be run separately by the Hindu Mahasabha nor would there be a separate Hindu Mahasabha Bloc in the Corporation. If any communal question came up before the Corporation in future, the Congress Municipal Association would not make it a party question but would allow liberty to the members to vote as they desired.

The afore-mentioned agreement did not last long. Differences arose over the selection of candidates and the agreement had to be abandoned.

Prior to the above understanding with the Hindu Mahasabha, I had made a public appeal to all organizations interested in the elections and particularly to the Hindu Mahasabha and the Muslim League, asking for their co-operation in the domain of civic affairs, in spite of any differences that might exist on other questions. I also addressed letters to several organizations in this connection. We naturally felt gratified when the Hindu Mahasabha responded in the above manner.

According to our reading of the situation, the temporary agreement was possible because of the pro-nationalist elements in the Hindu Mahasabha. The agreement fell through because the diehard communal elements in the Hindu Mahasabha who were throughout opposed to any understanding with the Congress, ultimately got the upper hand.

There has been a country-wide propaganda against us because of our understanding with the Hindu Mahasabha over civic affairs. Much of this propaganda is mendacious, while some of it is based on misunderstanding. We are convinced that the basis of the understanding was a sound one and was fully consonant with Congress principles. If the understanding had been implemented in due course, the principles of nationalism would have triumphed and not those of communalism. Unfortunately, to some politicians and political agents we are the *bete noire* and any stick is good enough to beat us with. But we desire to assert even at this late hour that the basis on which we arrived at a temporary understanding with the Hindu Mahasabha is a basis on which a similar understanding could be arrived at with any other organization.

The New Calcutta Municipal Act which is the result of the recent Amending Bill and according to which elections have just been held, has created a new situation for Calcutta which is fraught with danger. If the Indian members of the Corporation, both Hindu and Muslim, do not join hands, then the Corporation will pass into the hands of Britishers. A handful of Britishers will begin to dominate the Corporation as they have been dominating the Bengal Assembly.

We tried to avert this calamity by seeking the cooperation of the Hindu Mahasabha in civic affairs while adhering to Congress principles. We have been disappointed. Moreover, the tactics employed by some Hindu Mahasabha leaders for whom we had great personal regard, as also by some Hindu Mahasabha workers in connection with the elections, have caused us pain and sorrow. The Hindu Mahasabha did not fight a clean fight.

What is more, the Hindu Mahasabha candidates included men who had tried their level best to break the Congress Municipal Association and to that end had formed the United Party in the Corporation in cooperation with British and Nominated Groups of Councillors. Some of them have been re-elected and one could easily anticipate how they would behave in future. The Hindu Mahasabha has given evidence of greater desire to down the Congress than to save the Corporation from British domination.

It remains to be seen if any other Indian group in the Corporation will show more keenness to resist British domination than to fight the Congress.

The above action of the Hindu Mahasabha is the beginning of a new phase in its history. It has come forward to play a political role and to make a bid for the political leadership of Bengal, or at least of the Hindus of Bengal who have been the backbone of Nationalism in this country. With a real Hindu Mahasabha, we have no quarrel and no conflict. But with a political Hindu Mahasabha, that seeks to replace the Congress in the public life of Bengal and for that purpose has already taken the offensive against us, a fight is inevitable. This fight has just begun.

58. 'The Way to Communal Harmony': An Article by R.C. Das

Indian Social Reformer, 3 February 1940.

The Benares Fellowship is an inter-religious and inter-racial organization of eight years standing. Its chief object is to promote mutual understanding and goodwill among persons of different sects and communities by sharing the views and experience of one another and by encouraging social and intellectual fellowship through personal contact. In some of its meetings during the past few years, the Fellowship, in association with others in sympathy with its object has discussed the question of communal peace both from a religious and practical standpoint. Some of the views and important conclusions are here collected and presented in the form of a brief statement. An earnest hope is entertained that the public, especially those leaders in different communities who feel concerned about the communal situation in the country, will seriously ponder over the decisions of the Fellowship and see whether they supply any light to the problems that oppress us.

Causes of Communal Tension

In the opinion of the Fellowship these are many and complex and some very ancient. Many of them lie deep down in the human heart; others are not so fundamental but are due to the exigencies of times or related to narrow self-interest. Though the members of the Fellowship are not unanimous on every question, the following, they believe, are some of the root causes of communal troubles:

1. Social-religious viz. Untouchability on the part of Hindu and cow sacrifice on the part of Moslems. On account of caste a peculiar social structure of Hindu–Mussalmans have always been regarded as untouchable though they have ruled India. This Hindu treatment of Moslems has gnawed upon the susceptibilities of the latter and when opportunities have arrived the bitterness has expressed itself in violent thought, word and deed. Similarly, Hindus who have regarded the cow as a very useful and sacred animal and have worshipped her have seen her cruelly slaughtered throughout centuries and are no longer ready to tolerate it. Demonstrative religion, like Holi and Moharram and other festival processions and music provide occasions for misunderstanding, ending not infrequently in actual clashes and riots.

2. Lack of understanding of a fundamental unity of at least the main religions which are regarded as rivals. The similarities between religions are not brought out and

appreciated; differences are usually harped upon and emphasized; hence a jarring spirit arises in men's minds and suspicions grow.

3. The main cause of communal tension in modern India has recently developed and is political one viz. the Communal Electorate and the Communal Award which has aggravated communal consciousness and selfishness and for which the British Imperial Government is responsible.

4. Communal troubles in India are, from another standpoint, part of the world-madness in seeking power, wealth and prestige at the cost of the weak, unskilled and the ignorant. The statesmen of the world want worldly success based on expansion of their empire and exploitation of weaker races. Indian riots are a trifle compared to the gigantic world preparation for mutual destruction.

5. The Pandits of the Hindus and Mullahs among Moslems are to blame for the fight between the Hindus and Mussalmans. By false or ill-informed propaganda they fan ill-feeling and trouble to gain their personal ends.

6. Again, rioting is a very human symptom and religion is only a cloak. Mere 'difference' of any kind is often enough cause for a quarrel. A hundred years ago there were serious riots in London and other English cities.

7. The Police have sometimes not been quite impartial in discharging their duties. They have taken sides and thus a situation that could have been brought under control easily, has been allowed to grow serious. The Congress Governments have in this respect a solemn responsibility in moulding the old material and weapon with new ideals and principles and in making the Police the true servants of the public.

The Remedy

So much regarding the causes. The Fellowship suggest and offer the following remedies as calculated to improve the situation in the country.

1. The communal electorate and the communal award must be abolished. This is the duty of the Imperial Government. The country must make a united demand for it. Merit and unselfish service (appropriate qualification) alone not religion should be the criteria for distinction, leadership and office. Meanwhile good men of all communities can combine and frustrate the evil effects of communal election by choosing through mutual understanding those men as their representative who would take up a non-communal stand in all matters.

2. Cow slaughter by Moslems, one of the potent cause of ill-feeling and fighting, could not be stopped by agitation or legislation. That would merely aggravate the situation. It has to be recognized the poor man's staple food for a larger number of Moslems, just as the flesh of other animals and fish are the chief diet of millions of Hindus. The habit of eating cow's flesh might disappear gradually if Hindus, instead of using force, sent a friendly mission among Moslems preaching in a peaceful and persuasive manner the unsuitability of cow's meat in India. In the same way, Moslems could not force Hindus to give up caste and to treat all Moslems as touchable fellowmen in as much as caste formed an essential part of their very complex socio-religious order. Hindus could be enlightened and persuaded only by reason and friendship.

3. Right kind of education and re-writing of History showing many facts of Hindu–Moslem fraternity.

(a) A strict censure of all news regarding riots and Hindu–Moslem relations, restraining gossip and sensation.

(b) On the apprehension of any breach of the public peace, and, not after the mischief has been done, all regular goondas and criminally disposed persons might be arrested and locked up as is done with political detenues.

These three remedies are obviously the special duty of the Government and the police.

4. The State should be reconstructed on the basis of broad socialistic principles so that all persons will find employment and there will be no opportunity for the poor and unemployed to play into the hands of the devil.

5. A few minor solutions suggested are:

(i) The desirability of a uniform external life doing away with the distinctive marks of a Hindu or a Moslem (ii) Suppression of much of what is popularly known as religion. These will go some way to cement friendship. But, however much the exterior of life might be improved, the real trouble and the true remedy both lie inside the heart of man. We need more of love and fellowship, the higher religion which touches the springs of life. The disease being socio-religious as much as politico-economic, the cure must also be the purification of our hearts, convictions and sentiments. To stop consequences motives must be regulated.

6. Compilation and use in all schools, of text books dealing with the common elements of truth in different religions. This will produce citizens who will have a less exclusive outlook and a more tolerant attitude.

7. The evolution of a comprehensive casteless social order among Hindus according to ancient Indian tradition is an important and urgent need.

8. Toleration and respect for another's religion in spite of differences must be fostered by men of goodwill everywhere and by all means.

9. The remedies that proved successful in England in stamping out riots and quarrels might be useful in India too—viz. provision of social amenities and economic relief, such as Boys' clubs, Football Teams, the cinema, cheap transport, excursions, the Radio, Unemployment Insurance schemes, Increased salaries and wages, etc. In India, common dinners, meals, Reading Rooms might also be encouraged.

10. In cities throughout India Unity Boards and Peace Communities with branches in the villages might be usefully started. And in this work of reconciliation the services of those students who are less tainted with the communal virus might be effectively requisitioned.

11. To be practical and impressive in the work of peacemaking, small local areas should be selected for experiments.

12. The Provincial and Central Government might usefully and wisely take note of the following important matters in handling the communal situation in the country.

(a) They should issue with guarantees and assurance a statement on Fundamental Rights for the minority communities in India as to (a) Profession and (b) practice of faith. The majority community should extend hearty and public consent. This will allay suspicions and fears which are natural.

(b) General Principles and not local varying customs, should be followed by Government with regard to the question of cow-killing, music, processions and festivals etc.

(c) Special Police and not Punitive Police recruited locally should be entrusted with the preservation of peace in a disturbed area.

(d) Common and mutual observance of all the chief communal holidays both by Government and the public.

(e) Positive toleration and respect for religion and not indifference or negative neutrality or much less suppression of religion (unless it is immoral) to be exercised by Government.

(f) A common Civil Law—such as in marriage which will indirectly and steadily make for unity and concord between the communities.

(g) Impartial preservation and promotion, both by Government and the Public, of different cultures and languages.

59. Subhas Bose: Congress and Communal Organizations

Editorial in the *Forward Bloc*, 4 May 1940; Sisir Kumar Bose (ed.), *Crossroads: The Works of Subhas Chandra Bose, 1938–1940*, Calcutta, 1981 (2nd edition), pp. 308–10.

There was a time, not long ago, when prominent leaders of the Congress could be members and leaders of communal organizations like the Hindu Mahasabha and the Muslim League. In those days the communalism of such communal organizations was of a subdued character. Hence Lala Lajpat Rai could be a leader of the Hindu Mahasabha and the Ali Brothers could be leaders of the Muslim League. In Bengal, an ex-President of the Bengal Provincial Congress Committee and of the Bengal Provincial Conference, like Moulana Akram Khan, could be a leader of the Muslim League. But in recent times, circumstances have changed. These communal organizations have become more communal than before. As a reaction to this, the Indian National Congress has put into its Constitution a clause to the effect that no member of a communal organization like the Hindu Mahasabha or the Muslim League can be a member of an elective Committee of the Congress.

Since the Congress imposed this ban, a tendency has developed among certain circles to regard these communal organizations as untouchable. While trying to discard social untouchability, we are, as it were, encouraging political untouchability. Consequently, whenever an attempt is made to bring these organizations nearer to the Congress, many people are scandalized. This happened in the case of the Bengal Provincial Congress Committee when it attempted an understanding with the Hindu Mahasabha and later on, with the Muslim League, in the domain of civic affairs.

Two attempts were made at a rapprochement with the Hindu Mahasabha. The first was made towards the end of February last, prior to the Calcutta Municipal Elections. The second was made about the middle of April (last month), after the General Election and on the eve of the Alderman Election.

The basis of the first agreement was that the elections would be run in the name of the Congress alone and that after the elections, all the successful candidates would join the Congress Municipal Association. The election of candidates would be made by the representatives of the Hindu Mahasabha and the Congress jointly and the Congress Election Board would co-opt a number of representatives of the Hindu Mahasabha. This agreement broke down ultimately over the selection of candidates and in consequence thereof, the Congress and the Hindu Mahasabha fought a battle royal at the polls.

Judged in the light of Congress principles, the above understanding was unassailable. Nevertheless, a great deal of prejudice and resentment was in evidence not only among Muslims but also among orthodox Congressmen, including Gandhiites when the news was published. One can account for this only on the theory that of late we have been developing a species of political untouchability.

The second understanding with the Hindu Mahasabha broke down on the night of the 16th April at about 10 P.M. over the selection of five candidates for the posts of Aldermen to be elected by the Councillors in a body. After this final breach, negotiations between the Congress and the Muslim League were started at 11 P.M. and they culminated in an agreement at about 2 A.M. in the morning.

The agreement took place over the question of Aldermen and Mayor. If all goes well, the agreement will be extended to other municipal problems. And with good luck, the scope and sphere of such an understanding may one day be enlarged so as to embrace much larger questions concerning the province and the country.

Thanks to the Hindu Mahasabha and to papers like the *Amrita Bazar Patrika* that have suddenly developed a rabid communalism, communal venom is being emitted from day to day, with a view to poisoning the minds of the Hindus in Bengal and elsewhere. But all attempts to mislead the Hindus have so far failed. Two mammoth meetings of the citizens of Calcutta were held at Shraddhananda Park and Deshbandhu Park recently, for obtaining the verdict of the Calcutta public on the above Congress-League Pact. At the first meeting, at a modest estimate twenty thousand people were present and at the second meeting thirty thousand. At both meetings, a unanimous vote of confidence was given us. Nevertheless, one cannot ignore the fact that a certain number of communally-minded Hindus are furious over the above understanding.

We, on our part, do not regard the communal organizations as untouchable. On the contrary, we hold that the Congress should try continuously to woo them over to its side. During the last three years, repeated attempts have been made to bring about a rapprochement between the Congress and the Muslim League. At a certain stage, the writer, then President of the Congress, met Mr Jinnah, the President of the Muslim League, and several interviews took place. At that time, the attempt failed, though the writer had been blessed by the Congress Working Committee and by Mahatma Gandhi. Those who had not objected to that attempt, which failed ultimately, now strongly object to the present attempt, because it has succeeded. Can prejudice go any further?

We regard the present agreement with the Muslim League as a great achievement not in its actuality, but in its potentiality. During the last three years, we have been groping in the dark, but without success. Every time we have come up against a dead wall of communal prejudice and passion and we have been frustrated in our efforts. This time we have broken through the wall and through the fissure, a ray of light has poured in. There is now some hope that we may ultimately succeed in solving a problem which has proved well nigh insoluble to many. Great achievements are often born out of small beginnings.

60.   Different National Leaders' Views on the Pakistan Scheme
      Statesman, 29 March 1940.

Partitioning of India: Schemes Disapproved

Disapproval of the Muslim League's suggestion for the partitioning of India has been expressed by various Indian leaders.

Dr R.P. Paranjpye

'Indians cannot possibly accept this division of India into two—Moslem India and Hindu India and the constitution of autonomous States based on religion' says Dr R.P. Paranjpye, President of the National Liberal Federation.[1]

Continuing Dr Paranjpye says: 'The two communities are so completely mixed with each other that the minority problems will remain in spite of any such rearrangement of Indian provinces. I think that the Congress, the Muslim League and other organizations should meet together and arrive at a possible settlement instead of the kind of long-range declarations from the two sides. These tend to assume an extreme colour which is very unfavourable for any settlement by compromise. I do not think that the differences between Hindus and Moslems are more important than the points on which they agree with each other and one should stress the latter rather than emphasize the former'.

Mr Asaf Ali

'The scheme of Moslem segregation which the League has announced spells the maximum danger to Indian Moslems themselves', observes Mr Asaf Ali, member of the Congress Working Committee.

'India's unity may appear a dream to certain leaders of the League but the isolation which they have declared to be their aim is a positive nightmare.

'The League's reactionary leadership instead of working for an honourable settlement is obviously heading towards a fruitless civil war, the brunt of which will fall on the innocent masses'.

Sir C. Setalvad

'I am emphatically of opinion that Mr Jinnah's scheme is against the best interests of all concerned, including the Muslims themselves, and if adopted would lead to disaster', says Sir Chimanlal Setalvad.

'I grant that Moslems have not been properly treated by the Congress Governments. But it is not the Moslems alone who have to complain. Large sections of caste Hindus, the scheduled classes and various organizations have also complained bitterly against the rule of the Congress party. But granting fully the existence and extent of the evil, the remedy that Mr Jinnah proposes is infinitely worse than the disease'.

Mr M.C. Chagla

The view that Mr Jinnah's presidential address and the resolution passed by the League at Lahore have caused consternation in the minds of all those Moslems who look upon India as their motherland and who are proud to be part and parcel of the great nation, is expressed by Mr M.C. Chagla.

In his opinion only political bankruptcy can suggest that Moslem rights can be safeguarded only by the creation of an independent Moslem State. It is equally mischievous, says Mr Chagla, to suggest that Moslems need a homeland when the whole of India is their homeland.

Sir Homy Mody

Sir Homy Mody, who is on a visit to Peshawar, said that the resolution had vastly complicated the Indian situation. It was not for outsiders to criticize a resolution which had received the unanimous backing of all shades of Moslem political opinion. One could not without entering into the feelings of Moslems appreciate its full implications.

Master Tara Singh

'If the Moslems cannot trust the Hindu majority they should also presume that the Sikhs cannot trust the Moslem majority' said Master Tara Singh president of the Sikh Gurdwara Prabandhak Committee. He continued: 'In order to strengthen the Moslem demands the Muslim League claims to represent all the minorities in India but in reality it ignores all the minorities altogether as and when it suits its purpose'.

61. Suggestions for Solving the Communal Problem: Dr R.P. Paranjpye
Indian Social Reformer, 13 April 1940.

The Communal Question

Certain aspects of the communal problem are similar to those already referred to when we spoke of caste questions. But this whole matter is even more important as on a correct solution of it depends the future progress of our country. Some may consider it to be a purely political problem which has no place in any discussion on social reform. Political progress is, however, only one aspect of social progress and, just as no political reformer can shut his eyes to social and economic questions, so no social reformer can neglect to consider political and economic questions.

The gulf between the two communities has in recent years become wider and wider and there is even a talk of dividing India into a Hindu India and a Muslim India. There is no doubt that the bitterness between the two communities has been aggravated by the constitution of separate electorates which cuts the leader of one community entirely off from any contact with the sister community. Candidates for election naturally take the extreme communal line to ensure success and moderate opinion in both communities is at a discount.

The contest is mainly for power and for loaves and fishes on the part of the leaders, but these leaders are able to mislead their followers by harping on differences of religion, civilization and culture and the fundamental unity of outlook is lost sight of in the rough and tumble of political strife.

I have urged a complete divorce of religion from social reform; religion should be purely a personal matter and should not be mixed up with matters of mundane moment. It was, in my opinion, a great mistake to import religion into politics even though this offered a momentary advantage and appeared to bring the Hindus and Muslims on one platform in defence of the Khilafat. But the advantage was soon lost and we have only an increase of bitterness which threatens our future progress.

If an amicable solution of the problem is to be achieved, some simple principles have to be accepted first by the leaders and then by the mass of both communities. The first is that both of them have to live in one common country and that it is impossible to conceive of a time when one of them will disappear by conversion, migration or any other method. The second is that mutual understanding, rather than mutual conflict is necessary for peaceful progress, that conflict is sure to harm both sides in the end, whichever may be the nominal victor. The third is a lively realization of the fact that both communities have made their own contribution to India's past, that even if one were to wish some of the past happenings undone that it is not now possible and that it is best to stop harping on unpleasant events of history.

Then it must be understood that India of the present-day is neither Hindu India nor Muslim India but Indian India and that, therefore, every force which tends towards increasing Indian solidarity should be encouraged and any which tends to alienate the two should be consciously discouraged. Then again everybody must be convinced that by our conflicts we make the way of the foreigner easy and that, if Indians are to be the master of their own destiny, they must be united.

Finally leaders must realize that sacrifice of self is often the best contribution that they can make to the general good and that to ensure general progress selfish considerations must often give way. Every thinking person will probably give his intellectual assent to such propositions, but unless they form part of his whole moral being they will not have much practical effect.

Practical men will try to examine the various causes of conflict and then do their best to do away with them and create new opportunities of mutual understanding. Where there are existing any lines of division, they will not, however, try to erase them all at once as such attempts will not be successful and may lead to further trouble. But a social reformer will not deepen these lines but will do his best to smooth them out gradually. This means that while the present conditions of settlement between the communities will be gradually altered in the direction of national unity, no addition will in any case be allowed which will involve any new differentiation on purely communal consideration.

To carry out this policy a record must first be prepared of existing conditions in all fields with the consent of both parties and any alteration therein will only be in one direction and will be made after agreement. This record will serve as a kind of Doomsday Book and unless altered as aforesaid will be strictly adjudged by a tribunal which will consist at the desire of either party, of judges who are neither Hindus nor Muslims but may be Christians, Parsees, etc, but of Indian nationality, except perhaps in the highest court of appeal. The record will be made for each town and village and if there is a dispute about the present state of things, it will be adjudged as above.

The causes of conflict are of several kinds (1) Political relating to representation in legislatures and ministries, ... (2) regarding services and government employment (3) cultural and educational, (4) regarding music before mosques and processions generally (5) relating to cow slaughter, (6) relating to conversions (7) miscellaneous. We shall consider these briefly in order and suggest ways of reducing the causes of friction in a gradual manner.

Political

At present in the legislatures Muslims have separate electorates and also a certain weightage. From the democratic point of view both these are theoretically vicious principles and the ideal is to have these elections fought only on secular issues with all voters having equal rights. In the first place this principle should not be extended to any elections where they do not apply at present. Secondly, a very gradual effort must be made by successive steps according to a planned schedule so that, say, in fifty years, separate electorates will be abolished but the numbers of seats will not be touched until the results of joint electorates are observed, and the requisite number of Muslims will be secured by means of reserved seats.

To satisfy Muslims that men so elected will truly represent them, the constituencies will be multi-membered returning about five members each, the voting being by means of proportional representation with a transferable vote, no eliminations being made at the time of the counting of votes unless the proper number of Muslims are returned. At the end of every term of five years of a legislature, approximately one tenth of Muslim members will cease to be returned by separate electorates and joint electorates will be instituted in their place.

The constituencies to be selected for such joint electorates will be drawn by lot unless the Muslim members agree to any particular selection. In the ministries genuine representatives of Muslims should be included and strict party voting should often be relaxed by leaving many questions to a free vote of the members. Votes of census should be either against an individual minister or against the cabinet as a whole. Similar procedure will be used with the necessary modifications in the case of other election like those of local bodies. These proposals will be recognized as very modest but are in the right direction....

62. The Hindu–Muslim Problem: S. Srinivasa Iyengar's Scheme

Hindustan Times, 17 July 1940.

The full text of the scheme propounded by Mr S. Srinvasa Iyengar,[1] ex-President of the Indian National Congress for a solution of the Hindu–Muslim problem which was presented for consideration to the Congress President and other Congress leaders recently at Wardha by Mir Akbar Ali Khan of Hyderabad, has been released for publication. Mr Srinivasa Iyengar says:

'We need discuss neither Dominion Status nor Independence, neither a Constituent Assembly nor Pakistan. We have to go to the root of our national existence and any national organization or state should be built upon National bedrock. It must now be quite clear to the meanest intelligence that Hindus and Muslims cannot range themselves as political communities or parties. That they will continue in a sense to be separate communities for religious purposes must be conceded. Any feeling that the two are different peoples must be prevented from taking hold of us. Probably Muslims generally feel that the superiority of Hindus in numbers and perhaps also in economic position taking India as a whole will make the Hindus the dominant political caste and will result in an inferior position for themselves both in politics and in the economic ordering. The Hindus probably feel that the Muslims are not sufficiently national in their outlook and may resort to force against Hindus indulging in extra-territorial ambitions which modify the tempo of Indian patriotism. Probably each community feels that the other is or will be ordinarily against it. In other words, shortly put, the Hindus fear a Muslim Raj and the Muslims fear a Hindu Raj.

Wanted a Secular Basis

The Problem today by no means is so difficult as it used to be when the two communities regarded themselves with some passion as rival religious sects. The differences between the two communities are now more political than others. Reference is sometimes made to cultural differences but this is largely theoretical. The difference in religion and the consequent difference in the personal law together with some difference in language and in the script are about all. The culture in India is a blended culture and it can hardly be said to be pure Hindu or pure Muslim. There can be no doubt there is much more of secular culture in common between the Indian Muslim and the Hindu than between the former and the Turk or Arab. There is however, one difference between the Hindu and the Indian Muslim. The philosophy of Ahimsa has received enormous attention in these latter years and has been egregiously distorted and corrupted to unworthy ends. The Ahimsa philosophy of the ordinary secular Hindu was not in the past however, radically different from the humane culture of the Muslims. It is plain, however, that the Congress with its leadership and its philosophy can never win the permanent trust of Muslims as a body and its amazing ineptitude in this hour of crisis has been demonstrated beyond the shadow of a doubt. The polity of India must be built upon patriotism pure and undefined. Religion and politics must not be mixed. We must cultivate a sense of racial identity as between Hindu and Muslim without any meticulous investigation into past histories and genealogies or any idea of false prestige. Any feeling that the Hindus and Muslims in India are two distinct races or nations will always be a stumbling block to any scheme of Hindu–Muslim rule in India. The only basis upon which the two communities can be welded together indissolubly must be wholly secular and racial or national, whichever term is preferred.

Hindus and Defence

The secular state must rest upon the broad foundation of adequate military defence for India and upon the making the people of India reasonably military minded. The Hindus must have the same military mindedness as the Muslims and should not think there is anything wrong in that culture. Neither the ancient Kshatriya tradition nor the military tradition of Western countries has prevented the progress of arts and sciences, of industries or of the learned professions or of scholarship or anything that is vital in civilization. The present moment offers a supreme opportunity for the two communities to ask for the defence of India being made over to them on a basis of perfect equality of Hindus and Muslims. The Indian Army must consist of an equal number of Hindus and Muslims and no regiment should be on a communal as distinguished from a regional basis. Every military unit should consist of an equal number of Hindus and Muslims independently of recruits from other communities. We must guard against the result of progressive deterioration in the international situation by building the Indian State on the normal basis of an effective army, navy, air force and so on.

The Government of such a state can only be entrusted not to leaders or followers of the Ahimsa doctrine or to those who indulge in the demagogic crudities which are only disguised by verbal fireworks but to those who are realistic and believe that the world is still governed by force in the ultimate analysis and that righteousness will prevail against evil only when it is backed by force.

There are grades of military-mindedness and there is no fear for centuries to come of Indian becoming very aggressively military-minded. It is also abundantly clear now that party politics has been mainly responsible for the hopeless inadequacy of Western democracies and that it seriously undermines patriotism and consciously or unconsciously gets hold of foreign or international ideologies if not for the purpose but with the result of betraying the country to the invader.

Party politics in India has further the decisive disadvantage of keeping the average Hindu and the average Muslim apart. And political parties in India will be either wholly communal or fall on some spurious and decadent philosophy which will make them untrustworthy for all purposes of national advancement or of defence in times of crisis.

National Government

The Government at the provinces and at the Centre should, therefore, be wholly national governments composed of men who are reasonably military-minded. Having regard to the very large area of the communal differences in the country in every province as well as at the Centre subject to the special representation of important minorities, Hindu and Muslim ministries should be equal in number in the Executive Government of India and of the province. We have had enough of the rule of the majority in the West. It has only occasionally been true; often it has been a rule of minority. The Hindu in the Punjab, the Frontier, Bengal and Sind or the Muslim in Bombay, Madras, the United Provinces and Bihar, for instance, will have the feeling that he is effectively sharing in the administration of the country only if Hindus and Muslims are equal in number in the Cabinet, apart from the extra membership that may be given to any other minority community in any province or at the Centre. This is the only permanent solution which will compel the two communities to trust one another and to acquire the sense of complete racial and national identity. No amount of tinkering with representation in the legislatures or electorates or other arrangements will help to destroy the deep seated canker in our life. This equal representation in every executive Government will give ample confidence to the respective communities throughout India whether in respect of representation in the services or in connection with political or administrative measures. Of course, the Hindu Ministers must be selected by the Hindu members of the legislatures and the Muslim Ministers must be selected by the Muslim members of the Legislatures. I certainly favour joint electorates and this scheme will function most satisfactorily with the system of joint electorates. But experience has shown the intensity of communal feelings in joint electorates also. Whether the electorates be joint or separate the sharing of power equally in the executive Governments of every part of the country by the two communities is the one indispensable requisite for complete national consolidation. What is to happen when this equality in representation creates a dead-lock is not a matter which requires an anxious discussion. The Cabinet will be hammered into unity as it will be jointly responsible and there will be an extra number of members of the minority communities to give the casting vote. Muslims are apparently anxious that they should have equal representation at least in the Central legislature. This is not a vital matter when once the Cabinet is formed on national lines and with equal representation for both the major communities. All the entanglements and confusing proposals are due to our fondness for the system of party politics which should be discarded. The cabinet is to be removable only on an express vote of non-confidence against the Cabinet as a whole by two thirds majority of the Legislature. The two-thirds majority must be of Hindus and Muslims taken separately.

Safeguards Essential

The religion, language and personal law of each community should be safeguarded by a Paramount constitutional check enabling the majority of members representing that community in the legislature placing a veto upon any legislative or other measure effecting it. A similar veto must be provided against any measure designed or calculated to affect adversely the economic well-being of any community especially. Lastly, an adequate communal representation in the services must be agreed to as a practical measure of justice in the administration and in the distribution of patronage. The simpler the solution the wider and more lasting will be the trust and satisfaction enjoyed by both the communities.

The rule of equality in the executive Government is the one canon which will solve many of the difficulties in the present and all the difficulties of the future. I do not believe in the efficacy of percentages of communal representation in the Legislature which may keep the sore open or give rise to ever recurring points of dispute. Whether the electorates should be joint or separate or what should be the representation of each community in the legislature, Central or provincial, appears to be unessential and their value is largely historical. They are not essential to the satisfactory safeguarding of the rights and interests of the respective communities, either of the provinces or at the Centre on the basis of the scheme outlined above.

Joint Rule Needed

What the Hindus and Muslims want today is that they should be compelled to forget that they are two separate people and enabled to trust each other in the Government of the country. For this purpose neither the Pakistan Scheme nor the scheme of weightage or artificially enlarged representation will serve. What the Muslim wants is an equal share in the actual Government of the province in which his community is in a minority. What the Hindu wants is an equal share in the actual administration of the provinces in which his community is in a minority. No scheme should be set up which would perpetuate communal differences or bring about civil war. Both the major communities are together entitled to rule India. It is only by their joint and equal rule that the sense of common nationality and of undivided patriotism will develop. Today partly for want of a scope and largely owing to our outworn philosophy we are helpless and divided. If Hindus and Muslims cannot trust one another for the purpose of joint rule and if each has any *aviere pensee* that each can rule or outwit the other there is ro salvation for us. And democracy on the basis of a national Government will be the soundest of democracies and will prevent not only dictatorships but will canalize national endeavour solely for the benefit of the country.

Wanted a New Organization

At this moment with the foregoing aims in view a political organization of a national character is absolutely essential. It should sedulously uphold the spirit of non-party patriotism and should consist of an equal number of Muslims and Hindus. Any Hindu is entitled to be a member only if he brings a Muslim in and a Muslim is entitled to be a member only if he brings a Hindu in. It should steer clear equally of Congress leadership and policies and of the Muslim League and Hindu Sabha leadership and policies. It should devote itself exclusively to securing the establishment of national Government at the Centre and in the provinces outlined as above, unhampered by the ambitions of Congressmen who want to be ministers at all costs by the rule of majority and by the ideologues of Muslim League who wanted to create Islamic States and who do not acknowledge undivided allegiance to India.

The Congress does not command the confidence of the great majority of Muslims and there is no good therefore, in trying to reform it so long as its present leadership and philosophy are there making us a supine people. The Muslim League is not trusted by the Hindus and cannot, therefore, serve any national purpose. An entirely new organization is of the utmost urgency, if men of goodwill among the two communities are determined to cut a new path along which Indians generally may travel. Such an organization will embody a new type of patriotism determined to discard old party allegiances and to bring into existence an altogether new bond of union.

An Equitable Solution

What have the Muslims to fear in a system where the Muslim Minister cannot be removed except by a two third majority of the Muslim Members of the Legislature, where the powers of the Legislature do not extend to passing of laws by a majority which affect adversely the interests of any community especially its language or religion or personal law, where the Government by Muslim is joint and equal all over India with the Government by Hindu and where adequate communal representation in services is guaranteed. And what has the Hindu to fear in a system where he rules equally and jointly with the Muslim in all the provinces and at the centre and where every military unit must be composed of equal members of Hindus and Muslims and where Muslim communalism deserts the barren sands of extra-territorial allegiance and mingles with the Hindu on the basis of a secular non-party patriotism and leadership that do not seek to revive old and effective religious creeds but are only devoted to founding a stable polity and free India. The Muslim community in India must feel that its title to rule India in equal measures with the Hindu community is established. And the Hindu community must feel that any adjustments that are made to secure that object do not perpetuate distinctions that must be obliterated or are only starting points for fresh strife. When once this is achieved the rest does not matter'.

---

[1] He was President of the Indian National Congress, Gauhati Session, 1926.

63. M.N. Roy on Muslim League and Pakistan Scheme

Extracts from M.N. Roy's Presidential Address at the Inaugural Conference of Radical Democratic People's Party, Bombay, 21 December 1940.
Indian Annual Register, 1940, Vol. II, p. 331.

MUSLIM LEAGUE ATTITUDE

Having condemned the Congress policy as it deserves, it is necessary to make a few observations also about the attitude of the Muslim League, which has been causing misgivings. Although leading members of the Muslim League favour India's participation in the war, and are actually cooperating with the war efforts, the official policy of the organization still remains rather ambiguous. Most probably, that is a reaction to the Congress attitude. But in view of the fact that the Muslim countries of the Near East are menaced directly by Fascism even today, Indian Muslims cannot remain indifferent to the danger. The solution of the present political images very largely depends upon initiative on the part of the Muslim League. In the absence of the initiative on the part of the Muslim League, the effort for the formation of emergency ministries in the provinces does not arouse sufficient enthusiasm. The other opposition groups are doubtful about the attitude the Muslim League will take up at the last moment. In this situation, the responsibility to lead the entire country out of the crisis devolves upon the Muslim League. All fighters for Indian freedom, who are not influenced by any communal considerations therefore, must appeal to the Muslim League to rise up to the occasion. They are, however, discouraged by the latest announcement that members of the Muslim League will not cooperate with other political parties for ending the present constitutional deadlock unless the latter accept the idea of Pakistan. This highly controversial issue need not be raised on the occasion of the inauguration of a party which is committed to all the general principles of minority rights. But I venture to suggest that no useful purpose will be served by creating difficulties for ending the present constitutional deadlock by raising issues which cannot possibly be settled immediately.

PAKISTAN

As far as the Radical Democratic People's Party is concerned, the Pakistan scheme was adumbrated, its political and constitutional substance was incorporated in the programme of national reconstruction elaborated by the pioneers of our party for adoption by the Congress. The ethnic and linguistic structure of India precludes the establishment of a centralized democratic state. India is bound to be a federation of autonomous units to be built as far as possible on the basis of ethnic and linguistic homogeneity. This conclusion, deduced from the realities of the situation, cannot be avoided while framing the constitution for the democratic state of India. Therefore, the Pakistan scheme should not terrorize anybody who wants democratic freedom. Nevertheless, for the moment, it only serves as a scare-crow. What is the use of obstructing the solution of immediate issues by raising a distant issue which cannot be settled today, even if all the goodwill in the world was there.

64. Justice Party Demands Dravida Nad and Supports Pakistan Scheme

Fortnightly Report for the First Half of June 1940, Public (General) Department, Government of Madras to Secretary to the Government of India, Home Department, 19 June 1940, Tamil Nadu State Archives.

...The Justice Party organized a Dravida Nad Conference on 2nd June at Conjeevaram which was fairly well supported. A feature of the conference was the unveiling of a map of Dravida Nad by E.V. Ramaswami Naicker. Speakers appealed for support for the British Government in the war in all possible ways, forecast the division of British India into linguistic provinces after the war, and urged the formation at that time, of a Dravida Nad comprising the area where Tamil, Telugu, Canarese and Malayalam were spoken, together with Bengal. There were a number of meetings in connection with the conference and also the usual propaganda meetings in other districts in which the Pakistan Scheme was frequently commended.

At a moderately attended Hindu Mahasabha meeting in Madras, the speakers, while condemning the Pakistan Scheme, pleaded for the unconditional co-operation of Indians in waging the war....

65. Justice Party and Muslim League Work Together

Fortnightly Report for the First Half of October 1940, Public (General) Department, Government of Madras to Secretary to the Government of India, Home Department, 18 October 1940, Tamil Nadu State Archives.

...There have been the usual Justice Party and Muslim League meetings. The two organizations continue to work together closely, and the Justice Party leader Sri Ramaswami Naicker addressed the South Arcot district Muslim League Conference, supporting the Pakistan scheme and urging the partition of South India in favour of the Dravidians. These parties give consistent support to the War effort. Anti-Brahminism is of course, still prominent and it is not uncommon for Brahmins to be linked to 'their fellow Aryans in the Germans'.

The Government have declared that persons who were convicted in connection with the anti-Hindustani agitation will not for that reason be debarred from entering Government service.

The Hindu Mahasabha held a poorly attended meeting in Madras to observe 'Hindu Nation Day'. The speakers denounced the Pakistan scheme and criticized the Congress policy of appeasing the Mulsims.

66. Gathering Wind to 'Smash Congress'

Bombay Chronicle, 11 January 1940.

Justice Leader to Sail in Same Boat with Jinnah and Ambedkar

Plans for the formation of an anti-Congress front are being vigorously canvassed by Mr E.V. Ramaswami Naicker, leader of the Justice Party in Madras who has been in Bombay for the last five days.

Activating New Views

To a city which has recently been regaled with stories of 'atrocities' committed by the Congress against Muslims, Mr Naicker is trying to infuse the virus of a disease which had been troubling Madras for some time—Brahmanophobia but from which this province has been free to a considerable extent.

Mr Naicker is the leader of the Justice Party of Madras which counted among its leading lights men such as Sir Shanmukham Chetty, the present Dewan of Cochin, Sir A. Ramaswami Mudaliar, Commerce Member to the Government of India, Sir K.V. Reddi, who was for some time the Acting Governor of Madras and Premier of the interim Cabinet and the Raja of Bobbili. In the 1937 elections the Justice Party was swept off the field by the people, an overwhelming majority of whom are non-Brahmins, but who were sick of the antics of the party. With the eclipse of the party the big leaders gave up leadership of the party and passed on to more fruitful pastures. This has brought up Mr Naicker to the leadership of the Justicites.

Out to 'Smash Congress'

Mr Naicker used the anti-Hindi agitation in Madras to come into limelight and now that the Congress Ministry is out of power, he is trying to use the opportunity to resuscitate the Justice party and 'Smash the Congress'. And in this task he is trying to seek the help of Mr M.A. Jinnah and Dr B.R. Ambedkar.

Gathering Wind

Mr Naicker had lengthy talks with Mr M.A. Jinnah and Ambedkar in the course of which he is understood to have narrated to them, with the help of an interpreter, the alleged acts of oppression against the non-Brahmins. He is also understood to have explained that theirs was not a minority question in Madras. The non-Brahmins who formed about 97 per cent of the population were being subjected to the tyranny of the small Brahmin minority which was completely controlling the Congress policy in the province. Since the Muslim League and the Depressed Classes were also fighting against the same organization, he suggested that they should make common cause.

Mr Naicker's disapproval of the Constituent Assembly plan is understood to have evoked the sympathy and support of the League leader.

67. Bombay Governor's Report to Viceroy on Dr B.R. Ambedkar's Views on the Partition Scheme, 8 May 1940

Viceroy's Correspondence with Governor of Bombay and His Secretary, Linlithgow Papers, Acc. No. 1108, 1940, NAI.

1. I had occasion today to send for Dr Ambedkar over some minor matter, and I took the opportunity of sounding him on the present situation. You may be interested to hear his views.

2. I asked what he thought of Jinnah's partition scheme, and he replied that he was very much in favour of it and thought it an excellent plan. He had, in fact, been studying the question for some time and was writing a book about it, which he hoped would be out in a few weeks' time[1]. His view was that it would not be difficult either in the Punjab or in Bengal, to draw a line which would separate the Muslims from the Hindus in those localities, and that, once the Muslims had their own cultural home they would cease to be nerveracked and on the defensive and would turn their thoughts more to their own improvement than to the salvation of Islam. In fact, he would hope for development on the lines of modern Turkey. He took it for granted that the proposed North-Western bloc, if it came into being, would always remain within the British Empire, and that the rest of India could become a Dominion. On the more difficult question of what would happen to the Muslims in Provinces like this, his idea was that for a period, say of ten years, they should be given the option of migrating to Hyderabad State, and that it might be possible to find similar States in other parts of India which would serve the same purpose.

3. One of the reasons why he favoured a Pakistan scheme was that it was, in principle, what he wanted for his own people. His ideal was to have a Pakistan for untouchables, but he did not think that a practical proposition. The safeguard which he wanted, therefore, for his own people in any future constitution was an undertaking that the Provincial Governments would spend a certain sum of money, he mentioned five to ten lakhs, a year on Settlements for untouchables. The idea would be that, with Government assistance, new lands should be opened up for untouchable communities alone. Only if they lived in their own villages did he think that they would ever be able to rise out of the inferiority complex which at present kept them down.

4. I always find Dr Ambedkar stimulating to talk to, but I have noticed that he is apt to take things up with great enthusiasm and drop them very soon, and I feel very doubtful whether we shall hear much more of the ideas which he has outlined to me. Their interest, however, lies in the fact that he is at present evidently giving his full support to Jinnah.

5. I asked him whether he thought his party had made progress lately, and he told me he felt convinced that at the next Provincial election he would increase his numbers from 15 to 25, and possibly even to 30, mainly at the expense of Congress. He told me that the Harijans of Gujarat had now come over to him, mainly because of their dissatisfaction with Gandhi's refusal to accept an untouchable on the constitutional committee for Rajkot at the time of his fast. I accept these estimates of his increasing strength with considerable caution, but I think, on the whole, that the untouchable

community is more solidly behind him and that he would be likely to gain some seats in another election.

---

[1] Dr B.R. Ambedkar's book on Pakistan was first published in December 1940 and its corrected version in 1945 under the title *Pakistan or the Partition of India*. The reprint of its third edition (1946) was brought out in 1990 by the Government of Maharashtra under the title *Dr Babasahab Ambedkar— Writings and Speeches, Vol. 8, Reprint of Pakistan or The Partition of India*.

68. Congress Responsible for Minority Problem: Sir C.P. Ramaswami Iyer

Tribune, 24 August 1940.

The injurious idea of segregating India into Hindu India, Muslim India and Princes India was due to a great extent to the policy pursued by the Indian National Congress, said the Dewan of Travancore, Sir C.P. Ramaswamy Iyer, presiding at a meeting held under the auspices of the Travancore University last evening, when Mr S. Satyamurthi, Mayor of Madras, surveyed the Indian situation from the Congress viewpoint.

Sir Ramaswami Iyer stated that the discussion under the auspices of the University had been intended to be academic, but had ceased to be such. Hence, it was his duty to answer the points raised by Mr Satyamurthi.

Sir Ramaswamy Iyer said, that the Congress had done a great deal and had still to do a great deal, but it must use all its great organizations and its powers of persuasion to make friends with elements in the life of the country whose confidence it had lost or was fast losing. What was the use of talking of independence and resistance to this policy or that policy, when they knew the country was unarmed and could not resist any chance invader? India could defend herself only with the cooperation of England. She made a start on the programme of equipping herself for such self-defence spread over a period of say 5 or 7 years. The Congress must also use that period for making friends with Muslims and Princes and disabuse the public mind of its fears of a Congress 'Junta'.

Sir Ramaswami Iyer said many of the difficulties in India to-day were greatly due to the policy pursued by a saint in politics. The Muslim trouble was entirely a creation of the Congress. Mr Jinnah held to-day the position practically of a dictator because of lack of provision of Congress leaders and the intrusion of non-secular elements into the secular field of politics beginning from the era of the Khilafat agitation and the unwise concession then made. They owed the system of communal electorates to the compromising policy of Mahatma Gandhi and his friends, who yielded at every threat and yielded so much that they raised expectations they could not fulfil.

The position of the princes 'vis-à-vis' England and Indian politics to day was also the result of the Congress policy. Sir Ramaswamy Iyer accused Congress leaders of having stirred up differences between British India and Indian Princes. The Princes and their advisers and people of States were as patriotic as Mahatma Gandhi and British Indian politicians. If today the Congress retraced its path, saw the error of its ways and instead of instigating disunion, made for unity, for friendship between Indian India and British India then there was a great future for the country.

There was no point in blaming Mr Amery for his references to the minorities in his speeches in the Commons. As Mr Amery said, the Mussalman problem was there today but it need not have been there. Mussalmans were one with Mr Gandhi until recently. Whatever they asked Mr Gandhi yielded. Mr Gandhi then retraced his path, but they would not. Mr Gandhi was a very great person but one who having seen an ideal would pursue it to its logical goal notwithstanding its practicability or otherwise.

Sir Ramaswamy Iyer cited as an example the doctrine of non-violence which today was an impediment to the progress and organization of India's man-power. Sir Ramaswamy Iyer emphasized that he was one of those who considered that India had the right to govern herself as much as any other and that she had the capacity to do so.

The fundamental unity of India was something greater than unity ever evolved in Europe. Innate unity in India deserved all that could be deserved by any nation.

Concluding Sir Ramaswami Iyer said: nobody could dispute that if India had to be governed by any other nation, the most fitted was the British who had an innate sense of justice....

F.   NATIONALIST MUSLIMS

69.   Mr Yakub Hassan's (Former Minister of Madras) Views on the 'Two-Nation Theory'—A Letter to Prominent Muslims

Hindustan Times, 2 March 1940.

Danger of Two-Nation Theory

A move to mobilize nationalist Muslims who are outside the Muslim League is understood to have been started in an effort to bring about a settlement between Hindus and Muslims as well as between both of them and the Government.

Mr Yakub Hassan, former Minister of Madras, it is learned, has taken the first step and has addressed a letter to prominent Muslims suggesting the holding of a conference of them either at Allahabad or Delhi some time before the All India Congress Committee meets at Ramgarh on March 17.

Mr Yakub Hassan says in the letter:

'There are surely hundreds, if not thousands, of clear-sighted Muslims outside the Muslim League who take a more rational and patriotic view of Indian politics and whose minds are not clouded with communal narrowness, prejudices and mistrust of others. The circle of such broad-minded Muslims is not necessarily confined to the four corners of the Congress. They feel distressed over the unnatural and anti-national situation that has been created owing to the misguided, reactionary policy of a few leaders. They are sure to rally round any movement that is set on foot to counteract the reactionary propaganda of the Muslim League.

Unity of India

'It is only proper that the situation created by one section of the Muslim community should be rectified by the more progressive leaders of the same people and the present is the most opportune time for calling a meeting of prominent Muslims who stand for the unity of India and for a fully self-governing status for India. The considered views of such a meeting of prominent Muslims on the outstanding and burning questions of the day that are exercising the minds of all Indians at the present moment will not only remove the stigma of self-stultifying communalism and slavish attachment to British Imperialism from the fair name of the Muslim community, but they will also carry weight with the British Government and the general public.

Any reasonable demand that the proposed conference may also make on the Congress in the name of the Muslim community will receive the respectful consideration of that national organization. If the small conference that I suggest is conducted on proper lines and its recommendations command the confidence of the more advanced and thinking section of the Muslim community, it is sure to become a powerful factor at the present juncture and it may even play an important role in resolving the deadlock that has come in the negotiations between Gandhiji and the Viceroy.

'You are aware that in the opinion of some publicists the Congress can advance the cause of Indian independence more effectively and expeditiously by resuming and exercising responsibilities in eight provinces through benevolent administration calculated to dispel honest suspicion and mistrust and to win over the allegiance of the Muslim and other minorities more effectively than it can possibly do by remaining outside office indefinitely. The advice of the proposed conference on this and similar other matters is bound to carry weight with the Congress Working Committee.

'Among the questions that should engage the attention of the conference is the much-debated subject of the Constituent Assembly and the principle underlying it. The conference can make an important contribution to the defining of a proper course in the connection also.'

Turning Point

Earlier the letter observes 'The reply that the Viceroy has recently given to Mr Jinnah has provided a turning point in the Hindu–Muslim situation. The Viceroy has restricted his commitment definitely to the safeguarding of Muslims interests. This restricted assurance from the British Government is quite in keeping with the assurance that the Congress has given from time to time.

'The Viceroy has announced that India shall have Dominion Status as defined in the Westminster Statute and has also reiterated that the British Parliamentary system of democratic Government must prevail in India. This gives a quietus to the demand of Mr Jinnah for a recognition of separate nationality for Muslims in the framing of the constitution for India.

'The Congress may go any length to gain the goodwill and cooperation of the Muslim League, but it cannot and will not agree to any arrangement, permanent or temporary, that will divide the legislature into watertight communal groups, each having its proportionate representation in the Cabinet. Common sense as well as Parliamentary traditions will not allow the British Government to countenance any system that involves divided responsibility, and the Viceroy has made this fairly clear to Mr Jinnah.

'The present position is this, that the Congress is not prepared to discuss the question of the coalition Ministry with Mr Jinnah and Mr Jinnah will not discuss with the Congress High Command the more important and crucial question of removing the antagonism that now subsists between Hindus and Muslims, the Congress and the Muslim League.

'do not believe that Mr Jinnah's views that Muslims and Hindus should stand separated as two nations are shared by a majority of Muslim League and the League Working Committee resolutions are not always as unanimous as they pretend to be. Though the proposition adumbrated by Mr Jinnah has caught the imagination of the unthinking two-anna members of the Muslim League, the thinking section of Muslims are always alive to the danger of the two-nation theory and to the inevitable political consequence of it, namely, the permanent and effective continuance of British domination. The more reasonably minded Muslim Leaguers are, however, so entangled in a mesh of their own creation that they dare not differ from the new political creed of the League for fear of being denounced as traitors not to the League, but to Islam itself.'

70.   Asaf Ali's Statement to the Press Regarding the Pakistan Scheme
Hindustan Times, 29 March 1940.

League's Reactionary Leadership

Mr Asaf Ali, a member of the Congress Working Committee, in the statement to the Press, says:

The scheme of Muslim segregation, which the League has announced spells the maximum danger to Indian Muslims themselves. India's unity may appear a dream to certain leaders of the League, but the isolation which they have declared to be their aim is a positive nightmare. The insidiously specious argument which *The Times* of London has built up on the analogy of France and Germany to justify the League's tendencies is eloquently significant in the face of all the responsible pronouncements which point to the federalization of Europe and the World Federal Union. To fight Hitler in Europe and to encourage Hitlerian tactics among those in India who do not possess Hitler's military resources is a species of hypocrisy, the poisonous nature of which cannot be missed by those who have known the policy of divide and rule in many forms.

It is unfortunate that the present leadership of the League has perhaps quite unconsciously, and possibly with contrary intentions, but in a paroxysm of anti-Hindu rage, become an instrument of reactionary forces. While the forces of political sanity are moving toward continental and even world unity, the League has persuaded itself to commence a retrograde march. The American Republics are thinking of pooling their resources together. England and France have already begun to lay the foundations of a union, the small countries of the Near and Middle East are forming defensive leagues and in short, the whole world is beginning to think in terms of a federal union, but the Muslim League with no military or economic resources has started thinking of segregating half the Muslim population of India into defenceless units leaving the other half including all the Muslim public servants under the Central Government and in the Hindu-majority provinces to the logical consequences of being alien nationals. This by itself is sufficient for more than one half of the Muslim population of India to repudiate the League without a moment's hesitation.

It was under Mr Jinnah's guidance in 1916 that the League agreed to reduce the Muslim majority in the Punjab and Bengal to 50 per cent and now he has discovered two sovereign States in the North-East and the North-West, with a separate control of their external affairs, defence, communications, customs etc. The Railways are mortgaged upto the hilt and these so-called sovereign States, if ever allowed to be formed will inherit only heavy liabilities guaranteed by British bayonets. Again, the defence of these frontier provinces is at present costing nearly Rs 30 to 35 crores a year and as sovereign States they must also build up defences against the rest of India. Central revenues *pro rata* cannot yield one-fifth of this sum, and other liabilities will be equally heavy. All public servants now employed by the Central Government and the rest of India will naturally be liable to be thrown out and the ranks of the unemployed will swell to enormous proportions.

The Third Party

It is difficult to analyse within a short space the full implications of this hopelessly bad dream of the League. The reference in the League's Lahore resolution to mandatory safeguards for minorities, however, exposes the true significance of the kind of sovereignty they desire. Who but a third party can enforce the mandatory safeguards, and, if the third party is going to remain in a dominating enough position to enforce the safeguards, why deceive the credulous into believing that there is the slightest truth in the demand for independent sovereign States?

The League's reactionary leadership instead of working for an honourable settlement is obviously leading towards a fruitless civil war, the brunt of which will fall on the innocent masses. Independent and Nationalist Muslims can no longer remain silent spectators of so glaring a tragedy, and therefore, they must bestir themselves and save the situation from developing into a crisis. The old reactionaries now working in an unholy alliance with thoughtless visionaries, must not be allowed to play with the destiny of nine crores of Indian Muslims.

71. Resolution Passed by the South Indian Nationalist Muslim Association Condemning the Pakistan Scheme

Star of India, 4 April 1940.

'Divide and Rule' Policy of Muslim League—Its Effect on South Indian Muslims

A resolution strongly protesting against the attitude of Mr M.A. Jinnah and the Muslim League on the question of dividing India into Hindu India and Muslim India and characterizing the same as retrograde step was passed by the South Indian National Muslim Association which met here, Mr A.K. Abdul Rahim, Municipal Vice-Chairman presiding.

The meeting appealed to the Muslims of South India to follow the lead of Maulana Abul Kalam Azad and join the Congress in large numbers and declared that the Muslim League did not care for the interests of Muslims in South India who were in a minority but looked to the interests of Muslims in Provinces where they were in a majority.

72. On the Activities of Nationalist Muslims

Editorial, *Hindustan Times*, 19 April 1940.

We are glad that distinguished Muslim leaders are coming out one by one to repudiate the League plan for partitioning the country. The latest to do so is Sir Ghulam Hussain Hidayatullah, a former Premier of Sind[1]. He points out that the way out of the difficulty in which the Indian Muslims are finding themselves is not through carrying segregation one step further but through a retracting of their steps and the adoption of Joint electorates. Responsible government implies for its successful working the existence of the party system, but, if the parties are organized on lines on which it becomes impossible for any party to increase or decrease its strength, we are immediately confronted with the problem of permanent majorities and minorities which makes the system of ins and outs unworkable. Since responsible government began to be introduced even partially, this has been the position in the provinces though the malady became acute with the introduction of full provincial autonomy. The courageous course for Indian Muslims will be to renounce separate communal electorates and form political parties which will make inter-communal cooperation possible. Segregation of the communities, as Sir G.M. Hidayatullah states, will not only not make for peace and harmony but on the contrary will make for increased rivalry and hostility.

Not An Easy Matter

Those who have put forward the plan of partition and those who apparently speak of it as a practicable scheme, we are afraid, are either profoundly ignorant or willfully ignore the insurmountable obstacles in the way of giving effect to any such fantastic proposal. As Sir Ghulam Hussain points out, the allocation of territories will not at all be an easy matter as it will lead to complications with other communities and with Indian States. Lord Curzon attempted the partition of a province, but within a decade Lord Morley's settled fact became unsettled. Ajmer-Merwara is carrying on an agitation for amalgamation with the UP but nothing has come out of it. The separation of Sind was not brought about easily, and already those who took the most prominent part in the agitation are regretting it. The Andhras have been asking for a separate province all these years in vain. The partition of Palestine, a country much smaller than an Indian province, was the subject of enquiry by two commissions only to be ultimately abandoned. The dismemberment of Austria created as many problems as it solved and not one of them has been solved upto date. The vision of a country which has been functioning as a unit for many generations is not merely a question of redrawing the map and painting it red and green. It means so much in terms of human hardship and misery that none but the hard-hearted, to whom human suffering is as nothing compared to the realization of their own insensate ambitions and hatred, can put it forward light-heartedly, as a way of solving the communal problem.

Deplorable Feature

Nor is this all. Once Mr Jinnah and his accomplices are allowed to complete the crime the flood gates will be opened. If communalism is to form the basis of the new States, why stop short with Muslims? The Sikhs and other communities can put forward similar claims. If communalism is to have its own way, what about provincial ambitions? Men like Mr Subhas Bose will only be too ready to unfurl the banner of revolt. Instead of Hindu and Muslim Federations, which Mr Jinnah envisages, India will break up into a hundred and one independent and semi-independent States, the hand of each State being on its neighbour's throat. India will thus relapse into the anarchy from which it has been redeemed. Lord Lothian, when he was here on a study tour, contrasted the state of affairs in this country with those of Europe where the existence of sovereign independent States had spelt war and anarchy. While the best minds in the world are thinking in terms of European and even World Federation as the only way in which peace can be maintained and war exorcised from the face of the earth here in India we are asked to start the contrary process of disrupting our unity to form sovereign States which would be at daggers drawn with each other. That British statesmen who are paying so heavily in blood and money on account of the existence of these conditions in Europe should encourage such disruptive ideas in India is to us the most deplorable feature of the present situation.

Conference of Legislators

Finally, we see that Sir Ghulam Hussain supports the idea of convening a conference of members of legislatures for the purpose of considering the constitutional and communal problems. We have ourselves supported the idea though it is obvious that in view of the confused situation which has arisen in the country after the Congress Cabinets had resigned it will be well to hold a general election before convening such a conference. But whether such constructive suggestions are accepted or not depends on the attitude of the Government and so far as we can see the Government do not appear to be anxious to consider proposals likely to end the deadlock.

---

[1] Sir Shaikh Ghulam Hussain Hidayatullah was the first Premier of Sind in 1937–38. Later he rejoined Muslim League and was the Premier of Sind from 1942 to 1947.

73. Meeting of Nationalist Muslims Under the Auspices of Majlis-i-Ahrar

Hindustan Times, 20 April 1940.

Nationalist Muslims Condemnation

The proposal to partition India into Muslim and non-Muslim zones was criticized at a public meeting of Muslims held under the auspices of the Majlis-i-Ahrar[1] tonight.

Messrs Abid Ali, Ali Bahadur Khan and J. Bhokari addressed the meeting.

A resolution was passed condemning the partition scheme as 'fantastic and mischievous' and warning the Muslims of India 'against falling into the trap of communalists whose hymn of hate is bound to harm the best interests of the motherland in general and of Muslims in particular'. The resolution further called upon the Muslims of India to join other communities for the freedom and self-determination of a united India.

Calcutta

In observance of the Hindustan Day, nationalist Muslims of Calcutta held a meeting in Wellington Square under the presidency of Maulana Saif Siddiqui of Bareilly today.

A resolution protesting against the Lahore resolution of the All India Muslim League and opining that the said resolution was prejudicial to the interests of India in general and the Muslim community in particular was adopted.

The meeting also accorded support to the All India Nationalist Muslim Conference to be held in Delhi and nominated five delegates from Calcutta to the Delhi conference.

Lucknow

The UP Provincial Majlis-e-Ahrar observed the 'Hindustan Day' at a meeting held in Belachpura, Lucknow, under the presidentship of Maulana Husain Ahmad Madani. A resolution was adopted condemning the Pakistan scheme.

Patna

The Muslim League's Pakistan scheme was condemned by the local Ahrars at a meeting held at Patna today after Friday prayers in observance of 'Hindustan Day'.

Sylhet Disturbance

Confusion was caused at a meeting held in Sylhet today under the auspices of the Assam Provincial Jamait-ul-Ulema in observance of the Hindustan Day.

It is stated that when Maulana Abdul Mubashir was delivering his presidential speech one member of the audience interrupted him, giving rise to an altercation which culminated in an exchange of blows. Some Jamait leaders while returning from the meeting are stated to have received injuries as a result of hurling of brickbats. A resolution disapproving the partition scheme was however, passed by the meeting amidst confusion.

Another meeting was held under the auspices of the Muslim League where the Lahore resolution was endorsed.

---

[1] Majlis-i-Ahrar was formed in 1929 with the objectives of winning the country's freedom and promoting harmony between different communities. It also laid stress on improving the living conditions of the common people, particularly Muslims.

74. 'Anti-Partition Day' Meeting at Jama Masjid, New Delhi
Hindustan Times, 20 April 1940.

Delhi Muslims Condemn Pakistan Scheme

The absurdity and the utter impracticability of the partition scheme as outlined by the Muslim League was exposed by speakers at a crowded public meeting of the local Muslims held in the Jama Masjid to observe 'Anti-Partition Day'. More than 10,000 Muslims attended the meeting.

Maulana Hafizul Rahman, addressing the meeting, said that all sane people among the Muslims had already condemned the partition scheme. Even the Secretary of State for India who, when speaking of the so-called communal problem, seemed to have copied Mr Jinnah's style and language, thought it impracticable and made it clear beyond doubt that the British Government would not entertain any such scheme.

Proceeding, the speaker said that even among the Muslim Leaguers, a large section of opinion was totally opposed to the scheme and considered it as merely a nightmare. According to his information, the partition scheme had only the support of three members of the Working Committee of the Muslim League, namely Mr Jinnah, Nawabzada Liaqat Ali Khan and Sir Abdulla Haroon. The rest of the members had shown no enthusiasm for it, even after it was officially adopted as the goal of the Muslim League. Continuing, the speaker asked what had happened to the goal of Complete Independence for India which the Muslim League session at Lucknow had adopted.

In his opinion, the idea of partition was diametrically opposed to the basic idea of independence and therefore, the two could not go together.

Maulana Nur-ud-Din, who spoke next, said that Mr Jinnah had a peculiar position in the Muslim League Executive which was comparable to the position his group occupied in the Central Assembly. Further developing the analogy, the Maulana Sahib said that a majority of the members of the League Working Committee were ex-Executive Councillors and Ministers in the Provincial Government under the Montford Reforms Scheme, and had worked in that capacity under British masters in close alliance with their Hindu colleagues. They never thought of partition at any time as they had a share in power which was all they stood for. Then again there was a small minority in the League's Working Committee which till recently was prepared to accept the Wardha programme of the Congress and work as Ministers in the Congress Cabinets with minor adjustments. This small minority was now thoroughly disgusted with the barren policy of the Muslim League. Yet the fact remained that they had not the courage of their conviction. Between these two groups which had nothing in common between them, Mr Jinnah with one or two followers, held the balance in his hands and, in this way, was able to dictate to the Muslim League. The Maulana Sahib was sure that such patchwork unity could not last long. He thought that the slogan of partition which Mr Jinnah had raised was like a drowning man clutching at a straw. It was an attempt to hoodwink the Muslim intelligentsia who were asking the Muslim League to define their demands.

Maulana Samiullah said that the alliance of the Muslim League and the Hindu Mahasabha in Sind and the Forward Bloc and the League in Calcutta had unmasked its leaders.

These alliances had demonstrated beyond doubt that the League leaders did not feel concerned over Muslim rights but were after something else.

A resolution condemning the partition scheme was passed at the meeting.

75. Abdul Qaiyum Ansari Opposes Partition
Hindustan Times, 25 April 1940.

'It is a blasphemy to say that Islam is in danger here. It is a tragedy to place orders for a Pakistan for the segregation of Islam. It is a defeat of Islam to run away from the battle of life in search of privacy. It is a fantastic wavering of a fevered mind'.

Thus observed Mr Abdul Qaiyum Ansari, the noted Momin leader in the course of his presidential address delivered at the first session of the Bihar Provincial Momin Conference which held its session here. There was a huge gathering of Momins from all parts of the Province.

Mr Ansari pointed out that the whole scheme of partition was absurd, impracticable and against the true conception of Islam. He who wanted to cut up the country into parts was a traitor, he added.

Cultural Differences Among Muslims

He explained continuing that the plea of cultural dissimilarity between Hindus and Muslims of India did not hold any water. What had the Indian Muslims in common culturally with the Muslims of Arabia or Turkey? he asked. Take the Muslims of Bengal who, according to the Muslim League formula constituted a separate nation. What had these Muslims in common with their co-regionalists of the North-West Frontier, and how much in common have they with their Hindu brethren of Bengal? Racially they are much the same. They speak the same language, they dress alike, they live alike, they partake of much the same food.

Defects of Pakistan Scheme

Proceeding, the speaker dwelt on the defects of the Pakistan scheme. He said that it would not be able to protect the Muslims of a minority province as they would remain in the hands of the majority community with this difference that Muslims would have no control over the administration of the province which they have got in the present state of affairs. The plea that Muslim States in India would protect the Muslims in minority provinces was utterly useless. Even today there are Muslim states of Afghanistan, Turkey, Persia and many others but they could not interfere in the affairs of India even on the complaints made by the Muslim League that Muslims were being crushed by the Hindus. In the same way the Pakistan States would also be unable to do anything and the plea was simply meant to hide the reality and hoodwink the Muslims of the minority provinces.

Position Will be Worse

Further on he said that even the Muslims in general will not be in a better position if the scheme materialized. The Pakistan States would be scattered in the East, North-West and the extreme North and the Hindus would be able to make a compact state, organized on a sound basis. If antagonized the Hindu state would prove a great menace to the Muslim culture and language for the protection of which the League had been crying hoarse. Giving an example he said that if the Hindu State of Bihar invaded the Muslim State of Bengal, neither the Muslim states of Punjab or Hyderabad could help in any way because Hindus being consolidated would frustrate all attempts to do so. Besides, in the absence of any irresistible frontier lines, the fear of invasion would always loom large.

Holy Places in India

What would be the fate, Mr Ansari further asked, of most of the important holy places of the Muslims, ancient mosques, historical monuments and religious and secular institutions of the Muslims if they were given willingly to the absolute control of the Hindus situated as they were in the Hindu provinces? If this scheme materialized the Urdu language was gone because the Hindu states would ban it and the Pakistan States, each of which had its own language, would refuse to accept it. Besides, there was a very faint chance of the Muslims getting their religious freedom in the Hindu states which they had at present.

Key Industries and Resources

Proceeding he said that if the Pakistan scheme came to be realized, the Muslim States would have to depend upon Hindu States for industrial enterprises as most of the materials for the key industries such as iron, coal, mica etc. would fall in the Hindu States. The resources of the Pakistan States would be so limited that they would not be able to meet the expenditure of defence and railways etc.

Overthrow Capitalist Leaders

In view of these facts, it was clear that the Pakistan scheme was wholly injurious to the cause of the Muslims and Islam. It was simply designed to serve the purpose of those capitalist Muslims who wanted to dominate over the Muslim masses and who could thrive only on Hindu–Muslim hatred and rank communalism. In conclusion, the President exhorted the Momins to be on their guard against the propaganda of the Muslim League. The Muslim League, he said, was an organization of the Nawabs, the capitalists and the Zamindars. Poor Momins' voice could not be heard there. The Momins should have their own organization and it was the Momin conference. They should all strengthen it with the objective to unite all the poor working class Muslims, who numbered about eight crores, in order to overthrow the present capitalistic leadership of the Muslim League and lead India on the road to freedom.

76.   Azad Muslim Conference Advocates a United India

Tribune, 29 April 1940.

Azad Conference Subjects Committee's Resolution

The Subjects Committee consisting of the members elected by the delegates of the Azad Muslim Conference, commenced its session at 2 p.m. today under the presidency of Khan Bahadur

Allah Bux. Among those present at the meeting were Mr Nurie, Dr Syed Mahmud and Mr Nausher Ali.

The resolution[1] on the Indian independence evoked considerable discussion and was passed unanimously. A number of amendments were either rejected or withdrawn.

Text of Resolution

Following is the full text of the resolution passed by the Subjects Committee of the Azad Conference this evening:

'This conference of representatives of Indian Muslims, who desire to secure the fullest freedom of the country, consisting of delegates and representatives of every province, after having given its fullest and most careful consideration to all the vital questions affecting the interest of the Muslim community and the country as a whole declares the following:

'India will have geographical and political boundaries of an individual whole, and as such is the common homeland of all the citizens, irrespective of race or religion, who are joint owners of its resources. All nooks and corners of the country contain hearths and homes of Muslims, who cherish the historic eminence of their religion and culture which are dearer to them than their lives. From the national point of view every Muslim is an Indian. The common rights of all residents of the country and their responsibilities in every walk of life and in every sphere of human activity are the same. An Indian Muslim, by virtue of these rights and responsibilities is unquestionably an Indian national and in every part of the country is entitled to equal privileges, that of every Indian national, in every sphere of governmental, economic and other national activities and in public services. For that very reason Muslims own equal responsibilities with other Indians for striving and making sacrifices to achieve the country's independence. This is a well-evident proposition the truth of which no right-thinking Mussalman will question.

'This conference declares unequivocally and with all the emphasis at its command that the goal of Indian Muslims is complete independence along with protection of their religion and communal rights, and that they are anxious to attain this goal as early as possible. Inspired by this aim they have in the past made great sacrifices and are ever ready to make greater sacrifices.

'The Conference unreservedly and strongly repudiates the baseless charge levelled against Indian Muslims by the agents of British imperialism and others that they are an obstacle in the path of Indian freedom and emphatically declares that the Muslims are fully alive to their responsibilities and consider it inconsistent with their traditions and derogatory to their honour to lag behind others in the struggle for independence'.

---

[1] The resolution was moved by Mufti Kifayatulla, President of the Jamiat-ul-Ulema-i-Hind.

77. Khan Bahadur Allah Baksh's Presidential Address at All India Azad Muslim Conference, Delhi, 27 April 1940

Indian Annual Register, 1940, Vol. I, pp. 323–7.

In the course of his Presidential Address, Khan Bahadur Allah Baksh declared:

'If Germany's ruthless and brutal disregard of the right of other sovereign States to live peacefully is a challenge to civilization and therefore, Britain and France must stake their all in it, Britain should be the last to challenge India's right to exist as a sovereign and completely independent State and should, therefore, not obstruct its people if they desire to frame their own constitution'. Mr Baksh also condemned the Pakistan scheme of the Muslim League characterizing it as grotesque and observed that it was 'about the most indiscreet approach to a serious problem and as such has torpedoed the very basis of a reasonable settlement'.

Proceeding, Mr Baksh said, 'It is this conference and this conference alone today which is in a position to evolve a constructive scheme to bring the political deadlock to an end. If you can come to an agreement as regards the basis of a communal settlement, the Congress, which is undoubtedly the most influential and powerful organization in the country today, is bound to consider your proposals as the one golden bridge which leads not merely to communal and political harmony in the country but to the ultimate goal, namely, India's independence. Perhaps your decisions are being awaited both in the country and abroad with great impatience, because on them will depend a very great deal. I am perfectly confident in my mind that the Congress will not hesitate to endorse our reasonable proposals for the communal settlement. The Congress can no longer say that the scattered Muslim organizations and individuals who are eager to attain the country's freedom have not yet formulated their proposals on behalf of the Muslim community for the settlement of the entire communal problem.

'It is perfectly obvious that whatever scheme of settlement you may eventually evolve for safeguarding the rights and interests of the minorities, whether they happen to be in a Hindu or Muslim majority province, you keep in view the principle of equal and universal application of the same standard to all of them everywhere.

DANGER OF AGGRESSIVE COMMUNALISM

Warning his audience that aggressive communalism was fatal to the growth of that feeling of brotherliness, good neighbourliness and common nationality which were essential, not merely for the acceleration of a common national effort but also for the maintenance of an atmosphere of peace, progress and stability in the country, Mr Allah Baksh urged that a fair adjustment of the general needs of the country and the various communities should be undertaken in a spirit of generosity and toleration and of right brotherly affection for one another. 'Whatever our faiths, we must live together in our country in an atmosphere of perfect amity and our relations should be the relations of several brothers of a joint family, the various members of which are free to profess the faith they like without any let or hindrance and all of whom enjoy equal benefits of their joint property'.

To achieve the objects outlined by him, the President suggested the election of committees or boards consisting of a limited number of representatives of the delegates to consider the problem. He said: 'The question of formulating definite proposals for the communal settlement is scarcely a matter which can be disposed of quickly at a conference like this. It will require deep and anxious thought and continuous consultations for some time before the result of the Board's or sub-committee's labours can be presented to you in a convenient form. I, therefore, suggest that a board consisting of the representatives of different associations and others may be formed to undertake this onerous duty and they may be authorized to co-opt experts or others to help them to come to correct conclusions. Their report as soon as it is ready—and I take it that they will take some time to conclude their labours—should come up before another session of this conference and after it has been ratified with or without modifications, it should be released to the country for the consideration of all parties concerned. In the meantime we can appoint some executive of this conference for the purpose of carrying on intensive constructive work among the Mussalmans throughout the country. We can also name a day or days for echo-meeting throughout the country for making known to the millions of Mussalmans the result of deliberations of our conference. All this is essential because a great deal of educative work has to be done and Muslim electorates have to be prepared to consider the larger issues which their votes will ultimately have to decide'.

Mr Allah Baksh dealt at considerable length with the Muslim League's partition scheme, the League-Congress efforts for a settlement and with the background of a communal strife in India. He said, 'Not service but rule, not fruitful co-operation but domination, not a general elevation of the level of common prosperity and material benefits but the enrichment of a few families at the cost of millions of their supports, not a common willing effort to construct a comfortable world for all alike but a graded scale of benefits, the maximum to go to the most intriguing and the Hindu and Muslim masses to grovel in the dust and squalor of their villages and urban slums have been the main aspects of the history of all the Hindu, Muslim and British Empires in India upto now. Islam, on the other hand, does not prevent anyone from developing his natural gifts to the full and enjoying the fruits of his skill and labour. It does not work for a deal level but it forbids exploitation in all shapes and forms and all parties concerned will do well to note this as a fair warning against any attempt to found a structure of government in which domination, coercion or exploitation of the Muslim masses may be possible'.

BRITAIN AND INDIA

After reviewing rapidly the history of the events which had led to the present communal and constitutional impasse, the President said, 'By far the most disturbing feature for Great Britain in the present struggle, from the point of view of world opinion, is the anomalous relationship between England and India. If Germany's ruthless and brutal disregard of the right of other sovereign States to live peacefully is a challenge to civilization and therefore, Britain and France must stake their all on it, Britain should be the last to challenge India's right to exist as a sovereign and completely independent State and should, therefore, not obstruct it if they desire to frame their own constitution. Sooner or later this principle on which the whole of that civilization is based and for whose preservation millions of Englishmen and Frenchmen are ready to lay down their lives cannot fail to be recognized by Britain. Sooner or later, therefore, England must make up her mind to honour the cheque which she has proclaimed that she has drawn in India's favour. By the unwise action of the All India Muslim League however, England, for the time being, has found it possible to bring the Indian Muslims to the fore and has declared that since the Congress, whose representative position in eight out of eleven provinces cannot be constitutionally questioned, has not yet made its peace with the Muslim League, the encashment of the Dominion Status cheque must be deferred indefinitely'.

Proceeding, Mr Baksh pointed out that the Muslims of India appeared in the eyes of the world as the main obstacle in the way of India's progress as a whole. 'No Mussalmans with the sense slightest of realism and self-respect can possibly tolerate for a moment that he should be made a political scapegoat and the evil consequences of the process should be allowed to react unfavourably on his own and the coming generation's political and material future', he said. 'The proposal, if not promptly and authoritatively repudiated by a representative gathering like this, is calculated to cause infinite harm to our Indian co-religionists throughout the Muslim and non-Muslim parts of the world and much more so at home'.

LEAGUE'S CREDENTIAL QUESTIONED

Contesting the claim of the Muslim League as the sole representative body of the Indian Mussalmans, Mr Allah Baksh said that the representative character of the Congress as a political party with a majority in seven and controlling power in the eighth province was comprehensive. 'But what credentials beyond public meetings does the League present to be recognized as the representative of the majority of Indian Muslims? The only way to test its representative character would be to send the League to the polls on the specific issue of the policy it has declared at Lahore. For whatever may have been its support before in the provinces where the Muslims are in a minority, it has definitely injured it beyond repair by suddenly throwing the minority Muslims overboard and propounding a wholly impracticable scheme of creating a sovereign State of some crores of Punjabi, Sindhi, Pathan and Baluch Muslims in the North-West and another of about two and a half crores of Assamese and Bengali Muslims in the north-east separated by over a thousand miles. Only after these dreams have materialized will these sovereign and independent States begin to negotiate a treaty for the protection of the Muslim minorities throughout India. If the Muslim minorities in Hindu majority provinces are to wait for the protection of their rights till these independent and sovereign States of the Punjab and Bengal have come into existence, they will have to wait till the Greek Calends.

TWO NATIONS THEORY

Dealing with the 'two nations theory of certain leading Muslim politicians of admittedly Indian origin', Mr Allah Baksh said that Indian Muslims were proud to be the Indian nationals and they were equally proud that their spiritual level and credal realm was Islam. Every Muslim going for pilgrimage to the holy Mecca was invariably described as a Hindu by every Arab and all Indian Muslims were similarly known as Hindustani in Iran and Afghanistan and as Indians throughout the World. 'A majority of the ninety million Indian Muslims who are descendants of the earlier inhabitants of India are in no sense other than sons of soil with the Dravidian and the Aryan and have as much right to be reckoned among the earliest settlers of this common land. The nationals of different countries cannot divest themselves of their nationality merely by embracing one or the other faith. In its universal sweep, Islam, the faith, can run in and out of as many nationalities and regional cultures as may be found in the world'.

After describing the bounds that knitted the Hindus and the Muslims in various walks of human life, Mr Baksh declared that no segretated or isolated region but the whole of India was the homeland of all the Indian Muslims and no Hindu or Muslim or any other had the right to deprive them of their homeland.

PARTITION PROPOSALS EXAMINED

Analysing the Partition scheme, the speaker said that if the sixty lakhs of NWF Province, Baluchi and Sindhi Muslims were excluded from the North-west Pakistan because they had a more realistic sense of things, the Punjab, with a population of 1½ crore of Muslims, confined between Campbellpore and perhaps Lahore, would constitute a problematic little Pakistan with rather drastically curtailed financial resources and reduced to the position of one of the bigger Indian States. 'I have heard it said that the Sikhs and the Jats or at least Sikhs can be won over by fair concessions to remain in this Pakistan. Of Course, such an infantile assumption proceeds on the basis that the bargaining power of the others does not exist. Once again, if over a crore of Sikhs and Jats and other Hindus of the Punjab choose to stay in this Pakistan, one fails to see how it will be different in political composition and power from the present autonomous provinces and in what sense it will become an independent sovereign Islamic State. In the first place, the NWF Province, Baluchistan and Sind which now enjoy comfortable majorities in autonomous provinces helped by the centre financially and in the matter of defence would not care to exchange their present position for a minority in another unit, though overwhelmingly Muslim.

But if for the same of argument they did, who would bear, asked Mr Baksh, their deficit of over Rs 2½ crores and what guarantee, without efficient financial resources, would the Punjab offer regarding land, air and sea defences against not merely the external but the internal invaders? The total revenue of the proposed Pakistan, if all the units contemplated including Kashmir and Bahawalpur coalesced (excluding the region which is predominantly Hindu-cum-Sikh), would not exceed Rs 16 to 17 crores, all of which was required for daily administration. And if the railways and customs and other central revenues of Pakistan's share yielded, say, another five or six or even ten crores of net surplus, the whole of it would not be enough to maintain the defences of the unit against external invasions and to satisfy the interest charges and other liabilities. It was true that the unit if allowed a period of peace and prosperity might develop its industries and build up like Czechoslovakia a decent enough position and defence force but why should it be assumed that the rest of India would all this time stand still and so would the transborder neighbours including Russia and that their resources would not be put to the best use. Who then would defend this unit against Russia or Afghanistan in the meanwhile in case a new builder of a Russian or some other empire rose? If the British were asked to hold this baby until it was strong enough to stand on its own legs, in the first place what was the *quid pro quo*, and in the second what was this smokescreen of an independent sovereign and Islamic State for?

'The North-East Pakistan is ten times more fantastic and a hundred times more fragile', said Mr Baksh. 'In the conception of the North-Western Pakistan or the Punjab, there is at least a possibility of its being linked up with more powerful Afghan or Russian Muslim neighbours, but the Bengal and Assam Pakistan will be an isolation quarantine, with no superfluity of material races to its credit, and which, therefore, may not take long to be quickly absorbed by its more enterprising neighbours. But if the League does not contemplate anything better than Burma and Ceylon, the credulous should not be deceived into thinking of an independent Islamic State but they should be frankly told that another Palestine is sought to be created under the British Mandate. Let us not waste time on this part of the grotesque scheme.

'It is a matter for some satisfaction that responsible spokesmen of the British Government have scotched this scheme at the outset. We may, however, hope that the indirect and subtle encouragement some influential individual Englishmen have so far given to the sponsors of the scheme, for obvious reasons, will not continue to vitiate a perfectly straight issue. It should be carefully noted that no responsible Minister of the Punjab cared to lend the slightest support to the scheme nor has any popular support been forthcoming from either the Punjab or Bengal. It is quite obvious that if even a decision along these lines was ever likely to be taken, it would rest not with a political organization or a party but with the accredited representatives of the population concerned and, therefore, it is difficult to understand the League's objection to a Constituent Assembly in which Indian Mussalmans should decide the question of the form of constitution under which they would be prepared to live peacefully. If the population of the majority provinces do not want the League's Pakistan and if the Muslim minority in the Hindu majority provinces cannot dictate to the Muslim majority province, it is difficult to see on what constitutional basis the League can possibly advance its demand. To my mind it is perfectly obvious that a political personality of Mr Jinnah's distinction cannot but admit the force of this argument and therefore, I am inclined to believe that the Pakistan scheme is about the most indiscreet approach to a serious problem and as such has torpedoed the very basis of a reasonable settlement'.

Referring to the world situation, Khan Bahadur Allah Baksh described the present world war as the birth pangs of a new world order. He said that the aggressor had been condemned by all right thinking men as a menace to human freedom and civilization. 'Where ultimately all this will lead none can clearly foresee, but one thing is certain beyond a shadow of doubt, that unless the brutal and ruthless methods of the aggressor are checked and also the ambitious maps of all the empires are rolled up, whether they are based on democratic or totalitarian ideologies, the peace and prosperity for which the vast bulk of mankind has been pining for will not come into sight.'

78. Pakistan Scheme Denounced by Azad Muslim Conference, 29 April 1940

Indian Annual Register, 1940, Vol. I, pp. 329.

After a discussion lasting over a hundred and thirty minutes, the Conference passed unanimously tonight the resolution on the Pakistan scheme characterizing it as impracticable and harmful to the country's interest generally and of Muslims in particular. *Maulana Habibu Rehman* moved the following resolution:

'This Conference considers that any scheme which divides India into Hindu India and Moslem India is impracticable and harmful to the country's interest generally and those of Moslems in particular.

'This Conference is convinced that the inevitable result of such a scheme will be that obstacles will be created in the path of Indian freedom and British Imperialism will exploit it for its own purpose'.

The mover said that the Conference was one of the most representative gatherings held in India in recent years. Tracing the history of political agitation in India, he said, 'We want a democratic government, which would have representatives of all communities and interests. We want a government of the Indian masses and not of the British or the Rajas or Nawabs or of any religious group'. Proceeding, the Maulana said that communalism had been inflamed not only by Muslims but by Hindus also. Muslims were in the front rank in the freedom struggle as was seen in the Frontier in 1930. The Government of India Act 1935 had enhanced the power and prestige of Indian masses and electorates. It was alleged that under the present constitution, Muslims were oppressed by the Congress. But that was framed by non-Congressmen and by those who stood for separate electorates and safeguards for minorities. He challenged Mr Jinnah to come out in an open meeting and put his case before the audience. They would also put their case before the audience. 'We will leave the verdict to the community as to whether Mr Jinnah or we served the Muslims best'.

Criticizing the Pakistan scheme and the cry of 'Islam in danger', the speaker said that the demand for exchange of populations had now been given up and Muslim minorities would have to remain in Hindu India. He declared that the Pakistan scheme would never be accepted by any sensible Muslim as it would reduce autonomous provinces to the status of Indian States. Proceeding, the Maulana said that it was Hindus who were responsible for making the Muslim League strong. The Hindu press did Mr Jinnah's propaganda and weakened the cause of Nationalist Muslims. The Maulana asked the audience whether anyone was in favour of Pakistan. The audience signified their opposition to the scheme. The speaker, continuing, said that he did not want protection for Islam either from Hindus or any other community. He would protect it by his own strength and sacrifice. 'I could not be protected by Pakistan'.

The resolution was seconded by Maulvi Abdulla Ulkazi of Bengal, who said that no Muslim in Bengal was in favour of the partition. He added that the proposal was likely to deprive two to three crores of Muslims living in Hindu zones of their rights. The same would be the fate of Muslim buildings of worship and shrines.

Hafiz Mohamed Ibrahim, ex-Minister of the United Provinces, further supported the resolution. He said that the alleged oppression of Muslims in the Congress-governed provinces was claimed to be the reason for the partition scheme, but the question was whether oppression of Muslims, if any, would cease even under the Pakistan. He did not think so. Further, the allegation of oppression, he declared, was baseless and without any foundation. But the Muslim League had propagated these allegations amongst the Muslim masses, because some of the Leaguers were not included in the Ministries. Mr Ibrahim claimed that even if the League Ministries had been in power, they would not have done as much for the Muslims as the Congress Governments had done.

Mr Abdur Rehman Khan (Frontier), in lending support to the resolution, described the Pakistan scheme as a ruse to keep India under British domination.

The resolution was passed.

79. Pakistan Scheme 'Impracticable and Harmful': Report of the All India Muslim Independent Conference

Hindustan Times, 30 April 1940.

New Delhi,
Wednesday

Delhi Conference Votes for Constituent Assembly
NO SEPARATE ELECTORATES
'Pakistan' Fraud Exposed

AZAD MUSLIMS CONDEMN LEAGUE SCHEME
THE ALL INDIA MUSLIM INDEPENDENT CONFERENCE WHICH MET IN OPEN SESSION IN DELHI AGAIN LAST NIGHT AND CONTINUED ITS DELIBERATIONS TILL THE EARLY HOURS OF THIS MORNING PASSED UNANIMOUSLY AT 1 A.M. THE RESOLUTION WAS PASSED ON THE PAKISTAN SCHEME, CHARACTERIZING IT AS IMPRACTICABLE AND HARMFUL TO THE COUNTRY'S INTERESTS GENERALLY AND OF THE MUSLIMS IN PARTICULAR.

THE CONFERENCE ALSO PASSED A RESOLUTION DEMANDING A CONSTITUENT ASSEMBLY TO FRAME INDIA'S FUTURE CONSTITUTION.

In the Subjects Committee which had a prolonged sitting yesterday the resolution on the Constituent Assembly had been amended to clarify the point that the Muslims would not have separate electorates in the process of voting in the proposed Constituent Assembly. In the resolution as it stood originally there was a clause which could be interpreted to mean that the Muslim representatives of the Constituent Assembly would be elected by Muslims alone.

The open session has been extended for a day more, e.g., there will be another meeting today at which the resolution on the rights of the minorities which was inconclusively deliberated on by the Subjects Committee last night would be placed and discussed.

When the open session of the All India Muslim Independent Conference met last night at about 11 pm in a packed pandal a condolence resolution on the death of Maulana Mujib ul-Rahman was passed unanimously.

Maulana Habib-Ul-Rahman of the Majlis-i-Ahrar was given an ovation when he rose to move the resolution condemning the Partition scheme.

Tracing the history of the growth of the nationalist movement in India, Maulana Habib-Ul-Rahman said that since the nationalist movement became virile in India, the enemies of India's freedom had been trying to create divisions among the Hindus and Muslims. He wanted them to dispel from their minds the dreams of a Hindu Raj, Muslim Raj or Sikh Raj. The freedom for which they were fighting would be the freedom of the masses, the establishment of a Panchayati Raj in India. He emphasized that it was futile to think in terms of Hindu Raj or Muslim Raj which was an impossibility in the present democratic age in India. He recalled the sacrifices of the Muslims in the struggle for freedom.

The Maulana challenged Mr Jinnah to come and address a Muslims' meeting anywhere on the issue of the reactionary lead which had been given by the League.

Referring to the Deliverance Day celebrations organized by the Muslim League, the speaker declared that he would be with Mr Jinnah, if the latter succeeded in convincing the Governors and the Governor-General that the Mussalmans were really oppressed by the Congress Ministries. He demanded the impeachment of Mr Jinnah for misleading the Mussalmans. He said that it was the height of absurdity to talk of Muslim Raj and Hindu Raj as long as the whole India was under British yoke. The entire population of Sind and the NWF Province was not more than 60 lakhs. No single community could establish its rule in Bengal and the Punjab where the Muslims were not in a decisive majority.

He declared that no sane Muslim could accept the Pakistan scheme which was positively dangerous to their interests. The speaker felt that the sponsors of the Pakistan scheme were the same old allies of British imperialism who had been their opponents during the last 20 years. He thought that undue importance had been given to the Pakistan scheme which was a dead letter.

The speaker asked his audience to signify their disapproval of the Muslim League by raising their hands. The entire audience without a single exception raised their hands and shouted slogans of 'Pakistan Murdabad'.

'Unholy' Conception of Pakistan Scheme

Mr Abdulla Altafi of the Bengal Krishak Praja Party supporting the resolution said that his province was on the other end of India. He declared that the Muslims of his province were totally opposed to the scheme of partition which was detrimental to the political and economic interests of the Muslims. The speaker felt that the scheme, if carried into effect, will leave Muslims in predominantly Hindu provinces at the mercy of the majority community. He reminded them that the United Provinces and Bihar were centres of Islamic culture in India. He asked them as to whether they were prepared to accept an inferior status in these provinces. He warned them that the whole conception of Pakistan was 'Unholy' and designed to perpetuate India's slavery.

He asked them to repudiate it with all their force.

Hafiz Mohammed Ibrahim, ex-Minister, United Provinces, further supporting the resolution said that ever since the establishment of Congress Ministries in India, the stories of atrocities against Muslims in Congress provinces were circulated. Even admitting these stories as true for the sake of argument, the speaker asked whether the Pakistan scheme was a sufficient safeguard against the oppression of Muslims in the minority provinces. He thought that the division of India would make the position of the Muslims more insecure.

Reverting to the stories of atrocities, he said that, as he was one of the members of a Congress Cabinet, he could speak with some authority. Speaking as a Muslim as one of their brothers in faith, Hafiz Sahib said that these stories were absolutely baseless. It was, however, an open fact that the Muslim League carried on a campaign against the Congress Ministries. He felt that those in the Muslim League who could not secure ministerships, deliberately spread these stories. He claimed that the Muslim Ministers in the Congress cabinets did more for their co-religionists than what the Muslim Leaguers would have been able to do, if they had been in the Congress Cabinet. He felt that the conception of partition was based on fear. He said that it was a mere nightmare to hold out the prospect of Islamic rule. No Government other than a fully democratic Government could function in India as a whole or in the provinces. The majority could not deny to the minority its legitimate rights and share in the administration. He characterized the Lahore scheme as a shame and a huge fraud, a dream that could never be realized.

Bankruptcy of Statesmanship

Proceeding, Hafiz Ibrahim said that the partition scheme betrayed utter ignorance of the real state of affairs in India and the bankruptcy of statesmanship on the part of its authors. He emphasized that there was no escape from a democratic system of government at the centre. He was sure that all legitimate aspirations of the Indian Mussalmans could be realized within the framework of a democratic system.

Arbab Abdul Rahman, MLA of the NWF Province, further supporting the resolution, said that the Pakistan scheme was an absurdity and designed to put obstacles in the struggle for freedom. They will have to resist this and similar schemes. The world was on the verge of a revolution. No scheme, however attractive, could avert it. The division of India would make her more vulnerable to foreign attack. He declared that as long as one Pathan follower of Khan Abdul Gaffar Khan was alive, they would keep the flag of freedom flying. He condemned the false cry of 'Islam in Danger' raised by the Muslim League.

Referring to the latest developments in Sind, the speaker said that it had now been established beyond doubt that the Muslim Leaguers had raised the bogey of Islam in danger in order to secure ministerships....

80. Azad Muslim Conference on Safeguard to Minorities
   Hindustan Times, 1 May 1940.

The Azad Muslim Conference concluded its four day session late last night after passing a resolution setting up a board of 27 members, with the power to co-opt other Muslim leaders and experts, to draw up a charter of safeguards for the minorities.

By another resolution the conference made it clear that the Muslim members to the proposed Constituent Assembly would be elected by the Muslims themselves.

'I wish to make it clear beyond doubt that our resolution defining Complete Independence as the goal of Indian Mussalmans does not mean that we will not join the struggle for freedom till our religious and communal rights are safeguarded. On the other hand, our attitude on the question of participation in the struggle for freedom has always been unequivocal. We have taken full part in the past struggle for freedom, and are prepared to join the coming struggle. We want to reiterate that we would not rest content till we achieve Complete Independence'. This declaration was made by Hafiz Ibrahim, Ex-Minister, UP moving the resolution on the minorities' rights in the open session of the All India Independent Conference. The proceedings commenced with the recitation of the Quran. The Pandal was as usual overflowing with people. A large number of 'pardanashin' women watched the proceedings from the Zenana enclosure.

No Caste Barrier

Moving the resolution on the minorities' rights, which sought to set up a Board consisting of 27 members to be nominated by the President K.B. Allah Bux, for the purpose of defining the minorities' rights, Hafiz Ibrahim, in the course of his speech said that they had already a comprehensive resolution declaring Complete Independence as their goal. All the organizations represented in the Conference stood for Complete Independence which to them meant freedom for all the citizens, irrespective of caste and creed. They visualized that every citizen will have equal opportunities of rising to his or her full status in a free India. The Government would protect every citizen. No community would be able to oppress the other community. The Congress had accepted this position and has declared so time and again.

Problem of Safeguards

Continuing, Hafiz Sahib said that he wanted to remove another misunderstanding by making it clear that they did not rely on any foreign power for the protection of their rights. They believed that they could safeguard their rights effectively by mutual agreement. They were actuated by a burning desire to usher in freedom in their country in putting forward this resolution. They did not aim at anything more than incorporating in the future constitution of India effective safeguards for the protection of their cultural and religious rights. The goal of Complete Independence was not incompatible with that desire. They were always prepared to join the struggle for freedom. They did not seek concessions from any outside power. Referring to the obstructionist attitude adopted by the Muslim League, Hafiz Ibrahim said that the Lahore resolution on partition showed that the League had no constructive proposal for safeguarding the special rights of the Muslims. The Congress tried thrice to come to a settlement with the League, but the latter every time, refused to define its demands and insisted on its being accepted as the sole representative organization of the Muslims. Could any sensible man believe that this demand of the League had anything to do with the special rights of the Muslims. It seemed as if they looked to a foreign power for support. They relied on the British Government. That was why they felt the necessity of giving constructive lead to the Muslims on that question.

Continuing, Hafiz Sahib explained the different clauses of the resolution.

Bedrock of Unity

Referring to the negotiations between the Congress and Mr Jinnah, the speaker blamed Mr Jinnah for losing a unique opportunity for bringing about Hindu–Muslim unity. If Mr Jinnah had not insisted on his impossible demand of the recognition of the League as the sole representative organization of the Muslims, there would have been a settlement in twenty-four hours. He emphasized the necessity of preparing for the coming struggle.

League Criticized

Maulana Ahmed Said further supporting the resolution said that the decision of the Conference would be the common decision of seven powerful Muslim organizations, which in combination, represented a far larger body of Muslim opinion than the League. He thought that the League consisted of arm-chair politicians and they who had gathered there had a record of sacrifice and suffering in the struggle for freedom. He characterized the League's representative claim as totally false and untenable. He condemned the Pakistan Scheme as un-Islamic in its conception. He revealed that Maulana Zafar Ali Khan, a prominent leader of the League had confessed in private talks that the partition scheme was an absurdity. He was confident that no power on earth could resist the united decision of the proposed Board that will define the Muslims' demands.

The Resolution

The following is the text of the resolution as passed:

Whereas in the future constitution of India it would be essential, in order to ensure stability of Government and preservation of security, that individuals as well as communities should be contented, this Conference considers it necessary that a scheme of safeguards as regards vital matters mentioned below should be prepared to the satisfaction of the Muslims.

This Conference appoints a board consisting of 27 persons. This board should after the fullest investigation, consultation and consideration, make its recommendations for submission to the next session of the Conference so that the Conference may utilize the recommendations as a means of securing a permanent national settlement of the communal questions. These recommendations should be submitted within two months.

The matters referred to the Board are as follows:

Protection of Muslim culture, personal law and religious rights.

Political rights of Muslims and other protection.

The form of the future constitution of India to be non-unitary and federal with absolutely essential and unavoidable powers for the Federal Government.

Provision of safeguards will include economic, social and cultural rights of Muslims and their share in the public service.

The Board will be empowered to fill up the vacancy of a member in a suitable manner. The Board will have the right to co-opt other members by a unanimous vote. It will be empowered also to consult other Muslim bodies and if it considers necessary any responsible organization of the country.

The 27 members of the Board will be nominated by the President.

The quorum for the meeting of the Board will be five.

Constituent Assembly

Mr Asaf Ali then moved the following resolution:

Since the safeguards for the communal rights of different communities will be determined in the Constituent Assembly referred to in an earlier resolution, this conference considers it necessary to declare that the Muslim members of this Constituent Assembly will be elected by the Muslims themselves.

Mr Asaf Ali speaking as a member of the Congress Working Committee said that he wished to clear the misunderstanding that the proposed method of election was incompatible with the position taken up by the nationalist Muslims on the issue of separate versus joint electorates. He thought that by passing this resolution, they would not make themselves liable to a charge of inconsistency. He reminded them that the Congress had decided to give the right of self-determination to all the groups and the communities in the matter of framing safeguards for the protection of their special rights. The Muslims had their special cultural and religious needs and it was only proper that they alone should have a final say in the matter of framing safeguards for the satisfaction of their needs. He vigorously defended the position taken up by the Congress. It was open to the Constituent Assembly to abolish separate electorates or to retain them. The resolution was only in relation to the election of the Muslim members of the Constituent Assembly and therefore, strictly limited in its scope. He thought that no reasonable man could question the soundness of the proposition that the Hindus should not interfere in the matter of the nature of safeguards necessary for the protection of Muslim rights.

81. Mian Iftikhar-Ud-Din's Presidential Address at the 11th Session of the Kerala Provincial Political Conference

Hindustan Times, 10 May 1940.

Mian Iftikhar-Ud-Din of the Punjab, presiding over the 11th session of the Kerala Provincial Political Conference at Azad Nagar, Kottakal, observed in the course of his presidential address:

It is my belief that the communal problem, originally a creation of the British Imperialism, has assumed its present form on account of the clash in the interests of the various classes of our country and it is today being used as a weapon of defence by Imperialism and feudalism. To understand this I have not to go outside my own province where the communal and reactionary leaders of the three communities namely, the Muslims, the Hindus and the Sikhs, who inhabit the Punjab have come together and have arrayed themselves against the Congress. These leaders are co-operating with each other to safeguard their own landed interests as against the rising movement of the masses. If the Muslim League leader and his colleagues, the leaders of the Sikh communal reactionary organizations—the Khalsa Nationalist Party etc.—and the leaders of the Hindu feudal interests had gone to the masses of their respective communities for support in the maintenance of their jagirs, estates, etc., there would have been no response, nor the straight appeal for help to prolong the life of British Imperialism, with which the existence of Feudal India is linked, could have attracted the masses. The public, however uneducated as it is, is easily taken in by the communal appeal. It does not see the game and does not realize that, if such leaders or rather the exploiters of the masses, in spite of their communal differences can come together for the protection of their feudal or British Imperial interests, it is only just and logical for the exploited to make common cause for the furtherance of their class interests and for ending their exploitation.

In the Name of Religion

I have given a provincial example, but if you consider the major issues that face the country closely you will find that, generally speaking, the policies of the communalists of all countries coincide. Just consider the two most important questions that face us today in the sphere of national politics, the question of the Indian states and that of international politics, that of war. On these questions the policies of the Muslim League and the Hindu Mahasabha, of Mr Mohammad Ali Jinnah and Mr Savarkar, no matter what they say or write at times, in objective results are the same. They both aim at the prolongation of the barbarous rule of the Indian Princes on the one hand and of the exploitation by Britain of the Indian men and resources on the other. Naturally it comes to one's mind that if Mr Savarkar regards it detrimental to Hindu interests, vis-a-vis the Muslim interests, to oppose the autocratic rule of the Indian Princes or to deny support to Britain in this imperialist war, it must be beneficial for the Muslim communal interests to follow the opposite course. But we know in objective results their policies coincide. Both the League and the Mahasabha in practice are the tools of the Indian States and of British Imperialism. Actually it is calculated and considered policy that they follow for obtaining a further lease of life for feudalism and imperialism which I said are interdependent. If the leaders of those communal organizations had appealed to the masses in the name of their own anti-national and unpatriotic interests, they would have elicited no response. They therefore, wisely appealed to the masses in the name of religion.

Muslim Masses Misled

The question however, that rightly comes to one's mind is how is it that the Muslim masses in general have responded to the appeal of Mr Mohammad Ali Jinnah whereas Mr Savarkar and his colleagues have not been successful with their community. The answer to this question is the key to the understanding of the communal problem today.

As it is clear, the illiterate masses of India are being led today by the upper and the middle classes. It had so happened that the upper and middle classes amongst the Hindus are chiefly comprised of the rising capitalists to whose advantage it is to help the struggle for freedom in order to obtain concessions from British Imperialism and to exploit for their own advantage the resources of the country, the slogan of Swadeshi being of help to them. The middle classes amongst the Hindus too, having started education earlier than their Muslim brethren, would gain if the policy of the reservation of jobs gave place to free competition. The two upper classes amongst the Hindus, therefore, having found it beneficial to their class interests to support the Congress, the Hindu masses have not been misled and the result is that they have rallied round the Congress. On the contrary, the upper class in the Muslims which is mainly constituted of big land owners, having visualized their inevitable absence in the scheme of a free progressive and industrialized India, have come out as our opponents. The middle class amongst Muslims with its late start in education, thanks to the Mullahs, can get its share of jobs only through the protection of a communalist organization and by the reservation of services. The two upper classes amongst the Muslims, therefore, finding it harmful to their immediate class interests to join the freedom movement, have succeeded in dissuading a section of the Muslim masses from participating in our struggle.

In other words, the immediate interests of the masses amongst Hindus and their upper and middle classes being common, the Hindus in general have joined the Congress. On the other hand, the immediate class interests of the Muslim upper and lower classes being opposed to those of the poverty-stricken Mussalmans who constitute 90 per cent of the Muslim population, they have misled their poor brethren in the name of religion for their own interests. And the masses being simple-minded the Muslim League has succeeded in misleading them. This in short, is the reason of the lack of full response on the part of Mussalmans to the call of the Congress.

Refusal to Come to Terms

To understand that it is not really on account of communal considerations that the Muslim League has refused to come to terms with the Congress you have only to remember the Congress stand with regard to the communal question. The Congress has conceded to the Mussalmans or any other minority which wished to exercise that right, to elect their representatives on the basis of separate electorates in the future Constituent Assembly of India. In the event of there being a difference of opinion between the majority of the Muslim representatives and that of the Hindu representatives to the Constituent Assembly, the question of difference, it is further conceded, be referred to an independent international tribunal. This brings the minority on the same footing as the majority. The next step could only be that of reducing the majority to minority. And that, you will agree, no sane person could demand.

The Muslim League having then no answer to the fairness of this offer replied firstly by the Deliverance Day, but this alone was not sufficient to be the programme of the Muslim League. Hence the impossible demand to partition India. There was no other way to distract the attention of the masses and to prevent them from following the path of freedom and progress. There was no other weapon. Had there been an agreement on the communal question between the League and the Congress, the next step would logically have been that of struggle against British Imperialism, the fight for the liberation of India. That meant suffering and sacrifice. Of that the League leaders were not capable. On the other hand, they knew that their exposure would disillusion the Mussalmans who follow their party with some sincerity. That is why a new stunt was necessary and that the Lahore session of the All India Muslim League has given us in the form of a demand for autonomous Muslim States.

Giving Permanence to Foreign Rule

Before proceeding further it would not be out of place to pause for a moment and to ponder over the proposal to partition India. A hundred and one objections have been raised in the criticism of this scheme. I have no intention to go through them. I have only this much to say that any scheme to partition India at this juncture amounts to nothing less than keeping this country in permanent subjection. As we all know, the first attempt of British Imperialism would be to continue to rule over and to exploit a settled and more or less united India. Failing that, the British can only retain their hold or prolong our exploitation in a divided India.

If there were two or more autonomous States in India, the policy of an outside power would obviously be to enter into an alliance with one or the other and to exploit its resources on the promise of helping it against the other. If British Imperialism were to enter into alliance, say, with the Muslim India of Mr Jinnah's imagination, it would naturally demand a price for its help against the Hindu India. This leaving aside for the interest of the Hindu India for the moment would in itself result in the permanent dependence of Muslim India on Britain. On the other hand, if the Hindu India were prepared to pay a greater price for British help against the Muslim India and its friends, the Muslim India will find it difficult to live in peace or even to maintain it's independence. It is obvious therefore, that the proposal for partitioning India amounts to nothing less than the maintenance of permanent rule of British Imperialism over this country. It would lead the Hindus and Mussalmans of the so-called autonomous India to interminable conflicts with each other, not to mention the unimaginable plight of the minorities in the Hindu and the Muslim Indias. There could be no better scheme to make foreign rule in this country permanent.

Muslim Interests

With reference to the question of the Indian freedom in relation to the Mussalmans, allow me to touch on one or more points. To my mind, if we must look at it even from a purely Muslim communal angle, it is more in the interest of the Indian Mussalmans to fight for the freedom of their country than it is to the interests of the Hindu masses. The Muslims are generally poor and those who have any wealth of landed property are being left behind in the era of the rise of capitalism. Their future hopes, therefore, lie in the birth of a new world order, in the establishment of a more equitable economic structure and in the termination of exploitation both by foreign and Indian interests. The liquidation of British Imperialism is a prerequisite of any such change.

All those who are even slightly conversant with the history of the world during the last 50 years know that the present state of India has been the most important cause of the backwardness of the Islamic countries of the world. We all know that the British policy of interference in Egypt and Arabia has mainly been due to the desire on the part of British Imperialism to keep its sea route to India safe. Palestine was carved out and the Jews dumped there partly for the purpose of having under British control the base for a future land route to the Arabian and Indian seas and to India. This also explains the existence of dependent state of Iraq. On account of its affinity to the British sphere of interests, Iran too has never been able to raise its head and its natural wealth is being permanently drained away by the British capitalists. The history of Afghanistan is too near home to require a mention.

You will realize then that the Muslim League is impeding the march of India towards freedom and is not serving the cause of the Islamic world, not to mention the harm that its policy is doing to the people of India and other downtrodden nations. So to repeat, it is more necessary even for pure communal consideration for the Mussalmans of this country to fight for the freedom of India than it is for their Hindu brethren and a free India would bring better days not only for India but for the Muslims beyond the boundaries of this country also.

82. Extracts from *Tarikh Shia* (Urdu) by Hakim Muhammad Anwar Ali Khan

No. 141/VIII–1008, 12 January 1940, Records Office, Assam Secretariat.

Reality

It is a fact that until the country is free no one can have a breath of satisfaction.

Go and drown yourself somewhere and do not talk of life, if you cannot set your country free.

How painful is cold for the poor! How can he know it who cannot shiver with cold?

Address to the Youth

Get up, O Young and set right the degraded condition of the nation. Steer shore the boat of the nation's life.

Spread yourself in the form of the cloud of freedom on the country's horizon and hide behind it the sun of slavery.

O youngmen, mix your youth in dust for the honour of the country and the nation.

Set this mother India which is rolling in the dust of slavery on the throne of freedom.

If communalists obstruct your path mix your blood with their sweat.

If you listen to me, raze to the ground these mosques and temples where these dissensions are taught.

The Pledge of Young

I swear by my mother's milk that I will not only spill my sweat but my blood in the service of the country.

O Ali, not to speak of imprisonment, I will get my head severed for the freedom of India.

Confusion

If the love of one's country is a sin, I am a sinner. If the love of one's freedom is a fault, I am a defaulter.

There is the song of freedom on my lips and in my heart is the love of country.

I have committed this offence and I am a culprit.

If you are not free what use are the temple and the harem(Mecca).

O my dear country, I am one of your devotees.

Capitalist and the Labourer

O you capitalists who are steeped in luxury, may I tell on whom depend your riches?

He, who you see (toiling) in this scorching heat when you enjoy (breeze) of the electric fan.

That is the labourer who is toiling at this hour and with bowed head mixing his blood with his sweat (Lit. water).

He who does not get a hut to hide his head and who passes the night by the roadside.

He whose wife is clad in old rags and whose children wear the cloths cast off by your children.

The Writing of Fate

The sigh of the desperate is going to produce effect. A world is going to be topsy-turvy.

All oppression and tyranny of the aliens is going to end. The evening of sorrow is departing and the day of happiness is going to dawn.

O Ali, fearlessly tell the powers that the heedless India is going to be heedful.

The Evening of Poverty

The dogs of the rulers are fed with milk in England by the money earned by you.

But you do not get even barley bread, how can you live?

All the wealth is being plundered and going to England and Japan day and night.

O Ali, it is due to slavery that India is poor today.

Lesson of Nationalism

Go on taking goblet after goblet of the wine of freedom and in its ecstasy go on singing songs of patriotism.

Your intoxication itself will be your guide. Continue your forward march though at a stumbling gait.

Do not be involved in the quarrels of 'Jai Bhagwan' (Hindu Shout) and 'Allah-o-Akbar' (Muslim Shout). Go on shouting Jai (victory to the motherland).

Tear into shreds the flag of falsehood in the world and hoist the flags of truth.

O Ali any one may listen or not but you should go on singing the ecstatic songs of freedom.

Lesson of Freedom

Be disgusted with the world of the rich. Be the sympathizer of the world of the poor. If you want to be free then get up from profound slumber. Be that strong wall of steel against which the enemy may break his head by striking. If you want the relish of life.

Be a sinner of patriotism.

What is a life of slavery, it is not life.

Be a leader or a give up your life. If you want to set your country free.

Be brave and self-respecting.

O Ali, be ready to tear apart federation in India.

G.   SIKHS AND CHRISTIANS

83.   Repudiate Mr Jinnah and the League: A Letter by a Nationalist Sikh to the Editor

Hindustan Times, 3 February 1940.

Sir, Through the columns of your paper I beg to draw the attention of the leaders of the Sikhs, the Christians and the Harijan communities to the fact that Mr Jinnah has lately been dragging the fair name of the other minority communities in his crusade against the Congress. He has been preaching that the religion, culture and language of the Muslims and the minorities are in danger at the hands of the Congress and that the Congress is out to establish a Hindu Raj in India.

Mr Jinnah is trying to make the other minorities tools in furthering his anti-national activities. His efforts have brought the minority problem to the fore-front of our national life as if it is a problem of all the minorities in India. In fact, it is a problem of Muslim League leadership. Only the Leaguers, the Ambedkarites, Nawabs, and now the Justicites have joined his chorus. The majority of the Harijans, excepting Dr Ambedker's group, are with the Congress, and Mr Jinnah never received support from all parties of Harijans. The Sikhs have always been active nationalists and they are now a part of the Congress in Punjab. They have never held communal electorates and the communal award as highly detrimental to the growth of the Indian nation. The last session of the All India Conference of Indian Christians and the session of the UP Indian Christian Conference held at Mirzapur last November will prove that the Christians too have condemned communalism in unambiguous terms. Presiding over the All India Conference of Indian Christians at Nagpur, Dr H.C. Mukerji remarked that the stand taken by some of the Muslims was improper and unreasonable and regarded it as the result of encouragement received from the British Government. In his opinion, the Muslims, far from labouring under any special disabilities, have been favoured almost everywhere, and that too, at the expense of the majority community. That is exactly what the Sikh leaders have been saying till now.

It is therefore, apparent that the other minorities, referred to so often by Mr Jinnah, are opposed to his policy. Though individual leaders of these minorities have condemned his policy, this has not resulted in removing the impression formed in and outside India that the minorities are standing in the way of India's freedom. Therefore, the leaders of the Sikh, the Christian, the Harijan and the other minorities should immediately convene a conference representing these minorities. Such a conference should vigorously protest against being bracketed with the Muslim League and call upon the latter body not to speak on their behalf in the future. It should also chalk out a uniform policy towards the question of India's freedom, the Indian National Congress, and the communal electorates, etc. This will go a long way to remove the misunderstanding about the position of the minorities.

The urgency of carrying out such a suggestion is proved by the following abstract from an article under the head 'Obstacles to Indian Freedom' written by Mr Asaf Ali, MLA in the Hindustan Times dated October 22, 1939. He says: 'It is now for the League and its collaborators, the Hindu Mahasabha, the Liberal Federation and the leaders of the Scheduled Castes, the Sikh and the Parsis who have been charged with holding up India's progress to return, if they think it advisable in the interest of their own communities and the country, a fitting reply to Lord Zetland'.

As the honour of the other minorities is at stake it is hoped that their leaders and the nationalist Press will give earnest consideration to the above suggestion.

Yours etc.

Ajmer   A Nationalist Sikh

84.   Sikhs Opposed to Muslim League Partition Scheme
Hindustan Times, 5 April 1940.

The Shiromani Gurdwara Prabandhak Committee, which held a special meeting today lasting six hours, declared the determination of the Sikhs to oppose the Muslim League's demand for the creation of separate Muslim and Hindu States in India. Master Tara Singh presided. While expressing satisfaction at the recent resolution of the Khalsa Nationalist Party in this connection, the committee expressed the hope that the Sikh members of the Provincial Legislature, who are cooperating with the Ministerial Party would withdraw their support from the Ministry in case the Muslim members of the Punjab Ministry did not dissociate themselves from the Muslim League.

Jinnah's Pakistan Can Be in Arabia

Sardar Ravel Singh, Jathedar, UP Akali Dal, has issued the following statement regarding the Muslim League scheme of Pakistan:

'The decision of the Muslim League at Lahore demanding division of India into Hindu and Muslim States has come as a rude shock to every Sikh Akali in these provinces. The Punjab is our Dharmakshetra and Matrubhumi and we have a right of sovereignty over it, being the kinsmen of Maharaja Ranjit Singh from whom the British have retained it as a trust property. The Muslims claim Arabia as their holy land and homeland, and we will have no objection if Mr Jinnah and his admirers of the Muslim League evacuate India and go to reside in that land. But so far as the Punjab is concerned, it is ours and ours alone. Not only the Punjab but Afghanistan, the Frontier Province and Kashmir have been our domain and were maintained as such by the great sacrifices of our forefathers. Still the name of Hari Singh Nalva sounds heavily in this dreamland of Mr Jinnah. We Sikhs are a democratic people, and our religion has taught us the great slogan of 'equality, fraternity and liberty'. Therefore, we are always willing and ready to renounce our claim of sovereignty in the general interest of the national good, which, according to us, has only one logical culmination—the united democratic India. However, if communal claims are advanced and an attempt is made to seize our birthright, the Sikhs cannot remain sightseers. Let every Sikh be cautious and watch developments and keep ready for all consequences which the protection and defence of our rights and claims may require'.

85. Three-Nation Theory: Master Tara Singh's Reply to Jinnah

Hindustan Times, 29 March 1940.

Master Tara Singh's Reply to Jinnah

'If the Muslims cannot trust the Hindu majority they should also presume that the Sikhs cannot trust the Muslim majority', said Master Tara Singh, President of the SGPC commenting on the Muslim League resolution.

'I fear', added Master Tara Singh, 'that the Lahore session of the Muslim League has dealt a severe blow to our aspirations of Swaraj as without Muslim cooperation Swaraj is a misnomer'.

'In order to strengthen the Muslim demands the Muslim League claims to represent all the minorities in India, but in reality it ignores all the minorities altogether as and when it suits its purpose. The two nation theory is good as long as it benefits the Muslims, but when the Sikhs put forward the three nation theory it was bad, as it did not suit the communal Muslim leaders'.

Are Mr Jinnah and his associates, asks Master Tara Singh, prepared to admit the three-nation theory in the Punjab and agree to an equal share for each community in the administration of the Province?

'I know they will not' concludes Master Tara Singh.

86. Christian Leaders' Appeal to 'Follow Mahatma Gandhi' in Order to Abolish Communalism

Hindustan Times, 9 January 1940.

Follow Mahatma Gandhi

'Communal ill-feeling is bound to disappear once the recognized leaders of all communities set their faces against it and show by their example that toleration is not inconsistent with orthodoxy. Once this lesson is assimilated by our masses, communalism will no longer have any effect in creating misunderstandings among them'.

Thus observed Dr H.C. Mookerjee, President of the All India Conference of Indian Christians, in the course of a speech on 'Religion, Culture and Communal Harmony' at a public meeting today.

Continuing, Dr Mookerjee said: 'A cosmopolitan outlook has to be cultivated by both the Hindu and the Muslim. This will not come at once but the way can be shown by the leaders of the two communities.

'There is not the slightest doubt that one of the best and most logical of ways to abolish communal ill-feelings is to make the masses understand that at bottom the interests of all, whether Hindu or Muslim, are identical, and that, however, highly ingenious and politically powerful a communalist may be, it is impossible for him to really benefit one community at the cost of, or to the exclusion of, another. If the bulk of one community distrusts the bulk of the other, it is mainly because each community is desirous of securing more than its share of the good things which may be going round. Education, unselfish leadership and an enlightened self-interest will teach them the foolishness of this selfish attitude. No Hindu grudges the past glory of Muslim India, nor do I think that the ordinary Muslim of today puts on any offensive airs of superiority on the strength of a greatness which disappeared more than 200 years ago. This is never a factor in communal differences.'

Muslim Apprehension

Proceeding, the speaker dwelt at length on the question why nationalism among Muslims was discouraged in India by the politically backward section of the community, and said that it was owing to their apprehension that the majority community was aiming at the establishment of a Hindu Raj, in which they, as a minority community, would have to occupy an inferior position. 'They anticipate oppression and tyranny', said Dr Mookerjee, 'and probably interference with the practice of their religious rites and ceremonies. So far as the National Congress is concerned, it had made its position absolutely clear in the fundamental rights resolution carried unanimously at the Karachi Congress. It is, however, true that here and there intemperate language has been used by the Hindu rank and file. Such people cannot but be regarded as rank communalists and so far as I am aware, their conduct is always condemned by those higher up in the Congress organization. The pronouncements made from time to time from the platform of the Hindu Mahasabha have been unfortunate and have tended to increase the apprehensions of a section of the Muslim community. But may I remind them that some very prominent members of the Muslim League who happen to occupy very responsible positions in the provincial administrations have also been equally indiscreet'?

Propaganda

'Whatever the extremist section of the Mahasabha may state, I hold that it is said for propaganda purposes only and to discredit the Congress in the eyes of the Hindus who are supporting it in very much larger numbers than members of any other community. No one except a lunatic will believe that a purely Hindu Raj is practicable or even possible in India in the present day. The 80 odd millions of Muslims, in spite of their numerical inferiority, are a power to be reckoned with. Comparatively small in number, they possess a solidarity and a unity of purpose found in no other single community excepting probably the Sikhs. No minority community anywhere has ever been crushed by mere persecution so long as its members possessed these qualities. The great Muslim community has not only not been crushed but it is gaining strength with every year that passes. The apprehensions which some of them express are either hypocritical cries of alarm aimed at establishing a closer unity and a greater solidarity in the community, or, in the alternative, proof of a defeatist mentality to which I believe, the community as a whole is an utter stranger'. Concluding, Dr Mookerjee said, 'As for the present misunderstanding between the Hindu and the Muslim, which has most unfortunately assumed a communal complexion, we may safely follow Mahatma Gandhi'.

Mr A. Dharam Das observed in the course of his presidential speech at the thirty-fourth annual conference of the Indian Christian Association of the United Provinces, that the communal bogey is the creation of the British Government itself. The seed of separate communal electorates was sown by the Morley-Minto reforms and since then the communal differences have been growing deeper and deeper. Therefore, the Christians should try to remain faithful to their country and join any one of the two political bodies open to the people of all religious persuasions, namely, Congress and the Liberal Association. Their salvation will come through the political and economic independence of the country.

H.   COMMUNAL RIOTS AND TENSIONS

87.   Hindu–Muslim Clashes in Ballygunge, Calcutta

Statesman, 22 January 1940.

Hindu–Moslem Disturbance

About 15 persons were injured some seriously and several arrests were made as the result of a Hindu–Moslem disturbance yesterday at Tiljala, near the Ballygunge railway level-crossing. Prompt action by the police prevented the development of serious communal rioting.

Eight persons were admitted to the Campbell Hospital, Calcutta, several suffering from deep wounds in the scalp and shoulders.

Notifications under section 144 CrPC have been promulgated by the District Magistrate of 24 Parganas (Mr K.A.L. Hill) prohibiting the assemblage of more than five persons and the carrying of lathis, knives and other weapons and imposing a curfew between the hours of 6 pm and 6 am. The orders are to remain in force for three days.

The first clash occurred shortly before noon when there was fighting between groups who used brickbats and other weapons. With the arrival of armed police order was restored but throughout the early afternoon a tense atmosphere existed.

Some sporadic cases of assault were reported towards the evening in the neighbourhood of Rifle Road, and the prohibitory orders were put into force.

Mr A.K. Fazlul Huq, the Premier visited the area twice and conferred with local Moslem leaders.

It is stated that some Moslems wanted to sacrifice a cow in a mosque under construction on Picnic Garden Road, about a hundred yards to the east of the railway line. This was objected to by Hindus of the locality mostly upcountrymen. A settlement, it is said, was arrived at in the presence of Mr B. Rahman, Sub-divisional Officer of Alipore, Khan Bahadur Mr Hidayetulla, Chairman of the Tollygunge Municipality and other local leaders, both Hindu and Moslem, to the effect that as no sacrifice had taken place there in previous years and as Hindus objected to it the *qurbani* sacrifice should take place at a mosque some distance away.

Yesterday morning, however, after prayers it is alleged that some Moslems not belonging to the locality insisted that the sacrifice should take place at the mosque under construction. Hindus raised objections and soon excited mobs of Hindus and Moslems gathered in the neighbourhood and the efforts of the officers present including Mr S.N. Saha, Police Magistrate of Alipore and Mr D. Dutt, Officer-in-charge of the Tollygunge Police Station to pacify them proved unavailing. Brickbats and other missiles were thrown.

Crowds Dispersed

About 12 persons were injured and sent to hospital. Armed police were sent from Alipore and Lal Bazar and succeeded in dispersing the crowds before the situation took a more serious turn.

Later Mr K.A.L. Hill, District Magistrate of 24 Parganas, Mr B. Rahaman, Sub-Divisional Officer, Alipore, Raj Bahadur Rambehary Mukerji, Deputy Commissioner of Police,

South Division, Calcutta, Mr M.A. Khaleque, Superintendent, Government Railway Police, Mr P.E.S. Finney, Deputy Commissioner of Police, Special Branch, Mr P. Chakravarty, DSP Crime, 24 Parganas and Khan Bahadur M. Hidayatulla, Chairman, Tolygunge Municipality visited the area.

Mr Hill held an informal conference with Moslem leaders and the latter agreed to perform the sacrifice at the mosque mentioned in the agreement of the previous evening.

While the negotiations were in progress large crowds of Hindus drew near and apprehending that they might make a rush the police dispersed them.

Later, the *qurbani* took place at the mosque agreed upon without any hitch. Late in the afternoon a further disturbance occurred, three men were injured and several arrests were made.

In view of the tension prevailing in the neighbourhood, police pickets have been posted at strategic points and arrangements have been made for the patrolling of the area. The situation although tense was peaceful at a late hour last night....

In Calcutta proper Bakr-id was observed in the customary manner. No untoward incident occurred. In the morning thousands of Moslems offered prayers on the Maidan and at different mosques of the city. The afternoon was devoted to visiting and merry making.

The celebration also passed off smoothly in the mill areas. Additional police were posted in several areas as a precautionary measure. No disturbance was reported from the industrial area around Calcutta. In some areas extra police were posted on an all night guard.

88. District Magistrate's Report on the Sukkur Riots

Letter from the Governor of Sind, 11 March 1940, Correspondence with the Governor of Sind and his Secretary, 1940, Linlithgow Papers, Acc. No. 2230, NAI.

[Enclosure]

Bomb Explosion at the Muhammadan Procession at Sukkur on the 19th February

The usual Muhammadan procession was to pass through Sukkur on the 19th. On the 17th I came from Camp, met the District Superintendent of Police and found that the police arrangements were excellent, as they subsequently proved to be.

On the 19th I came over from camp in the morning and went with the District Superintendent of Police to the Foujdari before 2 pm. and we both were present when the various 'Tabuts' assembled to form this into a procession. Having seen the formation we went further up and watched it actually pass the Jubilee Tower. By this time, the procession was well-formed and was led by Mr Galbraith, the Additional District Superintendent of Police and the Deputy Superintendent of Police. We again met the procession at the Post Office where the last Tazia, which leads the procession was to join it. By this time the procession was in full swing and as usual the Muhammadans in religious fervour were beating their chests and lashing themselves with iron whips. Some 4 or 5 were actually seen bleeding on account of this frenzy. No danger in particular was apprehended upto this point as the procession passed more or less through Muhammadan localities. We met it again just before it entered the Bunder Road and walked along with it throughout the Bunder road as this road is almost entirely inhabited by Hindus. While going out to meet it we passed the crowded Hindu Bazar area and noticed that the shops were open and the business going on as usual.

When we reached the Nimun-Jo-Chowk, the procession halted as usual to offer prayers. It usually stops here for half an hour for this purpose but on this occasion the leaders had been requested, and they had agreed to restrict this period to 15 minutes. This spot was reached at about 5–30. The 'Tabuts' were placed on the ground and everyone sat down and offered prayers. At the head of the procession were the two District Superintendents of Police, the Deputy Superintendent of Police, a Magistrate and myself. The Police force was distributed at the entrance of the Nimun-Jo-Chowk and in the front and the rear of the procession. The usual prayers took about 15 minutes and as soon as they were over a couple of men got up to continue the procession. Just at this period, a loud report was heard about 12 feet from where Mr Moss and I stood and within 8 feet of Mr Galbraith, a column of smoke was seen to rise about 20 feet. When people realized what had happened there was a general scare and the Hindu sight-seers who had gathered there began to run while from the Muhammadan processionists rose up a cry of fury. When the smoke cleared we saw a man lying dead and three persons sitting near him with their faces bleeding profusely. Apparently the bomb had directly hit the head of the man whose head was completely shattered beyond all traces of recognition and the body lay in blood. The faces of the men who had been hurt also bled freely and presented a ghastly sight. This naturally infuriated the processionists and the fate of the city hung by hair again. No worse time could have been selected for this dastardly act. In a Muharram procession, the Mussalmans are naturally in a state of excited mourning and in that procession the time selected was just after prayers. Any affront to them is surely to court trouble with a will. As soon as the processionists saw the dead body and the bleeding and they rushed forward with one cry 'Let us get at the Hindus'. Had they got at them, there would have been a massacre as the Hindus were hemmed in between the walls of houses and the excited mob. Luckily before the mob could do anything, I asked the District Superintendent of Police to surround the houses to prevent any one from moving and went up to the processionists and asked them not to get excited and sit down as I myself was dealing with the people from whose direction the bomb had come. Luckily for us the procession was led by Mr Abdul Rahim, the retired Sub-Inspector of Police, a very reasonable man. The Khaksar Leaders promptly obeyed the instructions and the two Muslim leaders who were with us as J.Ps.—Mr Nizamuddin Agha and Mr Rasulbakhah Munshi behaved with exemplary courage. Mr Nizammuddin was actually sprayed with blood. They exhorted the processionists to remain quiet stating that the Police were apprehending all the suspects, and to the credit of everyone the excited mob listened to them and sat down. In the meantime the three houses just opposite the place from which the bomb could have been dropped were surrounded, those on the road were cleared and those on the varandas or in the houses were surrounded up and taken into custody. My object in doing this was two-fold—one was that if those persons had not immediately been taken into custody the infuriated mob would have lynched them on the spot and started a riot which would have spread throughout the town and perhaps the district. My other object was to get the names of all who were present at the site so that the investigation would have some basis for enquiry. 166 men were detained. The number appears to be a large one, but subsequent events show that the action was justified. The Houses run into each other like a rabbit warren and it is obvious that any of the persons apprehended must have seen the persons either throw the bomb or run away after the event. It is not unlikely that some of the culprits might even be among those detained.

After detaining these persons, a cordon of police was placed all round the locked up buildings. The Military who were standing by at the Foujdari were sent for and the whole block of buildings was cut off from external communication. The procession was then reformed as compactedly as possible and taken to the Foujdari under Military and Police escort along roads which led through Mussalman quarters, and there dispersed. After dispersing the procession a curfew order was imposed on the town and the local CID officer was asked to visit the houses. He went through them carefully and confirms the view that more than one persons were implicated and that from certain clues left by them they could have been seen by the persons who were arrested from the houses or in the courtyards. On getting this information all the 168 persons were detained under Section 2 of the Ordinance and the Superintendent, CID, was immediately phoned up. The District Superintendent of Police and I went thoroughly over the buildings and found that the conclusions arrived at by the local CID officers would justify us in detaining the men, and in keeping the whole block of the houses locked up. The CID officer arrived on the 21st and the position was explained to him. He has thoroughly combed the three houses and made panchanamas and has begun releasing those persons who obviously could not be related with the offence. The three houses which are suspected are the corner houses nearest the point at which the bomb exploded, which is vacant but had a door and couple of windows open, the house next to it which is more or less residential house and a third in which is situated a club which has the notoriety of being a gambling den.

The dead body and the wounded were taken to Hospital where their wounds have been treated. In all one man is dead and 19 have been wounded. Among those wounded are a Hindu, Inspector Lewis and two constables who were within 6 feet of the bomb. It was lucky that the bomb fell directly on the head of the unfortunate man as the explosion in mid-air dissipated the force of the explosion. Had it struck the ground and exploded the recoil would have increased its range of damage and might have included some of us.

The behaviour of the police was excellent. There was not only no scare, though the bomb exploded within a few feet of all of us injuring some of them, but on the contrary they immediately were alert and did their best to search houses, apprehend suspects and keep the crowd and the procession under control. Those detained were sent to Jail in Military lorries under the protection of a Sub-Inspector of Police and a Magistrate—both Hindu. Mukhi Gobindram who also accompanied the procession as J.P. deserves mention for the manner in which he helped us in arresting the Hindus, explaining to them the reasons for detaining them. This man without any fear kept himself at the spot, though an infuriated mob of Mussalmans was there calling out for vengeance. The reserve Military which were kept at Sukkur were immediately called out, patrols were organized in the town and throughout the district. That night 4 patrols left Shikarpur to visit the affected areas in the district, another under Sergeant Lewis left immediately for Ubauro and that area, and throughout the night Sukkur was patrolled by the Military and the police under the supervision of senior officers. The District Superintendent of Police and I patrolled till 3 am after which the Additional District Superintendent of Police carried on. Luckily the town and the district remained quiet.

The next day was full of anxiety on account of the funeral of the man who had lost his life. To have prohibited it totally would have only given cause for the excitement to find vent against the other community. It was therefore, decided to collect under stringent police protection as few members of the deceased's family and his friends as possible, and bring them to the civil Hospital from which place the funeral was allowed to start. It was taken under strong Police and Military escort along the outskirts of the town to the usual burial ground. The District Superintendent of Police, the Senior Military Officer and I accompanied the procession all along the route. After the burial the crowd was brought back to town under Police guard and sent home. Patrols were sent out throughout the city and the town.

Sir Ghulam Hussain Hidayatullah arrived at about 10 by air and after seeing the site and meeting a few leaders called a meeting of the leading Hindu and Muslim gentlemen in my office. He explained the futility and fatuity of these disturbances and the leaders of both the parties were vehement in expressing their abhorrence of this dastardly act and manifested apprehensions of the new direction in which communal antipathy found expression. To show their practical sympathy for the deceased the gentlemen on the spot led by the Hon'ble Minister immediately collected about Rs 300 for the family of the deceased. It was also resolved that leading Hindus and Muslims should visit Hindu and Muslim localities next morning and ask the public to remain calm. It was also agreed that leading gentlemen should tour throughout the district asking villagers not to get excited or to perpetrate communal disturbances.

In the morning the Hon'ble Minister for Law and Order accompanied by the President of the Municipality, local MLA and Dr Choithram and Professor Ghanshyam and the leading Hindu and Muslim gentlemen went throughout the town in Hindu and Muslim localities exhorting the people to remain quiet and live in unity. The Hindus demanded the release of those who had been apprehended. It was explained to them that the Superintendent of CID already had arrived and as soon as he found after enquiries that any person was unrelated with the offence, he would be released. The Mussalmans naturally were excited over this wanton irritation. They also pressed two points (1) that the bomb which had prematurely exploded on the 19th of January was obviously destined to mar the *Id* celebrations which were to take place the next day and (2) the unprovoked aggression by the Hindus on this occasion supported their claim that even on the 19th of November the disturbances started with them. Speeches were made both by Hindu and Muslim leaders pacifying the population. In the evening the Hon'ble Minister accompanied by 3 MLAs, the District Superintendent of Police, and myself left for the mofussil and Gosarji, Bagarji, Lakhi, Jehan Khan and Shikarpur were visited. At all these places the action taken was explained and the people asked to keep cool. The Hindus were requested to be calm and trust the Mussalman zamindars who were exhorted to protect and look after their Hindu brethren. Luckily there was a good response. While on way to Shikarpur we found that a rumour had spread that disturbances had started in Sukkur again. We rushed back but were told that the scare was started by entirely false rumours that 5 Hindus had been killed. Those responsible for the scare have been arrested and are being dealt with. The curfew was lifted from 8 am to 9 pm and imposed during the night. The military were asked to help in enforcing it.

89. Report on the Riot at Jabbulpore

Governor of the Central Provinces and Berar to Governor General, Telegram R., 30 March 1940, Linlithgow Papers, Acc. No. 2197, NAI.

I feel that it is necessary to warn Your Excellency that communal situation in Jubbulpore has assumed somewhat serious shape.

In 1938 and 1939 at time of Holi new practice arose of large crowd collecting in the centre of the city carrying lathis. Crowd which on both occasions contained considerable admixture of Hindu rowdies under the influence of strong communal excitement paraded through town indulging in extremely provocative behaviour. Both in 1938 and 1939 serious rioting followed.

On March 8th District Magistrate, Jubbulpore, took Government orders whether he should this year: (a) require to take out licence procession or (b) issue order under Section 144, CPC prohibiting carrying of lathis. District Magistrate very rightly pointed out that crowd on these occasions is not properly speaking, procession at all, it carried no object of veneration and has no traditional justification. He recommended therefore, that order under Section 144, CPC be promulgated prohibiting carrying of lathis.

I was due myself in Jubbulpore on March 20—Holi this year was on March 24th—and I arranged to discuss situation with local officers there on that date. Matter was one which required very careful handling as, due to fact that Misra who hails from Jubbulpore has been in Provincial Cabinet for two years and has repeatedly interfered with discretion of local officers on such occasions, Jubbulpore Hindus have become very arrogant and this fact has in no small measure contributed to communal tension in the town which is now chronic. I must reiterate however, that whatever may be the case at other festivals carrying of lathis is not essential part of Holi celebrations.

New feature in Jubbulpore communal situation is very recent emergence of Hindu volunteer organization known as Shakti Dal. This organization parades with lathis. While I was still on tour and had not yet reached Jubbulpore Shakti Dal parade fell foul of party of Muslims outside a mosque and there was a minor clash which was quickly put down by Police. Khaksars responded with opposition parade next day.

When I reached Jubbulpore I told local officers that this clash obviously rendered order under Section 144, CPC prohibiting carrying of lathis during Holi unavoidable. Real problem however, was not clash but innovation of 1938 and 1939 and I advised District Magistrate to frame his order in such a way that it would be clear that Government was not so much concerned with minor clash between Shakti Dal and Muslims as with this innovation.

Order making this point perfectly clear and prohibiting carrying of lathis from March 23rd to March 25th was accordingly passed by District Magistrate on March 22nd. Before order was passed District Magistrate saw leading Hindus who generally agreed that order was necessary if repetition of riots which had marred Holi celebrations in 1938 and 1939 was to be prevented.

Due to local rivalries for leadership of Hindu Mahasabha, principal Hindu leaders however, went back on this afterwards. Meetings were held in which real meaning of order was deliberately misrepresented and people were advised not to celebrate Holi at all. As a result Holi fires were lit in private houses and back streets only. *Phagwas* in main thoroughfares, though they had been built, were not ignited.

Hindu leaders then decided to hold celebration including procession with lathis after the date of expiry of the order. On March 24th therefore, District Magistrate on his own authority extended order till April 1st. In this he was, in my opinion, perfectly correct and I am myself quite clear that Hindu challenge to legitimate and necessary order must be firmly met.

I am informed that the local authorities are now considering the following alternatives (a) to allow order to expire on April 1st, and permit procession with lathis to be then taken out following fixed route, or (b) extend order for full period of 2 months.

90. Riot at Bahraich

Aaj, 20 April 1940.

4 Died, 25 Injured; Several Shops Looted and Burnt. Violent Attitude of Muslim Processionists

Bahraich, 16 April. It is reported that around 2000 Muslims, mainly Muslim Leaguers and Khaksars, started riots at Nanpara Zamindari on 14th April. They kept their shops closed on that day since morning and assembled at the 'Idgah' in the afternoon and after being armed, they marched on the roads shouting slogans condemning Hindus and officers. After reaching the centre of the market they attacked the Hindus and looted and burnt their shops. 32 shops were looted and 4 were burnt. Around 25 persons were injured. Among them the condition of some is said to be serious. So far 4 persons have died. It is reported that sticks, spears and knives were extensively used. The total loss accrued through this riot is said to be around one lakh (Rupees).

It is reported that the Muslims and Khaksars of Bahraich openly supported this riot. It is also rumoured that the officers of the 'estate' were also involved in this riot. As soon as the news spread, police officers and 3 contingents of police reached there and maintained peace. 50 people have been arrested so far and section 144 has been promulgated there.

Government Communique

The communique which the District Magistrate has issued in this connection states that the reason for these riots is the demonstration which they staged against the fight during the last Muharram. At that time the processionists, started looting the Bazar and attacking the passersby. The reason of the processionists getting violent is not known. We reached there as soon as we got the telegram but the riots had stopped by that time. It is sorrowful that 2 people died and numerous people were injured. Some shops were also looted. Many people have been arrested and the (area) is peaceful now. Section 144 has been promulgated.

Situation Peaceful Now!

A telegram from Bahraich, dated 18 April, says that the situation is totally peaceful and Section 144 has been promulgated.

91. Report from Provinces: Quarterly Survey of Political and Constitutional Positions in British India, No. 11–14, 1 February to 30 April 1940, 1 May to 31 July 1940, 1 August to 31 October 1940 and 1 November to 31 January 1941

Linlithgow Papers, Acc. No. 2325, NAI.

1 February to 30 April 1940

60. Bengal: On the occasion of the Moharram festival on February 19th the police had to open fire on an unruly mob in Kaliganj in Murshidabad district; three persons were killed and eleven injured in the firing.

On March 10th a Hindu–Muslim riot occurred at Bansberia in the Hooghly district; before the police could arrive four persons were killed and six injured.

61. Bihar: During February communal tension was evident all over the Province. Trouble broke out at Gaya on February 21st and during the next three days assaults were responsible for one death, and injuries to 10 Hindus and to 15 Muslims. Nothing very serious occurred in connection with the Holi festival in March.

62. Central Provinces: In Biswa murder case out of 43 persons prosecuted 6 have been sentenced to death, 24 to transportation for life, 9 were fined and the rest acquitted. Severe strictures were passed on the Hindu assessors who gave a verdict of guilty against all the accused; the judge remarked their communal bias had outrun their sense of justice.

The situation in Jubbulpore took a serious turn on the occasion of the Holi festival in March. Local Hindus have become arrogant as a result of the Congress Ministry's repeated interference with the discretion of local officers in past years, and communal tension has become chronic. A new practice of parading with lathis on the occasion of Holi has resulted in riots in both the last two years; and shortly before Holi this year a Hindu volunteer organization bearing lathis clashed with a party of Muslims. This made inevitable the issue of an order prohibiting the carrying of lathis. Local Hindu leaders deliberately misrepresented the order and advised the people not to celebrate the festival: the tension prevailing necessitated the extension of the order for two months.

On the Burhanpur riot (see para 63 of the last survey) an enquiry was held by a Session Judge. The report was submitted and orders were passed, with a promptitude strongly contrasting with the dilatoriness of the Congress Ministry in similar circumstances (viz. disturbances at Jubbulpore). The Governor decided reluctantly to quarter a force of additional police on the town, the cost of which will be borne by the Muslim community.

63. Sind: The province has been quite except for one incident when, on February 19th, a country-made bomb was thrown at a Moharram procession in Sukkur. One Muslim was killed and 17 injured; 1 Hindu was injured. Elaborate precautions were successfully taken to prevent disorder. The outrage is reported to have been the outcome of a carefully planned conspiracy with a purely communal objective. All the troops sent to Sukkur to restore order in connection with the riots of November had been withdrawn by March 1st.

An adjournment motion on February 5th in the Sind Assembly to discuss the Sukkur riots was not pressed to a division: the Premier (Allah Baksh) laid the responsibility for the disorders on a section of the Muslim League and on Hindu leaders who had indulged in provocative utterances. The subsidence of the Manzilgah agitation on the downfall of the Allah Baish Ministry is an indication that the motives of those who fomented it were political rather than religious. The Assembly has passed the Bill (mentioned in para 65 of the last survey) which extends to Sukkur district the system of trial by Jirga; and also the Bill providing for the constitution of courts of inquiry.

On March 26th the new Premier announced that Government had decided to refer the Manzilgah dispute to an independent court of inquiry consisting of a Judge of the Judicial Commissioner's court, who is to come to a conclusion as to whether the building should or should not be considered a mosque. The new Ministry have undertaken to take action on the decision of the tribunal; but it seems that the real intension is to arrive at some amicable agreement before the court has time to make a decision, which will result in the Muslims getting possession of the Manzilgah subject to certain safeguards. The local Muslim League threaten that in the event of an adverse finding by the tribunal ministers passing orders against the restoration of the Manzilgah to the Muslims will incur expulsion from the League. They have expressed alarm at the Hindu demand for greater representation in the police, and have proclaimed their distrust of all Hindu officials connected in any way with the aftermath of the Sukkur riots.

64. United Provinces: Moharram passed off peacefully except in Gonda where a Shia-Sunni riot resulted in the death of one person.

The Holi festival saw riots in Cawnpore and Allahabad. In the former 10 persons were killed and 20 injured; in Allahabad 4 were killed and 2 injured. Minor riots occurred elsewhere. In the middle of April small riots occurred in Bahraich and Gorakhpur districts; in the former two men were killed.

The Midhe-Sahaba dispute has again been the cause of trouble. Abul Kalam Azad, the Congress President, who during 1939 played a prominent part in efforts to effect a settlement of the dispute, issued a statement on April 19th saying that the UP Government's decision of March 30th, 1939 (see para 93 of Survey No. 7) was an error of judgment, and appealing to all Sunnis to persuade the organizers of the Barawafat Day Madhe-Sahaba procession to abandon it. However, the procession was taken out in Lucknow. The Government took the attitude that no imposed solution of the dispute could give satisfaction, and they would intervene only if it was necessary to preserve peace. Last year, thanks to elaborate precautions, the day passed off quietly; this year rioting broke out, and the police had to open fire. During 2 days rioting 9 persons were killed and a number injured.

65. Delhi: The Civil disobedience movement in connection with the 'Shiv Mandir' dispute has continued on a small scale.

1 May to 31 July 1940

Exhibitions of communal bitterness in the quarter have been mainly confined to parts of northern India.

49. Central Provinces: In Jubbulpore on May 7th Muslims attacked a Jain marriage procession while it was passing a mosque; about a dozen persons were injured and stray assaults accounted for the more injuries later. The situation was quickly brought under control. The prohibitory order issued at the time of the Holi festival in March has been further extended.

Previous Surveys have mentioned the Biswa murder case from time to time. On March 17th 1939, a prominent Congressman was murdered in broad day light by a party of Muslims; forty-three persons were prosecuted; of these six were sentenced to death, 24 to transportation for life, one was fined and the rest were acquitted. When the case came up on appeal to the High Court early in May all the persons sentenced were acquitted. The High Court severely criticized the conduct of the investigation by the police and the preparation of the case for trial. The behaviour of the late Premier (of which mention was made in para 90 of Survey No. 7) with regard to the case also came in for condemnation. Muslims in the Province naturally hailed the judgment with delight. The Government immediately instituted a public inquiry into the conduct of case, and obtained for the purpose of services of Mr Justice Macklin from the Bombay High Court. The terms of reference were to examine the whole conduct of the police investigation and the preparation of the case for trial and, if any defects or irregularities are disclosed, to report the persons responsible for them. The inquiry opened on June 17th and had not concluded by the end of July.

50. Punjab: The Khaksar agitation, caused some communal tension, particularly in Lahore. Among Hindus the British reverses in Europe gave rise to fears that public order in India

would be endangered, and that Muslims would resort to violence and looting, many Hindus are said to have made private arrangements for their personal security. But the collapse of the Khaksar movement, and the evidence of the strength and determination of Britain's resistance in the War, restored confidence, and such incidents as occurred had their origins in normal circumstances.

Early in May the Privy Council dismissed the Muslim appeal in the Shahidganj case. (This may be briefly summarized. In December 1937, an agitation was revived for the restoration to Muslims of the Shahidganj building in Lahore which was once a mosque but has long been in the possession of Sikhs. A civil suit relating to the right of possession was decided by the High Court early in 1938 in favour of the Sikhs. The Muslim agitation continued for some months, and was then held in abeyance pending decision of the appeal to the Privy Council). Both Muslims and Sikhs have shown commendable restraint, and no attempt has yet been made by the Sikhs to build on the site.

On July 7th communal tension in Sargodha between Sikhs and Hindus on one side and Muslims on the other, which had been smouldering for some time, flared up into an affray during which Muslims assaulted a number of Sikhs, two of whom died of their injuries. The trouble did not spread; but non-Muslims have, in the press and elsewhere, made a loud outcry and have not hesitated to impute partiality to the local offices.

On July 13th a Muslim fanatic attacked a prominent Sikh Congressman at Gujranwala and inflicted injuries which caused his death. The Muslim then attacked a group of Sikhs but was himself killed by them.

Sind: The Manzilgah riots which broke out in and around Sukkur about the middle of November last have been the subject of an enquiry by a Judge of the Chief Court. The hearing began in April and is over, but the Judge has not yet presented his report. At one stage in the enquiry Hindus threatened to boycott it unless the Government conceded various demands, which included the immediate transfer of officers who were in Sukkur during the riots, and the grant of immunity of witnesses. The Government declined to transfer the officers but assured Hindus of all reasonable protection for witnesses. Efforts were made to influence the special magistrate trying cases arising out of the Sukkur riots. The riots enquiry will be followed by another, to be held by the same Judge; this will be directed to the question whether the Manzilgah building was at one time a mosque as the Muslims claim.

Communal tension has continued in the Sukkur neighbourhood, and has recently been greatly aggravated throughout the Province by two outrages committed on Hindus who were also Congressmen. The second was the murder of a member of the Legislative Assembly, shot at close quarters by two assailants who escaped; he was returning from enquiry into the earlier outrage. Police investigations indicate that the responsibility for these two crimes rests on an adherent of the Pir of Baharchundi—the Pir is a 'holy man' of Sukkur district and sufficient evidence has by now been collected to implicate one of the same man's adherents in the murder of the Hindu saint on November 1st, 1939 (see paragraph 65 of Survey No. 10). There is reason to believe that the central culprit in all three outrages is the eldest son of the Pir of Baharchundi, but there is not enough evidence to prove this. The Ministers have come to the conclusion that there is a conspiracy afoot for the murder of prominent Hindus and officials who have taken part in proceedings connected with the Sukkur riots, but there appears to be no ground for this supposition. A special police staff has been proposed to examine the three crimes and to investigate the existence of such a conspiracy. Before any far-reaching action is taken the report of the Inquiring Officer is awaited. An additional police force of 250 men is being recruited.

1st August to 31 October 1940

The tension between the two major communities cannot be said to have much relaxed. The influence of the Muslim League and Hindu Mahasabha shows no sign of diminution; that of the latter, indeed, may be growing at the expense of Congress and there seems no likelihood of much improvement in communal feeling in the near future. But there have been no major disturbances during the quarter, and it is only in the province of Sind that the general situation is disquieting.

50. Bengal: On August 2nd a crowd of Muslims incited by a peripatetic Maulvi from Baghdad, attempted to take forcible possession of a mosque in Dacca District, standing on private land, which had been disused for a hundred years. An order under section 144 was defied by the mob, who attacked the police party at the mosque, and inflicted a number of injuries on them. The police were obliged to open fire, as a result of which one man was shot dead and three injured. The interest of the case lies in the fact that the Home Minister (in whose brother's constituency the incident occurred) desired to exculpate the accused completely, and would have had the prosecution withdrawn had not the Governor intervened. The incident has now been satisfactorily settled, the mosque having been attached and put in charge of a reliable local Muslim.

There was a serious affray at Kendua Bazar in the Burdwan District on the 22nd September, in connection with a Hindu procession. Owing to the usual route being flooded, a license was issued for this procession to go by a slightly different route, which took it near a mosque, but at a greater distance from it than the usual route. Despite this, the procession was attacked by a body of Muslims, who tried to break through the police cordon. The police halted the procession; the Hindus resented this, and attacked the police with brickbats. After 23 policemen had been injured, fire was opened, and four persons were killed; a Hindu was also hammered to death by the Muslims. There has been an outcry in the Hindu nationalist press, and a demand for an independent inquiry. The Governor is not in favour of departing from the ordinary practice, that is to say, a report by the District Magistrate, but it is possible that an exception may have to be made.

51. Central Provinces: Early in August the enquiry by Mr Justice Macklin, mentioned in para 49 of the last Survey, into the Biswa murder case was concluded. He found that the Police investigation in the case was open to criticism in three respects only: (a) the failure to make an immediate search for bloodstained articles, (b) the failure to push on the investigation in the first few days after the murder, and (c) the mass arrests of Muslims ordered by the Deputy Superintendent in charge of the investigation. Of these the third stricture is the most important; a departmental enquiry was started against the officer but he has since died of apoplexy. Still further publicity was given to this case by an open letter addressed by Mr Fazlul Huq, the Bengal Premier, to Mr Gandhi at the end of August in which he gave a distinctly biased account of it and criticized in particular the part played by the ex-Premier, Pandit Shukla. Mr Gandhi replied with an article in the '*Harijan*'. Neither can be said to have enhanced his reputation, or eased communal relations, by this controversy.

In the Jubbulpore Division the Provincial Government extended for a further period of six months from September 23rd the order under section 144 Criminal Procedure Code, prohibiting the carrying of lathis. Despite the clear statement of the Provincial Government that this order would not apply to the Dussehra and Ramlila processions, the Hindu community perversely announced their intention of not taking out those processions.

On September 2nd an incident occurred at the Satranjpura mosque at Nagpur. A procession was passing the mosque with music outside prayer hours, when some Mohammedans in the mosque attempted to rush out, and in so doing assaulted a police officer on duty at the entrance of the mosque. The police headed by the City Superintendent of Police entered the compound of the mosque and arrested 14 Muslims. The Muslim League gave a distorted version of this incident, alleging that it occurred during prayer hours and that the police desecrated the mosque. At a largely attended meeting held at Nagpur on September 5th, Khan Bahadur Siddiq Ali Khan, MLA (Central) made an inflammatory speech for which he is being prosecuted. He has refused to accept bail, written to the Governor renouncing his titles, and instigated a campaign of misrepresentation, for which he is trying to secure all India support. The Provincial Government after careful examination came to the conclusion that the Muslims had no real grievance.

52. Sind: The report of Mr Justice Weston on his enquiry into the causes of the Sukkur riots, referred to in para 51 of the last Survey, was published early in September. The Judge while offering his sympathy to the Hindus who suffered more seriously than the Muslims in life and loss of property, commented on the narrowly communal attitude of the Hindus in Sukkur town, where they are actually the majority community. The report exonerates the higher District officials. The cause of the disturbances is found to be the long Manzilgah agitation, ending with the evacuation of the building, operating upon 'the age-long antagonism of Hindus and Mohammedans'. The agitation was embittered by Hindu opposition, and by the political turn given to it when the Muslim League took up the quarrel for the purpose of strengthening its position and driving out the Allah Baksh Ministry. The Ministry was however, at a fault both in the indecision, delay, and lack of a sense of collective responsibility shown in its handling of the dispute, and in its interference with the executive officers, particularly the District Magistrate, which was one of the causes of the general lowering of respect for law and order.

'The root cause of the trouble is to be found, not in the final manoeuvres of the negotiations, but in the long period of inaction, a decision during which would have avoided the happenings both of October and of November 1939'. Communalism existed among both the armed and the unarmed police.

The report gives as the number of persons murdered and injured:

	Murdered		Injured	
	Hindus	Muslims	Hindus	Muslims
Sukkur Town	21	12	11	11
Elsewhere	130	2	47	1

In para 38 of the last Survey it was mentioned that the attempt of the present Ministry to relax the administration of the Arms Act had given occasion for intervention by the Central Government. A passage in the Weston report shows that the issue of gun licences in Sukkur in 1939 was made an occasion for obtaining subscriptions to a 'literacy fund' sponsored by the Education Minister. The Muslim members of the Ministry recently made an attempt to have the death sentence passed on a Muslim who had been convicted of murder in the Sukkur riots, commuted, but ultimately thought better of it.

The situation in Sukkur District showed signs of improvement in the early part of the quarter, thanks to stringent measures adopted by the District Magistrate under the Sind Frontier Regulations. The arrest of the Khalifas of the Pir of Baharchundi early in September passed off quietly. There was, however, a sudden and disquieting recrudescence of violence at the end of September. Three Hindus were shot dead on September 24th. On the following day three more Hindus were fired at and wounded, and on the 27th another Hindu was killed. These crimes are all thought to be in the nature of reprisals for the arrest of the Khalifas. The Pir of Baharchundi himself and his eldest son had moved with their families into Bahawalpur State before the murders were committed a highly suspicious move. The Pir was arrested at Sukkur on October 8th and is at present in Karachi Prison, detained under Bombay Regulation XXV of 1827. His son will be arrested if he can be found. The arrest of the Pir has been quietly received; but outrages on Hindus appear to be continuing.

The Working Committee of the Sind Provincial Muslim League issued a long statement on October 4th about present political conditions in Sind. This claimed that the ordinary crime rate in the Province is not so high as in certain other Provinces of India; and argued that the recent murders had been given undue publicity by the Hindu press, and were caused by a gang of irresponsible persons. It accused Hindus of intriguing to annul the constitution of Sind as a separate Province.

Hindu circles are, naturally, not so complacent about the state of public order; and the demand is still made that the Governor by some abnormal procedure shall take on himself the full responsibility for the security of the Province.

53. United Provinces: On October 10th a communal riot took place at Ghaziabad in the Meerut District, during the Dusserah celebrations. A Hindu procession approached a mosque during the taravi recitation of the Koran. Rioting and arson broke out, and the police were compelled to open fire, killing seven persons and wounding a number of others. Several people, including police officers, were also injured with brickbats. The cause of the riot was the insistence of the Hindus on taking out the procession before the time agreed on.

This was the only serious disturbance in British India at a time of particular danger, owing to the occurrence of the Dusserah in the month of Ramzan.

1 November to 31 January 1941

46. As far as outward disturbances go, the quarter has been a remarkably peaceful one; and the situation in Sind has improved. But the uncompromising attitude of the leaders of the two main communal parties, the Muslim League and the Hindu Mahasabha, reflects a spirit which throughout a great part of the country keeps alive the possibility of violence. The special communal problems arising out of the Census are dealt with in paragraph 64 below.

Bengal: The two incidents described in paragraph 50 of the last Survey have not yet been settled. (In both the police were compelled to fire on Muslims in one instance and on Hindus in the other). The Chief Minister interested himself in both cases, possibly in order to obtain Muslim support at the expense of the Home Minister, Sir Nazimuddin. In December he made a proposal in Cabinet that the prosecutions arising out of the riot at Kendua Bazar (where Hindus were the culprits) should be withdrawn subject to a number of conditions which included the withdrawal of the prosecution arising from the incident in Dacca district. In the Kendua Bazar case the cabinet decided to ask the Chief Justice to lend the services of a High Court Judge to examine the magisterial report and give his opinion whether the police were justified in opening fire. The Chief Justice in reply has enquired whether any prosecutions are pending. The Governor's special responsibility is attracted from the point of view both of the peace of the province and of the morale of the police service. These cases have been given much publicity and have tended to embitter communal feelings in the province. Though there may be little to fear from Political movements in Bengal at present, the communal situation presents a growing threat to the public peace. With the Mahasabha developing into a leading political force in a province torn by the factions of rival sections of the Congress, tension is unlikely to abate. Hindu prospects, influence and culture are held to be adversely affected by a number of measures showing a deliberate policy of the Government—the fixation of a communal ratio in the public service; the Calcutta Municipal (Amendment) Act, 1939 which widens the franchise and changes the basis of election of councilors in a manner which seems to favour the Muslims; the Calcutta Municipal (Amendment) Bill, providing for a greater degree of governmental, that is to say, Muslim control over the Calcutta Corporation; and the Secondary Education Bill. The frequent need for suppression of minor communal disturbances is beginning to have a demoralizing effect on the rank and file of the police. Communal feelings among the police are not serious at present, but the situation is potentially dangerous, and there is a feeling that the Ministry favours Muslim members of the force.

47. Bihar: The peace in Bhagalpur town, in which place the two communities appear to be constantly on the outlook for causes of offence, was badly disturbed on November 1st. The trouble arose in regard to the processional route to be followed for the immersion of certain images, but after some argument and persuasion the procession and ceremony were completed without incident. A little later, however, sporadic communal rioting was reported from various quarters of the towns. The situation was firmly handled by the local officials, but by the end of the day about 46 persons had been injured of whom 30 were Mohammedans and the rest Hindus. One of the Mohammedans afterwards died in hospital. On November 3rd the situation again deteriorated, and there was a murderous assault on 3 Hindus one of whom afterwards died. The following day a Mohammedan was found murdered on the outskirts of the town. The ordinary police were reinforced by the mounted military police and a warning was issued that punitive police, the cost which would be recovered from the public might be posted. Even then, it required a show of force by the mounted military police to restore quiet.

A clash between Hindus and Muslims near Muzaffarpur occurred on January 9th in connection with the Bakr-Id. A Hindu mob, reported to number about ten thousand, made repeated attacks on a Muslim village setting on fire a number of houses and haystacks; the Muslims retaliated using firearms; as the mob refused to disperse the Sub-Divisional Officer ordered the Police to open fire, which resulted in the death of two persons and the injury of two others.

48. Central Provinces: The Satranjpura incident of September 2nd was described in para 51 of the last Survey. The agitation continued during the first half of the quarter. Khan bahadur Siddiq Ali Khan was given a very light sentence of 4 months simple imprisonment on November 13th. The Chief Minister of Bengal and two of his Muslim colleagues asked the Governor to intervene. The Governor, who already felt that a compromise would be in the interest of permanent peace, if it could be secured without weakening the position of the police of respect of law and order, deputed the Chief Secretary to see Siddiq Ali Khan in Jail. Siddiq Ali Khan, however, obstinately refused to accept any arrangement involving an admission that he might have let his tongue run away with him, as he feared that would ruin his political standing with

the Muslims. His attitude was really inspired by party faction within the Provincial Muslim League, one section of which he controlled. At the beginning of December a number of Muslim leaders of the province, aided by a Central MLA sent by Mr Jinnah, waited upon the Governor and a satisfactory settlement was reached. Siddiq Ali Khan and another agitator were released on their making suitable statements in Court. At the bottom of the trouble is the fact that the Muslim community in the province were nursing a general sense of grievance, after two years of Congress rule, and wanted some gesture of goodwill and the treatment of this incident has made them well disposed towards the Government.

49. Sind: More violent crime against Hindus in the Sukkur district broke out during the first fortnight of November. The Hindu press throughout India has tended to give the impression that wholesale atrocities were being perpetrated throughout Sind on harmless Hindus. Actually the total Hindu causalities from the beginning of September 1940 till the middle of November were 16 killed and 14 wounded, and these were almost entirely confined to Sukkur District. At the same time, the murders were murders of Hindus as such, the victims being generally unknown to the murderers. The Premier against the Governor's advice issued in the press an exhortation to the public the main purpose of which seemed to be to whitewash the Muslims. This received some pungent criticism; in particular the Sind Branch of the European Association failed to find in it an assurance that the authority of district officials would be strengthened. The Premier, accompanied by two Ministers, held conferences at Sukkur of district officials and zamindars early in November. The Governor saw to it that the Ministers were cautioned not to interfere with the operations of the District Officers directed towards the capture of the murder gang. Though the main offender, the eldest son of the Pir of Baharchundi is still at large, these operations have been successful in that there have been no communal murders since the middle of November. The Pir of Baharchundi is still in detention.

The visit of the President of the Congress to Sind in November had as its published objects the study of the situation created by the murders of several Hindus and of the Ministerial position. The first object was subordinated to the second, and the visit is therefore, described in para 14 above as is the subsequent visit of the President of the Muslim League.

The order prohibiting the public from entering the Manzilgah was extended for a further two months at the end of December, as Mr Justice Weston was still pursuing his inquiry into the use and purpose of the buildings. The terms of reference of the inquiry were whether either of the domed buildings was consutructed for use as a mosque or had even been used as such. He ended his inquiry in the middle of January, and came to the conclusion that, in view of the overwhelming evidence of the features of the western building, it was constructed for use as a mosque. Having formed this conclusion, Mr Weston did not think it necessary to go fully into the question of user throughout the history of building which dates from about 1600 A.D. The conclusion as to the purpose for which it was built should prove conducive to a settlement. The report is under the consideration of the Provincial Government.

92. Delhi Riot: Sub-Inspector Stabbed to Death

Hindustan Times, 28 August 1940.

Trouble in Paharganj

Sardar Amar Singh, Sub-Inspector of Police in charge of Paharganj Police Station, was stabbed to death and about half a dozen policemen including a head constable were injured as the result of an attack on a police party accompanying a Janam Ashtami procession last night in front of the Bandhanionwali Masjid in Paharganj. An official version of the incident says: 'On the night of August 26 while a Janam Ashtami procession was in the vicinity of the Bandhanionwali Mosque in Chuna mandi Paharganj a scuffle started, the origin of which is not clear. In the course of this Singh received a stab wound to which he later succumbed. Today the request was made by representatives of the Sikh community that the body should be taken in procession through the city enroute to the cremation ground. This request was not acceded to by the authorities and so the body was cremated quietly outside Delhi in the presence and with the approval of the relatives and Sikh brother officers, the obsequies being performed by a *granthi* chosen by the bereaved.

'Inquiries into the circumstances of the crime are in progress'.

Inquiries made in this connection show that the procession reached near the Masjid at about 9–30 p.m. when the prayers had almost finished. The band accompanying the procession stopped playing near the mosque and only resumed playing when the *namazis* were coming out. Hardly had it reached in front of the mosque when a party of Muslims, armed with lathis, came out of the mosque and asked the processionists to stop the band. Confusion prevailed for some time, during which stones and brickbats were thrown at the processionists and the police party which was headed by Sardar Amar Singh. Finding the situation uncontrollable the Sub-Inspector took out his pistol, and while loading it, it is stated, a Muslim from among the assailants stabbed the Sub-Inspector in the ribs and he fell on the ground. By this time the procession had moved away from the mosque. The Sub-Inspector was mortally wounded and he was removed to hospital in a precarious condition where he succumbed to his injuries at about 11 p.m.

Immediately after the incident a large posse of police, headed by the DSP City reached the spot and restored order. Eight cartridges in possession of the Sub-Inspector were found missing. Police pickets were posted throughout the city and in front of the mosque on Tuesday morning.

Postmortem Exam

The dead body of the deceased was removed to the mortuary in the morning, where POSTMORTEM examination was held. There was a six-inch deep wound, apparently caused by a sharp knife. From the mortuary the dead body was taken to the Police Hospital which was guarded by armed police all the time it was there.

A large number of Sikhs, numbering about 1000 collected before the CID office and made a request to the authorities to hand over the body to them for being taken to Gurdwara Sisganj for necessary religious rites. After protracted negotiations the authorities turned down their request, as, in their opinion, there was a danger of a riot in case the body was allowed to be taken to the city. Meanwhile, the authorities took all the possible precautionary measures. A tear-gas squad was kept in readiness in the CID office. A large police force was requisitioned. Police pickets were placed on all important crossings.

Cremation

At about 2.30 pm the City Magistrate, S.B.S. Narinder Singh and Mr R.G. Mellor informed the people that the dead body had been cremated according to Sikh rites; in the presence of the relations of the deceased. A *granthi* was present. All ranks of the local police were represented.

It is learnt that sufficient financial assistance has been given to the widow of the deceased in order to tide over her immediate needs.

Section 144 Promulgated

Five persons have been so far arrested by the police in Paharganj as a security measure. An order under Section 144, CrPC has been promulgated by the City Magistrate, which says:

'Whereas it has been made to appear to me that there exists in the city of Delhi a communal tension threatening the public tranquility and likely to lead to a disturbance of the peace and whereas immediate prevention is desirable. Now, therefore, I, Narinder Singh, city Magistrate of Delhi, do prohibit under Section 144, Criminal Procedure Code, the assemblage or procession of five or more persons within the limits of the municipalities of Delhi and of New Delhi, and within the Notified Areas of Fort and Civil Station.

This order shall take effect immediately and shall remain in force for a period of four days'.

The situation in the city is quiet and there are no signs of panic anywhere. Paharganj and most of the shopping centres in the city observed hartal.

In the evening a meeting of the Sikhs was held in Gurdwara Sisganj when a resolution condoling the death of the Sub-Inspector was adopted and a telegram was sent to the Shiromani Gurdwara Prabandhak Committee at Amritsar informing it about the incident last night.

The Dharmik Leela Committee also passed a resolution mourning the death of Sub-Inspector Amar Singh.

Investigation Started

It is understood that the police have taken up in right earnest the investigation of the murder and rioting case registered in connection with the incident. Lala Dina Nath, a Senior Inspector of Police, has been put in charge of the investigation. It is learnt that several eye-witnesses have given the description of the assassin to the police who are quite confident of arresting the culprit.

The police officers were vigilant throughout the night.

93. Controversy Over a Film

(a) Report on a Film, 'Sandesa' or 'The Alarm Signal'

File No. 313–1940, Home Department, 26 August 1940, Maharashtra State Archives.

From:
R. Agarwalla,
President, Hindu Sabha Kalbadevi,
299, Kalbadevi Road, Bombay No. 2.

To:
The Secretary,
Bombay Board of Film Censors,
Old Customs House, Bombay.

'Sandesa' or 'the Alarm Signal'

Dear Sir,

After the 'Diamond Queen' the above is the second dirtiest picture of the year, produced by Hind Pictures, now running in the New West End Talkies. The story-writer, proprietor, directors and actors are almost all Muslims.

The picture is most objectionable and should be stopped immediately. The objectionable features are summarized as below:

1. A robust Muslim pays a visit to his Hindu friend, a fellow lean and advanced in age, devoid of manly power and unfit for cohabitation, after usual compliments he is pleased to ask his young and robust wife to entertain his friend, she gladly agrees.
2. The story begins with three friends Rafique (Muslim), Suresh and Miss Indira (Hindus) all college students enjoying life jointly on cycles, in a car and boat, Indira in the middle between two different arms.
3. The first line of synopsis 'All for one and one for all' i.e. Indira for both and both for Indira guides the whole story—a Hindu woman with two husbands one Hindu and one Muslim, one in name, the other real.
4. Suresh wants to marry parentless Indira, but father objects, describes her as a stray girl of loose character with a number of lovers including Muslims.
5. Indira entertains her boy and girl friends both Hindus and Muslims with dances in European dress, and style, rouses the sex appeal by decent and semi-decent jokes mutually—while Suresh the would-be husband stays outside.
6. Suresh is expelled from home, elopes with Indira, commits theft in father's house and subsists on earnings of Indira's dances for some time.
7. Indira is employed as tutoress to the daughter of her old friend Rafique and Suresh as the Manager in his office.
8. Suresh is busy with office files and Rafique with her keep (Indira) at home, eyes of Suresh are opened only after odiums from the office staff.
9. Throughout the picture Rafique enjoys full liberty with the person of Suresh's wife, but whenever Suresh goes to Rafique's house he sends his wife inside and cannot tolerate even to see her face by his confident friend.
10. Rafique is sick, his wife has already deserted him for his connection with Indira, who is a regular attendance and ever grateful for giving bread to the starving couple.

In acts as well as in conversation the producers have attempted to impress the public, that the Hindu ladies should have two homes—one Hindu, to be fed and clothed, the other Muslim for sexual enjoyment. The generous Hindus, inspite of sarcastic remarks from the society should never allow themselves to suspect the adultery and infidelity of their Muslim friends with their wives—because after all a Muslim is a true Muslim, cent per cent true to the polygamous laws of the Quoran and the Shariat and this is suggested as the only and the best solution of Hindu–Muslim unity if the dirty brains of Hindus and Muslims could understand.

Apart from the rascality of the producers we have to take pity and shed tears for Film Inspectors who do not seem to know the ABC of censorship and are proving themselves to be too stupid to grasp the wicked intentions of the producers.

Will the members of the Censor Board open their eyes, use their commonsense and moral courage not only to stop but finally to reject such nasty pictures as a lesson to other mischief makers and save the Indian Film Industry from its doom.

As such pictures create communal bitterness and likely to lead to riots and bloodshed, endanger the peace of the country, most harmful especially in time of war. We most respectfully appeal to Government and His Excellency, the Governor to be pleased to take drastic steps and stop this poisonous, mean and malicious anti-Hindu propaganda on the screen.

(b) Hind's 'Sandesa' Starring Nazir and Yasmin Preaches Hindu–Muslim Unity

Times of India, 23 November 1940.

'Sandesa', the Hindu Picture' release, now in its second week at West End Talkies, has a highly commendable theme in that it represents the first attempt on the Indian screen to deal directly with the country's major communal problem and to discuss frankly and in a commonsense manner the essentially human aspect of Hindu–Muslim relations. From this angle 'Sandesa' as well as those responsible for its production, from the story writer, Mr Munshi Dill Lucknovi (who incidentally also wrote the dialogue and the songs which both bear strongly upon the main theme) to the cast and director, deserve praise for opening up a new field of the most consuming interest and importance to Indian life and full of the most alluring potentialities for the industry as well as the public.

It is unfortunate that in technique, acting and other values the picture falls somewhat short of the best standards leaving one with the impression that the message deserved a better vehicle. This is due principally to the acting which displays an amateurish touch that robs the situations of most of their dramatic content and detracts from the tone of the picture.

The story is built around the lives of a pair of Hindu lovers Suresh and Indira and their college mate and bosom friend Rafique, a Muslim. When Suresh's father objects to his marriage with Indira, Rafique undertakes to persuade the old man. When the lovers elope and return penniless Rafique gives them work and stands by them in the face of his friends, relations, even his wife.

Even when Suresh misled by gossip entertains base thoughts of his friend's relations with Indira, Rafique is unswerving in his loyalty and at the last when a Hindu–Muslim riot breaks out in the town Rafique goes out into the streets to search for Indira and finally is himself slain, a victim upon the altar of friendship.

His death brings the two families together and some telling dialogue in the last sequence points the futility of bitterness between individuals who whatever their differences of faith and custom may be are children of the same soil and deriving a common sustenance from the same sources of life and prosperity.

Nazir as Rafique puts over a convincing portrayal of the high-minded Muslim expressing the true charity and democratic outlook of Islam. He also wrote the scenario and directed the picture. Ashik Hussain is passable as Suresh, Yasmin none too happy as Indira.

The supporting cast, headed by Majid, Shushila, Sadiq and others is mediocre, though a clever portrayal is given by Janardan as the Mehta. Baby Madhuri, a tiny tot knee-high to the proverbial grasshopper, is the most charming character in the whole picture and acts with a self-possession that experienced actors might envy. She is easily the liveliest child actor the Indian screen has yet presented.

The music is not remarkable though some of the songs are pretty and well rendered. Yasmin dances with attractive grace, but her dancing is of the type commonly described as oriental rather than Indian.

Index